# NORTH AMERICAN INDUSTRY CLASSIFICATION SYSTEM

United States, 2022

EXECUTIVE OFFICE OF THE PRESIDENT
OFFICE OF MANAGEMENT AND BUDGET

Published by Bernan Press
An imprint of The Rowman & Littlefield Publishing Group, Inc.
4501 Forbes Boulevard, Suite 200, Lanham, Maryland 20706
www.rowman.com

ISBN 978-1-63671-100-3 (cloth)

# Foreword

The Instituto Nacional de Estadística y Geografía (INEGI) of Mexico, Statistics Canada, and the United States Office of Management and Budget, through its Economic Classification Policy Committee, have jointly updated the system of classification of economic activities that makes the industrial statistics produced in the three countries comparable. The North American Industry Classification System (NAICS) revision for 2022 is scheduled to go into effect for reference year 2022 in Canada and the United States, and 2023 in Mexico. NAICS was originally developed to provide a consistent framework for the collection, analysis, and dissemination of industrial statistics used by government policy analysts, by academics and researchers, by the business community, and by the public. Revisions for 2022 were made to account for our rapidly changing economies.

Classifications serve as a lens through which to view the data they classify. NAICS was developed in accordance with a single principle of aggregation, the principle that producing units that use similar production processes should be grouped together. Though NAICS differs from other industry classification systems, the three countries continue to strive to create industries that do not cross two-digit Division boundaries of the United Nations' International Standard Industrial Classification of All Economic Activities (ISIC).

The actual classification reveals only the tip of the work carried out by dedicated staff from INEGI, Statistics Canada, and U.S. statistical agencies. It is through their efforts, painstaking analysis, and spirit of accommodation that NAICS serves as a harmonized international classification of economic activities in North America.

# Preface

The North American Industry Classification System (NAICS) represents a continuing cooperative effort among Statistics Canada, Mexico's Instituto Nacional de Estadística y Geografía (INEGI), and the Economic Classification Policy Committee (ECPC) of the United States, acting on behalf of the Office of Management and Budget, to create and maintain a common industry classification system. With its inception in 1997, NAICS replaced the Standard Industrial Classification (1980) of Canada, the Mexican Classification of Activities and Products (1994), and the Standard Industrial Classification (1987) of the United States. Since 1997, the countries have collaborated in producing five-year revisions to NAICS in order to keep the classification system current with changes in economic activities.

NAICS is unique among industry classifications in that it is constructed within a single conceptual framework. Economic units that have similar production processes are classified in the same industry, and the lines drawn between industries demarcate, to the extent practicable, differences in production processes. This supply-based, or production-oriented, economic concept was adopted for NAICS because an industry classification system is a framework for collecting and publishing information on both inputs and outputs, for statistical uses that require that inputs and outputs be used together and be classified consistently. Examples of such uses include measuring productivity, unit labor costs, and the capital intensity of production, estimating employment-output relationships, constructing input-output tables, and other uses that imply the analysis of production relationships in the economy. The classification concept for NAICS leads to production of data that facilitate such analyses.

In the design of NAICS, attention was given to developing production-oriented classifications for (a) new and emerging industries, (b) service industries in general, and (c) industries engaged in the production of advanced technologies. These special emphases are embodied in the particular features of NAICS, discussed below. These same areas of special emphasis account for many of the differences between the structure of NAICS and the structures of industry classification systems in use elsewhere. NAICS provides industry comparability among the three North American countries and maintains compatibility with the two-digit level of the United Nation's International Standard Industrial Classification of all Economic Activities (ISIC, Rev. 4).

NAICS divides the economy into 20 sectors. Industries within these sectors are grouped according to the production criterion. The NAICS Information sector brings together activities that transform information into commodities that are produced and distributed, and activities that provide the means for distributing those products, other than through traditional wholesale-retail distribution channels. Industries included in this sector are grouped into six subsectors: motion picture and sound recording industries; publishing industries; broadcasting and content providers; telecommunications; computing infrastructure providers, data processing, web hosting, and related services; and web search portals, libraries, archives, and other information services.

A sector for Professional, Scientific, and Technical Services comprises establishments engaged in activities where human capital is the major input. The industries within this sector are each defined by the expertise and training of the service provider. The sector includes such industries as offices of lawyers, engineering services, architectural services, advertising agencies, and interior design services.

A sector for Arts, Entertainment, and Recreation includes a wide range of establishments that operate facilities or provide services to meet varied cultural, entertainment, and recreational interests of their patrons.

Another key sector, Health Care and Social Assistance, recognizes the merging of the boundaries of health care and social assistance. The industries in this sector are arranged in an order that reflects the range and extent of health care and social assistance provided.

In the Manufacturing sector, an important subsector, Computer and Electronic Product Manufacturing, brings together industries producing electronic products and their components. The manufacturers of computers, communications equipment, and semiconductors, for example, are grouped into the same subsector because of the inherent technological similarities of their production processes. NAICS acknowledges the importance of these electronic industries in the economies of the three North American countries.

This NAICS structure reflects the levels at which data comparability was agreed upon by the three countries' statistical agencies. The boundaries of all the sectors of NAICS are delineated. In most sectors, NAICS provides for trilateral comparability at the industry (five-digit) level. However, three-country comparability occurs either at the industry group (four-digit) or subsector (three-digit) level for one subsector in Mining, Quarrying, and Oil and Gas Extraction, one industry group in Utilities, one industry group in Construction, two subsectors in Finance and Insurance, two industry groups in the Real Estate subsector, one subsector in Information, and two subsectors in Other Services (except Public Administration). For these sectors or subsectors, differences in the economies of the three countries prevent full comparability at the NAICS industry level. For Retail Trade, Wholesale Trade, and Public Administration, the three countries' statistical agencies have agreed only on the boundaries of the sector (two-digit level). Below the agreed upon level of comparability, each country may add additional detailed industries, as necessary to meet national needs, provided that this additional detail aggregates to the NAICS level.

The United States has adopted the revised classification in statistical programs for the reference year beginning in 2022.

# Acknowledgments

This 2022 revision of the North American Industry Classification System (NAICS) was an immense undertaking requiring the time, energy, creativity, and cooperation of numerous people and organizations throughout the three countries. The work that has been accomplished is a testament to the individual and collective willingness of many persons and organizations both inside and outside the government to contribute to the development of NAICS. Within the United States, NAICS was revised under the guidance of the Office of Management and Budget by the Economic Classification Policy Committee (ECPC). Members of the ECPC were **Dennis Fixler** and **Edward T. Morgan**, Bureau of Economic Analysis, U.S. Department of Commerce; **Nick Orsini** and **Fay Dorsett** (Co-Chair), Bureau of the Census, U.S. Department of Commerce; **David Talan** and **Vincent Russo** (Co-Chair), Bureau of Labor Statistics, U.S. Department of Labor; and **Kerrie Leslie**, Office of Management and Budget.

In addition to the parties listed above, OMB would like to acknowledge the dedicated staff of the Classification Development Branch at the Bureau of the Census. This staff was responsible for researching, summarizing, and making preliminary recommendations to the ECPC for comments received from the public on 2022 NAICS revisions; for preparing documents summarizing the ECPC position for use in negotiations with Canada and Mexico; and for preparing all of the manuscript files for the published manual. It was their hard work and dedication that resulted in this complete documentation of 2022 NAICS United States.

# Contents

# Explanation of Symbols

**In NAICS United States Structure**

| Symbol | Explanation |
|---|---|
| T | Canadian, Mexican, and United States industries are comparable |

**In Part I, Titles and Descriptions of Industries**

| Symbol | Explanation |
|---|---|
| T | Canadian, Mexican, and United States industries are comparable |

**In Appendix A**

| Symbol | Explanation |
|---|---|
| N | New NAICS industry/code for 2022 |
| * | Part of 2017 NAICS United States industry |
| R | 2017 NAICS industry code reused with different content |

**In Appendix B**

| Symbol | Explanation |
|---|---|
| pt. | Part of 2022 NAICS United States industry |

# Introduction

## Background

In 1937, the Central Statistical Board established an Interdepartmental Committee on Industrial Classification "to develop a plan of classification of various types of statistical data by industries and to promote the general adoption of such classification as the standard classification of the Federal Government."[1] The List of Industries for manufacturing was first available in 1938, with the List of Industries for nonmanufacturing following in 1939. These Lists of Industries became the first Standard Industrial Classification (SIC) for the United States.

The SIC was developed for use in the classification of establishments by type of activity in which they are primarily engaged; for purposes of facilitating the collection, tabulation, presentation, and analysis of data relating to establishments; and for promoting uniformity and comparability in the presentation of statistical data collected by various agencies of the United States Government, State agencies, trade associations, and private research organizations. The SIC covered the entire field of economic activities by defining industries in accordance with the composition and structure of the economy.

Since the inception of the SIC in the 1930's, the system was periodically revised to reflect the economy's changing industrial composition and organization. The last revision of the SIC was in 1987.

Rapid changes in both the U.S. and world economies brought the SIC under increasing criticism. In 1991, an International Conference on the Classification of Economic Activities was convened in Williamsburg, Virginia, to provide a forum for responding to such criticism and to explore new approaches to classifying economic activity. In July 1992, the Office of Management and Budget (OMB) established the Economic Classification Policy Committee (ECPC) and charged it with a "fresh slate" examination of economic classifications for statistical purposes. The ECPC prepared a number of issue papers regarding classification, consulted with outside users, and ultimately joined with Mexico's Instituto Nacional de Estadística, Geografía e Informática (now the Instituto Nacional de Estadística y Geografía) (INEGI) and Statistics Canada to develop the North American Industry Classification System (NAICS), which replaced the 1987 U.S. SIC and the classification systems of Canada (1980 SIC) and Mexico (1994 Mexican Classification of Activities and Products (CMAP)).

The dynamic nature of world economies continues to affect classification systems. The creators of NAICS agreed that the classification system should be reviewed every five years and revised as appropriate to reflect the changing economies of the three countries. The U.S. statistical programs implemented NAICS for the first time in 1997. NAICS was revised in 2002, 2007, 2012, and 2017. This 2022 NAICS revision was undertaken to achieve one main goal—to modify or create industries to reflect new, emerging, or changing activities and technologies.

The impact of NAICS on various countries has brought about a renewed effort for additional convergence with the many industry classifications used throughout the world. Future revisions of NAICS will continue to strive for greater global comparability.

---

[1] Pearce, Esther, History of the Standard Industrial Classification, Executive Office of the President, Office of Statistical Standards, U.S. Bureau of the Budget, Washington, DC, July 1957 (mimeograph).

**Purpose of NAICS**

NAICS is an industry classification system that groups establishments into industries based on the similarity of their production processes. It is a comprehensive system covering all economic activities. There are 20 sectors and 1,012 industries in 2022 NAICS United States.

NAICS was initially developed and subsequently revised by Mexico's INEGI, Statistics Canada, and the U.S. ECPC (the latter acting on behalf of OMB) to provide common industry definitions for Canada, Mexico, and the United States that will facilitate economic analyses of the economies of the three North American countries. The statistical agencies in the three countries produce information on inputs and outputs, industrial performance, productivity, unit labor costs, and employment. NAICS, which is based on a production-oriented concept, ensures maximum usefulness of industrial statistics for these and similar purposes.

NAICS United States is used by U.S. statistical agencies to facilitate the collection, tabulation, presentation, and analysis of data relating to establishments; and to provide uniformity and comparability in the presentation of statistical data describing the U.S. economy. NAICS United States is designed for statistical purposes. Although the classification also may be used for various administrative, regulatory, and taxation purposes, the requirements of government agencies that use it for nonstatistical purposes played no role in its development or subsequent revision.

**Development of NAICS as a Replacement for the U.S. SIC**

The U.S. ECPC established by OMB in 1992 was chaired by the Bureau of Economic Analysis, U.S. Department of Commerce, with representatives from the Bureau of the Census, U.S. Department of Commerce, and the Bureau of Labor Statistics, U.S. Department of Labor. The ECPC was asked to examine economic classifications for statistical purposes and to determine the desirability of developing a new industry classification system for the United States based on a single economic concept. On March 31, 1993, OMB published a **Federal Register** notice (58 FR 16990-17004) announcing the intention to revise the SIC for 1997, the establishment of the ECPC, and the process for revising the SIC.

In July 1994, OMB announced plans to develop a new industry classification system in cooperation with Mexico's INEGI and Statistics Canada. The new system—NAICS—replaced the U.S. SIC. The concepts of the new system and the principles upon which NAICS was to be developed were announced in a July 26, 1994, **Federal Register** notice (59 FR 38092-38096) and were as follows:

1.  NAICS will be erected on a production-oriented or supply-based conceptual framework. This means that producing units that use identical or similar production processes will be grouped together in NAICS.
2.  The system will give special attention to developing production-oriented classifications for (a) new and emerging industries, (b) service industries in general, and (c) industries engaged in the production of advanced technologies.
3.  Time series continuity will be maintained to the greatest extent possible. However, changes in the economy and proposals from data users must be considered. In addition, adjustments will be required for sectors where the United States, Canada, and Mexico have incompatible industry

classification definitions in order to produce a common industry system for all three North American countries.

4.   The system will strive for compatibility with the two-digit level of the International Standard Industrial Classification of All Economic Activities (ISIC, Rev. 3) of the United Nations.

The structure of NAICS was developed in a series of meetings among the three countries. Public proposals for individual industries from all three countries were considered for acceptance if the proposed industry was based on the production-oriented concept of the system. In the United States, public comments also were solicited as groups of subsectors of NAICS were completed and agreed upon by the three countries. The ECPC published the proposed industries for those subsectors in a series of five successive **Federal Register** notices, in 1995 and 1996, asking for comments from interested data users.

## Revision of NAICS for 2022

OMB published a notification of potential revision to NAICS for 2022 in a February 26, 2020, **Federal Register** notice (85 FR 11120-11124). This notice solicited comments on: 1) new and emerging industries for consideration in potential revisions to NAICS for 2022; 2) the NAICS treatment of electronic shopping in Retail Trade; and 3) the concept of Internet publishing and broadcasting and the potential to eliminate the industry in NAICS 2022.

After considering all proposals from the public, consulting with a number of U.S. data users and industry groups, and undertaking extensive discussions with Statistics Canada and Mexico's Instituto Nacional de Estadística y Geografía (INEGI), the ECPC formulated a set of recommendations for revisions to NAICS for 2022. OMB published a solicitation of public comments on these recommendations in a July 2, 2021, **Federal Register** notice (86 FR 35350-35365). After reviewing comments to that notice and conducting further consultation with data users and industry groups, OMB decided to adopt the ECPC recommendations presented in the July 2, 2021, notice. OMB published a notice of final decisions regarding NAICS revisions for 2022 in a December 21, 2021, **Federal Register** notice (86 FR 72277-72279).

## Conceptual Framework

NAICS is erected on a production-oriented or supply-based conceptual framework that groups establishments into industries according to similarity in the processes used to produce goods or services. A production-oriented industry classification system ensures that statistical agencies in the three countries can produce information on inputs and outputs, industrial performance, productivity, unit labor costs, employment, and other statistics and structural changes occurring in each of the three economies.

When an industry is defined on a production-oriented concept, producing units within the industry's boundaries share a basic production process; they use closely similar technology. In the language of economics, producing units within an industry share the same production functions; producing units in different industries have different production functions. The boundaries between industries thus demarcate, in principle, differences in production processes and production technologies.

The reasoning behind the three countries' decision to base NAICS on a production-oriented concept is summarized as follows: An industry is a grouping of economic activities. Though it inevitably groups the products of the economic activities that are included in the industry definition, it is not solely a grouping of products; put another way, an industry groups producing units. Accordingly, an industry classification system provides a framework for collecting data on inputs and outputs together.

The uses of economic data that require that data on inputs and outputs be used together and be collected on the same basis include production analyses, productivity measurement, and studying input usage and input intensities. The North American statistical agencies developed NAICS using a production-oriented concept as the framework for two reasons: (1) an industry classification system groups producing units, not products or services; and (2) groupings of producing units permit the collection of data on inputs and outputs on a comparable basis, which is required for production-oriented analysis, but do not facilitate a comprehensive collection of data on the total output of any particular good or service, which is required for market-oriented analysis. Thus, the efficient organizing concept of an industry classification system is production-oriented rather than market-oriented.

### Structure of NAICS

The structure of NAICS is hierarchical. The first two digits of the structure designate the NAICS sectors that represent general categories of economic activities.

NAICS classifies all economic activities into 20 sectors. The NAICS sectors, their two-digit codes or code ranges, and the distinguishing activities of each are:

**11 Agriculture, Forestry, Fishing and Hunting**—Activities of this sector are growing crops, raising animals, harvesting timber, and harvesting fish and other animals from farms, ranches, or the animals' natural habitats.

**21 Mining, Quarrying, and Oil and Gas Extraction**—Activities of this sector are extracting naturally occurring mineral solids, such as coal and ore; liquid minerals, such as crude petroleum; and gases, such as natural gas; and beneficiating (e.g., crushing, screening, washing, and flotation) and other preparation at the mine site, or as part of mining activity.

**22 Utilities**—Activities of this sector are generating, transmitting, and/or distributing electricity, gas, steam, and water and removing sewage through a permanent infrastructure of lines, mains, and pipe.

**23 Construction**—Activities of this sector are erecting buildings and other structures (including additions); heavy construction other than buildings; and alterations, reconstruction, installation, and maintenance and repairs.

**31-33 Manufacturing**—Activities of this sector are the mechanical, physical, or chemical transformation of materials, substances, or components into new products.

**42 Wholesale Trade**—Activities of this sector are selling or arranging for the purchase or sale of goods for resale; capital or durable nonconsumer goods; and raw and intermediate materials and supplies used in production, and providing services incidental to the sale of the merchandise.

**44-45 Retail Trade**—Activities of this sector are retailing merchandise generally in small quantities to the general public and providing services incidental to the sale of the merchandise.

**48-49 Transportation and Warehousing**—Activities of this sector are providing transportation of passengers and cargo, warehousing and storing goods, scenic and sightseeing transportation, and supporting these activities.

**51 Information**—Activities of this sector are distributing information and cultural products, providing the means to transmit or distribute these products as data or communications, and processing data.

**52 Finance and Insurance**—Activities of this sector involve the creation, liquidation, or change in ownership of financial assets (financial transactions) and/or facilitating financial transactions.

**53 Real Estate and Rental and Leasing**—Activities of this sector are renting, leasing, or otherwise allowing the use of tangible or intangible assets (except copyrighted works), and providing related services.

**54 Professional, Scientific, and Technical Services**—Activities of this sector are performing professional, scientific, and technical services for the operations of other organizations.

**55 Management of Companies and Enterprises**—Activities of this sector are the holding of securities of companies and enterprises, for the purpose of owning controlling interest or influencing their management decisions, or administering, overseeing, and managing other establishments of the same company or enterprise and normally undertaking the strategic or organizational planning and decision-making role of the company or enterprise.

**56 Administrative and Support and Waste Management and Remediation Services**—Activities of this sector are performing routine support activities for the day-to-day operations of other organizations.

**61 Educational Services**—Activities of this sector are providing instruction and training in a wide variety of subjects.

**62 Health Care and Social Assistance**—Activities of this sector are providing health care and social assistance for individuals.

**71 Arts, Entertainment, and Recreation**—Activities of this sector are operating or providing services to meet varied cultural, entertainment, and recreational interests of their patrons.

**72 Accommodation and Food Services**—Activities of this sector are providing customers with lodging and/or preparing meals, snacks, and beverages for immediate consumption.

**81 Other Services (except Public Administration)**—Activities of this sector are providing services not elsewhere specified, including repairs, religious activities, grantmaking, advocacy, laundry, personal care, death care, and other personal services.

**92 Public Administration**—Activities of this sector are administration, management, and oversight of public programs by Federal, State, and local governments.

NAICS uses a six-digit coding system to identify industries and their placement in this hierarchical structure of the classification system. The first two digits of the code designate the sector, the third digit designates the subsector, the fourth digit designates the industry group, the fifth digit designates the NAICS industry, and the sixth digit designates the national industry. A zero as the sixth digit generally indicates that the NAICS industry and the U.S. industry are the same.

The subsectors, industry groups, and NAICS industries, in accord with the conceptual principle of NAICS, are production-oriented combinations of establishments. However, the production distinctions become more narrowly defined as one moves down the hierarchy.

NAICS agreements permit each country to designate detailed industries, below the level of a NAICS industry, to meet national needs. The United States has such industry detail in many places in the classification system to recognize large, important U.S. industries that cannot be recognized in the other countries because of size, specialization, or organization of the industry.

Typically the level at which comparable data will be available for Canada, Mexico, and the United States is the five-digit NAICS industry; for some sectors (or subsectors or industry groups) however, the three countries agreed upon the boundaries at a higher level of detail rather than the detailed industry structure (five-digit). NAICS with U.S. detail is known as NAICS United States, while Canada and Mexico produce six-digit detail and publish that detail as NAICS Canada and NAICS (SCIAN in Spanish) Mexico.

## Definition of an Establishment

NAICS is a classification system for establishments. The establishment as a statistical unit is defined as the smallest operating entity for which records provide information on the cost of resources—materials, labor, and capital—employed to produce the units of output. The output may be sold to other establishments and receipts or sales recorded, or the output may be provided without explicit charge, that is, the good or service may be "sold" within the company itself.

The establishment, in NAICS United States, is generally a single physical location where business is conducted or where services or industrial operations are performed (for example, a factory, mill, store, hotel, movie theater, mine, farm, airline terminal, sales office, warehouse, or central administrative office). There are cases where records identify distinct and separate economic activities performed at a single physical location (e.g., shops in a hotel). These retailing activities, operated out of the same physical location as the hotel, are identified as separate establishments and classified in the Retail Trade sector, while the hotel is classified in the Accommodation subsector. In such cases, each activity is treated as a separate establishment provided: (1) no one industry description in the classification includes such combined activities; (2) separate reports can be prepared on the number of employees, their wages and salaries, sales or receipts, and expenses; and (3) employment and output are significant for both activities.

Exceptions to the single location exist for physically dispersed operations, such as construction, transportation, and telecommunications. For these activities the individual sites, projects, fields, networks, lines, or systems of such dispersed activities are not normally considered to be establishments. The establishment is represented by those relatively permanent main or branch offices, terminals, stations, and so forth, that are either (1) directly responsible for supervising such activities, or (2) the base from which personnel operate to carry out these activities.

Although an establishment may be identical with the enterprise (company), the two terms should not be confused. An enterprise (company) may consist of more than one establishment. Such multiunit enterprises may have establishments in more than one industry in NAICS. If such enterprises have a separate establishment primarily engaged in providing headquarters services, that establishment is classified in Sector 55, Management of Companies and Enterprises.

Although all establishments have output, they may or may not have receipts. In large enterprises, it is not unusual for establishments to exist to solely serve other establishments of the same enterprise (auxiliary, or enterprise support, establishments). In such cases, these units often do not collect receipts from the establishments they serve. This type of support (captive) activity is found throughout the economy and involves goods-producing activities as well as services. Units that carry out support activities for the enterprise to which they belong are classified, to the extent feasible, according to the NAICS code related to their own activity. This means that warehouses providing storage facilities for their own enterprise are classified as warehouses. For certain analytical purposes, an alternative code may be assigned corresponding to the activity of the enterprise that they support.

## Determining an Establishment's Industry Classification

An establishment is classified in an industry when its primary activity meets the definition for that industry. Because establishments may perform more than one activity, it is necessary to determine procedures for identifying the primary activity of the establishment.

In most cases, if an establishment is engaged in more than one activity, the industry code is assigned based on the establishment's principal product or group of products produced or distributed, or services rendered. Ideally, the principal good or service should be determined by its relative share of current production costs and capital investment at the establishment. In practice, however, it is often necessary to use other variables such as revenue, shipments, or employment as proxies for measuring significance.

There are two types of combined activities that are given special attention in NAICS. They are vertical integration and joint production. These combined activities have an economic basis and occur in both goods-producing and services-producing sectors. In some cases, there are efficiencies to be gained from combining certain activities in the same establishment. Some of these combinations occur so commonly or frequently that the combination can be treated as a third activity in its own right and explicitly classified in a specific industry.

Vertical integration involves consecutive stages of fabrication or production processes in which the output of one step is the input of the next. In general, establishments are classified based on the final process in a vertically integrated production environment, unless specifically identified as classified in another industry. For example, paper may be produced either by establishments that first produce pulp and then consume that pulp to produce paper or by those establishments producing paper from purchased pulp. NAICS explicitly specifies that both of these types of paper-producing processes should be classified in NAICS 32212, Paper Mills, the final step in paper manufacturing, rather than in NAICS 32211, Pulp Mills. In other cases, NAICS specifies that vertically integrated establishments are classified in the industry representing the first stage of the manufacturing process. For example, steel mills that make steel and also perform other activities such as producing steel castings are classified in NAICS 33111, Iron and Steel Mills and Ferroalloy Manufacturing, the first stage of the manufacturing process.

The joint production of goods or services represents the second type of combined activities. For example, automobile dealers both sell and repair automobiles; automotive parts dealers may both sell parts and repair automobiles; and musical instrument stores may both sell and rent instruments. In the Manufacturing sector, establishments may make two different products such as medical and dental supplies, activities that are classified in two different NAICS United States detailed industries. In general, receipts/sales and revenue data are used as a proxy to determine primary activity for these establishments. The assumption is that the activity generating the most receipts is also the activity using the most resources and most indicative of the production process.

In some cases, however, these combined activities have been assigned to a specific NAICS industry. Most of these activities involve either the sale and repair of goods or the sale and rental of goods in the same establishment. For example, establishments that both sell automobile parts and repair automobiles are classified in NAICS 44133, Automotive Parts and Accessories Retailers, and music stores that both sell and rent musical instruments are classified in NAICS 45914, Musical Instrument and Supplies Retailers. In other cases, specific industries identify combined activities, such as NAICS 45711, Gasoline Stations with Convenience Stores.

Classification rules related to the agreement to permit individual country detail at the six-digit level for NAICS sometimes result in less comparable NAICS industries at the five-digit level and above. For example in NAICS, the assignment of the industry code is at the most detailed level of the classification (the six-digit U.S. detail code), except for Agriculture. That is, if the value of an establishment's production consists of 30 percent from computers, 30 percent from computer storage devices, and 40 percent from semiconductors and related devices, it is classified in U.S. detail industry 334413, Semiconductor and Related Device Manufacturing, that is aggregated to NAICS 33441, Semiconductor and Other Electronic Component Manufacturing, the level that comparable information is shown for all three countries. If the classification for the above example were at the five-digit NAICS level, that establishment would be classified in NAICS 33411, Computer and Peripheral Equipment Manufacturing. There would then be more comparable information at the NAICS level, but it would be impossible to classify this establishment to a six-digit U.S. detail industry.

In Agriculture, however, NAICS coding begins at the top of the structure and continues down to the most detailed level (the six-digit U.S. detail code). The presence of combination industries based on families of related agricultural products with none accounting for 50 percent or more of production requires a top down coding procedure rather than coding at the most detailed level first as is done in the balance of the classification.

## Use of Reporting Units Other than Establishments

NAICS is based on the economic principle that establishments should be grouped together based on their production processes. The NAICS definition of the establishment ensures that, at some level, "establishments": (1) identify the most refined (generally smallest) individual entity possible; (2) can provide the information needed when surveying economic activity; and (3) when aggregated, approximate the statistical universe of economic activity. Each economic survey program, in practice, determines whether the establishment is the most appropriate reporting unit to meet the three criteria listed above with respect to the program's objectives. If not, an alternative reporting unit is identified.

For example, an economic survey of employment or wage data may choose the establishment—generally a physical location—as the reporting unit. Physical locations generally have records for the number of employees and their wages readily available. Therefore, it is reasonable to expect that separate wage and employment data are available for each switching station in a multiunit telecommunications carrier enterprise, and the physical location is a logical choice for the reporting unit.

If the economic survey collects output data, the individual switching stations would not have the total number of telephone calls or a complete accounting of inputs and outputs of the multiunit telecommunications carrier. If a telephone call is routed through three different switching stations and the price is determined at a fourth location, all of the related locations would need to be merged into an alternative reporting unit to measure the volume and value of the output. In this case, the physical location is not an appropriate reporting unit. The level of aggregation of physical units required to create reporting units will vary greatly depending on the business activity being studied. To efficiently define reporting units, statistical surveys need to evaluate the characteristics of the activities being studied and the organizational structure of the entities producing goods or services. In some cases, the physical location is appropriate, sometimes units will need to be grouped based on homogeneous production characteristics or geographical groupings, and in other cases, the enterprise (company) may form the most appropriate reporting unit.

The practical variation in reporting unit definitions affects comparability of data. A count of units defined as physical locations will be different from a count of units defined based on the need for complete input and output records in the telecommunications industries. It is critical that each data provider clearly identify the reporting unit definition used when presenting summary statistics. The analysis of statistical data from a variety of sources requires the transparency of clearly defined reporting units.

While the reporting unit definition can vary, NAICS is a classification system for establishments and is based on grouping establishments with similar production function characteristics.

## Comparison of NAICS to the International Standard Industrial Classification of All Economic Activities (ISIC)

Recognizing the need for international comparability of economic statistics, the United Nations (UN) first adopted an International Standard Industrial Classification system in 1948. Revisions to the ISIC structure and codes were adopted by the UN's Statistical Commission in 1958, 1968, 1989, 2002, and 2007.[2]

Similar to NAICS, ISIC was designed primarily to provide classifications for grouping activities (rather than enterprises or firms), and the primary focus for the ISIC classification system is the kind

---

[2] International Standard Industrial Classification of All Economic Activities, Statistical Papers, Series M, No. 4, Rev. 4, United Nations, New York, 2008.

of activity in which establishments or other statistical entities are engaged. The main criteria employed in delineating Divisions and Groups (the two- and three-digit categories, respectively) of ISIC are: (a) the character of the goods and services produced; (b) the uses to which the goods and services are put; and (c) the inputs, the process, and the technology of production.

The third classification criterion of the ISIC is the conceptual foundation of NAICS. However, there are differences between the NAICS and ISIC classification schemes. Most important, perhaps, is the single (production process) conceptual framework of NAICS. As noted elsewhere, this is unique among industry classifications.

ISIC, Rev. 4, groups economic activity into 21 Sections, 88 Divisions, 238 Groups, and 420 Classes. In the coding system, Sections are distinguished by the letters A through U, and the Divisions, Groups, and Classes are identified as the two-digit, three-digit, and four-digit groupings, respectively. In the development and subsequent revisions of NAICS industries, the three countries strove to create industries that did not cross ISIC two-digit Division boundaries.

# 2022 NAICS United States Structure

The following page contains a summary table of the 2022 NAICS United States structure. This table shows the counts of subsectors, industry groups, industries, and United States detail industries for each of the NAICS sectors.

Following the summary table is a complete listing of the 2022 NAICS United States structure. This list displays the codes and official full titles for the sectors, subsectors, industry groups, industries, and United States detail industries. A "T" superscript on the title indicates a level at which Canada, Mexico, and the United States formally agreed to maintain comparability. Detail below that level may or may not be comparable to detail for one or both of the other countries.

# 2022 NAICS United States Structure

| Sector | Name | Subsectors (3-digit) | Industry Groups (4-digit) | NAICS Industries (5-digit) | 6-digit Industries | | |
|--------|------|---------------------|---------------------------|----------------------------|-------------------|---|---|
| | | | | | U.S. Detail | Same as 5-digit | Total |
| 11 | Agriculture, Forestry, Fishing and Hunting | 5 | 19 | 42 | 32 | 32 | 64 |
| 21 | Mining, Quarrying, and Oil and Gas Extraction | 3 | 5 | 11 | 14 | 7 | 21 |
| 22 | Utilities | 1 | 3 | 6 | 10 | 4 | 14 |
| 23 | Construction | 3 | 10 | 28 | 4 | 27 | 31 |
| 31-33 | Manufacturing | 21 | 86 | 176 | 249 | 97 | 346 |
| 42 | Wholesale Trade | 3 | 19 | 69 | 0 | 69 | 69 |
| 44-45 | Retail Trade | 9 | 24 | 48 | 16 | 41 | 57 |
| 48-49 | Transportation and Warehousing | 11 | 29 | 42 | 25 | 32 | 57 |
| 51 | Information | 6 | 11 | 24 | 10 | 19 | 29 |
| 52 | Finance and Insurance | 5 | 11 | 27 | 13 | 22 | 35 |
| 53 | Real Estate and Rental and Leasing | 3 | 8 | 17 | 11 | 13 | 24 |
| 54 | Professional, Scientific, and Technical Services | 1 | 9 | 35 | 20 | 29 | 49 |
| 55 | Management of Companies and Enterprises | 1 | 1 | 1 | 3 | 0 | 3 |
| 56 | Administrative and Support and Waste Management and Remediation Services | 2 | 11 | 29 | 25 | 19 | 44 |
| 61 | Educational Services | 1 | 7 | 12 | 7 | 10 | 17 |
| 62 | Health Care and Social Assistance | 4 | 18 | 30 | 16 | 23 | 39 |
| 71 | Arts, Entertainment, and Recreation | 3 | 9 | 23 | 3 | 22 | 25 |
| 72 | Accommodation and Food Services | 2 | 6 | 10 | 8 | 7 | 15 |
| 81 | Other Services (except Public Administration) | 4 | 14 | 30 | 24 | 20 | 44 |
| 92 | Public Administration | 8 | 8 | 29 | 0 | 29 | 29 |
| | **Total** | **96** | **308** | **689** | **490** | **522** | **1012** |

# Sector 11--Agriculture, Forestry, Fishing and Hunting[T]

## 111 Crop Production[T]

### 1111 Oilseed and Grain Farming[T]
11111 Soybean Farming[T]
111110 Soybean Farming
11112 Oilseed (except Soybean) Farming[T]
111120 Oilseed (except Soybean) Farming
11113 Dry Pea and Bean Farming[T]
111130 Dry Pea and Bean Farming
11114 Wheat Farming[T]
111140 Wheat Farming
11115 Corn Farming[T]
111150 Corn Farming
11116 Rice Farming[T]
111160 Rice Farming
11119 Other Grain Farming[T]
111191 Oilseed and Grain Combination Farming
111199 All Other Grain Farming

### 1112 Vegetable and Melon Farming[T]
11121 Vegetable and Melon Farming[T]
111211 Potato Farming
111219 Other Vegetable (except Potato) and Melon Farming

### 1113 Fruit and Tree Nut Farming[T]
11131 Orange Groves[T]
111310 Orange Groves
11132 Citrus (except Orange) Groves[T]
111320 Citrus (except Orange) Groves
11133 Noncitrus Fruit and Tree Nut Farming[T]
111331 Apple Orchards
111332 Grape Vineyards
111333 Strawberry Farming
111334 Berry (except Strawberry) Farming
111335 Tree Nut Farming
111336 Fruit and Tree Nut Combination Farming
111339 Other Noncitrus Fruit Farming

### 1114 Greenhouse, Nursery, and Floriculture Production[T]
11141 Food Crops Grown Under Cover[T]
111411 Mushroom Production
111419 Other Food Crops Grown Under Cover
11142 Nursery and Floriculture Production[T]
111421 Nursery and Tree Production
111422 Floriculture Production

### 1119 Other Crop Farming[T]
11191 Tobacco Farming[T]
111910 Tobacco Farming
11192 Cotton Farming[T]
111920 Cotton Farming
11193 Sugarcane Farming[T]
111930 Sugarcane Farming

11194   Hay Farming$^T$
111940  Hay Farming
11199   All Other Crop Farming$^T$
111991  Sugar Beet Farming
111992  Peanut Farming
111998  All Other Miscellaneous Crop Farming

## 112   Animal Production and Aquaculture$^T$

### 1121   Cattle Ranching and Farming$^T$
11211   Beef Cattle Ranching and Farming, including Feedlots$^T$
112111  Beef Cattle Ranching and Farming
112112  Cattle Feedlots
11212   Dairy Cattle and Milk Production$^T$
112120  Dairy Cattle and Milk Production
11213   Dual-Purpose Cattle Ranching and Farming$^T$
112130  Dual-Purpose Cattle Ranching and Farming

### 1122   Hog and Pig Farming$^T$
11221   Hog and Pig Farming$^T$
112210  Hog and Pig Farming

### 1123   Poultry and Egg Production$^T$
11231   Chicken Egg Production$^T$
112310  Chicken Egg Production
11232   Broilers and Other Meat Type Chicken Production$^T$
112320  Broilers and Other Meat Type Chicken Production
11233   Turkey Production$^T$
112330  Turkey Production
11234   Poultry Hatcheries$^T$
112340  Poultry Hatcheries
11239   Other Poultry Production$^T$
112390  Other Poultry Production

### 1124   Sheep and Goat Farming$^T$
11241   Sheep Farming$^T$
112410  Sheep Farming
11242   Goat Farming$^T$
112420  Goat Farming

### 1125   Aquaculture$^T$
11251   Aquaculture$^T$
112511  Finfish Farming and Fish Hatcheries
112512  Shellfish Farming
112519  Other Aquaculture

### 1129   Other Animal Production$^T$
11291   Apiculture$^T$
112910  Apiculture
11292   Horses and Other Equine Production$^T$
112920  Horses and Other Equine Production
11293   Fur-Bearing Animal and Rabbit Production$^T$
112930  Fur-Bearing Animal and Rabbit Production
11299   All Other Animal Production$^T$
112990  All Other Animal Production

**113**     **Forestry and Logging**[T]

    **1131**     **Timber Tract Operations**[T]
       11311   Timber Tract Operations[T]
       113110   Timber Tract Operations

    **1132**     **Forest Nurseries and Gathering of Forest Products**[T]
       11321   Forest Nurseries and Gathering of Forest Products[T]
       113210   Forest Nurseries and Gathering of Forest Products

    **1133**     **Logging**[T]
       11331   Logging[T]
       113310   Logging

**114**     **Fishing, Hunting and Trapping**[T]

    **1141**     **Fishing**[T]
       11411   Fishing[T]
       114111   Finfish Fishing
       114112   Shellfish Fishing
       114119   Other Marine Fishing

    **1142**     **Hunting and Trapping**[T]
       11421   Hunting and Trapping[T]
       114210   Hunting and Trapping

**115**     **Support Activities for Agriculture and Forestry**[T]

    **1151**     **Support Activities for Crop Production**[T]
       11511   Support Activities for Crop Production[T]
       115111   Cotton Ginning
       115112   Soil Preparation, Planting, and Cultivating
       115113   Crop Harvesting, Primarily by Machine
       115114   Postharvest Crop Activities (except Cotton Ginning)
       115115   Farm Labor Contractors and Crew Leaders
       115116   Farm Management Services

    **1152**     **Support Activities for Animal Production**[T]
       11521   Support Activities for Animal Production[T]
       115210   Support Activities for Animal Production

    **1153**     **Support Activities for Forestry**[T]
       11531   Support Activities for Forestry[T]
       115310   Support Activities for Forestry

# Sector 21--Mining, Quarrying, and Oil and Gas Extraction[T]

**211**     **Oil and Gas Extraction**[T]

    **2111**     **Oil and Gas Extraction**[T]
       21112   Crude Petroleum Extraction
       211120   Crude Petroleum Extraction
       21113   Natural Gas Extraction
       211130   Natural Gas Extraction

## 212          Mining (except Oil and Gas)<sup>T</sup>

### 2121     Coal Mining<sup>T</sup>
21211    Coal Mining<sup>T</sup>
212114   Surface Coal Mining
212115   Underground Coal Mining

### 2122     Metal Ore Mining<sup>T</sup>
21221    Iron Ore Mining<sup>T</sup>
212210   Iron Ore Mining
21222    Gold Ore and Silver Ore Mining<sup>T</sup>
212220   Gold Ore and Silver Ore Mining
21223    Copper, Nickel, Lead, and Zinc Mining<sup>T</sup>
212230   Copper, Nickel, Lead, and Zinc Mining
21229    Other Metal Ore Mining<sup>T</sup>
212290   Other Metal Ore Mining

### 2123     Nonmetallic Mineral Mining and Quarrying<sup>T</sup>
21231    Stone Mining and Quarrying<sup>T</sup>
212311   Dimension Stone Mining and Quarrying
212312   Crushed and Broken Limestone Mining and Quarrying
212313   Crushed and Broken Granite Mining and Quarrying
212319   Other Crushed and Broken Stone Mining and Quarrying
21232    Sand, Gravel, Clay, and Ceramic and Refractory Minerals Mining and Quarrying<sup>T</sup>
212321   Construction Sand and Gravel Mining
212322   Industrial Sand Mining
212323   Kaolin, Clay, and Ceramic and Refractory Minerals Mining
21239    Other Nonmetallic Mineral Mining and Quarrying<sup>T</sup>
212390   Other Nonmetallic Mineral Mining and Quarrying

## 213          Support Activities for Mining<sup>T</sup>

### 2131     Support Activities for Mining<sup>T</sup>
21311    Support Activities for Mining<sup>T</sup>
213111   Drilling Oil and Gas Wells
213112   Support Activities for Oil and Gas Operations
213113   Support Activities for Coal Mining
213114   Support Activities for Metal Mining
213115   Support Activities for Nonmetallic Minerals (except Fuels) Mining

# Sector 22--Utilities<sup>T</sup>

## 221          Utilities<sup>T</sup>

### 2211     Electric Power Generation, Transmission and Distribution<sup>T</sup>
22111    Electric Power Generation<sup>T</sup>
221111   Hydroelectric Power Generation
221112   Fossil Fuel Electric Power Generation
221113   Nuclear Electric Power Generation
221114   Solar Electric Power Generation
221115   Wind Electric Power Generation
221116   Geothermal Electric Power Generation
221117   Biomass Electric Power Generation

    221118  Other Electric Power Generation
    22112   Electric Power Transmission, Control, and Distribution$^T$
    221121  Electric Bulk Power Transmission and Control
    221122  Electric Power Distribution

2212    **Natural Gas Distribution$^T$**
    22121   Natural Gas Distribution$^T$
    221210  Natural Gas Distribution

2213    **Water, Sewage and Other Systems$^T$**
    22131   Water Supply and Irrigation Systems
    221310  Water Supply and Irrigation Systems
    22132   Sewage Treatment Facilities
    221320  Sewage Treatment Facilities
    22133   Steam and Air-Conditioning Supply
    221330  Steam and Air-Conditioning Supply

# Sector 23--Construction$^T$

## 236    Construction of Buildings$^T$

2361    **Residential Building Construction$^T$**
    23611   Residential Building Construction$^T$
    236115  New Single-Family Housing Construction (except For-Sale Builders)
    236116  New Multifamily Housing Construction (except For-Sale Builders)
    236117  New Housing For-Sale Builders
    236118  Residential Remodelers

2362    **Nonresidential Building Construction$^T$**
    23621   Industrial Building Construction$^T$
    236210  Industrial Building Construction
    23622   Commercial and Institutional Building Construction$^T$
    236220  Commercial and Institutional Building Construction

## 237    Heavy and Civil Engineering Construction$^T$

2371    **Utility System Construction$^T$**
    23711   Water and Sewer Line and Related Structures Construction$^T$
    237110  Water and Sewer Line and Related Structures Construction
    23712   Oil and Gas Pipeline and Related Structures Construction$^T$
    237120  Oil and Gas Pipeline and Related Structures Construction
    23713   Power and Communication Line and Related Structures Construction$^T$
    237130  Power and Communication Line and Related Structures Construction

2372    **Land Subdivision$^T$**
    23721   Land Subdivision$^T$
    237210  Land Subdivision

2373    **Highway, Street, and Bridge Construction$^T$**
    23731   Highway, Street, and Bridge Construction$^T$
    237310  Highway, Street, and Bridge Construction

2379    **Other Heavy and Civil Engineering Construction$^T$**
    23799   Other Heavy and Civil Engineering Construction$^T$
    237990  Other Heavy and Civil Engineering Construction

**238          Specialty Trade Contractors[T]**

> **2381          Foundation, Structure, and Building Exterior Contractors[T]**
> 23811     Poured Concrete Foundation and Structure Contractors
> 238110   Poured Concrete Foundation and Structure Contractors
> 23812     Structural Steel and Precast Concrete Contractors
> 238120   Structural Steel and Precast Concrete Contractors
> 23813     Framing Contractors
> 238130   Framing Contractors
> 23814     Masonry Contractors
> 238140   Masonry Contractors
> 23815     Glass and Glazing Contractors
> 238150   Glass and Glazing Contractors
> 23816     Roofing Contractors
> 238160   Roofing Contractors
> 23817     Siding Contractors
> 238170   Siding Contractors
> 23819     Other Foundation, Structure, and Building Exterior Contractors
> 238190   Other Foundation, Structure, and Building Exterior Contractors

> **2382          Building Equipment Contractors[T]**
> 23821     Electrical Contractors and Other Wiring Installation Contractors[T]
> 238210   Electrical Contractors and Other Wiring Installation Contractors
> 23822     Plumbing, Heating, and Air-Conditioning Contractors[T]
> 238220   Plumbing, Heating, and Air-Conditioning Contractors
> 23829     Other Building Equipment Contractors[T]
> 238290   Other Building Equipment Contractors

> **2383          Building Finishing Contractors[T]**
> 23831     Drywall and Insulation Contractors[T]
> 238310   Drywall and Insulation Contractors
> 23832     Painting and Wall Covering Contractors[T]
> 238320   Painting and Wall Covering Contractors
> 23833     Flooring Contractors[T]
> 238330   Flooring Contractors
> 23834     Tile and Terrazzo Contractors[T]
> 238340   Tile and Terrazzo Contractors
> 23835     Finish Carpentry Contractors[T]
> 238350   Finish Carpentry Contractors
> 23839     Other Building Finishing Contractors[T]
> 238390   Other Building Finishing Contractors

> **2389          Other Specialty Trade Contractors[T]**
> 23891     Site Preparation Contractors[T]
> 238910   Site Preparation Contractors
> 23899     All Other Specialty Trade Contractors[T]
> 238990   All Other Specialty Trade Contractors

# Sector 31-33--Manufacturing[T]

**311          Food Manufacturing[T]**

> **3111          Animal Food Manufacturing[T]**
> 31111     Animal Food Manufacturing[T]

311111  Dog and Cat Food Manufacturing
311119  Other Animal Food Manufacturing

**3112    Grain and Oilseed Milling**[T]
  31121   Flour Milling and Malt Manufacturing[T]
  311211  Flour Milling
  311212  Rice Milling
  311213  Malt Manufacturing
  31122   Starch and Vegetable Fats and Oils Manufacturing[T]
  311221  Wet Corn Milling and Starch Manufacturing
  311224  Soybean and Other Oilseed Processing
  311225  Fats and Oils Refining and Blending
  31123   Breakfast Cereal Manufacturing[T]
  311230  Breakfast Cereal Manufacturing

**3113    Sugar and Confectionery Product Manufacturing**[T]
  31131   Sugar Manufacturing[T]
  311313  Beet Sugar Manufacturing
  311314  Cane Sugar Manufacturing
  31134   Nonchocolate Confectionery Manufacturing[T]
  311340  Nonchocolate Confectionery Manufacturing
  31135   Chocolate and Confectionery Manufacturing[T]
  311351  Chocolate and Confectionery Manufacturing from Cacao Beans
  311352  Confectionery Manufacturing from Purchased Chocolate

**3114    Fruit and Vegetable Preserving and Specialty Food Manufacturing**[T]
  31141   Frozen Food Manufacturing[T]
  311411  Frozen Fruit, Juice, and Vegetable Manufacturing
  311412  Frozen Specialty Food Manufacturing
  31142   Fruit and Vegetable Canning, Pickling, and Drying[T]
  311421  Fruit and Vegetable Canning
  311422  Specialty Canning
  311423  Dried and Dehydrated Food Manufacturing

**3115    Dairy Product Manufacturing**[T]
  31151   Dairy Product (except Frozen) Manufacturing[T]
  311511  Fluid Milk Manufacturing
  311512  Creamery Butter Manufacturing
  311513  Cheese Manufacturing
  311514  Dry, Condensed, and Evaporated Dairy Product Manufacturing
  31152   Ice Cream and Frozen Dessert Manufacturing[T]
  311520  Ice Cream and Frozen Dessert Manufacturing

**3116    Animal Slaughtering and Processing**[T]
  31161   Animal Slaughtering and Processing[T]
  311611  Animal (except Poultry) Slaughtering
  311612  Meat Processed from Carcasses
  311613  Rendering and Meat Byproduct Processing
  311615  Poultry Processing

**3117    Seafood Product Preparation and Packaging**[T]
  31171   Seafood Product Preparation and Packaging[T]
  311710  Seafood Product Preparation and Packaging

**3118    Bakeries and Tortilla Manufacturing**[T]
  31181   Bread and Bakery Product Manufacturing[T]

311811  Retail Bakeries
311812  Commercial Bakeries
311813  Frozen Cakes, Pies, and Other Pastries Manufacturing
31182   Cookie, Cracker, and Pasta Manufacturing[T]
311821  Cookie and Cracker Manufacturing
311824  Dry Pasta, Dough, and Flour Mixes Manufacturing from Purchased Flour
31183   Tortilla Manufacturing[T]
311830  Tortilla Manufacturing

**3119    Other Food Manufacturing[T]**
31191   Snack Food Manufacturing[T]
311911  Roasted Nuts and Peanut Butter Manufacturing
311919  Other Snack Food Manufacturing
31192   Coffee and Tea Manufacturing[T]
311920  Coffee and Tea Manufacturing
31193   Flavoring Syrup and Concentrate Manufacturing[T]
311930  Flavoring Syrup and Concentrate Manufacturing
31194   Seasoning and Dressing Manufacturing[T]
311941  Mayonnaise, Dressing, and Other Prepared Sauce Manufacturing
311942  Spice and Extract Manufacturing
31199   All Other Food Manufacturing[T]
311991  Perishable Prepared Food Manufacturing
311999  All Other Miscellaneous Food Manufacturing

# 312    Beverage and Tobacco Product Manufacturing[T]

**3121    Beverage Manufacturing[T]**
31211   Soft Drink and Ice Manufacturing[T]
312111  Soft Drink Manufacturing
312112  Bottled Water Manufacturing
312113  Ice Manufacturing
31212   Breweries[T]
312120  Breweries
31213   Wineries[T]
312130  Wineries
31214   Distilleries[T]
312140  Distilleries

**3122    Tobacco Manufacturing[T]**
31223   Tobacco Manufacturing
312230  Tobacco Manufacturing

# 313    Textile Mills[T]

**3131    Fiber, Yarn, and Thread Mills[T]**
31311   Fiber, Yarn, and Thread Mills[T]
313110  Fiber, Yarn, and Thread Mills

**3132    Fabric Mills[T]**
31321   Broadwoven Fabric Mills[T]
313210  Broadwoven Fabric Mills
31322   Narrow Fabric Mills and Schiffli Machine Embroidery[T]
313220  Narrow Fabric Mills and Schiffli Machine Embroidery
31323   Nonwoven Fabric Mills[T]
313230  Nonwoven Fabric Mills

31324   Knit Fabric Mills[T]
313240  Knit Fabric Mills

**3133    Textile and Fabric Finishing and Fabric Coating Mills[T]**
31331   Textile and Fabric Finishing Mills[T]
313310  Textile and Fabric Finishing Mills
31332   Fabric Coating Mills[T]
313320  Fabric Coating Mills

# 314    Textile Product Mills[T]

**3141    Textile Furnishings Mills[T]**
31411   Carpet and Rug Mills[T]
314110  Carpet and Rug Mills
31412   Curtain and Linen Mills[T]
314120  Curtain and Linen Mills

**3149    Other Textile Product Mills[T]**
31491   Textile Bag and Canvas Mills[T]
314910  Textile Bag and Canvas Mills
31499   All Other Textile Product Mills[T]
314994  Rope, Cordage, Twine, Tire Cord, and Tire Fabric Mills
314999  All Other Miscellaneous Textile Product Mills

# 315    Apparel Manufacturing[T]

**3151    Apparel Knitting Mills[T]**
31512   Apparel Knitting Mills[T]
315120  Apparel Knitting Mills

**3152    Cut and Sew Apparel Manufacturing[T]**
31521   Cut and Sew Apparel Contractors
315210  Cut and Sew Apparel Contractors
31525   Cut and Sew Apparel Manufacturing (except Contractors)
315250  Cut and Sew Apparel Manufacturing (except Contractors)

**3159    Apparel Accessories and Other Apparel Manufacturing[T]**
31599   Apparel Accessories and Other Apparel Manufacturing[T]
315990  Apparel Accessories and Other Apparel Manufacturing

# 316    Leather and Allied Product Manufacturing[T]

**3161    Leather and Hide Tanning and Finishing[T]**
31611   Leather and Hide Tanning and Finishing[T]
316110  Leather and Hide Tanning and Finishing

**3162    Footwear Manufacturing[T]**
31621   Footwear Manufacturing[T]
316210  Footwear Manufacturing

**3169    Other Leather and Allied Product Manufacturing[T]**
31699   Other Leather and Allied Product Manufacturing[T]
316990  Other Leather and Allied Product Manufacturing

## 321     Wood Product Manufacturing[T]

### 3211     Sawmills and Wood Preservation[T]
32111    Sawmills and Wood Preservation[T]
321113   Sawmills
321114   Wood Preservation

### 3212     Veneer, Plywood, and Engineered Wood Product Manufacturing[T]
32121    Veneer, Plywood, and Engineered Wood Product Manufacturing[T]
321211   Hardwood Veneer and Plywood Manufacturing
321212   Softwood Veneer and Plywood Manufacturing
321215   Engineered Wood Member Manufacturing
321219   Reconstituted Wood Product Manufacturing

### 3219     Other Wood Product Manufacturing[T]
32191    Millwork[T]
321911   Wood Window and Door Manufacturing
321912   Cut Stock, Resawing Lumber, and Planing
321918   Other Millwork (including Flooring)
32192    Wood Container and Pallet Manufacturing[T]
321920   Wood Container and Pallet Manufacturing
32199    All Other Wood Product Manufacturing[T]
321991   Manufactured Home (Mobile Home) Manufacturing
321992   Prefabricated Wood Building Manufacturing
321999   All Other Miscellaneous Wood Product Manufacturing

## 322     Paper Manufacturing[T]

### 3221     Pulp, Paper, and Paperboard Mills[T]
32211    Pulp Mills[T]
322110   Pulp Mills
32212    Paper Mills[T]
322120   Paper Mills
32213    Paperboard Mills[T]
322130   Paperboard Mills

### 3222     Converted Paper Product Manufacturing[T]
32221    Paperboard Container Manufacturing[T]
322211   Corrugated and Solid Fiber Box Manufacturing
322212   Folding Paperboard Box Manufacturing
322219   Other Paperboard Container Manufacturing
32222    Paper Bag and Coated and Treated Paper Manufacturing[T]
322220   Paper Bag and Coated and Treated Paper Manufacturing
32223    Stationery Product Manufacturing[T]
322230   Stationery Product Manufacturing
32229    Other Converted Paper Product Manufacturing[T]
322291   Sanitary Paper Product Manufacturing
322299   All Other Converted Paper Product Manufacturing

## 323     Printing and Related Support Activities[T]

### 3231     Printing and Related Support Activities[T]
32311    Printing[T]
323111   Commercial Printing (except Screen and Books)
323113   Commercial Screen Printing

323117  Books Printing
32312   Support Activities for Printing<sup>T</sup>
323120  Support Activities for Printing

# 324     Petroleum and Coal Products Manufacturing<sup>T</sup>

## 3241    Petroleum and Coal Products Manufacturing<sup>T</sup>
32411   Petroleum Refineries<sup>T</sup>
324110  Petroleum Refineries
32412   Asphalt Paving, Roofing, and Saturated Materials Manufacturing<sup>T</sup>
324121  Asphalt Paving Mixture and Block Manufacturing
324122  Asphalt Shingle and Coating Materials Manufacturing
32419   Other Petroleum and Coal Products Manufacturing<sup>T</sup>
324191  Petroleum Lubricating Oil and Grease Manufacturing
324199  All Other Petroleum and Coal Products Manufacturing

# 325     Chemical Manufacturing<sup>T</sup>

## 3251    Basic Chemical Manufacturing<sup>T</sup>
32511   Petrochemical Manufacturing<sup>T</sup>
325110  Petrochemical Manufacturing
32512   Industrial Gas Manufacturing<sup>T</sup>
325120  Industrial Gas Manufacturing
32513   Synthetic Dye and Pigment Manufacturing<sup>T</sup>
325130  Synthetic Dye and Pigment Manufacturing
32518   Other Basic Inorganic Chemical Manufacturing<sup>T</sup>
325180  Other Basic Inorganic Chemical Manufacturing
32519   Other Basic Organic Chemical Manufacturing<sup>T</sup>
325193  Ethyl Alcohol Manufacturing
325194  Cyclic Crude, Intermediate, and Gum and Wood Chemical Manufacturing
325199  All Other Basic Organic Chemical Manufacturing

## 3252    Resin, Synthetic Rubber, and Artificial and Synthetic Fibers and Filaments Manufacturing<sup>T</sup>
32521   Resin and Synthetic Rubber Manufacturing<sup>T</sup>
325211  Plastics Material and Resin Manufacturing
325212  Synthetic Rubber Manufacturing
32522   Artificial and Synthetic Fibers and Filaments Manufacturing<sup>T</sup>
325220  Artificial and Synthetic Fibers and Filaments Manufacturing

## 3253    Pesticide, Fertilizer, and Other Agricultural Chemical Manufacturing<sup>T</sup>
32531   Fertilizer and Compost Manufacturing<sup>T</sup>
325311  Nitrogenous Fertilizer Manufacturing
325312  Phosphatic Fertilizer Manufacturing
325314  Fertilizer (Mixing Only) Manufacturing
325315  Compost Manufacturing
32532   Pesticide and Other Agricultural Chemical Manufacturing<sup>T</sup>
325320  Pesticide and Other Agricultural Chemical Manufacturing

## 3254    Pharmaceutical and Medicine Manufacturing<sup>T</sup>
32541   Pharmaceutical and Medicine Manufacturing<sup>T</sup>
325411  Medicinal and Botanical Manufacturing
325412  Pharmaceutical Preparation Manufacturing
325413  In-Vitro Diagnostic Substance Manufacturing
325414  Biological Product (except Diagnostic) Manufacturing

**3255   Paint, Coating, and Adhesive Manufacturing**^T
32551   Paint and Coating Manufacturing^T
325510  Paint and Coating Manufacturing
32552   Adhesive Manufacturing^T
325520  Adhesive Manufacturing

**3256   Soap, Cleaning Compound, and Toilet Preparation Manufacturing**^T
32561   Soap and Cleaning Compound Manufacturing^T
325611  Soap and Other Detergent Manufacturing
325612  Polish and Other Sanitation Good Manufacturing
325613  Surface Active Agent Manufacturing
32562   Toilet Preparation Manufacturing^T
325620  Toilet Preparation Manufacturing

**3259   Other Chemical Product and Preparation Manufacturing**^T
32591   Printing Ink Manufacturing^T
325910  Printing Ink Manufacturing
32592   Explosives Manufacturing^T
325920  Explosives Manufacturing
32599   All Other Chemical Product and Preparation Manufacturing^T
325991  Custom Compounding of Purchased Resins
325992  Photographic Film, Paper, Plate, Chemical, and Copy Toner Manufacturing
325998  All Other Miscellaneous Chemical Product and Preparation Manufacturing

# 326   Plastics and Rubber Products Manufacturing^T

**3261   Plastics Product Manufacturing**^T
32611   Plastics Packaging Materials and Unlaminated Film and Sheet Manufacturing^T
326111  Plastics Bag and Pouch Manufacturing
326112  Plastics Packaging Film and Sheet (including Laminated) Manufacturing
326113  Unlaminated Plastics Film and Sheet (except Packaging) Manufacturing
32612   Plastics Pipe, Pipe Fitting, and Unlaminated Profile Shape Manufacturing^T
326121  Unlaminated Plastics Profile Shape Manufacturing
326122  Plastics Pipe and Pipe Fitting Manufacturing
32613   Laminated Plastics Plate, Sheet (except Packaging), and Shape Manufacturing^T
326130  Laminated Plastics Plate, Sheet (except Packaging), and Shape Manufacturing
32614   Polystyrene Foam Product Manufacturing^T
326140  Polystyrene Foam Product Manufacturing
32615   Urethane and Other Foam Product (except Polystyrene) Manufacturing^T
326150  Urethane and Other Foam Product (except Polystyrene) Manufacturing
32616   Plastics Bottle Manufacturing^T
326160  Plastics Bottle Manufacturing
32619   Other Plastics Product Manufacturing^T
326191  Plastics Plumbing Fixture Manufacturing
326199  All Other Plastics Product Manufacturing

**3262   Rubber Product Manufacturing**^T
32621   Tire Manufacturing^T
326211  Tire Manufacturing (except Retreading)
326212  Tire Retreading
32622   Rubber and Plastics Hoses and Belting Manufacturing^T
326220  Rubber and Plastics Hoses and Belting Manufacturing
32629   Other Rubber Product Manufacturing^T

326291  Rubber Product Manufacturing for Mechanical Use
326299  All Other Rubber Product Manufacturing

# 327    Nonmetallic Mineral Product Manufacturing[T]

### 3271    Clay Product and Refractory Manufacturing[T]
32711    Pottery, Ceramics, and Plumbing Fixture Manufacturing[T]
327110  Pottery, Ceramics, and Plumbing Fixture Manufacturing
32712    Clay Building Material and Refractories Manufacturing[T]
327120  Clay Building Material and Refractories Manufacturing

### 3272    Glass and Glass Product Manufacturing[T]
32721    Glass and Glass Product Manufacturing[T]
327211  Flat Glass Manufacturing
327212  Other Pressed and Blown Glass and Glassware Manufacturing
327213  Glass Container Manufacturing
327215  Glass Product Manufacturing Made of Purchased Glass

### 3273    Cement and Concrete Product Manufacturing[T]
32731    Cement Manufacturing[T]
327310  Cement Manufacturing
32732    Ready-Mix Concrete Manufacturing[T]
327320  Ready-Mix Concrete Manufacturing
32733    Concrete Pipe, Brick, and Block Manufacturing[T]
327331  Concrete Block and Brick Manufacturing
327332  Concrete Pipe Manufacturing
32739    Other Concrete Product Manufacturing[T]
327390  Other Concrete Product Manufacturing

### 3274    Lime and Gypsum Product Manufacturing[T]
32741    Lime Manufacturing[T]
327410  Lime Manufacturing
32742    Gypsum Product Manufacturing[T]
327420  Gypsum Product Manufacturing

### 3279    Other Nonmetallic Mineral Product Manufacturing[T]
32791    Abrasive Product Manufacturing[T]
327910  Abrasive Product Manufacturing
32799    All Other Nonmetallic Mineral Product Manufacturing[T]
327991  Cut Stone and Stone Product Manufacturing
327992  Ground or Treated Mineral and Earth Manufacturing
327993  Mineral Wool Manufacturing
327999  All Other Miscellaneous Nonmetallic Mineral Product Manufacturing

# 331    Primary Metal Manufacturing[T]

### 3311    Iron and Steel Mills and Ferroalloy Manufacturing[T]
33111    Iron and Steel Mills and Ferroalloy Manufacturing[T]
331110  Iron and Steel Mills and Ferroalloy Manufacturing

### 3312    Steel Product Manufacturing from Purchased Steel[T]
33121    Iron and Steel Pipe and Tube Manufacturing from Purchased Steel[T]
331210  Iron and Steel Pipe and Tube Manufacturing from Purchased Steel
33122    Rolling and Drawing of Purchased Steel[T]
331221  Rolled Steel Shape Manufacturing

331222  Steel Wire Drawing

**3313    Alumina and Aluminum Production and Processing**[T]
33131    Alumina and Aluminum Production and Processing[T]
331313  Alumina Refining and Primary Aluminum Production
331314  Secondary Smelting and Alloying of Aluminum
331315  Aluminum Sheet, Plate, and Foil Manufacturing
331318  Other Aluminum Rolling, Drawing, and Extruding

**3314    Nonferrous Metal (except Aluminum) Production and Processing**[T]
33141    Nonferrous Metal (except Aluminum) Smelting and Refining[T]
331410  Nonferrous Metal (except Aluminum) Smelting and Refining
33142    Copper Rolling, Drawing, Extruding, and Alloying[T]
331420  Copper Rolling, Drawing, Extruding, and Alloying
33149    Nonferrous Metal (except Copper and Aluminum) Rolling, Drawing, Extruding, and Alloying[T]
331491  Nonferrous Metal (except Copper and Aluminum) Rolling, Drawing, and Extruding
331492  Secondary Smelting, Refining, and Alloying of Nonferrous Metal (except Copper and Aluminum)

**3315    Foundries**[T]
33151    Ferrous Metal Foundries[T]
331511  Iron Foundries
331512  Steel Investment Foundries
331513  Steel Foundries (except Investment)
33152    Nonferrous Metal Foundries[T]
331523  Nonferrous Metal Die-Casting Foundries
331524  Aluminum Foundries (except Die-Casting)
331529  Other Nonferrous Metal Foundries (except Die-Casting)

# 332    Fabricated Metal Product Manufacturing[T]

**3321    Forging and Stamping**[I]
33211    Forging and Stamping[T]
332111  Iron and Steel Forging
332112  Nonferrous Forging
332114  Custom Roll Forming
332117  Powder Metallurgy Part Manufacturing
332119  Metal Crown, Closure, and Other Metal Stamping (except Automotive)

**3322    Cutlery and Handtool Manufacturing**[T]
33221    Cutlery and Handtool Manufacturing[T]
332215  Metal Kitchen Cookware, Utensil, Cutlery, and Flatware (except Precious) Manufacturing
332216  Saw Blade and Handtool Manufacturing

**3323    Architectural and Structural Metals Manufacturing**[T]
33231    Plate Work and Fabricated Structural Product Manufacturing[T]
332311  Prefabricated Metal Building and Component Manufacturing
332312  Fabricated Structural Metal Manufacturing
332313  Plate Work Manufacturing
33232    Ornamental and Architectural Metal Products Manufacturing[T]
332321  Metal Window and Door Manufacturing
332322  Sheet Metal Work Manufacturing

332323  Ornamental and Architectural Metal Work Manufacturing

**3324**  **Boiler, Tank, and Shipping Container Manufacturing**[T]
33241  Power Boiler and Heat Exchanger Manufacturing[T]
332410  Power Boiler and Heat Exchanger Manufacturing
33242  Metal Tank (Heavy Gauge) Manufacturing[T]
332420  Metal Tank (Heavy Gauge) Manufacturing
33243  Metal Can, Box, and Other Metal Container (Light Gauge) Manufacturing[T]
332431  Metal Can Manufacturing
332439  Other Metal Container Manufacturing

**3325**  **Hardware Manufacturing**[T]
33251  Hardware Manufacturing[T]
332510  Hardware Manufacturing

**3326**  **Spring and Wire Product Manufacturing**[T]
33261  Spring and Wire Product Manufacturing[T]
332613  Spring Manufacturing
332618  Other Fabricated Wire Product Manufacturing

**3327**  **Machine Shops; Turned Product; and Screw, Nut, and Bolt Manufacturing**[T]
33271  Machine Shops[T]
332710  Machine Shops
33272  Turned Product and Screw, Nut, and Bolt Manufacturing[T]
332721  Precision Turned Product Manufacturing
332722  Bolt, Nut, Screw, Rivet, and Washer Manufacturing

**3328**  **Coating, Engraving, Heat Treating, and Allied Activities**[T]
33281  Coating, Engraving, Heat Treating, and Allied Activities[T]
332811  Metal Heat Treating
332812  Metal Coating, Engraving (except Jewelry and Silverware), and Allied Services to Manufacturers
332813  Electroplating, Plating, Polishing, Anodizing, and Coloring

**3329**  **Other Fabricated Metal Product Manufacturing**[T]
33291  Metal Valve Manufacturing[T]
332911  Industrial Valve Manufacturing
332912  Fluid Power Valve and Hose Fitting Manufacturing
332913  Plumbing Fixture Fitting and Trim Manufacturing
332919  Other Metal Valve and Pipe Fitting Manufacturing
33299  All Other Fabricated Metal Product Manufacturing[T]
332991  Ball and Roller Bearing Manufacturing
332992  Small Arms Ammunition Manufacturing
332993  Ammunition (except Small Arms) Manufacturing
332994  Small Arms, Ordnance, and Ordnance Accessories Manufacturing
332996  Fabricated Pipe and Pipe Fitting Manufacturing
332999  All Other Miscellaneous Fabricated Metal Product Manufacturing

# 333  **Machinery Manufacturing**[T]

**3331**  **Agriculture, Construction, and Mining Machinery Manufacturing**[T]
33311  Agricultural Implement Manufacturing[T]
333111  Farm Machinery and Equipment Manufacturing
333112  Lawn and Garden Tractor and Home Lawn and Garden Equipment Manufacturing
33312  Construction Machinery Manufacturing[T]

333120  Construction Machinery Manufacturing
33313   Mining and Oil and Gas Field Machinery Manufacturing[T]
333131  Mining Machinery and Equipment Manufacturing
333132  Oil and Gas Field Machinery and Equipment Manufacturing

**3332    Industrial Machinery Manufacturing[T]**
33324   Industrial Machinery Manufacturing[T]
333241  Food Product Machinery Manufacturing
333242  Semiconductor Machinery Manufacturing
333243  Sawmill, Woodworking, and Paper Machinery Manufacturing
333248  All Other Industrial Machinery Manufacturing

**3333    Commercial and Service Industry Machinery Manufacturing[T]**
33331   Commercial and Service Industry Machinery Manufacturing[T]
333310  Commercial and Service Industry Machinery Manufacturing

**3334    Ventilation, Heating, Air-Conditioning, and Commercial Refrigeration Equipment Manufacturing[T]**
33341   Ventilation, Heating, Air-Conditioning, and Commercial Refrigeration Equipment Manufacturing[T]
333413  Industrial and Commercial Fan and Blower and Air Purification Equipment Manufacturing
333414  Heating Equipment (except Warm Air Furnaces) Manufacturing
333415  Air-Conditioning and Warm Air Heating Equipment and Commercial and Industrial Refrigeration Equipment Manufacturing

**3335    Metalworking Machinery Manufacturing[T]**
33351   Metalworking Machinery Manufacturing[T]
333511  Industrial Mold Manufacturing
333514  Special Die and Tool, Die Set, Jig, and Fixture Manufacturing
333515  Cutting Tool and Machine Tool Accessory Manufacturing
333517  Machine Tool Manufacturing
333519  Rolling Mill and Other Metalworking Machinery Manufacturing

**3336    Engine, Turbine, and Power Transmission Equipment Manufacturing[T]**
33361   Engine, Turbine, and Power Transmission Equipment Manufacturing[T]
333611  Turbine and Turbine Generator Set Units Manufacturing
333612  Speed Changer, Industrial High-Speed Drive, and Gear Manufacturing
333613  Mechanical Power Transmission Equipment Manufacturing
333618  Other Engine Equipment Manufacturing

**3339    Other General Purpose Machinery Manufacturing[T]**
33391   Pump and Compressor Manufacturing[T]
333912  Air and Gas Compressor Manufacturing
333914  Measuring, Dispensing, and Other Pumping Equipment Manufacturing
33392   Material Handling Equipment Manufacturing[T]
333921  Elevator and Moving Stairway Manufacturing
333922  Conveyor and Conveying Equipment Manufacturing
333923  Overhead Traveling Crane, Hoist, and Monorail System Manufacturing
333924  Industrial Truck, Tractor, Trailer, and Stacker Machinery Manufacturing
33399   All Other General Purpose Machinery Manufacturing[T]
333991  Power-Driven Handtool Manufacturing
333992  Welding and Soldering Equipment Manufacturing
333993  Packaging Machinery Manufacturing
333994  Industrial Process Furnace and Oven Manufacturing
333995  Fluid Power Cylinder and Actuator Manufacturing

333996   Fluid Power Pump and Motor Manufacturing
333998   All Other Miscellaneous General Purpose Machinery Manufacturing

## 334      Computer and Electronic Product Manufacturing[T]

### 3341      Computer and Peripheral Equipment Manufacturing[T]
33411    Computer and Peripheral Equipment Manufacturing[T]
334111   Electronic Computer Manufacturing
334112   Computer Storage Device Manufacturing
334118   Computer Terminal and Other Computer Peripheral Equipment Manufacturing

### 3342      Communications Equipment Manufacturing[T]
33421    Telephone Apparatus Manufacturing[T]
334210   Telephone Apparatus Manufacturing
33422    Radio and Television Broadcasting and Wireless Communications Equipment
           Manufacturing[T]
334220   Radio and Television Broadcasting and Wireless Communications Equipment
           Manufacturing
33429    Other Communications Equipment Manufacturing[T]
334290   Other Communications Equipment Manufacturing

### 3343      Audio and Video Equipment Manufacturing[T]
33431    Audio and Video Equipment Manufacturing[T]
334310   Audio and Video Equipment Manufacturing

### 3344      Semiconductor and Other Electronic Component Manufacturing[T]
33441    Semiconductor and Other Electronic Component Manufacturing[T]
334412   Bare Printed Circuit Board Manufacturing
334413   Semiconductor and Related Device Manufacturing
334416   Capacitor, Resistor, Coil, Transformer, and Other Inductor Manufacturing
334417   Electronic Connector Manufacturing
334418   Printed Circuit Assembly (Electronic Assembly) Manufacturing
334419   Other Electronic Component Manufacturing

### 3345      Navigational, Measuring, Electromedical, and Control Instruments
### Manufacturing[T]
33451    Navigational, Measuring, Electromedical, and Control Instruments
           Manufacturing[T]
334510   Electromedical and Electrotherapeutic Apparatus Manufacturing
334511   Search, Detection, Navigation, Guidance, Aeronautical, and Nautical System
           and Instrument Manufacturing
334512   Automatic Environmental Control Manufacturing for Residential,
           Commercial, and Appliance Use
334513   Instruments and Related Products Manufacturing for Measuring, Displaying,
           and Controlling Industrial Process Variables
334514   Totalizing Fluid Meter and Counting Device Manufacturing
334515   Instrument Manufacturing for Measuring and Testing Electricity and Electrical
           Signals
334516   Analytical Laboratory Instrument Manufacturing
334517   Irradiation Apparatus Manufacturing
334519   Other Measuring and Controlling Device Manufacturing

### 3346      Manufacturing and Reproducing Magnetic and Optical Media[T]
33461    Manufacturing and Reproducing Magnetic and Optical Media[T]
334610   Manufacturing and Reproducing Magnetic and Optical Media

## 335     Electrical Equipment, Appliance, and Component Manufacturing[T]

### 3351    Electric Lighting Equipment Manufacturing[T]
33513    Electric Lighting Equipment Manufacturing[T]
335131   Residential Electric Lighting Fixture Manufacturing
335132   Commercial, Industrial, and Institutional Electric Lighting Fixture
          Manufacturing
335139   Electric Lamp Bulb and Other Lighting Equipment Manufacturing

### 3352    Household Appliance Manufacturing[T]
33521    Small Electrical Appliance Manufacturing[T]
335210   Small Electrical Appliance Manufacturing
33522    Major Household Appliance Manufacturing[T]
335220   Major Household Appliance Manufacturing

### 3353    Electrical Equipment Manufacturing[T]
33531    Electrical Equipment Manufacturing[T]
335311   Power, Distribution, and Specialty Transformer Manufacturing
335312   Motor and Generator Manufacturing
335313   Switchgear and Switchboard Apparatus Manufacturing
335314   Relay and Industrial Control Manufacturing

### 3359    Other Electrical Equipment and Component Manufacturing[T]
33591    Battery Manufacturing[T]
335910   Battery Manufacturing
33592    Communication and Energy Wire and Cable Manufacturing[T]
335921   Fiber Optic Cable Manufacturing
335929   Other Communication and Energy Wire Manufacturing
33593    Wiring Device Manufacturing[T]
335931   Current-Carrying Wiring Device Manufacturing
335932   Noncurrent-Carrying Wiring Device Manufacturing
33599    All Other Electrical Equipment and Component Manufacturing[T]
335991   Carbon and Graphite Product Manufacturing
335999   All Other Miscellaneous Electrical Equipment and Component
          Manufacturing

## 336     Transportation Equipment Manufacturing[T]

### 3361    Motor Vehicle Manufacturing[T]
33611    Automobile and Light Duty Motor Vehicle Manufacturing[T]
336110   Automobile and Light Duty Motor Vehicle Manufacturing
33612    Heavy Duty Truck Manufacturing[T]
336120   Heavy Duty Truck Manufacturing

### 3362    Motor Vehicle Body and Trailer Manufacturing[T]
33621    Motor Vehicle Body and Trailer Manufacturing[T]
336211   Motor Vehicle Body Manufacturing
336212   Truck Trailer Manufacturing
336213   Motor Home Manufacturing
336214   Travel Trailer and Camper Manufacturing

### 3363    Motor Vehicle Parts Manufacturing[T]
33631    Motor Vehicle Gasoline Engine and Engine Parts Manufacturing[T]
336310   Motor Vehicle Gasoline Engine and Engine Parts Manufacturing
33632    Motor Vehicle Electrical and Electronic Equipment Manufacturing[T]

336320 Motor Vehicle Electrical and Electronic Equipment Manufacturing
33633   Motor Vehicle Steering and Suspension Components (except Spring) Manufacturing[T]
336330 Motor Vehicle Steering and Suspension Components (except Spring) Manufacturing
33634   Motor Vehicle Brake System Manufacturing[T]
336340 Motor Vehicle Brake System Manufacturing
33635   Motor Vehicle Transmission and Power Train Parts Manufacturing[T]
336350 Motor Vehicle Transmission and Power Train Parts Manufacturing
33636   Motor Vehicle Seating and Interior Trim Manufacturing[T]
336360 Motor Vehicle Seating and Interior Trim Manufacturing
33637   Motor Vehicle Metal Stamping[T]
336370 Motor Vehicle Metal Stamping
33639   Other Motor Vehicle Parts Manufacturing[T]
336390 Other Motor Vehicle Parts Manufacturing

**3364   Aerospace Product and Parts Manufacturing[T]**
33641   Aerospace Product and Parts Manufacturing[T]
336411 Aircraft Manufacturing
336412 Aircraft Engine and Engine Parts Manufacturing
336413 Other Aircraft Parts and Auxiliary Equipment Manufacturing
336414 Guided Missile and Space Vehicle Manufacturing
336415 Guided Missile and Space Vehicle Propulsion Unit and Propulsion Unit Parts Manufacturing
336419 Other Guided Missile and Space Vehicle Parts and Auxiliary Equipment Manufacturing

**3365   Railroad Rolling Stock Manufacturing[T]**
33651   Railroad Rolling Stock Manufacturing[T]
336510 Railroad Rolling Stock Manufacturing

**3366   Ship and Boat Building[T]**
33661   Ship and Boat Building[T]
336611 Ship Building and Repairing
336612 Boat Building

**3369   Other Transportation Equipment Manufacturing[T]**
33699   Other Transportation Equipment Manufacturing[T]
336991 Motorcycle, Bicycle, and Parts Manufacturing
336992 Military Armored Vehicle, Tank, and Tank Component Manufacturing
336999 All Other Transportation Equipment Manufacturing

# 337   Furniture and Related Product Manufacturing[T]

**3371   Household and Institutional Furniture and Kitchen Cabinet Manufacturing[T]**
33711   Wood Kitchen Cabinet and Countertop Manufacturing[T]
337110 Wood Kitchen Cabinet and Countertop Manufacturing
33712   Household and Institutional Furniture Manufacturing[T]
337121 Upholstered Household Furniture Manufacturing
337122 Nonupholstered Wood Household Furniture Manufacturing
337126 Household Furniture (except Wood and Upholstered) Manufacturing
337127 Institutional Furniture Manufacturing

**3372   Office Furniture (including Fixtures) Manufacturing[T]**
33721   Office Furniture (including Fixtures) Manufacturing[T]
337211 Wood Office Furniture Manufacturing

337212  Custom Architectural Woodwork and Millwork Manufacturing
337214  Office Furniture (except Wood) Manufacturing
337215  Showcase, Partition, Shelving, and Locker Manufacturing

**3379**  **Other Furniture Related Product Manufacturing**[T]
33791  Mattress Manufacturing[T]
337910  Mattress Manufacturing
33792  Blind and Shade Manufacturing[T]
337920  Blind and Shade Manufacturing

# 339  Miscellaneous Manufacturing[T]

**3391**  **Medical Equipment and Supplies Manufacturing**[T]
33911  Medical Equipment and Supplies Manufacturing[T]
339112  Surgical and Medical Instrument Manufacturing
339113  Surgical Appliance and Supplies Manufacturing
339114  Dental Equipment and Supplies Manufacturing
339115  Ophthalmic Goods Manufacturing
339116  Dental Laboratories

**3399**  **Other Miscellaneous Manufacturing**[T]
33991  Jewelry and Silverware Manufacturing[T]
339910  Jewelry and Silverware Manufacturing
33992  Sporting and Athletic Goods Manufacturing[T]
339920  Sporting and Athletic Goods Manufacturing
33993  Doll, Toy, and Game Manufacturing[T]
339930  Doll, Toy, and Game Manufacturing
33994  Office Supplies (except Paper) Manufacturing[T]
339940  Office Supplies (except Paper) Manufacturing
33995  Sign Manufacturing[T]
339950  Sign Manufacturing
33999  All Other Miscellaneous Manufacturing[T]
339991  Gasket, Packing, and Sealing Device Manufacturing
339992  Musical Instrument Manufacturing
339993  Fastener, Button, Needle, and Pin Manufacturing
339994  Broom, Brush, and Mop Manufacturing
339995  Burial Casket Manufacturing
339999  All Other Miscellaneous Manufacturing

# Sector 42--Wholesale Trade[T]

# 423  Merchant Wholesalers, Durable Goods

**4231**  **Motor Vehicle and Motor Vehicle Parts and Supplies Merchant Wholesalers**
42311  Automobile and Other Motor Vehicle Merchant Wholesalers
423110  Automobile and Other Motor Vehicle Merchant Wholesalers
42312  Motor Vehicle Supplies and New Parts Merchant Wholesalers
423120  Motor Vehicle Supplies and New Parts Merchant Wholesalers
42313  Tire and Tube Merchant Wholesalers
423130  Tire and Tube Merchant Wholesalers
42314  Motor Vehicle Parts (Used) Merchant Wholesalers
423140  Motor Vehicle Parts (Used) Merchant Wholesalers

**4232**  **Furniture and Home Furnishing Merchant Wholesalers**
42321  Furniture Merchant Wholesalers

423210 Furniture Merchant Wholesalers
42322 Home Furnishing Merchant Wholesalers
423220 Home Furnishing Merchant Wholesalers

**4233 Lumber and Other Construction Materials Merchant Wholesalers**
42331 Lumber, Plywood, Millwork, and Wood Panel Merchant Wholesalers
423310 Lumber, Plywood, Millwork, and Wood Panel Merchant Wholesalers
42332 Brick, Stone, and Related Construction Material Merchant Wholesalers
423320 Brick, Stone, and Related Construction Material Merchant Wholesalers
42333 Roofing, Siding, and Insulation Material Merchant Wholesalers
423330 Roofing, Siding, and Insulation Material Merchant Wholesalers
42339 Other Construction Material Merchant Wholesalers
423390 Other Construction Material Merchant Wholesalers

**4234 Professional and Commercial Equipment and Supplies Merchant Wholesalers**
42341 Photographic Equipment and Supplies Merchant Wholesalers
423410 Photographic Equipment and Supplies Merchant Wholesalers
42342 Office Equipment Merchant Wholesalers
423420 Office Equipment Merchant Wholesalers
42343 Computer and Computer Peripheral Equipment and Software Merchant Wholesalers
423430 Computer and Computer Peripheral Equipment and Software Merchant Wholesalers
42344 Other Commercial Equipment Merchant Wholesalers
423440 Other Commercial Equipment Merchant Wholesalers
42345 Medical, Dental, and Hospital Equipment and Supplies Merchant Wholesalers
423450 Medical, Dental, and Hospital Equipment and Supplies Merchant Wholesalers
42346 Ophthalmic Goods Merchant Wholesalers
423460 Ophthalmic Goods Merchant Wholesalers
42349 Other Professional Equipment and Supplies Merchant Wholesalers
423490 Other Professional Equipment and Supplies Merchant Wholesalers

**4235 Metal and Mineral (except Petroleum) Merchant Wholesalers**
42351 Metal Service Centers and Other Metal Merchant Wholesalers
423510 Metal Service Centers and Other Metal Merchant Wholesalers
42352 Coal and Other Mineral and Ore Merchant Wholesalers
423520 Coal and Other Mineral and Ore Merchant Wholesalers

**4236 Household Appliances and Electrical and Electronic Goods Merchant Wholesalers**
42361 Electrical Apparatus and Equipment, Wiring Supplies, and Related Equipment Merchant Wholesalers
423610 Electrical Apparatus and Equipment, Wiring Supplies, and Related Equipment Merchant Wholesalers
42362 Household Appliances, Electric Housewares, and Consumer Electronics Merchant Wholesalers
423620 Household Appliances, Electric Housewares, and Consumer Electronics Merchant Wholesalers
42369 Other Electronic Parts and Equipment Merchant Wholesalers
423690 Other Electronic Parts and Equipment Merchant Wholesalers

**4237 Hardware, and Plumbing and Heating Equipment and Supplies Merchant Wholesalers**
42371 Hardware Merchant Wholesalers

423710   Hardware Merchant Wholesalers
42372     Plumbing and Heating Equipment and Supplies (Hydronics) Merchant
              Wholesalers
423720   Plumbing and Heating Equipment and Supplies (Hydronics) Merchant
              Wholesalers
42373     Warm Air Heating and Air-Conditioning Equipment and Supplies Merchant
              Wholesalers
423730   Warm Air Heating and Air-Conditioning Equipment and Supplies Merchant
              Wholesalers
42374     Refrigeration Equipment and Supplies Merchant Wholesalers
423740   Refrigeration Equipment and Supplies Merchant Wholesalers

**4238      Machinery, Equipment, and Supplies Merchant Wholesalers**
42381     Construction and Mining (except Oil Well) Machinery and Equipment
              Merchant Wholesalers
423810   Construction and Mining (except Oil Well) Machinery and Equipment
              Merchant Wholesalers
42382     Farm and Garden Machinery and Equipment Merchant Wholesalers
423820   Farm and Garden Machinery and Equipment Merchant Wholesalers
42383     Industrial Machinery and Equipment Merchant Wholesalers
423830   Industrial Machinery and Equipment Merchant Wholesalers
42384     Industrial Supplies Merchant Wholesalers
423840   Industrial Supplies Merchant Wholesalers
42385     Service Establishment Equipment and Supplies Merchant Wholesalers
423850   Service Establishment Equipment and Supplies Merchant Wholesalers
42386     Transportation Equipment and Supplies (except Motor Vehicle) Merchant
              Wholesalers
423860   Transportation Equipment and Supplies (except Motor Vehicle) Merchant
              Wholesalers

**4239      Miscellaneous Durable Goods Merchant Wholesalers**
42391     Sporting and Recreational Goods and Supplies Merchant Wholesalers
423910   Sporting and Recreational Goods and Supplies Merchant Wholesalers
42392     Toy and Hobby Goods and Supplies Merchant Wholesalers
423920   Toy and Hobby Goods and Supplies Merchant Wholesalers
42393     Recyclable Material Merchant Wholesalers
423930   Recyclable Material Merchant Wholesalers
42394     Jewelry, Watch, Precious Stone, and Precious Metal Merchant Wholesalers
423940   Jewelry, Watch, Precious Stone, and Precious Metal Merchant Wholesalers
42399     Other Miscellaneous Durable Goods Merchant Wholesalers
423990   Other Miscellaneous Durable Goods Merchant Wholesalers

# 424     Merchant Wholesalers, Nondurable Goods

**4241      Paper and Paper Product Merchant Wholesalers**
42411     Printing and Writing Paper Merchant Wholesalers
424110   Printing and Writing Paper Merchant Wholesalers
42412     Stationery and Office Supplies Merchant Wholesalers
424120   Stationery and Office Supplies Merchant Wholesalers
42413     Industrial and Personal Service Paper Merchant Wholesalers
424130   Industrial and Personal Service Paper Merchant Wholesalers

**4242      Drugs and Druggists' Sundries Merchant Wholesalers**
42421     Drugs and Druggists' Sundries Merchant Wholesalers
424210   Drugs and Druggists' Sundries Merchant Wholesalers

**4243    Apparel, Piece Goods, and Notions Merchant Wholesalers**
    42431    Piece Goods, Notions, and Other Dry Goods Merchant Wholesalers
    424310  Piece Goods, Notions, and Other Dry Goods Merchant Wholesalers
    42434    Footwear Merchant Wholesalers
    424340  Footwear Merchant Wholesalers
    42435    Clothing and Clothing Accessories Merchant Wholesalers
    424350  Clothing and Clothing Accessories Merchant Wholesalers

**4244    Grocery and Related Product Merchant Wholesalers**
    42441    General Line Grocery Merchant Wholesalers
    424410  General Line Grocery Merchant Wholesalers
    42442    Packaged Frozen Food Merchant Wholesalers
    424420  Packaged Frozen Food Merchant Wholesalers
    42443    Dairy Product (except Dried or Canned) Merchant Wholesalers
    424430  Dairy Product (except Dried or Canned) Merchant Wholesalers
    42444    Poultry and Poultry Product Merchant Wholesalers
    424440  Poultry and Poultry Product Merchant Wholesalers
    42445    Confectionery Merchant Wholesalers
    424450  Confectionery Merchant Wholesalers
    42446    Fish and Seafood Merchant Wholesalers
    424460  Fish and Seafood Merchant Wholesalers
    42447    Meat and Meat Product Merchant Wholesalers
    424470  Meat and Meat Product Merchant Wholesalers
    42448    Fresh Fruit and Vegetable Merchant Wholesalers
    424480  Fresh Fruit and Vegetable Merchant Wholesalers
    42449    Other Grocery and Related Products Merchant Wholesalers
    424490  Other Grocery and Related Products Merchant Wholesalers

**4245    Farm Product Raw Material Merchant Wholesalers**
    42451    Grain and Field Bean Merchant Wholesalers
    424510  Grain and Field Bean Merchant Wholesalers
    42452    Livestock Merchant Wholesalers
    424520  Livestock Merchant Wholesalers
    42459    Other Farm Product Raw Material Merchant Wholesalers
    424590  Other Farm Product Raw Material Merchant Wholesalers

**4246    Chemical and Allied Products Merchant Wholesalers**
    42461    Plastics Materials and Basic Forms and Shapes Merchant Wholesalers
    424610  Plastics Materials and Basic Forms and Shapes Merchant Wholesalers
    42469    Other Chemical and Allied Products Merchant Wholesalers
    424690  Other Chemical and Allied Products Merchant Wholesalers

**4247    Petroleum and Petroleum Products Merchant Wholesalers**
    42471    Petroleum Bulk Stations and Terminals
    424710  Petroleum Bulk Stations and Terminals
    42472    Petroleum and Petroleum Products Merchant Wholesalers (except Bulk
          Stations and Terminals)
    424720  Petroleum and Petroleum Products Merchant Wholesalers (except Bulk
          Stations and Terminals)

**4248    Beer, Wine, and Distilled Alcoholic Beverage Merchant Wholesalers**
    42481    Beer and Ale Merchant Wholesalers
    424810  Beer and Ale Merchant Wholesalers
    42482    Wine and Distilled Alcoholic Beverage Merchant Wholesalers
    424820  Wine and Distilled Alcoholic Beverage Merchant Wholesalers

**4249    Miscellaneous Nondurable Goods Merchant Wholesalers**
42491    Farm Supplies Merchant Wholesalers
424910    Farm Supplies Merchant Wholesalers
42492    Book, Periodical, and Newspaper Merchant Wholesalers
424920    Book, Periodical, and Newspaper Merchant Wholesalers
42493    Flower, Nursery Stock, and Florists' Supplies Merchant Wholesalers
424930    Flower, Nursery Stock, and Florists' Supplies Merchant Wholesalers
42494    Tobacco Product and Electronic Cigarette Merchant Wholesalers
424940    Tobacco Product and Electronic Cigarette Merchant Wholesalers
42495    Paint, Varnish, and Supplies Merchant Wholesalers
424950    Paint, Varnish, and Supplies Merchant Wholesalers
42499    Other Miscellaneous Nondurable Goods Merchant Wholesalers
424990    Other Miscellaneous Nondurable Goods Merchant Wholesalers

## 425    Wholesale Trade Agents and Brokers

**4251    Wholesale Trade Agents and Brokers**
42512    Wholesale Trade Agents and Brokers
425120    Wholesale Trade Agents and Brokers

# Sector 44-45--Retail Trade[T]

## 441    Motor Vehicle and Parts Dealers

**4411    Automobile Dealers**
44111    New Car Dealers
441110    New Car Dealers
44112    Used Car Dealers
441120    Used Car Dealers

**4412    Other Motor Vehicle Dealers**
44121    Recreational Vehicle Dealers
441210    Recreational Vehicle Dealers
44122    Motorcycle, Boat, and Other Motor Vehicle Dealers
441222    Boat Dealers
441227    Motorcycle, ATV, and All Other Motor Vehicle Dealers

**4413    Automotive Parts, Accessories, and Tire Retailers**
44133    Automotive Parts and Accessories Retailers
441330    Automotive Parts and Accessories Retailers
44134    Tire Dealers
441340    Tire Dealers

## 444    Building Material and Garden Equipment and Supplies Dealers

**4441    Building Material and Supplies Dealers**
44411    Home Centers
444110    Home Centers
44412    Paint and Wallpaper Retailers
444120    Paint and Wallpaper Retailers
44414    Hardware Retailers
444140    Hardware Retailers
44418    Other Building Material Dealers
444180    Other Building Material Dealers

|   | 4442 | **Lawn and Garden Equipment and Supplies Retailers** |
|---|---|---|
|   | 44423 | Outdoor Power Equipment Retailers |
|   | 444230 | Outdoor Power Equipment Retailers |
|   | 44424 | Nursery, Garden Center, and Farm Supply Retailers |
|   | 444240 | Nursery, Garden Center, and Farm Supply Retailers |

## 445    Food and Beverage Retailers

|   | 4451 | **Grocery and Convenience Retailers** |
|---|---|---|
|   | 44511 | Supermarkets and Other Grocery Retailers (except Convenience Retailers) |
|   | 445110 | Supermarkets and Other Grocery Retailers (except Convenience Retailers) |
|   | 44513 | Convenience Retailers and Vending Machine Operators |
|   | 445131 | Convenience Retailers |
|   | 445132 | Vending Machine Operators |

|   | 4452 | **Specialty Food Retailers** |
|---|---|---|
|   | 44523 | Fruit and Vegetable Retailers |
|   | 445230 | Fruit and Vegetable Retailers |
|   | 44524 | Meat Retailers |
|   | 445240 | Meat Retailers |
|   | 44525 | Fish and Seafood Retailers |
|   | 445250 | Fish and Seafood Retailers |
|   | 44529 | Other Specialty Food Retailers |
|   | 445291 | Baked Goods Retailers |
|   | 445292 | Confectionery and Nut Retailers |
|   | 445298 | All Other Specialty Food Retailers |

|   | 4453 | **Beer, Wine, and Liquor Retailers** |
|---|---|---|
|   | 44532 | Beer, Wine, and Liquor Retailers |
|   | 445320 | Beer, Wine, and Liquor Retailers |

## 449    Furniture, Home Furnishings, Electronics, and Appliance Retailers

|   | 4491 | **Furniture and Home Furnishings Retailers** |
|---|---|---|
|   | 44911 | Furniture Retailers |
|   | 449110 | Furniture Retailers |
|   | 44912 | Home Furnishings Retailers |
|   | 449121 | Floor Covering Retailers |
|   | 449122 | Window Treatment Retailers |
|   | 449129 | All Other Home Furnishings Retailers |

|   | 4492 | **Electronics and Appliance Retailers** |
|---|---|---|
|   | 44921 | Electronics and Appliance Retailers |
|   | 449210 | Electronics and Appliance Retailers |

## 455    General Merchandise Retailers

|   | 4551 | **Department Stores** |
|---|---|---|
|   | 45511 | Department Stores |
|   | 455110 | Department Stores |

|   | 4552 | **Warehouse Clubs, Supercenters, and Other General Merchandise Retailers** |
|---|---|---|
|   | 45521 | Warehouse Clubs, Supercenters, and Other General Merchandise Retailers |
|   | 455211 | Warehouse Clubs and Supercenters |
|   | 455219 | All Other General Merchandise Retailers |

**456      Health and Personal Care Retailers**

    **4561      Health and Personal Care Retailers**
        45611     Pharmacies and Drug Retailers
        456110   Pharmacies and Drug Retailers
        45612     Cosmetics, Beauty Supplies, and Perfume Retailers
        456120   Cosmetics, Beauty Supplies, and Perfume Retailers
        45613     Optical Goods Retailers
        456130   Optical Goods Retailers
        45619     Other Health and Personal Care Retailers
        456191   Food (Health) Supplement Retailers
        456199   All Other Health and Personal Care Retailers

**457      Gasoline Stations and Fuel Dealers**

    **4571      Gasoline Stations**
        45711     Gasoline Stations with Convenience Stores
        457110   Gasoline Stations with Convenience Stores
        45712     Other Gasoline Stations
        457120   Other Gasoline Stations

    **4572      Fuel Dealers**
        45721     Fuel Dealers
        457210   Fuel Dealers

**458      Clothing, Clothing Accessories, Shoe, and Jewelry Retailers**

    **4581      Clothing and Clothing Accessories Retailers**
        45811     Clothing and Clothing Accessories Retailers
        458110   Clothing and Clothing Accessories Retailers

    **4582      Shoe Retailers**
        45821     Shoe Retailers
        458210   Shoe Retailers

    **4583      Jewelry, Luggage, and Leather Goods Retailers**
        45831     Jewelry Retailers
        458310   Jewelry Retailers
        45832     Luggage and Leather Goods Retailers
        458320   Luggage and Leather Goods Retailers

**459      Sporting Goods, Hobby, Musical Instrument, Book, and Miscellaneous Retailers**

    **4591      Sporting Goods, Hobby, and Musical Instrument Retailers**
        45911     Sporting Goods Retailers
        459110   Sporting Goods Retailers
        45912     Hobby, Toy, and Game Retailers
        459120   Hobby, Toy, and Game Retailers
        45913     Sewing, Needlework, and Piece Goods Retailers
        459130   Sewing, Needlework, and Piece Goods Retailers
        45914     Musical Instrument and Supplies Retailers
        459140   Musical Instrument and Supplies Retailers

    **4592**   **Book Retailers and News Dealers**
       45921  Book Retailers and News Dealers
       459210 Book Retailers and News Dealers

    **4593**   **Florists**
       45931  Florists
       459310 Florists

    **4594**   **Office Supplies, Stationery, and Gift Retailers**
       45941  Office Supplies and Stationery Retailers
       459410 Office Supplies and Stationery Retailers
       45942  Gift, Novelty, and Souvenir Retailers
       459420 Gift, Novelty, and Souvenir Retailers

    **4595**   **Used Merchandise Retailers**
       45951  Used Merchandise Retailers
       459510 Used Merchandise Retailers

    **4599**   **Other Miscellaneous Retailers**
       45991  Pet and Pet Supplies Retailers
       459910 Pet and Pet Supplies Retailers
       45992  Art Dealers
       459920 Art Dealers
       45993  Manufactured (Mobile) Home Dealers
       459930 Manufactured (Mobile) Home Dealers
       45999  All Other Miscellaneous Retailers
       459991 Tobacco, Electronic Cigarette, and Other Smoking Supplies Retailers
       459999 All Other Miscellaneous Retailers

# Sector 48-49--Transportation and Warehousing[T]

## 481   Air Transportation[T]

    **4811**   **Scheduled Air Transportation[T]**
       48111  Scheduled Air Transportation[T]
       481111 Scheduled Passenger Air Transportation
       481112 Scheduled Freight Air Transportation

    **4812**   **Nonscheduled Air Transportation[T]**
       48121  Nonscheduled Air Transportation[T]
       481211 Nonscheduled Chartered Passenger Air Transportation
       481212 Nonscheduled Chartered Freight Air Transportation
       481219 Other Nonscheduled Air Transportation

## 482   Rail Transportation[T]

    **4821**   **Rail Transportation[T]**
       48211  Rail Transportation[T]
       482111 Line-Haul Railroads
       482112 Short Line Railroads

## 483   Water Transportation[T]

    **4831**   **Deep Sea, Coastal, and Great Lakes Water Transportation[T]**
       48311  Deep Sea, Coastal, and Great Lakes Water Transportation[T]

483111  Deep Sea Freight Transportation
483112  Deep Sea Passenger Transportation
483113  Coastal and Great Lakes Freight Transportation
483114  Coastal and Great Lakes Passenger Transportation

### 4832    Inland Water Transportation[T]
48321   Inland Water Transportation[T]
483211  Inland Water Freight Transportation
483212  Inland Water Passenger Transportation

## 484    Truck Transportation[T]

### 4841    General Freight Trucking[T]
48411   General Freight Trucking, Local[T]
484110  General Freight Trucking, Local
48412   General Freight Trucking, Long-Distance[T]
484121  General Freight Trucking, Long-Distance, Truckload
484122  General Freight Trucking, Long-Distance, Less Than Truckload

### 4842    Specialized Freight Trucking[T]
48421   Used Household and Office Goods Moving[T]
484210  Used Household and Office Goods Moving
48422   Specialized Freight (except Used Goods) Trucking, Local[T]
484220  Specialized Freight (except Used Goods) Trucking, Local
48423   Specialized Freight (except Used Goods) Trucking, Long-Distance[T]
484230  Specialized Freight (except Used Goods) Trucking, Long-Distance

## 485    Transit and Ground Passenger Transportation[T]

### 4851    Urban Transit Systems[T]
48511   Urban Transit Systems[T]
485111  Mixed Mode Transit Systems
485112  Commuter Rail Systems
485113  Bus and Other Motor Vehicle Transit Systems
485119  Other Urban Transit Systems

### 4852    Interurban and Rural Bus Transportation[T]
48521   Interurban and Rural Bus Transportation[T]
485210  Interurban and Rural Bus Transportation

### 4853    Taxi and Limousine Service[T]
48531   Taxi and Ridesharing Services[T]
485310  Taxi and Ridesharing Services
48532   Limousine Service[T]
485320  Limousine Service

### 4854    School and Employee Bus Transportation[T]
48541   School and Employee Bus Transportation[T]
485410  School and Employee Bus Transportation

### 4855    Charter Bus Industry[T]
48551   Charter Bus Industry[T]
485510  Charter Bus Industry

4859 **Other Transit and Ground Passenger Transportation**[T]
  48599 Other Transit and Ground Passenger Transportation[T]
  485991 Special Needs Transportation
  485999 All Other Transit and Ground Passenger Transportation

# 486 Pipeline Transportation[T]

4861 **Pipeline Transportation of Crude Oil**[T]
  48611 Pipeline Transportation of Crude Oil[T]
  486110 Pipeline Transportation of Crude Oil

4862 **Pipeline Transportation of Natural Gas**[T]
  48621 Pipeline Transportation of Natural Gas[T]
  486210 Pipeline Transportation of Natural Gas

4869 **Other Pipeline Transportation**[T]
  48691 Pipeline Transportation of Refined Petroleum Products[T]
  486910 Pipeline Transportation of Refined Petroleum Products
  48699 All Other Pipeline Transportation[T]
  486990 All Other Pipeline Transportation

# 487 Scenic and Sightseeing Transportation[T]

4871 **Scenic and Sightseeing Transportation, Land**[T]
  48711 Scenic and Sightseeing Transportation, Land[T]
  487110 Scenic and Sightseeing Transportation, Land

4872 **Scenic and Sightseeing Transportation, Water**[T]
  48721 Scenic and Sightseeing Transportation, Water[T]
  487210 Scenic and Sightseeing Transportation, Water

4879 **Scenic and Sightseeing Transportation, Other**[T]
  48799 Scenic and Sightseeing Transportation, Other[T]
  487990 Scenic and Sightseeing Transportation, Other

# 488 Support Activities for Transportation[T]

4881 **Support Activities for Air Transportation**[T]
  48811 Airport Operations[T]
  488111 Air Traffic Control
  488119 Other Airport Operations
  48819 Other Support Activities for Air Transportation[T]
  488190 Other Support Activities for Air Transportation

4882 **Support Activities for Rail Transportation**[T]
  48821 Support Activities for Rail Transportation[T]
  488210 Support Activities for Rail Transportation

4883 **Support Activities for Water Transportation**[T]
  48831 Port and Harbor Operations[T]
  488310 Port and Harbor Operations
  48832 Marine Cargo Handling[T]
  488320 Marine Cargo Handling
  48833 Navigational Services to Shipping[T]
  488330 Navigational Services to Shipping

48839    Other Support Activities for Water Transportation[T]
488390  Other Support Activities for Water Transportation

**4884    Support Activities for Road Transportation[T]**
48841    Motor Vehicle Towing[T]
488410  Motor Vehicle Towing
48849    Other Support Activities for Road Transportation[T]
488490  Other Support Activities for Road Transportation

**4885    Freight Transportation Arrangement[T]**
48851    Freight Transportation Arrangement[T]
488510  Freight Transportation Arrangement

**4889    Other Support Activities for Transportation[T]**
48899    Other Support Activities for Transportation[T]
488991  Packing and Crating
488999  All Other Support Activities for Transportation

# 491    Postal Service[T]

**4911    Postal Service[T]**
49111    Postal Service[T]
491110  Postal Service

# 492    Couriers and Messengers[T]

**4921    Couriers and Express Delivery Services[T]**
49211    Couriers and Express Delivery Services[T]
492110  Couriers and Express Delivery Services

**4922    Local Messengers and Local Delivery[T]**
49221    Local Messengers and Local Delivery[T]
492210  Local Messengers and Local Delivery

# 493    Warehousing and Storage[T]

**4931    Warehousing and Storage[T]**
49311    General Warehousing and Storage[T]
493110  General Warehousing and Storage
49312    Refrigerated Warehousing and Storage[T]
493120  Refrigerated Warehousing and Storage
49313    Farm Product Warehousing and Storage[T]
493130  Farm Product Warehousing and Storage
49319    Other Warehousing and Storage[T]
493190  Other Warehousing and Storage

# Sector 51--Information[T]

# 512    Motion Picture and Sound Recording Industries[T]

**5121    Motion Picture and Video Industries[T]**
51211    Motion Picture and Video Production[T]
512110  Motion Picture and Video Production
51212    Motion Picture and Video Distribution[T]

512120  Motion Picture and Video Distribution
51213  Motion Picture and Video Exhibition$^T$
512131  Motion Picture Theaters (except Drive-Ins)
512132  Drive-In Motion Picture Theaters
51219  Postproduction Services and Other Motion Picture and Video Industries$^T$
512191  Teleproduction and Other Postproduction Services
512199  Other Motion Picture and Video Industries

### 5122  Sound Recording Industries$^T$
51223  Music Publishers$^T$
512230  Music Publishers
51224  Sound Recording Studios$^T$
512240  Sound Recording Studios
51225  Record Production and Distribution$^T$
512250  Record Production and Distribution
51229  Other Sound Recording Industries$^T$
512290  Other Sound Recording Industries

## 513  Publishing Industries$^T$

### 5131  Newspaper, Periodical, Book, and Directory Publishers$^T$
51311  Newspaper Publishers$^T$
513110  Newspaper Publishers
51312  Periodical Publishers$^T$
513120  Periodical Publishers
51313  Book Publishers$^T$
513130  Book Publishers
51314  Directory and Mailing List Publishers$^T$
513140  Directory and Mailing List Publishers
51319  Other Publishers$^T$
513191  Greeting Card Publishers
513199  All Other Publishers

### 5132  Software Publishers$^T$
51321  Software Publishers$^T$
513210  Software Publishers

## 516  Broadcasting and Content Providers$^T$

### 5161  Radio and Television Broadcasting Stations$^T$
51611  Radio Broadcasting Stations$^T$
516110  Radio Broadcasting Stations
51612  Television Broadcasting Stations$^T$
516120  Television Broadcasting Stations

### 5162  Media Streaming Distribution Services, Social Networks, and Other Media Networks and Content Providers$^T$
51621  Media Streaming Distribution Services, Social Networks, and Other Media Networks and Content Providers$^T$
516210  Media Streaming Distribution Services, Social Networks, and Other Media Networks and Content Providers

## 517  Telecommunications$^T$

### 5171  Wired and Wireless Telecommunications (except Satellite)

51711   Wired and Wireless Telecommunications Carriers (except Satellite)
517111  Wired Telecommunications Carriers
517112  Wireless Telecommunications Carriers (except Satellite)
51712   Telecommunications Resellers and Agents for Wireless Telecommunication Services
517121  Telecommunications Resellers
517122  Agents for Wireless Telecommunications Services

**5174    Satellite Telecommunications**[T]
51741   Satellite Telecommunications[T]
517410  Satellite Telecommunications

**5178    All Other Telecommunications**
51781   All Other Telecommunications
517810  All Other Telecommunications

# 518    Computing Infrastructure Providers, Data Processing, Web Hosting, and Related Services[T]

**5182    Computing Infrastructure Providers, Data Processing, Web Hosting, and Related Services**[T]
51821   Computing Infrastructure Providers, Data Processing, Web Hosting, and Related Services[T]
518210  Computing Infrastructure Providers, Data Processing, Web Hosting, and Related Services

# 519    Web Search Portals, Libraries, Archives, and Other Information Services[T]

**5192    Web Search Portals, Libraries, Archives, and Other Information Services**[T]
51921   Libraries and Archives[T]
519210  Libraries and Archives
51929   Web Search Portals and All Other Information Services[T]
519290  Web Search Portals and All Other Information Services

# Sector 52--Finance and Insurance[T]

# 521    Monetary Authorities-Central Bank[T]

**5211    Monetary Authorities-Central Bank**[T]
52111   Monetary Authorities-Central Bank[T]
521110  Monetary Authorities-Central Bank

# 522    Credit Intermediation and Related Activities[T]

**5221    Depository Credit Intermediation**
52211   Commercial Banking
522110  Commercial Banking
52213   Credit Unions
522130  Credit Unions
52218   Savings Institutions and Other Depository Credit Intermediation
522180  Savings Institutions and Other Depository Credit Intermediation

**5222    Nondepository Credit Intermediation**
52221   Credit Card Issuing
522210  Credit Card Issuing

52222    Sales Financing
522220   Sales Financing
52229    Other Nondepository Credit Intermediation
522291   Consumer Lending
522292   Real Estate Credit
522299   International, Secondary Market, and All Other Nondepository Credit Intermediation

**5223    Activities Related to Credit Intermediation**
52231    Mortgage and Nonmortgage Loan Brokers
522310   Mortgage and Nonmortgage Loan Brokers
52232    Financial Transactions Processing, Reserve, and Clearinghouse Activities
522320   Financial Transactions Processing, Reserve, and Clearinghouse Activities
52239    Other Activities Related to Credit Intermediation
522390   Other Activities Related to Credit Intermediation

# 523    Securities, Commodity Contracts, and Other Financial Investments and Related Activities[T]

**5231    Securities and Commodity Contracts Intermediation and Brokerage[T]**
52315    Investment Banking and Securities Intermediation
523150   Investment Banking and Securities Intermediation
52316    Commodity Contracts Intermediation
523160   Commodity Contracts Intermediation

**5232    Securities and Commodity Exchanges[T]**
52321    Securities and Commodity Exchanges[T]
523210   Securities and Commodity Exchanges

**5239    Other Financial Investment Activities[T]**
52391    Miscellaneous Intermediation
523910   Miscellaneous Intermediation
52394    Portfolio Management and Investment Advice
523940   Portfolio Management and Investment Advice
52399    All Other Financial Investment Activities
523991   Trust, Fiduciary, and Custody Activities
523999   Miscellaneous Financial Investment Activities

# 524    Insurance Carriers and Related Activities[T]

**5241    Insurance Carriers[T]**
52411    Direct Life, Health, and Medical Insurance Carriers
524113   Direct Life Insurance Carriers
524114   Direct Health and Medical Insurance Carriers
52412    Direct Insurance (except Life, Health, and Medical) Carriers
524126   Direct Property and Casualty Insurance Carriers
524127   Direct Title Insurance Carriers
524128   Other Direct Insurance (except Life, Health, and Medical) Carriers
52413    Reinsurance Carriers
524130   Reinsurance Carriers

**5242    Agencies, Brokerages, and Other Insurance Related Activities[T]**
52421    Insurance Agencies and Brokerages
524210   Insurance Agencies and Brokerages
52429    Other Insurance Related Activities
524291   Claims Adjusting

524292  Pharmacy Benefit Management and Other Third Party Administration of Insurance and Pension Funds
524298  All Other Insurance Related Activities

## 525     Funds, Trusts, and Other Financial Vehicles

### 5251     Insurance and Employee Benefit Funds
52511    Pension Funds
525110   Pension Funds
52512    Health and Welfare Funds
525120   Health and Welfare Funds
52519    Other Insurance Funds
525190   Other Insurance Funds

### 5259     Other Investment Pools and Funds
52591    Open-End Investment Funds
525910   Open-End Investment Funds
52592    Trusts, Estates, and Agency Accounts
525920   Trusts, Estates, and Agency Accounts
52599    Other Financial Vehicles
525990   Other Financial Vehicles

# Sector 53--Real Estate and Rental and Leasing[T]

## 531     Real Estate[T]

### 5311     Lessors of Real Estate[T]
53111    Lessors of Residential Buildings and Dwellings
531110   Lessors of Residential Buildings and Dwellings
53112    Lessors of Nonresidential Buildings (except Miniwarehouses)
531120   Lessors of Nonresidential Buildings (except Miniwarehouses)
53113    Lessors of Miniwarehouses and Self-Storage Units
531130   Lessors of Miniwarehouses and Self-Storage Units
53119    Lessors of Other Real Estate Property
531190   Lessors of Other Real Estate Property

### 5312     Offices of Real Estate Agents and Brokers[T]
53121    Offices of Real Estate Agents and Brokers[T]
531210   Offices of Real Estate Agents and Brokers

### 5313     Activities Related to Real Estate[T]
53131    Real Estate Property Managers
531311   Residential Property Managers
531312   Nonresidential Property Managers
53132    Offices of Real Estate Appraisers
531320   Offices of Real Estate Appraisers
53139    Other Activities Related to Real Estate
531390   Other Activities Related to Real Estate

## 532     Rental and Leasing Services[T]

### 5321     Automotive Equipment Rental and Leasing[T]
53211    Passenger Car Rental and Leasing[T]
532111   Passenger Car Rental
532112   Passenger Car Leasing

53212    Truck, Utility Trailer, and RV (Recreational Vehicle) Rental and Leasing[T]
532120  Truck, Utility Trailer, and RV (Recreational Vehicle) Rental and Leasing

**5322    Consumer Goods Rental[T]**
53221    Consumer Electronics and Appliances Rental[T]
532210  Consumer Electronics and Appliances Rental
53228    Other Consumer Goods Rental[T]
532281  Formal Wear and Costume Rental
532282  Video Tape and Disc Rental
532283  Home Health Equipment Rental
532284  Recreational Goods Rental
532289  All Other Consumer Goods Rental

**5323    General Rental Centers[T]**
53231    General Rental Centers[T]
532310  General Rental Centers

**5324    Commercial and Industrial Machinery and Equipment Rental and Leasing[T]**
53241    Construction, Transportation, Mining, and Forestry Machinery and Equipment Rental and Leasing[T]
532411  Commercial Air, Rail, and Water Transportation Equipment Rental and Leasing
532412  Construction, Mining, and Forestry Machinery and Equipment Rental and Leasing
53242    Office Machinery and Equipment Rental and Leasing[T]
532420  Office Machinery and Equipment Rental and Leasing
53249    Other Commercial and Industrial Machinery and Equipment Rental and Leasing[T]
532490  Other Commercial and Industrial Machinery and Equipment Rental and Leasing

# 533    Lessors of Nonfinancial Intangible Assets (except Copyrighted Works)[T]

**5331    Lessors of Nonfinancial Intangible Assets (except Copyrighted Works)[T]**
53311    Lessors of Nonfinancial Intangible Assets (except Copyrighted Works)[T]
533110  Lessors of Nonfinancial Intangible Assets (except Copyrighted Works)

# Sector 54--Professional, Scientific, and Technical Services[T]

## 541    Professional, Scientific, and Technical Services[T]

**5411    Legal Services[T]**
54111    Offices of Lawyers[T]
541110  Offices of Lawyers
54112    Offices of Notaries[T]
541120  Offices of Notaries
54119    Other Legal Services[T]
541191  Title Abstract and Settlement Offices
541199  All Other Legal Services

**5412    Accounting, Tax Preparation, Bookkeeping, and Payroll Services[T]**
54121    Accounting, Tax Preparation, Bookkeeping, and Payroll Services[T]
541211  Offices of Certified Public Accountants
541213  Tax Preparation Services
541214  Payroll Services

541219  Other Accounting Services

**5413    Architectural, Engineering, and Related Services**[T]
54131    Architectural Services[T]
541310  Architectural Services
54132    Landscape Architectural Services[T]
541320  Landscape Architectural Services
54133    Engineering Services[T]
541330  Engineering Services
54134    Drafting Services[T]
541340  Drafting Services
54135    Building Inspection Services[T]
541350  Building Inspection Services
54136    Geophysical Surveying and Mapping Services[T]
541360  Geophysical Surveying and Mapping Services
54137    Surveying and Mapping (except Geophysical) Services[T]
541370  Surveying and Mapping (except Geophysical) Services
54138    Testing Laboratories and Services[T]
541380  Testing Laboratories and Services

**5414    Specialized Design Services**[T]
54141    Interior Design Services[T]
541410  Interior Design Services
54142    Industrial Design Services[T]
541420  Industrial Design Services
54143    Graphic Design Services[T]
541430  Graphic Design Services
54149    Other Specialized Design Services[T]
541490  Other Specialized Design Services

**5415    Computer Systems Design and Related Services**[T]
54151    Computer Systems Design and Related Services[T]
541511  Custom Computer Programming Services
541512  Computer Systems Design Services
541513  Computer Facilities Management Services
541519  Other Computer Related Services

**5416    Management, Scientific, and Technical Consulting Services**[T]
54161    Management Consulting Services[T]
541611  Administrative Management and General Management Consulting
            Services
541612  Human Resources Consulting Services
541613  Marketing Consulting Services
541614  Process, Physical Distribution, and Logistics Consulting Services
541618  Other Management Consulting Services
54162    Environmental Consulting Services[T]
541620  Environmental Consulting Services
54169    Other Scientific and Technical Consulting Services[T]
541690  Other Scientific and Technical Consulting Services

**5417    Scientific Research and Development Services**[T]
54171    Research and Development in the Physical, Engineering, and Life Sciences[T]
541713  Research and Development in Nanotechnology
541714  Research and Development in Biotechnology (except Nanobiotechnology)
541715  Research and Development in the Physical, Engineering, and Life Sciences
            (except Nanotechnology and Biotechnology)

54172   Research and Development in the Social Sciences and Humanities[T]
541720  Research and Development in the Social Sciences and Humanities

**5418    Advertising, Public Relations, and Related Services[T]**
54181   Advertising Agencies[T]
541810  Advertising Agencies
54182   Public Relations Agencies[T]
541820  Public Relations Agencies
54183   Media Buying Agencies[T]
541830  Media Buying Agencies
54184   Media Representatives[T]
541840  Media Representatives
54185   Indoor and Outdoor Display Advertising[T]
541850  Indoor and Outdoor Display Advertising
54186   Direct Mail Advertising[T]
541860  Direct Mail Advertising
54187   Advertising Material Distribution Services[T]
541870  Advertising Material Distribution Services
54189   Other Services Related to Advertising[T]
541890  Other Services Related to Advertising

**5419    Other Professional, Scientific, and Technical Services[T]**
54191   Marketing Research and Public Opinion Polling[T]
541910  Marketing Research and Public Opinion Polling
54192   Photographic Services[T]
541921  Photography Studios, Portrait
541922  Commercial Photography
54193   Translation and Interpretation Services[T]
541930  Translation and Interpretation Services
54194   Veterinary Services[T]
541940  Veterinary Services
54199   All Other Professional, Scientific, and Technical Services[T]
541990  All Other Professional, Scientific, and Technical Services

# Sector 55--Management of Companies and Enterprises[T]

## 551    Management of Companies and Enterprises[T]

**5511    Management of Companies and Enterprises[T]**
55111   Management of Companies and Enterprises[T]
551111  Offices of Bank Holding Companies
551112  Offices of Other Holding Companies
551114  Corporate, Subsidiary, and Regional Managing Offices

# Sector 56--Administrative and Support and Waste Management and Remediation Services[T]

## 561    Administrative and Support Services[T]

**5611    Office Administrative Services[T]**
56111   Office Administrative Services[T]
561110  Office Administrative Services

**5612    Facilities Support Services**[T]
        56121    Facilities Support Services[T]
        561210  Facilities Support Services

**5613    Employment Services**[T]
        56131    Employment Placement Agencies and Executive Search Services[T]
        561311  Employment Placement Agencies
        561312  Executive Search Services
        56132    Temporary Help Services[T]
        561320  Temporary Help Services
        56133    Professional Employer Organizations[T]
        561330  Professional Employer Organizations

**5614    Business Support Services**[T]
        56141    Document Preparation Services[T]
        561410  Document Preparation Services
        56142    Telephone Call Centers[T]
        561421  Telephone Answering Services
        561422  Telemarketing Bureaus and Other Contact Centers
        56143    Business Service Centers[T]
        561431  Private Mail Centers
        561439  Other Business Service Centers (including Copy Shops)
        56144    Collection Agencies[T]
        561440  Collection Agencies
        56145    Credit Bureaus[T]
        561450  Credit Bureaus
        56149    Other Business Support Services[T]
        561491  Repossession Services
        561492  Court Reporting and Stenotype Services
        561499  All Other Business Support Services

**5615    Travel Arrangement and Reservation Services**[T]
        56151    Travel Agencies[T]
        561510  Travel Agencies
        56152    Tour Operators[T]
        561520  Tour Operators
        56159    Other Travel Arrangement and Reservation Services[T]
        561591  Convention and Visitors Bureaus
        561599  All Other Travel Arrangement and Reservation Services

**5616    Investigation and Security Services**[T]
        56161    Investigation, Guard, and Armored Car Services[T]
        561611  Investigation and Personal Background Check Services
        561612  Security Guards and Patrol Services
        561613  Armored Car Services
        56162    Security Systems Services[T]
        561621  Security Systems Services (except Locksmiths)
        561622  Locksmiths

**5617    Services to Buildings and Dwellings**[T]
        56171    Exterminating and Pest Control Services[T]
        561710  Exterminating and Pest Control Services
        56172    Janitorial Services[T]
        561720  Janitorial Services
        56173    Landscaping Services[T]
        561730  Landscaping Services

           56174   Carpet and Upholstery Cleaning Services[T]
           561740  Carpet and Upholstery Cleaning Services
           56179   Other Services to Buildings and Dwellings[T]
           561790  Other Services to Buildings and Dwellings

    **5619**   **Other Support Services**[T]
           56191   Packaging and Labeling Services[T]
           561910  Packaging and Labeling Services
           56192   Convention and Trade Show Organizers[T]
           561920  Convention and Trade Show Organizers
           56199   All Other Support Services[T]
           561990  All Other Support Services

**562**   **Waste Management and Remediation Services**[T]

    **5621**   **Waste Collection**
           56211   Waste Collection
           562111  Solid Waste Collection
           562112  Hazardous Waste Collection
           562119  Other Waste Collection

    **5622**   **Waste Treatment and Disposal**
           56221   Waste Treatment and Disposal
           562211  Hazardous Waste Treatment and Disposal
           562212  Solid Waste Landfill
           562213  Solid Waste Combustors and Incinerators
           562219  Other Nonhazardous Waste Treatment and Disposal

    **5629**   **Remediation and Other Waste Management Services**
           56291   Remediation Services
           562910  Remediation Services
           56292   Materials Recovery Facilities
           562920  Materials Recovery Facilities
           56299   All Other Waste Management Services
           562991  Septic Tank and Related Services
           562998  All Other Miscellaneous Waste Management Services

# Sector 61--Educational Services[T]

**611**   **Educational Services**[T]

    **6111**   **Elementary and Secondary Schools**[T]
           61111   Elementary and Secondary Schools
           611110  Elementary and Secondary Schools

    **6112**   **Junior Colleges**[T]
           61121   Junior Colleges[T]
           611210  Junior Colleges

    **6113**   **Colleges, Universities, and Professional Schools**[T]
           61131   Colleges, Universities, and Professional Schools[T]
           611310  Colleges, Universities, and Professional Schools

    **6114**   **Business Schools and Computer and Management Training**[T]
           61141   Business and Secretarial Schools[T]

611410  Business and Secretarial Schools
61142   Computer Training[T]
611420  Computer Training
61143   Professional and Management Development Training[T]
611430  Professional and Management Development Training

**6115    Technical and Trade Schools[T]**
61151   Technical and Trade Schools[T]
611511  Cosmetology and Barber Schools
611512  Flight Training
611513  Apprenticeship Training
611519  Other Technical and Trade Schools

**6116    Other Schools and Instruction[T]**
61161   Fine Arts Schools[T]
611610  Fine Arts Schools
61162   Sports and Recreation Instruction[T]
611620  Sports and Recreation Instruction
61163   Language Schools[T]
611630  Language Schools
61169   All Other Schools and Instruction[T]
611691  Exam Preparation and Tutoring
611692  Automobile Driving Schools
611699  All Other Miscellaneous Schools and Instruction

**6117    Educational Support Services[T]**
61171   Educational Support Services[T]
611710  Educational Support Services

# Sector 62--Health Care and Social Assistance[T]

## 621    Ambulatory Health Care Services[T]

**6211    Offices of Physicians[T]**
62111   Offices of Physicians[T]
621111  Offices of Physicians (except Mental Health Specialists)
621112  Offices of Physicians, Mental Health Specialists

**6212    Offices of Dentists[T]**
62121   Offices of Dentists[T]
621210  Offices of Dentists

**6213    Offices of Other Health Practitioners[T]**
62131   Offices of Chiropractors[T]
621310  Offices of Chiropractors
62132   Offices of Optometrists[T]
621320  Offices of Optometrists
62133   Offices of Mental Health Practitioners (except Physicians)[T]
621330  Offices of Mental Health Practitioners (except Physicians)
62134   Offices of Physical, Occupational and Speech Therapists, and Audiologists[T]
621340  Offices of Physical, Occupational and Speech Therapists, and Audiologists
62139   Offices of All Other Health Practitioners[T]
621391  Offices of Podiatrists
621399  Offices of All Other Miscellaneous Health Practitioners

**6214    Outpatient Care Centers[T]**
    62141    Family Planning Centers[T]
    621410  Family Planning Centers
    62142    Outpatient Mental Health and Substance Abuse Centers[T]
    621420  Outpatient Mental Health and Substance Abuse Centers
    62149    Other Outpatient Care Centers[T]
    621491  HMO Medical Centers
    621492  Kidney Dialysis Centers
    621493  Freestanding Ambulatory Surgical and Emergency Centers
    621498  All Other Outpatient Care Centers

**6215    Medical and Diagnostic Laboratories[T]**
    62151    Medical and Diagnostic Laboratories[T]
    621511  Medical Laboratories
    621512  Diagnostic Imaging Centers

**6216    Home Health Care Services[T]**
    62161    Home Health Care Services[T]
    621610  Home Health Care Services

**6219    Other Ambulatory Health Care Services[T]**
    62191    Ambulance Services[T]
    621910  Ambulance Services
    62199    All Other Ambulatory Health Care Services[T]
    621991  Blood and Organ Banks
    621999  All Other Miscellaneous Ambulatory Health Care Services

# 622    Hospitals[T]

**6221    General Medical and Surgical Hospitals[T]**
    62211    General Medical and Surgical Hospitals[T]
    622110  General Medical and Surgical Hospitals

**6222    Psychiatric and Substance Abuse Hospitals[T]**
    62221    Psychiatric and Substance Abuse Hospitals[T]
    622210  Psychiatric and Substance Abuse Hospitals

**6223    Specialty (except Psychiatric and Substance Abuse) Hospitals[T]**
    62231    Specialty (except Psychiatric and Substance Abuse) Hospitals[T]
    622310  Specialty (except Psychiatric and Substance Abuse) Hospitals

# 623    Nursing and Residential Care Facilities[T]

**6231    Nursing Care Facilities (Skilled Nursing Facilities)[T]**
    62311    Nursing Care Facilities (Skilled Nursing Facilities)[T]
    623110  Nursing Care Facilities (Skilled Nursing Facilities)

**6232    Residential Intellectual and Developmental Disability, Mental Health, and Substance Abuse Facilities[T]**
    62321    Residential Intellectual and Developmental Disability Facilities[T]
    623210  Residential Intellectual and Developmental Disability Facilities
    62322    Residential Mental Health and Substance Abuse Facilities[T]
    623220  Residential Mental Health and Substance Abuse Facilities

**6233    Continuing Care Retirement Communities and Assisted Living Facilities for the Elderly**[T]
62331    Continuing Care Retirement Communities and Assisted Living Facilities for the Elderly[T]
623311    Continuing Care Retirement Communities
623312    Assisted Living Facilities for the Elderly

**6239    Other Residential Care Facilities**[T]
62399    Other Residential Care Facilities[T]
623990    Other Residential Care Facilities

# 624    Social Assistance[T]

**6241    Individual and Family Services**[T]
62411    Child and Youth Services[T]
624110    Child and Youth Services
62412    Services for the Elderly and Persons with Disabilities[T]
624120    Services for the Elderly and Persons with Disabilities
62419    Other Individual and Family Services[T]
624190    Other Individual and Family Services

**6242    Community Food and Housing, and Emergency and Other Relief Services**[T]
62421    Community Food Services[T]
624210    Community Food Services
62422    Community Housing Services[T]
624221    Temporary Shelters
624229    Other Community Housing Services
62423    Emergency and Other Relief Services[T]
624230    Emergency and Other Relief Services

**6243    Vocational Rehabilitation Services**[T]
62431    Vocational Rehabilitation Services[T]
624310    Vocational Rehabilitation Services

**6244    Child Care Services**[T]
62441    Child Care Services[T]
624410    Child Care Services

# Sector 71--Arts, Entertainment, and Recreation[T]

## 711    Performing Arts, Spectator Sports, and Related Industries[T]

**7111    Performing Arts Companies**[T]
71111    Theater Companies and Dinner Theaters[T]
711110    Theater Companies and Dinner Theaters
71112    Dance Companies[T]
711120    Dance Companies
71113    Musical Groups and Artists[T]
711130    Musical Groups and Artists
71119    Other Performing Arts Companies[T]
711190    Other Performing Arts Companies

**7112    Spectator Sports**[T]
71121    Spectator Sports[T]
711211    Sports Teams and Clubs

711212 Racetracks
711219 Other Spectator Sports

**7113    Promoters of Performing Arts, Sports, and Similar Events[T]**
71131   Promoters of Performing Arts, Sports, and Similar Events with Facilities[T]
711310  Promoters of Performing Arts, Sports, and Similar Events with Facilities
71132   Promoters of Performing Arts, Sports, and Similar Events without Facilities[T]
711320  Promoters of Performing Arts, Sports, and Similar Events without Facilities

**7114    Agents and Managers for Artists, Athletes, Entertainers, and Other Public Figures[T]**
71141   Agents and Managers for Artists, Athletes, Entertainers, and Other Public Figures[T]
711410  Agents and Managers for Artists, Athletes, Entertainers, and Other Public Figures

**7115    Independent Artists, Writers, and Performers[T]**
71151   Independent Artists, Writers, and Performers[T]
711510  Independent Artists, Writers, and Performers

# 712    Museums, Historical Sites, and Similar Institutions[T]

**7121    Museums, Historical Sites, and Similar Institutions[T]**
71211   Museums[T]
712110  Museums
71212   Historical Sites[T]
712120  Historical Sites
71213   Zoos and Botanical Gardens[T]
712130  Zoos and Botanical Gardens
71219   Nature Parks and Other Similar Institutions[T]
712190  Nature Parks and Other Similar Institutions

# 713    Amusement, Gambling, and Recreation Industries[T]

**7131    Amusement Parks and Arcades[T]**
71311   Amusement and Theme Parks[T]
713110  Amusement and Theme Parks
71312   Amusement Arcades[T]
713120  Amusement Arcades

**7132    Gambling Industries[T]**
71321   Casinos (except Casino Hotels)[T]
713210  Casinos (except Casino Hotels)
71329   Other Gambling Industries[T]
713290  Other Gambling Industries

**7139    Other Amusement and Recreation Industries[T]**
71391   Golf Courses and Country Clubs[T]
713910  Golf Courses and Country Clubs
71392   Skiing Facilities[T]
713920  Skiing Facilities
71393   Marinas[T]
713930  Marinas
71394   Fitness and Recreational Sports Centers[T]
713940  Fitness and Recreational Sports Centers

71395   Bowling Centers[T]
713950  Bowling Centers
71399   All Other Amusement and Recreation Industries[T]
713990  All Other Amusement and Recreation Industries

# Sector 72--Accommodation and Food Services[T]

## 721      Accommodation[T]

### 7211      Traveler Accommodation[T]
72111   Hotels (except Casino Hotels) and Motels[T]
721110  Hotels (except Casino Hotels) and Motels
72112   Casino Hotels[T]
721120  Casino Hotels
72119   Other Traveler Accommodation[T]
721191  Bed-and-Breakfast Inns
721199  All Other Traveler Accommodation

### 7212      RV (Recreational Vehicle) Parks and Recreational Camps[T]
72121   RV (Recreational Vehicle) Parks and Recreational Camps[T]
721211  RV (Recreational Vehicle) Parks and Campgrounds
721214  Recreational and Vacation Camps (except Campgrounds)

### 7213      Rooming and Boarding Houses, Dormitories, and Workers' Camps[T]
72131   Rooming and Boarding Houses, Dormitories, and Workers' Camps[T]
721310  Rooming and Boarding Houses, Dormitories, and Workers' Camps

## 722      Food Services and Drinking Places[T]

### 7223      Special Food Services[T]
72231   Food Service Contractors[T]
722310  Food Service Contractors
72232   Caterers[I]
722320  Caterers
72233   Mobile Food Services[T]
722330  Mobile Food Services

### 7224      Drinking Places (Alcoholic Beverages)[T]
72241   Drinking Places (Alcoholic Beverages)[T]
722410  Drinking Places (Alcoholic Beverages)

### 7225      Restaurants and Other Eating Places[T]
72251   Restaurants and Other Eating Places[T]
722511  Full-Service Restaurants
722513  Limited-Service Restaurants
722514  Cafeterias, Grill Buffets, and Buffets
722515  Snack and Nonalcoholic Beverage Bars

# Sector 81--Other Services (except Public Administration)[T]

## 811      Repair and Maintenance[T]

### 8111      Automotive Repair and Maintenance[T]
81111   Automotive Mechanical and Electrical Repair and Maintenance[T]

811111  General Automotive Repair
811114  Specialized Automotive Repair
81112   Automotive Body, Paint, Interior, and Glass Repair[T]
811121  Automotive Body, Paint, and Interior Repair and Maintenance
811122  Automotive Glass Replacement Shops
81119   Other Automotive Repair and Maintenance[T]
811191  Automotive Oil Change and Lubrication Shops
811192  Car Washes
811198  All Other Automotive Repair and Maintenance

**8112    Electronic and Precision Equipment Repair and Maintenance[T]**
81121   Electronic and Precision Equipment Repair and Maintenance[T]
811210  Electronic and Precision Equipment Repair and Maintenance

**8113    Commercial and Industrial Machinery and Equipment (except Automotive and Electronic) Repair and Maintenance[T]**
81131   Commercial and Industrial Machinery and Equipment (except Automotive and Electronic) Repair and Maintenance[T]
811310  Commercial and Industrial Machinery and Equipment (except Automotive and Electronic) Repair and Maintenance

**8114    Personal and Household Goods Repair and Maintenance[T]**
81141   Home and Garden Equipment and Appliance Repair and Maintenance[T]
811411  Home and Garden Equipment Repair and Maintenance
811412  Appliance Repair and Maintenance
81142   Reupholstery and Furniture Repair[T]
811420  Reupholstery and Furniture Repair
81143   Footwear and Leather Goods Repair[T]
811430  Footwear and Leather Goods Repair
81149   Other Personal and Household Goods Repair and Maintenance[T]
811490  Other Personal and Household Goods Repair and Maintenance

# 812    Personal and Laundry Services[T]

**8121    Personal Care Services**
81211   Hair, Nail, and Skin Care Services
812111  Barber Shops
812112  Beauty Salons
812113  Nail Salons
81219   Other Personal Care Services
812191  Diet and Weight Reducing Centers
812199  Other Personal Care Services

**8122    Death Care Services**
81221   Funeral Homes and Funeral Services
812210  Funeral Homes and Funeral Services
81222   Cemeteries and Crematories
812220  Cemeteries and Crematories

**8123    Drycleaning and Laundry Services**
81231   Coin-Operated Laundries and Drycleaners
812310  Coin-Operated Laundries and Drycleaners
81232   Drycleaning and Laundry Services (except Coin-Operated)
812320  Drycleaning and Laundry Services (except Coin-Operated)
81233   Linen and Uniform Supply
812331  Linen Supply

812332  Industrial Launderers

**8129    Other Personal Services**
81291   Pet Care (except Veterinary) Services
812910  Pet Care (except Veterinary) Services
81292   Photofinishing
812921  Photofinishing Laboratories (except One-Hour)
812922  One-Hour Photofinishing
81293   Parking Lots and Garages
812930  Parking Lots and Garages
81299   All Other Personal Services
812990  All Other Personal Services

## 813    Religious, Grantmaking, Civic, Professional, and Similar Organizations[T]

**8131    Religious Organizations**
81311   Religious Organizations
813110  Religious Organizations

**8132    Grantmaking and Giving Services**
81321   Grantmaking and Giving Services
813211  Grantmaking Foundations
813212  Voluntary Health Organizations
813219  Other Grantmaking and Giving Services

**8133    Social Advocacy Organizations**
81331   Social Advocacy Organizations
813311  Human Rights Organizations
813312  Environment, Conservation and Wildlife Organizations
813319  Other Social Advocacy Organizations

**8134    Civic and Social Organizations**
81341   Civic and Social Organizations
813410  Civic and Social Organizations

**8139    Business, Professional, Labor, Political, and Similar Organizations**
81391   Business Associations
813910  Business Associations
81392   Professional Organizations
813920  Professional Organizations
81393   Labor Unions and Similar Labor Organizations
813930  Labor Unions and Similar Labor Organizations
81394   Political Organizations
813940  Political Organizations
81399   Other Similar Organizations (except Business, Professional, Labor, and
        Political Organizations)
813990  Other Similar Organizations (except Business, Professional, Labor, and
        Political Organizations)

## 814    Private Households[T]

**8141    Private Households[T]**
81411   Private Households[T]
814110  Private Households

# Sector 92--Public Administration[T]

## 921    Executive, Legislative, and Other General Government Support

### 9211    Executive, Legislative, and Other General Government Support
92111   Executive Offices
921110  Executive Offices
92112   Legislative Bodies
921120  Legislative Bodies
92113   Public Finance Activities
921130  Public Finance Activities
92114   Executive and Legislative Offices, Combined
921140  Executive and Legislative Offices, Combined
92115   American Indian and Alaska Native Tribal Governments
921150  American Indian and Alaska Native Tribal Governments
92119   Other General Government Support
921190  Other General Government Support

## 922    Justice, Public Order, and Safety Activities

### 9221    Justice, Public Order, and Safety Activities
92211   Courts
922110  Courts
92212   Police Protection
922120  Police Protection
92213   Legal Counsel and Prosecution
922130  Legal Counsel and Prosecution
92214   Correctional Institutions
922140  Correctional Institutions
92215   Parole Offices and Probation Offices
922150  Parole Offices and Probation Offices
92216   Fire Protection
922160  Fire Protection
92219   Other Justice, Public Order, and Safety Activities
922190  Other Justice, Public Order, and Safety Activities

## 923    Administration of Human Resource Programs

### 9231    Administration of Human Resource Programs
92311   Administration of Education Programs
923110  Administration of Education Programs
92312   Administration of Public Health Programs
923120  Administration of Public Health Programs
92313   Administration of Human Resource Programs (except Education, Public
            Health, and Veterans' Affairs Programs)
923130  Administration of Human Resource Programs (except Education, Public
            Health, and Veterans' Affairs Programs)
92314   Administration of Veterans' Affairs
923140  Administration of Veterans' Affairs

## 924    Administration of Environmental Quality Programs

### 9241    Administration of Environmental Quality Programs
92411   Administration of Air and Water Resource and Solid Waste Management
            Programs

924110  Administration of Air and Water Resource and Solid Waste Management
        Programs
92412   Administration of Conservation Programs
924120  Administration of Conservation Programs

## 925    Administration of Housing Programs, Urban Planning, and Community Development

### 9251   Administration of Housing Programs, Urban Planning, and Community Development
92511   Administration of Housing Programs
925110  Administration of Housing Programs
92512   Administration of Urban Planning and Community and Rural Development
925120  Administration of Urban Planning and Community and Rural Development

## 926    Administration of Economic Programs

### 9261   Administration of Economic Programs
92611   Administration of General Economic Programs
926110  Administration of General Economic Programs
92612   Regulation and Administration of Transportation Programs
926120  Regulation and Administration of Transportation Programs
92613   Regulation and Administration of Communications, Electric, Gas, and Other
        Utilities
926130  Regulation and Administration of Communications, Electric, Gas, and Other
        Utilities
92614   Regulation of Agricultural Marketing and Commodities
926140  Regulation of Agricultural Marketing and Commodities
92615   Regulation, Licensing, and Inspection of Miscellaneous Commercial
        Sectors
926150  Regulation, Licensing, and Inspection of Miscellaneous Commercial
        Sectors

## 927    Space Research and Technology

### 9271   Space Research and Technology
92711   Space Research and Technology
927110  Space Research and Technology

## 928    National Security and International Affairs

### 9281   National Security and International Affairs
92811   National Security
928110  National Security
92812   International Affairs
928120  International Affairs

# Frequently Asked Questions About Economic Classifications

1. What is the purpose of an industry classification system?
   - An industry classification system facilitates the collection, tabulation, presentation, and analysis of data relating to establishments and ensures that data about the U.S. economy published by U.S. statistical agencies are uniform and comparable. NAICS ensures that such data are uniform and comparable among Canada, Mexico, and the United States.

2. What is an establishment?
   - An establishment is generally a single, physical location at which economic activity occurs (e.g., store, factory, farm, etc.). An enterprise consists of one or more locations that are more than 50 percent owned by the same entity performing the same or different types of economic activities. Each establishment of that enterprise is assigned a NAICS code, based on its own primary activity.

3. How can I determine the correct NAICS code for my business?
   - To determine the correct NAICS code for your establishment, first identify the primary business activity. Then refer either to: 1) the NAICS United States Structure to search the titles from the 2-digit level down through the 6-digit, more detailed level, to find the appropriate code; or 2) the Alphabetic Index to search alphabetically for the primary activity and its corresponding code. Next, read the full description of the industry (including the narrative, cross-references, and illustrative examples), and determine if that description fits the primary business activity of your establishment. An electronic NAICS search and references are available at www.census.gov/naics.

4. Who assigns NAICS codes to businesses and how?
   - There is no central government agency with the role of assigning, monitoring, or approving NAICS codes for establishments. Different agencies maintain their own lists of business establishments to meet their own programmatic needs. These different agencies use their own methods for assigning NAICS codes to the establishments on their lists. Statistical agencies assign one NAICS code to each establishment based on its primary activity. For example, the Social Security Administration assigns a NAICS code to new businesses based on information provided on their application for an Employer Identification Number. The Census Bureau generally assigns NAICS codes to businesses on its list of establishments based on information provided by the business on a survey or census report form. The Bureau of Labor Statistics initially assigns NAICS codes based on business activity information provided on an application for unemployment insurance.

5. How do I apply for a NAICS code?
   - A business does not 'apply' for a NAICS code. As explained above, statistical agencies generally assign NAICS codes based on information provided by a business on an application form, an administrative report, or on a survey or census report form.

6. How can I get a new NAICS code created for my type of business?

- Every five years NAICS is reviewed for potential revisions, so that the classification system can keep pace with the changing economy. This is the only time that new NAICS codes can be considered. The Office of Management and Budget (OMB), through its Economic Classification Policy Committee (ECPC), will solicit public comments regarding changes to NAICS through a notice published in the **Federal Register**. The notice will provide details of the format in which comments should be submitted, how and to whom they should be submitted, and the deadline for submission. During the public comment period, suggestions for new and emerging industries can be submitted to the ECPC. The next scheduled review of NAICS will be for a potential 2027 revision.

7. What is the relationship between NAICS and the Small Business Administration's (SBA) size standards?

- NAICS categories do not distinguish between small and large business, or between for-profit and non-profit. The Small Business Administration (SBA) develops size standards for each NAICS category. To find more information about the SBA size standards, or when the SBA will update their size standards to reflect 2022 NAICS revisions, visit the SBA Web site at www.sba.gov/federal-contracting/contracting-guide/size-standards. You may also contact SBA's Office of Size Standards Answer Desk on 800-827-5722 or via email to answerdesk@sba.gov.

8. How do the NAICS codes affect federal procurement and regulatory activities, such as those carried out by the Environmental Protection Agency, OSHA, the Department of Defense, and the General Services Administration?

- NAICS was developed specifically for the collection and publication of statistical data to foster the comparability of economic estimates for Canada, Mexico, and the United States. The NAICS categories and definitions were not developed to meet the needs of procurement and/or regulatory applications. However, other federal agencies and other organizations have adopted NAICS for procurement and regulatory purposes even though it does not entirely fit their specific needs. For questions regarding these agencies' use of the NAICS system, contact the specific agency.

For answers to other NAICS questions, visit the NAICS Web site at www.census.gov/naics.

# Part I

# Titles and Descriptions of Industries

# Sector 11--Agriculture, Forestry, Fishing and Hunting[T]

## The Sector as a Whole

The Agriculture, Forestry, Fishing and Hunting sector comprises establishments primarily engaged in growing crops, raising animals, harvesting timber, and harvesting fish and other animals from a farm, ranch, or their natural habitats.

The establishments in this sector are often described as farms, ranches, dairies, greenhouses, nurseries, orchards, or hatcheries. A farm may consist of a single tract of land or a number of separate tracts which may be held under different tenures. For example, one tract may be owned by the farm operator and another rented. It may be operated by the operator alone or with the assistance of members of the household or hired employees, or it may be operated by a partnership, corporation, or other type of organization. When a landowner has one or more tenants, renters, croppers, or managers, the land operated by each is considered a farm.

The sector distinguishes two basic activities: agricultural production and agricultural support activities. Agricultural production includes establishments performing the complete farm or ranch operation, such as farm owner-operators and tenant farm operators. Agricultural support activities include establishments that perform one or more activities associated with farm operation, such as soil preparation, planting, harvesting, and management, on a contract or fee basis.

Excluded from the Agriculture, Forestry, Fishing and Hunting sector are establishments primarily engaged in agricultural research (e.g., experimental farms) and government establishments primarily engaged in administering programs for regulating and conserving land, mineral, wildlife, and forest use. These establishments are classified in Industry 54171, Research and Development in the Physical, Engineering, and Life Sciences; and Industry 92412, Administration of Conservation Programs, respectively.

## 111   Crop Production[T]

Industries in the Crop Production subsector grow crops mainly for food and fiber. The subsector comprises establishments, such as farms, orchards, groves, greenhouses, and nurseries, primarily engaged in growing crops, plants, vines, or trees and their seeds.

The industries in this subsector are grouped by similarity of production activity, including biological and physiological characteristics and economic requirements, the length of growing season, degree of crop rotation, extent of input specialization, labor requirements, and capital demands. The production process is typically completed when the raw product or commodity grown reaches the "farm gate" for market, that is, at the point of first sale or price determination.

Establishments are classified in the Crop Production subsector when crop production (i.e., value of crops for market) accounts for one-half or more of the establishment's total agricultural production. Within the subsector, establishments are classified in a specific industry when a product or industry family of products (i.e., oilseed and grain farming, vegetable and melon farming, fruit and tree nut farming) account for one-half or more of the establishment's agricultural production. Establishments with one-half or more crop production with no one product or family of products of an industry accounting for one-half of the establishment's agricultural production are treated as general combination crop farming and are classified in Industry 11199, All Other Crop Farming.

Industries in the Crop Production subsector include establishments that own, operate, and manage and those that operate and manage. Those that manage only are classified in Subsector 115, Support Activities for Agriculture and Forestry. Establishments that raise aquatic plants in controlled or selected aquatic environments are classified in Subsector 112, Animal Production and Aquaculture.

## 1111   Oilseed and Grain Farming[T]

This industry group comprises establishments primarily engaged in (1) growing oilseed and/or grain crops and/or (2) producing oilseed and grain seeds. These crops have an annual life cycle and are typically grown in open fields.

## 11111   Soybean Farming[T]
See industry description for 111110.

---

T—Canadian, Mexican, and United States industries are comparable.

**111110  Soybean Farming**

This industry comprises establishments primarily engaged in growing soybeans and/or producing soybean seeds.

*Cross-References.*

Establishments engaged in growing soybeans in combination with grain(s) with the soybeans or grain(s) not accounting for one-half of the establishment's agricultural production (value of crops for market) are classified in U.S. Industry 111191, Oilseed and Grain Combination Farming.

**11112   Oilseed (except Soybean) Farming**[T]
See industry description for 111120.

**111120  Oilseed (except Soybean) Farming**

This industry comprises establishments primarily engaged in growing fibrous oilseed producing plants and/or producing oilseed seeds, such as sunflower, safflower, flax, rape, canola, and sesame.

*Cross-References.*          Establishments primarily engaged in--

- Growing soybeans--are classified in Industry 111110, Soybean Farming; and
- Growing oilseed(s) in combination with grain(s) with no one oilseed (or family of oilseeds) or grain(s) (or family of grains) accounting for one-half of the establishment's agricultural production (value of crops for market)--are classified in U.S. Industry 111191, Oilseed and Grain Combination Farming.

**11113   Dry Pea and Bean Farming**[T]
See industry description for 111130.

**111130  Dry Pea and Bean Farming**

This industry comprises establishments primarily engaged in growing dry peas, beans, and/or lentils.

*Cross-References.*

Establishments primarily engaged in growing fresh green beans and peas are classified in U.S. Industry 111219, Other Vegetable (except Potato) and Melon Farming.

**11114   Wheat Farming**[T]
See industry description for 111140.

**111140  Wheat Farming**

This industry comprises establishments primarily engaged in growing wheat and/or producing wheat seeds.

*Cross-References.*

Establishments growing wheat in combination with oilseed(s) with the wheat or oilseed(s) not accounting for one-half of the establishment's agricultural production (value of crops for market) are classified in U.S. Industry 111191, Oilseed and Grain Combination Farming.

**11115   Corn Farming**[T]
See industry description for 111150.

---

T—Canadian, Mexican, and United States industries are comparable.

**111150  Corn Farming**

This industry comprises establishments primarily engaged in growing corn (except sweet corn) and/or producing corn seeds.

*Cross-References.*          Establishments primarily engaged in--

- Growing sweet corn--are classified in U.S. Industry 111219, Other Vegetable (except Potato) and Melon Farming; and
- Growing corn in combination with oilseed(s) with the corn or oilseed(s) not accounting for one-half of the establishment's production (value of crops for market)--are classified in U.S. Industry 111191, Oilseed and Grain Combination Farming.

**11116  Rice Farming[T]**
See industry description for 111160.

**111160  Rice Farming**

This industry comprises establishments primarily engaged in growing rice (except wild rice) and/or producing rice seeds.

*Cross-References.*          Establishments primarily engaged in--

- Growing wild rice--are classified in U.S. Industry 111199, All Other Grain Farming; and
- Growing rice in combination with oilseed(s) with the rice or oilseed(s) not accounting for one-half of the establishment's agricultural production (value of crops for market)--are classified in U.S. Industry 111191, Oilseed and Grain Combination Farming.

**11119  Other Grain Farming[T]**

This industry comprises establishments primarily engaged in (1) growing grain(s) and/or producing grain seeds (except wheat, corn, and rice) or (2) growing a combination of grain(s) and oilseed(s) with no one grain (or family of grains) or oilseed (or family of oilseeds) accounting for one-half of the establishment's agricultural production (i.e., value of crops for market).  Combination grain(s) and oilseed(s) establishments may produce oilseed(s) and grain(s) seeds and/or grow oilseed(s) and grain(s).

*Illustrative Examples:*

Barley farming                                        Oat farming
Rye farming                                           Wild rice farming
Milo farming                                          Oilseed and grain combination farming
Sorghum farming

*Cross-References.*          Establishments primarily engaged in--

- Growing wheat--are classified in Industry 11114, Wheat Farming;
- Growing corn (except sweet corn)--are classified in Industry 11115, Corn Farming;
- Growing sweet corn--are classified in Industry 11121, Vegetable and Melon Farming; and
- Growing rice (except wild rice)--are classified in Industry 11116, Rice Farming.

**111191  Oilseed and Grain Combination Farming**

This U.S. industry comprises establishments engaged in growing a combination of oilseed(s) and grain(s) with no one oilseed (or family of oilseeds) or grain (or family of grains) accounting for one-half of the establishment's

---

T—Canadian, Mexican, and United States industries are comparable.

agricultural production (value of crops for market). These establishments may produce oilseed(s) and grain(s) seeds and/or grow oilseed(s) and grain(s).

*Cross-References.*

Establishments engaged in growing one grain (or family of grains) or oilseed (or family of oilseeds) accounting for one-half of the establishment's agricultural production (i.e., value of crops for market) are classified in Industry Group 1111, Oilseed and Grain Farming, accordingly by the prominent grain(s) or oilseed(s) grown.

## 111199  All Other Grain Farming

This U.S. industry comprises establishments primarily engaged in growing grains and/or producing grain(s) seeds (except wheat, corn, rice, and oilseed(s) and grain(s) combinations).

*Illustrative Examples:*

Barley farming
Sorghum farming
Oat farming

Wild rice farming
Rye farming

*Cross-References.*          Establishments primarily engaged in--

- Growing wheat--are classified in Industry 111140, Wheat Farming;
- Growing corn (except sweet corn)--are classified in Industry 111150, Corn Farming;
- Growing rice (except wild rice)--are classified in Industry 111160, Rice Farming;
- Growing sweet corn--are classified in U.S. Industry 111219, Other Vegetable (except Potato) and Melon Farming; and
- Growing a combination of grain(s) and oilseed(s) with no one grain (or family of grains) or oilseed (or family of oilseeds) accounting for one-half of the establishment's agricultural production (value of crops for market)--are classified in U.S. Industry 111191, Oilseed and Grain Combination Farming.

## 1112  Vegetable and Melon Farming<sup>T</sup>

## 11121  Vegetable and Melon Farming<sup>T</sup>

This industry comprises establishments primarily engaged in one or more of the following: (1) growing vegetable and/or melon crops; (2) producing vegetable and/or melon seeds; and (3) growing vegetable and/or melon bedding plants. The crops included in this industry have an annual growth cycle and are grown in open fields. Climate and cultural practices limit producing areas but often permit the growing of a combination of crops in a year.

*Cross-References.*          Establishments primarily engaged in--

- Growing sugar beets--are classified in Industry 11199, All Other Crop Farming;
- Growing vegetables and melons under glass or protective cover--are classified in Industry 11141, Food Crops Grown Under Cover;
- Growing dry peas and beans--are classified in Industry 11113, Dry Pea and Bean Farming;
- Growing corn (except sweet corn)--are classified in Industry 11115, Corn Farming;
- Canning, pickling, and/or drying (artificially) vegetables--are classified in Industry 31142, Fruit and Vegetable Canning, Pickling, and Drying; and
- Growing fruit on trees and other fruit-bearing plants (except melons)--are classified in Industry Group 1113, Fruit and Tree Nut Farming.

---

T—Canadian, Mexican, and United States industries are comparable.

**census.gov/naics**

## 111211  Potato Farming

This U.S. industry comprises establishments primarily engaged in growing potatoes and/or producing seed potatoes.

*Cross-References.*

Establishments primarily engaged in canning or drying potatoes are classified in Industry 31142, Fruit and Vegetable Canning, Pickling, and Drying.

## 111219  Other Vegetable (except Potato) and Melon Farming

This U.S. industry comprises establishments primarily engaged in one or more of the following: (1) growing melons and/or vegetables (except potatoes; dry peas; dry beans; field, silage, or seed corn; and sugar beets); (2) producing vegetable and/or melon seeds; and (3) growing vegetable and/or melon bedding plants.

*Illustrative Examples:*

Carrot farming
Squash farming
Green bean farming
Tomato farming
Watermelon farming

Melon farming (e.g., cantaloupe, casaba, honeydew, watermelon)
Vegetable (except potato) farming
Pepper farming (e.g., bell, chili, green, red, sweet peppers)

*Cross-References.*        Establishments primarily engaged in--

- Growing potatoes, including sweet potatoes and yams--are classified in U.S. Industry 111211, Potato Farming;
- Growing sugar beets--are classified in U.S. Industry 111991, Sugar Beet Farming;
- Growing vegetables and melons under glass or protective cover--are classified in U.S. Industry 111419, Other Food Crops Grown Under Cover;
- Growing dry peas and beans--are classified in Industry 111130, Dry Pea and Bean Farming;
- Growing corn (except sweet corn)--are classified in Industry 111150, Corn Farming;
- Canning, pickling, and/or drying (artificially) vegetables--are classified in Industry 31142, Fruit and Vegetable Canning, Pickling, and Drying; and
- Growing fruit on trees and other fruit-bearing plants (except melons)--are classified in Industry Group 1113, Fruit and Tree Nut Farming.

## 1113     Fruit and Tree Nut Farming[T]

This industry group comprises establishments primarily engaged in growing fruit and/or tree nut crops.  The crops included in this industry group are generally not grown from seeds and have a perennial life cycle.

## 11131    Orange Groves[T]
See industry description for 111310.

## 111310  Orange Groves

This industry comprises establishments primarily engaged in growing oranges.

## 11132    Citrus (except Orange) Groves[T]
See industry description for 111320.

---

T—Canadian, Mexican, and United States industries are comparable.

## 111320 Citrus (except Orange) Groves

This industry comprises establishments primarily engaged in growing citrus fruits (except oranges).

*Illustrative Examples:*

Citrus groves (except oranges)
Mandarin groves
Grapefruit groves

Tangelo groves
Lemon groves
Tangerine groves

*Cross-References.*

Establishments primarily engaged in growing oranges are classified in Industry 111310, Orange Groves.

## 11133   Noncitrus Fruit and Tree Nut Farming[T]

This industry comprises establishments primarily engaged in one or more of the following: (1) growing noncitrus fruits (e.g., apples, grapes, berries, peaches); (2) growing tree nuts (e.g., pecans, almonds, pistachios); or (3) growing a combination of fruit(s) and tree nut(s) with no one fruit (or family of fruit) or family of tree nuts accounting for one-half of the establishment's agricultural production (i.e., value of crops for market).

*Cross-References.*          Establishments primarily engaged in--

- Harvesting berries or nuts from native and non-cultivated plants--are classified in Industry 11321, Forest Nurseries and Gathering of Forest Products;
- Canning and/or drying (artificially) fruit--are classified in Industry 31142, Fruit and Vegetable Canning, Pickling, and Drying;
- Growing apples and manufacturing alcoholic ciders or growing grapes and manufacturing wines and brandies--are classified in Industry 31213, Wineries; and
- Providing farm management or farm labor services on a contract or fee basis--are classified in Industry 11511, Support Activities for Crop Production.

## 111331 Apple Orchards

This U.S. industry comprises establishments primarily engaged in growing apples.

*Cross-References.*          Establishments primarily engaged in--

- Growing apples and manufacturing alcoholic ciders--are classified in Industry 312130, Wineries; and
- Growing apples in combination with tree nut(s) with the apples or family of tree nuts not accounting for one-half of the establishment's agricultural production (i.e., value of crops for market)--are classified in U.S. Industry 111336, Fruit and Tree Nut Combination Farming.

## 111332 Grape Vineyards

This U.S. industry comprises establishments primarily engaged in growing grapes and/or growing grapes to sun dry into raisins.

*Cross-References.*          Establishments primarily engaged in--

- Drying grapes artificially--are classified in U.S. Industry 311423, Dried and Dehydrated Food Manufacturing;
- Growing grapes and manufacturing wines and brandies--are classified in Industry 312130, Wineries; and

---

T—Canadian, Mexican, and United States industries are comparable.

- Growing grapes in combination with tree nut(s) with the grapes or family of tree nuts not accounting for one-half of the establishment's agricultural production (i.e., value of crops for market)--are classified in U.S. Industry 111336, Fruit and Tree Nut Combination Farming.

## 111333  Strawberry Farming

This U.S. industry comprises establishments primarily engaged in growing strawberries.

*Cross-References.*

Establishments engaged in growing strawberries in combination with tree nut(s) with the strawberries or family of tree nuts not accounting for one-half of the establishment's agricultural production (i.e., value of crops for market) are classified in U.S. Industry 111336, Fruit and Tree Nut Combination Farming.

## 111334  Berry (except Strawberry) Farming

This U.S. industry comprises establishments primarily engaged in growing berries.

*Illustrative Examples:*

| | |
|---|---|
| Berry (except strawberries) farming | Currant farming |
| Cranberry farming | Blueberry farming |
| Blackberry farming | Raspberry farming |

*Cross-References.*          Establishments primarily engaged in--

- Growing strawberries--are classified in U.S. Industry 111333, Strawberry Farming;
- Harvesting berries from native and non-cultivated bushes or vines--are classified in Industry 113210, Forest Nurseries and Gathering of Forest Products; and
- Growing berries in combination with tree nut(s) with the berries or family of tree nuts not accounting for one-half of the establishment's agricultural production (i.e., value of crops for market)--are classified in U.S. Industry 111336, Fruit and Tree Nut Combination Farming.

## 111335  Tree Nut Farming

This U.S. industry comprises establishments primarily engaged in growing tree nuts.

*Illustrative Examples:*

| | |
|---|---|
| Almond farming | Macadamia farming |
| Pistachio farming | Walnut farming |
| Filbert farming | Pecan farming |
| Tree nut farming | |

*Cross-References.*          Establishments primarily engaged in--

- Growing coconut and coffee--are classified in U.S. Industry 111339, Other Noncitrus Fruit Farming; and
- Growing tree nut(s) in combination with fruit(s) with no one fruit (or family of fruit or of tree nuts) accounting for one-half of the establishment's agricultural production (i.e., value of crops for market)--are classified in U.S. Industry 111336, Fruit and Tree Nut Combination Farming.

---

T—Canadian, Mexican, and United States industries are comparable.

### 111336 Fruit and Tree Nut Combination Farming

This U.S. industry comprises establishments primarily engaged in growing a combination of fruit(s) and tree nut(s) with no one fruit (or family of fruit) or family of tree nuts accounting for one-half of the establishment's agricultural production (i.e., value of crops for market).

*Cross-References.*

Establishments engaged in growing fruit(s) or the family of tree nut(s) accounting for one-half of the establishment's agricultural production (i.e., value of crops for market) are classified in Industry Group 1113, Fruit and Tree Nut Farming, accordingly by the prominent fruit(s) or tree nut(s) grown.

### 111339 Other Noncitrus Fruit Farming

This U.S. industry comprises establishments primarily engaged in growing noncitrus fruits (except apples, grapes, berries, and fruit(s) and tree nut(s) combinations).

*Illustrative Examples:*

| | |
|---|---|
| Apricot farming | Peach farming |
| Fig farming | Coffee farming |
| Banana farming | Pineapple farming |
| Noncitrus fruit farming | Date farming |
| Cherry farming | Prune farming |

*Cross-References.*　　　Establishments primarily engaged in--

- Growing apples--are classified in U.S. Industry 111331, Apple Orchards;
- Growing grapes including sun drying of grapes into raisins--are classified in U.S. Industry 111332, Grape Vineyards;
- Growing strawberries--are classified in U.S. Industry 111333, Strawberry Farming;
- Growing berries (except strawberries)--are classified in U.S. Industry 111334, Berry (except Strawberry) Farming;
- Drying fruit artificially--are classified in U.S. Industry 311423, Dried and Dehydrated Food Manufacturing; and
- Growing noncitrus fruit(s) in combination with tree nut(s) with no one fruit (or family of fruits) or family of tree nuts accounting for one-half of the establishment's agricultural production (i.e., value of crops for market)--are classified in U.S. Industry 111336, Fruit and Tree Nut Combination Farming.

### 1114　　Greenhouse, Nursery, and Floriculture Production[T]

This industry group comprises establishments primarily engaged in growing crops of any kind under cover and/or growing nursery stock and flowers. "Under cover" is generally defined as greenhouses, cold frames, cloth houses, and lath houses. The crops grown are removed at various stages of maturity and have annual and perennial life cycles. The nursery stock includes short rotation woody crops that have growth cycles of 10 years or less.

### 11141　　Food Crops Grown Under Cover[T]

This industry comprises establishments primarily engaged in growing food crops (e.g., fruits, melons, tomatoes) under glass or protective cover.

*Cross-References.*

Establishments primarily engaged in growing vegetable and melon bedding plants are classified in Industry 11121, Vegetable and Melon Farming.

---

T—Canadian, Mexican, and United States industries are comparable.

## 111411  Mushroom Production

This U.S. industry comprises establishments primarily engaged in growing mushrooms under cover in mines underground, or in other controlled environments.

## 111419  Other Food Crops Grown Under Cover

This U.S. industry comprises establishments primarily engaged in growing food crops (except mushrooms) under glass or protective cover.

*Illustrative Examples:*

Alfalfa sprout farming, grown under cover
Melon farming, grown under cover
Vegetable farming, grown under cover

Hydroponic crop farming
Fruit farming, grown under cover

*Cross-References.*

Establishments primarily engaged in growing mushrooms under cover are classified in U.S. Industry 111411, Mushroom Production.

## 11142   Nursery and Floriculture Production[T]

This industry comprises establishments primarily engaged in (1) growing nursery and floriculture products (e.g., nursery stock, shrubbery, cut flowers, flower seeds, foliage plants) under cover or in open fields and/or (2) growing short rotation woody trees with a growing and harvesting cycle of 10 years or less for pulp or tree stock (e.g., cut Christmas trees, cottonwoods).

*Cross-References.*          Establishments primarily engaged in--

- Growing vegetable and melon bedding plants--are classified in Industry 11121, Vegetable and Melon Farming;
- Operating timber tracts (i.e., growing cycle greater than 10 years)--are classified in Industry 11311, Timber Tract Operations;
- Retailing nursery, tree stock, and floriculture products primarily purchased from others--are classified in Industry 44424, Nursery, Garden Center, and Farm Supply Retailers;
- Merchant wholesale distribution of plant seeds and plant bulbs primarily purchased from others--are classified in Industry 42491, Farm Supplies Merchant Wholesalers; and
- Merchant wholesale distribution of nursery stock (except seeds and plant bulbs) primarily purchased from others--are classified in Industry 42493, Flower, Nursery Stock, and Florists' Supplies Merchant Wholesalers.

## 111421  Nursery and Tree Production

This U.S. industry comprises establishments primarily engaged in (1) growing nursery products, nursery stock, shrubbery, bulbs, fruit stock, sod, and so forth, under cover or in open fields and/or (2) growing short rotation woody trees with a growth and harvest cycle of 10 years or less for pulp or tree stock.

*Cross-References.*          Establishments primarily engaged in--

- Growing vegetable and melon bedding plants--are classified in Industry 11121, Vegetable and Melon Farming;
- Operating timber tracts (i.e., growing cycle greater than 10 years)--are classified in Industry 113110, Timber Tract Operations;

---

T—Canadian, Mexican, and United States industries are comparable.

- Retailing nursery, tree stock, and floriculture products primarily purchased from others--are classified in Industry 444240, Nursery, Garden Center, and Farm Supply Retailers;
- Merchant wholesale distribution of plant seeds and plant bulbs primarily purchased from others--are classified in Industry 424910, Farm Supplies Merchant Wholesalers; and
- Merchant wholesale distribution of nursery stock (except seeds and plant bulbs) primarily purchased from others--are classified in Industry 424930, Flower, Nursery Stock, and Florists' Supplies Merchant Wholesalers.

### 111422 Floriculture Production

This U.S. industry comprises establishments primarily engaged in growing and/or producing floriculture products (e.g., cut flowers and roses, cut cultivated greens, potted flowering and foliage plants, and flower seeds) under cover and in open fields.

*Cross-References.*

Establishments primarily engaged in retailing floriculture products primarily purchased from others are classified in Industry 444240, Nursery, Garden Center, and Farm Supply Retailers.

### 1119    Other Crop Farming<sup>T</sup>

This industry group comprises establishments primarily engaged in (1) growing crops (except oilseed and/or grain; vegetable and/or melon; fruit and tree nut; and greenhouse, nursery, and/or floriculture products), such as tobacco, cotton, sugarcane, hay, sugar beets, peanuts, agave, herbs and spices, and hay and grass seeds, or (2) growing a combination of crops (except a combination of oilseed(s) and grain(s) and a combination of fruit(s) and tree nut(s)).

### 11191    Tobacco Farming<sup>T</sup>
See industry description for 111910.

### 111910 Tobacco Farming

This industry comprises establishments primarily engaged in growing tobacco.

### 11192    Cotton Farming<sup>T</sup>
See industry description for 111920.

### 111920 Cotton Farming

This industry comprises establishments primarily engaged in growing cotton.

*Cross-References.*

Establishments primarily engaged in ginning cotton are classified in U.S. Industry 115111, Cotton Ginning.

### 11193    Sugarcane Farming<sup>T</sup>
See industry description for 111930.

### 111930 Sugarcane Farming

This industry comprises establishments primarily engaged in growing sugarcane.

### 11194    Hay Farming<sup>T</sup>
See industry description for 111940.

---

T—Canadian, Mexican, and United States industries are comparable.

**census.gov/naics**

**111940 Hay Farming**

This industry comprises establishments primarily engaged in growing hay, alfalfa, clover, and/or mixed hay.

*Cross-References.*        Establishments primarily engaged in--

- Growing grain hay--are classified in Industry Group 1111, Oilseed and Grain Farming; and
- Growing grass and hay seeds--are classified in U.S. Industry 111998, All Other Miscellaneous Crop Farming.

**11199    All Other Crop Farming[T]**

This industry comprises establishments primarily engaged in (1) growing crops (except oilseeds and/or grains; vegetables and/or melons; fruits and/or tree nuts; greenhouse, nursery, and/or floriculture products; tobacco; cotton; sugarcane; or hay) or (2) growing a combination of crops (except a combination of oilseed(s) and grain(s); and a combination of fruit(s) and tree nut(s)) with no one crop or family of crops accounting for one-half of the establishment's agricultural production (i.e., value of crops for market).

*Illustrative Examples:*

Agave farming
Spice farming
General combination crop farming (except oilseed and grain; vegetables and melons; fruit and nut combinations)
Tea farming

Hay seed farming
Maple sap gathering
Peanut farming
Sugar beet farming
Grass seed farming

*Cross-References.*        Establishments primarily engaged in--

- Growing oilseeds and/or wheat, corn, rice, or other grains--are classified in Industry Group 1111, Oilseed and Grain Farming;
- Growing vegetables and/or melons--are classified in Industry Group 1112, Vegetable and Melon Farming;
- Growing fruits and/or tree nuts--are classified in Industry Group 1113, Fruit and Tree Nut Farming;
- Growing greenhouse, nursery, and/or floriculture products--are classified in Industry Group 1114, Greenhouse, Nursery, and Floriculture Production;
- Growing tobacco--are classified in Industry 11191, Tobacco Farming;
- Growing cotton--are classified in Industry 11192, Cotton Farming;
- Growing sugarcane--are classified in Industry 11193, Sugarcane Farming;
- Growing hay--are classified in Industry 11194, Hay Farming; and
- Growing algae, seaweed, or other aquatic plants--are classified in Industry 11251, Aquaculture.

**111991 Sugar Beet Farming**

This U.S. industry comprises establishments primarily engaged in growing sugar beets.

*Cross-References.*

Establishments primarily engaged in growing beets (except sugar beets) are classified in U.S. Industry 111219, Other Vegetable (except Potato) and Melon Farming.

**111992 Peanut Farming**

This U.S. industry comprises establishments primarily engaged in growing peanuts.

---

T—Canadian, Mexican, and United States industries are comparable.

**111998  All Other Miscellaneous Crop Farming**

This U.S. industry comprises establishments primarily engaged in one of the following: (1) growing crops (except oilseeds and/or grains; vegetables and/or melons; fruits and/or tree nuts; greenhouse, nursery, and/or floriculture products; tobacco; cotton; sugarcane; hay; sugar beets; or peanuts); (2) growing a combination of crops (except a combination of oilseed(s) and grain(s); and a combination of fruit(s) and tree nut(s)) with no one crop or family of crops accounting for one-half of the establishment's agricultural production (i.e., value of crops for market); or (3) gathering tea or maple sap.

*Illustrative Examples:*

| | |
|---|---|
| Agave farming | Hay seed farming |
| Mint farming | Grass seed farming |
| General combination crop farming (except oilseed | Hop farming |
| and grain; vegetables and melons; fruit and tree nut | Spice farming |
| combinations) | |

*Cross-References.*          Establishments primarily engaged in--

- Growing oilseeds and/or wheat, corn, rice, or other grains--are classified in Industry Group 1111, Oilseed and Grain Farming;
- Growing vegetables and/or melons--are classified in Industry Group 1112, Vegetable and Melon Farming;
- Growing fruits and/or tree nuts--are classified in Industry Group 1113, Fruit and Tree Nut Farming;
- Growing greenhouse, nursery, and/or floriculture products--are classified in Industry Group 1114, Greenhouse, Nursery, and Floriculture Production;
- Growing tobacco--are classified in Industry 111910, Tobacco Farming;
- Growing cotton--are classified in Industry 111920, Cotton Farming;
- Growing sugarcane--are classified in Industry 111930, Sugarcane Farming;
- Growing hay--are classified in Industry 111940, Hay Farming;
- Growing sugar beets--are classified in U.S. Industry 111991, Sugar Beet Farming;
- Growing peanuts--are classified in U.S. Industry 111992, Peanut Farming; and
- Growing algae, seaweed, or other aquatic plants--are classified in U.S. Industry 112519, Other Aquaculture.

**112       Animal Production and Aquaculture[T]**

Industries in the Animal Production and Aquaculture subsector raise or fatten animals for the sale of animals or animal products and/or raise aquatic plants and animals in controlled or selected aquatic environments for the sale of aquatic plants, animals, or their products. The subsector includes establishments, such as ranches, farms, and feedlots, primarily engaged in keeping, grazing, breeding, or feeding animals. These animals are kept for the products they produce or for eventual sale. The animals are generally raised in various environments, from total confinement or captivity to feeding on an open range pasture.

The industries in this subsector are grouped by important factors, such as suitable grazing or pasture land, specialized buildings, type of equipment, and the amount and types of labor required. Establishments are classified in the Animal Production and Aquaculture subsector when animal production (i.e., value of animals for market) accounts for one-half or more of the establishment's total agricultural production. Establishments with one-half or more animal production with no one animal product or family of animal products of an industry accounting for one-half of the establishment's agricultural production are treated as combination animal farming classified in Industry 11299, All Other Animal Production.

**1121      Cattle Ranching and Farming[T]**

This industry group comprises establishments primarily engaged in raising cattle, milking dairy cattle, or feeding cattle for fattening.

---

T—Canadian, Mexican, and United States industries are comparable.

**11211 Beef Cattle Ranching and Farming, including Feedlots[T]**

This industry comprises establishments primarily engaged in raising cattle (including cattle for dairy herd replacements), or feeding cattle for fattening.

*Cross-References.*          Establishments primarily engaged in--

- Milking dairy cattle--are classified in Industry 11212, Dairy Cattle and Milk Production; and
- Operating stockyards for transportation and not buying, selling, or auctioning livestock--are classified in Industry 48899, Other Support Activities for Transportation.

**112111 Beef Cattle Ranching and Farming**

This U.S. industry comprises establishments primarily engaged in raising cattle (including cattle for dairy herd replacements).

*Cross-References.*

Establishments primarily engaged in milking dairy cattle are classified in Industry 112120, Dairy Cattle and Milk Production.

**112112 Cattle Feedlots**

This U.S. industry comprises establishments primarily engaged in feeding cattle for fattening.

*Cross-References.*

Establishments primarily engaged in operating stockyards for transportation and not buying, selling, or auctioning livestock are classified in U.S. Industry 488999, All Other Support Activities for Transportation.

**11212 Dairy Cattle and Milk Production[T]**
See industry description for 112120.

**112120 Dairy Cattle and Milk Production**

This industry comprises establishments primarily engaged in milking dairy cattle.

*Cross-References.*          Establishments primarily engaged in--

- Raising dairy herd replacements--are classified in U.S. Industry 112111, Beef Cattle Ranching and Farming; and
- Milking goats--are classified in Industry 112420, Goat Farming.

**11213 Dual-Purpose Cattle Ranching and Farming[T]**
See industry description for 112130.

**112130 Dual-Purpose Cattle Ranching and Farming**

This industry comprises establishments primarily engaged in raising cattle for both milking and meat production.

*Cross-References.*          Establishments primarily engaged in--

- Milking dairy cattle--are classified in Industry 112120, Dairy Cattle and Milk Production;
- Raising cattle or feeding cattle for fattening--are classified in Industry 11211, Beef Cattle Ranching and Farming, including Feedlots; and

---

T—Canadian, Mexican, and United States industries are comparable.

- Operating stockyards for transportation and not buying, selling, or auctioning livestock--are classified in U.S. Industry 488999, All Other Support Activities for Transportation.

## 1122	Hog and Pig Farming[T]

### 11221	Hog and Pig Farming[T]
See industry description for 112210.

### 112210	Hog and Pig Farming

This industry comprises establishments primarily engaged in raising hogs and pigs. These establishments may include farming activities, such as breeding, farrowing, and the raising of weanling pigs, feeder pigs, or market size hogs.

*Cross-References.*

Establishments primarily engaged in operating stockyards for transportation and not buying, selling, or auctioning livestock are classified in U.S. Industry 488999, All Other Support Activities for Transportation.

## 1123	Poultry and Egg Production[T]

This industry group comprises establishments primarily engaged in breeding, hatching, and raising poultry for meat or egg production.

### 11231	Chicken Egg Production[T]
See industry description for 112310.

### 112310	Chicken Egg Production

This industry comprises establishments primarily engaged in raising chickens for egg production. The eggs produced may be for use as table eggs or hatching eggs.

*Cross-References.*

Establishments primarily engaged in raising chickens for the production of meat are classified in Industry 112320, Broilers and Other Meat Type Chicken Production.

### 11232	Broilers and Other Meat Type Chicken Production[T]
See industry description for 112320.

### 112320	Broilers and Other Meat Type Chicken Production

This industry comprises establishments primarily engaged in raising broilers, fryers, roasters, and other meat type chickens.

*Cross-References.*

Establishments primarily engaged in raising chickens for egg production are classified in Industry 112310, Chicken Egg Production.

### 11233	Turkey Production[T]
See industry description for 112330.

---

T—Canadian, Mexican, and United States industries are comparable.

**112330  Turkey Production**

This industry comprises establishments primarily engaged in raising turkeys for meat or egg production.

**11234  Poultry Hatcheries[T]**
See industry description for 112340.

**112340  Poultry Hatcheries**

This industry comprises establishments primarily engaged in hatching poultry of any kind.

**11239  Other Poultry Production[T]**
See industry description for 112390.

**112390  Other Poultry Production**

This industry comprises establishments primarily engaged in raising poultry (except chickens for meat or egg production and turkeys).

*Illustrative Examples:*

Duck production                                     Pheasant production
Ostrich production                                 Geese production
Emu production                                     Quail production

*Cross-References.*          Establishments primarily engaged in--

- Raising aviary birds, such as parakeets, canaries, and love birds--are classified in Industry 112990, All Other Animal Production;
- Raising chickens for egg production--are classified in Industry 112310, Chicken Egg Production;
- Raising broilers and other meat type chickens--are classified in Industry 112320, Broilers and Other Meat Type Chicken Production;
- Raising turkeys--are classified in Industry 112330, Turkey Production; and
- Raising swans, peacocks, flamingos or other "adornment birds"--are classified in Industry 112990, All Other Animal Production.

**1124      Sheep and Goat Farming[T]**

This industry group comprises establishments primarily engaged in raising sheep, lambs, and goats, or feeding lambs for fattening.

**11241    Sheep Farming[T]**
See industry description for 112410.

**112410  Sheep Farming**

This industry comprises establishments primarily engaged in raising sheep and lambs, or feeding lambs for fattening.  The sheep or lambs may be raised for sale or wool production.

*Cross-References.*

Establishments primarily engaged in operating stockyards for transportation and not buying, selling, or auctioning livestock are classified in U.S. Industry 488999, All Other Support Activities for Transportation.

---

T—Canadian, Mexican, and United States industries are comparable.

**11242   Goat Farming<sup>T</sup>**

See industry description for 112420.

**112420  Goat Farming**

This industry comprises establishments primarily engaged in raising goats.

**1125    Aquaculture<sup>T</sup>**

**11251   Aquaculture<sup>T</sup>**

This industry comprises establishments primarily engaged in the farm raising and production of aquatic animals or plants in controlled or selected aquatic environments.  These establishments use some form of intervention in the rearing process to enhance production, such as holding in captivity, regular stocking, feeding, and protecting from predators, pests, and disease.

*Cross-References.*

Establishments primarily engaged in the catching or taking of fish and other aquatic animals from their natural habitat are classified in Industry 11411, Fishing.

**112511  Finfish Farming and Fish Hatcheries**

This U.S. industry comprises establishments primarily engaged in (1) farm raising finfish (e.g., catfish, trout, goldfish, tropical fish, minnows) and/or (2) hatching fish of any kind.

*Cross-References.*

Establishments primarily engaged in the catching or taking of finfish from their natural habitat are classified in U.S. Industry 114111, Finfish Fishing.

**112512  Shellfish Farming**

This U.S. industry comprises establishments primarily engaged in farm raising shellfish (e.g., crayfish, shrimp, oysters, clams, mollusks).

*Cross-References.*

Establishments primarily engaged in the catching or taking of shellfish from their natural habitat are classified in U.S. Industry 114112, Shellfish Fishing.

**112519  Other Aquaculture**

This U.S. industry comprises establishments primarily engaged in (1) farm raising of aquatic animals (except finfish and shellfish) and/or (2) farm raising of aquatic plants.  Alligator, algae, frog, seaweed, or turtle production is included in this industry.

*Cross-References.*        Establishments primarily engaged in--

- Miscellaneous fishing activities, such as catching or taking of terrapins, turtles, and frogs from their natural habitat--are classified in U.S. Industry 114119, Other Marine Fishing;
- Farm raising finfish--are classified in U.S. Industry 112511, Finfish Farming and Fish Hatcheries;
- Farm raising shellfish--are classified in U.S. Industry 112512, Shellfish Farming; and
- Growing hydroponic crops--are classified in U.S. Industry 111419, Other Food Crops Grown Under Cover.

---

T—Canadian, Mexican, and United States industries are comparable.

## 1129    Other Animal Production[T]

This industry group comprises establishments primarily engaged in raising animals and insects (except cattle, hogs and pigs, poultry, sheep and goats, and aquaculture) for sale or product production.  These establishments are primarily engaged in raising one of the following: bees, horses and other equines, rabbits and other fur-bearing animals, and so forth, and producing products, such as honey and other bee products.  Establishments primarily engaged in raising a combination of animals with no one animal or family of animals accounting for one-half of the establishment's agricultural production (i.e., value of animals for market) are included in this industry group.

### 11291    Apiculture[T]
See industry description for 112910.

### 112910  Apiculture

This industry comprises establishments primarily engaged in raising bees.  These establishments may collect and gather honey; and/or sell queen bees, packages of bees, royal jelly, bees' wax, propolis, venom, pollen, and/or other bee products.

### 11292    Horses and Other Equine Production[T]
See industry description for 112920.

### 112920  Horses and Other Equine Production

This industry comprises establishments primarily engaged in raising horses, mules, donkeys, and other equines.

*Cross-References.*

- Establishments primarily engaged in equine boarding and/or training (except racehorses) are classified in Industry 115210, Support Activities for Animal Production; and
- Equine owners entering horses in racing or other spectator sporting events are classified in U.S. Industry 711219, Other Spectator Sports.

### 11293    Fur-Bearing Animal and Rabbit Production[T]
See industry description for 112930.

### 112930  Fur-Bearing Animal and Rabbit Production

This industry comprises establishments primarily engaged in raising fur-bearing animals including rabbits.  These animals may be raised for sale or for their pelt production.

*Cross-References.*

Establishments primarily engaged in the trapping or hunting of wild fur-bearing animals are classified in Industry 114210, Hunting and Trapping.

### 11299    All Other Animal Production[T]
See industry description for 112990.

### 112990  All Other Animal Production

This industry comprises establishments primarily engaged in (1) raising animals (except cattle, hogs and pigs, poultry, sheep and goats, aquaculture, apiculture, horses and other equines; and fur-bearing animals including rabbits) or (2) raising a combination of animals, with no one animal or family of animals accounting for one-half of the establishment's agricultural production (i.e., value of animals for market).

---

T—Canadian, Mexican, and United States industries are comparable.

*Illustrative Examples:*

Bird production (e.g., canaries, parakeets, parrots)
Laboratory animal production (e.g., rats, mice, guinea pigs)
Deer production

Combination animal farming (except dairy, poultry)
Companion animals production (e.g., cats, dogs)
Worm production
Llama production

*Cross-References.*          Establishments primarily engaged in--

- Raising cattle, dairy cattle, or feeding cattle for fattening--are classified in Industry Group 1121, Cattle Ranching and Farming;
- Raising hogs and pigs--are classified in Industry Group 1122, Hog and Pig Farming;
- Raising poultry and raising poultry for egg production--are classified in Industry Group 1123, Poultry and Egg Production;
- Raising sheep and goats--are classified in Industry Group 1124, Sheep and Goat Farming;
- Animal aquaculture--are classified in Industry 11251, Aquaculture;
- Raising bees--are classified in Industry 112910, Apiculture;
- Raising horses and other equines--are classified in Industry 112920, Horses and Other Equine Production; and
- Raising fur-bearing animals including rabbits--are classified in Industry 112930, Fur-Bearing Animal and Rabbit Production.

## 113      Forestry and Logging[T]

Industries in the Forestry and Logging subsector grow and harvest timber on a long production cycle (i.e., of 10 years or more). Long production cycles use different production processes than short production cycles, which require more horticultural interventions prior to harvest, resulting in processes more similar to those found in the Crop Production subsector. Consequently, Christmas tree production and other production involving production cycles of less than 10 years, are classified in the Crop Production subsector.

Industries in this subsector specialize in different stages of the production cycle. Reforestation requires production of seedlings in specialized nurseries. Timber production requires natural forest or suitable areas of land that are available for a long duration. The maturation time for timber depends upon the species of tree, the climatic conditions of the region, and the intended purpose of the timber. The harvesting of timber (except when done on an extremely small scale) requires specialized machinery unique to the industry. Establishments gathering forest products, such as gums, barks, balsam needles, rhizomes, fibers, Spanish moss, and ginseng and truffles, are also included in this subsector.

## 1131      Timber Tract Operations[T]

### 11311      Timber Tract Operations[T]
See industry description for 113110.

### 113110  Timber Tract Operations

This industry comprises establishments primarily engaged in the operation of timber tracts for the purpose of selling standing timber.

*Cross-References.*          Establishments primarily engaged in--

- Acting as lessors of land with trees as real estate property--are classified in Industry 531190, Lessors of Other Real Estate Property;
- Growing short rotation woody trees (i.e., growing and harvesting cycle is 10 years or less)--are classified in U.S. Industry 111421, Nursery and Tree Production;
- Growing trees for reforestation--are classified in Industry 113210, Forest Nurseries and Gathering of Forest Products;

---

T—Canadian, Mexican, and United States industries are comparable.

- Cutting timber--are classified in Industry 113310, Logging; and
- Operating sawmills--are classified in U.S. Industry 321113, Sawmills.

## 1132    Forest Nurseries and Gathering of Forest Products<sup>T</sup>

## 11321    Forest Nurseries and Gathering of Forest Products<sup>T</sup>
See industry description for 113210.

## 113210  Forest Nurseries and Gathering of Forest Products

This industry comprises establishments primarily engaged in (1) growing trees for reforestation and/or (2) gathering forest products, such as gums, barks, balsam needles, rhizomes, fibers, Spanish moss, ginseng, and truffles.

*Cross-References.*          Establishments primarily engaged in--

- Gathering tea and maple sap--are classified in U.S. Industry 111998, All Other Miscellaneous Crop Farming;
- Processing maple syrup into other products--are classified in U.S. Industry 311999, All Other Miscellaneous Food Manufacturing; and
- Operating timber tracts for the purpose of selling standing timber--are classified in Industry 113110, Timber Tract Operations.

## 1133    Logging<sup>T</sup>

## 11331    Logging<sup>T</sup>
See industry description for 113310.

## 113310  Logging

This industry comprises establishments primarily engaged in one or more of the following: (1) cutting timber; (2) cutting and transporting timber; and (3) producing wood chips in the field.

*Cross-References.*          Establishments primarily engaged in--

- Trucking timber without cutting timber--are classified in Industry 484220, Specialized Freight (except Used Goods) Trucking, Local; and
- Producing wood chips in sawmills--are classified in U.S. Industry 321113, Sawmills.

## 114    Fishing, Hunting and Trapping<sup>T</sup>

Industries in the Fishing, Hunting and Trapping subsector harvest fish and other wild animals from their natural habitats and are dependent upon a continued supply of the natural resource. The harvesting of fish is the predominant economic activity of this subsector and it usually requires specialized vessels that, by the nature of their size, configuration and equipment, are not suitable for any other type of production, such as transportation.

Hunting and trapping activities utilize a wide variety of production processes and are classified in the same subsector as fishing because the availability of resources and the constraints imposed, such as conservation requirements and proper habitat maintenance, are similar.

## 1141    Fishing<sup>T</sup>

T—Canadian, Mexican, and United States industries are comparable.

## 11411   Fishing^T

This industry comprises establishments primarily engaged in the commercial catching or taking of finfish, shellfish, or miscellaneous marine products from a natural habitat, such as the catching of bluefish, eels, salmon, tuna, clams, crabs, lobsters, mussels, oysters, shrimp, frogs, sea urchins, and turtles.

*Cross-References.*          Establishments primarily engaged in--

- Farm raising finfish, shellfish or other marine animals and plants--are classified in Industry 11251, Aquaculture; and
- Gathering and processing seafood into canned seafood products--are classified in Industry 31171, Seafood Product Preparation and Packaging.

## 114111  Finfish Fishing

This U.S. industry comprises establishments primarily engaged in the commercial catching or taking of finfish (e.g., bluefish, salmon, trout, tuna) from their natural habitat.

*Cross-References.*          Establishments primarily engaged in--

- Farm raising finfish--are classified in U.S. Industry 112511, Finfish Farming and Fish Hatcheries; and
- Gathering and processing (known as "floating factory ships") seafood into canned seafood products--are classified in Industry 311710, Seafood Product Preparation and Packaging.

## 114112  Shellfish Fishing

This U.S. industry comprises establishments primarily engaged in the commercial catching or taking of shellfish (e.g., clams, crabs, lobsters, mussels, oysters, sea urchins, shrimp) from their natural habitat.

*Cross-References.*

Establishments primarily engaged in farm raising shellfish are classified in U.S. Industry 112512, Shellfish Farming.

## 114119  Other Marine Fishing

This U.S. industry comprises establishments primarily engaged in the commercial catching or taking of marine animals (except finfish and shellfish).

*Cross-References.*          Establishments primarily engaged in--

- Animal or plant aquaculture (except finfish and shellfish)--are classified in U.S. Industry 112519, Other Aquaculture;
- The commercial catching or taking of finfish from their natural habitat--are classified in U.S. Industry 114111, Finfish Fishing; and
- The commercial catching or taking of shellfish from their natural habitat--are classified in U.S. Industry 114112, Shellfish Fishing.

## 1142   Hunting and Trapping^T

## 11421   Hunting and Trapping^T
See industry description for 114210.

---

T—Canadian, Mexican, and United States industries are comparable.

## 114210 Hunting and Trapping

This industry comprises establishments primarily engaged in one or more of the following: (1) commercial hunting and trapping; (2) operating commercial game preserves, such as game retreats; and (3) operating hunting preserves.

*Cross-References.* Establishments primarily engaged in--

- Operating nature preserves--are classified in Industry 712190, Nature Parks and Other Similar Institutions;
- Farm raising rabbits and other fur-bearing animals--are classified in Industry 112930, Fur-Bearing Animal and Rabbit Production;
- Operating hunting camps with accommodation facilities--are classified in U.S. Industry 721214, Recreational and Vacation Camps (except Campgrounds);
- Providing hunting guide services without accommodation facilities--are classified in Industry 713990, All Other Amusement and Recreation Industries; and
- Providing bird and rodent control services--are classified in Industry 561710, Exterminating and Pest Control Services.

## 115 Support Activities for Agriculture and Forestry[T]

Industries in the Support Activities for Agriculture and Forestry subsector provide support services that are an essential part of agricultural and forestry production. These support activities may be performed by the agriculture or forestry producing establishment or conducted independently as an alternative source of inputs required for the production process for a given crop, animal, or forestry industry. Establishments that primarily perform these activities independent of the agriculture or forestry producing establishment are in this subsector.

## 1151 Support Activities for Crop Production[T]

## 11511 Support Activities for Crop Production[T]

This industry comprises establishments primarily engaged in providing support activities for growing crops.

*Illustrative Examples:*

Aerial crop dusting or spraying (i.e., using specialized or dedicated aircraft)
Farm management services
Cotton ginning

Planting crops
Cultivating services
Vineyard cultivation services

*Cross-References.* Establishments primarily engaged in--

- Performing crop production that are generally known as farms, orchards, groves, or vineyards (including tenant farms)--are classified in the appropriate crop industry within Subsector 111, Crop Production;
- Providing support activities for forestry--are classified in Industry 11531, Support Activities for Forestry;
- Landscaping services, such as lawn and maintenance care and ornamental tree and shrub services--are classified in Industry 56173, Landscaping Services;
- Land clearing, land leveling, and earth moving for terracing, ponds, and irrigation--are classified in Industry 23891, Site Preparation Contractors;
- Artificially drying and dehydrating fruits and vegetables--are classified in Industry 31142, Fruit and Vegetable Canning, Pickling, and Drying;
- Stemming and redrying tobacco--are classified in Industry 31223, Tobacco Manufacturing;
- Providing water for irrigation--are classified in Industry 22131, Water Supply and Irrigation Systems; and
- Buying farm products, such as fruits or vegetables, for resale to other wholesalers or retailers, and preparing them for market or further processing--are classified in Industry 42448, Fresh Fruit and Vegetable Merchant Wholesalers.

---

T—Canadian, Mexican, and United States industries are comparable.

### 115111  Cotton Ginning

This U.S. industry comprises establishments primarily engaged in ginning cotton.

### 115112  Soil Preparation, Planting, and Cultivating

This U.S. industry comprises establishments primarily engaged in performing a soil preparation activity or crop production service, such as plowing, fertilizing, seed bed preparation, planting, cultivating, and crop protecting services.

*Cross-References.*          Establishments primarily engaged in--

- Mulching and seeding burned forests from the air in support of reforestation or on an emergency basis--are classified in Industry 115310, Support Activities for Forestry;
- Land clearing, land leveling, and earth moving for terracing, ponds, and irrigation--are classified in Industry 238910, Site Preparation Contractors;
- Providing water for irrigation--are classified in Industry 221310, Water Supply and Irrigation Systems; and
- Landscaping services, such as lawn and maintenance care and ornamental tree and shrub services--are classified in Industry 561730, Landscaping Services.

### 115113  Crop Harvesting, Primarily by Machine

This U.S. industry comprises establishments primarily engaged in mechanical harvesting, picking, and combining of crops, and related activities.  The machinery used is provided by the servicing establishment.

*Cross-References.*          Establishments primarily engaged in--

- Providing personnel for manual harvesting--are classified in U.S. Industry 115115, Farm Labor Contractors and Crew Leaders; and
- Providing farm management services (i.e., on a contract or fee basis) and arranging or contracting crop mechanical or manual harvesting operations for the farm(s) they manage--are classified in U.S. Industry 115116, Farm Management Services.

### 115114  Postharvest Crop Activities (except Cotton Ginning)

This U.S. industry comprises establishments primarily engaged in performing services on crops, subsequent to their harvest, with the intent of preparing them for market or further processing.  These establishments provide postharvest activities, such as crop cleaning, sun drying, shelling, fumigating, curing, sorting, grading, packing, and cooling.

*Cross-References.*          Establishments primarily engaged in--

- Ginning cotton--are classified in U.S. Industry 115111, Cotton Ginning;
- Custom grain grinding for animal feed--are classified in U.S. Industry 311119, Other Animal Food Manufacturing;
- Artificially drying and dehydrating fruits and vegetables--are classified in U.S. Industry 311423, Dried and Dehydrated Food Manufacturing;
- Stemming and redrying tobacco--are classified in Industry 312230, Tobacco Manufacturing;
- Buying farm products for resale to other wholesalers or retailers and preparing them for market or further processing--are classified in Industry 424480, Fresh Fruit and Vegetable Merchant Wholesalers; and
- Providing farm management services (i.e., on a contract or fee basis) and arranging or contracting postharvesting crop activities for the farm(s) they manage--are classified in U.S. Industry 115116, Farm Management Services.

---

T--Canadian, Mexican, and United States industries are comparable.

## 115115 Farm Labor Contractors and Crew Leaders

This U.S. industry comprises establishments primarily engaged in supplying labor for agricultural production or harvesting.

*Cross-References.* Establishments primarily engaged in--

- Providing machine harvesting--are classified in U.S. Industry 115113, Crop Harvesting, Primarily by Machine; and
- Providing farm management services (i.e., on a contract or fee basis) and arranging or contracting farm labor for the farm(s) they manage--are classified in U.S. Industry 115116, Farm Management Services.

## 115116 Farm Management Services

This U.S. industry comprises establishments primarily engaged in providing farm management services on a contract or fee basis usually to citrus groves, orchards, or vineyards. These establishments always provide management and may arrange or contract for the partial or the complete operations of the farm establishment(s) they manage. Operational activities may include cultivating, harvesting, and/or other specialized agricultural support activities.

*Cross-References.*

Establishments primarily engaged in crop production that are generally known as farms, orchards, groves, or vineyards (including tenant farms), are classified in the appropriate crop industry within Subsector 111, Crop Production.

## 1152 Support Activities for Animal Production[T]

## 11521 Support Activities for Animal Production[T]
See industry description for 115210.

## 115210 Support Activities for Animal Production

This industry comprises establishments primarily engaged in performing support activities related to raising livestock (e.g., cattle, goats, hogs, horses, poultry, sheep). These establishments may perform one or more of the following: (1) breeding services for animals, including companion animals (e.g., cats, dogs, pet birds); (2) pedigree record services; (3) boarding horses; (4) dairy herd improvement activities; (5) livestock spraying; and (6) sheep dipping and shearing.

*Cross-References.*

- Establishments primarily engaged in raising companion animals (e.g., cats, dogs, pet birds) for sale are classified in Industry 112990, All Other Animal Production; and
- Equine owners entering horses in racing or other spectator sporting events are classified in U.S. Industry 711219, Other Spectator Sports.

## 1153 Support Activities for Forestry[T]

## 11531 Support Activities for Forestry[T]
See industry description for 115310.

## 115310 Support Activities for Forestry

This industry comprises establishments primarily engaged in performing particular support activities related to timber production, wood technology, forestry economics and marketing, and forest protection. These establishments

T—Canadian, Mexican, and United States industries are comparable.

may provide support activities for forestry, such as estimating timber, forest firefighting, forest pest control, treating burned forests from the air for reforestation or on an emergency basis, and consulting on wood attributes and reforestation.

*Cross-References.*            Establishments primarily engaged in--

- Public administration and conservation of forest lands--are classified in Industry 924120, Administration of Conservation Programs;
- Growing trees for reforestation--are classified in Industry 113210, Forest Nurseries and Gathering of Forest Products; and
- Individual activities as part of a restoration project--are classified according to the primary activity.

---

T—Canadian, Mexican, and United States industries are comparable.

# Sector 21--Mining, Quarrying, and Oil and Gas Extraction[T]

## The Sector as a Whole

The Mining, Quarrying, and Oil and Gas Extraction sector comprises establishments that extract naturally occurring mineral solids, such as coal and ores; liquid minerals, such as crude petroleum; and gases, such as natural gas. The term "mining" is used in the broad sense to include quarrying, well operations, beneficiating (e.g., crushing, screening, washing, and flotation), and other preparation customarily performed at the mine site, or as a part of mining activity.

The Mining, Quarrying, and Oil and Gas Extraction sector distinguishes two basic activities: mine operation and mining support activities. Mine operation includes establishments operating mines, quarries, or oil and gas wells on their own account or for others on a contract or fee basis. Mining support activities include establishments that perform exploration (except geophysical surveying and mapping) on a contract or fee basis and/or other mining services on a contract or fee basis (except mine site preparation, construction, and transportation activities).

Establishments in the Mining, Quarrying, and Oil and Gas Extraction sector are grouped and classified according to the natural resource mined or to be mined. Industries include establishments that develop and/or operate the mine site, extract the natural resources, beneficiate (i.e., prepare) the mineral mined, or provide mining support activities. Beneficiation is the process whereby the extracted material is reduced to particles that can be separated into mineral and waste, the former suitable for further processing or direct use. The operations that take place in beneficiation are primarily mechanical, such as grinding, washing, magnetic separation, and centrifugal separation. In contrast, manufacturing operations primarily use chemical and electrochemical processes, such as electrolysis and distillation. However, some treatments, such as heat treatments, take place in both the beneficiation and the manufacturing (i.e., smelting/refining) stages. The range of preparation activities varies by mineral and the purity of any given ore deposit. While some minerals, such as petroleum and natural gas, require little or no preparation, others are washed and screened, while yet others, such as gold and silver, can be transformed into bullion before leaving the mine site.

Mining, beneficiating, and manufacturing activities often occur in a single location. Separate receipts will be collected for these activities whenever possible. When receipts cannot be broken out between mining and manufacturing, establishments that mine or quarry nonmetallic minerals, and then beneficiate the nonmetallic minerals into more finished manufactured products are classified based on the primary activity of the establishment. A mine that manufactures a small amount of finished products will be classified in Sector 21, Mining, Quarrying, and Oil and Gas Extraction. An establishment that mines whose primary output is a more finished manufactured product will be classified in Sector 31-33, Manufacturing.

## 211 Oil and Gas Extraction[T]

Industries in the Oil and Gas Extraction subsector operate and/or develop oil and gas field properties. Operation and development activities include exploration for crude petroleum and natural gas; drilling, completing, and equipping wells; operating separators, emulsion breakers, desilting equipment, and field gathering lines for crude petroleum and natural gas; and all other activities in the preparation of oil and gas up to the point of shipment from the producing property. This subsector includes the production of crude petroleum, the mining and extraction of oil from oil shale and oil sands, the production of natural gas, sulfur recovery from natural gas, and recovery of hydrocarbon liquids.

Establishments in this subsector include those that operate oil and gas wells on their own account or for others on a contract or fee basis. Establishments primarily engaged in providing support services, on a contract or fee basis, required for the drilling or operation of oil and gas wells (except geophysical surveying and mapping, mine site preparation, construction of oil/gas pipelines, and transportation activities) are classified in Subsector 213, Support Activities for Mining.

## 2111 Oil and Gas Extraction[T]

## 21112 Crude Petroleum Extraction
See industry description for 211120.

---

T—Canadian, Mexican, and United States industries are comparable.

**211120  Crude Petroleum Extraction**

This industry comprises establishments primarily engaged in (1) the exploration, development, and/or the production of petroleum from wells in which the hydrocarbons will initially flow or can be produced using normal or enhanced drilling and extraction techniques or (2) the production of crude petroleum from surface shales or tar sands or from reservoirs in which the hydrocarbons are semisolids. Establishments in this industry operate oil wells on their own account or for others on a contract or fee basis.

*Cross-References.*          Establishments primarily engaged in--

- Performing oil field services for operators on a contract or fee basis--are classified in Industry 21311, Support Activities for Mining;
- The combined activities of crude petroleum and natural gas extraction--are classified in Industry Group 2111, Oil and Gas Extraction, based on the primary activity of the establishment; and
- Refining crude petroleum into refined petroleum and liquid hydrocarbons--are classified in Industry 324110, Petroleum Refineries.

**21113    Natural Gas Extraction**
          See industry description for 211130.

**211130  Natural Gas Extraction**

This industry comprises establishments primarily engaged in (1) the exploration, development, and/or the production of natural gas from wells in which the hydrocarbons will initially flow or can be produced using normal or enhanced drilling and extraction techniques or (2) the recovery of liquid hydrocarbons from oil and gas field gases. Establishments primarily engaged in sulfur recovery from natural gas are included in this industry.

*Cross-References.*          Establishments primarily engaged in--

- Performing gas field services for operators on a contract or fee basis--are classified in Industry 21311, Support Activities for Mining;
- The combined activities of crude petroleum and natural gas extraction--are classified in Industry Group 2111, Oil and Gas Extraction, based on the primary activity of the establishment;
- Manufacturing acyclic and cyclic hydrocarbons from refined petroleum or converting refined petroleum into liquid hydrocarbons (i.e., petrochemicals)--are classified in Industry 325110, Petrochemical Manufacturing;
- Refining crude petroleum into refined petroleum and liquid hydrocarbons--are classified in Industry 324110, Petroleum Refineries; and
- Recovering helium from natural gas--are classified in Industry 325120, Industrial Gas Manufacturing.

**212      Mining (except Oil and Gas)[T]**

Industries in the Mining (except Oil and Gas) subsector primarily engage in mining, mine site development, and beneficiating (i.e., preparing) metallic minerals and nonmetallic minerals, including coal. The term "mining" is used in the broad sense to include ore extraction, quarrying, and beneficiating (e.g., crushing, screening, washing, sizing, concentrating, and flotation), customarily done at the mine site.

Beneficiation is the process whereby the extracted material is reduced to particles which can be separated into mineral and waste, the former suitable for further processing or direct use. The operations that take place in beneficiation are primarily mechanical, such as grinding, washing, magnetic separation, centrifugal separation, and so on. In contrast, manufacturing operations primarily use chemical and electrochemical processes, such as electrolysis, distillation, and so on. However, some treatments, such as heat treatments, take place in both stages: the beneficiation and the manufacturing (i.e., smelting/refining) stages. The range of preparation activities varies by mineral and the purity of any given ore deposit. While some minerals, such as petroleum and natural gas, require little or no preparation, others are washed and screened, while yet others, such as gold and silver, can be transformed into bullion before leaving the mine site.

---

T—Canadian, Mexican, and United States industries are comparable.

Establishments in the Mining (except Oil and Gas) subsector include those that have complete responsibility for operating mines and quarries (except oil and gas wells) and those that operate mines and quarries (except oil and gas wells) for others on a contract or fee basis. Establishments primarily engaged in providing support services, on a contract or fee basis (except geophysical surveying and mapping, mine site preparation, construction, and transportation activities), required for the mining and quarrying of minerals are classified in Subsector 213, Support Activities for Mining.

## 2121 Coal Mining[T]

## 21211 Coal Mining[T]

This industry comprises establishments primarily engaged in one or more of the following: (1) mining bituminous coal, anthracite coal, and lignite by underground mining, auger mining, strip mining, culm bank mining, and other surface mining; (2) developing coal mine sites; and (3) beneficiating (i.e., preparing) coal (e.g., cleaning, washing, screening, and sizing).

*Cross-References.*        Establishments primarily engaged in--

- Manufacturing coke oven products in coke oven establishments--are classified in Industry 32419, Other Petroleum and Coal Products Manufacturing;
- Manufacturing coal products in steel mills--are classified in Industry 33111, Iron and Steel Mills and Ferroalloy Manufacturing; and
- Providing support activities (except geophysical surveying and mapping, site preparation, construction, and transportation) for the mining of coal on a contract or fee basis--are classified in Industry 21311, Support Activities for Mining.

## 212114 Surface Coal Mining

This U.S. industry comprises establishments primarily engaged in one or more of the following: (1) surface mining of bituminous coal, lignite, and anthracite coal; (2) developing bituminous coal, lignite, and anthracite coal surface mine sites; (3) surface mining and beneficiating (e.g., cleaning, washing, screening, and sizing) of bituminous coal, lignite, and anthracite coal; or (4) beneficiating (e.g., cleaning, washing, screening, and sizing), but not mining, bituminous coal, lignite, and anthracite coal.

*Cross-References.*        Establishments primarily engaged in--

- Underground mining and/or development of underground bituminous and anthracite coal mines--are classified in U.S. Industry 212115, Underground Coal Mining;
- Providing support activities (except geophysical surveying and mapping, site preparation, construction, and transportation) for the mining of coal on a contract or fee basis--are classified in U.S. Industry 213113, Support Activities for Coal Mining;
- Manufacturing coke oven products in coke oven establishments--are classified in U.S. Industry 324199, All Other Petroleum and Coal Products Manufacturing; and
- Manufacturing coal products in steel mills--are classified in Industry 331110, Iron and Steel Mills and Ferroalloy Manufacturing.

## 212115 Underground Coal Mining

This U.S. industry comprises establishments primarily engaged in one or more of the following: (1) underground mining of bituminous and anthracite coal; (2) developing bituminous and anthracite coal underground mine sites; and (3) underground mining and beneficiating (e.g., cleaning, washing, screening, and sizing) of bituminous and anthracite coal.

---

T—Canadian, Mexican, and United States industries are comparable.

*Cross-References.*        Establishments primarily engaged in--

- Surface mining and/or beneficiating of bituminous coal, lignite, and anthracite coal--are classified in U.S. Industry 212114, Surface Coal Mining;
- Providing support activities (except geophysical surveying and mapping, site preparation, construction, and transportation) for the mining of coal on a contract or fee basis--are classified in U.S. Industry 213113, Support Activities for Coal Mining;
- Manufacturing coke oven products in coke oven establishments--are classified in U.S. Industry 324199, All Other Petroleum and Coal Products Manufacturing; and
- Manufacturing coal products in steel mills--are classified in Industry 331110, Iron and Steel Mills and Ferroalloy Manufacturing.

## 2122    Metal Ore Mining[T]

This industry group comprises establishments primarily engaged in developing mine sites or mining metallic minerals, and establishments primarily engaged in ore dressing and beneficiating (i.e., preparing) operations, such as crushing, grinding, washing, drying, sintering, concentrating, calcining, and leaching.  Beneficiating may be performed at mills operated in conjunction with the mines served or at mills, such as custom mills, operated separately.

## 21221    Iron Ore Mining[T]
See industry description for 212210.

## 212210  Iron Ore Mining

This industry comprises establishments primarily engaged in (1) developing mine sites, mining, and/or beneficiating (i.e., preparing) iron ores and manganiferous ores valued chiefly for their iron content and/or (2) producing sinter iron ore (except iron ore produced in iron and steel mills) and other iron ore agglomerates.

*Cross-References.*

Establishments primarily engaged in manufacturing pig iron ore are classified in Industry 331110, Iron and Steel Mills and Ferroalloy Manufacturing.

## 21222    Gold Ore and Silver Ore Mining[T]
See industry description for 212220.

## 212220  Gold Ore and Silver Ore Mining

This industry comprises establishments primarily engaged in developing the mine site, mining, and/or beneficiating (i.e., preparing) ores valued chiefly for their gold and/or silver content.  Establishments primarily engaged in the transformation of the gold and silver into bullion or dore bar in combination with mining activities are included in this industry.

*Cross-References.*

Establishments primarily engaged in manufacturing gold or silver bullion or dore bar without mining are classified in Industry 331410, Nonferrous Metal (except Aluminum) Smelting and Refining.

## 21223    Copper, Nickel, Lead, and Zinc Mining[T]
See industry description for 212230.

T—Canadian, Mexican, and United States industries are comparable.

### 212230  Copper, Nickel, Lead, and Zinc Mining

This industry comprises establishments primarily engaged in developing the mine site, mining, and/or beneficiating (i.e., preparing) ores valued chiefly for their copper, nickel, lead, or zinc content. Beneficiating includes the transformation of ores into concentrates. Establishments primarily engaged in recovering copper concentrates by the precipitation, leaching, or electrowinning of copper ore are included in this industry.

*Cross-References.*          Establishments primarily engaged in--

- Refining copper concentrates--are classified in Industry 331410, Nonferrous Metal (except Aluminum) Smelting and Refining; and
- Developing the mine site, mining, and/or beneficiating iron and manganiferous ores valued for their iron content--are classified in Industry 212210, Iron Ore Mining.

### 21229  Other Metal Ore Mining[T]
See industry description for 212290.

### 212290  Other Metal Ore Mining

This industry comprises establishments primarily engaged in developing the mine site, mining, and/or beneficiating (i.e., preparing) metal ores (except iron and manganiferous ores valued for their iron content, gold ore, silver ore, copper, nickel, lead, and zinc ore).

*Illustrative Examples:*

Antimony ores mining and/or beneficiating
Tantalum ores mining and/or beneficiating
Columbite ores mining and/or beneficiating
Tungsten ores mining and/or beneficiating

Ilmenite ores mining and/or beneficiating
Uranium-radium-vanadium ores mining and/or beneficiating
Molybdenum ores mining and/or beneficiating

*Cross-References.*          Establishments primarily engaged in--

- Developing the mine site, mining, and/or beneficiating iron and manganiferous ores valued chiefly for their iron content--are classified in Industry 212210, Iron Ore Mining;
- Developing the mine site, mining, and/or beneficiating ores valued chiefly for their gold or silver content--are classified in Industry 212220, Gold Ore and Silver Ore Mining;
- Developing the mine site, mining, and/or beneficiating ores valued chiefly for their copper, nickel, lead, or zinc content--are classified in Industry 212230, Copper, Nickel, Lead, and Zinc Mining;
- Enriching uranium--are classified in Industry 325180, Other Basic Inorganic Chemical Manufacturing; and
- Providing support activities (except geophysical surveying and mapping, site preparation, construction, and transportation) for the mining of metallic minerals and ores on a contract or fee basis--are classified in U.S. Industry 213114, Support Activities for Metal Mining.

### 2123  Nonmetallic Mineral Mining and Quarrying[T]

This industry group comprises establishments primarily engaged in developing mine sites, or in mining or quarrying nonmetallic minerals (except fuels). Also included are certain well and brine operations, and preparation plants primarily engaged in beneficiating (e.g., crushing, grinding, washing, and concentrating) nonmetallic minerals.
Beneficiation is the process whereby the extracted material is reduced to particles which can be separated into mineral and waste, the former suitable for further processing or direct use. The operations that take place in beneficiation are primarily mechanical, such as grinding, washing, magnetic separation, and centrifugal separation. In contrast, manufacturing operations primarily use chemical and electrochemical processes, such as electrolysis and distillation. However, some treatments, such as heat treatments, take place in both the beneficiation and the manufacturing (i.e., smelting/refining) stages. The range of preparation activities varies by mineral and the purity of

T—Canadian, Mexican, and United States industries are comparable.

any given ore deposit. While some minerals, such as petroleum and natural gas, require little or no preparation, others are washed and screened, while yet others, such as gold and silver, can be transformed into bullion before leaving the mine site.

## 21231    Stone Mining and Quarrying[T]

This industry comprises (1) establishments primarily engaged in developing the mine site, mining or quarrying dimension stone (i.e., rough blocks and/or slabs of stone), or mining and quarrying crushed and broken stone and/or (2) preparation plants primarily engaged in beneficiating stone (e.g., crushing, grinding, washing, screening, pulverizing, and sizing).

*Cross-References.*          Establishments primarily engaged in--

- Producing lime--are classified in Industry 32741, Lime Manufacturing; and
- Quarrying and dressing dimension stone--are classified in Industry 32799, All Other Nonmetallic Mineral Product Manufacturing.

## 212311  Dimension Stone Mining and Quarrying

This U.S. industry comprises establishments primarily engaged in developing the mine site and/or mining or quarrying dimension stone (i.e., rough blocks and/or slabs of stone).

*Cross-References.*

Establishments primarily engaged in dressing dimension stone and manufacturing stone products are classified in U.S. Industry 327991, Cut Stone and Stone Product Manufacturing.

## 212312  Crushed and Broken Limestone Mining and Quarrying

This U.S. industry comprises (1) establishments primarily engaged in developing the mine site, mining or quarrying crushed and broken limestone (including related rocks, such as dolomite, cement rock, marl, travertine, and calcareous tufa) and (2) preparation plants primarily engaged in beneficiating limestone (e.g., grinding or pulverizing).

*Cross-References.*          Establishments primarily engaged in--

- Producing lime--are classified in Industry 327410, Lime Manufacturing; and
- Mining or quarrying bituminous limestone--are classified in U.S. Industry 212319, Other Crushed and Broken Stone Mining and Quarrying.

## 212313  Crushed and Broken Granite Mining and Quarrying

This U.S. industry comprises (1) establishments primarily engaged in developing the mine site, and/or mining or quarrying crushed and broken granite (including related rocks, such as gneiss, syenite (except nepheline), and diorite) and (2) preparation plants primarily engaged in beneficiating granite (e.g., grinding or pulverizing).

## 212319  Other Crushed and Broken Stone Mining and Quarrying

This U.S. industry comprises: (1) establishments primarily engaged in developing the mine site and/or mining or quarrying crushed and broken stone (except limestone and granite); (2) preparation plants primarily engaged in beneficiating (e.g., grinding and pulverizing) stone (except limestone and granite); and (3) establishments primarily engaged in mining or quarrying bituminous limestone and bituminous sandstone.

---

T—Canadian, Mexican, and United States industries are comparable.

*Illustrative Examples:*

Bituminous limestone mining and/or beneficiating
Marble crushed and broken stone mining and/or
beneficiating

Bituminous sandstone mining and/or beneficiating
Sandstone crushed and broken stone mining and/or
beneficiating

*Cross-References.*        Establishments primarily engaged in--

- Mining, quarrying, or beneficiating crushed and broken limestone--are classified in U.S. Industry 212312, Crushed and Broken Limestone Mining and Quarrying; and
- Mining, quarrying, or beneficiating crushed and broken granite--are classified in U.S. Industry 212313, Crushed and Broken Granite Mining and Quarrying.

## 21232   Sand, Gravel, Clay, and Ceramic and Refractory Minerals Mining and Quarrying[T]

This industry comprises (1) establishments primarily engaged in developing the mine site and/or mining, quarrying, dredging for sand and gravel, or mining clay (e.g., china clay, paper clay and slip clay) or ceramic and refractory minerals and (2) preparation plants primarily engaged in beneficiating (e.g., washing, screening, and grinding) sand and gravel, clay, and ceramic and refractory minerals.

*Cross-References.*        Establishments primarily engaged in--

- Manufacturing ready-mix concrete--are classified in Industry 32732, Ready-Mix Concrete Manufacturing;
- Calcining, dead burning, or otherwise processing (i.e., beyond basic preparation) clay or ceramic and refractory minerals--are classified in Industry 32799, All Other Nonmetallic Mineral Product Manufacturing;
- Shaping, molding, baking, burning, or hardening nonclay ceramics, clay and nonclay refractories, and structural clay products--are classified in Industry 32712, Clay Building Material and Refractories Manufacturing;
- Shaping, molding, glazing, and firing pottery, ceramics, and plumbing fixtures--are classified in Industry 32711, Pottery, Ceramics, and Plumbing Fixture Manufacturing;
- Oil shale mining and/or beneficiating--are classified in Industry 21112, Crude Petroleum Extraction; and
- Construction projects involving water resources (e.g., dredging and land drainage)--are classified in Industry 23799, Other Heavy and Civil Engineering Construction.

## 212321  Construction Sand and Gravel Mining

This U.S. industry comprises establishments primarily engaged in one or more of the following: (1) operating commercial grade (i.e., construction) sand and gravel pits; (2) dredging for commercial grade sand and gravel; and (3) washing, screening, or otherwise preparing commercial grade sand and gravel.

*Cross-References.*        Establishments primarily engaged in--

- Mining industrial grade sand--are classified in U.S. Industry 212322, Industrial Sand Mining;
- Manufacturing ready-mix concrete--are classified in Industry 327320, Ready-Mix Concrete Manufacturing; and
- Construction projects involving water resources (e.g., dredging and land drainage)--are classified in Industry 237990, Other Heavy and Civil Engineering Construction.

## 212322  Industrial Sand Mining

This U.S. industry comprises establishments primarily engaged in one or more of the following: (1) operating industrial grade sand pits; (2) dredging for industrial grade sand; and (3) washing, screening, or otherwise preparing industrial grade sand.

---

T—Canadian, Mexican, and United States industries are comparable.

*Cross-References.*          Establishments primarily engaged in--

- Mining commercial (i.e., construction) grade gravel--are classified in U.S. Industry 212321, Construction Sand and Gravel Mining; and
- Construction projects involving water resources (e.g., dredging and land drainage)--are classified in Industry 237990, Other Heavy and Civil Engineering Construction.

## 212323  Kaolin, Clay, and Ceramic and Refractory Minerals Mining

This U.S. industry comprises (1) establishments primarily engaged in developing the mine site and/or mining clay (e.g., china clay, paper clay and slip clay) or ceramic and refractory minerals and (2) establishments primarily engaged in beneficiating (i.e., preparing) clay or ceramic and refractory minerals.

*Illustrative Examples:*

Bentonite mining and/or beneficiating
Fuller's earth mining and/or beneficiating
Common clay mining and/or beneficiating
Kaolin mining and/or beneficiating

Feldspar mining and/or beneficiating
Ball clay mining and/or beneficiating
Fire clay mining and/or beneficiating
Shale (except oil shale) mining and/or beneficiating

*Cross-References.*          Establishments primarily engaged in--

- Shaping, molding, glazing, and firing pottery, ceramics, and plumbing fixtures--are classified in Industry 327110, Pottery, Ceramics, and Plumbing Fixture Manufacturing;
- Shaping, molding, baking, burning, or hardening clay and nonclay refractories, and structural clay products--are classified in Industry 327120, Clay Building Material and Refractories Manufacturing;
- Calcining, dead burning, or otherwise processing (i.e., beyond basic preparation) clay or ceramic and refractory minerals--are classified in U.S. Industry 327992, Ground or Treated Mineral and Earth Manufacturing; and
- Oil shale mining and/or beneficiating--are classified in Industry 211120, Crude Petroleum Extraction.

## 21239  Other Nonmetallic Mineral Mining and Quarrying[T]
See industry description for 212390.

## 212390  Other Nonmetallic Mineral Mining and Quarrying

This industry comprises establishments primarily engaged in developing the mine site, mining, and/or milling or otherwise beneficiating (i.e., preparing) nonmetallic minerals (except coal, stone, sand, gravel, clay, and ceramic and refractory minerals).  Drylake brine operations are included in this industry, as well as establishments engaged in producing the specified minerals from underground and open pit mines.

*Illustrative Examples:*

Barite mining and/or beneficiating
Phosphate rock mining and/or beneficiating
Borate, natural, mining and/or beneficiating

Potash mining and/or beneficiating
Peat mining and/or beneficiating
Rock salt mining and/or beneficiating

*Cross-References.*          Establishments primarily engaged in--

- Mining or quarrying stone--are classified in Industry 21231, Stone Mining and Quarrying;
- Mining, quarrying, or beneficiating sand, gravel, clay, and ceramic and refractory minerals--are classified in Industry 21232, Sand, Gravel, Clay, and Ceramic and Refractory Minerals Mining and Quarrying;
- Calcining, dead burning, or otherwise processing (i.e., beyond basic preparation) minerals, such as talc, mica, feldspar, barite, and soapstone--are classified in U.S. Industry 327992, Ground or Treated Mineral and Earth Manufacturing;

---

T—Canadian, Mexican, and United States industries are comparable.

- Manufacturing sodium carbonate, boron compounds, and/or potassium salts--are classified in Industry 325180, Other Basic Inorganic Chemical Manufacturing;
- Manufacturing table salt--are classified in U.S. Industry 311942, Spice and Extract Manufacturing;
- Manufacturing industrial salt--are classified in U.S. Industry 325998, All Other Miscellaneous Chemical Product and Preparation Manufacturing;
- Manufacturing phosphoric acid, superphosphates, or other phosphatic fertilizer materials--are classified in U.S. Industry 325312, Phosphatic Fertilizer Manufacturing; and
- Providing support activities (except geophysical surveying and mapping, site preparation, construction, and transportation) for the mining of nonmetallic minerals (except fuel) on a contract or fee basis--are classified in U.S. Industry 213115, Support Activities for Nonmetallic Minerals (except Fuels) Mining.

## 213    Support Activities for Mining[T]

Industries in the Support Activities for Mining subsector group establishments primarily providing support services, on a contract or fee basis (except geophysical surveying and mapping, mine site preparation, construction, and transportation activities), required for the mining and quarrying of minerals and for the extraction of oil and gas. Establishments performing exploration for minerals, on a contract or fee basis, are included in this subsector. Exploration services include traditional prospecting methods, such as taking core samples and making geological observations at prospective sites.

The activities performed on a contract or fee basis by establishments in the Support Activities for Mining subsector are also often performed in-house by mining operators. These activities include taking core samples, making geological observations at prospective sites, excavating slush pits and cellars, and such oil and gas operations as spudding in, drilling in, redrilling, directional drilling, and well surveying; running, cutting, and pulling casings, tubes, and rods; cementing and shooting wells; perforating well casings; acidizing and chemically treating wells; cleaning out, bailing, and swabbing wells; and operating oil and gas field gathering lines.

Establishments primarily engaged in providing site preparation and related construction activities on a contract or fee basis are classified in Sector 23, Construction. Establishments primarily engaged in providing transportation activities in support of mining, quarrying, or oil and gas extraction are classified in Sector 48-49, Transportation and Warehousing, based on the primary activity.

## 2131    Support Activities for Mining[T]

## 21311    Support Activities for Mining[T]

This industry comprises establishments primarily engaged in providing support services, on a contract or fee basis (except geophysical surveying and mapping, mine site preparation, construction, and transportation activities), required for the mining and quarrying of minerals and for the extraction of oil and gas. Drilling, taking core samples, and making geological observations at prospective sites for minerals, on a contract or fee basis, are included in this industry.

*Cross-References.*        Establishments primarily engaged in--

- Performing geophysical surveying and mapping services for minerals (i.e., coal, metal ores, oil and gas, and nonmetallic minerals) on a contract or fee basis--are classified in Industry 54136, Geophysical Surveying and Mapping Services;
- Mining, quarrying, and/or beneficiating on a contract or fee basis--are classified in Subsector 212, Mining (except Oil and Gas), based on the mineral mined;
- Operating oil and gas field properties on a contract or fee basis--are classified in Subsector 211, Oil and Gas Extraction, based on the primary activity;
- Oil and gas pipeline and related structures construction and repair--are classified in Industry 23712, Oil and Gas Pipeline and Related Structures Construction;
- Inspecting pipelines (i.e., visual)--are classified in Industry 54199, All Other Professional, Scientific, and Technical Services;
- Site preparation and related construction activities on a contract or fee basis--are classified in Industry 23891, Site Preparation Contractors;

---

T—Canadian, Mexican, and United States industries are comparable.

- Mining machinery and equipment repair and maintenance--are classified in Industry 81131, Commercial and Industrial Machinery and Equipment (except Automotive and Electronic) Repair and Maintenance;
- Providing transportation activities on a contract or fee basis--are classified in Sector 48-49, Transportation and Warehousing, based on the primary activity; and
- Providing landman services on a contract or fee basis--are classified in Industry 53139, Other Activities Related to Real Estate.

### 213111  Drilling Oil and Gas Wells

This U.S. industry comprises establishments primarily engaged in drilling oil and gas wells for others on a contract or fee basis.  This industry includes contractors that specialize in spudding in, drilling in, redrilling, and directional drilling.

*Cross-References.*            Establishments primarily engaged in--

- Performing exploration (except geophysical surveying and mapping) services for oil and gas on a contract or fee basis--are classified in U.S. Industry 213112, Support Activities for Oil and Gas Operations; and
- Performing geophysical surveying and mapping services for oil and gas on a contract or fee basis--are classified in Industry 541360, Geophysical Surveying and Mapping Services.

### 213112  Support Activities for Oil and Gas Operations

This U.S. industry comprises establishments primarily engaged in performing support activities, on a contract or fee basis, for oil and gas operations (except geophysical surveying and mapping, site preparation, construction, and transportation activities).  Services included are exploration; excavating slush pits and cellars, well surveying; running, cutting, and pulling casings, tubes, and rods; cementing wells, shooting wells; perforating well casings; acidizing and chemically treating wells; and cleaning out, bailing, and swabbing wells.

*Cross-References.*            Establishments primarily engaged in--

- Contract drilling for oil and gas--are classified in U.S. Industry 213111, Drilling Oil and Gas Wells;
- Operating oil and gas field properties on a contract or fee basis--are classified in Industry Group 2111, Oil and Gas Extraction;
- Performing geophysical surveying and mapping services for oil and gas on a contract or fee basis--are classified in Industry 541360, Geophysical Surveying and Mapping Services;
- Oil and gas pipeline and related structures construction and repair--are classified in Industry 237120, Oil and Gas Pipeline and Related Structures Construction;
- Inspecting pipelines (i.e., visual)--are classified in Industry 541990, All Other Professional, Scientific, and Technical Services;
- Site preparation and related construction activities on a contract or fee basis--are classified in Industry 238910, Site Preparation Contractors;
- Mining machinery and equipment repair and maintenance--are classified in Industry 811310, Commercial and Industrial Machinery and Equipment (except Automotive and Electronic) Repair and Maintenance;
- Providing transportation activities on a contract or fee basis--are classified in Sector 48-49, Transportation and Warehousing, based on the primary activity; and
- Providing landman services on a contract or fee basis--are classified in Industry 531390, Other Activities Related to Real Estate.

### 213113  Support Activities for Coal Mining

This U.S. industry comprises establishments primarily engaged in providing support activities for coal mining (except geophysical surveying and mapping, site preparation, construction, and transportation activities) on a contract or fee basis.  Exploration for coal is included in this industry.  Exploration services include traditional prospecting methods, such as taking core samples and making geological observations at prospective sites.

---

T—Canadian, Mexican, and United States industries are comparable.

*Cross-References.*        Establishments primarily engaged in--

- Performing geophysical surveying and mapping services for coal on a contract or fee basis--are classified in Industry 541360, Geophysical Surveying and Mapping Services;
- Operating coal mines or quarries on a contract or fee basis--are classified in Industry 21211, Coal Mining, based on the type of mine;
- Site preparation and related construction activities on a contract or fee basis--are classified in Industry 238910, Site Preparation Contractors; and
- Providing transportation activities on a contract or fee basis--are classified in Sector 48-49, Transportation and Warehousing, based on the primary activity.

## 213114  Support Activities for Metal Mining

This U.S. industry comprises establishments primarily engaged in providing support activities (except geophysical surveying and mapping, site preparation, construction, and transportation activities), on a contract or fee basis, for the mining and quarrying of metallic minerals and for the extraction of metal ores.  Exploration for these minerals is included in this industry.  Exploration services include traditional prospecting methods, such as taking core samples and making geological observations at prospective sites.

*Cross-References.*        Establishments primarily engaged in--

- Performing geophysical surveying and mapping services for metallic minerals on a contract or fee basis-- are classified in Industry 541360, Geophysical Surveying and Mapping Services;
- Operating metallic mineral mines or quarries on a contract or fee basis--are classified in Industry Group 2122, Metal Ore Mining, based on the type of ore mined;
- Site preparation and related construction activities on a contract or fee basis--are classified in Industry 238910, Site Preparation Contractors; and
- Providing transportation activities on a contract or fee basis--are classified in Sector 48-49, Transportation and Warehousing, based on the primary activity.

## 213115  Support Activities for Nonmetallic Minerals (except Fuels) Mining

This U.S. industry comprises establishments primarily engaged in providing support activities, on a contract or fee basis, for the mining and quarrying of nonmetallic minerals (except fuel) and for the extraction of nonmetallic minerals (except geophysical surveying and mapping, site preparation, construction, and transportation activities). Exploration for these minerals is included in this industry.  Exploration services include traditional prospecting methods, such as taking core samples and making geological observations at prospective sites.

*Cross-References.*        Establishments primarily engaged in--

- Performing geophysical surveying and mapping services for nonmetallic minerals on a contract or fee basis--are classified in Industry 541360, Geophysical Surveying and Mapping Services;
- Operating nonmetallic mineral mines or quarries on a contract or fee basis--are classified in Industry Group 2123, Nonmetallic Mineral Mining and Quarrying, based on the type of mineral mined or quarried;
- Site preparation and related construction activities on a contract or fee basis--are classified in Industry 238910, Site Preparation Contractors; and
- Providing transportation activities on a contract or fee basis--are classified in Sector 48-49, Transportation and Warehousing, based on the primary activity.

---

T—Canadian, Mexican, and United States industries are comparable.

# Sector 22--Utilities[T]

## The Sector as a Whole

The Utilities sector comprises establishments engaged in the provision of the following utility services: electric power, natural gas, steam supply, water supply, and sewage treatment and disposal. Within this sector, the specific activities associated with the utility services provided vary by utility: electric power includes generation, transmission, and distribution; natural gas includes distribution; steam supply includes provision and/or distribution; water supply includes treatment and distribution; and sewage removal includes collection, treatment, and disposal of waste through sewer systems and sewage treatment facilities.

Excluded from this sector are establishments primarily engaged in waste management services classified in Subsector 562, Waste Management and Remediation Services. These establishments also collect, treat, and dispose of waste materials; however, they do not use sewer systems or sewage treatment facilities.

## 221    Utilities[T]

Industries in the Utilities subsector provide electric power, natural gas, steam supply, water supply, and sewage treatment and disposal through a permanent infrastructure of lines, mains, and pipes. Establishments are grouped together based on the utility service provided and the particular system or facilities required to perform the service.

## 2211    Electric Power Generation, Transmission and Distribution[T]

This industry group comprises establishments primarily engaged in generating, transmitting, and/or distributing electric power. Establishments in this industry group may perform one or more of the following activities: (1) operate generation facilities that produce electric energy; (2) operate transmission systems that convey the electricity from the generation facility to the distribution system; and (3) operate distribution systems that convey electric power received from the generation facility or the transmission system to the final consumer.

## 22111    Electric Power Generation[T]

This industry comprises establishments primarily engaged in operating electric power generation facilities. These facilities convert other forms of energy, such as water power (i.e., hydroelectric), fossil fuels, nuclear power, and solar power, into electrical energy. The establishments in this industry produce electric energy and provide electricity to transmission systems or to electric power distribution systems.

*Cross-References.*         Establishments primarily engaged in--

- Operating trash incinerators that also generate electricity--are classified in Industry 56221, Waste Treatment and Disposal; and
- Installing solar panels or solar heating equipment--are classified in Industry Group 2382, Building Equipment Contractors.

## 221111  Hydroelectric Power Generation

This U.S. industry comprises establishments primarily engaged in operating hydroelectric power generation facilities. These facilities use water power to drive a turbine and produce electric energy. The electric energy produced in these establishments is provided to electric power transmission systems or to electric power distribution systems.

## 221112  Fossil Fuel Electric Power Generation

This U.S. industry comprises establishments primarily engaged in operating fossil fuel powered electric power generation facilities. These facilities use fossil fuels, such as coal, oil, or gas, in internal combustion or combustion

---

T—Canadian, Mexican, and United States industries are comparable.

turbine conventional steam process to produce electric energy. The electric energy produced in these establishments is provided to electric power transmission systems or to electric power distribution systems.

**221113  Nuclear Electric Power Generation**

This U.S. industry comprises establishments primarily engaged in operating nuclear electric power generation facilities. These facilities use nuclear power to produce electric energy. The electric energy produced in these establishments is provided to electric power transmission systems or to electric power distribution systems.

**221114  Solar Electric Power Generation**

This U.S. industry comprises establishments primarily engaged in operating solar electric power generation facilities. These facilities use energy from the sun to produce electric energy. The electric energy produced in these establishments is provided to electric power transmission systems or to electric power distribution systems.

*Cross-References.*

Establishments primarily engaged in installing solar panels or solar heating equipment are classified in Industry Group 2382, Building Equipment Contractors.

**221115  Wind Electric Power Generation**

This U.S. industry comprises establishments primarily engaged in operating wind electric power generation facilities. These facilities use wind power to drive a turbine and produce electric energy. The electric energy produced in these establishments is provided to electric power transmission systems or to electric power distribution systems.

**221116  Geothermal Electric Power Generation**

This U.S. industry comprises establishments primarily engaged in operating geothermal electric power generation facilities. These facilities use heat derived from the Earth to produce electric energy. The electric energy produced in these establishments is provided to electric power transmission systems or to electric power distribution systems.

**221117  Biomass Electric Power Generation**

This U.S. industry comprises establishments primarily engaged in operating biomass electric power generation facilities. These facilities use biomass (e.g., wood, waste, alcohol fuels) to produce electric energy. The electric energy produced in these establishments is provided to electric power transmission systems or to electric power distribution systems.

*Cross-References.*

Establishments primarily engaged in operating trash disposal incinerators that also generate electricity are classified in U.S. Industry 562213, Solid Waste Combustors and Incinerators.

**221118  Other Electric Power Generation**

This U.S. industry comprises establishments primarily engaged in operating electric power generation facilities (except hydroelectric, fossil fuel, nuclear, solar, wind, geothermal, biomass). These facilities convert other forms of energy, such as tidal power, into electric energy. The electric energy produced in these establishments is provided to electric power transmission systems or to electric power distribution systems.

T—Canadian, Mexican, and United States industries are comparable.

*Cross-References.* Establishments primarily engaged in--

- Operating trash disposal incinerators that also generate electricity--are classified in U.S. Industry 562213, Solid Waste Combustors and Incinerators;
- Operating hydroelectric power generation facilities--are classified in U.S. Industry 221111, Hydroelectric Power Generation;
- Operating fossil fuel powered electric power generation facilities--are classified in U.S. Industry 221112, Fossil Fuel Electric Power Generation;
- Operating nuclear electric power generation facilities--are classified in U.S. Industry 221113, Nuclear Electric Power Generation;
- Operating solar electric power generation facilities--are classified in U.S. Industry 221114, Solar Electric Power Generation;
- Operating wind electric power generation facilities--are classified in U.S. Industry 221115, Wind Electric Power Generation;
- Operating geothermal electric power generation facilities--are classified in U.S. Industry 221116, Geothermal Electric Power Generation; and
- Operating biomass electric power generation facilities--are classified in U.S. Industry 221117, Biomass Electric Power Generation.

## 22112 Electric Power Transmission, Control, and Distribution[T]

This industry comprises establishments primarily engaged in operating electric power transmission systems, controlling (i.e., regulating voltages) the transmission of electricity, and/or distributing electricity. The transmission system includes lines and transformer stations. These establishments arrange, facilitate, or coordinate the transmission of electricity from the generating source to the distribution centers, other electric utilities, or final consumers. The distribution system consists of lines, poles, meters, and wiring that deliver the electricity to final consumers.

*Cross-References.*

Establishments primarily engaged in generating electric energy are classified in Industry 22111, Electric Power Generation.

## 221121 Electric Bulk Power Transmission and Control

This U.S. industry comprises establishments primarily engaged in operating electric power transmission systems and/or controlling (i.e., regulating voltages) the transmission of electricity from the generating source to distribution centers or other electric utilities. The transmission system includes lines and transformer stations.

*Cross-References.* Establishments primarily engaged in--

- Generating electric energy--are classified in Industry 22111, Electric Power Generation; and
- Distributing electricity to final consumers--are classified in U.S. Industry 221122, Electric Power Distribution.

## 221122 Electric Power Distribution

This U.S. industry comprises electric power establishments primarily engaged in either (1) operating electric power distribution systems (i.e., consisting of lines, poles, meters, and wiring) or (2) operating as electric power brokers or agents that arrange the sale of electricity via power distribution systems operated by others.

*Cross-References.* Establishments primarily engaged in--

- Generating electric energy--are classified in Industry 22111, Electric Power Generation; and

---

T—Canadian, Mexican, and United States industries are comparable.

- Transmitting electricity between generating sources or distribution centers--are classified in U.S. Industry 221121, Electric Bulk Power Transmission and Control.

## 2212   Natural Gas Distribution[T]

## 22121   Natural Gas Distribution[T]
See industry description for 221210.

## 221210   Natural Gas Distribution

This industry comprises: (1) establishments primarily engaged in operating gas distribution systems (e.g., mains, meters); (2) establishments known as gas marketers that buy gas from the well and sell it to a distribution system; (3) establishments known as gas brokers or agents that arrange the sale of gas over gas distribution systems operated by others; and (4) establishments primarily engaged in transmitting and distributing gas to final consumers.

*Cross-References.*          Establishments primarily engaged in--

- Pipeline transportation of natural gas from process plants to local distribution systems--are classified in Industry 486210, Pipeline Transportation of Natural Gas;
- Operating liquefied natural gas (LNG) terminals without operating natural gas pipelines--are classified in U.S. Industry 488999, All Other Support Activities for Transportation; and
- Retailing liquefied petroleum (LP) gas via direct selling (i.e., home delivery)--are classified in Industry 457210, Fuel Dealers.

## 2213   Water, Sewage and Other Systems[T]

This industry group comprises establishments primarily engaged in: (1) operating water treatment plants and/or water supply systems; (2) operating sewer systems or sewage treatment facilities; or (3) providing steam, heated air, or cooled air.

## 22131   Water Supply and Irrigation Systems
See industry description for 221310.

## 221310   Water Supply and Irrigation Systems

This industry comprises establishments primarily engaged in operating water treatment plants and/or operating water supply systems.  The water supply system may include pumping stations, aqueducts, and/or distribution mains.  The water may be used for drinking, irrigation, or other uses.

*Cross-References.*

- Establishments primarily engaged in irrigation project construction (except lawn) are classified in Industry 237110, Water and Sewer Line and Related Structures Construction;
- Establishments primarily engaged in installing lawn sprinkler systems are classified in Industry 238220, Plumbing, Heating, and Air-Conditioning Contractors;
- Establishments primarily engaged in lawn irrigation services are classified in Industry 561730, Landscaping Services;
- Establishments primarily engaged in retailing bottled water are classified in U.S. Industry 445298, All Other Specialty Food Retailers; and
- Government establishments primarily engaged in administering irrigation districts are classified in Industry 926130, Regulation and Administration of Communications, Electric, Gas, and Other Utilities.

## 22132   Sewage Treatment Facilities
See industry description for 221320.

---

T—Canadian, Mexican, and United States industries are comparable.

**221320 Sewage Treatment Facilities**

This industry comprises establishments primarily engaged in operating sewer systems or sewage treatment facilities that collect, treat, and dispose of waste.

*Cross-References.*        Establishments primarily engaged in--

- Operating waste treatment or disposal facilities (except sewer systems or sewage treatment facilities)--are classified in Industry 56221, Waste Treatment and Disposal;
- Operating water treatment plants and/or operating water supply systems--are classified in Industry 221310, Water Supply and Irrigation Systems;
- Pumping (i.e., cleaning) cesspools, portable toilets, and septic tanks or renting portable toilets--are classified in U.S. Industry 562991, Septic Tank and Related Services; and
- Cleaning and rodding sewers and catch basins--are classified in U.S. Industry 562998, All Other Miscellaneous Waste Management Services.

**22133  Steam and Air-Conditioning Supply**
See industry description for 221330.

**221330  Steam and Air-Conditioning Supply**

This industry comprises establishments primarily engaged in providing steam, heated air, or cooled air. The steam distribution may be through mains.

*Cross-References.*        Establishments primarily engaged in--

- Selling and installing warm air heating and air-conditioning equipment--are classified in Industry 238220, Plumbing, Heating, and Air-Conditioning Contractors; and
- Merchant wholesale distribution of warm air heating and air-conditioning equipment--are classified in Industry 423730, Warm Air Heating and Air-Conditioning Equipment and Supplies Merchant Wholesalers.

T—Canadian, Mexican, and United States industries are comparable.

# Sector 23--Construction[T]

## The Sector as a Whole

The Construction sector comprises establishments primarily engaged in the construction of buildings or engineering projects (e.g., highways and utility systems).  Establishments primarily engaged in the preparation of sites for new construction and establishments primarily engaged in subdividing land for sale as building sites also are included in this sector.

Construction work done may include new work, additions, alterations, or maintenance and repairs.  Activities of these establishments generally are managed at a fixed place of business, but they usually perform construction activities at multiple project sites.  Production responsibilities for establishments in this sector are usually specified in (1) contracts with the owners of construction projects (prime contracts) or (2) contracts with other construction establishments (subcontracts).

Establishments primarily engaged in contracts that include responsibility for all aspects of individual construction projects are commonly known as general contractors, but also may be known as design-builders, construction managers, turnkey contractors, or (in cases where two or more establishments jointly secure a general contract) joint-venture contractors.  Construction managers that provide oversight and scheduling only (i.e., agency) as well as construction managers that are responsible for the entire project (i.e., at risk) are included as general contractor type establishments.  Establishments of the "general contractor type" frequently arrange construction of separate parts of their projects through subcontracts with other construction establishments.

Establishments primarily engaged in activities to produce a specific component (e.g., masonry, painting, and electrical work) of a construction project are commonly known as specialty trade contractors.  Activities of specialty trade contractors are usually subcontracted from other construction establishments, but especially in remodeling and repair construction, the work may be done directly for the owner of the property.

Establishments primarily engaged in activities to construct buildings to be sold on sites that they own are known as for-sale builders, but also may be known as speculative builders or merchant builders.  For-sale builders produce buildings in a manner similar to general contractors, but their production processes also include site acquisition and securing of financial backing.  For-sale builders are most often associated with the construction of residential buildings.  Like general contractors, they may subcontract all or part of the actual construction work on their buildings.

There are substantial differences in the types of equipment, work force skills, and other inputs required by establishments in this sector.  To highlight these differences and variations in the underlying production functions, this sector is divided into three subsectors.

Subsector 236, Construction of Buildings, comprises establishments of the general contractor type and for-sale builders involved in the construction of buildings.  Subsector 237, Heavy and Civil Engineering Construction, comprises establishments involved in the construction of engineering projects.  Subsector 238, Specialty Trade Contractors, comprises establishments engaged in specialty trade activities generally needed in the construction of all types of buildings.

Force account construction is construction work performed by an enterprise primarily engaged in some business other than construction for its own account, using employees of the enterprise.  This activity is not included in the construction sector unless the construction work performed is the primary activity of a separate establishment of the enterprise.  The installation and the ongoing repair and maintenance of telecommunications and utility networks is excluded from construction when the establishments performing the work are not independent contractors.  Although a growing proportion of this work is subcontracted to independent contractors in the Construction sector, the operating units of telecommunications and utility companies performing this work are included with the telecommunications or utility activities.

## 236    Construction of Buildings[T]

The Construction of Buildings subsector comprises establishments primarily responsible for the construction of buildings.  The work performed may include new work, additions, alterations, or maintenance and repairs.  The on-site assembly of precut, panelized, and prefabricated buildings and construction of temporary buildings are included in this subsector.  Part or all of the production work for which the establishments in this subsector have responsibility may be subcontracted to other construction establishments--usually specialty trade contractors.

---

T—Canadian, Mexican, and United States industries are comparable.

Establishments in this subsector are classified based on the types of buildings they construct. This classification reflects variations in the requirements of the underlying production processes.

**2361     Residential Building Construction^T**

**23611     Residential Building Construction^T**

This industry comprises establishments primarily responsible for the construction or remodeling and renovation of single-family and multifamily residential buildings. Included in this industry are residential housing general contractors (i.e., new construction, remodeling, or renovating existing residential structures), for-sale builders and remodelers of residential structures, residential project construction management firms, and residential design-build firms.

*Cross-References.*          Establishments primarily engaged in--

- Performing specialized construction work on houses and other residential buildings, generally on a subcontract basis--are classified in Subsector 238, Specialty Trade Contractors;
- Performing manufactured (mobile) home set up and tie-down work--are classified in Industry 23899, All Other Specialty Trade Contractors;
- Manufacturing prefabricated residential buildings and assembling/erecting them at the customers' site--are classified in Sector 31-33, Manufacturing, based on the primary material (wood, plastic, or metal); and
- Constructing and leasing residential buildings on their own account--are classified in Industry 53111, Lessors of Residential Buildings and Dwellings.

**236115  New Single-Family Housing Construction (except For-Sale Builders)**

This U.S. industry comprises general contractor establishments primarily responsible for the entire construction of new single-family housing, such as single-family detached houses and town houses or row houses where each housing unit (1) is separated from its neighbors by a ground-to-roof wall and (2) has no housing units constructed above or below. This industry includes general contractors responsible for the on-site assembly of modular and prefabricated houses. Single-family housing design-build firms and single-family construction management firms acting as general contractors are included in this industry.

*Cross-References.*          Establishments primarily engaged in--

- Building single-family houses on their own account for sale as speculative builders or merchant builders-- are classified in U.S. Industry 236117, New Housing For-Sale Builders;
- Remodeling or repairing existing houses and other residential buildings--are classified in U.S. Industry 236118, Residential Remodelers;
- Performing manufactured (mobile) home set up and tie-down work--are classified in Industry 238990, All Other Specialty Trade Contractors;
- Performing specialized construction work on houses and other residential buildings, generally on a subcontract basis--are classified in Subsector 238, Specialty Trade Contractors;
- Manufacturing prefabricated residential buildings and assembling/erecting them at the customers' site--are classified in Sector 31-33, Manufacturing, based on the primary material (wood, plastic, or metal); and
- Constructing and leasing residential buildings on their own account--are classified in Industry 531110, Lessors of Residential Buildings and Dwellings.

**236116  New Multifamily Housing Construction (except For-Sale Builders)**

This U.S. industry comprises general contractor establishments primarily responsible for the construction of new multifamily residential housing units (e.g., high-rise, garden, town house apartments, and condominiums where each unit is not separated from its neighbors by a ground-to-roof wall). Multifamily design-build firms and multifamily housing construction management firms acting as general contractors are included in this industry.

---

T—Canadian, Mexican, and United States industries are comparable.

*Cross-References.*        Establishments primarily engaged in--

- Building multifamily buildings on their own account for sale as speculative builders or merchant builders-- are classified in U.S. Industry 236117, New Housing For-Sale Builders;
- Remodeling or repairing existing multifamily housing and other residential buildings--are classified in U.S. Industry 236118, Residential Remodelers;
- Performing specialized construction work on multifamily housing and other residential buildings, generally on a subcontract basis--are classified in Subsector 238, Specialty Trade Contractors;
- Manufacturing prefabricated residential buildings and assembling/erecting them at the customers' site--are classified in Sector 31-33, Manufacturing, based on the primary material (wood, plastic, or metal); and
- Constructing and leasing residential buildings on their own account--are classified in Industry 531110, Lessors of Residential Buildings and Dwellings.

## 236117  New Housing For-Sale Builders

This U.S. industry comprises establishments primarily engaged in building new homes on land that is owned or controlled by the builder rather than the homebuyer or investor. The land is included with the sale of the home. Establishments in this industry build single-family and/or multifamily homes. These establishments are often referred to as merchant builders, but are also known as production or for-sale builders.

*Cross-References.*        Establishments primarily engaged in--

- Building single-family houses for others as general contractors--are classified in U.S. Industry 236115, New Single-Family Housing Construction (except For-Sale Builders);
- Building multifamily residential buildings for others as general contractors--are classified in U.S. Industry 236116, New Multifamily Housing Construction (except For-Sale Builders);
- Remodeling or repairing existing houses and other residential buildings, either for others or on own account for sale--are classified in U.S. Industry 236118, Residential Remodelers;
- Performing specialized construction work on houses or other residential buildings, generally on a subcontract basis--are classified in Subsector 238, Specialty Trade Contractors; and
- Constructing and leasing residential buildings on their own account--are classified in Industry 531110, Lessors of Residential Buildings and Dwellings.

## 236118  Residential Remodelers

This U.S. industry comprises establishments primarily responsible for the remodeling construction (including additions, alterations, reconstruction, maintenance, and repairs) of houses and other residential buildings, single-family and multifamily. Included in this industry are remodeling general contractors, for-sale remodelers, remodeling design-build firms, and remodeling project construction management firms.

*Cross-References.*        Establishments primarily engaged in--

- Building single-family houses for others as general contractors--are classified in U.S. Industry 236115, New Single-Family Housing Construction (except For-Sale Builders);
- Building multifamily buildings for others as general contractors--are classified in U.S. Industry 236116, New Multifamily Housing Construction (except For-Sale Builders);
- Building houses or other residential buildings, on their own account for sale as speculative builders or merchant builders--are classified in U.S. Industry 236117, New Housing For-Sale Builders;
- Remodeling nonresidential buildings--are classified in Industry Group 2362, Nonresidential Building Construction, based on the type of structure being remodeled;
- Performing specialized construction work on houses or other residential buildings, generally on a subcontract basis--are classified in Subsector 238, Specialty Trade Contractors; and
- Constructing and leasing residential buildings on their own account--are classified in Industry 531110, Lessors of Residential Buildings and Dwellings.

---

T—Canadian, Mexican, and United States industries are comparable.

## 2362    Nonresidential Building Construction[T]

This industry group comprises establishments primarily responsible for the construction (including new work, additions, alterations, maintenance, and repairs) of nonresidential buildings.  This industry group includes nonresidential general contractors, nonresidential for-sale builders, nonresidential design-build firms, and nonresidential project construction management firms.

### 23621    Industrial Building Construction[T]
See industry description for 236210.

### 236210  Industrial Building Construction

This industry comprises establishments primarily responsible for the construction (including new work, additions, alterations, maintenance, and repairs) of industrial buildings (except warehouses).  The construction of selected additional structures, whose production processes are similar to those for industrial buildings (e.g., incinerators, cement plants, blast furnaces, and similar nonbuilding structures), is included in this industry.  Included in this industry are industrial building general contractors, industrial building for-sale builders, industrial building design-build firms, and industrial building construction management firms.

*Illustrative Examples:*

Assembly plant construction
Furnace, industrial plant, construction
Cannery construction
Mine loading and discharging station construction
Cement plant construction
Paper or pulp mill construction
Steel mill construction

Chemical plant (except petrochemical) construction
Pharmaceutical manufacturing plant construction
Factory construction
Food processing plant construction
Waste disposal plant (except sewage treatment) construction

*Cross-References.*         Establishments primarily engaged in--

- Constructing oil refineries and petrochemical plants--are classified in Industry 237120, Oil and Gas Pipeline and Related Structures Construction;
- Constructing water treatment plants, sewage treatment plants, and pumping stations for water and sewer systems--are classified in Industry 237110, Water and Sewer Line and Related Structures Construction;
- Constructing power generation plants (except hydroelectric)--are classified in Industry 237130, Power and Communication Line and Related Structures Construction;
- Constructing hydroelectric generating facilities--are classified in Industry 237990, Other Heavy and Civil Engineering Construction;
- Constructing industrial warehouses--are classified in Industry 236220, Commercial and Institutional Building Construction;
- Performing specialized construction work on industrial buildings, generally on a subcontract basis--are classified in Subsector 238, Specialty Trade Contractors; and
- Manufacturing prefabricated industrial buildings and assembling/erecting them at the customers' site--are classified in Sector 31-33, Manufacturing, based on the primary material (wood, plastic, or metal).

### 23622    Commercial and Institutional Building Construction[T]
See industry description for 236220.

### 236220  Commercial and Institutional Building Construction

This industry comprises establishments primarily responsible for the construction (including new work, additions, alterations, maintenance, and repairs) of commercial and institutional buildings and related structures, such as stadiums, grain elevators, and indoor swimming facilities.  This industry includes establishments responsible for the on-site assembly of modular or prefabricated commercial and institutional buildings.  Included in this industry are

T—Canadian, Mexican, and United States industries are comparable.

commercial and institutional building general contractors, commercial and institutional building for-sale builders, commercial and institutional building design-build firms, and commercial and institutional building project construction management firms.

*Illustrative Examples:*

Airport building construction
Office building construction
Arena construction
Parking garage construction
Barrack construction
Prison construction
Farm building construction
Radio and television broadcast studio construction
Fire station construction
Grain elevator or bin construction
Data center construction

Religious building (e.g., church, synagogue, mosque, temple) construction
Restaurant construction
Hospital construction
School building construction
Hotel construction
Shopping mall construction
Indoor swimming facility construction
Warehouse construction (e.g., commercial, industrial, manufacturing, private)

*Cross-References.*          Establishments primarily engaged in--

- Constructing structures that are integral parts of utility systems (e.g., storage tanks, pumping stations) or are used to produce products for these systems (e.g., power plants, refineries)--are classified in Industry Group 2371, Utility System Construction, based on the type of construction project;
- Performing specialized construction work on commercial and institutional buildings, generally on a subcontract basis--are classified in Subsector 238, Specialty Trade Contractors;
- Manufacturing prefabricated commercial or institutional buildings and assembling/erecting them at the customers' site--are classified in Sector 31-33, Manufacturing, based on the primary material (wood, plastic, or metal); and
- Constructing buildings on their own account for rent or lease--are classified in Industry Group 5311, Lessors of Real Estate.

## 237     Heavy and Civil Engineering Construction[T]

   The Heavy and Civil Engineering Construction subsector comprises establishments whose primary activity is the construction of entire engineering projects (e.g., highways and dams), and specialty trade contractors, whose primary activity is the production of a specific component for such projects. Specialty trade contractors in the Heavy and Civil Engineering Construction subsector generally are performing activities that are specific to heavy and civil engineering construction projects and are not normally performed on buildings. The work performed may include new work, additions, alterations, or maintenance and repairs.

   Specialty trade activities are classified in this subsector if the skills and equipment present are specific to heavy or civil engineering construction projects. For example, specialized equipment is needed to paint lines on highways. This equipment is not normally used in building applications so the activity is classified in this subsector. Traffic signal installation, while specific to highways, uses much of the same skills and equipment that are needed for electrical work in building projects and is therefore classified in Subsector 238, Specialty Trade Contractors.

   Construction projects involving water resources (e.g., dredging and land drainage) and projects involving open space improvement (e.g., parks and trails) are included in this subsector. Establishments whose primary activity is the subdivision of land into individual building lots usually perform various additional site-improvement activities (e.g., road building and utility line installation) and are included in this subsector.

   Establishments in this subsector are classified based on the types of structures that they construct. This classification reflects variations in the requirements of the underlying production processes.

## 2371     Utility System Construction[T]

   This industry group comprises establishments primarily engaged in the construction of distribution lines and related buildings and structures for utilities (i.e., water, sewer, petroleum, gas, power, and communication). All

T—Canadian, Mexican, and United States industries are comparable.

structures (including buildings) that are integral parts of utility systems (e.g., storage tanks, pumping stations, power plants, and refineries) are included in this industry group.

**23711   Water and Sewer Line and Related Structures Construction[T]**
         See industry description for 237110.

**237110  Water and Sewer Line and Related Structures Construction**

This industry comprises establishments primarily engaged in the construction of water and sewer lines, mains, pumping stations, treatment plants, and storage tanks. The work performed may include new work, reconstruction, rehabilitation, and repairs. Specialty trade contractors are included in this industry if they are engaged in activities primarily related to water, sewer line, and related structures construction. All structures (including buildings) that are integral parts of water and sewer networks (e.g., storage tanks, pumping stations, water treatment plants, and sewage treatment plants) are included in this industry.

*Illustrative Examples:*

Distribution line, sewer and water, construction
Sewer main, pipe and connection, construction
Fire hydrant installation
Storm sewer construction
Irrigation systems construction
Water main and line construction
Sewage disposal plant construction

Water treatment plant construction
Pumping station, water and sewage system, construction
Water system storage tank and tower construction
Reservoir construction
Water well drilling, digging, boring, or sinking (except water intake wells in oil and gas fields)

*Cross-References.*          Establishments primarily engaged in--

- Constructing marine facilities (e.g., ports), flood control structures, dams, or hydroelectric power generation facilities--are classified in Industry 237990, Other Heavy and Civil Engineering Construction;
- Installing septic tanks--are classified in Industry 238910, Site Preparation Contractors;
- Drilling oil and gas field water intake wells--are classified in U.S. Industry 213111, Drilling Oil and Gas Wells; and
- Installing and maintaining water and sewer lines performed by water and sewage utilities companies--are classified in Industry Group 2213, Water, Sewage and Other Systems.

**23712   Oil and Gas Pipeline and Related Structures Construction[T]**
         See industry description for 237120.

**237120  Oil and Gas Pipeline and Related Structures Construction**

This industry comprises establishments primarily engaged in the construction of oil and gas lines, mains, refineries, and storage tanks. The work performed may include new work, reconstruction, rehabilitation, and repairs. Specialty trade contractors are included in this industry if they are engaged in activities primarily related to oil and gas pipeline and related structures construction. All structures (including buildings) that are integral parts of oil and gas networks (e.g., storage tanks, pumping stations, and refineries) are included in this industry.

*Illustrative Examples:*

Distribution line, gas and oil, construction
Oil refinery construction
Gas main construction
Petrochemical plant construction
Gathering line, gas and oil field, construction
Natural gas pipeline construction

Pumping station, gas and oil transmission, construction
Storage tank, natural gas or oil, tank farm or field, construction
Natural gas processing plant construction

---

T—Canadian, Mexican, and United States industries are comparable.

*Cross-References.*        Establishments primarily engaged in--

- Building chemical plants (except petrochemical) and similar process or batch facilities--are classified in Industry 236210, Industrial Building Construction;
- Oil well rig building, repairing, and dismantling, on a contract basis--are classified in U.S. Industry 213112, Support Activities for Oil and Gas Operations;
- Inspecting pipelines (i.e., visual)--are classified in Industry 541990, All Other Professional, Scientific, and Technical Services;
- Installing and maintaining natural gas distribution lines performed by natural gas utility companies--are classified in Subsector 221, Utilities;
- Mining machinery and equipment repair and maintenance--are classified in Industry 811310, Commercial and Industrial Machinery and Equipment (except Automotive and Electronic) Repair and Maintenance; and
- Manufacturing floating oil and gas drilling and production platforms--are classified in U.S. Industry 336611, Ship Building and Repairing.

## 23713    Power and Communication Line and Related Structures Construction[T]
See industry description for 237130.

## 237130   Power and Communication Line and Related Structures Construction

This industry comprises establishments primarily engaged in the construction of power lines and towers, power plants, and radio, television, and telecommunications transmitting/receiving towers. The work performed may include new work, reconstruction, rehabilitation, and repairs. Specialty trade contractors are included in this industry if they are engaged in activities primarily related to power and communication line and related structures construction. All structures (including buildings) that are integral parts of power and communication networks (e.g., transmitting towers, substations, and power plants) are included.

*Illustrative Examples:*

Alternative energy (e.g., geothermal, ocean wave, solar, wind) structure construction
Power line stringing
Cellular phone tower construction
Radio transmitting tower construction
Co-generation plant construction
Satellite receiving station construction
Communication tower construction
Nuclear power plant construction

Telephone line stringing
Electric light and power plant (except hydroelectric) construction
Transformer station and substation, electric power, construction
Electric power transmission line and tower construction
Underground cable (e.g., fiber optic, electricity, telephone, cable television) laying

*Cross-References.*        Establishments primarily engaged in--

- Constructing hydroelectric generating facilities--are classified in Industry 237990, Other Heavy and Civil Engineering Construction;
- Constructing broadcast studios and similar nonresidential buildings--are classified in Industry 236220, Commercial and Institutional Building Construction;
- Performing electrical work within buildings--are classified in Industry 238210, Electrical Contractors and Other Wiring Installation Contractors;
- Line slashing or cutting (except maintenance)--are classified in Industry 238910, Site Preparation Contractors;
- Installing and maintaining communication transmission lines and towers performed by telecommunications companies--are classified in Subsector 517, Telecommunications;
- Installing and maintaining electric power lines and towers performed by electric utility companies--are classified in Industry Group 2211, Electric Power Generation, Transmission and Distribution;
- Locating underground utility lines prior to digging--are classified in Industry 561990, All Other Support Services; and

T—Canadian, Mexican, and United States industries are comparable.

- Tree and brush trimming for overhead utility lines--are classified in Industry 561730, Landscaping Services.

## 2372    Land Subdivision[T]

### 23721    Land Subdivision[T]
See industry description for 237210.

### 237210   Land Subdivision

This industry comprises establishments primarily engaged in servicing land and subdividing real property into lots, for subsequent sale to builders. Servicing of land may include excavation work for the installation of roads and utility lines. The extent of work may vary from project to project. Land subdivision precedes building activity and the subsequent building is often residential, but may also be commercial tracts and industrial parks. These establishments may do all the work themselves or subcontract the work to others. Establishments that perform only the legal subdivision of land are not included in this industry.

*Cross-References.*        Establishments primarily engaged in--

- Constructing buildings, for sale, on lots they subdivide--are classified based on the primary type of construction project, in Industry Group 2361, Residential Building Construction, or Industry Group 2362, Nonresidential Building Construction;
- Installing roads on a subcontract basis for land subdividers--are classified in Industry 237310, Highway, Street, and Bridge Construction;
- Installing utilities (i.e., water, sewer, petroleum, gas, power, and communication) on a subcontract basis for land subdividers--are classified in Industry Group 2371, Utility System Construction;
- Preparing land owned by others for building construction--are classified in Industry 238910, Site Preparation Contractors;
- Constructing buildings, for rent or lease, on lots they subdivide--are classified in Industry Group 5311, Lessors of Real Estate;
- Subdividing and servicing land for cemetery development--are classified in Industry 812220, Cemeteries and Crematories; and
- Legal subdivision of land without land preparation--are classified elsewhere in the classification system based on the primary activity of the establishment.

## 2373    Highway, Street, and Bridge Construction[T]

### 23731    Highway, Street, and Bridge Construction[T]
See industry description for 237310.

### 237310   Highway, Street, and Bridge Construction

This industry comprises establishments primarily engaged in the construction of highways (including elevated), streets, roads, airport runways, public sidewalks, or bridges. The work performed may include new work, reconstruction, rehabilitation, and repairs. Specialty trade contractors are included in this industry if they are engaged in activities primarily related to highway, street, and bridge construction (e.g., installing guardrails on highways).

*Illustrative Examples:*

| | |
|---|---|
| Airport runway construction | Pothole filling, highway, road, street, or bridge |
| Highway line painting | Elevated highway construction |
| Causeway construction | Resurfacing, highway, road, street, or bridge |
| Painting traffic lanes or parking lot lines | Guardrail construction |
| Culverts, highway, road, and street, construction | Sign erection, highway, road, street, or bridge |

---

T—Canadian, Mexican, and United States industries are comparable.

*Cross-References.* Establishments primarily engaged in--

- Constructing tunnels--are classified in Industry 237990, Other Heavy and Civil Engineering Construction;
- Highway lighting and signal installation--are classified in Industry 238210, Electrical Contractors and Other Wiring Installation Contractors;
- Painting bridges--are classified in Industry 238320, Painting and Wall Covering Contractors;
- Road decommissioning or removing culverts or bridges--are classified in Industry 238910, Site Preparation Contractors;
- Constructing parking lots, private driveways, sidewalks, or erecting billboards--are classified in Industry 238990, All Other Specialty Trade Contractors; and
- Providing road cleaning or snow removal services--are classified in Industry 488490, Other Support Activities for Road Transportation.

**2379    Other Heavy and Civil Engineering Construction**[T]

**23799    Other Heavy and Civil Engineering Construction**[T]
See industry description for 237990.

**237990  Other Heavy and Civil Engineering Construction**

  This industry comprises establishments primarily engaged in heavy and civil engineering construction projects (excluding highway, street, bridge, and distribution line construction). The work performed may include new work, reconstruction, rehabilitation, and repairs. Specialty trade contractors are included in this industry if they are engaged in activities primarily related to heavy and civil engineering construction projects (excluding highway, street, bridge, distribution line, oil and gas structure, and utilities building and structure construction). Construction projects involving water resources (e.g., dredging and land drainage), development of marine facilities, and projects involving open space improvement (e.g., parks and trails) are included in this industry.

*Illustrative Examples:*

Channel construction
Land drainage contractors
Dam construction
Marine construction
Dock construction
Microtunneling contractors
Dredging (e.g., canal, channel, ditch, waterway)
Nuclear waste disposal site construction
Earth retention system construction
Flood control project construction

Park ground and recreational open space improvement construction
Railroad construction
Golf course construction
Subway construction
Horizontal drilling (e.g., cable, pipeline, sewer installation)
Trenching, underwater
Hydroelectric generating station construction
Tunnel construction

*Cross-References.* Establishments primarily engaged in--

- Constructing water mains, sewers, and related structures--are classified in Industry 237110, Water and Sewer Line and Related Structures Construction;
- Constructing oil and gas pipelines and related structures--are classified in Industry 237120, Oil and Gas Pipeline and Related Structures Construction;
- Constructing power and communication transmission lines and related structures--are classified in Industry 237130, Power and Communication Line and Related Structures Construction;
- Installing and maintaining electric power lines and towers performed by electric utility companies--are classified in Industry Group 2211, Electric Power Generation, Transmission and Distribution;
- Installing and maintaining communication transmission lines and towers performed by telecommunications companies--are classified in Subsector 517, Telecommunications;
- Constructing highways, streets, and bridges--are classified in Industry 237310, Highway, Street, and Bridge Construction;

T—Canadian, Mexican, and United States industries are comparable.

- Trenching (except underwater) or removing dams, dikes, and other heavy and civil engineering constructions--are classified in Industry 238910, Site Preparation Contractors; and
- Inspecting pipelines (i.e., visual)--are classified in Industry 541990, All Other Professional, Scientific, and Technical Services.

## 238          Specialty Trade Contractors[T]

The Specialty Trade Contractors subsector comprises establishments whose primary activity is performing specific activities (e.g., pouring concrete, site preparation, plumbing, painting, and electrical work) involved in building construction or other activities that are similar for all types of construction, but that are not responsible for the entire project. The work performed may include new work, additions, alterations, maintenance, and repairs. The production work performed by establishments in this subsector is usually subcontracted from establishments of the general contractor type or for-sale builders, but especially in remodeling and repair construction, work also may be done directly for the owner of the property. Specialty trade contractors usually perform most of their work at the construction site, although they may have shops where they perform prefabrication and other work. Establishments primarily engaged in preparing sites for new construction are also included in this subsector.

There are substantial differences in types of equipment, work force skills, and other inputs required by specialty trade contractors. Establishments in this subsector are classified based on the underlying production function for the specialty trade in which they specialize. Throughout the Specialty Trade Contractors subsector, establishments commonly provide both the parts and labor required to complete work. For example, electrical contractors supply the current-carrying and noncurrent-carrying wiring devices that are required to install a circuit. Plumbing, heating, and air-conditioning contractors also supply the parts required to complete a contract.

Establishments that specialize in activities primarily related to heavy and civil engineering construction that are not normally performed on buildings, such as the painting of lines on highways, are classified in Subsector 237, Heavy and Civil Engineering Construction.

Establishments that are primarily engaged in selling construction materials are classified in Sector 42, Wholesale Trade, or Sector 44-45, Retail Trade, based on the characteristics of the selling unit.

## 2381          Foundation, Structure, and Building Exterior Contractors[T]

This industry group comprises establishments primarily engaged in the specialty trades needed to complete the basic structure (i.e., foundation, frame, and shell) of buildings. The work performed may include new work, additions, alterations, maintenance, and repairs.

## 23811          Poured Concrete Foundation and Structure Contractors
See industry description for 238110.

## 238110  Poured Concrete Foundation and Structure Contractors

This industry comprises establishments primarily engaged in pouring and finishing concrete foundations and structural elements. This industry also includes establishments performing grout and shotcrete work. The work performed may include new work, additions, alterations, maintenance, and repairs.

*Illustrative Examples:*

| | |
|---|---|
| Concrete pouring and finishing | Concrete work (except paving) |
| Gunite contractors | Shotcrete contractors |
| Concrete pumping (i.e., placement) | Footing and foundation concrete contractors |
| Mud-jacking contractors | |

*Cross-References.*          Establishments primarily engaged in--

- Constructing or paving streets, highways, and public sidewalks--are classified in Industry 237310, Highway, Street, and Bridge Construction;

---

T—Canadian, Mexican, and United States industries are comparable.

- Concrete sealing, coating, waterproofing, or dampproofing--are classified in Industry 238390, Other Building Finishing Contractors;
- Paving residential driveways, commercial parking lots, and other private parking areas--are classified in Industry 238990, All Other Specialty Trade Contractors; and
- Mixing and delivering ready-mix concrete--are classified in Industry 327320, Ready-Mix Concrete Manufacturing.

## 23812 Structural Steel and Precast Concrete Contractors
See industry description for 238120.

## 238120 Structural Steel and Precast Concrete Contractors

This industry comprises establishments primarily engaged in (1) erecting and assembling structural parts made from steel or precast concrete (e.g., steel beams, structural steel components, and similar products of precast concrete) and/or (2) assembling and installing other steel construction products (e.g., steel rods, bars, rebar, mesh, and cages) to reinforce poured-in-place concrete. The work performed may include new work, additions, alterations, maintenance, and repairs.

*Illustrative Examples:*

Concrete product (e.g., structural precast, structural prestressed) installation
Rebar contractors
Erecting structural steel
Reinforcing steel contractors

Placing and tying reinforcing rod at a construction site
Structural steel contractors
Precast concrete panel, slab, or form installation

*Cross-References.*  Establishments primarily engaged in--

- Pouring concrete at the construction site for building foundations or structural elements--are classified in Industry 238110, Poured Concrete Foundation and Structure Contractors; and
- Masonry work--are classified in Industry 238140, Masonry Contractors.

## 23813 Framing Contractors
See industry description for 238130.

## 238130 Framing Contractors

This industry comprises establishments primarily engaged in structural framing and sheathing using materials other than structural steel or concrete. The work performed may include new work, additions, alterations, maintenance, and repairs.

*Illustrative Examples:*

Building framing (except structural steel)
Post framing contractors
Foundation, building, wood, contractors
Steel framing contractors

Framing contractors
Wood frame component (e.g., truss) fabrication on site

*Cross-References.*  Establishments primarily engaged in--

- Finish carpentry--are classified in Industry 238350, Finish Carpentry Contractors; and
- Installing structural steel, precast concrete framing, or structural elements--are classified in Industry 238120, Structural Steel and Precast Concrete Contractors.

---

T—Canadian, Mexican, and United States industries are comparable.

**23814   Masonry Contractors**
See industry description for 238140.

**238140  Masonry Contractors**

  This industry comprises establishments primarily engaged in masonry work, stone setting, bricklaying, and other stone work. The work performed may include new work, additions, alterations, maintenance, and repairs.

*Illustrative Examples:*

Block laying
Marble, granite, and slate, exterior, contractors
Bricklaying
Masonry pointing, cleaning, or caulking

Concrete block laying
Stucco contractors
Foundation (e.g., brick, block, stone), building, contractors

*Cross-References.*          Establishments primarily engaged in--

  • Erecting the basic structure of buildings by pouring concrete--are classified in Industry 238110, Poured Concrete Foundation and Structure Contractors;
  • Interior marble, granite, and slate work--are classified in Industry 238340, Tile and Terrazzo Contractors; and
  • Laying precast stones or bricks for patios, sidewalks, and driveways; or paving residential driveways, commercial parking lots, and other private parking areas--are classified in Industry 238990, All Other Specialty Trade Contractors.

**23815   Glass and Glazing Contractors**
See industry description for 238150.

**238150  Glass and Glazing Contractors**

  This industry comprises establishments primarily engaged in installing glass panes in prepared openings (i.e., glazing work) and other glass work for buildings.  The work performed may include new work, additions, alterations, maintenance, and repairs.

*Illustrative Examples:*

Decorative glass and mirror installation
Glazing contractors
Glass cladding installation
Stained glass installation

Window pane or sheet installation
Glass coating and tinting (except automotive) contractors
Glass installation (except automotive) contractors

*Cross-References.*          Establishments primarily engaged in--

  • Installing prefabricated window and door units--are classified in Industry 238350, Finish Carpentry Contractors; and
  • The replacement, repair, and/or tinting of automotive glass--are classified in U.S. Industry 811122, Automotive Glass Replacement Shops.

**23816   Roofing Contractors**
See industry description for 238160.

---

T—Canadian, Mexican, and United States industries are comparable.

**238160  Roofing Contractors**

This industry comprises establishments primarily engaged in roofing.  This industry also includes establishments treating roofs (i.e., spraying, painting, or coating) and installing skylights.  The work performed may include new work, additions, alterations, maintenance, and repairs.

*Illustrative Examples:*

Painting, spraying, or coating, roof                          Shake and shingle, roof, installation
Sheet metal roofing installation                               Skylight installation

*Cross-References.*          Establishments primarily engaged in--

- Installing roof trusses and sheathing attached to trusses--are classified in Industry 238130, Framing Contractors;
- Installing downspouts, gutters, fascia, and soffits--are classified in Industry 238170, Siding Contractors; and
- Installing solar panels--are classified in Industry 238210, Electrical Contractors and Other Wiring Installation Contractors.

**23817   Siding Contractors**
See industry description for 238170.

**238170  Siding Contractors**

This industry comprises establishments primarily engaged in installing siding of wood, aluminum, vinyl, or other exterior finish material (except brick, stone, stucco, or curtain wall).  This industry also includes establishments installing gutters and downspouts.  The work performed may include new work, additions, alterations, maintenance, and repairs.

*Illustrative Examples:*

Downspout, gutter, and gutter guard installation                 Siding (e.g., vinyl, wood, aluminum) installation
Fascia and soffit installation

*Cross-References.*          Establishments primarily engaged in--

- Installing brick, stone, or stucco building exterior finish materials--are classified in Industry 238140, Masonry Contractors;
- Installing curtain wall--are classified in Industry 238190, Other Foundation, Structure, and Building Exterior Contractors; and
- Installing sheet metal duct work--are classified in Industry 238220, Plumbing, Heating, and Air-Conditioning Contractors.

**23819   Other Foundation, Structure, and Building Exterior Contractors**
See industry description for 238190.

**238190  Other Foundation, Structure, and Building Exterior Contractors**

This industry comprises establishments primarily engaged in building foundation and structure trades work (except poured concrete, structural steel, precast concrete, framing, masonry, glass and glazing, roofing, and siding). The work performed may include new work, additions, alterations, maintenance, and repairs.

---

T—Canadian, Mexican, and United States industries are comparable.

*Illustrative Examples:*

Curtain wall, metal, installation
Forms for poured concrete, erecting and dismantling
Welding, on-site, contractors

Ornamental metal work installation
Fire escape installation
Decorative steel and wrought iron work installation

*Cross-References.*          Establishments primarily engaged in--

- Poured concrete foundation and structure work--are classified in Industry 238110, Poured Concrete Foundation and Structure Contractors;
- Installation of structural steel or precast concrete building components--are classified in Industry 238120, Structural Steel and Precast Concrete Contractors;
- Framing buildings--are classified in Industry 238130, Framing Contractors;
- Masonry work--are classified in Industry 238140, Masonry Contractors;
- Glass and glazing work--are classified in Industry 238150, Glass and Glazing Contractors;
- Installing or repairing roofs--are classified in Industry 238160, Roofing Contractors;
- Installing siding--are classified in Industry 238170, Siding Contractors; and
- Fireproofing buildings--are classified in Industry 238310, Drywall and Insulation Contractors.

## 2382    Building Equipment Contractors[T]

This industry group comprises establishments primarily engaged in installing or servicing equipment that forms part of a building mechanical system (e.g., electricity, water, heating, and cooling). The work performed may include new work, additions, alterations, maintenance, and repairs. Contractors installing specialized building equipment, such as elevators, escalators, service station equipment, and central vacuum cleaning systems, are also included.

### 23821    Electrical Contractors and Other Wiring Installation Contractors[T]
See industry description for 238210.

### 238210    Electrical Contractors and Other Wiring Installation Contractors

This industry comprises establishments primarily engaged in installing and servicing electrical wiring and equipment. Contractors included in this industry may include both the parts and labor when performing work. These contractors may perform new work, additions, alterations, maintenance, and repairs.

*Illustrative Examples:*

Airport runway lighting contractors
Fiber optic cable (except transmission line) contractors
Alarm system (e.g., fire, burglar), electric, installation only
Highway, street, and bridge lighting and electrical signal installation
Audio equipment (except automotive) installation contractors

Home automation system installation
Lighting system installation
Cable television hookup contractors
Telecommunications equipment and wiring (except transmission line) installation contractors
Computer and network cable installation
Traffic signal installation
Environmental control system installation
Cable splicing, electrical or fiber optic

*Cross-References.*          Establishments primarily engaged in--

- Installing and maintaining telecommunications lines performed by telecommunications companies--are classified in Subsector 517, Telecommunications;
- Installing and maintaining electric power lines performed by electric utility companies--are classified in Industry Group 2211, Electric Power Generation, Transmission and Distribution;

---

T—Canadian, Mexican, and United States industries are comparable.

- Constructing power and communication lines--are classified in Industry 237130, Power and Communication Line and Related Structures Construction;
- Burglar and fire alarm installation combined with sales, maintenance, or monitoring services--are classified in U.S. Industry 561621, Security Systems Services (except Locksmiths); and
- Retailing and installing automotive audio equipment--are classified in Industry 441330, Automotive Parts and Accessories Retailers.

## 23822 Plumbing, Heating, and Air-Conditioning Contractors[T]
See industry description for 238220.

## 238220 Plumbing, Heating, and Air-Conditioning Contractors

This industry comprises establishments primarily engaged in installing and servicing plumbing, heating, and air-conditioning equipment. Contractors in this industry may provide both parts and labor when performing work. The work performed may include new work, additions, alterations, maintenance, and repairs.

*Illustrative Examples:*

Cooling tower installation
Heating, ventilation, and air-conditioning (HVAC) contractors
Duct work (e.g., cooling, dust collection, exhaust, heating, ventilation) installation
Lawn sprinkler system installation
Fire sprinkler system installation

Mechanical contractors
Fireplace, natural gas, installation
Refrigeration system (e.g., commercial, industrial, scientific) installation
Furnace installation
Sewer hookup and connection, building

*Cross-References.* Establishments primarily engaged in--

- Installing electrical controls for HVAC systems--are classified in Industry 238210, Electrical Contractors and Other Wiring Installation Contractors;
- Duct cleaning--are classified in Industry 561790, Other Services to Buildings and Dwellings;
- Installing septic tanks and systems--are classified in Industry 238910, Site Preparation Contractors;
- Water well drilling (except water intake wells in oil and gas fields) and water well pump and piping system installation--are classified in Industry 237110, Water and Sewer Line and Related Structures Construction; and
- Repair and maintenance of commercial refrigeration equipment or fire extinguisher and waterless fire suppression systems, without installation--are classified in Industry 811310, Commercial and Industrial Machinery and Equipment (except Automotive and Electronic) Repair and Maintenance.

## 23829 Other Building Equipment Contractors[T]
See industry description for 238290.

## 238290 Other Building Equipment Contractors

This industry comprises establishments primarily engaged in installing or servicing building equipment (except electrical, plumbing, heating, cooling, or ventilation equipment). The repair and maintenance of miscellaneous building equipment is included in this industry. The work performed may include new work, additions, alterations, maintenance, and repairs.

*Illustrative Examples:*

Automated and revolving door installation
Lightning protection equipment (e.g., lightning rod) installation
Boiler and pipe insulation installation

Machine rigging
Commercial-type door installation
Millwrights
Conveyor system installation

---

T—Canadian, Mexican, and United States industries are comparable.

Revolving door installation
Overhead door, commercial- or industrial-type, installation
Dismantling large-scale machinery and equipment
Elevator installation

Satellite dish, household-type, installation
Escalator installation
Vacuum cleaning system, built-in, installation
Gasoline pump, service station, installation

*Cross-References.*　　　Establishments primarily engaged in--

- Manufacturing industrial equipment with incidental installation--are classified in Sector 31-33, Manufacturing;
- Repair and maintenance of commercial refrigeration equipment or production equipment--are classified in Industry 811310, Commercial and Industrial Machinery and Equipment (except Automotive and Electronic) Repair and Maintenance; and
- Installing prefabricated window and door units--are classified in Industry 238350, Finish Carpentry Contractors.

## 2383    Building Finishing Contractors[T]

This industry group comprises establishments primarily engaged in the specialty trades needed to finish buildings. The work performed may include new work, additions, alterations, maintenance, and repairs.

### 23831    Drywall and Insulation Contractors[T]
See industry description for 238310.

### 238310  Drywall and Insulation Contractors

This industry comprises establishments primarily engaged in drywall, plaster work, and building insulation work. Plaster work includes applying plain or ornamental plaster, and installation of lath to receive plaster. The work performed may include new work, additions, alterations, maintenance, and repairs. Establishments primarily engaged in providing firestop services are included in this industry.

*Illustrative Examples:*

Acoustical ceiling tile and panel installation
Lathing contractors
Drop ceiling installation
Plastering (i.e., ornamental, plain) contractors
Drywall contractors
Soundproofing contractors

Firestop contractors
Fresco (i.e., decorative plaster finishing) contractors
Taping and finishing drywall
Gypsum board installation
Wall cavity and attic space insulation installation

*Cross-References.*　　　Establishments primarily engaged in--

- Applying stucco--are classified in Industry 238140, Masonry Contractors; and
- Insulating pipes and boilers--are classified in Industry 238290, Other Building Equipment Contractors.

### 23832    Painting and Wall Covering Contractors[T]
See industry description for 238320.

### 238320  Painting and Wall Covering Contractors

This industry comprises establishments primarily engaged in interior or exterior painting or interior wall covering. The work performed may include new work, additions, alterations, maintenance, and repairs.

---

T—Canadian, Mexican, and United States industries are comparable.

*Illustrative Examples:*

Bridge painting
Paperhanging or removal contractors
House painting

Ship painting contractors
Paint and wallpaper stripping
Wallpaper hanging and removal contractors

*Cross-References.*　　Establishments primarily engaged in--

- Painting lines on highways, streets, and parking lots--are classified in Industry 237310, Highway, Street, and Bridge Construction;
- Roof painting--are classified in Industry 238160, Roofing Contractors;
- Installing wood paneling--are classified in Industry 238350, Finish Carpentry Contractors;
- Concrete coating, glazing, or sealing--are classified in Industry 238390, Other Building Finishing Contractors; and
- Painting and rustproofing automotive vehicles and trailer bodies--are classified in Industry Group 8111, Automotive Repair and Maintenance.

**23833　Flooring Contractors**[T]
See industry description for 238330.

**238330　Flooring Contractors**

This industry comprises establishments primarily engaged in the installation of resilient floor tile, carpeting, linoleum, and hardwood flooring. The work performed may include new work, additions, alterations, maintenance, and repairs.

*Illustrative Examples:*

Carpet, installation only
Resilient floor tile or sheet (e.g., linoleum, rubber, vinyl), installation only
Vinyl flooring contractors

Resurfacing hardwood flooring
Hardwood flooring, installation only
Floor laying, scraping, finishing, and refinishing

*Cross-References.*　　Establishments primarily engaged in--

- Laying concrete flooring--are classified in Industry 238110, Poured Concrete Foundation and Structure Contractors;
- Applying epoxy to concrete flooring--are classified in Industry 238190, Other Foundation, Structure, and Building Exterior Contractors;
- Installing fireproof flooring--are classified in Industry 238310, Drywall and Insulation Contractors;
- Installing stone or ceramic floor tile--are classified in Industry 238340, Tile and Terrazzo Contractors; and
- Retailing and installing carpet and other flooring products--are classified in Sector 44-45, Retail Trade.

**23834　Tile and Terrazzo Contractors**[T]
See industry description for 238340.

**238340　Tile and Terrazzo Contractors**

This industry comprises establishments primarily engaged in setting and installing ceramic tile, stone (interior only), and mosaic and/or mixing marble particles and cement to make terrazzo at the job site. The work performed may include new work, additions, alterations, maintenance, and repairs.

*Illustrative Examples:*

Ceramic tile installation

Mosaic work

T—Canadian, Mexican, and United States industries are comparable.

Mantel, marble or stone, installation
Tile (except resilient) laying and setting
Stone flooring installation

Marble, granite, and slate, interior installation
contractors

*Cross-References.*          Establishments primarily engaged in--

- Exterior marble, granite, and slate work--are classified in Industry 238140, Masonry Contractors;
- Manufacturing precast terrazzo products--are classified in Industry 327390, Other Concrete Product Manufacturing; and
- Installing, without selling resilient floor tile--are classified in Industry 238330, Flooring Contractors.

**23835   Finish Carpentry Contractors[T]**
See industry description for 238350.

**238350  Finish Carpentry Contractors**

   This industry comprises establishments primarily engaged in finish carpentry work.  The work performed may include new work, additions, alterations, maintenance, and repairs.

*Illustrative Examples:*

Built-in wood cabinets constructed on site
Molding or trim, wood or plastic, installation
Countertop (except ceramic tile or stone), residential-type, installation
Paneling installation
Door and window frame construction
Garage door, residential-type, installation

Prefabricated kitchen and bath cabinet, residential-type, installation
Ship joinery contractors
Millwork installation
Window and door, residential-type, of any material, prefabricated, installation

*Cross-References.*          Establishments primarily engaged in--

- Installing ceramic tile or stone countertops--are classified in Industry 238340, Tile and Terrazzo Contractors;
- Installing nonresidential-type metal countertops and cabinets--are classified in Industry 238390, Other Building Finishing Contractors;
- Installing skylights--are classified in Industry 238160, Roofing Contractors;
- Framing--are classified in Industry 238130, Framing Contractors; and
- Manufacturing custom kitchen and bath cabinets (except freestanding) in a shop--are classified in Industry 337110, Wood Kitchen Cabinet and Countertop Manufacturing.

**23839   Other Building Finishing Contractors[T]**
See industry description for 238390.

**238390  Other Building Finishing Contractors**

   This industry comprises establishments primarily engaged in building finishing trade work (except drywall, plaster, and insulation work; painting and wall covering work; flooring work; tile and terrazzo work; and finish carpentry work).  The work performed may include new work, additions, alterations, maintenance, and repairs.

*Illustrative Examples:*

Bathtub refinishing, on-site
Fabricating metal cabinets or countertops on site
Closet organizer system installation
Modular furniture system attachment and installation

Concrete coating, glazing, or sealing
Trade show exhibit installation and dismantling
Countertop and cabinet, metal (except residential-type), installation

---

T—Canadian, Mexican, and United States industries are comparable.

Waterproofing contractors
Window shade and blind installation

Drapery fixture (e.g., hardware, rods, tracks) installation

*Cross-References.* Establishments primarily engaged in--

- Installing drywall, plaster, or insulation--are classified in Industry 238310, Drywall and Insulation Contractors;
- Installing or removing paint or wall coverings--are classified in Industry 238320, Painting and Wall Covering Contractors;
- Installing or repairing wood floors, resilient flooring, and carpet--are classified in Industry 238330, Flooring Contractors;
- Setting tile or performing terrazzo work--are classified in Industry 238340, Tile and Terrazzo Contractors;
- Finish carpentry--are classified in Industry 238350, Finish Carpentry Contractors; and
- Retailing and installing window shades and blinds--are classified in U.S. Industry 449122, Window Treatment Retailers.

## 2389 Other Specialty Trade Contractors[T]

This industry group comprises establishments primarily engaged in site preparation activities and in specialized trades (except foundation, structure, and building exterior contractors; building equipment contractors; and building finishing contractors). The specialty trade work performed includes new work, additions, alterations, maintenance, and repairs.

### 23891 Site Preparation Contractors[T]
See industry description for 238910.

### 238910 Site Preparation Contractors

This industry comprises establishments primarily engaged in site preparation activities, such as excavating and grading, demolition of buildings and other structures, and septic system installation. Earthmoving and land clearing for all types of sites (e.g., building, nonbuilding, mining) is included in this industry. Establishments primarily engaged in construction equipment rental with operator (except cranes) are also included.

*Illustrative Examples:*

Blasting, building demolition
Building interior gutting and stripping
Concrete breaking and cutting for demolition
Cutting new rights of way
Demolition, building and structure
Exterior demolition contractors
Foundation digging (i.e., excavation)
Foundation drilling contractors
Grading construction sites
Interior demolition contractors
Dewatering contractors

Dirt moving for construction
Equipment rental (except crane), construction, with operator
Excavating, earthmoving, or land clearing contractors
Line slashing or cutting (except maintenance)
Septic system contractors
Trenching (except underwater)
Underground tank (except hazardous) removal
Wrecking, building or other structure
Whole building deconstruction

*Cross-References.* Establishments primarily engaged in--

- Servicing land and subdividing real property into lots for sale to builders--are classified in Industry 237210, Land Subdivision;
- Constructing distribution lines and related buildings and structures for utilities (i.e., water, sewer, petroleum, gas, power, and communication)--are classified in Industry Group 2371, Utility System Construction;

---

T—Canadian, Mexican, and United States industries are comparable.

- Earth retention or underwater trenching--are classified in Industry 237990, Other Heavy and Civil Engineering Construction;
- Crane rental with operator--are classified in Industry 238990, All Other Specialty Trade Contractors;
- Overburden removal as an activity prior to mineral removal from quarries or open pit mines--are classified in Sector 21, Mining, Quarrying, and Oil and Gas Extraction;
- Drilling oil and gas field water intake wells--are classified in U.S. Industry 213111, Drilling Oil and Gas Wells;
- Dismantling tanks in oil fields--are classified in U.S. Industry 213112, Support Activities for Oil and Gas Operations;
- Construction equipment rental without an operator--are classified in U.S. Industry 532412, Construction, Mining, and Forestry Machinery and Equipment Rental and Leasing;
- Tree and brush trimming for overhead utility lines--are classified in Industry 561730, Landscaping Services; and
- Nuclear power plant decommissioning and environmental remediation work, such as the removal of underground steel tanks for hazardous materials--are classified in Industry 562910, Remediation Services.

**23899    All Other Specialty Trade Contractors**[T]
See industry description for 238990.

**238990  All Other Specialty Trade Contractors**

  This industry comprises establishments primarily engaged in specialized trades (except foundation, structure, and building exterior contractors; building equipment contractors; building finishing contractors; and site preparation contractors).  The specialty trade work performed includes new work, additions, alterations, maintenance, and repairs.

*Illustrative Examples:*

Billboard erection
Outdoor swimming pool construction
Paver, brick (e.g., driveway, patio, sidewalk), installation
Crane rental with operator
Paving, residential and commercial driveway and parking lot
Sandblasting building exteriors

Fence installation
Scaffold erecting and dismantling
Interlocking brick and block installation
Steeplejack work
Manufactured (mobile) home set up and tie-down work
Driveway paving or sealing

*Cross-References.*        Establishments primarily engaged in--

- Foundation, structure, and building exterior work--are classified in Industry Group 2381, Foundation, Structure, and Building Exterior Contractors;
- Installing, repairing, or maintaining building mechanical systems--are classified in Industry Group 2382, Building Equipment Contractors;
- Finishing buildings--are classified in Industry Group 2383, Building Finishing Contractors;
- Paving public highways, streets, and roads--are classified in Industry 237310, Highway, Street, and Bridge Construction;
- Construction equipment rental with an operator (except cranes), preparing land for building construction, or building demolition--are classified in Industry 238910, Site Preparation Contractors;
- Construction equipment rental without an operator--are classified in U.S. Industry 532412, Construction, Mining, and Forestry Machinery and Equipment Rental and Leasing;
- Radon testing--are classified in Industry 541380, Testing Laboratories and Services;
- Swimming pool cleaning and maintenance, power washing, and other building exterior cleaning (except sandblasting)--are classified in Industry 561790, Other Services to Buildings and Dwellings;
- Environmental remediation work, such as asbestos and lead paint abatement--are classified in Industry 562910, Remediation Services;

---

T—Canadian, Mexican, and United States industries are comparable.

- Installing electronic containment fencing for pets--are classified in Industry 238210, Electrical Contractors and Other Wiring Installation Contractors; and
- Constructing indoor swimming pools--are classified in Industry 236220, Commercial and Institutional Building Construction.

---

T—Canadian, Mexican, and United States industries are comparable.

# Sector 31-33--Manufacturing<sup>T</sup>

## The Sector as a Whole

The Manufacturing sector comprises establishments engaged in the mechanical, physical, or chemical transformation of materials, substances, or components into new products. The assembling of component parts of manufactured products is considered manufacturing, except in cases where the activity is appropriately classified in Sector 23, Construction.

Establishments in the Manufacturing sector are often described as plants, factories, or mills and characteristically use power-driven machines and material handling equipment. However, establishments that transform materials or substances into new products by hand or in the worker's home and those engaged in selling to the general public products made on the same premises from which they are sold, such as bakeries, candy stores, and custom tailors, may also be included in this sector. Manufacturing establishments may process materials or may contract with other establishments to process their materials for them. Both types of establishments are included in manufacturing. Selected industries in the Manufacturing sector are comprised solely of establishments that process materials for other establishments on a contract or fee basis. Beyond these dedicated contract manufacturing industries, establishments that process materials for other establishments are generally classified in the Manufacturing industry of the processed materials.

The materials, substances, or components transformed by manufacturing establishments are raw materials that are products of agriculture, forestry, fishing, mining, or quarrying as well as products of other manufacturing establishments. The materials used may be purchased directly from producers, obtained through customary trade channels, or secured without recourse to the market by transferring the product from one establishment to another, under the same ownership.

The new product of a manufacturing establishment may be finished in the sense that it is ready for utilization or consumption, or it may be semi-finished to become an input for an establishment engaged in further manufacturing. For example, the product of the alumina refinery is the input used in the primary production of aluminum; primary aluminum is the input to an aluminum wire drawing plant; and aluminum wire is the input for a fabricated wire product manufacturing establishment.

The subsectors in the Manufacturing sector generally reflect distinct production processes related to material inputs, production equipment, and employee skills. In the machinery area, where assembling is a key activity, parts and accessories for manufactured products are classified in the industry of the finished manufactured item when they are made for separate sale. For example, an attachment for a piece of metalworking machinery would be classified with metalworking machinery. However, component inputs from other manufacturing establishments are classified based on the production function of the component manufacturer. For example, electronic components are classified in Subsector 334, Computer and Electronic Product Manufacturing, and stampings are classified in Subsector 332, Fabricated Metal Product Manufacturing.

Manufacturing establishments often perform one or more activities that are classified outside the Manufacturing sector of NAICS. For instance, almost all manufacturing has some captive research and development or administrative operations, such as accounting, payroll, or management. These captive services are treated the same as captive manufacturing activities. When the services are provided by separate establishments, they are classified in the NAICS sector where such services are primary, not in manufacturing.

The boundaries of manufacturing and the other sectors of the classification system can be somewhat blurry. The establishments in the Manufacturing sector are engaged in the transformation of materials into new products. Their output is a new product. However, the definition of what constitutes a new product can be somewhat subjective. As clarification, the following activities are considered manufacturing in NAICS:

Milk bottling and pasteurizing;
Water bottling and processing;
Fresh fish packaging (oyster shucking, fish filleting);
Apparel jobbing (assigning materials to contract factories or shops for fabrication or other contract operations) as well as contracting on materials owned by others;
Printing and related activities;

Ready-mix concrete production;
Leather converting;
Grinding lenses to prescription;
Wood preserving;
Electroplating, plating, metal heat treating, and polishing for the trade;
Lapidary work for the trade;
Fabricating signs and advertising displays;

T—Canadian, Mexican, and United States industries are comparable.

Rebuilding or remanufacturing machinery (i.e., automotive parts);
Ship repair and renovation;
Machine shops;

Making manufactured homes (i.e., mobile homes) or prefabricated buildings, whether or not assembling/erecting at the customers' site; and
Tire retreading.

Conversely, there are activities that are sometimes considered manufacturing, but which for NAICS are classified in another sector (i.e., not classified as manufacturing). They include:

1. Logging, classified in Sector 11, Agriculture, Forestry, Fishing and Hunting, is considered a harvesting operation;
2. Beneficiating ores and other minerals, classified in Sector 21, Mining, Quarrying, and Oil and Gas Extraction, is considered part of the activity of mining;
3. Constructing structures, assembling prefabricated buildings, and fabricating at the construction site by contractors are classified in Sector 23, Construction;
4. Breaking bulk and reselling in smaller lots, including packaging, repackaging, or bottling products, such as liquors or chemicals; assembling and selling computers on a custom basis; sorting and reselling scrap; mixing and selling paints to customer order; and cutting metals to customer order for resale are classified in Sector 42, Wholesale Trade, or Sector 44-45, Retail Trade; and
5. Publishing and the combined activity of publishing and printing, classified in Sector 51, Information, transform information into a product for which the value to the consumer lies in the information content, not in the format in which it is distributed (i.e., the book or software compact disc).

## 311    Food Manufacturing[T]

Industries in the Food Manufacturing subsector transform livestock and agricultural products into products for intermediate or final consumption.  The industry groups are distinguished by the raw materials (generally of animal or vegetable origin) processed into food products.
The food products manufactured in these establishments are typically sold to wholesalers or retailers for distribution to consumers, but establishments primarily engaged in retailing bakery and candy products made on the premises not for immediate consumption are included.
Establishments primarily engaged in manufacturing beverages are classified in Subsector 312, Beverage and Tobacco Product Manufacturing.

## 3111    Animal Food Manufacturing[T]

## 31111    Animal Food Manufacturing[T]

This industry comprises establishments primarily engaged in manufacturing food and feed for animals from ingredients, such as grains, oilseed mill products, and meat products.

*Cross-References.*          Establishments primarily engaged in--

- Slaughtering animals for feed--are classified in Industry 31161, Animal Slaughtering and Processing; and
- Manufacturing vitamins and minerals for animals--are classified in Industry 32541, Pharmaceutical and Medicine Manufacturing.

## 311111  Dog and Cat Food Manufacturing

This U.S. industry comprises establishments primarily engaged in manufacturing dog and cat food from ingredients, such as grains, oilseed mill products, and meat products.

*Cross-References.*          Establishments primarily engaged in--

- Manufacturing food for animals (except dog and cat)--are classified in U.S. Industry 311119, Other Animal Food Manufacturing;

---

T—Canadian, Mexican, and United States industries are comparable.

- Slaughtering animals for feed--are classified in Industry 31161, Animal Slaughtering and Processing; and
- Manufacturing vitamins and minerals for dogs and cats--are classified in Industry 32541, Pharmaceutical and Medicine Manufacturing.

## 311119  Other Animal Food Manufacturing

This U.S. industry comprises establishments primarily engaged in manufacturing animal food (except dog and cat) from ingredients, such as grains, oilseed mill products, and meat products.

*Cross-References.*            Establishments primarily engaged in--

- Manufacturing dog and cat foods--are classified in U.S. Industry 311111, Dog and Cat Food Manufacturing;
- Slaughtering animals for feed--are classified in Industry 31161, Animal Slaughtering and Processing; and
- Manufacturing vitamins and minerals for animals--are classified in Industry 32541, Pharmaceutical and Medicine Manufacturing.

## 3112     Grain and Oilseed Milling$^T$

This industry group comprises establishments primarily engaged in milling flour or meal from grains or vegetables, manufacturing malt, wet milling corn and other vegetables, crushing oilseeds and tree nuts, refining and/or blending vegetable oils, and manufacturing breakfast cereals.

## 31121    Flour Milling and Malt Manufacturing$^T$

This industry comprises establishments primarily engaged in one or more of the following: (1) milling flour or meal from grains or vegetables; (2) preparing flour mixes or doughs from flour milled in the same establishment; (3) milling, cleaning, and polishing rice; and (4) manufacturing malt from barley, rye, or other grains.

*Cross-References.*            Establishments primarily engaged in--

- Preparing breakfast cereals from flour milled in the same establishment--are classified in Industry 31123, Breakfast Cereal Manufacturing;
- Crushing soybeans or wet milling corn and vegetables--are classified in Industry 31122, Starch and Vegetable Fats and Oils Manufacturing;
- Manufacturing prepared flour mixes or doughs from flour ground elsewhere--are classified in Industry 31182, Cookie, Cracker, and Pasta Manufacturing;
- Brewing malt beverages--are classified in Industry 31212, Breweries;
- Mixing purchased dried and dehydrated ingredients with purchased rice--are classified in Industry 31199, All Other Food Manufacturing;
- Drying and/or dehydrating ingredients and packaging them with purchased rice--are classified in Industry 31142, Fruit and Vegetable Canning, Pickling, and Drying; and
- Manufacturing malt extract and syrups--are classified in Industry 31194, Seasoning and Dressing Manufacturing.

## 311211  Flour Milling

This U.S. industry comprises establishments primarily engaged in (1) milling flour or meal from grains (except rice) or vegetables and/or (2) milling flour and preparing flour mixes or doughs.

*Cross-References.*            Establishments primarily engaged in--

- Preparing breakfast cereals from flour milled in the same establishment--are classified in Industry 311230, Breakfast Cereal Manufacturing;

---

T—Canadian, Mexican, and United States industries are comparable.

- Manufacturing prepared flour mixes or doughs from flour ground elsewhere--are classified in U.S. Industry 311824, Dry Pasta, Dough, and Flour Mixes Manufacturing from Purchased Flour;
- Milling rice or cleaning and polishing rice--are classified in U.S. Industry 311212, Rice Milling;
- Wet milling corn and vegetables--are classified in U.S. Industry 311221, Wet Corn Milling and Starch Manufacturing; and
- Crushing soybeans and extracting soybean oil--are classified in U.S. Industry 311224, Soybean and Other Oilseed Processing.

## 311212  Rice Milling

This U.S. industry comprises establishments primarily engaged in one of the following: (1) milling rice; (2) cleaning and polishing rice; or (3) milling, cleaning, and polishing rice.  The establishments in this industry may package the rice they mill with other ingredients.

*Cross-References.*          Establishments primarily engaged in--

- Drying and/or dehydrating ingredients and packaging them with purchased rice--are classified in U.S. Industry 311423, Dried and Dehydrated Food Manufacturing; and
- Mixing purchased dried and/or dehydrated ingredients with purchased rice--are classified in U.S. Industry 311999, All Other Miscellaneous Food Manufacturing.

## 311213  Malt Manufacturing

This U.S. industry comprises establishments primarily engaged in manufacturing malt from barley, rye, or other grains.

*Cross-References.*          Establishments primarily engaged in--

- Brewing malt beverages--are classified in Industry 312120, Breweries; and
- Manufacturing malt extract and syrups--are classified in U.S. Industry 311942, Spice and Extract Manufacturing.

## 31122  Starch and Vegetable Fats and Oils Manufacturing[T]

This industry comprises establishments primarily engaged in one or more of the following: (1) wet milling corn and vegetables; (2) crushing oilseeds and tree nuts; (3) refining and/or blending vegetable oils; (4) manufacturing shortening and margarine; and (5) blending purchased animal fats with vegetable fats.

*Cross-References.*          Establishments primarily engaged in--

- Manufacturing table syrups from corn syrup and starch base dessert powders--are classified in Industry 31199, All Other Food Manufacturing;
- Reducing maple sap to maple syrup--are classified in Industry 11199, All Other Crop Farming;
- Milling flour or meal from grains and vegetables--are classified in Industry 31121, Flour Milling and Malt Manufacturing;
- Wet milling corn to produce nonpotable ethyl alcohol--are classified in Industry 32519, Other Basic Organic Chemical Manufacturing;
- Rendering or refining animal fats and oils--are classified in Industry 31161, Animal Slaughtering and Processing; and
- Manufacturing laundry starches--are classified in Industry 32561, Soap and Cleaning Compound Manufacturing.

---

T—Canadian, Mexican, and United States industries are comparable.

## 311221  Wet Corn Milling and Starch Manufacturing

This U.S. industry comprises establishments primarily engaged in wet milling corn and other vegetables (except to make ethyl alcohol).  Examples of products made in these establishments are corn sweeteners, such as glucose, dextrose, and fructose; corn oil; and starches (except laundry).

*Cross-References.*        Establishments primarily engaged in--

- Refining and/or blending corn oil from purchased oils--are classified in U.S. Industry 311225, Fats and Oils Refining and Blending;
- Manufacturing sweetening syrups from corn syrup and starch base dessert powders--are classified in U.S. Industry 311999, All Other Miscellaneous Food Manufacturing;
- Reducing maple sap to maple syrup--are classified in U.S. Industry 111998, All Other Miscellaneous Crop Farming;
- Milling (except wet milling) corn--are classified in U.S. Industry 311211, Flour Milling;
- Wet milling corn to produce nonpotable ethyl alcohol--are classified in U.S. Industry 325193, Ethyl Alcohol Manufacturing; and
- Manufacturing laundry starches--are classified in U.S. Industry 325612, Polish and Other Sanitation Good Manufacturing.

## 311224  Soybean and Other Oilseed Processing

This U.S. industry comprises establishments primarily engaged in crushing oilseeds and tree nuts, such as soybeans, cottonseeds, linseeds, peanuts, and sunflower seeds.  Examples of products produced in these establishments are oilseed oils, cakes, meals, and protein isolates and concentrates.

*Cross-References.*        Establishments primarily engaged in--

- Wet milling corn and other vegetables--are classified in U.S. Industry 311221, Wet Corn Milling and Starch Manufacturing; and
- Refining and/or blending vegetable, oilseed, and tree nut oils from purchased oils--are classified in U.S. Industry 311225, Fats and Oils Refining and Blending.

## 311225  Fats and Oils Refining and Blending

This U.S. industry comprises establishments primarily engaged in one or more of the following: (1) manufacturing shortening and margarine from purchased fats and oils; (2) refining and/or blending vegetable, oilseed, and tree nut oils from purchased oils; and (3) blending purchased animal fats with purchased vegetable fats.

*Cross-References.*        Establishments primarily engaged in--

- Refining and/or blending corn oil made by wet corn milling--are classified in U.S. Industry 311221, Wet Corn Milling and Starch Manufacturing;
- Refining and/or blending oilseed and tree nut oils in crushing mills--are classified in U.S. Industry 311224, Soybean and Other Oilseed Processing; and
- Rendering or refining animal fats and oils--are classified in Industry 31161, Animal Slaughtering and Processing.

## 31123  Breakfast Cereal Manufacturing[T]
See industry description for 311230.

## 311230  Breakfast Cereal Manufacturing

This industry comprises establishments primarily engaged in manufacturing breakfast cereal foods.

---

T—Canadian, Mexican, and United States industries are comparable.

*Cross-References.*    Establishments primarily engaged in--

- Manufacturing nonchocolate-coated granola bars and other types of breakfast bars--are classified in Industry 311340, Nonchocolate Confectionery Manufacturing;
- Manufacturing chocolate-coated granola bars from purchased chocolate--are classified in U.S. Industry 311352, Confectionery Manufacturing from Purchased Chocolate;
- Manufacturing chocolate-coated granola bars from cacao beans--are classified in U.S. Industry 311351, Chocolate and Confectionery Manufacturing from Cacao Beans; and
- Manufacturing coffee substitutes from grain--are classified in Industry 311920, Coffee and Tea Manufacturing.

### 3113    Sugar and Confectionery Product Manufacturing[T]

This industry group comprises (1) establishments that process agricultural inputs, such as sugarcane, beet, and cacao, to give rise to a new product (sugar or chocolate) and (2) establishments that begin with sugar and chocolate and process these further.

### 31131    Sugar Manufacturing[T]

This industry comprises establishments primarily engaged in manufacturing raw sugar, liquid sugar, and refined sugar from sugarcane, raw cane sugar and sugar beets.

*Cross-References.*    Establishments primarily engaged in--

- Manufacturing corn sweeteners by wet milling corn--are classified in Industry 31122, Starch and Vegetable Fats and Oils Manufacturing;
- Manufacturing table syrups from corn syrup and starch base dessert powders--are classified in Industry 31199, All Other Food Manufacturing;
- Reducing maple sap to maple syrup or maple sugar--are classified in Industry 11199, All Other Crop Farming; and
- Manufacturing synthetic sweeteners (i.e., sweetening agents), such as saccharin and sugar substitutes (i.e., synthetic sweetener blended with other ingredients)--are classified in Subsector 325, Chemical Manufacturing.

### 311313  Beet Sugar Manufacturing

This U.S. industry comprises establishments primarily engaged in manufacturing refined beet sugar from sugar beets.

*Cross-References.*    Establishments primarily engaged in--

- Manufacturing raw cane sugar and/or refined cane sugar--are classified in U.S. Industry 311314, Cane Sugar Manufacturing;
- Manufacturing corn sweeteners by wet milling corn--are classified in U.S. Industry 311221, Wet Corn Milling and Starch Manufacturing;
- Manufacturing table syrups from corn syrup--are classified in U.S. Industry 311999, All Other Miscellaneous Food Manufacturing;
- Reducing maple sap to maple syrup or maple sugar--are classified in U.S. Industry 111998, All Other Miscellaneous Crop Farming; and
- Manufacturing synthetic sweeteners (i.e., sweetening agents), such as saccharin and sugar substitutes (i.e., synthetic sweetener blended with other ingredients)--are classified in Subsector 325, Chemical Manufacturing.

T—Canadian, Mexican, and United States industries are comparable.

**census.gov/naics**

## 311314  Cane Sugar Manufacturing

This U.S. industry comprises establishments primarily engaged in (1) processing sugarcane and/or (2) refining cane sugar from raw cane sugar.

*Cross-References.*          Establishments primarily engaged in--

- Manufacturing beet sugar--are classified in U.S. Industry 311313, Beet Sugar Manufacturing;
- Manufacturing corn sweeteners by wet milling corn--are classified in U.S. Industry 311221, Wet Corn Milling and Starch Manufacturing;
- Reducing maple sap to maple syrup or maple sugar--are classified in U.S. Industry 111998, All Other Miscellaneous Crop Farming;
- Manufacturing table syrups from corn syrup--are classified in U.S. Industry 311999, All Other Miscellaneous Food Manufacturing; and
- Manufacturing synthetic sweeteners (i.e., sweetening agents), such as saccharin and sugar substitutes (i.e., synthetic sweetener blended with other ingredients)--are classified in Subsector 325, Chemical Manufacturing.

## 31134  Nonchocolate Confectionery Manufacturing[T]
See industry description for 311340.

## 311340  Nonchocolate Confectionery Manufacturing

This industry comprises establishments primarily engaged in manufacturing nonchocolate confectioneries. Included in this industry are establishments primarily engaged in retailing nonchocolate confectionery products not for immediate consumption made on the premises.

*Cross-References.*          Establishments primarily engaged in--

- Manufacturing chocolate confectioneries from cacao beans--are classified in U.S. Industry 311351, Chocolate and Confectionery Manufacturing from Cacao Beans;
- Manufacturing chocolate confectioneries from chocolate made elsewhere--are classified in U.S. Industry 311352, Confectionery Manufacturing from Purchased Chocolate;
- Retailing confectioneries not for immediate consumption made elsewhere--are classified in U.S. Industry 445292, Confectionery and Nut Retailers;
- Preparing and selling confectioneries for immediate consumption--are classified in U.S. Industry 722515, Snack and Nonalcoholic Beverage Bars; and
- Roasting, salting, drying, cooking, or canning nuts and seeds--are classified in U.S. Industry 311911, Roasted Nuts and Peanut Butter Manufacturing.

## 31135  Chocolate and Confectionery Manufacturing[T]

This industry comprises establishments primarily engaged in (1) manufacturing chocolate and chocolate confectioneries from cacao beans or (2) manufacturing chocolate confectioneries from chocolate produced elsewhere.  Included in this industry are establishments primarily engaged in retailing chocolate confectionery products not for immediate consumption made on the premises from chocolate made elsewhere.

*Cross-References.*          Establishments primarily engaged in--

- Manufacturing, not for immediate consumption, nonchocolate confectioneries--are classified in Industry 31134, Nonchocolate Confectionery Manufacturing;
- Retailing confectioneries not for immediate consumption made elsewhere--are classified in Industry 44529, Other Specialty Food Retailers; and
- Preparing and selling confectioneries for immediate consumption--are classified in Industry 72251, Restaurants and Other Eating Places.

---

T—Canadian, Mexican, and United States industries are comparable.

### 311351  Chocolate and Confectionery Manufacturing from Cacao Beans

This U.S. industry comprises establishments primarily engaged in shelling, roasting, and grinding cacao beans and making chocolate cacao products and chocolate confectioneries.

*Cross-References.*          Establishments primarily engaged in--

- Manufacturing, not for immediate consumption, chocolate confectioneries from chocolate made elsewhere--are classified in U.S. Industry 311352, Confectionery Manufacturing from Purchased Chocolate;
- Manufacturing, not for immediate consumption, nonchocolate candies--are classified in Industry 311340, Nonchocolate Confectionery Manufacturing;
- Preparing and selling confectioneries for immediate consumption--are classified in U.S. Industry 722515, Snack and Nonalcoholic Beverage Bars; and
- Retailing confectioneries not for immediate consumption made elsewhere--are classified in U.S. Industry 445292, Confectionery and Nut Retailers.

### 311352  Confectionery Manufacturing from Purchased Chocolate

This U.S. industry comprises establishments primarily engaged in manufacturing chocolate confectioneries from chocolate produced elsewhere.  Included in this industry are establishments primarily engaged in retailing chocolate confectionery products not for immediate consumption made on the premises from chocolate made elsewhere.

*Cross-References.*          Establishments primarily engaged in--

- Manufacturing chocolate confectioneries from cacao beans--are classified in U.S. Industry 311351, Chocolate and Confectionery Manufacturing from Cacao Beans;
- Manufacturing, not for immediate consumption, nonchocolate confectioneries--are classified in Industry 311340, Nonchocolate Confectionery Manufacturing;
- Retailing confectioneries not for immediate consumption made elsewhere--are classified in U.S. Industry 445292, Confectionery and Nut Retailers; and
- Preparing and selling confectioneries for immediate consumption--are classified in U.S. Industry 722515, Snack and Nonalcoholic Beverage Bars.

### 3114    Fruit and Vegetable Preserving and Specialty Food Manufacturing[T]

This industry group includes (1) establishments that freeze food and (2) establishments that use preservation processes, such as pickling, canning, and dehydrating.  Both types begin their production process with inputs of vegetable or animal origin.

### 31141   Frozen Food Manufacturing[T]

This industry comprises establishments primarily engaged in manufacturing frozen fruit, frozen juices, frozen vegetables, and frozen specialty foods (except seafood), such as frozen dinners, entrees, and side dishes; frozen pizza; frozen whipped toppings; and frozen waffles, pancakes, and French toast.

*Cross-References.*          Establishments primarily engaged in--

- Manufacturing frozen dairy specialties--are classified in Industry 31152, Ice Cream and Frozen Dessert Manufacturing;
- Manufacturing frozen bakery products--are classified in Industry 31181, Bread and Bakery Product Manufacturing;
- Manufacturing frozen seafood products--are classified in Industry 31171, Seafood Product Preparation and Packaging; and
- Manufacturing frozen meat products--are classified in Industry 31161, Animal Slaughtering and Processing.

---

T—Canadian, Mexican, and United States industries are comparable.

## 311411  Frozen Fruit, Juice, and Vegetable Manufacturing

This U.S. industry comprises establishments primarily engaged in manufacturing frozen fruits; frozen vegetables; and frozen fruit juices, ades, drinks, cocktail mixes and concentrates.

*Cross-References.*

Establishments primarily engaged in manufacturing frozen specialty foods are classified in U.S. Industry 311412, Frozen Specialty Food Manufacturing.

## 311412  Frozen Specialty Food Manufacturing

This U.S. industry comprises establishments primarily engaged in manufacturing frozen specialty foods (except seafood), such as frozen dinners, entrees, and side dishes; frozen pizza; frozen whipped topping; and frozen waffles, pancakes, and French toast.

*Cross-References.*          Establishments primarily engaged in--

- Manufacturing frozen dairy specialties--are classified in Industry 311520, Ice Cream and Frozen Dessert Manufacturing;
- Manufacturing frozen bakery products--are classified in U.S. Industry 311813, Frozen Cakes, Pies, and Other Pastries Manufacturing;
- Manufacturing frozen fruits, frozen fruit juices, and frozen vegetables--are classified in U.S. Industry 311411, Frozen Fruit, Juice, and Vegetable Manufacturing;
- Manufacturing frozen meat products--are classified in Industry 31161, Animal Slaughtering and Processing; and
- Manufacturing frozen seafood products--are classified in Industry 311710, Seafood Product Preparation and Packaging.

## 31142  Fruit and Vegetable Canning, Pickling, and Drying[T]

This industry comprises establishments primarily engaged in manufacturing canned, pickled, and dried fruits, vegetables, and specialty foods. Establishments in this industry may package the dried or dehydrated ingredients they make with other purchased ingredients. Examples of products made by these establishments are canned juices; canned baby foods; canned soups (except seafood); canned dry beans; canned tomato-based sauces, such as catsup, salsa, chili sauce, spaghetti sauce, barbeque sauce, and tomato paste; pickles and relishes; jams and jellies; dried soup mixes and bouillon; and sauerkraut.

*Cross-References.*          Establishments primarily engaged in--

- Manufacturing canned dairy products--are classified in Industry 31151, Dairy Product (except Frozen) Manufacturing;
- Manufacturing canned seafood soups and seafood products--are classified in Industry 31171, Seafood Product Preparation and Packaging;
- Manufacturing canned meat products--are classified in Industry 31161, Animal Slaughtering and Processing;
- Milling rice and packaging it with other ingredients or manufacturing vegetable flours and meals--are classified in Industry 31121, Flour Milling and Malt Manufacturing;
- Manufacturing dry pasta and packaging it with other ingredients--are classified in Industry 31182, Cookie, Cracker, and Pasta Manufacturing;
- Mixing purchased dried and/or dehydrated potatoes, rice, and pasta and packaging them with other purchased ingredients; mixing purchased dried and/or dehydrated ingredients for soup mixes and bouillon; and manufacturing canned puddings--are classified in Industry 31199, All Other Food Manufacturing;
- Manufacturing dry salad dressing and dry sauce mixes--are classified in Industry 31194, Seasoning and Dressing Manufacturing; and

---

T—Canadian, Mexican, and United States industries are comparable.

- Manufacturing canned fruit and vegetable drinks, cocktails, and ades (except juices)--are classified in Industry 31211, Soft Drink and Ice Manufacturing.

### 311421  Fruit and Vegetable Canning

This U.S. industry comprises establishments primarily engaged in manufacturing canned, pickled, and brined fruits and vegetables.  Examples of products made in these establishments are canned juices; canned jams and jellies; canned tomato-based sauces, such as catsup, salsa, chili sauce, spaghetti sauce, barbeque sauce, and tomato paste; and pickles, relishes, and sauerkraut.

*Cross-References.*          Establishments primarily engaged in--

- Manufacturing canned baby foods, canned soups (except seafood), and canned specialty foods (except seafood)--are classified in U.S. Industry 311422, Specialty Canning;
- Manufacturing canned seafood soups and canned seafood products--are classified in Industry 311710, Seafood Product Preparation and Packaging;
- Manufacturing canned meat products--are classified in Industry 31161, Animal Slaughtering and Processing; and
- Manufacturing canned fruit and vegetable drinks, cocktails, and ades (except juices)--are classified in U.S. Industry 312111, Soft Drink Manufacturing.

### 311422  Specialty Canning

This U.S. industry comprises establishments primarily engaged in manufacturing canned specialty foods. Examples of products made in these establishments are canned baby food, canned baked beans, canned soups (except seafood), canned spaghetti, and other canned nationality foods.

*Cross-References.*          Establishments primarily engaged in--

- Manufacturing canned dairy products--are classified in U.S. Industry 311514, Dry, Condensed, and Evaporated Dairy Product Manufacturing;
- Manufacturing canned fruits, canned vegetables, and canned juices--are classified in U.S. Industry 311421, Fruit and Vegetable Canning;
- Manufacturing canned seafood soups and canned seafood products--are classified in Industry 311710, Seafood Product Preparation and Packaging;
- Manufacturing canned meat products--are classified in Industry 31161, Animal Slaughtering and Processing; and
- Manufacturing canned puddings--are classified in U.S. Industry 311999, All Other Miscellaneous Food Manufacturing.

### 311423  Dried and Dehydrated Food Manufacturing

This U.S. industry comprises establishments primarily engaged in (1) drying (including freeze-dried) and/or dehydrating fruits, vegetables, and soup mixes and bouillon and/or (2) drying and/or dehydrating ingredients and packaging them with other purchased ingredients, such as rice and dry pasta.

*Cross-References.*          Establishments primarily engaged in--

- Milling rice and packaging it with other ingredients--are classified in U.S. Industry 311212, Rice Milling;
- Manufacturing dry pasta and packaging it with other ingredients--are classified in U.S. Industry 311824, Dry Pasta, Dough, and Flour Mixes Manufacturing from Purchased Flour;
- Manufacturing fruit, grain (except rice), and vegetable flours, meals, and powders--are classified in U.S. Industry 311211, Flour Milling;

---

T—Canadian, Mexican, and United States industries are comparable.

- Mixing purchased dried and/or dehydrated potatoes, rice, and pasta, and packaging them with other purchased ingredients, and mixing purchased dried and/or dehydrated ingredients for soup mixes and bouillon--are classified in U.S. Industry 311999, All Other Miscellaneous Food Manufacturing; and
- Manufacturing dry salad dressing and dry sauce mixes--are classified in U.S. Industry 311942, Spice and Extract Manufacturing.

### 3115    Dairy Product Manufacturing[T]

This industry group comprises establishments that manufacture dairy products from raw milk, processed milk, and dairy substitutes (except butter substitutes).

### 31151    Dairy Product (except Frozen) Manufacturing[T]

This industry comprises establishments primarily engaged in one or more of the following: (1) manufacturing dairy products (except frozen) from raw milk and/or processed milk products; (2) manufacturing dairy substitutes (except frozen) from soybeans and other nondairy substances; and (3) manufacturing dry, condensed, concentrated, and evaporated dairy and dairy substitute products.

*Cross-References.*          Establishments primarily engaged in--

- Manufacturing cheese-based salad dressings--are classified in Industry 31194, Seasoning and Dressing Manufacturing;
- Manufacturing margarine, margarine-butter blends, or butter substitutes--are classified in Industry 31122, Starch and Vegetable Fats and Oils Manufacturing;
- Manufacturing frozen whipped toppings--are classified in Industry 31141, Frozen Food Manufacturing;
- Manufacturing ice cream, frozen yogurt, and other frozen dairy desserts--are classified in Industry 31152, Ice Cream and Frozen Dessert Manufacturing; and
- Milking dairy cattle--are classified in Industry 11212, Dairy Cattle and Milk Production.

### 311511  Fluid Milk Manufacturing

This U.S. industry comprises establishments primarily engaged in (1) manufacturing processed milk products, such as pasteurized milk or cream and sour cream and/or (2) manufacturing fluid milk dairy substitutes from soybeans and other nondairy substances.

*Cross-References.*          Establishments primarily engaged in--

- Manufacturing dry mix whipped toppings, canned milk, and ultra high temperature milk--are classified in U.S. Industry 311514, Dry, Condensed, and Evaporated Dairy Product Manufacturing;
- Manufacturing frozen whipped toppings--are classified in U.S. Industry 311412, Frozen Specialty Food Manufacturing;
- Manufacturing ice cream and frozen yogurt and other frozen desserts--are classified in Industry 311520, Ice Cream and Frozen Dessert Manufacturing; and
- Milking dairy cattle--are classified in Industry 112120, Dairy Cattle and Milk Production.

### 311512  Creamery Butter Manufacturing

This U.S. industry comprises establishments primarily engaged in manufacturing creamery butter from milk and/or processed milk products.

*Cross-References.*

Establishments primarily engaged in manufacturing margarine, margarine-butter blends, or butter substitutes are classified in U.S. Industry 311225, Fats and Oils Refining and Blending.

---

T—Canadian, Mexican, and United States industries are comparable.

**311513 Cheese Manufacturing**

This U.S. industry comprises establishments primarily engaged in (1) manufacturing cheese products (except cottage cheese) from raw milk and/or processed milk products and/or (2) manufacturing cheese substitutes from soybean and other nondairy substances.

*Cross-References.*　　　Establishments primarily engaged in--

- Manufacturing cheese-based salad dressings--are classified in U.S. Industry 311941, Mayonnaise, Dressing, and Other Prepared Sauce Manufacturing; and
- Manufacturing cottage cheese--are classified in U.S. Industry 311511, Fluid Milk Manufacturing.

**311514 Dry, Condensed, and Evaporated Dairy Product Manufacturing**

This U.S. industry comprises establishments primarily engaged in manufacturing dry, condensed, and evaporated milk and dairy substitute products.

*Cross-References.*　　　Establishments primarily engaged in--

- Manufacturing fluid milk products--are classified in U.S. Industry 311511, Fluid Milk Manufacturing;
- Manufacturing creamery butter--are classified in U.S. Industry 311512, Creamery Butter Manufacturing; and
- Manufacturing cheese products--are classified in U.S. Industry 311513, Cheese Manufacturing.

**31152 Ice Cream and Frozen Dessert Manufacturing$^T$**
See industry description for 311520.

**311520 Ice Cream and Frozen Dessert Manufacturing**

This industry comprises establishments primarily engaged in manufacturing ice cream, frozen yogurts, frozen ices, sherbets, frozen tofu, and other frozen desserts (except bakery products).

*Cross-References.*　　　Establishments primarily engaged in--

- Manufacturing frozen bakery products--are classified in U.S. Industry 311813, Frozen Cakes, Pies, and Other Pastries Manufacturing; and
- Manufacturing ice cream and ice milk mixes--are classified in U.S. Industry 311514, Dry, Condensed, and Evaporated Dairy Product Manufacturing.

**3116 Animal Slaughtering and Processing$^T$**

**31161 Animal Slaughtering and Processing$^T$**

This industry comprises establishments primarily engaged in one or more of the following: (1) slaughtering animals; (2) preparing processed meats and meat byproducts; and (3) rendering and/or refining animal fat, bones, and meat scraps. This industry includes establishments primarily engaged in assembly cutting and packing of meats (i.e., boxed meats) from purchased carcasses.

*Cross-References.*　　　Establishments primarily engaged in--

- Manufacturing canned meat for baby food--are classified in Industry 31142, Fruit and Vegetable Canning, Pickling, and Drying;
- Manufacturing meat-based animal feeds from purchased carcasses--are classified in Industry 31111, Animal Food Manufacturing;

---

T—Canadian, Mexican, and United States industries are comparable.

- Blending purchased animal fats with vegetable fats--are classified in Industry 31122, Starch and Vegetable Fats and Oils Manufacturing;
- Manufacturing canned and frozen specialty foods containing meat, such as nationality foods (e.g., enchiladas, pizza, egg rolls) and frozen dinners--are classified in Industry Group 3114, Fruit and Vegetable Preserving and Specialty Food Manufacturing;
- Drying, freezing, or breaking eggs--are classified in Industry 31199, All Other Food Manufacturing; and
- Cutting purchased meat carcasses and wholesaling meat cuts (except boxed meat)--are classified in Industry 42447, Meat and Meat Product Merchant Wholesalers.

## 311611 Animal (except Poultry) Slaughtering

This U.S. industry comprises establishments primarily engaged in slaughtering animals (except poultry and small game). Establishments that slaughter and prepare meats are included in this industry.

*Cross-References.* Establishments primarily engaged in--

- Processing meat and meat byproducts (except poultry and small game) from purchased meats--are classified in U.S. Industry 311612, Meat Processed from Carcasses;
- Slaughtering and/or processing poultry and small game--are classified in U.S. Industry 311615, Poultry Processing;
- Rendering lard and other animal fats and oils, bones, and meat scraps--are classified in U.S. Industry 311613, Rendering and Meat Byproduct Processing; and
- Manufacturing canned and frozen specialty foods containing meat, such as nationality foods (e.g., enchiladas, egg rolls, pizza) and frozen dinners--are classified in Industry Group 3114, Fruit and Vegetable Preserving and Specialty Food Manufacturing.

## 311612 Meat Processed from Carcasses

This U.S. industry comprises establishments primarily engaged in processing or preserving meat and meat byproducts (except poultry and small game) from purchased meats. This industry includes establishments primarily engaged in assembly cutting and packing of meats (i.e., boxed meats) from purchased meats.

*Cross-References.* Establishments primarily engaged in--

- Slaughtering animals (except poultry and small game)--are classified in U.S. Industry 311611, Animal (except Poultry) Slaughtering;
- Slaughtering poultry and small game--are classified in U.S. Industry 311615, Poultry Processing;
- Rendering lard and other animal fats and oils, bones, and meat scraps--are classified in U.S. Industry 311613, Rendering and Meat Byproduct Processing;
- Manufacturing canned meats for baby food--are classified in U.S. Industry 311422, Specialty Canning;
- Manufacturing meat-based animal feeds from purchased carcasses--are classified in Industry 31111, Animal Food Manufacturing;
- Manufacturing canned and frozen specialty foods containing meat, such as nationality foods (e.g., enchiladas, egg rolls, pizza) and frozen dinners--are classified in Industry Group 3114, Fruit and Vegetable Preserving and Specialty Food Manufacturing; and
- Cutting purchased meat carcasses and wholesaling meat cuts (except boxed meat)--are classified in Industry 424470, Meat and Meat Product Merchant Wholesalers.

## 311613 Rendering and Meat Byproduct Processing

This U.S. industry comprises establishments primarily engaged in rendering animal fat, bones, and meat scraps.

---

T—Canadian, Mexican, and United States industries are comparable.

*Cross-References.*          Establishments primarily engaged in--

- Blending purchased animal fats with vegetable fats--are classified in U.S. Industry 311225, Fats and Oils Refining and Blending; and
- Manufacturing meat-based animal feeds from purchased carcasses--are classified in Industry 31111, Animal Food Manufacturing.

## 311615  Poultry Processing

This U.S. industry comprises establishments primarily engaged in (1) slaughtering poultry and small game and/or (2) preparing processed poultry and small game meat and meat byproducts.

*Cross-References.*          Establishments primarily engaged in--

- Slaughtering animals (except poultry and small game) and/or preparing meats--are classified in U.S. Industry 311611, Animal (except Poultry) Slaughtering;
- Preparing meat and meat byproducts (except poultry and small game) from purchased meats--are classified in U.S. Industry 311612, Meat Processed from Carcasses;
- Rendering animal fats and oils, bones, and meat scraps--are classified in U.S. Industry 311613, Rendering and Meat Byproduct Processing;
- Canning poultry and small game for baby food--are classified in U.S. Industry 311422, Specialty Canning;
- Manufacturing poultry-based animal feeds from purchased carcasses--are classified in Industry 31111, Animal Food Manufacturing;
- Manufacturing frozen meat and poultry products, such as nationality foods (e.g., enchiladas, egg rolls, pizza) and frozen dinners--are classified in U.S. Industry 311412, Frozen Specialty Food Manufacturing; and
- Drying, freezing, and breaking eggs--are classified in U.S. Industry 311999, All Other Miscellaneous Food Manufacturing.

## 3117    Seafood Product Preparation and Packaging[T]

## 31171   Seafood Product Preparation and Packaging[T]
See industry description for 311710.

## 311710  Seafood Product Preparation and Packaging

This industry comprises establishments primarily engaged in one or more of the following: (1) canning seafood (including soup); (2) smoking, salting, and drying seafood; (3) eviscerating fresh fish by removing heads, fins, scales, bones, and entrails; (4) shucking and packing fresh shellfish; (5) processing marine fats and oils; and (6) freezing seafood.  Establishments known as "floating factory ships" that are engaged in the gathering and processing of seafood into canned seafood products are included in this industry.

## 3118    Bakeries and Tortilla Manufacturing[T]

This industry group comprises establishments primarily engaged in one of the following: (1) manufacturing fresh and frozen bread and other bakery products; (2) retailing bread and other bakery products not for immediate consumption made on the premises from flour, not from prepared dough; (3) manufacturing cookies, crackers, and dry pasta; (4)  manufacturing prepared flour mixes or dough from flour ground elsewhere; or (5) manufacturing tortillas.

## 31181   Bread and Bakery Product Manufacturing[T]

This industry comprises establishments primarily engaged in manufacturing fresh and frozen bread and other bakery products.

---

T—Canadian, Mexican, and United States industries are comparable.

*Cross-References.*        Establishments primarily engaged in--

- Manufacturing cookies and crackers--are classified in Industry 31182, Cookie, Cracker, and Pasta Manufacturing;
- Preparing and selling bakery products (e.g., cookies, pretzels) for immediate consumption--are classified in Industry 72251, Restaurants and Other Eating Places;
- Retailing bakery products not for immediate consumption made elsewhere--are classified in Industry 44529, Other Specialty Food Retailers; and
- Manufacturing pretzels (except soft)--are classified in Industry 31191, Snack Food Manufacturing.

### 311811  Retail Bakeries

This U.S. industry comprises establishments primarily engaged in retailing bread and other bakery products not for immediate consumption made on the premises from flour, not from prepared dough.

*Cross-References.*        Establishments primarily engaged in--

- Retailing bakery products not for immediate consumption made elsewhere--are classified in U.S. Industry 445291, Baked Goods Retailers;
- Preparing and selling bakery products (e.g., cookies, pretzels) for immediate consumption--are classified in U.S. Industry 722515, Snack and Nonalcoholic Beverage Bars;
- Manufacturing fresh or frozen breads and other fresh bakery (except cookies and crackers) products--are classified in U.S. Industry 311812, Commercial Bakeries; and
- Manufacturing cookies and crackers--are classified in U.S. Industry 311821, Cookie and Cracker Manufacturing.

### 311812  Commercial Bakeries

This U.S. industry comprises establishments primarily engaged in manufacturing fresh and frozen bread and bread-type rolls and other fresh bakery (except cookies and crackers) products.

*Cross-References.*        Establishments primarily engaged in--

- Retailing bread and other bakery products not for immediate consumption made on the premises from flour, not from prepared dough--are classified in U.S. Industry 311811, Retail Bakeries;
- Manufacturing frozen bakery products (except bread)--are classified in U.S. Industry 311813, Frozen Cakes, Pies, and Other Pastries Manufacturing;
- Preparing and selling bakery products (e.g., cookies, pretzels) for immediate consumption--are classified in U.S. Industry 722515, Snack and Nonalcoholic Beverage Bars;
- Retailing bakery products not for immediate consumption made elsewhere--are classified in U.S. Industry 445291, Baked Goods Retailers;
- Manufacturing cookies and crackers--are classified in U.S. Industry 311821, Cookie and Cracker Manufacturing; and
- Manufacturing pretzels (except soft)--are classified in U.S. Industry 311919, Other Snack Food Manufacturing.

### 311813  Frozen Cakes, Pies, and Other Pastries Manufacturing

This U.S. industry comprises establishments primarily engaged in manufacturing frozen bakery products (except bread), such as cakes, pies, and doughnuts.

*Cross-References.*        Establishments primarily engaged in--

- Manufacturing frozen breads--are classified in U.S. Industry 311812, Commercial Bakeries;

---

T—Canadian, Mexican, and United States industries are comparable.

- Retailing bakery products not for immediate consumption made on the premises from flour, not from prepared dough--are classified in U.S. Industry 311811, Retail Bakeries;
- Preparing and selling bakery products (e.g., cookies, pretzels) for immediate consumption--are classified in U.S. Industry 722515, Snack and Nonalcoholic Beverage Bars;
- Manufacturing cookies and crackers--are classified in U.S. Industry 311821, Cookie and Cracker Manufacturing; and
- Retailing bakery products not for immediate consumption made elsewhere--are classified in U.S. Industry 445291, Baked Goods Retailers.

## 31182   Cookie, Cracker, and Pasta Manufacturing[T]

This industry comprises establishments primarily engaged in one of the following: (1) manufacturing cookies and crackers; (2) preparing flour and dough mixes and dough from flour ground elsewhere; and (3) manufacturing dry pasta.  The establishments in this industry may package the dry pasta they manufacture with other ingredients.

*Cross-References.*          Establishments primarily engaged in--

- Preparing and selling bakery products (e.g., cookies, pretzels) for immediate consumption--are classified in Industry 72251, Restaurants and Other Eating Places;
- Retailing bakery products not for immediate consumption made elsewhere--are classified in Industry 44529, Other Specialty Food Retailers;
- Manufacturing bakery products (e.g., bread, cookies, pies)--are classified in Industry 31181, Bread and Bakery Product Manufacturing;
- Milling flour and preparing flour mixes or doughs--are classified in Industry 31121, Flour Milling and Malt Manufacturing;
- Manufacturing fresh pasta--are classified in Industry 31199, All Other Food Manufacturing;
- Manufacturing pasta specialties--are classified in Industry Group 3114, Fruit and Vegetable Preserving and Specialty Food Manufacturing;
- Manufacturing pretzels (except soft)--are classified in Industry 31191, Snack Food Manufacturing;
- Mixing purchased dried and/or dehydrated ingredients with purchased dry pasta--are classified in Industry 31199, All Other Food Manufacturing; and
- Drying and/or dehydrating ingredients and packaging them with purchased dry pasta--are classified in Industry 31142, Fruit and Vegetable Canning, Pickling, and Drying.

## 311821  Cookie and Cracker Manufacturing

This U.S. industry comprises establishments primarily engaged in manufacturing cookies, crackers, and other products, such as ice cream cones.

*Cross-References.*          Establishments primarily engaged in--

- Preparing and selling bakery products (e.g., cookies, pretzels) for immediate consumption--are classified in U.S. Industry 722515, Snack and Nonalcoholic Beverage Bars;
- Retailing bakery products not for immediate consumption made elsewhere--are classified in U.S. Industry 445291, Baked Goods Retailers;
- Manufacturing bakery products (e.g., breads, cookies, pies)--are classified in Industry 31181, Bread and Bakery Product Manufacturing; and
- Manufacturing pretzels (except soft)--are classified in U.S. Industry 311919, Other Snack Food Manufacturing.

## 311824  Dry Pasta, Dough, and Flour Mixes Manufacturing from Purchased Flour

This U.S. industry comprises establishments primarily engaged in (1) manufacturing dry pasta and/or (2) manufacturing prepared flour mixes or dough from flour ground elsewhere.  The establishments in this industry may package the dry pasta they manufacture with other ingredients.

---

T—Canadian, Mexican, and United States industries are comparable.

*Cross-References.*          Establishments primarily engaged in--

- Milling flour and preparing flour mixes or doughs--are classified in U.S. Industry 311211, Flour Milling;
- Manufacturing fresh pasta--are classified in U.S. Industry 311991, Perishable Prepared Food Manufacturing;
- Manufacturing pasta specialties--are classified in Industry Group 3114, Fruit and Vegetable Preserving and Specialty Food Manufacturing;
- Mixing purchased dried and/or dehydrated ingredients with purchased dry pasta--are classified in U.S. Industry 311999, All Other Miscellaneous Food Manufacturing; and
- Drying and/or dehydrating ingredients packaged with purchased dry pasta--are classified in U.S. Industry 311423, Dried and Dehydrated Food Manufacturing.

## 31183   Tortilla Manufacturing[T]
See industry description for 311830.

## 311830  Tortilla Manufacturing

This industry comprises establishments primarily engaged in manufacturing tortillas.

*Cross-References.*          Establishments primarily engaged in--

- Manufacturing canned nationality foods using tortillas--are classified in U.S. Industry 311422, Specialty Canning;
- Manufacturing frozen nationality foods using tortillas--are classified in U.S. Industry 311412, Frozen Specialty Food Manufacturing; and
- Manufacturing tortilla chips--are classified in U.S. Industry 311919, Other Snack Food Manufacturing.

## 3119   Other Food Manufacturing[T]

This industry group comprises establishments primarily engaged in manufacturing food (except animal food; grain and oilseed milling; sugar and confectionery products; preserved fruits, vegetables, and specialty foods; dairy products; meat products; seafood products; and bakery products and tortillas).  This industry group includes industries with different production processes, such as snack food manufacturing; coffee and tea manufacturing; concentrate, syrup, condiment, and spice manufacturing; and, in general, an entire range of other miscellaneous food product manufacturing.

## 31191   Snack Food Manufacturing[T]

This industry comprises establishments primarily engaged in one or more of the following: (1) salting, roasting, drying, cooking, or canning nuts; (2) processing grains or seeds into snacks; (3) manufacturing peanut butter; and (4) manufacturing potato chips, corn chips, popped popcorn, pretzels (except soft), pork rinds, and similar snacks.

*Cross-References.*          Establishments primarily engaged in--

- Manufacturing crackers--are classified in Industry 31182, Cookie, Cracker, and Pasta Manufacturing;
- Manufacturing unpopped popcorn--are classified in Industry 31199, All Other Food Manufacturing;
- Manufacturing chocolate or candy-coated nuts and candy-covered popcorn--are classified in Industry Group 3113, Sugar and Confectionery Product Manufacturing;
- Manufacturing soybean, sunflower, and other oilseed butters--are classified in Industry 31122, Starch and Vegetable Fats and Oils Manufacturing;
- Manufacturing soft pretzels--are classified in Industry 31181, Bread and Bakery Product Manufacturing;
- Manufacturing dried and smoked meat snacks (except pork rinds)--are classified in Industry 31161, Animal Slaughtering and Processing; and
- Preparing and selling snacks (e.g., popcorn, pretzels) for immediate consumption--are classified in Industry 72251, Restaurants and Other Eating Places.

---

T—Canadian, Mexican, and United States industries are comparable.

**311911  Roasted Nuts and Peanut Butter Manufacturing**

This U.S. industry comprises establishments primarily engaged in one or more of the following: (1) salting, roasting, drying, cooking, or canning nuts; (2) processing grains or seeds into snacks; and (3) manufacturing peanut butter and other nut butters.

*Cross-References.*          Establishments primarily engaged in--

- Manufacturing chocolate or candy-coated nuts and candy-covered popcorn--are classified in Industry Group 3113, Sugar and Confectionery Product Manufacturing; and
- Manufacturing soybean, sunflower, and other oilseed butters--are classified in Industry 31122, Starch and Vegetable Fats and Oils Manufacturing.

**311919  Other Snack Food Manufacturing**

This U.S. industry comprises establishments primarily engaged in manufacturing snack foods (except roasted nuts and peanut butter).

*Illustrative Examples:*

| | |
|---|---|
| Corn chips and related corn snacks manufacturing | Potato chips manufacturing |
| Popped popcorn (except candy-covered) manufacturing | Pretzels (except soft) manufacturing |
| | Tortilla chips manufacturing |
| Pork rinds manufacturing | |

*Cross-References.*          Establishments primarily engaged in--

- Manufacturing cookies and crackers--are classified in U.S. Industry 311821, Cookie and Cracker Manufacturing;
- Manufacturing candy-covered popcorn and nonchocolate granola bars--are classified in Industry 311340, Nonchocolate Confectionery Manufacturing;
- Salting, roasting, drying, cooking, or canning nuts and seeds--are classified in U.S. Industry 311911, Roasted Nuts and Peanut Butter Manufacturing;
- Manufacturing unpopped popcorn--are classified in U.S. Industry 311999, All Other Miscellaneous Food Manufacturing;
- Manufacturing soft pretzels--are classified in U.S. Industry 311812, Commercial Bakeries;
- Manufacturing dried and smoked meat snacks (except pork rinds)--are classified in Industry 31161, Animal Slaughtering and Processing; and
- Preparing and selling snacks (e.g., popcorn, pretzels) for immediate consumption--are classified in U.S. Industry 722515, Snack and Nonalcoholic Beverage Bars.

**31192  Coffee and Tea Manufacturing**[T]
See industry description for 311920.

**311920  Coffee and Tea Manufacturing**

This industry comprises establishments primarily engaged in one or more of the following: (1) roasting coffee; (2) manufacturing coffee and tea concentrates (including instant and freeze-dried); (3) blending tea; (4) manufacturing herbal tea; and (5) manufacturing coffee extracts, flavorings, and syrups.

*Cross-References.*

Establishments primarily engaged in bottling and canning iced coffee or tea are classified in U.S. Industry 312111, Soft Drink Manufacturing.

---

T—Canadian, Mexican, and United States industries are comparable.

**31193   Flavoring Syrup and Concentrate Manufacturing**[T]
See industry description for 311930.

**311930   Flavoring Syrup and Concentrate Manufacturing**

This industry comprises establishments primarily engaged in manufacturing flavoring syrup drink concentrates and related products for soda fountain use or for the manufacture of soft drinks.

*Cross-References.*          Establishments primarily engaged in--

- Manufacturing chocolate syrup--are classified in Industry 31135, Chocolate and Confectionery Manufacturing;
- Manufacturing flavoring extracts (except coffee and meat) and natural food colorings--are classified in U.S. Industry 311942, Spice and Extract Manufacturing;
- Manufacturing coffee extracts and/or coffee-based syrups--are classified in Industry 311920, Coffee and Tea Manufacturing;
- Manufacturing liquid meat extracts from slaughtered or purchased carcasses--are classified in Industry 31161, Animal Slaughtering and Processing;
- Manufacturing canned gravies by mixing liquid meat extracts with other ingredients--are classified in U.S. Industry 311422, Specialty Canning;
- Manufacturing powdered drink mixes (except coffee, tea, chocolate, or milk based), table syrup from corn syrup, or sweetening syrups (except pure maple)--are classified in U.S. Industry 311999, All Other Miscellaneous Food Manufacturing;
- Reducing maple sap to maple syrup--are classified in U.S. Industry 111998, All Other Miscellaneous Crop Farming; and
- Manufacturing natural nonfood colorings--are classified in U.S. Industry 325199, All Other Basic Organic Chemical Manufacturing.

**31194   Seasoning and Dressing Manufacturing**[T]

This industry comprises establishments primarily engaged in one or more of the following: (1) manufacturing dressings and sauces, such as mayonnaise, salad dressing, vinegar, mustard, horseradish, soy sauce, tartar sauce, Worcestershire sauce, and other prepared sauces (except tomato-based and gravies); (2) manufacturing spices, table salt, seasoning, and flavoring extracts (except coffee and meat), and natural food colorings; and (3) manufacturing dry mix food preparations, such as salad dressing mixes, gravy and sauce mixes, frosting mixes, and other dry mix preparations.

*Cross-References.*          Establishments primarily engaged in--

- Manufacturing catsup and other tomato-based sauces--are classified in Industry 31142, Fruit and Vegetable Canning, Pickling, and Drying;
- Mixing purchased dried and/or dehydrated potato, rice, and pasta and packaging them with other purchased ingredients, and manufacturing prepared frosting--are classified in Industry 31199, All Other Food Manufacturing;
- Drying and/or dehydrating ingredients for dry soup mixes and bouillon--are classified in Industry 31142, Fruit and Vegetable Canning, Pickling, and Drying;
- Mixing purchased dried and/or dehydrated ingredients for dry soup mixes and bouillon--are classified in Industry 31199, All Other Food Manufacturing;
- Manufacturing industrial salts--are classified in Industry 32599, All Other Chemical Product and Preparation Manufacturing;
- Manufacturing flavoring syrups (except chocolate and coffee-based syrups)--are classified in Industry 31193, Flavoring Syrup and Concentrate Manufacturing;
- Manufacturing synthetic food colorings--are classified in Industry 32513, Synthetic Dye and Pigment Manufacturing;

---

T—Canadian, Mexican, and United States industries are comparable.

- Manufacturing natural organic colorings for nonfood uses--are classified in Industry 32519, Other Basic Organic Chemical Manufacturing;
- Manufacturing coffee extracts--are classified in Industry 31192, Coffee and Tea Manufacturing;
- Manufacturing liquid meat extracts from slaughtered or purchased carcasses--are classified in Industry 31161, Animal Slaughtering and Processing; and
- Manufacturing canned liquid gravies--are classified in Industry 31142, Fruit and Vegetable Canning, Pickling, and Drying.

## 311941 Mayonnaise, Dressing, and Other Prepared Sauce Manufacturing

This U.S. industry comprises establishments primarily engaged in manufacturing mayonnaise, salad dressing, vinegar, mustard, horseradish, soy sauce, tartar sauce, Worcestershire sauce, and other prepared sauces (except tomato-based and gravy).

*Cross-References.*        Establishments primarily engaged in--

- Manufacturing catsup and other tomato-based sauces--are classified in U.S. Industry 311421, Fruit and Vegetable Canning;
- Manufacturing dry salad dressing and dry sauce mixes--are classified in U.S. Industry 311942, Spice and Extract Manufacturing; and
- Manufacturing canned liquid gravies--are classified in U.S. Industry 311422, Specialty Canning.

## 311942 Spice and Extract Manufacturing

This U.S. industry comprises establishments primarily engaged in (1) manufacturing spices, table salt, seasonings, flavoring extracts (except coffee and meat), and natural food colorings and/or (2) manufacturing dry mix food preparations, such as salad dressing mixes, gravy and sauce mixes, frosting mixes, and other dry mix preparations.

*Cross-References.*        Establishments primarily engaged in--

- Manufacturing catsup and other tomato-based sauces--are classified in U.S. Industry 311421, Fruit and Vegetable Canning;
- Manufacturing mayonnaise, dressings, and prepared sauces (except tomato-based and gravy)--are classified in U.S. Industry 311941, Mayonnaise, Dressing, and Other Prepared Sauce Manufacturing;
- Manufacturing canned liquid gravies--are classified in U.S. Industry 311422, Specialty Canning;
- Manufacturing industrial salts--are classified in U.S. Industry 325998, All Other Miscellaneous Chemical Product and Preparation Manufacturing;
- Drying and/or dehydrating ingredients for dry soup mixes and bouillon--are classified in U.S. Industry 311423, Dried and Dehydrated Food Manufacturing;
- Mixing purchased dried and/or dehydrated ingredients for dry soup mixes and bouillon--are classified in U.S. Industry 311999, All Other Miscellaneous Food Manufacturing;
- Manufacturing flavoring syrups (except chocolate and coffee-based syrups)--are classified in Industry 311930, Flavoring Syrup and Concentrate Manufacturing;
- Mixing purchased dried and/or dehydrated potato, rice, and pasta and packaging them with other purchased ingredients, and manufacturing prepared frosting--are classified in U.S. Industry 311999, All Other Miscellaneous Food Manufacturing;
- Manufacturing coffee extracts and/or coffee-based syrups--are classified in Industry 311920, Coffee and Tea Manufacturing;
- Manufacturing liquid meat extracts from slaughtered or purchased carcasses--are classified in Industry 31161, Animal Slaughtering and Processing;
- Manufacturing synthetic food colorings--are classified in Industry 325130, Synthetic Dye and Pigment Manufacturing; and
- Manufacturing natural organic colorings for nonfood uses--are classified in U.S. Industry 325199, All Other Basic Organic Chemical Manufacturing.

T—Canadian, Mexican, and United States industries are comparable.

**31199    All Other Food Manufacturing<sup>T</sup>**

This industry comprises establishments primarily engaged in manufacturing food (except animal food; grain and oilseed milling; sugar and confectionery products; preserved fruits, vegetables, and specialty foods; dairy products; meat products; seafood products; baked goods and tortillas; snack foods; coffee and tea; flavoring syrups and concentrates; seasonings; and dressings). Included in this industry are establishments primarily engaged in mixing purchased dried and/or dehydrated ingredients, including those mixing purchased dried and/or dehydrated ingredients for soup mixes and bouillon.

*Illustrative Examples:*

Baking powder manufacturing
Cut or peeled fresh vegetables manufacturing
Dessert puddings manufacturing
Egg substitutes manufacturing
Sweetening syrups (except pure maple) manufacturing

Fresh pasta manufacturing
Fresh pizza manufacturing
Honey processing
Popcorn (except popped) manufacturing
Powdered drink mixes (except chocolate, coffee, tea, or milk based) manufacturing

*Cross-References.*        Establishments primarily engaged in--

- Manufacturing animal foods--are classified in Industry Group 3111, Animal Food Manufacturing;
- Milling grains and oilseeds--are classified in Industry Group 3112, Grain and Oilseed Milling;
- Manufacturing sugar and confectionery products--are classified in Industry Group 3113, Sugar and Confectionery Product Manufacturing;
- Preserving fruit, vegetables, and specialty foods--are classified in Industry Group 3114, Fruit and Vegetable Preserving and Specialty Food Manufacturing;
- Manufacturing dairy products--are classified in Industry Group 3115, Dairy Product Manufacturing;
- Manufacturing meat products--are classified in Industry Group 3116, Animal Slaughtering and Processing;
- Manufacturing seafood products--are classified in Industry Group 3117, Seafood Product Preparation and Packaging;
- Manufacturing bakery products and tortillas--are classified in Industry Group 3118, Bakeries and Tortilla Manufacturing;
- Manufacturing snack foods--are classified in Industry 31191, Snack Food Manufacturing;
- Manufacturing coffee and tea--are classified in Industry 31192, Coffee and Tea Manufacturing;
- Manufacturing flavoring syrups and concentrates (except chocolate and coffee-based)--are classified in Industry 31193, Flavoring Syrup and Concentrate Manufacturing;
- Manufacturing seasonings and dressings--are classified in Industry 31194, Seasoning and Dressing Manufacturing;
- Milling rice and packaging it with other ingredients--are classified in Industry 31121, Flour Milling and Malt Manufacturing;
- Manufacturing dry pasta and packaging it with other ingredients--are classified in Industry 31182, Cookie, Cracker, and Pasta Manufacturing;
- Drying and/or dehydrating ingredients and packaging them with other purchased ingredients--are classified in Industry 31142, Fruit and Vegetable Canning, Pickling, and Drying;
- Reducing maple sap to maple syrup--are classified in Industry 11199, All Other Crop Farming; and
- Preparing and selling food for immediate consumption--are classified in Industry 72251, Restaurants and Other Eating Places.

**311991  Perishable Prepared Food Manufacturing**

This U.S. industry comprises establishments primarily engaged in manufacturing perishable prepared foods, such as salads, sandwiches, prepared meals, fresh pizza, fresh pasta, and peeled or cut vegetables.

---

T—Canadian, Mexican, and United States industries are comparable.

*Cross-References.*

  Establishments primarily engaged in preparing and selling food for immediate consumption are classified in Industry 72251, Restaurants and Other Eating Places.

**311999  All Other Miscellaneous Food Manufacturing**

  This U.S. industry comprises establishments primarily engaged in manufacturing food (except animal food; grain and oilseed milling; sugar and confectionery products; preserved fruits, vegetables, and specialties; dairy products; meat products; seafood products; bakeries and tortillas; snack foods; coffee and tea; flavoring syrups and concentrates; seasonings and dressings; and perishable prepared food).  Included in this industry are establishments primarily engaged in mixing purchased dried and/or dehydrated ingredients including those mixing purchased dried and/or dehydrated ingredients for soup mixes and bouillon.

*Illustrative Examples:*

Baking powder manufacturing
Cake frosting, prepared, manufacturing
Dessert puddings manufacturing
Sweetening syrups (except pure maple) manufacturing
Egg substitutes manufacturing

Gelatin dessert preparations manufacturing
Honey processing
Powdered drink mixes (except chocolate, coffee, tea, or milk based) manufacturing
Popcorn (except popped) manufacturing
Yeast manufacturing

*Cross-References.*        Establishments primarily engaged in--

- Manufacturing animal foods--are classified in Industry Group 3111, Animal Food Manufacturing;
- Milling grains and oilseeds--are classified in Industry Group 3112, Grain and Oilseed Milling;
- Manufacturing sugar and confectionery products--are classified in Industry Group 3113, Sugar and Confectionery Product Manufacturing;
- Preserving fruit, vegetable, and specialty foods--are classified in Industry Group 3114, Fruit and Vegetable Preserving and Specialty Food Manufacturing;
- Manufacturing dairy products--are classified in Industry Group 3115, Dairy Product Manufacturing;
- Manufacturing meat products--are classified in Industry Group 3116, Animal Slaughtering and Processing;
- Manufacturing seafood products--are classified in Industry Group 3117, Seafood Product Preparation and Packaging;
- Manufacturing bakery products and tortillas--are classified in Industry Group 3118, Bakeries and Tortilla Manufacturing;
- Manufacturing snack foods--are classified in Industry 31191, Snack Food Manufacturing;
- Manufacturing coffee and tea--are classified in Industry 31192, Coffee and Tea Manufacturing;
- Manufacturing flavoring syrups and concentrates (except coffee-based)--are classified in Industry 31193, Flavoring Syrup and Concentrate Manufacturing;
- Manufacturing seasonings and dressings--are classified in Industry 31194, Seasoning and Dressing Manufacturing;
- Manufacturing perishable prepared foods--are classified in U.S. Industry 311991, Perishable Prepared Food Manufacturing;
- Milling rice and packaging it with other ingredients--are classified in U.S. Industry 311212, Rice Milling;
- Manufacturing dry pasta and packaging it with ingredients--are classified in U.S. Industry 311824, Dry Pasta, Dough, and Flour Mixes Manufacturing from Purchased Flour;
- Drying and/or dehydrating ingredients and packaging them with other purchased ingredients--are classified in U.S. Industry 311423, Dried and Dehydrated Food Manufacturing;
- Reducing maple sap to maple syrup--are classified in U.S. Industry 111998, All Other Miscellaneous Crop Farming; and
- Preparing and selling food (including popcorn) for immediate consumption--are classified in Industry 72251, Restaurants and Other Eating Places.

---

T—Canadian, Mexican, and United States industries are comparable.

## 312    Beverage and Tobacco Product Manufacturing[T]

Industries in the Beverage and Tobacco Product Manufacturing subsector manufacture beverages and tobacco products. The Beverage Manufacturing industry group includes three types of establishments: (1) those that manufacture nonalcoholic beverages; (2) those that manufacture alcoholic beverages through the fermentation process; and (3) those that produce distilled alcoholic beverages. Ice manufacturing, while not a beverage, is included with nonalcoholic beverage manufacturing because it uses the same production process as water purification.

In the case of activities related to the manufacture of beverages, the structure follows the defined production processes. Brandy, a distilled beverage, is not placed under distillery product manufacturing, but rather under winery product manufacturing since the production process used in the manufacturing of alcoholic grape-based beverages produces both wines (fermented beverage) and brandies (distilled beverage).

The Tobacco Manufacturing industry group includes two types of establishments: (1) those engaged in redrying and stemming tobacco and (2) those that manufacture tobacco products, such as cigarettes and cigars.

## 3121    Beverage Manufacturing[T]

This industry group comprises establishments primarily engaged in manufacturing soft drinks and ice; purifying and bottling water; and manufacturing brewery, winery, and distillery products.

## 31211    Soft Drink and Ice Manufacturing[T]

This industry comprises establishments primarily engaged in one or more of the following: (1) manufacturing soft drinks; (2) manufacturing ice; and (3) purifying and bottling water.

*Cross-References.*          Establishments primarily engaged in--

- Canning fruit and vegetable juices--are classified in Industry 31142, Fruit and Vegetable Canning, Pickling, and Drying;
- Manufacturing soft drink bases--are classified in Industry 31193, Flavoring Syrup and Concentrate Manufacturing;
- Manufacturing nonalcoholic cider--are classified in Industry 31194, Seasoning and Dressing Manufacturing;
- Manufacturing dry ice--are classified in Industry 32512, Industrial Gas Manufacturing;
- Retailing ice through vending machines that they service--are classified in Industry 44513, Convenience Retailers and Vending Machine Operators;
- Manufacturing milk-based drinks--are classified in Industry 31151, Dairy Product (except Frozen) Manufacturing;
- Manufacturing nonalcoholic beers--are classified in Industry 31212, Breweries;
- Manufacturing nonalcoholic wines--are classified in Industry 31213, Wineries; and
- Bottling purchased purified water and wholesaling bottled water--are classified in Industry 42449, Other Grocery and Related Products Merchant Wholesalers.

## 312111  Soft Drink Manufacturing

This U.S. industry comprises establishments primarily engaged in manufacturing soft drinks and artificially carbonated waters.

*Cross-References.*          Establishments primarily engaged in--

- Canning fruit and vegetable juices--are classified in U.S. Industry 311421, Fruit and Vegetable Canning;
- Manufacturing fruit syrups for flavoring--are classified in Industry 311930, Flavoring Syrup and Concentrate Manufacturing;
- Manufacturing nonalcoholic cider--are classified in U.S. Industry 311941, Mayonnaise, Dressing, and Other Prepared Sauce Manufacturing;

---

T—Canadian, Mexican, and United States industries are comparable.

- Purifying and bottling water (except artificially carbonated and flavored water)--are classified in U.S. Industry 312112, Bottled Water Manufacturing;
- Manufacturing milk-based drinks--are classified in U.S. Industry 311511, Fluid Milk Manufacturing;
- Manufacturing nonalcoholic beers--are classified in Industry 312120, Breweries; and
- Manufacturing nonalcoholic wines--are classified in Industry 312130, Wineries.

### 312112  Bottled Water Manufacturing

This U.S. industry comprises establishments primarily engaged in purifying and bottling water (including naturally carbonated).

*Cross-References.*          Establishments primarily engaged in--

- Manufacturing artificially carbonated or flavored waters--are classified in U.S. Industry 312111, Soft Drink Manufacturing; and
- Bottling purchased purified water and wholesaling bottled water--are classified in Industry 424490, Other Grocery and Related Products Merchant Wholesalers.

### 312113  Ice Manufacturing

This U.S. industry comprises establishments primarily engaged in manufacturing ice.

*Cross-References.*          Establishments primarily engaged in--

- Manufacturing dry ice--are classified in Industry 325120, Industrial Gas Manufacturing; and
- Retailing ice through vending machines that they service--are classified in U.S. Industry 445132, Vending Machine Operators.

### 31212  Breweries[T]
See industry description for 312120.

### 312120  Breweries

This industry comprises establishments primarily engaged in brewing beer, ale, lager, malt liquors, and nonalcoholic beer.

*Cross-References.*          Establishments primarily engaged in--

- Bottling or canning purchased malt liquors and wholesaling bottled or canned malt liquors--are classified in Industry 424810, Beer and Ale Merchant Wholesalers; and
- Manufacturing malt--are classified in U.S. Industry 311213, Malt Manufacturing.

### 31213  Wineries[T]
See industry description for 312130.

### 312130  Wineries

This industry comprises establishments primarily engaged in one or more of the following: (1) growing grapes and manufacturing wines and brandies; (2) manufacturing wines and brandies from grapes and other fruits grown elsewhere; and (3) blending wines and brandies.

*Cross-References.*          Establishments primarily engaged in--

- Bottling purchased wines and wholesaling bottled wines--are classified in Industry 424820, Wine and Distilled Alcoholic Beverage Merchant Wholesalers; and

---

T—Canadian, Mexican, and United States industries are comparable.

- Growing grapes without manufacturing wine--are classified in U.S. Industry 111332, Grape Vineyards.

## 31214 Distilleries[T]
See industry description for 312140.

## 312140 Distilleries

This industry comprises establishments primarily engaged in one or more of the following: (1) distilling potable liquors (except brandies); (2) distilling and blending liquors; and (3) blending and mixing liquors and other ingredients.

*Cross-References.*        Establishments primarily engaged in--

- Manufacturing nonpotable ethyl alcohol--are classified in U.S. Industry 325193, Ethyl Alcohol Manufacturing;
- Bottling purchased liquors and wholesaling bottled liquors--are classified in Industry 424820, Wine and Distilled Alcoholic Beverage Merchant Wholesalers; and
- Manufacturing brandies--are classified in Industry 312130, Wineries.

## 3122 Tobacco Manufacturing[T]

## 31223 Tobacco Manufacturing
See industry description for 312230.

## 312230 Tobacco Manufacturing

This industry comprises establishments primarily engaged in (1) stemming and redrying tobacco and/or (2) manufacturing cigarettes or other tobacco products.

*Illustrative Examples:*

Chewing tobacco manufacturing
Cigar manufacturing
Cigarettes manufacturing (except electronic)

Snuff manufacturing
Prepared pipe tobacco manufacturing
Tobacco leaf processing and aging

*Cross-References.*        Establishments primarily engaged in--

- Manufacturing tobacco pipes or electronic cigarettes--are classified in U.S. Industry 339999, All Other Miscellaneous Manufacturing;
- Manufacturing electronic cigarette vapor liquids, including closed refills--are classified in U.S. Industry 325998, All Other Miscellaneous Chemical Product and Preparation Manufacturing;
- Selling leaf tobacco as merchant wholesalers that also engage in stemming tobacco--are classified in Industry 424940, Tobacco Product and Electronic Cigarette Merchant Wholesalers; and
- Selling leaf tobacco as agents or brokers that also engage in stemming tobacco--are classified in Industry 425120, Wholesale Trade Agents and Brokers.

## 313 Textile Mills[T]

Industries in the Textile Mills subsector group establishments that transform a basic fiber (natural or synthetic) into a product, such as yarn or fabric that is further manufactured into usable items, such as apparel, sheets, towels, and textile bags for individual or industrial consumption. The further manufacturing may be performed in the same establishment and classified in this subsector, or it may be performed at a separate establishment and be classified elsewhere in the Manufacturing sector.

The main processes in this subsector include preparation and spinning of fiber, knitting or weaving of fabric, and the finishing of the textile. The NAICS structure follows and captures this process flow. Major industries in this

T--Canadian, Mexican, and United States industries are comparable.

flow, such as preparation of fibers, weaving of fabric, knitting of fabric, and fiber and fabric finishing, are uniquely identified. Texturizing, throwing, twisting, and winding of yarn contain aspects of both fiber preparation and fiber finishing and are classified with preparation of fibers rather than with finishing of fibers.

NAICS separates the manufacturing of primary textiles and the manufacturing of textile products (except apparel) produced from purchased primary textiles, such as fabric. The manufacturing of textile products (except apparel) from purchased fabric is classified in Subsector 314, Textile Product Mills, and apparel from purchased fabric is classified in Subsector 315, Apparel Manufacturing.

Excluded from this subsector are establishments that weave or knit fabric and make garments. These establishments are included in Subsector 315, Apparel Manufacturing.

**3131     Fiber, Yarn, and Thread Mills**[T]

**31311     Fiber, Yarn, and Thread Mills**[T]
          See industry description for 313110.

**313110     Fiber, Yarn, and Thread Mills**

This industry comprises establishments primarily engaged in one or more of the following: (1) spinning yarn; (2) manufacturing thread of any fiber; (3) texturizing, throwing, twisting, and winding purchased yarn or manmade fibers and filaments; and (4) producing hemp yarn and further processing into rope or bags.

*Cross-References.*

Establishments primarily engaged in manufacturing artificial and synthetic fibers and filaments and texturizing these filaments are classified in Industry 325220, Artificial and Synthetic Fibers and Filaments Manufacturing.

**3132     Fabric Mills**[T]

This industry group comprises establishments primarily engaged in one of the following: (1) weaving broadwoven fabrics and felts (except tire fabrics and rugs); (2) weaving or braiding narrow fabrics; (3) making fabric-covered elastic yarn and thread; (4) manufacturing Schiffli machine embroideries; (5) manufacturing nonwoven fabrics and felts; (6) knitting weft (i.e., circular) and warp (i.e., flat) fabric; (7) knitting and finishing weft and warp fabric; (8) manufacturing lace; or (9) manufacturing, dyeing, and finishing lace and lace goods.

**31321     Broadwoven Fabric Mills**[T]
          See industry description for 313210.

**313210     Broadwoven Fabric Mills**

This industry comprises establishments primarily engaged in weaving broadwoven fabrics and felts (except tire fabrics and rugs). Establishments in this industry may weave only, weave and finish, or weave, finish, and further fabricate fabric products.

*Cross-References.*          Establishments primarily engaged in--

- Weaving widths specifically constructed for cutting to narrow widths--are classified in Industry 313220, Narrow Fabric Mills and Schiffli Machine Embroidery;
- Weaving or tufting carpet and rugs--are classified in Industry 314110, Carpet and Rug Mills; and
- Making tire cord and tire fabrics--are classified in U.S. Industry 314994, Rope, Cordage, Twine, Tire Cord, and Tire Fabric Mills.

**31322     Narrow Fabric Mills and Schiffli Machine Embroidery**[T]
          See industry description for 313220.

---

T—Canadian, Mexican, and United States industries are comparable.

**313220  Narrow Fabric Mills and Schiffli Machine Embroidery**

This industry comprises establishments primarily engaged in one or more of the following: (1) weaving or braiding narrow fabrics in their final form or initially made in wider widths that are specially constructed for narrower widths; (2) making fabric-covered elastic yarn and thread; and (3) manufacturing Schiffli machine embroideries. Establishments in this industry may weave only; weave and finish; or weave, finish, and further fabricate fabric products.

**31323  Nonwoven Fabric Mills[T]**
See industry description for 313230.

**313230  Nonwoven Fabric Mills**

This industry comprises establishments primarily engaged in manufacturing nonwoven fabrics and felts. Processes used include bonding and/or interlocking fibers by mechanical, chemical, thermal, or solvent means, or by combinations thereof.

**31324  Knit Fabric Mills[T]**
See industry description for 313240.

**313240  Knit Fabric Mills**

This industry comprises establishments primarily engaged in one of the following: (1) knitting weft (i.e., circular) and warp (i.e., flat) fabric; (2) knitting and finishing weft and warp fabric; (3) manufacturing lace; or (4) manufacturing, dyeing, and finishing lace and lace goods. Establishments in this industry may knit only; knit and finish; or knit, finish, and further fabricate fabric products (except apparel).

*Cross-References.*

Establishments primarily engaged in knitting apparel are classified in Industry 315120, Apparel Knitting Mills.

**3133     Textile and Fabric Finishing and Fabric Coating Mills[T]**

This industry group comprises establishments primarily engaged in one of the following: (1) finishing textiles, fabrics, and apparel; (2) converting fabrics and textiles by buying fabric goods in the grey, having them finished on contract, and selling them at wholesale; or (3) coating, laminating, varnishing, waxing, and rubberizing textiles and apparel.

**31331   Textile and Fabric Finishing Mills[T]**
See industry description for 313310.

**313310  Textile and Fabric Finishing Mills**

This industry comprises (1) establishments primarily engaged in finishing textiles, fabrics, and apparel and (2) establishments of converters who buy fabric goods in the grey, have them finished on contract, and sell at wholesale. Finishing operations include: bleaching, dyeing, printing (e.g., roller, screen, flock, plisse), stonewashing, and other mechanical finishing, such as preshrinking, shrinking, sponging, calendering, mercerizing, and napping; as well as cleaning, scouring, and the preparation of natural fibers and raw stock.

*Cross-References.*          Establishments primarily engaged in--

- Coating or impregnating fabrics--are classified in Industry 313320, Fabric Coating Mills;
- Knitting or knitting and finishing fabric--are classified in Industry 313240, Knit Fabric Mills;
- Manufacturing and finishing apparel--are classified in Subsector 315, Apparel Manufacturing;
- Weaving and finishing fabrics--are classified in Industry Group 3132, Fabric Mills;

T—Canadian, Mexican, and United States industries are comparable.

- Manufacturing and finishing rugs and carpets--are classified in Industry 314110, Carpet and Rug Mills; and
- Printing on apparel--are classified in Industry 32311, Printing.

### 31332  Fabric Coating Mills[T]
See industry description for 313320.

### 313320  Fabric Coating Mills

This industry comprises establishments primarily engaged in coating, laminating, varnishing, waxing, and rubberizing textiles and apparel.

*Cross-References.*

Establishments primarily engaged in dyeing and finishing textiles are classified in Industry 313310, Textile and Fabric Finishing Mills.

### 314     Textile Product Mills[T]

Industries in the Textile Product Mills subsector group establishments that make textile products (except apparel). With a few exceptions, processes used by these establishments are generally cut and sew (i.e., purchasing fabric and cutting and sewing to make nonapparel textile products, such as sheets and towels).

### 3141    Textile Furnishings Mills[T]

This industry group comprises establishments primarily engaged in (1) manufacturing woven, tufted, and other carpets and rugs and (2) manufacturing household textile products from purchased materials. The household textile products may be made on a stock or custom basis for sale to individual retail customers.

### 31411   Carpet and Rug Mills[T]
See industry description for 314110.

### 314110  Carpet and Rug Mills

This industry comprises establishments primarily engaged in (1) manufacturing woven, tufted, and other carpets and rugs, such as art squares, floor mattings, needlepunch carpeting, and door mats and mattings, from textile materials or from twisted paper, grasses, reeds, sisal, jute, or rags and/or (2) finishing carpets and rugs.

### 31412   Curtain and Linen Mills[T]
See industry description for 314120.

### 314120  Curtain and Linen Mills

This industry comprises establishments primarily engaged in manufacturing household textile products, such as curtains, draperies, linens, bedspreads, sheets, tablecloths, towels, and shower curtains, from purchased materials. The household textile products may be made on a stock or custom basis for sale to individual retail customers.

*Cross-References.*          Establishments primarily engaged in--

- Weaving broadwoven fabrics--are classified in Industry 313210, Broadwoven Fabric Mills;
- Manufacturing lace curtains on lace machines--are classified in Industry 313240, Knit Fabric Mills;
- Manufacturing textile blanket, wardrobe, and laundry bags--are classified in Industry 314910, Textile Bag and Canvas Mills; and
- Manufacturing mops--are classified in U.S. Industry 339994, Broom, Brush, and Mop Manufacturing.

---

T—Canadian, Mexican, and United States industries are comparable.

## 3149  Other Textile Product Mills<sup>T</sup>

This industry group comprises establishments primarily engaged in making textile products (except carpets and rugs, curtains and draperies, and other household textile products) from purchased materials.

### 31491  Textile Bag and Canvas Mills<sup>T</sup>
See industry description for 314910.

### 314910  Textile Bag and Canvas Mills

This industry comprises establishments primarily engaged in manufacturing textile bags (except luggage) or other canvas and canvas-like products, such as awnings, sails, tarpaulins, and tents from purchased textile fabrics or yarns.

*Illustrative Examples:*

Covers (e.g., boat, swimming pool, truck) made from purchased fabrics
Laundry bags made from purchased woven or knitted materials

Seed bags made from purchased woven or knitted materials
Textile bags made from purchased woven or knitted materials

*Cross-References.*    Establishments primarily engaged in--

- Manufacturing plastic bags--are classified in U.S. Industry 326111, Plastics Bag and Pouch Manufacturing;
- Manufacturing canvas blinds and shades--are classified in Industry 337920, Blind and Shade Manufacturing; and
- Manufacturing luggage (all materials) and handbags and purses of leather or other material (except precious metal)--are classified in Industry 316990, Other Leather and Allied Product Manufacturing.

### 31499  All Other Textile Product Mills<sup>T</sup>

This industry comprises establishments primarily engaged in manufacturing nonapparel textile products (except carpet, rugs, curtains, linens, bags, and canvas products) from purchased materials.  This industry includes establishments primarily engaged in decorative stitching such as embroidery or other art needlework on textile products, including apparel.

*Illustrative Examples:*

Batts and batting (except nonwoven fabrics) manufacturing
Carpet cutting and binding
Diapers (except disposable) made from purchased materials
Fishing nets made from purchased materials

Embroidering on textile products or apparel for the trade
Ropes (except wire rope) manufacturing
Sleeping bags manufacturing
Tire cord and fabric, all materials, manufacturing
Twines manufacturing

*Cross-References.*    Establishments primarily engaged in--

- Manufacturing yarns and thread--are classified in Industry 31311, Fiber, Yarn, and Thread Mills;
- Manufacturing carpets and rugs--are classified in Industry 31411, Carpet and Rug Mills;
- Manufacturing apparel--are classified in Subsector 315, Apparel Manufacturing;
- Manufacturing curtains and linens--are classified in Industry 31412, Curtain and Linen Mills; and
- Manufacturing textile bags and canvas products--are classified in Industry 31491, Textile Bag and Canvas Mills.

---

T—Canadian, Mexican, and United States industries are comparable.

## 314994 Rope, Cordage, Twine, Tire Cord, and Tire Fabric Mills

This U.S. industry comprises establishments primarily engaged in (1) manufacturing rope, cable, cordage, twine, and related products from all materials (e.g., abaca, sisal, henequen, cotton, paper, jute, flax, manmade fibers including glass) and/or (2) manufacturing cord and fabric of polyester, rayon, cotton, glass, steel, or other materials for use in reinforcing rubber tires, industrial belting, and similar uses.

*Cross-References.*

Establishments primarily engaged in spinning yarns and filaments are classified in Industry 313110, Fiber, Yarn, and Thread Mills.

## 314999 All Other Miscellaneous Textile Product Mills

This U.S. industry comprises establishments primarily engaged in manufacturing textile products (except carpets and rugs; curtains and linens; textile bags and canvas products; rope, cordage, and twine; and tire cords and tire fabrics) from purchased materials. These establishments may further embellish the textile products they manufacture with decorative stitching. Establishments primarily engaged in adding decorative stitching such as embroidery or other art needlework on textile products, including apparel, on a contract or fee basis for the trade, are included in this industry.

*Illustrative Examples:*

Batts and batting (except nonwoven fabrics) manufacturing
Embroidering on textile products or apparel for the trade
Fishing nets made from purchased materials
Carpet cutting and binding

Sleeping bags manufacturing
Diapers (except disposable) made from purchased materials
Textile fire hoses made from purchased materials
Dust cloths made from purchased fabric
Weatherstripping made from purchased textiles

*Cross-References.*        Establishments primarily engaged in--

- Manufacturing yarns and thread--are classified in Industry 313110, Fiber, Yarn, and Thread Mills;
- Manufacturing carpets and rugs--are classified in Industry 314110, Carpet and Rug Mills;
- Manufacturing apparel--are classified in Subsector 315, Apparel Manufacturing;
- Manufacturing curtains and linens--are classified in Industry 314120, Curtain and Linen Mills;
- Manufacturing textile bags and canvas products--are classified in Industry 314910, Textile Bag and Canvas Mills; and
- Manufacturing rope, cordage, twine, tire cord, and tire fabrics--are classified in U.S. Industry 314994, Rope, Cordage, Twine, Tire Cord, and Tire Fabric Mills.

## 315    Apparel Manufacturing[T]

Industries in the Apparel Manufacturing subsector group establishments with two distinct manufacturing processes: (1) cut and sew (i.e., purchasing fabric and cutting and sewing to make a garment) and (2) the manufacture of garments in establishments that first knit fabric and then cut and sew the fabric into a garment. The Apparel Manufacturing subsector includes a diverse range of establishments manufacturing full lines of ready-to-wear apparel and custom apparel: apparel contractors, performing cutting or sewing operations on materials owned by others; jobbers, performing entrepreneurial functions involved in apparel manufacturing; and tailors, manufacturing custom garments for individual clients. Knitting fabric, when done alone, is classified in the Textile Mills subsector, but when knitting is combined with the production of complete garments, the activity is classified in the Apparel Manufacturing subsector.

## 3151    Apparel Knitting Mills[T]

---

T—Canadian, Mexican, and United States industries are comparable.

**31512    Apparel Knitting Mills<sup>T</sup>**
See industry description for 315120.

**315120   Apparel Knitting Mills**

This industry comprises establishments primarily engaged in knitting apparel or knitting fabric and then manufacturing apparel. Jobbers, performing entrepreneurial functions involved in knitting apparel and accessories, are included.

*Cross-References.*            Establishments primarily engaged in--

- Manufacturing outerwear, underwear, and nightwear from purchased fabric--are classified in Industry Group 3152, Cut and Sew Apparel Manufacturing;
- Finishing apparel products only--are classified in Industry 313310, Textile and Fabric Finishing Mills;
- Manufacturing slipper socks from purchased socks--are classified in Industry 316210, Footwear Manufacturing; and
- Manufacturing orthopedic hosiery--are classified in U.S. Industry 339113, Surgical Appliance and Supplies Manufacturing.

**3152     Cut and Sew Apparel Manufacturing<sup>T</sup>**

This industry group comprises establishments primarily engaged in manufacturing cut and sew apparel from woven fabric or purchased knit fabric. Included in this industry group is a diverse range of establishments manufacturing full lines of ready-to-wear apparel and custom apparel: apparel contractors, performing cutting or sewing operations on materials owned by others; jobbers, performing entrepreneurial functions involved in apparel manufacturing; and tailors, manufacturing custom garments for individual clients. Establishments weaving or knitting fabric, without manufacturing apparel, are classified in Subsector 313, Textile Mills.

**31521    Cut and Sew Apparel Contractors**
See industry description for 315210.

**315210   Cut and Sew Apparel Contractors**

This industry comprises establishments commonly referred to as contractors primarily engaged in (1) cutting materials owned by others for apparel and accessories and/or (2) sewing materials owned by others for apparel and accessories.

*Cross-References.*            Establishments primarily engaged in--

- Manufacturing cut and sew apparel from purchased fabric--are classified in Industry 315250, Cut and Sew Apparel Manufacturing (except Contractors);
- Manufacturing apparel accessories from purchased fabric--are classified in Industry 315990, Apparel Accessories and Other Apparel Manufacturing; and
- Embroidering apparel on a contract or fee basis for the trade--are classified in U.S. Industry 314999, All Other Miscellaneous Textile Product Mills.

**31525    Cut and Sew Apparel Manufacturing (except Contractors)**
See industry description for 315250.

**315250   Cut and Sew Apparel Manufacturing (except Contractors)**

This industry comprises establishments primarily engaged in manufacturing cut and sew apparel from purchased fabric. Clothing jobbers, who perform entrepreneurial functions involved in apparel manufacture, including buying raw materials, designing and preparing samples, arranging for apparel to be made from their materials, and marketing finished apparel, are included.

---

T—Canadian, Mexican, and United States industries are comparable.

*Cross-References.*          Establishments primarily engaged in--

- Cutting and/or sewing materials owned by others for apparel--are classified in Industry 315210, Cut and Sew Apparel Contractors;
- Knitting apparel or knitting fabric and manufacturing apparel--are classified in Industry 315120, Apparel Knitting Mills;
- Manufacturing fur and leather mittens and gloves--are classified in Industry 315990, Apparel Accessories and Other Apparel Manufacturing;
- Dyeing and dressing furs--are classified in Industry 316110, Leather and Hide Tanning and Finishing; and
- Manufacturing cloth diapers--are classified in U.S. Industry 314999, All Other Miscellaneous Textile Product Mills.

**3159      Apparel Accessories and Other Apparel Manufacturing<sup>T</sup>**

**31599    Apparel Accessories and Other Apparel Manufacturing<sup>T</sup>**
See industry description for 315990.

**315990  Apparel Accessories and Other Apparel Manufacturing**

This industry comprises establishments primarily engaged in manufacturing apparel and accessories (except apparel knitting mills, cut and sew apparel contractors, and cut and sew apparel manufacturing (except contractors)). Jobbers, who perform entrepreneurial functions involved in apparel accessories manufacture, including buying raw materials, designing and preparing samples, arranging for apparel accessories to be made from their materials, and marketing finished apparel accessories, are included. Examples of products made by these establishments are belts, caps, gloves (except medical, safety, sporting), hats, and neckties.

*Cross-References.*          Establishments primarily engaged in--

- Cutting and/or sewing materials owned by others for apparel and apparel accessories--are classified in Industry 315210, Cut and Sew Apparel Contractors;
- Manufacturing paper hats and caps--are classified in U.S. Industry 322299, All Other Converted Paper Product Manufacturing;
- Manufacturing plastics or rubber hats and caps (except bathing caps)--are classified in Subsector 326, Plastics and Rubber Products Manufacturing;
- Manufacturing athletic gloves, such as boxing gloves, baseball gloves, golf gloves, batting gloves, and racquetball gloves--are classified in Industry 339920, Sporting and Athletic Goods Manufacturing;
- Manufacturing metal fabric, metal mesh, or rubber gloves--are classified in U.S. Industry 339113, Surgical Appliance and Supplies Manufacturing;
- Knitting apparel, mittens, gloves, hats, and caps or knitting fabric and manufacturing apparel, mittens, gloves, hats, and caps--are classified in Industry 315120, Apparel Knitting Mills; and
- Manufacturing cut and sew apparel from purchased fabric, including manufacturing fur and leather apparel--are classified in Industry 315250, Cut and Sew Apparel Manufacturing (except Contractors).

**316      Leather and Allied Product Manufacturing<sup>T</sup>**

Establishments in the Leather and Allied Product Manufacturing subsector transform hides into leather by tanning or curing and fabricating the leather into products for final consumption. This subsector also includes the manufacture of similar products from other materials, including products (except apparel) made from "leather substitutes," such as rubber, plastics, or textiles. Rubber footwear, textile luggage, and plastics purses or wallets are examples of "leather substitute" products included in this subsector. The products made from leather substitutes are included in this subsector because they are made in similar ways leather products are made (e.g., luggage). They are made in the same establishments, so it is not practical to separate them.

The inclusion of leather and hide tanning and finishing in this subsector is partly because it is a relatively small industry that has few close neighbors as a production process, partly because leather is an input to some of the other products classified in this subsector, and partly for historical reasons.

---

T—Canadian, Mexican, and United States industries are comparable.

**3161  Leather and Hide Tanning and Finishing$^T$**

**31611  Leather and Hide Tanning and Finishing$^T$**
See industry description for 316110.

**316110  Leather and Hide Tanning and Finishing**

This industry comprises establishments primarily engaged in one or more of the following: (1) tanning, currying, and finishing hides and skins; (2) having others process hides and skins on a contract basis; and (3) dyeing or dressing furs.

**3162  Footwear Manufacturing$^T$**

**31621  Footwear Manufacturing$^T$**
See industry description for 316210.

**316210  Footwear Manufacturing**

This industry comprises establishments primarily engaged in manufacturing footwear (except orthopedic extension footwear).

*Illustrative Examples:*

Athletic shoes manufacturing
Ballet slippers manufacturing
Cleated athletic shoes manufacturing
Shoes, children's and infants' (except orthopedic extension), manufacturing

Shoes, men's (except orthopedic extension), manufacturing
Shoes, women's (except orthopedic extension), manufacturing

*Cross-References.*

Establishments primarily engaged in manufacturing orthopedic extension footwear are classified in U.S. Industry 339113, Surgical Appliance and Supplies Manufacturing.

**3169  Other Leather and Allied Product Manufacturing$^T$**

**31699  Other Leather and Allied Product Manufacturing$^T$**
See industry description for 316990.

**316990  Other Leather and Allied Product Manufacturing**

This industry comprises establishments primarily engaged in manufacturing leather products (except footwear and apparel) from purchased leather or leather substitutes (e.g., fabric, plastics).

*Illustrative Examples:*

Billfolds, all materials, manufacturing
Boot and shoe cut stock and findings, leather, manufacturing
Dog furnishings (e.g., collars, harnesses, leashes, muzzles), manufacturing
Luggage, all materials, manufacturing
Shoe soles, leather, manufacturing

Purses, women's, all materials (except metal), manufacturing
Toilet kits and cases (except metal) manufacturing
Watch bands (except metal) manufacturing
Welders' jackets, leggings, and sleeves, leather, manufacturing

---

T—Canadian, Mexican, and United States industries are comparable.

*Cross-References.*     Establishments primarily engaged in--

- Manufacturing leather apparel--are classified in Industry 315250, Cut and Sew Apparel Manufacturing (except Contractors);
- Manufacturing leather gloves, mittens, belts, and apparel accessories--are classified in Industry 315990, Apparel Accessories and Other Apparel Manufacturing;
- Manufacturing footwear--are classified in Industry 316210, Footwear Manufacturing;
- Manufacturing nonleather soles--are classified elsewhere based on the primary input material;
- Manufacturing small articles made of metal carried on or about the person, including precious metal handbags and purses--are classified in Industry 339910, Jewelry and Silverware Manufacturing; and
- Manufacturing leather gaskets--are classified in U.S. Industry 339991, Gasket, Packing, and Sealing Device Manufacturing.

## 321     Wood Product Manufacturing[T]

Establishments in the Wood Product Manufacturing subsector manufacture wood products, such as lumber, plywood, veneers, wood containers, wood flooring, wood trusses, manufactured homes (i.e., mobile homes), and prefabricated wood buildings. The production processes of the Wood Product Manufacturing subsector include sawing, planing, shaping, laminating, and assembling wood products starting from logs that are cut into bolts, or lumber that then may be further cut, or shaped by lathes or other shaping tools. The lumber or other transformed wood shapes may also be subsequently planed or smoothed, and assembled into finished products, such as wood containers. The Wood Product Manufacturing subsector includes establishments that make wood products from logs and bolts that are sawed and shaped, and establishments that purchase sawed lumber and make wood products. With the exception of sawmills and wood preservation establishments, the establishments are grouped into industries mainly based on the specific products manufactured.

## 3211     Sawmills and Wood Preservation[T]

## 32111     Sawmills and Wood Preservation[T]

This industry comprises establishments primarily engaged in one or more of the following: (1) sawing dimension lumber, boards, beams, timber, poles, ties, shingles, shakes, siding, and wood chips from logs or bolts; (2) sawing round wood poles, pilings, and posts and treating them with preservatives; and (3) treating wood sawed, planed, or shaped in other establishments with creosote or other preservatives to prevent decay and to protect against fire and insects. Sawmills may plane the rough lumber that they make with a planing machine to achieve smoothness and uniformity of size.

*Cross-References.*     Establishments primarily engaged in--

- Operating portable chipper mills in the field--are classified in Industry 11331, Logging;
- Manufacturing wood products (except round wood poles, pilings, and posts) and treating them with preservatives--are classified elsewhere in Subsector 321, Wood Product Manufacturing, based on the related production process;
- Manufacturing veneer from logs and bolts or manufacturing engineered lumber and structural members other than solid wood--are classified in Industry 32121, Veneer, Plywood, and Engineered Wood Product Manufacturing; and
- Planing purchased lumber or manufacturing cut stock or dimension stock (i.e., shapes) from logs or bolts--are classified in Industry 32191, Millwork.

## 321113  Sawmills

This U.S. industry comprises establishments primarily engaged in sawing dimension lumber, boards, beams, timbers, poles, ties, shingles, shakes, siding, and wood chips from logs or bolts. Sawmills may plane the rough lumber that they make with a planing machine to achieve smoothness and uniformity of size.

---

T—Canadian, Mexican, and United States industries are comparable.

*Cross-References.*          Establishments primarily engaged in--

- Planing purchased lumber or manufacturing cut stock or dimension stock (i.e., shapes) from logs or bolts-- are classified in Industry 32191, Millwork;
- Manufacturing veneer from logs or bolts--are classified in Industry 32121, Veneer, Plywood, and Engineered Wood Product Manufacturing; and
- Operating portable chipper mills in the field--are classified in Industry 113310, Logging.

## 321114  Wood Preservation

This U.S. industry comprises establishments primarily engaged in (1) treating wood sawed, planed, or shaped in other establishments with creosote or other preservatives, such as alkaline copper quat, copper azole, and sodium borates, to prevent decay and to protect against fire and insects and/or (2) sawing round wood poles, pilings, and posts and treating them with preservatives.

*Cross-References.*

Establishments primarily engaged in manufacturing wood products (except round wood poles, pilings, and posts) and treating them with preservatives are classified elsewhere in Subsector 321, Wood Product Manufacturing, based on the related production process.

## 3212    Veneer, Plywood, and Engineered Wood Product Manufacturing[T]

## 32121   Veneer, Plywood, and Engineered Wood Product Manufacturing[T]

This industry comprises establishments primarily engaged in one or more of the following: (1) manufacturing veneer and/or plywood; (2) manufacturing engineered wood members; and (3) manufacturing reconstituted wood products.  This industry includes manufacturing plywood from veneer made in the same establishment or from veneer made in other establishments, and manufacturing plywood faced with nonwood materials, such as plastics or metal.

*Illustrative Examples:*

| | |
|---|---|
| Fabricated structural wood members manufacturing | Plywood manufacturing |
| Laminated structural wood members manufacturing | Reconstituted wood sheets and boards manufacturing |
| Medium density fiberboard (MDF) manufacturing | Roof trusses, wood, manufacturing |
| Oriented strandboard (OSB) manufacturing | Veneer mills |
| Particleboard manufacturing | Waferboard manufacturing |

*Cross-References.*          Establishments primarily engaged in--

- Manufacturing veneer and further processing that veneer into wood containers or wood container parts in the same establishment--are classified in Industry 32192, Wood Container and Pallet Manufacturing;
- Manufacturing prefabricated wood buildings or wood sections and panels for buildings--are classified in Industry 32199, All Other Wood Product Manufacturing; and
- Manufacturing solid wood structural members, such as dimension lumber and timber from logs or bolts in sawmills--are classified in Industry 32111, Sawmills and Wood Preservation.

## 321211  Hardwood Veneer and Plywood Manufacturing

This U.S. industry comprises establishments primarily engaged in manufacturing hardwood veneer and/or hardwood plywood.

---

T—Canadian, Mexican, and United States industries are comparable.

*Cross-References.*         Establishments primarily engaged in--

- Manufacturing veneer and further processing that veneer into wood containers or wood container parts--are classified in Industry 321920, Wood Container and Pallet Manufacturing;
- Manufacturing softwood veneer and softwood plywood--are classified in U.S. Industry 321212, Softwood Veneer and Plywood Manufacturing; and
- Manufacturing reconstituted wood sheets and boards--are classified in U.S. Industry 321219, Reconstituted Wood Product Manufacturing.

## 321212  Softwood Veneer and Plywood Manufacturing

This U.S. industry comprises establishments primarily engaged in manufacturing softwood veneer and/or softwood plywood.

*Cross-References.*         Establishments primarily engaged in--

- Manufacturing veneer and further processing that veneer into wood containers or wood container parts--are classified in Industry 321920, Wood Container and Pallet Manufacturing;
- Manufacturing hardwood veneer and hardwood plywood--are classified in U.S. Industry 321211, Hardwood Veneer and Plywood Manufacturing; and
- Manufacturing reconstituted wood sheets and boards--are classified in U.S. Industry 321219, Reconstituted Wood Product Manufacturing.

## 321215  Engineered Wood Member Manufacturing

This U.S. industry comprises establishments primarily engaged in manufacturing fabricated or laminated wood arches, wood roof and floor trusses, and/or other fabricated or laminated wood structural members.

*Illustrative Examples:*

Finger joint lumber manufacturing
I-joists, wood, fabricating
Laminated veneer lumber (LVL) manufacturing
Parallel strand lumber manufacturing

Timbers, structural, glue laminated or pre-engineered wood, manufacturing
Trusses, wood roof or floor, manufacturing

*Cross-References.*         Establishments primarily engaged in--

- Manufacturing prefabricated wood buildings or wood sections and panels for buildings--are classified in U.S. Industry 321992, Prefabricated Wood Building Manufacturing; and
- Manufacturing solid wood structural members, such as dimension lumber and timber from logs or bolts-- are classified in U.S. Industry 321113, Sawmills.

## 321219  Reconstituted Wood Product Manufacturing

This U.S. industry comprises establishments primarily engaged in manufacturing reconstituted wood sheets and boards.

*Illustrative Examples:*

Medium density fiberboard (MDF) manufacturing
Oriented strandboard (OSB) manufacturing
Particleboard manufacturing

Reconstituted wood sheets and boards manufacturing
Waferboard manufacturing

---

T—Canadian, Mexican, and United States industries are comparable.

*Cross-References.* Establishments primarily engaged in--

- Manufacturing softwood plywood--are classified in U.S. Industry 321212, Softwood Veneer and Plywood Manufacturing; and
- Manufacturing hardwood plywood--are classified in U.S. Industry 321211, Hardwood Veneer and Plywood Manufacturing.

## 3219 Other Wood Product Manufacturing[T]

This industry group comprises establishments primarily engaged in manufacturing wood products (except establishments operating sawmills and wood preservation facilities; and establishments manufacturing veneer, plywood, or engineered wood products).

## 32191 Millwork[T]

This industry comprises establishments primarily engaged in manufacturing hardwood and softwood cut stock and dimension stock (i.e., shapes); wood windows and wood doors; and other millwork including wood flooring. Dimension stock or cut stock is defined as lumber and worked wood products cut or shaped to specialized sizes. These establishments generally use woodworking machinery, such as jointers, planers, lathes, and routers to shape wood.

*Cross-References.* Establishments primarily engaged in--

- Manufacturing dimension lumber, boards, beams, timbers, poles, ties, shingles, shakes, siding, and wood chips from logs and bolts--are classified in Industry 32111, Sawmills and Wood Preservation;
- Fabricating millwork at the construction site--are classified in Industry 23835, Finish Carpentry Contractors; and
- Manufacturing wood furniture frames and finished wood furniture parts--are classified in Industry 33721, Office Furniture (including Fixtures) Manufacturing.

## 321911 Wood Window and Door Manufacturing

This U.S. industry comprises establishments primarily engaged in manufacturing window and door units, sash, window and door frames, and doors from wood or wood clad with metal or plastics.

*Cross-References.*

Establishments primarily engaged in fabricating wood windows or wood doors at the construction site are classified in Industry 238350, Finish Carpentry Contractors.

## 321912 Cut Stock, Resawing Lumber, and Planing

This U.S. industry comprises establishments primarily engaged in one or more of the following: (1) manufacturing dimension lumber from purchased lumber; (2) manufacturing dimension stock (i.e., shapes) or cut stock; (3) resawing the output of sawmills; and (4) planing purchased lumber. These establishments generally use woodworking machinery, such as jointers, planers, lathes, and routers to shape wood.

*Cross-References.* Establishments primarily engaged in--

- Manufacturing dimension lumber, boards, beams, timbers, poles, ties, shingles, shakes, siding, and wood chips from logs or bolts--are classified in U.S. Industry 321113, Sawmills;
- Manufacturing wood stairwork, wood molding, wood trim, and other millwork--are classified in U.S. Industry 321918, Other Millwork (including Flooring); and
- Manufacturing wood furniture frames and finished wood furniture parts--are classified in U.S. Industry 337215, Showcase, Partition, Shelving, and Locker Manufacturing.

T—Canadian, Mexican, and United States industries are comparable.

**321918  Other Millwork (including Flooring)**

This U.S. industry comprises establishments primarily engaged in manufacturing millwork (except wood windows, wood doors, and cut stock).

*Illustrative Examples:*

Clear and finger joint wood moldings manufacturing
Decorative wood moldings (e.g., base, chair rail, crown, shoe) manufacturing
Ornamental woodwork (e.g., cornices, mantel) manufacturing

Planing mills, millwork
Stairwork (e.g., newel posts, railings, stairs, staircases), wood, manufacturing
Wood flooring manufacturing
Wood shutters manufacturing

*Cross-References.*        Establishments primarily engaged in--

- Manufacturing wood windows and doors--are classified in U.S. Industry 321911, Wood Window and Door Manufacturing; and
- Manufacturing cut stock, resawing lumber, and/or planing purchased lumber--are classified in U.S. Industry 321912, Cut Stock, Resawing Lumber, and Planing.

**32192    Wood Container and Pallet Manufacturing[T]**
See industry description for 321920.

**321920  Wood Container and Pallet Manufacturing**

This industry comprises establishments primarily engaged in manufacturing wood pallets, wood box shook, wood boxes, other wood containers, and wood parts for pallets and containers.

*Cross-References.*

Establishments primarily engaged in manufacturing wood burial caskets are classified in U.S. Industry 339995, Burial Casket Manufacturing.

**32199    All Other Wood Product Manufacturing[T]**

This industry comprises establishments primarily engaged in manufacturing wood products (except establishments operating sawmills and wood preservation facilities; and establishments manufacturing veneer, plywood, engineered wood products, millwork, wood containers, or pallets).

*Illustrative Examples:*

Mobile homes manufacturing
Panels, prefabricated wood building, manufacturing
Prefabricated wood buildings manufacturing
Wood dowels manufacturing

Sections, prefabricated wood building, manufacturing
Wood handles (e.g., broom, handtool, mop) manufacturing

*Cross-References.*        Establishments primarily engaged in--

- Operating sawmills or preserving wood--are classified in Industry 32111, Sawmills and Wood Preservation;
- Manufacturing veneer, plywood, and engineered wood products--are classified in Industry 32121, Veneer, Plywood, and Engineered Wood Product Manufacturing;
- Manufacturing millwork--are classified in Industry 32191, Millwork;
- Manufacturing wood containers, pallets, and wood container parts--are classified in Industry 32192, Wood Container and Pallet Manufacturing;

---

T—Canadian, Mexican, and United States industries are comparable.

- Manufacturing travel trailers with self-contained facilities for storage of water and waste--are classified in Industry 33621, Motor Vehicle Body and Trailer Manufacturing; and
- Fabricating wood buildings or wood sections and panels for buildings at the construction site, or setting up manufactured homes (i.e., mobile homes) at the construction site--are classified in Sector 23, Construction.

## 321991  Manufactured Home (Mobile Home) Manufacturing

This U.S. industry comprises establishments primarily engaged in making manufactured homes (i.e., mobile homes) and nonresidential mobile buildings.  Manufactured homes are designed to accept permanent water, sewer, and utility connections and although equipped with wheels, they are not intended for regular highway movement.

*Cross-References.*          Establishments primarily engaged in--

- Manufacturing prefabricated wood buildings not equipped with wheels--are classified in U.S. Industry 321992, Prefabricated Wood Building Manufacturing;
- Manufacturing travel trailers with self-contained facilities for storage of water and waste--are classified in U.S. Industry 336214, Travel Trailer and Camper Manufacturing; and
- Setting up manufactured homes (i.e., mobile homes) at the construction site--are classified in Industry 238990, All Other Specialty Trade Contractors.

## 321992  Prefabricated Wood Building Manufacturing

This U.S. industry comprises establishments primarily engaged in manufacturing prefabricated wood buildings and wood sections and panels for prefabricated wood buildings.

*Cross-References.*          Establishments primarily engaged in--

- Fabricating wood buildings or wood sections and panels for buildings at the construction site--are classified in Sector 23, Construction;
- Making manufactured homes (i.e., mobile homes)--are classified in U.S. Industry 321991, Manufactured Home (Mobile Home) Manufacturing; and
- Setting up manufactured homes (i.e., mobile homes) at the construction site--are classified in Industry 238990, All Other Specialty Trade Contractors.

## 321999  All Other Miscellaneous Wood Product Manufacturing

This U.S. industry comprises establishments primarily engaged in manufacturing wood products (except establishments operating sawmills and preservation facilities; establishments manufacturing veneer, engineered wood products, millwork, wood containers, pallets, and wood container parts; and establishments making manufactured homes (i.e., mobile homes) and prefabricated buildings and components).

*Illustrative Examples:*

Cabinets (i.e., housings), wood (e.g., sewing machines, stereo, television), manufacturing
Cork products (except gaskets) manufacturing
Kiln drying lumber
Shoe trees manufacturing
Wood dowels manufacturing
Wood extension ladders manufacturing

Wood handles (e.g., broom, handtool, mop), manufacturing
Wood kitchenware manufacturing
Wood stepladders manufacturing
Wood toilet seats manufacturing
Wood toothpicks manufacturing

*Cross-References.*          Establishments primarily engaged in--

- Operating sawmills and preserving wood--are classified in Industry 32111, Sawmills and Wood Preservation;

_____

T—Canadian, Mexican, and United States industries are comparable.

- Manufacturing veneer and engineered wood products--are classified in Industry 32121, Veneer, Plywood, and Engineered Wood Product Manufacturing;
- Manufacturing millwork--are classified in Industry 32191, Millwork;
- Manufacturing boxes, box shook, wood containers, pallets, and wood parts for containers--are classified in Industry 321920, Wood Container and Pallet Manufacturing;
- Making manufactured homes (i.e., mobile homes)--are classified in U.S. Industry 321991, Manufactured Home (Mobile Home) Manufacturing; and
- Manufacturing prefabricated wood buildings or wood sections and panels for buildings--are classified in U.S. Industry 321992, Prefabricated Wood Building Manufacturing.

## 322　　Paper Manufacturing[T]

Industries in the Paper Manufacturing subsector make pulp, paper, or converted paper products. The manufacturing of these products is grouped together because they constitute a series of vertically connected processes. More than one is often carried out in a single establishment. There are essentially three activities. The manufacturing of pulp involves separating the cellulose fibers from other impurities in wood or used paper. The manufacturing of paper involves matting these fibers into a sheet. The manufacturing of converted paper products involves converting paper and other materials by various cutting and shaping techniques and includes coating and laminating activities.

The Paper Manufacturing subsector is subdivided into two industry groups, the first for the manufacturing of pulp and paper and the second for the manufacturing of converted paper products. Paper making is treated as the core activity of the subsector. Therefore, any establishment that makes paper (including paperboard), either alone or in combination with pulp manufacturing or paper converting, is classified as a paper or paperboard mill. Establishments that make pulp without making paper are classified as pulp mills. Pulp mills, paper mills, and paperboard mills comprise the first industry group.

Establishments that make products from purchased paper and other materials make up the second industry group, Converted Paper Product Manufacturing. This general activity is then subdivided based, for the most part, on process distinctions. Paperboard container manufacturing uses corrugating, cutting, and shaping machinery to form paperboard into containers. Paper bag and coated and treated paper manufacturing establishments cut and coat paper and foil. Stationery product manufacturing establishments make a variety of paper products used for writing, filing, and similar applications. Other converted paper product manufacturing includes, in particular, the conversion of sanitary paper stock into such things as tissue paper and disposable diapers.

An important process used in the Paper Bag and Coated and Treated Paper Manufacturing industry is lamination, often combined with coating. Lamination and coating make a composite material with improved properties of strength, impermeability, and so on. The laminated materials may be paper, metal foil, or plastics film. While paper is often one of the components, it is not always. Lamination of plastics film to plastics film is classified in Subsector 326, Plastics and Rubber Products Manufacturing, because establishments that do this often first make the film. The same situation holds with respect to bags. The manufacturing of bags from plastics only, whether or not laminated, is classified in Subsector 326, Plastics and Rubber Products Manufacturing.

Excluded from this subsector are photosensitive papers. These papers are chemically treated and are classified in Industry 32599, All Other Chemical Product and Preparation Manufacturing.

## 3221　　Pulp, Paper, and Paperboard Mills[T]

This industry group comprises establishments primarily engaged in manufacturing pulp, paper, or paperboard.

## 32211　　Pulp Mills[T]
See industry description for 322110.

## 322110　Pulp Mills

This industry comprises establishments primarily engaged in manufacturing pulp without manufacturing paper or paperboard. The pulp is made by separating the cellulose fibers from the other impurities in wood or other materials, such as used or recycled rags, linters, scrap paper, and straw.

---

T—Canadian, Mexican, and United States industries are comparable.

*Cross-References.*          Establishments primarily engaged in--

- Manufacturing both pulp and paper--are classified in Industry 322120, Paper Mills; and
- Manufacturing both pulp and paperboard--are classified in Industry 322130, Paperboard Mills.

**32212   Paper Mills**$^T$
See industry description for 322120.

**322120   Paper Mills**

This industry comprises establishments primarily engaged in manufacturing paper from pulp. These establishments may manufacture or purchase pulp.  In addition, the establishments may convert the paper they make. The activity of making paper classifies an establishment into this industry regardless of the output.

*Cross-References.*          Establishments primarily engaged in--

- Manufacturing pulp without manufacturing paper--are classified in Industry 322110, Pulp Mills;
- Manufacturing paperboard--are classified in Industry 322130, Paperboard Mills;
- Converting paper without manufacturing paper--are classified in Industry Group 3222, Converted Paper Product Manufacturing; and
- Manufacturing photographic sensitized paper from purchased paper--are classified in U.S. Industry 325992, Photographic Film, Paper, Plate, Chemical, and Copy Toner Manufacturing.

**32213   Paperboard Mills**$^T$
See industry description for 322130.

**322130   Paperboard Mills**

This industry comprises establishments primarily engaged in manufacturing paperboard (e.g., can/drum stock, container board, corrugating medium, folding carton stock, linerboard, tube) from pulp.  These establishments may manufacture or purchase pulp.  In addition, the establishments may also convert the paperboard they make.

*Cross-References.*          Establishments primarily engaged in--

- Manufacturing pulp without manufacturing paperboard--are classified in Industry 322110, Pulp Mills;
- Converting paperboard without manufacturing paperboard--are classified in Industry Group 3222, Converted Paper Product Manufacturing; and
- Manufacturing insulation board and other reconstituted wood fiberboard--are classified in U.S. Industry 321219, Reconstituted Wood Product Manufacturing.

**3222   Converted Paper Product Manufacturing**$^T$

This industry group comprises establishments primarily engaged in converting paper or paperboard without manufacturing paper or paperboard.

**32221   Paperboard Container Manufacturing**$^T$

This industry comprises establishments primarily engaged in converting paperboard into containers without manufacturing paperboard.  These establishments use corrugating, cutting, and shaping machinery to form paperboard into containers.  Products made by these establishments include boxes, corrugated sheets, pads, pallets, paper dishes, and fiber drums and reels.

---

T—Canadian, Mexican, and United States industries are comparable.

*Cross-References.*          Establishments primarily engaged in--

- Manufacturing similar items of plastics materials--are classified in Industry Group 3261, Plastics Product Manufacturing;
- Manufacturing paperboard and converting paperboard into containers--are classified in Industry 32213, Paperboard Mills;
- Manufacturing egg cartons, food trays, and other food containers from molded pulp--are classified in Industry 32229, Other Converted Paper Product Manufacturing;
- Manufacturing paper and converting paper into containers--are classified in Industry 32212, Paper Mills; and
- Manufacturing paper bags without manufacturing paper--are classified in Industry 32222, Paper Bag and Coated and Treated Paper Manufacturing.

## 322211  Corrugated and Solid Fiber Box Manufacturing

This U.S. industry comprises establishments primarily engaged in laminating purchased paper or paperboard into corrugated or solid fiber boxes and related products, such as pads, partitions, pallets, and corrugated paper without manufacturing paperboard.  These boxes are generally used for shipping.

*Cross-References.*          Establishments primarily engaged in--

- Manufacturing setup paperboard boxes (except corrugated or laminated solid fiber boxes)--are classified in U.S. Industry 322219, Other Paperboard Container Manufacturing;
- Manufacturing folding paperboard boxes (except corrugated or laminated solid fiber boxes)--are classified in U.S. Industry 322212, Folding Paperboard Box Manufacturing; and
- Manufacturing paperboard and converting paperboard into boxes--are classified in Industry 322130, Paperboard Mills.

## 322212  Folding Paperboard Box Manufacturing

This U.S. industry comprises establishments primarily engaged in converting paperboard (except corrugated) into folding paperboard boxes without manufacturing paper and paperboard.

*Cross-References.*          Establishments primarily engaged in--

- Manufacturing setup paperboard boxes (except corrugated or laminated solid fiber boxes) or milk cartons--are classified in U.S. Industry 322219, Other Paperboard Container Manufacturing;
- Manufacturing corrugated and solid fiber boxes--are classified in U.S. Industry 322211, Corrugated and Solid Fiber Box Manufacturing;
- Manufacturing paperboard and converting paperboard into containers--are classified in Industry 322130, Paperboard Mills;
- Manufacturing paper and converting paper into containers--are classified in Industry 322120, Paper Mills; and
- Manufacturing paper bags--are classified in Industry 322220, Paper Bag and Coated and Treated Paper Manufacturing.

## 322219  Other Paperboard Container Manufacturing

This U.S. industry comprises establishments primarily engaged in converting paperboard into paperboard containers (except corrugated, solid fiber, and folding paperboard boxes) without manufacturing paperboard.

*Illustrative Examples:*

Fiber cans and drums (i.e., all-fiber, nonfiber ends of any material) made from purchased paperboard

Milk cartons made from purchased paper or paperboard

---

T—Canadian, Mexican, and United States industries are comparable.

**census.gov/naics**

Sanitary food containers (except folding) made from purchased paper or paperboard

Setup (i.e., not shipped flat) boxes made from purchased paperboard

*Cross-References.*        Establishments primarily engaged in--

- Manufacturing sanitary food containers of solely plastics materials--are classified in Industry Group 3261, Plastics Product Manufacturing;
- Manufacturing paperboard and converting paperboard into containers--are classified in Industry 322130, Paperboard Mills;
- Manufacturing corrugated and solid fiber boxes--are classified in U.S. Industry 322211, Corrugated and Solid Fiber Box Manufacturing;
- Manufacturing folding paperboard boxes (except corrugated or laminated solid fiber boxes)--are classified in U.S. Industry 322212, Folding Paperboard Box Manufacturing; and
- Manufacturing egg cartons, food trays, and other food containers from molded pulp--are classified in U.S. Industry 322299, All Other Converted Paper Product Manufacturing.

## 32222    Paper Bag and Coated and Treated Paper Manufacturing[T]
See industry description for 322220.

## 322220  Paper Bag and Coated and Treated Paper Manufacturing

This industry comprises establishments primarily engaged in one or more of the following: (1) cutting and coating paper and paperboard; (2) cutting and laminating paper, paperboard, and other flexible materials (except plastics film to plastics film); (3) manufacturing bags, multiwall bags, sacks of paper, metal foil, coated paper, laminates, or coated combinations of paper and foil with plastics film; (4) manufacturing laminated aluminum and other converted metal foils from purchased foils; and (5) surface coating paper or paperboard.

*Cross-References.*        Establishments primarily engaged in--

- Manufacturing paper from pulp--are classified in Industry 322120, Paper Mills;
- Manufacturing textile bags--are classified in Industry 314910, Textile Bag and Canvas Mills;
- Manufacturing single wall and multiwall plastics bags--are classified in U.S. Industry 326111, Plastics Bag and Pouch Manufacturing;
- Manufacturing plastics to plastics packaging laminations--are classified in U.S. Industry 326112, Plastics Packaging Film and Sheet (including Laminated) Manufacturing;
- Manufacturing unsupported plastic film--are classified in U.S. Industry 326113, Unlaminated Plastics Film and Sheet (except Packaging) Manufacturing;
- Manufacturing photographic sensitized paper from purchased paper--are classified in U.S. Industry 325992, Photographic Film, Paper, Plate, Chemical, and Copy Toner Manufacturing;
- Printing on purchased packaging materials--are classified in Industry 32311, Printing, based on the printing process used;
- Manufacturing foil cookware, dinnerware, and other semi-rigid metal containers--are classified in U.S. Industry 332999, All Other Miscellaneous Fabricated Metal Product Manufacturing;
- Making aluminum and aluminum foil--are classified in Industry 33131, Alumina and Aluminum Production and Processing; and
- Cutting purchased aluminum foil into smaller lengths and widths--are classified in U.S. Industry 332999, All Other Miscellaneous Fabricated Metal Product Manufacturing.

## 32223    Stationery Product Manufacturing[T]
See industry description for 322230.

## 322230  Stationery Product Manufacturing

This industry comprises establishments primarily engaged in converting paper or paperboard into products used for writing, filing, art work, and similar applications.

---

T—Canadian, Mexican, and United States industries are comparable.

*Illustrative Examples:*

Computer paper, die-cut, made from purchased paper
Die-cut paper products for office use made from
purchased paper or paperboard
Envelopes (i.e., mailing, stationery) made from any
material

Stationery made from purchased paper
Tablets (e.g., memo, note, writing) made from
purchased paper
Tapes (e.g., adding machine, calculator, cash register)
made from purchased paper

*Cross-References.*

   Establishments primarily engaged in manufacturing die-cut paper and paperboard products other than office
supplies are classified in U.S. Industry 322299, All Other Converted Paper Product Manufacturing.

**32229   Other Converted Paper Product Manufacturing[T]**

   This industry comprises establishments primarily engaged in (1) converting paper and paperboard into products
(except containers, bags, coated and treated paper and paperboard, and stationery products) or (2) converting pulp
into pulp products, such as disposable diapers, or molded pulp egg cartons, food trays, and dishes.  Processes used
include laminating or lining purchased paper or paperboard.

*Illustrative Examples:*

Crepe paper made from purchased paper
Die-cut paper products (except for office use) made
from purchased paper or paperboard
Paper novelties made from purchased paper

Molded pulp products (e.g., egg cartons, food
containers, food trays) manufacturing
Sanitary products made from purchased sanitary
paper stock

*Cross-References.*          Establishments primarily engaged in--

- Manufacturing pulp from wood or from other materials--are classified in Industry 32211, Pulp Mills;
- Manufacturing paper from pulp or making pulp and manufacturing paper--are classified in Industry 32212, Paper Mills;
- Manufacturing paperboard from pulp or making pulp and manufacturing paperboard--are classified in Industry 32213, Paperboard Mills;
- Manufacturing paperboard containers--are classified in Industry 32221, Paperboard Container Manufacturing;
- Manufacturing bags of coated, laminated, or uncoated paper, of metal foil, or combinations thereof--are classified in Industry 32222, Paper Bag and Coated and Treated Paper Manufacturing; and
- Manufacturing stationery and other related office supplies--are classified in Industry 32223, Stationery Product Manufacturing.

**322291  Sanitary Paper Product Manufacturing**

   This U.S. industry comprises establishments primarily engaged in converting purchased sanitary paper stock or
wadding into sanitary paper products, such as facial tissues, handkerchiefs, table napkins, toilet paper, towels,
disposable diapers, sanitary napkins, and tampons.

**322299  All Other Converted Paper Product Manufacturing**

   This U.S. industry comprises establishments primarily engaged in converting paper or paperboard into products
(except containers, bags, coated and treated paper, stationery products, and sanitary paper products) or converting
pulp into pulp products, such as egg cartons, food trays, and other food containers from molded pulp.

---

T—Canadian, Mexican, and United States industries are comparable.

*Illustrative Examples:*

Crepe paper made from purchased paper
Die-cut paper products (except for office use) made
from purchased paper or paperboard

Molded pulp products (e.g., egg cartons, food
containers, food trays) manufacturing
Paper novelties made from purchased paper

*Cross-References.*          Establishments primarily engaged in--

- Manufacturing pulp from wood or from other materials--are classified in Industry 322110, Pulp Mills;
- Manufacturing paper from pulp or making pulp and manufacturing paper--are classified in Industry 322120, Paper Mills;
- Manufacturing paperboard from pulp or making pulp and manufacturing paperboard--are classified in Industry 322130, Paperboard Mills;
- Manufacturing paperboard containers--are classified in Industry 32221, Paperboard Container Manufacturing;
- Manufacturing bags of coated, laminated, or uncoated paper, of metal foil, or combinations thereof--are classified in Industry 322220, Paper Bag and Coated and Treated Paper Manufacturing; and
- Manufacturing stationery and other related office supplies--are classified in Industry 322230, Stationery Product Manufacturing.

## 323     Printing and Related Support Activities[T]

Industries in the Printing and Related Support Activities subsector print products, such as newspapers, books, labels, business cards, stationery, business forms, and other materials, and perform support activities, such as data imaging, platemaking services, and bookbinding. The support activities included here are an integral part of the printing industry, and a product (a printing plate, a bound book, or a computer disk or file) that is an integral part of the printing industry is almost always provided by these operations.

Processes used in printing include a variety of methods used to transfer an image from a plate, screen, film, or computer file to some medium, such as paper, plastics, metal, textile articles, or wood. The printing processes employed include, but are not limited to, lithographic, gravure, screen, flexographic, digital, and letterpress.

In contrast to many other classification systems that locate publishing of printed materials in manufacturing, NAICS classifies the publishing of printed products in Subsector 513, Publishing Industries. Though printing and publishing are often carried out by the same enterprise, it is less and less the case that these distinct activities are carried out in the same establishment. When publishing and printing are done in the same establishment, the establishment is classified in Subsector 513, Publishing Industries, in the appropriate NAICS industry even if the receipts for printing exceed those for publishing.

This subsector includes printing on clothing because the production process for that activity is printing, not clothing manufacturing. For instance, the printing of T-shirts is included in this subsector. In contrast, printing on fabric (or grey goods) is not included. This activity is part of the process of finishing the fabric and is included in Industry 31331, Textile and Fabric Finishing Mills.

Excluded from this subsector are establishment primarily engaged in manufacturing bare printed circuit boards. These establishments print, perforate, plate, screen, etch, or photoprint interconnecting pathways for electric current on laminates and are classified in Industry 33441, Semiconductor and Other Electronic Component Manufacturing. Establishments primarily providing printing brokerage services are classified in Industry 56199, All Other Support Services.

## 3231     Printing and Related Support Activities[T]

## 32311     Printing[T]

This industry comprises establishments primarily engaged in printing on apparel and textile products, paper, metal, glass, plastics, and other materials, except fabric (grey goods). The printing processes employed include, but are not limited to, lithographic, gravure, screen, flexographic, digital, and letterpress. Establishments in this industry do not manufacture the stock that they print, but may perform postprinting activities, such as folding, cutting, or laminating the materials they print, and mailing.

---

T—Canadian, Mexican, and United States industries are comparable.

*Cross-References.*          Establishments primarily engaged in--

- Providing photocopying services on photocopy equipment without performing traditional printing activities--are classified in Industry 56143, Business Service Centers;
- Printing on fabric grey goods--are classified in Industry 31331, Textile and Fabric Finishing Mills;
- Printing and publishing, known as publishers--are classified in Subsector 513, Publishing Industries;
- Performing prepress or postpress services without performing traditional printing activities--are classified in Industry 32312, Support Activities for Printing;
- Manufacturing and printing advertising specialties--are classified in the Manufacturing sector according to the products made;
- Manufacturing bare printed circuit boards--are classified in Industry 33441, Semiconductor and Other Electronic Component Manufacturing; and
- Providing printing brokerage services--are classified in Industry 56199, All Other Support Services.

## 323111  Commercial Printing (except Screen and Books)

This U.S. industry comprises establishments primarily engaged in commercial printing (except screen printing, books printing) without publishing (except fabric grey goods printing).  The printing processes used in this industry include, but are not limited to, lithographic, gravure, flexographic, letterpress, engraving, and various digital printing technologies.  This industry includes establishments engaged in commercial printing on purchased stock materials, such as stationery, invitations, labels, and similar items, on a job-order basis.  Establishments primarily engaged in traditional printing activities combined with document photocopying services (i.e., quick printers) or primarily engaged in printing graphical materials using digital printing equipment are included in this industry.

*Cross-References.*          Establishments primarily engaged in--

- Screen printing on purchased stock materials (except books, grey goods, and manifold business forms)--are classified in U.S. Industry 323113, Commercial Screen Printing;
- Printing on fabric grey goods--are classified in Industry 313310, Textile and Fabric Finishing Mills;
- Printing books and pamphlets--are classified in U.S. Industry 323117, Books Printing;
- Manufacturing paper stock materials, including stationery, invitations, labels, and similar items--are classified in Subsector 322, Paper Manufacturing;
- Manufacturing and printing advertising specialties--are classified in the Manufacturing sector according to the products made;
- Providing photocopying services on photocopy equipment without performing traditional printing activities--are classified in U.S. Industry 561439, Other Business Service Centers (including Copy Shops);
- Printing and publishing, known as publishers--are classified in Subsector 513, Publishing Industries;
- Manufacturing bare printed circuit boards--are classified in U.S. Industry 334412, Bare Printed Circuit Board Manufacturing; and
- Providing printing brokerage services--are classified in Industry 561990, All Other Support Services.

## 323113  Commercial Screen Printing

This U.S. industry comprises establishments primarily engaged in screen printing without publishing (except books, fabric grey goods, and manifold business forms).  This industry includes establishments engaged in screen printing on purchased stock materials, such as stationery, invitations, labels, and similar items, on a job-order basis. Establishments primarily engaged in printing on apparel and textile products, such as T-shirts, caps, jackets, towels, and napkins, are included in this industry.

*Cross-References.*          Establishments primarily engaged in--

- Printing on fabric grey goods--are classified in Industry 313310, Textile and Fabric Finishing Mills;
- Printing books and pamphlets--are classified in U.S. Industry 323117, Books Printing;
- Printing manifold business forms including checkbooks--are classified in U.S. Industry 323111, Commercial Printing (except Screen and Books);

---

T—Canadian, Mexican, and United States industries are comparable.

- Manufacturing paper stock materials, including invitations, labels, and similar items--are classified in Subsector 322, Paper Manufacturing;
- Manufacturing and printing advertising specialties--are classified in the Manufacturing sector according to the products made; and
- Printing and publishing, known as publishers--are classified in Subsector 513, Publishing Industries.

## 323117  Books Printing

This U.S. industry comprises establishments primarily engaged in printing or printing and binding books and pamphlets without publishing.

*Cross-References.*                 Establishments primarily engaged in--

- Printing and publishing, known as publishers--are classified in Subsector 513, Publishing Industries; and
- Binding books without printing in the same establishment--are classified in Industry 323120, Support Activities for Printing.

## 32312  Support Activities for Printing[T]
See industry description for 323120.

## 323120  Support Activities for Printing

This industry comprises establishments primarily engaged in performing prepress and postpress services in support of printing activities.  Prepress services may include such things as platemaking, typesetting, trade binding, and sample mounting.  Postpress services include such things as book or paper bronzing, die cutting, edging, embossing, folding, gilding, gluing, and indexing.

*Cross-References.*                 Establishments primarily engaged in--

- Engraving on metal--are classified in U.S. Industry 332812, Metal Coating, Engraving (except Jewelry and Silverware), and Allied Services to Manufacturers;
- Manufacturing photosensitive plates for printing--are classified in U.S. Industry 325992, Photographic Film, Paper, Plate, Chemical, and Copy Toner Manufacturing;
- Manufacturing blank plates (except photosensitive plates) for printing--are classified in U.S. Industry 333248, All Other Industrial Machinery Manufacturing; and
- Printing books or printing and binding books--are classified in U.S. Industry 323117, Books Printing.

## 324      Petroleum and Coal Products Manufacturing[T]

The Petroleum and Coal Products Manufacturing subsector is based on the transformation of crude petroleum and coal into usable products.  The dominant process is petroleum refining that involves the separation of crude petroleum into component products through such techniques as cracking and distillation.

In addition, this subsector includes establishments that primarily further process refined petroleum and coal products and produce products, such as asphalt coatings and petroleum lubricating oils.  However, establishments that manufacture petrochemicals from refined petroleum are classified in Industry 32511, Petrochemical Manufacturing.

## 3241     Petroleum and Coal Products Manufacturing[T]

## 32411    Petroleum Refineries[T]
See industry description for 324110.

---

T—Canadian, Mexican, and United States industries are comparable.

### 324110  Petroleum Refineries

This industry comprises establishments primarily engaged in refining crude petroleum into refined petroleum. Petroleum refining involves one or more of the following activities: (1) fractionation; (2) straight distillation of crude oil; and (3) cracking.

*Cross-References.*          Establishments primarily engaged in--

- Manufacturing asphalt paving, roofing, and saturated materials from refined petroleum--are classified in Industry 32412, Asphalt Paving, Roofing, and Saturated Materials Manufacturing;
- Manufacturing paper mats and felts and saturating them with asphalt or tar into rolls and sheets--are classified in Industry 322120, Paper Mills;
- Blending or compounding refined petroleum to make lubricating oils and greases and/or re-refining used petroleum lubricating oils--are classified in U.S. Industry 324191, Petroleum Lubricating Oil and Grease Manufacturing;
- Manufacturing biofuels blended with purchased refined petroleum--are classified in U.S. Industry 324199, All Other Petroleum and Coal Products Manufacturing;
- Manufacturing biofuels not blended with refined petroleum--are classified in U.S. Industry 325199, All Other Basic Organic Chemical Manufacturing;
- Manufacturing synthetic lubricating oils and greases--are classified in U.S. Industry 325998, All Other Miscellaneous Chemical Product and Preparation Manufacturing;
- Recovering natural gasoline and/or liquid hydrocarbons from oil and gas field gases--are classified in Industry 211130, Natural Gas Extraction;
- Manufacturing acyclic and cyclic aromatic hydrocarbons (i.e., petrochemicals) from refined petroleum or liquid hydrocarbons--are classified in Industry 325110, Petrochemical Manufacturing;
- Manufacturing cyclic and acyclic chemicals (except petrochemicals)--are classified in Industry 32519, Other Basic Organic Chemical Manufacturing;
- Manufacturing coke oven products in steel mills--are classified in Industry 331110, Iron and Steel Mills and Ferroalloy Manufacturing; and
- Manufacturing coke oven products in coke oven establishments--are classified in U.S. Industry 324199, All Other Petroleum and Coal Products Manufacturing.

### 32412  Asphalt Paving, Roofing, and Saturated Materials Manufacturing[T]

This industry comprises establishments primarily engaged in (1) manufacturing asphalt and tar paving mixtures and blocks and roofing cements and coatings from purchased asphaltic materials and/or (2) saturating purchased mats and felts with asphalt or tar from purchased asphaltic materials.

*Cross-References.*          Establishments primarily engaged in--

- Refining crude petroleum and manufacturing asphalt and tar paving, roofing, and saturated materials--are classified in Industry 32411, Petroleum Refineries; and
- Manufacturing paper mats and felts and saturating them with asphalt or tar--are classified in Industry 32212, Paper Mills.

### 324121  Asphalt Paving Mixture and Block Manufacturing

This U.S. industry comprises establishments primarily engaged in manufacturing asphalt and tar paving mixtures and blocks from purchased asphaltic materials.

*Cross-References.*

Establishments primarily engaged in refining crude petroleum and manufacturing asphalt and tar paving mixtures and blocks are classified in Industry 324110, Petroleum Refineries.

---

T—Canadian, Mexican, and United States industries are comparable.

## 324122 Asphalt Shingle and Coating Materials Manufacturing

This U.S. industry comprises establishments primarily engaged in (1) saturating purchased mats and felts with asphalt or tar from purchased asphaltic materials and (2) manufacturing asphalt and tar and roofing cements and coatings from purchased asphaltic materials.

*Cross-References.*      Establishments primarily engaged in--

- Refining crude petroleum and saturating purchased mats and felts with asphalt or tar into rolls and sheets and/or refining crude petroleum and manufacturing asphalt and tar roofing cements and coatings--are classified in Industry 324110, Petroleum Refineries; and
- Manufacturing paper mats and felts and saturating them with asphalt or tar into rolls and sheets--are classified in Industry 322120, Paper Mills.

## 32419   Other Petroleum and Coal Products Manufacturing[T]

This industry comprises establishments primarily engaged in manufacturing petroleum products (except asphalt paving, roofing, and saturated materials) from refined petroleum or coal products made in coke ovens not integrated with a steel mill.

*Illustrative Examples:*

Biodiesel fuels not made in petroleum refineries and blended with purchased refined petroleum
Coke oven products (e.g., coke, gases, tars) made in coke oven establishments
Petroleum brake fluids made from refined petroleum
Petroleum jelly made from refined petroleum

Petroleum briquettes made from refined petroleum
Petroleum lubricating oils and greases made from refined petroleum
Petroleum waxes made from refined petroleum
Re-refining used petroleum lubricating oils

*Cross-References.*      Establishments primarily engaged in--

- Manufacturing petroleum products by refining crude petroleum--are classified in Industry 32411, Petroleum Refineries;
- Manufacturing biofuels not blended with refined petroleum--are classified in Industry 32519, Other Basic Organic Chemical Manufacturing;
- Manufacturing asphalt and tar paving, roofing, and saturated materials from refined petroleum--are classified in Industry 32412, Asphalt Paving, Roofing, and Saturated Materials Manufacturing;
- Manufacturing coke oven products in steel mills--are classified in Industry 33111, Iron and Steel Mills and Ferroalloy Manufacturing;
- Manufacturing acyclic and cyclic aromatic hydrocarbons (i.e., petrochemicals) from refined petroleum or liquid hydrocarbons--are classified in Industry 32511, Petrochemical Manufacturing;
- Manufacturing cyclic and acyclic organic chemicals (except petrochemicals)--are classified in Industry 32519, Other Basic Organic Chemical Manufacturing;
- Manufacturing petroleum polymer resins--are classified in Industry 32521, Resin and Synthetic Rubber Manufacturing; and
- Manufacturing synthetic lubricating oils and greases--are classified in Industry 32599, All Other Chemical Product and Preparation Manufacturing.

## 324191  Petroleum Lubricating Oil and Grease Manufacturing

This U.S. industry comprises establishments primarily engaged in blending or compounding refined petroleum to make lubricating oils and greases and/or re-refining used petroleum lubricating oils.

---

T—Canadian, Mexican, and United States industries are comparable.

*Cross-References.*　　　　　Establishments primarily engaged in--

- Refining crude petroleum and manufacturing lubricating oils and greases--are classified in Industry 324110, Petroleum Refineries; and
- Manufacturing synthetic lubricating oils and greases--are classified in U.S. Industry 325998, All Other Miscellaneous Chemical Product and Preparation Manufacturing.

## 324199　All Other Petroleum and Coal Products Manufacturing

This U.S. industry comprises establishments primarily engaged in manufacturing petroleum products (except asphalt paving, roofing, and saturated materials and lubricating oils and greases) from refined petroleum and coal products made in coke ovens not integrated with a steel mill.

*Illustrative Examples:*

Biodiesel fuels not made in petroleum refineries and blended with purchased refined petroleum
Coke oven products (e.g., coke, gases, tars) made in coke oven establishments

Petroleum briquettes made from refined petroleum
Petroleum jelly made from refined petroleum
Petroleum waxes made from refined petroleum

*Cross-References.*　　　　　Establishments primarily engaged in--

- Manufacturing petroleum products by refining crude petroleum--are classified in Industry 324110, Petroleum Refineries;
- Manufacturing biofuels not blended with refined petroleum--are classified in U.S. Industry 325199, All Other Basic Organic Chemical Manufacturing;
- Manufacturing asphalt paving and roofing materials from refined petroleum--are classified in Industry 32412, Asphalt Paving, Roofing, and Saturated Materials Manufacturing;
- Blending and compounding petroleum lubricating oils and greases and/or re-refining used petroleum lubrication oils and greases--are classified in U.S. Industry 324191, Petroleum Lubricating Oil and Grease Manufacturing;
- Manufacturing coke oven products in steel mills--are classified in Industry 331110, Iron and Steel Mills and Ferroalloy Manufacturing;
- Manufacturing acyclic and cyclic aromatic hydrocarbons (i.e., petrochemicals) from refined petroleum or liquid hydrocarbons--are classified in Industry 325110, Petrochemical Manufacturing;
- Manufacturing cyclic and acyclic organic chemicals (except petrochemicals)--are classified in Industry 32519, Other Basic Organic Chemical Manufacturing; and
- Manufacturing petroleum polymer resins--are classified in U.S. Industry 325211, Plastics Material and Resin Manufacturing.

## 325　Chemical Manufacturing[T]

The Chemical Manufacturing subsector is based on the transformation of organic and inorganic raw materials by a chemical process and the formulation of products. This subsector distinguishes the production of basic chemicals that comprise the first industry group from the production of intermediate and end products produced by further processing of basic chemicals that make up the remaining industry groups.

This subsector does not include all industries transforming raw materials by a chemical process. It is common for some chemical processing to occur during mining operations. These beneficiating operations, such as copper concentrating, are classified in Sector 21, Mining, Quarrying, and Oil and Gas Extraction. Furthermore, the refining of crude petroleum is included in Subsector 324, Petroleum and Coal Products Manufacturing. In addition, the manufacturing of aluminum oxide is included in Subsector 331, Primary Metal Manufacturing; and beverage distilleries are classified in Subsector 312, Beverage and Tobacco Product Manufacturing. As is the case of these two activities, the grouping of industries into subsectors may take into account the association of the activities performed with other activities in the subsector.

---

T—Canadian, Mexican, and United States industries are comparable.

**3251    Basic Chemical Manufacturing<sup>T</sup>**

This industry group comprises establishments primarily engaged in manufacturing chemicals using basic processes, such as thermal cracking and distillation. Chemicals manufactured in this industry group are usually separate chemical elements or separate chemically-defined compounds.

**32511    Petrochemical Manufacturing<sup>T</sup>**
See industry description for 325110.

**325110  Petrochemical Manufacturing**

This industry comprises establishments primarily engaged in (1) manufacturing acyclic (i.e., aliphatic) hydrocarbons such as ethylene, propylene, and butylene made from refined petroleum or liquid hydrocarbons and/or (2) manufacturing cyclic aromatic hydrocarbons such as benzene, toluene, styrene, xylene, ethyl benzene, and cumene made from refined petroleum or liquid hydrocarbons.

*Cross-References.*         Establishments primarily engaged in--

- Manufacturing petrochemicals by refining crude petroleum--are classified in Industry 324110, Petroleum Refineries;
- Manufacturing acetylene--are classified in Industry 325120, Industrial Gas Manufacturing;
- Manufacturing basic organic chemicals (except petrochemicals)--are classified in Industry 32519, Other Basic Organic Chemical Manufacturing; and
- Recovering liquid hydrocarbons from oil and gas field gases--are classified in Industry 211130, Natural Gas Extraction.

**32512    Industrial Gas Manufacturing<sup>T</sup>**
See industry description for 325120.

**325120  Industrial Gas Manufacturing**

This industry comprises establishments primarily engaged in manufacturing industrial organic and inorganic gases in compressed, liquid, and solid forms.

*Cross-References.*         Establishments primarily engaged in--

- Manufacturing chlorine gas--are classified in Industry 325180, Other Basic Inorganic Chemical Manufacturing; and
- Manufacturing ethane and butane gases made from refined petroleum or liquid hydrocarbons--are classified in Industry 325110, Petrochemical Manufacturing.

**32513    Synthetic Dye and Pigment Manufacturing<sup>T</sup>**
See industry description for 325130.

**325130  Synthetic Dye and Pigment Manufacturing**

This industry comprises establishments primarily engaged in manufacturing synthetic organic and inorganic dyes and pigments, such as lakes and toners (except electrostatic and photographic).

*Cross-References.*         Establishments primarily engaged in--

- Manufacturing natural food colorings--are classified in U.S. Industry 311942, Spice and Extract Manufacturing;
- Manufacturing natural organic colorings for nonfood uses (except wood byproducts)--are classified in U.S. Industry 325199, All Other Basic Organic Chemical Manufacturing;

------------------------------

T—Canadian, Mexican, and United States industries are comparable.

- Manufacturing electrostatic and photographic toners--are classified in U.S. Industry 325992, Photographic Film, Paper, Plate, Chemical, and Copy Toner Manufacturing;
- Manufacturing wood byproducts used as dyeing materials--are classified in U.S. Industry 325194, Cyclic Crude, Intermediate, and Gum and Wood Chemical Manufacturing; and
- Manufacturing carbon, bone, and lamp black--are classified in Industry 325180, Other Basic Inorganic Chemical Manufacturing.

### 32518    Other Basic Inorganic Chemical Manufacturing[T]
See industry description for 325180.

### 325180    Other Basic Inorganic Chemical Manufacturing

This industry comprises establishments primarily engaged in manufacturing basic inorganic chemicals (except industrial gases and synthetic dyes and pigments).

*Illustrative Examples:*

Alkalies manufacturing
Aluminum compounds, not specified elsewhere by process, manufacturing
Carbides (e.g., baron, calcium, silicon, tungsten) manufacturing
Carbon black manufacturing
Chlorine manufacturing

Hydrochloric acid manufacturing
Potassium inorganic compounds, not specified elsewhere by process, manufacturing
Radioactive isotopes manufacturing
Sulfides and sulfites manufacturing
Sulfuric acid manufacturing

*Cross-References.*        Establishments primarily engaged in--

- Manufacturing industrial gases--are classified in Industry 325120, Industrial Gas Manufacturing;
- Manufacturing inorganic dyes and pigments--are classified in Industry 325130, Synthetic Dye and Pigment Manufacturing;
- Manufacturing household bleaches--are classified in U.S. Industry 325612, Polish and Other Sanitation Good Manufacturing;
- Mining and/or beneficiating alkalies--are classified in Industry 212390, Other Nonmetallic Mineral Mining and Quarrying;
- Manufacturing chlorine preparations (e.g., for swimming pools)--are classified in U.S. Industry 325998, All Other Miscellaneous Chemical Product and Preparation Manufacturing;
- Manufacturing nitrogenous and phosphoric fertilizers and fertilizer materials--are classified in Industry 32531, Fertilizer and Compost Manufacturing;
- Manufacturing pharmaceuticals, medicines, and dietary supplements--are classified in Industry Group 3254, Pharmaceutical and Medicine Manufacturing;
- Manufacturing aluminum oxide (alumina)--are classified in U.S. Industry 331313, Alumina Refining and Primary Aluminum Production;
- Manufacturing inorganic insecticidal, herbicidal, fungicidal and pesticidal preparations--are classified in Industry 325320, Pesticide and Other Agricultural Chemical Manufacturing; and
- Manufacturing photographic chemicals--are classified in U.S. Industry 325992, Photographic Film, Paper, Plate, Chemical, and Copy Toner Manufacturing.

### 32519    Other Basic Organic Chemical Manufacturing[T]

This industry comprises establishments primarily engaged in manufacturing basic organic chemicals (except petrochemicals, industrial gases, and synthetic dyes and pigments).

---

T—Canadian, Mexican, and United States industries are comparable.

*Illustrative Examples:*

Biodiesel fuels not made in petroleum refineries and
not blended with petroleum
Carbon organic compounds, not specified elsewhere
by process, manufacturing
Cyclic intermediates made from refined petroleum or
natural gas (except aromatic petrochemicals)
Enzyme proteins (i.e., basic synthetic chemicals)
(except pharmaceutical use) manufacturing
Gum and wood chemicals manufacturing

Fatty acids (e.g., margaric, oleic, stearic)
manufacturing
Organo-inorganic compound manufacturing
Plasticizers (i.e., basic synthetic chemical)
manufacturing
Silicone (except resins) manufacturing
Synthetic sweeteners (i.e., sweetening agents)
manufacturing

*Cross-References.*        Establishments primarily engaged in--

- Manufacturing petrochemicals from refined petroleum or liquid hydrocarbons--are classified in Industry 32511, Petrochemical Manufacturing;
- Manufacturing petrochemicals by refining crude petroleum--are classified in Industry 32411, Petroleum Refineries;
- Blending purchased biodiesel fuels and purchased refined petroleum--are classified in Industry 32419, Other Petroleum and Coal Products Manufacturing;
- Manufacturing organic industrial gases--are classified in Industry 32512, Industrial Gas Manufacturing;
- Manufacturing synthetic organic dyes and pigments--are classified in Industry 32513, Synthetic Dye and Pigment Manufacturing;
- Manufacturing natural glycerin--are classified in Industry 32561, Soap and Cleaning Compound Manufacturing;
- Manufacturing activated charcoal--are classified in Industry 32599, All Other Chemical Product and Preparation Manufacturing;
- Manufacturing organic insecticidal, herbicidal, fungicidal, and pesticidal preparations--are classified in Industry 32532, Pesticide and Other Agricultural Chemical Manufacturing;
- Manufacturing elastomers--are classified in Industry 32521, Resin and Synthetic Rubber Manufacturing;
- Manufacturing urea--are classified in Industry 32531, Fertilizer and Compost Manufacturing;
- Manufacturing pharmaceuticals, medicines, and dietary supplements--are classified in Industry Group 3254, Pharmaceutical and Medicine Manufacturing;
- Manufacturing coal tar crudes in integrated steel mills with coke ovens--are classified in Industry 33111, Iron and Steel Mills and Ferroalloy Manufacturing;
- Manufacturing coal tar crudes in coke ovens not integrated with steel mills and fuel briquettes from refined petroleum--are classified in Industry 32419, Other Petroleum and Coal Products Manufacturing; and
- Manufacturing natural food colorings--are classified in Industry 31194, Seasoning and Dressing Manufacturing.

## 325193 Ethyl Alcohol Manufacturing

This U.S. industry comprises establishments primarily engaged in manufacturing nonpotable ethyl alcohol.

*Cross-References.*        Establishments primarily engaged in--

- Distilling liquors (except brandy)--are classified in Industry 312140, Distilleries; and
- Manufacturing brandies--are classified in Industry 312130, Wineries.

## 325194 Cyclic Crude, Intermediate, and Gum and Wood Chemical Manufacturing

This U.S. industry comprises establishments primarily engaged in one or more of the following: (1) distilling wood or gum into products, such as tall oil and wood distillates; (2) distilling coal tars; (3) manufacturing wood or gum chemicals, such as naval stores, natural tanning materials, charcoal briquettes, and charcoal (except activated);

T—Canadian, Mexican, and United States industries are comparable.

and (4) manufacturing cyclic crudes or cyclic intermediates (i.e., hydrocarbons, except aromatic petrochemicals) from refined petroleum or natural gas.

*Cross-references.*          Establishments primarily engaged in--

- Manufacturing cyclic chemicals (except aromatic and intermediates)--are classified in U.S. Industry 325199, All Other Basic Organic Chemical Manufacturing;
- Manufacturing aromatic petrochemicals from refined petroleum or natural gas--are classified in Industry 325110, Petrochemical Manufacturing;
- Manufacturing aromatic petrochemicals by refining crude petroleum--are classified in Industry 324110, Petroleum Refineries;
- Manufacturing coal tar crudes in steel mills with coke ovens--are classified in Industry 331110, Iron and Steel Mills and Ferroalloy Manufacturing;
- Manufacturing fuel briquettes from refined petroleum--are classified in U.S. Industry 324199, All Other Petroleum and Coal Products Manufacturing; and
- Manufacturing activated charcoal--are classified in U.S. Industry 325998, All Other Miscellaneous Chemical Product and Preparation Manufacturing.

## 325199  All Other Basic Organic Chemical Manufacturing

This U.S. industry comprises establishments primarily engaged in manufacturing basic organic chemical products (except aromatic petrochemicals, industrial gases, synthetic organic dyes and pigments, gum and wood chemicals, cyclic crudes and intermediates, and ethyl alcohol).

*Illustrative Examples:*

Biodiesel fuels not made in petroleum refineries and not blended with petroleum
Calcium organic compounds, not specified elsewhere by process, manufacturing
Carbon organic compounds, not specified elsewhere by process, manufacturing
Enzyme proteins (i.e., basic synthetic chemicals) (except pharmaceutical use) manufacturing
Organo-inorganic compound manufacturing

Fatty acids (e.g., margaric, oleic, stearic) manufacturing
Plasticizers (i.e., basic synthetic chemicals) manufacturing
Raw organic waxes manufacturing
Refrigerant mixtures and blends manufacturing
Silicone (except resins) manufacturing
Synthetic sweeteners (i.e., sweetening agents) manufacturing

*Cross-References.*          Establishments primarily engaged in--

- Manufacturing aromatic petrochemicals from refined petroleum or natural gas--are classified in Industry 325110, Petrochemical Manufacturing;
- Manufacturing aromatic petrochemicals or biodiesel fuels by refining crude petroleum--are classified in Industry 324110, Petroleum Refineries;
- Blending purchased biodiesel fuels and purchased refined petroleum--are classified in U.S. Industry 324199, All Other Petroleum and Coal Products Manufacturing;
- Manufacturing organic industrial gases--are classified in Industry 325120, Industrial Gas Manufacturing;
- Manufacturing synthetic organic dyes and pigments--are classified in Industry 325130, Synthetic Dye and Pigment Manufacturing;
- Manufacturing ethyl alcohol--are classified in U.S. Industry 325193, Ethyl Alcohol Manufacturing;
- Manufacturing organic insecticidal, herbicidal, fungicidal, and pesticidal preparations--are classified in Industry 325320, Pesticide and Other Agricultural Chemical Manufacturing;
- Manufacturing elastomers--are classified in Industry 32521, Resin and Synthetic Rubber Manufacturing;
- Manufacturing urea--are classified in U.S. Industry 325311, Nitrogenous Fertilizer Manufacturing;
- Manufacturing pharmaceuticals, medicines, and dietary supplements--are classified in Industry Group 3254, Pharmaceutical and Medicine Manufacturing;

---

T—Canadian, Mexican, and United States industries are comparable.

- Manufacturing natural glycerin--are classified in U.S. Industry 325611, Soap and Other Detergent Manufacturing; and
- Manufacturing natural food colorings--are classified in U.S. Industry 311942, Spice and Extract Manufacturing.

## 3252    Resin, Synthetic Rubber, and Artificial and Synthetic Fibers and Filaments Manufacturing[T]

This industry group comprises establishments primarily engaged in one of the following: (1) manufacturing synthetic resins, plastics materials, and nonvulcanizable elastomers and mixing and blending resins on a custom basis; (2) manufacturing noncustomized synthetic resins; (3) manufacturing synthetic rubber; (4) manufacturing cellulosic (e.g., rayon, acetate) and noncellulosic (e.g., nylon, polyolefin, polyester) fibers and filaments in the form of monofilament, filament yarn, staple, or tow; or (5) manufacturing and texturizing cellulosic and noncellulosic fibers and filaments.

## 32521    Resin and Synthetic Rubber Manufacturing[T]

This industry comprises establishments primarily engaged in one or more of the following: (1) manufacturing synthetic resins, plastics materials, and nonvulcanizable elastomers and mixing and blending resins on a custom basis; (2) manufacturing noncustomized synthetic resins; and (3) manufacturing synthetic rubber.

*Cross-References.*          Establishments primarily engaged in--

- Manufacturing plastics resins and converting resins into plastics products--are classified in Industry Group 3261, Plastics Product Manufacturing;
- Processing natural, synthetic, or reclaimed rubber into intermediate or final products--are classified in Industry Group 3262, Rubber Product Manufacturing;
- Custom compounding resins made elsewhere--are classified in Industry 32599, All Other Chemical Product and Preparation Manufacturing; and
- Manufacturing resin adhesives--are classified in Industry 32552, Adhesive Manufacturing.

## 325211  Plastics Material and Resin Manufacturing

This U.S. industry comprises establishments primarily engaged in (1) manufacturing resins, plastics materials, and nonvulcanizable thermoplastic elastomers and mixing and blending resins on a custom basis and/or (2) manufacturing noncustomized synthetic resins.

*Cross-References.*          Establishments primarily engaged in--

- Manufacturing plastics resins and converting resins into plastics products--are classified in Industry Group 3261, Plastics Product Manufacturing;
- Custom compounding resins made elsewhere--are classified in U.S. Industry 325991, Custom Compounding of Purchased Resins; and
- Manufacturing plastics adhesives--are classified in Industry 325520, Adhesive Manufacturing.

## 325212  Synthetic Rubber Manufacturing

This U.S. industry comprises establishments primarily engaged in manufacturing synthetic rubber.

*Cross-References.*          Establishments primarily engaged in--

- Processing natural, synthetic, or reclaimed rubber into intermediate or final products (except adhesives)--are classified in Industry Group 3262, Rubber Product Manufacturing; and
- Manufacturing rubber adhesives--are classified in Industry 325520, Adhesive Manufacturing.

---

T—Canadian, Mexican, and United States industries are comparable.

### 32522 Artificial and Synthetic Fibers and Filaments Manufacturing[T]
See industry description for 325220.

### 325220 Artificial and Synthetic Fibers and Filaments Manufacturing

This industry comprises establishments primarily engaged in (1) manufacturing cellulosic (e.g., rayon, acetate) and noncellulosic (e.g., nylon, polyolefin, polyester) fibers and filaments in the form of monofilament, filament yarn, staple, or tow or (2) manufacturing and texturizing cellulosic and noncellulosic fibers and filaments.

*Cross-References.*        Establishments primarily engaged in--

- Texturizing cellulosic and noncellulosic fibers and filaments made elsewhere--are classified in Industry 313110, Fiber, Yarn, and Thread Mills; and
- Manufacturing textile glass fibers--are classified in U.S. Industry 327212, Other Pressed and Blown Glass and Glassware Manufacturing.

### 3253 Pesticide, Fertilizer, and Other Agricultural Chemical Manufacturing[T]

This industry group comprises establishments primarily engaged in one or more of the following: (1) manufacturing nitrogenous or phosphatic fertilizer materials; (2) manufacturing fertilizers from sewage or animal waste; (3) manufacturing nitrogenous or phosphatic materials and mixing with other ingredients into fertilizers; (4) mixing ingredients made elsewhere into fertilizers; (5) manufacturing compost; and (6) formulating and preparing pesticides and other agricultural chemicals.

### 32531 Fertilizer and Compost Manufacturing[T]

This industry comprises establishments primarily engaged in one or more of the following: (1) manufacturing nitrogenous or phosphatic fertilizer materials; (2) manufacturing fertilizers from sewage or animal waste; (3) manufacturing nitrogenous or phosphatic materials and mixing with other ingredients into fertilizers; (4) mixing ingredients made elsewhere into fertilizers; and (5) manufacturing compost.

### 325311 Nitrogenous Fertilizer Manufacturing

This U.S. industry comprises establishments primarily engaged in one or more of the following: (1) manufacturing nitrogenous fertilizer materials; (2) manufacturing fertilizers from sewage or animal waste; and (3) manufacturing nitrogenous materials and mixing with other ingredients into fertilizers.

*Cross-References.*

Establishments primarily engaged in mixing ingredients made elsewhere into nitrogenous fertilizers are classified in U.S. Industry 325314, Fertilizer (Mixing Only) Manufacturing.

### 325312 Phosphatic Fertilizer Manufacturing

This U.S. industry comprises establishments primarily engaged in (1) manufacturing phosphatic fertilizer materials or (2) manufacturing phosphatic materials and mixing with other ingredients into fertilizers.

*Cross-References.*

Establishments primarily engaged in mixing ingredients made elsewhere into phosphatic fertilizers are classified in U.S. Industry 325314, Fertilizer (Mixing Only) Manufacturing.

---

T—Canadian, Mexican, and United States industries are comparable.

## 325314  Fertilizer (Mixing Only) Manufacturing

This U.S. industry comprises establishments primarily engaged in mixing ingredients made elsewhere into fertilizers.

*Cross-References.*        Establishments primarily engaged in--

- Manufacturing nitrogenous fertilizer materials or fertilizer materials from sewage or animal waste and mixing these ingredients into nitrogenous fertilizers--are classified in U.S. Industry 325311, Nitrogenous Fertilizer Manufacturing;
- Manufacturing phosphatic fertilizer materials and mixing these ingredients into phosphatic fertilizers--are classified in U.S. Industry 325312, Phosphatic Fertilizer Manufacturing; and
- Manufacturing compost--are classified in U.S. Industry 325315, Compost Manufacturing.

## 325315  Compost Manufacturing

This U.S. industry comprises establishments primarily engaged in manufacturing compost through the controlled aerobic, biological decomposition and curing of biodegradable materials.

*Cross-References.*        Establishments primarily engaged in--

- Manufacturing nitrogenous fertilizer materials or fertilizer materials from sewage or animal waste and mixing these ingredients into nitrogenous fertilizers--are classified in U.S. Industry 325311, Nitrogenous Fertilizer Manufacturing;
- Manufacturing phosphatic fertilizer materials and mixing these ingredients into phosphatic fertilizers--are classified in U.S. Industry 325312, Phosphatic Fertilizer Manufacturing; and
- Mixing ingredients made elsewhere into fertilizers--are classified in U.S. Industry 325314, Fertilizer (Mixing Only) Manufacturing.

## 32532  Pesticide and Other Agricultural Chemical Manufacturing[T]
See industry description for 325320.

## 325320  Pesticide and Other Agricultural Chemical Manufacturing

This industry comprises establishments primarily engaged in the formulation and preparation of agricultural and household pest control chemicals (except fertilizers).

*Cross-References.*        Establishments primarily engaged in--

- Manufacturing basic chemicals requiring further processing before use as agricultural chemicals--are classified in Industry Group 3251, Basic Chemical Manufacturing;
- Manufacturing fertilizers--are classified in Industry 32531, Fertilizer and Compost Manufacturing; and
- Manufacturing agricultural lime products--are classified in Industry 327410, Lime Manufacturing.

## 3254  Pharmaceutical and Medicine Manufacturing[T]

## 32541  Pharmaceutical and Medicine Manufacturing[T]

This industry comprises establishments primarily engaged in one or more of the following: (1) manufacturing biological and medicinal products; (2) processing (i.e., grading, grinding, and milling) botanical drugs and herbs; (3) isolating active medicinal principals from botanical drugs and herbs; and (4) manufacturing pharmaceutical products intended for internal and external consumption in such forms as ampoules, tablets, capsules, vials, ointments, powders, solutions, and suspensions.

---

T—Canadian, Mexican, and United States industries are comparable.

### 325411  Medicinal and Botanical Manufacturing

This U.S. industry comprises establishments primarily engaged in (1) manufacturing uncompounded medicinal chemicals and their derivatives (i.e., generally for use by pharmaceutical preparation manufacturers) and/or (2) grading, grinding, and milling uncompounded botanicals.

*Cross-References.*          Establishments primarily engaged in--

- Manufacturing packaged compounded medicinals and botanicals--are classified in U.S. Industry 325412, Pharmaceutical Preparation Manufacturing; and
- Manufacturing vaccines, toxoids, blood fractions, and culture media of plant or animal origin (except for diagnostic use)--are classified in U.S. Industry 325414, Biological Product (except Diagnostic) Manufacturing.

### 325412  Pharmaceutical Preparation Manufacturing

This U.S. industry comprises establishments primarily engaged in manufacturing in-vivo diagnostic substances and pharmaceutical preparations (except biological) intended for internal and external consumption in dose forms, such as ampoules, tablets, capsules, vials, ointments, powders, solutions, and suspensions.

*Cross-References.*          Establishments primarily engaged in--

- Manufacturing uncompounded medicinal chemicals and their derivatives--are classified in U.S. Industry 325411, Medicinal and Botanical Manufacturing;
- Manufacturing in-vitro diagnostic substances--are classified in U.S. Industry 325413, In-Vitro Diagnostic Substance Manufacturing; and
- Manufacturing vaccines, toxoids, blood fractions, and culture media of plant or animal origin (except for diagnostic use)--are classified in U.S. Industry 325414, Biological Product (except Diagnostic) Manufacturing.

### 325413  In-Vitro Diagnostic Substance Manufacturing

This U.S. industry comprises establishments primarily engaged in manufacturing in-vitro (i.e., not taken internally) diagnostic substances, such as chemical, biological, or radioactive substances. The substances are used for diagnostic tests that are performed in test tubes, petri dishes, machines, and other diagnostic test-type devices.

*Cross-References.*

Establishments primarily engaged in manufacturing in-vivo diagnostic substances are classified in U.S. Industry 325412, Pharmaceutical Preparation Manufacturing.

### 325414  Biological Product (except Diagnostic) Manufacturing

This U.S. industry comprises establishments primarily engaged in manufacturing vaccines, toxoids, blood fractions, and culture media of plant or animal origin (except diagnostic).

*Cross-References.*          Establishments primarily engaged in--

- Manufacturing in-vitro diagnostic substances--are classified in U.S. Industry 325413, In-Vitro Diagnostic Substance Manufacturing; and
- Manufacturing pharmaceutical preparations (except biological and in-vitro diagnostic substances)--are classified in U.S. Industry 325412, Pharmaceutical Preparation Manufacturing.

---

T—Canadian, Mexican, and United States industries are comparable.

## 3255    Paint, Coating, and Adhesive Manufacturing[T]

This industry group comprises establishments primarily engaged in one or more of the following: (1) mixing pigments, solvents, and binders into paints and other coatings; (2) manufacturing allied paint products; and (3) manufacturing adhesives, glues, and caulking compounds.

## 32551    Paint and Coating Manufacturing[T]
See industry description for 325510.

## 325510    Paint and Coating Manufacturing

This industry comprises establishments primarily engaged in (1) mixing pigments, solvents, and binders into paints and other coatings, such as stains, varnishes, lacquers, enamels, shellacs, and water-repellent coatings for concrete and masonry, and/or (2) manufacturing allied paint products, such as putties, paint and varnish removers, paint brush cleaners, and frit.

*Cross-References.*          Establishments primarily engaged in--

- Manufacturing creosote or turpentine--are classified in U.S. Industry 325194, Cyclic Crude, Intermediate, and Gum and Wood Chemical Manufacturing;
- Manufacturing caulking compounds and sealants--are classified in Industry 325520, Adhesive Manufacturing; and
- Manufacturing artists' paints--are classified in Industry 339940, Office Supplies (except Paper) Manufacturing.

## 32552    Adhesive Manufacturing[T]
See industry description for 325520.

## 325520    Adhesive Manufacturing

This industry comprises establishments primarily engaged in manufacturing adhesives, glues, and caulking compounds.

*Cross-References.*          Establishments primarily engaged in--

- Manufacturing asphalt and tar roofing cements from purchased asphaltic materials--are classified in U.S. Industry 324122, Asphalt Shingle and Coating Materials Manufacturing; and
- Manufacturing gypsum based caulking compounds--are classified in Industry 327420, Gypsum Product Manufacturing.

## 3256    Soap, Cleaning Compound, and Toilet Preparation Manufacturing[T]

This industry group comprises establishments primarily engaged in (1) manufacturing and packaging soaps, detergents, polishes, surface active agents, textile and leather finishing agents, and other sanitation goods or (2) preparing, blending, compounding, and packaging toilet preparations.

## 32561    Soap and Cleaning Compound Manufacturing[T]

This industry comprises establishments primarily engaged in manufacturing and packaging soaps and other cleaning compounds, surface active agents, and textile and leather finishing agents used to reduce tension or speed the drying process.

---

T—Canadian, Mexican, and United States industries are comparable.

*Cross-References.*          Establishments primarily engaged in--

- Manufacturing synthetic glycerin or raw organic waxes--are classified in Industry 32519, Other Basic Organic Chemical Manufacturing;
- Manufacturing industrial bleaches--are classified in Industry 32518, Other Basic Inorganic Chemical Manufacturing; and
- Manufacturing shampoos and shaving preparations--are classified in Industry 32562, Toilet Preparation Manufacturing.

## 325611  Soap and Other Detergent Manufacturing

This U.S. industry comprises establishments primarily engaged in manufacturing and packaging bath, facial, and hand soaps, hand sanitizers, and other detergents, such as laundry and dishwashing detergents; toothpaste gels and tooth powders; and natural glycerin.

*Cross-References.*          Establishments primarily engaged in--

- Manufacturing synthetic glycerin--are classified in U.S. Industry 325199, All Other Basic Organic Chemical Manufacturing; and
- Manufacturing shampoos and shaving preparations--are classified in Industry 325620, Toilet Preparation Manufacturing.

## 325612  Polish and Other Sanitation Good Manufacturing

This U.S. industry comprises establishments primarily engaged in manufacturing and packaging polishes and specialty cleaning preparations.

*Cross-References.*          Establishments primarily engaged in--

- Manufacturing chlorine dioxide (i.e., industrial bleaching agent)--are classified in Industry 325180, Other Basic Inorganic Chemical Manufacturing; and
- Manufacturing raw organic waxes--are classified in U.S. Industry 325199, All Other Basic Organic Chemical Manufacturing.

## 325613  Surface Active Agent Manufacturing

This U.S. industry comprises establishments primarily engaged in (1) manufacturing bulk surface active agents for use as wetting agents, emulsifiers, and penetrants and/or (2) manufacturing textile and leather finishing agents used to reduce tension or speed the drying process.

## 32562    Toilet Preparation Manufacturing[T]
See industry description for 325620.

## 325620  Toilet Preparation Manufacturing

This industry comprises establishments primarily engaged in preparing, blending, compounding, and packaging toilet preparations, such as perfumes, shaving preparations, hair preparations, face creams, lotions (including sunscreens), and other cosmetic preparations.

*Cross-References.*

Establishments primarily engaged in manufacturing toothpaste are classified in U.S. Industry 325611, Soap and Other Detergent Manufacturing.

---

T—Canadian, Mexican, and United States industries are comparable.

**3259    Other Chemical Product and Preparation Manufacturing**[T]

This industry group comprises establishments primarily engaged in manufacturing chemical products (except basic chemicals; resins, synthetic rubber, cellulosic and noncellulosic fibers and filaments; pesticides, fertilizers, and other agricultural chemicals; pharmaceuticals and medicines; paints, coatings, and adhesives; soaps and cleaning compounds; and toilet preparations).

**32591    Printing Ink Manufacturing**[T]
See industry description for 325910.

**325910  Printing Ink Manufacturing**

This industry comprises establishments primarily engaged in manufacturing printing and inkjet inks and inkjet cartridges.

*Cross-References.*        Establishments primarily engaged in--

*   Manufacturing writing, drawing, and stamping inks--are classified in U.S. Industry 325998, All Other Miscellaneous Chemical Product and Preparation Manufacturing;
*   Manufacturing toners and toner cartridges for photocopiers, fax machines, computer printers, and similar office machines--are classified in U.S. Industry 325992, Photographic Film, Paper, Plate, Chemical, and Copy Toner Manufacturing; and
*   Purchasing used inkjet cartridges and reselling them to manufacturers for remanufacturing--are classified in Industry 423930, Recyclable Material Merchant Wholesalers.

**32592    Explosives Manufacturing**[T]
See industry description for 325920.

**325920  Explosives Manufacturing**

This industry comprises establishments primarily engaged in manufacturing explosives.

*Cross-References.*        Establishments primarily engaged in--

*   Manufacturing ammunition, ammunition detonators, and percussion caps--are classified in U.S. Industry 332992, Small Arms Ammunition Manufacturing; and
*   Manufacturing pyrotechnics--are classified in U.S. Industry 325998, All Other Miscellaneous Chemical Product and Preparation Manufacturing.

**32599    All Other Chemical Product and Preparation Manufacturing**[T]

This industry comprises establishments primarily engaged in manufacturing chemical products (except basic chemicals, resins, and synthetic rubber; cellulosic and noncellulosic fibers and filaments; pesticides, fertilizers, and other agricultural chemicals; pharmaceuticals and medicines; paints, coatings, and adhesives; soaps, cleaning compounds, and toilet preparations; printing inks; and explosives).

*Illustrative Examples:*

Activated carbon and charcoal manufacturing
Antifreeze preparations manufacturing
Custom compounding (i.e., blending and mixing) of purchased plastics resins
Electronic cigarette vapor liquids, including closed refills, manufacturing
Industrial salt manufacturing

Matches and matchbook manufacturing
Photographic chemicals manufacturing
Pyrotechnics (e.g., flares, flashlight bombs, signals) manufacturing
Sugar substitutes (i.e., synthetic sweeteners blended with other ingredients) made from purchased synthetic sweeteners

---

T—Canadian, Mexican, and United States industries are comparable.

Swimming pool chemical preparations manufacturing          Writing inks manufacturing

*Cross-References.*          Establishments primarily engaged in--

- Manufacturing basic chemicals--are classified in Industry Group 3251, Basic Chemical Manufacturing;
- Manufacturing resins, synthetic rubber, and artificial and synthetic fibers and filaments--are classified in Industry Group 3252, Resin, Synthetic Rubber, and Artificial and Synthetic Fibers and Filaments Manufacturing;
- Manufacturing pesticides, fertilizers, and other agricultural chemicals--are classified in Industry Group 3253, Pesticide, Fertilizer, and Other Agricultural Chemical Manufacturing;
- Manufacturing pharmaceuticals and medicines, including medicinal gelatins (e.g., agar-agar)--are classified in Industry Group 3254, Pharmaceutical and Medicine Manufacturing;
- Manufacturing paints, coatings, and adhesives--are classified in Industry Group 3255, Paint, Coating, and Adhesive Manufacturing;
- Manufacturing soaps and cleaning compounds--are classified in Industry Group 3256, Soap, Cleaning Compound, and Toilet Preparation Manufacturing;
- Manufacturing printing and inkjet inks--are classified in Industry 32591, Printing Ink Manufacturing;
- Manufacturing explosives--are classified in Industry 32592, Explosives Manufacturing;
- Manufacturing photographic paper stock (i.e., unsensitized) and paper mats, mounts, easels, and folders for photographic use--are classified in Subsector 322, Paper Manufacturing;
- Manufacturing dessert gelatins--are classified in Industry 31199, All Other Food Manufacturing; and
- Purchasing used toner cartridges and reselling them to manufacturers for remanufacturing--are classified in Industry 42393, Recyclable Material Merchant Wholesalers.

### 325991  Custom Compounding of Purchased Resins

This U.S. industry comprises establishments primarily engaged in (1) custom mixing and blending plastics resins made elsewhere or (2) reformulating plastics resins from recycled plastics products.

*Cross-References.*

Establishments primarily engaged in manufacturing synthetic resins and custom mixing and blending resins are classified in U.S. Industry 325211, Plastics Material and Resin Manufacturing.

### 325992  Photographic Film, Paper, Plate, Chemical, and Copy Toner Manufacturing

This U.S. industry comprises establishments primarily engaged in manufacturing sensitized film, sensitized paper, sensitized cloth, sensitized plates, toners (i.e., for photocopiers, laser printers, and similar electrostatic printing devices), toner cartridges, and photographic chemicals.

*Cross-References.*          Establishments primarily engaged in--

- Manufacturing photographic paper stock (i.e., unsensitized) and paper mats, mounts, easels, and folders for photographic use--are classified in Subsector 322, Paper Manufacturing; and
- Purchasing used toner cartridges and reselling them to manufacturers for remanufacturing--are classified in Industry 423930, Recyclable Material Merchant Wholesalers.

### 325998  All Other Miscellaneous Chemical Product and Preparation Manufacturing

This U.S. industry comprises establishments primarily engaged in manufacturing chemical products (except basic chemicals, resins, and synthetic rubber; cellulosic and noncellulosic fibers and filaments; pesticides, fertilizers, and other agricultural chemicals; pharmaceuticals and medicines; paints, coatings and adhesives; soaps, cleaning compounds, and toilet preparations; printing inks; explosives; custom compounding of purchased resins; and photographic films, papers, plates, chemicals, and copy toners).

---

T—Canadian, Mexican, and United States industries are comparable.

*Illustrative Examples:*

Activated carbon and charcoal manufacturing
Antifreeze preparations manufacturing
Electronic cigarette vapor liquids, including closed refills, manufacturing
Industrial salt manufacturing
Lighter fluids (e.g., charcoal, cigarette) manufacturing
Matches and matchbook manufacturing

Pyrotechnics (e.g., flares, flashlight bombs, signals) manufacturing
Sugar substitutes (i.e., synthetic sweeteners blended with other ingredients) made from purchased synthetic sweeteners
Swimming pool chemical preparations manufacturing
Writing inks manufacturing

*Cross-References.*          Establishments primarily engaged in--

- Manufacturing basic chemicals--are classified in Industry Group 3251, Basic Chemical Manufacturing;
- Manufacturing resins, synthetic rubber, and artificial and synthetic fibers and filaments--are classified in Industry Group 3252, Resin, Synthetic Rubber, and Artificial and Synthetic Fibers and Filaments Manufacturing;
- Manufacturing pesticides, fertilizers, and other agricultural chemicals--are classified in Industry Group 3253, Pesticide, Fertilizer, and Other Agricultural Chemical Manufacturing;
- Manufacturing pharmaceuticals and medicines, including medicinal gelatins (e.g., agar-agar)--are classified in Industry Group 3254, Pharmaceutical and Medicine Manufacturing;
- Manufacturing paints, coatings, and adhesives--are classified in Industry Group 3255, Paint, Coating, and Adhesive Manufacturing;
- Manufacturing soaps and cleaning compounds--are classified in Industry 32561, Soap and Cleaning Compound Manufacturing;
- Manufacturing printing and inkjet inks--are classified in Industry 325910, Printing Ink Manufacturing;
- Manufacturing explosives--are classified in Industry 325920, Explosives Manufacturing;
- Custom compounding purchased plastics resins--are classified in U.S. Industry 325991, Custom Compounding of Purchased Resins;
- Manufacturing photographic films, papers, plates, chemicals, and copy toners--are classified in U.S. Industry 325992, Photographic Film, Paper, Plate, Chemical, and Copy Toner Manufacturing; and
- Manufacturing dessert gelatin--are classified in U.S. Industry 311999, All Other Miscellaneous Food Manufacturing.

## 326    Plastics and Rubber Products Manufacturing[T]

Industries in the Plastics and Rubber Products Manufacturing subsector make goods by processing plastics materials and raw rubber. The core technology employed by establishments in this subsector is that of plastics or rubber product production. Plastics and rubber are combined in the same subsector because plastics are increasingly being used as a substitute for rubber; however, the subsector is generally restricted to the production of products made of just one material, either solely plastics or rubber.

Many manufacturing activities use plastics or rubber, for example the manufacture of footwear or furniture. Typically, the production process of these products involves more than one material. In these cases, technologies that allow disparate materials to be formed and combined are of central importance in describing the manufacturing activity. In NAICS, such activities (footwear and furniture manufacturing) are not classified in the Plastics and Rubber Products Manufacturing subsector because the core technologies for these activities are diverse and involve multiple materials.

Within the Plastics and Rubber Products Manufacturing subsector, a distinction is made between plastics and rubber products at the industry group level, although it is not a rigid distinction, as can be seen from the definition of Industry 32622, Rubber and Plastics Hoses and Belting Manufacturing. In the case of hoses and belting, plastics are used as a substitute for rubber, and the distinction in materials is not useful as a basis for establishment classification.

In keeping with the core technology focus of plastics, lamination of plastics film to plastics film as well as the production of bags from plastics only is classified in this subsector. Lamination and bag production involving plastics and materials other than plastics are classified in Subsector 322, Paper Manufacturing.

---

T—Canadian, Mexican, and United States industries are comparable.

## 3261    Plastics Product Manufacturing[T]

This industry group comprises establishments primarily engaged in processing new or spent (i.e., recycled) plastics resins into intermediate or final products, using such processes as compression molding; extrusion molding; injection molding; blow molding; and casting.  Within most of these industries, the production process is such that a wide variety of products can be made.

## 32611   Plastics Packaging Materials and Unlaminated Film and Sheet Manufacturing[T]

This industry comprises establishments primarily engaged in (1) converting plastics resins into unsupported plastics film and sheet and/or (2) forming, coating, or laminating plastics film and sheet into plastics bags.

*Cross-References.*          Establishments primarily engaged in--

- Laminating plastics sheet (except for packaging)--are classified in Industry 32613, Laminated Plastics Plate, Sheet (except Packaging), and Shape Manufacturing;
- Manufacturing plastics blister and bubble packaging--are classified in Industry 32619, Other Plastics Product Manufacturing; and
- Coating or laminating combinations of plastics, foils, and paper (except plastics film to plastics film) into film, sheet or bags--are classified in Industry 32222, Paper Bag and Coated and Treated Paper Manufacturing.

### 326111  Plastics Bag and Pouch Manufacturing

This U.S. industry comprises establishments primarily engaged in (1) converting plastics resins into plastics bags or pouches and/or (2) forming, coating, or laminating plastics film or sheet into single-web or multiweb plastics bags or pouches.  Establishments in this industry may print on the bags or pouches they manufacture.

*Cross-References.*          Establishments primarily engaged in--

- Manufacturing laminated or coated combinations of plastics, foils, and paper (except plastics film to plastics film) materials into single wall or multiwall bags--are classified in Industry 322220, Paper Bag and Coated and Treated Paper Manufacturing; and
- Printing on purchased packaging materials--are classified in Industry Group 3231, Printing and Related Support Activities, based on the printing process used.

### 326112  Plastics Packaging Film and Sheet (including Laminated) Manufacturing

This U.S. industry comprises establishments primarily engaged in converting plastics resins into plastics packaging (flexible) film and packaging sheet.

*Cross-References.*          Establishments primarily engaged in--

- Converting plastics resins into plastics film and unlaminated sheet (except packaging)--are classified in U.S. Industry 326113, Unlaminated Plastics Film and Sheet (except Packaging) Manufacturing;
- Laminating or coating combinations of plastics, foils, and paper (except plastics film to plastics film) film and sheet, packaging or nonpackaging--are classified in Industry 322220, Paper Bag and Coated and Treated Paper Manufacturing;
- Laminating plastics sheet (except for packaging)--are classified in Industry 326130, Laminated Plastics Plate, Sheet (except Packaging), and Shape Manufacturing; and
- Manufacturing plastics bags--are classified in U.S. Industry 326111, Plastics Bag and Pouch Manufacturing.

---

T—Canadian, Mexican, and United States industries are comparable.

### 326113 Unlaminated Plastics Film and Sheet (except Packaging) Manufacturing

This U.S. industry comprises establishments primarily engaged in converting plastics resins into plastics film and unlaminated sheet (except packaging).

*Cross-References.*　　　Establishments primarily engaged in--

- Converting plastics resins into plastics packaging film and unlaminated packaging sheet--are classified in U.S. Industry 326112, Plastics Packaging Film and Sheet (including Laminated) Manufacturing;
- Laminating plastics sheet (except for packaging)--are classified in Industry 326130, Laminated Plastics Plate, Sheet (except Packaging), and Shape Manufacturing;
- Laminating or coating combinations of plastics, foils, and paper (except plastics film to plastics film) film and sheet, packaging or nonpackaging--are classified in Industry 322220, Paper Bag and Coated and Treated Paper Manufacturing; and
- Manufacturing plastics bags--are classified in U.S. Industry 326111, Plastics Bag and Pouch Manufacturing.

### 32612　Plastics Pipe, Pipe Fitting, and Unlaminated Profile Shape Manufacturing[T]

This industry comprises establishments primarily engaged in manufacturing plastics pipes and pipe fittings, and plastics profile shapes such as rod, tube, and sausage casings.

*Cross-References.*　　　Establishments primarily engaged in--

- Manufacturing plastics hose--are classified in Industry 32622, Rubber and Plastics Hoses and Belting Manufacturing;
- Manufacturing noncurrent-carrying plastics conduit--are classified in Industry 33593, Wiring Device Manufacturing;
- Manufacturing plastics plumbing fixtures--are classified in Industry 32619, Other Plastics Product Manufacturing; and
- Manufacturing plastics film, plastics unlaminated sheet, and plastics bags--are classified in Industry 32611, Plastics Packaging Materials and Unlaminated Film and Sheet Manufacturing.

### 326121　Unlaminated Plastics Profile Shape Manufacturing

This U.S. industry comprises establishments primarily engaged in converting plastics resins into nonrigid plastics profile shapes (except film, sheet, bags, and hoses), such as rod, tube, and sausage casings.

*Cross-References.*　　　Establishments primarily engaged in--

- Manufacturing plastics film, plastics unlaminated sheet, and plastics bags--are classified in Industry 32611, Plastics Packaging Materials and Unlaminated Film and Sheet Manufacturing; and
- Manufacturing plastics hoses--are classified in Industry 326220, Rubber and Plastics Hoses and Belting Manufacturing.

### 326122　Plastics Pipe and Pipe Fitting Manufacturing

This U.S. industry comprises establishments primarily engaged in converting plastics resins into plastics pipes and pipe fittings.

*Cross-References.*　　　Establishments primarily engaged in--

- Manufacturing plastics hose--are classified in Industry 326220, Rubber and Plastics Hoses and Belting Manufacturing;

---

T—Canadian, Mexican, and United States industries are comparable.

- Manufacturing noncurrent-carrying plastics conduit--are classified in U.S. Industry 335932, Noncurrent-Carrying Wiring Device Manufacturing; and
- Manufacturing plastics plumbing fixtures--are classified in U.S. Industry 326191, Plastics Plumbing Fixture Manufacturing.

**32613    Laminated Plastics Plate, Sheet (except Packaging), and Shape Manufacturing**[T]
See industry description for 326130.

**326130  Laminated Plastics Plate, Sheet (except Packaging), and Shape Manufacturing**

This industry comprises establishments primarily engaged in laminating plastics profile shapes such as plate, sheet (except packaging), and rod. The lamination process generally involves bonding or impregnating profiles with plastics resins and compressing them under heat.

*Cross-References.*          Establishments primarily engaged in--

- Manufacturing plastics film, plastics unlaminated sheet, and plastics bags--are classified in Industry 32611, Plastics Packaging Materials and Unlaminated Film and Sheet Manufacturing; and
- Coating or laminating nonplastics film, sheet, or bags with plastics--are classified in Industry 322220, Paper Bag and Coated and Treated Paper Manufacturing.

**32614    Polystyrene Foam Product Manufacturing**[T]
See industry description for 326140.

**326140  Polystyrene Foam Product Manufacturing**

This industry comprises establishments primarily engaged in manufacturing polystyrene foam products.

*Cross-References.*

Establishments primarily engaged in manufacturing plastics foam products (except polystyrene) are classified in Industry 326150, Urethane and Other Foam Product (except Polystyrene) Manufacturing.

**32615    Urethane and Other Foam Product (except Polystyrene) Manufacturing**[T]
See industry description for 326150.

**326150  Urethane and Other Foam Product (except Polystyrene) Manufacturing**

This industry comprises establishments primarily engaged in manufacturing plastics foam products (except polystyrene).

*Cross-References.*

Establishments primarily engaged in manufacturing polystyrene foam products are classified in Industry 326140, Polystyrene Foam Product Manufacturing.

**32616    Plastics Bottle Manufacturing**[T]
See industry description for 326160.

**326160  Plastics Bottle Manufacturing**

This industry comprises establishments primarily engaged in manufacturing plastics bottles.

---

T—Canadian, Mexican, and United States industries are comparable.

*Cross-References.*

Establishments primarily engaged in manufacturing plastics containers (except bottles) and plastics bottle caps are classified in U.S. Industry 326199, All Other Plastics Product Manufacturing.

**32619   Other Plastics Product Manufacturing**$^T$

This industry comprises establishments primarily engaged in manufacturing plastics plumbing fixtures and other plastics products (except film, sheet, bags, profile shapes, pipes, pipe fittings, laminates, foam products, bottles, and hoses).

*Illustrative Examples:*

Inflatable plastics swimming pool rafts and similar flotation devices manufacturing
Plastics air mattresses manufacturing
Plastics bottle caps and lids manufacturing
Plastics bowls and bowl covers manufacturing
Plastics clothes hangers manufacturing
Plastics cups (except foam) manufacturing
Plastics dinnerware (except foam) manufacturing
Plastics gloves manufacturing
Plastics hardware manufacturing

Plastics ice chests or coolers (except plastics foam) manufacturing
Plastics or fiberglass plumbing fixtures (e.g., toilets, shower stalls, urinals) manufacturing
Plastics prefabricated buildings manufacturing
Plastics siding manufacturing
Plastics trash containers manufacturing
Resilient floor coverings (e.g., sheet, tiles) manufacturing

*Cross-References.*          Establishments primarily engaged in--

- Manufacturing plastics film, plastics unlaminated sheet, and plastics bags--are classified in Industry 32611, Plastics Packaging Materials and Unlaminated Film and Sheet Manufacturing;
- Manufacturing plastics pipes, pipe fittings, and plastics profile shapes (except film, sheet, bags)--are classified in Industry 32612, Plastics Pipe, Pipe Fitting, and Unlaminated Profile Shape Manufacturing;
- Laminating plastics profile shapes, such as plate, sheet, and rod--are classified in Industry 32613, Laminated Plastics Plate, Sheet (except Packaging), and Shape Manufacturing;
- Manufacturing polystyrene foam products--are classified in Industry 32614, Polystyrene Foam Product Manufacturing;
- Manufacturing foam products (except polystyrene)--are classified in Industry 32615, Urethane and Other Foam Product (except Polystyrene) Manufacturing;
- Manufacturing plastics bottles--are classified in Industry 32616, Plastics Bottle Manufacturing;
- Manufacturing plastics hoses--are classified in Industry 32622, Rubber and Plastics Hoses and Belting Manufacturing;
- Manufacturing plastics furniture parts--are classified in Industry 33721, Office Furniture (including Fixtures) Manufacturing;
- Assembling plastics components into plumbing fixture fittings, such as faucets--are classified in Industry 33291, Metal Valve Manufacturing; and
- Manufacturing rubber floor mats and rubber treads--are classified in Industry 32629, Other Rubber Product Manufacturing.

**326191  Plastics Plumbing Fixture Manufacturing**

This U.S. industry comprises establishments primarily engaged in manufacturing plastics or fiberglass plumbing fixtures. Examples of products made by these establishments are plastics or fiberglass bathtubs, hot tubs, portable toilets, and shower stalls.

---

T—Canadian, Mexican, and United States industries are comparable.

*Cross-References.*          Establishments primarily engaged in--

- Assembling plastics components into plumbing fixture fittings, such as faucets--are classified in U.S. Industry 332913, Plumbing Fixture Fitting and Trim Manufacturing; and
- Manufacturing plastics pipe and pipe fittings--are classified in U.S. Industry 326122, Plastics Pipe and Pipe Fitting Manufacturing.

## 326199  All Other Plastics Product Manufacturing

  This U.S. industry comprises establishments primarily engaged in manufacturing plastics products (except film, sheet, bags, profile shapes, pipes, pipe fittings, laminates, foam products, bottles, plumbing fixtures, and hoses).

*Illustrative Examples:*

Inflatable plastics swimming pool rafts and similar flotation devices manufacturing
Plastics air mattresses manufacturing
Plastics bottle caps and lids manufacturing
Plastics bowls and bowl covers manufacturing
Plastics clothes hangers manufacturing
Plastics cups (except foam) manufacturing

Plastics dinnerware (except foam) manufacturing
Plastics gloves manufacturing
Plastics hardware manufacturing
Plastics siding manufacturing
Plastics trash containers manufacturing
Resilient floor coverings (e.g., sheet, tiles) manufacturing

*Cross-References.*          Establishments primarily engaged in--

- Manufacturing plastics film, plastics unlaminated sheet, and plastics bags--are classified in Industry 32611, Plastics Packaging Materials and Unlaminated Film and Sheet Manufacturing;
- Manufacturing plastics pipes, pipe fittings, and plastics profile shapes (except film, sheet, bags)--are classified in Industry 32612, Plastics Pipe, Pipe Fitting, and Unlaminated Profile Shape Manufacturing;
- Laminating plastics profile shapes, such as plate, sheet, and rod--are classified in Industry 326130, Laminated Plastics Plate, Sheet (except Packaging), and Shape Manufacturing;
- Manufacturing polystyrene foam products--are classified in Industry 326140, Polystyrene Foam Product Manufacturing;
- Manufacturing foam (except polystyrene) products--are classified in Industry 326150, Urethane and Other Foam Product (except Polystyrene) Manufacturing;
- Manufacturing plastics bottles--are classified in Industry 326160, Plastics Bottle Manufacturing;
- Manufacturing plastics hoses--are classified in Industry 326220, Rubber and Plastics Hoses and Belting Manufacturing;
- Manufacturing heavy-duty inflatable plastics boats--are classified in U.S. Industry 336612, Boat Building;
- Manufacturing plastics furniture parts and components--are classified in U.S. Industry 337215, Showcase, Partition, Shelving, and Locker Manufacturing;
- Manufacturing rubber floor mats and rubber treads--are classified in U.S. Industry 326299, All Other Rubber Product Manufacturing;
- Manufacturing plastics plumbing fixtures--are classified in U.S. Industry 326191, Plastics Plumbing Fixture Manufacturing; and
- Assembling plastics components into plumbing fixture fittings, such as faucets--are classified in U.S. Industry 332913, Plumbing Fixture Fitting and Trim Manufacturing.

## 3262    Rubber Product Manufacturing[T]

  This industry group comprises establishments primarily engaged in processing natural, synthetic, or reclaimed rubber materials into intermediate or final products using processes, such as vulcanizing, cementing, molding, extruding, and lathe-cutting.

---

T—Canadian, Mexican, and United States industries are comparable.

## 32621 Tire Manufacturing[T]

This industry comprises establishments primarily engaged in manufacturing tires and inner tubes from natural and synthetic rubber and retreading or rebuilding tires.

*Cross-References.*        Establishments primarily engaged in--

- Repairing tires, such as plugging--are classified in Industry 81119, Other Automotive Repair and Maintenance; and
- Retailing tires--are classified in Industry 44134, Tire Dealers.

## 326211 Tire Manufacturing (except Retreading)

This U.S. industry comprises establishments primarily engaged in manufacturing tires and inner tubes from natural and synthetic rubber.

*Cross-References.*

Establishments primarily engaged in retreading or rebuilding tires are classified in U.S. Industry 326212, Tire Retreading.

## 326212 Tire Retreading

This U.S. industry comprises establishments primarily engaged in retreading or rebuilding tires.

*Cross-References.*        Establishments primarily engaged in--

- Repairing tires, such as plugging--are classified in U.S. Industry 811198, All Other Automotive Repair and Maintenance;
- Retailing tires--are classified in Industry 441340, Tire Dealers; and
- Manufacturing tires and inner tubes from natural and synthetic rubber--are classified in U.S. Industry 326211, Tire Manufacturing (except Retreading).

## 32622 Rubber and Plastics Hoses and Belting Manufacturing[T]
See industry description for 326220.

## 326220 Rubber and Plastics Hoses and Belting Manufacturing

This industry comprises establishments primarily engaged in manufacturing rubber hose and/or plastics (reinforced) hose and belting from natural and synthetic rubber and/or plastics resins. Establishments manufacturing garden hoses from purchased hose are included in this industry.

*Cross-References.*        Establishments primarily engaged in--

- Manufacturing rubber tubing--are classified in U.S. Industry 326299, All Other Rubber Product Manufacturing;
- Manufacturing plastics tubing--are classified in U.S. Industry 326121, Unlaminated Plastics Profile Shape Manufacturing;
- Manufacturing extruded, lathe-cut, or molded rubber goods (except tubing) for mechanical applications-- are classified in U.S. Industry 326291, Rubber Product Manufacturing for Mechanical Use; and
- Manufacturing fluid power hose assemblies--are classified in U.S. Industry 332912, Fluid Power Valve and Hose Fitting Manufacturing.

---

T—Canadian, Mexican, and United States industries are comparable.

## 32629   Other Rubber Product Manufacturing[T]

This industry comprises establishments primarily engaged in manufacturing rubber products (except tires, hoses, and belting) from natural and synthetic rubber.

*Illustrative Examples:*

Birth control devices (e.g., diaphragms, prophylactics) manufacturing
Latex foam rubber manufacturing
Mechanical rubber goods (i.e., molded, extruded, lathe-cut) manufacturing
Reclaiming rubber from waste and scrap

Rubber balloons manufacturing
Rubber bands manufacturing
Rubber floor mats (e.g., door, bath) manufacturing
Rubber hair care products (e.g., combs, curlers) manufacturing
Rubber tubing manufacturing

*Cross-References.*        Establishments primarily engaged in--

- Manufacturing tires and inner tubes--are classified in Industry 32621, Tire Manufacturing;
- Manufacturing rubber hoses and belting--are classified in Industry 32622, Rubber and Plastics Hoses and Belting Manufacturing;
- Rubberizing fabric--are classified in Industry 31332, Fabric Coating Mills;
- Manufacturing rubber gaskets, packing, and sealing devices--are classified in Industry 33999, All Other Miscellaneous Manufacturing;
- Manufacturing rubber gloves--are classified in Industry 33911, Medical Equipment and Supplies Manufacturing;
- Manufacturing rubber clothing accessories (e.g., bathing caps)--are classified in Industry 31599, Apparel Accessories and Other Apparel Manufacturing; and
- Manufacturing rubber toys--are classified in Industry 33993, Doll, Toy, and Game Manufacturing.

### 326291  Rubber Product Manufacturing for Mechanical Use

This U.S. industry comprises establishments primarily engaged in manufacturing rubber goods (except tubing) for mechanical applications, using the processes of molding, extruding or lathe-cutting. Products of this industry are generally parts for motor vehicles, machinery, and equipment.

*Cross-References.*

Establishments primarily engaged in manufacturing rubber tubing from natural and synthetic rubber or in manufacturing rubber products for mechanical applications using processes other than molding, extruding or lathe-cutting are classified in U.S. Industry 326299, All Other Rubber Product Manufacturing.

### 326299  All Other Rubber Product Manufacturing

This U.S. industry comprises establishments primarily engaged in manufacturing rubber products (except tires; hoses and belting; and molded, extruded, and lathe-cut rubber goods for mechanical applications (except rubber tubing)) from natural and synthetic rubber. Establishments manufacturing rubber tubing made from natural and synthetic rubber, regardless of process used, are included in this industry.

*Illustrative Examples:*

Birth control devices (i.e., diaphragms, prophylactics) manufacturing
Latex foam rubber manufacturing
Reclaiming rubber from waste and scrap
Rubber balloons manufacturing

Rubber bands manufacturing
Rubber floor mats (e.g., door, bath) manufacturing
Rubber hair care products (e.g., combs, curlers) manufacturing
Rubber tubing manufacturing

---

T—Canadian, Mexican, and United States industries are comparable.

*Cross-References.*          Establishments primarily engaged in--

- Manufacturing tires and inner tubes and rebuilding tires--are classified in Industry 32621, Tire Manufacturing;
- Manufacturing rubber hoses and belting--are classified in Industry 326220, Rubber and Plastics Hoses and Belting Manufacturing;
- Manufacturing heavy-duty inflatable rubber boats--are classified in U.S. Industry 336612, Boat Building;
- Molding, extruding, and lathe-cutting rubber to manufacture rubber goods (except tubing) for mechanical applications--are classified in U.S. Industry 326291, Rubber Product Manufacturing for Mechanical Use;
- Rubberizing fabrics--are classified in Industry 313320, Fabric Coating Mills;
- Manufacturing rubber gasket, packing, and sealing devices--are classified in U.S. Industry 339991, Gasket, Packing, and Sealing Device Manufacturing;
- Manufacturing rubber toys--are classified in Industry 339930, Doll, Toy, and Game Manufacturing;
- Manufacturing rubber gloves--are classified in U.S. Industry 339113, Surgical Appliance and Supplies Manufacturing; and
- Manufacturing rubber clothing accessories (e.g., bathing caps)--are classified in Industry 315990, Apparel Accessories and Other Apparel Manufacturing.

## 327    Nonmetallic Mineral Product Manufacturing[T]

The Nonmetallic Mineral Product Manufacturing subsector is based on the transformation of mined or quarried nonmetallic minerals, such as sand, gravel, stone, clay, and refractory materials, into products for intermediate or final consumption. Processes used include grinding, mixing, cutting, shaping, and honing. Heat often is used in the process and chemicals are frequently mixed to change the composition, purity, and chemical properties for the intended product. For example, glass is produced by heating silica sand to the melting point (sometimes combined with cullet or recycled glass) and then drawn, floated, or blow molded to the desired shape or thickness. Refractory materials are heated and then formed into bricks or other shapes for use in industrial applications.

The Nonmetallic Mineral Product Manufacturing subsector includes establishments that manufacture bricks, refractories, ceramic products, and glass and glass products, such as plate glass and containers. Also included are cement and concrete products, lime, gypsum, and other nonmetallic mineral products including abrasive products, ceramic plumbing fixtures, statuary, cut stone products, and mineral wool. The products are used in a wide range of activities from construction and heavy and light manufacturing to articles for personal use.

Mining, beneficiating, and manufacturing activities often occur in a single location. Separate receipts will be collected for these activities whenever possible. When receipts cannot be broken out between mining and manufacturing, establishments that mine or quarry nonmetallic minerals, beneficiate the nonmetallic minerals, and further process the nonmetallic minerals into a more finished manufactured product are classified based on the primary activity of the establishment. A mine that manufactures a small amount of finished products is classified in Sector 21, Mining, Quarrying, and Oil and Gas Extraction. An establishment that mines whose primary output is a more finished manufactured product is classified in the Manufacturing sector.

Excluded from the Nonmetallic Mineral Product Manufacturing subsector are establishments that primarily beneficiate mined nonmetallic minerals. Beneficiation is the process whereby the extracted material is reduced to particles that can be separated into mineral and waste, the former suitable for further processing or direct use. Beneficiation establishments are included in Sector 21, Mining, Quarrying, and Oil and Gas Extraction.

## 3271    Clay Product and Refractory Manufacturing[T]

This industry group comprises establishments primarily engaged in (1) shaping, molding, glazing, and firing pottery, ceramics, and plumbing fixtures, and electrical supplies made entirely or partly of clay or other ceramic materials or (2) shaping, molding, baking, burning, or hardening clay refractories, nonclay refractories, ceramic tile, structural clay tile, brick, and other structural clay building materials.

## 32711    Pottery, Ceramics, and Plumbing Fixture Manufacturing[T]
See industry description for 327110.

---

T—Canadian, Mexican, and United States industries are comparable.

### 327110 Pottery, Ceramics, and Plumbing Fixture Manufacturing

This industry comprises establishments primarily engaged in shaping, molding, glazing, and firing pottery, ceramics, plumbing fixtures, and electrical supplies made entirely or partly of clay or other ceramic materials.

*Illustrative Examples:*

Bathroom accessories, vitreous china and earthenware, manufacturing
Ceramic or ferrite permanent magnets manufacturing
Chemical stoneware (i.e., pottery products) manufacturing

Clay and ceramic statuary manufacturing
Earthenware table and kitchen articles, coarse, manufacturing
Porcelain electrical insulators manufacturing
Vitreous china plumbing fixtures manufacturing

*Cross-References.*          Establishments primarily engaged in--

- Manufacturing enameled iron and steel plumbing fixtures--are classified in U.S. Industry 332999, All Other Miscellaneous Fabricated Metal Product Manufacturing;
- Manufacturing metal bathroom accessories--are classified in Subsector 332, Fabricated Metal Product Manufacturing;
- Manufacturing cultured marble and other plastics plumbing fixtures--are classified in U.S. Industry 326191, Plastics Plumbing Fixture Manufacturing;
- Manufacturing clay building materials, such as ceramic tile, bricks, and clay roofing tiles, and refractories--are classified in Industry 327120, Clay Building Material and Refractories Manufacturing;
- Manufacturing ferrite microwave devices and electronic components--are classified in Subsector 334, Computer and Electronic Product Manufacturing; and
- Manufacturing plastics bathroom accessories--are classified in U.S. Industry 326199, All Other Plastics Product Manufacturing.

### 32712 Clay Building Material and Refractories Manufacturing[T]
See industry description for 327120.

### 327120 Clay Building Material and Refractories Manufacturing

This industry comprises establishments primarily engaged in shaping, molding, baking, burning, or hardening clay refractories, nonclay refractories, ceramic tile, structural clay tile, brick, and other structural clay building materials. A refractory is a material that will retain its shape and chemical identity when subjected to high temperatures and is used in applications that require extreme resistance to heat, such as furnace linings.

*Cross-References.*          Establishments primarily engaged in--

- Manufacturing resilient flooring and asphalt floor tiles--are classified in U.S. Industry 326199, All Other Plastics Product Manufacturing;
- Manufacturing concrete bricks--are classified in U.S. Industry 327331, Concrete Block and Brick Manufacturing; and
- Manufacturing glass bricks and blocks--are classified in Industry 32721, Glass and Glass Product Manufacturing.

### 3272 Glass and Glass Product Manufacturing[T]

### 32721 Glass and Glass Product Manufacturing[T]

This industry comprises establishments primarily engaged in manufacturing glass and/or glass products. Establishments in this industry may manufacture glass and/or glass products by melting silica sand or cullet, or from purchased glass.

---

T—Canadian, Mexican, and United States industries are comparable.

*Cross-References.*          Establishments primarily engaged in--

- Manufacturing glass wool (i.e., fiberglass) insulation products--are classified in Industry 32799, All Other Nonmetallic Mineral Product Manufacturing;
- Manufacturing optical lenses (except ophthalmic), such as magnifying, photographic, and projection lenses--are classified in Industry 33331, Commercial and Service Industry Machinery Manufacturing;
- Grinding ophthalmic (i.e., eyeglass) lenses for the trade--are classified in Industry 33911, Medical Equipment and Supplies Manufacturing; and
- Manufacturing fiber optic cable from purchased fiber optic strand--are classified in Industry 33592, Communication and Energy Wire and Cable Manufacturing.

## 327211  Flat Glass Manufacturing

This U.S. industry comprises establishments primarily engaged in (1) manufacturing flat glass by melting silica sand or cullet or (2) manufacturing both flat glass and laminated glass by melting silica sand or cullet.

*Cross-References.*

Establishments primarily engaged in manufacturing laminated glass from purchased flat glass are classified in U.S. Industry 327215, Glass Product Manufacturing Made of Purchased Glass.

## 327212  Other Pressed and Blown Glass and Glassware Manufacturing

This U.S. industry comprises establishments primarily engaged in manufacturing glass by melting silica sand or cullet and making pressed, blown, or shaped glass or glassware (except glass packaging containers).

*Cross-References.*          Establishments primarily engaged in--

- Manufacturing flat glass--are classified in U.S. Industry 327211, Flat Glass Manufacturing;
- Manufacturing glass packaging containers--are classified in U.S. Industry 327213, Glass Container Manufacturing;
- Manufacturing glass wool (i.e., fiberglass) insulation--are classified in U.S. Industry 327993, Mineral Wool Manufacturing;
- Manufacturing glassware from purchased glass--are classified in U.S. Industry 327215, Glass Product Manufacturing Made of Purchased Glass; and
- Manufacturing fiber optic cable from purchased fiber optic strand--are classified in U.S. Industry 335921, Fiber Optic Cable Manufacturing.

## 327213  Glass Container Manufacturing

This U.S. industry comprises establishments primarily engaged in manufacturing glass packaging, bottling, and canning containers.

## 327215  Glass Product Manufacturing Made of Purchased Glass

This U.S. industry comprises establishments primarily engaged in coating, laminating, tempering, or shaping purchased glass.

*Cross-References.*          Establishments primarily engaged in--

- Manufacturing glass packaging containers--are classified in U.S. Industry 327213, Glass Container Manufacturing;
- Manufacturing optical lenses (except ophthalmic), such as magnifying, photographic, and projection lenses--are classified in Industry 333310, Commercial and Service Industry Machinery Manufacturing;

T—Canadian, Mexican, and United States industries are comparable.

- Manufacturing ophthalmic (i.e., eyeglass) lenses--are classified in U.S. Industry 339115, Ophthalmic Goods Manufacturing; and
- Manufacturing fiber optic cable from purchased fiber optic strand--are classified in U.S. Industry 335921, Fiber Optic Cable Manufacturing.

### 3273    Cement and Concrete Product Manufacturing[T]

This industry group comprises establishments primarily engaged in one of the following: (1) manufacturing Portland, natural, masonry, pozzolanic, and other hydraulic cements; (2) acting as batch or mixing plants, manufacturing concrete delivered to a purchaser in a plastic and unhardened state; (3) manufacturing concrete pipe, brick, and block; or (4) manufacturing other concrete products (except block, brick, and pipe).

### 32731    Cement Manufacturing[T]
See industry description for 327310.

### 327310    Cement Manufacturing

This industry comprises establishments primarily engaged in manufacturing Portland, natural, masonry, pozzolanic, and other hydraulic cements.  Cement manufacturing establishments may calcine earths or mine, quarry, manufacture, or purchase lime.

*Cross-References.*          Establishments primarily engaged in--

- Mining or quarrying limestone--are classified in U.S. Industry 212312, Crushed and Broken Limestone Mining and Quarrying;
- Manufacturing lime--are classified in Industry 327410, Lime Manufacturing;
- Manufacturing ready-mix concrete--are classified in Industry 327320, Ready-Mix Concrete Manufacturing; and
- Manufacturing dry mix concrete--are classified in U.S. Industry 327999, All Other Miscellaneous Nonmetallic Mineral Product Manufacturing.

### 32732    Ready-Mix Concrete Manufacturing[T]
See industry description for 327320.

### 327320    Ready-Mix Concrete Manufacturing

This industry comprises establishments, such as batch plants or mix plants, primarily engaged in manufacturing concrete delivered to a purchaser in a plastic and unhardened state.  Ready-mix concrete manufacturing establishments may mine, quarry, or purchase sand and gravel.

*Cross-References.*          Establishments primarily engaged in--

- Operating sand or gravel pits--are classified in U.S. Industry 212321, Construction Sand and Gravel Mining; and
- Manufacturing dry mix concrete--are classified in U.S. Industry 327999, All Other Miscellaneous Nonmetallic Mineral Product Manufacturing.

### 32733    Concrete Pipe, Brick, and Block Manufacturing[T]

This industry comprises establishments primarily engaged in manufacturing concrete pipe, brick, and block.

*Cross-References.*

Establishments primarily engaged in manufacturing concrete products (except block, brick, and pipe) are classified in Industry 32739, Other Concrete Product Manufacturing.

---

T—Canadian, Mexican, and United States industries are comparable.

### 327331  Concrete Block and Brick Manufacturing

This U.S. industry comprises establishments primarily engaged in manufacturing concrete block and brick.

### 327332  Concrete Pipe Manufacturing

This U.S. industry comprises establishments primarily engaged in manufacturing concrete pipe.

### 32739  Other Concrete Product Manufacturing<sup>T</sup>
See industry description for 327390.

### 327390  Other Concrete Product Manufacturing

This industry comprises establishments primarily engaged in manufacturing concrete products (except block, brick, and pipe).

*Cross-References.*          Establishments primarily engaged in--

- Manufacturing concrete block and brick--are classified in U.S. Industry 327331, Concrete Block and Brick Manufacturing; and
- Manufacturing concrete pipe--are classified in U.S. Industry 327332, Concrete Pipe Manufacturing.

### 3274  Lime and Gypsum Product Manufacturing<sup>T</sup>

This industry group comprises establishments primarily engaged in (1) manufacturing lime from calcitic limestone, dolomitic limestone, or other calcareous materials or (2) manufacturing gypsum products.

### 32741  Lime Manufacturing<sup>T</sup>
See industry description for 327410.

### 327410  Lime Manufacturing

This industry comprises establishments primarily engaged in manufacturing lime from calcitic limestone, dolomitic limestone, or other calcareous materials, such as coral, chalk, and shells.  Lime manufacturing establishments may mine, quarry, collect, or purchase the sources of calcium carbonate.

*Cross-References.*

Establishments primarily engaged in manufacturing dolomite refractories are classified in Industry 327120, Clay Building Material and Refractories Manufacturing.

### 32742  Gypsum Product Manufacturing<sup>T</sup>
See industry description for 327420.

### 327420  Gypsum Product Manufacturing

This industry comprises establishments primarily engaged in manufacturing gypsum products, such as wallboard, plaster, plasterboard, molding, ornamental moldings, statuary, and architectural plaster work.  Gypsum product manufacturing establishments may mine, quarry, or purchase gypsum.

*Cross-References.*

Establishments primarily engaged in operating gypsum mines or quarries are classified in Industry 212390, Other Nonmetallic Mineral Mining and Quarrying.

---

T—Canadian, Mexican, and United States industries are comparable.

### 3279    Other Nonmetallic Mineral Product Manufacturing[T]

This industry group comprises establishments manufacturing nonmetallic mineral products (except clay products, refractory products, glass products, cement and concrete products, lime, and gypsum products).

### 32791   Abrasive Product Manufacturing[T]
See industry description for 327910.

### 327910  Abrasive Product Manufacturing

This industry comprises establishments primarily engaged in manufacturing abrasive grinding wheels of natural or synthetic materials, abrasive-coated products, and other abrasive products.

*Illustrative Examples:*

Aluminum oxide (fused) abrasives manufacturing
Buffing and polishing wheels, abrasive and
nonabrasive, manufacturing
Diamond dressing wheels manufacturing

Sandpaper manufacturing
Silicon carbide abrasives manufacturing
Whetstones manufacturing

*Cross-References.*          Establishments primarily engaged in--

- Mining and cutting grindstones, pulpstones, and whetstones--are classified in Industry 212390, Other Nonmetallic Mineral Mining and Quarrying;
- Manufacturing plastic scouring pads--are classified in U.S. Industry 326199, All Other Plastics Product Manufacturing; and
- Manufacturing metallic scouring pads and steel wool--are classified in U.S. Industry 332999, All Other Miscellaneous Fabricated Metal Product Manufacturing.

### 32799   All Other Nonmetallic Mineral Product Manufacturing[T]

This industry comprises establishments primarily engaged in manufacturing nonmetallic mineral products (except pottery and plumbing fixtures; clay building materials and refractories; glass and glass products; cement; ready-mix concrete; concrete products; lime; gypsum products; and abrasive products).

*Cross-References.*          Establishments primarily engaged in--

- Manufacturing pottery, ceramics, and plumbing fixtures--are classified in Industry 32711, Pottery, Ceramics, and Plumbing Fixture Manufacturing;
- Mining or quarrying stone, earth, or other nonmetallic minerals--are classified in Industry Group 2123, Nonmetallic Mineral Mining and Quarrying;
- Buying and selling semi-finished monuments and tombstones with no work other than polishing, lettering, or shaping to custom order--are classified in Sector 42, Wholesale Trade, or Sector 44-45, Retail Trade;
- Manufacturing clay building materials and refractories--are classified in Industry 32712, Clay Building Material and Refractories Manufacturing;
- Manufacturing glass and glass products--are classified in Industry 32721, Glass and Glass Product Manufacturing;
- Manufacturing cement--are classified in Industry 32731, Cement Manufacturing;
- Mixing and delivering ready-mix concrete--are classified in Industry 32732, Ready-Mix Concrete Manufacturing;
- Manufacturing concrete pipe, brick, and block--are classified in Industry 32733, Concrete Pipe, Brick, and Block Manufacturing;
- Manufacturing concrete products (except pipe, brick, and block)--are classified in Industry 32739, Other Concrete Product Manufacturing;
- Manufacturing lime--are classified in Industry 32741, Lime Manufacturing;

---

T—Canadian, Mexican, and United States industries are comparable.

- Manufacturing gypsum products--are classified in Industry 32742, Gypsum Product Manufacturing;
- Manufacturing abrasive products--are classified in Industry 32791, Abrasive Product Manufacturing; and
- Manufacturing metallic scouring pads and steel wool--are classified in Industry 33299, All Other Fabricated Metal Product Manufacturing.

## 327991  Cut Stone and Stone Product Manufacturing

This U.S. industry comprises establishments primarily engaged in cutting, shaping, and finishing granite, marble, limestone, slate, and other stone for building and miscellaneous uses.  Stone product manufacturing establishments may mine, quarry, or purchase stone.

*Cross-References.*            Establishments primarily engaged in--

- Mining or quarrying stone--are classified in Industry Group 2123, Nonmetallic Mineral Mining and Quarrying; and
- Buying and selling semi-finished monuments and tombstones with no work other than polishing, lettering, or shaping to custom order--are classified in Sector 42, Wholesale Trade, or Sector 44-45, Retail Trade.

## 327992  Ground or Treated Mineral and Earth Manufacturing

This U.S. industry comprises establishments primarily engaged in calcining, dead burning, or otherwise processing beyond beneficiation, clays, ceramic and refractory minerals, barite, and miscellaneous nonmetallic minerals.

*Cross-References.*

Establishments primarily engaged in crushing, grinding, pulverizing, washing, screening, sizing, or otherwise beneficiating mined clays, ceramics and refractory, and other miscellaneous nonmetallic minerals are classified in Industry Group 2123, Nonmetallic Mineral Mining and Quarrying.

## 327993  Mineral Wool Manufacturing

This U.S. industry comprises establishments primarily engaged in manufacturing mineral wool and mineral wool (i.e., fiberglass) insulation products made of such siliceous materials as rock, slag, and glass or combinations thereof.

*Cross-References.*

Establishments primarily engaged in manufacturing metallic scouring pads and steel wool are classified in U.S. Industry 332999, All Other Miscellaneous Fabricated Metal Product Manufacturing.

## 327999  All Other Miscellaneous Nonmetallic Mineral Product Manufacturing

This U.S. industry comprises establishments primarily engaged in manufacturing nonmetallic mineral products (except pottery, ceramics, and plumbing fixtures; clay building materials and refractories; glass and glass products; cement; ready-mix concrete; concrete products; lime; gypsum products; abrasive products; cut stone and stone products; ground and treated minerals and earth; and mineral wool).

*Illustrative Examples:*

| | |
|---|---|
| Dry mix concrete manufacturing | Stucco and stucco products manufacturing |
| Mica products manufacturing | Synthetic stones, for gem stones and industrial use, |
| Manmade and engineered proppants (e.g., resin-coated sand, ceramic materials) manufacturing | manufacturing |

---

T—Canadian, Mexican, and United States industries are comparable.

*Cross-References.*          Establishments primarily engaged in--

- Manufacturing pottery, ceramics, and plumbing fixtures--are classified in Industry 327110, Pottery, Ceramics, and Plumbing Fixture Manufacturing;
- Manufacturing clay building materials and refractories--are classified in Industry 327120, Clay Building Material and Refractories Manufacturing;
- Manufacturing glass and glass products--are classified in Industry 32721, Glass and Glass Product Manufacturing;
- Manufacturing cement--are classified in Industry 327310, Cement Manufacturing;
- Mixing and delivering ready-mix concrete--are classified in Industry 327320, Ready-Mix Concrete Manufacturing;
- Manufacturing concrete pipe, brick, and block--are classified in Industry 32733, Concrete Pipe, Brick, and Block Manufacturing;
- Manufacturing concrete products (except pipe, brick, and block)--are classified in Industry 327390, Other Concrete Product Manufacturing;
- Manufacturing lime--are classified in Industry 327410, Lime Manufacturing;
- Manufacturing gypsum products--are classified in Industry 327420, Gypsum Product Manufacturing;
- Manufacturing abrasives and abrasive products--are classified in Industry 327910, Abrasive Product Manufacturing;
- Manufacturing cut stone and stone products--are classified in U.S. Industry 327991, Cut Stone and Stone Product Manufacturing;
- Manufacturing ground and treated minerals and earth (i.e., not at the mine site)--are classified in U.S. Industry 327992, Ground or Treated Mineral and Earth Manufacturing; and
- Manufacturing mineral wool and fiberglass insulation products--are classified in U.S. Industry 327993, Mineral Wool Manufacturing.

### 331    Primary Metal Manufacturing[T]

Industries in the Primary Metal Manufacturing subsector smelt and/or refine ferrous and nonferrous metals from ore, pig, or scrap, using electrometallurgical and other process metallurgical techniques.  Establishments in this subsector also manufacture metal alloys and superalloys by introducing other chemical elements to pure metals.  The output of smelting and refining, usually in ingot form, is used in rolling, drawing, and extruding operations to make sheet, strip, bar, rod, or wire, and in molten form to make castings and other basic metal products.

Primary manufacturing of ferrous and nonferrous metals begins with ore or concentrate as the primary input. Establishments manufacturing primary metals from ore and/or concentrate remain classified in the primary smelting, primary refining, or iron and steel mill industries regardless of the form of their output.  Establishments primarily engaged in secondary smelting and/or secondary refining recover ferrous and nonferrous metals from scrap and/or dross.  The output of the secondary smelting and/or secondary refining industries is limited to shapes such as ingot or billet that will be further processed.  Recovery of metals from scrap often occurs in establishments that are primarily engaged in activities, such as rolling, drawing, extruding, or similar processes.

Excluded from the Primary Metal Manufacturing subsector are establishments primarily engaged in manufacturing ferrous and nonferrous forgings (except ferrous forgings made in steel mills) and stampings.  Although forging, stamping, and casting are all methods used to make metal shapes, forging and stamping do not use molten metals and are included in Subsector 332, Fabricated Metal Product Manufacturing.  Establishments primarily engaged in operating coke ovens are classified in Industry 32419, Other Petroleum and Coal Products Manufacturing.

### 3311    Iron and Steel Mills and Ferroalloy Manufacturing[T]

### 33111    Iron and Steel Mills and Ferroalloy Manufacturing[T]
See industry description for 331110.

### 331110  Iron and Steel Mills and Ferroalloy Manufacturing

This industry comprises establishments primarily engaged in one or more of the following: (1) direct reduction of iron ore; (2) manufacturing pig iron in molten or solid form; (3) converting pig iron into steel; (4) making steel; (5)

---

T—Canadian, Mexican, and United States industries are comparable.

making steel and manufacturing shapes (e.g., bar, plate, rod, sheet, strip, wire); (6) making steel and forming pipe and tube; and (7) manufacturing electrometallurgical ferroalloys. Ferroalloys add critical elements, such as silicon and manganese for carbon steel and chromium, vanadium, tungsten, titanium, and molybdenum for low- and high-alloy metals. Ferroalloys include iron-rich alloys and more pure forms of elements added during the steel manufacturing process that alter or improve the characteristics of the metal.

*Cross-References.*          Establishments primarily engaged in--

- Operating coke ovens--are classified in U.S. Industry 324199, All Other Petroleum and Coal Products Manufacturing;
- Manufacturing nonferrous superalloys, such as cobalt or nickel-based superalloys--are classified in U.S. Industry 331492, Secondary Smelting, Refining, and Alloying of Nonferrous Metal (except Copper and Aluminum);
- Manufacturing concrete reinforcing bar by rolling and drawing steel from purchased steel--are classified in U.S. Industry 331221, Rolled Steel Shape Manufacturing; and
- Manufacturing fabricated structural metal products from concrete reinforcing bars and fabricated bar joists--are classified in U.S. Industry 332312, Fabricated Structural Metal Manufacturing.

## 3312    Steel Product Manufacturing from Purchased Steel[T]

This industry group comprises establishments primarily engaged in manufacturing iron and steel tube and pipe, drawing steel wire, and rolling or drawing shapes from purchased iron or steel.

## 33121    Iron and Steel Pipe and Tube Manufacturing from Purchased Steel[T]
See industry description for 331210.

## 331210  Iron and Steel Pipe and Tube Manufacturing from Purchased Steel

This industry comprises establishments primarily engaged in manufacturing welded, riveted, or seamless pipe and tube from purchased iron or steel.

*Cross-References.*

Establishments primarily engaged in making steel and further processing the steel into steel pipe and tube are classified in Industry 331110, Iron and Steel Mills and Ferroalloy Manufacturing.

## 33122    Rolling and Drawing of Purchased Steel[T]

This industry comprises establishments primarily engaged in rolling and/or drawing steel shapes, such as plate, sheet, strip, rod, and bar, from purchased steel.

*Cross-References.*          Establishments primarily engaged in--

- Making steel and rolling and/or drawing steel--are classified in Industry 33111, Iron and Steel Mills and Ferroalloy Manufacturing; and
- Manufacturing wire products from purchased wire--are classified in Industry 33261, Spring and Wire Product Manufacturing.

## 331221  Rolled Steel Shape Manufacturing

This U.S. industry comprises establishments primarily engaged in rolling or drawing shapes (except wire), such as plate, sheet, strip, rod, and bar, from purchased steel.

---

T—Canadian, Mexican, and United States industries are comparable.

*Cross-References.*              Establishments primarily engaged in--

- Making steel and rolling or drawing steel shapes, or manufacturing concrete reinforcing bars in an iron and steel mill--are classified in Industry 331110, Iron and Steel Mills and Ferroalloy Manufacturing;
- Drawing wire from purchased steel--are classified in U.S. Industry 331222, Steel Wire Drawing; and
- Manufacturing fabricated structural metal products from concrete reinforcing bars and fabricated bar joists--are classified in U.S. Industry 332312, Fabricated Structural Metal Manufacturing.

## 331222  Steel Wire Drawing

This U.S. industry comprises establishments primarily engaged in drawing wire from purchased steel.

*Cross-References.*              Establishments primarily engaged in--

- Making steel and drawing steel wire--are classified in Industry 331110, Iron and Steel Mills and Ferroalloy Manufacturing; and
- Manufacturing wire products, such as nails, spikes, and paper clips, from purchased steel wire--are classified in Industry 33261, Spring and Wire Product Manufacturing.

## 3313    Alumina and Aluminum Production and Processing[T]

## 33131   Alumina and Aluminum Production and Processing[T]

This industry comprises establishments primarily engaged in one or more of the following: (1) refining alumina; (2) making (i.e., the primary production) aluminum from alumina; (3) recovering aluminum from scrap or dross; (4) alloying purchased aluminum; and (5) manufacturing aluminum primary forms (e.g., bar, foil, pipe, plate, rod, sheet, tube, wire).

*Cross-References.*              Establishments primarily engaged in--

- Manufacturing aluminum oxide abrasives and refractories--are classified in Subsector 327, Nonmetallic Mineral Product Manufacturing;
- Sorting, breaking up, and wholesaling scrap aluminum metal without also smelting or refining--are classified in Industry 42393, Recyclable Material Merchant Wholesalers; and
- Operating facilities where commingled recyclable materials, such as paper, plastics, used beverage cans, and metals, are sorted into distinct categories without also smelting or refining--are classified in Industry 56292, Materials Recovery Facilities.

## 331313  Alumina Refining and Primary Aluminum Production

This U.S. industry comprises establishments primarily engaged in one or more of the following: (1) refining alumina (i.e., aluminum oxide) generally from bauxite; (2) making aluminum from alumina; and/or (3) making aluminum from alumina and rolling, drawing, extruding, or casting the aluminum they make into primary forms. Establishments in this industry may make primary aluminum or aluminum-based alloys from alumina.

*Cross-references.*              Establishments primarily engaged in--

- Manufacturing aluminum oxide abrasives and refractories--are classified in Subsector 327, Nonmetallic Mineral Product Manufacturing; and
- Recovering aluminum from scrap or alloying purchased aluminum--are classified in U.S. Industry 331314, Secondary Smelting and Alloying of Aluminum.

---

T—Canadian, Mexican, and United States industries are comparable.

## 331314  Secondary Smelting and Alloying of Aluminum

This U.S. industry comprises establishments primarily engaged in (1) recovering aluminum and aluminum alloys from scrap and/or dross (i.e., secondary smelting) and making billet or ingot (except by rolling) and/or (2) manufacturing alloys, powder, paste, or flake from purchased aluminum.

*Cross-References.*          Establishments primarily engaged in--

- Refining alumina or making aluminum and/or aluminum alloys from alumina--are classified in U.S. Industry 331313, Alumina Refining and Primary Aluminum Production;
- Manufacturing aluminum sheet, plate, and foil from purchased aluminum or by recovering aluminum from scrap and flat rolling or continuous casting--are classified in U.S. Industry 331315, Aluminum Sheet, Plate, and Foil Manufacturing;
- Manufacturing aluminum extruded products or rolled ingot or billet from purchased aluminum or by recovering aluminum from scrap and extruding, rolling, or drawing--are classified in U.S. Industry 331318, Other Aluminum Rolling, Drawing, and Extruding;
- Sorting, breaking up, and wholesaling scrap metal without also smelting or refining--are classified in Industry 423930, Recyclable Material Merchant Wholesalers; and
- Operating facilities where commingled recyclable materials, such as paper, plastics, used beverage cans, and metals, are sorted into distinct categories without also smelting or refining--are classified in Industry 562920, Materials Recovery Facilities.

## 331315  Aluminum Sheet, Plate, and Foil Manufacturing

This U.S. industry comprises establishments primarily engaged in (1) flat rolling or continuous casting sheet, plate, foil and welded tube from purchased aluminum and/or (2) recovering aluminum from scrap and flat rolling or continuous casting sheet, plate, foil, and welded tube in integrated mills.

*Cross-References.*

Establishments primarily engaged in making aluminum from alumina and flat rolling or continuous casting aluminum sheet, plate, foil, and welded tube are classified in U.S. Industry 331313, Alumina Refining and Primary Aluminum Production.

## 331318  Other Aluminum Rolling, Drawing, and Extruding

This U.S. industry comprises establishments primarily engaged in (1) rolling, drawing, or extruding shapes (except flat rolled sheet, plate, foil, and welded tube) from purchased aluminum and/or (2) recovering aluminum from scrap and rolling, drawing, or extruding shapes (except flat rolled sheet, plate, foil, and welded tube) in integrated mills.

*Illustrative Examples:*

Aluminum bar made by extruding purchased aluminum
Nails, aluminum, made in wire drawing plants
Structural shapes made by rolling purchased aluminum

Rod made by extruding purchased aluminum
Tube made by drawing or extruding purchased aluminum
Wire, bare, made in aluminum wire drawing plants

*Cross-References.*          Establishments primarily engaged in--

- Flat rolling sheet, plate, foil, and welded tube from either purchased aluminum or by recovering aluminum from scrap and flat rolling or continuous casting--are classified in U.S. Industry 331315, Aluminum Sheet, Plate, and Foil Manufacturing; and
- Making aluminum from alumina and making aluminum shapes--are classified in U.S. Industry 331313, Alumina Refining and Primary Aluminum Production.

---

T—Canadian, Mexican, and United States industries are comparable.

**3314 Nonferrous Metal (except Aluminum) Production and Processing[T]**

This industry group comprises establishments primarily engaged in nonferrous metal (except aluminum) smelting, refining, rolling, drawing, extruding, and alloying.

**33141 Nonferrous Metal (except Aluminum) Smelting and Refining[T]**
See industry description for 331410.

**331410 Nonferrous Metal (except Aluminum) Smelting and Refining**

This industry comprises establishments primarily engaged in (1) smelting ores into nonferrous metals and/or (2) the primary refining of nonferrous metals (except aluminum) by electrolytic methods or other processes.

*Cross-References.* Establishments primarily engaged in--

- Mining and making copper and other nonferrous concentrates (including gold and silver bullion), by processes, such as solvent extraction or electrowinning--are classified in Industry Group 2122, Metal Ore Mining;
- Recovering copper or copper alloys from scrap or dross and/or alloying, rolling, drawing, and extruding purchased copper--are classified in Industry 331420, Copper Rolling, Drawing, Extruding, and Alloying;
- Rolling, drawing, and/or extruding nonferrous metal shapes (except copper and aluminum) from purchased nonferrous metals (except copper and aluminum) or by recovering nonferrous metals (except copper and aluminum) and rolling, drawing, or extruding--are classified in U.S. Industry 331491, Nonferrous Metal (except Copper and Aluminum) Rolling, Drawing, and Extruding;
- Recovering nonferrous metals (except copper and aluminum) from scrap and making primary forms and/or alloying purchased nonferrous metals (except copper and aluminum)--are classified in U.S. Industry 331492, Secondary Smelting, Refining, and Alloying of Nonferrous Metal (except Copper and Aluminum);
- Making aluminum from alumina--are classified in U.S. Industry 331313, Alumina Refining and Primary Aluminum Production;
- Operating facilities where commingled recyclable materials, such as paper, plastics, used beverage cans, and metals, are sorted into distinct categories without also smelting or refining--are classified in Industry 562920, Materials Recovery Facilities; and
- Sorting, breaking up, and wholesaling scrap metal without also smelting or refining--are classified in Industry 423930, Recyclable Material Merchant Wholesalers.

**33142 Copper Rolling, Drawing, Extruding, and Alloying[T]**
See industry description for 331420.

**331420 Copper Rolling, Drawing, Extruding, and Alloying**

This industry comprises establishments primarily engaged in one or more of the following: (1) recovering copper or copper alloys from scraps; (2) alloying purchased copper; (3) rolling, drawing, or extruding shapes (e.g., bar, plate, sheet, strip, tube, wire) from purchased copper; and (4) recovering copper or copper alloys from scrap and rolling, drawing, or extruding shapes (e.g., bar, plate, sheet, strip, tube, wire).

*Cross-References.* Establishments primarily engaged in--

- Smelting copper ore, primary copper refining, and/or rolling, drawing, or extruding primary copper made in the same establishment--are classified in Industry 331410, Nonferrous Metal (except Aluminum) Smelting and Refining;
- Manufacturing wire products from purchased copper wire--are classified in Industry 33261, Spring and Wire Product Manufacturing;
- Die-casting purchased copper--are classified in U.S. Industry 331523, Nonferrous Metal Die-Casting Foundries;

T—Canadian, Mexican, and United States industries are comparable.

**census.gov/naics**

- Rolling, drawing, or extruding shapes from purchased nonferrous metals (except copper and aluminum) or recovering nonferrous metals (except copper and aluminum) from scrap and rolling, drawing, or extruding- -are classified in U.S. Industry 331491, Nonferrous Metal (except Copper and Aluminum) Rolling, Drawing, and Extruding;
- Recovering nonferrous metals (except copper, aluminum) from scrap and making primary forms and/or alloying purchased nonferrous metals (except copper and aluminum)--are classified in U.S. Industry 331492, Secondary Smelting, Refining, and Alloying of Nonferrous Metal (except Copper and Aluminum);
- Insulating purchased copper wire--are classified in U.S. Industry 335929, Other Communication and Energy Wire Manufacturing;
- Operating facilities where commingled recyclable materials, such as paper, plastics, used beverage cans, and metals, are sorted into distinct categories without also smelting or refining--are classified in Industry 562920, Materials Recovery Facilities; and
- Sorting, breaking up, and wholesaling scrap metal without also smelting or refining--are classified in Industry 423930, Recyclable Material Merchant Wholesalers.

## 33149 Nonferrous Metal (except Copper and Aluminum) Rolling, Drawing, Extruding, and Alloying[T]

This industry comprises establishments primarily engaged in one or more of the following: (1) recovering nonferrous metals (except copper and aluminum) and nonferrous metal alloys from scrap; (2) alloying purchased nonferrous metals (except copper and aluminum); (3) rolling, drawing, and extruding shapes from purchased nonferrous metals (except copper and aluminum); and (4) recovering nonferrous metals from scrap (except copper and aluminum) and rolling, drawing, or extruding shapes in integrated facilities.

*Cross-References.*     Establishments primarily engaged in--

- Rolling, drawing, and/or extruding aluminum or secondary smelting and alloying of aluminum--are classified in Industry 33131, Alumina and Aluminum Production and Processing;
- Recovering copper and copper alloys from scrap, alloying purchased copper, rolling, drawing, or extruding shapes from purchased copper, and recovering copper or copper alloys from scrap and rolling, drawing, or extruding shapes in integrated mills--are classified in Industry 33142, Copper Rolling, Drawing, Extruding, and Alloying;
- Insulating purchased nonferrous wire--are classified in Industry 33592, Communication and Energy Wire and Cable Manufacturing;
- Making primary nonferrous metals and rolling, drawing, or extruding nonferrous metal shapes--are classified in Industry 33141, Nonferrous Metal (except Aluminum) Smelting and Refining;
- Manufacturing products from purchased wire--are classified in Industry 33261, Spring and Wire Product Manufacturing;
- Sorting, breaking up, and wholesaling scrap metal without also smelting or refining--are classified in Industry 42393, Recyclable Material Merchant Wholesalers; and
- Operating facilities where commingled recyclable materials, such as paper, plastics, used beverage cans, and metals, are sorted into distinct categories without also smelting or refining--are classified in Industry 56292, Materials Recovery Facilities.

## 331491 Nonferrous Metal (except Copper and Aluminum) Rolling, Drawing, and Extruding

This U.S. industry comprises establishments primarily engaged in (1) rolling, drawing, or extruding shapes (e.g., bar, plate, sheet, strip, tube) from purchased nonferrous metals and/or (2) recovering nonferrous metals from scrap and rolling, drawing, and/or extruding shapes (e.g., bar, plate, sheet, strip, tube) in integrated mills.

*Cross-References.*     Establishments primarily engaged in--

- Rolling, drawing, and/or extruding shapes from purchased copper or recovering copper from scrap and rolling, drawing, or extruding shapes--are classified in Industry 331420, Copper Rolling, Drawing, Extruding, and Alloying;

---

T—Canadian, Mexican, and United States industries are comparable.

- Recovering nonferrous metals (except copper and aluminum) from scrap and making primary forms and/or alloying purchased nonferrous metals--are classified in U.S. Industry 331492, Secondary Smelting, Refining, and Alloying of Nonferrous Metal (except Copper and Aluminum);
- Rolling, drawing, and/or extruding aluminum--are classified in Industry 33131, Alumina and Aluminum Production and Processing;
- Making primary nonferrous metals and rolling, drawing, or extruding nonferrous metal shapes--are classified in Industry 331410, Nonferrous Metal (except Aluminum) Smelting and Refining; and
- Insulating purchased nonferrous wire--are classified in U.S. Industry 335929, Other Communication and Energy Wire Manufacturing.

### 331492 Secondary Smelting, Refining, and Alloying of Nonferrous Metal (except Copper and Aluminum)

This U.S. industry comprises establishments primarily engaged in (1) alloying purchased nonferrous metals and/or (2) recovering nonferrous metals from scrap. Establishments in this industry make primary forms (e.g., bar, billet, bloom, cake, ingot, slab, slug, wire) using smelting or refining processes.

*Cross-References.*          Establishments primarily engaged in--

- Recovering aluminum and aluminum alloys from scrap and/or alloying purchased aluminum--are classified in U.S. Industry 331314, Secondary Smelting and Alloying of Aluminum;
- Sorting, breaking up, and wholesaling scrap metal without also smelting or refining--are classified in Industry 423930, Recyclable Material Merchant Wholesalers;
- Recovering nonferrous metals from scrap and rolling, drawing, or extruding shapes in integrated facilities-- are classified in U.S. Industry 331491, Nonferrous Metal (except Copper and Aluminum) Rolling, Drawing, and Extruding;
- Operating facilities where commingled recyclable materials, such as paper, plastics, used beverage cans, and metals, are sorted into distinct categories without also smelting or refining--are classified in Industry 562920, Materials Recovery Facilities; and
- Recovering copper and copper alloys from scrap and making primary forms, and/or alloying purchased copper--are classified in Industry 331420, Copper Rolling, Drawing, Extruding, and Alloying.

### 3315 Foundries[T]

This industry group comprises establishments primarily engaged in pouring molten metal into molds or dies to form castings. Establishments making castings and further manufacturing, such as machining or assembling, a specific manufactured product are classified in the industry of the finished product. Foundries may perform operations, such as cleaning and deburring, on the castings they manufacture. More involved processes, such as tapping, threading, milling, or machining to tight tolerances, that transform castings into more finished products are classified elsewhere in the Manufacturing sector based on the product made.

Establishments in this industry group make castings from purchased metals or in integrated secondary smelting and casting facilities. When the production of primary metals is combined with making castings, the establishment is classified in Subsector 331, Primary Metal Manufacturing, with the primary metal made.

### 33151 Ferrous Metal Foundries[T]

This industry comprises establishments primarily engaged in pouring molten iron and steel into molds of a desired shape to make castings. Establishments in this industry purchase iron and steel made in other establishments.

*Cross-References.*

Establishments primarily engaged in manufacturing iron or steel castings and further manufacturing them into finished products are classified based on the specific finished product.

---

T—Canadian, Mexican, and United States industries are comparable.

## 331511  Iron Foundries

This U.S. industry comprises establishments primarily engaged in pouring molten pig iron or iron alloys into molds to manufacture castings (e.g., cast iron manhole covers, cast iron pipe, cast iron skillets).  Establishments in this industry purchase iron made in other establishments.

*Cross-References.*

Establishments primarily engaged in manufacturing iron castings and further manufacturing them into finished products are classified based on the specific finished product.

## 331512  Steel Investment Foundries

This U.S. industry comprises establishments primarily engaged in manufacturing steel investment castings. Investment molds are formed by covering a wax shape with a refractory slurry.  After the refractory slurry hardens, the wax is melted, leaving a seamless mold.  Investment molds provide highly detailed, consistent castings. Establishments in this industry purchase steel made in other establishments.

*Cross-References.*          Establishments primarily engaged in--

- Manufacturing steel castings (except steel investment castings)--are classified in U.S. Industry 331513, Steel Foundries (except Investment); and
- Manufacturing steel investment castings and further manufacturing them into finished products--are classified based on the specific finished product.

## 331513  Steel Foundries (except Investment)

This U.S. industry comprises establishments primarily engaged in manufacturing steel castings (except steel investment castings).  Establishments in this industry purchase steel made in other establishments.

*Cross-References.*          Establishments primarily engaged in--

- Manufacturing steel investment castings--are classified in U.S. Industry 331512, Steel Investment Foundries; and
- Manufacturing steel castings and further manufacturing them into finished products--are classified based on the specific finished product.

## 33152  Nonferrous Metal Foundries[T]

This industry comprises establishments primarily engaged in pouring and/or introducing molten nonferrous metal, under high pressure, into metal molds or dies to manufacture castings.  Establishments in this industry purchase nonferrous metals made in other establishments.

*Cross-References.*          Establishments primarily engaged in--

- Manufacturing iron or steel castings--are classified in Industry 33151, Ferrous Metal Foundries; and
- Manufacturing nonferrous metal castings and further manufacturing them into finished products--are classified based on the specific finished product.

## 331523  Nonferrous Metal Die-Casting Foundries

This U.S. industry comprises establishments primarily engaged in introducing molten nonferrous metal, under high pressure, into molds or dies to make nonferrous metal die-castings.  Establishments in this industry purchase nonferrous metals made in other establishments.

---

T—Canadian, Mexican, and United States industries are comparable.

*Cross-references.* Establishments primarily engaged in--

- Pouring molten aluminum into molds to manufacture aluminum castings--are classified in U.S. Industry 331524, Aluminum Foundries (except Die-Casting);
- Pouring molten nonferrous metal (except aluminum) into molds to manufacture nonferrous (except aluminum) castings--are classified in U.S. Industry 331529, Other Nonferrous Metal Foundries (except Die-Casting); and
- Manufacturing nonferrous die-castings and further manufacturing them into finished products--are classified based on the specific finished product.

## 331524 Aluminum Foundries (except Die-Casting)

This U.S. industry comprises establishments primarily engaged in pouring molten aluminum into molds to manufacture aluminum castings (except nonferrous die-castings). Establishments in this industry purchase aluminum made in other establishments.

*Cross-References.* Establishments primarily engaged in--

- Manufacturing aluminum die-castings--are classified in U.S. Industry 331523, Nonferrous Metal Die-Casting Foundries; and
- Manufacturing aluminum or aluminum alloy castings and further manufacturing them into finished products--are classified based on the specific finished product.

## 331529 Other Nonferrous Metal Foundries (except Die-Casting)

This U.S. industry comprises establishments primarily engaged in pouring molten nonferrous metals (except aluminum) into molds to manufacture nonferrous castings (except nonferrous die-castings and aluminum castings). Establishments in this industry purchase nonferrous metals, such as copper, nickel, lead, and zinc, made in other establishments.

*Cross-references.* Establishments primarily engaged in--

- Manufacturing nonferrous die-castings--are classified in U.S. Industry 331523, Nonferrous Metal Die-Casting Foundries;
- Pouring molten aluminum into molds to manufacture aluminum castings--are classified in U.S. Industry 331524, Aluminum Foundries (except Die-Casting); and
- Manufacturing nonferrous castings and further manufacturing them into finished products--are classified based on the specific finished product.

## 332 Fabricated Metal Product Manufacturing[T]

Industries in the Fabricated Metal Product Manufacturing subsector transform metal into intermediate or end products, other than machinery, computers and electronics, and metal furniture, or treat metals and metal formed products fabricated elsewhere. Important fabricated metal processes are forging, stamping, bending, forming, and machining, used to shape individual pieces of metal; and other processes, such as welding and assembling, used to join separate parts together. Establishments in this subsector may use one of these processes or a combination of these processes.

The NAICS structure for this subsector distinguishes the forging and stamping processes in a single industry. The remaining industries in the subsector group establishments based on similar combinations of processes used to make products.

The manufacturing performed in the Fabricated Metal Product Manufacturing subsector begins with manufactured metal shapes. The establishments in this subsector further fabricate the purchased metal shapes into a product. For instance, the Spring and Wire Product Manufacturing industry starts with wire and fabricates such items.

Within the Manufacturing sector there are other establishments that make the same products made by this subsector; only these establishments begin production further back in the production process. These establishments

---

T—Canadian, Mexican, and United States industries are comparable.

have a more integrated operation. For instance, one establishment may manufacture steel, draw it into wire, and make wire products in the same establishment. Such operations are classified in the Primary Metal Manufacturing subsector.

## 3321 Forging and Stamping[T]

## 33211 Forging and Stamping[T]

This industry comprises establishments primarily engaged in one or more of the following: (1) manufacturing forgings from purchased metals; (2) manufacturing metal custom roll forming products; (3) manufacturing metal stamped and spun products (except automotive, cans, coins); and (4) manufacturing powder metallurgy products. Establishments making metal forgings, metal stampings, and metal spun products and further manufacturing (e.g., machining, assembling) a specific manufactured product are classified in the industry of the finished product. Metal forging, metal stamping, and metal spun products establishments may perform surface finishing operations, such as cleaning and deburring, on the products they manufacture.

*Cross-References.* Establishments primarily engaged in--

- Manufacturing metal forgings in integrated primary metal establishments--are classified in Subsector 331, Primary Metal Manufacturing;
- Manufacturing automotive stampings--are classified in Industry 33637, Motor Vehicle Metal Stamping;
- Forming and installing seamless gutters at construction sites--are classified in Industry 23817, Siding Contractors; and
- Stamping coins--are classified in Industry 33991, Jewelry and Silverware Manufacturing.

## 332111 Iron and Steel Forging

This U.S. industry comprises establishments primarily engaged in manufacturing iron and steel forgings from purchased iron and steel by hammering mill shapes. Establishments making iron and steel forgings and further manufacturing (e.g., machining, assembling) a specific manufactured product are classified in the industry of the finished product. Iron and steel forging establishments may perform surface finishing operations, such as cleaning and deburring, on the forgings they manufacture.

*Cross-References.* Establishments primarily engaged in--

- Manufacturing iron and steel forgings in integrated iron and steel mills--are classified in Industry 331110, Iron and Steel Mills and Ferroalloy Manufacturing; and
- Manufacturing nonferrous forgings--are classified in U.S. Industry 332112, Nonferrous Forging.

## 332112 Nonferrous Forging

This U.S. industry comprises establishments primarily engaged in manufacturing nonferrous forgings from purchased nonferrous metals by hammering mill shapes. Establishments making nonferrous forgings and further manufacturing (e.g., machining, assembling) a specific manufactured product are classified in the industry of the finished product. Nonferrous forging establishments may perform surface finishing operations, such as cleaning and deburring, on the forgings they manufacture.

*Cross-References.* Establishments primarily engaged in--

- Manufacturing iron and steel forgings--are classified in U.S. Industry 332111, Iron and Steel Forging; and
- Manufacturing nonferrous forgings in integrated primary or secondary nonferrous metal production facilities--are classified in Subsector 331, Primary Metal Manufacturing.

---

T—Canadian, Mexican, and United States industries are comparable.

### 332114  Custom Roll Forming

This U.S. industry comprises establishments primarily engaged in custom roll forming metal products by use of rotary motion of rolls with various contours to bend or shape the products.

*Cross-References.*

Establishments primarily engaged in forming and installing seamless gutters at construction sites are classified in Industry 238170, Siding Contractors.

### 332117  Powder Metallurgy Part Manufacturing

This U.S. industry comprises establishments primarily engaged in manufacturing powder metallurgy products using any of the various powder metallurgy processing techniques, such as pressing and sintering or metal injection molding.  Establishments in this industry generally make a wide range of parts on a job or order basis.

### 332119  Metal Crown, Closure, and Other Metal Stamping (except Automotive)

This U.S. industry comprises establishments primarily engaged in (1) stamping metal crowns and closures, such as bottle caps and home canning lids and rings, and/or (2) manufacturing other unfinished metal stampings and spinning unfinished metal products (except automotive, cans, and coins).  Establishments making metal stampings and metal spun products and further manufacturing (e.g., machining, assembling) a specific product are classified in the industry of the finished product.  Metal stamping and metal spun products establishments may perform surface finishing operations, such as cleaning and deburring, on the products they manufacture.

*Cross-References.*          Establishments primarily engaged in--

- Manufacturing automotive stampings--are classified in Industry 336370, Motor Vehicle Metal Stamping;
- Manufacturing metal cans--are classified in U.S. Industry 332431, Metal Can Manufacturing; and
- Stamping coins--are classified in Industry 339910, Jewelry and Silverware Manufacturing.

## 3322  Cutlery and Handtool Manufacturing[T]

### 33221  Cutlery and Handtool Manufacturing[T]

This industry comprises establishments primarily engaged in one or more of the following: (1) manufacturing metal kitchen cookware (except by casting (e.g., cast iron skillets) or stamped without further fabrication), utensils, and/or nonprecious and precious plated metal cutlery and flatware; (2) manufacturing saw blades, all types (including those for power sawing machines); and (3) manufacturing nonpowered handtools and edge tools.

*Cross-References.*          Establishments primarily engaged in--

- Manufacturing precious (except precious plated) metal cutlery and flatware--are classified in Industry 33991, Jewelry and Silverware Manufacturing;
- Manufacturing electric razors and hair clippers for use on humans--are classified in Industry 33521, Small Electrical Appliance Manufacturing;
- Manufacturing power hedge shears and trimmers and electric hair clippers for use on animals--are classified in Industry 33311, Agricultural Implement Manufacturing;
- Manufacturing metal cutting dies, attachments, and accessories for machine tools--are classified in Industry 33351, Metalworking Machinery Manufacturing;
- Manufacturing power-driven handtools--are classified in Industry 33399, All Other General Purpose Machinery Manufacturing;
- Manufacturing finished cast iron kitchen utensils and cookware (i.e., cast iron skillets) and castings for kitchen utensils and cookware--are classified in Industry Group 3315, Foundries; and

---

T—Canadian, Mexican, and United States industries are comparable.

- Manufacturing stampings for kitchen utensils, pots, and pans--are classified in Industry 33211, Forging and Stamping.

## 332215   Metal Kitchen Cookware, Utensil, Cutlery, and Flatware (except Precious) Manufacturing

This U.S. industry comprises establishments primarily engaged in manufacturing metal kitchen cookware (except by casting (e.g., cast iron skillets) or stamped without further fabrication), utensils, and/or nonprecious and precious plated metal cutlery and flatware.

*Cross-References.*          Establishments primarily engaged in--

- Manufacturing precious (except precious plated) metal cutlery and flatware--are classified in Industry 339910, Jewelry and Silverware Manufacturing;
- Manufacturing electric razors and hair clippers for use on humans--are classified in Industry 335210, Small Electrical Appliance Manufacturing;
- Manufacturing power hedge shears and trimmers--are classified in U.S. Industry 333112, Lawn and Garden Tractor and Home Lawn and Garden Equipment Manufacturing;
- Manufacturing nonelectric hair clippers for use on animals--are classified in U.S. Industry 332216, Saw Blade and Handtool Manufacturing;
- Manufacturing finished cast iron kitchen utensils and cookware (i.e., cast iron skillets) and castings for kitchen utensils and cookware--are classified in Industry Group 3315, Foundries; and
- Manufacturing stampings for kitchen utensils, pots, and pans--are classified in U.S. Industry 332119, Metal Crown, Closure, and Other Metal Stamping (except Automotive).

## 332216   Saw Blade and Handtool Manufacturing

This U.S. industry comprises establishments primarily engaged in (1) manufacturing saw blades, all types (including those for power sawing machines) and/or (2) manufacturing nonpowered handtools and edge tools.

*Cross-References.*          Establishments primarily engaged in--

- Manufacturing metal cutting dies, attachments, and accessories for machine tools--are classified in Industry 33351, Metalworking Machinery Manufacturing;
- Manufacturing power-driven handtools--are classified in U.S. Industry 333991, Power-Driven Handtool Manufacturing;
- Manufacturing electric razors and hair clippers for use on humans--are classified in Industry 335210, Small Electrical Appliance Manufacturing;
- Manufacturing electric hair clippers for use on animals--are classified in U.S. Industry 333111, Farm Machinery and Equipment Manufacturing; and
- Manufacturing nonelectric household-type scissors and shears--are classified in U.S. Industry 332215, Metal Kitchen Cookware, Utensil, Cutlery, and Flatware (except Precious) Manufacturing.

## 3323   Architectural and Structural Metals Manufacturing[T]

This industry group comprises establishments primarily engaged in manufacturing one or more of the following: (1) prefabricated metal buildings, panels, and sections; (2) structural metal products; (3) metal plate work products; (4) metal framed windows (i.e., typically using purchased glass) and metal doors; (5) sheet metal work; and (6) ornamental and architectural metal products.

## 33231   Plate Work and Fabricated Structural Product Manufacturing[T]

This industry comprises establishments primarily engaged in manufacturing one or more of the following: (1) prefabricated metal buildings, panels, and sections; (2) structural metal products; and (3) metal plate work products.

---

T—Canadian, Mexican, and United States industries are comparable.

*Cross-References.*          Establishments primarily engaged in--

- Making manufactured homes (i.e., mobile homes) and prefabricated wood buildings--are classified in Industry 32199, All Other Wood Product Manufacturing;
- Constructing buildings, bridges, and other heavy construction projects on site--are classified in Sector 23, Construction;
- Building ships, boats, and barges--are classified in Industry 33661, Ship and Boat Building;
- Manufacturing power boilers and heat exchangers--are classified in Industry 33241, Power Boiler and Heat Exchanger Manufacturing;
- Manufacturing heavy gauge tanks--are classified in Industry 33242, Metal Tank (Heavy Gauge) Manufacturing;
- Manufacturing metal plate cooling towers--are classified in Industry 33341, Ventilation, Heating, Air-Conditioning, and Commercial Refrigeration Equipment Manufacturing; and
- Manufacturing metal windows, doors, and studs--are classified in Industry 33232, Ornamental and Architectural Metal Products Manufacturing.

## 332311  Prefabricated Metal Building and Component Manufacturing

This U.S. industry comprises establishments primarily engaged in manufacturing prefabricated metal buildings, panels, and sections.

*Cross-References.*          Establishments primarily engaged in--

- Making manufactured homes (i.e., mobile homes) and prefabricated wood buildings--are classified in Industry 32199, All Other Wood Product Manufacturing;
- Constructing prefabricated buildings on site--are classified in Subsector 236, Construction of Buildings; and
- Manufacturing metal windows and doors--are classified in U.S. Industry 332321, Metal Window and Door Manufacturing.

## 332312  Fabricated Structural Metal Manufacturing

This U.S. industry comprises establishments primarily engaged in fabricating structural metal products, such as assemblies of concrete reinforcing bars and fabricated bar joists.

*Cross-References.*          Establishments primarily engaged in--

- Manufacturing concrete reinforcing bars in an iron and steel mill--are classified in Industry 331110, Iron and Steel Mills and Ferroalloy Manufacturing;
- Manufacturing metal windows and doors--are classified in U.S. Industry 332321, Metal Window and Door Manufacturing;
- Manufacturing metal studs--are classified in U.S. Industry 332322, Sheet Metal Work Manufacturing;
- Constructing buildings, bridges, and other heavy construction projects on site--are classified in Sector 23, Construction;
- Manufacturing concrete reinforcing bar by rolling and drawing steel from purchased steel--are classified in U.S. Industry 331221, Rolled Steel Shape Manufacturing;
- Building ships, boats, and barges--are classified in Industry 33661, Ship and Boat Building; and
- Prefabricating metal buildings, panels, and sections--are classified in U.S. Industry 332311, Prefabricated Metal Building and Component Manufacturing.

## 332313  Plate Work Manufacturing

This U.S. industry comprises establishments primarily engaged in manufacturing fabricated metal plate work by cutting, punching, bending, shaping, and welding purchased metal plate.

---

T—Canadian, Mexican, and United States industries are comparable.

*Cross-References.*        Establishments primarily engaged in--

- Manufacturing power boilers and heat exchangers--are classified in Industry 332410, Power Boiler and Heat Exchanger Manufacturing;
- Manufacturing heavy gauge tanks--are classified in Industry 332420, Metal Tank (Heavy Gauge) Manufacturing; and
- Manufacturing metal plate cooling towers--are classified in U.S. Industry 333415, Air-Conditioning and Warm Air Heating Equipment and Commercial and Industrial Refrigeration Equipment Manufacturing.

## 33232   Ornamental and Architectural Metal Products Manufacturing[T]

This industry comprises establishments primarily engaged in manufacturing one or more of the following: (1) metal framed windows (i.e., typically using purchased glass) and metal doors; (2) sheet metal work; and (3) ornamental and architectural metal products.

*Cross-References.*        Establishments primarily engaged in--

- Manufacturing metal covered (i.e., clad) wood windows and doors--are classified in Industry 32191, Millwork;
- Manufacturing bins, cans, vats, and light tanks of sheet metal--are classified in Industry 33243, Metal Can, Box, and Other Metal Container (Light Gauge) Manufacturing;
- Manufacturing prefabricated metal buildings, panels, and sections--are classified in Industry 33231, Plate Work and Fabricated Structural Product Manufacturing;
- Fabricating sheet metal work on site--are classified in Subsector 238, Specialty Trade Contractors;
- Manufacturing metal stampings (except automotive, coins) and custom roll forming products--are classified in Industry 33211, Forging and Stamping;
- Manufacturing automotive stampings--are classified in Industry 33637, Motor Vehicle Metal Stamping; and
- Stamping coins--are classified in Industry 33991, Jewelry and Silverware Manufacturing.

## 332321   Metal Window and Door Manufacturing

This U.S. industry comprises establishments primarily engaged in manufacturing metal framed windows (i.e., typically using purchased glass) and metal doors.  Examples of products made by these establishments are metal door frames; metal framed window and door screens; and metal molding and trim (except automotive).

*Cross-References.*        Establishments primarily engaged in--

- Manufacturing wood or metal covered (i.e., clad) wood framed windows and doors--are classified in U.S. Industry 321911, Wood Window and Door Manufacturing; and
- Manufacturing metal automotive molding and trim--are classified in Industry 336370, Motor Vehicle Metal Stamping.

## 332322   Sheet Metal Work Manufacturing

This U.S. industry comprises establishments primarily engaged in manufacturing sheet metal work (except stampings).

*Cross-References.*        Establishments primarily engaged in--

- Manufacturing sheet metal bins, vats, and light tanks--are classified in U.S. Industry 332439, Other Metal Container Manufacturing;
- Manufacturing metal cans, lids, and ends--are classified in U.S. Industry 332431, Metal Can Manufacturing;
- Fabricating sheet metal work on site--are classified in Subsector 238, Specialty Trade Contractors;

---

T—Canadian, Mexican, and United States industries are comparable.

- Manufacturing metal stampings (except automotive, coins) and custom roll forming products--are classified in Industry 33211, Forging and Stamping;
- Manufacturing automotive stampings--are classified in Industry 336370, Motor Vehicle Metal Stamping; and
- Stamping coins--are classified in Industry 339910, Jewelry and Silverware Manufacturing.

### 332323  Ornamental and Architectural Metal Work Manufacturing

This U.S. industry comprises establishments primarily engaged in manufacturing ornamental and architectural metal work, such as staircases, metal open steel flooring, fire escapes, railings, and scaffolding.

*Cross-References.*

Establishments primarily engaged in manufacturing prefabricated metal buildings, panels, and sections are classified in U.S. Industry 332311, Prefabricated Metal Building and Component Manufacturing.

### 3324     Boiler, Tank, and Shipping Container Manufacturing[T]

This industry group comprises establishments primarily engaged in one of the following: (1) manufacturing power boilers and heat exchangers; (2) cutting, forming, and joining heavy gauge metal to manufacture tanks, vessels, and other containers; or (3) forming light gauge metal containers.

### 33241   Power Boiler and Heat Exchanger Manufacturing[T]
See industry description for 332410.

### 332410  Power Boiler and Heat Exchanger Manufacturing

This industry comprises establishments primarily engaged in manufacturing power boilers and heat exchangers. Establishments in this industry may perform installation in addition to manufacturing power boilers and heat exchangers.

*Cross-References.*          Establishments primarily engaged in--

- Manufacturing heavy gauge metal tanks--are classified in Industry 332420, Metal Tank (Heavy Gauge) Manufacturing;
- Manufacturing steam or hot water low pressure heating boilers--are classified in U.S. Industry 333414, Heating Equipment (except Warm Air Furnaces) Manufacturing; and
- Installing power boilers and heat exchangers without manufacturing--are classified in Industry 238220, Plumbing, Heating, and Air-Conditioning Contractors.

### 33242   Metal Tank (Heavy Gauge) Manufacturing[T]
See industry description for 332420.

### 332420  Metal Tank (Heavy Gauge) Manufacturing

This industry comprises establishments primarily engaged in cutting, forming, and joining heavy gauge metal to manufacture tanks, vessels, and other containers.

*Cross-References.*          Establishments primarily engaged in--

- Manufacturing power boilers--are classified in Industry 332410, Power Boiler and Heat Exchanger Manufacturing;
- Manufacturing light gauge metal containers--are classified in Industry 33243, Metal Can, Box, and Other Metal Container (Light Gauge) Manufacturing; and

---

T—Canadian, Mexican, and United States industries are comparable.

- Installing heavy gauge metal tanks without manufacturing--are classified in Industry 238120, Structural Steel and Precast Concrete Contractors.

## 33243  Metal Can, Box, and Other Metal Container (Light Gauge) Manufacturing[T]

This industry comprises establishments primarily engaged in forming light gauge metal containers.

*Cross-References.*          Establishments primarily engaged in--

- Manufacturing foil containers--are classified in Industry 33299, All Other Fabricated Metal Product Manufacturing;
- Reconditioning barrels and drums--are classified in Industry 81131, Commercial and Industrial Machinery and Equipment (except Automotive and Electronic) Repair and Maintenance; and
- Manufacturing heavy gauge metal containers--are classified in Industry 33242, Metal Tank (Heavy Gauge) Manufacturing.

## 332431  Metal Can Manufacturing

This U.S. industry comprises establishments primarily engaged in manufacturing metal cans, lids, and ends.

*Cross-References.*          Establishments primarily engaged in--

- Manufacturing foil containers--are classified in U.S. Industry 332999, All Other Miscellaneous Fabricated Metal Product Manufacturing; and
- Manufacturing light gauge metal containers (except cans)--are classified in U.S. Industry 332439, Other Metal Container Manufacturing.

## 332439  Other Metal Container Manufacturing

This U.S. industry comprises establishments primarily engaged in manufacturing metal (light gauge) containers (except cans).

*Illustrative Examples:*

Light gauge metal bins manufacturing
Light gauge metal drums manufacturing
Light gauge metal garbage cans manufacturing
Light gauge metal lunch boxes manufacturing
Light gauge metal mailboxes manufacturing
Light gauge metal tool boxes manufacturing
Light gauge metal vats manufacturing
Metal air cargo containers manufacturing
Metal barrels manufacturing
Vacuum bottles and jugs manufacturing

*Cross-References.*          Establishments primarily engaged in--

- Manufacturing foil containers--are classified in U.S. Industry 332999, All Other Miscellaneous Fabricated Metal Product Manufacturing;
- Manufacturing metal cans--are classified in U.S. Industry 332431, Metal Can Manufacturing;
- Reconditioning barrels and drums--are classified in Industry 811310, Commercial and Industrial Machinery and Equipment (except Automotive and Electronic) Repair and Maintenance; and
- Manufacturing heavy gauge metal containers--are classified in Industry 332420, Metal Tank (Heavy Gauge) Manufacturing.

## 3325  Hardware Manufacturing[T]

## 33251  Hardware Manufacturing[T]
See industry description for 332510.

---

T—Canadian, Mexican, and United States industries are comparable.

## 332510  Hardware Manufacturing

This industry comprises establishments primarily engaged in manufacturing metal hardware, such as metal hinges, metal handles, keys, and locks (except coin- or card-operated, time locks).

*Cross-References.*          Establishments primarily engaged in--

- Manufacturing bolts, nuts, screws, rivets, washers, hose clamps, and turnbuckles--are classified in U.S. Industry 332722, Bolt, Nut, Screw, Rivet, and Washer Manufacturing;
- Manufacturing nails and spikes from wire drawn elsewhere--are classified in U.S. Industry 332618, Other Fabricated Wire Product Manufacturing;
- Manufacturing metal furniture parts (except hardware)--are classified in U.S. Industry 337215, Showcase, Partition, Shelving, and Locker Manufacturing;
- Drawing wire and manufacturing nails and spikes--are classified in Subsector 331, Primary Metal Manufacturing;
- Manufacturing pole line and transmission hardware--are classified in U.S. Industry 335932, Noncurrent-Carrying Wiring Device Manufacturing;
- Manufacturing coin- or card-operated locking mechanisms--are classified in Industry 333310, Commercial and Service Industry Machinery Manufacturing;
- Manufacturing time locks--are classified in U.S. Industry 334519, Other Measuring and Controlling Device Manufacturing;
- Manufacturing fireplace fixtures and equipment, traps, handcuffs and leg irons, ladder jacks, and other like metal products--are classified in U.S. Industry 332999, All Other Miscellaneous Fabricated Metal Product Manufacturing;
- Manufacturing fire hose nozzles and metal hose couplings (except fluid power)--are classified in U.S. Industry 332919, Other Metal Valve and Pipe Fitting Manufacturing; and
- Manufacturing automotive luggage racks and utility racks--are classified in Industry 336390, Other Motor Vehicle Parts Manufacturing.

## 3326     Spring and Wire Product Manufacturing[T]

## 33261    Spring and Wire Product Manufacturing[T]

This industry comprises establishments primarily engaged in (1) manufacturing steel springs by forming, such as cutting, bending, and heat winding, metal rod or strip stock and/or (2) manufacturing wire springs and fabricated wire products from wire drawn elsewhere (except watch and clock springs).

*Cross-References.*          Establishments primarily engaged in--

- Manufacturing watch and clock springs from purchased wire--are classified in Industry 33451, Navigational, Measuring, Electromedical, and Control Instruments Manufacturing;
- Drawing wire and manufacturing wire products--are classified in Subsector 331, Primary Metal Manufacturing; and
- Manufacturing nonferrous insulated wire from wire drawn elsewhere--are classified in Industry 33592, Communication and Energy Wire and Cable Manufacturing.

## 332613  Spring Manufacturing

This U.S. industry comprises establishments primarily engaged in manufacturing springs from purchased wire, strip, or rod.

*Cross-References.*          Establishments primarily engaged in--

- Manufacturing watch and clock springs--are classified in U.S. Industry 334519, Other Measuring and Controlling Device Manufacturing; and

---

T—Canadian, Mexican, and United States industries are comparable.

**census.gov/naics**

- Producing wire, strip, or rod and further fabricating springs--are classified in Subsector 331, Primary Metal Manufacturing.

## 332618  Other Fabricated Wire Product Manufacturing

This U.S. industry comprises establishments primarily engaged in manufacturing fabricated wire products (except springs) made from purchased wire.

*Illustrative Examples:*

Barbed wire made from purchased wire
Chain link fencing and fence gates made from purchased wire
Metal baskets made from purchased wire

Paper clips made from purchased wire
Nails, brads, and staples made from purchased wire
Noninsulated wire cable made from purchased wire
Woven wire cloth made from purchased wire

*Cross-References.*       Establishments primarily engaged in--

- Drawing wire and manufacturing wire products--are classified in Subsector 331, Primary Metal Manufacturing;
- Manufacturing springs from purchased wire, strip, or rod--are classified in U.S. Industry 332613, Spring Manufacturing; and
- Insulating nonferrous wire from wire drawn elsewhere--are classified in U.S. Industry 335929, Other Communication and Energy Wire Manufacturing.

## 3327    Machine Shops; Turned Product; and Screw, Nut, and Bolt Manufacturing[T]

This industry group comprises establishments primarily engaged in one of the following: (1) operating machine shops primarily engaged in machining metal and plastic parts and parts of other composite materials on a job or order basis; (2) machining precision turned products; or (3) manufacturing metal bolts, nuts, screws, rivets, and other industrial fasteners.

## 33271    Machine Shops[T]
See industry description for 332710.

## 332710  Machine Shops

This industry comprises establishments known as machine shops primarily engaged in machining metal and plastic parts and parts of other composite materials on a job or order basis.  Generally machine shop jobs are low volume using machine tools, such as lathes (including computer numerically controlled); automatic screw machines; and machines for boring, grinding, milling, and additive manufacturing.

*Cross-References.*       Establishments primarily engaged in--

- Machining precision products, known as precision turned manufacturers--are classified in U.S. Industry 332721, Precision Turned Product Manufacturing;
- Manufacturing metal bolts, nuts, screws, rivets, washers, and other industrial fasteners using machines, such as headers, threaders, and nut forming machines--are classified in U.S. Industry 332722, Bolt, Nut, Screw, Rivet, and Washer Manufacturing;
- Manufacturing stampings (except motor vehicle)--are classified in U.S. Industry 332119, Metal Crown, Closure, and Other Metal Stamping (except Automotive);
- Manufacturing weldments and fabricated metal plate products--are classified in U.S. Industry 332313, Plate Work Manufacturing;
- Coating, engraving, and heat treating metals and metal formed products fabricated elsewhere--are classified in Industry 33281, Coating, Engraving, Heat Treating, and Allied Activities;

T—Canadian, Mexican, and United States industries are comparable.

- Manufacturing foundry patterns--are classified in U.S. Industry 332999, All Other Miscellaneous Fabricated Metal Product Manufacturing;
- Manufacturing motor vehicle stampings--are classified in Industry 336370, Motor Vehicle Metal Stamping; and
- Repairing industrial machinery and equipment--are classified in Industry 811310, Commercial and Industrial Machinery and Equipment (except Automotive and Electronic) Repair and Maintenance.

### 33272   Turned Product and Screw, Nut, and Bolt Manufacturing[T]

This industry comprises establishments primarily engaged in (1) machining precision turned products or (2) manufacturing metal bolts, nuts, screws, rivets, and other industrial fasteners. Included in this industry are establishments primarily engaged in manufacturing parts for machinery and equipment on a custom basis.

*Cross-References.*        Establishments primarily engaged in--

- Machining parts, known as machine shops--are classified in Industry 33271, Machine Shops; and
- Manufacturing plastics fasteners--are classified in Industry 32619, Other Plastics Product Manufacturing.

### 332721   Precision Turned Product Manufacturing

This U.S. industry comprises establishments known as precision turned manufacturers primarily engaged in machining precision products of all materials on a job or order basis. Generally precision turned product jobs are large volume using machines, such as automatic screw machines, rotary transfer machines, computer numerically controlled (CNC) lathes, or turning centers.

*Cross-References.*        Establishments primarily engaged in--

- Manufacturing metal bolts, nuts, screws, rivets, washers, and other industrial fasteners using machines, such as headers, threaders, and nut forming machines--are classified in U.S. Industry 332722, Bolt, Nut, Screw, Rivet, and Washer Manufacturing; and
- Machining parts, known as machine shops--are classified in Industry 332710, Machine Shops.

### 332722   Bolt, Nut, Screw, Rivet, and Washer Manufacturing

This U.S. industry comprises establishments primarily engaged in manufacturing metal bolts, nuts, screws, rivets, washers, and other industrial fasteners using machines, such as headers, threaders, and nut forming machines.

*Cross-References.*        Establishments primarily engaged in--

- Manufacturing precision turned products--are classified in U.S. Industry 332721, Precision Turned Product Manufacturing; and
- Manufacturing plastics fasteners--are classified in U.S. Industry 326199, All Other Plastics Product Manufacturing.

### 3328   Coating, Engraving, Heat Treating, and Allied Activities[T]

### 33281   Coating, Engraving, Heat Treating, and Allied Activities[T]

This industry comprises establishments primarily engaged in one or more of the following: (1) heat treating metals and metal products; (2) enameling, lacquering, and varnishing metals and metal products; (3) hot dip galvanizing metals and metal products; (4) engraving, chasing, or etching metals and metal products (except jewelry; personal goods carried on or about the person, such as compacts and cigarette cases; precious metal products (except precious plated flatware and other plated ware); and printing plates); (5) powder coating metals and metal products; (6) electroplating, plating, anodizing, coloring, and finishing metals and metal products; and (7) providing other metal surfacing services for the trade. Establishments in this industry coat, engrave, and heat treat metals and metal

---

T—Canadian, Mexican, and United States industries are comparable.

formed products fabricated elsewhere. Included in this industry are establishments that perform these processes on other materials, such as plastics, in addition to metals.

*Cross-References.* Establishments primarily engaged in--

- Engraving, chasing, or etching jewelry, metal personal goods, or precious metal products (except precious plated flatware and other plated ware)--are classified in Industry 33991, Jewelry and Silverware Manufacturing;
- Engraving, chasing, or etching printing plates--are classified in Industry 32312, Support Activities for Printing; and
- Both fabricating and coating, engraving, and heat treating metals and metal products--are classified in the Manufacturing sector according to the product made.

## 332811 Metal Heat Treating

This U.S. industry comprises establishments primarily engaged in heat treating, such as annealing, tempering, and brazing, and cryogenically treating metals and metal products for the trade.

*Cross-References.*

Establishments primarily engaged in both fabricating and heat treating metal products are classified in the Manufacturing sector according to the product made.

## 332812 Metal Coating, Engraving (except Jewelry and Silverware), and Allied Services to Manufacturers

This U.S. industry comprises establishments primarily engaged in one or more of the following: (1) enameling, lacquering, and varnishing metals and metal products; (2) hot dip galvanizing metals and metal products; (3) engraving, chasing, or etching metals and metal products (except jewelry; personal goods carried on or about the person, such as compacts and cigarette cases; precious metal products (except precious plated flatware and other plated ware); and printing plates); (4) powder coating metals and metal products; and (5) providing other metal surfacing services for the trade. Included in this industry are establishments that perform these processes on other materials, such as plastics, in addition to metals.

*Cross-References.* Establishments primarily engaged in--

- Both fabricating and coating and engraving products--are classified in the Manufacturing sector according to the product made;
- Engraving, chasing, or etching jewelry, metal personal goods, or precious metal products (except precious plated flatware and other plated ware)--are classified in Industry 339910, Jewelry and Silverware Manufacturing; and
- Engraving, chasing, or etching printing plates--are classified in Industry 323120, Support Activities for Printing.

## 332813 Electroplating, Plating, Polishing, Anodizing, and Coloring

This U.S. industry comprises establishments primarily engaged in electroplating, plating, anodizing, coloring, buffing, polishing, cleaning, and sandblasting metals and metal products for the trade. Included in this industry are establishments that perform these processes on other materials, such as plastics, in addition to metals.

*Cross-References.*

Establishments primarily engaged in both fabricating and electroplating, plating, polishing, anodizing, and coloring products are classified in the Manufacturing sector according to the product made.

---

T—Canadian, Mexican, and United States industries are comparable.

### 3329 Other Fabricated Metal Product Manufacturing[T]

This industry group comprises establishments primarily engaged in manufacturing fabricated metal products (except forgings and stampings, cutlery and handtools, architectural and structural metals, boilers, tanks, shipping containers, hardware, spring and wire products, machine shop products, turned products, screws, and nuts and bolts).

### 33291 Metal Valve Manufacturing[T]

This industry comprises establishments primarily engaged in manufacturing one or more of the following metal valves: (1) industrial valves; (2) fluid power valves and hose fittings; (3) plumbing fixture fittings and trim; and (4) other metal valves and pipe fittings.

*Cross-References.* Establishments primarily engaged in--

- Manufacturing fluid power cylinders and pumps--are classified in Industry 33399, All Other General Purpose Machinery Manufacturing;
- Manufacturing intake and exhaust valves for internal combustion engines--are classified in Industry 33631, Motor Vehicle Gasoline Engine and Engine Parts Manufacturing;
- Manufacturing metal shower rods and metal couplings from purchased metal pipe--are classified in Industry 33299, All Other Fabricated Metal Product Manufacturing;
- Manufacturing plastics aerosol spray nozzles--are classified in Industry 32619, Other Plastics Product Manufacturing;
- Casting iron pipe fittings and couplings without machining--are classified in Industry 33151, Ferrous Metal Foundries; and
- Manufacturing plastics pipe fittings and couplings--are classified in Industry 32612, Plastics Pipe, Pipe Fitting, and Unlaminated Profile Shape Manufacturing.

### 332911 Industrial Valve Manufacturing

This U.S. industry comprises establishments primarily engaged in manufacturing industrial valves and valves for water works and municipal water systems.

*Illustrative Examples:*

Complete fire hydrants manufacturing
Industrial-type ball valves manufacturing
Industrial-type butterfly valves manufacturing
Industrial-type check valves manufacturing
Industrial-type gate valves manufacturing
Industrial-type globe valves manufacturing

Industrial-type plug valves manufacturing
Industrial-type solenoid valves (except fluid power) manufacturing
Industrial-type steam traps manufacturing
Valves for nuclear applications manufacturing

*Cross-References.* Establishments primarily engaged in--

- Manufacturing fluid power valves--are classified in U.S. Industry 332912, Fluid Power Valve and Hose Fitting Manufacturing; and
- Manufacturing plumbing and heating inline valves--are classified in U.S. Industry 332919, Other Metal Valve and Pipe Fitting Manufacturing.

### 332912 Fluid Power Valve and Hose Fitting Manufacturing

This U.S. industry comprises establishments primarily engaged in manufacturing fluid power valves and hose fittings.

---

T—Canadian, Mexican, and United States industries are comparable.

55Table.

*Illustrative Examples:*

Fluid power aircraft subassemblies manufacturing
Hose assemblies for fluid power systems manufacturing

Hydraulic and pneumatic hose and tube fittings manufacturing
Hydraulic and pneumatic valves manufacturing

*Cross-References.*     Establishments primarily engaged in--

- Manufacturing fluid power cylinders--are classified in U.S. Industry 333995, Fluid Power Cylinder and Actuator Manufacturing;
- Manufacturing fluid power pumps--are classified in U.S. Industry 333996, Fluid Power Pump and Motor Manufacturing;
- Manufacturing intake and exhaust valves for internal combustion engines--are classified in Industry 336310, Motor Vehicle Gasoline Engine and Engine Parts Manufacturing;
- Manufacturing industrial-type valves--are classified in U.S. Industry 332911, Industrial Valve Manufacturing; and
- Manufacturing plumbing and heating inline valves--are classified in U.S. Industry 332919, Other Metal Valve and Pipe Fitting Manufacturing.

## 332913 Plumbing Fixture Fitting and Trim Manufacturing

This U.S. industry comprises establishments primarily engaged in manufacturing plumbing fixture fittings and trim of all materials, such as faucets, flush valves, and shower heads.

*Cross-References.*     Establishments primarily engaged in--

- Manufacturing metal shower rods--are classified in U.S. Industry 332999, All Other Miscellaneous Fabricated Metal Product Manufacturing; and
- Manufacturing fire hose nozzles, lawn hose nozzles, water traps, metal hose couplings (except fluid power), and plumbing and heating inline valves--are classified in U.S. Industry 332919, Other Metal Valve and Pipe Fitting Manufacturing.

## 332919 Other Metal Valve and Pipe Fitting Manufacturing

This U.S. industry comprises establishments primarily engaged in manufacturing metal valves (except industrial valves, fluid power valves, fluid power hose fittings, and plumbing fixture fittings and trim).

*Illustrative Examples:*

Aerosol valves manufacturing
Firefighting nozzles manufacturing
Lawn hose nozzles manufacturing
Lawn sprinklers manufacturing
Water traps manufacturing

Metal hose couplings (except fluid power) manufacturing
Metal pipe flanges and flange unions manufacturing
Plumbing and heating inline valves (e.g., check, cutoff, stop) manufacturing

*Cross-References.*     Establishments primarily engaged in--

- Manufacturing fluid power valves and hose fittings--are classified in U.S. Industry 332912, Fluid Power Valve and Hose Fitting Manufacturing;
- Manufacturing industrial valves--are classified in U.S. Industry 332911, Industrial Valve Manufacturing;
- Manufacturing plumbing fixture fittings and trim--are classified in U.S. Industry 332913, Plumbing Fixture Fitting and Trim Manufacturing;
- Manufacturing plastics aerosol spray nozzles--are classified in U.S. Industry 326199, All Other Plastics Product Manufacturing;

T—Canadian, Mexican, and United States industries are comparable.

- Casting iron pipe fittings and couplings without machining--are classified in U.S. Industry 331511, Iron Foundries;
- Manufacturing metal couplings from purchased metal pipe--are classified in U.S. Industry 332996, Fabricated Pipe and Pipe Fitting Manufacturing; and
- Manufacturing plastics pipe fittings and couplings--are classified in U.S. Industry 326122, Plastics Pipe and Pipe Fitting Manufacturing.

## 33299   All Other Fabricated Metal Product Manufacturing[T]

This industry comprises establishments primarily engaged in manufacturing fabricated metal products (except forgings and stampings, cutlery and handtools, architectural and structural metal products, boilers, tanks, shipping containers, hardware, spring and wire products, machine shop products, turned products, screws, nuts and bolts, and metal valves).

*Illustrative Examples:*

Ammunition manufacturing
Ball and roller bearing manufacturing
Enameled iron and metal sanitary ware manufacturing
Fabricated pipe and pipe fittings made from purchased metal pipe

Foil containers (except bags) manufacturing
Industrial pattern manufacturing
Metal safes manufacturing
Portable metal ladders manufacturing
Small arms and other ordnance manufacturing
Steel wool manufacturing

*Cross-References.*          Establishments primarily engaged in--

- Manufacturing forgings, stampings, and powder metallurgy parts--are classified in Industry 33211, Forging and Stamping;
- Manufacturing cutlery and handtools--are classified in Industry 33221, Cutlery and Handtool Manufacturing;
- Manufacturing architectural and structural metals--are classified in Industry Group 3323, Architectural and Structural Metals Manufacturing;
- Manufacturing boilers, tanks, and shipping containers--are classified in Industry Group 3324, Boiler, Tank, and Shipping Container Manufacturing;
- Manufacturing hardware and safe and vault locks--are classified in Industry 33251, Hardware Manufacturing;
- Manufacturing spring and wire products--are classified in Industry 33261, Spring and Wire Product Manufacturing;
- Manufacturing machine shop products, turned products, screws, and nuts and bolts--are classified in Industry Group 3327, Machine Shops; Turned Product; and Screw, Nut, and Bolt Manufacturing;
- Coating, engraving, heat treating, and allied activities--are classified in Industry 33281, Coating, Engraving, Heat Treating, and Allied Activities;
- Manufacturing plain bearings--are classified in Industry 33361, Engine, Turbine, and Power Transmission Equipment Manufacturing;
- Manufacturing military tanks--are classified in Industry 33699, Other Transportation Equipment Manufacturing;
- Manufacturing guided missiles--are classified in Industry 33641, Aerospace Product and Parts Manufacturing;
- Manufacturing cast iron pipe and fittings--are classified in Industry 33151, Ferrous Metal Foundries;
- Manufacturing pipe system fittings (except cast iron couplings and couplings made from purchased pipe) and metal aerosol spray nozzles--are classified in Industry 33291, Metal Valve Manufacturing;
- Manufacturing welded and seamless steel pipes from purchased steel--are classified in Industry 33121, Iron and Steel Pipe and Tube Manufacturing from Purchased Steel;
- Manufacturing plastics plumbing fixtures and plastics portable chemical toilets--are classified in Industry 32619, Other Plastics Product Manufacturing;

T--Canadian, Mexican, and United States industries are comparable.

- Manufacturing vitreous and semivitreous pottery sanitary ware--are classified in Industry 32711, Pottery, Ceramics, and Plumbing Fixture Manufacturing;
- Manufacturing blasting caps, detonating caps, and safety fuses--are classified in Industry 32592, Explosives Manufacturing;
- Manufacturing fireworks--are classified in Industry 32599, All Other Chemical Product and Preparation Manufacturing;
- Manufacturing metal furniture frames--are classified in Industry 33721, Office Furniture (including Fixtures) Manufacturing;
- Manufacturing metal mechanically refrigerated drinking fountains--are classified in Industry 33341, Ventilation, Heating, Air-Conditioning, and Commercial Refrigeration Equipment Manufacturing;
- Manufacturing metal foil bags--are classified in Industry 32222, Paper Bag and Coated and Treated Paper Manufacturing;
- Manufacturing aluminum foil--are classified in Industry 33131, Alumina and Aluminum Production and Processing;
- Manufacturing metal foil (except aluminum)--are classified in Industry Group 3314, Nonferrous Metal (except Aluminum) Production and Processing; and
- Manufacturing metal burial vaults--are classified in Industry 33999, All Other Miscellaneous Manufacturing.

## 332991  Ball and Roller Bearing Manufacturing

This U.S. industry comprises establishments primarily engaged in manufacturing ball and roller bearings of all materials.

*Cross-References.*

Establishments primarily engaged in manufacturing plain bearings are classified in U.S. Industry 333613, Mechanical Power Transmission Equipment Manufacturing.

## 332992  Small Arms Ammunition Manufacturing

This U.S. industry comprises establishments primarily engaged in manufacturing small arms ammunition.

*Cross-References.*          Establishments primarily engaged in--

- Manufacturing ammunition (except small arms)--are classified in U.S. Industry 332993, Ammunition (except Small Arms) Manufacturing;
- Manufacturing blasting and detonating caps and safety fuses--are classified in Industry 325920, Explosives Manufacturing; and
- Manufacturing fireworks--are classified in U.S. Industry 325998, All Other Miscellaneous Chemical Product and Preparation Manufacturing.

## 332993  Ammunition (except Small Arms) Manufacturing

This U.S. industry comprises establishments primarily engaged in manufacturing ammunition (except small arms). Examples of products made by these establishments are bombs, depth charges, rockets (except guided missiles), grenades, mines, and torpedoes.

*Cross-References.*          Establishments primarily engaged in--

- Manufacturing small arms ammunition--are classified in U.S. Industry 332992, Small Arms Ammunition Manufacturing;
- Manufacturing blasting and detonating caps and safety fuses--are classified in Industry 325920, Explosives Manufacturing;

---

T—Canadian, Mexican, and United States industries are comparable.

- Manufacturing fireworks--are classified in U.S. Industry 325998, All Other Miscellaneous Chemical Product and Preparation Manufacturing; and
- Manufacturing guided missiles--are classified in U.S. Industry 336414, Guided Missile and Space Vehicle Manufacturing.

## 332994  Small Arms, Ordnance, and Ordnance Accessories Manufacturing

This U.S. industry comprises establishments primarily engaged in manufacturing small arms, other ordnance, and/or ordnance accessories.

*Cross-References.*          Establishments primarily engaged in--

- Manufacturing military tanks--are classified in U.S. Industry 336992, Military Armored Vehicle, Tank, and Tank Component Manufacturing; and
- Manufacturing guided missiles--are classified in U.S. Industry 336414, Guided Missile and Space Vehicle Manufacturing.

## 332996  Fabricated Pipe and Pipe Fitting Manufacturing

This U.S. industry comprises establishments primarily engaged in fabricating, such as cutting, threading, and bending, metal pipes and pipe fittings made from purchased metal pipe.

*Cross-References.*          Establishments primarily engaged in--

- Manufacturing cast iron pipe and fittings--are classified in U.S. Industry 331511, Iron Foundries;
- Manufacturing pipe system fittings (except cast iron couplings and couplings made from purchased pipe)--are classified in U.S. Industry 332919, Other Metal Valve and Pipe Fitting Manufacturing; and
- Manufacturing welded and seamless steel pipes from purchased steel--are classified in Industry 331210, Iron and Steel Pipe and Tube Manufacturing from Purchased Steel.

## 332999  All Other Miscellaneous Fabricated Metal Product Manufacturing

This U.S. industry comprises establishments primarily engaged in manufacturing fabricated metal products (except forgings and stampings, cutlery and handtools, architectural and structural metals, boilers, tanks, shipping containers, hardware, spring and wire products, machine shop products, turned products, screws, nuts and bolts, metal valves, ball and roller bearings, ammunition, small arms and other ordnances and accessories, and fabricated pipes and pipe fittings).

*Illustrative Examples:*

Foil containers (except bags) manufacturing
Industrial pattern manufacturing
Metal hair curlers manufacturing
Metal ironing boards manufacturing
Metal pallets manufacturing
Metal pipe hangers and supports manufacturing
Metal safes manufacturing

Metal vaults (except burial) manufacturing
Permanent metallic magnets manufacturing
Portable metal ladders manufacturing
Sanitary ware (e.g., bathtubs, lavatories, sinks), metal and enameled metal, manufacturing
Steel wool manufacturing

*Cross-References.*          Establishments primarily engaged in--

- Manufacturing forgings and stampings--are classified in Industry 33211, Forging and Stamping;
- Manufacturing cutlery and handtools--are classified in Industry 33221, Cutlery and Handtool Manufacturing;
- Manufacturing architectural and structural metals--are classified in Industry Group 3323, Architectural and Structural Metals Manufacturing;

---

T—Canadian, Mexican, and United States industries are comparable.

- Manufacturing boilers, tanks, and shipping containers--are classified in Industry Group 3324, Boiler, Tank, and Shipping Container Manufacturing;
- Manufacturing hardware and safe and vault locks--are classified in Industry 332510, Hardware Manufacturing;
- Manufacturing spring and wire products--are classified in Industry 33261, Spring and Wire Product Manufacturing;
- Manufacturing machine shop products, turned products, screws, and nuts and bolts--are classified in Industry Group 3327, Machine Shops; Turned Product; and Screw, Nut, and Bolt Manufacturing;
- Coating, engraving, heat treating, and allied activities--are classified in Industry 33281, Coating, Engraving, Heat Treating, and Allied Activities;
- Manufacturing ball and roller bearings--are classified in U.S. Industry 332991, Ball and Roller Bearing Manufacturing;
- Manufacturing small arms ammunition--are classified in U.S. Industry 332992, Small Arms Ammunition Manufacturing;
- Manufacturing ammunition (except small arms)--are classified in U.S. Industry 332993, Ammunition (except Small Arms) Manufacturing;
- Manufacturing small firearms that are carried and fired by the individual and/or other ordnance and accessories--are classified in U.S. Industry 332994, Small Arms, Ordnance, and Ordnance Accessories Manufacturing;
- Manufacturing metal pipes and pipe fittings from metal pipe produced elsewhere--are classified in U.S. Industry 332996, Fabricated Pipe and Pipe Fitting Manufacturing;
- Manufacturing cast iron pipe and fittings--are classified in U.S. Industry 331511, Iron Foundries;
- Manufacturing welded and seamless steel pipes from purchased steel--are classified in Industry 331210, Iron and Steel Pipe and Tube Manufacturing from Purchased Steel;
- Manufacturing metal furniture frames--are classified in U.S. Industry 337215, Showcase, Partition, Shelving, and Locker Manufacturing;
- Manufacturing powder metallurgy parts--are classified in U.S. Industry 332117, Powder Metallurgy Part Manufacturing;
- Manufacturing metal boxes--are classified in U.S. Industry 332439, Other Metal Container Manufacturing;
- Manufacturing metal nozzles, hose couplings, and aerosol valves--are classified in U.S. Industry 332919, Other Metal Valve and Pipe Fitting Manufacturing;
- Manufacturing metal foil bags--are classified in Industry 322220, Paper Bag and Coated and Treated Paper Manufacturing;
- Manufacturing aluminum foil--are classified in Industry 33131, Alumina and Aluminum Production and Processing;
- Manufacturing metal foil (except aluminum)--are classified in Industry Group 3314, Nonferrous Metal (except Aluminum) Production and Processing;
- Manufacturing metal burial vaults--are classified in U.S. Industry 339995, Burial Casket Manufacturing;
- Manufacturing plastics plumbing fixtures--are classified in U.S. Industry 326191, Plastics Plumbing Fixture Manufacturing;
- Manufacturing vitreous and semivitreous pottery sanitary ware--are classified in Industry 327110, Pottery, Ceramics, and Plumbing Fixture Manufacturing;
- Manufacturing plastics portable chemical toilets--are classified in U.S. Industry 326199, All Other Plastics Product Manufacturing; and
- Manufacturing metal mechanically refrigerated drinking fountains--are classified in U.S. Industry 333415, Air-Conditioning and Warm Air Heating Equipment and Commercial and Industrial Refrigeration Equipment Manufacturing.

## 333    Machinery Manufacturing[T]

Industries in the Machinery Manufacturing subsector create end products that apply mechanical force, for example, the application of gears and levers, to perform work. Some important processes for the manufacture of machinery are forging, stamping, bending, forming, and machining that are used to shape individual pieces of metal. Processes, such as welding and assembling are used to join separate parts together. Although these processes are similar to those used in metal fabricating establishments, machinery manufacturing is different because it typically

---

T—Canadian, Mexican, and United States industries are comparable.

employs multiple metal forming processes in manufacturing the various parts of the machine. Moreover, complex assembly operations are an inherent part of the production process.

In general, design considerations are very important in machinery production. Establishments specialize in making machinery designed for particular applications. Thus, design is considered to be part of the production process for the purpose of implementing NAICS. The NAICS structure reflects this by defining industries and industry groups that make machinery for different applications. A broad distinction exists between machinery that is generally used in a variety of industrial applications (i.e., general purpose machinery) and machinery that is designed to be used in a particular industry (i.e., special purpose machinery). Three industry groups consist of special purpose machinery--Agriculture, Construction, and Mining Machinery Manufacturing; Industrial Machinery Manufacturing; and Commercial and Service Industry Machinery Manufacturing. The other industry groups make general purpose machinery: Ventilation, Heating, Air-Conditioning, and Commercial Refrigeration Equipment Manufacturing; Metalworking Machinery Manufacturing; Engine, Turbine, and Power Transmission Equipment Manufacturing; and Other General Purpose Machinery Manufacturing.

### 3331    Agriculture, Construction, and Mining Machinery Manufacturing[T]

This industry group comprises establishments primarily engaged in manufacturing one or more of the following: (1) farm machinery and equipment, power mowing equipment, and other powered home lawn and garden equipment; (2) construction machinery, surface mining machinery, and logging equipment; and (3) oil and gas field and underground mining machinery and equipment.

### 33311    Agricultural Implement Manufacturing[T]

This industry comprises establishments primarily engaged in manufacturing farm machinery and equipment, powered mowing equipment, and other powered home lawn and garden equipment.

*Illustrative Examples:*

| | |
|---|---|
| Combines (i.e., harvester-threshers) manufacturing | Powered lawnmowers manufacturing |
| Cotton ginning machinery manufacturing | Poultry brooders, feeders, and waterers |
| Fertilizing machinery, farm-type, manufacturing | manufacturing |
| Haying machines manufacturing | Snowblowers and throwers, residential-type, |
| Milking machines manufacturing | manufacturing |
| Planting machines, farm-type, manufacturing | Tractors and attachments, lawn and garden-type and |
| Plows, farm-type, manufacturing | farm-type, manufacturing |

*Cross-References.*        Establishments primarily engaged in--

- Manufacturing agricultural handtools and nonpowered lawnmowers--are classified in Industry 33221, Cutlery and Handtool Manufacturing;
- Manufacturing farm conveyors--are classified in Industry 33392, Material Handling Equipment Manufacturing; and
- Manufacturing forestry machinery and equipment, such as brush, limb, and log chippers; log splitters; and construction equipment--are classified in Industry 33312, Construction Machinery Manufacturing.

### 333111  Farm Machinery and Equipment Manufacturing

This U.S. industry comprises establishments primarily engaged in manufacturing agricultural and farm machinery and equipment, and other turf and grounds care equipment, including planting, harvesting, and grass mowing equipment (except lawn and garden-type).

*Illustrative Examples:*

| | |
|---|---|
| Combines (i.e., harvester-threshers) manufacturing | Feed processing equipment, farm-type, |
| Cotton ginning machinery manufacturing | manufacturing |

---

T—Canadian, Mexican, and United States industries are comparable.

Fertilizing machinery, farm-type, manufacturing
Grass mowing equipment (except lawn and garden)
manufacturing
Haying machines manufacturing
Milking machines manufacturing

Planting machines, farm-type, manufacturing
Plows, farm-type, manufacturing
Poultry brooders, feeders, and waterers
manufacturing
Tractors and attachments, farm-type, manufacturing

*Cross-References.*        Establishments primarily engaged in--

- Manufacturing farm conveyors--are classified in U.S. Industry 333922, Conveyor and Conveying Equipment Manufacturing;
- Manufacturing tractors and lawnmowers for home lawn and garden care--are classified in U.S. Industry 333112, Lawn and Garden Tractor and Home Lawn and Garden Equipment Manufacturing; and
- Manufacturing construction-type tractors--are classified in Industry 333120, Construction Machinery Manufacturing.

### 333112  Lawn and Garden Tractor and Home Lawn and Garden Equipment Manufacturing

This U.S. industry comprises establishments primarily engaged in manufacturing powered lawnmowers, lawn and garden tractors, and other home lawn and garden equipment, such as tillers, shredders, yard vacuums, and leaf blowers.

*Cross-References.*        Establishments primarily engaged in--

- Manufacturing commercial mowing and other turf and grounds care equipment--are classified in U.S. Industry 333111, Farm Machinery and Equipment Manufacturing; and
- Manufacturing nonpowered lawn and garden shears, edgers, pruners, and lawnmowers--are classified in U.S. Industry 332216, Saw Blade and Handtool Manufacturing.

### 33312   Construction Machinery Manufacturing[T]
See industry description for 333120.

### 333120  Construction Machinery Manufacturing

This industry comprises establishments primarily engaged in manufacturing construction machinery, surface mining machinery, and logging equipment.

*Illustrative Examples:*

Backhoes manufacturing
Bulldozers manufacturing
Construction and surface mining-type rock drill bits
manufacturing
Construction-type tractors and attachments
manufacturing
Off-highway trucks manufacturing

Pile-driving equipment manufacturing
Portable crushing, pulverizing, and screening
machinery manufacturing
Powered post hole diggers manufacturing
Road graders manufacturing
Surface mining machinery (except drilling)
manufacturing

*Cross-References.*        Establishments primarily engaged in--

- Manufacturing drilling and underground mining machinery and equipment--are classified in Industry 33313, Mining and Oil and Gas Field Machinery Manufacturing;
- Manufacturing industrial plant overhead traveling cranes and hoists, truck-type cranes and hoists, winches, aerial work platforms, and automotive wrecker hoists--are classified in Industry 33392, Material Handling Equipment Manufacturing; and
- Manufacturing rail layers, ballast distributors, and other railroad track-laying equipment--are classified in Industry 336510, Railroad Rolling Stock Manufacturing.

T—Canadian, Mexican, and United States industries are comparable.

## 33313   Mining and Oil and Gas Field Machinery Manufacturing[T]

This industry comprises establishments primarily engaged in manufacturing oil and gas field and underground mining machinery and equipment.

*Illustrative Examples:*

Coal breakers, cutters, and pulverizers manufacturing
Core drills, underground mining-type, manufacturing
Mineral processing and beneficiating machinery manufacturing
Mining cars manufacturing
Oil and gas field-type derricks manufacturing

Oil and gas field-type drilling machinery and equipment (except offshore floating platforms) manufacturing
Stationary rock crushing machinery manufacturing
Water well drilling machinery manufacturing

*Cross-References.*          Establishments primarily engaged in--

- Manufacturing offshore oil and gas well drilling and production floating platforms--are classified in Industry 33661, Ship and Boat Building;
- Manufacturing surface mining machinery and equipment--are classified in Industry 33312, Construction Machinery Manufacturing;
- Manufacturing coal and ore conveyors--are classified in Industry 33392, Material Handling Equipment Manufacturing;
- Manufacturing underground mining locomotives--are classified in Industry 33651, Railroad Rolling Stock Manufacturing; and
- Manufacturing pumps and pumping equipment--are classified in Industry 33391, Pump and Compressor Manufacturing.

## 333131   Mining Machinery and Equipment Manufacturing

This U.S. industry comprises establishments primarily engaged in (1) manufacturing underground mining machinery and equipment, such as coal breakers, mining cars, core drills, coal cutters, and rock drills, and (2) manufacturing mineral beneficiating machinery and equipment used in surface or underground mines.

*Cross-References.*          Establishments primarily engaged in--

- Manufacturing surface mining machinery and equipment--are classified in Industry 333120, Construction Machinery Manufacturing;
- Manufacturing well drilling machinery--are classified in U.S. Industry 333132, Oil and Gas Field Machinery and Equipment Manufacturing;
- Manufacturing coal and ore conveyors--are classified in U.S. Industry 333922, Conveyor and Conveying Equipment Manufacturing; and
- Manufacturing underground mining locomotives--are classified in Industry 336510, Railroad Rolling Stock Manufacturing.

## 333132   Oil and Gas Field Machinery and Equipment Manufacturing

This U.S. industry comprises establishments primarily engaged in (1) manufacturing oil and gas field machinery and equipment, such as oil and gas field drilling machinery and equipment; oil and gas field production machinery and equipment; and oil and gas field derricks, and (2) manufacturing water well drilling machinery.

*Cross-References.*          Establishments primarily engaged in--

- Manufacturing offshore oil and gas well drilling and production floating platforms--are classified in U.S. Industry 336611, Ship Building and Repairing;

---

T—Canadian, Mexican, and United States industries are comparable.

- Manufacturing underground mining drills--are classified in U.S. Industry 333131, Mining Machinery and Equipment Manufacturing; and
- Manufacturing pumps and pumping equipment--are classified in U.S. Industry 333914, Measuring, Dispensing, and Other Pumping Equipment Manufacturing.

## 3332    Industrial Machinery Manufacturing[T]

## 33324    Industrial Machinery Manufacturing[T]

This industry comprises establishments primarily engaged in manufacturing industrial machinery, such as food and beverage manufacturing machinery, semiconductor manufacturing machinery, sawmill and woodworking machinery (except handheld), machinery for making paper and paper products, printing and binding machinery and equipment, textile making machinery, and machinery for making plastics and rubber products.

*Cross-References.*        Establishments primarily engaged in--

- Manufacturing agricultural and farm-type, construction, and mining machinery--are classified in Industry Group 3331, Agriculture, Construction, and Mining Machinery Manufacturing;
- Manufacturing food and beverage packaging machinery or power-driven handtools--are classified in Industry 33399, All Other General Purpose Machinery Manufacturing;
- Manufacturing commercial and industrial refrigeration and freezer equipment--are classified in Industry 33341, Ventilation, Heating, Air-Conditioning, and Commercial Refrigeration Equipment Manufacturing;
- Manufacturing commercial-type cooking and food warming equipment, automotive maintenance equipment (except mechanics' handtools), or photocopiers--are classified in Industry 33331, Commercial and Service Industry Machinery Manufacturing; and
- Manufacturing mechanics' handtools and other nonpowered handtools--are classified in Industry 33221, Cutlery and Handtool Manufacturing.

## 333241  Food Product Machinery Manufacturing

This U.S. industry comprises establishments primarily engaged in manufacturing food and beverage manufacturing-type machinery and equipment, such as dairy product plant machinery and equipment (e.g., homogenizers, pasteurizers, ice cream freezers), bakery machinery and equipment (e.g., dough mixers, bake ovens, pastry rolling machines), meat and poultry processing and preparation machinery, and other commercial food products machinery (e.g., slicers, choppers, and mixers).

*Cross-References.*        Establishments primarily engaged in--

- Manufacturing food and beverage packaging machinery--are classified in U.S. Industry 333993, Packaging Machinery Manufacturing;
- Manufacturing commercial and industrial refrigeration and freezer equipment--are classified in U.S. Industry 333415, Air-Conditioning and Warm Air Heating Equipment and Commercial and Industrial Refrigeration Equipment Manufacturing; and
- Manufacturing commercial-type cooking and food warming equipment--are classified in Industry 333310, Commercial and Service Industry Machinery Manufacturing.

## 333242  Semiconductor Machinery Manufacturing

This U.S. industry comprises establishments primarily engaged in manufacturing wafer processing equipment, semiconductor assembly and packaging equipment, and other semiconductor making machinery.

*Cross-References.*        Establishments primarily engaged in--

- Manufacturing printed circuit board manufacturing machinery--are classified in U.S. Industry 333248, All Other Industrial Machinery Manufacturing; and

---

T—Canadian, Mexican, and United States industries are comparable.

- Manufacturing semiconductor testing instruments--are classified in U.S. Industry 334515, Instrument Manufacturing for Measuring and Testing Electricity and Electrical Signals.

### 333243  Sawmill, Woodworking, and Paper Machinery Manufacturing

This U.S. industry comprises establishments primarily engaged in (1) manufacturing sawmill and woodworking machinery (except handheld), such as circular and band sawing equipment, planing machinery, and sanding machinery, and/or (2) manufacturing paper industry machinery for making paper and paper products, such as pulp making machinery, paper and paperboard making machinery, and paper and paperboard converting machinery.

*Cross-References.*        Establishments primarily engaged in--

- Manufacturing planes, axes, drawknives, and handsaws--are classified in U.S. Industry 332216, Saw Blade and Handtool Manufacturing;
- Manufacturing power-driven handtools--are classified in U.S. Industry 333991, Power-Driven Handtool Manufacturing; and
- Manufacturing printing machinery--are classified in U.S. Industry 333248, All Other Industrial Machinery Manufacturing.

### 333248  All Other Industrial Machinery Manufacturing

This U.S. industry comprises establishments primarily engaged in manufacturing industrial machinery (except agricultural and farm-type; construction and mining machinery; food manufacturing-type machinery; semiconductor making machinery; and sawmill, woodworking, and paper making machinery).

*Illustrative Examples:*

Additive manufacturing machinery manufacturing
Bookbinding machines manufacturing
Chemical processing machinery and equipment manufacturing
Cigarette making machinery manufacturing
Glass making machinery (e.g., blowing, forming, molding) manufacturing
Petroleum refining machinery manufacturing

Plastics working machinery manufacturing
Printing presses manufacturing
Rubber working machinery manufacturing
Sewing machines (including household-type) manufacturing
Shoe making and repairing machinery manufacturing
Tannery machinery manufacturing
Textile making machinery manufacturing

*Cross-References.*        Establishments primarily engaged in--

- Manufacturing agricultural and farm-type, construction, and mining machinery--are classified in Industry Group 3331, Agriculture, Construction, and Mining Machinery Manufacturing;
- Manufacturing food and beverage manufacturing-type machinery--are classified in U.S. Industry 333241, Food Product Machinery Manufacturing;
- Manufacturing semiconductor making machinery--are classified in U.S. Industry 333242, Semiconductor Machinery Manufacturing;
- Manufacturing sawmill, woodworking, and paper and paperboard making machinery--are classified in U.S. Industry 333243, Sawmill, Woodworking, and Paper Machinery Manufacturing;
- Manufacturing automotive maintenance equipment (except mechanics' handtools) or photocopiers--are classified in Industry 333310, Commercial and Service Industry Machinery Manufacturing;
- Manufacturing mechanics' handtools--are classified in U.S. Industry 332216, Saw Blade and Handtool Manufacturing; and
- Manufacturing industrial metal molds for plastics and rubber products making machinery--are classified in U.S. Industry 333511, Industrial Mold Manufacturing.

---

T—Canadian, Mexican, and United States industries are comparable.

**census.gov/naics**

**3333    Commercial and Service Industry Machinery Manufacturing[T]**

**33331   Commercial and Service Industry Machinery Manufacturing[T]**
See industry description for 333310.

**333310 Commercial and Service Industry Machinery Manufacturing**

This industry comprises establishments primarily engaged in manufacturing commercial and service industry machinery, such as optical instruments and lenses (except ophthalmic), photographic and photocopying equipment, automatic vending machinery, commercial laundry and drycleaning machinery, office machinery, automotive maintenance equipment (except mechanics' handtools), and commercial-type cooking equipment.

*Cross-References.*          Establishments primarily engaged in--

- Manufacturing household-type appliances--are classified in Industry Group 3352, Household Appliance Manufacturing;
- Manufacturing and/or assembling electronic computers--are classified in U.S. Industry 334111, Electronic Computer Manufacturing;
- Manufacturing computer terminals and other computer peripheral equipment (except storage devices), including point-of-sale terminals and automated teller machines (ATMs)--are classified in U.S. Industry 334118, Computer Terminal and Other Computer Peripheral Equipment Manufacturing;
- Manufacturing facsimile equipment--are classified in Industry 334210, Telephone Apparatus Manufacturing;
- Manufacturing radio and television broadcast equipment--are classified in Industry 334220, Radio and Television Broadcasting and Wireless Communications Equipment Manufacturing;
- Manufacturing electron and proton microscopes--are classified in U.S. Industry 334516, Analytical Laboratory Instrument Manufacturing;
- Manufacturing time clocks and time stamps--are classified in U.S. Industry 334519, Other Measuring and Controlling Device Manufacturing;
- Manufacturing sensitized film, paper, cloth, and plates, toners, and prepared photographic chemicals--are classified in U.S. Industry 325992, Photographic Film, Paper, Plate, Chemical, and Copy Toner Manufacturing;
- Manufacturing pencil sharpeners and staplers--are classified in Industry 339940, Office Supplies (except Paper) Manufacturing;
- Manufacturing coin- or card-operated arcade games--are classified in U.S. Industry 339999, All Other Miscellaneous Manufacturing;
- Manufacturing mechanics' handtools--are classified in U.S. Industry 332216, Saw Blade and Handtool Manufacturing;
- Manufacturing ophthalmic focus lenses--are classified in U.S. Industry 339115, Ophthalmic Goods Manufacturing;
- Manufacturing molded plastics lens blanks--are classified in U.S. Industry 326199, All Other Plastics Product Manufacturing; and
- Manufacturing molded glass lens blanks--are classified in U.S. Industry 327212, Other Pressed and Blown Glass and Glassware Manufacturing.

**3334    Ventilation, Heating, Air-Conditioning, and Commercial Refrigeration Equipment Manufacturing[T]**

**33341   Ventilation, Heating, Air-Conditioning, and Commercial Refrigeration Equipment Manufacturing[T]**

This industry comprises establishments primarily engaged in manufacturing ventilating, heating, air-conditioning, and commercial and industrial refrigeration and freezer equipment.

---

T—Canadian, Mexican, and United States industries are comparable.

*Illustrative Examples:*

Air-conditioner filters manufacturing
Air-conditioning and warm air heating combination units manufacturing
Attic fans manufacturing
Dust and fume collecting equipment manufacturing
Gas fireplaces manufacturing

Heating boilers manufacturing
Industrial and commercial-type fans manufacturing
Refrigerated counter and display cases manufacturing
Refrigerated drinking fountains manufacturing
Space heaters (except portable electric) manufacturing

*Cross-References.*        Establishments primarily engaged in--

- Manufacturing household-type fans (except attic), portable electric space heaters, humidifiers, dehumidifiers, and air purification equipment--are classified in Industry 33521, Small Electrical Appliance Manufacturing;
- Manufacturing household-type appliances, such as cooking stoves, ranges, refrigerators, and freezers--are classified in Industry 33522, Major Household Appliance Manufacturing;
- Manufacturing commercial-type cooking equipment--are classified in Industry 33331, Commercial and Service Industry Machinery Manufacturing;
- Manufacturing industrial, power, and marine boilers--are classified in Industry 33241, Power Boiler and Heat Exchanger Manufacturing;
- Manufacturing industrial process furnaces and ovens--are classified in Industry 33399, All Other General Purpose Machinery Manufacturing; and
- Manufacturing motor vehicle air-conditioning systems and compressors--are classified in Industry 33639, Other Motor Vehicle Parts Manufacturing.

### 333413  Industrial and Commercial Fan and Blower and Air Purification Equipment Manufacturing

This U.S. industry comprises establishments primarily engaged in (1) manufacturing stationary air purification equipment, such as industrial dust and fume collection equipment, electrostatic precipitation equipment, warm air furnace filters, air washers, and other dust collection equipment, and/or (2) manufacturing attic fans and industrial and commercial fans and blowers, such as commercial exhaust fans and commercial ventilating fans.

*Cross-References.*        Establishments primarily engaged in--

- Manufacturing air-conditioning equipment (except motor vehicle)--are classified in U.S. Industry 333415, Air-Conditioning and Warm Air Heating Equipment and Commercial and Industrial Refrigeration Equipment Manufacturing;
- Manufacturing motor vehicle air-conditioning systems and compressors--are classified in Industry 336390, Other Motor Vehicle Parts Manufacturing; and
- Manufacturing household-type fans (except attic) and portable air purification equipment--are classified in Industry 335210, Small Electrical Appliance Manufacturing.

### 333414  Heating Equipment (except Warm Air Furnaces) Manufacturing

This U.S. industry comprises establishments primarily engaged in manufacturing heating equipment (except electric and warm air furnaces), such as heating boilers, heating stoves, floor and wall furnaces, and wall and baseboard heating units.

*Cross-References.*        Establishments primarily engaged in--

- Manufacturing warm air furnaces--are classified in U.S. Industry 333415, Air-Conditioning and Warm Air Heating Equipment and Commercial and Industrial Refrigeration Equipment Manufacturing;
- Manufacturing electric space heaters--are classified in Industry 335210, Small Electrical Appliance Manufacturing;

---

T—Canadian, Mexican, and United States industries are comparable.

- Manufacturing household-type cooking stoves and ranges--are classified in Industry 335220, Major Household Appliance Manufacturing;
- Manufacturing industrial, power, and marine boilers--are classified in Industry 332410, Power Boiler and Heat Exchanger Manufacturing;
- Manufacturing industrial process furnaces and ovens--are classified in U.S. Industry 333994, Industrial Process Furnace and Oven Manufacturing; and
- Manufacturing commercial-type cooking equipment--are classified in Industry 333310, Commercial and Service Industry Machinery Manufacturing.

### 333415 Air-Conditioning and Warm Air Heating Equipment and Commercial and Industrial Refrigeration Equipment Manufacturing

This U.S. industry comprises establishments primarily engaged in (1) manufacturing air-conditioning (except motor vehicle) and warm air furnace equipment and/or (2) manufacturing commercial and industrial refrigeration and freezer equipment.

*Illustrative Examples:*

Air-conditioning and warm air heating combination units manufacturing
Air-conditioning compressors (except motor vehicle) manufacturing
Air-conditioning condensers and condensing units manufacturing
Dehumidifiers (except portable electric) manufacturing

Heat pumps manufacturing
Humidifying equipment (except portable) manufacturing
Refrigerated counter and display cases manufacturing
Refrigerated drinking fountains manufacturing
Snow making machinery manufacturing
Soda fountain cooling and dispensing equipment manufacturing

*Cross-References.* Establishments primarily engaged in--

- Manufacturing motor vehicle air-conditioning systems and compressors--are classified in Industry 336390, Other Motor Vehicle Parts Manufacturing;
- Manufacturing household-type refrigerators and freezers--are classified in Industry 335220, Major Household Appliance Manufacturing;
- Manufacturing portable electric space heaters, humidifiers, and dehumidifiers--are classified in Industry 335210, Small Electrical Appliance Manufacturing;
- Manufacturing heating boilers, heating stoves, floor and wall mount furnaces, and electric wall and baseboard heating units--are classified in U.S. Industry 333414, Heating Equipment (except Warm Air Furnaces) Manufacturing; and
- Manufacturing furnace air filters--are classified in U.S. Industry 333413, Industrial and Commercial Fan and Blower and Air Purification Equipment Manufacturing.

### 3335 Metalworking Machinery Manufacturing[T]

### 33351 Metalworking Machinery Manufacturing[T]

This industry comprises establishments primarily engaged in manufacturing metalworking machinery, such as metal cutting and metal forming machine tools; cutting tools; accessories for metalworking machinery; special dies, tools, jigs, and fixtures; industrial molds; rolling mill machinery; assembly machinery; coil handling, conversion, or straightening equipment; and wire drawing and fabricating machines.

*Cross-References.* Establishments primarily engaged in--

- Manufacturing handtools (except power-driven), cutting dies (except metal cutting), saw blades, and handsaws--are classified in Industry 33221, Cutlery and Handtool Manufacturing;

---

T—Canadian, Mexican, and United States industries are comparable.

- Manufacturing casting molds for heavy steel ingots--are classified in Industry 33151, Ferrous Metal Foundries; and
- Manufacturing power-driven handtools and welding and soldering equipment--are classified in Industry 33399, All Other General Purpose Machinery Manufacturing.

### 333511  Industrial Mold Manufacturing

This U.S. industry comprises establishments primarily engaged in manufacturing industrial molds for casting metals or forming other materials, such as plastics, glass, or rubber.

*Cross-References.*

Establishments primarily engaged in manufacturing casting molds for steel ingots are classified in U.S. Industry 331511, Iron Foundries.

### 333514  Special Die and Tool, Die Set, Jig, and Fixture Manufacturing

This U.S. industry comprises establishments, known as tool and die shops, primarily engaged in manufacturing special tools and fixtures, such as cutting dies and jigs.

*Cross-References.*            Establishments primarily engaged in--

- Manufacturing molds for die-casting and foundry casting; and metal molds for plaster working, rubber working, plastics working, and glass working machinery--are classified in U.S. Industry 333511, Industrial Mold Manufacturing;
- Manufacturing molds for heavy steel ingots--are classified in U.S. Industry 331511, Iron Foundries; and
- Manufacturing cutting dies for materials other than metal--are classified in U.S. Industry 332216, Saw Blade and Handtool Manufacturing.

### 333515  Cutting Tool and Machine Tool Accessory Manufacturing

This U.S. industry comprises establishments primarily engaged in manufacturing accessories and attachments for metal cutting and metal forming machine tools.

*Illustrative Examples:*

| | |
|---|---|
| Knives and bits for metalworking lathes, planers, and shapers manufacturing | Metalworking drill bits manufacturing |
| Measuring attachments (e.g., sine bars) for machine tool manufacturing | Taps and dies (i.e., machine tool accessories) manufacturing |

*Cross-References.*

Establishments primarily engaged in manufacturing saw blades, handsaws, and accessories and attachments for saw blades and for nonpowered metal cutting and forming handtools are classified in U.S. Industry 332216, Saw Blade and Handtool Manufacturing.

### 333517  Machine Tool Manufacturing

This U.S. industry comprises establishments primarily engaged in (1) manufacturing metal cutting machine tools (except handtools) and/or (2) manufacturing metal forming machine tools (except handtools), such as punching, sheering, bending, forming, pressing, forging and die-casting machines.

---

T—Canadian, Mexican, and United States industries are comparable.

*Illustrative Examples:*

Bending and forming machines, metalworking, manufacturing
Buffing and polishing machines, metalworking, manufacturing
Drilling machines, metalworking, manufacturing
Grinding machines, metalworking, manufacturing

Home workshop metal cutting machine tools (except handtools, welding equipment) manufacturing
Metalworking lathes manufacturing
Milling machines, metalworking, manufacturing
Stamping machines, metalworking, manufacturing

*Cross-References.*        Establishments primarily engaged in--

- Manufacturing welding and soldering equipment--are classified in U.S. Industry 333992, Welding and Soldering Equipment Manufacturing;
- Manufacturing power-driven handtools--are classified in U.S. Industry 333991, Power-Driven Handtool Manufacturing;
- Manufacturing rolling mill machinery and equipment--are classified in U.S. Industry 333519, Rolling Mill and Other Metalworking Machinery Manufacturing; and
- Manufacturing accessories and attachments for metal cutting and forming machine tools (except saw blades)--are classified in U.S. Industry 333515, Cutting Tool and Machine Tool Accessory Manufacturing.

## 333519 Rolling Mill and Other Metalworking Machinery Manufacturing

This U.S. industry comprises establishments primarily engaged in manufacturing rolling mill machinery and equipment and/or other metalworking machinery (except industrial molds; special dies and tools, die sets, jigs, and fixtures; cutting tools and machine tool accessories; and machine tools).

*Illustrative Examples:*

Assembly machines (i.e., wire making equipment) manufacturing
Cradle assembly machinery (i.e., wire making equipment) manufacturing
Metalworking coil winding and cutting machinery manufacturing

Rolling mill roll machines, metalworking, manufacturing
Wire drawing and fabricating machinery and equipment (except dies) manufacturing

*Cross-References.*        Establishments primarily engaged in--

- Manufacturing industrial molds--are classified in U.S. Industry 333511, Industrial Mold Manufacturing;
- Manufacturing metal cutting and metal forming machine tools--are classified in U.S. Industry 333517, Machine Tool Manufacturing;
- Manufacturing special dies and tools, die sets, jigs, and fixtures--are classified in U.S. Industry 333514, Special Die and Tool, Die Set, Jig, and Fixture Manufacturing; and
- Manufacturing accessories and attachments for metal cutting and forming machine tools (except saw blades)--are classified in U.S. Industry 333515, Cutting Tool and Machine Tool Accessory Manufacturing.

## 3336 Engine, Turbine, and Power Transmission Equipment Manufacturing[T]

## 33361 Engine, Turbine, and Power Transmission Equipment Manufacturing[T]

This industry comprises establishments primarily engaged in manufacturing turbines, power transmission equipment, and internal combustion engines (except automotive gasoline and aircraft).

T—Canadian, Mexican, and United States industries are comparable.

*Illustrative Examples:*

Clutches and brakes (except electromagnetic industrial controls, motor vehicle) manufacturing
Diesel and semidiesel engines manufacturing
Electric outboard motors manufacturing
Internal combustion engines for hybrid drive systems (except automotive) manufacturing
Plain bearings (except internal combustion engine) manufacturing
Power transmission pulleys manufacturing

Plain bushings (except internal combustion engine) manufacturing
Speed changers (i.e., power transmission equipment) manufacturing
Speed reducers (i.e., power transmission equipment) manufacturing
Turbine generator set units manufacturing
Universal joints (except aircraft, motor vehicle) manufacturing

*Cross-References.*          Establishments primarily engaged in--

- Manufacturing motor vehicle power transmission equipment--are classified in Industry 33635, Motor Vehicle Transmission and Power Train Parts Manufacturing;
- Manufacturing aircraft engines and aircraft power transmission equipment--are classified in Industry 33641, Aerospace Product and Parts Manufacturing;
- Manufacturing ball and roller bearings--are classified in Industry 33299, All Other Fabricated Metal Product Manufacturing;
- Manufacturing gasoline automotive engines--are classified in Industry 33631, Motor Vehicle Gasoline Engine and Engine Parts Manufacturing; and
- Manufacturing electric power transmission, electric power distribution equipment, generators, or prime mover generator sets (except turbines)--are classified in Industry 33531, Electrical Equipment Manufacturing.

**333611  Turbine and Turbine Generator Set Units Manufacturing**

This U.S. industry comprises establishments primarily engaged in manufacturing turbines (except aircraft); and complete turbine generator set units, such as steam, hydraulic, gas, and wind.

*Cross-References.*          Establishments primarily engaged in--

- Manufacturing aircraft turbines--are classified in U.S. Industry 336412, Aircraft Engine and Engine Parts Manufacturing; and
- Manufacturing generators or prime mover generator sets (except turbines)--are classified in U.S. Industry 335312, Motor and Generator Manufacturing.

**333612  Speed Changer, Industrial High-Speed Drive, and Gear Manufacturing**

This U.S. industry comprises establishments primarily engaged in manufacturing gears, speed changers, and industrial high-speed drives (except hydrostatic).

*Cross-References.*          Establishments primarily engaged in--

- Manufacturing motor vehicle power transmission equipment--are classified in Industry 336350, Motor Vehicle Transmission and Power Train Parts Manufacturing;
- Manufacturing aircraft power transmission equipment--are classified in U.S. Industry 336413, Other Aircraft Parts and Auxiliary Equipment Manufacturing; and
- Manufacturing industrial hydrostatic transmissions--are classified in U.S. Industry 333996, Fluid Power Pump and Motor Manufacturing.

---

T—Canadian, Mexican, and United States industries are comparable.

## 333613  Mechanical Power Transmission Equipment Manufacturing

This U.S. industry comprises establishments primarily engaged in manufacturing mechanical power transmission equipment (except motor vehicle and aircraft), such as plain bearings, clutches (except motor vehicle and electromagnetic industrial control), couplings, joints, and drive chains.

*Cross-References.*          Establishments primarily engaged in--

- Manufacturing motor vehicle power transmission equipment--are classified in Industry 336350, Motor Vehicle Transmission and Power Train Parts Manufacturing;
- Manufacturing aircraft power transmission equipment--are classified in U.S. Industry 336413, Other Aircraft Parts and Auxiliary Equipment Manufacturing;
- Manufacturing ball and roller bearings--are classified in U.S. Industry 332991, Ball and Roller Bearing Manufacturing; and
- Manufacturing gears, speed changers, and industrial high-speed drives (except hydrostatic)--are classified in U.S. Industry 333612, Speed Changer, Industrial High-Speed Drive, and Gear Manufacturing.

## 333618  Other Engine Equipment Manufacturing

This U.S. industry comprises establishments primarily engaged in manufacturing internal combustion engines (except automotive gasoline and aircraft).

*Cross-References.*          Establishments primarily engaged in--

- Manufacturing gasoline motor vehicle engines and motor vehicle transmissions--are classified in Industry Group 3363, Motor Vehicle Parts Manufacturing;
- Manufacturing gasoline aircraft engines and aircraft transmissions--are classified in Industry 33641, Aerospace Product and Parts Manufacturing;
- Manufacturing turbine and turbine generator set units--are classified in U.S. Industry 333611, Turbine and Turbine Generator Set Units Manufacturing;
- Manufacturing speed changers and industrial high-speed drives and gears--are classified in U.S. Industry 333612, Speed Changer, Industrial High-Speed Drive, and Gear Manufacturing; and
- Manufacturing mechanical power transmission equipment (except motor vehicle and aircraft)--are classified in U.S. Industry 333613, Mechanical Power Transmission Equipment Manufacturing.

## 3339    Other General Purpose Machinery Manufacturing[T]

This industry group comprises establishments primarily engaged in manufacturing pumps and compressors, material handling equipment, and all other general purpose machinery (except ventilation, heating, air-conditioning, and commercial refrigeration equipment; metalworking machinery; and engines, turbines, and power transmission equipment).

## 33391   Pump and Compressor Manufacturing[T]

This industry comprises establishments primarily engaged in manufacturing pumps and compressors, such as general purpose air and gas compressors, nonagricultural spraying and dusting equipment, general purpose pumps and pumping equipment (except fluid power pumps and motors), and measuring and dispensing pumps.

*Cross-References.*          Establishments primarily engaged in--

- Manufacturing fluid power pumps and motors and handheld pneumatic spray guns--are classified in Industry 33399, All Other General Purpose Machinery Manufacturing;
- Manufacturing agricultural spraying and dusting equipment--are classified in Industry 33311, Agricultural Implement Manufacturing;

---

T—Canadian, Mexican, and United States industries are comparable.

- Manufacturing laboratory vacuum pumps--are classified in Industry 33911, Medical Equipment and Supplies Manufacturing;
- Manufacturing pumps and air-conditioning systems and compressors for motor vehicles--are classified in Industry Group 3363, Motor Vehicle Parts Manufacturing; and
- Manufacturing air-conditioning systems and compressors (except motor vehicle)--are classified in Industry 33341, Ventilation, Heating, Air-Conditioning, and Commercial Refrigeration Equipment Manufacturing.

## 333912  Air and Gas Compressor Manufacturing

This U.S. industry comprises establishments primarily engaged in manufacturing general purpose air and gas compressors, such as reciprocating compressors, centrifugal compressors, vacuum pumps (except laboratory), and nonagricultural spraying and dusting compressors and spray gun units.

*Cross-References.*        Establishments primarily engaged in--

- Manufacturing refrigeration and air-conditioning (except motor vehicle) systems and compressors--are classified in U.S. Industry 333415, Air-Conditioning and Warm Air Heating Equipment and Commercial and Industrial Refrigeration Equipment Manufacturing;
- Manufacturing motor vehicle air-conditioning systems and compressors--are classified in Industry 336390, Other Motor Vehicle Parts Manufacturing;
- Manufacturing fluid power pumps and motors--are classified in U.S. Industry 333996, Fluid Power Pump and Motor Manufacturing;
- Manufacturing agricultural spraying and dusting equipment--are classified in U.S. Industry 333111, Farm Machinery and Equipment Manufacturing;
- Manufacturing laboratory vacuum pumps--are classified in U.S. Industry 339113, Surgical Appliance and Supplies Manufacturing; and
- Manufacturing handheld pneumatic spray guns--are classified in U.S. Industry 333991, Power-Driven Handtool Manufacturing.

## 333914  Measuring, Dispensing, and Other Pumping Equipment Manufacturing

This U.S. industry comprises establishments primarily engaged in (1) manufacturing measuring and dispensing pumps, such as gasoline pumps and lubricating oil measuring and dispensing pumps and/or (2) manufacturing general purpose pumps and pumping equipment (except fluid power pumps and motors), such as reciprocating pumps, turbine pumps, centrifugal pumps, rotary pumps, diaphragm pumps, domestic water system pumps, oil well and oil field pumps, and sump pumps.

*Cross-References.*        Establishments primarily engaged in--

- Manufacturing fluid power pumps and motors--are classified in U.S. Industry 333996, Fluid Power Pump and Motor Manufacturing;
- Manufacturing vacuum pumps (except laboratory)--are classified in U.S. Industry 333912, Air and Gas Compressor Manufacturing;
- Manufacturing laboratory vacuum pumps--are classified in U.S. Industry 339113, Surgical Appliance and Supplies Manufacturing; and
- Manufacturing fluid pumps for motor vehicles, such as oil pumps, water pumps, and power steering pumps--are classified in Industry Group 3363, Motor Vehicle Parts Manufacturing.

## 33392  Material Handling Equipment Manufacturing[T]

This industry comprises establishments primarily engaged in manufacturing material handling equipment, such as elevators and moving stairs; conveyors and conveying equipment; overhead traveling cranes, hoists, and monorail systems; and industrial trucks, tractors, trailers, and stacker machinery.

---

T—Canadian, Mexican, and United States industries are comparable.

*Cross-References.*            Establishments primarily engaged in--

- Manufacturing motor vehicle-type trailers--are classified in Industry 33621, Motor Vehicle Body and Trailer Manufacturing;
- Manufacturing farm-type tractors--are classified in Industry 33311, Agricultural Implement Manufacturing;
- Manufacturing construction-type tractors and cranes--are classified in Industry 33312, Construction Machinery Manufacturing; and
- Manufacturing power transmission pulleys--are classified in Industry 33361, Engine, Turbine, and Power Transmission Equipment Manufacturing.

## 333921  Elevator and Moving Stairway Manufacturing

This U.S. industry comprises establishments primarily engaged in manufacturing elevators and moving stairways.

*Illustrative Examples:*

Automobile lifts (i.e., garage-type, service station) manufacturing
Escalators manufacturing

Moving walkways manufacturing
Passenger and freight elevators manufacturing

*Cross-References.*

Establishments primarily engaged in manufacturing commercial conveyor systems and equipment are classified in U.S. Industry 333922, Conveyor and Conveying Equipment Manufacturing.

## 333922  Conveyor and Conveying Equipment Manufacturing

This U.S. industry comprises establishments primarily engaged in manufacturing conveyors and conveying equipment, such as gravity conveyors, trolley conveyors, tow conveyors, pneumatic tube conveyors, carousel conveyors, farm conveyors, and belt conveyors.

*Cross-References.*            Establishments primarily engaged in--

- Manufacturing passenger or freight elevators, dumbwaiters, and moving stairways--are classified in U.S. Industry 333921, Elevator and Moving Stairway Manufacturing; and
- Manufacturing overhead traveling cranes and monorail systems--are classified in U.S. Industry 333923, Overhead Traveling Crane, Hoist, and Monorail System Manufacturing.

## 333923  Overhead Traveling Crane, Hoist, and Monorail System Manufacturing

This U.S. industry comprises establishments primarily engaged in manufacturing overhead traveling cranes, hoists, and monorail systems.

*Illustrative Examples:*

Aerial work platforms manufacturing
Automobile wrecker (i.e., tow truck) hoists manufacturing
Block and tackle manufacturing

Metal pulleys (except power transmission) manufacturing
Winches manufacturing

*Cross-References.*        Establishments primarily engaged in--

- Manufacturing construction-type cranes--are classified in Industry 333120, Construction Machinery Manufacturing;

_____

T—Canadian, Mexican, and United States industries are comparable.

- Manufacturing aircraft loading hoists--are classified in U.S. Industry 333924, Industrial Truck, Tractor, Trailer, and Stacker Machinery Manufacturing; and
- Manufacturing power transmission pulleys--are classified in U.S. Industry 333613, Mechanical Power Transmission Equipment Manufacturing.

## 333924  Industrial Truck, Tractor, Trailer, and Stacker Machinery Manufacturing

This U.S. industry comprises establishments primarily engaged in manufacturing industrial trucks, tractors, trailers, and stackers (i.e., truck-type) such as forklifts, pallet loaders and unloaders, and portable loading docks.

*Cross-References.*          Establishments primarily engaged in--

- Manufacturing motor vehicle-type trailers--are classified in Industry 33621, Motor Vehicle Body and Trailer Manufacturing;
- Manufacturing farm-type tractors--are classified in U.S. Industry 333111, Farm Machinery and Equipment Manufacturing; and
- Manufacturing construction-type tractors--are classified in Industry 333120, Construction Machinery Manufacturing.

## 33399    All Other General Purpose Machinery Manufacturing[T]

This industry comprises establishments primarily engaged in manufacturing general purpose machinery (except ventilation, heating, air-conditioning, and commercial refrigeration equipment; metalworking machinery; engines, turbines, and power transmission equipment; pumps and compressors; and material handling equipment).

*Illustrative Examples:*

| | |
|---|---|
| Automatic fire sprinkler systems manufacturing | Industrial-type furnaces manufacturing |
| Bridge and gate lifting machinery manufacturing | Packaging machinery manufacturing |
| Fluid power cylinders manufacturing | Power-driven handtools manufacturing |
| Fluid power pumps manufacturing | Scales and balances manufacturing |
| Hydraulic and pneumatic jacks manufacturing | Welding equipment manufacturing |

*Cross-References.*          Establishments primarily engaged in--

- Manufacturing ventilating, heating, air-conditioning (except motor vehicle), commercial refrigeration, and furnace filters--are classified in Industry 33341, Ventilation, Heating, Air-Conditioning, and Commercial Refrigeration Equipment Manufacturing;
- Manufacturing engine, turbine, and power transmission equipment--are classified in Industry Group 3336, Engine, Turbine, and Power Transmission Equipment Manufacturing;
- Manufacturing pumps and compressors--are classified in Industry 33391, Pump and Compressor Manufacturing;
- Manufacturing material handling equipment--are classified in Industry 33392, Material Handling Equipment Manufacturing;
- Manufacturing motor vehicle air-conditioning systems and compressors, engine filters, and pumps--are classified in Industry Group 3363, Motor Vehicle Parts Manufacturing;
- Manufacturing metal cutting, metal forming, and other metalworking machinery--are classified in Industry 33351, Metalworking Machinery Manufacturing;
- Manufacturing power-driven heavy construction or mining hand operated tools, such as tampers, jackhammers, and augers--are classified in Industry 33312, Construction Machinery Manufacturing, or Industry 33313, Mining and Oil and Gas Field Machinery Manufacturing;
- Manufacturing bakery ovens and industrial kilns, such as cement, wood, and chemical--are classified in Industry 33324, Industrial Machinery Manufacturing;

---

T—Canadian, Mexican, and United States industries are comparable.

- Manufacturing mechanical jacks, handheld soldering irons, countersink bits, drill bits, router bits, milling cutters, and other machine tools for woodcutting--are classified in Industry 33221, Cutlery and Handtool Manufacturing;
- Manufacturing carnival and amusement park equipment, automotive maintenance equipment, and coin- or card-operated vending machines--are classified in Industry 33331, Commercial and Service Industry Machinery Manufacturing; and
- Manufacturing arc-welding transformers--are classified in Industry 33531, Electrical Equipment Manufacturing.

## 333991 Power-Driven Handtool Manufacturing

This U.S. industry comprises establishments primarily engaged in manufacturing power-driven (e.g., battery, corded, pneumatic) handtools, such as drills, screwguns, circular saws, chain saws, staplers, and nailers.

*Cross-References.*        Establishments primarily engaged in--

- Manufacturing metal cutting and metal forming machines (including home workshop)--are classified in Industry 33351, Metalworking Machinery Manufacturing;
- Manufacturing countersink bits, drill bits, router bits, milling cutters, and other machine tools for woodcutting--are classified in U.S. Industry 332216, Saw Blade and Handtool Manufacturing;
- Manufacturing power-driven heavy construction or mining hand operated tools, such as tampers, jackhammers, and augers--are classified in Industry 333120, Construction Machinery Manufacturing, or Industry 33313, Mining and Oil and Gas Field Machinery Manufacturing; and
- Manufacturing powered home lawn and garden equipment--are classified in U.S. Industry 333112, Lawn and Garden Tractor and Home Lawn and Garden Equipment Manufacturing.

## 333992 Welding and Soldering Equipment Manufacturing

This U.S. industry comprises establishments primarily engaged in manufacturing welding and soldering equipment and accessories (except transformers), such as arc, resistance, gas, plasma, laser, electron beam, and ultrasonic welding equipment; welding electrodes; coated or cored welding wire; and soldering equipment (except handheld).

*Cross-References.*        Establishments primarily engaged in--

- Manufacturing handheld soldering irons--are classified in U.S. Industry 332216, Saw Blade and Handtool Manufacturing; and
- Manufacturing arc-welding transformers--are classified in U.S. Industry 335311, Power, Distribution, and Specialty Transformer Manufacturing.

## 333993 Packaging Machinery Manufacturing

This U.S. industry comprises establishments primarily engaged in manufacturing packaging machinery, such as wrapping, bottling, canning, and labeling machinery.

## 333994 Industrial Process Furnace and Oven Manufacturing

This U.S. industry comprises establishments primarily engaged in manufacturing industrial process ovens, induction and dielectric heating equipment, and kilns (except cement, chemical, wood). Included in this industry are establishments manufacturing laboratory furnaces and ovens.

*Cross-References.*        Establishments primarily engaged in--

- Manufacturing bakery ovens--are classified in U.S. Industry 333241, Food Product Machinery Manufacturing;

---

T—Canadian, Mexican, and United States industries are comparable.

- Manufacturing cement, wood, and chemical kilns--are classified in U.S. Industry 333248, All Other Industrial Machinery Manufacturing; and
- Manufacturing cremating ovens--are classified in U.S. Industry 333998, All Other Miscellaneous General Purpose Machinery Manufacturing.

### 333995  Fluid Power Cylinder and Actuator Manufacturing

This U.S. industry comprises establishments primarily engaged in manufacturing fluid power (i.e., hydraulic and pneumatic) cylinders and actuators.

*Cross-References.*

Establishments primarily engaged in manufacturing general purpose air and gas compressors are classified in U.S. Industry 333912, Air and Gas Compressor Manufacturing.

### 333996  Fluid Power Pump and Motor Manufacturing

This U.S. industry comprises establishments primarily engaged in manufacturing fluid power (i.e., hydraulic and pneumatic) pumps and motors.

*Cross-References.*          Establishments primarily engaged in--

- Manufacturing fluid pumps for motor vehicles, such as oil pumps, water pumps, and power steering pumps--are classified in Industry Group 3363, Motor Vehicle Parts Manufacturing;
- Manufacturing general purpose pumps (except fluid power)--are classified in U.S. Industry 333914, Measuring, Dispensing, and Other Pumping Equipment Manufacturing; and
- Manufacturing air compressors--are classified in U.S. Industry 333912, Air and Gas Compressor Manufacturing.

### 333998  All Other Miscellaneous General Purpose Machinery Manufacturing

This U.S. industry comprises establishments primarily engaged in manufacturing general purpose machinery (except ventilating, heating, air-conditioning, and commercial refrigeration equipment; metalworking machinery; engines, turbines, and power transmission equipment; pumps and compressors; material handling equipment; power-driven handtools; welding and soldering equipment; packaging machinery; industrial process furnaces and ovens; fluid power cylinders and actuators; and fluid power pumps and motors).

*Illustrative Examples:*

Automatic fire sprinkler systems manufacturing
Baling machinery (e.g., paper, scrap metal)
manufacturing
Bridge and gate lifting machinery manufacturing
Centrifuges, industrial and laboratory-type,
manufacturing
Cremating ovens manufacturing

General purpose-type sieves and screening equipment
manufacturing
Hydraulic and pneumatic jacks manufacturing
Industrial and general purpose-type filters (except
internal combustion engine, warm air furnace)
manufacturing
Scales and balances manufacturing

*Cross-References.*          Establishments primarily engaged in--

- Manufacturing ventilating, heating, air-conditioning (except motor vehicle), and commercial refrigeration equipment--are classified in Industry 33341, Ventilation, Heating, Air-Conditioning, and Commercial Refrigeration Equipment Manufacturing;
- Manufacturing motor vehicle air-conditioning systems and compressors--are classified in Industry 336390, Other Motor Vehicle Parts Manufacturing;

---

T—Canadian, Mexican, and United States industries are comparable.

- Manufacturing material handling equipment--are classified in Industry 33392, Material Handling Equipment Manufacturing;
- Manufacturing power-driven handtools--are classified in U.S. Industry 333991, Power-Driven Handtool Manufacturing;
- Manufacturing welding and soldering equipment (except handheld soldering irons)--are classified in U.S. Industry 333992, Welding and Soldering Equipment Manufacturing;
- Manufacturing packaging machinery--are classified in U.S. Industry 333993, Packaging Machinery Manufacturing;
- Manufacturing bakery ovens--are classified in U.S. Industry 333241, Food Product Machinery Manufacturing;
- Manufacturing cement, wood, and chemical kilns--are classified in U.S. Industry 333248, All Other Industrial Machinery Manufacturing;
- Manufacturing industrial process furnaces and ovens (except bakery)--are classified in U.S. Industry 333994, Industrial Process Furnace and Oven Manufacturing;
- Manufacturing fluid power cylinders and actuators--are classified in U.S. Industry 333995, Fluid Power Cylinder and Actuator Manufacturing;
- Manufacturing fluid power pumps and motors--are classified in U.S. Industry 333996, Fluid Power Pump and Motor Manufacturing;
- Manufacturing carnival and amusement park equipment, automotive maintenance equipment, and coin- or card-operated vending machines--are classified in Industry 333310, Commercial and Service Industry Machinery Manufacturing;
- Manufacturing motor vehicle engine filters and pumps--are classified in Industry Group 3363, Motor Vehicle Parts Manufacturing; and
- Manufacturing mechanical jacks--are classified in U.S. Industry 332216, Saw Blade and Handtool Manufacturing.

## 334    Computer and Electronic Product Manufacturing[T]

Industries in the Computer and Electronic Product Manufacturing subsector group establishments that manufacture computers, computer peripherals, communications equipment, and similar electronic products, and establishments that manufacture components for such products. The Computer and Electronic Product Manufacturing industries are combined in the hierarchy of NAICS because of their economic significance to the economies of all three North American countries. For industries in this subsector, the manufacturing processes are fundamentally different from the manufacturing processes of other machinery and equipment. The design and use of integrated circuits and the application of highly specialized miniaturization technologies are common elements in the production technologies of the Computer and Electronic Product Manufacturing subsector.

## 3341    Computer and Peripheral Equipment Manufacturing[T]

## 33411    Computer and Peripheral Equipment Manufacturing[T]

This industry comprises establishments primarily engaged in manufacturing and/or assembling electronic computers, such as mainframes, personal computers, workstations, laptops, and computer servers; and computer peripheral equipment, such as storage devices, printers, monitors, and input/output devices and terminals. Computers can be analog, digital, or hybrid. Digital computers, the most common type, are devices that do all of the following: (1) store the processing program or programs and the data immediately necessary for the execution of the program; (2) can be freely programmed in accordance with the requirements of the user; (3) perform arithmetical computations specified by the user; and (4) execute, without human intervention, a processing program that requires the computer to modify its execution by logical decision during the processing run. Analog computers are capable of simulating mathematical models and comprise at least analog, control, and programming elements.

---

T—Canadian, Mexican, and United States industries are comparable.

*Cross-References.*          Establishments primarily engaged in--

- Manufacturing digital telecommunications switches, and local area network and wide area network communications equipment, such as bridges, routers, and gateways--are classified in Industry 33421, Telephone Apparatus Manufacturing;
- Manufacturing blank magnetic and optical recording media--are classified in Industry 33461, Manufacturing and Reproducing Magnetic and Optical Media;
- Manufacturing machinery or equipment that incorporates electronic computers for operation or control purposes and embedded control applications--are classified in the Manufacturing sector based on the classification of the complete machinery or equipment;
- Manufacturing external audio speakers for computer use--are classified in Industry 33431, Audio and Video Equipment Manufacturing;
- Manufacturing internal loaded printed circuit board devices, such as sound, video, controller, and network interface cards; internal and external computer modems; and semiconductor storage devices, such as memory chips--are classified in Industry 33441, Semiconductor and Other Electronic Component Manufacturing;
- Manufacturing other parts, such as casings, stampings, cable sets, and switches, for computers, storage devices and other peripheral equipment--are classified in the Manufacturing sector based on their associated production processes;
- Manufacturing digital cameras--are classified in Industry 33331, Commercial and Service Industry Machinery Manufacturing; and
- Retailing computers with on-site assembly--are classified in Industry 44921, Electronics and Appliance Retailers.

## 334111  Electronic Computer Manufacturing

This U.S. industry comprises establishments primarily engaged in manufacturing and/or assembling electronic computers, such as mainframes, personal computers, workstations, laptops, and computer servers. Computers can be analog, digital, or hybrid. Digital computers, the most common type, are devices that do all of the following: (1) store the processing program or programs and the data immediately necessary for the execution of the program; (2) can be freely programmed in accordance with the requirements of the user; (3) perform arithmetical computations specified by the user; and (4) execute, without human intervention, a processing program that requires the computer to modify its execution by logical decision during the processing run. Analog computers are capable of simulating mathematical models and contain at least analog, control, and programming elements. The manufacture of computers includes the assembly or integration of processors, coprocessors, memory, storage, and input/output devices into a user-programmable final product.

*Cross-References.*          Establishments primarily engaged in--

- Manufacturing digital telecommunications switches, and local area network and wide area network communication equipment, such as bridges, routers, and gateways--are classified in Industry 334210, Telephone Apparatus Manufacturing;
- Manufacturing blank magnetic and optical recording media--are classified in Industry 334610, Manufacturing and Reproducing Magnetic and Optical Media;
- Manufacturing machinery or equipment that incorporates electronic computers for operation or control purposes and embedded control applications--are classified in the Manufacturing sector based on the classification of the complete machinery or equipment;
- Manufacturing internal, loaded, printed circuit board devices, such as sound, video, controller, and network interface cards; internal and external computer modems; and semiconductor storage devices, such as memory chips--are classified in Industry 33441, Semiconductor and Other Electronic Component Manufacturing;
- Manufacturing other parts, such as casings, stampings, cable sets, and switches, for computers--are classified in the Manufacturing sector based on their associated production processes; and
- Retailing computers with on-site assembly--are classified in Industry 449210, Electronics and Appliance Retailers.

---

T—Canadian, Mexican, and United States industries are comparable.

## 334112 Computer Storage Device Manufacturing

This U.S. industry comprises establishments primarily engaged in manufacturing computer storage devices that allow the storage and retrieval of data from a phase change, magnetic, optical, or magnetic/optical media. Examples of products made by these establishments are computer disk drives, USB flash drives, and tape storage and backup units.

*Cross-References.*          Establishments primarily engaged in--

- Manufacturing blank magnetic and optical recording media, such as flash memory cards--are classified in Industry 334610, Manufacturing and Reproducing Magnetic and Optical Media;
- Manufacturing semiconductor storage devices, such as memory chips--are classified in U.S. Industry 334413, Semiconductor and Related Device Manufacturing;
- Manufacturing drive controller cards, internal or external to the storage device--are classified in U.S. Industry 334418, Printed Circuit Assembly (Electronic Assembly) Manufacturing; and
- Manufacturing other parts, such as casings, stampings, cable sets, and switches, for computer storage devices--are classified in the Manufacturing sector based on their associated production processes.

## 334118 Computer Terminal and Other Computer Peripheral Equipment Manufacturing

This U.S. industry comprises establishments primarily engaged in manufacturing computer terminals and other computer peripheral equipment (except storage devices).

*Illustrative Examples:*

Automated teller machines (ATM) manufacturing
Computer terminals manufacturing
Joystick devices manufacturing
Keyboards, computer peripheral equipment, manufacturing
Monitors, computer peripheral equipment, manufacturing

Mouse devices, computer peripheral equipment, manufacturing
Optical readers and scanners manufacturing
Plotters, computer, manufacturing
Point-of-sale terminals manufacturing
Printers, computer, manufacturing

*Cross-References.*          Establishments primarily engaged in--

- Manufacturing local area network and wide area network communications equipment, such as bridges, routers, and gateways--are classified in Industry 334210, Telephone Apparatus Manufacturing;
- Manufacturing computer storage devices--are classified in U.S. Industry 334112, Computer Storage Device Manufacturing;
- Manufacturing external audio speakers for computer use--are classified in Industry 334310, Audio and Video Equipment Manufacturing;
- Manufacturing internal, loaded, printed circuit board devices, such as sound, video, controller, and network interface cards; and internal and external computer modems used as computer peripherals--are classified in U.S. Industry 334418, Printed Circuit Assembly (Electronic Assembly) Manufacturing;
- Manufacturing other parts, such as casings, stampings, cable sets, and switches, for computer peripheral equipment--are classified in the Manufacturing sector based on their associated production processes; and
- Manufacturing digital cameras--are classified in Industry 333310, Commercial and Service Industry Machinery Manufacturing.

## 3342    Communications Equipment Manufacturing[T]

This industry group comprises establishments primarily engaged in manufacturing wire telephone and data communications equipment, radio and television broadcast and wireless communications equipment, and all other communications equipment.

---

T—Canadian, Mexican, and United States industries are comparable.

**33421   Telephone Apparatus Manufacturing**[T]
See industry description for 334210.

**334210   Telephone Apparatus Manufacturing**

This industry comprises establishments primarily engaged in manufacturing wire telephone and data communications equipment.  These products may be stand-alone or board-level components of a larger system.  Examples of products made by these establishments are central office switching equipment, cordless and wire telephones (except cellular), PBX equipment, telephone answering machines, LAN modems, multi-user modems, and other data communications equipment, such as bridges, routers, and gateways.

*Cross-References.*          Establishments primarily engaged in--

- Manufacturing internal and external computer modems, single-user fax/modems, and electronic components used in telephone apparatus--are classified in Industry 33441, Semiconductor and Other Electronic Component Manufacturing; and
- Manufacturing cellular telephones--are classified in Industry 334220, Radio and Television Broadcasting and Wireless Communications Equipment Manufacturing.

**33422   Radio and Television Broadcasting and Wireless Communications Equipment Manufacturing**[T]
See industry description for 334220.

**334220   Radio and Television Broadcasting and Wireless Communications Equipment Manufacturing**

This industry comprises establishments primarily engaged in manufacturing radio and television broadcast and wireless communications equipment.  Examples of products made by these establishments are transmitting and receiving antennas, cable television equipment, GPS equipment, pagers, cellular phones, mobile communications equipment, and radio and television studio and broadcasting equipment.

*Cross-References.*          Establishments primarily engaged in--

- Manufacturing household-type audio and video equipment, such as televisions and radio sets--are classified in Industry 334310, Audio and Video Equipment Manufacturing;
- Manufacturing wired and wireless intercommunications equipment (i.e., intercoms)--are classified in Industry 334290, Other Communications Equipment Manufacturing;
- Manufacturing equipment for measuring and testing communications signals--are classified in U.S. Industry 334515, Instrument Manufacturing for Measuring and Testing Electricity and Electrical Signals; and
- Manufacturing tablet computers--are classified in U.S. Industry 334111, Electronic Computer Manufacturing.

**33429   Other Communications Equipment Manufacturing**[T]
See industry description for 334290.

**334290   Other Communications Equipment Manufacturing**

This industry comprises establishments primarily engaged in manufacturing communications equipment (except telephone apparatus, radio and television broadcast equipment, and wireless communications equipment).

*Illustrative Examples:*

Fire detection and alarm systems manufacturing
Signals (e.g., highway, pedestrian, railway, traffic) manufacturing

Intercom systems and equipment manufacturing
Video-based stadium displays manufacturing

---

T—Canadian, Mexican, and United States industries are comparable.

*Cross-References.*        Establishments primarily engaged in--

- Manufacturing telephone apparatus--are classified in Industry 334210, Telephone Apparatus Manufacturing;
- Manufacturing radio and television broadcast and wireless communications equipment (except wireless intercoms)--are classified in Industry 334220, Radio and Television Broadcasting and Wireless Communications Equipment Manufacturing; and
- Manufacturing automobile audio and related equipment--are classified in Industry 334310, Audio and Video Equipment Manufacturing.

**3343    Audio and Video Equipment Manufacturing**[T]

**33431   Audio and Video Equipment Manufacturing**[T]
See industry description for 334310.

**334310  Audio and Video Equipment Manufacturing**

This industry comprises establishments primarily engaged in manufacturing electronic audio and video equipment for home entertainment, motor vehicles, and public address and musical instrument amplification. Examples of products made by these establishments are digital video recorders, televisions, stereo equipment, speaker systems, household-type video cameras, jukeboxes, and amplifiers for musical instruments and public address systems.

*Cross-References.*        Establishments primarily engaged in--

- Manufacturing photographic (i.e., still and motion picture) equipment--are classified in Industry 333310, Commercial and Service Industry Machinery Manufacturing;
- Manufacturing phonograph needles and cartridges--are classified in Industry 33441, Semiconductor and Other Electronic Component Manufacturing;
- Manufacturing auto theft alarms or video-based stadium displays--are classified in Industry 334290, Other Communications Equipment Manufacturing; and
- Manufacturing mobile radios, such as citizens band and FM transceivers for household or motor vehicle uses; studio and broadcast video cameras; and cable decoders and satellite television equipment--are classified in Industry 334220, Radio and Television Broadcasting and Wireless Communications Equipment Manufacturing.

**3344    Semiconductor and Other Electronic Component Manufacturing**[T]

**33441   Semiconductor and Other Electronic Component Manufacturing**[T]

This industry comprises establishments primarily engaged in manufacturing semiconductors and other components for electronic applications. Examples of products made by these establishments are capacitors, resistors, microprocessors, bare and loaded printed circuit boards, electron tubes, electronic connectors, and computer modems.

*Cross-References.*        Establishments primarily engaged in--

- Manufacturing X-ray tubes--are classified in Industry 33451, Navigational, Measuring, Electromedical, and Control Instruments Manufacturing;
- Manufacturing glass blanks for electron tubes--are classified in Industry 32721, Glass and Glass Product Manufacturing;
- Manufacturing telephone system components or modules--are classified in Industry 33421, Telephone Apparatus Manufacturing;
- Manufacturing finished products that incorporate loaded printed circuit boards--are classified in the Manufacturing sector based on the production process of making the final product;

---

T—Canadian, Mexican, and United States industries are comparable.

- Manufacturing communications antennas--are classified in Industry 33422, Radio and Television Broadcasting and Wireless Communications Equipment Manufacturing; and
- Manufacturing coils, switches, transformers, connectors, capacitors, rheostats, and similar devices for electrical applications--are classified in Subsector 335, Electrical Equipment, Appliance, and Component Manufacturing.

### 334412  Bare Printed Circuit Board Manufacturing

This U.S. industry comprises establishments primarily engaged in manufacturing bare (i.e., rigid or flexible) printed circuit boards without mounted electronic components. These establishments print, perforate, plate, screen, etch, or photoprint interconnecting pathways for electric current on laminates.

*Cross-References.*            Establishments primarily engaged in--

- Loading components onto printed circuit boards or manufacturing loaded printed circuit boards--are classified in U.S. Industry 334418, Printed Circuit Assembly (Electronic Assembly) Manufacturing; and
- Manufacturing printed circuit laminates--are classified in U.S. Industry 334419, Other Electronic Component Manufacturing.

### 334413  Semiconductor and Related Device Manufacturing

This U.S. industry comprises establishments primarily engaged in manufacturing semiconductors and related solid-state devices. Examples of products made by these establishments are integrated circuits, memory chips, microprocessors, diodes, transistors, solar cells, and other optoelectronic devices.

### 334416  Capacitor, Resistor, Coil, Transformer, and Other Inductor Manufacturing

This U.S. industry comprises establishments primarily engaged in one or more of the following: (1) manufacturing electronic fixed and variable capacitors and condensers; (2) manufacturing electronic resistors, such as fixed and variable resistors, resistor networks, thermistors, and varistors; and (3) manufacturing electronic inductors, such as coils and transformers.

*Cross-References.*            Establishments primarily engaged in--

- Manufacturing electrical capacitors for power generation and distribution, heavy industrial equipment, induction heating and melting, and similar industrial applications--are classified in U.S. Industry 335999, All Other Miscellaneous Electrical Equipment and Component Manufacturing;
- Manufacturing electronic rheostats--are classified in U.S. Industry 334419, Other Electronic Component Manufacturing; and
- Manufacturing electrical transformers used in the generation, storage, transmission, transformation, distribution, and utilization of electrical energy--are classified in U.S. Industry 335311, Power, Distribution, and Specialty Transformer Manufacturing.

### 334417  Electronic Connector Manufacturing

This U.S. industry comprises establishments primarily engaged in manufacturing electronic connectors, such as coaxial, cylindrical, rack and panel, pin and sleeve, printed circuit, and fiber optic.

*Cross-References.*

Establishments primarily engaged in manufacturing electrical connectors, such as plugs, bus bars, twist on wire connectors and terminals, are classified in U.S. Industry 335931, Current-Carrying Wiring Device Manufacturing.

---

T—Canadian, Mexican, and United States industries are comparable.

## 334418  Printed Circuit Assembly (Electronic Assembly) Manufacturing

This U.S. industry comprises establishments primarily engaged in loading components onto printed circuit boards or who manufacture and ship loaded printed circuit boards.  Also known as printed circuit assemblies, electronics assemblies, or modules, these products are printed circuit boards that have some or all of the semiconductor and electronic components inserted or mounted and are inputs to a wide variety of electronic systems and devices.

*Cross-References.*        Establishments primarily engaged in--

- Manufacturing printed circuit laminates--are classified in U.S. Industry 334419, Other Electronic Component Manufacturing;
- Manufacturing bare printed circuit boards--are classified in U.S. Industry 334412, Bare Printed Circuit Board Manufacturing;
- Manufacturing telephone system components or modules--are classified in Industry 334210, Telephone Apparatus Manufacturing; and
- Manufacturing finished products that incorporate loaded printed circuit boards--are classified in the Manufacturing sector based on the production process of making the final product.

## 334419  Other Electronic Component Manufacturing

This U.S. industry comprises establishments primarily engaged in manufacturing electronic components (except bare printed circuit boards; semiconductors and related devices; electronic capacitors; electronic resistors; coils, transformers, and other inductors; connectors; and loaded printed circuit boards).

*Illustrative Examples:*

Crystals and crystal assemblies, electronic, manufacturing
Electron tubes manufacturing
LCD (liquid crystal display) unit screens manufacturing

Microwave components manufacturing
Piezoelectric devices manufacturing
Printed circuit laminates manufacturing
Switches for electronic applications manufacturing
Transducers (except pressure) manufacturing

*Cross-References.*        Establishments primarily engaged in--

- Manufacturing bare printed circuit boards--are classified in U.S. Industry 334412, Bare Printed Circuit Board Manufacturing;
- Manufacturing semiconductors, photonic integrated circuits, and/or silicon wave guides--are classified in U.S. Industry 334413, Semiconductor and Related Device Manufacturing;
- Manufacturing electronic capacitors, electronic resistors, and electronic inductors--are classified in U.S. Industry 334416, Capacitor, Resistor, Coil, Transformer, and Other Inductor Manufacturing;
- Manufacturing electronic connectors--are classified in U.S. Industry 334417, Electronic Connector Manufacturing;
- Loading components onto printed circuit boards or manufacturing loaded printed circuit boards--are classified in U.S. Industry 334418, Printed Circuit Assembly (Electronic Assembly) Manufacturing;
- Manufacturing communications antennas--are classified in Industry 334220, Radio and Television Broadcasting and Wireless Communications Equipment Manufacturing;
- Manufacturing X-ray tubes--are classified in U.S. Industry 334517, Irradiation Apparatus Manufacturing; and
- Manufacturing glass blanks for electron tubes--are classified in Industry 32721, Glass and Glass Product Manufacturing.

## 3345    Navigational, Measuring, Electromedical, and Control Instruments Manufacturing[T]

---

T—Canadian, Mexican, and United States industries are comparable.

### 33451    Navigational, Measuring, Electromedical, and Control Instruments Manufacturing[T]

This industry comprises establishments primarily engaged in manufacturing navigational, measuring, electromedical, and control instruments. Examples of products made by these establishments are aeronautical instruments, appliance regulators and controls (except switches), laboratory analytical instruments, navigation and guidance systems, and physical properties testing equipment.

*Cross-References.*          Establishments primarily engaged in--

- Manufacturing global positioning system (GPS) equipment--are classified in Industry 33422, Radio and Television Broadcasting and Wireless Communications Equipment Manufacturing;
- Manufacturing motor control switches and relays (including timing relays)--are classified in Industry 33531, Electrical Equipment Manufacturing;
- Manufacturing switches for appliances--are classified in Industry 33593, Wiring Device Manufacturing;
- Manufacturing optical instruments--are classified in Industry 33331, Commercial and Service Industry Machinery Manufacturing;
- Manufacturing glass watch and clock crystals--are classified in Industry 32721, Glass and Glass Product Manufacturing;
- Manufacturing plastics watch and clock crystals--are classified in Industry 32619, Other Plastics Product Manufacturing;
- Manufacturing smartwatches--are classified in Industry 33422, Radio and Television Broadcasting and Wireless Communications Equipment Manufacturing; and
- Manufacturing medical thermometers and other nonelectrical medical apparatus--are classified in Industry 33911, Medical Equipment and Supplies Manufacturing.

### 334510   Electromedical and Electrotherapeutic Apparatus Manufacturing

This U.S. industry comprises establishments primarily engaged in manufacturing electromedical and electrotherapeutic apparatus, such as magnetic resonance imaging equipment, medical ultrasound equipment, pacemakers, hearing aids, electrocardiographs, and electromedical endoscopic equipment.

*Cross-References.*          Establishments primarily engaged in--

- Manufacturing medical irradiation apparatus--are classified in U.S. Industry 334517, Irradiation Apparatus Manufacturing; and
- Manufacturing nonelectrical medical and therapeutic apparatus--are classified in Industry 33911, Medical Equipment and Supplies Manufacturing.

### 334511   Search, Detection, Navigation, Guidance, Aeronautical, and Nautical System and Instrument Manufacturing

This U.S. industry comprises establishments primarily engaged in manufacturing search, detection, navigation, guidance, aeronautical, and nautical systems and instruments. Examples of products made by these establishments are aircraft instruments (except engine), flight recorders, navigational instruments and systems, radar systems and equipment, and sonar systems and equipment.

*Cross-References.*          Establishments primarily engaged in--

- Manufacturing global positioning system (GPS) equipment--are classified in Industry 334220, Radio and Television Broadcasting and Wireless Communications Equipment Manufacturing; and
- Manufacturing aircraft engine instruments and meteorological systems and equipment--are classified in U.S. Industry 334519, Other Measuring and Controlling Device Manufacturing.

---

T—Canadian, Mexican, and United States industries are comparable.

### 334512 Automatic Environmental Control Manufacturing for Residential, Commercial, and Appliance Use

This U.S. industry comprises establishments primarily engaged in manufacturing automatic controls and regulators for applications, such as heating, air-conditioning, refrigeration, and appliances.

*Cross-References.*       Establishments primarily engaged in--

- Manufacturing industrial process controls--are classified in U.S. Industry 334513, Instruments and Related Products Manufacturing for Measuring, Displaying, and Controlling Industrial Process Variables;
- Manufacturing motor control switches and relays--are classified in U.S. Industry 335314, Relay and Industrial Control Manufacturing;
- Manufacturing switches for appliances--are classified in U.S. Industry 335931, Current-Carrying Wiring Device Manufacturing; and
- Manufacturing appliance timers--are classified in U.S. Industry 334519, Other Measuring and Controlling Device Manufacturing.

### 334513 Instruments and Related Products Manufacturing for Measuring, Displaying, and Controlling Industrial Process Variables

This U.S. industry comprises establishments primarily engaged in manufacturing instruments and related devices for measuring, displaying, indicating, recording, transmitting, and controlling industrial process variables. These instruments measure, display, or control (monitor, analyze, and so forth) industrial process variables, such as temperature, humidity, pressure, vacuum, combustion, flow, level, viscosity, density, acidity, concentration, and rotation.

*Cross-References.*       Establishments primarily engaged in--

- Manufacturing instruments for measuring or testing electricity and electrical signals--are classified in U.S. Industry 334515, Instrument Manufacturing for Measuring and Testing Electricity and Electrical Signals;
- Manufacturing medical thermometers--are classified in U.S. Industry 339112, Surgical and Medical Instrument Manufacturing;
- Manufacturing glass hydrometers and thermometers for other non-medical uses--are classified in U.S. Industry 334519, Other Measuring and Controlling Device Manufacturing;
- Manufacturing instruments and instrumentation systems for laboratory analysis of samples--are classified in U.S. Industry 334516, Analytical Laboratory Instrument Manufacturing; and
- Manufacturing optical alignment and display instruments, optical comparators, and optical test and inspection equipment--are classified in Industry 333310, Commercial and Service Industry Machinery Manufacturing.

### 334514 Totalizing Fluid Meter and Counting Device Manufacturing

This U.S. industry comprises establishments primarily engaged in manufacturing totalizing (i.e., registering) fluid meters and counting devices. Examples of products made by these establishments are gas consumption meters, water consumption meters, parking meters, taxi meters, motor vehicle gauges, and fare collection equipment.

*Cross-References.*       Establishments primarily engaged in--

- Manufacturing integrating meters and counters for measuring the characteristics of electricity and electrical signals--are classified in U.S. Industry 334515, Instrument Manufacturing for Measuring and Testing Electricity and Electrical Signals; and
- Manufacturing instruments and devices that measure, display, or control (i.e., monitor or analyze) related industrial process variables--are classified in U.S. Industry 334513, Instruments and Related Products Manufacturing for Measuring, Displaying, and Controlling Industrial Process Variables.

T—Canadian, Mexican, and United States industries are comparable.

### 334515 Instrument Manufacturing for Measuring and Testing Electricity and Electrical Signals

This U.S. industry comprises establishments primarily engaged in manufacturing instruments for measuring and testing the characteristics of electricity and electrical signals. Examples of products made by these establishments are circuit and continuity testers, voltmeters, ohm meters, wattmeters, multimeters, and semiconductor test equipment.

*Cross-References.*

Establishments primarily engaged in manufacturing electronic monitoring, evaluating, and other electronic support equipment for navigational, radar, and sonar systems are classified in U.S. Industry 334511, Search, Detection, Navigation, Guidance, Aeronautical, and Nautical System and Instrument Manufacturing.

### 334516 Analytical Laboratory Instrument Manufacturing

This U.S. industry comprises establishments primarily engaged in manufacturing instruments and instrumentation systems for laboratory analysis of the chemical or physical composition or concentration of samples of solid, fluid, gaseous, or composite material.

*Cross-References.*        Establishments primarily engaged in--

- Manufacturing instruments for monitoring and analyzing continuous samples from medical patients--are classified in U.S. Industry 334510, Electromedical and Electrotherapeutic Apparatus Manufacturing; and
- Manufacturing instruments and related devices that measure, display, or control (i.e., monitor or analyze) industrial process variables--are classified in U.S. Industry 334513, Instruments and Related Products Manufacturing for Measuring, Displaying, and Controlling Industrial Process Variables.

### 334517 Irradiation Apparatus Manufacturing

This U.S. industry comprises establishments primarily engaged in manufacturing irradiation apparatus and tubes for applications, such as medical diagnostic, medical therapeutic, industrial, research, and scientific evaluation. Irradiation can take the form of beta-rays, gamma-rays, X-rays, or other ionizing radiation.

### 334519 Other Measuring and Controlling Device Manufacturing

This U.S. industry comprises establishments primarily engaged in manufacturing measuring and controlling devices (except search, detection, navigation, guidance, aeronautical, and nautical instruments and systems; automatic environmental controls for residential, commercial, and appliance use; instruments for measurement, display, and control of industrial process variables; totalizing fluid meters and counting devices; instruments for measuring and testing electricity and electrical signals; analytical laboratory instruments; irradiation equipment; and electromedical and electrotherapeutic apparatus).

*Illustrative Examples:*

Aircraft engine instruments manufacturing
Automotive emissions testing equipment manufacturing
Clocks assembling
Meteorological instruments manufacturing
Physical properties testing and inspection equipment manufacturing
Polygraph machines manufacturing

Radiation detection and monitoring instruments manufacturing
Surveying instruments manufacturing
Thermometers, liquid-in-glass and bimetal types (except medical), manufacturing
Watches (except smartwatches) and parts (except crystals) manufacturing

---

T—Canadian, Mexican, and United States industries are comparable.

*Cross-References.*        Establishments primarily engaged in--

- Manufacturing medical thermometers--are classified in U.S. Industry 339112, Surgical and Medical Instrument Manufacturing;
- Manufacturing search, detection, navigation, guidance, aeronautical, and nautical systems and instruments-- are classified in U.S. Industry 334511, Search, Detection, Navigation, Guidance, Aeronautical, and Nautical System and Instrument Manufacturing;
- Manufacturing automatic controls and regulators for applications, such as heating, air-conditioning, refrigeration and appliances--are classified in U.S. Industry 334512, Automatic Environmental Control Manufacturing for Residential, Commercial, and Appliance Use;
- Manufacturing instruments and related devices that measure, display, or control (i.e., monitor or analyze) industrial process variables--are classified in U.S. Industry 334513, Instruments and Related Products Manufacturing for Measuring, Displaying, and Controlling Industrial Process Variables;
- Manufacturing totalizing (i.e., registering) fluid meters and counting devices, including motor vehicle gauges--are classified in U.S. Industry 334514, Totalizing Fluid Meter and Counting Device Manufacturing;
- Manufacturing instruments for measuring and testing the characteristics of electricity and electrical signals- -are classified in U.S. Industry 334515, Instrument Manufacturing for Measuring and Testing Electricity and Electrical Signals;
- Manufacturing instruments for laboratory analysis of the physical composition or concentration of samples of solid, fluid, gaseous, or composite materials--are classified in U.S. Industry 334516, Analytical Laboratory Instrument Manufacturing;
- Manufacturing X-ray apparatus, tubes, or related irradiation apparatus--are classified in U.S. Industry 334517, Irradiation Apparatus Manufacturing;
- Manufacturing electromedical and electrotherapeutic apparatus--are classified in U.S. Industry 334510, Electromedical and Electrotherapeutic Apparatus Manufacturing;
- Manufacturing glass watch and clock crystals--are classified in Industry 32721, Glass and Glass Product Manufacturing;
- Manufacturing plastics watch and clock crystals--are classified in U.S. Industry 326199, All Other Plastics Product Manufacturing;
- Manufacturing timing relays--are classified in U.S. Industry 335314, Relay and Industrial Control Manufacturing; and
- Manufacturing smartwatches--are classified in Industry 334220, Radio and Television Broadcasting and Wireless Communications Equipment Manufacturing.

## 3346     Manufacturing and Reproducing Magnetic and Optical Media[T]

## 33461    Manufacturing and Reproducing Magnetic and Optical Media[T]
See industry description for 334610.

## 334610  Manufacturing and Reproducing Magnetic and Optical Media

This industry comprises establishments primarily engaged in (1) manufacturing optical and magnetic media, such as blank audio tapes, blank video tapes, and blank diskettes, and/or (2) mass duplicating (i.e., making copies) audio, video, software, and other data on magnetic, optical, and similar media. These establishments do not generally develop software or produce audio or video content.

*Cross-References.*        Establishments primarily engaged in--

- Designing, developing, and publishing software--are classified in Industry 513210, Software Publishers; and
- Motion picture and sound recording production and distribution--are classified in Subsector 512, Motion Picture and Sound Recording Industries.

---

T—Canadian, Mexican, and United States industries are comparable.

## 335    Electrical Equipment, Appliance, and Component Manufacturing[T]

Industries in the Electrical Equipment, Appliance, and Component Manufacturing subsector manufacture products that generate, distribute, and use electrical power.  Electric Lighting Equipment Manufacturing establishments produce lighting fixtures, electric light bulbs, and parts (except glass parts and light emitting diodes (LEDs)), and other lighting equipment.  Household Appliance Manufacturing establishments make both small and major electrical appliances and parts.  Electrical Equipment Manufacturing establishments make goods, such as electric motors, generators, transformers, and switchgear apparatus.  Other Electrical Equipment and Component Manufacturing establishments make devices for storing electrical power (e.g., batteries), for transmitting electricity (e.g., insulated wire), and wiring devices (e.g., electrical outlets, fuse boxes, and light switches).

## 3351    Electric Lighting Equipment Manufacturing[T]

## 33513    Electric Lighting Equipment Manufacturing[T]

This industry comprises establishments primarily engaged in manufacturing electric lighting fixtures (except vehicular), nonelectric lighting equipment, lamp shades (except glass and plastics), electric light bulbs, tubes, and parts (except glass blanks for electric light bulbs and light emitting diodes (LEDs)), and lighting fixture components (except current-carrying wiring devices).

*Cross-References.*          Establishments primarily engaged in--

- Manufacturing vehicular lighting fixtures--are classified in Industry 33632, Motor Vehicle Electrical and Electronic Equipment Manufacturing;
- Manufacturing current-carrying wiring devices for lighting fixtures--are classified in Industry 33593, Wiring Device Manufacturing;
- Manufacturing ceiling fans or bath fans with integrated lighting fixtures--are classified in Industry 33521, Small Electrical Appliance Manufacturing;
- Manufacturing plastics lamp shades--are classified in Industry 32619, Other Plastics Product Manufacturing;
- Manufacturing glassware and glass parts for lighting fixtures, including glass blanks for electric light bulbs--are classified in Industry 32721, Glass and Glass Product Manufacturing;
- Manufacturing light emitting diodes (LEDs)--are classified in Industry 33441, Semiconductor and Other Electronic Component Manufacturing; and
- Manufacturing signaling devices that incorporate electric light bulbs, such as traffic and railway signals--are classified in Industry 33429, Other Communications Equipment Manufacturing.

## 335131  Residential Electric Lighting Fixture Manufacturing

This U.S. industry comprises establishments primarily engaged in manufacturing fixed or portable residential electric lighting fixtures and lamp shades of metal, paper, or textiles.  Residential electric lighting fixtures include those for use both inside and outside the residence.

*Illustrative Examples:*

Ceiling lighting fixtures, residential, manufacturing          Table lamps (i.e., lighting fixtures) manufacturing
Chandeliers, residential, manufacturing

*Cross-References.*          Establishments primarily engaged in--

- Manufacturing glassware and glass parts for residential lighting fixtures, including glass blanks for electric light bulbs--are classified in Industry 32721, Glass and Glass Product Manufacturing;
- Manufacturing plastics lamp shades--are classified in U.S. Industry 326199, All Other Plastics Product Manufacturing;

---

T—Canadian, Mexican, and United States industries are comparable.

- Manufacturing ceiling fans or bath fans with integrated lighting fixtures--are classified in Industry 335210, Small Electrical Appliance Manufacturing;
- Manufacturing current-carrying wiring devices for lighting fixtures--are classified in U.S. Industry 335931, Current-Carrying Wiring Device Manufacturing;
- Manufacturing commercial, industrial, and institutional electric lighting fixtures--are classified in U.S. Industry 335132, Commercial, Industrial, and Institutional Electric Lighting Fixture Manufacturing;
- Manufacturing electric light bulbs, tubes, and parts (except glass parts and light emitting diodes (LEDs)), and other lighting fixtures, such as street lights (except traffic signals), flashlights, and nonelectric lighting fixtures--are classified in U.S. Industry 335139, Electric Lamp Bulb and Other Lighting Equipment Manufacturing; and
- Manufacturing light emitting diodes (LEDs)--are classified in U.S. Industry 334413, Semiconductor and Related Device Manufacturing.

### 335132 Commercial, Industrial, and Institutional Electric Lighting Fixture Manufacturing

This U.S. industry comprises establishments primarily engaged in manufacturing commercial, industrial, and institutional electric lighting fixtures.

*Cross-References.*        Establishments primarily engaged in--

- Manufacturing glassware and glass parts for commercial, industrial, and institutional electric lighting fixtures, including glass blanks for electric light bulbs--are classified in Industry 32721, Glass and Glass Product Manufacturing;
- Manufacturing residential electric lighting fixtures--are classified in U.S. Industry 335131, Residential Electric Lighting Fixture Manufacturing;
- Manufacturing current-carrying wiring devices for lighting fixtures--are classified in U.S. Industry 335931, Current-Carrying Wiring Device Manufacturing;
- Manufacturing vehicular lighting fixtures--are classified in Industry 336320, Motor Vehicle Electrical and Electronic Equipment Manufacturing;
- Manufacturing electric light bulbs, tubes, and parts (except glass parts and light emitting diodes (LEDs)), and other lighting fixtures, such as street lights (except traffic signals), flashlights, and nonelectric lighting equipment--are classified in U.S. Industry 335139, Electric Lamp Bulb and Other Lighting Equipment Manufacturing;
- Manufacturing light emitting diodes (LEDs)--are classified in U.S. Industry 334413, Semiconductor and Related Device Manufacturing; and
- Manufacturing signaling devices that incorporate electric light bulbs, such as traffic and railway signals--are classified in Industry 334290, Other Communications Equipment Manufacturing.

### 335139 Electric Lamp Bulb and Other Lighting Equipment Manufacturing

This U.S. industry comprises establishments primarily engaged in manufacturing electric light bulbs, tubes, and parts (except glass blanks for electric light bulbs and light emitting diodes (LEDs)), electric lighting fixtures (except residential, commercial, industrial, institutional, and vehicular electric lighting fixtures), and nonelectric lighting equipment.

*Illustrative Examples:*

Christmas tree lighting sets, electric, manufacturing
Electric light bulbs, complete, manufacturing
Fireplace logs, electric, manufacturing
Flashlights manufacturing
Insect lamps, electric, manufacturing
Spotlights (except vehicular) manufacturing

Lanterns (e.g., carbide, electric, gas, gasoline, kerosene) manufacturing
LED (light emitting diode) light bulbs manufacturing
Street lighting fixtures (except traffic signals) manufacturing

---

T—Canadian, Mexican, and United States industries are comparable.

*Cross-References.*          Establishments primarily engaged in--

- Manufacturing glassware and glass parts for lighting fixtures, including glass blanks for electric light bulbs--are classified in Industry 32721, Glass and Glass Product Manufacturing;
- Manufacturing current-carrying wiring devices for lighting fixtures--are classified in U.S. Industry 335931, Current-Carrying Wiring Device Manufacturing;
- Manufacturing residential electric lighting fixtures--are classified in U.S. Industry 335131, Residential Electric Lighting Fixture Manufacturing;
- Manufacturing commercial, industrial, and institutional electric lighting fixtures--are classified in U.S. Industry 335132, Commercial, Industrial, and Institutional Electric Lighting Fixture Manufacturing;
- Manufacturing vehicular lighting fixtures--are classified in Industry 336320, Motor Vehicle Electrical and Electronic Equipment Manufacturing;
- Manufacturing light emitting diodes (LEDs)--are classified in U.S. Industry 334413, Semiconductor and Related Device Manufacturing; and
- Manufacturing signaling devices that incorporate electric light bulbs, such as traffic and railway signals--are classified in Industry 334290, Other Communications Equipment Manufacturing.

### 3352    Household Appliance Manufacturing[T]

This industry group comprises establishments primarily engaged in manufacturing small electric appliances, electric housewares, and major household appliances.

### 33521    Small Electrical Appliance Manufacturing[T]
See industry description for 335210.

### 335210  Small Electrical Appliance Manufacturing

This industry comprises establishments primarily engaged in manufacturing small electric appliances and electric housewares, household-type fans (except attic fans), household-type vacuum cleaners, and other electric household-type floor care machines.

*Illustrative Examples:*

Bath fans, residential, manufacturing
Carpet and floor cleaning equipment, household-type electric, manufacturing
Ceiling fans, residential, manufacturing
Curling irons, household-type electric, manufacturing
Electric blankets manufacturing
Portable electric space heaters manufacturing
Portable hair dryers, electric, manufacturing

Portable cooking appliances (except microwave, convection ovens), household-type electric, manufacturing
Portable humidifiers and dehumidifiers manufacturing
Scissors, electric, manufacturing
Ventilating and exhaust fans (except attic fans), household-type, manufacturing

*Cross-References.*          Establishments primarily engaged in--

- Manufacturing attic fans--are classified in U.S. Industry 333413, Industrial and Commercial Fan and Blower and Air Purification Equipment Manufacturing;
- Manufacturing wall and baseboard heating units for permanent installation--are classified in U.S. Industry 333414, Heating Equipment (except Warm Air Furnaces) Manufacturing;
- Manufacturing room air-conditioners--are classified in U.S. Industry 333415, Air-Conditioning and Warm Air Heating Equipment and Commercial and Industrial Refrigeration Equipment Manufacturing;
- Manufacturing microwave and convection ovens--are classified in Industry 335220, Major Household Appliance Manufacturing;
- Manufacturing electric vacuum cleaners for commercial, industrial, and institutional uses, and mechanical carpet sweepers--are classified in Industry 333310, Commercial and Service Industry Machinery Manufacturing; and

---

T—Canadian, Mexican, and United States industries are comparable.

- Installing central vacuum cleaning systems--are classified in Industry 238290, Other Building Equipment Contractors.

## 33522   Major Household Appliance Manufacturing[T]
See industry description for 335220.

## 335220   Major Household Appliance Manufacturing

This industry comprises establishments primarily engaged in manufacturing household-type cooking appliances, household-type laundry equipment, household-type refrigerators, upright and chest freezers, and other electrical and nonelectrical major household-type appliances, such as dishwashers, water heaters, and garbage disposal units.

*Cross-References.*           Establishments primarily engaged in--

- Manufacturing small electric appliances and electric housewares, such as hot plates, griddles, toasters, and electric irons--are classified in Industry 335210, Small Electrical Appliance Manufacturing;
- Manufacturing commercial and industrial refrigerators and freezers--are classified in U.S. Industry 333415, Air-Conditioning and Warm Air Heating Equipment and Commercial and Industrial Refrigeration Equipment Manufacturing;
- Manufacturing commercial-type cooking equipment and commercial-type laundry, drycleaning, and pressing equipment--are classified in Industry 333310, Commercial and Service Industry Machinery Manufacturing; and
- Manufacturing household-type sewing machines--are classified in U.S. Industry 333248, All Other Industrial Machinery Manufacturing.

## 3353   Electrical Equipment Manufacturing[T]

## 33531   Electrical Equipment Manufacturing[T]

This industry comprises establishments primarily engaged in manufacturing power, distribution, and specialty transformers; electric motors, generators, and motor generator sets; switchgear and switchboard apparatus; relays; and industrial controls.

*Cross-References.*           Establishments primarily engaged in--

- Manufacturing turbine generator set units and electric outboard motors--are classified in Industry 33361, Engine, Turbine, and Power Transmission Equipment Manufacturing;
- Manufacturing electronic component-type transformers and switches--are classified in Industry 33441, Semiconductor and Other Electronic Component Manufacturing;
- Manufacturing environmental controls and industrial process control instruments--are classified in Industry 33451, Navigational, Measuring, Electromedical, and Control Instruments Manufacturing;
- Manufacturing switches for electrical circuits, such as pushbutton and snap switches--are classified in Industry 33593, Wiring Device Manufacturing;
- Manufacturing welding and soldering equipment (except handheld soldering irons)--are classified in Industry 33399, All Other General Purpose Machinery Manufacturing; and
- Manufacturing starting motors and generators for internal combustion engines--are classified in Industry 33632, Motor Vehicle Electrical and Electronic Equipment Manufacturing.

## 335311   Power, Distribution, and Specialty Transformer Manufacturing

This U.S. industry comprises establishments primarily engaged in manufacturing power, distribution, and specialty transformers (except electronic components). Industrial-type and consumer-type transformers in this industry vary (e.g., step up or step down) voltage but do not convert alternating to direct or direct to alternating current.

---

T—Canadian, Mexican, and United States industries are comparable.

*Illustrative Examples:*

Fluorescent ballasts (i.e., transformers) manufacturing
Substation transformers, electric power distribution, manufacturing

Distribution transformers, electric, manufacturing
Transmission and distribution voltage regulators manufacturing

*Cross-References.*

   Establishments primarily engaged in manufacturing electronic component-type transformers are classified in U.S. Industry 334416, Capacitor, Resistor, Coil, Transformer, and Other Inductor Manufacturing.

**335312  Motor and Generator Manufacturing**

   This U.S. industry comprises establishments primarily engaged in manufacturing electric motors (except internal combustion engine starting motors), power generators (except battery charging alternators for internal combustion engines), and motor generator sets (except turbine generator set units).  This industry includes establishments rewinding armatures on a factory basis.

*Cross-References.*          Establishments primarily engaged in--

- Manufacturing electric outboard motors--are classified in U.S. Industry 333618, Other Engine Equipment Manufacturing;
- Manufacturing gas, steam, or hydraulic turbine generator set units--are classified in U.S. Industry 333611, Turbine and Turbine Generator Set Units Manufacturing;
- Manufacturing starting motors and battery charging alternators for internal combustion engines--are classified in Industry 336320, Motor Vehicle Electrical and Electronic Equipment Manufacturing;
- Rewinding armatures, not on a factory basis--are classified in Industry 811310, Commercial and Industrial Machinery and Equipment (except Automotive and Electronic) Repair and Maintenance; and
- Manufacturing welding and soldering equipment (except handheld soldering irons)--are classified in U.S. Industry 333992, Welding and Soldering Equipment Manufacturing.

**335313  Switchgear and Switchboard Apparatus Manufacturing**

   This U.S. industry comprises establishments primarily engaged in manufacturing switchgear and switchboard apparatus.

*Illustrative Examples:*

Circuit breakers, power, manufacturing
Control panels, electric power distribution, manufacturing
Ducts for electrical switchboard apparatus manufacturing

Fuses, electric, manufacturing
Power switching equipment manufacturing
Switches, electric power (except pushbutton, snap, solenoid, tumbler), manufacturing

*Cross-References.*      Establishments primarily engaged in--

- Manufacturing relays--are classified in U.S. Industry 335314, Relay and Industrial Control Manufacturing;
- Manufacturing switches for electronic applications--are classified in U.S. Industry 334419, Other Electronic Component Manufacturing; and
- Manufacturing snap, pushbutton, and similar switches for electrical circuits--are classified in U.S. Industry 335931, Current-Carrying Wiring Device Manufacturing.

T—Canadian, Mexican, and United States industries are comparable.

**census.gov/naics**

### 335314 Relay and Industrial Control Manufacturing

This U.S. industry comprises establishments primarily engaged in manufacturing relays, motor starters and controllers, and other industrial controls and control accessories.

*Cross-References.* Establishments primarily engaged in--

- Manufacturing environmental and appliance control equipment--are classified in U.S. Industry 334512, Automatic Environmental Control Manufacturing for Residential, Commercial, and Appliance Use; and
- Manufacturing instruments for controlling industrial process variables--are classified in U.S. Industry 334513, Instruments and Related Products Manufacturing for Measuring, Displaying, and Controlling Industrial Process Variables.

### 3359 Other Electrical Equipment and Component Manufacturing[T]

This industry group comprises establishments manufacturing electrical equipment and components (except electric lighting equipment, household-type appliances, transformers, switchgear, relays, motors, and generators).

### 33591 Battery Manufacturing[T]
See industry description for 335910.

### 335910 Battery Manufacturing

This industry comprises establishments primarily engaged in manufacturing primary and storage batteries.

*Illustrative Examples:*

Disposable flashlight batteries manufacturing
Dry cells, primary (e.g., AAA, AA, C, D, 9V), manufacturing
Lead acid storage batteries manufacturing

Lithium batteries manufacturing
Rechargeable nickel-cadmium (NICAD) batteries manufacturing
Watch batteries manufacturing

### 33592 Communication and Energy Wire and Cable Manufacturing[T]

This industry comprises establishments primarily engaged in insulating fiber optic cable, and manufacturing insulated nonferrous wire and cable from nonferrous wire drawn in other establishments.

*Cross-References.* Establishments primarily engaged in--

- Drawing nonferrous wire--are classified in Subsector 331, Primary Metal Manufacturing;
- Manufacturing cable sets consisting of insulated wire and various connectors for electronic applications--are classified in Industry 33441, Semiconductor and Other Electronic Component Manufacturing;
- Manufacturing extension cords, appliance cords, and similar electrical cord sets from purchased insulated wire or cable--are classified in Industry 33599, All Other Electrical Equipment and Component Manufacturing; and
- Manufacturing unsheathed fiber optic materials--are classified in Industry 32721, Glass and Glass Product Manufacturing.

### 335921 Fiber Optic Cable Manufacturing

This U.S. industry comprises establishments primarily engaged in manufacturing insulated fiber optic cable from purchased fiber optic strand.

---

T—Canadian, Mexican, and United States industries are comparable.

*Cross-References.*          Establishments primarily engaged in--

- Manufacturing unsheathed fiber optic materials--are classified in Industry 32721, Glass and Glass Product Manufacturing; and
- Manufacturing insulated nonferrous wire and cable from purchased wire--are classified in U.S. Industry 335929, Other Communication and Energy Wire Manufacturing.

## 335929  Other Communication and Energy Wire Manufacturing

This U.S. industry comprises establishments primarily engaged in manufacturing insulated wire and cable of nonferrous metals from purchased wire.

*Cross-References.*          Establishments primarily engaged in--

- Manufacturing cable sets consisting of insulated wire and various connectors for electronic applications--are classified in U.S. Industry 334419, Other Electronic Component Manufacturing;
- Manufacturing extension cords, appliance cords, and similar electrical cord sets from purchased insulated wire--are classified in U.S. Industry 335999, All Other Miscellaneous Electrical Equipment and Component Manufacturing;
- Drawing and insulating copper wire in the same establishment--are classified in Industry 331420, Copper Rolling, Drawing, Extruding, and Alloying;
- Drawing and insulating aluminum wire in the same establishment--are classified in U.S. Industry 331318, Other Aluminum Rolling, Drawing, and Extruding; and
- Drawing nonferrous wire (except copper and aluminum)--are classified in U.S. Industry 331491, Nonferrous Metal (except Copper and Aluminum) Rolling, Drawing, and Extruding.

## 33593  Wiring Device Manufacturing[T]

This industry comprises establishments primarily engaged in manufacturing current-carrying wiring devices and noncurrent-carrying wiring devices for wiring electrical circuits.

*Cross-References.*          Establishments primarily engaged in--

- Manufacturing ceramic and glass insulators--are classified in Subsector 327, Nonmetallic Mineral Product Manufacturing; and
- Manufacturing electronic component-type connectors, sockets, and switches--are classified in Industry 33441, Semiconductor and Other Electronic Component Manufacturing.

## 335931  Current-Carrying Wiring Device Manufacturing

This U.S. industry comprises establishments primarily engaged in manufacturing current-carrying wiring devices.

*Illustrative Examples:*

Bus bars, electrical conductors (except switchgear-type), manufacturing
GFCI (ground fault circuit interrupters) manufacturing
Lamp holders manufacturing

Lightning arrestors and coils manufacturing
Receptacles (i.e., outlets), electrical, manufacturing
Switches for electrical wiring (e.g., pressure, pushbutton, snap, tumbler) manufacturing

*Cross-References.*          Establishments primarily engaged in--

- Manufacturing electronic component-type connectors--are classified in U.S. Industry 334417, Electronic Connector Manufacturing;

---

T—Canadian, Mexican, and United States industries are comparable.

- Manufacturing noncurrent-carrying wiring devices--are classified in U.S. Industry 335932, Noncurrent-Carrying Wiring Device Manufacturing; and
- Manufacturing electronic component-type sockets and switches--are classified in U.S. Industry 334419, Other Electronic Component Manufacturing.

## 335932  Noncurrent-Carrying Wiring Device Manufacturing

This U.S. industry comprises establishments primarily engaged in manufacturing noncurrent-carrying wiring devices.

*Illustrative Examples:*

Boxes, electrical wiring (e.g., junction, outlet, switch), manufacturing
Conduits and fittings, electrical, manufacturing

Face plates (i.e., outlet or switch covers) manufacturing
Transmission pole and line hardware manufacturing

*Cross-References.*          Establishments primarily engaged in--

- Manufacturing porcelain and ceramic insulators--are classified in Industry 327110, Pottery, Ceramics, and Plumbing Fixture Manufacturing;
- Manufacturing current-carrying wiring devices--are classified in U.S. Industry 335931, Current-Carrying Wiring Device Manufacturing; and
- Manufacturing glass insulators--are classified in Industry 32721, Glass and Glass Product Manufacturing.

## 33599  All Other Electrical Equipment and Component Manufacturing[T]

This industry comprises establishments primarily engaged in manufacturing electrical equipment (except electric lighting equipment, household-type appliances, transformers, motors, generators, switchgear, relays, industrial controls, batteries, communication and energy wire and cable, and wiring devices).

*Illustrative Examples:*

Carbon and graphite electrodes and brushes manufacturing
Extension cords made from purchased insulated wire

Door opening and closing devices, electrical, manufacturing
Surge suppressors manufacturing

*Cross-References.*          Establishments primarily engaged in--

- Manufacturing lighting equipment--are classified in Industry 33513, Electric Lighting Equipment Manufacturing;
- Manufacturing household-type appliances--are classified in Industry Group 3352, Household Appliance Manufacturing;
- Manufacturing transformers, motors, generators, switchgear, relays, and industrial controls--are classified in Industry 33531, Electrical Equipment Manufacturing;
- Manufacturing batteries--are classified in Industry 33591, Battery Manufacturing;
- Manufacturing communication and energy wire--are classified in Industry 33592, Communication and Energy Wire and Cable Manufacturing;
- Manufacturing current-carrying and noncurrent-carrying wiring devices--are classified in Industry 33593, Wiring Device Manufacturing;
- Manufacturing carbon or graphite gaskets--are classified in Industry 33999, All Other Miscellaneous Manufacturing;
- Manufacturing electronic component-type rectifiers, voltage regulating integrated circuits, power converting integrated circuits, electronic capacitors, electronic resistors, and similar devices--are classified in Industry 33441, Semiconductor and Other Electronic Component Manufacturing; and

---

T—Canadian, Mexican, and United States industries are comparable.

- Manufacturing equipment incorporating lasers--are classified in the Manufacturing sector based on the associated production process of the finished equipment.

### 335991  Carbon and Graphite Product Manufacturing

This U.S. industry comprises establishments primarily engaged in manufacturing carbon, graphite, and metal-graphite brushes and brush stock; carbon or graphite electrodes for thermal and electrolytic uses; carbon and graphite fibers; and other carbon, graphite, and metal-graphite products.

*Cross-References.*

Establishments primarily engaged in manufacturing carbon or graphite gaskets are classified in U.S. Industry 339991, Gasket, Packing, and Sealing Device Manufacturing.

### 335999  All Other Miscellaneous Electrical Equipment and Component Manufacturing

This U.S. industry comprises establishments primarily engaged in manufacturing industrial and commercial electric apparatus and other equipment (except lighting equipment, household appliances, transformers, motors, generators, switchgear, relays, industrial controls, batteries, communication and energy wire and cable, wiring devices, and carbon and graphite products).  Examples of products made by these establishments are power converters (i.e., AC to DC and DC to AC), power supplies, surge suppressors, and similar equipment for industrial-type and consumer-type equipment.

*Illustrative Examples:*

| | |
|---|---|
| Appliance cords made from purchased insulated wire | Extension cords made from purchased insulated wire |
| Battery chargers, solid-state, manufacturing | Inverters manufacturing |
| Door opening and closing devices, electrical, manufacturing | Surge suppressers manufacturing |
| | Uninterruptible power supplies (UPS) manufacturing |
| Electric bells manufacturing | |

*Cross-References.*          Establishments primarily engaged in--

- Manufacturing lighting equipment--are classified in Industry 33513, Electric Lighting Equipment Manufacturing;
- Manufacturing household-type appliances--are classified in Industry Group 3352, Household Appliance Manufacturing;
- Manufacturing transformers, motors, generators, switchgear, relays, and industrial controls--are classified in Industry 33531, Electrical Equipment Manufacturing;
- Manufacturing primary and storage batteries--are classified in Industry 335910, Battery Manufacturing;
- Manufacturing communication and energy wire and cable from purchased wire or fiber optic strand--are classified in Industry 33592, Communication and Energy Wire and Cable Manufacturing;
- Manufacturing current-carrying and noncurrent-carrying wiring devices--are classified in Industry 33593, Wiring Device Manufacturing;
- Manufacturing electronic component-type rectifiers (except semiconductor)--are classified in U.S. Industry 334419, Other Electronic Component Manufacturing;
- Manufacturing semiconductor rectifiers, voltage regulating integrated circuits, power converting integrated circuits, and similar semiconductor devices--are classified in U.S. Industry 334413, Semiconductor and Related Device Manufacturing;
- Manufacturing electronic component-type capacitors and condensers--are classified in U.S. Industry 334416, Capacitor, Resistor, Coil, Transformer, and Other Inductor Manufacturing;
- Manufacturing carbon and graphite products--are classified in U.S. Industry 335991, Carbon and Graphite Product Manufacturing; and
- Manufacturing equipment incorporating lasers--are classified in the Manufacturing sector based on the associated production process of the finished equipment.

---

T—Canadian, Mexican, and United States industries are comparable.

## 336      Transportation Equipment Manufacturing<sup>T</sup>

Industries in the Transportation Equipment Manufacturing subsector produce equipment for transporting people and goods. Transportation equipment is a type of machinery. An entire subsector is devoted to this activity because of the significance of its economic size in all three North American countries.

Establishments in this subsector utilize production processes similar to those of other machinery manufacturing establishments—bending, forming, welding, machining, and assembling metal or plastic parts into components and finished products. However, the assembly of components and subassemblies and their further assembly into finished vehicles tends to be a more common production process in this subsector than in the Machinery Manufacturing subsector.

NAICS has industry groups for the manufacture of equipment for each mode of transport—road, rail, air, and water. Parts for motor vehicles warrant a separate industry group because of their importance and because they require less assembly than complete vehicles.

Land use motor vehicle equipment not designed for highway operation (e.g., agricultural equipment, construction equipment, and material handling equipment) is classified in the appropriate NAICS subsector based on the type and use of the equipment.

## 3361    Motor Vehicle Manufacturing<sup>T</sup>

This industry group comprises establishments primarily engaged in (1) manufacturing complete automobiles, light duty motor vehicles, and heavy duty trucks (i.e., body and chassis or unibody) or (2) manufacturing motor vehicle chassis only.

## 33611   Automobile and Light Duty Motor Vehicle Manufacturing<sup>T</sup>
       See industry description for 336110.

## 336110  Automobile and Light Duty Motor Vehicle Manufacturing

This industry comprises establishments primarily engaged in (1) manufacturing complete automobiles and light duty motor vehicles (i.e., body and chassis or unibody) or (2) manufacturing automobile and light duty motor vehicle chassis only. Vehicles made include passenger cars, light duty trucks, light duty vans, pick-up trucks, minivans, and sport utility vehicles.

*Cross-References.*          Establishments primarily engaged in--

- Manufacturing car, truck, and bus bodies and assembling vehicles on purchased chassis and manufacturing kit cars for highway use--are classified in U.S. Industry 336211, Motor Vehicle Body Manufacturing;
- Manufacturing motor homes on purchased light duty truck chassis--are classified in U.S. Industry 336213, Motor Home Manufacturing; and
- Manufacturing race cars--are classified in U.S. Industry 336999, All Other Transportation Equipment Manufacturing.

## 33612   Heavy Duty Truck Manufacturing<sup>T</sup>
       See industry description for 336120.

## 336120  Heavy Duty Truck Manufacturing

This industry comprises establishments primarily engaged in (1) manufacturing heavy duty truck chassis and assembling complete heavy duty trucks, buses, heavy duty motor homes, and other special purpose heavy duty motor vehicles for highway use or (2) manufacturing heavy duty truck chassis only.

*Cross-References.*          Establishments primarily engaged in--

- Manufacturing truck and bus bodies and assembling vehicles on purchased chassis--are classified in U.S. Industry 336211, Motor Vehicle Body Manufacturing;

---

T—Canadian, Mexican, and United States industries are comparable.

- Manufacturing motor homes on purchased heavy truck chassis--are classified in U.S. Industry 336213, Motor Home Manufacturing;
- Manufacturing vans, minivans, and light trucks--are classified in Industry 336110, Automobile and Light Duty Motor Vehicle Manufacturing;
- Manufacturing military armored vehicles--are classified in U.S. Industry 336992, Military Armored Vehicle, Tank, and Tank Component Manufacturing; and
- Manufacturing off-highway construction equipment--are classified in Industry 333120, Construction Machinery Manufacturing.

**3362     Motor Vehicle Body and Trailer Manufacturing[T]**

**33621     Motor Vehicle Body and Trailer Manufacturing[T]**

This industry comprises establishments primarily engaged in (1) manufacturing motor vehicle bodies and cabs or (2) manufacturing truck, automobile and utility trailers, truck trailer chassis, detachable trailer bodies, and detachable trailer chassis. The products made may be sold separately or may be assembled on purchased chassis and sold as complete vehicles. Motor homes are units where the motor and the living quarters are contained in the same integrated unit, while travel trailers are designed to be towed by a motor unit, such as an automobile or a light truck.

*Illustrative Examples:*

Bodies and cabs, truck, manufacturing
Camper units, slide-in, for pick-up trucks, manufacturing
Pick-up canopies, caps, or covers manufacturing

Motor homes, self-contained, assembling on purchased chassis
Semi-trailers manufacturing
Travel trailers, recreational, manufacturing

*Cross-References.*          Establishments primarily engaged in--

- Making manufactured homes (i.e., mobile homes)--are classified in Industry 32199, All Other Wood Product Manufacturing;
- Customizing automotive vehicle and trailer interiors (i.e., van conversions) on an individual basis--are classified in Industry 81112, Automotive Body, Paint, Interior, and Glass Repair;

- Manufacturing complete automobiles and light duty motor vehicles (i.e., body and chassis or unibody) or manufacturing automobile and light duty motor vehicle chassis only--are classified in Industry 33611, Automobile and Light Duty Motor Vehicle Manufacturing; and
- Manufacturing heavy duty trucks, buses, motor homes, and other special purpose heavy duty motor vehicles for highway use (i.e., body and chassis) or manufacturing heavy duty truck chassis only--are classified in Industry 33612, Heavy Duty Truck Manufacturing.

**336211  Motor Vehicle Body Manufacturing**

This U.S. industry comprises establishments primarily engaged in manufacturing truck and bus bodies and cabs and automobile bodies. The products made may be sold separately or may be assembled on purchased chassis and sold as complete vehicles.

*Cross-References.*          Establishments primarily engaged in--

- Manufacturing complete automobiles and light duty motor vehicles (i.e., body and chassis or unibody) or manufacturing automobile and light duty motor vehicle chassis only--are classified in Industry 336110, Automobile and Light Duty Motor Vehicle Manufacturing; and
- Manufacturing heavy duty trucks, buses, motor homes, and other special purpose heavy duty motor vehicles for highway use (i.e., body and chassis) or manufacturing heavy duty truck chassis only--are classified in Industry 336120, Heavy Duty Truck Manufacturing.

---

T—Canadian, Mexican, and United States industries are comparable.

## 336212  Truck Trailer Manufacturing

This U.S. industry comprises establishments primarily engaged in manufacturing truck trailers, truck trailer chassis, cargo container chassis, detachable trailer bodies, and detachable trailer chassis for sale separately.

*Cross-References.*

Establishments primarily engaged in manufacturing utility trailers, light-truck trailers, and travel trailers are classified in U.S. Industry 336214, Travel Trailer and Camper Manufacturing.

## 336213  Motor Home Manufacturing

This U.S. industry comprises establishments primarily engaged in (1) manufacturing motor homes on purchased chassis and/or (2) manufacturing conversion vans on an assembly line basis.  Motor homes are units where the motor and the living quarters are integrated in the same unit.

*Cross-References.*          Establishments primarily engaged in--

- Manufacturing complete motor homes (i.e., body and chassis) or manufacturing light duty motor home chassis only--are classified in Industry 336110, Automobile and Light Duty Motor Vehicle Manufacturing;
- Manufacturing complete heavy duty motor homes (i.e., body and chassis) or manufacturing heavy duty motor home chassis only--are classified in Industry 336120, Heavy Duty Truck Manufacturing;
- Customizing automotive vehicle and trailer interiors (i.e., van conversions) on an individual basis--are classified in U.S. Industry 811121, Automotive Body, Paint, and Interior Repair and Maintenance; and
- Making manufactured homes (i.e., mobile homes) designed to accept permanent water, sewer, and utility connections and equipped with wheels, but not intended for regular highway use--are classified in U.S. Industry 321991, Manufactured Home (Mobile Home) Manufacturing.

## 336214  Travel Trailer and Camper Manufacturing

This U.S. industry comprises establishments primarily engaged in one or more of the following: (1) manufacturing travel trailers and campers designed to attach to motor vehicles; (2) manufacturing pick-up coaches (i.e., campers) and caps (i.e., covers) for mounting on pick-up trucks; and (3) manufacturing automobile, utility, and light-truck trailers.  Travel trailers do not have their own motor but are designed to be towed by a motor unit, such as an automobile or a light truck.

*Illustrative Examples:*

| | |
|---|---|
| Automobile transporter trailers, single car, manufacturing | Horse trailers (except fifth-wheel-type) manufacturing |
| Camper units, slide-in, for pick-up trucks, manufacturing | Pick-up canopies, caps, or covers manufacturing |
| Camping trailers and chassis manufacturing | Travel trailers, recreational, manufacturing |
| | Utility trailers manufacturing |

*Cross-References.*          Establishments primarily engaged in--

- Manufacturing truck trailers, truck trailer chassis, cargo container chassis, detachable trailer bodies, and detachable trailer chassis for sale separately--are classified in U.S. Industry 336212, Truck Trailer Manufacturing; and
- Making manufactured homes (i.e., mobile homes) designed to accept permanent water, sewer, and utility connections and equipped with wheels, but not intended for regular highway use--are classified in U.S. Industry 321991, Manufactured Home (Mobile Home) Manufacturing.

---

T—Canadian, Mexican, and United States industries are comparable.

### 3363    Motor Vehicle Parts Manufacturing[T]

This industry group comprises establishments primarily engaged in manufacturing motor vehicle gasoline engines and engine parts, motor vehicle electrical and electronic equipment, motor vehicle steering and suspension components (except springs), motor vehicle brake systems, motor vehicle transmission and power train parts, motor vehicle seating and interior trim, motor vehicle metal stampings, and other motor vehicle parts and accessories. This industry group includes establishments that rebuild motor vehicle parts.

### 33631   Motor Vehicle Gasoline Engine and Engine Parts Manufacturing[T]
See industry description for 336310.

### 336310  Motor Vehicle Gasoline Engine and Engine Parts Manufacturing

This industry comprises establishments primarily engaged in (1) manufacturing and/or rebuilding motor vehicle gasoline engines and engine parts and/or (2) manufacturing and/or rebuilding carburetors, pistons, piston rings, and engine valves, whether or not for vehicular use.

*Illustrative Examples:*

Carburetors, all types, manufacturing
Crankshaft assemblies, automotive and truck gasoline engine, manufacturing
Cylinder heads, automotive and truck gasoline engine, manufacturing
Fuel injection systems and parts, automotive and truck gasoline engine, manufacturing
Gasoline engines for hybrid automotive vehicles manufacturing

Pistons and piston rings manufacturing
Manifolds (i.e., intake and exhaust), automotive and truck gasoline engine, manufacturing
Pumps (e.g., fuel, oil, water), mechanical, automotive and truck gasoline engine (except power steering), manufacturing
Timing gears and chains, automotive and truck gasoline engine, manufacturing
Valves, engine, intake and exhaust, manufacturing

*Cross-References.*          Establishments primarily engaged in--

- Manufacturing wiring harnesses and other vehicular electrical and electronic equipment--are classified in Industry 336320, Motor Vehicle Electrical and Electronic Equipment Manufacturing;
- Manufacturing transmission and power train equipment--are classified in Industry 336350, Motor Vehicle Transmission and Power Train Parts Manufacturing;
- Manufacturing radiators--are classified in Industry 336390, Other Motor Vehicle Parts Manufacturing;
- Manufacturing steering and suspension components--are classified in Industry 336330, Motor Vehicle Steering and Suspension Components (except Spring) Manufacturing;
- Manufacturing parts for machine repair and equipment parts (except electric) on a job or shop basis--are classified in Industry 332710, Machine Shops;
- Manufacturing rubber and plastic belts and hoses without fittings--are classified in Industry 326220, Rubber and Plastics Hoses and Belting Manufacturing; and
- Manufacturing stationary and diesel engines--are classified in U.S. Industry 333618, Other Engine Equipment Manufacturing.

### 33632   Motor Vehicle Electrical and Electronic Equipment Manufacturing[T]
See industry description for 336320.

### 336320  Motor Vehicle Electrical and Electronic Equipment Manufacturing

This industry comprises establishments primarily engaged in manufacturing and/or rebuilding electrical and electronic equipment for motor vehicles and internal combustion engines. The products made can be used for all types of transportation equipment (i.e., aircraft, automobiles, trucks, trains, ships) or stationary internal combustion engine applications.

---

T—Canadian, Mexican, and United States industries are comparable.

*Illustrative Examples:*

Alternators and generators for internal combustion engines manufacturing

Automotive lighting fixtures manufacturing

Coils, ignition, internal combustion engines, manufacturing

Distributors for internal combustion engines manufacturing

Electrical control chips (modules), motor vehicle, manufacturing

Electrical ignition cable sets for internal combustion engines manufacturing

Generators for internal combustion engines manufacturing

Ignition wiring harness for internal combustion engines manufacturing

Instrument control panels (i.e., assembling purchased gauges), automotive, truck, and bus, manufacturing

Spark plugs for internal combustion engines manufacturing

Windshield washer pumps, automotive, truck, and bus, manufacturing

*Cross-References.*          Establishments primarily engaged in--

- Manufacturing automotive lamps (i.e., bulbs)--are classified in U.S. Industry 335139, Electric Lamp Bulb and Other Lighting Equipment Manufacturing;
- Manufacturing automotive batteries--are classified in Industry 335910, Battery Manufacturing;
- Manufacturing electric motors for electric vehicles--are classified in U.S. Industry 335312, Motor and Generator Manufacturing;
- Manufacturing railway traffic control signals and passenger car alarms--are classified in Industry 334290, Other Communications Equipment Manufacturing; and
- Manufacturing motor vehicle electronic audio and video equipment, including car stereos--are classified in Industry 334310, Audio and Video Equipment Manufacturing.

**33633    Motor Vehicle Steering and Suspension Components (except Spring) Manufacturing[T]**
See industry description for 336330.

**336330  Motor Vehicle Steering and Suspension Components (except Spring) Manufacturing**

This industry comprises establishments primarily engaged in manufacturing and/or rebuilding motor vehicle steering mechanisms and suspension components (except springs).

*Illustrative Examples:*

Rack and pinion steering assemblies manufacturing

Shock absorbers, automotive, truck, and bus, manufacturing

Steering columns, automotive, truck, and bus, manufacturing

Steering wheels, automotive, truck, and bus, manufacturing

Struts, automotive, truck, and bus, manufacturing

Power steering pumps manufacturing

*Cross-References.*

Establishments primarily engaged in manufacturing springs are classified in Industry 33261, Spring and Wire Product Manufacturing.

**33634    Motor Vehicle Brake System Manufacturing[T]**
See industry description for 336340.

**336340  Motor Vehicle Brake System Manufacturing**

This industry comprises establishments primarily engaged in manufacturing and/or rebuilding motor vehicle brake systems and related components.

---

T—Canadian, Mexican, and United States industries are comparable.

*Illustrative Examples:*

Brake cylinders, master and wheel, automotive, truck, and bus, manufacturing
Brake drums, automotive, truck, and bus, manufacturing
Brake hose assemblies manufacturing

Brake pads and shoes, automotive, truck, and bus, manufacturing
Calipers, brake, automotive, truck, and bus, manufacturing

*Cross-References.*

   Establishments primarily engaged in manufacturing rubber and plastics belts and hoses without fittings are classified in Industry 326220, Rubber and Plastics Hoses and Belting Manufacturing.

**33635   Motor Vehicle Transmission and Power Train Parts Manufacturing**[T]
      See industry description for 336350.

**336350  Motor Vehicle Transmission and Power Train Parts Manufacturing**

   This industry comprises establishments primarily engaged in manufacturing and/or rebuilding motor vehicle transmissions and power train parts.

*Illustrative Examples:*

Automatic transmissions, automotive, truck, and bus, manufacturing
Axle bearings, automotive, truck, and bus, manufacturing
Constant velocity joints, automotive, truck, and bus, manufacturing

Differential and rear axle assemblies, automotive, truck, and bus, manufacturing
Torque converters, automotive, truck, and bus, manufacturing
Universal joints, automotive, truck, and bus, manufacturing

**33636   Motor Vehicle Seating and Interior Trim Manufacturing**[T]
      See industry description for 336360.

**336360  Motor Vehicle Seating and Interior Trim Manufacturing**

   This industry comprises establishments primarily engaged in manufacturing motor vehicle seating, seats, seat frames, seat belts, and interior trimmings.

*Cross-References.*          Establishments primarily engaged in--

   • Manufacturing vehicle convertible tops and air bags--are classified in Industry 336390, Other Motor Vehicle Parts Manufacturing;
   • Manufacturing automobile and aircraft carpets and rugs--are classified in Industry 314110, Carpet and Rug Mills; and
   • Manufacturing automotive pads and upholstery filling (except foam rubber and plastics)--are classified in U.S. Industry 314999, All Other Miscellaneous Textile Product Mills.

**33637   Motor Vehicle Metal Stamping**[T]
      See industry description for 336370.

**336370  Motor Vehicle Metal Stamping**

   This industry comprises establishments primarily engaged in manufacturing motor vehicle stampings, such as fenders, tops, body parts, trim, and molding.

_____

T—Canadian, Mexican, and United States industries are comparable.

*Cross-References.*            Establishments primarily engaged in--

- Manufacturing stampings and further processing the stampings--are classified according to the process of the specific product made; and
- Manufacturing stampings (except motor vehicle)--are classified in U.S. Industry 332119, Metal Crown, Closure, and Other Metal Stamping (except Automotive).

**33639    Other Motor Vehicle Parts Manufacturing$^T$**
See industry description for 336390.

**336390   Other Motor Vehicle Parts Manufacturing**

 This industry comprises establishments primarily engaged in manufacturing and/or rebuilding motor vehicle parts and accessories (except motor vehicle gasoline engines and engine parts, motor vehicle electrical and electronic equipment, motor vehicle steering and suspension components, motor vehicle brake systems, motor vehicle transmissions and power train parts, motor vehicle seating and interior trim, and motor vehicle stampings).

*Illustrative Examples:*

Air bag assemblies manufacturing
Air-conditioners, motor vehicle, manufacturing
Air filters, automotive, truck, and bus, manufacturing
Radiators and cores manufacturing
Catalytic converters, engine exhaust, automotive, truck, and bus, manufacturing

Compressors, motor vehicle air-conditioning, manufacturing
Mufflers and resonators, motor vehicle, manufacturing
Wheels (i.e., rims), automotive, truck, and bus, manufacturing

*Cross-References.*            Establishments primarily engaged in--

- Manufacturing motor vehicle gasoline engines and engine parts--are classified in Industry 336310, Motor Vehicle Gasoline Engine and Engine Parts Manufacturing;
- Manufacturing motor vehicle electrical and electronic equipment--are classified in Industry 336320, Motor Vehicle Electrical and Electronic Equipment Manufacturing;
- Manufacturing motor vehicle steering and suspension components--are classified in Industry 336330, Motor Vehicle Steering and Suspension Components (except Spring) Manufacturing;
- Manufacturing motor vehicle brake systems--are classified in Industry 336340, Motor Vehicle Brake System Manufacturing;
- Manufacturing motor vehicle transmissions and power train parts--are classified in Industry 336350, Motor Vehicle Transmission and Power Train Parts Manufacturing;
- Manufacturing motor vehicle seating and interior trim--are classified in Industry 336360, Motor Vehicle Seating and Interior Trim Manufacturing;
- Manufacturing motor vehicle stampings--are classified in Industry 336370, Motor Vehicle Metal Stamping;
- Manufacturing air-conditioning systems and compressors (except motor vehicle air-conditioning systems)--are classified in U.S. Industry 333415, Air-Conditioning and Warm Air Heating Equipment and Commercial and Industrial Refrigeration Equipment Manufacturing; and
- Manufacturing motor vehicle electronic audio and video equipment, including car stereos--are classified in Industry 334310, Audio and Video Equipment Manufacturing.

**3364    Aerospace Product and Parts Manufacturing$^T$**

**33641   Aerospace Product and Parts Manufacturing$^T$**

 This industry comprises establishments primarily engaged in one or more of the following: (1) manufacturing complete aircraft, missiles, or space vehicles; (2) manufacturing aerospace engines, propulsion units, auxiliary equipment, or parts; (3) developing and making prototypes of aerospace products; (4) aircraft conversion (i.e., major

---

T—Canadian, Mexican, and United States industries are comparable.

modifications to systems); and (5) complete aircraft or propulsion systems overhaul and rebuilding (i.e., periodic restoration of aircraft to original design specifications).

*Cross-References.*

- Establishments primarily engaged in manufacturing space satellites are classified in Industry 33422, Radio and Television Broadcasting and Wireless Communications Equipment Manufacturing;
- Establishments primarily engaged in manufacturing flight simulators are classified in Industry 33331, Commercial and Service Industry Machinery Manufacturing;
- Establishments primarily engaged in the repair of aircraft or aircraft engines (except overhauling, conversion, and rebuilding) are classified in Industry 48819, Other Support Activities for Air Transportation;
- Research and development establishments primarily engaged in aerospace R&D (except prototype production) are classified in Industry 54171, Research and Development in the Physical, Engineering, and Life Sciences;
- Establishments primarily engaged in manufacturing aircraft engine intake and exhaust valves, pistons, or engine filters are classified in Industry 33631, Motor Vehicle Gasoline Engine and Engine Parts Manufacturing;
- Establishments primarily engaged in manufacturing aircraft seating are classified in Industry 33636, Motor Vehicle Seating and Interior Trim Manufacturing;
- Establishments primarily engaged in manufacturing aeronautical, navigational, and guidance systems and instruments are classified in Industry 33451, Navigational, Measuring, Electromedical, and Control Instruments Manufacturing;
- Establishment primarily engaged in manufacturing aircraft engine electrical (aeronautical electrical) equipment or aircraft lighting fixtures are classified in Industry 33632, Motor Vehicle Electrical and Electronic Equipment Manufacturing; and
- Establishments primarily engaged in manufacturing aircraft fluid power subassemblies are classified in Industry 33291, Metal Valve Manufacturing.

### 336411 Aircraft Manufacturing

This U.S. industry comprises establishments primarily engaged in one or more of the following: (1) manufacturing or assembling complete aircraft; (2) developing and making aircraft prototypes; (3) aircraft conversion (i.e., major modifications to systems); and (4) complete aircraft overhaul and rebuilding (i.e., periodic restoration of aircraft to original design specifications).

*Cross-References.*

- Establishments primarily engaged in manufacturing guided missiles and space vehicles are classified in U.S. Industry 336414, Guided Missile and Space Vehicle Manufacturing;
- Establishments primarily engaged in manufacturing flight simulators are classified in Industry 333310, Commercial and Service Industry Machinery Manufacturing;
- Establishments primarily engaged in the repair of aircraft (except overhauling, conversion, and rebuilding) are classified in Industry 488190, Other Support Activities for Air Transportation; and
- Research and development establishments primarily engaged in aircraft R&D (except prototype production) are classified in U.S. Industry 541715, Research and Development in the Physical, Engineering, and Life Sciences (except Nanotechnology and Biotechnology).

### 336412 Aircraft Engine and Engine Parts Manufacturing

This U.S. industry comprises establishments primarily engaged in one or more of the following: (1) manufacturing aircraft engines and engine parts; (2) developing and making prototypes of aircraft engines and engine parts; (3) aircraft propulsion system conversion (i.e., major modifications to systems); and (4) aircraft propulsion systems overhaul and rebuilding (i.e., periodic restoration of aircraft propulsion system to original design specifications).

---

T—Canadian, Mexican, and United States industries are comparable.

*Cross-References.*

- Establishments primarily engaged in manufacturing guided missile and space vehicle propulsion units and parts are classified in U.S. Industry 336415, Guided Missile and Space Vehicle Propulsion Unit and Propulsion Unit Parts Manufacturing;
- Establishments primarily engaged in manufacturing aircraft intake and exhaust valves and pistons and aircraft internal combustion engine filters are classified in Industry 336310, Motor Vehicle Gasoline Engine and Engine Parts Manufacturing;
- Establishments primarily engaged in the repair of aircraft engines (except overhauling, conversion, and rebuilding) are classified in Industry 488190, Other Support Activities for Air Transportation;
- Research and development establishments primarily engaged in aircraft engine and engine parts R&D (except prototype production) are classified in U.S. Industry 541715, Research and Development in the Physical, Engineering, and Life Sciences (except Nanotechnology and Biotechnology); and
- Establishments primarily engaged in manufacturing aeronautical instruments are classified in U.S. Industry 334511, Search, Detection, Navigation, Guidance, Aeronautical, and Nautical System and Instrument Manufacturing.

## 336413 Other Aircraft Parts and Auxiliary Equipment Manufacturing

This U.S. industry comprises establishments primarily engaged in (1) manufacturing aircraft parts or auxiliary equipment (except engines and aircraft fluid power subassemblies) and/or (2) developing and making prototypes of aircraft parts and auxiliary equipment. Auxiliary equipment includes such items as crop dusting apparatus, armament racks, inflight refueling equipment, and external fuel tanks.

*Cross-References.*

- Establishments primarily engaged in manufacturing aircraft engines and engine parts are classified in U.S. Industry 336412, Aircraft Engine and Engine Parts Manufacturing;
- Establishments primarily engaged in manufacturing aeronautical instruments are classified in U.S. Industry 334511, Search, Detection, Navigation, Guidance, Aeronautical, and Nautical System and Instrument Manufacturing;
- Establishments primarily engaged in manufacturing aircraft lighting fixtures and aircraft engine electrical (aeronautical electrical) equipment are classified in Industry 336320, Motor Vehicle Electrical and Electronic Equipment Manufacturing;
- Establishments primarily engaged in manufacturing guided missile and space vehicle parts and auxiliary equipment are classified in U.S. Industry 336419, Other Guided Missile and Space Vehicle Parts and Auxiliary Equipment Manufacturing;
- Establishments primarily engaged in manufacturing aircraft fluid power subassemblies are classified in U.S. Industry 332912, Fluid Power Valve and Hose Fitting Manufacturing;
- Establishments primarily engaged in manufacturing aircraft seating are classified in Industry 336360, Motor Vehicle Seating and Interior Trim Manufacturing; and
- Research and development establishments primarily engaged in aircraft parts and auxiliary equipment R&D (except prototype production) are classified in U.S. Industry 541715, Research and Development in the Physical, Engineering, and Life Sciences (except Nanotechnology and Biotechnology).

## 336414 Guided Missile and Space Vehicle Manufacturing

This U.S. industry comprises establishments primarily engaged in (1) manufacturing complete guided missiles and space vehicles and/or (2) developing and making prototypes of guided missiles or space vehicles.

*Cross-References.*

- Establishments primarily engaged in manufacturing space satellites are classified in Industry 334220, Radio and Television Broadcasting and Wireless Communications Equipment Manufacturing; and

---

T—Canadian, Mexican, and United States industries are comparable.

- Research and development establishments primarily engaged in guided missile and space vehicle R&D (except prototype production) are classified in U.S. Industry 541715, Research and Development in the Physical, Engineering, and Life Sciences (except Nanotechnology and Biotechnology).

**336415 Guided Missile and Space Vehicle Propulsion Unit and Propulsion Unit Parts Manufacturing**

This U.S. industry comprises establishments primarily engaged in (1) manufacturing guided missile and/or space vehicle propulsion units and propulsion unit parts and/or (2) developing and making prototypes of guided missile and space vehicle propulsion units and propulsion unit parts.

*Cross-References.*

Research and development establishments primarily engaged in guided missile and space propulsion unit and propulsion unit parts R&D (except prototype production) are classified in U.S. Industry 541715, Research and Development in the Physical, Engineering, and Life Sciences (except Nanotechnology and Biotechnology).

**336419 Other Guided Missile and Space Vehicle Parts and Auxiliary Equipment Manufacturing**

This U.S. industry comprises establishments primarily engaged in (1) manufacturing guided missile and space vehicle parts and auxiliary equipment (except guided missile and space vehicle propulsion units and propulsion unit parts) and/or (2) developing and making prototypes of guided missile and space vehicle parts and auxiliary equipment.

*Cross-References.*

- Establishments primarily engaged in manufacturing navigational and guidance systems are classified in U.S. Industry 334511, Search, Detection, Navigation, Guidance, Aeronautical, and Nautical System and Instrument Manufacturing;
- Establishments primarily engaged in manufacturing guided missile and space vehicle propulsion units and propulsion unit parts are classified in U.S. Industry 336415, Guided Missile and Space Vehicle Propulsion Unit and Propulsion Unit Parts Manufacturing; and
- Research and development establishments primarily engaged in guided missile and space vehicle parts and auxiliary equipment R&D (except prototype production) are classified in U.S. Industry 541715, Research and Development in the Physical, Engineering, and Life Sciences (except Nanotechnology and Biotechnology).

**3365    Railroad Rolling Stock Manufacturing**[T]

**33651    Railroad Rolling Stock Manufacturing**[T]
See industry description for 336510.

**336510    Railroad Rolling Stock Manufacturing**

This industry comprises establishments primarily engaged in one or more of the following: (1) manufacturing and/or rebuilding locomotives, locomotive frames, and parts; (2) manufacturing railroad, street, and rapid transit cars and car equipment for operation on rails for freight and passenger service; and (3) manufacturing rail layers, ballast distributors, rail tamping equipment, and other railway track maintenance equipment.

*Cross-References.*

- Establishments primarily engaged in manufacturing mining rail cars are classified in U.S. Industry 333131, Mining Machinery and Equipment Manufacturing;
- Establishments primarily engaged in manufacturing locomotive fuel lubricating or cooling medium pumps are classified in U.S. Industry 333914, Measuring, Dispensing, and Other Pumping Equipment Manufacturing;

---

T—Canadian, Mexican, and United States industries are comparable.

- Repair establishments of railroad and local transit companies primarily engaged in repairing railroad and transit cars are classified in Industry 488210, Support Activities for Rail Transportation; and
- Establishments not owned by railroad or local transit companies engaged in repairing railroad cars and locomotive engines are classified in Industry 811310, Commercial and Industrial Machinery and Equipment (except Automotive and Electronic) Repair and Maintenance.

**3366    Ship and Boat Building$^T$**

**33661    Ship and Boat Building$^T$**

This industry comprises establishments primarily engaged in operating shipyards or boat yards (i.e., ship or boat manufacturing facilities). Shipyards are fixed facilities with drydocks and fabrication equipment capable of building a ship, defined as watercraft typically suitable or intended for other than personal or recreational use. Boats are defined as watercraft typically suitable or intended for personal use. Activities of shipyards include the construction of ships, their repair, conversion and alteration, production of prefabricated ship and barge sections, and specialized services, such as ship scaling.

*Illustrative Examples:*

| | |
|---|---|
| Barge building | Inflatable plastic boats, heavy-duty, manufacturing |
| Boat yards (i.e., boat manufacturing facilities) | Inflatable rubber boats, heavy-duty, manufacturing |
| Cargo ship building | Rigid inflatable boats (RIBs) manufacturing |
| Drilling and production platforms, floating, oil and gas, building | Boats (e.g., motorboats, rowboats, canoes, kayaks) manufacturing |
| Passenger ship building | |

*Cross-References.*      Establishments primarily engaged in--

- Manufacturing inflatable rubber swimming pool rafts and similar flotation devices--are classified in Industry 32629, Other Rubber Product Manufacturing;
- Manufacturing inflatable plastic swimming pool rafts and similar flotation devices--are classified in Industry 32619, Other Plastics Product Manufacturing;
- Fabricating structural assemblies or components for ships, or subcontractors engaged in ship painting, joinery, carpentry work, and electrical wiring installation--are classified based on the production process used; and
- Ship repairs performed in floating drydocks--are classified in Industry 48839, Other Support Activities for Water Transportation.

**336611  Ship Building and Repairing**

This U.S. industry comprises establishments primarily engaged in operating shipyards. Shipyards are fixed facilities with drydocks and fabrication equipment capable of building a ship, defined as watercraft typically suitable or intended for other than personal or recreational use. Activities of shipyards include the construction of ships, their repair, conversion and alteration, the production of prefabricated ship and barge sections, and specialized services, such as ship scaling.

*Illustrative Examples:*

| | |
|---|---|
| Barge building | Passenger ship building |
| Cargo ship building | Submarine building |
| Drilling and production platforms, floating, oil and gas, building | Yachts built in shipyards |

---

T—Canadian, Mexican, and United States industries are comparable.

*Cross-References.*        Establishments primarily engaged in--

- Fabricating structural assemblies or components for ships, or subcontractors engaged in ship painting, joinery, carpentry work, and electrical wiring installation--are classified based on the production process used; and
- Ship repairs performed in floating drydocks--are classified in Industry 488390, Other Support Activities for Water Transportation.

## 336612  Boat Building

This U.S. industry comprises establishments primarily engaged in building boats. Boats are defined as watercraft not built in shipyards and typically of the type suitable or intended for personal use. Included in this industry are establishments that manufacture heavy-duty inflatable rubber or inflatable plastic boats (RIBs).

*Illustrative Examples:*

Inflatable plastic boats, heavy-duty, manufacturing
Inflatable rubber boats, heavy-duty, manufacturing
Boats (e.g., motorboats, rowboats, canoes, kayaks) manufacturing

Rigid inflatable boats (RIBs) manufacturing
Sailboat building, not done in shipyards
Yacht building, not done in shipyards

*Cross-References.*        Establishments primarily engaged in--

- Ship building or ship repairs performed in a shipyard--are classified in U.S. Industry 336611, Ship Building and Repairing;
- Ship repairs performed in floating drydocks--are classified in Industry 488390, Other Support Activities for Water Transportation;
- Manufacturing inflatable rubber swimming pool rafts and similar flotation devices--are classified in U.S. Industry 326299, All Other Rubber Product Manufacturing; and
- Manufacturing inflatable plastic swimming pool rafts and similar flotation devices--are classified in U.S. Industry 326199, All Other Plastics Product Manufacturing.

## 3369    Other Transportation Equipment Manufacturing[T]

## 33699    Other Transportation Equipment Manufacturing[T]

This industry comprises establishments primarily engaged in manufacturing motorcycles, bicycles, metal tricycles, complete military armored vehicles, tanks, self-propelled weapons, vehicles pulled by draft animals, and other transportation equipment (except motor vehicles, boats, ships, railroad rolling stock, and aerospace products), including parts thereof.

*Cross-References.*        Establishments primarily engaged in--

- Manufacturing ships and boats--are classified in Industry 33661, Ship and Boat Building;
- Manufacturing aerospace products and parts--are classified in Industry 33641, Aerospace Product and Parts Manufacturing;
- Manufacturing motor vehicle parts--are classified in Industry Group 3363, Motor Vehicle Parts Manufacturing;
- Manufacturing children's vehicles (except bicycles and metal tricycles)--are classified in Industry 33993, Doll, Toy, and Game Manufacturing;
- Manufacturing railroad rolling stock--are classified in Industry 33651, Railroad Rolling Stock Manufacturing; and
- Manufacturing motor vehicles--are classified in Industry Group 3361, Motor Vehicle Manufacturing.

---

T—Canadian, Mexican, and United States industries are comparable.

## 336991 Motorcycle, Bicycle, and Parts Manufacturing

This U.S. industry comprises establishments primarily engaged in manufacturing motorcycles, bicycles, tricycles and similar equipment, and parts.

*Cross-References.*     Establishments primarily engaged in--

- Manufacturing children's vehicles (except bicycles and metal tricycles)--are classified in Industry 339930, Doll, Toy, and Game Manufacturing; and
- Manufacturing powered golf carts and other similar motorized passenger carriers--are classified in U.S. Industry 336999, All Other Transportation Equipment Manufacturing.

## 336992 Military Armored Vehicle, Tank, and Tank Component Manufacturing

This U.S. industry comprises establishments primarily engaged in manufacturing complete military armored vehicles, combat tanks, specialized components for combat tanks, and self-propelled weapons.

*Cross-References.*

Establishments primarily engaged in manufacturing nonarmored military universal carriers are classified in Industry 336110, Automobile and Light Duty Motor Vehicle.

## 336999 All Other Transportation Equipment Manufacturing

This U.S. industry comprises establishments primarily engaged in manufacturing transportation equipment (except motor vehicles, motor vehicle parts, boats, ships, railroad rolling stock, aerospace products, motorcycles, bicycles, armored vehicles, and tanks).

*Illustrative Examples:*

All-terrain vehicles (ATVs), wheeled or tracked, manufacturing
Animal-drawn vehicles and parts manufacturing
Gocarts (except children's) manufacturing

Golf carts and similar motorized passenger carriers manufacturing
Race cars manufacturing
Snowmobiles and parts manufacturing

*Cross-References.*     Establishments primarily engaged in--

- Manufacturing motorcycles, bicycles, and parts--are classified in U.S. Industry 336991, Motorcycle, Bicycle, and Parts Manufacturing;
- Manufacturing military armored vehicles, tanks, and tank components--are classified in U.S. Industry 336992, Military Armored Vehicle, Tank, and Tank Component Manufacturing;
- Manufacturing ships and boats--are classified in Industry 33661, Ship and Boat Building;
- Manufacturing aerospace products and parts--are classified in Industry 33641, Aerospace Product and Parts Manufacturing;
- Manufacturing motor vehicle parts--are classified in Industry Group 3363, Motor Vehicle Parts Manufacturing;
- Manufacturing railroad rolling stock--are classified in Industry 336510, Railroad Rolling Stock Manufacturing;
- Manufacturing motor vehicles--are classified in Industry Group 3361, Motor Vehicle Manufacturing; and
- Manufacturing children's gocarts and other children's vehicles (except bicycles and metal tricycles)--are classified in Industry 339930, Doll, Toy, and Game Manufacturing.

---

T—Canadian, Mexican, and United States industries are comparable.

## 337    Furniture and Related Product Manufacturing[T]

Industries in the Furniture and Related Product Manufacturing subsector make furniture and related articles, such as mattresses, window blinds, cabinets, and fixtures. The processes used in the manufacture of furniture include the cutting, bending, molding, laminating, and assembly of such materials as wood, metal, glass, plastics, and rattan. However, the production process for furniture is not solely bending metal, cutting and shaping wood, or extruding and molding plastics. Design and fashion trends play an important part in the production of furniture. The integrated design of the article for both esthetic and functional qualities is also a major part of the process of manufacturing furniture. Design services may be performed by the furniture establishment's work force or may be purchased from industrial designers.

Furniture may be made of any material, but the most common ones used in North America are metal and wood. Furniture manufacturing establishments may specialize in making articles primarily from one material. Some of the equipment required to make a wooden table, for example, is different from that used to make a metal one. However, furniture is usually made from several materials. A wooden table might have metal brackets, and a wooden chair a fabric or plastics seat. Therefore, in NAICS, furniture initially is classified based on the type of furniture (application for which it is designed) rather than the material used. For example, an upholstered sofa is treated as household furniture, although it may also be used in hotels or offices.

When classifying furniture according to the component material from which it is made, furniture made from more than one material is classified based on the material used in the frame, or if there is no frame, the predominant component material. Upholstered household furniture (excluding kitchen and dining room chairs with upholstered seats) is classified without regard to the frame material. Kitchen or dining room chairs with upholstered seats are classified according to the frame material.

Furniture may be made on a stock or custom basis and may be shipped assembled or unassembled (i.e., knockdown). The manufacture of furniture parts and frames is included in this subsector.

Some of the processes used in furniture manufacturing are similar to processes that are used in other segments of manufacturing. For example, cutting and assembly occurs in the production of wood trusses that are classified in Subsector 321, Wood Product Manufacturing. However, the multiple processes that distinguish wood furniture manufacturing from wood product manufacturing warrant inclusion of wooden furniture manufacturing in the Furniture and Related Product Manufacturing subsector. Metal furniture manufacturing uses techniques that are also employed in the manufacturing of roll formed products classified in Subsector 332, Fabricated Metal Product Manufacturing. The molding process for plastics furniture is similar to the molding of other plastics products. However, plastics furniture producing establishments tend to specialize in furniture.

NAICS attempts to keep furniture manufacturing together, but there are notable exceptions: concrete, ceramic, or stone furniture; seating for transportation equipment; and specialized hospital furniture (e.g., hospital beds and operating tables). These are classified in Subsector 327, Nonmetallic Mineral Product Manufacturing; Subsector 336, Transportation Equipment Manufacturing; and Subsector 339, Miscellaneous Manufacturing, respectively.

## 3371    Household and Institutional Furniture and Kitchen Cabinet Manufacturing[T]

This industry group comprises establishments manufacturing household-type furniture, such as living room, kitchen and bedroom furniture and institutional (i.e., public building) furniture, such as furniture for schools, theaters, and churches.

### 33711    Wood Kitchen Cabinet and Countertop Manufacturing[T]
See industry description for 337110.

### 337110  Wood Kitchen Cabinet and Countertop Manufacturing

This industry comprises establishments primarily engaged in manufacturing wood or plastics laminated on wood kitchen cabinets, bathroom vanities, and countertops (except freestanding). The cabinets and counters may be made on a stock or custom basis.

---

T—Canadian, Mexican, and United States industries are comparable.

*Cross-References.*          Establishments primarily engaged in--

- Manufacturing metal kitchen and bathroom cabinets (except freestanding)--are classified in U.S. Industry 337126, Household Furniture (except Wood and Upholstered) Manufacturing;
- Manufacturing plastics countertops--are classified in U.S. Industry 326199, All Other Plastics Product Manufacturing;
- Manufacturing stone countertops--are classified in U.S. Industry 327991, Cut Stone and Stone Product Manufacturing;
- Manufacturing wood or plastics laminated on wood countertops (except kitchen and bathroom)--are classified in U.S. Industry 337215, Showcase, Partition, Shelving, and Locker Manufacturing;
- Constructing built-in wood cabinets on site--are classified in Industry 238350, Finish Carpentry Contractors; and
- Manufacturing freestanding household-type wood cabinets--are classified in U.S. Industry 337122, Nonupholstered Wood Household Furniture Manufacturing.

## 33712   Household and Institutional Furniture Manufacturing[T]

This industry comprises establishments primarily engaged in manufacturing household-type and public building furniture (e.g., library, school, theater, and church furniture).  This industry includes establishments that manufacture general purpose hospital, laboratory, and/or dental furniture (e.g., stools, tables, benches).  The furniture may be made on a stock or custom basis and may be assembled or unassembled (i.e., knockdown).

*Cross-References.*          Establishments primarily engaged in--

- Manufacturing specialized hospital and/or dental furniture (e.g., hospital beds, operating tables, dental chairs)--are classified in Industry 33911, Medical Equipment and Supplies Manufacturing;
- Manufacturing wood or plastics laminated on wood kitchen cabinets, bathroom vanities, and countertops (except freestanding)--are classified in Industry 33711, Wood Kitchen Cabinet and Countertop Manufacturing;
- Manufacturing office-type furniture and/or office or store fixtures--are classified in Industry 33721, Office Furniture (including Fixtures) Manufacturing;
- Manufacturing concrete, ceramic, or stone furniture--are classified in Subsector 327, Nonmetallic Mineral Product Manufacturing, according to the materials used;
- Installing modular furniture systems--are classified in Industry 23839, Other Building Finishing Contractors; and
- Repairing or refinishing furniture, or restoring antique furniture--are classified in Industry 81142, Reupholstery and Furniture Repair.

## 337121  Upholstered Household Furniture Manufacturing

This U.S. industry comprises establishments primarily engaged in manufacturing upholstered household-type furniture.  The furniture may be made on a stock or custom basis.

*Cross-References.*          Establishments primarily engaged in--

- Reupholstering furniture or upholstering frames to individual order--are classified in Industry 811420, Reupholstery and Furniture Repair;
- Manufacturing wood kitchen and dining room chairs with upholstered seats or backs--are classified in U.S. Industry 337122, Nonupholstered Wood Household Furniture Manufacturing; and
- Manufacturing kitchen and dining room chairs (except wood) with upholstered seats or backs--are classified in U.S. Industry 337126, Household Furniture (except Wood and Upholstered) Manufacturing.

---

T—Canadian, Mexican, and United States industries are comparable.

### 337122  Nonupholstered Wood Household Furniture Manufacturing

This U.S. industry comprises establishments primarily engaged in manufacturing nonupholstered wood household-type furniture and freestanding cabinets (except television, stereo, and sewing machine cabinets).  The furniture may be made on a stock or custom basis and may be assembled or unassembled (i.e., knockdown).

*Cross-References.*          Establishments primarily engaged in--

- Manufacturing reed, rattan, plastics, and similar furniture--are classified in U.S. Industry 337126, Household Furniture (except Wood and Upholstered) Manufacturing;
- Manufacturing wood television, stereo, and sewing machine cabinets (i.e., housings)--are classified in U.S. Industry 321999, All Other Miscellaneous Wood Product Manufacturing;
- Manufacturing wood or plastics laminated on wood kitchen cabinets, bathroom vanities, and countertops (except freestanding)--are classified in Industry 337110, Wood Kitchen Cabinet and Countertop Manufacturing; and
- Repairing or refinishing furniture, or restoring antique furniture--are classified in Industry 811420, Reupholstery and Furniture Repair.

### 337126  Household Furniture (except Wood and Upholstered) Manufacturing

This U.S. industry comprises establishments primarily engaged in manufacturing nonupholstered household-type furniture of materials other than wood, such as metal, plastics, reed, rattan, wicker, and fiberglass.  The furniture may be partially upholstered (e.g., chairs with upholstered seats or backs), made on a stock or custom basis, and may be assembled or unassembled (i.e., knockdown).

*Cross-References.*          Establishments primarily engaged in--

- Manufacturing upholstered household-type furniture--are classified in U.S. Industry 337121, Upholstered Household Furniture Manufacturing;
- Manufacturing nonupholstered or partially upholstered wood household-type furniture--are classified in U.S. Industry 337122, Nonupholstered Wood Household Furniture Manufacturing;
- Manufacturing concrete, ceramic, or stone furniture--are classified in Subsector 327, Nonmetallic Mineral Product Manufacturing, according to the materials used; and
- Manufacturing specialized hospital and/or dental furniture (e.g., hospital beds, operating tables, dental chairs)--are classified in Industry 33911, Medical Equipment and Supplies Manufacturing.

### 337127  Institutional Furniture Manufacturing

This U.S. industry comprises establishments primarily engaged in manufacturing institutional-type furniture (e.g., library, school, theater, and church furniture).  Included in this industry are establishments primarily engaged in manufacturing general purpose hospital, laboratory, and dental furniture (e.g., tables, stools, and benches).  The furniture may be made on a stock or custom basis and may be assembled or unassembled (i.e., knockdown).

*Cross-References.*          Establishments primarily engaged in--

- Manufacturing specialized hospital furniture (e.g., hospital beds, operating tables)--are classified in U.S. Industry 339113, Surgical Appliance and Supplies Manufacturing;
- Manufacturing specialized dental furniture (e.g., dental chairs)--are classified in U.S. Industry 339114, Dental Equipment and Supplies Manufacturing;
- Manufacturing wood or plastics laminated on wood kitchen cabinets, bathroom vanities, and countertops (except freestanding)--are classified in Industry 337110, Wood Kitchen Cabinet and Countertop Manufacturing;
- Installing modular furniture systems--are classified in Industry 238390, Other Building Finishing Contractors;

---

T—Canadian, Mexican, and United States industries are comparable.

- Manufacturing office-type furniture and/or office or store fixtures--are classified in Industry 33721, Office Furniture (including Fixtures) Manufacturing; and
- Repairing or refinishing furniture--are classified in Industry 811420, Reupholstery and Furniture Repair.

## 3372    Office Furniture (including Fixtures) Manufacturing[T]

## 33721    Office Furniture (including Fixtures) Manufacturing[T]

This industry comprises establishments primarily engaged in manufacturing office furniture and/or office and store fixtures. The furniture may be made on a stock or custom basis and may be assembled or unassembled (i.e., knockdown).

*Cross-References.*          Establishments primarily engaged in--

- Manufacturing millwork on a factory basis--are classified in Industry 32191, Millwork;
- Manufacturing household-type and institutional-type furniture--are classified in Industry 33712, Household and Institutional Furniture Manufacturing;
- Manufacturing refrigerated cabinets, showcases, and display cases--are classified in Industry 33341, Ventilation, Heating, Air-Conditioning, and Commercial Refrigeration Equipment Manufacturing;
- Manufacturing metal safes and vaults--are classified in Industry 33299, All Other Fabricated Metal Product Manufacturing;
- Constructing wood shelving on site--are classified in Industry 23835, Finish Carpentry Contractors; and
- Installing modular office furniture systems and partitions, and constructing metal shelving on site--are classified in Industry 23839, Other Building Finishing Contractors.

## 337211  Wood Office Furniture Manufacturing

This U.S. industry comprises establishments primarily engaged in manufacturing wood office-type furniture. The furniture may be made on a stock or custom basis and may be assembled or unassembled (i.e., knockdown).

## 337212  Custom Architectural Woodwork and Millwork Manufacturing

This U.S. industry comprises establishments primarily engaged in manufacturing custom designed interiors consisting of architectural woodwork and fixtures utilizing wood, wood products, and plastics laminates. All of the industry output is made to individual order on a job shop basis and requires skilled craftsmen as a labor input. A job might include custom manufacturing of display fixtures, gondolas, wall shelving units, entrance and window architectural detail, sales and reception counters, wall paneling, and matching furniture.

*Cross-References.*          Establishments primarily engaged in--

- Manufacturing millwork on a factory basis--are classified in U.S. Industry 321918, Other Millwork (including Flooring);
- Manufacturing wood office-type furniture on a stock or custom basis--are classified in U.S. Industry 337211, Wood Office Furniture Manufacturing; and
- Manufacturing wood office-type and store fixtures on a stock or custom basis--are classified in U.S. Industry 337215, Showcase, Partition, Shelving, and Locker Manufacturing.

## 337214  Office Furniture (except Wood) Manufacturing

This U.S. industry comprises establishments primarily engaged in manufacturing nonwood office-type furniture. The furniture may be made on a stock or custom basis and may be assembled or unassembled (i.e., knockdown).

---

T—Canadian, Mexican, and United States industries are comparable.

*Cross-References.*

Establishments primarily engaged in installing modular office furniture systems and partitions, and constructing metal shelving on site are classified in Industry 238390, Other Building Finishing Contractors.

## 337215  Showcase, Partition, Shelving, and Locker Manufacturing

This U.S. industry comprises establishments primarily engaged in manufacturing wood and nonwood office and store fixtures, shelving, lockers, frames, partitions, and related fabricated products of wood and nonwood materials, including plastics laminated fixture tops.  The products are made on a stock or custom basis and may be assembled or unassembled (i.e., knockdown).  Establishments exclusively making furniture parts (e.g., frames) are included in this industry.

*Cross-References.*          Establishments primarily engaged in--

- Manufacturing refrigerated cabinets, showcases, and display cases--are classified in U.S. Industry 333415, Air-Conditioning and Warm Air Heating Equipment and Commercial and Industrial Refrigeration Equipment Manufacturing;
- Manufacturing metal safes and vaults--are classified in U.S. Industry 332999, All Other Miscellaneous Fabricated Metal Product Manufacturing;
- Manufacturing wood or plastics laminated kitchen and bathroom countertops--are classified in Industry 337110, Wood Kitchen Cabinet and Countertop Manufacturing;
- Constructing wood shelving on site--are classified in Industry 238350, Finish Carpentry Contractors; and
- Installing modular office furniture systems and partitions, and constructing metal shelving on site--are classified in Industry 238390, Other Building Finishing Contractors.

## 3379     Other Furniture Related Product Manufacturing[T]

This industry group comprises establishments manufacturing furniture related products, such as mattresses, blinds, and shades.

## 33791   Mattress Manufacturing[T]
See industry description for 337910.

## 337910  Mattress Manufacturing

This industry comprises establishments primarily engaged in manufacturing innerspring, box spring, and noninnerspring mattresses.

*Cross-References.*          Establishments primarily engaged in--

- Manufacturing individual wire springs--are classified in Industry 33261, Spring and Wire Product Manufacturing; and
- Manufacturing inflatable mattresses--are classified in Subsector 326, Plastics and Rubber Products Manufacturing.

## 33792   Blind and Shade Manufacturing[T]
See industry description for 337920.

## 337920  Blind and Shade Manufacturing

This industry comprises establishments primarily engaged in manufacturing one or more of the following: venetian blinds, other window blinds, and shades; curtain and drapery rods and poles; and/or curtain and drapery fixtures.  The blinds and shades may be made on a stock or custom basis and may be made of any material.

---

T—Canadian, Mexican, and United States industries are comparable.

*Cross-References.*        Establishments primarily engaged in--

- Manufacturing canvas awnings--are classified in Industry 314910, Textile Bag and Canvas Mills; and
- Manufacturing curtains and draperies--are classified in Industry 314120, Curtain and Linen Mills.

## 339      Miscellaneous Manufacturing[T]

Industries in the Miscellaneous Manufacturing subsector make a wide range of products that cannot readily be classified in specific NAICS subsectors in manufacturing. Processes used by these establishments vary significantly, both among and within industries. For example, a variety of manufacturing processes are used in manufacturing sporting and athletic goods that include products such as tennis rackets and golf balls. The processes for these products differ from each other, and the processes differ significantly from the fabrication processes used in making dolls or toys, the melting and shaping of precious metals to make jewelry, and the bending, forming, and assembly used in making medical products.

The industries in this subsector are defined by what is made rather than how it is made. Although individual establishments might be appropriately classified elsewhere in the NAICS structure, for historical continuity, these product-based industries were maintained. In most cases, no one process or material predominates for an industry.

Establishments in this subsector manufacture products as diverse as medical equipment and supplies, jewelry, sporting goods, toys, and office supplies.

## 3391      Medical Equipment and Supplies Manufacturing[T]

## 33911      Medical Equipment and Supplies Manufacturing[T]

This industry comprises establishments primarily engaged in manufacturing medical equipment and supplies. Examples of products made by these establishments are surgical and medical instruments, surgical appliances and supplies, dental equipment and supplies, orthodontic goods, ophthalmic goods, dentures, and orthodontic appliances.

*Cross-References.*        Establishments primarily engaged in--

- Manufacturing laboratory instruments, X-ray apparatus, electromedical apparatus (including electronic hearing aids), and thermometers (except medical)--are classified in Industry 33451, Navigational, Measuring, Electromedical, and Control Instruments Manufacturing;
- Manufacturing molded glass lens blanks--are classified in Industry 32721, Glass and Glass Product Manufacturing;
- Manufacturing molded plastics lens blanks--are classified in Industry 32619, Other Plastics Product Manufacturing;
- Retailing and grinding prescription eyeglasses--are classified in Industry 45613, Optical Goods Retailers;
- Manufacturing sporting goods helmets and protective equipment--are classified in Industry 33992, Sporting and Athletic Goods Manufacturing;
- Manufacturing general purpose hospital, laboratory, and/or dental furniture (e.g., stools, tables, benches)--are classified in Industry 33712, Household and Institutional Furniture Manufacturing;
- Manufacturing laboratory scales and balances, laboratory furnaces and ovens, and/or laboratory centrifuges--are classified in Industry 33399, All Other General Purpose Machinery Manufacturing;
- Manufacturing laboratory distilling equipment--are classified in Industry 33324, Industrial Machinery Manufacturing; and
- Manufacturing laboratory freezers--are classified in Industry 33341, Ventilation, Heating, Air-Conditioning, and Commercial Refrigeration Equipment Manufacturing.

## 339112  Surgical and Medical Instrument Manufacturing

This U.S. industry comprises establishments primarily engaged in manufacturing medical, surgical, ophthalmic, and veterinary instruments and apparatus (except electrotherapeutic, electromedical, and irradiation apparatus). Examples of products made by these establishments are syringes, hypodermic needles, anesthesia apparatus, blood transfusion equipment, catheters, surgical clamps, and medical thermometers.

---

T—Canadian, Mexican, and United States industries are comparable.

*Cross-References.*          Establishments primarily engaged in--

- Manufacturing electromedical and electrotherapeutic apparatus--are classified in U.S. Industry 334510, Electromedical and Electrotherapeutic Apparatus Manufacturing;
- Manufacturing irradiation apparatus--are classified in U.S. Industry 334517, Irradiation Apparatus Manufacturing;
- Manufacturing surgical (except dental) and orthopedic appliances or specialized hospital furniture (e.g., hospital beds, operating tables)--are classified in U.S. Industry 339113, Surgical Appliance and Supplies Manufacturing;
- Manufacturing dental equipment, dental supplies, dental laboratory apparatus, and dental laboratory furniture--are classified in U.S. Industry 339114, Dental Equipment and Supplies Manufacturing;
- Manufacturing general purpose hospital, laboratory, and/or dental furniture (e.g., stools, tables, benches)--are classified in U.S. Industry 337127, Institutional Furniture Manufacturing;
- Manufacturing thermometers (except medical)--are classified in U.S. Industry 334519, Other Measuring and Controlling Device Manufacturing; and
- Manufacturing ophthalmic goods--are classified in U.S. Industry 339115, Ophthalmic Goods Manufacturing.

## 339113  Surgical Appliance and Supplies Manufacturing

This U.S. industry comprises establishments primarily engaged in manufacturing surgical appliances and supplies. Examples of products made by these establishments are orthopedic devices, prosthetic appliances, surgical dressings, crutches, surgical sutures, personal industrial safety devices (except protective eyewear), hospital beds, and operating room tables.

*Cross-References.*          Establishments primarily engaged in--

- Manufacturing medical, surgical, ophthalmic, and veterinary instruments and apparatus (except electrotherapeutic, electromedical, and irradiation apparatus)--are classified in U.S. Industry 339112, Surgical and Medical Instrument Manufacturing;
- Manufacturing dental equipment, dental supplies, dental laboratory apparatus, and specialized dental laboratory furniture (e.g., dental chairs)--are classified in U.S. Industry 339114, Dental Equipment and Supplies Manufacturing;
- Manufacturing general purpose hospital, laboratory, and/or dental furniture (e.g., stools, tables, benches)--are classified in U.S. Industry 337127, Institutional Furniture Manufacturing;
- Manufacturing electronic hearing aids--are classified in U.S. Industry 334510, Electromedical and Electrotherapeutic Apparatus Manufacturing;
- Manufacturing industrial protective eyewear--are classified in U.S. Industry 339115, Ophthalmic Goods Manufacturing; and
- Manufacturing sporting goods helmets and protective equipment--are classified in Industry 339920, Sporting and Athletic Goods Manufacturing.

## 339114  Dental Equipment and Supplies Manufacturing

This U.S. industry comprises establishments primarily engaged in manufacturing dental equipment and supplies used by dental laboratories and offices of dentists, such as dental chairs, dental instrument delivery systems, dental hand instruments, dental impression material, and dental cements.

*Cross-References.*

Establishments primarily engaged in manufacturing dentures, crowns, bridges, and orthodontic appliances customized for individual application are classified in U.S. Industry 339116, Dental Laboratories.

---

T—Canadian, Mexican, and United States industries are comparable.

## 339115 Ophthalmic Goods Manufacturing

This U.S. industry comprises establishments primarily engaged in manufacturing ophthalmic goods. Examples of products made by these establishments are prescription eyeglasses (except grinding lenses in a retail setting), contact lenses, sunglasses, eyeglass frames, reading glasses made to standard powers, and protective eyewear.

*Cross-References.*        Establishments primarily engaged in--

- Manufacturing intraocular lenses--are classified in U.S. Industry 339113, Surgical Appliance and Supplies Manufacturing;
- Manufacturing molded glass lens blanks--are classified in U.S. Industry 327212, Other Pressed and Blown Glass and Glassware Manufacturing;
- Manufacturing molded plastics lens blanks--are classified in U.S. Industry 326199, All Other Plastics Product Manufacturing; and
- Retailing and grinding prescription eyeglasses--are classified in Industry 456130, Optical Goods Retailers.

## 339116 Dental Laboratories

This U.S. industry comprises establishments primarily engaged in manufacturing dentures, crowns, bridges, and orthodontic appliances customized for individual application.

*Cross-References.*

Establishments primarily engaged in manufacturing dental equipment and supplies are classified in U.S. Industry 339114, Dental Equipment and Supplies Manufacturing.

## 3399      Other Miscellaneous Manufacturing[T]

This industry group comprises establishments primarily engaged in miscellaneous manufacturing, such as jewelry and silverware manufacturing, sporting and athletic goods manufacturing, doll, toy, and game manufacturing, office supplies (except paper) manufacturing, sign manufacturing, and all other miscellaneous manufacturing.

## 33991   Jewelry and Silverware Manufacturing[T]
See industry description for 339910.

## 339910  Jewelry and Silverware Manufacturing

This industry comprises establishments primarily engaged in one or more of the following: (1) manufacturing, engraving, chasing, or etching fine and costume jewelry; (2) manufacturing, engraving, chasing, or etching metal personal goods (i.e., small articles carried on or about the person, such as compacts or cigarette cases); (3) manufacturing, engraving, chasing, or etching precious metal solid, precious metal clad, or pewter flatware and other hollowware; (4) stamping coins; (5) manufacturing unassembled jewelry parts and stock shop products, such as sheet, wire, and tubing; (6) cutting, slabbing, tumbling, carving, engraving, polishing, or faceting precious or semiprecious stones and gems; (7) recutting, repolishing, and setting gem stones; and (8) drilling, sawing, and peeling cultured and costume pearls. This industry includes establishments primarily engaged in manufacturing precious solid, precious clad, and precious plated jewelry and personal goods.

*Cross-References.*        Establishments primarily engaged in--

- Manufacturing nonprecious and precious plated metal cutlery and flatware--are classified in U.S. Industry 332215, Metal Kitchen Cookware, Utensil, Cutlery, and Flatware (except Precious) Manufacturing;
- Manufacturing nonprecious metal plated ware (except cutlery and flatware)--are classified in U.S. Industry 332999, All Other Miscellaneous Fabricated Metal Product Manufacturing;

---

T—Canadian, Mexican, and United States industries are comparable.

- Engraving, chasing, or etching nonprecious and precious plated metal cutlery, flatware, and other plated ware--are classified in U.S. Industry 332812, Metal Coating, Engraving (except Jewelry and Silverware), and Allied Services to Manufacturers;
- Plating jewelry--are classified in U.S. Industry 332813, Electroplating, Plating, Polishing, Anodizing, and Coloring;
- Manufacturing synthetic stones--are classified in U.S. Industry 327999, All Other Miscellaneous Nonmetallic Mineral Product Manufacturing; and
- Manufacturing personal goods (except metal) carried on or about the person, such as compacts and cigarette cases--are classified in Industry 316990, Other Leather and Allied Product Manufacturing.

**33992 Sporting and Athletic Goods Manufacturing**[T]
See industry description for 339920.

**339920 Sporting and Athletic Goods Manufacturing**

This industry comprises establishments primarily engaged in manufacturing sporting and athletic goods (except apparel and footwear).

*Cross-References.* Establishments primarily engaged in--

- Manufacturing athletic apparel--are classified in Subsector 315, Apparel Manufacturing;
- Manufacturing athletic footwear--are classified in Industry 316210, Footwear Manufacturing;
- Manufacturing small arms and small arms ammunition--are classified in Industry 33299, All Other Fabricated Metal Product Manufacturing;
- Manufacturing sleeping bags, backpacks, and tents from purchased fabrics--are classified in Industry Group 3149, Other Textile Product Mills;
- Manufacturing bicycles--are classified in U.S. Industry 336991, Motorcycle, Bicycle, and Parts Manufacturing; and
- Manufacturing boats (including heavy-duty inflatables)--are classified in U.S. Industry 336612, Boat Building.

**33993 Doll, Toy, and Game Manufacturing**[T]
See industry description for 339930.

**339930 Doll, Toy, and Game Manufacturing**

This industry comprises establishments primarily engaged in manufacturing complete dolls, doll parts, doll clothes, action figures, toys, games (including electronic, such as gaming consoles and devices and handheld video games), hobby kits, and children's vehicles (except metal bicycles and tricycles).

*Cross-References.* Establishments primarily engaged in--

- Manufacturing metal tricycles and bicycles--are classified in U.S. Industry 336991, Motorcycle, Bicycle, and Parts Manufacturing;
- Manufacturing sporting and athletic goods--are classified in Industry 339920, Sporting and Athletic Goods Manufacturing;
- Manufacturing coin- or card-operated game machines--are classified in U.S. Industry 339999, All Other Miscellaneous Manufacturing;
- Manufacturing electronic video game cartridges and reproducing video game software--are classified in Industry 334610, Manufacturing and Reproducing Magnetic and Optical Media; and
- Publishing or publishing and reproducing game software--are classified in Industry 513210, Software Publishers.

**33994 Office Supplies (except Paper) Manufacturing**[T]
See industry description for 339940.

---

T—Canadian, Mexican, and United States industries are comparable.

### 339940 Office Supplies (except Paper) Manufacturing

This industry comprises establishments primarily engaged in manufacturing office supplies. Examples of products made by these establishments are pens, pencils, felt tip markers, crayons, chalk, pencil sharpeners, staplers, modeling clay, hand operated stamps, stamp pads, stencils, carbon paper, and inked ribbons.

*Cross-References.*          Establishments primarily engaged in--

- Manufacturing writing and drawing inks--are classified in U.S. Industry 325998, All Other Miscellaneous Chemical Product and Preparation Manufacturing;
- Manufacturing rubber erasers--are classified in U.S. Industry 326299, All Other Rubber Product Manufacturing;
- Manufacturing paper office supplies--are classified in Subsector 322, Paper Manufacturing;
- Printing manifold business forms and manufacturing blankbooks, looseleaf binders, and looseleaf devices-- are classified in U.S. Industry 323111, Commercial Printing (except Screen and Books);
- Manufacturing drafting tables and boards--are classified in U.S. Industry 337127, Institutional Furniture Manufacturing; and
- Manufacturing inkjet and toner cartridges--are classified in Industry Group 3259, Other Chemical Product and Preparation Manufacturing.

### 33995 Sign Manufacturing[T]
See industry description for 339950.

### 339950 Sign Manufacturing

This industry comprises establishments primarily engaged in manufacturing signs and related displays of all materials (except printing paper and paperboard signs, notices, displays).

*Cross-References.*          Establishments primarily engaged in--

- Printing advertising specialties or printing paper and paperboard signs, notices, and displays--are classified in Industry 32311, Printing;
- Manufacturing and printing advertising specialties--are classified in the Manufacturing sector according to the products made;
- Manufacturing die-cut paperboard displays--are classified in U.S. Industry 322299, All Other Converted Paper Product Manufacturing; and
- Sign lettering and painting--are classified in Industry 541890, Other Services Related to Advertising.

### 33999 All Other Miscellaneous Manufacturing[T]

This industry comprises establishments primarily engaged in miscellaneous manufacturing (except medical equipment and supplies, jewelry and silverware, sporting and athletic goods, dolls, toys, games, office supplies, and signs).

*Illustrative Examples:*

Artificial Christmas trees manufacturing
Burial caskets and cases manufacturing
Candles manufacturing
Coin- or card-operated amusement machines (except jukebox) manufacturing
Electronic cigarettes manufacturing
Floor and dust mops manufacturing

Musical instruments (except toy) manufacturing
Fasteners, buttons, needles, and pins (except precious metals or precious and semiprecious stones and gems) manufacturing
Gasket, packing, and sealing devices manufacturing
Portable fire extinguishers manufacturing
Umbrellas manufacturing

---

T—Canadian, Mexican, and United States industries are comparable.

*Cross-References.*        Establishments primarily engaged in--

- Manufacturing medical equipment and supplies--are classified in Industry Group 3391, Medical Equipment and Supplies Manufacturing;
- Manufacturing jewelry and silverware--are classified in Industry 33991, Jewelry and Silverware Manufacturing;
- Manufacturing sporting and athletic goods--are classified in Industry 33992, Sporting and Athletic Goods Manufacturing;
- Manufacturing dolls, toys, and games--are classified in Industry 33993, Doll, Toy, and Game Manufacturing;
- Manufacturing office supplies (except paper)--are classified in Industry 33994, Office Supplies (except Paper) Manufacturing;
- Manufacturing signs--are classified in Industry 33995, Sign Manufacturing;
- Manufacturing concrete burial vaults--are classified in Industry 32739, Other Concrete Product Manufacturing;
- Manufacturing Christmas tree glass ornaments and glass lamp shades--are classified in Industry 32721, Glass and Glass Product Manufacturing;
- Manufacturing Christmas tree lighting sets--are classified in Industry 33513, Electric Lighting Equipment Manufacturing;
- Manufacturing beauty and barber chairs--are classified in Industry 33712, Household and Institutional Furniture Manufacturing;
- Manufacturing burnt wood articles--are classified in Industry 32199, All Other Wood Product Manufacturing;
- Dressing and bleaching furs--are classified in Industry 31611, Leather and Hide Tanning and Finishing;
- Manufacturing paper, textile, and metal lamp shades--are classified in Industry 33513, Electric Lighting Equipment Manufacturing;
- Manufacturing plastics lamp shades and other plastics products, such as plastics combs and hair curlers--are classified in Industry 32619, Other Plastics Product Manufacturing;
- Manufacturing metal products, such as metal combs and hair curlers--are classified in Industry 33299, All Other Fabricated Metal Product Manufacturing;
- Manufacturing electric hair clippers for use on humans--are classified in Industry 33521, Small Electrical Appliance Manufacturing;
- Manufacturing jukeboxes--are classified in Industry 33431, Audio and Video Equipment Manufacturing;
- Growing Christmas trees--are classified in Industry 11142, Nursery and Floriculture Production; and
- Manufacturing matches and electronic cigarette vapor liquids, including closed refills--are classified in Industry 32599, All Other Chemical Product and Preparation Manufacturing.

### 339991  Gasket, Packing, and Sealing Device Manufacturing

This U.S. industry comprises establishments primarily engaged in manufacturing gaskets, packing, and sealing devices of all materials.

### 339992  Musical Instrument Manufacturing

This U.S. industry comprises establishments primarily engaged in manufacturing musical instruments (except toys).

*Cross-References.*

Establishments primarily engaged in manufacturing toy musical instruments are classified in Industry 339930, Doll, Toy, and Game Manufacturing.

---

T—Canadian, Mexican, and United States industries are comparable.

## 339993  Fastener, Button, Needle, and Pin Manufacturing

This U.S. industry comprises establishments primarily engaged in manufacturing fasteners, buttons, needles, pins, and buckles (except made of precious metals or precious and semiprecious stones and gems).

*Cross-References.*          Establishments primarily engaged in--

- Manufacturing buttons, pins, and buckles made of precious metals or precious and semiprecious stones and gems--are classified in Industry 339910, Jewelry and Silverware Manufacturing;
- Manufacturing hypodermic and suture needles--are classified in U.S. Industry 339112, Surgical and Medical Instrument Manufacturing; and
- Manufacturing phonograph and styli needles--are classified in U.S. Industry 334419, Other Electronic Component Manufacturing.

## 339994  Broom, Brush, and Mop Manufacturing

This U.S. industry comprises establishments primarily engaged in manufacturing brooms, mops, and brushes.

## 339995  Burial Casket Manufacturing

This U.S. industry comprises establishments primarily engaged in manufacturing burial caskets, cases, and vaults (except concrete).

*Cross-References.*

Establishments primarily engaged in manufacturing concrete burial vaults are classified in Industry 327390, Other Concrete Product Manufacturing.

## 339999  All Other Miscellaneous Manufacturing

This U.S. industry comprises establishments primarily engaged in miscellaneous manufacturing (except medical equipment and supplies, jewelry and silverware, sporting and athletic goods, dolls, toys, games, office supplies, signs, gaskets, packing, and sealing devices, musical instruments, fasteners, buttons, needles, pins, brooms, brushes, mops, and burial caskets).

*Illustrative Examples:*

Artificial Christmas trees manufacturing
Candles manufacturing
Christmas tree ornaments (except glass and electric) manufacturing
Cigarette lighters (except precious metal) manufacturing
Coin- or card-operated amusement machines (except jukebox) manufacturing

Electronic cigarettes manufacturing
Hairpieces (e.g., wigs, toupees, wiglets) manufacturing
Portable fire extinguishers manufacturing
Potpourri manufacturing
Tobacco pipes manufacturing
Umbrellas manufacturing

*Cross-References.*          Establishments primarily engaged in--

- Manufacturing medical equipment and supplies--are classified in Industry Group 3391, Medical Equipment and Supplies Manufacturing;
- Manufacturing jewelry and silverware--are classified in Industry 339910, Jewelry and Silverware Manufacturing;
- Manufacturing sporting and athletic goods--are classified in Industry 339920, Sporting and Athletic Goods Manufacturing;

---

T—Canadian, Mexican, and United States industries are comparable.

- Manufacturing dolls, toys, and games--are classified in Industry 339930, Doll, Toy, and Game Manufacturing;
- Manufacturing office supplies (except paper)--are classified in Industry 339940, Office Supplies (except Paper) Manufacturing;
- Manufacturing signs--are classified in Industry 339950, Sign Manufacturing;
- Manufacturing gasket, packing, and sealing devices--are classified in U.S. Industry 339991, Gasket, Packing, and Sealing Device Manufacturing;
- Manufacturing musical instruments--are classified in U.S. Industry 339992, Musical Instrument Manufacturing;
- Manufacturing fasteners, buttons, needles, and pins--are classified in U.S. Industry 339993, Fastener, Button, Needle, and Pin Manufacturing;
- Manufacturing brooms, brushes, and mops--are classified in U.S. Industry 339994, Broom, Brush, and Mop Manufacturing;
- Manufacturing burial caskets--are classified in U.S. Industry 339995, Burial Casket Manufacturing;
- Manufacturing Christmas tree glass ornaments and glass lamp shades--are classified in U.S. Industry 327215, Glass Product Manufacturing Made of Purchased Glass;
- Manufacturing Christmas tree lighting sets--are classified in U.S. Industry 335139, Electric Lamp Bulb and Other Lighting Equipment Manufacturing;
- Manufacturing beauty and barber chairs--are classified in U.S. Industry 337127, Institutional Furniture Manufacturing;
- Manufacturing burnt wood articles--are classified in U.S. Industry 321999, All Other Miscellaneous Wood Product Manufacturing;
- Dressing and bleaching furs--are classified in Industry 316110, Leather and Hide Tanning and Finishing;
- Manufacturing paper, textile, and metal lamp shades--are classified in U.S. Industry 335131, Residential Electric Lighting Fixture Manufacturing;
- Manufacturing plastics lamp shades and other plastics products, such as plastics combs and hair curlers--are classified in U.S. Industry 326199, All Other Plastics Product Manufacturing;
- Manufacturing metal products, such as metal combs and hair curlers--are classified in U.S. Industry 332999, All Other Miscellaneous Fabricated Metal Product Manufacturing;
- Manufacturing electric hair clippers for use on humans--are classified in Industry 335210, Small Electrical Appliance Manufacturing;
- Manufacturing jukeboxes--are classified in Industry 334310, Audio and Video Equipment Manufacturing;
- Growing Christmas trees--are classified in U.S. Industry 111421, Nursery and Tree Production; and
- Manufacturing matches and electronic cigarette vapor liquids, including closed refills--are classified in U.S. Industry 325998, All Other Miscellaneous Chemical Product and Preparation Manufacturing.

T—Canadian, Mexican, and United States industries are comparable.

# Sector 42--Wholesale Trade[T]

## The Sector as a Whole

The Wholesale Trade sector comprises establishments engaged in wholesaling merchandise, generally without transformation, and rendering services incidental to the sale of merchandise. The merchandise described in this sector includes the outputs of agriculture, mining, manufacturing, and certain information industries, such as publishing.

The wholesaling process is an intermediate step in the distribution of merchandise. Wholesalers are organized to sell or arrange the purchase or sale of (a) goods for resale (i.e., goods sold to other wholesalers or retailers), (b) capital or durable nonconsumer goods, and (c) raw and intermediate materials and supplies used in production.

Wholesalers sell merchandise to other businesses and normally operate from a warehouse or office. These warehouses and offices are characterized by having little or no display of merchandise. In addition, neither the design nor the location of the premises is intended to solicit walk-in traffic. Wholesalers do not normally use advertising directed to the general public. Customers are generally reached initially via telephone, in-person marketing, or by specialized advertising that may include Internet and other electronic means. Follow-up orders are either vendor-initiated or client-initiated, generally based on previous sales, and typically exhibit strong ties between sellers and buyers. In fact, transactions are often conducted between wholesalers and clients that have long-standing business relationships.

This sector comprises two main types of wholesalers: merchant wholesalers that sell goods on their own account and agents and brokers that arrange sales and purchases for others generally for a commission or fee.

(1)  Establishments that sell goods on their own account are known as wholesale merchants, distributors, jobbers, drop shippers, and import/export merchants. Also included as wholesale merchants are sales offices and sales branches (but not retail stores) maintained by manufacturing, refining, or mining enterprises apart from their plants or mines for the purpose of marketing their products, and group purchasing organizations primarily purchasing and selling goods on their own account. Merchant wholesale establishments typically maintain their own warehouse, where they receive and handle goods for their customers. Goods are generally sold without transformation, but may include integral functions, such as sorting, packaging, labeling, and other marketing services.

(2)  Establishments arranging for the purchase or sale of goods owned by others or purchasing goods, generally on a commission basis are known as business-to-business electronic markets, agents and brokers, commission merchants, import/export agents and brokers, auction companies, group purchasing organizations (acting as agents), and manufacturers' representatives. These establishments operate from offices and generally do not own or handle the goods they sell.

Some wholesale establishments may be connected with a single manufacturer and promote and sell the particular manufacturer's products to a wide range of other wholesalers or retailers. Other wholesalers may be connected to a retail chain, or limited number of retail chains, and only provide a variety of products needed by that particular retail operation(s). These wholesalers may obtain the products from a wide range of manufacturers. Still other wholesalers may not take title to the goods, but act as agents and brokers for a commission.

Although, in general, wholesaling normally denotes sales in large volumes, durable nonconsumer goods may be sold in single units. Sales of capital or durable nonconsumer goods used in the production of goods and services, such as farm machinery, medium- and heavy-duty trucks, and industrial machinery, are always included in wholesale trade.

## 423    Merchant Wholesalers, Durable Goods

Industries in the Merchant Wholesalers, Durable Goods subsector sell capital or durable goods to other businesses. Merchant wholesalers generally take title to the goods that they sell; in other words, they buy and sell goods on their own account. Durable goods are new or used items generally with a normal life expectancy of three years or more. Durable goods merchant wholesale trade establishments are engaged in wholesaling products, such as motor vehicles, furniture, construction materials, machinery and equipment (including household-type appliances), metals and minerals (except petroleum), sporting goods, toys and hobby goods, recyclable materials, and parts.

Agents and brokers primarily engaged in wholesaling durable goods, generally on a commission or fee basis, are classified in Subsector 425, Wholesale Trade Agents and Brokers.

---

T—Canadian, Mexican, and United States industries are comparable.

**4231    Motor Vehicle and Motor Vehicle Parts and Supplies Merchant Wholesalers**

This industry group comprises establishments primarily engaged in the merchant wholesale distribution of automobiles and other motor vehicles, motor vehicle supplies, tires, and new and used parts.

**42311    Automobile and Other Motor Vehicle Merchant Wholesalers**
       See industry description for 423110.

**423110  Automobile and Other Motor Vehicle Merchant Wholesalers**

This industry comprises establishments primarily engaged in the merchant wholesale distribution of new and used passenger automobiles, trucks, trailers, and other motor vehicles, such as motorcycles, motor homes, and snowmobiles.

**42312    Motor Vehicle Supplies and New Parts Merchant Wholesalers**
       See industry description for 423120.

**423120  Motor Vehicle Supplies and New Parts Merchant Wholesalers**

This industry comprises establishments primarily engaged in the merchant wholesale distribution of motor vehicle supplies, accessories, tools, and equipment; and new motor vehicle parts (except new tires and tubes).

*Cross-References.*          Establishments primarily engaged in--

- Merchant wholesale distribution of new and/or used tires and tubes--are classified in Industry 423130, Tire and Tube Merchant Wholesalers;
- Merchant wholesale distribution of automotive chemicals (except lubricating oils and greases)--are classified in Industry 424690, Other Chemical and Allied Products Merchant Wholesalers;
- Merchant wholesale distribution of lubricating oils and greases--are classified in Industry 424720, Petroleum and Petroleum Products Merchant Wholesalers (except Bulk Stations and Terminals); and
- Merchant wholesale distribution of used motor vehicle parts--are classified in Industry 423140, Motor Vehicle Parts (Used) Merchant Wholesalers.

**42313    Tire and Tube Merchant Wholesalers**
       See industry description for 423130.

**423130  Tire and Tube Merchant Wholesalers**

This industry comprises establishments primarily engaged in the merchant wholesale distribution of new and/or used tires and tubes for passenger and commercial vehicles.

*Cross-References.*          Establishments primarily engaged in--

- Merchant wholesale distribution of other new automobile parts and accessories (including wheels)--are classified in Industry 423120, Motor Vehicle Supplies and New Parts Merchant Wholesalers;
- Merchant wholesale distribution of other used automobile parts and accessories--are classified in Industry 423140, Motor Vehicle Parts (Used) Merchant Wholesalers; and
- Retreading or rebuilding tires--are classified in U.S. Industry 326212, Tire Retreading.

**42314    Motor Vehicle Parts (Used) Merchant Wholesalers**
       See industry description for 423140.

---

T—Canadian, Mexican, and United States industries are comparable.

## 423140  Motor Vehicle Parts (Used) Merchant Wholesalers

This industry comprises establishments primarily engaged in the merchant wholesale distribution of used motor vehicle parts (except used tires and tubes) and establishments primarily engaged in dismantling motor vehicles for the purpose of selling the parts.

*Cross-References.*          Establishments primarily engaged in--

- Dismantling motor vehicles for the purpose of selling scrap--are classified in Industry 423930, Recyclable Material Merchant Wholesalers; and
- Merchant wholesale distribution of new and/or used tires and tubes--are classified in Industry 423130, Tire and Tube Merchant Wholesalers.

## 4232    Furniture and Home Furnishing Merchant Wholesalers

This industry group comprises establishments primarily engaged in the merchant wholesale distribution of furniture (except hospital beds, medical furniture, and drafting tables), home furnishings, and/or housewares.

## 42321   Furniture Merchant Wholesalers
See industry description for 423210.

## 423210  Furniture Merchant Wholesalers

This industry comprises establishments primarily engaged in the merchant wholesale distribution of furniture (except hospital beds, medical furniture, and drafting tables).

*Illustrative Examples*:

Household-type furniture merchant wholesalers
Outdoor furniture merchant wholesalers
Mattresses merchant wholesalers

Public building furniture merchant wholesalers
Office furniture merchant wholesalers
Religious furniture merchant wholesalers

*Cross-References.*          Establishments primarily engaged in--

- Merchant wholesale distribution of partitions, shelving, lockers, and store fixtures--are classified in Industry 423440, Other Commercial Equipment Merchant Wholesalers;
- Merchant wholesale distribution of hospital beds and medical furniture--are classified in Industry 423450, Medical, Dental, and Hospital Equipment and Supplies Merchant Wholesalers; and
- Merchant wholesale distribution of drafting tables--are classified in Industry 423490, Other Professional Equipment and Supplies Merchant Wholesalers.

## 42322   Home Furnishing Merchant Wholesalers
See industry description for 423220.

## 423220  Home Furnishing Merchant Wholesalers

This industry comprises establishments primarily engaged in the merchant wholesale distribution of home furnishings and/or housewares.

*Illustrative Examples:*

Carpet merchant wholesalers
Floor coverings (except wood flooring) merchant wholesalers
Glassware, household-type, merchant wholesalers

Chinaware, household-type, merchant wholesalers
Lamps (i.e., lighting fixtures) merchant wholesalers
Household-type cooking utensils merchant wholesalers

---

T—Canadian, Mexican, and United States industries are comparable.

| Curtains merchant wholesalers | Linens (e.g., bath, bed, table) merchant wholesalers |
| Draperies merchant wholesalers | Window shades and blinds merchant wholesalers |

*Cross-References.*        Establishments primarily engaged in--

- Merchant wholesale distribution of wood flooring--are classified in Industry 423310, Lumber, Plywood, Millwork, and Wood Panel Merchant Wholesalers;
- Merchant wholesale distribution of household-type gas and electric appliances (except water heaters and heating stoves (i.e., noncooking))--are classified in Industry 423620, Household Appliances, Electric Housewares, and Consumer Electronics Merchant Wholesalers;
- Merchant wholesale distribution of precious metal flatware--are classified in Industry 423940, Jewelry, Watch, Precious Stone, and Precious Metal Merchant Wholesalers; and
- Merchant wholesale distribution of disposable paper and plastics tableware and containers--are classified in Industry 424130, Industrial and Personal Service Paper Merchant Wholesalers.

## 4233    Lumber and Other Construction Materials Merchant Wholesalers

This industry group comprises establishments primarily engaged in the merchant wholesale distribution of lumber, plywood, millwork, and wood panels; brick, stone, and related construction materials; roofing, siding, and insulation materials; and other construction materials, including manufactured homes (i.e., mobile homes) and/or prefabricated buildings.

### 42331    Lumber, Plywood, Millwork, and Wood Panel Merchant Wholesalers
See industry description for 423310.

### 423310  Lumber, Plywood, Millwork, and Wood Panel Merchant Wholesalers

This industry comprises establishments primarily engaged in the merchant wholesale distribution of lumber; plywood; reconstituted wood fiber products; wood fencing; doors and windows and their frames (all materials); wood roofing and siding; and/or other wood or metal millwork.

*Cross-References.*        Establishments primarily engaged in--

- Merchant wholesale distribution of nonwood roofing and siding materials--are classified in Industry 423330, Roofing, Siding, and Insulation Material Merchant Wholesalers;
- Merchant wholesale distribution of timber and timber products, such as railroad ties, logs, firewood, and pulpwood--are classified in Industry 423990, Other Miscellaneous Durable Goods Merchant Wholesalers; and
- Installing doors and windows--are classified in Subsector 238, Specialty Trade Contractors.

### 42332    Brick, Stone, and Related Construction Material Merchant Wholesalers
See industry description for 423320.

### 423320  Brick, Stone, and Related Construction Material Merchant Wholesalers

This industry comprises establishments primarily engaged in the merchant wholesale distribution of stone, cement, lime, construction sand, and gravel; brick; asphalt and concrete mixtures; and/or concrete, stone, and structural clay products.

*Cross-References.*        Establishments primarily engaged in--

- Merchant wholesale distribution of refractory brick and other refractory products or industrial sand--are classified in Industry 423840, Industrial Supplies Merchant Wholesalers;
- Selling ready-mix concrete--are classified in Industry 327320, Ready-Mix Concrete Manufacturing; and

---

T—Canadian, Mexican, and United States industries are comparable.

- Quarrying, dredging, and/or beneficiating construction sand and gravel--are classified in U.S. Industry 212321, Construction Sand and Gravel Mining.

## 42333 Roofing, Siding, and Insulation Material Merchant Wholesalers
See industry description for 423330.

## 423330 Roofing, Siding, and Insulation Material Merchant Wholesalers

This industry comprises establishments primarily engaged in the merchant wholesale distribution of nonwood roofing and nonwood siding and insulation materials.

*Cross-References.*

Establishments primarily engaged in the merchant wholesale distribution of wood roofing and wood siding are classified in Industry 423310, Lumber, Plywood, Millwork, and Wood Panel Merchant Wholesalers.

## 42339 Other Construction Material Merchant Wholesalers
See industry description for 423390.

## 423390 Other Construction Material Merchant Wholesalers

This industry comprises (1) establishments primarily engaged in the merchant wholesale distribution of manufactured homes (i.e., mobile homes) and/or prefabricated buildings and (2) establishments primarily engaged in the merchant wholesale distribution of construction materials (except lumber, plywood, millwork, wood panels, brick, stone, roofing, siding, electrical and wiring supplies, and insulation materials).

*Illustrative Examples:*

Flat glass merchant wholesalers
Prefabricated buildings (except wood) merchant wholesalers
Ornamental ironwork merchant wholesalers

Fencing and fencing accessories (except wood) merchant wholesalers
Plate glass merchant wholesalers
Storage bins merchant wholesalers

*Cross-References.*     Establishments primarily engaged in--

- Merchant wholesale distribution of products of the primary metals industries--are classified in Industry 423510, Metal Service Centers and Other Metal Merchant Wholesalers;
- Merchant wholesale distribution of lumber; plywood; reconstituted wood fiber products; wood fencing; doors, windows, and their frames; wood roofing and wood siding; and other wood or metal millwork--are classified in Industry 423310, Lumber, Plywood, Millwork, and Wood Panel Merchant Wholesalers;
- Merchant wholesale distribution of stone, cement, lime, construction sand and gravel; brick; asphalt and concrete mixtures (except ready-mix concrete); and/or concrete, stone, and structural clay products--are classified in Industry 423320, Brick, Stone, and Related Construction Material Merchant Wholesalers;
- Merchant wholesale distribution of nonwood roofing and nonwood siding and insulation materials--are classified in Industry 423330, Roofing, Siding, and Insulation Material Merchant Wholesalers;
- Merchant wholesale distribution of electrical supplies and wiring supplies--are classified in Industry 423610, Electrical Apparatus and Equipment, Wiring Supplies, and Related Equipment Merchant Wholesalers; and
- Selling ready-mix concrete--are classified in Industry 327320, Ready-Mix Concrete Manufacturing.

## 4234 Professional and Commercial Equipment and Supplies Merchant Wholesalers

This industry group comprises establishments primarily engaged in the merchant wholesale distribution of photographic equipment and supplies; office, computer, and computer peripheral equipment; and medical, dental, hospital, ophthalmic, and other commercial and professional equipment and supplies.

---

T—Canadian, Mexican, and United States industries are comparable.

**42341  Photographic Equipment and Supplies Merchant Wholesalers**
See industry description for 423410.

**423410  Photographic Equipment and Supplies Merchant Wholesalers**

This industry comprises establishments primarily engaged in the merchant wholesale distribution of photographic equipment and supplies (except office equipment).

*Illustrative Examples:*

Photofinishing equipment merchant wholesalers
Television cameras merchant wholesalers
Photographic camera equipment and supplies merchant wholesalers

Video cameras (except household-type) merchant wholesalers
Photographic film and plates merchant wholesalers

*Cross-References.*          Establishments primarily engaged in--

- Merchant wholesale distribution of household-type video cameras--are classified in Industry 423620, Household Appliances, Electric Housewares, and Consumer Electronics Merchant Wholesalers;
- Merchant wholesale distribution of office equipment, such as photocopy and microfilm equipment--are classified in Industry 423420, Office Equipment Merchant Wholesalers; and
- Selling video security systems and providing system installation, repair, or monitoring services (except closed-circuit (CCTV))--are classified in U.S. Industry 561621, Security Systems Services (except Locksmiths).

**42342  Office Equipment Merchant Wholesalers**
See industry description for 423420.

**423420  Office Equipment Merchant Wholesalers**

This industry comprises establishments primarily engaged in the merchant wholesale distribution of office machines and related equipment (except computers and computer peripheral equipment).

*Illustrative Examples:*

Automated teller machines (ATM) merchant wholesalers
Calculators and calculating machines merchant wholesalers
Cash registers merchant wholesalers

Security safes merchant wholesalers
Copying machines merchant wholesalers
Point of sale terminals merchant wholesalers
Paper shredders merchant wholesalers

*Cross-References.*          Establishments primarily engaged in--

- Merchant wholesale distribution of office furniture--are classified in Industry 423210, Furniture Merchant Wholesalers;
- Merchant wholesale distribution of computers and computer peripheral equipment (including printers)--are classified in Industry 423430, Computer and Computer Peripheral Equipment and Software Merchant Wholesalers;
- Merchant wholesale distribution of office supplies--are classified in Industry 424120, Stationery and Office Supplies Merchant Wholesalers; and
- Merchant wholesale distribution of facsimile (fax) machines, modems, and communications equipment--are classified in Industry 423690, Other Electronic Parts and Equipment Merchant Wholesalers.

**42343  Computer and Computer Peripheral Equipment and Software Merchant Wholesalers**
See industry description for 423430.

T—Canadian, Mexican, and United States industries are comparable.

**423430 Computer and Computer Peripheral Equipment and Software Merchant Wholesalers**

This industry comprises establishments primarily engaged in the merchant wholesale distribution of computers, computer peripheral equipment, loaded computer boards, and/or computer software.

*Cross-References.*        Establishments primarily engaged in--

- Merchant wholesale distribution of modems, routers, printed circuit boards, semiconductor devices, and other electronic communications equipment--are classified in Industry 423690, Other Electronic Parts and Equipment Merchant Wholesalers; and
- Selling, planning, and designing computer systems that integrate computer hardware, software, and communication technologies--are classified in U.S. Industry 541512, Computer Systems Design Services.

**42344    Other Commercial Equipment Merchant Wholesalers**
See industry description for 423440.

**423440  Other Commercial Equipment Merchant Wholesalers**

This industry comprises establishments primarily engaged in the merchant wholesale distribution of commercial and related machines and equipment (except photographic equipment and supplies; office equipment; and computers and computer peripheral equipment and software) generally used in restaurants and stores.

*Illustrative Examples:*

Balances and scales (except laboratory) merchant wholesalers
Commercial shelving merchant wholesalers
Coin- or card-operated merchandising machine merchant wholesalers
Electrical signs merchant wholesalers

Commercial chinaware merchant wholesalers
Partitions merchant wholesalers
Commercial cooking equipment merchant wholesalers
Store fixtures (except refrigerated) merchant wholesalers

*Cross-References.*        Establishments primarily engaged in--

- Merchant wholesale distribution of photographic equipment and supplies--are classified in Industry 423410, Photographic Equipment and Supplies Merchant Wholesalers;
- Merchant wholesale distribution of office machines and related equipment--are classified in Industry 423420, Office Equipment Merchant Wholesalers;
- Merchant wholesale distribution of computers, computer peripheral equipment, and packaged computer software--are classified in Industry 423430, Computer and Computer Peripheral Equipment and Software Merchant Wholesalers;
- Merchant wholesale distribution of laboratory scales and balances (except medical and dental)--are classified in Industry 423490, Other Professional Equipment and Supplies Merchant Wholesalers; and
- Merchant wholesale distribution of refrigerated store fixtures--are classified in Industry 423740, Refrigeration Equipment and Supplies Merchant Wholesalers.

**42345    Medical, Dental, and Hospital Equipment and Supplies Merchant Wholesalers**
See industry description for 423450.

**423450  Medical, Dental, and Hospital Equipment and Supplies Merchant Wholesalers**

This industry comprises establishments primarily engaged in the merchant wholesale distribution of professional medical equipment, instruments, and supplies (except ophthalmic equipment and instruments and goods used by ophthalmologists, optometrists, and opticians).

T—Canadian, Mexican, and United States industries are comparable.

*Illustrative Examples*:

Dental equipment and supplies merchant wholesalers
Surgical dressings merchant wholesalers
Electromedical equipment merchant wholesalers
Patient monitoring equipment merchant wholesalers
Hospital beds merchant wholesalers
Prosthetic appliances and supplies merchant wholesalers
Hospital furniture merchant wholesalers

Surgical instruments and apparatus merchant wholesalers
Medical and dental X-ray machines and parts merchant wholesalers
First-aid kits (except household) merchant wholesalers
Surgical and medical masks merchant wholesalers

*Cross-References.*        Establishments primarily engaged in--

- Merchant wholesale distribution of professional equipment, instruments, and/or goods sold, prescribed, or used by ophthalmologists, optometrists, and opticians--are classified in Industry 423460, Ophthalmic Goods Merchant Wholesalers;
- Merchant wholesale distribution of personal safety devices and supplies (e.g., eye shields, face shields, nonelectric respirators)--are classified in Industry 423990, Other Miscellaneous Durable Goods Merchant Wholesalers; and
- Merchant wholesale distribution of household first-aid kits and nonsurgical bandages--are classified in Industry 424210, Drugs and Druggists' Sundries Merchant Wholesalers.

**42346   Ophthalmic Goods Merchant Wholesalers**
See industry description for 423460.

**423460  Ophthalmic Goods Merchant Wholesalers**

This industry comprises establishments primarily engaged in the merchant wholesale distribution of professional equipment, instruments, and/or goods sold, prescribed, or used by ophthalmologists, optometrists, and opticians.

*Illustrative Examples:*

Binoculars merchant wholesalers
Optometric equipment and supplies merchant wholesalers

Ophthalmic frames merchant wholesalers
Sunglasses merchant wholesalers
Ophthalmic lenses merchant wholesalers

**42349   Other Professional Equipment and Supplies Merchant Wholesalers**
See industry description for 423490.

**423490  Other Professional Equipment and Supplies Merchant Wholesalers**

This industry comprises establishments primarily engaged in the merchant wholesale distribution of professional equipment and supplies (except ophthalmic goods and medical, dental, and hospital equipment and supplies).

*Illustrative Examples*:

Church supplies (except silverware, plated ware) merchant wholesalers
School equipment and supplies (except books, furniture) merchant wholesalers
Drafting tables and instruments merchant wholesalers

Scientific instruments merchant wholesalers
Laboratory equipment (except medical, dental) merchant wholesalers
Surveying equipment and supplies merchant wholesalers

---

T—Canadian, Mexican, and United States industries are comparable.

*Cross-References.*        Establishments primarily engaged in--

- Merchant wholesale distribution of professional equipment, instruments, and/or goods sold, prescribed, or used by ophthalmologists, optometrists, and opticians, such as ophthalmic frames and lenses, and sunglasses--are classified in Industry 423460, Ophthalmic Goods Merchant Wholesalers;
- Merchant wholesale distribution of professional medical equipment, instruments, and supplies used by medical and dental practitioners (except ophthalmic equipment, instruments, and goods used by ophthalmologists, optometrists, and opticians) and medical facilities--are classified in Industry 423450, Medical, Dental, and Hospital Equipment and Supplies Merchant Wholesalers;
- Merchant wholesale distribution of silverware and plated flatware--are classified in Industry 423940, Jewelry, Watch, Precious Stone, and Precious Metal Merchant Wholesalers;
- Merchant wholesale distribution of books--are classified in Industry 424920, Book, Periodical, and Newspaper Merchant Wholesalers; and
- Merchant wholesale distribution of school furniture--are classified in Industry 423210, Furniture Merchant Wholesalers.

## 4235    Metal and Mineral (except Petroleum) Merchant Wholesalers

This industry group comprises establishments primarily engaged in the merchant wholesale distribution of products of the primary metals industries (including metal service centers) and coal, coke, metal ores, and/or nonmetallic minerals (except precious and semiprecious stones and minerals used in construction).

## 42351    Metal Service Centers and Other Metal Merchant Wholesalers
See industry description for 423510.

## 423510    Metal Service Centers and Other Metal Merchant Wholesalers

This industry comprises establishments primarily engaged in the merchant wholesale distribution of products of the primary metals industries.  Service centers maintain inventory and may perform functions, such as sawing, shearing, bending, leveling, cleaning, or edging, on a custom basis as part of sales transactions.

*Illustrative Examples:*

| | |
|---|---|
| Cast iron pipe merchant wholesalers | Metal ingots (except precious) merchant wholesalers |
| Metal rods merchant wholesalers | Metal pipe merchant wholesalers |
| Metal bars (except precious) merchant wholesalers | Nails merchant wholesalers |
| Metal sheets merchant wholesalers | Metal plates merchant wholesalers |
| Metal spikes merchant wholesalers | Noninsulated wire merchant wholesalers |

*Cross-References.*        Establishments primarily engaged in--

- Merchant wholesale distribution of gold, silver, and platinum--are classified in Industry 423940, Jewelry, Watch, Precious Stone, and Precious Metal Merchant Wholesalers;
- Merchant wholesale distribution of automotive, industrial, and other recyclable metal scrap--are classified in Industry 423930, Recyclable Material Merchant Wholesalers; and
- Merchant wholesale distribution of insulated wire--are classified in Industry 423610, Electrical Apparatus and Equipment, Wiring Supplies, and Related Equipment Merchant Wholesalers.

## 42352    Coal and Other Mineral and Ore Merchant Wholesalers
See industry description for 423520.

---

T—Canadian, Mexican, and United States industries are comparable.

**423520  Coal and Other Mineral and Ore Merchant Wholesalers**

This industry comprises establishments primarily engaged in the merchant wholesale distribution of coal, coke, metal ores, and/or nonmetallic minerals (except precious and semiprecious stones and minerals used in construction, such as sand and gravel).

*Cross-References.*           Establishments primarily engaged in--

- Merchant wholesale distribution of nonmetallic minerals used in construction, such as sand and gravel--are classified in Industry 423320, Brick, Stone, and Related Construction Material Merchant Wholesalers;
- Merchant wholesale distribution of industrial sand--are classified in Industry 423840, Industrial Supplies Merchant Wholesalers;
- Merchant wholesale distribution of crude petroleum--are classified in Industry Group 4247, Petroleum and Petroleum Products Merchant Wholesalers;
- Merchant wholesale distribution of precious and semiprecious stones and metals--are classified in Industry 423940, Jewelry, Watch, Precious Stone, and Precious Metal Merchant Wholesalers; and
- Quarrying, dredging, and/or beneficiating construction sand and gravel--are classified in U.S. Industry 212321, Construction Sand and Gravel Mining.

**4236    Household Appliances and Electrical and Electronic Goods Merchant Wholesalers**

This industry group comprises establishments primarily engaged in the merchant wholesale distribution of electrical apparatus and equipment, wiring supplies, and related equipment; household appliances, electric housewares, and consumer electronics; and other electronic parts and equipment.

**42361    Electrical Apparatus and Equipment, Wiring Supplies, and Related Equipment Merchant Wholesalers**
See industry description for 423610.

**423610  Electrical Apparatus and Equipment, Wiring Supplies, and Related Equipment Merchant Wholesalers**

This industry comprises establishments primarily engaged in the merchant wholesale distribution of electrical construction materials; wiring supplies; electric light fixtures; light bulbs; and/or electrical power equipment for the generation, transmission, distribution, or control of electric energy.

**42362    Household Appliances, Electric Housewares, and Consumer Electronics Merchant Wholesalers**
See industry description for 423620.

**423620  Household Appliances, Electric Housewares, and Consumer Electronics Merchant Wholesalers**

This industry comprises establishments primarily engaged in the merchant wholesale distribution of household-type gas and electric appliances (except water heaters and heating stoves (i.e., noncooking)), room air-conditioners, and/or household-type audio or video equipment.

*Illustrative Examples:*

Household-type sewing machines merchant wholesalers

Household-type radios (including automotive) merchant wholesalers

Household-type video cameras merchant wholesalers

Household-type refrigerators merchant wholesalers

Television sets merchant wholesalers

Toothbrushes, electric, merchant wholesalers

Curling irons, electric, merchant wholesalers

---

T—Canadian, Mexican, and United States industries are comparable.

*Cross-References.*    Establishments primarily engaged in--

- Merchant wholesale distribution of gas and electric water heaters and heating stoves (i.e., noncooking)--are classified in Industry 423720, Plumbing and Heating Equipment and Supplies (Hydronics) Merchant Wholesalers;
- Merchant wholesale distribution of warm air heating and air-conditioning equipment (except room units)--are classified in Industry 423730, Warm Air Heating and Air-Conditioning Equipment and Supplies Merchant Wholesalers;
- Selling and installing warm air heating and air-conditioning equipment--are classified in Industry 238220, Plumbing, Heating, and Air-Conditioning Contractors;
- Merchant wholesale distribution of nonhousehold-type video cameras--are classified in Industry 423410, Photographic Equipment and Supplies Merchant Wholesalers; and
- Selling video security systems and providing system installation, repair, or monitoring services (except closed-circuit (CCTV))--are classified in U.S. Industry 561621, Security Systems Services (except Locksmiths).

## 42369    Other Electronic Parts and Equipment Merchant Wholesalers
See industry description for 423690.

## 423690    Other Electronic Parts and Equipment Merchant Wholesalers

This industry comprises establishments primarily engaged in the merchant wholesale distribution of electronic parts and equipment (except electrical apparatus and equipment, wiring supplies, and construction materials; electrical and electronic appliances; and television sets and radios).

*Illustrative Examples:*

Blank compact discs (CDs) merchant wholesalers
Blank digital video discs (DVDs) merchant wholesalers
Broadcasting equipment merchant wholesalers
Cellular telephones merchant wholesalers

Communications equipment merchant wholesalers
Modems and routers merchant wholesalers
Radar equipment merchant wholesalers
Teleconferencing equipment merchant wholesalers
Unloaded computer boards merchant wholesalers

*Cross-References.*    Establishments primarily engaged in--

- Merchant wholesale distribution of household-type gas and electric appliances (except water heaters and heating stoves (i.e., noncooking)), room air-conditioners, clothes dryers, and/or household-type audio or video equipment--are classified in Industry 423620, Household Appliances, Electric Housewares, and Consumer Electronics Merchant Wholesalers;
- Merchant wholesale distribution of computers, computer peripheral equipment, and loaded computer boards--are classified in Industry 423430, Computer and Computer Peripheral Equipment and Software Merchant Wholesalers; and
- Merchant wholesale distribution of electrical construction materials, wiring supplies, electric light fixtures, light bulbs, and/or electrical power equipment for generation, transmission, distribution, or control of electric energy--are classified in Industry 423610, Electrical Apparatus and Equipment, Wiring Supplies, and Related Equipment Merchant Wholesalers.

## 4237    Hardware, and Plumbing and Heating Equipment and Supplies Merchant Wholesalers

This industry group comprises establishments primarily engaged in the merchant wholesale distribution of hardware; plumbing and heating equipment and supplies (hydronics); warm air heating and air-conditioning equipment and supplies; and refrigeration equipment and supplies.

## 42371    Hardware Merchant Wholesalers
See industry description for 423710.

---

T—Canadian, Mexican, and United States industries are comparable.

**423710  Hardware Merchant Wholesalers**

This industry comprises establishments primarily engaged in the merchant wholesale distribution of hardware, knives, or handtools.

*Illustrative Examples:*

Brads merchant wholesalers
Cutlery merchant wholesalers
Knives (except disposable plastics) merchant wholesalers
Power handtools (e.g., drills, saws, sanders) merchant wholesalers
Fasteners (e.g., bolts, nuts, rivets, screws) merchant wholesalers

Staples merchant wholesalers
Handtools (except motor vehicle, machinists' precision) merchant wholesalers
Hardware (except motor vehicle) merchant wholesalers
Tacks merchant wholesalers
Keys and locks merchant wholesalers

*Cross-References.*      Establishments primarily engaged in--

- Merchant wholesale distribution of nails, noninsulated wire, and screening--are classified in Industry 423510, Metal Service Centers and Other Metal Merchant Wholesalers;
- Merchant wholesale distribution of motor vehicle handtools, hardware, and equipment--are classified in Industry 423120, Motor Vehicle Supplies and New Parts Merchant Wholesalers;
- Merchant wholesale distribution of machinists' precision handtools--are classified in Industry 423830, Industrial Machinery and Equipment Merchant Wholesalers; and
- Merchant wholesale distribution of disposable plastics knives and eating utensils--are classified in Industry 424130, Industrial and Personal Service Paper Merchant Wholesalers.

**42372  Plumbing and Heating Equipment and Supplies (Hydronics) Merchant Wholesalers**
See industry description for 423720.

**423720  Plumbing and Heating Equipment and Supplies (Hydronics) Merchant Wholesalers**

This industry comprises establishments primarily engaged in the merchant wholesale distribution of plumbing equipment, hydronic heating equipment, household-type water heaters, and/or supplies.

*Cross-References.*      Establishments primarily engaged in--

- Selling and installing plumbing, heating, and air-conditioning equipment--are classified in Industry 238220, Plumbing, Heating, and Air-Conditioning Contractors;
- Merchant wholesale distribution of warm air heating and air-conditioning equipment--are lclassified in Industry 423730, Warm Air Heating and Air-Conditioning Equipment and Supplies Merchant Wholesalers; and
- Merchant wholesale distribution of household-type gas and electric appliances (except water heaters and heating stoves (i.e., noncooking)), room air-conditioners, clothes dryers, and/or household-type audio or video equipment--are classified in Industry 423620, Household Appliances, Electric Housewares, and Consumer Electronics Merchant Wholesalers.

**42373  Warm Air Heating and Air-Conditioning Equipment and Supplies Merchant Wholesalers**
See industry description for 423730.

**423730  Warm Air Heating and Air-Conditioning Equipment and Supplies Merchant Wholesalers**

This industry comprises establishments primarily engaged in the merchant wholesale distribution of warm air heating and air-conditioning equipment and supplies.

T—Canadian, Mexican, and United States industries are comparable.

*Illustrative Examples:*

Air pollution control equipment and supplies merchant wholesalers

Nonportable electric baseboard heaters merchant wholesalers

Air-conditioning equipment (except room units) merchant wholesalers

Warm air central heating equipment merchant wholesalers

Automotive air-conditioners merchant wholesalers

Ductless heating and air-conditioning system equipment merchant wholesalers

*Cross-References.*          Establishments primarily engaged in--

- Merchant wholesale distribution of household-type gas and electric appliances (except water heaters and heating stoves (i.e., noncooking)) and room air-conditioners--are classified in Industry 423620, Household Appliances, Electric Housewares, and Consumer Electronics Merchant Wholesalers;
- Merchant wholesale distribution of hydronic heating equipment--are classified in Industry 423720, Plumbing and Heating Equipment and Supplies (Hydronics) Merchant Wholesalers;
- Merchant wholesale distribution of commercial-type refrigeration equipment--are classified in Industry 423740, Refrigeration Equipment and Supplies Merchant Wholesalers;
- Merchant wholesale distribution of refrigerants--are classified in Industry 424690, Other Chemical and Allied Products Merchant Wholesalers; and
- Selling and installing warm air heating and air-conditioning equipment--are classified in Industry 238220, Plumbing, Heating, and Air-Conditioning Contractors.

## 42374    Refrigeration Equipment and Supplies Merchant Wholesalers
See industry description for 423740.

## 423740   Refrigeration Equipment and Supplies Merchant Wholesalers

This industry comprises establishments primarily engaged in the merchant wholesale distribution of refrigeration equipment (except household-type refrigerators, freezers, and air-conditioners).

*Illustrative Examples:*

Cold storage machinery merchant wholesalers

Refrigerated display cases merchant wholesalers

Commercial refrigerators merchant wholesalers

Water coolers merchant wholesalers

*Cross-References.*          Establishments primarily engaged in--

- Merchant wholesale distribution of household-type refrigerators, freezers, and room air-conditioners--are classified in Industry 423620, Household Appliances, Electric Housewares, and Consumer Electronics Merchant Wholesalers;
- Merchant wholesale distribution of air-conditioning equipment (except room units)--are classified in Industry 423730, Warm Air Heating and Air-Conditioning Equipment and Supplies Merchant Wholesalers;
- Merchant wholesale distribution of refrigerants--are classified in Industry 424690, Other Chemical and Allied Products Merchant Wholesalers; and
- Repairing and maintaining commercial refrigeration equipment--are classified in Industry 811310, Commercial and Industrial Machinery and Equipment (except Automotive and Electronic) Repair and Maintenance.

## 4238    Machinery, Equipment, and Supplies Merchant Wholesalers

This industry group comprises establishments primarily engaged in the merchant wholesale distribution of construction, mining, farm, garden, industrial, service establishment, and transportation machinery, equipment, and supplies.

---

T—Canadian, Mexican, and United States industries are comparable.

**42381 Construction and Mining (except Oil Well) Machinery and Equipment Merchant Wholesalers**
See industry description for 423810.

**423810 Construction and Mining (except Oil Well) Machinery and Equipment Merchant Wholesalers**

This industry comprises establishments primarily engaged in the merchant wholesale distribution of specialized machinery, equipment, and related parts generally used in construction, mining (except oil well), and logging activities.

*Illustrative Examples:*

Excavating machinery and equipment merchant wholesalers

Road construction and maintenance machinery merchant wholesalers

Forestry machinery and equipment merchant wholesalers

Scaffolding merchant wholesalers

Mining cranes merchant wholesalers

*Cross-References.*

Establishments primarily engaged in the merchant wholesale distribution of oil well machinery and equipment are classified in Industry 423830, Industrial Machinery and Equipment Merchant Wholesalers.

**42382 Farm and Garden Machinery and Equipment Merchant Wholesalers**
See industry description for 423820.

**423820 Farm and Garden Machinery and Equipment Merchant Wholesalers**

This industry comprises establishments primarily engaged in the merchant wholesale distribution of specialized machinery, equipment, and related parts generally used in agricultural, farm, and lawn and garden activities.

*Illustrative Examples:*

Animal feeders merchant wholesalers

Lawnmowers merchant wholesalers

Milking machinery and equipment merchant wholesalers

Harvesting machinery and equipment merchant wholesalers

Planting machinery and equipment merchant wholesalers

**42383 Industrial Machinery and Equipment Merchant Wholesalers**
See industry description for 423830.

**423830 Industrial Machinery and Equipment Merchant Wholesalers**

This industry comprises establishments primarily engaged in the merchant wholesale distribution of specialized machinery, equipment, and related parts generally used in manufacturing, oil well, and warehousing activities.

*Illustrative Examples:*

Fluid power transmission equipment merchant wholesalers

Metalworking machinery and equipment merchant wholesalers

Food processing machinery and equipment merchant wholesalers

Oil well machinery and equipment merchant wholesalers

Material handling machinery and equipment merchant wholesalers

---

T—Canadian, Mexican, and United States industries are comparable.

*Cross-References.*          Establishments primarily engaged in--

- Merchant wholesale distribution of specialized machinery, equipment, and related parts generally used in construction, mining (except oil well), and logging activities--are classified in Industry 423810, Construction and Mining (except Oil Well) Machinery and Equipment Merchant Wholesalers; and
- Merchant wholesale distribution of supplies used in machinery and equipment generally used in manufacturing, oil well, and warehousing activities--are classified in Industry 423840, Industrial Supplies Merchant Wholesalers.

## 42384    Industrial Supplies Merchant Wholesalers
See industry description for 423840.

## 423840    Industrial Supplies Merchant Wholesalers

This industry comprises establishments primarily engaged in the merchant wholesale distribution of supplies for machinery and equipment generally used in manufacturing, oil well, and warehousing activities.

*Illustrative Examples:*

Industrial containers merchant wholesalers
Industrial diamonds merchant wholesalers
Printing inks merchant wholesalers
Industrial sand merchant wholesalers

Refractory materials (e.g., brick, blocks, shapes) merchant wholesalers
Welding supplies (except welding gases) merchant wholesalers

*Cross-References.*          Establishments primarily engaged in--

- Merchant wholesale distribution of hydraulic and pneumatic (fluid power) pumps, motors, pistons, and valves--are classified in Industry 423830, Industrial Machinery and Equipment Merchant Wholesalers; and
- Merchant wholesale distribution of welding gases and other industrial gases--are classified in Industry 424690, Other Chemical and Allied Products Merchant Wholesalers.

## 42385    Service Establishment Equipment and Supplies Merchant Wholesalers
See industry description for 423850.

## 423850    Service Establishment Equipment and Supplies Merchant Wholesalers

This industry comprises establishments primarily engaged in the merchant wholesale distribution of specialized equipment and supplies of the type used by service establishments (except specialized equipment and supplies used in offices, stores, hotels, restaurants, schools, health and medical facilities, photographic facilities, and specialized equipment used in transportation and construction activities).

*Illustrative Examples:*

Amusement park equipment merchant wholesalers
Beauty parlor equipment and supplies merchant wholesalers
Car wash equipment and supplies merchant wholesalers
Drycleaning equipment and supplies merchant wholesalers
Voting machines merchant wholesalers

Janitorial equipment and supplies merchant wholesalers
Undertakers' equipment and supplies merchant wholesalers
Upholsterers' equipment and supplies (except fabrics) merchant wholesalers
Water treatment equipment, municipal, merchant wholesalers

---

T—Canadian, Mexican, and United States industries are comparable.

*Cross-References.*          Establishments primarily engaged in--

- Merchant wholesale distribution of janitorial and automotive chemicals--are classified in Industry 424690, Other Chemical and Allied Products Merchant Wholesalers;
- Merchant wholesale distribution of piece goods, fabrics, knitting yarns (except industrial), thread and other notions--are classified in Industry 424310, Piece Goods, Notions, and Other Dry Goods Merchant Wholesalers;
- Merchant wholesale distribution of industrial yarns--are classified in Industry 424990, Other Miscellaneous Nondurable Goods Merchant Wholesalers;
- Merchant wholesale distribution of plumbing and hydronic heating equipment--are classified in Industry 423720, Plumbing and Heating Equipment and Supplies (Hydronics) Merchant Wholesalers; and
- Merchant wholesale distribution of grave markers, monuments, and tombstones--are classified in Industry 423990, Other Miscellaneous Durable Goods Merchant Wholesalers.

**42386    Transportation Equipment and Supplies (except Motor Vehicle) Merchant Wholesalers**
See industry description for 423860.

**423860   Transportation Equipment and Supplies (except Motor Vehicle) Merchant Wholesalers**

  This industry comprises establishments primarily engaged in the merchant wholesale distribution of transportation equipment and supplies (except marine pleasure craft and motor vehicles).

*Illustrative Examples:*

Aircraft merchant wholesalers                          Motorized passenger golf carts merchant wholesalers
Railroad cars merchant wholesalers                 Boats (except pleasure) merchant wholesalers
Ships merchant wholesalers

*Cross-References.*          Establishments primarily engaged in--

- Merchant wholesale distribution of motor vehicles and motor vehicle parts--are classified in Industry Group 4231, Motor Vehicle and Motor Vehicle Parts and Supplies Merchant Wholesalers; and
- Merchant wholesale distribution of marine pleasure craft--are classified in Industry 423910, Sporting and Recreational Goods and Supplies Merchant Wholesalers.

**4239    Miscellaneous Durable Goods Merchant Wholesalers**

  This industry group comprises establishments primarily engaged in the merchant wholesale distribution of sporting, recreational, toy, hobby, and jewelry goods and supplies, and precious stones and metals.

**42391    Sporting and Recreational Goods and Supplies Merchant Wholesalers**
See industry description for 423910.

**423910   Sporting and Recreational Goods and Supplies Merchant Wholesalers**

  This industry comprises establishments primarily engaged in the merchant wholesale distribution of sporting goods and accessories; billiard and pool supplies; sporting firearms and ammunition; and/or marine pleasure craft, equipment, and supplies.

*Cross-References.*          Establishments primarily engaged in--

- Merchant wholesale distribution of motor vehicles and trailers--are classified in Industry 423110, Automobile and Other Motor Vehicle Merchant Wholesalers;
- Merchant wholesale distribution of motorized passenger golf carts--are classified in Industry 423860, Transportation Equipment and Supplies (except Motor Vehicle) Merchant Wholesalers; and

---

T—Canadian, Mexican, and United States industries are comparable.

- Merchant wholesale distribution of athletic apparel (except athletic uniforms) and athletic footwear (except specialty athletic footwear, such as golf shoes, bowling shoes, and cleated footwear)--are classified in Industry Group 4243, Apparel, Piece Goods, and Notions Merchant Wholesalers.

## 42392 Toy and Hobby Goods and Supplies Merchant Wholesalers
See industry description for 423920.

## 423920 Toy and Hobby Goods and Supplies Merchant Wholesalers

This industry comprises establishments primarily engaged in the merchant wholesale distribution of games, toys, fireworks, playing cards, hobby goods and supplies, and/or related goods.

## 42393 Recyclable Material Merchant Wholesalers
See industry description for 423930.

## 423930 Recyclable Material Merchant Wholesalers

This industry comprises establishments primarily engaged in the merchant wholesale distribution of automotive scrap, industrial scrap, and other recyclable materials. Included in this industry are auto wreckers primarily engaged in dismantling motor vehicles for the purpose of wholesaling scrap.

*Cross-References.*     Establishments primarily engaged in--

- Dismantling motor vehicles for the purpose of selling used parts--are classified in Industry 423140, Motor Vehicle Parts (Used) Merchant Wholesalers; and
- Operating facilities where commingled recyclable materials, such as paper, plastics, used beverage cans, and metals, are sorted into distinct categories--are classified in Industry 562920, Materials Recovery Facilities.

## 42394 Jewelry, Watch, Precious Stone, and Precious Metal Merchant Wholesalers
See industry description for 423940.

## 423940 Jewelry, Watch, Precious Stone, and Precious Metal Merchant Wholesalers

This industry comprises establishments primarily engaged in the merchant wholesale distribution of jewelry, precious and semiprecious stones, precious metals and metal flatware, costume jewelry, watches, clocks, silverware, and/or jewelers' findings.

*Cross-References.*     Establishments primarily engaged in--

- Merchant wholesale distribution of precious metal ores or concentrates--are classified in Industry 423520, Coal and Other Mineral and Ore Merchant Wholesalers; and
- Merchant wholesale distribution of nonprecious flatware--are classified in Industry 423220, Home Furnishing Merchant Wholesalers.

## 42399 Other Miscellaneous Durable Goods Merchant Wholesalers
See industry description for 423990.

## 423990 Other Miscellaneous Durable Goods Merchant Wholesalers

This industry comprises establishments primarily engaged in the merchant wholesale distribution of durable goods (except motor vehicles and motor vehicle parts and supplies; furniture and home furnishings; lumber and other construction materials; professional and commercial equipment and supplies; metals and minerals (except petroleum); electrical goods; hardware, and plumbing and heating equipment and supplies; machinery, equipment,

---

T—Canadian, Mexican, and United States industries are comparable.

and supplies; sporting and recreational goods and supplies; toy and hobby goods and supplies; recyclable materials; and jewelry, watches, precious stones, and precious metals).

*Illustrative Examples:*

Firearms (except sporting) merchant wholesalers
Musical instruments merchant wholesalers
Luggage merchant wholesalers
Monuments and grave markers merchant wholesalers
Prerecorded compact discs (CDs) and digital video discs (DVDs) merchant wholesalers

Timber and timber products (except lumber) merchant wholesalers
Personal safety devices and supplies (e.g., eye shields, face shields, nonelectric respirators) merchant wholesalers
Signs (except electrical) merchant wholesalers

*Cross-References.*          Establishments primarily engaged in--

- Merchant wholesale distribution of automobiles and other motor vehicles, motor vehicle supplies, tires, and new and used parts--are classified in Industry Group 4231, Motor Vehicle and Motor Vehicle Parts and Supplies Merchant Wholesalers;
- Merchant wholesale distribution of furniture and home furnishings--are classified in Industry Group 4232, Furniture and Home Furnishing Merchant Wholesalers;
- Merchant wholesale distribution of lumber, plywood, millwork, wood panels, brick, stone, roofing, siding, and other nonelectrical construction materials--are classified in Industry Group 4233, Lumber and Other Construction Materials Merchant Wholesalers;
- Merchant wholesale distribution of photographic, office, computer and computer peripheral, medical, dental, hospital, ophthalmic, and other commercial and professional equipment and supplies--are classified in Industry Group 4234, Professional and Commercial Equipment and Supplies Merchant Wholesalers;
- Merchant wholesale distribution of coal and other minerals and ores and semi-finished metal products--are classified in Industry Group 4235, Metal and Mineral (except Petroleum) Merchant Wholesalers;
- Merchant wholesale distribution of household appliances and electrical goods--are classified in Industry Group 4236, Household Appliances and Electrical and Electronic Goods Merchant Wholesalers;
- Merchant wholesale distribution of hardware; and plumbing, heating, air-conditioning, and refrigeration equipment and supplies--are classified in Industry Group 4237, Hardware, and Plumbing and Heating Equipment and Supplies Merchant Wholesalers;
- Merchant wholesale distribution of construction, mining, farm, garden, industrial, service establishment, and transportation machinery, equipment, and supplies--are classified in Industry Group 4238, Machinery, Equipment, and Supplies Merchant Wholesalers;
- Merchant wholesale distribution of sporting goods and accessories; billiard and pool supplies; sporting firearms and ammunition; and/or marine pleasure craft, equipment, and supplies--are classified in Industry 423910, Sporting and Recreational Goods and Supplies Merchant Wholesalers;
- Merchant wholesale distribution of toys, fireworks, playing cards, hobby goods and supplies and/or related goods--are classified in Industry 423920, Toy and Hobby Goods and Supplies Merchant Wholesalers;
- Merchant wholesale distribution of automotive, industrial, and other recyclable materials--are classified in Industry 423930, Recyclable Material Merchant Wholesalers;
- Merchant wholesale distribution of jewelry, precious and semiprecious stones, precious metals and metal flatware, costume jewelry, watches, clocks, silverware, and/or jewelers' findings--are classified in Industry 423940, Jewelry, Watch, Precious Stone, and Precious Metal Merchant Wholesalers;
- Merchant wholesale distribution of electrical signs--are classified in Industry 423440, Other Commercial Equipment Merchant Wholesalers; and
- Selling and installing fire suppression systems and fire extinguishers--are classified in Industry 238220, Plumbing, Heating, and Air-Conditioning Contractors.

## 424     Merchant Wholesalers, Nondurable Goods

Industries in the Merchant Wholesalers, Nondurable Goods subsector sell nondurable goods to other businesses. Nondurable goods are items generally with a normal life expectancy of less than three years. Nondurable goods merchant wholesale trade establishments are engaged in wholesaling products, such as paper and paper products,

---

T—Canadian, Mexican, and United States industries are comparable.

chemicals and chemical products, drugs, textiles and textile products, apparel, footwear, groceries, farm products, petroleum and petroleum products, alcoholic beverages, books, magazines, newspapers, flowers and nursery stock, and tobacco products.

The detailed industries within the subsector are organized in the classification structure based on the products sold.

Agents and brokers primarily engaged in wholesaling nondurable goods, generally on a commission or fee basis, are classified in Subsector 425, Wholesale Trade Agents and Brokers.

## 4241 Paper and Paper Product Merchant Wholesalers

This industry group comprises establishments primarily engaged in the merchant wholesale distribution of bulk printing and writing paper; stationery and office supplies; and industrial and personal service paper.

### 42411 Printing and Writing Paper Merchant Wholesalers
See industry description for 424110.

### 424110 Printing and Writing Paper Merchant Wholesalers

This industry comprises establishments primarily engaged in the merchant wholesale distribution of bulk printing and/or writing paper generally on rolls for further processing.

*Illustrative Examples*:

Bulk envelope paper merchant wholesalers
Bulk paper (e.g., fine, printing, writing) merchant wholesalers

Bulk groundwood paper merchant wholesalers
Newsprint merchant wholesalers

*Cross-References*.

Establishments primarily engaged in the merchant wholesale distribution of stationery and office paper (e.g., printer, copier) are classified in Industry 424120, Stationery and Office Supplies Merchant Wholesalers.

### 42412 Stationery and Office Supplies Merchant Wholesalers
See industry description for 424120.

### 424120 Stationery and Office Supplies Merchant Wholesalers

This industry comprises establishments primarily engaged in the merchant wholesale distribution of stationery, office supplies, and/or gift wrap.

*Illustrative Examples:*

Photocopy supplies merchant wholesalers
Envelopes merchant wholesalers
Social stationery merchant wholesalers
File cards and folders merchant wholesalers
Greeting cards merchant wholesalers

Office paper (e.g., printer, copier) merchant wholesalers
Writing pens merchant wholesalers
Pencils merchant wholesalers

*Cross-References*.

Establishments primarily engaged in the merchant wholesale distribution of bulk printing and/or writing paper are classified in Industry 424110, Printing and Writing Paper Merchant Wholesalers.

### 42413 Industrial and Personal Service Paper Merchant Wholesalers
See industry description for 424130.

---

T—Canadian, Mexican, and United States industries are comparable.

**424130  Industrial and Personal Service Paper Merchant Wholesalers**

This industry comprises establishments primarily engaged in the merchant wholesale distribution of kraft wrapping and other coarse paper, paperboard, converted paper (except stationery and office supplies), and/or related disposable plastics products.

*Illustrative Examples:*

Corrugated paper merchant wholesalers
Paper and disposable plastics tableware (e.g., utensils, dishes, cups) merchant wholesalers
Paper napkins merchant wholesalers
Paperboard and disposable plastics boxes and containers merchant wholesalers
Plastics bags merchant wholesalers
Paper and disposable plastics shipping supplies merchant wholesalers

Paper towels merchant wholesalers
Paper bags merchant wholesalers
Sanitary paper products merchant wholesalers
Wrapping paper (except gift wrap) merchant wholesalers
Waxed paper merchant wholesalers
Plastics foam products, disposable (except packaging, packing), merchant wholesalers

*Cross-References.*          Establishments primarily engaged in--

- Merchant wholesale distribution of stationery, office supplies, and/or gift wrap--are classified in Industry 424120, Stationery and Office Supplies Merchant Wholesalers; and
- Merchant wholesale distribution of plastics foam packing and packaging materials--are classified in Industry 423840, Industrial Supplies Merchant Wholesalers.

**4242     Drugs and Druggists' Sundries Merchant Wholesalers**

**42421    Drugs and Druggists' Sundries Merchant Wholesalers**
          See industry description for 424210.

**424210  Drugs and Druggists' Sundries Merchant Wholesalers**

This industry comprises establishments primarily engaged in the merchant wholesale distribution of biological and medical products; botanical drugs and herbs; and pharmaceutical products intended for internal and/or external consumption in such forms as ampoules, tablets, capsules, vials, ointments, powders, solutions, and suspensions.

*Illustrative Examples:*

Antibiotics merchant wholesalers
Endocrine substances merchant wholesalers
Blood derivatives merchant wholesalers
In-vitro and in-vivo diagnostics merchant wholesalers
Drugs merchant wholesalers

Botanicals merchant wholesalers
Vaccines merchant wholesalers
Cosmetics merchant wholesalers
Vitamins merchant wholesalers
Veterinarians' medicines merchant wholesalers

*Cross-References.*

Establishments primarily engaged in the merchant wholesale distribution of surgical, dental, and hospital equipment are classified in Industry 423450, Medical, Dental, and Hospital Equipment and Supplies Merchant Wholesalers.

**4243     Apparel, Piece Goods, and Notions Merchant Wholesalers**

This industry group comprises establishments primarily engaged in the merchant wholesale distribution of piece goods, notions, and other dry goods; footwear; and clothing and clothing accessories.

---

T—Canadian, Mexican, and United States industries are comparable.

**42431 Piece Goods, Notions, and Other Dry Goods Merchant Wholesalers**
See industry description for 424310.

**424310 Piece Goods, Notions, and Other Dry Goods Merchant Wholesalers**

This industry comprises establishments primarily engaged in the merchant wholesale distribution of piece goods, fabrics, knitting yarns (except industrial), thread and other notions, and/or hair accessories.

*Cross-References.*

- Establishments primarily engaged as converters who buy fabric goods in the grey, have them finished on a contract basis, and sell at wholesale are classified in Industry 313310, Textile and Fabric Finishing Mills; and
- Establishments primarily engaged in merchant wholesale distribution of industrial yarns are classified in Industry 424990, Other Miscellaneous Nondurable Goods Merchant Wholesalers.

**42434 Footwear Merchant Wholesalers**
See industry description for 424340.

**424340 Footwear Merchant Wholesalers**

This industry comprises establishments primarily engaged in the merchant wholesale distribution of footwear of leather, rubber, and other materials, including athletic footwear (except specialty athletic footwear).

*Cross-References.*

Establishments primarily engaged in the merchant wholesale distribution of specialty athletic footwear, such as golf shoes, bowling shoes, and cleated footwear, are classified in Industry 423910, Sporting and Recreational Goods and Supplies Merchant Wholesalers.

**42435 Clothing and Clothing Accessories Merchant Wholesalers**
See industry description for 424350.

**424350 Clothing and Clothing Accessories Merchant Wholesalers**

This industry comprises establishments primarily engaged in the merchant wholesale distribution of clothing and clothing accessories.

*Illustrative Examples:*

| | |
|---|---|
| Baby bottles merchant wholesalers | Lingerie merchant wholesalers |
| Diapers (except disposable) merchant wholesalers | Millinery merchant wholesalers |
| Dresses merchant wholesalers | Nightwear merchant wholesalers |
| Fur clothing merchant wholesalers | Outerwear merchant wholesalers |
| Handbags merchant wholesalers | Sportswear merchant wholesalers |
| Hosiery merchant wholesalers | Swimwear merchant wholesalers |

*Cross-References.*

Establishments primarily engaged in the merchant wholesale distribution of footwear are classified in Industry 424340, Footwear Merchant Wholesalers.

---

T—Canadian, Mexican, and United States industries are comparable.

## 4244    Grocery and Related Product Merchant Wholesalers

This industry group comprises establishments primarily engaged in the merchant wholesale distribution of (1) a general line of groceries; (2) packaged frozen food; (3) dairy products; (4) poultry and poultry products; (5) confectioneries; (6) fish and seafood; (7) meats and meat products; (8) fresh fruits and vegetables; and (9) other grocery and related products.

### 42441    General Line Grocery Merchant Wholesalers
See industry description for 424410.

### 424410  General Line Grocery Merchant Wholesalers

This industry comprises establishments primarily engaged in the merchant wholesale distribution of a general line (wide range) of groceries.

*Cross-References.*

Establishments primarily engaged in the merchant wholesale distribution of a specialized line of groceries are classified elsewhere in Sector 42, Wholesale Trade, according to the product sold.

### 42442    Packaged Frozen Food Merchant Wholesalers
See industry description for 424420.

### 424420  Packaged Frozen Food Merchant Wholesalers

This industry comprises establishments primarily engaged in the merchant wholesale distribution of packaged frozen foods (except dairy products).

*Illustrative Examples:*

| | |
|---|---|
| Frozen bakery products merchant wholesalers | Packaged frozen meats merchant wholesalers |
| Packaged frozen fish merchant wholesalers | Frozen vegetables merchant wholesalers |
| Frozen juices merchant wholesalers | Packaged frozen poultry merchant wholesalers |

*Cross-References.*

Establishments primarily engaged in the merchant wholesale distribution of frozen dairy products are classified in Industry 424430, Dairy Product (except Dried or Canned) Merchant Wholesalers.

### 42443    Dairy Product (except Dried or Canned) Merchant Wholesalers
See industry description for 424430.

### 424430  Dairy Product (except Dried or Canned) Merchant Wholesalers

This industry comprises establishments primarily engaged in the merchant wholesale distribution of dairy products (except dried or canned).

*Illustrative Examples:*

| | |
|---|---|
| Butter merchant wholesalers | Ice cream and ices merchant wholesalers |
| Fluid milk (except canned) merchant wholesalers | Cream merchant wholesalers |
| Cheese merchant wholesalers | Yogurt merchant wholesalers |

---

T—Canadian, Mexican, and United States industries are comparable.

*Cross-References.*        Establishments primarily engaged in--

- Merchant wholesale distribution of dried or canned dairy products and dairy substitutes--are classified in Industry 424490, Other Grocery and Related Products Merchant Wholesalers; and
- Pasteurizing and bottling milk--are classified in U.S. Industry 311511, Fluid Milk Manufacturing.

## 42444   Poultry and Poultry Product Merchant Wholesalers
See industry description for 424440.

## 424440   Poultry and Poultry Product Merchant Wholesalers

This industry comprises establishments primarily engaged in the merchant wholesale distribution of poultry and/or poultry products (except canned and packaged frozen).

*Cross-References.*        Establishments primarily engaged in--

- Merchant wholesale distribution of packaged frozen poultry--are classified in Industry 424420, Packaged Frozen Food Merchant Wholesalers;
- Merchant wholesale distribution of canned poultry--are classified in Industry 424490, Other Grocery and Related Products Merchant Wholesalers;
- Merchant wholesale distribution of live chicks--are classified in Industry 424590, Other Farm Product Raw Material Merchant Wholesalers; and
- Slaughtering and dressing poultry--are classified in U.S. Industry 311615, Poultry Processing.

## 42445   Confectionery Merchant Wholesalers
See industry description for 424450.

## 424450   Confectionery Merchant Wholesalers

This industry comprises establishments primarily engaged in the merchant wholesale distribution of confectioneries; salted or roasted nuts; popcorn; potato, corn, and similar chips; and/or fountain fruits and syrups.

*Cross-References.*        Establishments primarily engaged in--

- Merchant wholesale distribution of frozen pretzels--are classified in Industry 424420, Packaged Frozen Food Merchant Wholesalers;
- Merchant wholesale distribution of pretzels (except frozen) or soft drinks--are classified in Industry 424490, Other Grocery and Related Products Merchant Wholesalers; and
- Manufacturing and bottling soft drinks--are classified in U.S. Industry 312111, Soft Drink Manufacturing.

## 42446   Fish and Seafood Merchant Wholesalers
See industry description for 424460.

## 424460   Fish and Seafood Merchant Wholesalers

This industry comprises establishments primarily engaged in the merchant wholesale distribution of fish and seafood (except canned or packaged frozen).

*Cross-References.*        Establishments primarily engaged in--

- Merchant wholesale distribution of packaged frozen fish and seafood--are classified in Industry 424420, Packaged Frozen Food Merchant Wholesalers;
- Merchant wholesale distribution of canned fish and seafood--are classified in Industry 424490, Other Grocery and Related Products Merchant Wholesalers; and

---

T—Canadian, Mexican, and United States industries are comparable.

- Canning, smoking, salting, drying, or freezing seafood and shucking and packing fresh shellfish--are classified in Industry 311710, Seafood Product Preparation and Packaging.

### 42447   Meat and Meat Product Merchant Wholesalers
See industry description for 424470.

### 424470   Meat and Meat Product Merchant Wholesalers

This industry comprises establishments primarily engaged in the merchant wholesale distribution of meats and meat products (except canned and packaged frozen) and/or lard.

*Cross-References.*          Establishments primarily engaged in--

- Merchant wholesale distribution of packaged frozen meats--are classified in Industry 424420, Packaged Frozen Food Merchant Wholesalers;
- Merchant wholesale distribution of canned meats--are classified in Industry 424490, Other Grocery and Related Products Merchant Wholesalers;
- Preparing boxed beef from purchased carcasses--are classified in U.S. Industry 311612, Meat Processed from Carcasses;
- Merchant wholesale distribution of poultry and/or poultry products (except canned and packaged frozen)--are classified in Industry 424440, Poultry and Poultry Product Merchant Wholesalers; and
- Merchant wholesale distribution of fish and seafood (except canned and packaged frozen)--are classified in Industry 424460, Fish and Seafood Merchant Wholesalers.

### 42448   Fresh Fruit and Vegetable Merchant Wholesalers
See industry description for 424480.

### 424480   Fresh Fruit and Vegetable Merchant Wholesalers

This industry comprises establishments primarily engaged in the merchant wholesale distribution of fresh fruits and vegetables.

### 42449   Other Grocery and Related Products Merchant Wholesalers
See industry description for 424490.

### 424490   Other Grocery and Related Products Merchant Wholesalers

This industry comprises establishments primarily engaged in the merchant wholesale distribution of groceries and related products (except a general line of groceries; packaged frozen food; dairy products (except dried and canned); poultry products (except canned); confectioneries; fish and seafood (except canned); meat products (except canned); and fresh fruits and vegetables). Included in this industry are establishments primarily engaged in the bottling and merchant wholesale distribution of spring and mineral waters processed by others.

*Illustrative Examples:*

| | |
|---|---|
| Bakery products (except frozen) merchant wholesalers | Canned fruits merchant wholesalers |
| | Dried milk merchant wholesalers |
| Canned seafood merchant wholesalers | Canned meats merchant wholesalers |
| Canned fish merchant wholesalers | Soft drinks merchant wholesalers |
| Canned vegetables merchant wholesalers | Canned milk merchant wholesalers |

*Cross-References.*          Establishments primarily engaged in--

- Merchant wholesale distribution of grains, field beans, livestock, and other farm product raw materials--are classified in Industry Group 4245, Farm Product Raw Material Merchant Wholesalers;

---

T—Canadian, Mexican, and United States industries are comparable.

- Merchant wholesale distribution of beer, wine, and distilled alcoholic beverages--are classified in Industry Group 4248, Beer, Wine, and Distilled Alcoholic Beverage Merchant Wholesalers;
- Manufacturing and bottling soft drinks--are classified in U.S. Industry 312111, Soft Drink Manufacturing;
- Merchant wholesale distribution of a general line of groceries--are classified in Industry 424410, General Line Grocery Merchant Wholesalers;
- Merchant wholesale distribution of packaged frozen foods (except dairy)--are classified in Industry 424420, Packaged Frozen Food Merchant Wholesalers;
- Merchant wholesale distribution of dairy products--are classified in Industry 424430, Dairy Product (except Dried or Canned) Merchant Wholesalers;
- Merchant wholesale distribution of poultry and poultry products (except canned and packaged frozen)--are classified in Industry 424440, Poultry and Poultry Product Merchant Wholesalers;
- Merchant wholesale distribution of confectioneries; salted or roasted nuts; popcorn; potato, corn, and similar chips; and/or fountain fruits and syrups--are classified in Industry 424450, Confectionery Merchant Wholesalers;
- Merchant wholesale distribution of fish and seafood (except canned and packaged frozen)--are classified in Industry 424460, Fish and Seafood Merchant Wholesalers;
- Merchant wholesale distribution of meats (except canned and packaged frozen)--are classified in Industry 424470, Meat and Meat Product Merchant Wholesalers;
- Merchant wholesale distribution of fresh fruits and vegetables--are classified in Industry 424480, Fresh Fruit and Vegetable Merchant Wholesalers;
- Purifying and bottling water--are classified in U.S. Industry 312112, Bottled Water Manufacturing; and
- Roasting coffee--are classified in Industry 311920, Coffee and Tea Manufacturing.

## 4245 Farm Product Raw Material Merchant Wholesalers

This industry group comprises establishments primarily engaged in the merchant wholesale distribution of agricultural products (except raw milk, live poultry, and fresh fruits and vegetables), such as grains, field beans, livestock, and other farm product raw materials (excluding seeds).

## 42451 Grain and Field Bean Merchant Wholesalers
See industry description for 424510.

## 424510 Grain and Field Bean Merchant Wholesalers

This industry comprises establishments primarily engaged in the merchant wholesale distribution of grains, such as corn, wheat, oats, barley, and unpolished rice; dry beans; and soybeans and other inedible beans. Included in this industry are establishments primarily engaged in operating country or terminal grain elevators primarily for the purpose of wholesaling.

*Cross-References.* Establishments primarily engaged in--

- Merchant wholesale distribution of field and garden seeds--are classified in Industry 424910, Farm Supplies Merchant Wholesalers; and
- Operating grain elevators for storage only--are classified in Industry 493130, Farm Product Warehousing and Storage.

## 42452 Livestock Merchant Wholesalers
See industry description for 424520.

## 424520 Livestock Merchant Wholesalers

This industry comprises establishments primarily engaged in the merchant wholesale distribution of livestock (except horses and mules).

---

T—Canadian, Mexican, and United States industries are comparable.

*Illustrative Examples:*

Cattle merchant wholesalers
Hogs merchant wholesalers

Goats merchant wholesalers
Sheep merchant wholesalers

*Cross-References.*

Establishments primarily engaged in the merchant wholesale distribution of horses and mules are classified in Industry 424590, Other Farm Product Raw Material Merchant Wholesalers.

**42459 Other Farm Product Raw Material Merchant Wholesalers**
See industry description for 424590.

**424590 Other Farm Product Raw Material Merchant Wholesalers**

This industry comprises establishments primarily engaged in the merchant wholesale distribution of farm products (except grain and field beans, livestock, raw milk, live poultry, and fresh fruits and vegetables).

*Illustrative Examples:*

Chicks, live, merchant wholesalers
Hemp merchant wholesalers
Mules merchant wholesalers
Hides merchant wholesalers
Raw cotton merchant wholesalers
Horses merchant wholesalers

Nuts, unprocessed or shelled only, merchant wholesalers
Raw pelts merchant wholesalers
Leaf tobacco merchant wholesalers
Sod merchant wholesalers

*Cross-References.* Establishments primarily engaged in--

- Merchant wholesale distribution of raw milk--are classified in Industry 424430, Dairy Product (except Dried or Canned) Merchant Wholesalers;
- Merchant wholesale distribution of live poultry (except chicks)--are classified in Industry 424440, Poultry and Poultry Product Merchant Wholesalers;
- Merchant wholesale distribution of grain, dry beans, and soybeans and other inedible beans--are classified in Industry 424510, Grain and Field Bean Merchant Wholesalers;
- Merchant wholesale distribution of livestock (except horses and mules), such as cattle, hogs, sheep, and goats--are classified in Industry 424520, Livestock Merchant Wholesalers;
- Merchant wholesale distribution of fresh fruits and vegetables--are classified in Industry 424480, Fresh Fruit and Vegetable Merchant Wholesalers; and
- Merchant wholesale distribution of leaf tobacco that also engage in stemming tobacco--are classified in Industry 424940, Tobacco Product and Electronic Cigarette Merchant Wholesalers.

**4246 Chemical and Allied Products Merchant Wholesalers**

This industry group comprises establishments primarily engaged in the merchant wholesale distribution of chemicals, plastics materials and basic forms and shapes, and allied products.

**42461 Plastics Materials and Basic Forms and Shapes Merchant Wholesalers**
See industry description for 424610.

**424610 Plastics Materials and Basic Forms and Shapes Merchant Wholesalers**

This industry comprises establishments primarily engaged in the merchant wholesale distribution of plastics materials and resins, and unsupported plastics film, sheet, sheeting, rod, tube, and other basic forms and shapes.

---

T—Canadian, Mexican, and United States industries are comparable.

**42469    Other Chemical and Allied Products Merchant Wholesalers**
See industry description for 424690.

**424690    Other Chemical and Allied Products Merchant Wholesalers**

This industry comprises establishments primarily engaged in the merchant wholesale distribution of chemicals and allied products (except agricultural and medicinal chemicals, paints and varnishes, fireworks, and plastics materials and basic forms and shapes).

*Illustrative Examples:*

Acids merchant wholesalers
Industrial chemicals merchant wholesalers
Automotive chemicals (except lubricating oils and greases) merchant wholesalers
Industrial salts merchant wholesalers

Dyestuffs merchant wholesalers
Rosins merchant wholesalers
Explosives (except ammunition and fireworks) merchant wholesalers
Turpentine merchant wholesalers

*Cross-References.*          Establishments primarily engaged in--

- Merchant wholesale distribution of ammunition--are classified in Industry Group 4239, Miscellaneous Durable Goods Merchant Wholesalers;
- Merchant wholesale distribution of biological and medical products; botanical drugs and herbs; and pharmaceutical products intended for internal and external consumption in such forms as ampoules, tablets, capsules, vials, ointments, powders, solutions, and suspensions--are classified in Industry 424210, Drugs and Druggists' Sundries Merchant Wholesalers;
- Merchant wholesale distribution of farm supplies, such as animal feeds, fertilizers, agricultural chemicals, pesticides, seeds, and plant bulbs--are classified in Industry 424910, Farm Supplies Merchant Wholesalers;
- Merchant wholesale distribution of paints, varnishes, and similar coatings, pigments, wallpaper, and supplies, such as paintbrushes and rollers--are classified in Industry 424950, Paint, Varnish, and Supplies Merchant Wholesalers;
- Merchant wholesale distribution of lubricating oils and greases--are classified in Industry 424720, Petroleum and Petroleum Products Merchant Wholesalers (except Bulk Stations and Terminals);
- Merchant wholesale distribution of fireworks--are classified in Industry 423920, Toy and Hobby Goods and Supplies Merchant Wholesalers; and
- Merchant wholesale distribution of plastics materials and resins, and unsupported plastics film, sheet, sheeting, rod, tube, and other basic forms and shapes--are classified in Industry 424610, Plastics Materials and Basic Forms and Shapes Merchant Wholesalers.

**4247    Petroleum and Petroleum Products Merchant Wholesalers**

This industry group comprises establishments primarily engaged in the merchant wholesale distribution of petroleum and petroleum products, including liquefied petroleum gas.

**42471    Petroleum Bulk Stations and Terminals**
See industry description for 424710.

**424710    Petroleum Bulk Stations and Terminals**

This industry comprises establishments with bulk liquid storage facilities primarily engaged in the merchant wholesale distribution of crude petroleum and petroleum products, including liquefied petroleum gas.

*Cross-References.*

Establishments primarily engaged in bulk storage of petroleum are classified in Industry 493190, Other Warehousing and Storage.

---

T—Canadian, Mexican, and United States industries are comparable.

**42472   Petroleum and Petroleum Products Merchant Wholesalers (except Bulk Stations and Terminals)**
See industry description for 424720.

**424720   Petroleum and Petroleum Products Merchant Wholesalers (except Bulk Stations and Terminals)**

This industry comprises establishments primarily engaged in the merchant wholesale distribution of petroleum and petroleum products (except from bulk liquid storage facilities).

*Illustrative Examples:*

Gasoline merchant wholesalers (except bulk stations, terminals)
Lubricating oil and grease merchant wholesalers (except bulk stations, terminals)

Bottled liquid petroleum gas merchant wholesalers
Fuel oil merchant wholesalers (except bulk stations, terminals)

*Cross-References.*          Establishments primarily engaged in--

- Merchant wholesale distribution of crude petroleum and petroleum products from bulk liquid storage facilities--are classified in Industry 424710, Petroleum Bulk Stations and Terminals; and
- Fueling aircraft on a contract or fee basis--are classified in Industry 488190, Other Support Activities for Air Transportation.

**4248   Beer, Wine, and Distilled Alcoholic Beverage Merchant Wholesalers**

This industry group comprises establishments primarily engaged in the merchant wholesale distribution of beer, ale, wine, and/or distilled alcoholic beverages.

**42481   Beer and Ale Merchant Wholesalers**
See industry description for 424810.

**424810   Beer and Ale Merchant Wholesalers**

This industry comprises establishments primarily engaged in the merchant wholesale distribution of beer, ale, porter, and other fermented malt beverages.

**42482   Wine and Distilled Alcoholic Beverage Merchant Wholesalers**
See industry description for 424820.

**424820   Wine and Distilled Alcoholic Beverage Merchant Wholesalers**

This industry comprises establishments primarily engaged in the merchant wholesale distribution of wine, distilled alcoholic beverages, and/or neutral spirits and ethyl alcohol used in blended wines and distilled liquors.

**4249   Miscellaneous Nondurable Goods Merchant Wholesalers**

This industry group comprises establishments primarily engaged in the merchant wholesale distribution of nondurable goods, such as farm supplies; books, periodicals, and newspapers; flowers; nursery stock; paints; varnishes; tobacco and tobacco products; and other miscellaneous nondurable goods, such as cut Christmas trees and pet supplies.

**42491   Farm Supplies Merchant Wholesalers**
See industry description for 424910.

---

T—Canadian, Mexican, and United States industries are comparable.

**424910  Farm Supplies Merchant Wholesalers**

This industry comprises establishments primarily engaged in the merchant wholesale distribution of farm supplies, such as animal feeds, fertilizers, agricultural chemicals, pesticides, plant seeds, and plant bulbs.

*Cross-References.*          Establishments primarily engaged in--

- Merchant wholesale distribution of pet food--are classified in Industry 424490, Other Grocery and Related Products Merchant Wholesalers;
- Merchant wholesale distribution of grains--are classified in Industry 424510, Grain and Field Bean Merchant Wholesalers;
- Merchant wholesale distribution of pet supplies--are classified in Industry 424990, Other Miscellaneous Nondurable Goods Merchant Wholesalers; and
- Merchant wholesale distribution of nursery stock (except seeds and plant bulbs)--are classified in Industry 424930, Flower, Nursery Stock, and Florists' Supplies Merchant Wholesalers.

**42492     Book, Periodical, and Newspaper Merchant Wholesalers**
See industry description for 424920.

**424920  Book, Periodical, and Newspaper Merchant Wholesalers**

This industry comprises establishments primarily engaged in the merchant wholesale distribution of books, periodicals, and newspapers.

**42493     Flower, Nursery Stock, and Florists' Supplies Merchant Wholesalers**
See industry description for 424930.

**424930  Flower, Nursery Stock, and Florists' Supplies Merchant Wholesalers**

This industry comprises establishments primarily engaged in the merchant wholesale distribution of flowers, florists' supplies, and/or nursery stock (except plant seeds and plant bulbs).

*Cross-References.*          Establishments primarily engaged in--

- Merchant wholesale distribution of cut Christmas trees--are classified in Industry 424990, Other Miscellaneous Nondurable Goods Merchant Wholesalers;
- Merchant wholesale distribution of plant seeds and plant bulbs--are classified in Industry 424910, Farm Supplies Merchant Wholesalers; and
- Growing nursery products, nursery stock, and short rotation woody trees (i.e., growing and harvesting cycle is 10 years or less)--are classified in U.S. Industry 111421, Nursery and Tree Production.

**42494     Tobacco Product and Electronic Cigarette Merchant Wholesalers**
See industry description for 424940.

**424940  Tobacco Product and Electronic Cigarette Merchant Wholesalers**

This industry comprises establishments primarily engaged in the merchant wholesale distribution of tobacco products, such as cigarettes, snuff, cigars, pipe tobacco, and electronic cigarettes (including related parts and accessories).

*Cross-References.*          Establishments primarily engaged in--

- Merchant wholesale distribution of leaf tobacco and hemp--are classified in Industry 424590, Other Farm Product Raw Material Merchant Wholesalers; and

---

T—Canadian, Mexican, and United States industries are comparable.

- Merchant wholesale distribution of electronic cigarette vapor liquids--are classified in Industry 424690, Other Chemical and Allied Products Merchant Wholesalers.

**42495   Paint, Varnish, and Supplies Merchant Wholesalers**
See industry description for 424950.

**424950  Paint, Varnish, and Supplies Merchant Wholesalers**

This industry comprises establishments primarily engaged in the merchant wholesale distribution of paints, varnishes, and similar coatings; pigments; wallpaper; and supplies, such as paintbrushes and rollers.

*Cross-References.*

Establishments primarily engaged in the merchant wholesale distribution of artists' paints are classified in Industry 424990, Other Miscellaneous Nondurable Goods Merchant Wholesalers.

**42499   Other Miscellaneous Nondurable Goods Merchant Wholesalers**
See industry description for 424990.

**424990  Other Miscellaneous Nondurable Goods Merchant Wholesalers**

This industry comprises establishments primarily engaged in the merchant wholesale distribution of nondurable goods (except printing and writing paper; stationery and office supplies; industrial and personal service paper; drugs and druggists' sundries; apparel, piece goods, and notions; grocery and related products; farm product raw materials; chemical and allied products; petroleum and petroleum products; beer, wine, and distilled alcoholic beverages; farm supplies; books, periodicals, and newspapers; flowers, nursery stock, and florists' supplies; tobacco and tobacco products; and paint, varnishes, wallpaper, and supplies).

*Illustrative Examples:*

Artists' supplies merchant wholesalers
Pet supplies (except pet food) merchant wholesalers
Burlap merchant wholesalers
Statuary (except religious) merchant wholesalers

Christmas trees (e.g., artificial, cut) merchant wholesalers
Textile bags merchant wholesalers
Industrial yarns merchant wholesalers

*Cross-References.*          Establishments primarily engaged in--

- Distribution of advertising specialties--are classified in Industry 541890, Other Services Related to Advertising;
- Merchant wholesale distribution of farm supplies--are classified in Industry 424910, Farm Supplies Merchant Wholesalers;
- Merchant wholesale distribution of books, periodicals, and newspapers--are classified in Industry 424920, Book, Periodical, and Newspaper Merchant Wholesalers;
- Merchant wholesale distribution of flowers, nursery stock, and florists' supplies--are classified in Industry 424930, Flower, Nursery Stock, and Florists' Supplies Merchant Wholesalers;
- Merchant wholesale distribution of tobacco products--are classified in Industry 424940, Tobacco Product and Electronic Cigarette Merchant Wholesalers;
- Merchant wholesale distribution of paints, varnishes, and similar coatings; pigments; wallpaper; and supplies--are classified in Industry 424950, Paint, Varnish, and Supplies Merchant Wholesalers;
- Merchant wholesale distribution of bulk printing and/or writing paper--are classified in Industry 424110, Printing and Writing Paper Merchant Wholesalers;
- Merchant wholesale distribution of stationery, office supplies, and/or gift wrap--are classified in Industry 424120, Stationery and Office Supplies Merchant Wholesalers;

---

T—Canadian, Mexican, and United States industries are comparable.

- Merchant wholesale distribution of kraft wrapping and other coarse paper, paperboard, converted paper (except stationery and office supplies), and related disposable plastics products--are classified in Industry 424130, Industrial and Personal Service Paper Merchant Wholesalers;
- Merchant wholesale distribution of biological and medical products; botanical drugs and herbs; and pharmaceutical products intended for internal and external consumption--are classified in Industry 424210, Drugs and Druggists' Sundries Merchant Wholesalers;
- Merchant wholesale distribution of piece goods, yard goods, notions, hair accessories, footwear, and clothing and clothing accessories--are classified in Industry Group 4243, Apparel, Piece Goods, and Notions Merchant Wholesalers;
- Merchant wholesale distribution of meat, poultry, seafood, confectioneries, fruits and vegetables; and other groceries and related products--are classified in Industry Group 4244, Grocery and Related Product Merchant Wholesalers;
- Merchant wholesale distribution of grains, field beans, livestock, and other farm product raw materials--are classified in Industry Group 4245, Farm Product Raw Material Merchant Wholesalers;
- Merchant wholesale distribution of chemicals; plastics materials and basic forms and shapes; and allied products--are classified in Industry Group 4246, Chemical and Allied Products Merchant Wholesalers;
- Merchant wholesale distribution of petroleum and petroleum products--are classified in Industry Group 4247, Petroleum and Petroleum Products Merchant Wholesalers;
- Merchant wholesale distribution of beer, ale, wine, and distilled alcoholic beverages--are classified in Industry Group 4248, Beer, Wine, and Distilled Alcoholic Beverage Merchant Wholesalers;
- Merchant wholesale distribution of pet foods--are classified in Industry 424490, Other Grocery and Related Products Merchant Wholesalers;
- Merchant wholesale distribution of religious statuary--are classified in Industry 423490, Other Professional Equipment and Supplies Merchant Wholesalers;
- Merchant wholesale distribution of knitting yarns (except industrial)--are classified in Industry 424310, Piece Goods, Notions, and Other Dry Goods Merchant Wholesalers; and
- Growing Christmas trees--are classified in U.S. Industry 111421, Nursery and Tree Production.

## 425 Wholesale Trade Agents and Brokers

The Wholesale Trade Agents and Brokers subsector groups establishments that arrange for the sale of goods owned by others, generally on a fee or commission basis. They act on behalf of the buyers and sellers of goods to facilitate wholesale trade.

## 4251 Wholesale Trade Agents and Brokers

## 42512 Wholesale Trade Agents and Brokers
See industry description for 425120.

## 425120 Wholesale Trade Agents and Brokers

This industry comprises wholesale trade agents and brokers acting on behalf of buyers or sellers in the wholesale distribution of goods, including those that use the Internet or other electronic means to bring together buyers and sellers. Agents and brokers do not take title to the goods being sold but rather receive a commission or fee for their service. Agents and brokers for all durable and nondurable goods are included in this industry.

*Illustrative Examples:*

Independent sales representatives
Manufacturers' sales representatives

Group purchasing organizations (acting as agents for goods distribution)

---

T—Canadian, Mexican, and United States industries are comparable.

*Cross-References.*

- Group purchasing organizations purchasing and selling goods on their own account are classified in Subsector 423, Merchant Wholesalers, Durable Goods, or Subsector 424, Merchant Wholesalers, Nondurable Goods; and
- Group purchasing organizations acting as agents for services are classified in Industry 561990, All Other Support Services.

---

T—Canadian, Mexican, and United States industries are comparable.

# Sector 44-45--Retail Trade[T]

## The Sector as a Whole

The Retail Trade sector comprises establishments primarily engaged in retailing merchandise, generally without transformation, and rendering services incidental to the sale of merchandise.

The retailing process is the final step in the distribution of merchandise; retailers are, therefore, organized to sell merchandise in small quantities to the general public. Retail stores are fixed point-of-sale locations, located and designed to attract a high volume of walk-in customers. In general, retail stores have extensive displays of merchandise and use mass-media advertising to attract customers. Retailers often reach customers and market merchandise with methods other than, or in addition to, physical stores, such as Internet websites, the broadcasting of "infomercials," the broadcasting and publishing of direct-response advertising, the publishing of paper and electronic catalogs, door-to-door solicitation, in-home demonstration, selling from portable stalls (street vendors, except food), and distribution through vending machines. Establishments engaged in the direct sale and home delivery of products, such as home heating oil dealers and home delivery newspaper routes, are included here.

Retail establishments typically sell merchandise to the general public for personal or household consumption, but some also serve business and institutional clients. These include office supply retailers, computer and software retailers, building materials dealers, plumbing supply retailers, and electrical supply retailers.

In addition to retailing merchandise, some retailers are also engaged in the provision of after-sales services, such as repair and installation. For example, new automobile dealers, electronics and appliance retailers, and musical instrument and supplies retailers often provide repair services. As a general rule, establishments engaged in retailing merchandise and providing after-sales services are classified in this sector.

Retail trade establishments are grouped into industries and industry groups typically based on one or more of the following criteria:

(a) The merchandise line or lines carried; for example, specialty retailers are distinguished from general-line retailers.

(b) The usual trade designation of the establishments. This criterion applies in cases where a retailer is well recognized by the industry and the public, but difficult to define strictly in terms of merchandise lines carried; for example, pharmacies and department stores.

(c) Human resource requirements in terms of expertise; for example, the staff of an automobile dealer requires knowledge in financing, registering, and licensing issues that are not necessary in other retail industries.

The buying of goods for resale is a characteristic of retail trade establishments that particularly distinguishes them from establishments in the agriculture, manufacturing, and construction industries. For example, farms that sell their products at or from the point of production are not classified in retail, but rather in agriculture. Similarly, establishments that both manufacture and sell their products to the general public are not classified in retail, but rather in manufacturing. However, establishments that engage in processing activities incidental to retailing are classified in retail. This includes optical goods retailers that grind lenses, and meat and seafood retailers that process carcasses into cuts.

Wholesalers also engage in the buying of goods for resale, but they are not usually organized to serve the general public. They typically operate from a warehouse or office, and neither the design nor the location of these premises is intended to solicit a high volume of walk-in traffic. Wholesalers supply institutional, industrial, wholesale, and retail clients; their operations are, therefore, generally organized to purchase, sell, and deliver merchandise in larger quantities. However, dealers of durable nonconsumer goods, such as farm machinery and heavy-duty trucks, are included in wholesale trade even if they often sell these products in single units.

## 441    Motor Vehicle and Parts Dealers

Industries in the Motor Vehicle and Parts Dealers subsector retail motor vehicles and parts. Establishments in this subsector often operate from a showroom and/or an open lot where the vehicles are on display. The display of vehicles and the related parts require little by way of display equipment. The personnel generally include both the

---

T—Canadian, Mexican, and United States industries are comparable.

sales and sales support staff familiar with the requirements for registering and financing a vehicle as well as a staff of parts experts and mechanics trained to provide repair and maintenance services for the vehicles. Specific industries included in this subsector identify the type of vehicle being retailed.

Sales of capital or durable nonconsumer goods, such as medium- and heavy-duty trucks, are always included in wholesale trade.

**4411    Automobile Dealers**

This industry group comprises establishments primarily engaged in retailing new and used automobiles and light trucks, such as sport utility vehicles, and passenger and cargo vans.

**44111   New Car Dealers**
     See industry description for 441110.

**441110  New Car Dealers**

This industry comprises establishments primarily engaged in retailing new automobiles and light trucks, such as sport utility vehicles, and passenger and cargo vans, or retailing these new vehicles in combination with activities, such as repair services, retailing used cars, and selling replacement parts and accessories.

*Illustrative Examples:*

Automobile dealers, new only, or new and used          Light utility truck dealers, new only, or new and used

*Cross-References.*        Establishments primarily engaged in--

- Retailing used automobiles and light trucks without retailing new automobiles and light trucks--are classified in Industry 441120, Used Car Dealers;
- Providing automotive repair services without retailing new automotive vehicles--are classified in Industry Group 8111, Automotive Repair and Maintenance; and
- Merchant wholesale distribution of new medium- and heavy-duty trucks, buses, and other motor vehicles--are classified in Industry 423110, Automobile and Other Motor Vehicle Merchant Wholesalers.

**44112   Used Car Dealers**
     See industry description for 441120.

**441120  Used Car Dealers**

This industry comprises establishments primarily engaged in retailing used automobiles and light trucks, such as sport utility vehicles, and passenger and cargo vans.

*Illustrative Examples:*

Antique auto dealers                               Automobile dealers, used only
Light truck dealers, used only

*Cross-References.*        Establishments primarily engaged in--

- Retailing new automobiles and light trucks--are classified in Industry 441110, New Car Dealers;
- Merchant wholesale distribution of used medium- and heavy-duty trucks, buses, and other motor vehicles--are classified in Industry 423110, Automobile and Other Motor Vehicle Merchant Wholesalers; and
- Renting passenger cars without drivers, generally for short periods of time--are classified in U.S. Industry 532111, Passenger Car Rental.

---

T—Canadian, Mexican, and United States industries are comparable.

**4412    Other Motor Vehicle Dealers**

This industry group comprises establishments primarily engaged in retailing new and used vehicles (except automobiles, light trucks, such as sport utility vehicles, and passenger and cargo vans).

**44121    Recreational Vehicle Dealers**
    See industry description for 441210.

**441210    Recreational Vehicle Dealers**

This industry comprises establishments primarily engaged in retailing new and/or used recreational vehicles commonly referred to as RVs or retailing these new vehicles in combination with activities, such as repair services and selling replacement parts and accessories.

*Illustrative Examples:*

Motor home dealers
Recreational vehicle (RV) parts and accessories stores

Recreational vehicle (RV) dealers
Travel trailer dealers

*Cross-References.*        Establishments primarily engaged in--

- Retailing new or used boat trailers and utility trailers--are classified in Industry 44122, Motorcycle, Boat, and Other Motor Vehicle Dealers; and
- Retailing manufactured homes (i.e., mobile homes), parts, and equipment--are classified in Industry 459930, Manufactured (Mobile) Home Dealers.

**44122    Motorcycle, Boat, and Other Motor Vehicle Dealers**

This industry comprises establishments primarily engaged in retailing new and used motorcycles, boats, and other vehicles (except automobiles, light trucks, and recreational vehicles), or retailing these new vehicles in combination with activities, such as repair services and selling replacement parts and accessories.

*Illustrative Examples:*

Aircraft dealers
Motorcycle dealers
All-terrain vehicle (ATV) dealers

Utility trailer dealers
Boat dealers, new and used

*Cross-References.*        Establishments primarily engaged in--

- Retailing new nonmotorized bicycles, surfboards, or wind sailboards--are classified in Industry 45911, Sporting Goods Retailers;
- Retailing used nonmotorized bicycles, surfboards, or wind sailboards--are classified in Industry 45951, Used Merchandise Retailers;
- Retailing new or used automobiles and light trucks--are classified in Industry Group 4411, Automobile Dealers;
- Retailing new or used recreational vehicles, such as travel trailers--are classified in Industry 44121, Recreational Vehicle Dealers;
- Providing repair services for vehicles without retailing new vehicles--are classified in the appropriate industry for the repair services; and
- Operating docking and/or storage facilities for pleasure craft owners--are classified in Industry 71393, Marinas.

---

T—Canadian, Mexican, and United States industries are comparable.

**441222  Boat Dealers**

This U.S. industry comprises establishments primarily engaged in (1) retailing new and/or used boats or retailing new boats in combination with activities, such as repair services and selling replacement parts and accessories, and/or (2) retailing new and/or used outboard motors, boat trailers, marine supplies, parts, and accessories.

*Illustrative Examples:*

Boat dealers (e.g., power boats, rowboats, sailboats)          Marine supply dealers
Outboard motor dealers

*Cross-References.*          Establishments primarily engaged in--

- Retailing new surfboards or wind sailboards--are classified in Industry 459110, Sporting Goods Retailers;
- Retailing used surfboards or wind sailboards--are classified in Industry 459510, Used Merchandise Retailers;
- Providing boat repair services without retailing new boats--are classified in Industry 811490, Other Personal and Household Goods Repair and Maintenance;
- Retailing new or used personal watercraft--are classified in U.S. Industry 441227, Motorcycle, ATV, and All Other Motor Vehicle Dealers; and
- Operating docking and/or storage facilities for pleasure craft owners--are classified in Industry 713930, Marinas.

**441227  Motorcycle, ATV, and All Other Motor Vehicle Dealers**

This U.S. industry comprises establishments primarily engaged in retailing new and/or used motorcycles, motor scooters, motorbikes, mopeds, off-road all-terrain vehicles (ATV), personal watercraft, utility trailers, and other motor vehicles (except automobiles, light trucks, recreational vehicles, and boats) or retailing these new vehicles in combination with activities, such as repair services and selling replacement parts and accessories.

*Illustrative Examples:*

All-terrain vehicle (ATV) dealers                Aircraft dealers
Motorcycle dealers                               Snowmobile dealers
Moped dealers                                    Powered golf cart dealers
Motorcycle parts and accessories dealers         Utility trailer dealers
Personal watercraft dealers

*Cross-References.*          Establishments primarily engaged in--

- Retailing new automobiles and light trucks--are classified in Industry 441110, New Car Dealers;
- Retailing used automobiles and light trucks--are classified in Industry 441120, Used Car Dealers;
- Retailing new or used recreational vehicles, such as travel trailers--are classified in Industry 441210, Recreational Vehicle Dealers;
- Retailing new or used boats, outboard motors, boat trailers, and marine supplies--are classified in U.S. Industry 441222, Boat Dealers;
- Retailing new nonmotorized bicycles--are classified in Industry 459110, Sporting Goods Retailers;
- Retailing used nonmotorized bicycles--are classified in Industry 459510, Used Merchandise Retailers; and
- Providing vehicle repair services without retailing new vehicles--are classified in the appropriate industry for the repair services.

---

T—Canadian, Mexican, and United States industries are comparable.

**4413    Automotive Parts, Accessories, and Tire Retailers**

This industry group comprises establishments primarily engaged in retailing new, used, and/or rebuilt automotive parts and accessories, including tires and tubes.  Included in this industry group are establishments primarily engaged in retailing automotive parts and accessories in combination with automotive repair services.

**44133    Automotive Parts and Accessories Retailers**
See industry description for 441330.

**441330  Automotive Parts and Accessories Retailers**

This industry comprises establishments primarily engaged in retailing new, used, and/or rebuilt automotive parts and accessories, with or without repairing automobiles; and/or establishments primarily engaged in retailing and installing automotive accessories.

*Illustrative Examples*:

Automotive parts and supply retailers                Automotive stereo retailers
Truck cap retailers                                              Used automotive parts retailers

*Cross-References.*          Establishments primarily engaged in--

- Retailing new or used tires--are classified in Industry 441340, Tire Dealers; and
- Repairing and replacing automotive parts, such as transmissions, mufflers, and brake linings (except establishments known as automotive supply retailers)--are classified in Industry 81111, Automotive Mechanical and Electrical Repair and Maintenance.

**44134   Tire Dealers**
See industry description for 441340.

**441340  Tire Dealers**

This industry comprises establishments primarily engaged in retailing new and/or used tires and tubes or retailing new tires in combination with automotive repair services.

*Cross-References.*          Establishments primarily engaged in--

- Tire retreading or recapping--are classified in U.S. Industry 326212, Tire Retreading; and
- Merchant wholesale distribution of new/used tires for medium- and heavy-duty trucks, buses, and other motor vehicles--are classified in Industry 423130, Tire and Tube Merchant Wholesalers.

**444    Building Material and Garden Equipment and Supplies Dealers**

Industries in the Building Material and Garden Equipment and Supplies Dealers subsector retail new building materials, hardware, paint, and garden and outdoor power equipment and supplies.  Establishments in this subsector with fixed point-of-sale locations, including home centers and retail lumber yards, may display merchandise either indoors or outdoors under covered areas.  The staff is usually knowledgeable in the use of the specific products being retailed in the construction, repair, and maintenance of the home and associated grounds.

**4441    Building Material and Supplies Dealers**

This industry group comprises establishments primarily engaged in retailing new building materials and supplies.

**44411   Home Centers**
See industry description for 444110.

---

T—Canadian, Mexican, and United States industries are comparable.

**444110  Home Centers**

This industry comprises establishments generally known as home centers primarily engaged in retailing a general line of new home repair and improvement materials and supplies, such as lumber, plumbing goods, electrical goods, tools, housewares, hardware, and lawn and garden supplies, with no one merchandise line predominating.

*Cross-References.*

Establishments primarily engaged in retailing a general line of new hardware items, such as tools and builders' hardware, are classified in Industry 444140, Hardware Retailers.

**44412    Paint and Wallpaper Retailers**
        See industry description for 444120.

**444120  Paint and Wallpaper Retailers**

This industry comprises establishments primarily engaged in retailing paint, wallpaper, and related supplies.

*Cross-References.*

Establishments primarily engaged in retailing automotive paints are classified in Industry 441330, Automotive Parts and Accessories Retailers.

**44414    Hardware Retailers**
        See industry description for 444140.

**444140  Hardware Retailers**

This industry comprises establishments primarily engaged in retailing a general line of new hardware items, such as tools and builders' hardware.

*Cross-References.*          Establishments primarily engaged in--

- Retailing a general line of home repair and improvement materials and supplies, generally known as home centers--are classified in Industry 444110, Home Centers; and
- Retailing used hardware items--are classified in Industry 459510, Used Merchandise Retailers.

**44418    Other Building Material Dealers**
        See industry description for 444180.

**444180  Other Building Material Dealers**

This industry comprises establishments (except home centers, paint and wallpaper retailers, and hardware retailers) primarily engaged in retailing specialized lines of new building materials, such as lumber, fencing, glass, doors, plumbing fixtures and supplies, electrical supplies, prefabricated buildings and kits, and kitchen and bath cabinets and countertops to be installed.

*Illustrative Examples:*

| | |
|---|---|
| Electrical supply retailers | Plumbing supply retailers |
| Kitchen cabinet (except custom) retailers | Garage door dealers |
| Fencing dealers | Prefabricated building (except manufactured home) |
| Lumber yards, retail | dealers |
| Floor covering retailers, hardwood or ceramic tile only | Glass (except automotive) retailers |

---

T—Canadian, Mexican, and United States industries are comparable.

*Cross-References.* Establishments primarily engaged in--

- Retailing used building materials--are classified in Industry 459510, Used Merchandise Retailers;
- Providing carpentry/installation services for products--are classified in Industry 238350, Finish Carpentry Contractors;
- Installing plumbing fixtures and supplies--are classified in Industry 238220, Plumbing, Heating, and Air-Conditioning Contractors;
- Installing electrical supplies, such as lighting fixtures and ceiling fans--are classified in Industry 238210, Electrical Contractors and Other Wiring Installation Contractors;
- Making custom furniture (e.g., kitchen cabinets)--are classified in Subsector 337, Furniture and Related Product Manufacturing;
- Retailing a general line of new hardware items--are classified in Industry 444140, Hardware Retailers;
- Retailing paint and wallpaper--are classified in Industry 444120, Paint and Wallpaper Retailers;
- Retailing floor coverings (except hardwood or ceramic tile only)--are classified in U.S. Industry 449121, Floor Covering Retailers; and
- Retailing a general line of home repair and improvement materials and supplies, generally known as home centers--are classified in Industry 444110, Home Centers.

## 4442 Lawn and Garden Equipment and Supplies Retailers

This industry group comprises establishments primarily engaged in retailing new lawn and garden equipment and supplies.

### 44423 Outdoor Power Equipment Retailers
See industry description for 444230.

### 444230 Outdoor Power Equipment Retailers

This industry comprises establishments primarily engaged in retailing new outdoor power equipment or retailing new outdoor power equipment in combination with activities, such as repair services and selling replacement parts.

*Cross-References.* Establishments primarily engaged in--

- Retailing used outdoor power equipment--are classified in Industry 459510, Used Merchandise Retailers;
- Providing outdoor power equipment repair services without retailing new outdoor power equipment--are classified in U.S. Industry 811411, Home and Garden Equipment Repair and Maintenance;
- Merchant wholesale distribution of agricultural and lawn and garden equipment--are classified in Industry 423820, Farm and Garden Machinery and Equipment Merchant Wholesalers; and
- Installing home standby power generators and providing other low voltage electrical contract work--are classified in Industry 238210, Electrical Contractors and Other Wiring Installation Contractors.

### 44424 Nursery, Garden Center, and Farm Supply Retailers
See industry description for 444240.

### 444240 Nursery, Garden Center, and Farm Supply Retailers

This industry comprises establishments primarily engaged in retailing nursery and garden products, such as trees, shrubs, plants, seeds, bulbs, and sod, that are predominantly grown elsewhere. These establishments may sell a limited amount of a product they grow themselves. Also included in this industry are establishments primarily engaged in retailing farm supplies, such as animal (except pet) feed, fertilizers, agricultural chemicals, and pesticides.

---

T—Canadian, Mexican, and United States industries are comparable.

*Cross-References.*          Establishments primarily engaged in--

- Merchant wholesale distribution of farm supplies--are classified in Industry 424910, Farm Supplies Merchant Wholesalers;
- Providing landscaping services--are classified in Industry 561730, Landscaping Services; and
- Growing and retailing nursery stock--are classified in U.S. Industry 111421, Nursery and Tree Production.

## 445      Food and Beverage Retailers

Industries in the Food and Beverage Retailers subsector primarily retail general or specialized lines of food and beverage products.  Establishments in this subsector with fixed point-of-sale locations have special equipment (e.g., freezers, refrigerated display cases, refrigerators) for displaying food and beverage products and have staff trained in the processing of food products to guarantee the proper storage and sanitary conditions required by regulatory authority.  Vending machine operators are also included in this subsector.

## 4451     Grocery and Convenience Retailers

This industry group comprises establishments primarily engaged in retailing a general line of food products. This industry group also includes vending machine operators.

## 44511    Supermarkets and Other Grocery Retailers (except Convenience Retailers)
See industry description for 445110.

## 445110   Supermarkets and Other Grocery Retailers (except Convenience Retailers)

This industry comprises establishments generally known as supermarkets and other grocery retailers (except convenience retailers) primarily engaged in retailing a general line of food, such as canned and frozen foods; fresh fruits and vegetables; and fresh and prepared meats, fish, and poultry.  Included in this industry are delicatessen-type establishments primarily engaged in retailing a general line of food.

*Cross-References.*          Establishments primarily engaged in--

- Retailing automotive fuels in combination with a convenience store or food mart--are classified in Industry 457110, Gasoline Stations with Convenience Stores;
- Retailing a limited line of groceries, such as convenience stores or food marts (except those operating fuel pumps)--are classified in U.S. Industry 445131, Convenience Retailers;
- Providing food services in delicatessen-type establishments--are classified in U.S. Industry 722513, Limited-Service Restaurants;
- Retailing fresh meat in delicatessen-type establishments--are classified in Industry 445240, Meat Retailers; and
- Grocery order and delivery services on behalf of grocery retailers--are classified in Industry 492210, Local Messengers and Local Delivery.

## 44513    Convenience Retailers and Vending Machine Operators

This industry comprises establishments primarily engaged in retailing a limited line of groceries that generally includes milk, bread, soda, and snacks.  Included in this industry are convenience retailers, such as convenience stores or food marts (except those operating fuel pumps), and vending machine operators.

*Cross-References.*          Establishments primarily engaged in--

- Retailing a general line of food, such as supermarkets and grocery stores--are classified in Industry 44511, Supermarkets and Other Grocery Retailers (except Convenience Retailers);
- Retailing automotive fuels in combination with a convenience store or food mart--are classified in Industry 45711, Gasoline Stations with Convenience Stores;

T—Canadian, Mexican, and United States industries are comparable.

- Supplying and servicing coin- or card-operated personal service machines, such as photobooths and lockers--are classified in Industry 81299, All Other Personal Services;
- Supplying and servicing coin- or card-operated amusement and gambling devices in places of business operated by others--are classified in Subsector 713, Amusement, Gambling, and Recreation Industries; and
- Renting prerecorded digital video discs (DVDs) through vending machines--are classified in Industry 53228, Other Consumer Goods Rental.

## 445131 Convenience Retailers

This U.S. industry comprises establishments primarily engaged in retailing a limited line of groceries that generally includes milk, bread, soda, and snacks, such as convenience stores or food marts (except those operating fuel pumps).

*Cross-References.*        Establishments primarily engaged in--

- Retailing a general line of food, such as supermarkets and grocery stores--are classified in Industry 445110, Supermarkets and Other Grocery Retailers (except Convenience Retailers);
- Retailing automotive fuels in combination with a convenience store or food mart--are classified in Industry 457110, Gasoline Stations with Convenience Stores; and
- Retailing merchandise through vending machines--are classified in U.S. Industry 445132, Vending Machine Operators.

## 445132 Vending Machine Operators

This U.S. industry comprises establishments primarily engaged in retailing merchandise through vending machines that they service.

*Cross-References.*        Establishments primarily engaged in--

- Supplying and servicing coin- or card-operated personal service machines, such as photobooths and lockers--are classified in Industry 812990, All Other Personal Services;
- Supplying and servicing coin- or card-operated amusement and gambling devices in places of business operated by others--are classified in Subsector 713, Amusement, Gambling, and Recreation Industries; and
- Renting prerecorded digital video discs (DVDs) through vending machines--are classified in U.S. Industry 532282, Video Tape and Disc Rental.

## 4452    Specialty Food Retailers

This industry group comprises establishments primarily engaged in retailing specialized lines of food not for immediate consumption.

## 44523    Fruit and Vegetable Retailers
See industry description for 445230.

## 445230    Fruit and Vegetable Retailers

This industry comprises establishments primarily engaged in retailing fresh fruits and vegetables.

*Cross-References.*        Establishments primarily engaged in--

- Growing vegetables and/or fruits and selling them at roadside stands--are classified in Subsector 111, Crop Production; and
- Retailing fruit baskets and bouquets--are classified in Industry 459420, Gift, Novelty, and Souvenir Retailers.

---

T—Canadian, Mexican, and United States industries are comparable.

**44524    Meat Retailers**
　　　　See industry description for 445240.

**445240    Meat Retailers**

　This industry comprises establishments primarily engaged in retailing fresh, frozen, or cured meats and poultry not for immediate consumption.  Delicatessen-type establishments primarily engaged in retailing fresh meat are included in this industry.

*Illustrative Examples:*

Baked ham retailers                                    Poultry dealers
Meat retailers                                            Frozen meat retailers
Butcher shops

*Cross-References.*          Establishments primarily engaged in--

- Retailing a general line of food, such as supermarkets and grocery stores--are classified in Industry 445110, Supermarkets and Other Grocery Retailers (except Convenience Retailers);
- Providing food services in delicatessen-type establishments--are classified in U.S. Industry 722513, Limited-Service Restaurants; and
- Raising livestock for meat production--are classified in Subsector 112, Animal Production and Aquaculture.

**44525    Fish and Seafood Retailers**
　　　　See industry description for 445250.

**445250    Fish and Seafood Retailers**

　This industry comprises establishments primarily engaged in retailing fresh, frozen, or cured fish and seafood products not for immediate consumption.

*Cross-References.*

　Establishments primarily engaged in raising or harvesting fish or seafood and selling them live, fresh, frozen, or cured at roadside stands or market stalls are classified in Sector 11, Agriculture, Forestry, Fishing and Hunting.

**44529    Other Specialty Food Retailers**

　This industry comprises establishments primarily engaged in retailing specialty foods (except fruits and vegetables, meat, fish, and seafood) not for immediate consumption and not made on the premises.

*Illustrative Examples:*

Baked goods (not made on premises) retailers          Gourmet food retailers
Dairy product retailers                                          Confectionery (i.e., packaged) retailers
Coffee and tea (i.e., packaged) retailers                 Nut (i.e., packaged) retailers

*Cross-References.*          Establishments primarily engaged in--

- Retailing baked goods made on the premises but not for immediate consumption--are classified in Industry 31181, Bread and Bakery Product Manufacturing;
- Retailing fresh fruits and vegetables--are classified in Industry 44523, Fruit and Vegetable Retailers;
- Retailing fresh, frozen, or cured meats and poultry--are classified in Industry 44524, Meat Retailers;

---

T—Canadian, Mexican, and United States industries are comparable.

- Retailing fresh, frozen, or cured fish and seafood products--are classified in Industry 44525, Fish and Seafood Retailers;
- Retailing fruit baskets and bouquets--are classified in Industry 45942, Gift, Novelty, and Souvenir Retailers;
- Selling candy and confectionery products not for immediate consumption and made on the premises--are classified in Industry Group 3113, Sugar and Confectionery Product Manufacturing;
- Preparing and/or serving snack foods (e.g., doughnuts, bagels, ice cream, popcorn) for immediate consumption on or near the premises--are classified in Industry 72251, Restaurants and Other Eating Places; and
- Dairy farming, making dairy products, and selling them at roadside stands or market stalls--are classified in Industry 11212, Dairy Cattle and Milk Production.

## 445291  Baked Goods Retailers

This U.S. industry comprises establishments primarily engaged in retailing baked goods not for immediate consumption and not made on the premises.

*Cross-References.*          Establishments primarily engaged in--

- Preparing and/or serving snack foods (e.g., doughnuts, bagels, ice cream, popcorn) for immediate consumption on or near the premises--are classified in U.S. Industry 722515, Snack and Nonalcoholic Beverage Bars; and
- Retailing baked goods made on the premises but not for immediate consumption--are classified in U.S. Industry 311811, Retail Bakeries.

## 445292  Confectionery and Nut Retailers

This U.S. industry comprises establishments primarily engaged in retailing candy and other confections, nuts, and popcorn not for immediate consumption and not made on the premises.

*Cross-References.*          Establishments primarily engaged in--

- Selling confectionery goods and nuts made on the premises and not packaged for immediate consumption--are classified in Industry Group 3113, Sugar and Confectionery Product Manufacturing;
- Preparing and/or serving snack foods (e.g., doughnuts, bagels, ice cream, popcorn) for immediate consumption on or near the premises--are classified in U.S. Industry 722515, Snack and Nonalcoholic Beverage Bars; and
- Retailing baked goods made on the premises but not for immediate consumption--are classified in U.S. Industry 311811, Retail Bakeries.

## 445298  All Other Specialty Food Retailers

This U.S. industry comprises establishments primarily engaged in retailing miscellaneous specialty foods (except fruit and vegetables, meat, fish, seafood, confections, nuts, popcorn, and baked goods) not for immediate consumption and not made on the premises.

*Illustrative Examples:*

Coffee and tea (i.e., packaged) retailers
Soft drink (i.e., bottled) retailers
Dairy product retailers

Spice retailers
Gourmet food retailers
Water (i.e., bottled) retailers

---

T—Canadian, Mexican, and United States industries are comparable.

*Cross-References.*          Establishments primarily engaged in--

- Preparing and/or serving snack foods (e.g., doughnuts, bagels, ice cream, popcorn) for immediate consumption on or near the premises--are classified in U.S. Industry 722515, Snack and Nonalcoholic Beverage Bars;
- Retailing fresh fruits and vegetables--are classified in Industry 445230, Fruit and Vegetable Retailers;
- Retailing fresh, frozen, or cured meats and poultry--are classified in Industry 445240, Meat Retailers;
- Retailing fresh, frozen, or cured fish and seafood products--are classified in Industry 445250, Fish and Seafood Retailers;
- Retailing baked goods not for immediate consumption and not made on the premises--are classified in U.S. Industry 445291, Baked Goods Retailers;
- Retailing candy and other confections, nuts, and popcorn not for immediate consumption and not made on the premises--are classified in U.S. Industry 445292, Confectionery and Nut Retailers;
- Retailing fruit baskets and bouquets--are classified in Industry 459420, Gift, Novelty, and Souvenir Retailers; and
- Dairy farming, making dairy products, and selling them at roadside stands or market stalls--are classified in Industry 112120, Dairy Cattle and Milk Production.

## 4453     Beer, Wine, and Liquor Retailers

## 44532    Beer, Wine, and Liquor Retailers
See industry description for 445320.

## 445320  Beer, Wine, and Liquor Retailers

This industry comprises establishments primarily engaged in retailing packaged alcoholic beverages, such as ale, beer, wine, and liquor.

*Cross-References.*          Establishments primarily engaged in--

- Retailing packaged liquor in combination with providing prepared drinks for immediate consumption on the premises--are classified in Industry 722410, Drinking Places (Alcoholic Beverages);
- Manufacturing brewery, winery, and distillery products for consumption off the premises--are classified in Industry Group 3121, Beverage Manufacturing; and
- Manufacturing brewery, winery, and distillery products in combination with providing prepared food and drinks for immediate consumption on the premises--are classified in Subsector 722, Food Services and Drinking Places.

## 449     Furniture, Home Furnishings, Electronics, and Appliance Retailers

Industries in the Furniture, Home Furnishings, Electronics, and Appliance Retailers subsector retail new furniture, home furnishings, electronics, and appliances. Establishments in this subsector with fixed point-of-sale locations may operate from showrooms or other locations that have substantial areas for the presentation or demonstration of their products. Establishments in this subsector may provide incidental services, including interior decorating, product assembly, installation, or repair services.

## 4491    Furniture and Home Furnishings Retailers

This industry group comprises establishments primarily engaged in retailing new furniture and home furnishings. Establishments in this industry group with fixed point-of-sale locations may operate from showrooms and have substantial areas for the presentation of their products. Establishments in this industry group may provide incidental services, including interior decorating, product assembly, installation, or repair services.

## 44911   Furniture Retailers
See industry description for 449110.

---

T—Canadian, Mexican, and United States industries are comparable.

**449110  Furniture Retailers**

This industry comprises establishments primarily engaged in retailing new furniture, such as household furniture (e.g., baby furniture, box springs, and mattresses) and outdoor furniture; office furniture (except sold in combination with office supplies and equipment); and/or furniture sold in combination with major appliances, home electronics, home furnishings, or floor coverings.

*Cross-References.*          Establishments primarily engaged in--

- Retailing used furniture--are classified in Industry 459510, Used Merchandise Retailers;
- Selling custom furniture made on the premises--are classified in Subsector 337, Furniture and Related Product Manufacturing;
- Retailing new office furniture and a range of new office equipment and supplies--are classified in Industry 459410, Office Supplies and Stationery Retailers; and
- Renting furniture--are classified in Subsector 532, Rental and Leasing Services.

**44912  Home Furnishings Retailers**

This industry comprises establishments primarily engaged in retailing new home furnishings (except furniture).

*Illustrative Examples:*

Bath shops
Chinaware retailers
Floor covering retailers (except hardwood or ceramic tile only)

Glassware retailers
Kitchenware retailers
Window treatment retailers

*Cross-References.*          Establishments primarily engaged in--

- Installing floor coverings without retailing new floor coverings--are classified in Industry 23833, Flooring Contractors;
- Selling custom curtains and draperies made on the premises--are classified in Industry 31412, Curtain and Linen Mills;
- Manufacturing window blinds and shades--are classified in Industry 33792, Blind and Shade Manufacturing;
- Retailing new furniture--are classified in Industry 44911, Furniture Retailers;
- Retailing new mirrored glass, lighting fixtures, and new ceramic floor tile or hardwood floor coverings only--are classified in Industry 44418, Other Building Material Dealers; and
- Retailing used home furnishings--are classified in Industry 45951, Used Merchandise Retailers.

**449121  Floor Covering Retailers**

This U.S. industry comprises establishments primarily engaged in retailing new floor coverings, such as rugs and carpets, laminate and vinyl floor coverings, linoleum flooring, and floor tile (except ceramic tile or hardwood floor coverings only); or retailing new floor coverings in combination with installation and repair services.

*Cross-References.*          Establishments primarily engaged in--

- Installing floor coverings without retailing new floor coverings--are classified in Industry 238330, Flooring Contractors;
- Retailing new ceramic floor tile or hardwood floor coverings only--are classified in Industry 444180, Other Building Material Dealers; and
- Retailing used rugs and carpets--are classified in Industry 459510, Used Merchandise Retailers.

---

T—Canadian, Mexican, and United States industries are comparable.

**449122  Window Treatment Retailers**

This U.S. industry comprises establishments primarily engaged in retailing new window treatments, such as curtains, drapes, blinds, and shades.

*Cross-References.*          Establishments primarily engaged in--

- Selling custom curtains and draperies made on the premises--are classified in Industry 314120, Curtain and Linen Mills; and
- Manufacturing window blinds and shades--are classified in Industry 337920, Blind and Shade Manufacturing.

**449129  All Other Home Furnishings Retailers**

This U.S. industry comprises establishments primarily engaged in retailing new home furnishings (except furniture, floor coverings, and window treatments).

*Illustrative Examples:*

Bath shops
Kitchenware retailers
Chinaware retailers
Linen retailers
Electric lamp retailers

Picture frame retailers, custom
Glassware retailers
Wood-burning stove retailers
Housewares retailers

*Cross-References.*          Establishments primarily engaged in--

- Retailing new mirrored glass or lighting fixtures--are classified in Industry 444180, Other Building Material Dealers;
- Retailing new furniture--are classified in Industry 449110, Furniture Retailers;
- Retailing new floor coverings (except hardwood or ceramic tile only)--are classified in U.S. Industry 449121, Floor Covering Retailers;
- Retailing new window treatments--are classified in U.S. Industry 449122, Window Treatment Retailers;
- Manufacturing window blinds and shades--are classified in Industry 337920, Blind and Shade Manufacturing; and
- Retailing used home furnishings--are classified in Industry 459510, Used Merchandise Retailers.

**4492    Electronics and Appliance Retailers**

**44921    Electronics and Appliance Retailers**
          See industry description for 449210.

**449210  Electronics and Appliance Retailers**

This industry comprises establishments primarily engaged in one of the following: (1) retailing an array of new household-type appliances and consumer-type electronic products, such as televisions, computers, electronic tablets, and cameras; (2) specializing in retailing a single line of new consumer-type electronic products; (3) retailing these new products in combination with repair and support services; (4) retailing new prepackaged or downloadable computer software (without publishing); and/or (5) retailing prerecorded audio and video media, such as downloadable digital music and video files (without production or publishing), CDs, and DVDs.

*Illustrative Examples*:

Appliance retailers, household-type                    Cellular telephone accessories retailers

---

T—Canadian, Mexican, and United States industries are comparable.

Consumer-type electronics retailers (e.g., televisions, computers, cameras)

Stereo and sound system retailers (except automotive)

*Cross-References.* Establishments primarily engaged in--

- Retailing used appliance and electronic products--are classified in Industry 459510, Used Merchandise Retailers;
- Retailing automotive electronic sound systems--are classified in Industry 441330, Automotive Parts and Accessories Retailers;
- Retailing new electronic toys, such as dedicated gaming consoles and handheld electronic games--are classified in Industry 459120, Hobby, Toy, and Game Retailers;
- Retailing new sewing machines in combination with selling new sewing supplies, fabrics, patterns, yarns, and other needlework accessories--are classified in Industry 459130, Sewing, Needlework, and Piece Goods Retailers;
- Retailing new computers, computer peripherals, and prepackaged software in combination with retailing new office equipment, office furniture, and office supplies--are classified in Industry 459410, Office Supplies and Stationery Retailers;
- Selling wireless communication service plans and cellular telephones, as agents for wireless telecommunications carriers and resellers--are classified in U.S. Industry 517122, Agents for Wireless Telecommunications Services;
- Providing television, computer, or other electronic equipment repair services without retailing new televisions, computers, or electronic equipment--are classified in Industry 811210, Electronic and Precision Equipment Repair and Maintenance;
- Providing household-type appliance repair services without retailing new appliances--are classified in U.S. Industry 811412, Appliance Repair and Maintenance;
- Developing film and/or making photographic slides, prints, and enlargements without retailing a range of new photographic equipment and supplies--are classified in Industry 81292, Photofinishing;
- Renting prerecorded digital video discs (DVDs)--are classified in U.S. Industry 532282, Video Tape and Disc Rental;
- Publishing and distributing software through subscriptions and/or downloads--are classified in Industry 513210, Software Publishers;
- Producing and distributing motion pictures and videos--are classified in Industry 512110, Motion Picture and Video Production; and
- Producing records and/or releasing, promoting, and distributing sound recordings to wholesalers, retailers, or directly to the public--are classified in Industry 512250, Record Production and Distribution.

## 455 General Merchandise Retailers

Industries in the General Merchandise Retailers subsector retail new general merchandise. This subsector includes new and used general merchandise auction retailers and establishments generally known as department stores, warehouse clubs, superstores, or supercenters.

## 4551 Department Stores

## 45511 Department Stores
See industry description for 455110.

## 455110 Department Stores

This industry comprises establishments generally known as department stores that have separate departments for general lines of new merchandise, such as apparel, jewelry, home furnishings, and toys, with no one merchandise line predominating. Department stores may sell perishable groceries, such as fresh fruits, vegetables, and dairy products, but such sales are insignificant. Department stores with fixed point-of-sale locations may have separate customer checkout areas in each department, central customer checkout areas, or both.

---

T—Canadian, Mexican, and United States industries are comparable.

census.gov/naics

*Cross-References.*        Establishments primarily engaged in--

- Retailing apparel without a significant amount of housewares or general merchandise--are classified in Industry 458110, Clothing and Clothing Accessories Retailers;
- Retailing a general line of merchandise in combination with a significant amount and variety of perishable groceries, generally known as warehouse clubs, superstores, or supercenters--are classified in U.S. Industry 455211, Warehouse Clubs and Supercenters;
- Retailing a general line of merchandise and not generally known as department stores, warehouse clubs, superstores, or supercenters--are classified in U.S. Industry 455219, All Other General Merchandise Retailers; and
- Retailing used merchandise--are classified in Industry 459510, Used Merchandise Retailers.

**4552    Warehouse Clubs, Supercenters, and Other General Merchandise Retailers**

**45521    Warehouse Clubs, Supercenters, and Other General Merchandise Retailers**

   This industry comprises establishments primarily engaged in retailing new general merchandise (except department stores).  These establishments retail a general line of new merchandise, such as apparel, automotive parts, dry goods, hardware, groceries, housewares, and home furnishings, with no one merchandise line predominating.  Establishments generally known as warehouse clubs, superstores, or supercenters, and retailing a general line of merchandise in combination with a significant amount and variety of perishable groceries, are included in this industry.  This industry also includes establishments primarily engaged in retailing a general line of new and used merchandise on an auction basis.

*Illustrative Examples:*

Dollar stores

General merchandise (new and used) auction houses

General merchandise showrooms

General merchandise trading posts

General stores

Home and auto supply stores

Superstores (i.e., food and general merchandise)

Variety stores

Warehouse clubs (i.e., food and general merchandise)

*Cross-References.*        Establishments primarily engaged in--

- Auctioning on the location of others as independent auctioneers--are classified in Industry 56199, All Other Support Services;
- Retailing a general line of groceries, such as supermarkets and grocery stores--are classified in Industry 44511, Supermarkets and Other Grocery Retailers (except Convenience Retailers);
- Retailing automotive parts--are classified in Industry 44133, Automotive Parts and Accessories Retailers;
- Retailing a general line of new merchandise, generally known as department stores--are classified in Industry 45511, Department Stores;
- Retailing farm supplies--are classified in Industry 44424, Nursery, Garden Center, and Farm Supply Retailers;
- Retailing a general line of new home repair and improvement materials and supplies, generally known as home centers--are classified in Industry 44411, Home Centers;
- Retailing used merchandise, including by auction--are classified in Industry 45951, Used Merchandise Retailers; and
- Providing warehousing services for goods owned by others--are classified in Industry Group 4931, Warehousing and Storage.

**455211  Warehouse Clubs and Supercenters**

   This U.S. industry comprises establishments generally known as warehouse clubs, superstores, or supercenters, primarily engaged in retailing a general line of groceries, including a significant amount and variety of fresh fruits,

---

T—Canadian, Mexican, and United States industries are comparable.

vegetables, dairy products, meats, and other perishable groceries, in combination with a general line of new merchandise, such as apparel, furniture, and appliances.

*Cross-References.* Establishments primarily engaged in--

- Retailing a general line of groceries, such as supermarkets and grocery stores--are classified in Industry 445110, Supermarkets and Other Grocery Retailers (except Convenience Retailers);
- Retailing a general line of new merchandise, generally known as department stores--are classified in Industry 455110, Department Stores;
- Retailing a general line of new merchandise, except department stores, warehouse clubs, superstores, and supercenters--are classified in U.S. Industry 455219, All Other General Merchandise Retailers;
- Retailing a general line of new home repair and improvement materials and supplies, generally known as home centers--are classified in Industry 444110, Home Centers; and
- Retailing used merchandise--are classified in Industry 459510, Used Merchandise Retailers.

## 455219  All Other General Merchandise Retailers

This U.S. industry comprises establishments primarily engaged in retailing new and used general merchandise (except department stores, warehouse clubs, superstores, and supercenters). These establishments retail a general line of new and used merchandise, such as apparel, automotive parts, dry goods, groceries, hardware, housewares or home furnishings, and other lines in limited amounts, with none of the lines predominating. This industry also includes establishments primarily engaged in retailing a general line of new and used merchandise on an auction basis.

*Illustrative Examples:*

Dollar stores
General merchandise (new and used) auction houses
General merchandise showrooms
General merchandise trading posts

General stores
Home and auto supply stores
Variety stores

*Cross-References.* Establishments primarily engaged in--

- Auctioning on the location of others as independent auctioneers--are classified in Industry 561990, All Other Support Services;
- Retailing automotive parts--are classified in Industry 441330, Automotive Parts and Accessories Retailers;
- Retailing a general line of new merchandise, generally known as department stores--are classified in Industry 455110, Department Stores;
- Retailing a general line of merchandise in combination with a significant amount and variety of perishable groceries, generally known as warehouse clubs, superstores, or supercenters--are classified in U.S. Industry 455211, Warehouse Clubs and Supercenters;
- Retailing farm supplies--are classified in Industry 444240, Nursery, Garden Center, and Farm Supply Retailers;
- Retailing a general line of new home repair and improvement materials and supplies, generally known as home centers--are classified in Industry 444110, Home Centers;
- Retailing used merchandise, including by auction--are classified in Industry 459510, Used Merchandise Retailers; and
- Providing warehousing services for goods owned by others--are classified in Industry Group 4931, Warehousing and Storage.

## 456  Health and Personal Care Retailers

Industries in the Health and Personal Care Retailers subsector retail health and personal care merchandise. Establishments in this subsector are characterized principally by the products they retail, and some health and

---

T—Canadian, Mexican, and United States industries are comparable.

personal care retailers have specialized staff including pharmacists, opticians, and other professionals engaged in retailing, advising customers, and/or fitting the product sold to the customer's needs.

**4561    Health and Personal Care Retailers**

**45611   Pharmacies and Drug Retailers**
See industry description for 456110.

**456110  Pharmacies and Drug Retailers**

This industry comprises establishments generally known as pharmacies and drug retailers engaged in retailing prescription or nonprescription drugs and medicines.

*Cross-References.*          Establishments primarily engaged in--

- Retailing food supplement products, such as vitamins, nutrition supplements, and body enhancing supplements--are classified in U.S. Industry 456191, Food (Health) Supplement Retailers; and
- Providing pharmacy benefit management (PBM) services--are classified in U.S. Industry 524292, Pharmacy Benefit Management and Other Third Party Administration of Insurance and Pension Funds.

**45612   Cosmetics, Beauty Supplies, and Perfume Retailers**
See industry description for 456120.

**456120  Cosmetics, Beauty Supplies, and Perfume Retailers**

This industry comprises establishments primarily engaged in retailing cosmetics, perfumes, toiletries, and personal grooming products.

*Cross-References.*

Establishments primarily engaged in providing beauty salon services are classified in U.S. Industry 812112, Beauty Salons.

**45613   Optical Goods Retailers**
See industry description for 456130.

**456130  Optical Goods Retailers**

This industry comprises establishments primarily engaged in one or more of the following: (1) retailing and fitting prescription eyeglasses and contact lenses; (2) retailing prescription eyeglasses in combination with the grinding of lenses to order on the premises; and (3) retailing nonprescription eyeglasses.

*Cross-References.*          Establishments primarily engaged in--

- Grinding ophthalmic lenses without retailing lenses--are classified in U.S. Industry 339115, Ophthalmic Goods Manufacturing; and
- The independent private or group practice of optometry or ophthalmology, with or without the sale of glasses and contact lenses--are classified in Subsector 621, Ambulatory Health Care Services.

**45619   Other Health and Personal Care Retailers**

This industry comprises establishments primarily engaged in retailing health and personal care items (except drugs, medicines, cosmetics, beauty supplies, perfumes, and optical goods).

---

T—Canadian, Mexican, and United States industries are comparable.

*Illustrative Examples:*

Convalescent supply retailers                           Hearing aid retailers
Vitamin retailers                                       Wheelchair retailers
Sick room supply retailers

*Cross-References.*        Establishments primarily engaged in--

- The independent private or group practice of orthotics or prosthetics, with or without the sale of orthopedic and prosthetic appliances--are classified in Industry 62139, Offices of All Other Health Practitioners;
- The independent private or group practice of audiology, with or without the sale of hearing aid devices--are classified in Industry 62134, Offices of Physical, Occupational and Speech Therapists, and Audiologists;
- The independent private or group practice of optometry or ophthalmology, with or without the sale of glasses and contact lenses--are classified in Subsector 621, Ambulatory Health Care Services;
- Retailing orthopedic shoes--are classified in Industry 45821, Shoe Retailers;
- Selling orthopedic and prosthetic appliances made on the premises--are classified in Industry 33911, Medical Equipment and Supplies Manufacturing;
- Selling hearing aid devices made on the premises--are classified in Industry 33451, Navigational, Measuring, Electromedical, and Control Instruments Manufacturing;
- Retailing prescription and nonprescription drugs and medicines--are classified in Industry 45611, Pharmacies and Drug Retailers;
- Retailing cosmetics, beauty supplies, and perfumes--are classified in Industry 45612, Cosmetics, Beauty Supplies, and Perfume Retailers;
- Retailing eyeglasses and contact lenses (except offices of optometrists and ophthalmologists)--are classified in Industry 45613, Optical Goods Retailers;
- Retailing naturally organic foods, such as fruits and vegetables, dairy products, and cereals and grains--are classified in Subsector 445, Food and Beverage Retailers; and
- Renting home health furniture and equipment--are classified in Industry 53228, Other Consumer Goods Rental.

## 456191  Food (Health) Supplement Retailers

This U.S. industry comprises establishments primarily engaged in retailing food supplement products, such as vitamins, nutrition supplements, and body enhancing supplements.

*Cross-References.*        Establishments primarily engaged in--

- Retailing prescription and nonprescription drugs and medicines--are classified in Industry 456110, Pharmacies and Drug Retailers; and
- Retailing naturally organic foods, such as fruits and vegetables, dairy products, and cereals and grains--are classified in Subsector 445, Food and Beverage Retailers.

## 456199  All Other Health and Personal Care Retailers

This U.S. industry comprises establishments primarily engaged in retailing specialized lines of health and personal care merchandise (except drugs, medicines, cosmetics, beauty supplies, perfumes, optical goods, and food supplement products).

*Illustrative Examples:*

Convalescent supply retailers                           Hearing aid retailers
Sick room supply retailers                              Wheelchair retailers

---

T—Canadian, Mexican, and United States industries are comparable.

*Cross-References.*          Establishments primarily engaged in--

- Retailing vitamins, nutrition supplements, and body enhancing supplements--are classified in U.S. Industry 456191, Food (Health) Supplement Retailers;
- Retailing prescription and nonprescription drugs and medicines--are classified in Industry 456110, Pharmacies and Drug Retailers;
- Retailing cosmetics, beauty supplies, and perfumes--are classified in Industry 456120, Cosmetics, Beauty Supplies, and Perfume Retailers;
- Retailing eyeglasses and contact lenses (except offices of optometrists and ophthalmologists)--are classified in Industry 456130, Optical Goods Retailers;
- The independent private or group practice of optometry or ophthalmology, with or without the sale of glasses and contact lenses--are classified in Subsector 621, Ambulatory Health Care Services;
- The independent private or group practice of orthotics or prosthetics, with or without the sale of orthopedic and prosthetic appliances--are classified in U.S. Industry 621399, Offices of All Other Miscellaneous Health Practitioners;
- The independent private or group practice of audiology, with or without the sale of hearing aid devices--are classified in Industry 621340, Offices of Physical, Occupational and Speech Therapists, and Audiologists;
- Selling hearing aid devices made on the premises--are classified in U.S. Industry 334510, Electromedical and Electrotherapeutic Apparatus Manufacturing;
- Retailing orthopedic shoes--are classified in Industry 458210, Shoe Retailers;
- Selling orthopedic and prosthetic appliances made on the premises--are classified in U.S. Industry 339113, Surgical Appliance and Supplies Manufacturing; and
- Renting home health furniture and equipment--are classified in U.S. Industry 532283, Home Health Equipment Rental.

## 457    Gasoline Stations and Fuel Dealers

Industries in the Gasoline Stations and Fuel Dealers subsector retail automotive fuels (e.g., gasoline, diesel fuel, gasohol, alternative fuels) and automotive oils, without or in combination with convenience store items; or retail heating oil, liquefied petroleum (LP) gas, and other fuels via direct selling (i.e., home delivery).  Gasoline stations have specialized equipment for storing and dispensing automotive fuels.

## 4571    Gasoline Stations

This industry group comprises establishments primarily engaged in retailing automotive fuels (e.g., gasoline, diesel fuel, gasohol, alternative fuels) and automotive oils or retailing these products in combination with convenience store items.  These establishments have specialized equipment for storing and dispensing automotive fuels.

## 45711    Gasoline Stations with Convenience Stores
See industry description for 457110.

## 457110  Gasoline Stations with Convenience Stores

This industry comprises establishments primarily engaged in retailing automotive fuels (e.g., gasoline, diesel fuel, gasohol, alternative fuels) in combination with a limited line of groceries.  These establishments can either be in a convenience store (i.e., food mart) setting or a gasoline station setting.  These establishments may also provide automotive repair services.

*Cross-References.*          Establishments primarily engaged in--

- Operating truck stops or retailing automotive fuels without a convenience store--are classified in Industry 457120, Other Gasoline Stations;
- Retailing a limited line of groceries, such as convenience stores or food marts (except those operating fuel pumps)--are classified in U.S. Industry 445131, Convenience Retailers; and

---

T—Canadian, Mexican, and United States industries are comparable.

- Direct selling of heating oil, liquefied petroleum (LP) gas, and other fuels--are classified in Industry 457210, Fuel Dealers.

**45712  Other Gasoline Stations**
See industry description for 457120.

**457120  Other Gasoline Stations**

This industry comprises establishments generally known as gasoline stations (except those with convenience stores) or truck stops primarily engaged in (1) retailing automotive fuels (e.g., gasoline, diesel fuel, gasohol, alternative fuels) or (2) retailing these fuels in combination with activities, such as providing repair services; selling automotive oils, replacement parts, and accessories; and/or providing food services.

*Illustrative Examples:*

Gasoline stations without convenience stores
Truck stops

Marine service stations

*Cross-References.*        Establishments primarily engaged in--

- Repairing motor vehicles without retailing automotive fuels--are classified in Industry Group 8111, Automotive Repair and Maintenance;
- Retailing automotive fuels in combination with a convenience store or food mart--are classified in Industry 457110, Gasoline Stations with Convenience Stores;
- Direct selling of heating oil, liquefied petroleum (LP) gas, and other fuels--are classified in Industry 457210, Fuel Dealers;
- Retailing a limited line of groceries, such as convenience stores or food marts (except those operating fuel pumps)--are classified in U.S. Industry 445131, Convenience Retailers;
- Providing food services to patrons for immediate on-premises and off-premises consumption--are classified in Subsector 722, Food Services and Drinking Places; and
- Operating marinas--are classified in Industry 713930, Marinas.

**4572    Fuel Dealers**

**45721   Fuel Dealers**
See industry description for 457210.

**457210  Fuel Dealers**

This industry comprises establishments primarily engaged in retailing heating oil, liquefied petroleum (LP) gas, and other fuels via direct selling (i.e., home delivery).

*Cross-References.*        Establishments primarily engaged in--

- Retailing automotive fuels in combination with a convenience store or food mart--are classified in Industry 457110, Gasoline Stations with Convenience Stores;
- Operating truck stops or retailing automotive fuels without a convenience store--are classified in Industry 457120, Other Gasoline Stations; and
- Merchant wholesale distribution of petroleum and petroleum products, including liquefied petroleum (LP) gas, with or without bulk liquid storage facilities--are classified in Industry Group 4247, Petroleum and Petroleum Products Merchant Wholesalers.

---

T—Canadian, Mexican, and United States industries are comparable.

**458 Clothing, Clothing Accessories, Shoe, and Jewelry Retailers**

Industries in the Clothing, Clothing Accessories, Shoe, and Jewelry Retailers subsector retail new clothing, clothing accessories, shoes, jewelry, luggage, and leather goods.

**4581 Clothing and Clothing Accessories Retailers**

**45811 Clothing and Clothing Accessories Retailers**
See industry description for 458110.

**458110 Clothing and Clothing Accessories Retailers**

This industry comprises establishments primarily engaged in retailing general or specialized lines of new clothing and clothing accessories, such as hats and caps, costume jewelry, gloves, handbags, ties, wigs, toupees, and belts. These establishments may provide basic alterations, such as hemming, taking in or letting out seams, or lengthening or shortening sleeves.

*Cross-References.*          Establishments primarily engaged in--

- Selling custom apparel and accessories made on the premises--are classified in Subsector 315, Apparel Manufacturing;
- Retailing new shoes (except specialty sports footwear, such as golf shoes, bowling shoes, and cleated shoes)--are classified in Industry 458210, Shoe Retailers;
- Retailing precious jewelry and watches--are classified in Industry 458310, Jewelry Retailers;
- Retailing new luggage, briefcases, trunks, or these products in combination with a general line of leather items (except leather apparel)--are classified in Industry 458320, Luggage and Leather Goods Retailers;
- Retailing athletic uniforms--are classified in Industry 459110, Sporting Goods Retailers;
- Retailing secondhand clothes and used clothing accessories--are classified in Industry 459510, Used Merchandise Retailers; and
- Providing clothing alterations and repair--are classified in Industry 811490, Other Personal and Household Goods Repair and Maintenance.

**4582 Shoe Retailers**

**45821 Shoe Retailers**
See industry description for 458210.

**458210 Shoe Retailers**

This industry comprises establishments primarily engaged in retailing all types of new footwear (except hosiery and specialty sports footwear, such as golf shoes, bowling shoes, and cleated shoes). Establishments primarily engaged in retailing new tennis shoes or sneakers are included in this industry.

*Cross-References.*          Establishments primarily engaged in--

- Retailing hosiery and socks--are classified in Industry 458110, Clothing and Clothing Accessories Retailers;
- Retailing new specialty sports footwear (e.g., bowling shoes, golf shoes, cleated shoes)--are classified in Industry 459110, Sporting Goods Retailers; and
- Retailing used footwear--are classified in Industry 459510, Used Merchandise Retailers.

T—Canadian, Mexican, and United States industries are comparable.

## 4583 Jewelry, Luggage, and Leather Goods Retailers

This industry group comprises establishments primarily engaged in retailing new jewelry (except costume jewelry); new sterling and plated silverware; new watches and clocks; and new luggage with or without a general line of new leather goods and accessories, such as hats, gloves, handbags, ties, and belts.

### 45831 Jewelry Retailers
See industry description for 458310.

### 458310 Jewelry Retailers

This industry comprises establishments primarily engaged in retailing one or more of the following items: (1) new jewelry (except costume jewelry); (2) new sterling and plated silverware; and (3) new watches and clocks. Also included are establishments retailing these new products in combination with lapidary work and/or repair services.

*Cross-References.*  Establishments primarily engaged in--

- Retailing new costume jewelry--are classified in Industry 458110, Clothing and Clothing Accessories Retailers;
- Retailing antique or used jewelry, silverware, and watches and clocks--are classified in Industry 459510, Used Merchandise Retailers;
- Providing jewelry or watch and clock repair--are classified in Industry 811490, Other Personal and Household Goods Repair and Maintenance; and
- Cutting and setting gem stones--are classified in Industry 339910, Jewelry and Silverware Manufacturing.

### 45832 Luggage and Leather Goods Retailers
See industry description for 458320.

### 458320 Luggage and Leather Goods Retailers

This industry comprises establishments primarily engaged in retailing new luggage, briefcases, and trunks, or retailing these new products in combination with a general line of leather items (except leather apparel), such as belts, gloves, and handbags.

*Cross-References.*  Establishments primarily engaged in--

- Retailing used luggage and leather goods--are classified in Industry 459510, Used Merchandise Retailers;
- Retailing general or specialized lines of new clothing accessories (e.g., gloves, handbags, or leather belts)--are classified in Industry 458110, Clothing and Clothing Accessories Retailers; and
- Retailing new leather coats and other leather apparel--are classified in Industry 458110, Clothing and Clothing Accessories Retailers.

## 459 Sporting Goods, Hobby, Musical Instrument, Book, and Miscellaneous Retailers

Industries in the Sporting Goods, Hobby, Musical Instrument, Book, and Miscellaneous Retailers subsector retail new sporting goods; new toys, games, and hobby supplies; new sewing supplies and needlework accessories; new musical instruments; new books, newspapers, magazines, and other periodicals; and other specialized lines of merchandise, such as cut flowers and floral arrangements, new office supplies and stationery, new gifts, novelty merchandise, and souvenirs, used merchandise, pets and pet supplies, art, new or used manufactured (mobile) homes, and tobacco, electronic cigarettes, and other smoking supplies.

## 4591 Sporting Goods, Hobby, and Musical Instrument Retailers

This industry group comprises establishments primarily engaged in retailing new sporting goods, toys, games, hobby supplies, sewing supplies, needlework accessories, and musical instruments.

T—Canadian, Mexican, and United States industries are comparable.

**45911    Sporting Goods Retailers**
See industry description for 459110.

**459110  Sporting Goods Retailers**

This industry comprises establishments primarily engaged in retailing new sporting goods, such as bicycles and bicycle parts; camping equipment; exercise and fitness equipment; athletic uniforms; specialty sports footwear; and other sporting goods, equipment, and accessories.

*Illustrative Examples:*

| | |
|---|---|
| Athletic uniform supply retailers | Diving equipment retailers |
| Fishing supply retailers | Sporting goods (e.g., scuba, skiing, ball sports) |
| Bicycle (except motorized) retailers | retailers |
| Golf pro shops | Exercise equipment retailers |
| Bowling equipment and supply retailers | Sporting gun and hunting equipment retailers |
| Tack shops | Camping and hiking equipment retailers |

*Cross-References.*          Establishments primarily engaged in--

- Retailing new or used truck campers and camping trailers--are classified in Industry 441210, Recreational Vehicle Dealers;
- Retailing new or used snowmobiles, all-terrain vehicles (ATVs), motorcycles, motorized bicycles, utility trailers, personal watercraft, and motorized golf carts--are classified in U.S. Industry 441227, Motorcycle, ATV, and All Other Motor Vehicle Dealers;
- Retailing new or used boats, outboard motors, and boat trailers--are classified in U.S. Industry 441222, Boat Dealers;
- Retailing new shoes (except specialty sports footwear, such as golf shoes, bowling shoes, and cleated shoes)--are classified in Industry 458210, Shoe Retailers;
- Repairing or servicing sporting goods--are classified in Industry 811490, Other Personal and Household Goods Repair and Maintenance;
- Retailing used sporting goods and used bicycles (except motorized)--are classified in Industry 459510, Used Merchandise Retailers;
- Operating marinas--are classified in Industry 713930, Marinas;
- Operating shooting ranges--are classified in Industry 713990, All Other Amusement and Recreation Industries; and
- Operating golf courses (except miniature)--are classified in Industry 713910, Golf Courses and Country Clubs.

**45912    Hobby, Toy, and Game Retailers**
See industry description for 459120.

**459120  Hobby, Toy, and Game Retailers**

This industry comprises establishments primarily engaged in retailing new toys, games, and hobby and craft supplies (except needlecraft).

*Cross-References.*          Establishments primarily engaged in--

- Retailing artists' supplies or collectors' items (except used rare collectors' items), such as coins, stamps, autographs, and cards--are classified in U.S. Industry 459999, All Other Miscellaneous Retailers;
- Retailing new gaming software, including downloadable software (without publishing)--are classified in Industry 449210, Electronics and Appliance Retailers;
- Retailing used toys, games, and hobby supplies or used rare collectors' items, such as coins, stamps, autographs, and cards--are classified in Industry 459510, Used Merchandise Retailers;

---

T—Canadian, Mexican, and United States industries are comparable.

- Retailing new sewing supplies, fabrics, and needlework accessories--are classified in Industry 459130, Sewing, Needlework, and Piece Goods Retailers;
- Retailing new musical instruments and supplies--are classified in Industry 459140, Musical Instrument and Supplies Retailers;
- Publishing gaming sites--are classified in Subsector 513, Publishing Industries;
- Streaming games without publishing--are classified in Industry 516210, Media Streaming Distribution Services, Social Networks, and Other Media Networks and Content Providers; and
- Renting prerecorded gaming digital video discs (DVDs)--are classified in U.S. Industry 532282, Video Tape and Disc Rental.

**45913 Sewing, Needlework, and Piece Goods Retailers**
See industry description for 459130.

**459130 Sewing, Needlework, and Piece Goods Retailers**

This industry comprises establishments primarily engaged in retailing new sewing supplies, fabrics, patterns, yarns, and other needlework accessories or retailing these products in combination with new sewing machines.

*Illustrative Examples:*

Fabric retailers
Sewing supply retailers
Needlecraft sewing supply retailers

Upholstery materials retailers
Quilting supply retailers

*Cross-References.*        Establishments primarily engaged in--

- Retailing new sewing machines only and in combination with retailing other new appliances--are classified in Industry 449210, Electronics and Appliance Retailers;
- Retailing used sewing, needlework, and piece goods--are classified in Industry 459510, Used Merchandise Retailers; and
- Providing furniture upholstery repair services--are classified in Industry 811420, Reupholstery and Furniture Repair.

**45914 Musical Instrument and Supplies Retailers**
See industry description for 459140.

**459140 Musical Instrument and Supplies Retailers**

This industry comprises establishments primarily engaged in retailing new musical instruments, sheet music, and related supplies; or retailing these new products in combination with musical instrument repair, rental, or music instruction.

*Illustrative Examples*:

Musical instrument retailers
Sheet music retailers

Piano retailers

*Cross-References.*        Establishments primarily engaged in--

- Retailing new musical recordings, including downloadable music (without publishing)--are classified in Industry 449210, Electronics and Appliance Retailers;
- Streaming music without publishing--are classified in Industry 516210, Media Streaming Distribution Services, Social Networks, and Other Media Networks and Content Providers;
- Retailing used musical instruments (including used rare musical instruments), sheet music, and related supplies--are classified in Industry 459510, Used Merchandise Retailers;

T—Canadian, Mexican, and United States industries are comparable.

- Repairing musical instruments without retailing new instruments--are classified in Industry 811490, Other Personal and Household Goods Repair and Maintenance;
- Renting musical instruments without retailing new instruments--are classified in U.S. Industry 532289, All Other Consumer Goods Rental; and
- Providing musical instruction without retailing new instruments--are classified in Industry 611610, Fine Arts Schools.

**4592     Book Retailers and News Dealers**

**45921     Book Retailers and News Dealers**
See industry description for 459210.

**459210     Book Retailers and News Dealers**

This industry comprises establishments primarily engaged in retailing new books, newspapers, magazines, and other periodicals (without publishing).

*Cross-References.*          Establishments primarily engaged in--

- Retailing used books (including used rare books), newspapers, magazines, and other periodicals--are classified in Industry 459510, Used Merchandise Retailers;
- Publishing books, newspapers, and periodicals--are classified in Industry Group 5131, Newspaper, Periodical, Book, and Directory Publishers;
- Streaming audio books, news, and periodical content without publishing--are classified in Industry 516210, Media Streaming Distribution Services, Social Networks, and Other Media Networks and Content Providers; and
- Independently authoring books and other written works and acting as their own publisher--are classified in Industry 711510, Independent Artists, Writers, and Performers.

**4593     Florists**

**45931     Florists**
See industry description for 459310.

**459310     Florists**

This industry comprises establishments generally known as florists primarily engaged in retailing cut flowers, floral arrangements, and potted plants grown elsewhere.  These establishments may prepare the arrangements they sell.

*Cross-References.*          Establishments primarily engaged in--

- Retailing flowers or nursery stock grown on premises--are classified in Industry 11142, Nursery and Floriculture Production; and
- Retailing trees, shrubs, plants, seeds, bulbs, and sod grown elsewhere--are classified in Industry 444240, Nursery, Garden Center, and Farm Supply Retailers.

**4594     Office Supplies, Stationery, and Gift Retailers**

This industry group comprises establishments primarily engaged in retailing new office supplies, stationery, gifts, novelty merchandise, and souvenirs.

**45941     Office Supplies and Stationery Retailers**
See industry description for 459410.

---

T—Canadian, Mexican, and United States industries are comparable.

## 459410  Office Supplies and Stationery Retailers

This industry comprises establishments primarily engaged in one or more of the following: (1) retailing new office supplies, stationery, and school supplies; (2) retailing a combination of new office equipment, furniture, and supplies; and (3) retailing new office equipment, furniture, and supplies in combination with selling new computers.

*Cross-References.*          Establishments primarily engaged in--

- Retailing greeting cards--are classified in Industry 459420, Gift, Novelty, and Souvenir Retailers;
- Retailing new computers without retailing office equipment, furniture, and supplies--are classified in Industry 449210, Electronics and Appliance Retailers;
- Printing business forms--are classified in Industry 32311, Printing;
- Retailing new office furniture without retailing new office equipment and supplies--are classified in Industry 449110, Furniture Retailers;
- Retailing used office and school supplies--are classified in Industry 459510, Used Merchandise Retailers; and
- Providing document copying services (without printing) and other office support services--are classified in Industry 56143, Business Service Centers.

## 45942  Gift, Novelty, and Souvenir Retailers
See industry description for 459420.

## 459420  Gift, Novelty, and Souvenir Retailers

This industry comprises establishments primarily engaged in retailing new gifts, novelty merchandise, souvenirs, greeting cards, seasonal and holiday decorations, and curios.

*Illustrative Examples:*

Greeting card retailers
Seasonal and holiday decoration retailers
Novelty retailers

Souvenir retailers
Gift retailers
Fruit basket or fruit bouquet retailers

*Cross-References.*          Establishments primarily engaged in--

- Retailing stationery--are classified in Industry 459410, Office Supplies and Stationery Retailers;
- Retailing used gifts, novelties, and souvenirs (including used rare collectors' items)--are classified in Industry 459510, Used Merchandise Retailers; and
- Retailing new collectors' items, such as coins, stamps, autographs, and cards--are classified in U.S. Industry 459999, All Other Miscellaneous Retailers.

## 4595  Used Merchandise Retailers

## 45951  Used Merchandise Retailers
See industry description for 459510.

## 459510  Used Merchandise Retailers

This industry comprises establishments primarily engaged in retailing used merchandise, antiques, and secondhand goods (except motor vehicles, such as automobiles, RVs, motorcycles, and boats; motor vehicle parts; tires; and mobile homes).  This industry includes establishments retailing used merchandise on an auction basis.

*Illustrative Examples:*

Antique retailers

Used household appliance retailers

---

T—Canadian, Mexican, and United States industries are comparable.

| | |
|---|---|
| Used book retailers | Used clothing retailers |
| Used merchandise thrift shops | Used sporting goods retailers |

*Cross-References.*        Establishments primarily engaged in--

- Operating pawnshops--are classified in U.S. Industry 522299, International, Secondary Market, and All Other Nondepository Credit Intermediation;
- Retailing used automobiles--are classified in Industry 441120, Used Car Dealers;
- Retailing used automobile parts (except tires and tubes)--are classified in Industry 441330, Automotive Parts and Accessories Retailers;
- Retailing used tires--are classified in Industry 441340, Tire Dealers;
- Retailing used mobile homes--are classified in Industry 459930, Manufactured (Mobile) Home Dealers;
- Retailing used recreational vehicles--are classified in Industry 441210, Recreational Vehicle Dealers;
- Retailing used boats--are classified in U.S. Industry 441222, Boat Dealers;
- Retailing used motorcycles, all-terrain vehicles (ATVs), aircraft, snowmobiles, and utility trailers--are classified in U.S. Industry 441227, Motorcycle, ATV, and All Other Motor Vehicle Dealers; and
- Retailing a general line of new and used merchandise on an auction basis--are classified in U.S. Industry 455219, All Other General Merchandise Retailers.

## 4599    Other Miscellaneous Retailers

This industry group comprises establishments primarily engaged in retailing miscellaneous specialized lines of merchandise (except motor vehicle and parts dealers; building material and garden equipment and supplies dealers; food and beverage retailers; furniture, home furnishings, electronics, and appliance retailers; general merchandise retailers; health and personal care retailers; gasoline stations and fuel dealers; clothing, clothing accessories, shoe, and jewelry retailers; sporting goods, hobby, and musical instrument retailers; book retailers and news dealers; florists; office supplies, stationery, and gift retailers; and used merchandise retailers).

### 45991    Pet and Pet Supplies Retailers
See industry description for 459910.

### 459910  Pet and Pet Supplies Retailers

This industry comprises establishments primarily engaged in retailing pets, pet foods, and pet supplies.

*Cross-References.*        Establishments primarily engaged in--

- Providing pet grooming, walking, and boarding services--are classified in Industry 812910, Pet Care (except Veterinary) Services;
- Providing veterinary services--are classified in Industry 541940, Veterinary Services;
- Boarding horses (except racehorses), pedigree record services, and pet breeding services--are classified in Industry 115210, Support Activities for Animal Production; and
- Raising companion animals (e.g., cats, dogs, pet birds) for sale--are classified in Industry 112990, All Other Animal Production.

### 45992    Art Dealers
See industry description for 459920.

### 459920  Art Dealers

This industry comprises establishments primarily engaged in retailing original and limited edition art works created by others.  Included in this industry are establishments primarily engaged in displaying works of art for retail sale in art galleries.

---

T—Canadian, Mexican, and United States industries are comparable.

**census.gov/naics**

*Cross-References.*          Establishments primarily engaged in--

- Retailing art reproductions (except limited editions)--are classified in U.S. Industry 449129, All Other Home Furnishings Retailers;
- Creating original art works (except musical, commercial, or medical) or restoring art works for others--are classified in Industry 711510, Independent Artists, Writers, and Performers;
- Retailing artists' supplies--are classified in U.S. Industry 459999, All Other Miscellaneous Retailers; and
- Displaying works of art not for retail sale in art galleries--are classified in Industry 712110, Museums.

## 45993   Manufactured (Mobile) Home Dealers
See industry description for 459930.

## 459930   Manufactured (Mobile) Home Dealers

This industry comprises establishments primarily engaged in retailing new and/or used manufactured homes (i.e., mobile homes), parts, and equipment.

*Cross-References.*          Establishments primarily engaged in--

- Retailing new or used motor homes, campers, and travel trailers--are classified in Industry 441210, Recreational Vehicle Dealers;
- Retailing prefabricated buildings and kits without construction--are classified in Industry 444180, Other Building Material Dealers;
- Performing manufactured (mobile) home set up and tie-down work--are classified in Industry 238990, All Other Specialty Trade Contractors; and
- Manufacturing prefabricated residential buildings and assembling/erecting them at the customers' site--are classified in Sector 31-33, Manufacturing, based on the primary material (wood, plastic, or metal).

## 45999   All Other Miscellaneous Retailers

This industry comprises establishments primarily engaged in retailing miscellaneous specialized lines of merchandise (except motor vehicle and parts dealers; building material and garden equipment and supplies dealers; food and beverage retailers; furniture, home furnishings, electronics, and appliance retailers; general merchandise retailers; health and personal care retailers; gasoline stations and fuel dealers; clothing, clothing accessories, shoe, and jewelry retailers; sporting goods, hobby, and musical instrument retailers; book retailers and news dealers; florists; office supplies, stationery, and gift retailers; used merchandise retailers; pet and pet supplies retailers; art dealers; and manufactured (mobile) home dealers).

*Illustrative Examples:*

| | |
|---|---|
| Art supply retailers | Tobacco retailers |
| Swimming pool (above-ground) and supply retailers | Cigar retailers |
| Cemetery memorial (e.g., headstones, markers, vaults) dealers | E-cigarette retailers |
| Home security equipment retailers | Vape shops |

*Cross-References.*          Establishments primarily engaged in--

- Retailing pets and pet supplies--are classified in Industry 45991, Pet and Pet Supplies Retailers;
- Retailing original and limited edition art works created by others--are classified in Industry 45992, Art Dealers;
- Retailing manufactured homes (i.e., mobile homes)--are classified in Industry 45993, Manufactured (Mobile) Home Dealers;
- Retailing new books--are classified in Industry 45921, Book Retailers and News Dealers;
- Retailing new jewelry (except costume jewelry)--are classified in Industry 45831, Jewelry Retailers;

---

T—Canadian, Mexican, and United States industries are comparable.

- Retailing new costume jewelry--are classified in Industry 45811, Clothing and Clothing Accessories Retailers;
- Retailing used merchandise (except automobiles, RVs, mobile homes, motorcycles, all-terrain vehicles (ATVs), boats, motor vehicle parts, tires, aircraft, snowmobiles, and utility trailers)--are classified in Industry 45951, Used Merchandise Retailers;
- Constructing outdoor below-ground swimming pools--are classified in Industry 23899, All Other Specialty Trade Contractors;
- Selling security alarm systems combined with installation, repair, and/or remote alarm monitoring--are classified in Industry 56162, Security Systems Services; and
- Operating funeral homes, cemeteries, and crematories--are classified in Industry Group 8122, Death Care Services.

### 459991 Tobacco, Electronic Cigarette, and Other Smoking Supplies Retailers

This U.S. industry comprises establishments primarily engaged in retailing cigarettes, electronic cigarettes, cigars, tobacco, pipes, and other smokers' supplies.

*Illustrative Examples:*

| | |
|---|---|
| Cigar retailers | Cigarette retailers |
| E-cigarette retailers | Tobacco retailers |
| Smokers' supply retailers | Vape shops |

### 459999 All Other Miscellaneous Retailers

This U.S. industry comprises establishments primarily engaged in retailing miscellaneous specialized lines of merchandise (except motor vehicle and parts dealers; building material and garden equipment and supplies dealers; food and beverage retailers; furniture, home furnishings, electronics, and appliance retailers; general merchandise retailers; health and personal care retailers; gasoline stations and fuel dealers; clothing, clothing accessories, shoe, and jewelry retailers; sporting goods, hobby, and musical instrument retailers; book retailers and news dealers; florists; office supplies, stationery, and gift retailers; used merchandise retailers; pet and pet supplies retailers; art dealers; manufactured (mobile) home dealers; and tobacco, electronic cigarette, and other smoking supplies retailers).

*Illustrative Examples:*

| | |
|---|---|
| Art supply retailers | Fireworks retailers |
| Candle retailers | Collectors' items (e.g., autograph, coin, card, stamp) |
| Home security equipment retailers | retailers (except used rare items) |
| Cemetery memorial (e.g., headstones, markers, | Swimming pool (above-ground) and supply retailers |
| vaults) dealers | Trophy (e.g., awards and plaques) retailers |
| Hot tub retailers | Flower retailers, artificial or dried |

*Cross-References.*          Establishments primarily engaged in--

- Retailing pets and pet supplies--are classified in Industry 459910, Pet and Pet Supplies Retailers;
- Retailing original and limited edition art works created by others--are classified in Industry 459920, Art Dealers;
- Retailing manufactured homes (i.e., mobile homes)--are classified in Industry 459930, Manufactured (Mobile) Home Dealers;
- Retailing cigarettes, electronic cigarettes, cigars, tobacco, pipes, and other smokers' supplies--are classified in U.S. Industry 459991, Tobacco, Electronic Cigarette, and Other Smoking Supplies Retailers;
- Retailing new books--are classified in Industry 459210, Book Retailers and News Dealers;
- Retailing new jewelry (except costume jewelry)--are classified in Industry 458310, Jewelry Retailers;

---

T—Canadian, Mexican, and United States industries are comparable.

- Retailing new costume jewelry--are classified in Industry 458110, Clothing and Clothing Accessories Retailers;
- Retailing antiques--are classified in Industry 459510, Used Merchandise Retailers;
- Constructing outdoor below-ground swimming pools--are classified in Industry 238990, All Other Specialty Trade Contractors;
- Selling security alarm systems combined with installation, repair, and/or remote alarm monitoring--are classified in U.S. Industry 561621, Security Systems Services (except Locksmiths); and
- Operating funeral homes, cemeteries, and crematories--are classified in Industry Group 8122, Death Care Services.

---

T—Canadian, Mexican, and United States industries are comparable.

# Sector 48-49--Transportation and Warehousing[T]

## The Sector as a Whole

The Transportation and Warehousing sector includes industries providing transportation of passengers and cargo, warehousing and storage for goods, scenic and sightseeing transportation, and support activities related to modes of transportation. Establishments in these industries use transportation equipment or transportation-related facilities as a productive asset. The type of equipment depends on the mode of transportation. The modes of transportation are air, rail, water, road, and pipeline.

The Transportation and Warehousing sector distinguishes three basic types of activities: subsectors for each mode of transportation, a subsector for warehousing and storage, and a subsector for establishments providing support activities for transportation. In addition, there are subsectors for establishments that provide passenger transportation for scenic and sightseeing purposes, postal services, and courier services.

A separate subsector for support activities is established in the sector because, first, support activities for transportation are inherently multimodal, such as freight transportation arrangement, or have multimodal aspects. Secondly, there are production process similarities among the support activity industries.

One of the support activities identified in the Support Activities for Transportation subsector is the routine repair and maintenance of transportation equipment (e.g., aircraft at an airport, railroad rolling stock at a railroad terminal, or ships at a harbor or port facility). Such establishments do not perform complete overhauling or rebuilding of transportation equipment (i.e., periodic restoration of transportation equipment to original design specifications) or transportation equipment conversion (i.e., major modification to systems). An establishment that primarily performs factory (or shipyard) overhauls, rebuilding, or conversions of aircraft, railroad rolling stock, or ships is classified in Subsector 336, Transportation Equipment Manufacturing, according to the type of equipment.

Many of the establishments in this sector often operate on networks, with physical facilities, labor forces, and equipment spread over an extensive geographic area.

Warehousing establishments in this sector are distinguished from merchant wholesaling in that the warehouse establishments do not sell the goods.

Excluded from this sector are establishments primarily engaged in providing travel agent, travel arrangement, and reservation services that support transportation establishments, hotels, other businesses, and government agencies. These establishments are classified in Sector 56, Administrative and Support and Waste Management and Remediation Services. Establishments primarily engaged in providing rental and leasing of transportation equipment without operator are classified in Subsector 532, Rental and Leasing Services. Establishments primarily engaged in providing medical care with transportation are classified in Sector 62, Health Care and Social Assistance.

## 481    Air Transportation[T]

Industries in the Air Transportation subsector provide air transportation of passengers and/or cargo using aircraft, such as airplanes, helicopters, and spacecraft. The subsector distinguishes scheduled from nonscheduled air transportation. Scheduled air carriers fly regular routes on regular schedules and operate even if flights are only partially loaded. Nonscheduled carriers often operate during nonpeak time slots at busy airports. These establishments have more flexibility with respect to choice of airport, hours of operation, load factors, and similar operational characteristics. Nonscheduled carriers provide chartered air transportation of passengers, cargo, or specialty flying services. Specialty flying services establishments use general purpose aircraft to provide a variety of specialized flying services.

Scenic and sightseeing air transportation and air courier services are not included in this subsector but are included in Subsector 487, Scenic and Sightseeing Transportation, and in Subsector 492, Couriers and Messengers, respectively. Although these activities may use aircraft, they are different from the activities included in air transportation. Air sightseeing does not usually involve place-to-place transportation; the passenger's flight (e.g., balloon ride, aerial sightseeing) typically starts and ends at the same location. Courier services (individual package or cargo delivery) include more than air transportation; road transportation is usually required to deliver the cargo to the intended recipient.

## 4811    Scheduled Air Transportation[T]

---

T—Canadian, Mexican, and United States industries are comparable.

## 48111  Scheduled Air Transportation[T]

This industry comprises establishments primarily engaged in providing air transportation of passengers and/or cargo over regular routes and on regular schedules. Establishments in this industry operate flights even if partially loaded. Establishments primarily engaged in providing scheduled air transportation of mail on a contract basis are included in this industry.

*Illustrative Examples:*

Air commuter carriers, scheduled

Scheduled air passenger carriers

Scheduled air cargo carriers (except air couriers)

Scheduled helicopter passenger carriers

*Cross-References.*  Establishments primarily engaged in--

- Providing air courier services--are classified in Industry 49211, Couriers and Express Delivery Services;
- Providing air transportation of passengers, cargo, or specialty flying services with no regular routes and regular schedules--are classified in Industry 48121, Nonscheduled Air Transportation; and
- Providing helicopter rides for scenic and sightseeing transportation--are classified in Industry 48799, Scenic and Sightseeing Transportation, Other.

## 481111  Scheduled Passenger Air Transportation

This U.S. industry comprises establishments primarily engaged in providing air transportation of passengers or passengers and freight over regular routes and on regular schedules. Establishments in this industry operate flights even if partially loaded. Scheduled air passenger carriers including commuter and helicopter carriers (except scenic and sightseeing) are included in this industry.

*Cross-References.*  Establishments primarily engaged in--

- Providing air transportation of passengers or passengers and cargo with no regular routes and regular schedules--are classified in U.S. Industry 481211, Nonscheduled Chartered Passenger Air Transportation;
- Providing helicopter rides for scenic and sightseeing transportation--are classified in Industry 487990, Scenic and Sightseeing Transportation, Other; and
- Providing air transportation of cargo (without transporting passengers) over regular routes and on regular schedules--are classified in U.S. Industry 481112, Scheduled Freight Air Transportation.

## 481112  Scheduled Freight Air Transportation

This U.S. industry comprises establishments primarily engaged in providing air transportation of cargo without transporting passengers over regular routes and on regular schedules. Establishments in this industry operate flights even if partially loaded. Establishments primarily engaged in providing scheduled air transportation of mail on a contract basis are included in this industry.

*Cross-References.*  Establishments primarily engaged in--

- Providing air courier services--are classified in Industry 492110, Couriers and Express Delivery Services;
- Providing air transportation of cargo with no regular routes and regular schedules--are classified in U.S. Industry 481212, Nonscheduled Chartered Freight Air Transportation; and
- Providing air transportation of passengers or passengers and cargo over regular routes and on regular schedules--are classified in U.S. Industry 481111, Scheduled Passenger Air Transportation.

## 4812  Nonscheduled Air Transportation[T]

---

T—Canadian, Mexican, and United States industries are comparable.

## 48121   Nonscheduled Air Transportation[T]

This industry comprises establishments primarily engaged in (1) providing air transportation of passengers and/or cargo with no regular routes and regular schedules or (2) providing specialty flying services with no regular routes and regular schedules using general purpose aircraft. These establishments have more flexibility with respect to choice of airports, hours of operation, load factors, and similar operational characteristics.

*Illustrative Examples:*

Air taxi services                                              Aircraft charter services
Nonscheduled air freight transportation services              Nonscheduled air passenger transportation services

*Cross-References.*          Establishments primarily engaged in--

- Crop dusting using specialized aircraft--are classified in Industry 11511, Support Activities for Crop Production;
- Fighting forest fires using specialized water bombers--are classified in Industry 11531, Support Activities for Forestry;
- Providing air transportation of passengers and/or cargo over regular routes and on regular schedules--are classified in Industry 48111, Scheduled Air Transportation;
- Providing specialized air sightseeing services--are classified in Industry 48799, Scenic and Sightseeing Transportation, Other;
- Aerial gathering of geophysical data--are classified in Industry 54136, Geophysical Surveying and Mapping Services;
- Providing aerial and/or other surveying and mapping services--are classified in Industry 54137, Surveying and Mapping (except Geophysical) Services;
- Providing air ambulance services using specialized equipment--are classified in Industry 62191, Ambulance Services;
- Operating specialized flying schools, including all training for commercial pilots--are classified in Industry 61151, Technical and Trade Schools;
- Operating recreational aviation clubs--are classified in Industry 71399, All Other Amusement and Recreation Industries;
- Operating advocacy aviation clubs--are classified in Industry 81331, Social Advocacy Organizations;
- Providing air courier services--are classified in Industry 49211, Couriers and Express Delivery Services;
- Independent air pilot services (except owner-operators)--are classified in Industry 48819, Other Support Activities for Air Transportation; and
- Renting or leasing aircraft without an operator--are classified in Industry 53241, Construction, Transportation, Mining, and Forestry Machinery and Equipment Rental and Leasing.

## 481211   Nonscheduled Chartered Passenger Air Transportation

This U.S. industry comprises establishments primarily engaged in providing air transportation of passengers or passengers and cargo with no regular routes and regular schedules.

*Cross-References.*          Establishments primarily engaged in--

- Providing specialty air transportation or flying services with no regular routes and regular schedules using general purpose aircraft--are classified in U.S. Industry 481219, Other Nonscheduled Air Transportation;
- Providing specialized air sightseeing services--are classified in Industry 487990, Scenic and Sightseeing Transportation, Other;
- Providing air transportation of passengers or passengers and cargo over regular routes and on regular schedules--are classified in U.S. Industry 481111, Scheduled Passenger Air Transportation;
- Providing air transportation of cargo (without transporting passengers) with no regular routes and schedules--are classified in U.S. Industry 481212, Nonscheduled Chartered Freight Air Transportation;

---

T—Canadian, Mexican, and United States industries are comparable.

- Independent air pilot services (except owner-operators)--are classified in Industry 488190, Other Support Activities for Air Transportation; and
- Renting or leasing aircraft without an operator--are classified in U.S. Industry 532411, Commercial Air, Rail, and Water Transportation Equipment Rental and Leasing.

## 481212 Nonscheduled Chartered Freight Air Transportation

This U.S. industry comprises establishments primarily engaged in providing air transportation of cargo without transporting passengers with no regular routes and regular schedules.

*Cross-References.* Establishments primarily engaged in--

- Providing specialty air transportation or flying services with no regular routes and regular schedules using general purpose aircraft--are classified in U.S. Industry 481219, Other Nonscheduled Air Transportation;
- Providing air courier services--are classified in Industry 492110, Couriers and Express Delivery Services;
- Providing air transportation of cargo without transporting passengers over regular routes and on regular schedules--are classified in U.S. Industry 481112, Scheduled Freight Air Transportation;
- Providing air transportation of cargo and passengers with no regular routes and schedules--are classified in U.S. Industry 481211, Nonscheduled Chartered Passenger Air Transportation; and
- Independent air pilot services (except owner-operators)--are classified in Industry 488190, Other Support Activities for Air Transportation.

## 481219 Other Nonscheduled Air Transportation

This U.S. industry comprises establishments primarily engaged in providing air transportation with no regular routes and regular schedules (except nonscheduled chartered passenger and/or cargo air transportation). These establishments provide a variety of specialty air transportation or flying services based on individual customer needs using general purpose aircraft.

*Illustrative Examples:*

Aircraft charter services (i.e., general purpose aircraft used for a variety of specialty air and flying services)

Aviation clubs providing a variety of air transportation activities to the general public

*Cross-References.* Establishments primarily engaged in--

- Providing air transportation of passengers or passengers and cargo with no regular routes and regular schedules--are classified in U.S. Industry 481211, Nonscheduled Chartered Passenger Air Transportation;
- Providing air transportation of cargo without transporting passengers with no regular routes and regular schedules--are classified in U.S. Industry 481212, Nonscheduled Chartered Freight Air Transportation;
- Crop dusting using specialized aircraft--are classified in U.S. Industry 115112, Soil Preparation, Planting, and Cultivating;
- Fighting forest fires using specialized water bombers--are classified in Industry 115310, Support Activities for Forestry;
- Providing specialized air sightseeing services--are classified in Industry 487990, Scenic and Sightseeing Transportation, Other;
- Operating specialized flying schools, including all training for commercial pilots--are classified in U.S. Industry 611512, Flight Training;
- Providing specialized air ambulance services using specialized equipment--are classified in Industry 621910, Ambulance Services;
- Operating recreational aviation clubs--are classified in Industry 713990, All Other Amusement and Recreation Industries;
- Operating advocacy aviation clubs--are classified in U.S. Industry 813319, Other Social Advocacy Organizations;

T--Canadian, Mexican, and United States industries are comparable.

- Aerial gathering of geophysical data for surveying and mapping--are classified in Industry 541360, Geophysical Surveying and Mapping Services;
- Providing aerial and/or other surveying and mapping services--are classified in Industry 541370, Surveying and Mapping (except Geophysical) Services; and
- Independent air pilot services (except owner-operators)--are classified in Industry 488190, Other Support Activities for Air Transportation.

## 482    Rail Transportation[T]

Industries in the Rail Transportation subsector provide rail transportation of passengers and/or cargo using railroad rolling stock.  The railroads in this subsector primarily either operate on networks, with physical facilities, labor force, and equipment spread over an extensive geographic area, or operate over a short distance on a local rail line.

Scenic and sightseeing rail transportation and street railroads, commuter rail, and rapid transit are not included in this subsector but are included in Subsector 487, Scenic and Sightseeing Transportation, and Subsector 485, Transit and Ground Passenger Transportation, respectively.  Although these activities use railroad rolling stock, they are different from the activities included in rail transportation.  Sightseeing and scenic railroads do not usually involve place-to-place transportation; the passenger's trip typically starts and ends at the same location.  Commuter railroads operate in a manner more consistent with local and urban transit and are often part of integrated transit systems.

## 4821    Rail Transportation[T]

## 48211    Rail Transportation[T]

This industry comprises establishments primarily engaged in operating railroads (except street railroads, commuter rail, urban rapid transit, and scenic and sightseeing trains).  Line-haul railroads and short-line railroads are included in this industry.

*Cross-References.*        Establishments primarily engaged in--

- Operating street railroads, commuter rail, and urban rapid transit systems--are classified in Industry Group 4851, Urban Transit Systems;
- Operating scenic and sightseeing trains--are classified in Industry 48711, Scenic and Sightseeing Transportation, Land; and
- Operating switching and terminal facilities as separate establishments--are classified in Industry 48821, Support Activities for Rail Transportation.

## 482111  Line-Haul Railroads

This U.S. industry comprises establishments known as line-haul railroads primarily engaged in operating railroads for the transport of passengers and/or cargo over a long distance within a rail network.  These establishments provide for the intercity movement of trains between the terminals and stations on main and branch lines of a line-haul rail network (except for local switching services).

*Cross-References.*        Establishments primarily engaged in--

- Operating switching and terminal facilities as separate establishments--are classified in Industry 488210, Support Activities for Rail Transportation;
- Operating railroads over a short distance on local rail lines--are classified in U.S. Industry 482112, Short Line Railroads; and
- Operating commuter rail systems--are classified in U.S. Industry 485112, Commuter Rail Systems.

## 482112  Short Line Railroads

This U.S. industry comprises establishments known as short-line railroads primarily engaged in operating railroads for the transport of cargo over a short distance on local rail lines not part of a rail network.

T—Canadian, Mexican, and United States industries are comparable.

*Cross-References.*          Establishments primarily engaged in--

- Operating street railroads, commuter rail, and urban rapid transit systems--are classified in Industry Group 4851, Urban Transit Systems;
- Operating scenic and sightseeing trains--are classified in Industry 487110, Scenic and Sightseeing Transportation, Land;
- Operating switching and terminal facilities as separate establishments--are classified in Industry 488210, Support Activities for Rail Transportation; and
- Operating railroads for the transport of passengers and/or cargo over a long distance--are classified in U.S. Industry 482111, Line-Haul Railroads.

### 483      Water Transportation[T]

Industries in the Water Transportation subsector provide water transportation of passengers and cargo using watercraft, such as ships, barges, and boats.

The subsector is composed of two industry groups: (1) one for deep sea, coastal, and Great Lakes water transportation; and (2) one for inland water transportation. This split typically reflects the difference in equipment used.

Scenic and sightseeing water transportation services are not included in this subsector but are included in Subsector 487, Scenic and Sightseeing Transportation. Although these activities use watercraft, they are different from the activities included in water transportation. Water sightseeing does not usually involve place-to-place transportation; the passenger's trip starts and ends at the same location.

### 4831    Deep Sea, Coastal, and Great Lakes Water Transportation[T]

### 48311   Deep Sea, Coastal, and Great Lakes Water Transportation[T]

This industry comprises establishments primarily engaged in providing deep sea, coastal, Great Lakes, and St. Lawrence Seaway water transportation. Marine transportation establishments using the facilities of the St. Lawrence Seaway Authority Commission are considered to be using the Great Lakes Water Transportation System.

*Cross-References.*          Establishments primarily engaged in--

- Providing inland water transportation on lakes, rivers, or intracoastal waterways (except on the Great Lakes System)--are classified in Industry 48321, Inland Water Transportation;
- Providing scenic and sightseeing water transportation, such as harbor cruises and charter fishing boat operations--are classified in Industry 48721, Scenic and Sightseeing Transportation, Water;
- Operating tugboats in harbors--are classified in Industry 48833, Navigational Services to Shipping;
- Operating floating casinos (i.e., gambling cruises, riverboat gambling casinos)--are classified in Industry 71321, Casinos (except Casino Hotels);
- Renting yachts and pleasure boats, such as houseboats and sailboats, without crew--are classified in Industry 53228, Other Consumer Goods Rental; and
- Renting or leasing commercial boats (including vessel supply services), without crew--are classified in Industry 53241, Construction, Transportation, Mining, and Forestry Machinery and Equipment Rental and Leasing.

### 483111  Deep Sea Freight Transportation

This U.S. industry comprises establishments primarily engaged in providing deep sea transportation of cargo to or from foreign ports.

*Cross-References.*

Establishments primarily engaged in providing deep sea transportation of cargo to and from domestic ports are classified in U.S. Industry 483113, Coastal and Great Lakes Freight Transportation.

---

T—Canadian, Mexican, and United States industries are comparable.

## 483112  Deep Sea Passenger Transportation

This U.S. industry comprises establishments primarily engaged in providing deep sea transportation of passengers to or from foreign ports.

*Cross-References.*          Establishments primarily engaged in--

- Providing deep sea transportation of passengers to and from domestic ports--are classified in U.S. Industry 483114, Coastal and Great Lakes Passenger Transportation; and
- Operating floating casinos (i.e., gambling cruises)--are classified in Industry 713210, Casinos (except Casino Hotels).

## 483113  Coastal and Great Lakes Freight Transportation

This U.S. industry comprises establishments primarily engaged in providing water transportation of cargo in coastal waters, on the Great Lakes System, or deep seas between ports of the United States, Puerto Rico, and United States island possessions or protectorates.  Marine transportation establishments using the facilities of the St. Lawrence Seaway Authority Commission are considered to be using the Great Lakes Water Transportation System. Establishments primarily engaged in providing coastal and/or Great Lakes barge transportation services are included in this industry.

*Cross-References.*          Establishments primarily engaged in--

- Providing deep sea transportation of cargo to or from foreign ports--are classified in U.S. Industry 483111, Deep Sea Freight Transportation;
- Providing inland water transportation of cargo on lakes, rivers, or intracoastal waterways (except on the Great Lakes System)--are classified in U.S. Industry 483211, Inland Water Freight Transportation; and
- Operating tugboats in harbors--are classified in Industry 488330, Navigational Services to Shipping.

## 483114  Coastal and Great Lakes Passenger Transportation

This U.S. industry comprises establishments primarily engaged in providing water transportation of passengers in coastal waters, the Great Lakes System, or deep seas between ports of the United States, Puerto Rico, and United States island possessions and protectorates.  Marine transportation establishments using the facilities of the St. Lawrence Seaway Authority Commission are considered to be using the Great Lakes Water Transportation System.

*Cross-References.*          Establishments primarily engaged in--

- Providing inland water transportation of passengers on lakes, rivers, or intracoastal waterways (except on the Great Lakes System)--are classified in U.S. Industry 483212, Inland Water Passenger Transportation;
- Providing scenic and sightseeing water transportation, such as harbor cruises and charter fishing boat operations--are classified in Industry 487210, Scenic and Sightseeing Transportation, Water;
- Operating floating casinos (i.e., gambling cruises)--are classified in Industry 713210, Casinos (except Casino Hotels);
- Renting yachts and pleasure boats, such as houseboats and sailboats, without crew--are classified in U.S. Industry 532284, Recreational Goods Rental; and
- Renting or leasing commercial boats (including vessel supply services), without crew--are classified in U.S. Industry 532411, Commercial Air, Rail, and Water Transportation Equipment Rental and Leasing.

## 4832  Inland Water Transportation[T]

## 48321  Inland Water Transportation[T]

This industry comprises establishments primarily engaged in providing inland water transportation of passengers and/or cargo on lakes, rivers, or intracoastal waterways (except on the Great Lakes System).

---

T—Canadian, Mexican, and United States industries are comparable.

*Cross-References.*          Establishments primarily engaged in--

- Providing water transportation in deep sea, coastal, or on the Great Lakes System--are classified in Industry Group 4831, Deep Sea, Coastal, and Great Lakes Water Transportation;
- Providing scenic and sightseeing water transportation, such as harbor cruises and charter fishing boat operations--are classified in Industry 48721, Scenic and Sightseeing Transportation, Water;
- Operating floating casinos (i.e., gambling cruises, riverboat gambling casinos)--are classified in Industry 71321, Casinos (except Casino Hotels);
- Renting yachts and pleasure boats, such as houseboats and sailboats, without crew--are classified in Industry 53228, Other Consumer Goods Rental; and
- Renting or leasing commercial boats (including vessel supply services), without crew--are classified in Industry 53241, Construction, Transportation, Mining, and Forestry Machinery and Equipment Rental and Leasing.

## 483211  Inland Water Freight Transportation

This U.S. industry comprises establishments primarily engaged in providing inland water transportation of cargo on lakes, rivers, or intracoastal waterways (except on the Great Lakes System).

*Cross-References.*          Establishments primarily engaged in--

- Providing deep sea transportation of cargo to and from foreign ports--are classified in U.S. Industry 483111, Deep Sea Freight Transportation;
- Providing water transportation of cargo in coastal waters or on the Great Lakes System--are classified in U.S. Industry 483113, Coastal and Great Lakes Freight Transportation; and
- Renting or leasing commercial boats (including vessel supply services), without crew--are classified in U.S. Industry 532411, Commercial Air, Rail, and Water Transportation Equipment Rental and Leasing.

## 483212  Inland Water Passenger Transportation

This U.S. industry comprises establishments primarily engaged in providing inland water transportation of passengers on lakes, rivers, or intracoastal waterways (except on the Great Lakes System).

*Cross-References.*          Establishments primarily engaged in--

- Providing deep sea transportation of passengers to and from foreign ports--are classified in U.S. Industry 483112, Deep Sea Passenger Transportation;
- Operating floating casinos (i.e., gambling cruises, riverboat gambling casinos)--are classified in Industry 713210, Casinos (except Casino Hotels);
- Operating cruise ships or ferries in coastal waters or on the Great Lakes System--are classified in U.S. Industry 483114, Coastal and Great Lakes Passenger Transportation;
- Providing scenic and sightseeing water transportation, such as harbor cruises and charter fishing boat operations--are classified in Industry 487210, Scenic and Sightseeing Transportation, Water;
- Renting yachts and pleasure boats, such as houseboats and sailboats, without crew--are classified in U.S. Industry 532284, Recreational Goods Rental; and
- Renting or leasing commercial boats (including vessel supply services), without crew--are classified in U.S. Industry 532411, Commercial Air, Rail, and Water Transportation Equipment Rental and Leasing.

## 484     Truck Transportation[T]

Industries in the Truck Transportation subsector provide over-the-road transportation of cargo using motor vehicles, such as trucks and tractor trailers.  The subsector is subdivided into general freight trucking and specialized freight trucking.  This distinction reflects differences in equipment used, type of load carried, scheduling, terminal, and other networking services.  General freight transportation establishments handle a wide variety of general commodities, generally palletized, and transported in a container or van trailer.  Specialized freight transportation is

---

T—Canadian, Mexican, and United States industries are comparable.

the transportation of cargo that, because of size, weight, shape, or other inherent characteristics, requires specialized equipment for transportation.

Each of these industry groups is further subdivided based on distance traveled. Local trucking establishments primarily carry goods within a single metropolitan area and its adjacent nonurban areas. Long-distance trucking establishments carry goods between metropolitan areas.

The Specialized Freight Trucking industry group includes a separate industry for Used Household and Office Goods Moving. The household and office goods movers are separated because of the substantial network of establishments that has developed to deal with local and long-distance moving and the associated storage. In this area, the same establishment provides both local and long-distance services, while other specialized freight establishments generally limit their services to either local or long-distance hauling.

## 4841   General Freight Trucking[T]

This industry group comprises establishments primarily engaged in providing general freight trucking. General freight trucking establishments handle a wide variety of commodities, generally palletized, and transported in a container or van trailer. The establishments of this industry group provide a combination of the following network activities: local pick-up, local sorting and terminal operations, line-haul, destination sorting and terminal operations, and local delivery.

## 48411   General Freight Trucking, Local[T]
See industry description for 484110.

## 484110  General Freight Trucking, Local

This industry comprises establishments primarily engaged in providing local general freight trucking. General freight trucking establishments handle a wide variety of commodities, generally palletized and transported in a container or van trailer. Local general freight trucking establishments usually provide trucking within a metropolitan area which may cross state lines. Generally the trips are same-day return.

*Cross-References.*          Establishments primarily engaged in--

- Operating independent trucking terminals--are classified in Industry 488490, Other Support Activities for Road Transportation; and
- Providing general freight long-distance trucking, including all North American international travel--are classified in Industry 48412, General Freight Trucking, Long-Distance.

## 48412   General Freight Trucking, Long-Distance[T]

This industry comprises establishments primarily engaged in providing long-distance general freight trucking. General freight trucking establishments handle a wide variety of commodities, generally palletized and transported in a container or van trailer. Long-distance general freight trucking establishments usually provide trucking between metropolitan areas which may cross North American country borders. Included in this industry are establishments operating as truckload (TL) or less than truckload (LTL) carriers.

*Cross-References.*          Establishments primarily engaged in--

- Providing courier services--are classified in Industry 49211, Couriers and Express Delivery Services;
- Providing warehousing services of general freight without transportation--are classified in Industry 49311, General Warehousing and Storage;
- Providing specialized freight trucking--are classified in Industry Group 4842, Specialized Freight Trucking;
- Operating independent trucking terminals--are classified in Industry 48849, Other Support Activities for Road Transportation;
- Providing local general freight trucking services--are classified in Industry 48411, General Freight Trucking, Local; and

---

T—Canadian, Mexican, and United States industries are comparable.

- Providing independent truck driving services (except owner-operators)--are classified in Industry 48849, Other Support Activities for Road Transportation.

### 484121   General Freight Trucking, Long-Distance, Truckload

This U.S. industry comprises establishments primarily engaged in providing long-distance general freight truckload (TL) trucking.  These long-distance general freight truckload carrier establishments provide full truck movement of freight from origin to destination.  The shipment of freight on a truck is characterized as a full single load not combined with other shipments.

*Cross-References.*          Establishments primarily engaged in--

- Providing general freight long-distance, less than truckload trucking--are classified in U.S. Industry 484122, General Freight Trucking, Long-Distance, Less Than Truckload;
- Providing specialized freight trucking--are classified in Industry Group 4842, Specialized Freight Trucking;
- Operating independent trucking terminals--are classified in Industry 488490, Other Support Activities for Road Transportation;
- Providing local general freight trucking services--are classified in Industry 484110, General Freight Trucking, Local; and
- Providing independent truck driving services (except owner-operators)--are classified in Industry 488490, Other Support Activities for Road Transportation.

### 484122   General Freight Trucking, Long-Distance, Less Than Truckload

This U.S. industry comprises establishments primarily engaged in providing long-distance, general freight, less than truckload (LTL) trucking.  LTL carriage is characterized as multiple shipments combined onto a single truck for multiple deliveries within a network.  These establishments are generally characterized by the following network activities: local pick-up, local sorting and terminal operations, line-haul, destination sorting and terminal operations, and local delivery.

*Cross-References.*          Establishments primarily engaged in--

- Providing courier services--are classified in Industry 492110, Couriers and Express Delivery Services;
- Providing warehousing services of general freight without transportation--are classified in Industry 493110, General Warehousing and Storage;
- Providing specialized freight trucking--are classified in Industry Group 4842, Specialized Freight Trucking;
- Operating independent trucking terminals--are classified in Industry 488490, Other Support Activities for Road Transportation;
- Providing general freight long-distance truckload trucking--are classified in U.S. Industry 484121, General Freight Trucking, Long-Distance, Truckload;
- Providing local general freight trucking services--are classified in Industry 484110, General Freight Trucking, Local; and
- Providing independent truck driving services (except owner-operators)--are classified in Industry 488490, Other Support Activities for Road Transportation.

### 4842   Specialized Freight Trucking[T]

This industry group comprises establishments primarily engaged in providing local or long-distance specialized freight trucking.  The establishments of this industry are primarily engaged in the transportation of freight which, because of size, weight, shape, or other inherent characteristics, requires specialized equipment, such as flatbeds, tankers, or refrigerated trailers.  This industry includes the transportation of used household, institutional, and commercial furniture and equipment.

### 48421   Used Household and Office Goods Moving[T]
      See industry description for 484210.

---

T—Canadian, Mexican, and United States industries are comparable.

**484210  Used Household and Office Goods Moving**

This industry comprises establishments primarily engaged in providing local or long-distance trucking of used household, used institutional, or used commercial furniture and equipment.  Incidental packing and storage activities are often provided by these establishments.

**48422    Specialized Freight (except Used Goods) Trucking, Local<sup>T</sup>**
See industry description for 484220.

**484220  Specialized Freight (except Used Goods) Trucking, Local**

This industry comprises establishments primarily engaged in providing local, specialized trucking.  Local trucking establishments provide trucking within a metropolitan area that may cross state lines.  Generally the trips are same-day return.

*Illustrative Examples:*

Local agricultural products trucking                    Local livestock trucking
Local dump trucking (e.g., gravel, sand, top-soil)      Local bulk liquids trucking
Local boat hauling

*Cross-References.*        Establishments primarily engaged in--

- Providing long-distance specialized freight (except used goods) trucking including all North American international travel--are classified in Industry 484230, Specialized Freight (except Used Goods) Trucking, Long-Distance;
- Providing local general freight trucking--are classified in Industry 484110, General Freight Trucking, Local;
- Providing trucking of used household and office goods--are classified in Industry 484210, Used Household and Office Goods Moving;
- Providing waste collection--are classified in Industry Group 5621, Waste Collection;
- Providing independent truck driving services (except owner-operators)--are classified in Industry 488490, Other Support Activities for Road Transportation; and
- Providing hot shot oil field services (on- and off-road) on a contract basis--are classified in U.S. Industry 213112, Support Activities for Oil and Gas Operations.

**48423    Specialized Freight (except Used Goods) Trucking, Long-Distance<sup>T</sup>**
See industry description for 484230.

**484230  Specialized Freight (except Used Goods) Trucking, Long-Distance**

This industry comprises establishments primarily engaged in providing long-distance specialized trucking.  These establishments provide trucking between metropolitan areas that may cross North American country borders.

*Illustrative Examples:*

Long-distance automobile carrier trucking               Long-distance trucking of waste
Long-distance refrigerated product trucking             Long-distance hazardous material trucking
Long-distance bulk liquid trucking

*Cross-References.*        Establishments primarily engaged in--

- Providing local specialized freight trucking (except used goods)--are classified in Industry 484220, Specialized Freight (except Used Goods) Trucking, Local;

---

T—Canadian, Mexican, and United States industries are comparable.

- Providing long-distance general freight trucking, including all North American international travel--are classified in Industry 48412, General Freight Trucking, Long-Distance;
- Providing trucking of used household and office goods--are classified in Industry 484210, Used Household and Office Goods Moving;
- Collecting and/or hauling hazardous waste, nonhazardous waste, and/or recyclable materials within a local area--are classified in Industry 56211, Waste Collection;
- Providing independent truck driving services (except owner-operators)--are classified in Industry 488490, Other Support Activities for Road Transportation; and
- Providing hot shot oil field services (on- and off-road) on a contract basis--are classified in U.S. Industry 213112, Support Activities for Oil and Gas Operations.

## 485     Transit and Ground Passenger Transportation[T]

Industries in the Transit and Ground Passenger Transportation subsector include a variety of passenger transportation activities, such as urban transit systems; chartered bus, school bus, and interurban bus transportation; and taxis. These activities are distinguished based primarily on such production process factors as vehicle types, routes, and schedules.

In this subsector, the principal splits identify scheduled transportation as separate from nonscheduled transportation. The scheduled transportation industry groups are Urban Transit Systems, Interurban and Rural Bus Transportation, and School and Employee Bus Transportation. The nonscheduled industry groups are the Charter Bus Industry and Taxi and Limousine Service. The Other Transit and Ground Passenger Transportation industry group includes both scheduled and nonscheduled transportation.

Scenic and sightseeing ground transportation services are not included in this subsector but are included in Subsector 487, Scenic and Sightseeing Transportation. Sightseeing does not usually involve place-to-place transportation; the passenger's trip starts and ends at the same location.

## 4851     Urban Transit Systems[T]

## 48511     Urban Transit Systems[T]

This industry comprises establishments primarily engaged in operating local and suburban passenger transit systems over regular routes and on regular schedules within a metropolitan area and its adjacent nonurban areas. Such transportation systems involve the use of one or more modes of transport including light rail, commuter rail, subways, and streetcars, as well as buses and other motor vehicles.

*Cross-References.*          Establishments primarily engaged in--

- Providing scenic and sightseeing transportation on land--are classified in Industry 48711, Scenic and Sightseeing Transportation, Land;
- Providing support services to transit and ground transportation--are classified in Industry Group 4884, Support Activities for Road Transportation;
- Providing interurban and rural bus transportation--are classified in Industry 48521, Interurban and Rural Bus Transportation;
- Providing bus transportation for students and employees--are classified in Industry 48541, School and Employee Bus Transportation; and
- Providing bus shuttle services (except school and employee bus)--are classified in Industry 48599, Other Transit and Ground Passenger Transportation.

## 485111   Mixed Mode Transit Systems

This U.S. industry comprises establishments primarily engaged in operating local and suburban ground passenger transit systems using more than one mode of transport over regular routes and on regular schedules within a metropolitan area and its adjacent nonurban areas.

---

T—Canadian, Mexican, and United States industries are comparable.

*Cross-References.*      Establishments primarily engaged in--

- Operating local and suburban passenger transit systems using only one mode of transportation--are classified according to the mode of transport; and
- Providing support services to transit and ground passenger transportation--are classified in Industry Group 4884, Support Activities for Road Transportation.

## 485112  Commuter Rail Systems

This U.S. industry comprises establishments primarily engaged in operating local and suburban commuter rail systems over regular routes and on a regular schedule within a metropolitan area and its adjacent nonurban areas. Commuter rail is usually characterized by reduced fares, multiple ride and commutation tickets, and mostly used by passengers during the morning and evening peak periods.

*Cross-References.*      Establishments primarily engaged in--

- Operating local and suburban mass passenger transit systems using both commuter rail and another mode of transport--are classified in U.S. Industry 485111, Mixed Mode Transit Systems;
- Operating stand-alone subway or light rail systems--are classified in U.S. Industry 485119, Other Urban Transit Systems; and
- Providing scenic and sightseeing transportation on land--are classified in Industry 487110, Scenic and Sightseeing Transportation, Land.

## 485113  Bus and Other Motor Vehicle Transit Systems

This U.S. industry comprises establishments primarily engaged in operating local and suburban passenger transportation systems using buses or other motor vehicles over regular routes and on regular schedules within a metropolitan area and its adjacent nonurban areas.

*Cross-References.*      Establishments primarily engaged in--

- Operating local and suburban passenger transportation systems using both a bus or other motor vehicle and another mode of transport--are classified in U.S. Industry 485111, Mixed Mode Transit Systems;
- Providing interurban and rural bus transportation--are classified in Industry 485210, Interurban and Rural Bus Transportation;
- Providing bus transportation for students and employees--are classified in Industry 485410, School and Employee Bus Transportation;
- Providing scenic and sightseeing transportation using buses or other motor vehicles--are classified in Industry 487110, Scenic and Sightseeing Transportation, Land; and
- Providing bus shuttle services (except school and employee bus)--are classified in U.S. Industry 485999, All Other Transit and Ground Passenger Transportation.

## 485119  Other Urban Transit Systems

This U.S. industry comprises establishments primarily engaged in operating local and suburban ground passenger transit systems (except mixed mode transit systems, commuter rail systems, and buses and other motor vehicles) over regular routes and on regular schedules within a metropolitan area and its adjacent nonurban areas.

*Illustrative Examples:*

Commuter cable car systems (i.e., stand-alone)
Light rail systems (i.e., stand-alone)
Commuter tramway systems (i.e., stand-alone)

Monorail transit systems (i.e., stand-alone)
Commuter trolley systems (i.e., stand-alone)
Subway systems (i.e., stand-alone)

---

T—Canadian, Mexican, and United States industries are comparable.

*Cross-References.*          Establishments primarily engaged in--

- Operating local and suburban ground passenger transit systems using more than one mode of transport--are classified in U.S. Industry 485111, Mixed Mode Transit Systems;
- Providing local and suburban passenger transportation using commuter rail systems--are classified in U.S. Industry 485112, Commuter Rail Systems; and
- Operating local and suburban bus transit systems (except mixed mode)--are classified in U.S. Industry 485113, Bus and Other Motor Vehicle Transit Systems.

**4852   Interurban and Rural Bus Transportation<sup>T</sup>**

**48521   Interurban and Rural Bus Transportation<sup>T</sup>**
See industry description for 485210.

**485210  Interurban and Rural Bus Transportation**

This industry comprises establishments primarily engaged in providing bus passenger transportation over regular routes and on regular schedules, principally outside a single metropolitan area and its adjacent nonurban areas.

*Cross-References.*          Establishments primarily engaged in--

- Providing scenic and sightseeing transportation using buses--are classified in Industry 487110, Scenic and Sightseeing Transportation, Land;
- Providing buses for charter--are classified in Industry 485510, Charter Bus Industry;
- Operating local and suburban bus transit systems (except mixed mode)--are classified in U.S. Industry 485113, Bus and Other Motor Vehicle Transit Systems; and
- Operating independent bus terminals--are classified in Industry 488490, Other Support Activities for Road Transportation.

**4853   Taxi and Limousine Service<sup>T</sup>**

This industry group comprises establishments primarily engaged in providing passenger transportation by automobile or van or providing an array of specialty and luxury passenger transportation services via limousine or luxury sedan generally on a reserved basis.  These establishments do not operate over regular routes and on regular schedules.

**48531   Taxi and Ridesharing Services<sup>T</sup>**
See industry description for 485310.

**485310  Taxi and Ridesharing Services**

This industry comprises establishments primarily engaged in providing passenger transportation by automobile or van, not operated over regular routes and on regular schedules.  Establishments of taxicab owner/operators, taxicab fleet operators, taxicab organizations, ridesharing services (including arrangement services), and ride hailing services (including arrangement services) are included in this industry.

*Cross-References.*          Establishments primarily engaged in--

- Providing special needs transportation services (except to and from school or work) for the disabled or elderly--are classified in U.S. Industry 485991, Special Needs Transportation;
- Providing limousine services--are classified in Industry 485320, Limousine Service;
- Providing scheduled shuttle services between hotels, airports, or other destination points or operating car pools and vanpools--are classified in U.S. Industry 485999, All Other Transit and Ground Passenger Transportation;

T—Canadian, Mexican, and United States industries are comparable.

- Arranging car pools and vanpools--are classified in U.S. Industry 488999, All Other Support Activities for Transportation; and
- Renting passenger cars without drivers, generally for short periods of time--are classified in U.S. Industry 532111, Passenger Car Rental.

## 48532 Limousine Service[T]
See industry description for 485320.

## 485320 Limousine Service

This industry comprises establishments primarily engaged in providing an array of specialty and luxury passenger transportation services via limousine or luxury sedan generally on a reserved basis. These establishments do not operate over regular routes and on regular schedules.

*Cross-References.*          Establishments primarily engaged in--

- Providing taxi and ridesharing services--are classified in Industry 485310, Taxi and Ridesharing Services; and
- Providing scheduled shuttle services between hotels, airports, or other destination points--are classified in U.S. Industry 485999, All Other Transit and Ground Passenger Transportation.

## 4854 School and Employee Bus Transportation[T]

## 48541 School and Employee Bus Transportation[T]
See industry description for 485410.

## 485410 School and Employee Bus Transportation

This industry comprises establishments primarily engaged in providing buses and other motor vehicles to transport pupils to and from school or employees to and from work.

*Cross-References.*          Establishments primarily engaged in--

- Operating local and suburban bus transit systems (except mixed mode)--are classified in U.S. Industry 485113, Bus and Other Motor Vehicle Transit Systems;
- Providing interurban and rural bus transportation--are classified in Industry 485210, Interurban and Rural Bus Transportation; and
- Providing buses for charter--are classified in Industry 485510, Charter Bus Industry.

## 4855 Charter Bus Industry[T]

## 48551 Charter Bus Industry[T]
See industry description for 485510.

## 485510 Charter Bus Industry

This industry comprises establishments primarily engaged in providing buses for charter. These establishments provide bus services to meet customers' road transportation needs and generally do not operate over fixed routes and on regular schedules.

*Cross-References.*          Establishments primarily engaged in--

- Providing scenic and local sightseeing transportation using buses--are classified in Industry 487110, Scenic and Sightseeing Transportation, Land; and

---

T—Canadian, Mexican, and United States industries are comparable.

- Providing interurban and rural bus transportation--are classified in Industry 485210, Interurban and Rural Bus Transportation.

**4859    Other Transit and Ground Passenger Transportation**[T]

**48599    Other Transit and Ground Passenger Transportation**[T]

This industry comprises establishments primarily engaged in providing other transit and ground passenger transportation (except urban transit systems, interurban and rural bus transportation, taxi and ridesharing services, school and employee bus transportation, charter bus services, and limousine services (except shuttle services)). Shuttle services (except school and employee bus) and special needs transportation services are included in this industry. Shuttle services establishments generally travel within a metropolitan area and its adjacent nonurban areas on regular routes, on regular schedules and provide services between hotels, airports, or other destination points. Establishments in the Special Needs Transportation industry provide passenger transportation for the disabled or elderly. These establishments may use specially equipped vehicles to provide passenger transportation.

*Cross-References.*    Establishments primarily engaged in--

- Providing school or employee bus transportation for the disabled or elderly--are classified in Industry 48541, School and Employee Bus Transportation;
- Providing ambulance services for emergency and medical purposes--are classified in Industry 62191, Ambulance Services;
- Operating urban transit systems--are classified in Industry 48511, Urban Transit Systems;
- Providing interurban and rural bus transportation--are classified in Industry 48521, Interurban and Rural Bus Transportation;
- Providing taxi services, ridesharing services, and/or limousine services (except shuttle services)--are classified in Industry Group 4853, Taxi and Limousine Service; and
- Providing buses for charter--are classified in Industry 48551, Charter Bus Industry.

**485991  Special Needs Transportation**

This U.S. industry comprises establishments primarily engaged in providing special needs transportation (except to and from school or work) for the disabled or elderly. These establishments may use specially equipped vehicles to provide passenger transportation.

*Cross-References.*    Establishments primarily engaged in--

- Providing school or employee bus transportation for the disabled or elderly--are classified in Industry 485410, School and Employee Bus Transportation; and
- Providing ambulance services for emergency and medical purposes--are classified in Industry 621910, Ambulance Services.

**485999  All Other Transit and Ground Passenger Transportation**

This U.S. industry comprises establishments primarily engaged in providing ground passenger transportation (except urban transit systems; interurban and rural bus transportation, taxi and/or limousine services (except shuttle services), school and employee bus transportation, charter bus services, and special needs transportation). Establishments primarily engaged in operating shuttle services and car pools or vanpools (except ridesharing and ridesharing arrangement services) are included in this industry. Shuttle services establishments generally provide travel on regular routes and on regular schedules between hotels, airports, or other destination points.

*Cross-References.*    Establishments primarily engaged in--

- Operating urban transit systems--are classified in Industry 48511, Urban Transit Systems;

---

T—Canadian, Mexican, and United States industries are comparable.

- Providing interurban and rural bus transportation--are classified in Industry 485210, Interurban and Rural Bus Transportation;
- Providing taxi services, ridesharing services, and/or limousine services (except shuttle services)--are classified in Industry Group 4853, Taxi and Limousine Service;
- Providing school and employee bus transportation (including for the disabled or elderly)--are classified in Industry 485410, School and Employee Bus Transportation;
- Providing buses for charter--are classified in Industry 485510, Charter Bus Industry;
- Providing special needs transportation (except to and from school or work) for the disabled or elderly--are classified in U.S. Industry 485991, Special Needs Transportation; and
- Providing ambulance services for emergency and medical purposes--are classified in Industry 621910, Ambulance Services.

## 486      Pipeline Transportation<sup>T</sup>

Industries in the Pipeline Transportation subsector use transmission pipelines to transport products, such as crude oil, natural gas, refined petroleum products, and slurry.  Industries are identified based on the products transported (i.e., pipeline transportation of crude oil, natural gas, refined petroleum products, and other products).

The Pipeline Transportation of Natural Gas industry includes the storage of natural gas because the storage is usually done by the pipeline establishment and because a pipeline is inherently a network in which all the nodes are interdependent.

## 4861      Pipeline Transportation of Crude Oil<sup>T</sup>

## 48611      Pipeline Transportation of Crude Oil<sup>T</sup>
See industry description for 486110.

## 486110  Pipeline Transportation of Crude Oil

This industry comprises establishments primarily engaged in the pipeline transportation of crude oil.

*Cross-References.*          Establishments primarily engaged in--

- Providing the pipeline transportation of natural gas--are classified in Industry 486210, Pipeline Transportation of Natural Gas;
- Providing the pipeline transportation of refined petroleum products--are classified in Industry 486910, Pipeline Transportation of Refined Petroleum Products; and
- Operating oil and gas field gathering lines--are classified in Sector 21, Mining, Quarrying, and Oil and Gas Extraction.

## 4862      Pipeline Transportation of Natural Gas<sup>T</sup>

## 48621      Pipeline Transportation of Natural Gas<sup>T</sup>
See industry description for 486210.

## 486210  Pipeline Transportation of Natural Gas

This industry comprises establishments primarily engaged in the pipeline transportation of natural gas from processing plants to local distribution systems.  This industry includes the storage of natural gas because the storage is usually done by the pipeline establishment and because a pipeline is inherently a network in which all the nodes are interdependent.

*Cross-References.*          Establishments primarily engaged in--

- Operating oil and gas field gathering lines--are classified in Sector 21, Mining, Quarrying, and Oil and Gas Extraction; and

---

T—Canadian, Mexican, and United States industries are comparable.

- Providing natural gas to the end consumer--are classified in Industry 221210, Natural Gas Distribution.

## 4869 Other Pipeline Transportation[T]

This industry group comprises establishments primarily engaged in the pipeline transportation of products (except crude oil and natural gas).

### 48691 Pipeline Transportation of Refined Petroleum Products[T]
See industry description for 486910.

### 486910 Pipeline Transportation of Refined Petroleum Products

This industry comprises establishments primarily engaged in the pipeline transportation of refined petroleum products.

### 48699 All Other Pipeline Transportation[T]
See industry description for 486990.

### 486990 All Other Pipeline Transportation

This industry comprises establishments primarily engaged in the pipeline transportation of products (except crude oil, natural gas, and refined petroleum products).

*Cross-References.*          Establishments primarily engaged in--

- Providing pipeline transportation of crude oil--are classified in Industry 486110, Pipeline Transportation of Crude Oil;
- Providing pipeline transportation of natural gas--are classified in Industry 486210, Pipeline Transportation of Natural Gas;
- Providing pipeline transportation of refined petroleum products--are classified in Industry 486910, Pipeline Transportation of Refined Petroleum Products; and
- Operating water distribution systems--are classified in Industry 221310, Water Supply and Irrigation Systems.

## 487 Scenic and Sightseeing Transportation[T]

Industries in the Scenic and Sightseeing Transportation subsector utilize transportation equipment to provide recreation and entertainment. These activities have a production process distinct from passenger transportation carried out for the purpose of other types of for-hire transportation. This process does not emphasize efficient transportation; in fact, such activities often use obsolete vehicles, such as steam trains, to provide some extra ambience. The activity is local in nature, usually involving a same-day return to the point of departure.

The Scenic and Sightseeing Transportation subsector is separated into three industries based on the mode: land, water, and other.

Activities that are recreational in nature and involve participation by the customer, such as white water rafting, are generally excluded from this subsector, unless they impose an impact on part of the transportation system. Charter boat fishing, for example, is included in the Scenic and Sightseeing Transportation, Water industry.

## 4871 Scenic and Sightseeing Transportation, Land[T]

### 48711 Scenic and Sightseeing Transportation, Land[T]
See industry description for 487110.

---

T—Canadian, Mexican, and United States industries are comparable.

**487110  Scenic and Sightseeing Transportation, Land**

  This industry comprises establishments primarily engaged in providing scenic and sightseeing transportation on land, such as sightseeing buses and trolleys, steam train excursions, and horse-drawn sightseeing rides.  The services provided are usually local and involve same-day return to place of origin.

*Cross-References.*          Establishments primarily engaged in--

- Operating aerial trams or aerial cable cars--are classified in Industry 487990, Scenic and Sightseeing Transportation, Other;
- Providing sporting services, such as recreational pack trains and horseback riding--are classified in Industry 713990, All Other Amusement and Recreation Industries;
- Providing intercity and rural bus transportation--are classified in Industry 485210, Interurban and Rural Bus Transportation;
- Providing buses for charter--are classified in Industry 485510, Charter Bus Industry;
- Operating local and suburban passenger transit systems--are classified in Industry 48511, Urban Transit Systems; and
- Providing travel arrangement and reservation services and arranging and assembling tours--are classified in Industry Group 5615, Travel Arrangement and Reservation Services.

**4872     Scenic and Sightseeing Transportation, Water**[T]

**48721    Scenic and Sightseeing Transportation, Water**[T]
          See industry description for 487210.

**487210  Scenic and Sightseeing Transportation, Water**

  This industry comprises establishments primarily engaged in providing scenic and sightseeing transportation on water.  The services provided are usually local and involve same-day return to place of origin.

*Illustrative Examples:*

| | |
|---|---|
| Airboat (i.e., swamp buggy) operation | Harbor sightseeing tours |
| Excursion boat operation | Dinner cruises |
| Charter fishing boat services | |

*Cross-References.*          Establishments primarily engaged in--

- Providing recreational services, such as fishing guide services (except charter boat), white water rafting, parasailing, and water skiing--are classified in Industry 713990, All Other Amusement and Recreation Industries;
- Providing water taxi services--are classified in Industry 48321, Inland Water Transportation;
- Providing water transportation of passengers--are classified in Subsector 483, Water Transportation;
- Operating floating casinos (i.e., gambling cruises or riverboat casinos)--are classified in Industry 713210, Casinos (except Casino Hotels); and
- Providing boat rental without operators--are classified in U.S. Industry 532284, Recreational Goods Rental.

**4879     Scenic and Sightseeing Transportation, Other**[T]

**48799    Scenic and Sightseeing Transportation, Other**[T]
          See industry description for 487990.

---

T—Canadian, Mexican, and United States industries are comparable.

**487990  Scenic and Sightseeing Transportation, Other**

This industry comprises establishments primarily engaged in providing scenic and sightseeing transportation (except on land and water).  The services provided are usually local and involve same-day return to place of departure.

*Illustrative Examples:*

| | |
|---|---|
| Aerial cable cars, scenic and sightseeing operation | Aerial tramways, scenic and sightseeing operation |
| Helicopter rides, scenic and sightseeing operation | Hot air balloon rides, scenic and sightseeing |
| Glider excursions | operation |

*Cross-References.*          Establishments primarily engaged in--

- Providing recreational activities, such as hang gliding--are classified in Industry 713990, All Other Amusement and Recreation Industries; and
- Providing scheduled or nonscheduled air transportation of passengers or specialty flying services--are classified in Subsector 481, Air Transportation.

**488      Support Activities for Transportation**[T]

Industries in the Support Activities for Transportation subsector provide services which support transportation.  These services may be provided to transportation carrier establishments or to the general public.  This subsector includes a wide array of establishments, including air traffic control services, marine cargo handling, and motor vehicle towing.

The Support Activities for Transportation subsector includes services to transportation, separated by type of mode serviced.  The Support Activities for Rail Transportation industry includes services to the rail industry (e.g., railroad switching and terminal establishments).  Ship repair and maintenance services not done in a shipyard are included in the Other Support Activities for Water Transportation industry.  An example would be floating drydock services in a harbor.

Excluded from this subsector are establishments primarily engaged in providing factory conversion and overhaul of transportation equipment, which are classified in Subsector 336, Transportation Equipment Manufacturing.  Establishments primarily engaged in providing rental and leasing of transportation equipment without operator are classified in Subsector 532, Rental and Leasing Services. Also, establishments primarily engaged in providing travel arrangement and reservation services are classified in Industry Group 5615, Travel Arrangement and Reservation Services.

**4881      Support Activities for Air Transportation**[T]

This industry group comprises establishments primarily engaged in providing services to the air transportation industry.  These services include airport operation, servicing, repairing (except factory conversion and overhaul of aircraft), maintaining and storing aircraft, and ferrying aircraft.

**48811   Airport Operations**[T]

This industry comprises establishments primarily engaged in (1) operating international, national, or civil airports or public flying fields or (2) supporting airport operations (except special food services contractors), such as rental of hangar space, air traffic control (except military) services, baggage handling services, and cargo handling services.

*Cross-References.*

- Establishments primarily engaged in providing factory conversion, overhaul, and rebuilding of aircraft are classified in Industry 33641, Aerospace Product and Parts Manufacturing;

---

T—Canadian, Mexican, and United States industries are comparable.

- Establishments primarily engaged in wholesaling fuel at airports are classified in Industry 42472, Petroleum and Petroleum Products Merchant Wholesalers (except Bulk Stations and Terminals);
- Establishments primarily engaged in providing airport janitorial services are classified in Industry 56172, Janitorial Services;
- Establishments primarily engaged in providing food services at airports on a contractual arrangement (i.e., food service contractors) are classified in Industry 72231, Food Service Contractors; and
- Establishments of the Armed Forces, including the National Guard, primarily engaged in providing military air traffic control services are classified in Industry 92811, National Security.

## 488111  Air Traffic Control

This U.S. industry comprises establishments primarily engaged in providing air traffic control (except military) services to regulate the flow of air traffic.

*Cross-References.*

Establishments of the Armed Forces, including the National Guard, primarily engaged in providing military air traffic control services are classified in Industry 928110, National Security.

## 488119  Other Airport Operations

This U.S. industry comprises establishments primarily engaged in (1) operating international, national, or civil airports, or public flying fields or (2) supporting airport operations, such as rental of hangar space, and providing baggage handling and/or cargo handling services.

*Cross-References.*          Establishments primarily engaged in--

- Providing air traffic control (except military) services--are classified in U.S. Industry 488111, Air Traffic Control;
- Providing factory conversion, overhaul, and rebuilding of aircraft--are classified in Industry 33641, Aerospace Product and Parts Manufacturing;
- Wholesaling fuel at airports--are classified in Industry 424720, Petroleum and Petroleum Products Merchant Wholesalers (except Bulk Stations and Terminals);
- Providing airport janitorial services--are classified in Industry 561720, Janitorial Services; and
- Providing food services at airports on a contractual arrangement (i.e., food service contractors)--are classified in Industry 722310, Food Service Contractors.

## 48819    Other Support Activities for Air Transportation[T]
See industry description for 488190.

## 488190  Other Support Activities for Air Transportation

This industry comprises establishments primarily engaged in providing specialized services for air transportation (except air traffic control and other airport operations).

*Illustrative Examples:*

| | |
|---|---|
| Aircraft maintenance and repair services (except factory conversions, overhauls, rebuilding) | Aircraft passenger screening security services<br>Aircraft testing services |

*Cross-References.*          Establishments primarily engaged in--

- Wholesaling fuel at airports--are classified in Industry 424720, Petroleum and Petroleum Products Merchant Wholesalers (except Bulk Stations and Terminals);
- Providing aircraft janitorial services--are classified in Industry 561720, Janitorial Services;

---

T—Canadian, Mexican, and United States industries are comparable.

- Providing air traffic control (except military) services--are classified in U.S. Industry 488111, Air Traffic Control;
- Providing airport operations (except air traffic control)--are classified in U.S. Industry 488119, Other Airport Operations;
- Providing factory conversion, overhaul, and rebuilding of aircraft--are classified in Industry 33641, Aerospace Product and Parts Manufacturing; and
- Providing food services to airlines on a contractual arrangement (i.e., food service contractors)--are classified in Industry 722310, Food Service Contractors.

## 4882    Support Activities for Rail Transportation[T]

## 48821    Support Activities for Rail Transportation[T]
See industry description for 488210.

## 488210  Support Activities for Rail Transportation

This industry comprises establishments primarily engaged in providing specialized services for railroad transportation, including servicing, routine repairing (except factory conversion, overhaul, or rebuilding of rolling stock), and maintaining rail cars; loading and unloading rail cars; and operating independent terminals.

*Cross-References.*          Establishments primarily engaged in--

- Providing railroad car rental--are classified in U.S. Industry 532411, Commercial Air, Rail, and Water Transportation Equipment Rental and Leasing;
- Factory conversion, overhaul, or rebuilding of railroad rolling stock--are classified in Industry 336510, Railroad Rolling Stock Manufacturing; and
- Providing rail car janitorial services--are classified in Industry 561720, Janitorial Services.

## 4883    Support Activities for Water Transportation[T]

This industry group comprises establishments primarily engaged in one of the following: (1) operating ports, harbors (including docking and pier facilities), or canals; (2) providing stevedoring and other marine cargo handling services (except warehousing); (3) providing navigational services to shipping; or (4) providing other services to water transportation.

## 48831    Port and Harbor Operations[T]
See industry description for 488310.

## 488310  Port and Harbor Operations

This industry comprises establishments primarily engaged in operating ports, harbors (including docking and pier facilities), or canals.

*Cross-References.*          Establishments primarily engaged in--

- Providing stevedoring and other marine cargo handling services (except warehousing)--are classified in Industry 488320, Marine Cargo Handling;
- Providing navigational services to shipping--are classified in Industry 488330, Navigational Services to Shipping; and
- Operating docking and/or storage facilities, known as marinas--are classified in Industry 713930, Marinas.

## 48832    Marine Cargo Handling[T]
See industry description for 488320.

---

T—Canadian, Mexican, and United States industries are comparable.

**census.gov/naics**

## 488320  Marine Cargo Handling

This industry comprises establishments primarily engaged in providing stevedoring and other marine cargo handling services (except warehousing).

*Cross-References.*          Establishments primarily engaged in--

- Preparing freight for transportation (except warehousing)--are classified in U.S. Industry 488991, Packing and Crating;
- Operating general merchandise, refrigerated, or other warehousing and storage facilities--are classified in Subsector 493, Warehousing and Storage; and
- Operating docking and pier facilities--are classified in Industry 488310, Port and Harbor Operations.

## 48833   Navigational Services to Shipping[T]
See industry description for 488330.

## 488330  Navigational Services to Shipping

This industry comprises establishments primarily engaged in providing navigational services to shipping.  Marine salvage establishments are included in this industry.

*Illustrative Examples:*

Docking and undocking marine vessel services
Piloting services, water transportation

Marine vessel traffic reporting services
Tugboat services, harbor operation

*Cross-References.*          Establishments primarily engaged in--

- Providing barge transportation and towing services on inland waters--are classified in U.S. Industry 483211, Inland Water Freight Transportation; and
- Providing coastal and/or Great Lakes barge transportation services--are classified in U.S. Industry 483113, Coastal and Great Lakes Freight Transportation.

## 48839   Other Support Activities for Water Transportation[T]
See industry description for 488390.

## 488390  Other Support Activities for Water Transportation

This industry comprises establishments primarily engaged in providing services to water transportation (except port and harbor operations; marine cargo handling services; and navigational services to shipping).

*Illustrative Examples:*

Floating drydocks (i.e., routine repair and maintenance of ships)

Ship scaling services
Marine cargo checkers and surveyors

*Cross-References.*          Establishments primarily engaged in--

- Ship painting--are classified in Industry 238320, Painting and Wall Covering Contractors;
- Providing ship janitorial services--are classified in Industry 561720, Janitorial Services;
- Operating port, harbor, or canal facilities--are classified in Industry 488310, Port and Harbor Operations;
- Providing dredging services--are classified in Industry 237990, Other Heavy and Civil Engineering Construction;
- Providing stevedoring and other marine cargo handling services (except warehousing)--are classified in Industry 488320, Marine Cargo Handling;

---

T—Canadian, Mexican, and United States industries are comparable.

- Providing navigational services to shipping--are classified in Industry 488330, Navigational Services to Shipping;
- Providing ship overhauling or repairs in a shipyard--are classified in U.S. Industry 336611, Ship Building and Repairing; and
- Providing towing services on inland waters--are classified in U.S. Industry 483211, Inland Water Freight Transportation.

## 4884   Support Activities for Road Transportation[T]

This industry group comprises establishments primarily engaged in (1) towing light or heavy motor vehicles, both local and long-distance, or (2) providing other services to road network users.

### 48841   Motor Vehicle Towing[T]
See industry description for 488410.

### 488410  Motor Vehicle Towing

This industry comprises establishments primarily engaged in towing light or heavy motor vehicles, both local and long-distance.  These establishments may provide incidental services, such as storage and emergency road repair services.

*Cross-References.*          Establishments primarily engaged in--

- Operating gasoline stations--are classified in Industry Group 4571, Gasoline Stations;
- Providing automotive repair and maintenance--are classified in Industry Group 8111, Automotive Repair and Maintenance;
- Both retailing automotive parts and accessories, and repairing automobiles--are classified in Industry 441330, Automotive Parts and Accessories Retailers; and
- Repossessing motor vehicles--are classified in U.S. Industry 561491, Repossession Services.

### 48849   Other Support Activities for Road Transportation[T]
See industry description for 488490.

### 488490  Other Support Activities for Road Transportation

This industry comprises establishments primarily engaged in providing services (except motor vehicle towing) to road network users.

*Illustrative Examples:*

Bridge, tunnel, and highway operations
Pilot car services (i.e., wide load warning services)
Truck or weighing station operations

Driving services, independent (e.g., automobile, truck delivery)

*Cross-References.*          Establishments primarily engaged in--

- Providing automotive repair and maintenance--are classified in Industry Group 8111, Automotive Repair and Maintenance;
- Providing towing services to motor vehicles--are classified in Industry 488410, Motor Vehicle Towing;
- Providing a network for busing in combination with providing terminal services--are classified in Industry 485210, Interurban and Rural Bus Transportation;
- Providing a network for trucking in combination with providing terminal services--are classified in Subsector 484, Truck Transportation; and
- Providing transportation services as owner-operators--are classified in Sector 48-49, Transportation and Warehousing, according to primary activity.

---

T—Canadian, Mexican, and United States industries are comparable.

**4885    Freight Transportation Arrangement**[T]

**48851   Freight Transportation Arrangement**[T]
See industry description for 488510.

**488510  Freight Transportation Arrangement**

This industry comprises establishments primarily engaged in arranging transportation of freight between shippers and carriers.  These establishments are usually known as freight forwarders, marine shipping agents, or customs brokers and offer a combination of services spanning transportation modes but do not directly provide shipping services.

*Cross-References.*

Establishments primarily engaged in tariff and freight rate consulting services are classified in U.S. Industry 541614, Process, Physical Distribution, and Logistics Consulting Services.

**4889    Other Support Activities for Transportation**[T]

**48899   Other Support Activities for Transportation**[T]

This industry comprises establishments primarily engaged in providing support activities to transportation (except for air transportation; rail transportation; water transportation; road transportation; and freight transportation arrangement).

*Illustrative Examples:*

| | |
|---|---|
| Arrangement of vanpools or car pools (except ridesharing arrangement services) | Independent pipeline terminal facilities |
| | Stockyards (i.e., not for fattening or selling livestock) |

*Cross-References.*          Establishments primarily engaged in--

- Providing support activities for air transportation--are classified in Industry Group 4881, Support Activities for Air Transportation;
- Providing support activities for rail transportation--are classified in Industry Group 4882, Support Activities for Rail Transportation;
- Providing support activities for water transportation--are classified in Industry Group 4883, Support Activities for Water Transportation;
- Providing support activities for road transportation--are classified in Industry Group 4884, Support Activities for Road Transportation;
- Arranging transportation of freight between shippers and carriers--are classified in Industry 48851, Freight Transportation Arrangement;
- Operating car pools and vanpools--are classified in Industry 48599, Other Transit and Ground Passenger Transportation;
- Providing pipeline transportation and storage of natural gas--are classified in Industry 48621, Pipeline Transportation of Natural Gas;
- Providing ridesharing arrangement services and taxicab dispatch services--are classified in Industry 48531, Taxi and Ridesharing Services;
- Providing tariff and freight rate consulting services--are classified in Industry 54161, Management Consulting Services;
- Operating stockyards for fattening livestock--are classified in Subsector 112, Animal Production and Aquaculture;
- Providing packaging and labeling services (except warehousing)--are classified in Industry 56191, Packaging and Labeling Services;
- Providing warehousing services--are classified in Industry Group 4931, Warehousing and Storage; and

T—Canadian, Mexican, and United States industries are comparable.

- Providing packing and crating services for agricultural products--are classified in Industry 11511, Support Activities for Crop Production.

## 488991  Packing and Crating

This U.S. industry comprises establishments primarily engaged in packing, crating, and otherwise preparing goods for transportation.

*Cross-References.*          Establishments primarily engaged in--

- Providing packaging and labeling services (except warehousing)--are classified in Industry 561910, Packaging and Labeling Services;
- Providing warehousing services--are classified in Industry Group 4931, Warehousing and Storage; and
- Providing packing and crating services for agricultural products--are classified in U.S. Industry 115114, Postharvest Crop Activities (except Cotton Ginning).

## 488999  All Other Support Activities for Transportation

This U.S. industry comprises establishments primarily engaged in providing support activities to transportation (except for air transportation; rail transportation; water transportation; road transportation; freight transportation arrangement; and packing and crating).

*Illustrative Examples:*

Arrangement of vanpools or car pools (except ridesharing arrangement services)

Independent pipeline terminal facilities
Stockyards (i.e., not for fattening or selling livestock)

*Cross-References.*          Establishments primarily engaged in--

- Operating stockyards for fattening livestock--are classified in Subsector 112, Animal Production and Aquaculture;
- Providing tariff and freight rate consulting services--are classified in U.S. Industry 541614, Process, Physical Distribution, and Logistics Consulting Services;
- Providing packing and crating services for transportation (except warehousing)--are classified in U.S. Industry 488991, Packing and Crating;
- Providing warehousing services--are classified in Industry Group 4931, Warehousing and Storage;
- Operating car pools and vanpools--are classified in U.S. Industry 485999, All Other Transit and Ground Passenger Transportation;
- Providing pipeline transportation and storage of natural gas--are classified in Industry 486210, Pipeline Transportation of Natural Gas;
- Providing support activities for air transportation--are classified in Industry Group 4881, Support Activities for Air Transportation;
- Providing support activities for rail transportation--are classified in Industry 488210, Support Activities for Rail Transportation;
- Providing support activities for water transportation--are classified in Industry Group 4883, Support Activities for Water Transportation;
- Providing support activities for road transportation--are classified in Industry Group 4884, Support Activities for Road Transportation;
- Arranging transportation of freight between shippers and carriers--are classified in Industry 488510, Freight Transportation Arrangement; and
- Providing ridesharing arrangement services and taxicab dispatch services--are classified in Industry 485310, Taxi and Ridesharing Services.

---

T—Canadian, Mexican, and United States industries are comparable.

## 491    Postal Service[T]

The Postal Service subsector includes the activities of the National Post Office and its subcontractors operating under a universal service obligation to provide mail services, and using the infrastructure required to fulfill that obligation. These services include delivering letters and small parcels. These articles can be described as those that can be handled by one person without using special equipment. This allows the collection, pick-up, and delivery operations to be done with limited labor costs and minimal equipment. Sorting and transportation activities, where necessary, are generally mechanized. The restriction to small parcels distinguishes these establishments from those in the transportation industries. These establishments may also provide express delivery services using the infrastructure established for provision of basic mail services.

The traditional activity of the National Postal Service is described in this subsector. Subcontractors include rural post offices on contract to the Postal Service.

Bulk transportation of mail on contract to the Postal Service is not included here, because it is usually done by transportation establishments that carry other customers' cargo as well. Establishments that provide courier and express delivery services without operating under a universal service obligation are classified in Subsector 492, Couriers and Messengers.

## 4911    Postal Service[T]

## 49111    Postal Service[T]
See industry description for 491110.

## 491110  Postal Service

This industry comprises establishments primarily engaged in providing mail services under a universal service obligation. Mail services include the carriage of letters, printed matter, or mailable packages, including acceptance, collection, processing, and delivery. Due to the infrastructure requirements of providing mail service under a universal service obligation, postal service establishments often provide parcel and express delivery services in addition to the mail service. Establishments primarily engaged in performing one or more parts of the basic mail service, such as sorting, routing and/or delivery (except bulk transportation of mail) are included in this industry.

*Cross-References.*          Establishments primarily engaged in--

- Providing bulk transportation of mail on a contract basis to and from postal service establishments--are classified in Industry Group 4841, General Freight Trucking;
- Providing services outside of the basic mail service, such as mail presort, mail consolidation, or address bar coding services, on a contract or fee basis--are classified in U.S. Industry 561499, All Other Business Support Services;
- Providing courier services and express delivery of parcels without operating under a universal service obligation--are classified in Industry 492110, Couriers and Express Delivery Services;
- Providing mailbox services along with other business services--are classified in U.S. Industry 561431, Private Mail Centers; and
- Providing local messenger and delivery services--are classified in Industry 492210, Local Messengers and Local Delivery.

## 492    Couriers and Messengers[T]

Industries in the Couriers and Messengers subsector provide intercity, local, and/or international delivery of parcels and documents (including express delivery services) without operating under a universal service obligation. These articles may originate in the U.S. but be delivered to another country and can be described as those that may be handled by one person without using special equipment. This allows the collection, pick-up, and delivery operations to be done with limited labor costs and minimal equipment. Sorting and transportation activities, where necessary, are generally mechanized. The restriction to small parcels partly distinguishes these establishments from those in the transportation industries. The complete network of courier services establishments also distinguishes these transportation services from local messenger and delivery establishments in this subsector. This includes the

---

T—Canadian, Mexican, and United States industries are comparable.

establishments that perform intercity transportation as well as establishments that, under contract to them, perform local pick-up and delivery. Messengers, which usually deliver within a metropolitan or single urban area, may use bicycle, foot, car, small truck, or van.

**4921     Couriers and Express Delivery Services**[T]

**49211   Couriers and Express Delivery Services**[T]
          See industry description for 492110.

**492110  Couriers and Express Delivery Services**

This industry comprises establishments primarily engaged in providing air, surface, or combined mode courier and express delivery services of parcels, but not operating under a universal service obligation. These parcels can include goods and documents, but the express delivery services are not part of the normal mail service. These services are generally between metropolitan areas, urban centers, or international, but the establishments of this industry form a network that includes local pick-up and delivery to serve their customers' needs.

*Illustrative Examples:*

Air courier services, except establishments operating under a universal service obligation
Express delivery services, except establishments operating under a universal service obligation

Courier services (i.e., intercity network), except establishments operating under a universal service obligation

*Cross-References.*          Establishments primarily engaged in--

- Providing parcel and express delivery services in addition to mail services under a universal service obligation--are classified in Industry 491110, Postal Service;
- Providing messenger and delivery services within a metropolitan area or within an urban center--are classified in Industry 492210, Local Messengers and Local Delivery; and
- Providing the truck transportation of palletized general freight--are classified in Industry Group 4841, General Freight Trucking.

**4922     Local Messengers and Local Delivery**[T]

**49221   Local Messengers and Local Delivery**[T]
          See industry description for 492210.

**492210  Local Messengers and Local Delivery**

This industry comprises establishments primarily engaged in providing local messenger and delivery services of small items within a single metropolitan area or within an urban center. These establishments generally provide point-to-point pick-up and delivery and do not operate as part of an intercity courier network.

*Illustrative Examples:*

Letters, documents, or small parcels local delivery services
Grocery delivery services (i.e., independent service from grocery store)

Alcoholic beverages delivery services
Restaurant meals order and delivery services (i.e., independent order and delivery services)

*Cross-References.*          Establishments primarily engaged in--

- Providing local letter and parcel delivery services as part of an intercity courier network--are classified in Industry 492110, Couriers and Express Delivery Services;

---

T—Canadian, Mexican, and United States industries are comparable.

- Operating the National Postal Service or providing postal services on a contract basis (except the bulk transportation of mail)--are classified in Industry 491110, Postal Service; and
- Providing the bulk transportation of mail on a contract basis to and from Postal Service establishments--are classified in Industry Group 4841, General Freight Trucking.

## 493     Warehousing and Storage<sup>T</sup>

Industries in the Warehousing and Storage subsector are primarily engaged in operating warehousing and storage facilities for general merchandise, refrigerated goods, and other warehouse products. These establishments provide facilities to store goods. They do not sell the goods they handle. These establishments take responsibility for storing the goods and keeping them secure. They may also provide a range of services, often referred to as logistics services, related to the distribution of goods. Logistics services can include labeling, breaking bulk, inventory control and management, light assembly, order entry and fulfillment, packaging, pick and pack, price marking and ticketing, and transportation arrangement. However, establishments in this industry group always provide warehousing or storage services in addition to any logistic services. Furthermore, the warehousing or storage of goods must be more than incidental to the performance of services, such as price marking.

Bonded warehousing and storage services and warehouses located in free trade zones are included in the industries of this subsector.

## 4931     Warehousing and Storage<sup>T</sup>

## 49311     General Warehousing and Storage<sup>T</sup>
See industry description for 493110.

## 493110   General Warehousing and Storage

This industry comprises establishments primarily engaged in operating merchandise warehousing and storage facilities. These establishments generally handle goods in containers, such as boxes, barrels, and/or drums, using equipment, such as forklifts, pallets, and racks. They are not specialized in handling bulk products of any particular type, size, or quantity of goods or products.

*Cross-References.*          Establishments primarily engaged in--

- Renting or leasing space for self-storage--are classified in Industry 531130, Lessors of Miniwarehouses and Self-Storage Units; and
- Wholesale or retail sales in combination with handling and/or distributing goods--are classified in Sector 42, Wholesale Trade, or in Sector 44-45, Retail Trade.

## 49312     Refrigerated Warehousing and Storage<sup>T</sup>
See industry description for 493120.

## 493120   Refrigerated Warehousing and Storage

This industry comprises establishments primarily engaged in operating refrigerated warehousing and storage facilities. Establishments primarily engaged in the storage of furs for the trade are included in this industry. The services provided by these establishments include blast freezing, tempering, and modified atmosphere storage services.

*Cross-References.*

Establishments primarily engaged in cleaning and storing furs (except for the trade) and garments are classified in Industry 812320, Drycleaning and Laundry Services (except Coin-Operated).

## 49313     Farm Product Warehousing and Storage<sup>T</sup>
See industry description for 493130.

---

T—Canadian, Mexican, and United States industries are comparable.

**493130  Farm Product Warehousing and Storage**

This industry comprises establishments primarily engaged in operating bulk farm product warehousing and storage facilities (except refrigerated).  Grain elevators primarily engaged in storage are included in this industry.

*Cross-References.*            Establishments primarily engaged in--

- Operating refrigerated warehousing and storage facilities--are classified in Industry 493120, Refrigerated Warehousing and Storage; and
- Storing grains and field beans (i.e., grain elevators) as an incidental activity to sales--are classified in Industry 424510, Grain and Field Bean Merchant Wholesalers.

**49319   Other Warehousing and Storage[T]**
See industry description for 493190.

**493190  Other Warehousing and Storage**

This industry comprises establishments primarily engaged in operating warehousing and storage facilities (except general merchandise, refrigerated, and farm product warehousing and storage).

*Illustrative Examples:*

Bulk petroleum storage                                          Document storage and warehousing
Lumber storage terminals                                    Whiskey warehousing

*Cross-References.*            Establishments primarily engaged in--

- Renting or leasing space for self-storage--are classified in Industry 531130, Lessors of Miniwarehouses and Self-Storage Units;
- Storing hazardous materials for treatment and disposal--are classified in U.S. Industry 562211, Hazardous Waste Treatment and Disposal;
- Operating general warehousing and storage facilities--are classified in Industry 493110, General Warehousing and Storage;
- Wholesaling crude petroleum and petroleum products from bulk liquid storage facilities--are classified in Industry 424710, Petroleum Bulk Stations and Terminals;
- Operating refrigerated warehousing and storage facilities--are classified in Industry 493120, Refrigerated Warehousing and Storage;
- Operating farm product warehousing and storage facilities (except refrigerated)--are classified in Industry 493130, Farm Product Warehousing and Storage;
- Pipeline transportation and storage of natural gas--are classified in Industry 486210, Pipeline Transportation of Natural Gas;
- Operating docking and/or storage facilities for pleasure craft owners--are classified in Industry 713930, Marinas; and
- Renting or leasing vacant lots for storage--are classified in Industry 531190, Lessors of Other Real Estate Property.

---

T—Canadian, Mexican, and United States industries are comparable.

# Sector 51--Information[T]

## The Sector as a Whole

The Information sector comprises establishments engaged in the following processes: (a) producing and distributing information and cultural products, (b) providing the means to transmit or distribute these products as well as data or communications, and (c) processing data.

The main components of this sector are motion picture and sound recording industries; publishing industries, including software publishing; broadcasting and content providers; telecommunications industries; computing infrastructure providers, data processing, Web hosting, and related services; and Web search portals, libraries, archives, and other information services.

The unique characteristics of information and cultural products, and of the processes involved in their production and distribution, distinguish the Information sector from the goods-producing and service-producing sectors. Some of these characteristics are:

1. Unlike traditional goods, an "information or cultural product," such as an online newspaper or a television program, does not necessarily have tangible qualities, nor is it necessarily associated with a particular form. A movie can be viewed at a movie theater or through television broadcast, video-on-demand, or streaming services. A sound recording can be aired on radio, embedded in multimedia products, streamed, or sold at a record store.

2. Unlike traditional services, the delivery of these products does not require direct contact between the supplier and the consumer.

3. The value of these products to the consumer lies in their informational, educational, cultural, or entertainment content, not in the format in which they are distributed. Most of these products are protected from unlawful reproduction by copyright laws.

4. The intangible property aspect of information and cultural products makes the processes involved in their production and distribution very different from goods and services. Only those possessing the rights to these works are authorized to reproduce, alter, improve, and distribute them. Acquiring and using these rights often involves significant costs. In addition, technology has revolutionized the distribution of these products. It is possible to distribute them in a physical form, via broadcast, or online.

5. Distributors of information and cultural products can easily add value to the products they distribute. For instance, broadcasters add advertising not contained in the original product. This capacity means that unlike traditional goods distributors, they derive revenue not from sale of the distributed product to the final consumer, but from those who pay for the privilege of adding information to the original product. Similarly, a directory and mailing list publisher can acquire the rights to thousands of previously published newspaper and periodical articles and add new value by providing search and software and organizing the information in a way that facilitates research and retrieval. These products often command a much higher price than the original information.

Excluded from this sector are establishments primarily engaged in custom design of software; mass reproducing software or other prerecorded audio and video material on magnetic or optical media; producing live artistic and cultural works or productions; and performing in or creating artistic and cultural works or productions as independent (i.e., freelance) individuals.

## 512   Motion Picture and Sound Recording Industries[T]

Industries in the Motion Picture and Sound Recording Industries subsector group establishments involved in the production and distribution of motion pictures and sound recordings. While producers and distributors of motion pictures and sound recordings issue works for sale as traditional publishers do, the processes are sufficiently different to warrant placing establishments engaged in these activities in a separate subsector. Production is typically a complex process that involves several distinct types of establishments that are engaged in activities, such as contracting with performers, creating the film or sound content, and providing technical postproduction services. Film distribution is often to exhibitors, such as theaters and broadcasters, rather than through the wholesale and

---

T—Canadian, Mexican, and United States industries are comparable.

retail distribution chain. When the product is in a mass-produced form, NAICS treats production and distribution as the major economic activity as it does in the Publishing Industries subsector, rather than as a subsidiary activity to the manufacture of such products.

This subsector does not include establishments primarily engaged in the wholesale distribution of video and sound recordings, such as compact discs and audio tapes; these establishments are included in the Wholesale Trade sector. Reproduction of video and sound recordings that is carried out separately from establishments engaged in production and distribution is treated in NAICS as a manufacturing activity. Establishments that primarily acquire the rights to distribute video and sound recordings to the public via television or radio broadcast or streaming distribution services are classified in Subsector 516, Broadcasting and Content Providers. Establishments using facilities and infrastructure that they operate to distribute cable and satellite television subscription programming are included in Subsector 517, Telecommunications.

## 5121 Motion Picture and Video Industries[T]

This industry group comprises establishments primarily engaged in the production and/or distribution of motion pictures, videos, television programs, or commercials; in the exhibition of motion pictures; or in the provision of postproduction and related services.

## 51211 Motion Picture and Video Production[T]
See industry description for 512110.

## 512110 Motion Picture and Video Production

This industry comprises establishments primarily engaged in producing, or producing and distributing motion pictures, videos, television programs, or television commercials.

*Cross-References.*        Establishments primarily engaged in--

- Producing motion pictures and videos on contract as independent producers--are classified in Industry 711510, Independent Artists, Writers, and Performers;
- Providing teleproduction and other postproduction services--are classified in U.S. Industry 512191, Teleproduction and Other Postproduction Services;
- Providing video recording of weddings, special events, and/or business inventories--are classified in Industry 54192, Photographic Services;
- Providing motion picture laboratory services--are classified in U.S. Industry 512199, Other Motion Picture and Video Industries;
- Providing mass duplication and packaging of video discs, tapes, and film--are classified in Industry 334610, Manufacturing and Reproducing Magnetic and Optical Media; and
- Acquiring distribution rights and distributing motion pictures and videos--are classified in Industry 512120, Motion Picture and Video Distribution.

## 51212 Motion Picture and Video Distribution[T]
See industry description for 512120.

## 512120 Motion Picture and Video Distribution

This industry comprises establishments primarily engaged in acquiring distribution rights and distributing film and video productions to motion picture theaters, television networks and stations, other media broadcast and streaming outlets, and exhibitors.

*Cross-References.*        Establishments primarily engaged in--

- Producing and distributing motion pictures and videos--are classified in Industry 512110, Motion Picture and Video Production;

---

T—Canadian, Mexican, and United States industries are comparable.

- Operating television broadcasting stations, that may acquire the right to distribute content and subsequently broadcast or distribute that content--are classified in Industry 516120, Television Broadcasting Stations;
- Providing media streaming distribution services or operating media broadcasting and cable television networks, that may acquire the right to distribute content and subsequently broadcast or distribute that content--are classified in Industry 516210, Media Streaming Distribution Services, Social Networks, and Other Media Networks and Content Providers;
- Providing cable and satellite television distribution services using facilities and infrastructure that they operate--are classified in U.S. Industry 517111, Wired Telecommunications Carriers;
- Merchant wholesale distribution of blank digital video discs (DVDs)--are classified in Industry 423690, Other Electronic Parts and Equipment Merchant Wholesalers;
- Merchant wholesale distribution of prerecorded digital video discs (DVDs)--are classified in Industry 423990, Other Miscellaneous Durable Goods Merchant Wholesalers;
- Providing mass duplication and packaging of video tapes and discs--are classified in Industry 334610, Manufacturing and Reproducing Magnetic and Optical Media;
- Providing motion picture footage (via film libraries) to producers--are classified in U.S. Industry 512199, Other Motion Picture and Video Industries;
- Renting video tapes and discs to the general public, including through vending machines--are classified in U.S. Industry 532282, Video Tape and Disc Rental; and
- Retailing digital video discs (DVDs) to the general public--are classified in Sector 44-45, Retail Trade.

## 51213 Motion Picture and Video Exhibition[T]

This industry comprises establishments primarily engaged in operating motion picture theaters and/or exhibiting motion pictures or videos at film festivals, and so forth.

## 512131 Motion Picture Theaters (except Drive-Ins)

This U.S. industry comprises establishments primarily engaged in operating motion picture theaters (except drive-ins) and/or exhibiting motion pictures or videos at film festivals, and so forth.

## 512132 Drive-In Motion Picture Theaters

This U.S. industry comprises establishments primarily engaged in operating drive-in motion picture theaters.

## 51219 Postproduction Services and Other Motion Picture and Video Industries[T]

This industry comprises establishments primarily engaged in providing postproduction services and other services to the motion picture industry, including specialized motion picture or video postproduction services, such as editing, film/tape transfers, titling, subtitling, credits, closed captioning, and computer-produced graphics, animation and special effects, as well as developing and processing motion picture film.

*Illustrative Examples:*

Motion picture film laboratories
Stock footage film libraries

Postproduction facilities
Teleproduction services

*Cross-References.*        Establishments primarily engaged in--

- Mass duplicating video discs, tapes, and film--are classified in Industry 33461, Manufacturing and Reproducing Magnetic and Optical Media;
- Motion picture and video production--are classified in Industry 51211, Motion Picture and Video Production;
- Acquiring distribution rights and distributing film and video productions to motion picture theaters, television networks and stations, other media broadcast and streaming outlets, and exhibitors--are classified in Industry 51212, Motion Picture and Video Distribution;

---

T—Canadian, Mexican, and United States industries are comparable.

- Motion picture and video exhibition--are classified in Industry 51213, Motion Picture and Video Exhibition;
- Providing audio services for film, television, and video productions--are classified in Industry 51224, Sound Recording Studios;
- Formatting content, provided by a customer, for streaming and providing hosting and infrastructure support on behalf of the content owner, generally on a contract or fee basis--are classified in Industry 51821, Computing Infrastructure Providers, Data Processing, Web Hosting, and Related Services;
- Renting wardrobes and costumes for motion picture production--are classified in Industry 53228, Other Consumer Goods Rental;
- Renting studio equipment--are classified in Industry 53249, Other Commercial and Industrial Machinery and Equipment Rental and Leasing; and
- Casting actors and actresses for employment with production companies--are classified in Industry 56131, Employment Placement Agencies and Executive Search Services.

### 512191  Teleproduction and Other Postproduction Services

This U.S. industry comprises establishments primarily engaged in providing specialized motion picture or video postproduction services, such as editing, film/tape transfers, subtitling, credits, closed captioning, and animation and special effects.

*Cross-References.*          Establishments primarily engaged in--

- Mass duplicating video discs, tapes, and film--are classified in Industry 334610, Manufacturing and Reproducing Magnetic and Optical Media;
- Developing and processing motion picture film--are classified in U.S. Industry 512199, Other Motion Picture and Video Industries;
- Providing audio services for film, television, and video productions--are classified in Industry 512240, Sound Recording Studios;
- Acquiring distribution rights and distributing film and video productions to motion picture theaters, television networks and stations, other media broadcast and streaming outlets, and exhibitors--are classified in Industry 512120, Motion Picture and Video Distribution; and
- Formatting content, provided by a customer, for streaming and providing hosting and infrastructure support on behalf of the content owner, generally on a contract or fee basis--are classified in Industry 518210, Computing Infrastructure Providers, Data Processing, Web Hosting, and Related Services.

### 512199  Other Motion Picture and Video Industries

This U.S. industry comprises establishments primarily engaged in providing motion picture and video services (except motion picture and video production, distribution, exhibition, and teleproduction and other postproduction services).

*Illustrative Examples:*

Motion picture film laboratories                    Film preservation services
Stock footage film libraries

*Cross-References.*          Establishments primarily engaged in--

- Renting wardrobes and costumes for motion picture production--are classified in U.S. Industry 532281, Formal Wear and Costume Rental;
- Renting studio equipment--are classified in Industry 532490, Other Commercial and Industrial Machinery and Equipment Rental and Leasing;
- Casting actors and actresses for employment with production companies--are classified in U.S. Industry 561311, Employment Placement Agencies;

---

T—Canadian, Mexican, and United States industries are comparable.

- Motion picture and video production--are classified in Industry 512110, Motion Picture and Video Production;
- Acquiring distribution rights and distributing film and video productions to motion picture theaters, television networks and stations, other media broadcast and streaming outlets, and exhibitors--are classified in Industry 512120, Motion Picture and Video Distribution;
- Teleproduction and other postproduction services--are classified in U.S. Industry 512191, Teleproduction and Other Postproduction Services; and
- Motion picture and video exhibition--are classified in Industry 51213, Motion Picture and Video Exhibition.

## 5122 Sound Recording Industries[T]

This industry group comprises establishments primarily engaged in producing and distributing musical recordings, publishing music, or providing sound recording and related services.

### 51223 Music Publishers[T]
See industry description for 512230.

### 512230 Music Publishers

This industry comprises establishments primarily engaged in acquiring and registering copyrights for musical compositions in accordance with law and promoting and authorizing the use of these compositions in recordings, radio, television, motion pictures, live performances, print, or other media. Establishments in this industry represent the interests of the songwriter or other owners of musical compositions to produce revenues from the use of such works, generally through licensing agreements. These establishments may own the copyright or act as administrator of the music copyrights on behalf of copyright owners. Publishers of music books and sheet music are included in this industry.

*Cross-References.*

Establishments primarily engaged as independent songwriters who act as their own publishers are classified in Industry 711510, Independent Artists, Writers, and Performers.

### 51224 Sound Recording Studios[T]
See industry description for 512240.

### 512240 Sound Recording Studios

This industry comprises establishments primarily engaged in providing the facilities and technical expertise for sound recording in a studio. This industry includes establishments that provide audio production and postproduction services to produce master recordings. These establishments may provide audio services for film, television, and video productions.

*Cross-References.*          Establishments primarily engaged in--

- Record production and/or releasing, promoting, and distributing sound recordings--are classified in Industry 512250, Record Production and Distribution; and
- Providing mass duplication of recorded products--are classified in Industry 334610, Manufacturing and Reproducing Magnetic and Optical Media.

### 51225 Record Production and Distribution[T]
See industry description for 512250.

---

T—Canadian, Mexican, and United States industries are comparable.

## 512250  Record Production and Distribution

This industry comprises establishments primarily engaged in record production and/or releasing, promoting, and distributing sound recordings to wholesalers, retailers, or directly to the public.  These establishments contract with artists, arrange and finance the production of original master recordings, and/or produce master recordings themselves, such as digital music and compact discs.  Establishments in this industry hold the copyright to the master recording, or obtain reproduction and distribution rights to master recordings produced by others, and derive most of their revenues from the sales, leasing, licensing, or distribution of master recordings.

*Cross-References.*        Establishments primarily engaged in--

- Promoting and authorizing the use of musical works in various media--are classified in Industry 512230, Music Publishers;
- Providing facilities and technical expertise for recording musical performances--are classified in Industry 512240, Sound Recording Studios;
- Operating radio broadcasting stations, that may acquire the right to distribute content and subsequently broadcast or distribute that content--are classified in Industry 516110, Radio Broadcasting Stations;
- Operating radio broadcasting networks, including satellite radio networks, that may acquire the right to distribute content and subsequently broadcast or distribute that content--are classified in Industry 516210, Media Streaming Distribution Services, Social Networks, and Other Media Networks and Content Providers;
- Mass duplication of recorded products--are classified in Industry 334610, Manufacturing and Reproducing Magnetic and Optical Media;
- Merchant wholesale distribution of blank audio compact discs--are classified in Industry 423690, Other Electronic Parts and Equipment Merchant Wholesalers;
- Merchant wholesale distribution of prerecorded audio compact discs--are classified in Industry 423990, Other Miscellaneous Durable Goods Merchant Wholesalers;
- Retailing downloadable music files and compact discs without producing recordings--are classified in Sector 44-45, Retail Trade;
- Managing the careers of artists--are classified in Industry 711410, Agents and Managers for Artists, Athletes, Entertainers, and Other Public Figures;
- Producing albums on contract as independent producers--are classified in Industry 711510, Independent Artists, Writers, and Performers; and
- Producing live musical entertainment (except theatrical musical or opera productions) and independent (i.e., freelance) artists primarily engaged in providing live musical entertainment--are classified in Industry 711130, Musical Groups and Artists.

## 51229  Other Sound Recording Industries[T]
See industry description for 512290.

## 512290  Other Sound Recording Industries

This industry comprises establishments primarily engaged in providing sound recording services (except record production, distribution, music publishing, and sound recording in a studio).  Establishments in this industry provide services, such as the audio recording of meetings and conferences.

*Cross-References.*        Establishments primarily engaged in--

- Promoting and authorizing the use of musical works in various media--are classified in Industry 512230, Music Publishers;
- Providing facilities and technical expertise for recording musical performances--are classified in Industry 512240, Sound Recording Studios;
- Record production and/or releasing, promoting, and distributing sound recordings--are classified in Industry 512250, Record Production and Distribution;

---

T—Canadian, Mexican, and United States industries are comparable.

- Providing mass duplication of recorded products--are classified in Industry 334610, Manufacturing and Reproducing Magnetic and Optical Media; and
- Organizing and promoting the presentation of performing arts productions--are classified in Industry Group 7113, Promoters of Performing Arts, Sports, and Similar Events.

## 513    Publishing Industries[T]

Industries in the Publishing Industries subsector group establishments engaged in publishing newspapers, magazines, other periodicals, books, directories, and software. In general, establishments known as publishers issue copies of works for which they usually possess copyright. Works may be in one or more formats including print form, CD-ROM, proprietary electronic networks, or exclusively on the Internet. Publishers may publish works originally created by others for which they have obtained the rights and/or works that they have created in-house. Publishers may publish only and license rights to others to distribute their content, or they may publish and distribute content they create or own. Software publishing is included here because the activity, creation of a copyrighted product and bringing it to market, is equivalent to the creation process for other types of intellectual products.

In NAICS, publishing--the reporting, writing, editing, and other processes that are required to create an edition of a newspaper, for example--is treated as a major economic activity in its own right, rather than as a subsidiary activity to a manufacturing activity, printing. Thus, publishing is classified in the Information sector; whereas, printing is in the Manufacturing sector. The Publishing Industries subsector excludes printed products, such as manifold business forms and appointment books, for which information is not the essential component. Establishments producing these items are included in Subsector 323, Printing and Related Support Activities.

Reproduction of prepackaged software is treated in NAICS as a manufacturing activity, and custom design of software to client specifications is included in the Professional, Scientific, and Technical Services sector. These distinctions arise because of the different ways that software is created, reproduced, and distributed.

Music publishers and establishments primarily engaged in the production, or production and distribution, of motion pictures and sound recordings are included in Subsector 512, Motion Picture and Sound Recording Industries. Establishments not engaged in publishing and exclusively obtaining rights from publishers to broadcast and distribute content are included in Subsector 516, Broadcasting and Content Providers.

## 5131    Newspaper, Periodical, Book, and Directory Publishers[T]

This industry group comprises establishments primarily engaged in publishing newspapers, magazines, other periodicals, books, directories and mailing lists, and other works, such as calendars, greeting cards, and maps. These works are characterized by the intellectual creativity required in their development and are usually protected by copyright. Publishers distribute or arrange for the distribution of these works.

Publishing establishments may create the works in-house, or contract for, purchase, or compile works that were originally created by others. These works may be published in one or more formats, such as print and/or electronic form, including proprietary electronic networks or exclusively on the Internet. Establishments in this industry may print, reproduce, or offer direct access to the works themselves or may arrange with others to carry out such functions.

Establishments that both print and publish may fill excess capacity with commercial or job printing. However, the publishing activity is still considered to be the primary activity of these establishments.

## 51311    Newspaper Publishers[T]
See industry description for 513110.

## 513110  Newspaper Publishers

This industry comprises establishments known as newspaper publishers. Establishments in this industry carry out operations necessary for producing and distributing newspapers, including gathering news; writing news columns, feature stories, and editorials; and selling and preparing advertisements. These establishments may publish newspapers in print or electronic form, including exclusively on the Internet.

---

T—Canadian, Mexican, and United States industries are comparable.

*Cross-References.*

- Establishments primarily engaged in printing newspapers without publishing are classified in Industry 32311, Printing;
- Establishments, such as trade associations, schools and universities, financial institutions, and social welfare organizations, that publish newsletters or newspapers for distribution to their membership, but that are not commonly known as newspaper publishers, are classified according to their primary activity;
- Establishments primarily engaged in streaming news without publishing are classified in Industry 516210, Media Streaming Distribution Services, Social Networks, and Other Media Networks and Content Providers;
- Establishments primarily engaged in supplying the news media with information, such as news, reports, and pictures, are classified in Industry 516210, Media Streaming Distribution Services, Social Networks, and Other Media Networks and Content Providers; and
- Establishments of independent representatives primarily engaged in selling advertising space are classified in Industry 541840, Media Representatives.

## 51312   Periodical Publishers[T]
See industry description for 513120.

## 513120  Periodical Publishers

This industry comprises establishments known either as magazine publishers or periodical publishers. These establishments carry out the operations necessary for producing and distributing magazines and other periodicals, such as gathering, writing, and editing articles, and selling and preparing advertisements. These establishments may publish magazines and other periodicals in print or electronic form, including exclusively on the Internet.

*Illustrative Examples:*

| | |
|---|---|
| Comic book publishers | Newsletter publishers |
| Magazine publishers | Trade journal publishers |
| Scholarly journal publishers | |

*Cross-References.*

- Establishments primarily engaged in printing periodicals without publishing are classified in Industry 32311, Printing;
- Establishments, such as trade associations, schools and universities, financial institutions, and social welfare organizations, that publish magazines and periodicals for distribution to their membership, but that are not commonly known as periodical publishers, are classified according to their primary activity;
- Establishments primarily engaged in publishing directories and mailing lists are classified in Industry 513140, Directory and Mailing List Publishers;
- Establishments primarily engaged in streaming periodical content without publishing are classified in Industry 516210, Media Streaming Distribution Services, Social Networks, and Other Media Networks and Content Providers; and
- Establishments of independent representatives primarily engaged in selling advertising space are classified in Industry 541840, Media Representatives.

## 51313   Book Publishers[T]
See industry description for 513130.

## 513130  Book Publishers

This industry comprises establishments known as book publishers. Establishments in this industry carry out design, editing, and marketing activities necessary for producing and distributing books. These establishments may publish books in print, electronic, or audio form, including exclusively on the Internet.

---

T—Canadian, Mexican, and United States industries are comparable.

**census.gov/naics**

*Illustrative Examples:*

| | |
|---|---|
| Atlas publishers | Encyclopedia publishers |
| Religious book publishers | Technical manual publishers |
| Graphic novel publishers | Map publishers |
| School textbook publishers | Travel guide book publishers |

*Cross-References.*

- Establishments primarily engaged in printing books without publishing are classified in U.S. Industry 323117, Books Printing;
- Establishments known as music publishers are classified in Industry 512230, Music Publishers;
- Establishments, such as trade associations, schools and universities, and social welfare organizations, that publish books for distribution to their membership, that are not commonly known as book publishers, are classified according to their primary activity;
- Establishments primarily engaged in retailing new books (including downloads) without publishing, including book clubs primarily engaged in direct sales, are classified in Industry 459210, Book Retailers and News Dealers;
- Establishments primarily engaged in streaming audio books without publishing are classified in Industry 516210, Media Streaming Distribution Services, Social Networks, and Other Media Networks and Content Providers; and
- Establishments primarily engaged as independent authors who act as their own publishers are classified in Industry 711510, Independent Artists, Writers, and Performers.

**51314    Directory and Mailing List Publishers[T]**
See industry description for 513140.

**513140  Directory and Mailing List Publishers**

This industry comprises establishments primarily engaged in publishing directories, mailing lists, and collections or compilations of fact. The products are typically protected in their selection, arrangement and/or presentation. Examples are lists of mailing addresses, telephone directories, directories of businesses, collections or compilations of proprietary drugs or legal case results, compilations of public records, etc. These establishments may publish directories and mailing lists in print or electronic form, including exclusively on the Internet.

*Illustrative Examples:*

| | |
|---|---|
| Business directory publishers | Directory publishers |
| Mailing list publishers | Telephone directory publishers |

*Cross-References.*          Establishments primarily engaged in--

- Operating Web search portals--are classified in Industry 519290, Web Search Portals and All Other Information Services;
- Compiling mailing lists in conjunction with providing advertising and public relations services--are classified in Industry Group 5418, Advertising, Public Relations, and Related Services;
- Printing without publishing directories and mailing lists--are classified in Industry 32311, Printing;
- Publishing computer software--are classified in Industry 513210, Software Publishers;
- Creating and publishing encyclopedias and similar collections of creative works in print and/or electronic media--are classified in Industry 513130, Book Publishers; and
- Creating and publishing collections of creative works that are periodically updated--are classified in Industry 513120, Periodical Publishers.

---

T—Canadian, Mexican, and United States industries are comparable.

## 51319 Other Publishers<sup>T</sup>

This industry comprises establishments known as publishers (except newspaper, magazine, book, directory, mailing list, music, and software publishers). These establishments may publish works in print or electronic form, including exclusively on the Internet.

*Illustrative Examples:*

Art publishers                                         Calendar publishers
Greeting card publishers

*Cross-References.*

- Establishments known as newspaper publishers are classified in Industry 51311, Newspaper Publishers;
- Establishments known as magazine and other periodical publishers are classified in Industry 51312, Periodical Publishers;
- Establishments known as book publishers are classified in Industry 51313, Book Publishers;
- Establishments primarily engaged in publishing directories and mailing lists are classified in Industry 51314, Directory and Mailing List Publishers;
- Establishments known as music publishers are classified in Industry 51223, Music Publishers;
- Establishments primarily engaged in publishing computer software are classified in Industry 51321, Software Publishers;
- Establishments primarily engaged in manufacturing appointment books and/or manifold business forms are classified in Industry 32311, Printing; and
- Establishments primarily engaged in educational test development services that publish tests, but that are not commonly known as publishers, are classified in Industry 61171, Educational Support Services.

### 513191  Greeting Card Publishers

This U.S. industry comprises establishments primarily engaged in publishing greeting cards. These establishments may publish works in print or electronic form, including exclusively on the Internet.

*Cross-References.*

Establishments primarily engaged in printing greeting cards without publishing are classified in Industry 32311, Printing.

### 513199  All Other Publishers

This U.S. industry comprises establishments generally known as publishers (except newspaper, magazine, book, directory, mailing list, music, software, and greeting card publishers). These establishments may publish works in print or electronic form, including exclusively on the Internet.

*Illustrative Examples:*

Art publishers                                         Calendar publishers

*Cross-References.*

- Establishments known as newspaper publishers are classified in Industry 513110, Newspaper Publishers;
- Establishments known as magazine or other periodical publishers are classified in Industry 513120, Periodical Publishers;
- Establishments known as book publishers are classified in Industry 513130, Book Publishers;
- Establishments primarily engaged in publishing directories and mailing lists are classified in Industry 513140, Directory and Mailing List Publishers;

T—Canadian, Mexican, and United States industries are comparable.

- Establishments primarily engaged in publishing greeting cards are classified in U.S. Industry 513191, Greeting Card Publishers;
- Establishments known as music publishers are classified in Industry 512230, Music Publishers;
- Establishments primarily engaged in publishing computer software are classified in Industry 513210, Software Publishers;
- Establishments primarily engaged in manufacturing appointment books and/or manifold business forms are classified in U.S. Industry 323111, Commercial Printing (except Screen and Books); and
- Establishments primarily engaged in educational test development services that publish tests, but that are not commonly known as publishers, are classified in Industry 611710, Educational Support Services.

**5132**	**Software Publishers<sup>T</sup>**

**51321**	**Software Publishers<sup>T</sup>**
See industry description for 513210.

**513210	Software Publishers**

This industry comprises establishments primarily engaged in software publishing. Establishments in this industry carry out operations necessary for producing and distributing computer software, such as designing, providing documentation, assisting in installation, and providing support services to software purchasers. These establishments may design, develop, and publish, or publish only. These establishments may publish and distribute software through subscriptions and/or downloads.

*Cross-References.*		Establishments primarily engaged in--

- Reselling packaged software without publishing--are classified in Sector 42, Wholesale Trade, or Sector 44-45, Retail Trade;
- Providing hosting and infrastructure support to software publishers, generally on a contract or fee basis, including game server hosting providers--are classified in Industry 518210, Computing Infrastructure Providers, Data Processing, Web Hosting, and Related Services;
- Designing custom software to meet the needs of specific users--are classified in U.S. Industry 541511, Custom Computer Programming Services;
- Mass duplication of software without publishing--are classified in Industry 334610, Manufacturing and Reproducing Magnetic and Optical Media;
- Operating Internet gaming sites without publishing--are classified in Industry 516210, Media Streaming Distribution Services, Social Networks, and Other Media Networks and Content Providers; and
- Operating online gambling sites--are classified in Industry 713290, Other Gambling Industries.

**516**	**Broadcasting and Content Providers<sup>T</sup>**

Industries in the Broadcasting and Content Providers subsector include establishments that create content or acquire the right to distribute content and subsequently broadcast or distribute that content. The industry groups (Radio and Television Broadcasting Stations and Media Streaming Distribution Services, Social Networks, and Other Media Networks and Content Providers) are based on differences in the methods of communication and the nature of services provided. The Radio and Television Broadcasting Stations industry group includes establishments that operate radio or television broadcasting stations for the programming and transmission of programs to the public. Programming may originate in their own studio, from an affiliated network, or from external sources. The Media Streaming Distribution Services, Social Networks, and Other Media Networks and Content Providers industry group includes establishments providing media streaming distribution services, operating social network sites, operating media broadcasting and cable television networks, and supplying information, such as news reports, articles, pictures, and features, to the news media. The establishments classified in this subsector are often engaged in the production and purchase of programs and other textual, audio, and/or video content, and they typically generate revenues from the sale of advertising space and air time, subscriptions, donations, subsidies, and/or the sale of programs.

---

T—Canadian, Mexican, and United States industries are comparable.

Establishments operating telecommunications facilities and infrastructure and distributing audio and video programming, including cable and satellite television subscription programming, are included in Subsector 517, Telecommunications. Establishments primarily engaged as independent contractors in the installation and maintenance of broadcasting systems are classified in Sector 23, Construction. Establishments primarily engaged in the production, or production and distribution, of motion pictures and sound recordings are included in Subsector 512, Motion Picture and Sound Recording Industries.

### 5161    Radio and Television Broadcasting Stations[T]

This industry group comprises establishments operating radio or television broadcasting stations for the programming and transmission of programs to the public. Programming may originate in their own studio, from an affiliated network, or from external sources.

### 51611   Radio Broadcasting Stations[T]
See industry description for 516110.

### 516110  Radio Broadcasting Stations

This industry comprises establishments primarily engaged in broadcasting aural programs by radio to the public. These establishments operate radio broadcasting studios and facilities for the programming and transmission of programs to the public. Programming may originate in their own studio, from an affiliated network, or from external sources.

*Cross-References.*          Establishments primarily engaged in--

- Operating radio broadcasting networks, including satellite radio networks--are classified in Industry 516210, Media Streaming Distribution Services, Social Networks, and Other Media Networks and Content Providers; and
- Producing radio program recordings--are classified in Industry 512290, Other Sound Recording Industries.

### 51612   Television Broadcasting Stations[T]
See industry description for 516120.

### 516120  Television Broadcasting Stations

This industry comprises establishments primarily engaged in broadcasting images together with sound. These establishments operate television broadcasting studios and facilities for the programming and transmission of programs to the public. Programming may originate in their own studio, from an affiliated network, or from external sources.

*Cross-References.*          Establishments primarily engaged in--

- Providing cable and satellite television distribution services using facilities and infrastructure that they operate--are classified in U.S. Industry 517111, Wired Telecommunications Carriers;
- Producing television programs--are classified in Industry 512110, Motion Picture and Video Production; and
- Producing and broadcasting television programs for cable and satellite television systems--are classified in Industry 516210, Media Streaming Distribution Services, Social Networks, and Other Media Networks and Content Providers.

### 5162    Media Streaming Distribution Services, Social Networks, and Other Media Networks and Content Providers[T]

---

T—Canadian, Mexican, and United States industries are comparable.

**51621    Media Streaming Distribution Services, Social Networks, and Other Media Networks and Content Providers[T]**
See industry description for 516210.

**516210    Media Streaming Distribution Services, Social Networks, and Other Media Networks and Content Providers**

This industry comprises establishments primarily providing media streaming distribution services, operating social network sites, operating media broadcasting and cable television networks, and supplying information, such as news reports, articles, pictures, and features, to the news media. These establishments distribute textual, audio, and/or video content of general or specific interest.

*Illustrative Examples:*

Broadcasting networks, radio
Broadcasting networks, television
Cable broadcasting networks
Cable television networks
Internet broadcasting
Pay-per-view cable programming
Satellite radio networks
Satellite television networks

Social network sites, Internet
Stand-alone streaming services
Subscription Video on Demand (SVOD) services
Syndicates, news
Virtual Multichannel Video Programming Distributors (vMVPDs)
Web broadcasting
Wiki sites, Internet

*Cross-References.*        Establishments primarily engaged in--

- Operating radio and television broadcasting stations--are classified in Industry Group 5161, Radio and Television Broadcasting Stations;
- Providing cable and satellite television distribution services using facilities and infrastructure that they operate--are classified in U.S. Industry 517111, Wired Telecommunications Carriers;
- Operating Web sites that use search engines to allow for searching information on the Internet--are classified in Industry 519290, Web Search Portals and All Other Information Services;
- Producing radio program recordings--are classified in Industry 512290, Other Sound Recording Industries;
- Producing television programs--are classified in Industry 512110, Motion Picture and Video Production;
- Acquiring distribution rights and distributing motion pictures and videos to motion picture theaters, television networks and stations, other media broadcast and streaming outlets, and exhibitors--are classified in Industry 512120, Motion Picture and Video Distribution;
- Publishing, or publishing and distributing, content they create or own, including game software and gaming site publishers--are classified in Subsector 513, Publishing Industries;
- Formatting content, provided by a customer, for streaming and providing hosting and infrastructure support on behalf of the content owner, generally on a contract or fee basis, including game server hosting providers--are classified in Industry 518210, Computing Infrastructure Providers, Data Processing, Web Hosting, and Related Services; and
- Independent performing, writing, and journalism, including photojournalists and musicians--are classified in Subsector 711, Performing Arts, Spectator Sports, and Related Industries.

**517    Telecommunications[T]**

Industries in the Telecommunications subsector group establishments that provide telecommunications and the services related to that activity (e.g., telephony, including Voice over Internet Protocol (VoIP); cable and satellite television distribution services; Internet access; telecommunications reselling services). The Telecommunications subsector is primarily engaged in operating and/or providing access to facilities for the transmission of voice, data, text, sound, and video. Transmission facilities may be based on a single technology or a combination of technologies.

Establishments primarily engaged as independent contractors in the installation and maintenance of telecommunications systems are classified in Sector 23, Construction.

---

T—Canadian, Mexican, and United States industries are comparable.

**5171    Wired and Wireless Telecommunications (except Satellite)**

This industry group comprises establishments primarily engaged in (1) operating transmission facilities and infrastructure that they own and/or lease, and providing telecommunications services using wired and wireless telecommunications networks; (2) reselling wired and wireless telecommunications services (except satellite); and (3) acting as agents for wireless telecommunications services.

**51711    Wired and Wireless Telecommunications Carriers (except Satellite)**

This industry comprises establishments primarily engaged in operating, maintaining, and/or providing access to switching and transmission facilities and infrastructure that they own and/or lease for the transmission of voice, data, text, sound, and video using wired and wireless telecommunications networks (except satellite). Transmission facilities may be based on a single technology or a combination of technologies. By exception, establishments providing satellite television distribution services using facilities and infrastructure that they operate are included in this industry.

*Illustrative Examples:*

Broadband Internet service providers, wired (e.g., cable, DSL)
Cable television distribution services
Cellular telephone service carriers
Direct-to-home satellite system (DTH) services
Satellite television distribution systems
Telecommunications carriers, wired and wireless

VoIP service providers, using own operated wired telecommunications infrastructure
Wireless Internet service providers, except satellite
Wireless telecommunications carriers, except satellite
Wireless telephone communications carriers, except satellite

*Cross-References.*      Establishments primarily engaged in--

- Operating television and radio broadcasting networks, including satellite television and radio networks, that produce media programming for distribution through cable, satellite, streaming, or Internet broadcasting-- are classified in Industry 51621, Media Streaming Distribution Services, Social Networks, and Other Media Networks and Content Providers;
- Operating radio and television broadcasting stations--are classified in Industry Group 5161, Radio and Television Broadcasting Stations;
- Reselling telecommunications services (except satellite telecommunications), without operating a network, and/or acting as agents for wireless telecommunications services, including operating as mobile virtual network operators (MVNOs)--are classified in Industry 51712, Telecommunications Resellers and Agents for Wireless Telecommunication Services;
- Operating and maintaining satellite network infrastructure that they own and/or lease and/or reselling satellite telecommunications services--are classified in Industry 51741, Satellite Telecommunications;
- Providing Internet access services via client-supplied telecommunications connections (e.g., dial-up ISPs)-- are classified in Industry 51781, All Other Telecommunications;
- Providing voice over Internet protocol (VoIP) services via client-supplied telecommunications connections- -are classified in Industry 51781, All Other Telecommunications; and
- Providing expert advice in the field of information technology or in integrating communication and computer systems--are classified in Industry 54151, Computer Systems Design and Related Services.

**517111  Wired Telecommunications Carriers**

This U.S. industry comprises establishments primarily engaged in operating, maintaining, and/or providing access to transmission facilities and infrastructure that they own and/or lease for the transmission of voice, data, text, sound, and video using wired telecommunications networks. Transmission facilities may be based on a single technology or a combination of technologies. Establishments in this industry use the wired telecommunications network facilities that they operate to provide a variety of services, such as wired telephony services, including VoIP services; wired (cable) audio and video programming distribution; and wired broadband Internet services. By

---

T—Canadian, Mexican, and United States industries are comparable.

exception, establishments providing satellite television distribution services using facilities and infrastructure that they operate are included in this industry.

*Illustrative Examples:*

Broadband Internet service providers, wired (e.g., cable, DSL)
Cable television distribution services
Closed-circuit television (CCTV) services
Direct-to-home satellite system (DTH) services
Local telephone carriers, wired
Long-distance telephone carriers, wired

Multichannel multipoint distribution services (MMDS)
Satellite television distribution systems
Telecommunications carriers, wired
VoIP service providers, using own operated wired telecommunications infrastructure

*Cross-References.*　　　　Establishments primarily engaged in--

- Operating and maintaining wireless telecommunications networks--are classified in U.S. Industry 517112, Wireless Telecommunications Carriers (except Satellite);
- Operating television and radio broadcasting networks, including satellite television and radio networks, that produce media programming for distribution through cable, satellite, streaming, or Internet broadcasting-- are classified in Industry 516210, Media Streaming Distribution Services, Social Networks, and Other Media Networks and Content Providers;
- Operating radio and television broadcasting stations--are classified in Industry Group 5161, Radio and Television Broadcasting Stations;
- Reselling telecommunications services (except satellite telecommunications and agents for wireless telecommunications services), without operating a network--are classified in U.S. Industry 517121, Telecommunications Resellers;
- Acting as agents for wireless telecommunications services, including operating as agents for mobile virtual network operators (MVNOs)--are classified in U.S. Industry 517122, Agents for Wireless Telecommunications Services;
- Reselling satellite telecommunications services--are classified in Industry 517410, Satellite Telecommunications;
- Providing Internet access services via client-supplied telecommunications connections (e.g., dial-up ISPs)-- are classified in Industry 517810, All Other Telecommunications;
- Providing voice over Internet protocol (VoIP) services via client-supplied telecommunications connections- -are classified in Industry 517810, All Other Telecommunications; and
- Providing expert advice in the field of information technology or in integrating communication and computer systems--are classified in Industry 54151, Computer Systems Design and Related Services.

## 517112　Wireless Telecommunications Carriers (except Satellite)

This U.S. industry comprises establishments primarily engaged in operating and maintaining switching and transmission facilities to provide communications via the airwaves. Establishments in this industry have spectrum licenses and provide services using that spectrum, such as cellular phone services, paging services, wireless Internet access, and wireless video services.

*Illustrative Examples:*

Cellular telephone service carriers
Wireless Internet service providers, except satellite
Paging services, except satellite

Wireless telephone communications carriers, except satellite

*Cross-References.*　　　　Establishments primarily engaged in--

- Operating and maintaining wired telecommunications networks--are classified in U.S. Industry 517111, Wired Telecommunications Carriers;

---

T—Canadian, Mexican, and United States industries are comparable.

- Operating and maintaining satellite network infrastructure that they own and/or lease--are classified in Industry 517410, Satellite Telecommunications;
- Providing satellite television distribution services--are classified in U.S. Industry 517111, Wired Telecommunications Carriers;
- Acting as agents for wireless telecommunications services, including operating as agents for mobile virtual network operators (MVNOs)--are classified in U.S. Industry 517122, Agents for Wireless Telecommunications Services; and
- Providing expert advice in the field of information technology or in integrating communication and computer systems--are classified in Industry 54151, Computer Systems Design and Related Services.

### 51712 Telecommunications Resellers and Agents for Wireless Telecommunication Services

This industry comprises establishments primarily engaged in (1) purchasing access and network capacity from owners and operators of telecommunications networks and reselling wired and wireless telecommunications services to businesses and households (except satellite telecommunications) or (2) acting as agents for wireless telecommunications carriers and resellers, selling wireless plans on a commission basis. Establishments in this industry do not operate as telecommunications carriers. Mobile virtual network operators (MVNOs) are included in this industry.

*Illustrative Examples:*

Agents for wireless telecommunications carriers
Cellular telephone stores, selling cellular phone service plans on an agent basis
Mobile phone stores, selling mobile phone service plans on an agent basis

Wired telecommunications resellers
Wireless phone service plan sales agents, selling on behalf of wireless telecommunications carriers
Wireless telecommunications resellers (except satellite telecommunications)

*Cross-References.* Establishments primarily engaged in--

- Operating and maintaining wired and wireless telecommunications networks (except satellite)--are classified in Industry 51711, Wired and Wireless Telecommunications Carriers (except Satellite);
- Reselling satellite telecommunications services--are classified in Industry 51741, Satellite Telecommunications; and
- Reselling cellular telephones and accessories without selling service plans--are classified in Sector 42, Wholesale Trade, or Sector 44-45, Retail Trade.

### 517121 Telecommunications Resellers

This U.S. industry comprises establishments engaged in purchasing access and network capacity from owners and operators of telecommunications networks and reselling wired and wireless telecommunications services to businesses and households (except satellite telecommunications and agents for wireless telecommunications services). Establishments in this industry resell telecommunications; they do not operate transmission facilities and infrastructure.

*Illustrative Examples:*

Mobile virtual network operators (MVNOs) (except agents)
Pre-paid calling cards, telecommunications resellers

Wired telecommunications resellers
Wireless telecommunications resellers (except satellite telecommunications and agents)

*Cross-References.* Establishments primarily engaged in--

- Acting as agents for wireless telecommunications carriers and resellers--are classified in U.S. Industry 517122, Agents for Wireless Telecommunications Services;

---

T—Canadian, Mexican, and United States industries are comparable.

- Operating and maintaining wired telecommunications networks--are classified in U.S. Industry 517111, Wired Telecommunications Carriers;
- Operating and maintaining wireless telecommunications networks--are classified in U.S. Industry 517112, Wireless Telecommunications Carriers (except Satellite); and
- Reselling satellite telecommunications services--are classified in Industry 517410, Satellite Telecommunications.

## 517122 Agents for Wireless Telecommunications Services

This U.S. industry comprises establishments primarily engaged in acting as agents for wireless telecommunications carriers and resellers, selling wireless plans on a commission basis.

*Illustrative Examples:*

Agents for mobile virtual network operators (MVNOs)
Agents for wireless telecommunications carriers
Cellular telephone stores, selling cellular phone service plans on an agent basis

Mobile phone stores, selling mobile phone service plans on an agent basis
Wireless phone service plan sales agents, selling on behalf of wireless telecommunications carriers

*Cross-References.*          Establishments primarily engaged in--

- Operating and maintaining wireless telecommunications networks--are classified in U.S. Industry 517112, Wireless Telecommunications Carriers (except Satellite);
- Reselling telecommunications services (except satellite telecommunications and agents for wireless telecommunications carriers and resellers), without operating a network--are classified in U.S. Industry 517121, Telecommunications Resellers; and
- Reselling cellular telephones and accessories without selling service plans--are classified in Sector 42, Wholesale Trade, or Sector 44-45, Retail Trade.

## 5174      Satellite Telecommunications[T]

## 51741    Satellite Telecommunications[T]
See industry description for 517410.

## 517410  Satellite Telecommunications

This industry comprises establishments primarily engaged in providing telecommunications services to other establishments in the telecommunications and broadcasting industries by forwarding and receiving communications signals via a system of satellites or reselling satellite telecommunications.

*Cross-References.*          Establishments primarily engaged in--

- Providing direct-to-home satellite television services to individual households or consumers--are classified in U.S. Industry 517111, Wired Telecommunications Carriers;
- Operating television and radio broadcasting networks, including satellite television and radio networks, that produce media programming for distribution through cable, satellite, streaming, or Internet broadcasting--are classified in Industry 516210, Media Streaming Distribution Services, Social Networks, and Other Media Networks and Content Providers;
- Operating satellite tracking stations and associated facilities--are classified in Industry 517810, All Other Telecommunications; and
- Providing expert advice in the field of information technology or in integrating communication and computer systems--are classified in Industry 54151, Computer Systems Design and Related Services.

---

T—Canadian, Mexican, and United States industries are comparable.

**5178     All Other Telecommunications**

**51781    All Other Telecommunications**
         See industry description for 517810.

**517810  All Other Telecommunications**

   This industry comprises establishments primarily engaged in providing specialized telecommunications services, such as satellite tracking, communications telemetry, and radar station operation.  This industry also includes establishments primarily engaged in providing satellite terminal stations and associated facilities connected with one or more terrestrial systems and capable of transmitting telecommunications to, and receiving telecommunications from, satellite systems.  Establishments providing Internet services or Voice over Internet protocol (VoIP) services via client-supplied telecommunications connections are also included in this industry.  Establishments in this industry do not operate as telecommunications carriers.

*Illustrative Examples:*

Dial-up Internet service providers                        Satellite tracking stations
Internet service providers, using client-supplied         VoIP service providers, using client-supplied
telecommunications connections (e.g., dial-up ISPs)       telecommunications connections

*Cross-References.*          Establishments primarily engaged in--

   • Providing wired broadband Internet services, direct-to-home satellite television distribution services, or
     wired VoIP services via own operated telecommunications infrastructure--are classified in U.S. Industry
     517111, Wired Telecommunications Carriers;
   • Providing expert advice in the field of information technology or in integrating communication and
     computer systems--are classified in Industry 54151, Computer Systems Design and Related Services; and
   • Providing satellite telecommunications services--are classified in Industry 517410, Satellite
     Telecommunications.

**518     Computing Infrastructure Providers, Data Processing, Web Hosting, and Related Services[T]**

   The Computing Infrastructure Providers, Data Processing, Web Hosting, and Related Services subsector groups establishments that provide computing infrastructure, data processing services, Web hosting services (except software publishing), and related services, including streaming support services (except streaming distribution services).

**5182    Computing Infrastructure Providers, Data Processing, Web Hosting, and Related Services[T]**

**51821   Computing Infrastructure Providers, Data Processing, Web Hosting, and Related Services[T]**
         See industry description for 518210.

**518210  Computing Infrastructure Providers, Data Processing, Web Hosting, and Related Services**

   This industry comprises establishments primarily engaged in providing computing infrastructure, data processing services, Web hosting services (except software publishing), and related services, including streaming support services (except streaming distribution services).  Data processing establishments provide complete processing and specialized reports from data supplied by clients or provide automated data processing and data entry services.

*Illustrative Examples:*

Application hosting                                        Computing platform infrastructure provision
Cloud storage services                                    Infrastructure as a service (IaaS)
Computer data storage services                            Optical scanning services

---

T—Canadian, Mexican, and United States industries are comparable.

**census.gov/naics**

Platform as a service (PaaS)                                                    Web hosting
Video and audio technical streaming support services

*Cross-References.*          Establishments primarily engaged in--

- Providing video and audio streaming distribution services--are classified in Industry 516210, Media Streaming Distribution Services, Social Networks, and Other Media Networks and Content Providers;
- Providing audiovisual postproduction services, including film/tape transfers and digitization (except digitization as a technical streaming support service)--are classified in U.S. Industry 512191, Teleproduction and Other Postproduction Services;
- Providing text processing and related document preparation activities--are classified in Industry 561410, Document Preparation Services;
- Software design, development, and publishing, or software publishing only--are classified in Industry 513210, Software Publishers;
- Developing custom software to meet the needs of a particular customer, without providing infrastructure or hosting services--are classified in U.S. Industry 541511, Custom Computer Programming Services;
- Providing computer hardware, software, and communication technologies integration services, with or without product sales--are classified in U.S. Industry 541512, Computer Systems Design Services;
- Selling computer hardware, packaged software, and communications equipment without providing systems integration services--are classified in Sector 42, Wholesale Trade, or Sector 44-45, Retail Trade;
- Providing on-site management and operation of a client's data processing facilities--are classified in U.S. Industry 541513, Computer Facilities Management Services;
- Providing wired broadband Internet access services using own operated telecommunications infrastructure, in combination with Web hosting--are classified in U.S. Industry 517111, Wired Telecommunications Carriers;
- Providing Internet access via client-supplied telecommunications connections in combination with Web hosting--are classified in Industry 517810, All Other Telecommunications;
- Operating Web search portals--are classified in Industry 519290, Web Search Portals and All Other Information Services;
- Providing access to computers and office equipment, as well as other office support services--are classified in Industry 56143, Business Service Centers;
- Processing financial transactions--are classified in Industry 522320, Financial Transactions Processing, Reserve, and Clearinghouse Activities; and
- Providing payroll processing services--are classified in U.S. Industry 541214, Payroll Services.

## 519       Web Search Portals, Libraries, Archives, and Other Information Services[T]

Industries in the Web Search Portals, Libraries, Archives, and Other Information Services subsector group establishments supplying information, storing and providing access to information, searching and retrieving information, and operating Web sites that use search engines to allow for searching information on the Internet. The main components of the subsector are libraries, archives, and Web search portals.

## 5192     Web Search Portals, Libraries, Archives, and Other Information Services[T]

## 51921   Libraries and Archives[T]
See industry description for 519210.

## 519210  Libraries and Archives

This industry comprises establishments primarily engaged in providing library or archive services. These establishments are engaged in maintaining collections of documents (e.g., books, journals, newspapers, and music) and facilitating the use of such documents (recorded information regardless of its physical form and characteristics) as required to meet the informational, research, educational, or recreational needs of their user. These establishments may also acquire, research, store, preserve, and generally make accessible to the public historical

---

T—Canadian, Mexican, and United States industries are comparable.

documents, photographs, maps, audio material, audiovisual material, and other archival material of historical interest. All or portions of these collections may be accessible electronically.

*Cross-References.*          Establishments primarily engaged in--

- Providing stock film and video footage (via motion picture and video tape libraries) to the media, multimedia, and advertising industries--are classified in U.S. Industry 512199, Other Motion Picture and Video Industries;
- Providing stock music to the media, multimedia, and advertising industries--are classified in Industry 512290, Other Sound Recording Industries;
- Providing stock photos to the media, multimedia, and advertising industries--are classified in Industry 519290, Web Search Portals and All Other Information Services; and
- Acquiring distribution rights and distributing motion pictures and videos to motion picture theaters, television networks and stations, other media broadcast and streaming outlets, and exhibitors--are classified in Industry 512120, Motion Picture and Video Distribution.

**51929    Web Search Portals and All Other Information Services**[T]
See industry description for 519290.

**519290  Web Search Portals and All Other Information Services**

This industry comprises establishments primarily engaged in operating Web sites that use a search engine to generate and maintain extensive databases of Internet addresses and content in an easily searchable format (and known as Web search portals) or providing other information services not elsewhere classified. Establishments known as Web search portals often provide additional Internet services, such as email, connections to other Web sites, auctions, news, and other limited content.

*Illustrative Examples:*

News clipping services                                  Stock photo agencies
Telephone-based recorded information services           Web search portals

*Cross-References.*          Establishments primarily engaged in--

- Providing wired broadband Internet access services using own operated telecommunications infrastructure--are classified in U.S. Industry 517111, Wired Telecommunications Carriers;
- Providing Internet access via client-supplied telecommunications connections--are classified in Industry 517810, All Other Telecommunications;
- Publishing and distributing content they create or own, including gaming site publishers--are classified in Subsector 513, Publishing Industries;
- Formatting content, provided by a customer, for streaming and providing hosting and infrastructure support on behalf of the content owner, generally on a contract or fee basis--are classified in Industry 518210, Computing Infrastructure Providers, Data Processing, Web Hosting, and Related Services;
- Operating news syndicates--are classified in Industry 516210, Media Streaming Distribution Services, Social Networks, and Other Media Networks and Content Providers; and
- Operating libraries and archives--are classified in Industry 519210, Libraries and Archives.

---

T—Canadian, Mexican, and United States industries are comparable.

# Sector 52--Finance and Insurance[T]

## The Sector as a Whole

The Finance and Insurance sector comprises establishments primarily engaged in financial transactions (transactions involving the creation, liquidation, or change in ownership of financial assets) and/or in facilitating financial transactions. Three principal types of activities are identified:

1. Raising funds by taking deposits and/or issuing securities and, in the process, incurring liabilities. Establishments engaged in this activity use raised funds to acquire financial assets by making loans and/or purchasing securities. Putting themselves at risk, they channel funds from lenders to borrowers and transform or repackage the funds with respect to maturity, scale, and risk. This activity is known as financial intermediation.

2. Pooling of risk by underwriting insurance and annuities. Establishments engaged in this activity collect fees, insurance premiums, or annuity considerations; build up reserves; invest those reserves; and make contractual payments. Fees are based on the expected incidence of the insured risk and the expected return on investment.

3. Providing specialized services facilitating or supporting financial intermediation, insurance, and employee benefit programs.

In addition, monetary authorities charged with monetary control are included in this sector.

The subsectors, industry groups, and industries within the Finance and Insurance sector are defined on the basis of their unique production processes. As with all industries, the production processes are distinguished by their use of specialized human resources and specialized physical capital. In addition, the way in which these establishments acquire and allocate financial capital, their source of funds, and the use of those funds provides a third basis for distinguishing characteristics of the production process. For instance, the production process in raising funds through deposit-taking is different from the process of raising funds in bond or money markets. The process of making loans to individuals also requires different production processes than does the creation of investment pools or the underwriting of securities.

Most of the Finance and Insurance subsectors contain one or more industry groups of (1) intermediaries with similar patterns of raising and using funds and (2) establishments engaged in activities that facilitate, or are otherwise related to, that type of financial or insurance intermediation. Industries within this sector are defined in terms of activities for which a production process can be specified, and many of these activities are not exclusive to a particular type of financial institution. To deal with the varied activities taking place within existing financial institutions, the approach is to split these institutions into components performing specialized services. This requires defining the units engaged in providing those services and developing procedures that allow for their delineation. These units are the equivalents for finance and insurance of the establishments defined for other industries.

The output of many financial services, as well as the inputs and the processes by which they are combined, cannot be observed at a single location and can only be defined at a higher level of the organizational structure of the enterprise. Additionally, a number of independent activities that represent separate and distinct production processes may take place at a single location belonging to a multilocation financial firm. Activities are more likely to be homogeneous with respect to production characteristics than are locations, at least in financial services. The classification defines activities broadly enough that it can be used both by those classifying by location and by those employing a more top-down approach to the delineation of the establishment.

Establishments engaged in activities that facilitate, or are otherwise related to, the various types of intermediation are included in multiple subsectors, rather than in a separate subsector dedicated to services alone, because these services are performed by intermediaries, as well as by specialist establishments, and the extent to which the activity of the intermediaries can be separately identified is not clear.

Financial industries are extensive users of electronic means for facilitating the verification of financial balances, authorizing transactions, transferring funds to and from transactors' accounts, notifying banks (or credit card issuers) of the individual transactions, and providing daily summaries. Since these transaction processing activities are integral to the production of finance and insurance services, establishments that principally provide a financial transaction processing service are classified in this sector, rather than in the data processing industry in the Information sector.

---

T—Canadian, Mexican, and United States industries are comparable.

Legal entities that hold portfolios of assets on behalf of others are significant and data on them are required for a variety of purposes.  Thus, for NAICS, these funds, trusts, and other financial vehicles are the fifth subsector of the Finance and Insurance sector.  These entities earn interest, dividends, and other property income, but have little or no employment and no revenue from the sale of services.  Separate establishments and employees devoted to the management of funds are classified in Industry Group 5239, Other Financial Investment Activities.

### 521      Monetary Authorities-Central Bank<sup>T</sup>

The Monetary Authorities-Central Bank subsector groups establishments that engage in performing central banking functions, such as issuing currency, managing the Nation's money supply and international reserves, holding deposits that represent the reserves of other banks and other central banks, and acting as a fiscal agent for the central government.

### 5211      Monetary Authorities-Central Bank<sup>T</sup>

### 52111      Monetary Authorities-Central Bank<sup>T</sup>
See industry description for 521110.

### 521110  Monetary Authorities-Central Bank

This industry comprises establishments primarily engaged in performing central banking functions, such as issuing currency, managing the Nation's money supply and international reserves, holding deposits that represent the reserves of other banks and other central banks, and acting as a fiscal agent for the central government.

*Cross-References.*

Establishments of the Board of Governors of the Federal Reserve System are classified in Industry 921130, Public Finance Activities.

### 522      Credit Intermediation and Related Activities<sup>T</sup>

Industries in the Credit Intermediation and Related Activities subsector group establishments that (1) lend funds raised from depositors; (2) lend funds raised from credit market borrowing; or (3) facilitate the lending of funds or issuance of credit by engaging in such activities as mortgage and loan brokerage, clearinghouse and reserve services, and check cashing services.

### 5221      Depository Credit Intermediation

This industry group comprises establishments primarily engaged in accepting deposits (or share deposits) and in lending funds from these deposits.  Within this group, industries are defined on the basis of differences in the types of deposit liabilities assumed and in the nature of the credit extended.

### 52211      Commercial Banking
See industry description for 522110.

### 522110  Commercial Banking

This industry comprises establishments primarily engaged in accepting demand and other deposits and making commercial, industrial, and consumer loans.  Commercial banks and branches of foreign banks are included in this industry.

*Cross-References.*

- Establishments primarily engaged in credit card banking are classified in Industry 522210, Credit Card Issuing;

---

T—Canadian, Mexican, and United States industries are comparable.

**census.gov/naics**

- Establishments known as industrial banks and primarily engaged in accepting deposits are classified in Industry 522180, Savings Institutions and Other Depository Credit Intermediation; and
- Establishments of depository institutions primarily engaged in trust activities are classified in U.S. Industry 523991, Trust, Fiduciary, and Custody Activities.

## 52213 Credit Unions
See industry description for 522130.

## 522130 Credit Unions

This industry comprises establishments primarily engaged in accepting members' share deposits in cooperatives that are organized to offer consumer loans to their members.

## 52218 Savings Institutions and Other Depository Credit Intermediation
See industry description for 522180.

## 522180 Savings Institutions and Other Depository Credit Intermediation

This industry comprises establishments primarily engaged in accepting deposits, making mortgage, real estate, and other consumer and commercial loans, and investing in high-grade securities (except commercial banking and credit unions). Savings and loan associations, savings banks, private banks (i.e., unincorporated banks), and establishments known as industrial banks or Morris Plans and primarily engaged in accepting deposits are included in this industry.

*Cross-References.*        Establishments primarily engaged in--

- Accepting demand and other deposits and making all types of loans--are classified in Industry 522110, Commercial Banking;
- Accepting members' share deposits in cooperatives--are classified in Industry 522130, Credit Unions; and
- Buying, pooling, and repackaging loans for sale to others on the secondary market and establishments known as industrial banks and Morris Plans and primarily engaged in providing nondepository credit--are classified in U.S. Industry 522299, International, Secondary Market, and All Other Nondepository Credit Intermediation.

## 5222 Nondepository Credit Intermediation

This industry group comprises establishments, both public (government-sponsored enterprises) and private, primarily engaged in extending credit or lending funds raised by credit market borrowing, such as issuing commercial paper or other debt instruments or by borrowing from other financial intermediaries. Within this group, industries are defined on the basis of the type of credit being extended.

## 52221 Credit Card Issuing
See industry description for 522210.

## 522210 Credit Card Issuing

This industry comprises establishments primarily engaged in providing credit by issuing credit cards. Credit card issuance provides the funds required to purchase goods and services in return for payment of the full balance or payments on an installment basis. Credit card banks are included in this industry.

*Cross-References.*        Establishments primarily engaged in--

- Factoring accounts receivables--are classified in U.S. Industry 522299, International, Secondary Market, and All Other Nondepository Credit Intermediation; and

---

T—Canadian, Mexican, and United States industries are comparable.

- Issuing cards that contain a stored pre-paid value--are classified with the industry providing the service represented by the cards, such as transit fare cards in Subsector 482, Rail Transportation, and long-distance telephone cards in Subsector 517, Telecommunications.

## 52222   Sales Financing
See industry description for 522220.

## 522220  Sales Financing

This industry comprises establishments primarily engaged in sales financing or sales financing in combination with leasing.  Sales financing establishments are primarily engaged in lending money for the purpose of providing collateralized goods through a contractual installment sales agreement, either directly from or through arrangements with dealers.

*Cross-References.*

Establishments not engaged in sales financing, but primarily engaged in providing leases for equipment and other assets are classified in Subsector 532, Rental and Leasing Services.

## 52229    Other Nondepository Credit Intermediation

This industry comprises establishments primarily engaged in making cash loans or extending credit through credit instruments (except credit cards and sales finance agreements).

*Illustrative Examples:*

| | |
|---|---|
| Consumer finance companies (i.e., unsecured cash loans) | International trade financing |
| Mortgage companies | Secondary market financing |

*Cross-References.*          Establishments primarily engaged in--

- Providing credit sales by issuing credit cards--are classified in Industry 52221, Credit Card Issuing;
- Providing leases for equipment and other assets without sales financing--are classified in Subsector 532, Rental and Leasing Services;
- Accepting deposits and lending funds from these deposits--are classified in Industry Group 5221, Depository Credit Intermediation;
- Arranging loans for others on a commission or fee basis--are classified in Industry 52231, Mortgage and Nonmortgage Loan Brokers;
- Servicing loans or providing check cashing services--are classified in Industry 52239, Other Activities Related to Credit Intermediation; and
- Guaranteeing international trade loans--are classified in Industry 52412, Direct Insurance (except Life, Health, and Medical) Carriers.

## 522291  Consumer Lending

This U.S. industry comprises establishments primarily engaged in making unsecured cash loans to consumers.

*Illustrative Examples:*

| | |
|---|---|
| Finance companies (i.e., unsecured cash loans) | Loan companies (i.e., consumer, personal, student, small) |
| Personal credit institutions (i.e., unsecured cash loans) | Student loan companies |

---

T—Canadian, Mexican, and United States industries are comparable.

*Cross-References.*          Establishments primarily engaged in--

- Accepting deposits and lending funds from these deposits--are classified in Industry Group 5221, Depository Credit Intermediation;
- Arranging loans for others on a commission or fee basis--are classified in Industry 522310, Mortgage and Nonmortgage Loan Brokers;
- Servicing loans or providing check cashing services--are classified in Industry 522390, Other Activities Related to Credit Intermediation;
- Providing credit sales by issuing credit cards--are classified in Industry 522210, Credit Card Issuing; and
- Factoring accounts receivables--are classified in U.S. Industry 522299, International, Secondary Market, and All Other Depository Credit Intermediation.

## 522292  Real Estate Credit

This U.S. industry comprises establishments primarily engaged in lending funds with real estate as collateral.

*Illustrative Examples:*

Home equity credit lending
Mortgage companies
Reverse mortgage lending

Mortgage banking (i.e., nondepository mortgage lending)

*Cross-References.*          Establishments primarily engaged in--

- Servicing loans--are classified in Industry 522390, Other Activities Related to Credit Intermediation;
- Arranging loans for others on a commission or fee basis--are classified in Industry 522310, Mortgage and Nonmortgage Loan Brokers;
- Accepting deposits and lending funds secured by real estate--are classified in Industry Group 5221, Depository Credit Intermediation; and
- Buying, pooling, and repackaging mortgage loans for sale to others on the secondary market--are classified in U.S. Industry 522299, International, Secondary Market, and All Other Nondepository Credit Intermediation.

## 522299  International, Secondary Market, and All Other Nondepository Credit Intermediation

This U.S. industry comprises (1) establishments primarily engaged in providing working capital funds to U.S. exporters, lending funds to foreign buyers of U.S. goods, and/or lending funds to domestic buyers of imported goods; (2) establishments primarily engaged in buying, pooling, and repackaging loans for sale to others on the secondary market; and (3) establishments primarily providing other nondepository credit (except credit card issuing, sales financing, consumer lending, and real estate credit). Examples of types of lending in this industry are short-term inventory credit, agricultural lending (except real estate and sales financing), and consumer cash lending secured by personal property.

*Illustrative Examples:*

Commodity Credit Corporation
Factoring accounts receivable
Industrial banks (i.e., known as), nondepository
International trade financing

Morris Plans (i.e., known as), nondepository
Pawnshops
Secondary market financing

*Cross-References.*

- Establishments primarily engaged in providing credit sales funding are classified in Industry 522210, Credit Card Issuing;

---

T—Canadian, Mexican, and United States industries are comparable.

- Establishments primarily engaged in sales financing or sales financing in combination with leasing are classified in Industry 522220, Sales Financing;
- Establishments primarily engaged in making unsecured cash loans to consumers are classified in U.S. Industry 522291, Consumer Lending;
- Establishments primarily engaged in lending funds with real estate as collateral are classified in U.S. Industry 522292, Real Estate Credit;
- Establishments primarily engaged in accepting deposits and lending funds from these deposits are classified in Industry Group 5221, Depository Credit Intermediation;
- Establishments known as industrial banks or Morris Plans and primarily engaged in accepting deposits are classified in Industry 522180, Savings Institutions and Other Depository Credit Intermediation;
- Establishments primarily engaged in arranging loans, including international trade loans, for others on a commission or fee basis are classified in Industry 522310, Mortgage and Nonmortgage Loan Brokers; and
- Establishments primarily engaged in guaranteeing international trade loans are classified in U.S. Industry 524126, Direct Property and Casualty Insurance Carriers.

## 5223     Activities Related to Credit Intermediation

This industry group comprises establishments primarily engaged in facilitating credit intermediation by performing activities, such as arranging loans by bringing borrowers and lenders together and clearing checks and credit card transactions.

## 52231     Mortgage and Nonmortgage Loan Brokers
See industry description for 522310.

## 522310   Mortgage and Nonmortgage Loan Brokers

This industry comprises establishments primarily engaged in arranging loans by bringing borrowers and lenders together on a commission or fee basis.

*Cross-References.*          Establishments primarily engaged in--

- Lending funds with real estate as collateral--are classified in U.S. Industry 522292, Real Estate Credit;
- Accepting deposits and lending funds secured by real estate--are classified in Industry Group 5221, Depository Credit Intermediation;
- Servicing loans--are classified in Industry 522390, Other Activities Related to Credit Intermediation; and
- Buying, pooling, and repackaging mortgage loans for sale to others on the secondary market--are classified in U.S. Industry 522299, International, Secondary Market, and All Other Nondepository Credit Intermediation.

## 52232     Financial Transactions Processing, Reserve, and Clearinghouse Activities
See industry description for 522320.

## 522320   Financial Transactions Processing, Reserve, and Clearinghouse Activities

This industry comprises establishments primarily engaged in providing one or more of the following: (1) financial transaction processing (except central bank); (2) reserve and liquidity services (except central bank); and/or (3) check or other financial instrument clearinghouse services (except central bank).

*Illustrative Examples:*

Automated clearinghouses, bank or check (except central bank)
Credit card processing services

Check clearing services (except central bank)
Electronic funds transfer services, including peer-to-peer payment services

---

T—Canadian, Mexican, and United States industries are comparable.

*Cross-References.*

- Establishments primarily engaged in nonfinancial data and electronic transaction processing (except payroll processing services) are classified in Industry 518210, Computing Infrastructure Providers, Data Processing, Web Hosting, and Related Services;
- Establishments primarily engaged in providing payroll processing services are classified in U.S. Industry 541214, Payroll Services;
- Establishments of the central bank primarily engaged in check clearing and other financial transaction processing are classified in Industry 521110, Monetary Authorities-Central Bank;
- Establishments primarily engaged in credit card issuing and related financial transaction processing are classified in Industry 522210, Credit Card Issuing;
- Establishment primarily engaged in furnishing physical or electronic marketplaces for the purpose of facilitating the buying and selling of securities and commodities are classified in Industry 523210, Securities and Commodity Exchanges; and
- Establishments primarily engaged in operating commodity or securities exchange clearinghouses are classified in U.S. Industry 523999, Miscellaneous Financial Investment Activities.

**52239   Other Activities Related to Credit Intermediation**
See industry description for 522390.

**522390  Other Activities Related to Credit Intermediation**

This industry comprises establishments primarily engaged in facilitating credit intermediation (except mortgage and loan brokerage; and financial transactions processing, reserve, and clearinghouse activities).

*Illustrative Examples:*

Check cashing services
Money order issuance services
Loan servicing

Travelers' check issuance services
Money transmission services
Payday lending services

*Cross-References.*          Establishments primarily engaged in--

- Arranging loans for others on a commission or fee basis--are classified in Industry 522310, Mortgage and Nonmortgage Loan Brokers;
- Financial transactions processing, reserve, and clearinghouse activities (except commodity or securities exchange services)--are classified in Industry 522320, Financial Transactions Processing, Reserve, and Clearinghouse Activities;
- Furnishing physical or electronic marketplaces for the purpose of facilitating the buying and selling of securities and commodities--are classified in Industry 523210, Securities and Commodity Exchanges;
- Operating commodity or securities exchange clearinghouses--are classified in U.S. Industry 523999, Miscellaneous Financial Investment Activities;
- Foreign currency exchange dealing and brokering--are classified in Industry 523160, Commodity Contracts Intermediation;
- Providing escrow services (except real estate)--are classified in U.S. Industry 523991, Trust, Fiduciary, and Custody Activities; and
- Operating pawnshops--are classified in U.S. Industry 522299, International, Secondary Market, and All Other Nondepository Credit Intermediation.

**523   Securities, Commodity Contracts, and Other Financial Investments and Related Activities[T]**

Industries in the Securities, Commodity Contracts, and Other Financial Investments and Related Activities subsector group establishments that are primarily engaged in one of the following: (1) underwriting securities issues and/or making markets for securities and commodities; (2) acting as agents (i.e., brokers) between buyers and sellers of securities and commodities; (3) providing securities and commodity exchange services; and (4) providing other

---

T—Canadian, Mexican, and United States industries are comparable.

services, such as managing portfolios of assets; providing investment advice; and trust, fiduciary, and custody services.

### 5231 Securities and Commodity Contracts Intermediation and Brokerage[T]

This industry group comprises establishments primarily engaged in putting capital at risk in the process of underwriting securities issues or in making markets for securities and commodities; and those acting as agents and/or brokers between buyers and sellers of securities and commodities, usually charging a commission.

### 52315 Investment Banking and Securities Intermediation
See industry description for 523150.

### 523150 Investment Banking and Securities Intermediation

This industry comprises establishments primarily engaged in underwriting, originating, and/or maintaining markets for issues of securities, or acting as agents (i.e., brokers) between buyers and sellers in buying or selling securities on a commission or transaction fee basis. Investment bankers act as principals (i.e., investors who buy or sell on their own account) in firm commitment transactions or act as agents in best effort and standby commitments. This industry also includes establishments acting as principals in buying or selling securities generally on a spread basis, such as securities dealers or stock option dealers.

*Illustrative Examples:*

Bond dealing (i.e., acting as a principal in dealing securities to investors)
Mutual fund agencies (i.e., brokerages)
Securities brokerages

Securities underwriting
Stock brokerages
Stock options dealing

*Cross-References.*

- Investment clubs or individual investors primarily engaged in buying or selling financial contracts (e.g., securities) on their own account are classified in Industry 523910, Miscellaneous Intermediation; and
- Establishments primarily engaged in accepting deposits and lending funds from these deposits are classified in Industry Group 5221, Depository Credit Intermediation.

### 52316 Commodity Contracts Intermediation
See industry description for 523160.

### 523160 Commodity Contracts Intermediation

This industry comprises establishments primarily engaged in acting as principals (i.e., investors who buy or sell for their own account) in buying or selling spot or futures commodity contracts or options, such as precious metals, foreign currency, oil, or agricultural products, generally on a spread basis, or acting as agents (i.e., brokers) in buying or selling spot or futures commodity contracts or options on a commission or transaction fee basis.

*Illustrative Examples:*

Commodity contract trading companies
Commodity contracts brokerages
Commodity futures brokerages

Futures commodity contracts dealing (i.e., acting as a principal in dealing commodities to investors)

*Cross-References.*          Establishments primarily engaged in--

- Operating commodity or securities exchange clearinghouses (including virtual currency trading exchange clearinghouses)--are classified in U.S. Industry 523999, Miscellaneous Financial Investment Activities; and

---

T—Canadian, Mexican, and United States industries are comparable.

- Reselling physical commodities--are classified in Sector 42, Wholesale Trade, or in Sector 44-45, Retail Trade.

## 5232 Securities and Commodity Exchanges[T]

### 52321 Securities and Commodity Exchanges[T]
See industry description for 523210.

### 523210 Securities and Commodity Exchanges

This industry comprises establishments primarily engaged in furnishing physical or electronic marketplaces for the purpose of facilitating the buying and selling of stocks, stock options, bonds, or commodity contracts.

*Cross-References.*        Establishments primarily engaged in--

- Investment banking, securities dealing, securities brokering, commodity contracts dealing, or commodity contracts brokering--are classified in Industry Group 5231, Securities and Commodity Contracts Intermediation and Brokerage; and
- Operating commodity or securities exchange clearinghouses--are classified in U.S. Industry 523999, Miscellaneous Financial Investment Activities.

## 5239 Other Financial Investment Activities[T]

This industry group comprises establishments primarily engaged in one of the following: (1) acting as principals in buying or selling financial contracts (except investment bankers, securities dealers, and commodity contracts dealers); (2) acting as agents (i.e., brokers) (except securities brokerages and commodity contracts brokerages) in buying or selling financial contracts; or (3) providing other investment services (except securities and commodity exchanges), such as portfolio management; investment advice; and trust, fiduciary, and custody services.

### 52391 Miscellaneous Intermediation
See industry description for 523910.

### 523910 Miscellaneous Intermediation

This industry comprises establishments primarily engaged in acting as principals (except investment bankers, securities dealers, and commodity contracts dealers) in buying or selling financial contracts generally on a spread basis. Principals are investors that buy or sell for their own account.

*Illustrative Examples:*

Investment clubs
Tax liens dealing (i.e., acting as a principal in dealing tax liens to investors)

Venture capital companies
Mineral royalties or leases dealing (i.e., acting as a principal in dealing royalties or leases to investors)

*Cross-References.*        Establishments primarily engaged in--

- Investment banking, securities dealing, securities brokering, commodity contracts dealing, or commodity contracts brokering--are classified in Industry Group 5231, Securities and Commodity Contracts Intermediation and Brokerage; and
- Managing the portfolio assets (i.e., funds) of others and/or providing customized investment advice--are classified in Industry 523940, Portfolio Management and Investment Advice.

## 52394 Portfolio Management and Investment Advice
See industry description for 523940.

---

T—Canadian, Mexican, and United States industries are comparable.

**523940  Portfolio Management and Investment Advice**

This industry comprises establishments primarily engaged in managing the portfolio assets (i.e., funds) of others on a fee or commission basis and/or providing customized investment advice to clients on a fee basis. Establishments providing portfolio management have the authority to make investment decisions, and they derive fees based on the size and/or overall performance of the portfolio. Establishments providing investment advice provide financial planning advice and investment counseling to meet the goals and needs of specific clients, but do not have the authority to execute trades.

*Illustrative Examples:*

Financial planning services, customized, fees paid by client

Managing trusts

Investment advisory services, customized, fees paid by client

Portfolio fund managing

*Cross-References.*

- Establishments primarily engaged in investment banking, securities intermediation, and commodity contracts intermediation are classified in Industry Group 5231, Securities and Commodity Contracts Intermediation and Brokerage;
- Establishments primarily engaged in acting as principals (except investment bankers, securities dealers, and commodity contracts dealers) in buying or selling financial contracts are classified in Industry 523910, Miscellaneous Intermediation;
- Establishments primarily engaged in administering personal estates are classified in U.S. Industry 523991, Trust, Fiduciary, and Custody Activities;
- Legal entities (i.e., trusts, estates, or agency accounts) administered on behalf of the beneficiaries under the terms of a trust agreement, will, or agency agreement are classified in Industry 525920, Trusts, Estates, and Agency Accounts;
- Establishments providing investment advice in conjunction with their primary activity, such as the sale of stocks, bonds, annuities, and real estate, are classified according to their primary activity; and
- Establishments known as publishers providing generalized investment information to subscribers are classified in Subsector 513, Publishing Industries.

**52399  All Other Financial Investment Activities**

This industry comprises establishments primarily engaged in acting as agents or brokers (except securities brokerages and commodity contracts brokerages) in buying and selling financial contracts and those providing financial investment services (except securities and commodity exchanges, portfolio management, and investment advice).

*Illustrative Examples:*

Bank trust offices

Fiduciary agencies (except real estate)

Exchange clearinghouses, commodities or securities

Escrow agencies (except real estate)

Stock quotation services

*Cross-References.*

- Establishments primarily engaged in investment banking, securities dealing, securities brokerage, commodity contracts dealing, or commodity contracts brokering are classified in Industry Group 5231, Securities and Commodity Contracts Intermediation and Brokerage;
- Establishments primarily engaged in acting as principals (except investment bankers, securities dealers, and commodity contracts dealers) in buying or selling financial contracts are classified in Industry 52391, Miscellaneous Intermediation;

---

T—Canadian, Mexican, and United States industries are comparable.

- Establishments primarily engaged in furnishing physical or electronic marketplaces for the purpose of facilitating the buying and selling of securities and commodities are classified in Industry 52321, Securities and Commodity Exchanges;
- Establishments primarily engaged in managing the portfolio assets (i.e., funds) of others and/or providing customized investment advice are classified in Industry 52394, Portfolio Management and Investment Advice;
- Legal entities (i.e., trusts, estates, or agency accounts) administered on behalf of the beneficiaries under the terms of a trust agreement, will, or agency agreement are classified in Industry 52592, Trusts, Estates, and Agency Accounts;
- Establishments primarily engaged in awarding grants from trust funds are classified in Industry 81321, Grantmaking and Giving Services;
- Establishments primarily engaged in performing real estate escrow or real estate fiduciary activities are classified in Industry 53139, Other Activities Related to Real Estate; and
- Establishments primarily engaged in financial transactions processing, reserve, and clearinghouse activities (except commodity or securities exchange services) are classified in Industry 52232, Financial Transactions Processing, Reserve, and Clearinghouse Activities.

## 523991 Trust, Fiduciary, and Custody Activities

This U.S. industry comprises establishments primarily engaged in providing trust, fiduciary, and custody services to others, as instructed, on a fee or contract basis, such as bank trust offices and escrow agencies (except real estate).

*Cross-References.*

- Establishments primarily engaged in managing the portfolio assets (e.g., trusts, funds) of others are classified in Industry 523940, Portfolio Management and Investment Advice;
- Legal entities (i.e., trusts, estates, or agency accounts) administered on behalf of the beneficiaries under the terms of a trust agreement, will, or agency agreement are classified in Industry 525920, Trusts, Estates, and Agency Accounts;
- Establishments primarily engaged in performing real estate escrow or real estate fiduciary activities are classified in Industry 531390, Other Activities Related to Real Estate; and
- Establishments primarily engaged in awarding grants from trust funds are classified in Industry 81321, Grantmaking and Giving Services.

## 523999 Miscellaneous Financial Investment Activities

This U.S. industry comprises establishments primarily engaged in acting as agents and/or brokers (except securities brokerages and commodity contracts brokerages) in buying or selling financial contracts and those providing financial investment services (except securities and commodity exchanges; portfolio management; investment advice; and trust, fiduciary, and custody services) on a fee or commission basis.

*Illustrative Examples:*

Exchange clearinghouses, commodities or securities
Stock quotation services

Gas lease brokers' offices

*Cross-References.* Establishments primarily engaged in--

- Investment banking, securities dealing, securities brokering, commodity contracts dealing, or commodity contracts brokering--are classified in Industry Group 5231, Securities and Commodity Contracts Intermediation and Brokerage;
- Acting as principals or agents (i.e., brokers) in buying or selling virtual currency (cryptocurrency)--are classified in Industry 523160, Commodity Contracts Intermediation;
- Acting as principals (except investment bankers, securities dealers, and commodity contracts dealers) in buying or selling financial contracts--are classified in Industry 523910, Miscellaneous Intermediation;

T—Canadian, Mexican, and United States industries are comparable.

- Furnishing physical or electronic marketplaces for the purpose of facilitating the buying and selling of securities and commodities--are classified in Industry 523210, Securities and Commodity Exchanges;
- Managing the portfolio assets (i.e., funds) of others and/or providing customized investment advice--are classified in Industry 523940, Portfolio Management and Investment Advice;
- Providing trust, fiduciary, and custody services to others--are classified in U.S. Industry 523991, Trust, Fiduciary, and Custody Activities; and
- Financial transactions processing, reserve, and clearinghouse activities (except commodity or securities exchange services)--are classified in Industry 522320, Financial Transactions Processing, Reserve, and Clearinghouse Activities.

## 524    Insurance Carriers and Related Activities[T]

Industries in the Insurance Carriers and Related Activities subsector group establishments that are primarily engaged in one of the following: (1) underwriting (assuming the risk, assigning premiums, and so forth) annuities and insurance policies or (2) facilitating such underwriting by selling insurance policies and by providing other insurance and employee benefit related services.

## 5241    Insurance Carriers[T]

This industry group comprises establishments primarily engaged in underwriting (assuming the risk, assigning premiums, and so forth) annuities and insurance policies and investing premiums to build up a portfolio of financial assets to be used against future claims. Direct insurance carriers are establishments that are primarily engaged in initially underwriting and assuming the risk of annuities and insurance policies. Reinsurance carriers are establishments that are primarily engaged in assuming all or part of the risk associated with an existing insurance policy (or set of policies) originally underwritten by another insurance carrier.

Industries are defined in terms of the type of risk being insured against, such as death, loss of employment because of age or disability, and/or property damage. Contributions and premiums are set on the basis of actuarial calculations of probable payouts based on risk factors from experience tables and expected investment returns on reserves.

## 52411    Direct Life, Health, and Medical Insurance Carriers

This industry comprises establishments primarily engaged in initially underwriting (i.e., assuming the risk and assigning premiums) annuities and life insurance policies, disability income insurance policies, accidental death and dismemberment insurance policies, and health and medical insurance policies.

*Cross-References.*

- Establishments primarily engaged in reinsuring insurance policies are classified in Industry 52413, Reinsurance Carriers;
- Legal entities (i.e., funds, plans, and/or programs) organized to provide insurance and employee benefits exclusively for the sponsor, firm, or its employees or members are classified in Industry Group 5251, Insurance and Employee Benefit Funds; and
- HMO establishments providing health care services are classified in Industry 62149, Other Outpatient Care Centers.

## 524113  Direct Life Insurance Carriers

This U.S. industry comprises establishments primarily engaged in initially underwriting (i.e., assuming the risk and assigning premiums) annuities and life insurance policies, disability income insurance policies, and accidental death and dismemberment insurance policies.

---

T—Canadian, Mexican, and United States industries are comparable.

*Cross-References.*

- Establishments primarily engaged in reinsuring life insurance policies, disability income insurance policies, and accidental death and dismemberment insurance policies are classified in Industry 524130, Reinsurance Carriers; and
- Legal entities (i.e., funds, plans, and/or programs) organized to provide insurance and employee benefits exclusively for the sponsor, firm, or its employees or members are classified in Industry Group 5251, Insurance and Employee Benefit Funds.

**524114  Direct Health and Medical Insurance Carriers**

This U.S. industry comprises establishments primarily engaged in initially underwriting (i.e., assuming the risk and assigning premiums) health and medical insurance policies. Group hospitalization plans and HMO establishments that provide health and medical insurance policies without providing health care services are included in this industry.

*Cross-References.*

- HMO establishments that provide both health care services and underwrite health and medical insurance are classified in U.S. Industry 621491, HMO Medical Centers;
- Establishments primarily engaged in reinsuring health insurance policies are classified in Industry 524130, Reinsurance Carriers; and
- Legal entities (i.e., funds, plans, and/or programs) organized to provide health- and welfare-related employee benefits exclusively for the sponsor's employees or members are classified in Industry 525120, Health and Welfare Funds.

**52412  Direct Insurance (except Life, Health, and Medical) Carriers**

This industry comprises establishments primarily engaged in initially underwriting (i.e., assuming the risk and assigning premiums) various types of insurance policies (except life, disability income, accidental death and dismemberment, and health and medical insurance policies).

*Illustrative Examples:*

Automobile insurance carriers, direct
Property and casualty insurance carriers, direct
Bank deposit insurance carriers, direct
Title insurance carriers, real estate, direct

Mortgage guaranty insurance carriers, direct
Warranty insurance carriers (e.g., appliance, automobile, homeowners', product), direct

*Cross-References.*

- Establishments primarily engaged in reinsuring insurance policies are classified in Industry 52413, Reinsurance Carriers;
- Legal entities (i.e., funds, plans, and/or programs) organized to provide insurance and employee benefits exclusively for the sponsor, firm, or its employees or members are classified in Industry Group 5251, Insurance and Employee Benefit Funds;
- Establishments primarily engaged in initially underwriting annuities and life insurance policies, disability income insurance policies, accidental death and dismemberment insurance policies, and health and medical insurance policies are classified in Industry 52411, Direct Life, Health, and Medical Insurance Carriers; and
- Establishments primarily engaged in researching public land records for ownership of titles and/or conveying real estate titles are classified in Industry 54119, Other Legal Services.

T—Canadian, Mexican, and United States industries are comparable.

### 524126 Direct Property and Casualty Insurance Carriers

This U.S. industry comprises establishments primarily engaged in initially underwriting (i.e., assuming the risk and assigning premiums) insurance policies that protect policyholders against losses that may occur as a result of property damage or liability.

*Illustrative Examples:*

Automobile insurance carriers, direct
Malpractice insurance carriers, direct
Fidelity insurance carriers, direct
Mortgage guaranty insurance carriers, direct

Homeowners' insurance carriers, direct
Surety insurance carriers, direct
Liability insurance carriers, direct

*Cross-References.*

Establishments primarily engaged in reinsuring property and casualty insurance policies are classified in Industry 524130, Reinsurance Carriers.

### 524127 Direct Title Insurance Carriers

This U.S. industry comprises establishments primarily engaged in initially underwriting (i.e., assuming the risk and assigning premiums) insurance policies to protect the owners of real estate or real estate creditors against loss sustained by reason of any title defect to real property.

*Cross-References.*          Establishments primarily engaged in--

- Reinsuring title insurance policies--are classified in Industry 524130, Reinsurance Carriers; and
- Researching public land records for ownership of titles and/or conveying real estate titles--are classified in U.S. Industry 541191, Title Abstract and Settlement Offices.

### 524128 Other Direct Insurance (except Life, Health, and Medical) Carriers

This U.S. industry comprises establishments primarily engaged in initially underwriting (e.g., assuming the risk, assigning premiums) insurance policies (except life, disability income, accidental death and dismemberment, health and medical, property and casualty, and title insurance policies).

*Illustrative Examples:*

Bank deposit insurance carriers, direct
Product warranty insurance carriers, direct
Deposit or share insurance carriers, direct

Warranty insurance carriers (e.g., appliance, automobile, homeowners', product), direct

*Cross-References.*          Establishments primarily engaged in--

- Reinsuring insurance policies--are classified in Industry 524130, Reinsurance Carriers;
- Initially underwriting annuities and life insurance policies, disability income insurance policies, and accidental death and dismemberment insurance policies--are classified in U.S. Industry 524113, Direct Life Insurance Carriers;
- Initially underwriting health and medical insurance policies--are classified in U.S. Industry 524114, Direct Health and Medical Insurance Carriers;
- Initially underwriting property and casualty insurance policies--are classified in U.S. Industry 524126, Direct Property and Casualty Insurance Carriers; and
- Initially underwriting title insurance policies--are classified in U.S. Industry 524127, Direct Title Insurance Carriers.

---

T—Canadian, Mexican, and United States industries are comparable.

**52413   Reinsurance Carriers**
      See industry description for 524130.

**524130  Reinsurance Carriers**

   This industry comprises establishments primarily engaged in assuming all or part of the risk associated with existing insurance policies originally underwritten by other insurance carriers.

*Cross-References.*          Establishments primarily engaged in--

   - Initially underwriting annuities and life insurance policies, disability income insurance policies, accidental death and dismemberment insurance policies, and health and medical insurance policies--are classified in Industry 52411, Direct Life, Health, and Medical Insurance Carriers; and
   - Initially underwriting various types of insurance policies (except life, disability income, accidental death and dismemberment, and health and medical insurance policies)--are classified in Industry 52412, Direct Insurance (except Life, Health, and Medical) Carriers.

**5242   Agencies, Brokerages, and Other Insurance Related Activities[T]**

   This industry group comprises establishments primarily engaged in (1) acting as agents (i.e., brokers) in selling annuities and insurance policies or (2) providing other employee benefits and insurance related services, such as claims adjustment and third party administration.

**52421   Insurance Agencies and Brokerages**
      See industry description for 524210.

**524210  Insurance Agencies and Brokerages**

   This industry comprises establishments primarily engaged in acting as agents (i.e., brokers) in selling annuities and insurance policies.

*Cross-References.*          Establishments primarily engaged in--

   - Underwriting annuities and insurance policies--are classified in Industry Group 5241, Insurance Carriers; and
   - Researching public land records for ownership of titles and/or conveying real estate titles--are classified in U.S. Industry 541191, Title Abstract and Settlement Offices.

**52429   Other Insurance Related Activities**

   This industry comprises establishments primarily engaged in providing services related to insurance (except insurance agencies and brokerages).

*Illustrative Examples:*

Claims adjusting, insurance                          Insurance actuarial services
Insurance plan administrative services, third party  Insurance claims adjusting

*Cross-References.*          Establishments primarily engaged in--

   - Managing the portfolio assets (i.e., funds) of others--are classified in Industry 52394, Portfolio Management and Investment Advice;
   - Acting as agents (i.e., brokers) in selling annuities and insurance policies--are classified in Industry 52421, Insurance Agencies and Brokerages; and
   - Providing actuarial consulting services--are classified in Industry 54161, Management Consulting Services.

---

T—Canadian, Mexican, and United States industries are comparable.

**524291  Claims Adjusting**

This U.S. industry comprises establishments primarily engaged in investigating, appraising, and settling insurance claims.

**524292  Pharmacy Benefit Management and Other Third Party Administration of Insurance and Pension Funds**

This U.S. industry comprises establishments primarily engaged in providing pharmacy benefit management (PBM) services and other third party administration services of insurance and pension funds, such as claims processing and other administrative services to insurance carriers, employee benefit plans, and self-insurance funds.

*Cross-References.*          Establishments primarily engaged in--

- Managing the portfolio assets (i.e., funds) of others--are classified in Industry 523940, Portfolio Management and Investment Advice;
- Initially underwriting health and medical insurance policies--are classified in U.S. Industry 524114, Direct Health and Medical Insurance Carriers;
- Retailing prescription and nonprescription drugs and medicines--are classified in Industry 456110, Pharmacies and Drug Retailers;
- Providing insurance actuarial services--are classified in U.S. Industry 524298, All Other Insurance Related Activities; and
- Providing actuarial consulting services--are classified in U.S. Industry 541612, Human Resources Consulting Services.

**524298  All Other Insurance Related Activities**

This U.S. industry comprises establishments primarily engaged in providing insurance services on a contract or fee basis (except insurance agencies and brokerages, claims adjusting, and third party administration). Insurance advisory services, insurance actuarial services, and insurance ratemaking services are included in this industry.

*Cross-References.*          Establishments primarily engaged in--

- Providing actuarial consulting services--are classified in U.S. Industry 541612, Human Resources Consulting Services;
- Acting as agents (i.e., brokers) in selling annuities and insurance policies--are classified in Industry 524210, Insurance Agencies and Brokerages;
- Insurance claims adjusting--are classified in U.S. Industry 524291, Claims Adjusting; and
- Providing pharmacy benefit management services and other third party administration services of insurance and pension funds--are classified in U.S. Industry 524292, Pharmacy Benefit Management and Other Third Party Administration of Insurance and Pension Funds.

**525        Funds, Trusts, and Other Financial Vehicles**

Industries in the Funds, Trusts, and Other Financial Vehicles subsector group legal entities (i.e., funds, plans, and/or programs) organized to pool securities or other assets on behalf of shareholders or beneficiaries of employee benefit or other trust funds. The portfolios are customized to achieve specific investment characteristics, such as diversification, risk, rate of return, and price volatility. These entities earn interest, dividends, and other investment income, but have little or no employment and no revenue from the sale of services. Establishments with employees devoted to the management of funds are classified in Industry Group 5239, Other Financial Investment Activities.

Establishments primarily engaged in holding the securities of (or other equity interests in) other firms are classified in Sector 55, Management of Companies and Enterprises. Equity real estate investment trusts (REITs) that are primarily engaged in leasing buildings, dwellings, or other real estate property to others are classified in Subsector 531, Real Estate.

---

T—Canadian, Mexican, and United States industries are comparable.

**5251    Insurance and Employee Benefit Funds**

This industry group comprises legal entities (i.e., funds, plans, and/or programs) organized to provide insurance and employee benefits exclusively for the sponsor, firm, or its employees or members.

**52511    Pension Funds**
See industry description for 525110.

**525110  Pension Funds**

This industry comprises legal entities (i.e., funds, plans, and/or programs) organized to provide retirement income benefits exclusively for the sponsor's employees or members.

*Illustrative Examples:*

Employee benefit plans                              Pension funds and plans
Retirement plans

*Cross-References.*          Establishments primarily engaged in--

- Managing portfolios of pension funds--are classified in Industry 523940, Portfolio Management and Investment Advice; and
- Initially underwriting annuities--are classified in U.S. Industry 524113, Direct Life Insurance Carriers.

**52512    Health and Welfare Funds**
See industry description for 525120.

**525120  Health and Welfare Funds**

This industry comprises legal entities (i.e., funds, plans, and/or programs) organized to provide medical, surgical, hospital, vacation, training, and other health- and welfare-related employee benefits exclusively for the sponsor's employees or members.

*Cross-References.*          Establishments primarily engaged in--

- Managing portfolios of health and welfare funds--are classified in Industry 523940, Portfolio Management and Investment Advice; and
- Providing pharmacy benefit management services and other third party claims administration of health and welfare plans--are classified in U.S. Industry 524292, Pharmacy Benefit Management and Other Third Party Administration of Insurance and Pension Funds.

**52519    Other Insurance Funds**
See industry description for 525190.

**525190  Other Insurance Funds**

This industry comprises legal entities (i.e., funds (except pension, and health- and welfare-related employee benefit funds)) organized to provide insurance exclusively for the sponsor, firm, or its employees or members. Self-insurance funds (except employee benefit funds) and workers' compensation insurance funds are included in this industry.

*Cross-References.*

- Legal entities (i.e., funds, plans, and/or programs) organized to provide retirement income benefits exclusively for the sponsor's employees or members are classified in Industry 525110, Pension Funds;

T—Canadian, Mexican, and United States industries are comparable.

- Legal entities (i.e., funds, plans, and/or programs) organized to provide health- and welfare-related employee benefits exclusively for the sponsor's employees or members are classified in Industry 525120, Health and Welfare Funds;
- Establishments primarily engaged in managing portfolios of insurance funds are classified in Industry 523940, Portfolio Management and Investment Advice;
- Establishments primarily engaged in providing pharmacy benefit management services and other third party claims administration of insurance and other employee benefit funds are classified in U.S. Industry 524292, Pharmacy Benefit Management and Other Third Party Administration of Insurance and Pension Funds; and
- Establishments primarily engaged in providing insurance on a fee or contract basis are classified in Industry Group 5241, Insurance Carriers.

**5259     Other Investment Pools and Funds**

This industry group comprises legal entities (i.e., investment pools and/or funds) organized to pool securities or other assets (except insurance and employee benefit funds) on behalf of shareholders, unitholders, or beneficiaries.

**52591    Open-End Investment Funds**
See industry description for 525910.

**525910  Open-End Investment Funds**

This industry comprises legal entities (i.e., open-end investment funds) organized to pool assets that consist of securities or other financial instruments. Shares in these pools are offered to the public in an initial offering with additional shares offered continuously and perpetually and redeemed at a specific price determined by the net asset value.

*Illustrative Examples:*

Investment funds, open-ended                    Money market mutual funds, open-ended

**52592    Trusts, Estates, and Agency Accounts**
See industry description for 525920.

**525920  Trusts, Estates, and Agency Accounts**

This industry comprises legal entities, trusts, estates, or agency accounts, administered on behalf of the beneficiaries under the terms of a trust agreement, will, or agency agreement.

*Illustrative Examples:*

Bankruptcy estates                               Personal investment trusts
Private estates (i.e., administering on behalf of       Testamentary trusts
beneficiaries)

*Cross-References.*         Establishments primarily engaged in--

- Managing portfolios of trusts--are classified in Industry 523940, Portfolio Management and Investment Advice;
- Administering personal estates--are classified in U.S. Industry 523991, Trust, Fiduciary, and Custody Activities; and
- Operating businesses of trusts and bankruptcy estates--are classified according to the kind of business operated.

---

T—Canadian, Mexican, and United States industries are comparable.

**52599   Other Financial Vehicles**
  See industry description for 525990.

**525990   Other Financial Vehicles**

  This industry comprises legal entities (i.e., funds (except insurance and employee benefit funds; open-end investment funds; trusts, estates, and agency accounts)).  Included in this industry are mortgage real estate investment trusts (REITs).

*Illustrative Examples:*

Closed-end investment funds
Special purpose financial vehicles
Collateralized mortgage obligations (CMOs)
Unit investment trust funds

Face-amount certificate funds
Mortgage real estate investment trusts (REITs)
Real estate mortgage investment conduits (REMICs)

*Cross-References.*

- Legal entities (i.e., funds, plans, and programs) that provide insurance and employee benefits exclusively for the sponsor, firm, or its employees or members are classified in Industry Group 5251, Insurance and Employee Benefit Funds;
- Legal entities (i.e., open-end investment funds) organized to pool assets that consist of securities or other financial instruments, where the pools are offered to the public in an initial offering with additional shares offered continuously and perpetually at a specific price determined by the net asset value, are classified in Industry 525910, Open-End Investment Funds;
- Legal entities (i.e., trusts, estates, or agency accounts) administered on behalf of the beneficiaries under the terms of a trust agreement, will, or agency agreement are classified in Industry 525920, Trusts, Estates, and Agency Accounts; and
- Equity real estate investment trusts (REITs) that are primarily engaged in leasing buildings, dwellings, or other real estate property to others are classified in Industry Group 5311, Lessors of Real Estate, based on primary type of real estate property leased.

---

T—Canadian, Mexican, and United States industries are comparable.

# Sector 53--Real Estate and Rental and Leasing[T]

## The Sector as a Whole

The Real Estate and Rental and Leasing sector comprises establishments primarily engaged in renting, leasing, or otherwise allowing the use of tangible or intangible assets, and establishments providing related services. The major portion of this sector comprises establishments that rent, lease, or otherwise allow the use of their own assets by others. The assets may be tangible, as is the case of real estate and equipment, or intangible, as is the case with patents and trademarks.

This sector also includes establishments primarily engaged in managing real estate for others, selling, renting, and/or buying real estate for others, and appraising real estate. These activities are closely related to this sector's main activity, and from a production basis they are included here. In addition, a substantial proportion of property management is self-performed by lessors.

The main components of this sector are the real estate lessors industries (including equity real estate investment trusts (REITs)); equipment lessors industries (including motor vehicles, computers, and consumer goods); and lessors of nonfinancial intangible assets (except copyrighted works).

Excluded from this sector are establishments primarily engaged in renting or leasing equipment with operators. Establishments renting or leasing equipment with operators are classified in various subsectors of NAICS depending on the nature of the services provided (e.g., transportation, construction, agriculture). These activities are excluded from this sector because the client is paying for the expertise and knowledge of the equipment operator, in addition to the rental of the equipment. In many cases, such as the rental of heavy construction equipment, the operator is essential to operate the equipment. Also excluded from this sector are mortgage REITs and establishments primarily engaged in managing the financial portfolio assets of REITs on a fee or commission basis. These establishments are classified in Sector 52, Finance and Insurance.

## 531    Real Estate[T]

Industries in the Real Estate subsector group establishments primarily engaged in renting or leasing real estate to others; managing real estate for others; selling, buying, or renting real estate for others; and providing other real estate related services, such as appraisal services.

This subsector includes equity real estate investment trusts (REITs) primarily engaged in leasing buildings, dwellings, or other real estate property to others. Mortgage REITs are classified in Subsector 525, Funds, Trusts, and Other Financial Vehicles.

Establishments primarily engaged in subdividing and developing unimproved real estate and constructing buildings for sale are classified in Subsector 236, Construction of Buildings. Establishments primarily engaged in subdividing and improving raw land for subsequent sale to builders are classified in Subsector 237, Heavy and Civil Engineering Construction.

## 5311    Lessors of Real Estate[T]

This industry group comprises establishments primarily engaged in acting as lessors of (1) residential buildings and dwellings; (2) nonresidential buildings (except miniwarehouses); (3) miniwarehouses and self-storage units; and (4) other real estate property. This industry group includes equity real estate investment trusts (REITs) primarily engaged in leasing buildings, dwellings, or other real estate property to others.

### 53111   Lessors of Residential Buildings and Dwellings
See industry description for 531110.

### 531110  Lessors of Residential Buildings and Dwellings

This industry comprises establishments primarily engaged in acting as lessors of buildings used as residences or dwellings, such as single-family homes, apartment buildings, and town homes. Included in this industry are owner-lessors and establishments renting real estate and then acting as lessors in subleasing it to others. The establishments in this industry may manage the property themselves or have another establishment manage it for them.

---

T—Canadian, Mexican, and United States industries are comparable.

*Cross-References.*          Establishments primarily engaged in--

- Managing residential real estate for others--are classified in U.S. Industry 531311, Residential Property Managers; and
- Providing short-term lodging in facilities, such as hotels, motels, casino hotels, and bed-and-breakfast inns--are classified in Industry Group 7211, Traveler Accommodation.

**53112    Lessors of Nonresidential Buildings (except Miniwarehouses)**
See industry description for 531120.

**531120  Lessors of Nonresidential Buildings (except Miniwarehouses)**

  This industry comprises establishments primarily engaged in acting as lessors of buildings (except miniwarehouses and self-storage units) that are not used as residences or dwellings.  Included in this industry are: (1) owner-lessors of nonresidential buildings; (2) establishments renting real estate and then acting as lessors in subleasing it to others; and (3) establishments providing full service office space, whether on a lease or service contract basis.  The establishments in this industry may manage the property themselves or have another establishment manage it for them.

*Cross-References.*          Establishments primarily engaged in--

- Acting as lessors of buildings used as residences or dwellings--are classified in Industry 531110, Lessors of Residential Buildings and Dwellings;
- Renting or leasing space for self-storage--are classified in Industry 531130, Lessors of Miniwarehouses and Self-Storage Units;
- Managing nonresidential real estate for others--are classified in U.S. Industry 531312, Nonresidential Property Managers;
- Providing a range of office support services, such as mailbox rental, other postal and mailing (except direct mail advertising) services, document copying services, facsimile services, word processing services or on-site personal computer rental, that are not providing office space--are classified in Industry 56143, Business Service Centers;
- Managing and operating arenas, stadiums, theaters, or other related facilities and promoting and organizing performing arts productions, sports events, and similar events at those facilities--are classified in Industry 711310, Promoters of Performing Arts, Sports, and Similar Events with Facilities;
- Operating public and contract warehousing and storage facilities (except self-storage)--are classified in Industry Group 4931, Warehousing and Storage; and
- Providing colocation services (i.e., rental of server and networking space in data centers)--are classified in Industry 518210, Computing Infrastructure Providers, Data Processing, Web Hosting, and Related Services.

**53113    Lessors of Miniwarehouses and Self-Storage Units**
See industry description for 531130.

**531130  Lessors of Miniwarehouses and Self-Storage Units**

  This industry comprises establishments primarily engaged in renting or leasing space for self-storage.  These establishments provide secure space (i.e., rooms, compartments, lockers, containers, or outdoor space) where clients can store and retrieve their goods.

*Cross-References.*          Establishments primarily engaged in--

- Operating public and contract warehousing and storage facilities (except self-storage)--are classified in Industry Group 4931, Warehousing and Storage; and
- Operating coin- or card-operated lockers--are classified in Industry 812990, All Other Personal Services.

---

T—Canadian, Mexican, and United States industries are comparable.

**53119   Lessors of Other Real Estate Property**
See industry description for 531190.

**531190  Lessors of Other Real Estate Property**

This industry comprises establishments primarily engaged in acting as lessors of real estate (except buildings), such as manufactured home (i.e., mobile home) sites, vacant lots, and grazing land.

*Cross-References.*        Establishments primarily engaged in--

- Acting as lessors of buildings used as residences or dwellings, including on-site manufactured (mobile) homes--are classified in Industry 531110, Lessors of Residential Buildings and Dwellings;
- Acting as lessors of buildings (except miniwarehouses and self-storage units) that are not used as residences or dwellings--are classified in Industry 531120, Lessors of Nonresidential Buildings (except Miniwarehouses);
- Renting or leasing space for self-storage--are classified in Industry 531130, Lessors of Miniwarehouses and Self-Storage Units;
- Operating public and contract warehousing and storage facilities (except self-storage)--are classified in Industry Group 4931, Warehousing and Storage;
- Providing colocation services (i.e., rental of server and networking space in data centers)--are classified in Industry 518210, Computing Infrastructure Providers, Data Processing, Web Hosting, and Related Services;
- Operating docking and/or storage facilities for pleasure craft owners--are classified in Industry 713930, Marinas; and
- Providing parking space for motor vehicles--are classified in Industry 812930, Parking Lots and Garages.

**5312   Offices of Real Estate Agents and Brokers**[T]

**53121   Offices of Real Estate Agents and Brokers**[T]
See industry description for 531210.

**531210  Offices of Real Estate Agents and Brokers**

This industry comprises establishments primarily engaged in acting as agents and/or brokers in one or more of the following: (1) selling real estate for others; (2) buying real estate for others; and (3) renting real estate for others.

**5313   Activities Related to Real Estate**[T]

This industry group comprises establishments primarily engaged in providing real estate services (except lessors of real estate and offices of real estate agents and brokers). Included in this industry group are establishments primarily engaged in managing real estate for others and appraising real estate.

**53131   Real Estate Property Managers**

This industry comprises establishments primarily engaged in managing real property for others. Management includes ensuring that various activities associated with the overall operation of the property are performed, such as collecting rents and overseeing other services (e.g., maintenance, security, trash removal).

*Cross-References.*

- Establishments primarily engaged in acting as lessors of real estate are classified in Industry Group 5311, Lessors of Real Estate;
- Establishments formed as associations on behalf of individual condominium owners or homeowners are classified in Industry 81399, Other Similar Organizations (except Business, Professional, Labor, and Political Organizations);

---

T—Canadian, Mexican, and United States industries are comparable.

- Establishments primarily engaged in providing operating staff to perform a combination of services to support operations within a client's facilities are classified in Industry 56121, Facilities Support Services;
- Establishments primarily engaged in renting real estate on behalf of owners are classified in Industry 53121, Offices of Real Estate Agents and Brokers;
- Establishments primarily engaged in providing individual activities related to property management (e.g., maintenance, security, landscaping, etc.) are classified in the appropriate industry according to the service provided; and
- Establishments primarily engaged in operating short-term lodging facilities, such as hotels, motels, casino hotels, and bed-and-breakfast inns are classified in Industry Group 7211, Traveler Accommodation.

## 531311 Residential Property Managers

This U.S. industry comprises establishments primarily engaged in managing residential real estate for others.

*Cross-References.*

- Establishments primarily engaged in managing nonresidential real estate for others are classified in U.S. Industry 531312, Nonresidential Property Managers;
- Establishments primarily engaged in acting as lessors of buildings used as residences or dwellings are classified in Industry 531110, Lessors of Residential Buildings and Dwellings;
- Establishments formed as associations on behalf of individual residential condominium owners or homeowners are classified in Industry 813990, Other Similar Organizations (except Business, Professional, Labor, and Political Organizations);
- Establishments primarily engaged in renting real estate on behalf of owners are classified in Industry 531210, Offices of Real Estate Agents and Brokers; and
- Establishments primarily engaged in providing individual activities related to property management (e.g., maintenance, security, landscaping, etc.) are classified in the appropriate industry according to the service provided.

## 531312 Nonresidential Property Managers

This U.S. industry comprises establishments primarily engaged in managing nonresidential real estate for others.

*Cross-References.*

- Establishments primarily engaged in managing residential real estate for others are classified in U.S. Industry 531311, Residential Property Managers;
- Establishments primarily engaged in acting as lessors of buildings (except miniwarehouses and self-storage units) that are not used as residences or dwellings are classified in Industry 531120, Lessors of Nonresidential Buildings (except Miniwarehouses);
- Establishments primarily engaged in renting or leasing space for self-storage are classified in Industry 531130, Lessors of Miniwarehouses and Self-Storage Units;
- Establishments formed as associations on behalf of individual nonresidential condominium owners are classified in Industry 813990, Other Similar Organizations (except Business, Professional, Labor, and Political Organizations);
- Establishments primarily engaged in providing operating staff to perform a combination of services to support operations within a client's facilities are classified in Industry 561210, Facilities Support Services;
- Establishments primarily engaged in renting real estate on behalf of owners are classified in Industry 531210, Offices of Real Estate Agents and Brokers;
- Establishments primarily engaged in providing individual activities related to property management (e.g., maintenance, security, landscaping, etc.) are classified in the appropriate industry according to the service provided; and
- Establishments primarily engaged in operating short-term lodging facilities, such as hotels, motels, casino hotels, and bed-and-breakfast inns are classified in Industry Group 7211, Traveler Accommodation.

---

T—Canadian, Mexican, and United States industries are comparable.

**53132 Offices of Real Estate Appraisers**
See industry description for 531320.

**531320 Offices of Real Estate Appraisers**

This industry comprises establishments primarily engaged in estimating the fair market value of real estate.

**53139 Other Activities Related to Real Estate**
See industry description for 531390.

**531390 Other Activities Related to Real Estate**

This industry comprises establishments primarily engaged in performing real estate related services (except lessors of real estate, offices of real estate agents and brokers, real estate property managers, and offices of real estate appraisers).

*Illustrative Examples:*

Real estate escrow agencies
Real estate listing services

Real estate fiduciaries' offices
Landman services

*Cross-References.*     Establishments primarily engaged in--

- Acting as lessors of real estate--are classified in Industry Group 5311, Lessors of Real Estate;
- Selling, buying, and/or renting real estate for others--are classified in Industry 531210, Offices of Real Estate Agents and Brokers;
- Managing real estate for others--are classified in Industry 53131, Real Estate Property Managers;
- Estimating fair market value of real estate--are classified in Industry 531320, Offices of Real Estate Appraisers;
- Researching public land records for ownership of titles and/or conveying real estate titles--are classified in U.S. Industry 541191, Title Abstract and Settlement Offices; and
- Underwriting or acting as agents in selling real estate title insurance policies--are classified in Subsector 524, Insurance Carriers and Related Activities.

**532     Rental and Leasing Services[T]**

Industries in the Rental and Leasing Services subsector include establishments that provide a wide array of tangible goods, such as automobiles, computers, consumer goods, and industrial machinery and equipment, to customers in return for a periodic rental or lease payment.

The subsector includes two main types of establishments: (1) those that are engaged in renting consumer goods and equipment and (2) those that are engaged in leasing machinery and equipment often used for business operations. The first type typically operates from a retail-like or storefront facility and maintains inventories of goods that are rented for short periods of time. The latter type typically does not operate from retail-like locations or maintain inventories, and usually offers longer-term leases. These establishments work directly with clients to enable them to acquire the use of equipment on a lease basis, or they work with equipment vendors or dealers to support the marketing of equipment to their customers under lease arrangements. Equipment lessors generally structure lease contracts to meet the specialized needs of their clients and use their remarketing expertise to find other users for previously leased equipment. Establishments that provide operating and capital (i.e., finance) leases are included in this subsector.

Establishments primarily engaged in leasing in combination with providing loans are classified in Sector 52, Finance and Insurance. Establishments primarily engaged in leasing real property are classified in Subsector 531, Real Estate. Establishments primarily engaged in renting or leasing equipment with operators are classified in various subsectors of NAICS depending on the nature of the services provided (e.g., transportation, construction, agriculture). These activities are excluded from this subsector since the client is paying for the expertise and knowledge of the equipment operator, in addition to the rental of the equipment. In many cases, such as the rental of

T—Canadian, Mexican, and United States industries are comparable.

heavy construction equipment, the operator is essential to operate the equipment. Likewise, since the provision of crop harvesting services includes both the equipment and operator, it is included in Subsector 115, Support Activities for Agriculture and Forestry. The rental or leasing of copyrighted works is classified in Sector 51, Information, and the rental or leasing of nonfinancial intangible assets, such as patents, trademarks, and/or licensing agreements, is classified in Subsector 533, Lessors of Nonfinancial Intangible Assets (except Copyrighted Works).

## 5321    Automotive Equipment Rental and Leasing[T]

This industry group comprises establishments primarily engaged in renting or leasing passenger cars and trucks without drivers and utility trailers. These establishments generally operate from a retail-like facility. Some establishments offer only short-term rental, others only longer-term leases, and some provide both types of services.

## 53211    Passenger Car Rental and Leasing[T]

This industry comprises establishments primarily engaged in renting or leasing passenger cars without drivers.

*Illustrative Examples:*

Passenger car rental or leasing                          Passenger van rental or leasing
Passenger truck (light duty) rental or leasing           Sport utility vehicle rental or leasing

*Cross-References.*          Establishments primarily engaged in--

- Renting or leasing passenger cars with drivers (e.g., limousines, hearses, taxis)--are classified in Industry Group 4853, Taxi and Limousine Service;
- Retailing passenger cars through sales or lease arrangements--are classified in Industry Group 4411, Automobile Dealers; and
- Leasing passenger cars in combination with providing loans to buyers of such vehicles--are classified in Sector 52, Finance and Insurance.

## 532111   Passenger Car Rental

This U.S. industry comprises establishments primarily engaged in renting passenger cars without drivers, generally for short periods of time.

*Illustrative Examples:*

Passenger car rental                                     Passenger van rental
Passenger truck (light duty) rental                      Sport utility vehicle rental

*Cross-References.*          Establishments primarily engaged in--

- Leasing passenger cars without drivers, generally for long periods of time--are classified in U.S. Industry 532112, Passenger Car Leasing; and
- Renting or leasing passenger cars with drivers (e.g., limousines, hearses, taxis)--are classified in Industry Group 4853, Taxi and Limousine Service.

## 532112   Passenger Car Leasing

This U.S. industry comprises establishments primarily engaged in leasing passenger cars without drivers, generally for long periods of time.

*Illustrative Examples:*

Passenger car leasing                                    Passenger truck (light duty) leasing

---

T—Canadian, Mexican, and United States industries are comparable.

Passenger van leasing                                    Sport utility vehicle leasing

*Cross-References.*          Establishments primarily engaged in--

- Renting passenger cars without drivers, generally for short periods of time--are classified in U.S. Industry 532111, Passenger Car Rental;
- Renting or leasing passenger cars with drivers (e.g., limousines, hearses, taxis)--are classified in Industry Group 4853, Taxi and Limousine Service;
- Retailing passenger cars through sales or lease arrangements--are classified in Industry Group 4411, Automobile Dealers; and
- Leasing passenger cars in combination with providing loans to buyers of such vehicles--are classified in Sector 52, Finance and Insurance.

## 53212   Truck, Utility Trailer, and RV (Recreational Vehicle) Rental and Leasing[T]
See industry description for 532120.

## 532120  Truck, Utility Trailer, and RV (Recreational Vehicle) Rental and Leasing

This industry comprises establishments primarily engaged in renting or leasing, without drivers, one or more of the following: trucks, truck tractors, buses, semi-trailers, utility trailers, or RVs (recreational vehicles).

*Cross-References.*          Establishments primarily engaged in--

- Renting or leasing light duty passenger trucks and sport utility vehicles without drivers--are classified in Industry 53211, Passenger Car Rental and Leasing;
- Renting recreational goods, such as pleasure boats, canoes, motorcycles, mopeds, or bicycles--are classified in U.S. Industry 532284, Recreational Goods Rental;
- Renting or leasing farm tractors, industrial equipment, and industrial trucks, such as forklifts and other material handling equipment--are classified in Industry 532490, Other Commercial and Industrial Machinery and Equipment Rental and Leasing;
- Renting or leasing mobile home sites--are classified in Industry 531190, Lessors of Other Real Estate Property;
- Retailing vehicles commonly referred to as RVs through sales or lease arrangements--are classified in Industry 441210, Recreational Vehicle Dealers; and
- Leasing trucks, utility trailers, and RVs in combination with providing loans to buyers of such vehicles--are classified in Sector 52, Finance and Insurance.

## 5322   Consumer Goods Rental[T]

This industry group comprises establishments primarily engaged in renting personal and household-type goods. Establishments classified in this industry group generally provide short-term rental although in some instances, the goods may be leased for longer periods of time. These establishments often operate from a retail-like or storefront facility.

## 53221   Consumer Electronics and Appliances Rental[T]
See industry description for 532210.

## 532210  Consumer Electronics and Appliances Rental

This industry comprises establishments primarily engaged in renting consumer electronics equipment and appliances, such as televisions, stereos, and refrigerators. Included in this industry are appliance rental centers.

---

T—Canadian, Mexican, and United States industries are comparable.

*Cross-References.*        Establishments primarily engaged in--

- Renting or leasing computers--are classified in Industry 532420, Office Machinery and Equipment Rental and Leasing; and
- Renting a range of consumer, commercial, and industrial equipment, such as lawn and garden equipment, home repair tools, and party and banquet equipment--are classified in Industry 532310, General Rental Centers.

## 53228   Other Consumer Goods Rental[T]

This industry comprises establishments primarily engaged in renting consumer goods (except consumer electronics and appliances).

*Illustrative Examples:*

Costume rental

Formal wear rental

Furniture (i.e., residential) rental centers

Hospital bed rental and leasing (i.e., home use)

Party rental supply centers

Sporting goods rental

Video disc rental for home electronic equipment (e.g., DVD)

*Cross-References.*        Establishments primarily engaged in--

- Renting consumer electronics and appliances--are classified in Industry 53221, Consumer Electronics and Appliances Rental;
- Renting a general line of products, such as lawn and garden equipment, home repair tools, and party and banquet equipment--are classified in Industry 53231, General Rental Centers;
- Renting medical equipment (except home health equipment), such as electromedical and electrotherapeutic apparatus--are classified in Industry 53249, Other Commercial and Industrial Machinery and Equipment Rental and Leasing;
- Retailing prerecorded video discs (e.g., DVDs)--are classified in Industry 44921, Electronics and Appliance Retailers;
- Retailing and renting musical instruments--are classified in Industry 45914, Musical Instrument and Supplies Retailers;
- Theatrical distribution of motion pictures and videos--are classified in Industry 51213, Motion Picture and Video Exhibition;
- Providing video streaming distribution services or operating Internet gaming sites without publishing--are classified in Industry 51621, Media Streaming Distribution Services, Social Networks, and Other Media Networks and Content Providers;
- Publishing video games and other software--are classified in Industry 51321, Software Publishers;
- Providing home health care services and home health equipment--are classified in Industry 62161, Home Health Care Services;
- Retailing home health care equipment--are classified in Industry 45619, Other Health and Personal Care Retailers; and
- Laundering and supplying uniforms, other work apparel, and linens--are classified in Industry 81233, Linen and Uniform Supply.

## 532281  Formal Wear and Costume Rental

This U.S. industry comprises establishments primarily engaged in renting clothing, such as formal wear, costumes (e.g., theatrical), or other clothing (except laundered uniforms and work apparel).

*Cross-References.*

Establishments primarily engaged in laundering and supplying uniforms and other work apparel are classified in U.S. Industry 812332, Industrial Launderers.

---

T—Canadian, Mexican, and United States industries are comparable.

## 532282  Video Tape and Disc Rental

This U.S. industry comprises establishments primarily engaged in renting prerecorded video tapes and discs for home electronic equipment, including renting through vending machines.

*Cross-References.*          Establishments primarily engaged in--

- Renting video gaming consoles, video recorders, and media players--are classified in Industry 532210, Consumer Electronics and Appliances Rental;
- Retailing prerecorded video discs (e.g., DVDs)--are classified in Industry 449210, Electronics and Appliance Retailers;
- Theatrical distribution of motion pictures and videos--are classified in Industry 51213, Motion Picture and Video Exhibition;
- Providing video streaming distribution services or operating Internet gaming sites without publishing--are classified in Industry 516210, Media Streaming Distribution Services, Social Networks, and Other Media Networks and Content Providers; and
- Publishing video games and other software--are classified in Industry 513210, Software Publishers.

## 532283  Home Health Equipment Rental

This U.S. industry comprises establishments primarily engaged in renting home-type health and invalid equipment, such as wheelchairs, hospital beds, oxygen tanks, walkers, and crutches.

*Cross-References.*          Establishments primarily engaged in--

- Renting medical equipment (except home health equipment), such as electromedical and electrotherapeutic apparatus--are classified in Industry 532490, Other Commercial and Industrial Machinery and Equipment Rental and Leasing;
- Providing home health care services and home health equipment--are classified in Industry 621610, Home Health Care Services; and
- Retailing home health care equipment--are classified in U.S. Industry 456199, All Other Health and Personal Care Retailers.

## 532284  Recreational Goods Rental

This U.S. industry comprises establishments primarily engaged in renting recreational goods, such as bicycles, canoes, motorcycles, skis, sailboats, beach chairs, and beach umbrellas.

## 532289  All Other Consumer Goods Rental

This U.S. industry comprises establishments primarily engaged in renting consumer goods and products (except consumer electronics and appliances; formal wear and costumes; prerecorded video tapes and discs for home electronic equipment; home health furniture and equipment; and recreational goods).  Included in this industry are furniture rental centers and party rental supply centers.

*Cross-References.*          Establishments primarily engaged in--

- Renting consumer electronics and appliances--are classified in Industry 532210, Consumer Electronics and Appliances Rental;
- Renting formal wear and costumes--are classified in U.S. Industry 532281, Formal Wear and Costume Rental;
- Renting video discs (DVDs), including through vending machines--are classified in U.S. Industry 532282, Video Tape and Disc Rental;
- Renting home health furniture and equipment--are classified in U.S. Industry 532283, Home Health Equipment Rental;

T—Canadian, Mexican, and United States industries are comparable.

- Renting recreational goods--are classified in U.S. Industry 532284, Recreational Goods Rental;
- Renting a range of consumer, commercial, and industrial equipment, such as lawn and garden equipment, home repair tools, and party and banquet equipment--are classified in Industry 532310, General Rental Centers; and
- Retailing and renting musical instruments--are classified in Industry 459140, Musical Instrument and Supplies Retailers.

**5323    General Rental Centers**[T]

**53231    General Rental Centers**[T]
See industry description for 532310.

**532310  General Rental Centers**

This industry comprises establishments primarily engaged in renting a range of consumer, commercial, and industrial equipment. Establishments in this industry typically operate from conveniently located facilities where they maintain inventories of goods and equipment that they rent for short periods of time. The type of equipment that establishments in this industry provide often includes, but is not limited to: audio visual equipment, contractors' and builders' tools and equipment, home repair tools, lawn and garden equipment, moving equipment and supplies, and party and banquet equipment and supplies.

*Cross-References.*           Establishments primarily engaged in--

- Renting trucks and trailers without drivers--are classified in Industry 532120, Truck, Utility Trailer, and RV (Recreational Vehicle) Rental and Leasing;
- Renting party and banquet equipment--are classified in U.S. Industry 532289, All Other Consumer Goods Rental;
- Renting consumer electronics and appliances--are classified in Industry 532210, Consumer Electronics and Appliances Rental;
- Renting heavy construction equipment without operators--are classified in U.S. Industry 532412, Construction, Mining, and Forestry Machinery and Equipment Rental and Leasing; and
- Renting specialized types of commercial and industrial equipment, such as garden tractors or public address systems--are classified in Industry 532490, Other Commercial and Industrial Machinery and Equipment Rental and Leasing.

**5324    Commercial and Industrial Machinery and Equipment Rental and Leasing**[T]

This industry group comprises establishments primarily engaged in renting or leasing commercial-type and industrial-type machinery and equipment. Establishments included in this industry group are generally involved in providing capital or investment-type equipment that clients use in their business operations. These establishments typically cater to a business clientele and do not generally operate a retail-like or storefront facility.

**53241    Construction, Transportation, Mining, and Forestry Machinery and Equipment Rental and Leasing**[T]

This industry comprises establishments primarily engaged in renting or leasing one or more of the following without operators: heavy construction, off-highway transportation, mining, and forestry machinery and equipment. Establishments in this industry may rent or lease products, such as aircraft, railroad cars, steamships, tugboats, bulldozers, earthmoving equipment, well drilling machinery and equipment, or cranes.

*Cross-References.*           Establishments primarily engaged in--

- Renting or leasing automobiles or trucks without operators--are classified in Industry Group 5321, Automotive Equipment Rental and Leasing;
- Renting or leasing air, rail, highway, and water transportation equipment with operators--are classified in Sector 48-49, Transportation and Warehousing, based on their primary activity;

---

T—Canadian, Mexican, and United States industries are comparable.

- Renting or leasing heavy construction equipment with operators--are classified in Industry Group 2389, Other Specialty Trade Contractors;
- Renting or leasing heavy equipment for mining with operators--are classified in Industry 21311, Support Activities for Mining;
- Renting or leasing heavy equipment for forestry with operators--are classified in Industry 11531, Support Activities for Forestry; and
- Leasing heavy equipment in combination with providing loans to buyers of such equipment--are classified in Sector 52, Finance and Insurance.

## 532411 Commercial Air, Rail, and Water Transportation Equipment Rental and Leasing

This U.S. industry comprises establishments primarily engaged in renting or leasing off-highway transportation equipment without operators, such as aircraft, railroad cars, steamships, or tugboats.

*Cross-References.*          Establishments primarily engaged in--

- Renting or leasing air, rail, highway, and water transportation equipment with operators--are classified in Sector 48-49, Transportation and Warehousing, based on their primary activity;
- Renting pleasure boats--are classified in U.S. Industry 532284, Recreational Goods Rental; and
- Renting or leasing automobiles or trucks without drivers--are classified in Industry Group 5321, Automotive Equipment Rental and Leasing.

## 532412 Construction, Mining, and Forestry Machinery and Equipment Rental and Leasing

This U.S. industry comprises establishments primarily engaged in renting or leasing heavy equipment without operators that may be used for construction, mining, or forestry, such as bulldozers, earthmoving equipment, well drilling machinery and equipment, or cranes.

*Cross-References.*          Establishments primarily engaged in--

- Renting or leasing cranes with operators--are classified in Industry 238990, All Other Specialty Trade Contractors;
- Renting or leasing construction equipment with operators (except cranes)--are classified in Industry 238910, Site Preparation Contractors;
- Renting or leasing heavy equipment for mining with operators--are classified in Industry 21311, Support Activities for Mining;
- Renting or leasing heavy equipment for forestry with operators--are classified in Industry 115310, Support Activities for Forestry; and
- Leasing heavy equipment in combination with providing loans to buyers of such equipment--are classified in Sector 52, Finance and Insurance.

## 53242 Office Machinery and Equipment Rental and Leasing[T]
See industry description for 532420.

## 532420 Office Machinery and Equipment Rental and Leasing

This industry comprises establishments primarily engaged in renting or leasing office machinery and equipment, such as computers, office furniture, duplicating machines (i.e., copiers), or facsimile machines.

*Cross-References.*          Establishments primarily engaged in--

- Renting or leasing residential furniture--are classified in U.S. Industry 532289, All Other Consumer Goods Rental; and
- Leasing office machinery and equipment in combination with providing loans to buyers of such equipment--are classified in Sector 52, Finance and Insurance.

T—Canadian, Mexican, and United States industries are comparable.

**53249   Other Commercial and Industrial Machinery and Equipment Rental and Leasing**[T]
See industry description for 532490.

**532490   Other Commercial and Industrial Machinery and Equipment Rental and Leasing**

This industry comprises establishments primarily engaged in renting or leasing nonconsumer-type machinery and equipment (except heavy construction, transportation, mining, and forestry machinery and equipment without operators; and office machinery and equipment). Establishments in this industry rent or lease products, such as manufacturing equipment; metalworking, telecommunications, motion picture, theatrical machinery and equipment, or service industry machinery; institutional (i.e., public building) furniture, such as furniture for schools, theaters, or buildings; or agricultural equipment without operators.

*Cross-References.*          Establishments primarily engaged in--

- Renting or leasing heavy construction, off-highway transportation, mining, and forestry machinery and equipment without operators--are classified in Industry 53241, Construction, Transportation, Mining, and Forestry Machinery and Equipment Rental and Leasing;
- Renting or leasing office machinery and equipment--are classified in Industry 532420, Office Machinery and Equipment Rental and Leasing;
- Renting or leasing agricultural machinery and equipment with operators--are classified in Subsector 115, Support Activities for Agriculture and Forestry;
- Renting or leasing dump trucks without operator--are classified in Industry 532120, Truck, Utility Trailer, and RV (Recreational Vehicle) Rental and Leasing;
- Renting home furniture or medical equipment for home use--are classified in Industry 53228, Other Consumer Goods Rental; and
- Leasing nonconsumer machinery and equipment in combination with providing loans to buyers of such equipment--are classified in Sector 52, Finance and Insurance.

**533      Lessors of Nonfinancial Intangible Assets (except Copyrighted Works)**[T]

Industries in the Lessors of Nonfinancial Intangible Assets (except Copyrighted Works) subsector include establishments primarily engaged in assigning rights to assets, such as patents, trademarks, brand names, and/or franchise agreements, for which a royalty payment or licensing fee is paid to the asset holder. Establishments in this subsector own the patents, trademarks, and/or franchise agreements that they allow others to use or reproduce for a fee and may or may not have created those assets.

Establishments that allow franchisees the use of the franchise name, contingent on the franchisee buying products or services from the franchisor, are classified elsewhere.

Excluded from this subsector are establishments primarily engaged in leasing real property and establishments primarily engaged in leasing tangible assets, such as automobiles, computers, consumer goods, and industrial machinery and equipment. These establishments are classified in Subsector 531, Real Estate, and Subsector 532, Rental and Leasing Services, respectively.

**5331    Lessors of Nonfinancial Intangible Assets (except Copyrighted Works)**[T]

**53311   Lessors of Nonfinancial Intangible Assets (except Copyrighted Works)**[T]
See industry description for 533110.

**533110  Lessors of Nonfinancial Intangible Assets (except Copyrighted Works)**

This industry comprises establishments primarily engaged in assigning rights to assets, such as patents, trademarks, brand names, and/or franchise agreements, for which a royalty payment or licensing fee is paid to the asset holder.

---

T—Canadian, Mexican, and United States industries are comparable.

*Cross-References.*

- Establishments primarily engaged in producing, reproducing, and/or distributing copyrighted works are classified in Sector 51, Information;
- Independent artists, writers, and performers primarily engaged in creating copyrighted works are classified in Industry 711510, Independent Artists, Writers, and Performers;
- Establishments primarily engaged in leasing real property are classified in Subsector 531, Real Estate;
- Establishments primarily engaged in leasing tangible assets, such as automobiles, computers, consumer goods, and industrial machinery and equipment, are classified in Subsector 532, Rental and Leasing Services; and
- Establishments that allow franchisees the use of the franchise name, contingent on the franchisee buying products or services from the franchisor, are classified elsewhere.

---

T—Canadian, Mexican, and United States industries are comparable.

# Sector 54--Professional, Scientific, and Technical Services[T]

## The Sector as a Whole

The Professional, Scientific, and Technical Services sector comprises establishments that specialize in performing professional, scientific, and technical activities for others. These activities require a high degree of expertise and training. The establishments in this sector specialize according to expertise and provide these services to clients in a variety of industries and, in some cases, to households. Activities performed include: legal advice and representation; accounting, bookkeeping, and payroll services; architectural, engineering, and specialized design services; computer services; consulting services; research services; advertising services; photographic services; translation and interpretation services; veterinary services; and other professional, scientific, and technical services.

This sector excludes establishments primarily engaged in providing a range of day-to-day office administrative services, such as financial planning, billing and recordkeeping, personnel supply, and physical distribution and logistics. These establishments are classified in Sector 56, Administrative and Support and Waste Management and Remediation Services.

## 541    Professional, Scientific, and Technical Services[T]

Industries in the Professional, Scientific, and Technical Services subsector group establishments engaged in processes where human capital is the major input. These establishments make available the knowledge and skills of their employees, often on an assignment basis, where an individual or team is responsible for the delivery of services to the client. The individual industries of this subsector are defined on the basis of the particular expertise and training of the services provider.

The distinguishing feature of the Professional, Scientific, and Technical Services subsector is the fact that most of the industries grouped in it have production processes that are almost wholly dependent on worker skills. Thus, the establishments classified in this subsector sell expertise. Much of the expertise requires degrees, though not in every case.

## 5411    Legal Services[T]

This industry group comprises establishments primarily engaged in offering legal services, such as those offered by offices of lawyers, offices of notaries, and title abstract and settlement offices, and paralegal services.

## 54111   Offices of Lawyers[T]
See industry description for 541110.

## 541110  Offices of Lawyers

This industry comprises offices of legal practitioners known as lawyers or attorneys (i.e., counselors-at-law) primarily engaged in the practice of law. Establishments in this industry may provide expertise in a range or in specific areas of law, such as criminal law, corporate law, family and estate law, patent law, real estate law, or tax law.

*Cross-References.*

Establishments of legal practitioners (except lawyers or attorneys) primarily engaged in providing specialized legal or paralegal services are classified in Industry 54119, Other Legal Services.

## 54112   Offices of Notaries[T]
See industry description for 541120.

---

T—Canadian, Mexican, and United States industries are comparable.

### 541120  Offices of Notaries

This industry comprises establishments (except offices of lawyers and attorneys) primarily engaged in drafting, approving, and executing legal documents, such as real estate transactions, wills, and contracts; and in receiving, indexing, and storing such documents.

*Cross-References.*

- Establishments of lawyers and attorneys primarily engaged in the practice of law are classified in Industry 541110, Offices of Lawyers; and
- Establishments of notaries public engaged in activities, such as administering oaths and taking affidavits and depositions, witnessing and certifying signatures on documents, but not empowered to draw and approve legal documents and contracts, are classified in U.S. Industry 541199, All Other Legal Services.

### 54119  Other Legal Services[T]

This industry comprises establishments of legal practitioners (except lawyers and attorneys) primarily engaged in providing specialized legal or paralegal services.

*Illustrative Examples:*

Notary public services
Process serving services
Paralegal services
Real estate settlement offices

Patent agent services (i.e., patent filing and searching services)
Real estate title abstract companies

*Cross-References.*

- Establishments of lawyers and attorneys primarily engaged in the practice of law are classified in Industry 54111, Offices of Lawyers;
- Establishments (except offices of lawyers, attorneys, and paralegals) primarily engaged in providing arbitration and conciliation services are classified in Industry 54199, All Other Professional, Scientific, and Technical Services;
- Establishments primarily engaged in underwriting or acting as agents in selling real estate title insurance policies are classified in Subsector 524, Insurance Carriers and Related Activities; and
- Establishments primarily engaged in providing landman services or real estate escrow and fiduciary services are classified in Industry 53139, Other Activities Related to Real Estate.

### 541191  Title Abstract and Settlement Offices

This U.S. industry comprises establishments (except offices of lawyers and attorneys) primarily engaged in one or more of the following activities: (1) researching public land records to gather information relating to real estate titles; (2) preparing documents necessary for the transfer of the title, financing, and settlement; (3) conducting final real estate settlements and closings; and (4) filing legal and other documents relating to the sale of real estate. Real estate settlement offices, title abstract companies, and title search companies are included in this industry.

*Cross-References.*

- Establishments of lawyers and attorneys primarily engaged in the practice of law are classified in Industry 541110, Offices of Lawyers;
- Establishments primarily engaged in underwriting or acting as agents in selling real estate title insurance policies are classified in Subsector 524, Insurance Carriers and Related Activities; and
- Establishments primarily engaged in providing real estate escrow and fiduciary services are classified in Industry 531390, Other Activities Related to Real Estate.

---

T—Canadian, Mexican, and United States industries are comparable.

**541199  All Other Legal Services**

This U.S. industry comprises establishments of legal practitioners (except offices of lawyers and attorneys, settlement offices, and title abstract offices).  These establishments are primarily engaged in providing specialized legal or paralegal services.

*Illustrative Examples:*

Notary public services                                    Paralegal services
Patent agent services (i.e., patent filing and searching  Process serving services
services)

*Cross-References.*

- Establishments of lawyers and attorneys primarily engaged in the practice of law are classified in Industry 541110, Offices of Lawyers;
- Establishments (except offices of lawyers and attorneys) primarily engaged in researching public land records for ownership or title; preparing documents necessary for the transfer of the title, financing, and settlement; conducting final real estate settlements and closings; and/or filing legal and other documents relating to the sale of real estate are classified in U.S. Industry 541191, Title Abstract and Settlement Offices;
- Establishments (except offices of lawyers, attorneys, and paralegals) primarily engaged in providing arbitration and conciliation services are classified in Industry 541990, All Other Professional, Scientific, and Technical Services; and
- Establishments primarily engaged in providing landman services or real estate escrow and fiduciary services are classified in Industry 531390, Other Activities Related to Real Estate.

**5412    Accounting, Tax Preparation, Bookkeeping, and Payroll Services**[T]

**54121   Accounting, Tax Preparation, Bookkeeping, and Payroll Services**[T]

This industry comprises establishments primarily engaged in providing services, such as auditing of accounting records, designing accounting systems, preparing financial statements, developing budgets, preparing tax returns, processing payrolls, bookkeeping, and billing.

*Illustrative Examples:*

Accountants' offices                                      Bookkeeping services
Payroll processing services                               Tax return preparation services

*Cross-References.*          Establishments primarily engaged in--

- Providing data processing services (except payroll processing services and financial transaction processing services) at their own facility for others--are classified in Industry 51821, Computing Infrastructure Providers, Data Processing, Web Hosting, and Related Services; and
- Processing financial transactions (except central bank)--are classified in Industry 52232, Financial Transactions Processing, Reserve, and Clearinghouse Activities.

**541211  Offices of Certified Public Accountants**

This U.S. industry comprises establishments of accountants that are certified to audit the accounting records of public and private organizations and to attest to compliance with generally accepted accounting practices.  Offices of certified public accountants (CPAs) may provide one or more of the following accounting services: (1) auditing financial statements; (2) designing accounting systems; (3) preparing financial statements; (4) developing budgets;

---

T—Canadian, Mexican, and United States industries are comparable.

and (5) providing advice on matters related to accounting. These establishments may also provide related services, such as bookkeeping, tax return preparation, and payroll processing.

*Cross-References.*          Establishments primarily engaged in--

- Providing tax return preparation services only--are classified in U.S. Industry 541213, Tax Preparation Services;
- Providing payroll processing services only--are classified in U.S. Industry 541214, Payroll Services; and
- Providing accounting, bookkeeping, and billing services--are classified in U.S. Industry 541219, Other Accounting Services.

**541213  Tax Preparation Services**

  This U.S. industry comprises establishments (except offices of CPAs) engaged in providing tax return preparation services without also providing accounting, bookkeeping, billing, or payroll processing services. Basic knowledge of tax law and filing requirements is required.

*Cross-References.*

- Establishments of CPAs are classified in U.S. Industry 541211, Offices of Certified Public Accountants;
- Establishments of non-CPAs providing payroll processing services along with tax return preparation services are classified in U.S. Industry 541214, Payroll Services;
- Establishments of non-CPAs providing accounting, bookkeeping, or billing services along with tax return preparation services are classified in U.S. Industry 541219, Other Accounting Services;
- Establishments primarily engaged in processing financial transactions (except central bank) are classified in Industry 522320, Financial Transactions Processing, Reserve, and Clearinghouse Activities; and
- Establishments primarily engaged in providing data processing services (except payroll processing services and financial transaction processing services) at their own facility for others are classified in Industry 518210, Computing Infrastructure Providers, Data Processing, Web Hosting, and Related Services.

**541214  Payroll Services**

  This U.S. industry comprises establishments (except offices of CPAs) engaged in the following without also providing accounting, bookkeeping, or billing services: (1) collecting information on hours worked, pay rates, deductions, and other payroll-related data from their clients and (2) using that information to generate paychecks, payroll reports, and tax filings. These establishments may use data processing and tabulating techniques as part of providing their services.

*Cross-References.*

- Establishments of CPAs are classified in U.S. Industry 541211, Offices of Certified Public Accountants;
- Establishments of non-CPAs providing tax return preparation services only are classified in U.S. Industry 541213, Tax Preparation Services;
- Establishments of non-CPAs providing accounting, bookkeeping, or billing services along with payroll services are classified in U.S. Industry 541219, Other Accounting Services;
- Establishments primarily engaged in processing financial transactions (except central bank) are classified in Industry 522320, Financial Transactions Processing, Reserve, and Clearinghouse Activities; and
- Establishments primarily engaged in providing data processing services (except payroll processing services and financial transaction processing services) at their own facility for others are classified in Industry 518210, Computing Infrastructure Providers, Data Processing, Web Hosting, and Related Services.

**541219  Other Accounting Services**

  This U.S. industry comprises establishments (except offices of CPAs) engaged in providing accounting services (except tax return preparation services only or payroll services only). These establishments may also provide tax

---

T—Canadian, Mexican, and United States industries are comparable.

return preparation or payroll services. Accountant (except CPA) offices, bookkeeper offices, and billing offices are included in this industry.

*Cross-References.*

- Establishments of CPAs are classified in U.S. Industry 541211, Offices of Certified Public Accountants;
- Establishments of non-CPAs engaged in providing tax return preparation services only are classified in U.S. Industry 541213, Tax Preparation Services; and
- Establishments of non-CPAs engaged in providing payroll processing services only are classified in U.S. Industry 541214, Payroll Services.

## 5413  Architectural, Engineering, and Related Services[T]

This industry group comprises establishments primarily engaged in architectural, engineering, and related services, such as drafting services, building inspection services, geophysical surveying and mapping services, surveying and mapping (except geophysical) services, and testing services.

### 54131  Architectural Services[T]
See industry description for 541310.

### 541310  Architectural Services

This industry comprises establishments primarily engaged in planning and designing residential, institutional, leisure, commercial, and industrial buildings and structures by applying knowledge of design, construction procedures, zoning regulations, building codes, and building materials.

*Cross-References.*        Establishments primarily engaged in--

- Planning and designing the development of land areas--are classified in Industry 541320, Landscape Architectural Services; and
- Both the design and construction of buildings, highways, or other structures or in managing construction projects--are classified in Sector 23, Construction, according to the type of project.

### 54132  Landscape Architectural Services[T]
See industry description for 541320.

### 541320  Landscape Architectural Services

This industry comprises establishments primarily engaged in planning and designing the development of land areas for projects, such as parks and other recreational areas; airports; highways; hospitals; schools; land subdivisions; and commercial, industrial, and residential areas, by applying knowledge of land characteristics, location of buildings and structures, use of land areas, and design of landscape projects.

*Illustrative Examples:*

Garden planning services
Landscape architects' offices
Golf course or ski area design services

Landscape consulting services
Industrial land use planning services
Landscape design services

*Cross-References.*

- Establishments primarily engaged in providing landscape care and maintenance services and/or installing trees, shrubs, plants, lawns, or gardens along with the design of landscape plans are classified in Industry 561730, Landscaping Services; and

---

T—Canadian, Mexican, and United States industries are comparable.

- Government establishments primarily engaged in the administration and planning of the development of urban and rural areas, such as urban planning commissions, are classified in Industry 925120, Administration of Urban Planning and Community and Rural Development.

## 54133   Engineering Services[T]
See industry description for 541330.

## 541330   Engineering Services

This industry comprises establishments primarily engaged in applying physical laws and principles of engineering in the design, development, and utilization of machines, materials, instruments, structures, processes, and systems. The assignments undertaken by these establishments may involve any of the following activities: provision of advice, preparation of feasibility studies, preparation of preliminary and final plans and designs, provision of technical services during the construction or installation phase, inspection and evaluation of engineering projects, and related services.

*Illustrative Examples:*

| | |
|---|---|
| Civil engineering services | Mechanical engineering services |
| Environmental engineering services | Engineers' offices |
| Construction engineering services | Robotics automation engineering services |

*Cross-References.*          Establishments primarily engaged in--

- Planning and designing computer systems that integrate computer hardware, software, and communication technologies--are classified in U.S. Industry 541512, Computer Systems Design Services;
- Designing and writing custom software to meet the needs of a particular customer--are classified in U.S. Industry 541511, Custom Computer Programming Services;
- Software design, development, and publishing, or software publishing only--are classified in Industry 513210, Software Publishers;
- Performing surveying and mapping services of the surface of the earth, including the sea floor--are classified in Industry 541370, Surveying and Mapping (except Geophysical) Services;
- Gathering, interpreting, and mapping geophysical data--are classified in Industry 541360, Geophysical Surveying and Mapping Services;
- Creating and developing designs and specifications that optimize the use, value, and appearance of products--are classified in Industry 541420, Industrial Design Services;
- Providing advice and assistance to others on environmental issues, such as the control of environmental contamination from pollutants, toxic substances, and hazardous materials--are classified in Industry 541620, Environmental Consulting Services;
- Engineering research and development--are classified in U.S. Industry 541715, Research and Development in the Physical, Engineering, and Life Sciences (except Nanotechnology and Biotechnology); and
- Both the design and construction of buildings, highways, and other structures or in managing construction projects--are classified in Sector 23, Construction, according to the type of project.

## 54134   Drafting Services[T]
See industry description for 541340.

## 541340   Drafting Services

This industry comprises establishments primarily engaged in drawing detailed layouts, plans, and illustrations of buildings, structures, systems, or components from engineering and architectural specifications.

## 54135   Building Inspection Services[T]
See industry description for 541350.

---

T—Canadian, Mexican, and United States industries are comparable.

## 541350  Building Inspection Services

This industry comprises establishments primarily engaged in providing building inspection services. These establishments typically evaluate all aspects of the building structure and component systems and prepare a report on the physical condition of the property, generally for buyers or others involved in real estate transactions. Building inspection bureaus and establishments providing home inspection services are included in this industry.

*Cross-References.*          Establishments primarily engaged in--

- Inspecting buildings for termites and other pests--are classified in Industry 561710, Exterminating and Pest Control Services;
- Inspecting buildings for hazardous materials--are classified in Industry 541620, Environmental Consulting Services;
- Waterless fire suppression system testing and/or inspection, without sales, service, or installation--are classified in Industry 541990, All Other Professional, Scientific, and Technical Services;
- Estimating the fair market value of real estate--are classified in Industry 531320, Offices of Real Estate Appraisers; and
- Conducting building inspections and enforcing building codes and standards--are classified in Industry 926150, Regulation, Licensing, and Inspection of Miscellaneous Commercial Sectors.

## 54136  Geophysical Surveying and Mapping Services[T]
See industry description for 541360.

## 541360  Geophysical Surveying and Mapping Services

This industry comprises establishments primarily engaged in gathering, interpreting, and mapping geophysical data. Establishments in this industry often specialize in locating and measuring the extent of subsurface resources, such as oil, gas, and minerals, but they may also conduct surveys for engineering purposes. Establishments in this industry use a variety of surveying techniques depending on the purpose of the survey, including magnetic surveys, gravity surveys, seismic surveys, or electrical and electromagnetic surveys.

*Cross-References.*

Establishments primarily engaged in taking core samples, drilling test wells, or other mine development activities (except geophysical surveying and mapping) on a contract basis for others are classified in Industry 21311, Support Activities for Mining.

## 54137  Surveying and Mapping (except Geophysical) Services[T]
See industry description for 541370.

## 541370  Surveying and Mapping (except Geophysical) Services

This industry comprises establishments primarily engaged in performing surveying and mapping services of the surface of the earth, including the sea floor. These services may include surveying and mapping of areas above or below the surface of the earth, such as the creation of view easements or segregating rights in parcels of land by creating underground utility easements.

*Illustrative Examples:*

Cadastral surveying services
Mapping (except geophysical) services
Cartographic surveying services

Topographic surveying services
Geodetic surveying services

---

T—Canadian, Mexican, and United States industries are comparable.

*Cross-References.*            Establishments primarily engaged in--

- Providing geophysical surveying and mapping services--are classified in Industry 541360, Geophysical Surveying and Mapping Services; and
- Publishing atlases and maps--are classified in Industry 513130, Book Publishers.

## 54138    Testing Laboratories and Services[T]
See industry description for 541380.

## 541380  Testing Laboratories and Services

This industry comprises establishments primarily engaged in performing physical, chemical, and other analytical testing services, such as acoustics or vibration testing, assaying, biological testing (except medical and veterinary), calibration testing, electrical and electronic testing, geotechnical testing, mechanical testing, nondestructive testing, or thermal testing.  The testing may occur in a laboratory or on-site.

*Cross-References.*            Establishments primarily engaged in--

- Laboratory testing for the medical profession--are classified in Industry 62151, Medical and Diagnostic Laboratories;
- Veterinary testing services--are classified in Industry 541940, Veterinary Services; and
- Auto emissions testing--are classified in U.S. Industry 811198, All Other Automotive Repair and Maintenance.

## 5414    Specialized Design Services[T]

This industry group comprises establishments providing specialized design services (except architectural, engineering, and computer systems design).

## 54141    Interior Design Services[T]
See industry description for 541410.

## 541410  Interior Design Services

This industry comprises establishments primarily engaged in planning, designing, and administering projects in interior spaces to meet the physical and aesthetic needs of people using them, taking into consideration building codes, health and safety regulations, traffic patterns and floor planning, mechanical and electrical needs, and interior fittings and furniture.  Interior designers and interior design consultants work in areas, such as hospitality design, health care design, institutional design, commercial and corporate design, and residential design.  This industry also includes interior decorating consultants engaged exclusively in providing aesthetic services associated with interior spaces.

## 54142    Industrial Design Services[T]
See industry description for 541420.

## 541420  Industrial Design Services

This industry comprises establishments primarily engaged in creating and developing designs and specifications that optimize the use, value, and appearance of products.  These services can include the determination of the materials, construction, mechanisms, shape, color, and surface finishes of the product, taking into consideration human characteristics and needs, safety, market appeal, and efficiency in production, distribution, use, and maintenance.  Establishments providing automobile or furniture industrial design services or industrial design consulting services are included in this industry.

---

T—Canadian, Mexican, and United States industries are comparable.

*Cross-References.* Establishments primarily engaged in--

- Applying physical laws and principles of engineering in the design, development, and utilization of machines, materials, instruments, structures, processes, and systems--are classified in Industry 541330, Engineering Services;
- Designing clothing, shoes, or jewelry--are classified in Industry 541490, Other Specialized Design Services; and
- Industrial research and development--are classified in U.S. Industry 541715, Research and Development in the Physical, Engineering, and Life Sciences (except Nanotechnology and Biotechnology).

**54143 Graphic Design Services[T]**
See industry description for 541430.

**541430 Graphic Design Services**

This industry comprises establishments primarily engaged in planning, designing, and managing the production of visual communication in order to convey specific messages or concepts, clarify complex information, or project visual identities. These services can include the design of printed materials, packaging, advertising, signage systems, and corporate identification (logos). This industry also includes commercial artists engaged exclusively in generating drawings and illustrations requiring technical accuracy or interpretative skills.

*Illustrative Examples:*

Commercial art studios
Corporate identification (i.e., logo) design services
Independent commercial or graphic artists

Medical art or illustration services
Graphic design consulting services

*Cross-References.*

- Establishments primarily engaged in creating and/or placing public display advertising material are classified in Industry 541850, Indoor and Outdoor Display Advertising; and
- Independent artists primarily engaged in creating and selling visual artwork for noncommercial use and independent cartoonists are classified in Industry 711510, Independent Artists, Writers, and Performers.

**54149 Other Specialized Design Services[T]**
See industry description for 541490.

**541490 Other Specialized Design Services**

This industry comprises establishments primarily engaged in providing professional design services (except architectural, landscape architecture, engineering, interior, industrial, graphic, and computer systems design).

*Illustrative Examples:*

Costume design services (except independent theatrical costume designers)
Jewelry design services
Fashion design services

Float design services
Shoe design services
Lighting design services
Textile design services

*Cross-References.* Establishments primarily engaged in--

- Providing architectural design services--are classified in Industry 541310, Architectural Services;
- Providing landscape architecture design services--are classified in Industry 541320, Landscape Architectural Services;
- Providing engineering design services--are classified in Industry 541330, Engineering Services;

---

T—Canadian, Mexican, and United States industries are comparable.

- Providing interior design services--are classified in Industry 541410, Interior Design Services;
- Providing industrial design services--are classified in Industry 541420, Industrial Design Services;
- Providing graphic design services--are classified in Industry 541430, Graphic Design Services;
- Providing computer systems design services--are classified in U.S. Industry 541512, Computer Systems Design Services;
- Designing and writing custom software to meet the needs of a particular customer--are classified in U.S. Industry 541511, Custom Computer Programming Services; and
- Operating as independent theatrical costume or set designers--are classified in Industry 711510, Independent Artists, Writers, and Performers.

**5415    Computer Systems Design and Related Services[T]**

**54151    Computer Systems Design and Related Services[T]**

This industry comprises establishments primarily engaged in providing expertise in the field of information technologies through one or more of the following activities: (1) writing, modifying, testing, and supporting software to meet the needs of a particular customer; (2) planning and designing computer systems that integrate computer hardware, software, and communication technologies; (3) on-site management and operation of clients' computer systems and/or data processing facilities; and (4) other professional and technical computer related advice and services.

*Illustrative Examples:*

Computer facilities management services
Custom computer programming services
Computer systems integration design services

Computer hardware or software consulting services
Software installation services

*Cross-References.*        Establishments primarily engaged in--

- Providing robotics engineering design, integration, and related consulting services for industrial and manufacturing facilities and processes--are classified in Industry 54133, Engineering Services;
- Retailing computer hardware or software products and systems and providing supporting services, such as customized assembly of personal computers--are classified in Industry 44921, Electronics and Appliance Retailers;
- Merchant wholesaling computer hardware or software products and providing supporting services, such as customized assembly of personal computers--are classified in Industry 42343, Computer and Computer Peripheral Equipment and Software Merchant Wholesalers;
- Software design, development, and publishing, or software publishing only--are classified in Industry 51321, Software Publishers;
- Providing computer data processing services at their own facility for others--are classified in Industry 51821, Computing Infrastructure Providers, Data Processing, Web Hosting, and Related Services;
- Providing computer training (except computer repair), such as programming, software, systems, and network management training--are classified in Industry 61142, Computer Training; and
- Repairing computer, computer peripheral, and communication equipment--are classified in Industry 81121, Electronic and Precision Equipment Repair and Maintenance.

**541511  Custom Computer Programming Services**

This U.S. industry comprises establishments primarily engaged in writing, modifying, testing, and supporting software to meet the needs of a particular customer.

*Cross-References.*        Establishments primarily engaged in--

- Software design, development, and publishing, or software publishing only--are classified in Industry 513210, Software Publishers;

---

T—Canadian, Mexican, and United States industries are comparable.

- Providing computing infrastructure, data processing services, Web hosting services (except software publishing), and related services, including streaming support services (except streaming distribution services)--are classified in Industry 518210, Computing Infrastructure Providers, Data Processing, Web Hosting, and Related Services; and
- Planning and designing computer systems that integrate computer hardware, software, and communication technologies, even though such establishments may provide custom software as an integral part of their services--are classified in U.S. Industry 541512, Computer Systems Design Services.

## 541512  Computer Systems Design Services

This U.S. industry comprises establishments primarily engaged in planning and designing computer systems that integrate computer hardware, software, and communication technologies.  The hardware and software components of the system may be provided by this establishment or company as part of integrated services or may be provided by third parties or vendors.  These establishments often install the system and train and support users of the system.

*Illustrative Examples:*

Computer systems integration design consulting services
Local area network (LAN) computer systems integration design services

Information management computer systems integration design services
Office automation computer systems integration design services

*Cross-References.*        Establishments primarily engaged in--

- Providing robotics engineering design, integration, and related consulting services for industrial and manufacturing facilities and processes--are classified in Industry 541330, Engineering Services;
- Designing and writing custom software to meet the needs of a particular customer--are classified in U.S. Industry 541511, Custom Computer Programming Services;
- Retailing computer hardware or software products and systems and providing supporting services, such as customized assembly of personal computers--are classified in Industry 449210, Electronics and Appliance Retailers; and
- Merchant wholesaling computer hardware or software products and providing supporting services, such as customized assembly of personal computers--are classified in Industry 423430, Computer and Computer Peripheral Equipment and Software Merchant Wholesalers.

## 541513  Computer Facilities Management Services

This U.S. industry comprises establishments primarily engaged in providing on-site management and operation of clients' computer systems and/or data processing facilities.  Establishments providing computer systems or data processing facilities support services are included in this industry.

*Cross-References.*

Establishments primarily engaged in providing computer data processing services at their own facility for others are classified in Industry 518210, Computing Infrastructure Providers, Data Processing, Web Hosting, and Related Services.

## 541519  Other Computer Related Services

This U.S. industry comprises establishments primarily engaged in providing computer related services (except custom programming, systems integration design, and facilities management services). Establishments providing computer disaster recovery services or software installation services are included in this industry.

---

T—Canadian, Mexican, and United States industries are comparable.

*Cross-References.* Establishments primarily engaged in--

- Providing custom computer programming services--are classified in U.S. Industry 541511, Custom Computer Programming Services;
- Providing computer systems integration design services--are classified in U.S. Industry 541512, Computer Systems Design Services;
- Providing computer systems and/or data processing facilities management services--are classified in U.S. Industry 541513, Computer Facilities Management Services;
- Software publishing--are classified in Industry 513210, Software Publishers;
- Providing computing infrastructure, data processing services, Web hosting services (except software publishing), and related services, including streaming support services (except streaming distribution services)--are classified in Industry 518210, Computing Infrastructure Providers, Data Processing, Web Hosting, and Related Services;
- Providing computer training (except computer repair), such as programming, software, systems, and network management training--are classified in Industry 611420, Computer Training; and
- Repairing computer, computer peripheral, and communication equipment--are classified in Industry 811210, Electronic and Precision Equipment Repair and Maintenance.

## 5416 Management, Scientific, and Technical Consulting Services[T]

This industry group comprises establishments primarily engaged in providing advice and assistance to businesses and other organizations on management, environmental, scientific, and technical issues.

## 54161 Management Consulting Services[T]

This industry comprises establishments primarily engaged in providing advice and assistance to businesses and other organizations on management issues, such as strategic and organizational planning; financial planning and budgeting; marketing objectives and policies; human resource policies, practices, and planning; production scheduling; and control planning.

*Illustrative Examples:*

Actuarial, benefit, and compensation consulting services
Human resources consulting services
Marketing consulting services

Administrative and general management consulting services
Process, physical distribution, and logistics consulting services

*Cross-References.*

- Establishments primarily engaged in providing a range of day-to-day office administrative services, such as financial planning, billing and recordkeeping, personnel, and physical distribution and logistics, are classified in Industry 56111, Office Administrative Services;
- Establishments primarily engaged in providing executive search, recruitment, and placement services are classified in Industry 56131, Employment Placement Agencies and Executive Search Services;
- Establishments primarily engaged in administering, overseeing, and managing other establishments of the company or enterprise (except government establishments) are classified in Industry 55111, Management of Companies and Enterprises;
- Government establishments primarily engaged in administering, overseeing, and managing governmental programs are classified in Sector 92, Public Administration;
- Establishments primarily engaged in professional and management development training are classified in Industry 61143, Professional and Management Development Training;
- Establishments primarily engaged in listing employment vacancies and in recruiting, referring, and placing applicants in employment are classified in Industry 56131, Employment Placement Agencies and Executive Search Services;

---

T—Canadian, Mexican, and United States industries are comparable.

- Establishments primarily engaged in advertising and public relations are classified in Industry Group 5418, Advertising, Public Relations, and Related Services;
- Establishments primarily engaged in developing and conducting marketing research or public opinion polling are classified in Industry 54191, Marketing Research and Public Opinion Polling;
- Establishments primarily engaged in planning and designing industrial processes and systems are classified in Industry 54133, Engineering Services;
- Establishments primarily engaged in planning and designing computer systems are classified in Industry 54151, Computer Systems Design and Related Services;
- Establishments primarily engaged in providing financial investment advice services are classified in Industry 52394, Portfolio Management and Investment Advice;
- Establishments primarily engaged in arranging transportation of freight between shippers and carriers are classified in Industry 48851, Freight Transportation Arrangement; and
- Establishments primarily engaged in operating warehousing and storage facilities and providing related logistics services are classified in Industry Group 4931, Warehousing and Storage.

## 541611 Administrative Management and General Management Consulting Services

This U.S. industry comprises establishments primarily engaged in providing operating advice and assistance to businesses and other organizations on administrative management issues, such as financial planning and budgeting, equity and asset management, records management, office planning, strategic and organizational planning, site selection, new business start-up, and business process improvement. This industry also includes establishments of general management consultants that provide a full range of administrative, human resource, marketing, process, physical distribution, logistics, or other management consulting services to clients.

*Illustrative Examples:*

Administrative management consulting services
Financial management (except investment advice)
consulting services

General management consulting services
Site selection consulting services
Strategic planning consulting services

*Cross-References.*

- Establishments primarily engaged in providing a range of day-to-day office administrative services, such as financial planning, billing and recordkeeping, personnel, and physical distribution and logistics, are classified in Industry 561110, Office Administrative Services;
- Establishments providing operations consulting services are classified in U.S. Industry 541614, Process, Physical Distribution, and Logistics Consulting Services;
- Establishments primarily engaged in administering, overseeing, and managing other establishments of the company or enterprise (except government establishments) are classified in U.S. Industry 551114, Corporate, Subsidiary, and Regional Managing Offices;
- Government establishments primarily engaged in administering, overseeing, and managing governmental programs are classified in Sector 92, Public Administration;
- Establishments primarily engaged in providing investment advice are classified in Industry 523940, Portfolio Management and Investment Advice;
- Establishments primarily engaged in providing professional and management development training are classified in Industry 611430, Professional and Management Development Training; and
- Establishments primarily engaged in providing executive search, recruitment, and placement services are classified in U.S. Industry 561312, Executive Search Services.

## 541612 Human Resources Consulting Services

This U.S. industry comprises establishments primarily engaged in providing advice and assistance to businesses and other organizations in one or more of the following areas: (1) human resource and personnel policies, practices, and procedures; (2) employee benefits planning, communication, and administration; (3) compensation systems planning; and (4) wage and salary administration.

---

T—Canadian, Mexican, and United States industries are comparable.

*Illustrative Examples:*

Benefit or compensation consulting services          Personnel management consulting services
Employee assessment consulting services              Human resources consulting services

*Cross-References.*          Establishments primarily engaged in--

- Providing professional and management development training--are classified in Industry 611430, Professional and Management Development Training;
- Listing employment vacancies and recruiting, referring, and placing applicants in employment--are classified in U.S. Industry 561311, Employment Placement Agencies; and
- Providing executive search, recruitment, and placement services--are classified in U.S. Industry 561312, Executive Search Services.

### 541613  Marketing Consulting Services

This U.S. industry comprises establishments primarily engaged in providing operating advice and assistance to businesses and other organizations on marketing issues, such as developing marketing objectives and policies, sales forecasting, new product developing and pricing, licensing and franchise planning, and marketing planning and strategy.

*Illustrative Examples:*

Customer services management consulting services          Marketing management consulting services
New product development consulting services               Sales management consulting services

*Cross-References.*          Establishments primarily engaged in--

- Creating advertising campaigns and placing such advertising in media--are classified in Industry 541810, Advertising Agencies;
- Developing and implementing public relations plans--are classified in Industry 541820, Public Relations Agencies;
- Creating direct mail advertising campaigns--are classified in Industry 541860, Direct Mail Advertising; and
- Developing and conducting marketing research or public opinion polling--are classified in Industry 541910, Marketing Research and Public Opinion Polling.

### 541614  Process, Physical Distribution, and Logistics Consulting Services

This U.S. industry comprises establishments primarily engaged in providing operating advice and assistance to businesses and other organizations in: (1) manufacturing operations improvement; (2) productivity improvement; (3) production planning and control; (4) quality assurance and quality control; (5) inventory management; (6) distribution networks; (7) warehouse use, operations, and utilization; (8) transportation and shipment of goods and materials; and (9) materials management and handling.

*Illustrative Examples:*

Freight rate or tariff rate consulting services          Inventory planning and control management
Productivity improvement consulting services             consulting services
Manufacturing management consulting services             Transportation management consulting services

*Cross-References.*          Establishments primarily engaged in--

- Planning and designing industrial processes and systems--are classified in Industry 541330, Engineering Services;

---

T—Canadian, Mexican, and United States industries are comparable.

**census.gov/naics**

- Providing computer systems integration design services--are classified in U.S. Industry 541512, Computer Systems Design Services;
- Arranging transportation of freight between shippers and carriers--are classified in Industry 488510, Freight Transportation Arrangement; and
- Operating warehousing and storage facilities and providing related logistics services--are classified in Industry Group 4931, Warehousing and Storage.

## 541618 Other Management Consulting Services

This U.S. industry comprises establishments primarily engaged in providing management consulting services (except administrative and general management consulting; human resources consulting; marketing consulting; or process, physical distribution, and logistics consulting). Establishments providing telecommunications or utilities management consulting services are included in this industry.

*Cross-References.*        Establishments primarily engaged in--

- Providing administrative and general management consulting services--are classified in U.S. Industry 541611, Administrative Management and General Management Consulting Services;
- Providing human resources consulting services--are classified in U.S. Industry 541612, Human Resources Consulting Services;
- Providing marketing consulting services--are classified in U.S. Industry 541613, Marketing Consulting Services; and
- Providing process, physical distribution, and logistics consulting services--are classified in U.S. Industry 541614, Process, Physical Distribution, and Logistics Consulting Services.

## 54162  Environmental Consulting Services[T]
See industry description for 541620.

## 541620 Environmental Consulting Services

This industry comprises establishments primarily engaged in providing advice and assistance to businesses and other organizations on environmental issues, such as the control of environmental contamination from pollutants, toxic substances, and hazardous materials. These establishments identify problems (e.g., inspect buildings for hazardous materials), measure and evaluate risks, and recommend solutions. They employ a multidisciplined staff of scientists, engineers, and other technicians with expertise in areas, such as air and water quality, asbestos contamination, remediation, ecological restoration, and environmental law. Establishments providing sanitation or site remediation consulting services are included in this industry.

*Cross-References.*

- Establishments primarily engaged in environmental remediation are classified in Industry 562910, Remediation Services;
- Establishments primarily engaged in providing environmental engineering services are classified in Industry 541330, Engineering Services;
- Establishments primarily engaged in providing environmental testing services are classified in Industry 541380, Testing Laboratories and Services;
- Establishments primarily engaged in promoting the preservation and protection of the environment are classified in U.S. Industry 813312, Environment, Conservation and Wildlife Organizations;
- Establishments primarily engaged in individual activities as part of an ecological restoration project are classified according to the primary activity; and
- Government establishments primarily engaged in administering, overseeing, and managing governmental ecological restoration programs are classified in Industry 924110, Administration of Air and Water Resource and Solid Waste Management Programs.

---

T—Canadian, Mexican, and United States industries are comparable.

**54169   Other Scientific and Technical Consulting Services**ᵀ
See industry description for 541690.

**541690  Other Scientific and Technical Consulting Services**

This industry comprises establishments primarily engaged in providing advice and assistance to businesses and other organizations on scientific and technical issues (except environmental).

*Illustrative Examples:*

| | |
|---|---|
| Agricultural consulting services | Radio consulting services |
| Motion picture consulting services | Economic consulting services |
| Biological consulting services | Safety consulting services |
| Physics consulting services | Energy consulting services |
| Chemical consulting services | Security consulting services |

*Cross-References.*       Establishments primarily engaged in--

- Providing advice and assistance to businesses and other organizations on management issues--are classified in Industry 54161, Management Consulting Services;
- Environmental consulting--are classified in Industry 541620, Environmental Consulting Services;
- Providing architectural (except landscape) consulting services--are classified in Industry 541310, Architectural Services;
- Providing landscape consulting services--are classified in Industry 541320, Landscape Architectural Services;
- Providing engineering consulting services--are classified in Industry 541330, Engineering Services;
- Providing building inspection services--are classified in Industry 541350, Building Inspection Services;
- Providing computer software and hardware consulting services--are classified in U.S. Industry 541512, Computer Systems Design Services;
- Providing insurance advisory services--are classified in U.S. Industry 524298, All Other Insurance Related Activities; and
- Providing construction activities or managing construction projects--are classified in Sector 23, Construction, according to the type of project.

**5417     Scientific Research and Development Services**ᵀ

This industry group comprises establishments engaged in conducting original investigation undertaken on a systematic basis to gain new knowledge (research) and/or the application of research findings or other scientific knowledge for the creation of new or significantly improved products or processes (experimental development). Techniques may include modeling and simulation. The industries within this industry group are defined on the basis of the domain of research; that is, on the scientific expertise of the establishment.

**54171   Research and Development in the Physical, Engineering, and Life Sciences**ᵀ

This industry comprises establishments primarily engaged in conducting research and experimental development in the physical, engineering, and life sciences, such as agriculture, electronics, environmental, biology, botany, biotechnology, computers, chemistry, food, fisheries, forests, geology, health, mathematics, medicine, nanotechnology, oceanography, pharmacy, physics, veterinary, and other allied subjects.

*Cross-References.*       Establishments primarily engaged in--

- Providing veterinary testing services--are classified in Industry 54194, Veterinary Services;
- Providing medical laboratory testing for humans--are classified in Industry 62151, Medical and Diagnostic Laboratories;

---

T—Canadian, Mexican, and United States industries are comparable.

- Raising funds for health related research--are classified in Industry 81321, Grantmaking and Giving Services;
- Providing physical, chemical, or other analytical testing services (except medical or veterinary), such as acoustics or vibration testing, calibration testing, electrical and electronic testing, geotechnical testing, mechanical testing, nondestructive testing, or thermal testing--are classified in Industry 54138, Testing Laboratories and Services;
- Creating and developing industrial designs and specifications that optimize the use, value, and appearance of automobiles, furniture, and other products--are classified in Industry 54142, Industrial Design Services;
- Manufacturing products (e.g., apparel, electronic equipment, automotive equipment) using nanomaterials--are classified in Sector 31-33, Manufacturing, according to the process of the specific product made;
- Manufacturing vaccines, toxoids, blood fractions, and culture media of plant or animal origin (except diagnostic use) and/or uncompounded medicinal chemicals and their derivatives (i.e., enzyme proteins and antibiotics for pharmaceutical use)--are classified in Industry 32541, Pharmaceutical and Medicine Manufacturing; and
- Laboratory animal production (e.g., guinea pigs, mice, rats)--are classified in Industry 11299, All Other Animal Production.

## 541713 Research and Development in Nanotechnology

This U.S. industry comprises establishments primarily engaged in conducting nanotechnology research and experimental development. Nanotechnology research and experimental development involves the study of matter at the nanoscale (i.e., a scale of about 1 to 100 nanometers). This research and development in nanotechnology may result in development of new nanotechnology processes or in prototypes of new or altered materials and/or products that may be reproduced, utilized, or implemented by various industries.

*Cross-References.*        Establishments primarily engaged in--

- Conducting research and experimental development in biotechnology (except nanobiotechnology)--are classified in U.S. Industry 541714, Research and Development in Biotechnology (except Nanobiotechnology);
- Conducting research and experimental development in the physical, engineering, and life sciences (except nanotechnology and biotechnology)--are classified in U.S. Industry 541715, Research and Development in the Physical, Engineering, and Life Sciences (except Nanotechnology and Biotechnology);
- Providing veterinary testing services--are classified in Industry 541940, Veterinary Services;
- Providing physical, chemical, or other analytical testing services (except medical or veterinary), such as acoustics or vibration testing, calibration testing, electrical and electronic testing, geotechnical testing, mechanical testing, nondestructive testing, or thermal testing--are classified in Industry 541380, Testing Laboratories and Services;
- Providing medical laboratory testing for humans--are classified in U.S. Industry 621511, Medical Laboratories;
- Raising funds for health related research--are classified in U.S. Industry 813212, Voluntary Health Organizations; and
- Manufacturing products (e.g., apparel, electronic equipment, automotive equipment) using nanomaterials--are classified in Sector 31-33, Manufacturing, according to the process of the specific product made.

## 541714 Research and Development in Biotechnology (except Nanobiotechnology)

This U.S. industry comprises establishments primarily engaged in conducting biotechnology (except nanobiotechnology) research and experimental development. Biotechnology (except nanobiotechnology) research and experimental development involves the study of the use of microorganisms and cellular and biomolecular processes to develop or alter living or non-living materials. This research and development in biotechnology (except nanobiotechnology) may result in development of new biotechnology (except nanobiotechnology) processes or in prototypes of new or genetically-altered products that may be reproduced, utilized, or implemented by various industries.

---

T—Canadian, Mexican, and United States industries are comparable.

*Illustrative Examples:*

Cloning research and experimental development laboratories

DNA technologies (e.g., microarrays) research and experimental development laboratories

Nucleic acid chemistry research and experimental development laboratories

Protein engineering research and experimental development laboratories

Recombinant DNA research and experimental development laboratories

*Cross-References.* Establishments primarily engaged in--

- Conducting research and experimental development in nanotechnology (e.g., nanobiotechnology)--are classified in U.S. Industry 541713, Research and Development in Nanotechnology;
- Conducting research and experimental development in the physical, engineering, and life sciences (except nanotechnology and biotechnology)--are classified in U.S. Industry 541715, Research and Development in the Physical, Engineering, and Life Sciences (except Nanotechnology and Biotechnology);
- Providing physical, chemical, or other analytical testing services (except medical or veterinary), such as acoustics or vibration testing, calibration testing, electrical and electronic testing, geotechnical testing, mechanical testing, nondestructive testing, or thermal testing--are classified in Industry 541380, Testing Laboratories and Services;
- Providing veterinary testing services--are classified in Industry 541940, Veterinary Services;
- Providing medical laboratory testing for humans--are classified in U.S. Industry 621511, Medical Laboratories;
- Raising funds for health related research--are classified in U.S. Industry 813212, Voluntary Health Organizations;
- Manufacturing vaccines, toxoids, blood fractions, and culture media of plant or animal origin (except diagnostic use)--are classified in U.S. Industry 325414, Biological Product (except Diagnostic) Manufacturing; and
- Manufacturing uncompounded medicinal chemicals and their derivatives (i.e., enzyme proteins and antibiotics for pharmaceutical use)--are classified in U.S. Industry 325411, Medicinal and Botanical Manufacturing.

### 541715 Research and Development in the Physical, Engineering, and Life Sciences (except Nanotechnology and Biotechnology)

This U.S. industry comprises establishments primarily engaged in conducting research and experimental development (except nanotechnology and biotechnology research and experimental development) in the physical, engineering, and life sciences, such as agriculture, electronics, environmental, biology, botany, computers, chemistry, food, fisheries, forests, geology, health, mathematics, medicine, oceanography, pharmacy, physics, veterinary, and other allied subjects.

*Cross-References.* Establishments primarily engaged in--

- Conducting research and experimental development in nanotechnology--are classified in U.S. Industry 541713, Research and Development in Nanotechnology;
- Conducting research and experimental development in biotechnology (except nanobiotechnology)--are classified in U.S. Industry 541714, Research and Development in Biotechnology (except Nanobiotechnology);
- Providing physical, chemical, or other analytical testing services (except medical or veterinary), such as acoustics or vibration testing, calibration testing, electrical and electronic testing, geotechnical testing, mechanical testing, nondestructive testing, or thermal testing--are classified in Industry 541380, Testing Laboratories and Services;
- Creating and developing industrial designs and specifications that optimize the use, value, and appearance of automobiles, furniture, and other products--are classified in Industry 541420, Industrial Design Services;
- Providing veterinary testing services--are classified in Industry 541940, Veterinary Services;

---

T—Canadian, Mexican, and United States industries are comparable.

- Providing medical laboratory testing for humans--are classified in U.S. Industry 621511, Medical Laboratories;
- Raising funds for health related research--are classified in U.S. Industry 813212, Voluntary Health Organizations; and
- Laboratory animal production (e.g., guinea pigs, mice, rats)--are classified in Industry 112990, All Other Animal Production.

## 54172 Research and Development in the Social Sciences and Humanities[T]
See industry description for 541720.

## 541720 Research and Development in the Social Sciences and Humanities

This industry comprises establishments primarily engaged in conducting research and analyses in cognitive development, sociology, psychology, language, behavior, economic, and other social science and humanities research.

*Cross-References.*          Establishments primarily engaged in--

- Marketing research--are classified in Industry 541910, Marketing Research and Public Opinion Polling; and
- Raising funds for disease awareness--are classified in U.S. Industry 813212, Voluntary Health Organizations.

## 5418 Advertising, Public Relations, and Related Services[T]

This industry group comprises establishments primarily engaged in advertising, public relations, and related services, such as media buying, independent media representation, indoor and outdoor display advertising, direct mail advertising, advertising material distribution services, and other services related to advertising.

## 54181 Advertising Agencies[T]
See industry description for 541810.

## 541810 Advertising Agencies

This industry comprises establishments primarily engaged in creating advertising campaigns and placing such advertising in print and digital periodicals, newspapers, radio and television, or other media. These establishments are organized to provide a full range of services (i.e., through in-house capabilities or subcontracting), including advice, creative services, account management, production of advertising content, media planning, and buying (i.e., placing advertising).

*Cross-References.*          Establishments primarily engaged in--

- Purchasing advertising space from media outlets and reselling it directly to advertising agencies or individual companies--are classified in Industry 541830, Media Buying Agencies;
- Conceptualizing and producing artwork or graphic designs without providing other advertising agency services--are classified in Industry 541430, Graphic Design Services;
- Creating direct mail advertising campaigns--are classified in Industry 541860, Direct Mail Advertising;
- Providing marketing consulting services--are classified in U.S. Industry 541613, Marketing Consulting Services;
- Selling media time or space for media owners as independent representatives--are classified in Industry 541840, Media Representatives; and
- Providing access for clients to advertising servers and/or real-time bidding marketplaces from a central host site (except by publishers, Web search portals, and other content providers)--are classified in Industry 518210, Computing Infrastructure Providers, Data Processing, Web Hosting, and Related Services.

T—Canadian, Mexican, and United States industries are comparable.

**54182 Public Relations Agencies**[T]
See industry description for 541820.

**541820 Public Relations Agencies**

This industry comprises establishments primarily engaged in designing and implementing public relations campaigns. These campaigns are designed to promote the interests and image of their clients. Establishments providing lobbying, political consulting, or public relations consulting are included in this industry.

**54183 Media Buying Agencies**[T]
See industry description for 541830.

**541830 Media Buying Agencies**

This industry comprises establishments primarily engaged in purchasing advertising time or space from media outlets and reselling it to advertising agencies or individual companies directly.

*Cross-References.* Establishments primarily engaged in--

- Selling time and space to advertisers for media owners as independent representatives--are classified in Industry 541840, Media Representatives; and
- Creating advertising campaigns and placing such advertising in media--are classified in Industry 541810, Advertising Agencies.

**54184 Media Representatives**[T]
See industry description for 541840.

**541840 Media Representatives**

This industry comprises establishments of independent representatives primarily engaged in selling media time or space for media owners.

*Illustrative Examples:*

Newspaper advertising representatives (i.e., independent of media owners)
Radio advertising representatives (i.e., independent of media owners)

Publishers' advertising representatives (i.e., independent of media owners)
Television advertising representatives (i.e., independent of media owners)

*Cross-References.* Establishments primarily engaged in--

- Purchasing advertising time or space from media outlets and reselling it directly to advertising agencies or individual companies--are classified in Industry 541830, Media Buying Agencies; and
- Creating advertising campaigns and placing such advertising in media--are classified in Industry 541810, Advertising Agencies.

**54185 Indoor and Outdoor Display Advertising**[T]
See industry description for 541850.

**541850 Indoor and Outdoor Display Advertising**

This industry comprises establishments primarily engaged in creating and designing public display advertising campaign materials, such as printed, painted, or electronic displays; and/or placing such displays on indoor or outdoor billboards and panels, or on or within transit vehicles or facilities, shopping malls, retail (in-store) displays, and other display structures or sites.

---

T—Canadian, Mexican, and United States industries are comparable.

*Cross-References.* Establishments primarily engaged in--

- Providing sign lettering and painting services--are classified in Industry 541890, Other Services Related to Advertising;
- Creating advertising campaigns and placing such advertising in print and digital media (except indoor and outdoor display structures and sites)--are classified in Industry 541810, Advertising Agencies;
- Providing access for clients to advertising servers and/or real-time bidding marketplaces from a central host site (except by publishers, Web search portals, and other content providers)--are classified in Industry 518210, Computing Infrastructure Providers, Data Processing, Web Hosting, and Related Services;
- Printing paper or paperboard signs--are classified in Industry 32311, Printing;
- Erecting display boards--are classified in Industry 238990, All Other Specialty Trade Contractors; and
- Manufacturing electrical, mechanical, or plate signs and point-of-sale advertising displays--are classified in Industry 339950, Sign Manufacturing.

## 54186  Direct Mail Advertising[T]
See industry description for 541860.

## 541860  Direct Mail Advertising

This industry comprises establishments primarily engaged in (1) creating and designing advertising campaigns for the purpose of distributing advertising materials (e.g., coupons, flyers, samples) or specialties (e.g., keychains, magnets, pens with customized messages imprinted) by mail or other direct distribution and/or (2) preparing such advertising materials or specialties for mailing or other direct distribution. These establishments may also compile, maintain, sell, and rent mailing lists.

*Cross-References.* Establishments primarily engaged in--

- The direct distribution or delivery (e.g., door-to-door, windshield placement) of advertisements or samples--are classified in Industry 541870, Advertising Material Distribution Services;
- Distributing advertising specialties for clients who wish to use such materials for promotional purposes--are classified in Industry 541890, Other Services Related to Advertising;
- Creating advertising campaigns and placing such advertising in media--are classified in Industry 541810, Advertising Agencies; and
- Compiling and selling mailing lists without providing direct mail advertising services--are classified in Industry 513140, Directory and Mailing List Publishers.

## 54187  Advertising Material Distribution Services[T]
See industry description for 541870.

## 541870  Advertising Material Distribution Services

This industry comprises establishments primarily engaged in the direct distribution or delivery of advertisements (e.g., circulars, coupons, handbills) or samples. Establishments in this industry use methods, such as delivering advertisements or samples door-to-door, placing flyers or coupons on car windshields in parking lots, or handing out samples in retail stores.

*Cross-References.* Establishments primarily engaged in--

- Creating and designing advertising campaigns for the purpose of distributing advertising materials or samples through the mail--are classified in Industry 541860, Direct Mail Advertising;
- Publishing newspapers or operating television stations or online information services--are classified in Sector 51, Information;
- Distributing advertising specialties (e.g., keychains, magnets, or pens with customized messages imprinted) to clients who wish to use such materials for promotional purposes--are classified in Industry 541890, Other Services Related to Advertising; and

---

T—Canadian, Mexican, and United States industries are comparable.

- Creating advertising campaigns and placing such advertising in print and digital media--are classified in Industry 541810, Advertising Agencies.

## 54189    Other Services Related to Advertising[T]
See industry description for 541890.

## 541890    Other Services Related to Advertising

This industry comprises establishments primarily engaged in providing advertising services (except advertising agency services, public relations agency services, media buying agency services, media representative services, display advertising services, direct mail advertising services, advertising material distribution services, and marketing consulting services).

*Illustrative Examples:*

Advertising specialties (e.g., keychains, magnets, pens) distribution services (except direct mail)
Sign lettering and painting services
Display lettering services

Store window dressing or trimming services
Mannequin decorating services
Welcoming services (i.e., advertising services)
Merchandise demonstration services

*Cross-References.*        Establishments primarily engaged in--

- Creating advertising campaigns and placing such advertising in newspapers, television, or other media--are classified in Industry 541810, Advertising Agencies;
- Designing and implementing public relations campaigns--are classified in Industry 541820, Public Relations Agencies;
- Purchasing advertising time or space from media outlets and reselling it directly to advertising agencies or individual companies--are classified in Industry 541830, Media Buying Agencies;
- Selling media time or space for media owners as independent representatives--are classified in Industry 541840, Media Representatives;
- Providing display advertising services--are classified in Industry 541850, Indoor and Outdoor Display Advertising;
- Providing direct distribution or delivery (e.g., door-to-door, windshield placement) of advertisements or samples--are classified in Industry 541870, Advertising Material Distribution Services;
- Providing direct mail advertising services--are classified in Industry 541860, Direct Mail Advertising;
- Publishing newspapers or operating television stations or online information services--are classified in Sector 51, Information;
- Providing access for clients to advertising servers and/or real-time bidding marketplaces from a central host site (except by publishers, Web search portals, and other content providers)--are classified in Industry 518210, Computing Infrastructure Providers, Data Processing, Web Hosting, and Related Services;
- Providing custom search engine optimization (SEO) services--are classified in U.S. Industry 541511, Custom Computer Programming Services;
- Providing marketing consulting services--are classified in U.S. Industry 541613, Marketing Consulting Services;
- Printing advertising specialties--are classified in Industry 32311, Printing; and
- Manufacturing and printing advertising specialties--are classified in the Manufacturing sector according to the products made.

## 5419    Other Professional, Scientific, and Technical Services[T]

This industry group comprises establishments engaged in professional, scientific, and technical services (except legal services; accounting, tax preparation, bookkeeping, and related services; architectural, engineering, and related services; specialized design services; computer systems design and related services; management, scientific, and technical consulting services; scientific research and development services; and advertising, public relations, and related services).

---

T—Canadian, Mexican, and United States industries are comparable.

**census.gov/naics**

**54191    Marketing Research and Public Opinion Polling**[T]
See industry description for 541910.

**541910  Marketing Research and Public Opinion Polling**

This industry comprises establishments primarily engaged in systematically gathering, recording, tabulating, and presenting marketing and public opinion data.

*Illustrative Examples:*

Broadcast media rating services
Political opinion polling services
Marketing analysis or research services

Statistical sampling services
Opinion research services

*Cross-References.*          Establishments primarily engaged in--

- Providing research and analysis in economics, sociology, and related fields--are classified in Industry 541720, Research and Development in the Social Sciences and Humanities; and
- Providing advice and counsel on marketing strategies--are classified in U.S. Industry 541613, Marketing Consulting Services.

**54192    Photographic Services**[T]

This industry comprises establishments primarily engaged in providing still, video, or digital photography services.  These establishments may specialize in a particular field of photography, such as commercial and industrial photography, portrait photography, and special events photography.  Commercial or portrait photography studios are included in this industry.

*Cross-References.*          Establishments primarily engaged in--

- Producing film and videotape for commercial exhibition or sale--are classified in Industry 51211, Motion Picture and Video Production;
- Developing still photographs--are classified in Industry 81292, Photofinishing;
- Developing motion picture film--are classified in Industry 51219, Postproduction Services and Other Motion Picture and Video Industries;
- Taking, developing, and selling artistic, news, or other types of photographs on a freelance basis, such as photojournalists--are classified in Industry 71151, Independent Artists, Writers, and Performers; and
- Supplying and servicing automatic photography machines in places of business operated by others--are classified in Industry 81299, All Other Personal Services.

**541921  Photography Studios, Portrait**

This U.S. industry comprises establishments known as portrait studios primarily engaged in providing still, video, or digital portrait photography services.

*Illustrative Examples:*

Home photography services
School photography services
Passport photography services

Videotaping services for special events (e.g., weddings)

*Cross-References.*          Establishments primarily engaged in--

- Producing film and videotape for commercial exhibition or sale--are classified in Industry 512110, Motion Picture and Video Production;

---

T—Canadian, Mexican, and United States industries are comparable.

- Developing still photographs--are classified in Industry 81292, Photofinishing;
- Developing motion picture film--are classified in U.S. Industry 512199, Other Motion Picture and Video Industries;
- Taking, developing, and selling artistic, news, or other types of photographs on a freelance basis, such as photojournalists--are classified in Industry 711510, Independent Artists, Writers, and Performers; and
- Supplying and servicing automatic photography machines in places of business operated by others--are classified in Industry 812990, All Other Personal Services.

**541922 Commercial Photography**

This U.S. industry comprises establishments primarily engaged in providing commercial photography services, generally for advertising agencies, publishers, and other business and industrial users.

*Cross-References.* Establishments primarily engaged in--

- Producing film and videotape for commercial exhibition or sale--are classified in Industry 512110, Motion Picture and Video Production;
- Developing still photographs--are classified in Industry 81292, Photofinishing;
- Developing motion picture film--are classified in U.S. Industry 512199, Other Motion Picture and Video Industries;
- Taking, developing, and selling artistic, news, or other types of photographs on a freelance basis, such as photojournalists--are classified in Industry 711510, Independent Artists, Writers, and Performers; and
- Supplying and servicing automatic photography machines in places of business operated by others--are classified in Industry 812990, All Other Personal Services.

**54193 Translation and Interpretation Services**[T]
See industry description for 541930.

**541930 Translation and Interpretation Services**

This industry comprises establishments primarily engaged in translating written material and interpreting speech from one language to another and establishments primarily engaged in providing sign language services.

*Cross-References.* Establishments primarily engaged in--

- Providing transcription services--are classified in Industry 561410, Document Preparation Services;
- Providing real-time (i.e., simultaneous) closed captioning services for live television performances, at meetings and conferences--are classified in U.S. Industry 561492, Court Reporting and Stenotype Services;
- Providing film or tape closed captioning services--are classified in U.S. Industry 512191, Teleproduction and Other Postproduction Services; and
- Analyzing handwriting--are classified in Industry 541990, All Other Professional, Scientific, and Technical Services.

**54194 Veterinary Services**[T]
See industry description for 541940.

**541940 Veterinary Services**

This industry comprises establishments of licensed veterinary practitioners primarily engaged in the practice of veterinary medicine, dentistry, or surgery for animals; and establishments primarily engaged in providing testing services for licensed veterinary practitioners.

*Illustrative Examples:*

Animal hospitals                    Veterinary clinics

---

T--Canadian, Mexican, and United States industries are comparable.

**census.gov/naics**

Veterinarians' offices                                    Veterinary testing laboratories

*Cross-References.*          Establishments primarily engaged in--

- Providing veterinary research and development services--are classified in Industry 54171, Research and Development in the Physical, Engineering, and Life Sciences;
- Providing nonveterinary pet care services, such as boarding or grooming pets--are classified in Industry 812910, Pet Care (except Veterinary) Services;
- Providing animal breeding services or boarding horses--are classified in Industry 115210, Support Activities for Animal Production; and
- Transporting pets--are classified in U.S. Industry 485991, Special Needs Transportation.

**54199    All Other Professional, Scientific, and Technical Services**[T]
See industry description for 541990.

**541990   All Other Professional, Scientific, and Technical Services**

  This industry comprises establishments primarily engaged in the provision of professional, scientific, or technical services (except legal services; accounting, tax preparation, bookkeeping, and related services; architectural, engineering, and related services; specialized design services; computer systems design and related services; management, scientific, and technical consulting services; scientific research and development services; advertising, public relations, and related services; market research and public opinion polling; photographic services; translation and interpretation services; and veterinary services).

*Illustrative Examples:*

Appraisal (except real estate) services
Marine surveyor (i.e., appraiser) services
Arbitration and conciliation services (except by lawyer, attorney, or paralegal offices)
Patent broker services (i.e., patent marketing services)

Commodity inspector services
Pipeline or power line inspection (i.e., visual) services
Consumer credit counseling services
Weather forecasting services
Handwriting analysis services

*Cross-References.*          Establishments primarily engaged in--

- Providing legal services--are classified in Industry Group 5411, Legal Services;
- Providing accounting, tax preparation, bookkeeping, and payroll services--are classified in Industry Group 5412, Accounting, Tax Preparation, Bookkeeping, and Payroll Services;
- Providing architectural, engineering, and related services--are classified in Industry Group 5413, Architectural, Engineering, and Related Services;
- Providing specialized design services--are classified in Industry Group 5414, Specialized Design Services;
- Providing computer systems design and related services--are classified in Industry Group 5415, Computer Systems Design and Related Services;
- Providing management, scientific, and technical consulting services--are classified in Industry Group 5416, Management, Scientific, and Technical Consulting Services;
- Providing scientific research and development services--are classified in Industry Group 5417, Scientific Research and Development Services;
- Providing advertising and related services--are classified in Industry Group 5418, Advertising, Public Relations, and Related Services;
- Providing marketing research and public opinion polling--are classified in Industry 541910, Marketing Research and Public Opinion Polling;
- Providing photographic services--are classified in Industry 54192, Photographic Services;
- Providing translation and interpretation services--are classified in Industry 541930, Translation and Interpretation Services;
- Providing veterinary services--are classified in Industry 541940, Veterinary Services; and

---

T—Canadian, Mexican, and United States industries are comparable.

- Providing real estate appraisal services--are classified in Industry 531320, Offices of Real Estate Appraisers.

---

# Sector 55--Management of Companies and Enterprises[T]

## The Sector as a Whole

The Management of Companies and Enterprises sector comprises (1) establishments that hold the securities of (or other equity interests in) companies and enterprises for the purpose of owning a controlling interest or influencing management decisions or (2) establishments (except government establishments) that administer, oversee, and manage establishments of the company or enterprise and that normally undertake the strategic or organizational planning and decision-making role of the company or enterprise. Establishments that administer, oversee, and manage may hold the securities of the company or enterprise.

Establishments in this sector perform essential activities that are often undertaken in-house by establishments in many sectors of the economy. By consolidating the performance of these activities of the enterprise at one establishment, economies of scale are achieved.

Government establishments primarily engaged in administering, overseeing, and managing governmental programs are classified in Sector 92, Public Administration. Establishments primarily engaged in providing a range of day-to-day office administrative services for other companies or enterprises on a contract or fee basis, such as financial planning, billing and recordkeeping, personnel, and physical distribution and logistics, are classified in Industry 56111, Office Administrative Services.

## 551 Management of Companies and Enterprises[T]

Industries in the Management of Companies and Enterprises subsector include three main types of establishments: (1) those that hold the securities of (or other equity interests in) companies and enterprises; (2) those (except government establishments) that administer, oversee, and manage other establishments of the company or enterprise but do not hold the securities of these establishments; and (3) those that both administer, oversee, and manage other establishments of the company or enterprise and hold the securities of (or other equity interests in) these establishments. Those establishments that administer, oversee, and manage normally undertake the strategic or organizational planning and decision-making role of the company or enterprise.

## 5511 Management of Companies and Enterprises[T]

## 55111 Management of Companies and Enterprises[T]

This industry comprises (1) establishments primarily engaged in holding the securities of (or other equity interests in) companies and enterprises for the purpose of owning a controlling interest or influencing management decisions or (2) establishments (except government establishments) that administer, oversee, and manage other establishments of the company or enterprise and that normally undertake the strategic or organizational planning and decision-making role of the company or enterprise. Establishments that administer, oversee, and manage may hold the securities of the company or enterprise.

*Cross-References.*

- Establishments primarily engaged in holding the securities of companies or enterprises and operating these entities are classified according to the business operated;
- Establishments primarily engaged in holding the securities of depository banks and operating these entities are classified in Industry Group 5221, Depository Credit Intermediation;
- Establishments primarily engaged in patent buying and licensing are classified in Industry 53311, Lessors of Nonfinancial Intangible Assets (except Copyrighted Works);
- Establishments primarily engaged in providing a range of day-to-day office administrative services for other companies or enterprises on a contract or fee basis are classified in Industry 56111, Office Administrative Services;
- Establishments primarily engaged in providing a single service to other establishments of the company or enterprise, such as trucking, warehousing, research and development, and data processing, are classified according to the service provided; and

---

T—Canadian, Mexican, and United States industries are comparable.

- Government establishments primarily engaged in administering, overseeing, and managing governmental programs are classified in Sector 92, Public Administration.

## 551111  Offices of Bank Holding Companies

This U.S. industry comprises legal entities known as bank holding companies primarily engaged in holding the securities of (or other equity interests in) companies and enterprises for the purpose of owning a controlling interest or influencing the management decisions of these firms.  The holding companies in this industry do not administer, oversee, and manage other establishments of the company or enterprise whose securities they hold.

*Cross-References.*          Establishments primarily engaged in--

- Holding the securities of (or other equity interests in) a company or enterprise and administering, overseeing, and managing establishments of the company or enterprise whose securities they hold--are classified in U.S. Industry 551114, Corporate, Subsidiary, and Regional Managing Offices; and
- Holding the securities of depository banks and operating these entities--are classified in Industry Group 5221, Depository Credit Intermediation.

## 551112  Offices of Other Holding Companies

This U.S. industry comprises legal entities known as holding companies (except bank holding) primarily engaged in holding the securities of (or other equity interests in) companies and enterprises for the purpose of owning a controlling interest or influencing the management decisions of these firms.  The holding companies in this industry do not administer, oversee, and manage other establishments of the company or enterprise whose securities they hold.

*Cross-References.*          Establishments primarily engaged in--

- Holding the securities of (or other equity interests in) depository banks for the purpose of owning a controlling interest or influencing the management decisions of these firms--are classified in U.S. Industry 551111, Offices of Bank Holding Companies;
- Holding the securities of (or other equity interests in) a company or enterprise and administering, overseeing, and managing establishments of the company or enterprise whose securities they hold--are classified in U.S. Industry 551114, Corporate, Subsidiary, and Regional Managing Offices;
- Patent buying and licensing--are classified in Industry 533110, Lessors of Nonfinancial Intangible Assets (except Copyrighted Works); and
- Holding the securities of companies or enterprises and operating these entities--are classified according to the business operated.

## 551114  Corporate, Subsidiary, and Regional Managing Offices

This U.S. industry comprises establishments (except government establishments) primarily engaged in administering, overseeing, and managing other establishments of the company or enterprise.  These establishments normally undertake the strategic or organizational planning and decision-making role of the company or enterprise.  Establishments in this industry may hold the securities of the company or enterprise.

*Illustrative Examples:*

| | |
|---|---|
| Centralized administrative offices | Holding companies that manage |
| Head offices | District and regional offices |
| Corporate offices | Subsidiary management offices |

------------------------------

T—Canadian, Mexican, and United States industries are comparable.

**census.gov/naics**

*Cross-References.*

- Government establishments primarily engaged in administering, overseeing, and managing governmental programs are classified in Sector 92, Public Administration;
- Legal entities known as bank holding companies that do not administer, oversee, and manage other establishments of the companies or enterprises whose securities they hold are classified in U.S. Industry 551111, Offices of Bank Holding Companies;
- Legal entities known as holding companies (except bank holding) that do not administer, oversee, and manage other establishments of the companies or enterprises whose securities they hold are classified in U.S. Industry 551112, Offices of Other Holding Companies; and
- Establishments primarily engaged in providing a range of day-to-day office administrative services for other companies or enterprises on a contract or fee basis are classified in Industry 561110, Office Administrative Services.

---

T—Canadian, Mexican, and United States industries are comparable.

# Sector 56--Administrative and Support and Waste Management and Remediation Services[T]

## The Sector as a Whole

The Administrative and Support and Waste Management and Remediation Services sector comprises establishments performing routine support activities for the day-to-day operations of other organizations. These essential activities are often undertaken in-house by establishments in many sectors of the economy. The establishments in this sector specialize in one or more of these support activities and provide these services to clients in a variety of industries and, in some cases, to households. Activities performed include: office administration, hiring and placing of personnel, document preparation and similar clerical services, solicitation, collection, security and surveillance services, cleaning, and waste disposal services.

The administrative and management activities performed by establishments in this sector are typically on a contract or fee basis. These activities may also be performed by establishments that are part of the company or enterprise. However, establishments involved in administering, overseeing, and managing other establishments of the company or enterprise are classified in Sector 55, Management of Companies and Enterprises. Establishments in Sector 55, Management of Companies and Enterprises, normally undertake the strategic and organizational planning and decision-making role of the company or enterprise. Government establishments engaged in administering, overseeing, and managing governmental programs are classified in Sector 92, Public Administration.

## 561    Administrative and Support Services[T]

Industries in the Administrative and Support Services subsector group establishments engaged in activities that support the day-to-day operations of other organizations. The processes employed in this sector (e.g., general management, personnel administration, clerical activities, cleaning activities) are often integral parts of the activities of establishments found in all sectors of the economy. The establishments classified in this subsector have specialization in one or more of these activities and can, therefore, provide services to clients in a variety of industries and, in some cases, to households. The individual industries of this subsector are defined on the basis of the particular process that they are engaged in and the particular services they provide.

Many of the activities in this subsector are ongoing routine support functions that businesses and organizations perform in-house. However, it is common to contract or purchase services from businesses that specialize in such activities and can, therefore, provide the services more efficiently.

The industries in this subsector cannot be viewed as strictly "support." The Travel Arrangement and Reservation Services industry group includes travel agents, tour operators, and providers of other travel arrangement services, such as hotel and restaurant reservations and arranging the purchase of tickets, serving many types of clients, including individual consumers. This group was placed in this subsector because the services are often of the "support" nature (e.g., travel arrangement) to businesses and other organizations that purchase such services.

The administrative and management activities performed by establishments in this sector are typically on a contract or fee basis. These activities may also be performed by establishments that are part of the company or enterprise. However, establishments involved in administering, overseeing, and managing other establishments of the company or enterprise are classified in Sector 55, Management of Companies and Enterprises. Establishments in Sector 55, Management of Companies and Enterprises, normally undertake the strategic and organizational planning and decision-making role of the company or enterprise. Government establishments engaged in administering, overseeing, and managing governmental programs are classified in Sector 92, Public Administration.

## 5611    Office Administrative Services[T]

## 56111    Office Administrative Services[T]
See industry description for 561110.

## 561110  Office Administrative Services

This industry comprises establishments primarily engaged in providing a range of day-to-day office administrative services, such as financial planning; billing and recordkeeping; personnel; and physical distribution and logistics, for

---

T—Canadian, Mexican, and United States industries are comparable.

others on a contract or fee basis.  These establishments do not provide operating staff to carry out the complete operations of a business.

*Cross-References.*          Establishments primarily engaged in--

- Holding the securities or financial assets of companies and enterprises for the purpose of controlling them and influencing their management decisions--are classified in U.S. Industry 551111, Offices of Bank Holding Companies, or U.S. Industry 551112, Offices of Other Holding Companies;
- Administering, overseeing, and managing other establishments of the company or enterprise (except government establishments)--are classified in U.S. Industry 551114, Corporate, Subsidiary, and Regional Managing Offices;
- Providing computer facilities management--are classified in U.S. Industry 541513, Computer Facilities Management Services;
- Providing construction management--are classified in Sector 23, Construction, by type of construction project managed;
- Providing farm management--are classified in U.S. Industry 115116, Farm Management Services;
- Managing real property for others--are classified in Industry 53131, Real Estate Property Managers;
- Providing food services management at institutional, governmental, commercial, or industrial locations--are classified in Industry 722310, Food Service Contractors;
- Providing management advice without day-to-day management--are classified in Industry 54161, Management Consulting Services;
- Providing both management and operating staff for the complete operation of a client's business, such as a hotel, restaurant, mine site, or hospital--are classified according to the industry of the establishment operated; and
- Providing only one of the support services (e.g., accounting services) that establishments in this industry provide--are classified in the appropriate industry according to the service provided.

**5612    Facilities Support Services**[T]

**56121    Facilities Support Services**[T]
See industry description for 561210.

**561210  Facilities Support Services**

  This industry comprises establishments primarily engaged in providing operating staff to perform a combination of support services within a client's facilities.  Establishments in this industry typically provide a combination of services, such as janitorial, maintenance, trash disposal, guard and security, mail routing, reception, laundry, and related services to support operations within facilities.  These establishments provide operating staff to carry out these support activities, but are not involved with or responsible for the core business or activities of the client. Establishments providing facilities (except computer and/or data processing) operation support services and establishments providing private jail services or operating correctional facilities (i.e., jails) on a contract or fee basis are included in this industry.

*Cross-References.*

- Establishments primarily engaged in providing only one of the support services (e.g., janitorial services) that establishments in this industry provide are classified in the appropriate industry according to the service provided;
- Establishments primarily engaged in providing management and operating staff for the complete operation of a client's establishment, such as a hotel, restaurant, mine, or hospital, are classified according to the industry of the establishment operated;
- Establishments primarily engaged in providing ambulatory health care services within a client's facilities are classified in Subsector 621, Ambulatory Health Care Services;
- Establishments primarily engaged in managing nonresidential property for others without providing operating staff are classified in U.S. Industry 531312, Nonresidential Property Managers;

T—Canadian, Mexican, and United States industries are comparable.

- Establishments primarily engaged in providing on-site management and operation of a client's computer systems and/or data processing facilities are classified in U.S. Industry 541513, Computer Facilities Management Services; and
- Governmental correctional institutions are classified in Industry 922140, Correctional Institutions.

## 5613    Employment Services[T]

This industry group comprises establishments primarily engaged in one of the following: (1) listing employment vacancies and referring or placing applicants for employment; (2) providing executive search, recruitment, and placement services; (3) supplying workers to clients' businesses for limited periods of time to supplement the working force of the client; or (4) providing human resources and human resource management services to client businesses and households.

## 56131    Employment Placement Agencies and Executive Search Services[T]

This industry comprises establishments primarily engaged in one of the following: (1) listing employment vacancies and referring or placing applicants for employment; or (2) providing executive search, recruitment, and placement services.

*Illustrative Examples:*

Employment agencies                                          Executive search services
Executive placement agencies or services

*Cross-References.*          Establishments primarily engaged in--

- Supplying their own employees for limited periods of time to supplement the working force of a client's business--are classified in Industry 56132, Temporary Help Services;
- Providing human resources and human resource management services to client businesses and households-- are classified in Industry 56133, Professional Employer Organizations;
- Providing advice and assistance on human resource and personnel policies, practices, and procedures; and employee benefits and compensation systems--are classified in Industry 54161, Management Consulting Services; and
- Representing models, entertainers, athletes, and other public figures as their agent or manager--are classified in Industry 71141, Agents and Managers for Artists, Athletes, Entertainers, and Other Public Figures.

## 561311    Employment Placement Agencies

This U.S. industry comprises establishments primarily engaged in listing employment vacancies and in recruiting, referring, or placing applicants for employment. The individuals referred or placed are not employees of the employment agencies.

*Illustrative Examples:*

Babysitting bureaus (i.e., registries)                        Casting agencies or bureaus (i.e., motion picture,
Employment registries                                         theatrical, video)
Model registries                                              Employment agencies

*Cross-References.*          Establishments primarily engaged in--

- Providing executive search, recruitment, and placement services--are classified in U.S. Industry 561312, Executive Search Services;
- Supplying their own employees for limited periods of time to supplement the working force of a client's business--are classified in Industry 561320, Temporary Help Services;

---

T—Canadian, Mexican, and United States industries are comparable.

- Providing human resources and human resource management services to client businesses and households--are classified in Industry 561330, Professional Employer Organizations; and
- Representing models, entertainers, athletes, and other public figures as their agent or manager--are classified in Industry 711410, Agents and Managers for Artists, Athletes, Entertainers, and Other Public Figures.

## 561312  Executive Search Services

This U.S. industry comprises establishments primarily engaged in providing executive search, recruitment, and placement services for clients with specific executive and senior management position requirements.  The range of services provided by these establishments may include developing a search strategy and position specification based on the culture and needs of the client; researching, identifying, screening, and interviewing candidates; verifying candidate qualifications; and assisting in final offer negotiations and assimilation of the selected candidate.  The individuals identified, recruited, or placed are not employees of the executive search services establishments.

*Illustrative Examples:*

Senior executive search services                           Executive search services
Executive placement services

*Cross-References.*        Establishments primarily engaged in--

- Listing employment vacancies and in recruiting, referring, or placing applicants for employment--are classified in U.S. Industry 561311, Employment Placement Agencies;
- Supplying their own employees for limited periods of time to supplement the working force of a client's business--are classified in Industry 561320, Temporary Help Services;
- Providing human resources and human resource management services to client businesses and households--are classified in Industry 561330, Professional Employer Organizations;
- Providing administrative and general management consulting services--are classified in U.S. Industry 541611, Administrative Management and General Management Consulting Services;
- Providing advice and assistance on human resource and personnel policies, practices, and procedures; and employee benefits and compensation systems--are classified in U.S. Industry 541612, Human Resources Consulting Services;
- Providing professional and management development training--are classified in Industry 611430, Professional and Management Development Training; and
- Representing models, entertainers, athletes, and other public figures as their agent or manager--are classified in Industry 711410, Agents and Managers for Artists, Athletes, Entertainers, and Other Public Figures.

## 56132    Temporary Help Services[T]
See industry description for 561320.

## 561320  Temporary Help Services

This industry comprises establishments primarily engaged in supplying workers to clients' businesses for limited periods of time to supplement the working force of the client.  The individuals provided are employees of the temporary help services establishment.  However, these establishments do not provide direct supervision of their employees at the clients' work sites.

*Illustrative Examples:*

Help supply services                                Temporary employment or temporary staffing
Model supply services                               services
Labor (except farm) contractors (i.e., personnel    Manpower pools
suppliers)

---

T—Canadian, Mexican, and United States industries are comparable.

**census.gov/naics**

*Cross-References.*          Establishments primarily engaged in--

- Providing human resources and human resource management services to client businesses and households--are classified in Industry 561330, Professional Employer Organizations;
- Supplying farm labor--are classified in U.S. Industry 115115, Farm Labor Contractors and Crew Leaders;
- Providing operating staff to perform a combination of services to support operations within a client's facilities--are classified in Industry 561210, Facilities Support Services;
- Providing executive search, recruitment, and placement services--are classified in U.S. Industry 561312, Executive Search Services;
- Listing employment vacancies and in recruiting, referring, or placing applicants for employment--are classified in U.S. Industry 561311, Employment Placement Agencies; and
- Representing models, entertainers, athletes, and other public figures as their agent or manager--are classified in Industry 711410, Agents and Managers for Artists, Athletes, Entertainers, and Other Public Figures.

## 56133    Professional Employer Organizations[T]
See industry description for 561330.

## 561330  Professional Employer Organizations

This industry comprises establishments primarily engaged in providing human resources and human resource management services to client businesses and households.  Establishments in this industry operate in a co-employment relationship with client businesses or organizations and are specialized in performing a wide range of human resource and personnel management duties, such as payroll, payroll tax, benefits administration, workers' compensation, unemployment, and human resource administration.  Professional employer organizations (PEOs) are responsible for payroll, including withholding and remitting employment-related taxes, for some or all of the employees of their clients, and also serve as the employer of those employees for benefits and related purposes.

*Cross-References.*          Establishments primarily engaged in--

- Supplying their own employees for limited periods of time to supplement the working force of a client's business--are classified in Industry 561320, Temporary Help Services; and
- Listing employment vacancies and referring or placing applicants for employment--are classified in U.S. Industry 561311, Employment Placement Agencies.

## 5614    Business Support Services[T]

This industry group comprises establishments engaged in performing activities that are ongoing routine business support functions for clients on a contract or fee basis, or serving other establishments of the same enterprise.

## 56141    Document Preparation Services[T]
See industry description for 561410.

## 561410  Document Preparation Services

This industry comprises establishments primarily engaged in one or more of the following: (1) letter or resume writing; (2) document editing or proofreading; (3) typing, word processing, or desktop publishing; and (4) stenography (except court reporting or stenotype recording), transcription, and other secretarial services.

*Cross-References.*          Establishments primarily engaged in--

- Providing verbatim reporting and stenotype recording of live legal proceedings and transcribing subsequent recorded materials--are classified in U.S. Industry 561492, Court Reporting and Stenotype Services;
- Performing prepress and postpress services in support of printing activities--are classified in Industry 323120, Support Activities for Printing;

---

T—Canadian, Mexican, and United States industries are comparable.

- Providing document translation services--are classified in Industry 541930, Translation and Interpretation Services;
- Providing data entry and other data processing services--are classified in Industry 518210, Computing Infrastructure Providers, Data Processing, Web Hosting, and Related Services;
- Independent (freelance) writing, including technical and advertising copy writing--are classified in Industry 711510, Independent Artists, Writers, and Performers;
- Photocopying, duplicating, and other document copying services, with or without a range of other office support services (except printing)--are classified in U.S. Industry 561439, Other Business Service Centers (including Copy Shops); and
- Providing document copying services in combination with printing services, with or without a range of other office support services, and establishments known as quick or digital printers--are classified in U.S. Industry 323111, Commercial Printing (except Screen and Books).

## 56142   Telephone Call Centers[T]

This industry comprises (1) establishments primarily engaged in answering telephone calls and relaying messages and (2) establishments primarily engaged in providing telemarketing services, such as promoting products or services by telephone; taking orders by telephone, facsimile, email, or other communication modes; and soliciting contributions or providing information by telephone. Telephone call centers provide these services on behalf of clients and do not own the products or provide the services that they are representing, or they serve other establishments of the same enterprise.

*Cross-References.*          Establishments primarily engaged in--

- Wholesale or retail sales--are classified in Sector 42, Wholesale Trade, or Sector 44-45, Retail Trade;
- Providing automated data processing services and computing infrastructure for call centers--are classified in Industry 51821, Computing Infrastructure Providers, Data Processing, Web Hosting, and Related Services;
- Providing restaurant meal and grocery order and delivery services (i.e., independent order and delivery services)--are classified in Industry 49221, Local Messengers and Local Delivery;
- Providing paging and beeper transmission services--are classified in Industry 51711, Wired and Wireless Telecommunications Carriers (except Satellite);
- Organizing and conducting charitable fundraising campaigns on a contract or fee basis, that may include telephone solicitation services--are classified in Industry 56149, Other Business Support Services; and
- Gathering, recording, tabulating, and presenting marketing and public opinion data, that may include telephone canvassing services--are classified in Industry 54191, Marketing Research and Public Opinion Polling.

## 561421  Telephone Answering Services

This U.S. industry comprises establishments primarily engaged in answering telephone calls and relaying messages on behalf of clients or for other establishments of the same enterprise.

*Cross-References.*

Establishments primarily engaged in providing paging or beeper transmission services are classified in U.S. Industry 517112, Wireless Telecommunications Carriers (except Satellite).

## 561422  Telemarketing Bureaus and Other Contact Centers

This U.S. industry comprises establishments primarily engaged in operating call centers that initiate or receive communications via telephone, facsimile, email, or other communication modes for purposes such as: (1) promoting products or services, (2) taking orders, (3) soliciting contributions, and (4) providing information or assistance regarding products or services. Telemarketing bureaus and other contact centers provide these services on behalf of

---

T—Canadian, Mexican, and United States industries are comparable.

clients and do not own the products or provide the services that they are representing, or they serve other establishments of the same enterprise.

*Cross-References.*        Establishments primarily engaged in--

- Answering telephone calls and relaying messages--are classified in U.S. Industry 561421, Telephone Answering Services;
- Wholesale or retail sales--are classified in Sector 42, Wholesale Trade, or Sector 44-45, Retail Trade;
- Providing automated data processing services and computing infrastructure for call centers--are classified in Industry 518210, Computing Infrastructure Providers, Data Processing, Web Hosting, and Related Services;
- Providing restaurant meal and grocery order and delivery services (i.e., independent order and delivery services)--are classified in Industry 492210, Local Messengers and Local Delivery;
- Organizing and conducting charitable fundraising campaigns on a contract or fee basis, that may include telephone solicitation services--are classified in U.S. Industry 561499, All Other Business Support Services; and
- Gathering, recording, tabulating, and presenting marketing and public opinion data, that may include telephone canvassing services--are classified in Industry 541910, Marketing Research and Public Opinion Polling.

## 56143   Business Service Centers[T]

This industry comprises (1) establishments primarily engaged in providing mailbox rental and other postal and mailing services (except direct mail advertising); (2) establishments, generally known as copy centers or shops, primarily engaged in providing photocopying, duplicating, blueprinting, and other document copying services without also providing printing services (i.e., offset printing, quick printing, digital printing, prepress services); and (3) establishments that provide a range of office support services (except printing services), such as mailing services, document copying services, facsimile services, word processing services, on-site PC rental services, and office product sales.

*Cross-References.*        Establishments primarily engaged in--

- Operating contract post offices--are classified in Industry 49111, Postal Service;
- Delivering letters and parcels (except under a universal service obligation)--are classified in Subsector 492, Couriers and Messengers;
- Providing voice mailbox services--are classified in Industry 56142, Telephone Call Centers;
- Providing direct mail advertising services--are classified in Industry 54186, Direct Mail Advertising;
- Providing full service office space, whether on a lease or service contract basis--are classified in Industry 53112, Lessors of Nonresidential Buildings (except Miniwarehouses);
- Providing document copying services in combination with printing services, with or without a range of other office support services, and establishments known as quick or digital printers--are classified in Industry 32311, Printing; and
- Providing only one of the support services (e.g., word processing services) that establishments in this industry provide--are classified in the appropriate industry according to the service provided.

## 561431  Private Mail Centers

This U.S. industry comprises (1) establishments primarily engaged in providing mailbox rental and other postal and mailing (except direct mail advertising) services or (2) establishments engaged in providing these mailing services along with one or more other office support services, such as facsimile services, word processing services, on-site PC rental services, and office product sales.

*Cross-References.*        Establishments primarily engaged in--

- Operating contract post offices--are classified in Industry 491110, Postal Service;

---

T—Canadian, Mexican, and United States industries are comparable.

- Delivering letters and parcels (except under a universal service obligation)--are classified in Subsector 492, Couriers and Messengers;
- Providing voice mailbox services--are classified in U.S. Industry 561421, Telephone Answering Services;
- Providing direct mail advertising services--are classified in Industry 541860, Direct Mail Advertising;
- Providing only one of the support services (e.g., word processing services) that establishments in this industry provide--are classified in the appropriate industry according to the service provided; and
- Providing full service office space, whether on a lease or service contract basis--are classified in Industry 531120, Lessors of Nonresidential Buildings (except Miniwarehouses).

### 561439 Other Business Service Centers (including Copy Shops)

This U.S. industry comprises (1) establishments generally known as copy centers or shops primarily engaged in providing photocopying, duplicating, blueprinting, and other document copying services, without also providing printing services (e.g., offset printing, quick printing, digital printing, prepress services) and (2) establishments (except private mail centers) engaged in providing a range of office support services (except printing services), such as document copying services, facsimile services, word processing services, on-site PC rental services, and office product sales.

*Cross-References.*

- Establishments primarily engaged in providing document copying services in combination with printing services, with or without a range of other office support services, and establishments known as quick or digital printers are classified in U.S. Industry 323111, Commercial Printing (except Screen and Books);
- Establishments primarily engaged in providing mailbox rental and other postal and mailing services, with or without one or more other office support services (except printing), are classified in U.S. Industry 561431, Private Mail Centers;
- Establishments exclusively engaged in providing a single office support service (except document copying) to clients, but not the range of office support services that establishments in this industry may provide, are classified according to the service provided; and
- Establishments primarily engaged in providing full service office space, whether on a lease or service contract basis, are classified in Industry 531120, Lessors of Nonresidential Buildings (except Miniwarehouses).

### 56144 Collection Agencies[T]
See industry description for 561440.

### 561440 Collection Agencies

This industry comprises establishments primarily engaged in collecting payments for claims and remitting payments collected to their clients.

*Illustrative Examples:*

Account or delinquent account collection services
Tax collection services on a contract or fee basis

Bill or debt collection services

*Cross-References.*     Establishments primarily engaged in--

- Repossessing tangible assets--are classified in U.S. Industry 561491, Repossession Services;
- Providing financing to others by factoring accounts receivables (i.e., assuming the risk of collection and credit losses)--are classified in U.S. Industry 522299, International, Secondary Market, and All Other Nondepository Credit Intermediation; and
- Providing legal services for debt collection by offices of lawyers--are classified in Industry 541110, Offices of Lawyers.

---

T—Canadian, Mexican, and United States industries are comparable.

**56145   Credit Bureaus**[T]
   See industry description for 561450.

**561450   Credit Bureaus**

  This industry comprises establishments primarily engaged in compiling information, such as credit and employment histories, and providing the information to financial institutions, retailers, and others who have a need to evaluate the creditworthiness of individuals and businesses.

*Illustrative Examples:*

Credit agencies
Credit rating services

Credit investigation services
Credit reporting bureaus

**56149   Other Business Support Services**[T]

  This industry comprises establishments primarily engaged in providing business support services (except secretarial and other document preparation services; telephone answering or telemarketing services; private mail services or document copying services conducted as separate activities or in conjunction with other office support services; monetary debt collection services; and credit reporting services).

*Illustrative Examples:*

Address bar coding services
Mail presorting services
Bar code imprinting services
Court reporting services
Repossession services

Real-time (i.e., simultaneous) closed captioning of live television performances, meetings, conferences
Charitable fundraising campaign organization services on a contract or fee basis

*Cross-References.*         Establishments primarily engaged in--

- Providing secretarial and other document preparation services--are classified in Industry 56141, Document Preparation Services;
- Providing telephone answering or telemarketing services--are classified in Industry 56142, Telephone Call Centers;
- Providing private mail services; document copying services (except printing services); and/or a range of office support services (except printing)--are classified in Industry 56143, Business Service Centers;
- Providing document copying services in combination with printing services, with or without a range of other office support services, and establishments known as quick or digital printers--are classified in Industry 32311, Printing;
- Providing monetary debt collection services--are classified in Industry 56144, Collection Agencies;
- Providing credit reporting services--are classified in Industry 56145, Credit Bureaus;
- Providing towing services to motor vehicles--are classified in Industry 48841, Motor Vehicle Towing;
- Providing document translation services--are classified in Industry 54193, Translation and Interpretation Services; and
- Providing film or tape captioning or subtitling services--are classified in Industry 51219, Postproduction Services and Other Motion Picture and Video Industries.

**561491   Repossession Services**

  This U.S. industry comprises establishments primarily engaged in repossessing tangible assets (e.g., automobiles, boats, equipment, planes, furniture, appliances) for the creditor as a result of delinquent debts.

---

T—Canadian, Mexican, and United States industries are comparable.

*Cross-References.*      Establishments primarily engaged in--

- Providing monetary debt collection services--are classified in Industry 561440, Collection Agencies; and
- Providing towing services to motor vehicles--are classified in Industry 488410, Motor Vehicle Towing.

## 561492  Court Reporting and Stenotype Services

This U.S. industry comprises establishments primarily engaged in providing verbatim reporting and stenotype recording of live legal proceedings and transcribing subsequent recorded materials.

*Illustrative Examples:*

Real-time (i.e., simultaneous) closed captioning of live television performances, meetings, conferences

Court reporting or stenotype recording services
Public stenography services

*Cross-References.*      Establishments primarily engaged in--

- Providing stenotype recording of correspondence, reports, and other documents or in providing document transcription services--are classified in Industry 561410, Document Preparation Services;
- Providing document translation services--are classified in Industry 541930, Translation and Interpretation Services; and
- Providing film or tape captioning or subtitling services--are classified in U.S. Industry 512191, Teleproduction and Other Postproduction Services.

## 561499  All Other Business Support Services

This U.S. industry comprises establishments primarily engaged in providing business support services (except secretarial and other document preparation services; telephone answering and telemarketing services; private mail services or document copying services conducted as separate activities or in conjunction with other office support services; monetary debt collection services; credit reporting services; repossession services; and court reporting and stenotype recording services).

*Illustrative Examples:*

Address bar coding services
Charitable fundraising campaign organization services on a contract or fee basis

Bar code imprinting services
Mail presorting services

*Cross-References.*      Establishments primarily engaged in--

- Providing secretarial and other document preparation services--are classified in Industry 561410, Document Preparation Services;
- Providing telephone answering or telemarketing services--are classified in Industry 56142, Telephone Call Centers;
- Providing private mail services, document copying services without printing services, and/or a range of office support services--are classified in Industry 56143, Business Service Centers;
- Providing document copying services in combination with printing services, with or without one or more other office support services, and establishments known as quick or digital printers--are classified in U.S. Industry 323111, Commercial Printing (except Screen and Books);
- Providing monetary debt collection services--are classified in Industry 561440, Collection Agencies;
- Providing credit reporting services--are classified in Industry 561450, Credit Bureaus;
- Providing repossession services--are classified in U.S. Industry 561491, Repossession Services; and
- Providing court reporting and stenotype services--are classified in U.S. Industry 561492, Court Reporting and Stenotype Services.

---

T—Canadian, Mexican, and United States industries are comparable.

## 5615 Travel Arrangement and Reservation Services[T]

This industry group comprises establishments primarily engaged in one of the following: (1) travel agency services; (2) arranging and assembling tours; or (3) other travel arrangement and reservation services.

## 56151 Travel Agencies[T]
See industry description for 561510.

## 561510 Travel Agencies

This industry comprises establishments primarily engaged in acting as agents in selling travel, tour, and accommodation services to the general public and commercial clients.

*Cross-References.*       Establishments primarily engaged in--

- Arranging and assembling tours that they generally sell through travel agencies or on their own account-- are classified in Industry 561520, Tour Operators;
- Providing guide services, such as archeological, museum, tourist, hunting, or fishing--are classified in Industry 713990, All Other Amusement and Recreation Industries; and
- Providing reservation services (e.g., accommodations, entertainment events, travel)--are classified in U.S. Industry 561599, All Other Travel Arrangement and Reservation Services.

## 56152 Tour Operators[T]
See industry description for 561520.

## 561520 Tour Operators

This industry comprises establishments primarily engaged in arranging and assembling tours. The tours are sold through travel agencies or tour operators. Travel or wholesale tour operators are included in this industry.

*Cross-References.*       Establishments primarily engaged in--

- Acting as agents in selling travel, tour, and accommodation services to the general public and commercial clients--are classified in Industry 561510, Travel Agencies;
- Conducting scenic and sightseeing tours--are classified in Subsector 487, Scenic and Sightseeing Transportation; and
- Providing guide services, such as archeological, museum, tourist, hunting, or fishing--are classified in Industry 713990, All Other Amusement and Recreation Industries.

## 56159 Other Travel Arrangement and Reservation Services[T]

This industry comprises establishments (except travel agencies and tour operators) primarily engaged in providing travel arrangement and reservation services.

*Illustrative Examples:*

Condominium time-share exchange services
Road and travel services automobile clubs
Convention or visitors bureaus
Ticket (e.g., amusement, sports, theatrical) agencies

Ticket (e.g., airline, bus, cruise ship, sports, theatrical) offices
Reservation (e.g., airline, car rental, hotel, restaurant) services

*Cross-References.*

- Establishments primarily engaged in acting as agents and/or brokers in renting real estate for others are classified in Industry 53121, Offices of Real Estate Agents and Brokers;

---

T—Canadian, Mexican, and United States industries are comparable.

- Travel agencies are classified in Industry 56151, Travel Agencies;
- Tour operators are classified in Industry 56152, Tour Operators;
- Automobile clubs (i.e., enthusiasts' clubs, except road and travel services) are classified in Industry 81341, Civic and Social Organizations;
- Establishments primarily engaged in organizing, promoting, and/or managing events, such as business and trade shows, conventions, conferences, and meetings (whether or not they manage and provide the staff to operate the facilities in which these events take place), are classified in Industry 56192, Convention and Trade Show Organizers; and
- Establishments primarily engaged in organizing, promoting, and/or managing live performing arts productions, sports events, and similar events, such as festivals (whether or not they manage and provide the staff to operate the facilities in which these events take place), are classified in Industry Group 7113, Promoters of Performing Arts, Sports, and Similar Events.

### 561591 Convention and Visitors Bureaus

This U.S. industry comprises establishments primarily engaged in marketing and promoting communities and facilities to businesses and leisure travelers through a range of activities, such as assisting organizations in locating meeting and convention sites; providing travel information on area attractions, lodging accommodations, restaurants; providing maps; and organizing group tours of local historical, recreational, and cultural attractions.

*Cross-References.*          Establishments primarily engaged in--

- Organizing, promoting, and/or managing events, such as business and trade shows, conventions, conferences, and meetings (whether or not they manage and provide the staff to operate the facilities in which these events take place)--are classified in Industry 561920, Convention and Trade Show Organizers; and
- Organizing, promoting, and/or managing live performing arts productions, sports events, and similar events, such as festivals (whether or not they manage and provide the staff to operate the facilities in which these events take place)--are classified in Industry Group 7113, Promoters of Performing Arts, Sports, and Similar Events.

### 561599 All Other Travel Arrangement and Reservation Services

This U.S. industry comprises establishments (except travel agencies, tour operators, and convention and visitors bureaus) primarily engaged in providing travel arrangement and reservation services.

*Illustrative Examples:*

Condominium time-share exchange services
Ticket (e.g., airline, bus, cruise ship, sports, theatrical) offices
Road and travel services automobile clubs

Reservation (e.g., airline, car rental, hotel, restaurant) services
Ticket (e.g., amusement, sports, theatrical) agencies

*Cross-References.*

- Establishments primarily engaged in acting as agents and/or brokers in renting real estate for others are classified in Industry 531210, Offices of Real Estate Agents and Brokers;
- Travel agencies are classified in Industry 561510, Travel Agencies;
- Tour operators are classified in Industry 561520, Tour Operators;
- Convention and visitors bureaus are classified in U.S. Industry 561591, Convention and Visitors Bureaus;
- Establishments primarily engaged in organizing, promoting, and/or managing events, such as business and trade shows, conventions, conferences, and meetings (whether or not they manage and provide the staff to operate the facilities in which these events take place), are classified in Industry 561920, Convention and Trade Show Organizers;

---

T—Canadian, Mexican, and United States industries are comparable.

- Establishments primarily engaged in organizing, promoting, and/or managing live performing arts productions, sports events, and similar events, such as festivals (whether or not they manage and provide the staff to operate the facilities in which these events take place), are classified in Industry Group 7113, Promoters of Performing Arts, Sports, and Similar Events; and
- Automobile clubs (i.e., enthusiasts' clubs, except road and travel services) are classified in Industry 813410, Civic and Social Organizations.

## 5616    Investigation and Security Services[T]

This industry group comprises establishments primarily engaged in one of the following: (1) investigation, guard, and armored car services; (2) selling security systems, such as burglar and fire alarms and locking devices, along with installation, repair, or monitoring services; or (3) remote monitoring of electronic security alarm systems.

## 56161    Investigation, Guard, and Armored Car Services[T]

This industry comprises establishments primarily engaged in providing one or more of the following: (1) investigation, detective, and personal background check services; (2) guard and patrol services; and (3) picking up and delivering money, receipts, or other valuable items with personnel and equipment to protect such properties while in transit.

*Illustrative Examples:*

Armored car services
Private detective services
Bodyguard services

Security guard services
Polygraph services

*Cross-References.*

- Establishments primarily engaged in providing credit checks are classified in Industry 56145, Credit Bureaus;
- Establishments primarily engaged in selling, installing, monitoring, and maintaining security systems and devices (e.g., burglar and fire alarm systems) are classified in Industry 56162, Security Systems Services; and
- Government establishments primarily engaged in criminal and civil law enforcement, police, traffic safety, and similar activities related to the enforcement of law are classified in Industry 92212, Police Protection.

## 561611  Investigation and Personal Background Check Services

This U.S. industry comprises establishments primarily engaged in providing investigation, detective, and personal background check services.

*Illustrative Examples:*

Fingerprint services
Private detective services

Polygraph services
Private investigative services (except credit)

*Cross-References.*

Establishments primarily engaged in providing credit checks are classified in Industry 561450, Credit Bureaus.

## 561612  Security Guards and Patrol Services

This U.S. industry comprises establishments primarily engaged in providing guard and patrol services, such as bodyguard, guard dog, and parking security services.

---

T—Canadian, Mexican, and United States industries are comparable.

*Cross-References.*

- Establishments primarily engaged in picking up and delivering money, receipts, or other valuable items are classified in U.S. Industry 561613, Armored Car Services;
- Establishments primarily engaged in selling, installing, monitoring, and maintaining security systems and devices, such as burglar and fire alarms and locking devices, are classified in Industry 56162, Security Systems Services; and
- Government establishments primarily engaged in criminal and civil law enforcement, police, traffic safety, and similar activities related to the enforcement of law are classified in Industry 922120, Police Protection.

## 561613 Armored Car Services

This U.S. industry comprises establishments primarily engaged in picking up and delivering money, receipts, or other valuable items. These establishments maintain personnel and equipment to protect such properties while in transit.

## 56162 Security Systems Services[T]

This industry comprises establishments engaged in (1) selling security systems, such as burglar and fire alarms and locking devices, along with installation, repair, or monitoring services or (2) remote monitoring of electronic security alarm systems.

*Cross-References.*          Establishments primarily engaged in--

- Selling security systems for buildings without installation, repair, or monitoring services--are classified in Sector 42, Wholesale Trade, or Sector 44-45, Retail Trade;
- Installing alarm systems (e.g., fire, burglar), without selling or monitoring services--are classified in Industry 23821, Electrical Contractors and Other Wiring Installation Contractors;
- Retailing motor vehicle security systems, with or without installation or repair services--are classified in Industry 44133, Automotive Parts and Accessories Retailers; and
- Providing key duplication services--are classified in Industry 81149, Other Personal and Household Goods Repair and Maintenance.

## 561621 Security Systems Services (except Locksmiths)

This U.S. industry comprises establishments primarily engaged in (1) selling security alarm systems, such as burglar and fire alarms, along with installation, repair, or monitoring services or (2) remote monitoring of electronic security alarm systems.

*Cross-References.*          Establishments primarily engaged in--

- Selling security alarm systems for buildings, without installation, repair, or monitoring services--are classified in Sector 42, Wholesale Trade, or Sector 44-45, Retail Trade;
- Installing alarm systems (e.g., fire, burglar), without selling or monitoring services--are classified in Industry 238210, Electrical Contractors and Other Wiring Installation Contractors; and
- Retailing motor vehicle security systems, with or without installation or repair services--are classified in Industry 441330, Automotive Parts and Accessories Retailers.

## 561622 Locksmiths

This U.S. industry comprises establishments primarily engaged in (1) selling mechanical or electronic locking devices, safes, and security vaults, along with installation, repair, rebuilding, or adjusting services or (2) installing, repairing, rebuilding, and adjusting mechanical or electronic locking devices, safes, and security vaults.

---

T—Canadian, Mexican, and United States industries are comparable.

**census.gov/naics**

*Cross-References.*  Establishments primarily engaged in--

- Selling security systems, such as locking devices, safes, and vaults, without installation or maintenance services--are classified in Sector 42, Wholesale Trade, or Sector 44-45, Retail Trade; and
- Providing key duplication services--are classified in Industry 811490, Other Personal and Household Goods Repair and Maintenance.

## 5617    Services to Buildings and Dwellings[T]

This industry group comprises establishments primarily engaged in one of the following: (1) exterminating and pest control services; (2) janitorial services; (3) landscaping services; (4) carpet and upholstery cleaning services; or (5) other services to buildings and dwellings.

## 56171    Exterminating and Pest Control Services[T]
See industry description for 561710.

## 561710  Exterminating and Pest Control Services

This industry comprises establishments primarily engaged in exterminating and controlling birds, mosquitoes, rodents, termites, and other insects and pests (except for crop production and forestry production).  Establishments providing fumigation services are included in this industry.

*Cross-References.*

Establishments primarily engaged in providing pest control for crop or forestry production are classified in Subsector 115, Support Activities for Agriculture and Forestry.

## 56172    Janitorial Services[T]
See industry description for 561720.

## 561720  Janitorial Services

This industry comprises establishments primarily engaged in cleaning building interiors, interiors of transportation equipment (e.g., aircraft, rail cars, ships), and/or windows.

*Illustrative Examples:*

Custodial services
Service station cleaning and degreasing services
Housekeeping (i.e., cleaning) services

Washroom sanitation services
Maid (i.e., cleaning) services

*Cross-References.*  Establishments primarily engaged in--

- Cleaning building exteriors (except sandblasting and window cleaning) or chimneys--are classified in Industry 561790, Other Services to Buildings and Dwellings;
- Sandblasting building exteriors--are classified in Industry 238990, All Other Specialty Trade Contractors; and
- Crime scene cleanup services--are classified in Industry 562910, Remediation Services.

## 56173    Landscaping Services[T]
See industry description for 561730.

---

T—Canadian, Mexican, and United States industries are comparable.

**561730  Landscaping Services**

This industry comprises (1) establishments primarily engaged in providing landscape care and maintenance services and/or installing trees, shrubs, plants, lawns, or gardens and (2) establishments primarily engaged in providing these services along with the design of landscape plans and/or the construction (i.e., installation) of walkways, retaining walls, decks, fences, ponds, and similar structures.

*Cross-References.*        Establishments primarily engaged in--

- Installing artificial turf, constructing (i.e., installing) walkways, retaining walls, decks, fences, ponds, or similar structures, or right of way cutting (except maintenance)--are classified in Sector 23, Construction;
- Planning and designing the development of land areas for projects, such as parks and other recreational areas; airports; highways; hospitals; schools; land subdivisions; and commercial, industrial, and residential areas (without also installing trees, shrubs, plants, lawns/gardens, walkways, retaining walls, decks, and similar items or structures)--are classified in Industry 541320, Landscape Architectural Services; and
- Retailing landscaping materials and providing the installation and maintenance of these materials--are classified in Industry 444240, Nursery, Garden Center, and Farm Supply Retailers.

**56174    Carpet and Upholstery Cleaning Services**[T]
See industry description for 561740.

**561740  Carpet and Upholstery Cleaning Services**

This industry comprises establishments primarily engaged in cleaning and dyeing used rugs, carpets, and upholstery.

*Cross-References.*        Establishments primarily engaged in--

- Rug repair not associated with rug cleaning--are classified in Industry 811490, Other Personal and Household Goods Repair and Maintenance; and
- Reupholstering and repairing furniture--are classified in Industry 811420, Reupholstery and Furniture Repair.

**56179    Other Services to Buildings and Dwellings**[T]
See industry description for 561790.

**561790  Other Services to Buildings and Dwellings**

This industry comprises establishments primarily engaged in providing services to buildings and dwellings (except exterminating and pest control; janitorial; landscaping care and maintenance; and carpet and upholstery cleaning).

*Illustrative Examples:*

Building exterior cleaning services (except sandblasting, window cleaning)
Swimming pool cleaning and maintenance services

Chimney cleaning services
Ventilation duct cleaning services
Drain or gutter cleaning services

*Cross-References.*        Establishments primarily engaged in--

- Providing exterminating and pest control services--are classified in Industry 561710, Exterminating and Pest Control Services;
- Providing janitorial services--are classified in Industry 561720, Janitorial Services;
- Providing landscaping care and maintenance--are classified in Industry 561730, Landscaping Services;
- Providing carpet and upholstery cleaning services--are classified in Industry 561740, Carpet and Upholstery Cleaning Services;

---

T—Canadian, Mexican, and United States industries are comparable.

- Installing gutters, downspouts, and siding--are classified in Industry 238170, Siding Contractors;
- Resurfacing hardwood flooring and/or wood floor finishing--are classified in Industry 238330, Flooring Contractors; and
- Sandblasting building exteriors--are classified in Industry 238990, All Other Specialty Trade Contractors.

## 5619    Other Support Services[T]

This industry group comprises establishments primarily engaged in providing day-to-day business and other organizational support services (except office administrative services; facilities support services; employment services; business support services; travel arrangement and reservation services; security and investigation services; and services to buildings and dwellings).

### 56191    Packaging and Labeling Services[T]
See industry description for 561910.

### 561910  Packaging and Labeling Services

This industry comprises establishments primarily engaged in packaging client-owned materials.  The services may include labeling and/or imprinting the package.

*Illustrative Examples:*

Apparel and textile folding and packaging services
Kit assembling and packaging services
Blister packaging services

Shrink wrapping services
Gift wrapping services

*Cross-References.*        Establishments primarily engaged in--

- Providing aerosol packaging services--are classified in U.S. Industry 325998, All Other Miscellaneous Chemical Product and Preparation Manufacturing;
- Providing packing and crating services incidental to transportation--are classified in U.S. Industry 488991, Packing and Crating;
- Providing warehousing services, as well as packaging or other logistics services--are classified in Industry Group 4931, Warehousing and Storage;
- Providing packing and crating services for agricultural products--are classified in U.S. Industry 115114, Postharvest Crop Activities (except Cotton Ginning); and
- Processing client-owned materials into new products, such as mixing water and concentrate to produce soft drinks--are classified in Sector 31-33, Manufacturing.

### 56192    Convention and Trade Show Organizers[T]
See industry description for 561920.

### 561920  Convention and Trade Show Organizers

This industry comprises establishments primarily engaged in organizing, promoting, and/or managing events, such as business and trade shows, conventions, conferences, and meetings (whether or not they manage and provide the staff to operate the facilities in which these events take place).

*Cross-References.*

Establishments primarily engaged in organizing, promoting, and/or managing live performing arts productions, sports events, and similar events, such as festivals (whether or not they manage and provide the staff to operate the facilities in which these events take place), are classified in Industry Group 7113, Promoters of Performing Arts, Sports, and Similar Events.

---

T—Canadian, Mexican, and United States industries are comparable.

**56199 All Other Support Services[T]**
See industry description for 561990.

**561990 All Other Support Services**

This industry comprises establishments primarily engaged in providing day-to-day business and other organizational support services (except office administrative services, facilities support services, employment services, business support services, travel arrangement and reservation services, security and investigation services, services to buildings and other structures, packaging and labeling services, and convention and trade show organizing services).

*Illustrative Examples:*

Bartering services
Flagging (i.e., traffic control) services
Bottle exchanges
Float decorating services

Inventory taking services
Contract meter reading services
Lumber grading services
Diving services on a contract or fee basis

*Cross-References.*　　　Establishments primarily engaged in--

- Providing office administrative services--are classified in Industry 561110, Office Administrative Services;
- Providing facilities support services--are classified in Industry 561210, Facilities Support Services;
- Providing employment services--are classified in Industry Group 5613, Employment Services;
- Providing business support services--are classified in Industry Group 5614, Business Support Services;
- Providing travel arrangement and reservation services--are classified in Industry Group 5615, Travel Arrangement and Reservation Services;
- Providing security and investigation services--are classified in Industry Group 5616, Investigation and Security Services;
- Providing services to buildings and other structures--are classified in Industry Group 5617, Services to Buildings and Dwellings;
- Providing packaging and labeling services--are classified in Industry 561910, Packaging and Labeling Services;
- Organizing, promoting, and/or managing conferences, conventions, and trade shows (whether or not they manage and provide the staff to operate the facilities in which these events take place)--are classified in Industry 561920, Convention and Trade Show Organizers;
- Retailing bottled water--are classified in U.S. Industry 445298, All Other Specialty Food Retailers;
- Providing operating advice and assistance to businesses and other organizations on administrative management issues, such as business start-up consulting services--are classified in U.S. Industry 541611, Administrative Management and General Management Consulting Services; and
- Promoting the business interests of their members--are classified in Industry 813910, Business Associations.

**562　Waste Management and Remediation Services[T]**

Industries in the Waste Management and Remediation Services subsector group establishments engaged in the collection, treatment, and disposal of waste materials. This includes establishments engaged in local hauling of waste materials; operating materials recovery facilities (i.e., those that sort recyclable materials from the trash stream); providing remediation services (i.e., those that provide for the cleanup of contaminated buildings, mine sites, soil, or ground water); and providing septic pumping and other miscellaneous waste management services. There are three industry groups within the subsector that separate these activities into waste collection, waste treatment and disposal, and remediation and other waste management.

Excluded from this subsector are establishments primarily engaged in collecting, treating, and disposing waste through sewer systems or sewage treatment facilities that are classified in Industry 22132, Sewage Treatment Facilities, and establishments primarily engaged in long-distance hauling of waste materials that are classified in Industry 48423, Specialized Freight (except Used Goods) Trucking, Long-Distance. Also, there are some activities

---

T—Canadian, Mexican, and United States industries are comparable.

that appear to be related to waste management, but that are not included in this subsector. For example, establishments primarily engaged in providing waste management consulting services are classified in Industry 54162, Environmental Consulting Services.

## 5621    Waste Collection

## 56211    Waste Collection

This industry comprises establishments primarily engaged in (1) collecting and/or hauling hazardous waste, nonhazardous waste, and/or recyclable materials within a local area and/or (2) operating hazardous or nonhazardous waste transfer stations. Hazardous waste collection establishments may be responsible for the identification, treatment, packaging, and labeling of waste for the purposes of transport.

*Cross-References.*          Establishments primarily engaged in--

- Long-distance trucking of waste--are classified in Industry 48423, Specialized Freight (except Used Goods) Trucking, Long-Distance;
- Operating facilities for separating and sorting recyclable materials from nonhazardous waste streams (i.e., garbage) and/or for sorting commingled recyclable materials, such as paper, plastics, and metal cans, into distinct categories--are classified in Industry 56292, Materials Recovery Facilities;
- Merchant wholesaling automotive, industrial, and other recyclable materials--are classified in Industry 42393, Recyclable Material Merchant Wholesalers; and
- Collecting and/or hauling in combination with disposal of waste materials--are classified in Industry 56221, Waste Treatment and Disposal.

## 562111  Solid Waste Collection

This U.S. industry comprises establishments primarily engaged in one or more of the following: (1) collecting and/or hauling nonhazardous solid waste (i.e., garbage) within a local area; (2) operating nonhazardous solid waste transfer stations; and (3) collecting and/or hauling mixed recyclable materials within a local area.

*Cross-References.*          Establishments primarily engaged in--

- Long-distance trucking of waste--are classified in Industry 484230, Specialized Freight (except Used Goods) Trucking, Long-Distance;
- Collecting and/or hauling in combination with disposal of nonhazardous waste materials--are classified in Industry 56221, Waste Treatment and Disposal;
- Collecting and/or hauling hazardous waste within a local area and/or operating hazardous waste transfer stations--are classified in U.S. Industry 562112, Hazardous Waste Collection;
- Collecting and removing debris, such as brush or rubble, within a local area--are classified in U.S. Industry 562119, Other Waste Collection;
- Operating facilities for separating and sorting recyclable materials from nonhazardous waste streams (i.e., garbage) and/or for sorting commingled recyclable materials, such as paper, plastics, and metal cans, into distinct categories--are classified in Industry 562920, Materials Recovery Facilities; and
- Merchant wholesaling automotive, industrial, and other recyclable materials--are classified in Industry 423930, Recyclable Material Merchant Wholesalers.

## 562112  Hazardous Waste Collection

This U.S. industry comprises establishments primarily engaged in collecting and/or hauling hazardous waste within a local area and/or operating hazardous waste transfer stations. Hazardous waste collection establishments may be responsible for the identification, treatment, packaging, and labeling of waste for the purposes of transport.

---

T—Canadian, Mexican, and United States industries are comparable.

*Cross-References.*          Establishments primarily engaged in--

- Long-distance trucking of waste--are classified in Industry 484230, Specialized Freight (except Used Goods) Trucking, Long-Distance;
- Collecting and/or hauling in combination with disposal of hazardous waste materials--are classified in U.S. Industry 562211, Hazardous Waste Treatment and Disposal;
- Collecting and/or hauling nonhazardous solid waste (i.e., garbage) and/or recyclable materials within a local area and/or operating nonhazardous solid waste transfer stations--are classified in U.S. Industry 562111, Solid Waste Collection; and
- Collecting and removing debris, such as brush or rubble, within a local area--are classified in U.S. Industry 562119, Other Waste Collection.

## 562119  Other Waste Collection

This U.S. industry comprises establishments primarily engaged in collecting and/or hauling waste (except nonhazardous solid waste and hazardous waste) within a local area.  Establishments engaged in brush or rubble removal services are included in this industry.

*Cross-References.*          Establishments primarily engaged in--

- Long-distance trucking of waste--are classified in Industry 484230, Specialized Freight (except Used Goods) Trucking, Long-Distance;
- Collecting and/or hauling in combination with disposal of waste materials--are classified in Industry 56221, Waste Treatment and Disposal;
- Collecting and/or hauling nonhazardous solid waste (i.e., garbage) or mixed recyclable materials within a local area or operating nonhazardous solid waste transfer stations--are classified in U.S. Industry 562111, Solid Waste Collection;
- Collecting and/or hauling hazardous waste within a local area or operating hazardous waste transfer stations--are classified in U.S. Industry 562112, Hazardous Waste Collection; and
- Operating facilities for separating and sorting recyclable materials from nonhazardous waste streams (i.e., garbage) and/or for sorting commingled recyclable materials, such as paper, plastics, and metal cans, into distinct categories--are classified in Industry 562920, Materials Recovery Facilities.

## 5622    Waste Treatment and Disposal

## 56221    Waste Treatment and Disposal

This industry comprises establishments primarily engaged in (1) operating waste treatment or disposal facilities (except sewer systems or sewage treatment facilities) or (2) the combined activity of collecting and/or hauling of waste materials within a local area and operating waste treatment or disposal facilities.  Waste combustors or incinerators (including those that may produce byproducts, such as electricity), solid waste landfills, and compost dumps are included in this industry.

*Cross-References.*          Establishments primarily engaged in--

- Collecting, treating, and disposing waste through sewer systems or sewage treatment facilities--are classified in Industry 22132, Sewage Treatment Facilities;
- Manufacturing compost--are classified in Industry 32531, Fertilizer and Compost Manufacturing; and
- Pumping (i.e., cleaning) cesspools, portable toilets, and septic tanks or renting portable toilets--are classified in Industry 56299, All Other Waste Management Services.

---

T—Canadian, Mexican, and United States industries are comparable.

**562211 Hazardous Waste Treatment and Disposal**

This U.S. industry comprises establishments primarily engaged in (1) operating treatment and/or disposal facilities for hazardous waste or (2) the combined activity of collecting and/or hauling of hazardous waste materials within a local area and operating treatment or disposal facilities for hazardous waste.

*Cross-References.*        Establishments primarily engaged in--

- Operating landfills for the disposal of nonhazardous solid waste--are classified in U.S. Industry 562212, Solid Waste Landfill;
- Operating combustors and incinerators for the disposal of nonhazardous solid waste--are classified in U.S. Industry 562213, Solid Waste Combustors and Incinerators;
- Collecting, treating, and disposing waste through sewer systems or sewage treatment facilities--are classified in Industry 221320, Sewage Treatment Facilities;
- Operating nonhazardous waste treatment and disposal facilities (except landfills, combustors, incinerators, and sewer systems or sewage treatment facilities)--are classified in U.S. Industry 562219, Other Nonhazardous Waste Treatment and Disposal; and
- Pumping (i.e., cleaning) cesspools, portable toilets, and septic tanks or renting portable toilets--are classified in U.S. Industry 562991, Septic Tank and Related Services.

**562212 Solid Waste Landfill**

This U.S. industry comprises establishments primarily engaged in (1) operating landfills for the disposal of nonhazardous solid waste or (2) the combined activity of collecting and/or hauling nonhazardous waste materials within a local area and operating landfills for the disposal of nonhazardous solid waste. These establishments may produce byproducts, such as methane.

*Cross-References.*        Establishments primarily engaged in--

- Operating treatment and/or disposal facilities for hazardous waste--are classified in U.S. Industry 562211, Hazardous Waste Treatment and Disposal;
- Operating combustors and incinerators for the disposal of nonhazardous solid waste--are classified in U.S. Industry 562213, Solid Waste Combustors and Incinerators;
- Collecting, treating, and disposing waste through sewer systems or sewage treatment facilities--are classified in Industry 221320, Sewage Treatment Facilities;
- Operating nonhazardous waste treatment and disposal facilities (except landfills, combustors, incinerators, and sewer systems or sewage treatment facilities)--are classified in U.S. Industry 562219, Other Nonhazardous Waste Treatment and Disposal; and
- Manufacturing compost--are classified in U.S. Industry 325315, Compost Manufacturing.

**562213 Solid Waste Combustors and Incinerators**

This U.S. industry comprises establishments primarily engaged in operating combustors and incinerators for the disposal of nonhazardous solid waste. These establishments may produce byproducts, such as electricity and steam.

*Cross-References.*        Establishments primarily engaged in--

- Operating treatment and/or disposal facilities for hazardous waste--are classified in U.S. Industry 562211, Hazardous Waste Treatment and Disposal;
- Operating landfills for the disposal of nonhazardous solid waste--are classified in U.S. Industry 562212, Solid Waste Landfill;
- Collecting, treating, and disposing waste through sewer systems or sewage treatment facilities--are classified in Industry 221320, Sewage Treatment Facilities; and

---

T—Canadian, Mexican, and United States industries are comparable.

- Operating nonhazardous waste treatment and disposal facilities (except landfills, combustors, incinerators, and sewer systems or sewage treatment facilities)--are classified in U.S. Industry 562219, Other Nonhazardous Waste Treatment and Disposal.

### 562219 Other Nonhazardous Waste Treatment and Disposal

This U.S. industry comprises establishments primarily engaged in (1) operating nonhazardous waste treatment and disposal facilities (except landfills, combustors, incinerators, and sewer systems or sewage treatment facilities) or (2) the combined activity of collecting and/or hauling of nonhazardous waste materials within a local area and operating waste treatment or disposal facilities (except landfills, combustors, incinerators, and sewer systems or sewage treatment facilities). Compost dumps are included in this industry.

*Cross-References.*     Establishments primarily engaged in--

- Operating landfills for the disposal of nonhazardous solid waste--are classified in U.S. Industry 562212, Solid Waste Landfill;
- Operating combustors and incinerators for the disposal of nonhazardous solid waste--are classified in U.S. Industry 562213, Solid Waste Combustors and Incinerators;
- Collecting, treating, and disposing waste through sewer systems or sewage treatment facilities--are classified in Industry 221320, Sewage Treatment Facilities; and
- Manufacturing compost--are classified in U.S. Industry 325315, Compost Manufacturing.

### 5629     Remediation and Other Waste Management Services

This industry group comprises establishments primarily engaged in remediation and other waste management services (except waste collection, waste treatment and disposal, and waste management consulting services).

### 56291     Remediation Services
See industry description for 562910.

### 562910 Remediation Services

This industry comprises establishments primarily engaged in one or more of the following: (1) remediation and cleanup of contaminated buildings, mine sites, soil, or ground water; (2) integrated mine reclamation activities, including demolition, soil remediation, waste water treatment, hazardous material removal, contouring land, and revegetation; and (3) asbestos, lead paint, and other toxic material abatement.

*Cross-References.*     Establishments primarily engaged in--

- Environmental engineering services--are classified in Industry 541330, Engineering Services;
- Developing remedial action plans--are classified in Industry 541620, Environmental Consulting Services;
- Providing janitorial services, including for transportation equipment (e.g., aircraft, rail cars, ships)--are classified in Industry 561720, Janitorial Services;
- Pumping (i.e., cleaning) cesspools, portable toilets, and septic tanks or renting portable toilets--are classified in U.S. Industry 562991, Septic Tank and Related Services;
- Fire and flood restoration of buildings--are classified in Subsector 236, Construction of Buildings;
- Excavating soil--are classified in Industry 238910, Site Preparation Contractors;
- Individual activities as part of a reclamation, remediation, or restoration project--are classified according to the primary activity;
- Building modifications to alleviate radon gas--are classified in Industry 238990, All Other Specialty Trade Contractors; and
- Collecting, treating, and disposing waste water through sewer systems or sewage treatment facilities--are classified in Industry 221320, Sewage Treatment Facilities.

---

T—Canadian, Mexican, and United States industries are comparable.

**56292    Materials Recovery Facilities**
See industry description for 562920.

**562920  Materials Recovery Facilities**

This industry comprises establishments primarily engaged in (1) operating facilities for separating and sorting recyclable materials from nonhazardous waste streams (i.e., garbage) and/or (2) operating facilities where commingled recyclable materials, such as paper, plastics, used beverage cans, and metals, are sorted into distinct categories.

*Cross-References.*

Establishments primarily engaged in merchant wholesaling automotive, industrial, and other recyclable materials are classified in Industry 423930, Recyclable Material Merchant Wholesalers.

**56299    All Other Waste Management Services**

This industry comprises establishments primarily engaged in waste management services (except waste collection, waste treatment and disposal, remediation, operation of materials recovery facilities, and waste management consulting services).

*Illustrative Examples:*

Beach cleaning and maintenance services
Pumping (i.e., cleaning) cesspools, portable toilets, or
septic tanks
Cesspool cleaning services

Sewer cleaning and rodding services
Portable toilet renting and/or servicing
Sewer or storm basin cleanout services

*Cross-References.*         Establishments primarily engaged in--

- Collecting and/or hauling waste within a local area--are classified in Industry 56211, Waste Collection;
- Long-distance trucking of waste--are classified in Industry 48423, Specialized Freight (except Used Goods) Trucking, Long-Distance;
- Operating treatment or disposal facilities (except sewer systems or sewage treatment facilities) for waste-- are classified in Industry 56221, Waste Treatment and Disposal;
- Collecting, treating, and disposing waste through sewer systems or sewage treatment facilities--are classified in Industry 22132, Sewage Treatment Facilities;
- Remediation and cleanup of contaminated buildings, mine sites, soil, or ground water--are classified in Industry 56291, Remediation Services;
- Operating facilities for separating and sorting recyclable materials from nonhazardous waste streams (i.e., garbage) or where commingled recyclable materials, such as paper, plastics, and metal cans, are sorted into distinct categories--are classified in Industry 56292, Materials Recovery Facilities;
- Installing septic tanks--are classified in Industry 23891, Site Preparation Contractors;
- Providing waste management consulting services, such as developing remedial action plans--are classified in Industry 54162, Environmental Consulting Services;
- Providing street cleaning services--are classified in Industry 48849, Other Support Activities for Road Transportation; and
- Merchant wholesaling waste oil--are classified in Industry 42393, Recyclable Material Merchant Wholesalers.

**562991  Septic Tank and Related Services**

This U.S. industry comprises establishments primarily engaged in (1) pumping (i.e., cleaning) septic tanks and cesspools and/or (2) renting and/or servicing portable toilets.

---

T—Canadian, Mexican, and United States industries are comparable.

*Cross-References.*          Establishments primarily engaged in--

- Installing septic tanks--are classified in Industry 238910, Site Preparation Contractors; and
- Cleaning and rodding sewers and catch basins--are classified in U.S. Industry 562998, All Other Miscellaneous Waste Management Services.

## 562998  All Other Miscellaneous Waste Management Services

This U.S. industry comprises establishments primarily engaged in providing waste management services (except waste collection, waste treatment and disposal, remediation, operation of materials recovery facilities, septic tank pumping and related services, and waste management consulting services).

*Illustrative Examples:*

Beach cleaning and maintenance services
Sewer or storm basin cleanout services
Catch basin cleaning services

Tank cleaning and disposal services, commercial or industrial
Sewer cleaning and rodding services

*Cross-References.*          Establishments primarily engaged in--

- Collecting and/or hauling waste within a local area--are classified in Industry 56211, Waste Collection;
- Long-distance trucking of waste--are classified in Industry 484230, Specialized Freight (except Used Goods) Trucking, Long-Distance;
- Operating treatment or disposal facilities (except sewer systems or sewage treatment facilities) for waste--are classified in Industry 56221, Waste Treatment and Disposal;
- Collecting, treating, and disposing waste through sewer systems or sewage treatment facilities--are classified in Industry 221320, Sewage Treatment Facilities;
- Remediation and cleanup of contaminated buildings, mine sites, soil, or ground water--are classified in Industry 562910, Remediation Services;
- Operating facilities for separating and sorting recyclable materials from nonhazardous waste streams (i.e., garbage) or for sorting commingled recyclable materials, such as paper, plastics, and metal cans, into distinct categories--are classified in Industry 562920, Materials Recovery Facilities;
- Pumping (i.e., cleaning) cesspools, portable toilets, and septic tanks or renting portable toilets--are classified in U.S. Industry 562991, Septic Tank and Related Services;
- Providing waste management consulting services, such as developing remedial action plans--are classified in Industry 541620, Environmental Consulting Services;
- Providing street cleaning services--are classified in Industry 488490, Other Support Activities for Road Transportation; and
- Merchant wholesaling waste oil--are classified in Industry 423930, Recyclable Material Merchant Wholesalers.

T—Canadian, Mexican, and United States industries are comparable.

**census.gov/naics**

# Sector 61--Educational Services<sup>T</sup>

## The Sector as a Whole

The Educational Services sector comprises establishments that provide instruction and training in a wide variety of subjects. This instruction and training is provided by specialized establishments, such as schools, colleges, universities, and training centers. These establishments may be privately owned and operated for profit or not for profit, or they may be publicly owned and operated. They may also offer food and/or accommodation services to their students.

Educational services are usually delivered by teachers or instructors that explain, tell, demonstrate, supervise, and direct learning. Instruction is imparted in diverse settings, such as educational institutions, the workplace, or the home, and through diverse means, such as correspondence, television, the Internet, or other electronic and distance-learning methods. The training provided by these establishments may include the use of simulators and simulation methods. It can be adapted to the particular needs of the students, for example sign language can replace verbal language for teaching students with hearing impairments. All industries in the sector share this commonality of process, namely, labor inputs of instructors with the requisite subject matter expertise and teaching ability.

### 611 Educational Services<sup>T</sup>

Industries in the Educational Services subsector provide instruction and training in a wide variety of subjects. The instruction and training is provided by specialized establishments, such as schools, colleges, universities, and training centers.

The subsector is structured according to level and type of educational services. Elementary and secondary schools, junior colleges, and colleges, universities, and professional schools correspond to a recognized series of formal levels of education designated by diplomas, associate degrees (including equivalent certificates), and degrees. The remaining industry groups are based more on the type of instruction or training offered, and the levels are not always as formally defined. The establishments are often highly specialized, many offering instruction in a very limited subject matter, for example ski lessons or one specific computer software application. Within the subsector, the level and types of training that are required of the instructors and teachers vary depending on the industry.

Establishments that manage schools and other educational establishments on a contractual basis are classified in this subsector if they both manage the operation and provide the operating staff. Such establishments are classified in the Educational Services subsector based on the type of facility managed and operated.

Excluded from this subsector are establishments primarily engaged in publishing educational software or other educational materials without providing instruction. These establishments are classified in Subsector 513, Publishing Industries. Establishments that manage schools and other educational establishments on a contract or fee basis without providing the operating staff are classified in Subsector 561, Administrative and Support Services. Establishments primarily engaged in providing vocational rehabilitation services and establishments primarily engaged in providing child care services are classified in Subsector 624, Social Assistance.

### 6111 Elementary and Secondary Schools<sup>T</sup>

### 61111 Elementary and Secondary Schools
See industry description for 611110.

### 611110 Elementary and Secondary Schools

This industry comprises establishments primarily engaged in furnishing academic courses and associated course work that comprise a basic preparatory education. A basic preparatory education ordinarily constitutes kindergarten through 12th grade. This industry includes school boards and school districts.

*Illustrative Examples:*

Elementary schools

Parochial schools, elementary or secondary

---

T—Canadian, Mexican, and United States industries are comparable.

| | |
|---|---|
| High schools | Military academies, elementary or secondary |
| Primary schools | Schools for the physically disabled, elementary or |
| Charter schools | secondary |
| Kindergartens | |

*Cross-References.*

- Establishments primarily engaged in providing care and early learning opportunities for infants and children and also offering pre-kindergarten, kindergarten, and/or before- or after-school educational programs are classified in Industry 624410, Child Care Services; and
- College-level military academies are classified in Industry 611310, Colleges, Universities, and Professional Schools.

**6112    Junior Colleges<sup>T</sup>**

**61121    Junior Colleges<sup>T</sup>**
See industry description for 611210.

**611210  Junior Colleges**

This industry comprises establishments primarily engaged in furnishing academic, or academic and technical, courses and granting associate degrees, certificates, or diplomas below the baccalaureate level.  The requirement for admission to an associate or equivalent degree program is at least a high school diploma or equivalent general academic training.  Instruction may be provided in diverse settings, such as the establishment's or client's training facilities, educational institutions, the workplace, or the home, and through diverse means, such as correspondence, television, the Internet, or other electronic and distance-learning methods.  The training provided by these establishments may include the use of simulators and simulation methods.

*Cross-References.*

Establishments primarily engaged in providing technical training without offering academic courses are classified in Industry 61151, Technical and Trade Schools.

**6113    Colleges, Universities, and Professional Schools<sup>T</sup>**

**61131    Colleges, Universities, and Professional Schools<sup>T</sup>**
See industry description for 611310.

**611310  Colleges, Universities, and Professional Schools**

This industry comprises establishments primarily engaged in furnishing academic courses and granting degrees at baccalaureate or graduate levels.  The requirement for admission is at least a high school diploma or equivalent general academic training.  Instruction may be provided in diverse settings, such as the establishment's or client's training facilities, educational institutions, the workplace, or the home, and through diverse means, such as correspondence, television, the Internet, or other electronic and distance-learning methods.  The training provided by these establishments may include the use of simulators and simulation methods.

*Illustrative Examples:*

| | |
|---|---|
| Colleges (except junior colleges) | Universities |
| Theological seminaries offering baccalaureate or | Professional schools (e.g., business administration, |
| graduate degrees | dental, law, medical) |
| Military academies, college-level | |

---

T—Canadian, Mexican, and United States industries are comparable.

*Cross-References.*

Establishments primarily engaged in furnishing academic, or academic and technical, courses and granting associate degrees, certificates, or diplomas below the baccalaureate level are classified in Industry 611210, Junior Colleges.

**6114    Business Schools and Computer and Management Training$^T$**

This industry group comprises establishments primarily engaged in one of the following: (1) offering courses in office procedures and secretarial and stenographic skills and may offer courses in basic office skills, such as word processing; (2) conducting computer training (except computer repair); or (3) offering an array of short duration courses and seminars for management and professional development. Instruction may be provided in diverse settings, such as the establishment's or client's training facilities, educational institutions, the workplace, or the home, and through diverse means, such as correspondence, television, the Internet, or other electronic and distance-learning methods. The training provided by these establishments may include the use of simulators and simulation methods.

**61141    Business and Secretarial Schools$^T$**
See industry description for 611410.

**611410    Business and Secretarial Schools**

This industry comprises establishments primarily engaged in offering courses in office procedures and secretarial and stenographic skills and may offer courses in basic office skills, such as word processing. In addition, these establishments may offer such classes as office machine operation, reception, communications, and other skills designed for individuals pursuing a clerical or secretarial career. Instruction may be provided in diverse settings, such as the establishment's or client's training facilities, educational institutions, the workplace, or the home, and through diverse means, such as correspondence, television, the Internet, or other electronic and distance-learning methods. The training provided by these establishments may include the use of simulators and simulation methods.

*Cross-References.*        Establishments primarily engaged in--

- Offering computer training (except computer repair)--are classified in Industry 611420, Computer Training;
- Offering academic degrees (e.g., baccalaureate, graduate) in business education--are classified in Industry 611310, Colleges, Universities, and Professional Schools;
- Offering training in the maintenance and repair of computers--are classified in U.S. Industry 611519, Other Technical and Trade Schools; and
- Providing job training for the unemployed, underemployed, disabled, and persons who have a job market disadvantage because of lack of education, job skill, or experience--are classified in Industry 624310, Vocational Rehabilitation Services.

**61142    Computer Training$^T$**
See industry description for 611420.

**611420    Computer Training**

This industry comprises establishments primarily engaged in conducting computer training (except computer repair), such as instruction in computer programming, software applications, computerized business systems, computer electronics technology, computer operations, and local area network management. Instruction may be provided in diverse settings, such as the establishment's or client's training facilities, educational institutions, the workplace, or the home, and through diverse means, such as correspondence, television, the Internet, or other electronic and distance-learning methods. The training provided by these establishments may include the use of simulators and simulation methods.

---

T—Canadian, Mexican, and United States industries are comparable.

*Cross-References.*          Establishments primarily engaged in--

- Offering training in the maintenance and repair of computers--are classified in U.S. Industry 611519, Other Technical and Trade Schools;
- Computer retailing, wholesaling, or computer system designing that may also provide computer training-- are classified in their appropriate industries; and
- Providing job training for the unemployed, underemployed, disabled, and persons who have a job market disadvantage because of lack of education, job skill, or experience--are classified in Industry 624310, Vocational Rehabilitation Services.

**61143    Professional and Management Development Training**[T]
See industry description for 611430.

**611430  Professional and Management Development Training**

This industry comprises establishments primarily engaged in offering an array of short duration courses and seminars for management and professional development. Training for career development may be provided directly to individuals or through employers' training programs, and courses may be customized or modified to meet the special needs of customers. Instruction may be provided in diverse settings, such as the establishment's or client's training facilities, educational institutions, the workplace, or the home, and through diverse means, such as correspondence, television, the Internet, or other electronic and distance-learning methods. The training provided by these establishments may include the use of simulators and simulation methods.

*Cross-References.*          Establishments primarily engaged in--

- Advising clients on management and training issues without providing the training--are classified in Industry Group 5416, Management, Scientific, and Technical Consulting Services;
- Offering computer software training--are classified in Industry 611420, Computer Training;
- Offering academic degrees (e.g., baccalaureate, graduate)--are classified in Industry 611310, Colleges, Universities, and Professional Schools; and
- Publishing software without providing instruction--are classified in Industry 513210, Software Publishers.

**6115    Technical and Trade Schools**[T]

**61151   Technical and Trade Schools**[T]

This industry comprises establishments primarily engaged in offering vocational and technical training in a variety of technical subjects and trades. The training often leads to job-specific certification. Instruction may be provided in diverse settings, such as the establishment's or client's training facilities, educational institutions, the workplace, or the home, and through diverse means, such as correspondence, television, the Internet, or other electronic and distance-learning methods. The training provided by these establishments may include the use of simulators and simulation methods.

*Illustrative Examples:*

| | |
|---|---|
| Apprenticeship training programs | Nursing schools (except academic) |
| Graphic arts schools | Cosmetology schools |
| Aviation and flight training schools | Real estate schools |
| Modeling schools | Electronic equipment repair training |
| Computer repair training | Truck driving schools |

*Cross-References.*       Establishments primarily engaged in--

- Offering courses in office procedures and secretarial and stenographic skills--are classified in Industry 61141, Business and Secretarial Schools;

---

T—Canadian, Mexican, and United States industries are comparable.

- Offering computer training (except computer repair)--are classified in Industry 61142, Computer Training;
- Offering professional and management development training--are classified in Industry 61143, Professional and Management Development Training;
- Offering academic courses that may also offer technical and trade courses--are classified according to the type of school;
- Providing air transportation services that may also provide flight training--are classified in Subsector 481, Air Transportation;
- Offering registered nursing training with academic degrees (e.g., associate, baccalaureate)--are classified in Industry 61121, Junior Colleges, or Industry 61131, Colleges, Universities, and Professional Schools; and
- Providing job training for the unemployed, underemployed, disabled, and persons who have a job market disadvantage because of lack of education, job skill, or experience--are classified in Industry 62431, Vocational Rehabilitation Services.

## 611511 Cosmetology and Barber Schools

This U.S. industry comprises establishments primarily engaged in offering training in barbering, hair styling, or the cosmetic arts, such as makeup or skin care. These schools provide job-specific certification.

## 611512 Flight Training

This U.S. industry comprises establishments primarily engaged in offering aviation and flight training. These establishments may offer vocational training, recreational training, or both.

*Cross-References.* Establishments primarily engaged in--

- Offering specialized military training (except flight instruction, academies, and basic training)--are classified in U.S. Industry 611519, Other Technical and Trade Schools;
- Operating college-level military academies--are classified in Industry 611310, Colleges, Universities, and Professional Schools;
- National security and military basic training (except academies)--are classified in Industry 928110, National Security; and
- Providing air transportation services that may also provide flight training--are classified in Subsector 481, Air Transportation.

## 611513 Apprenticeship Training

This U.S. industry comprises establishments primarily engaged in offering apprenticeship training programs. These programs involve applied training as well as course work.

*Cross-References.*

Establishments primarily engaged in providing job training for the unemployed, underemployed, disabled, and persons who have a job market disadvantage because of lack of education, job skill, or experience are classified in Industry 624310, Vocational Rehabilitation Services.

## 611519 Other Technical and Trade Schools

This U.S. industry comprises establishments primarily engaged in offering job or career vocational or technical courses (except cosmetology and barber training, aviation and flight training, and apprenticeship training). The curriculums offered by these schools are highly structured and specialized and lead to job-specific certification.

*Illustrative Examples:*

Bartending schools
Modeling schools

Broadcasting schools
Real estate schools

---

T—Canadian, Mexican, and United States industries are comparable.

Computer repair training
Truck driving schools
Graphic arts schools

Specialized military training (except flight instruction, academies, and basic training)

*Cross-References.*      Establishments primarily engaged in--

- Offering courses in office procedures and secretarial and stenographic skills--are classified in Industry 611410, Business and Secretarial Schools;
- Offering computer training (except computer repair)--are classified in Industry 611420, Computer Training;
- Offering professional and management development training--are classified in Industry 611430, Professional and Management Development Training;
- Offering registered nursing training with academic degrees (e.g., associate, baccalaureate)--are classified in Industry 611210, Junior Colleges, or Industry 611310, College, Universities, and Professional Schools;
- Offering aviation and flight training, including military flight instruction--are classified in U.S. Industry 611512, Flight Training;
- Operating college-level military academies--are classified in Industry 611310, Colleges, Universities, and Professional Schools;
- National security and military basic training (except academies)--are classified in Industry 928110, National Security;
- Offering cosmetology and barber training--are classified in U.S. Industry 611511, Cosmetology and Barber Schools;
- Offering academic courses that may also offer technical and trade courses--are classified according to the type of school;
- Offering apprenticeship training programs--are classified in U.S. Industry 611513, Apprenticeship Training; and
- Providing job training for the unemployed, underemployed, disabled, and persons who have a job market disadvantage because of lack of education, job skill, or experience--are classified in Industry 624310, Vocational Rehabilitation Services.

## 6116    Other Schools and Instruction[T]

This industry group comprises establishments primarily engaged in offering or providing instruction (except academic schools, colleges, and universities; business, computer, and management instruction; and technical and trade instruction). Instruction may be provided in diverse settings, such as the establishment's or client's training facilities, educational institutions, the workplace, or the home, and through diverse means, such as correspondence, television, the Internet, or other electronic and distance-learning methods. The training provided by these establishments may include the use of simulators and simulation methods.

### 61161    Fine Arts Schools[T]
See industry description for 611610.

### 611610  Fine Arts Schools

This industry comprises establishments primarily engaged in offering instruction in the arts, including dance, art, drama, and music.

*Illustrative Examples:*

Art (except commercial and graphic) instruction
Music instruction (e.g., piano, guitar)
Dance instruction
Music schools (except academic)
Dance studios

Performing arts schools (except academic)
Drama schools (except academic)
Photography schools (except commercial photography)
Fine arts schools (except academic)

---

T—Canadian, Mexican, and United States industries are comparable.

*Cross-References.*

- Establishments offering high school diplomas or academic degrees (i.e., even if they specialize in fine arts) are classified elsewhere in this subsector according to the type of school; and
- Establishments primarily engaged in offering courses in commercial and graphic arts and commercial photography are classified in U.S. Industry 611519, Other Technical and Trade Schools.

**61162   Sports and Recreation Instruction**[T]
See industry description for 611620.

**611620   Sports and Recreation Instruction**

This industry comprises establishments, such as camps and schools, primarily engaged in offering instruction in athletic activities.  Overnight and day sports instruction camps are included in this industry.

*Illustrative Examples:*

| | |
|---|---|
| Camps, sports instruction | Gymnastics instruction |
| Professional sports instructors (i.e., not participating in sporting events) | Sports (e.g., baseball, basketball, football, golf) instruction |
| Cheerleading instruction | Martial arts instruction, camps or schools |
| Riding instruction academies or schools | Swimming instruction |

*Cross-References.*

- Establishments primarily engaged in operating overnight recreational camps that may offer some athletic instruction in addition to other activities are classified in U.S. Industry 721214, Recreational and Vacation Camps (except Campgrounds);
- Establishments primarily engaged in operating sports and recreation establishments that also offer athletic instruction are classified in Sector 71, Arts, Entertainment, and Recreation;
- Independent (i.e., freelance) athletes engaged in providing sports instruction and participating in spectator sporting events are classified in U.S. Industry 711219, Other Spectator Sports;
- Establishments primarily engaged in offering academic courses that may also offer athletic instruction are classified according to the type of school; and
- Establishments primarily engaged in providing personal fitness training services without operating physical fitness centers are classified in Industry 812990, All Other Personal Services.

**61163   Language Schools**[T]
See industry description for 611630.

**611630   Language Schools**

This industry comprises establishments primarily engaged in offering foreign language instruction (including sign language).  These establishments are designed to offer language instruction ranging from conversational skills for personal enrichment to intensive training courses for career or educational opportunities.

*Cross-References.*          Establishments primarily engaged in--

- Offering academic courses that may also offer language instruction--are classified according to type of school; and
- Providing translation and interpretation services--are classified in Industry 541930, Translation and Interpretation Services.

---

T—Canadian, Mexican, and United States industries are comparable.

## 61169    All Other Schools and Instruction[T]

This industry comprises establishments primarily engaged in offering instruction (except academic schools, colleges, and universities; business, computer, and management instruction; technical and trade instruction; and fine arts, sports, recreation, and language instruction).

*Illustrative Examples:*

Academic tutoring services
Public speaking training
Automobile driving schools

Speed reading instruction
Exam preparation services

*Cross-References.*          Establishments primarily engaged in--

- Offering elementary and secondary school instruction--are classified in Industry 61111, Elementary and Secondary Schools;
- Offering junior college instruction--are classified in Industry 61121, Junior Colleges;
- Offering college, university, and professional school instruction with academic degrees (e.g., baccalaureate, graduate)--are classified in Industry 61131, Colleges, Universities, and Professional Schools;
- Offering business, computer (except computer repair), and management training--are classified in Industry Group 6114, Business Schools and Computer and Management Training;
- Offering vocational and technical instruction (e.g., computer repair and maintenance)--are classified in Industry 61151, Technical and Trade Schools;
- Offering fine arts instruction--are classified in Industry 61161, Fine Arts Schools;
- Offering sports and recreation instruction--are classified in Industry 61162, Sports and Recreation Instruction; and
- Offering language instruction--are classified in Industry 61163, Language Schools.

## 611691  Exam Preparation and Tutoring

This U.S. industry comprises establishments primarily engaged in offering preparation for standardized examinations and/or academic tutoring services.

*Illustrative Examples:*

Academic tutoring services
Learning centers offering remedial courses

College board preparation centers
Professional examination review instruction

## 611692  Automobile Driving Schools

This U.S. industry comprises establishments primarily engaged in offering automobile driving instruction.

*Cross-References.*

Establishments primarily engaged in offering truck and bus driving instruction are classified in U.S. Industry 611519, Other Technical and Trade Schools.

## 611699  All Other Miscellaneous Schools and Instruction

This U.S. industry comprises establishments primarily engaged in offering instruction (except academic schools, colleges, and universities; business, computer, and management instruction; technical and trade instruction; and fine arts, sports, recreation, language, exam preparation, tutoring, and automobile driving instruction).

---

T—Canadian, Mexican, and United States industries are comparable.

*Illustrative Examples:*

Public speaking training                                    Speed reading instruction
Survival training                                           Yoga instruction, camps or schools

*Cross-References.*          Establishments primarily engaged in--

- Offering elementary and secondary school instruction--are classified in Industry 611110, Elementary and Secondary Schools;
- Offering junior college instruction--are classified in Industry 611210, Junior Colleges;
- Offering college, university, and professional school instruction with academic degrees (e.g., baccalaureate, graduate)--are classified in Industry 611310, Colleges, Universities, and Professional Schools;
- Offering business, computer (except computer repair), and management training--are classified in Industry Group 6114, Business Schools and Computer and Management Training;
- Offering vocational and technical instruction (e.g., computer repair and maintenance)--are classified in Industry 61151, Technical and Trade Schools;
- Offering fine arts instruction--are classified in Industry 611610, Fine Arts Schools;
- Offering sports and recreation instruction--are classified in Industry 611620, Sports and Recreation Instruction;
- Offering language instruction--are classified in Industry 611630, Language Schools;
- Offering exam preparation and tutoring services--are classified in U.S. Industry 611691, Exam Preparation and Tutoring; and
- Offering automobile driving instruction--are classified in U.S. Industry 611692, Automobile Driving Schools.

## 6117    Educational Support Services[T]

## 61171    Educational Support Services[T]
See industry description for 611710.

## 611710    Educational Support Services

  This industry comprises establishments primarily engaged in providing non-instructional services that support educational processes or systems.

*Illustrative Examples:*

Educational consultants                                     Student exchange programs
Educational testing services                               Educational testing evaluation services
Educational guidance counseling services

*Cross-References.*          Establishments primarily engaged in--

- Providing job training for the unemployed, underemployed, physically disabled, and persons who have a job market disadvantage because of lack of education or job skills--are classified in Industry 624310, Vocational Rehabilitation Services;
- Conducting research and analyses in cognitive development--are classified in Industry 541720, Research and Development in the Social Sciences and Humanities; and
- Publishing educational materials, including educational tests and assessments, and known as publishers-- are classified in Subsector 513, Publishing Industries.

---

T—Canadian, Mexican, and United States industries are comparable.

# Sector 62--Health Care and Social Assistance[T]

## The Sector as a Whole

The Health Care and Social Assistance sector comprises establishments providing health care and social assistance for individuals. The sector includes both health care and social assistance because it is sometimes difficult to distinguish between the boundaries of these two activities. The industries in this sector are arranged on a continuum starting with establishments providing medical care exclusively, continuing with those providing health care and social assistance, and finally finishing with those providing only social assistance. Establishments in this sector deliver services by trained professionals. All industries in the sector share this commonality of process, namely, labor inputs of health practitioners or social workers with the requisite expertise. Many of the industries in the sector are defined based on the educational degree held by the practitioners included in the industry.

Excluded from this sector are yoga and aerobics instruction in Subsector 611, Educational Services, physical fitness facilities in Subsector 713, Amusement, Gambling, and Recreation Industries, and personal fitness training services and non-medical diet and weight reducing centers in Subsector 812, Personal and Laundry Services. Although these can be viewed as health services, these services are not typically delivered by health practitioners.

## 621    Ambulatory Health Care Services[T]

Industries in the Ambulatory Health Care Services subsector provide health care services directly or indirectly to ambulatory patients and do not usually provide inpatient services. Health practitioners in this subsector provide outpatient services, with the facilities and equipment not usually being the most significant part of the production process.

## 6211    Offices of Physicians[T]

## 62111    Offices of Physicians[T]

This industry comprises establishments of health practitioners having the degree of M.D. (Doctor of Medicine) or D.O. (Doctor of Osteopathic Medicine) primarily engaged in the independent practice of general or specialized medicine (e.g., anesthesiology, oncology, ophthalmology, psychiatry) or surgery. These practitioners operate private or group practices in their own offices (e.g., centers, clinics) or in the facilities of others, such as hospitals or HMO medical centers.

*Cross-References.*

- Health maintenance organization (HMO) medical centers; freestanding medical centers primarily engaged in providing emergency medical care for accident or trauma victims and freestanding ambulatory surgical centers primarily engaged in providing surgery on an outpatient basis; and outpatient community health clinics with health practitioners from multiple industries are classified in Industry 62149, Other Outpatient Care Centers;
- Establishments of oral pathologists are classified in Industry 62121, Offices of Dentists;
- Establishments of independent mental health practitioners (except physicians) are classified in Industry 62133, Offices of Mental Health Practitioners (except Physicians);
- Establishments of speech or voice pathologists are classified in Industry 62134, Offices of Physical, Occupational and Speech Therapists, and Audiologists;
- Outpatient mental health and substance abuse centers are classified in Industry 62142, Outpatient Mental Health and Substance Abuse Centers; and
- Establishments primarily engaged in providing nonresidential counseling services for substance abuse, mental health, suicide intervention, and other crisis intervention social services to children and youth, the elderly, persons with disabilities, and all other individuals and families are classified in Industry Group 6241, Individual and Family Services.

---

T—Canadian, Mexican, and United States industries are comparable.

### 621111  Offices of Physicians (except Mental Health Specialists)

This U.S. industry comprises establishments of health practitioners having the degree of M.D. (Doctor of Medicine) or D.O. (Doctor of Osteopathic Medicine) primarily engaged in the independent practice of general or specialized medicine (except psychiatry or psychoanalysis) or surgery. These practitioners operate private or group practices in their own offices (e.g., centers, clinics) or in the facilities of others, such as hospitals or HMO medical centers.

*Cross-References.*

- Establishments of physicians primarily engaged in the independent practice of psychiatry or psychoanalysis are classified in U.S. Industry 621112, Offices of Physicians, Mental Health Specialists;
- Freestanding medical centers primarily engaged in providing emergency medical care for accident or trauma victims and freestanding ambulatory surgical centers primarily engaged in providing surgery on an outpatient basis are classified in U.S. Industry 621493, Freestanding Ambulatory Surgical and Emergency Centers;
- Health maintenance organization (HMO) medical centers are classified in U.S. Industry 621491, HMO Medical Centers;
- Outpatient community health clinics with health practitioners from multiple industries are classified in U.S. Industry 621498, All Other Outpatient Care Centers;
- Establishments of oral pathologists are classified in Industry 621210, Offices of Dentists; and
- Establishments of speech or voice pathologists are classified in Industry 621340, Offices of Physical, Occupational and Speech Therapists, and Audiologists.

### 621112  Offices of Physicians, Mental Health Specialists

This U.S. industry comprises establishments of health practitioners having the degree of M.D. (Doctor of Medicine) or D.O. (Doctor of Osteopathic Medicine) primarily engaged in the independent practice of psychiatry or psychoanalysis. These practitioners operate private or group practices in their own offices (e.g., centers, clinics) or in the facilities of others, such as hospitals or HMO medical centers.

*Cross-References.*

- Establishments of independent mental health practitioners (except physicians) are classified in Industry 621330, Offices of Mental Health Practitioners (except Physicians);
- Outpatient mental health and substance abuse centers are classified in Industry 621420, Outpatient Mental Health and Substance Abuse Centers; and
- Establishments primarily engaged in providing nonresidential counseling services for substance abuse, mental health, suicide intervention, and other crisis intervention social services to children and youth, the elderly, persons with disabilities, and all other individuals and families are classified in Industry Group 6241, Individual and Family Services.

### 6212  Offices of Dentists<sup>T</sup>

### 62121  Offices of Dentists<sup>T</sup>
See industry description for 621210.

### 621210  Offices of Dentists

This industry comprises establishments of health practitioners having the degree of D.M.D. (Doctor of Dental Medicine), D.D.S. (Doctor of Dental Surgery), or D.D.Sc. (Doctor of Dental Science) primarily engaged in the independent practice of general or specialized dentistry or dental surgery. These practitioners operate private or group practices in their own offices (e.g., centers, clinics) or in the facilities of others, such as hospitals or HMO medical centers. They can provide either comprehensive preventive, cosmetic, or emergency care, or specialize in a single field of dentistry.

---

T—Canadian, Mexican, and United States industries are comparable.

*Cross-References.*

- Establishments known as dental laboratories primarily engaged in making dentures, artificial teeth, and orthodontic appliances to order for dentists are classified in U.S. Industry 339116, Dental Laboratories;
- Establishments of dental hygienists primarily engaged in cleaning teeth and gums or establishments of denturists primarily engaged in taking impressions for and fitting dentures are classified in U.S. Industry 621399, Offices of All Other Miscellaneous Health Practitioners; and
- Outpatient community health clinics with health practitioners from multiple industries are classified in U.S. Industry 621498, All Other Outpatient Care Centers.

## 6213 Offices of Other Health Practitioners[T]

This industry group comprises establishments of independent health practitioners (except physicians and dentists).

### 62131 Offices of Chiropractors[T]
See industry description for 621310.

### 621310 Offices of Chiropractors

This industry comprises establishments of health practitioners having the degree of D.C. (Doctor of Chiropractic) primarily engaged in the independent practice of chiropractic. These practitioners provide diagnostic and therapeutic treatment of neuromusculoskeletal and related disorders through the manipulation and adjustment of the spinal column and extremities, and operate private or group practices in their own offices (e.g., centers, clinics) or in the facilities of others, such as hospitals or HMO medical centers.

### 62132 Offices of Optometrists[T]
See industry description for 621320.

### 621320 Offices of Optometrists

This industry comprises establishments of health practitioners having the degree of O.D. (Doctor of Optometry) primarily engaged in the independent practice of optometry. These practitioners examine, diagnose, treat, and manage diseases and disorders of the visual system, the eye, and associated structures as well as diagnose related systemic conditions. Offices of optometrists prescribe and/or provide eyeglasses, contact lenses, low vision aids, and vision therapy. They operate private or group practices in their own offices (e.g., centers, clinics) or in the facilities of others, such as hospitals or HMO medical centers, and may also provide the same services as opticians, such as selling and fitting prescription eyeglasses and contact lenses.

*Cross-References.*

- Offices of opticians primarily engaged in selling and fitting prescription eyeglasses and contact lenses are classified in Industry 456130, Optical Goods Retailers; and
- Offices of physicians primarily engaged in the independent practice of ophthalmology are classified in U.S. Industry 621111, Offices of Physicians (except Mental Health Specialists).

### 62133 Offices of Mental Health Practitioners (except Physicians)[T]
See industry description for 621330.

### 621330 Offices of Mental Health Practitioners (except Physicians)

This industry comprises establishments of independent mental health practitioners (except physicians) primarily engaged in (1) the diagnosis and treatment of mental, emotional, and behavioral disorders and/or (2) the diagnosis and treatment of individual or group social dysfunction brought about by such causes as mental illness, alcohol and substance abuse, physical and emotional trauma, or stress. These practitioners operate private or group practices in their own offices (e.g., centers, clinics) or in the facilities of others, such as hospitals or HMO medical centers.

T—Canadian, Mexican, and United States industries are comparable.

*Cross-References.*

- Establishments of psychiatrists, psychoanalysts, and psychotherapists having the degree of M.D. (Doctor of Medicine) or D.O. (Doctor of Osteopathic Medicine) are classified in U.S. Industry 621112, Offices of Physicians, Mental Health Specialists;
- Outpatient mental health and substance abuse centers are classified in Industry 621420, Outpatient Mental Health and Substance Abuse Centers; and
- Establishments primarily engaged in providing nonresidential counseling services for substance abuse, mental health, suicide intervention, and other crisis intervention social services to children and youth, the elderly, persons with disabilities, and all other individuals and families are classified in Industry Group 6241, Individual and Family Services.

### 62134   Offices of Physical, Occupational and Speech Therapists, and Audiologists[T]

See industry description for 621340.

### 621340   Offices of Physical, Occupational and Speech Therapists, and Audiologists

This industry comprises establishments of independent health practitioners primarily engaged in one of the following: (1) providing physical therapy services to patients who have impairments, functional limitations, disabilities, or changes in physical functions and health status resulting from injury, disease or other causes, or who require prevention, wellness or fitness services; (2) planning and administering educational, recreational, and social activities designed to help patients or individuals with disabilities regain physical or mental functioning or adapt to their disabilities; and (3) diagnosing and treating speech, language, or hearing problems. These practitioners operate private or group practices in their own offices (e.g., centers, clinics) or in the facilities of others, such as hospitals or HMO medical centers.

*Illustrative Examples:*

Audiologists' offices
Recreational (e.g., art, dance, music) therapists' offices
Industrial therapists' offices

Speech pathologists' offices
Occupational therapists' offices
Physical therapists' offices

*Cross-References.*

Establishments primarily engaged in providing skilled nursing services in the home are classified in Industry 621610, Home Health Care Services.

### 62139   Offices of All Other Health Practitioners[T]

This industry comprises establishments of independent health practitioners (except physicians; dentists; chiropractors; optometrists; mental health specialists; physical, occupational, and speech therapists; and audiologists). These practitioners operate private or group practices in their own offices (e.g., centers, clinics) or in the facilities of others, such as hospitals or HMO medical centers.

*Illustrative Examples:*

Acupuncturists' (except MDs or DOs) offices
Inhalation or respiratory therapists' offices
Dental hygienists' offices
Midwives' offices
Denturists' offices

Naturopaths' offices
Dietitians' offices
Podiatrists' offices
Homeopaths' offices
Registered or licensed practical nurses' offices

---

T—Canadian, Mexican, and United States industries are comparable.

*Cross-References.*        Establishments primarily engaged in--

- The independent practice of medicine (i.e., physicians)--are classified in Industry 62111, Offices of Physicians;
- The independent practice of dentistry--are classified in Industry 62121, Offices of Dentists;
- The independent practice of chiropractic--are classified in Industry 62131, Offices of Chiropractors;
- The independent practice of optometry--are classified in Industry 62132, Offices of Optometrists;
- The independent practice of mental health (except physicians)--are classified in Industry 62133, Offices of Mental Health Practitioners (except Physicians);
- The independent practice of physical, occupational, and speech therapy, and audiology--are classified in Industry 62134, Offices of Physical, Occupational and Speech Therapists, and Audiologists; and
- Operating outpatient community health clinics with health practitioners from multiple industries--are classified in Industry 62149, Other Outpatient Care Centers.

## 621391  Offices of Podiatrists

This U.S. industry comprises establishments of health practitioners having the degree of D.P.M. (Doctor of Podiatric Medicine) primarily engaged in the independent practice of podiatry.  These practitioners diagnose and treat diseases and deformities of the foot and operate private or group practices in their own offices (e.g., centers, clinics) or in the facilities of others, such as hospitals or HMO medical centers.

*Cross-References.*

Establishments primarily engaged in the independent practice of orthotics or prosthetics are classified in U.S. Industry 621399, Offices of All Other Miscellaneous Health Practitioners.

## 621399  Offices of All Other Miscellaneous Health Practitioners

This U.S. industry comprises establishments of independent health practitioners (except physicians; dentists; chiropractors; optometrists; mental health specialists; physical, occupational, and speech therapists; audiologists; and podiatrists).  These practitioners operate private or group practices in their own offices (e.g., centers, clinics) or in the facilities of others, such as hospitals or HMO medical centers.

*Illustrative Examples*:

| | |
|---|---|
| Acupuncturists' (except MDs or DOs) offices | Midwives' offices |
| Hypnotherapists' offices | Dietitians' offices |
| Dental hygienists' offices | Naturopaths' offices |
| Inhalation or respiratory therapists' offices | Homeopaths' offices |
| Denturists' offices | Registered or licensed practical nurses' offices |

*Cross-References.*        Establishments primarily engaged in--

- The independent practice of medicine (i.e., physicians)--are classified in Industry 62111, Offices of Physicians;
- The independent practice of dentistry--are classified in Industry 621210, Offices of Dentists;
- The independent practice of chiropractic--are classified in Industry 621310, Offices of Chiropractors;
- The independent practice of optometry--are classified in Industry 621320, Offices of Optometrists;
- The independent practice of mental health (except physicians)--are classified in Industry 621330, Offices of Mental Health Practitioners (except Physicians);
- The independent practice of physical, occupational, and speech therapy, and audiology--are classified in Industry 621340, Offices of Physical, Occupational and Speech Therapists, and Audiologists;
- The independent practice of podiatry--are classified in U.S. Industry 621391, Offices of Podiatrists; and
- Operating outpatient community health clinics with health practitioners from multiple industries--are classified in U.S. Industry 621498, All Other Outpatient Care Centers.

T—Canadian, Mexican, and United States industries are comparable.

**6214    Outpatient Care Centers**[T]

This industry group comprises establishments with medical staff primarily engaged in providing a range of outpatient services, such as family planning, diagnosis and treatment of mental health disorders and alcohol and other substance abuse, and other general or specialized outpatient care.

**62141    Family Planning Centers**[T]
See industry description for 621410.

**621410  Family Planning Centers**

This industry comprises establishments with medical staff primarily engaged in providing a range of family planning services on an outpatient basis, such as contraceptive services, genetic and prenatal counseling, voluntary sterilization, and therapeutic and medically induced termination of pregnancy.

*Illustrative Examples:*

Birth control clinics
Fertility clinics

Childbirth preparation classes
Pregnancy counseling centers

**62142    Outpatient Mental Health and Substance Abuse Centers**[T]
See industry description for 621420.

**621420  Outpatient Mental Health and Substance Abuse Centers**

This industry comprises establishments with medical staff primarily engaged in providing outpatient services related to the diagnosis and treatment of mental health disorders and alcohol and other substance abuse. These establishments generally treat patients who do not require inpatient treatment. They may provide a counseling staff and information regarding a wide range of mental health and substance abuse issues and/or refer patients to more extensive treatment programs, if necessary.

*Illustrative Examples*:

Outpatient alcoholism treatment centers and clinics (except hospitals)
Outpatient mental health centers and clinics (except hospitals)
Outpatient detoxification centers and clinics (except hospitals)

Outpatient substance abuse treatment centers and clinics (except hospitals)
Outpatient drug addiction treatment centers and clinics (except hospitals)

*Cross-References.*

- Establishments known and licensed as hospitals primarily engaged in the inpatient treatment of mental health and substance abuse illnesses with an emphasis on medical treatment and monitoring are classified in Industry 622210, Psychiatric and Substance Abuse Hospitals;
- Establishments primarily engaged in the inpatient treatment of mental health and substance abuse illnesses with an emphasis on residential care and counseling rather than medical treatment are classified in Industry 623220, Residential Mental Health and Substance Abuse Facilities;
- Establishments of physicians primarily engaged in the independent practice of psychiatry or psychoanalysis are classified in U.S. Industry 621112, Offices of Physicians, Mental Health Specialists;
- Establishments of independent mental health practitioners (except physicians) are classified in Industry 621330, Offices of Mental Health Practitioners (except Physicians); and
- Establishments primarily engaged in providing nonresidential counseling services for substance abuse, mental health, suicide intervention, and other crisis intervention social services to children and youth, the

T—Canadian, Mexican, and United States industries are comparable.

elderly, persons with disabilities, and all other individuals and families are classified in Industry Group 6241, Individual and Family Services.

## 62149 Other Outpatient Care Centers[T]

This industry comprises establishments with medical staff primarily engaged in providing general or specialized outpatient care (except family planning centers and outpatient mental health and substance abuse centers). Centers or clinics of health practitioners with different degrees from more than one industry practicing within the same establishment (e.g., Doctor of Medicine and Doctor of Dental Medicine) are included in this industry.

*Illustrative Examples:*

Dialysis centers and clinics
Outpatient biofeedback centers and clinics
Freestanding ambulatory surgical centers and clinics
Outpatient community health centers and clinics

Freestanding emergency medical centers and clinics
Outpatient sleep disorder centers and clinics
Health maintenance organization (HMO) medical centers and clinics

*Cross-References.*

- Centers and clinics of health practitioners from the same industry primarily engaged in the independent practice of their profession are classified in Industry 62111, Offices of Physicians; Industry 62121, Offices of Dentists; and Industry Group 6213, Offices of Other Health Practitioners;
- Family planning centers are classified in Industry 62141, Family Planning Centers;
- Outpatient mental health and substance abuse centers are classified in Industry 62142, Outpatient Mental Health and Substance Abuse Centers;
- HMO establishments (except those providing health care services) primarily engaged in underwriting health and medical insurance policies are classified in Industry 52411, Direct Life, Health, and Medical Insurance Carriers; and
- Establishments known and licensed as hospitals that also perform ambulatory surgery and emergency room services are classified in Subsector 622, Hospitals.

## 621491 HMO Medical Centers

This U.S. industry comprises establishments with physicians and other medical staff primarily engaged in providing a range of outpatient medical services to the health maintenance organization (HMO) subscribers with a focus generally on primary health care. These establishments are owned by the HMO. Included in this industry are HMO establishments that both provide health care services and underwrite health and medical insurance policies.

*Cross-References.*

- Health practitioners or health practitioner groups contracting to provide their services to subscribers of pre-paid health plans are classified in Industry 62111, Offices of Physicians; Industry 621210, Offices of Dentists; and Industry Group 6213, Offices of Other Health Practitioners; and
- HMO establishments (except those providing health care services) primarily engaged in underwriting and administering health and medical insurance policies are classified in U.S. Industry 524114, Direct Health and Medical Insurance Carriers.

## 621492 Kidney Dialysis Centers

This U.S. industry comprises establishments with medical staff primarily engaged in providing outpatient kidney or renal dialysis services.

---

T—Canadian, Mexican, and United States industries are comparable.

**621493 Freestanding Ambulatory Surgical and Emergency Centers**

This U.S. industry comprises establishments with physicians and other medical staff primarily engaged in (1) providing surgical services (e.g., orthoscopic and cataract surgery) on an outpatient basis or (2) providing emergency care services (e.g., setting broken bones, treating lacerations, or tending to patients suffering injuries as a result of accidents, trauma, or medical conditions necessitating immediate medical care) on an outpatient basis. Outpatient surgical establishments have specialized facilities, such as operating and recovery rooms, and specialized equipment, such as anesthetic or X-ray equipment.

*Illustrative Examples*:

Freestanding ambulatory surgical centers and clinics
Freestanding emergency medical centers and clinics
Freestanding trauma centers (except hospitals)

Urgent medical care centers and clinics (except hospitals)

*Cross-References.*

- Outpatient community health clinics with health practitioners from multiple industries are classified in U.S. Industry 621498, All Other Outpatient Care Centers; and
- Establishments known and licensed as hospitals that also perform ambulatory surgery and emergency room services are classified in Subsector 622, Hospitals.

**621498 All Other Outpatient Care Centers**

This U.S. industry comprises establishments with medical staff primarily engaged in providing general or specialized outpatient care (except family planning centers, outpatient mental health and substance abuse centers, HMO medical centers, kidney dialysis centers, and freestanding ambulatory surgical and emergency centers). Centers or clinics of health practitioners with different degrees from more than one industry practicing within the same establishment (e.g., Doctor of Medicine and Doctor of Dental Medicine) are included in this industry.

*Illustrative Examples:*

Outpatient biofeedback centers and clinics
Outpatient pain therapy centers and clinics

Outpatient community health centers and clinics
Outpatient sleep disorder centers and clinics

*Cross-References.*

- Centers and clinics of health practitioners from the same industry primarily engaged in the independent practice of their profession are classified in Industry 62111, Offices of Physicians; Industry 621210, Offices of Dentists; and Industry Group 6213, Offices of Other Health Practitioners;
- Family planning centers are classified in Industry 621410, Family Planning Centers;
- Outpatient mental health and substance abuse centers are classified in Industry 621420, Outpatient Mental Health and Substance Abuse Centers;
- HMO medical centers are classified in U.S. Industry 621491, HMO Medical Centers;
- Dialysis centers are classified in U.S. Industry 621492, Kidney Dialysis Centers; and
- Freestanding ambulatory surgical and emergency centers are classified in U.S. Industry 621493, Freestanding Ambulatory Surgical and Emergency Centers.

**6215 Medical and Diagnostic Laboratories[T]**

**62151 Medical and Diagnostic Laboratories[T]**

This industry comprises establishments known as medical and diagnostic laboratories primarily engaged in providing analytic or diagnostic services, including body fluid analysis and diagnostic imaging, generally to the medical profession or to the patient on referral from a health practitioner.

T—Canadian, Mexican, and United States industries are comparable.

*Illustrative Examples*:

Dental or medical X-ray laboratories          Medical testing laboratories
Medical pathology laboratories                Medical forensic laboratories
Diagnostic imaging centers

*Cross-References.*

- Establishments, such as dental, optical, and orthopedic laboratories, primarily engaged in providing the following activities to the medical profession, respectively: making dentures, artificial teeth, and orthodontic appliances to prescription; grinding lenses to prescription; and making orthopedic or prosthetic appliances to prescription are classified in Industry 33911, Medical Equipment and Supplies Manufacturing; and
- Establishments primarily engaged in providing health screening or physical fitness evaluation services (except by offices of health practitioners) are classified in Industry 62199, All Other Ambulatory Health Care Services.

## 621511  Medical Laboratories

This U.S. industry comprises establishments known as medical laboratories primarily engaged in providing analytic or diagnostic services, including body fluid analysis, generally to the medical profession or to the patient on referral from a health practitioner.

*Illustrative Examples:*

Blood analysis laboratories                   Medical testing laboratories
Medical pathology laboratories                Medical forensic laboratories
Medical bacteriological laboratories

*Cross-References.*

- Establishments known as dental laboratories primarily engaged in making dentures, artificial teeth, and orthodontic appliances to prescription are classified in U.S. Industry 339116, Dental Laboratories;
- Establishments known as optical laboratories primarily engaged in grinding lenses to prescription are classified in U.S. Industry 339115, Ophthalmic Goods Manufacturing;
- Establishments known as orthopedic laboratories primarily engaged in making orthopedic or prosthetic appliances to prescription are classified in U.S. Industry 339113, Surgical Appliance and Supplies Manufacturing; and
- Establishments primarily engaged in providing health screening or physical fitness evaluation services (except by offices of health practitioners) are classified in U.S. Industry 621999, All Other Miscellaneous Ambulatory Health Care Services.

## 621512  Diagnostic Imaging Centers

This U.S. industry comprises establishments known as diagnostic imaging centers primarily engaged in producing images of the patient generally on referral from a health practitioner.

*Illustrative Examples:*

Computer tomography (CT-scan) centers         Ultrasound imaging centers
Medical radiological laboratories             Magnetic resonance imaging (MRI) centers
Dental or medical X-ray laboratories

---

T—Canadian, Mexican, and United States industries are comparable.

**6216    Home Health Care Services**<sup>T</sup>

**62161    Home Health Care Services**<sup>T</sup>
See industry description for 621610.

**621610  Home Health Care Services**

This industry comprises establishments primarily engaged in providing skilled nursing services in the home, along with a range of the following: personal care services; homemaker and companion services; physical therapy; medical social services; medications; medical equipment and supplies; counseling; 24-hour home care; occupation and vocational therapy; dietary and nutritional services; speech therapy; audiology; and high-tech care, such as intravenous therapy.

*Illustrative Examples*:

Home health care agencies                    Home infusion therapy services
Visiting nurse associations                   In-home hospice care services

*Cross-References.*

- In-home health services provided by establishments of health practitioners and others primarily engaged in the independent practice of their profession are classified in Industry 62111, Offices of Physicians; Industry 621210, Offices of Dentists; Industry Group 6213, Offices of Other Health Practitioners; and U.S. Industry 621999, All Other Miscellaneous Ambulatory Health Care Services;
- Establishments primarily engaged in providing non-medical home care or homemaker services for the elderly or persons with disabilities are classified in Industry 624120, Services for the Elderly and Persons with Disabilities;
- Establishments primarily engaged in renting or leasing products for home health care are classified in U.S. Industry 532283, Home Health Equipment Rental; and
- Establishments primarily engaged in retailing home health care equipment are classified in U.S. Industry 456199, All Other Health and Personal Care Retailers.

**6219    Other Ambulatory Health Care Services**<sup>T</sup>

This industry group comprises establishments primarily engaged in providing ambulatory health care services (except offices of physicians, dentists, and other health practitioners; outpatient care centers; medical laboratories and diagnostic imaging centers; and home health care providers).

**62191    Ambulance Services**<sup>T</sup>
See industry description for 621910.

**621910  Ambulance Services**

This industry comprises establishments primarily engaged in providing transportation of patients by ground or air, along with medical care. These services are often provided during a medical emergency but are not restricted to emergencies. The vehicles are equipped with lifesaving equipment operated by medically trained personnel.

*Cross-References.*

Establishments primarily engaged in providing transportation of the disabled or elderly (without medical care) are classified in U.S. Industry 485991, Special Needs Transportation.

## 62199 All Other Ambulatory Health Care Services[T]

This industry comprises establishments primarily engaged in providing ambulatory health care services (except offices of physicians, dentists, and other health practitioners; outpatient care centers; medical and diagnostic laboratories; home health care providers; and ambulances).

*Illustrative Examples:*

Blood donor stations
Pacemaker monitoring services
Blood or body organ banks
Physical fitness evaluation services (except by offices of health practitioners)

Health screening services (except by offices of health practitioners)
Smoking cessation programs
Hearing testing services (except by offices of audiologists)

*Cross-References.*

- Establishments primarily engaged in the independent practice of medicine are classified in Industry 62111, Offices of Physicians;
- Establishments primarily engaged in the independent practice of dentistry are classified in Industry 62121, Offices of Dentists;
- Establishments primarily engaged in the independent practice of health care (except offices of physicians and dentists) are classified in Industry Group 6213, Offices of Other Health Practitioners;
- Establishments primarily engaged in providing general or specialized outpatient care services are classified in Industry Group 6214, Outpatient Care Centers;
- Establishments primarily engaged in providing home health care services are classified in Industry 62161, Home Health Care Services;
- Establishments primarily engaged in transportation of patients by ground or air, along with medical care, are classified in Industry 62191, Ambulance Services;
- Establishments known as medical and diagnostic laboratories primarily engaged in providing analytic or diagnostic services are classified in Industry 62151, Medical and Diagnostic Laboratories; and
- Establishments primarily engaged in providing courier and express delivery services for blood, blood products, and body organs without storage are classified in Industry 49211, Couriers and Express Delivery Services.

## 621991 Blood and Organ Banks

This U.S. industry comprises establishments primarily engaged in collecting, storing, and distributing blood and blood products and storing and distributing body organs.

*Cross-References.*

Establishments primarily engaged in providing courier and express delivery services for blood, blood products, and body organs without storage are classified in Industry 492110, Couriers and Express Delivery Services.

## 621999 All Other Miscellaneous Ambulatory Health Care Services

This U.S. industry comprises establishments primarily engaged in providing ambulatory health care services (except offices of physicians, dentists, and other health practitioners; outpatient care centers; medical and diagnostic laboratories; home health care providers; ambulances; and blood and organ banks).

*Illustrative Examples*:

Health screening services (except by offices of health practitioners)

Physical fitness evaluation services (except by offices of health practitioners)

---

T—Canadian, Mexican, and United States industries are comparable.

Hearing testing services (except by offices of
audiologists)

Smoking cessation programs
Pacemaker monitoring services

*Cross-References.*

- Establishments primarily engaged in the independent practice of medicine are classified in Industry 62111, Offices of Physicians;
- Establishments primarily engaged in the independent practice of dentistry are classified in Industry 621210, Offices of Dentists;
- Establishments primarily engaged in the independent practice of health care (except offices of physicians and dentists) are classified in Industry Group 6213, Offices of Other Health Practitioners;
- Establishments primarily engaged in providing general or specialized outpatient care services are classified in Industry Group 6214, Outpatient Care Centers;
- Establishments primarily engaged in providing home health care services are classified in Industry 621610, Home Health Care Services;
- Establishments primarily engaged in the transportation of patients by ground or air, along with medical care, are classified in Industry 621910, Ambulance Services;
- Establishments known as medical and diagnostic laboratories primarily engaged in providing analytic or diagnostic services are classified in Industry 62151, Medical and Diagnostic Laboratories; and
- Blood and organ banks are classified in U.S. Industry 621991, Blood and Organ Banks.

## 622     Hospitals[T]

Industries in the Hospitals subsector provide medical, diagnostic, and treatment services that include physician, nursing, and other health services to inpatients and the specialized accommodation services required by inpatients. Hospitals may also provide outpatient services as a secondary activity. Establishments in the Hospitals subsector provide inpatient health services, many of which can only be provided using the specialized facilities and equipment that form a significant and integral part of the production process.

## 6221     General Medical and Surgical Hospitals[T]

### 62211     General Medical and Surgical Hospitals[T]
See industry description for 622110.

### 622110  General Medical and Surgical Hospitals

This industry comprises establishments known and licensed as general medical and surgical hospitals primarily engaged in providing diagnostic and medical treatment (both surgical and nonsurgical) to inpatients with any of a wide variety of medical conditions. These establishments maintain inpatient beds and provide patients with food services that meet their nutritional requirements. These hospitals have an organized staff of physicians and other medical staff to provide patient care services. These establishments usually provide other services, such as outpatient services, anatomical pathology services, diagnostic X-ray services, clinical laboratory services, operating room services for a variety of procedures, and pharmacy services.

## 6222     Psychiatric and Substance Abuse Hospitals[T]

### 62221     Psychiatric and Substance Abuse Hospitals[T]
See industry description for 622210.

### 622210  Psychiatric and Substance Abuse Hospitals

This industry comprises establishments known and licensed as psychiatric and substance abuse hospitals primarily engaged in providing diagnostic, medical treatment, and monitoring services for inpatients who suffer from mental illness or substance abuse disorders. The treatment often requires an extended stay in the hospital. These establishments maintain inpatient beds and provide patients with food services that meet their nutritional

---

T—Canadian, Mexican, and United States industries are comparable.

requirements.  They have an organized staff of physicians and other medical staff to provide patient care services.  Psychiatric, psychological, and social work services are available at the facility.  These hospitals usually provide other services, such as outpatient services, clinical laboratory services, diagnostic X-ray services, and electroencephalograph services.

*Cross-References.*

- Establishments primarily engaged in providing treatment of mental health and substance abuse illnesses on an exclusively outpatient basis are classified in Industry 621420, Outpatient Mental Health and Substance Abuse Centers;
- Establishments referred to as hospitals but primarily engaged in providing inpatient treatment of mental health and substance abuse illnesses with the emphasis on counseling rather than medical treatment are classified in Industry 623220, Residential Mental Health and Substance Abuse Facilities; and
- Establishments referred to as hospitals but primarily engaged in providing residential care for persons with intellectual and developmental disabilities are classified in Industry 623210, Residential Intellectual and Developmental Disability Facilities.

**6223      Specialty (except Psychiatric and Substance Abuse) Hospitals[T]**

**62231     Specialty (except Psychiatric and Substance Abuse) Hospitals[T]**
See industry description for 622310.

**622310  Specialty (except Psychiatric and Substance Abuse) Hospitals**

  This industry comprises establishments known and licensed as specialty hospitals primarily engaged in providing diagnostic and medical treatment to inpatients with a specific type of disease or medical condition (except psychiatric or substance abuse).  Hospitals providing long-term care for the chronically ill and hospitals providing rehabilitation, restorative, and adjustive services to physically challenged or disabled people are included in this industry.  These establishments maintain inpatient beds and provide patients with food services that meet their nutritional requirements.  They have an organized staff of physicians and other medical staff to provide patient care services.  These hospitals may provide other services, such as outpatient services, diagnostic X-ray services, clinical laboratory services, operating room services, physical therapy services, educational and vocational services, and psychological and social work services.

*Cross-References.*

- Establishments known and licensed as hospitals primarily engaged in providing diagnostic and therapeutic inpatient services for a variety of medical conditions, both surgical and nonsurgical, are classified in Industry 622110, General Medical and Surgical Hospitals;
- Establishments known and licensed as hospitals primarily engaged in providing diagnostic and treatment services for inpatients with psychiatric or substance abuse illnesses are classified in Industry 622210, Psychiatric and Substance Abuse Hospitals;
- Establishments referred to as hospitals but primarily engaged in providing inpatient nursing and rehabilitative services to persons requiring convalescence are classified in Industry 623110, Nursing Care Facilities (Skilled Nursing Facilities);
- Establishments referred to as hospitals but primarily engaged in providing residential care of persons with intellectual and developmental disabilities are classified in Industry 623210, Residential Intellectual and Developmental Disability Facilities; and
- Establishments referred to as hospitals but primarily engaged in providing inpatient treatment for mental health and substance abuse illnesses with the emphasis on counseling rather than medical treatment are classified in Industry 623220, Residential Mental Health and Substance Abuse Facilities.

---

T—Canadian, Mexican, and United States industries are comparable.

**623     Nursing and Residential Care Facilities**[T]

Industries in the Nursing and Residential Care Facilities subsector provide residential care combined with either nursing, supervisory, or other types of care as required by the residents. In this subsector, the facilities are a significant part of the production process, and the care provided is a mix of health and social services with the health services being largely some level of nursing services.

**6231     Nursing Care Facilities (Skilled Nursing Facilities)**[T]

**62311     Nursing Care Facilities (Skilled Nursing Facilities)**[T]
See industry description for 623110.

**623110  Nursing Care Facilities (Skilled Nursing Facilities)**

This industry comprises establishments primarily engaged in providing inpatient nursing and rehabilitative services. The care is generally provided for an extended period of time to individuals requiring nursing care. These establishments have a permanent core staff of registered or licensed practical nurses who, along with other staff, provide nursing and continuous personal care services.

*Illustrative Examples:*

Convalescent homes or convalescent
hospitals (except psychiatric)
Nursing homes
Rest homes with nursing care

Assisted living facilities (without nursing facilities)
for the elderly with nursing care
Inpatient care hospices

*Cross-References.*

- Assisted living facilities with on-site nursing care facilities are classified in U.S. Industry 623311, Continuing Care Retirement Communities; and
- Psychiatric convalescent homes and other establishments primarily engaged in providing inpatient treatment of mental health and substance abuse illnesses with an emphasis on counseling rather than medical treatment are classified in Industry 623220, Residential Mental Health and Substance Abuse Facilities.

**6232     Residential Intellectual and Developmental Disability, Mental Health, and Substance Abuse Facilities**[T]

This industry group comprises establishments primarily engaged in providing residential care (but not licensed hospital care) to people with intellectual and developmental disabilities, mental illness, or substance abuse problems.

**62321     Residential Intellectual and Developmental Disability Facilities**[T]
See industry description for 623210.

**623210  Residential Intellectual and Developmental Disability Facilities**

This industry comprises establishments (e.g., group homes, hospitals, intermediate care facilities) primarily engaged in providing residential care services for persons with intellectual and developmental disabilities. These facilities may provide some health care, though the focus is room, board, protective supervision, and counseling.

*Cross-References.*

- Establishments primarily engaged in providing inpatient treatment of mental health and substance abuse illnesses with an emphasis on counseling rather than medical treatment are classified in Industry 623220, Residential Mental Health and Substance Abuse Facilities;

---

T—Canadian, Mexican, and United States industries are comparable.

- Establishments primarily engaged in providing treatment of mental health and substance abuse illnesses on an exclusively outpatient basis are classified in Industry 621420, Outpatient Mental Health and Substance Abuse Centers;
- Establishments known and licensed as hospitals primarily engaged in providing inpatient treatment of mental health and substance abuse illnesses with an emphasis on medical treatment and monitoring are classified in Industry 622210, Psychiatric and Substance Abuse Hospitals; and
- Establishments primarily engaged in operating group homes for the hearing or visually impaired are classified in Industry 623990, Other Residential Care Facilities.

## 62322 Residential Mental Health and Substance Abuse Facilities[T]
See industry description for 623220.

## 623220 Residential Mental Health and Substance Abuse Facilities

This industry comprises establishments primarily engaged in providing residential care and treatment for patients with mental health and substance abuse illnesses. These establishments provide room, board, supervision, and counseling services. Although medical services may be available at these establishments, they are incidental to the counseling, mental rehabilitation, and support services offered. These establishments generally provide a wide range of social services in addition to counseling.

*Illustrative Examples:*

Alcoholism or drug addiction rehabilitation facilities (except licensed hospitals)
Psychiatric convalescent homes or hospitals

Mental health halfway houses
Residential group homes for the emotionally disturbed

*Cross-References.*

- Establishments primarily engaged in providing treatment of mental health and substance abuse illnesses on an exclusively outpatient basis are classified in Industry 621420, Outpatient Mental Health and Substance Abuse Centers;
- Establishments primarily engaged in providing residential care for persons with intellectual and developmental disabilities are classified in Industry 623210, Residential Intellectual and Developmental Disability Facilities;
- Establishments known and licensed as hospitals primarily engaged in providing inpatient treatment of mental health and substance abuse illnesses with an emphasis on medical treatment and monitoring are classified in Industry 622210, Psychiatric and Substance Abuse Hospitals; and
- Establishments primarily engaged in operating halfway group homes for delinquents and ex-offenders are classified in Industry 623990, Other Residential Care Facilities.

## 6233 Continuing Care Retirement Communities and Assisted Living Facilities for the Elderly[T]

## 62331 Continuing Care Retirement Communities and Assisted Living Facilities for the Elderly[T]

This industry comprises establishments primarily engaged in providing residential and personal care services for (1) the elderly and other persons who are unable to fully care for themselves and/or (2) the elderly and other persons who do not desire to live independently. The care typically includes room, board, supervision, and assistance in daily living, such as housekeeping services. In some instances, these establishments provide skilled nursing care for residents in separate on-site facilities.

*Illustrative Examples:*

Assisted living facilities with on-site nursing care facilities
Continuing care retirement communities

Assisted living facilities for the elderly without nursing care
Rest homes without nursing care

---

T—Canadian, Mexican, and United States industries are comparable.

*Cross-References.*

- Establishments primarily engaged in providing inpatient nursing and rehabilitative services are classified in Industry 62311, Nursing Care Facilities (Skilled Nursing Facilities); and
- Apartment or condominium complexes where people live independently in rented housing units are classified in Industry 53111, Lessors of Residential Buildings and Dwellings.

### 623311 Continuing Care Retirement Communities

This U.S. industry comprises establishments primarily engaged in providing a range of residential and personal care services with on-site nursing care facilities for (1) the elderly and other persons who are unable to fully care for themselves and/or (2) the elderly and other persons who do not desire to live independently. Individuals live in a variety of residential settings with meals, housekeeping, social, leisure, and other services available to assist residents in daily living. Assisted living facilities with on-site nursing care facilities are included in this industry.

*Cross-References.*

- Establishments primarily engaged in providing inpatient nursing and rehabilitative services are classified in Industry 623110, Nursing Care Facilities (Skilled Nursing Facilities);
- Assisted living facilities without nursing care are classified in U.S. Industry 623312, Assisted Living Facilities for the Elderly; and
- Apartment or condominium complexes where people live independently in rented housing units are classified in Industry 531110, Lessors of Residential Buildings and Dwellings.

### 623312 Assisted Living Facilities for the Elderly

This U.S. industry comprises establishments primarily engaged in providing residential and personal care services without nursing care for (1) the elderly or other persons who are unable to fully care for themselves and/or (2) the elderly or other persons who do not desire to live independently. The care typically includes room, board, supervision, and assistance in daily living, such as housekeeping services.

*Illustrative Examples*:

Assisted living facilities for the elderly without nursing care

Rest homes without nursing care

*Cross-References.*

- Assisted living facilities with on-site nursing care facilities are classified in U.S. Industry 623311, Continuing Care Retirement Communities;
- Assisted living facilities for the elderly with nursing care or rest homes with nursing care are classified in Industry 623110, Nursing Care Facilities (Skilled Nursing Facilities); and
- Apartment or condominium complexes where people live independently in rented or owned housing units are classified in Industry 531110, Lessors of Residential Buildings and Dwellings.

### 6239 Other Residential Care Facilities[T]

### 62399 Other Residential Care Facilities[T]
See industry description for 623990.

### 623990 Other Residential Care Facilities

This industry comprises establishments primarily engaged in providing residential care (except residential intellectual and developmental disability facilities, residential mental health and substance abuse facilities,

---

T—Canadian, Mexican, and United States industries are comparable.

continuing care retirement communities, and assisted living facilities for the elderly). These establishments also provide supervision and personal care services.

*Illustrative Examples*:

Boot or disciplinary camps (except correctional) for delinquent youth
Group homes for the hearing or visually impaired
Child group foster homes
Delinquent youth halfway group homes

Halfway group homes for delinquents or ex-offenders
Homes for unwed mothers
Group homes for the disabled without nursing care
Orphanages

*Cross-References.*

- Residential intellectual and developmental disability facilities are classified in Industry 623210, Residential Intellectual and Developmental Disability Facilities;
- Continuing care retirement communities are classified in U.S. Industry 623311, Continuing Care Retirement Communities;
- Residential mental health and substance abuse facilities are classified in Industry 623220, Residential Mental Health and Substance Abuse Facilities;
- Assisted living facilities for the elderly without nursing care are classified in U.S. Industry 623312, Assisted Living Facilities for the Elderly;
- Establishments primarily engaged in providing inpatient nursing and rehabilitative services are classified in Industry 623110, Nursing Care Facilities (Skilled Nursing Facilities);
- Establishments primarily engaged in providing temporary shelter are classified in U.S. Industry 624221, Temporary Shelters;
- Privately operated correctional facilities are classified in Industry 561210, Facilities Support Services; and
- Government operated correctional facilities and camps are classified in Industry 922140, Correctional Institutions.

## 624     Social Assistance[T]

Industries in the Social Assistance subsector provide a wide variety of social assistance services directly to their clients. These services do not include residential or accommodation services, except on a short-stay basis.

## 6241     Individual and Family Services[T]

This industry group comprises establishments primarily engaged in providing nonresidential social assistance to children and youth, the elderly, persons with disabilities, and all other individuals and families.

### 62411   Child and Youth Services[T]
See industry description for 624110.

### 624110  Child and Youth Services

This industry comprises establishments primarily engaged in providing nonresidential social assistance services for children and youth. These establishments provide for the welfare of children in such areas as adoption and foster care, drug prevention, life skills training, and positive social development.

*Illustrative Examples:*

Adoption agencies
Youth centers (except recreational only)
Child guidance organizations

Youth self-help organizations
Foster care placement services

---

T—Canadian, Mexican, and United States industries are comparable.

*Cross-References.*

- Youth recreational centers are classified in Industry 713940, Fitness and Recreational Sports Centers;
- Youth recreational sports teams and leagues are classified in Industry 713990, All Other Amusement and Recreation Industries;
- Scouting organizations are classified in Industry 813410, Civic and Social Organizations;
- Establishments primarily engaged in providing child care services are classified in Industry 624410, Child Care Services; and
- Child group foster homes and juvenile halfway group homes are classified in Industry 623990, Other Residential Care Facilities.

**62412    Services for the Elderly and Persons with Disabilities<sup>T</sup>**
See industry description for 624120.

**624120  Services for the Elderly and Persons with Disabilities**

This industry comprises establishments primarily engaged in providing nonresidential social assistance services to improve the quality of life for the elderly or persons with intellectual and/or developmental disabilities. These establishments provide for the welfare of these individuals in such areas as day care, non-medical home care or homemaker services, social activities, group support, and companionship.

*Cross-References.*          Establishments primarily engaged in--

- Providing job training for persons with intellectual and/or developmental disabilities--are classified in Industry 624310, Vocational Rehabilitation Services;
- Providing residential care for the elderly or persons with intellectual and/or developmental disabilities--are classified in Subsector 623, Nursing and Residential Care Facilities;
- Providing in-home health care services--are classified in Subsector 621, Ambulatory Health Care Services; and
- Providing transportation of the disabled or elderly (without medical care) are classified in U.S. Industry 485991, Special Needs Transportation.

**62419    Other Individual and Family Services<sup>T</sup>**
See industry description for 624190.

**624190  Other Individual and Family Services**

This industry comprises establishments primarily engaged in providing nonresidential individual and family social assistance services (except those specifically directed toward children, the elderly, or persons with intellectual and/or developmental disabilities).

*Illustrative Examples:*

| | |
|---|---|
| Community action services agencies | Family welfare services |
| Marriage counseling services (except by offices of mental health practitioners) | Self-help organizations (except for disabled persons, the elderly) |
| Crisis intervention centers | Suicide crisis centers |
| Multi-purpose social services centers | Hotline centers |
| Family social services agencies | Telephone counseling services |

*Cross-References.*          Establishments primarily engaged in--

- Providing clinical psychological and psychiatric counseling services (except by offices of physicians)--are classified in Industry 621330, Offices of Mental Health Practitioners (except Physicians);

---

T—Canadian, Mexican, and United States industries are comparable.

- Providing child and youth social assistance services (except child care services)--are classified in Industry 624110, Child and Youth Services;
- Providing child care services--are classified in Industry 624410, Child Care Services;
- Providing social assistance services for the elderly and persons with intellectual and/or developmental disabilities--are classified in Industry 624120, Services for the Elderly and Persons with Disabilities;
- Community action advocacy--are classified in U.S. Industry 813319, Other Social Advocacy Organizations; and
- Providing in-home health care services--are classified in Subsector 621, Ambulatory Health Care Services.

## 6242 Community Food and Housing, and Emergency and Other Relief Services[T]

This industry group comprises establishments primarily engaged in one of the following: (1) collecting, preparing, and delivering food for the needy; (2) providing short-term emergency shelter, temporary residential shelter, transitional housing, volunteer construction or repair of low-cost housing, and/or repair of homes for individuals or families in need; or (3) providing food, shelter, clothing, medical relief, resettlement, and counseling to victims of domestic or international disasters or conflicts (e.g., wars).

## 62421 Community Food Services[T]
See industry description for 624210.

## 624210 Community Food Services

This industry comprises establishments primarily engaged in the collection, preparation, and delivery of food for the needy. Establishments in this industry may also distribute clothing and blankets to the poor. These establishments may prepare and deliver meals to persons who by reason of age, disability, or illness are unable to prepare meals for themselves; collect and distribute salvageable or donated food; or prepare and provide meals at fixed or mobile locations. Food banks, meal delivery programs, and soup kitchens are included in this industry.

## 62422 Community Housing Services[T]

This industry comprises establishments primarily engaged in providing one or more of the following community housing services: (1) short-term emergency shelter for victims of domestic violence, sexual assault, or child abuse; (2) temporary residential shelter for the homeless, runaway youths, and patients and families caught in medical crises; (3) transitional housing for low-income individuals and families; (4) volunteer construction or repair of low-cost housing, in partnership with the homeowner who may assist in construction or repair work; and (5) repair of homes for elderly or disabled homeowners. These establishments may operate their own shelter, they may subsidize housing using existing homes, apartments, hotels, or motels, or they may require a low-cost mortgage or work (sweat) equity.

*Cross-References.*

- Establishments primarily engaged in providing emergency shelter for victims of domestic or international disasters or conflicts are classified in Industry 62423, Emergency and Other Relief Services;
- Halfway group homes for delinquents and ex-offenders and homes for unwed mothers are classified in Industry 62399, Other Residential Care Facilities;
- General contractors, specialty trade contractors, and similar construction establishments primarily responsible for the construction of buildings or performing specialized construction work on houses and other residential buildings, generally on a subcontract basis, are classified in Sector 23, Construction;
- Establishments primarily engaged in leasing residential buildings on their own account are classified in Industry 53111, Lessors of Residential Buildings and Dwellings; and
- Central offices of government housing programs are classified in Industry 92511, Administration of Housing Programs.

---

T—Canadian, Mexican, and United States industries are comparable.

**624221　Temporary Shelters**

This U.S. industry comprises establishments primarily engaged in providing (1) short-term emergency shelter for victims of domestic violence, sexual assault, or child abuse and/or (2) temporary residential shelter for homeless individuals or families, runaway youth, and patients and families caught in medical crises.  These establishments may operate their own shelters or may subsidize housing using existing homes, apartments, hotels, or motels.

*Cross-References.*

- Establishments primarily engaged in providing emergency shelter for victims of domestic or international disasters or conflicts are classified in Industry 624230, Emergency and Other Relief Services; and
- Halfway group homes for delinquents and ex-offenders and homes for unwed mothers are classified in Industry 623990, Other Residential Care Facilities.

**624229　Other Community Housing Services**

This U.S. industry comprises establishments primarily engaged in providing one or more of the following community housing services: (1) transitional housing to low-income individuals and families; (2) volunteer construction or repair of low-cost housing, in partnership with the homeowner who may assist in the construction or repair work; and (3) the repair of homes for elderly or disabled homeowners.  These establishments may subsidize housing using existing homes, apartments, hotels, or motels or may require a low-cost mortgage or sweat equity.  These establishments may also provide low-income families with furniture and household supplies.

*Cross-References.*

- Halfway group homes for delinquents and ex-offenders and homes for unwed mothers are classified in Industry 623990, Other Residential Care Facilities;
- General contractors, specialty trade contractors, and similar construction establishments primarily responsible for the construction of buildings or performing specialized construction work on houses and other residential buildings, generally on a subcontract basis, are classified in Sector 23, Construction;
- Establishments primarily engaged in leasing residential buildings on their own account are classified in Industry 531110, Lessors of Residential Buildings and Dwellings; and
- Central offices of government housing programs are classified in Industry 925110, Administration of Housing Programs.

**62423　Emergency and Other Relief Services**[T]
See industry description for 624230.

**624230　Emergency and Other Relief Services**

This industry comprises establishments primarily engaged in providing food, shelter, clothing, medical relief, resettlement, and counseling to victims of domestic or international disasters or conflicts (e.g., wars).

**6243　Vocational Rehabilitation Services**[T]

**62431　Vocational Rehabilitation Services**[T]
See industry description for 624310.

**624310　Vocational Rehabilitation Services**

This industry comprises (1) establishments primarily engaged in providing vocational rehabilitation or habilitation services, such as job counseling, job training, and work experience, to unemployed and underemployed persons, persons with disabilities, and persons who have a job market disadvantage because of lack of education, job skill, or experience and (2) establishments primarily engaged in providing training and employment to persons with

---

T—Canadian, Mexican, and United States industries are comparable.

disabilities.  Vocational rehabilitation job training facilities (except schools) and sheltered workshops (i.e., work experience centers) are included in this industry.

*Cross-References.*

- Schools (except high schools) primarily engaged in providing vocational training are classified in Industry 61151, Technical and Trade Schools;
- Vocational high schools are classified in Industry 611110, Elementary and Secondary Schools;
- Apprenticeship training programs are classified in U.S. Industry 611513, Apprenticeship Training; and
- Establishments primarily engaged in providing career and vocational counseling (except rehabilitative) are classified in Industry 611710, Educational Support Services.

**6244    Child Care Services**[T]

**62441    Child Care Services**[T]
See industry description for 624410.

**624410  Child Care Services**

  This industry comprises establishments primarily engaged in providing care and early learning opportunities for infants and children.  These establishments generally care for children from birth through school age and may also offer pre-kindergarten, kindergarten, and/or before- or after-school educational programs.  The care and early learning provided by these establishments may include opportunities for development in health, social and emotional learning, and family engagement.

*Illustrative Examples:*

Before-school and after-school educational programs, separate from schools
Child care babysitting services
Child or infant care centers

Head Start and Early Head Start programs, separate from schools
Nursery schools
Preschool centers

*Cross-References.*        Establishments primarily engaged in--

- Offering kindergarten educational programs--are classified in Industry 611110, Elementary and Secondary Schools; and
- Providing child and youth social assistance services--are classified in Industry 624110, Child and Youth Services.

T—Canadian, Mexican, and United States industries are comparable.

# Sector 71--Arts, Entertainment, and Recreation[T]

## The Sector as a Whole

The Arts, Entertainment, and Recreation sector includes a wide range of establishments that operate facilities or provide services to meet varied cultural, entertainment, and recreational interests of their patrons. This sector comprises (1) establishments that are involved in producing, promoting, or participating in live performances, events, or exhibits intended for public viewing; (2) establishments that preserve and exhibit objects and sites of historical, cultural, or educational interest; and (3) establishments that operate facilities or provide services that enable patrons to participate in recreational activities or pursue amusement, hobby, and leisure-time interests.

Some establishments that provide cultural, entertainment, or recreational facilities and services are classified in other sectors. Excluded from this sector are: (1) establishments that provide both accommodations and recreational facilities, such as hunting and fishing camps and resort and casino hotels, are classified in Subsector 721, Accommodation; (2) restaurants and night clubs that provide live entertainment in addition to the sale of food and beverages are classified in Subsector 722, Food Services and Drinking Places; (3) motion picture theaters, libraries and archives, and publishers of newspapers, magazines, books, periodicals, and computer software are classified in Sector 51, Information; and (4) establishments using transportation equipment to provide recreational and entertainment services, such as those operating sightseeing buses, dinner cruises, or helicopter rides, are classified in Subsector 487, Scenic and Sightseeing Transportation.

## 711    Performing Arts, Spectator Sports, and Related Industries[T]

Industries in the Performing Arts, Spectator Sports, and Related Industries subsector group establishments that produce or organize and promote live presentations involving the performances of actors and actresses, singers, dancers, musical groups and artists, athletes, and other entertainers, including independent (i.e., freelance) entertainers and the establishments that manage their careers. The classification recognizes four basic processes: (1) producing (i.e., presenting) events; (2) organizing, managing, and/or promoting events; (3) managing and representing entertainers; and (4) providing the artistic, creative, and technical skills necessary to the production of these live events. Also, this subsector contains four industries for performing arts companies. Each is defined on the basis of the particular skills of the entertainers involved in the presentations.

The industry structure for this subsector makes a clear distinction between performing arts companies and performing artists (i.e., independent or freelance). Although not unique to arts and entertainment, freelancing is a particularly important phenomenon in this Performing Arts, Spectator Sports, and Related Industries subsector. Distinguishing this activity from the production activity is a meaningful process differentiation. This approach, however, is difficult to implement in the case of musical groups (i.e., companies) and artists. These establishments tend to be more loosely organized and it can be difficult to distinguish companies from freelancers. For this reason, NAICS includes one industry that covers both musical groups and musical artists.

This subsector contains two industries for Industry Group 7113, Promoters of Performing Arts, Sports, and Similar Events, one for those that operate facilities and another for those that do not. This is because there are significant differences in cost structures between those promoters that manage and provide the staff to operate facilities and those that do not. In addition to promoters without facilities, other industries in this subsector include establishments that may operate without permanent facilities. These types of establishments include performing arts companies; musical groups and artists; spectator sports; and independent (i.e., freelance) artists, writers, and performers.

Excluded from this subsector are nightclubs. Some nightclubs promote live entertainment on a regular basis and it can be argued that they could be classified in Industry Group 7113, Promoters of Performing Arts, Sports, and Similar Events. However, since most of these establishments function as any other drinking place when they do not promote entertainment and because most of their revenue is derived from sale of food and beverages, they are classified in Subsector 722, Food Services and Drinking Places.

## 7111    Performing Arts Companies[T]

This industry group comprises establishments primarily engaged in producing live presentations involving the performances of actors and actresses, singers, dancers, musical groups and artists, and other performing artists.

---

T—Canadian, Mexican, and United States industries are comparable.

**71111   Theater Companies and Dinner Theaters**[T]
See industry description for 711110.

**711110  Theater Companies and Dinner Theaters**

This industry comprises (1) companies, groups, or theaters primarily engaged in producing the following live theatrical presentations: musicals; operas; plays; and comedy, improvisational, mime, and puppet shows and (2) establishments, commonly known as dinner theaters, engaged in producing live theatrical productions and in providing food and beverages for consumption on the premises.  Theater groups or companies may or may not operate their own theater or other facility for staging their shows.

*Illustrative Examples:*

Comedy troupes                              Theatrical stock or repertory companies
Opera companies                            Musical theater companies
Live theatrical productions (except dance)

*Cross-References.*

- Establishments, such as nightclubs, primarily engaged in providing food and beverages for consumption on the premises and that also present live nontheatrical entertainment are classified in Subsector 722, Food Services and Drinking Places;
- Establishments primarily engaged in organizing, managing, and/or promoting performing arts productions without producing their own shows are classified in Industry Group 7113, Promoters of Performing Arts, Sports, and Similar Events;
- Companies, groups, or theaters primarily engaged in producing all types of live theatrical dance presentations are classified in Industry 711120, Dance Companies;
- Freelance producers and performing artists (except musicians and vocalists) primarily engaged in theatrical activities independent of a company or group are classified in Industry 711510, Independent Artists, Writers, and Performers; and
- Musicians and vocalists are classified in Industry 711130, Musical Groups and Artists.

**71112   Dance Companies**[T]
See industry description for 711120.

**711120  Dance Companies**

This industry comprises companies, groups, or theaters primarily engaged in producing all types of live theatrical dance (e.g., ballet, contemporary dance, folk dance) presentations.  Dance companies or groups may or may not operate their own theater or other facility for staging their shows.

*Cross-References.*

- Establishments, such as exotic dance clubs, primarily engaged in providing food and beverages for consumption on the premises and that also present live dance entertainment are classified in Subsector 722, Food Services and Drinking Places;
- Establishments primarily engaged in organizing, promoting, and/or managing dance productions without producing their own shows are classified in Industry Group 7113, Promoters of Performing Arts, Sports, and Similar Events; and
- Freelance producers and dancers primarily engaged in theatrical activities independent of a company or group are classified in Industry 711510, Independent Artists, Writers, and Performers.

**71113   Musical Groups and Artists**[T]
See industry description for 711130.

---

T—Canadian, Mexican, and United States industries are comparable.

**711130  Musical Groups and Artists**

This industry comprises (1) groups primarily engaged in producing live musical entertainment (except theatrical musical or opera productions) and (2) independent (i.e., freelance) artists primarily engaged in providing live musical entertainment.  Musical groups and artists may perform in front of a live audience or in a studio, and may or may not operate their own facilities for staging their shows.

*Illustrative Examples:*

Bands
Musical groups (except theatrical musical groups)
Drum and bugle corps (i.e., drill teams)

Orchestras
Independent musicians or vocalists

*Cross-References.*

- Establishments primarily engaged in organizing, promoting, and/or managing concerts and other musical performances without producing their own shows are classified in Industry Group 7113, Promoters of Performing Arts, Sports, and Similar Events;
- Companies, groups, or theaters primarily engaged in producing theatrical musicals and opera productions are classified in Industry 711110, Theater Companies and Dinner Theaters; and
- Freelance producers, song writers, composers, music arrangers, and directors (except musical groups and artists) primarily engaged in musical activities independent of a company or group are classified in Industry 711510, Independent Artists, Writers, and Performers.

**71119    Other Performing Arts Companies[T]**
See industry description for 711190.

**711190  Other Performing Arts Companies**

This industry comprises companies or groups (except theater companies, dance companies, and musical groups and artists) primarily engaged in producing live theatrical presentations.

*Illustrative Examples:*

Carnival traveling shows
Ice skating companies

Circuses
Magic shows

*Cross-References.*

- Establishments, such as nightclubs, primarily engaged in providing food and beverages for consumption on the premises and that also present live nontheatrical entertainment are classified in Subsector 722, Food Services and Drinking Places;
- Establishments primarily engaged in organizing, promoting, and/or managing ice skating shows, circuses, and other live performing arts presentations without producing their own shows are classified in Industry Group 7113, Promoters of Performing Arts, Sports, and Similar Events;
- Theater companies and groups (except dance) or dinner theaters engaged in producing musicals; plays; operas; and comedy, improvisational, mime, and puppet shows are classified in Industry 711110, Theater Companies and Dinner Theaters;
- Dance companies or groups are classified in Industry 711120, Dance Companies;
- Freelance producers and performing artists (except musicians and vocalists) are classified in Industry 711510, Independent Artists, Writers, and Performers;
- Musical groups and independent musicians and vocalists are classified in Industry 711130, Musical Groups and Artists; and
- Carnival ride concession operators (i.e., supplying and servicing in others' facilities) are classified in Industry 713990, All Other Amusement and Recreation Industries.

---

T—Canadian, Mexican, and United States industries are comparable.

**7112    Spectator Sports**[T]

**71121    Spectator Sports**[T]

This industry comprises (1) sports teams or clubs primarily participating in live sporting events before a paying audience; (2) establishments primarily engaged in operating racetracks without casinos; (3) independent athletes engaged in participating in live sporting or racing events before a paying audience; (4) owners of racing participants, such as cars, dogs, and horses, primarily engaged in entering them in racing events or other spectator sports events; and (5) establishments, such as sports trainers, primarily engaged in providing specialized services to support participants in sports events or competitions. The sports teams and clubs included in this industry may or may not operate their own arena, stadium, or other facility for presenting their games or other spectator sports events.

*Cross-References.*

- Establishments primarily engaged in promoting sporting events without participating in sporting events are classified in Industry Group 7113, Promoters of Performing Arts, Sports, and Similar Events;
- Recreational sports clubs (i.e., sports teams) not operating sports facilities are classified in Industry 71399, All Other Amusement and Recreation Industries;
- Amateur, semiprofessional, or professional athletic associations or leagues are classified in Industry 81399, Other Similar Organizations (except Business, Professional, Labor, and Political Organizations);
- Establishments primarily engaged in operating casinos (except casino hotels), with or without racetracks, are classified in Industry 71321, Casinos (except Casino Hotels);
- Establishments primarily engaged in operating casino hotels, with or without racetracks, are classified in Industry 72112, Casino Hotels;
- Establishments primarily engaged in representing or managing the careers of sports figures are classified in Industry 71141, Agents and Managers for Artists, Athletes, Entertainers, and Other Public Figures;
- Independent athletes engaged in providing sports instruction without participating in sporting events before a paying audience are classified in Industry 61162, Sports and Recreation Instruction;
- Independent athletes exclusively engaged in endorsing products or making speeches are classified in Industry 71151, Independent Artists, Writers, and Performers;
- Establishments primarily engaged in operating off-track betting parlors or online sports betting sites are classified in Industry 71329, Other Gambling Industries; and
- Establishments primarily engaged in raising horses, mules, donkeys, and other equines are classified in Industry 11292, Horses and Other Equine Production.

**711211    Sports Teams and Clubs**

This U.S. industry comprises professional or semiprofessional sports teams or clubs primarily engaged in participating in live sporting events, such as baseball, basketball, football, hockey, soccer, and jai alai games, before a paying audience. These establishments may or may not operate their own arena, stadium, or other facility for presenting these events.

*Cross-References.*

- Establishments primarily engaged in promoting sporting events without participating in sporting events are classified in Industry Group 7113, Promoters of Performing Arts, Sports, and Similar Events;
- Recreational sports clubs (i.e., sports teams) not operating sports facilities are classified in Industry 713990, All Other Amusement and Recreation Industries;
- Amateur, semiprofessional, or professional athletic associations or leagues are classified in Industry 813990, Other Similar Organizations (except Business, Professional, Labor, and Political Organizations); and
- Establishments primarily engaged in operating off-track betting parlors or online sports betting sites are classified in Industry 713290, Other Gambling Industries.

---

T—Canadian, Mexican, and United States industries are comparable.

## 711212 Racetracks

This U.S. industry comprises establishments primarily engaged in operating racetracks without casinos. These establishments may also present and/or promote the events, such as auto, dog, and horse races, held in these facilities.

*Cross-References.*

- Owners of racing participants, such as cars, dogs, and horses, primarily engaged in entering them in racing events; trainers of racing participants; and independent athletes, such as jockeys and race car drivers, primarily engaged in participating in racing events are classified in U.S. Industry 711219, Other Spectator Sports;
- Establishments primarily engaged in operating casinos (except casino hotels), with or without racetracks, are classified in Industry 713210, Casinos (except Casino Hotels);
- Establishments primarily engaged in operating casino hotels, with or without racetracks, are classified in Industry 721120, Casino Hotels; and
- Establishments primarily engaged in operating off-track betting parlors or online sports betting sites are classified in Industry 713290, Other Gambling Industries.

## 711219 Other Spectator Sports

This U.S. industry comprises (1) independent athletes, such as professional or semiprofessional golfers, boxers, and race car drivers, primarily engaged in participating in live sporting or racing events before a paying audience; (2) owners of racing participants, such as cars, dogs, and horses, primarily engaged in entering them in racing events or other spectator events; and (3) establishments, such as sports trainers, primarily engaged in providing specialized services required to support participants in sports events or competitions.

*Cross-References.*

- Establishments primarily engaged in operating racetracks without casinos are classified in U.S. Industry 711212, Racetracks;
- Establishments primarily engaged in representing or managing the careers of sports figures are classified in Industry 711410, Agents and Managers for Artists, Athletes, Entertainers, and Other Public Figures;
- Independent athletes engaged in providing sports instruction without participating in sporting events before a paying audience are classified in Industry 611620, Sports and Recreation Instruction;
- Independent athletes exclusively engaged in endorsing products or making speeches are classified in Industry 711510, Independent Artists, Writers, and Performers;
- Establishments primarily engaged in operating off-track betting parlors or online sports betting sites are classified in Industry 713290, Other Gambling Industries; and
- Establishments primarily engaged in raising horses, mules, donkeys, and other equines are classified in Industry 112920, Horses and Other Equine Production.

## 7113  Promoters of Performing Arts, Sports, and Similar Events[T]

This industry group comprises establishments primarily engaged in organizing, promoting, and/or managing live performing arts productions, sports events, and similar events, held in facilities that they manage and operate or in facilities that are managed and operated by others.

## 71131  Promoters of Performing Arts, Sports, and Similar Events with Facilities[T]
See industry description for 711310.

## 711310  Promoters of Performing Arts, Sports, and Similar Events with Facilities

This industry comprises establishments primarily engaged in (1) organizing, promoting, and/or managing live performing arts productions, sports events, and similar events, such as state fairs, county fairs, agricultural fairs,

---

T—Canadian, Mexican, and United States industries are comparable.

concerts, and festivals, held in facilities that they manage and operate and/or (2) managing and providing the staff to operate arenas, stadiums, theaters, or other related facilities for rent to other promoters.

*Cross-References.*            Establishments primarily engaged in--

- Producing live performances (but may also promote the performances and/or operate the facilities where the performances take place)--are classified in Industry Group 7111, Performing Arts Companies;
- Operating racetracks without casinos (but may also promote the events held in these facilities)--are classified in U.S. Industry 711212, Racetracks;
- Presenting sporting events (but may also promote the sporting events and/or operate the stadiums or arenas where the sporting events take place)--are classified in U.S. Industry 711211, Sports Teams and Clubs;
- Organizing, promoting, and/or managing conventions, conferences, and trade shows (but may also operate the facilities where these events take place)--are classified in Industry 561920, Convention and Trade Show Organizers;
- Organizing, promoting, and/or managing performing arts productions, sports events, and similar events in facilities managed and operated by others--are classified in Industry 711320, Promoters of Performing Arts, Sports, and Similar Events without Facilities; and
- Leasing stadiums, arenas, theaters, and other related facilities to others without operating the facilities--are classified in Industry 531120, Lessors of Nonresidential Buildings (except Miniwarehouses).

**71132    Promoters of Performing Arts, Sports, and Similar Events without Facilities[T]**
See industry description for 711320.

**711320  Promoters of Performing Arts, Sports, and Similar Events without Facilities**

This industry comprises promoters primarily engaged in organizing, promoting, and/or managing live performing arts productions, sports events, and similar events, such as state fairs, county fairs, agricultural fairs, concerts, and festivals, in facilities that are managed and operated by others. Theatrical (except motion picture) booking agencies are included in this industry.

*Cross-References.*            Establishments primarily engaged in--

- Booking motion pictures or videos--are classified in U.S. Industry 512199, Other Motion Picture and Video Industries;
- Producing live performances (but may also promote the performances)--are classified in Industry Group 7111, Performing Arts Companies;
- Operating racetracks without casinos (but may also promote the events held in these facilities)--are classified in U.S. Industry 711212, Racetracks;
- Presenting sporting events (but may also promote the sporting events)--are classified in U.S. Industry 711211, Sports Teams and Clubs;
- Organizing, promoting, and/or managing conventions, conferences, and trade shows (but may also operate the facilities where these events take place)--are classified in Industry 561920, Convention and Trade Show Organizers;
- Organizing, promoting, and/or managing performing arts, sports, and similar events in facilities they manage or operate--are classified in Industry 711310, Promoters of Performing Arts, Sports, and Similar Events with Facilities; and
- Operating amateur, semiprofessional, or professional athletic associations or leagues--are classified in Industry 813990, Other Similar Organizations (except Business, Professional, Labor, and Political Organizations).

**7114    Agents and Managers for Artists, Athletes, Entertainers, and Other Public Figures[T]**

**71141   Agents and Managers for Artists, Athletes, Entertainers, and Other Public Figures[T]**
See industry description for 711410.

---

T—Canadian, Mexican, and United States industries are comparable.

**711410  Agents and Managers for Artists, Athletes, Entertainers, and Other Public Figures**

This industry comprises establishments of agents and managers primarily engaged in representing and/or managing creative and performing artists, sports figures, entertainers, and other public figures. The representation and management includes activities, such as representing clients in contract negotiations; managing or organizing clients' financial affairs; and generally promoting the careers of their clients.

*Illustrative Examples:*

Celebrities' agents or managers
Sports figures' agents or managers
Literary agents

Talent agents
Modeling agents

*Cross-References.*

- Establishments primarily engaged in supplying models to clients are classified in Industry 561320, Temporary Help Services; and
- Establishments known as model registries primarily engaged in recruiting and placing models for clients are classified in U.S. Industry 561311, Employment Placement Agencies.

**7115    Independent Artists, Writers, and Performers<sup>T</sup>**

**71151    Independent Artists, Writers, and Performers<sup>T</sup>**
See industry description for 711510.

**711510  Independent Artists, Writers, and Performers**

This industry comprises independent (i.e., freelance) individuals primarily engaged in performing in artistic productions, in creating artistic and cultural works or productions, or in providing technical expertise necessary for these productions. This industry also includes athletes and other celebrities exclusively engaged in endorsing products and making speeches or public appearances for which they receive a fee.

*Illustrative Examples:*

Independent actors or actresses
Independent producers
Independent art restorers
Independent recording technicians
Independent artists (except musical, commercial, medical)
Independent speakers

Independent cartoonists
Independent theatrical costume designers
Independent dancers
Independent theatrical lighting technicians
Independent journalists
Independent technical writers

*Cross-References.*

- Freelance musicians and vocalists are classified in Industry 711130, Musical Groups and Artists;
- Independent commercial artists, medical illustrators, and graphic designers are classified in Industry 541430, Graphic Design Services; and
- Artisans and craftspersons are classified in Sector 31-33, Manufacturing.

**712    Museums, Historical Sites, and Similar Institutions<sup>T</sup>**

Industries in the Museums, Historical Sites, and Similar Institutions subsector engage in the preservation and exhibition of objects, sites, and natural wonders of historical, cultural, and/or educational value.

**7121    Museums, Historical Sites, and Similar Institutions<sup>T</sup>**

---

T—Canadian, Mexican, and United States industries are comparable.

**71211   Museums<sup>T</sup>**
See industry description for 712110.

**712110  Museums**

This industry comprises establishments primarily engaged in the preservation and exhibition of objects of historical, cultural, and/or educational value.

*Illustrative Examples:*

Art galleries (except retail)                           Science or technology museums
Planetariums                                            Halls of fame
Art museums                                             Wax museums

*Cross-References.*

- Establishments primarily engaged as independent museum exhibit designers are classified in Industry 711510, Independent Artists, Writers, and Performers;
- Establishments primarily engaged in the preservation and exhibition of historical sites are classified in Industry 712120, Historical Sites; and
- Commercial art galleries primarily engaged in selling art objects are classified in Industry 459920, Art Dealers.

**71212   Historical Sites<sup>T</sup>**
See industry description for 712120.

**712120  Historical Sites**

This industry comprises establishments primarily engaged in the preservation and exhibition of sites, buildings, forts, or communities that describe events or persons of particular historical interest.  Archeological sites, battlefields, historical ships, and pioneer villages are included in this industry.

**71213   Zoos and Botanical Gardens<sup>T</sup>**
See industry description for 712130.

**712130  Zoos and Botanical Gardens**

This industry comprises establishments primarily engaged in the preservation and exhibition of live plant and animal life displays.

*Illustrative Examples:*

Aquariums                                               Zoological gardens
Wild animal parks                                       Aviaries
Arboreta

*Cross-References.*

Government establishments primarily engaged in administering natural areas are classified in Industry 924120, Administration of Conservation Programs.

**71219   Nature Parks and Other Similar Institutions<sup>T</sup>**
See industry description for 712190.

---

T—Canadian, Mexican, and United States industries are comparable.

**712190 Nature Parks and Other Similar Institutions**

This industry comprises establishments primarily engaged in the preservation and exhibition of natural areas or settings.

*Illustrative Examples:*

Bird or wildlife sanctuaries
Natural wonder tourist attractions (e.g., caverns, waterfalls)

Conservation areas
Nature centers or preserves
National parks

*Cross-References.*

- Establishments primarily engaged in operating commercial hunting or fishing preserves without accommodations (e.g., game farms) are classified in Industry 114210, Hunting and Trapping;
- Establishments primarily engaged in operating commercial hunting, fishing, or nature preserves combined with accommodations are classified in Industry Group 7211, Traveler Accommodation; and
- Government establishments primarily engaged in administering natural areas are classified in Industry 924120, Administration of Conservation Programs.

**713      Amusement, Gambling, and Recreation Industries[T]**

Industries in the Amusement, Gambling, and Recreation Industries subsector (1) operate facilities where patrons can primarily engage in sports, recreation, amusement, or gambling activities and/or (2) provide other amusement and recreation services, such as supplying and servicing amusement devices in places of business operated by others; operating sports teams, clubs, or leagues engaged in playing games for recreational purposes; and guiding tours without using transportation equipment.

This subsector does not cover all establishments providing recreational services. Other sectors of NAICS also provide recreational services. Providers of recreational services are often engaged in processes classified in other sectors of NAICS. For example, operators of resorts and hunting and fishing camps provide both accommodation and recreational facilities and services. These establishments are classified in Subsector 721, Accommodation, partly to reflect the significant costs associated with the provision of accommodation services and partly to ensure consistency with international standards. Likewise, establishments using transportation equipment to provide recreational and entertainment services, such as those operating sightseeing buses, dinner cruises, or helicopter rides, are classified in Subsector 487, Scenic and Sightseeing Transportation.

The industry groups in this subsector highlight particular types of activities: amusement parks and arcades, gambling industries, and other amusement and recreation industries. The groups, however, are not all-inclusive of the activity. The Gambling Industries industry group does not provide for full coverage of gambling activities. For example, casino hotels are classified in Subsector 721, Accommodation; and horse and dog racing tracks without casinos are classified in Industry Group 7112, Spectator Sports.

**7131      Amusement Parks and Arcades[T]**

This industry group comprises establishments primarily engaged in operating amusement parks and amusement arcades and parlors.

**71311    Amusement and Theme Parks[T]**
         See industry description for 713110.

**713110 Amusement and Theme Parks**

This industry comprises establishments, known as amusement or theme parks, primarily engaged in operating a variety of attractions, such as mechanical rides, water rides, games, shows, theme exhibits, refreshment stands, and picnic grounds. These establishments may lease space to others on a concession basis.

---

T—Canadian, Mexican, and United States industries are comparable.

*Cross-References.*        Establishments primarily engaged in--

- Operating mechanical or water rides on a concession basis in amusement parks, fairs, and carnivals or operating recreation attractions, such as waterslides, miniature golf courses, and gocart raceways--are classified in Industry 713990, All Other Amusement and Recreation Industries;
- Operating refreshment stands on a concession basis--are classified in Industry 72251, Restaurants and Other Eating Places;
- Supplying and servicing coin- or card-operated amusement (except gambling) devices in places of business operated by others--are classified in Industry 713990, All Other Amusement and Recreation Industries;
- Supplying and servicing coin- or card-operated gambling devices (e.g., slot machines or video gambling terminals) in places of business operated by others--are classified in Industry 713290, Other Gambling Industries; and
- Organizing, promoting, and/or managing events, such as carnivals and fairs, with or without facilities--are classified in Industry Group 7113, Promoters of Performing Arts, Sports, and Similar Events.

### 71312    Amusement Arcades[T]
See industry description for 713120.

### 713120   Amusement Arcades

This industry comprises establishments primarily engaged in operating amusement (except gambling, billiard, or pool) arcades and parlors.

*Cross-References.*        Establishments primarily engaged in--

- Operating a variety of attractions, such as mechanical rides, water rides, games, shows, theme exhibits, refreshment stands, and picnic grounds, known as amusement or theme parks--are classified in Industry 713110, Amusement and Theme Parks;
- Supplying and servicing coin- or card-operated amusement (except gambling) devices or rides in places of business operated by others, operating billiard or pool parlors, or operating recreation attractions, such as waterslides, miniature golf courses, and gocart raceways--are classified in Industry 713990, All Other Amusement and Recreation Industries;
- Operating bingo, off-track betting, or slot machine parlors or in supplying and servicing coin- or card-operated gambling devices (e.g., slot machines or video gambling terminals) in places of business operated by others--are classified in Industry 713290, Other Gambling Industries;
- Operating casinos (except casino hotels)--are classified in Industry 713210, Casinos (except Casino Hotels); and
- Operating casino hotels--are classified in Industry 721120, Casino Hotels.

### 7132    Gambling Industries[T]

This industry group comprises establishments (except casino hotels) primarily engaged in operating gambling facilities, such as casinos, bingo halls, and video gaming terminals, or in the provision of gambling services, such as lotteries and off-track betting. Casino hotels are classified in Industry 72112, Casino Hotels.

### 71321    Casinos (except Casino Hotels)[T]
See industry description for 713210.

### 713210   Casinos (except Casino Hotels)

This industry comprises establishments primarily engaged in operating gambling facilities that offer table wagering games along with other gambling activities, such as slot machines and sports betting. These establishments often provide food and beverage services. Included in this industry are floating casinos (i.e., gambling cruises, riverboat casinos) and casinos with racetracks.

---

T--Canadian, Mexican, and United States industries are comparable.

*Cross-References.* Establishments primarily engaged in--

- Operating bingo, off-track betting, or slot machine parlors or in supplying and servicing coin- or card-operated gambling devices, such as slot machines and video gaming terminals, in places of business operated by others--are classified in Industry 713290, Other Gambling Industries; and
- Operating casino hotels--are classified in Industry 721120, Casino Hotels.

## 71329 Other Gambling Industries[T]
See industry description for 713290.

## 713290 Other Gambling Industries

This industry comprises establishments primarily engaged in operating gambling facilities (except casinos or casino hotels) or providing gambling services.

*Illustrative Examples:*

Bingo, off-track betting, or slot machine parlors
Coin- or card-operated gambling device concession operators (i.e., supplying and servicing in others' facilities)

Bookmakers
Lottery ticket sales agents (except retail stores)
Card rooms (e.g., poker rooms)

*Cross-References.* Establishments primarily engaged in--

- Operating casinos--are classified in Industry 713210, Casinos (except Casino Hotels);
- Operating casino hotels--are classified in Industry 721120, Casino Hotels;
- Operating facilities with coin- or card-operated amusement (except gambling) devices--are classified in Industry 713120, Amusement Arcades;
- Supplying and servicing coin- or card-operated amusement (except gambling) devices in places of business operated by others--are classified in Industry 713990, All Other Amusement and Recreation Industries; and
- Operating racetracks without casinos or presenting live racing or sporting events--are classified in Industry 71121, Spectator Sports.

## 7139 Other Amusement and Recreation Industries[T]

This industry group comprises establishments primarily engaged in operating golf courses and country clubs; skiing facilities; marinas; fitness and recreational sports centers; bowling centers; and providing other amusement and recreation services.

## 71391 Golf Courses and Country Clubs[T]
See industry description for 713910.

## 713910 Golf Courses and Country Clubs

This industry comprises (1) establishments primarily engaged in operating golf courses (except miniature) and (2) establishments primarily engaged in operating golf courses, along with dining facilities and other recreational facilities that are known as country clubs. These establishments often provide food and beverage services, equipment rental services, and golf instruction services.

*Cross-References.* Establishments primarily engaged in--

- Operating driving ranges and miniature golf courses--are classified in Industry 713990, All Other Amusement and Recreation Industries; and
- Operating resorts where golf facilities are combined with accommodations--are classified in Industry Group 7211, Traveler Accommodation.

---

T—Canadian, Mexican, and United States industries are comparable.

**71392   Skiing Facilities[T]**
        See industry description for 713920.

**713920   Skiing Facilities**

   This industry comprises establishments engaged in (1) operating downhill, cross country, or related skiing areas and/or (2) operating equipment, such as ski lifts and tows.  These establishments often provide food and beverage services, equipment rental services, and ski instruction services.  Four season resorts without accommodations are included in this industry.

*Cross-References.*

   Establishments primarily engaged in operating resorts where skiing facilities are combined with accommodations are classified in Industry Group 7211, Traveler Accommodation.

**71393   Marinas[T]**
        See industry description for 713930.

**713930   Marinas**

   This industry comprises establishments, commonly known as marinas, engaged in operating docking and/or storage facilities for pleasure craft owners, with or without one or more related activities, such as retailing fuel and marine supplies; and repairing, maintaining, or renting pleasure boats.

*Cross-References.*         Establishments primarily engaged in--

   - Building ships--are classified in U.S. Industry 336611, Ship Building and Repairing;
   - Building boats--are classified in U.S. Industry 336612, Boat Building;
   - Renting pleasure boats without operating a marina--are classified in U.S. Industry 532284, Recreational Goods Rental;
   - Repairing pleasure boats without operating a marina--are classified in Industry 811490, Other Personal and Household Goods Repair and Maintenance;
   - Retailing marine supplies without operating a marina--are classified in U.S. Industry 441222, Boat Dealers;
   - Retailing fuel for boats without operating a marina--are classified in Industry 457120, Other Gasoline Stations; and
   - Renting or leasing space for self-storage without operating a marina--are classified in Industry 531130, Lessors of Miniwarehouses and Self-Storage Units.

**71394   Fitness and Recreational Sports Centers[T]**
        See industry description for 713940.

**713940   Fitness and Recreational Sports Centers**

   This industry comprises establishments primarily engaged in operating fitness and recreational sports facilities featuring exercise and other active physical fitness conditioning or recreational sports activities, such as swimming, skating, or racquet sports.

*Illustrative Examples:*

Aerobic dance or exercise centers                    Physical fitness centers
Ice or roller skating rinks                          Handball, racquetball, or tennis club facilities
Gymnasiums                                           Swimming or wave pools

---

T—Canadian, Mexican, and United States industries are comparable.

*Cross-References.*

- Establishments primarily engaged in providing non-medical services to assist clients in attaining or maintaining a desired weight are classified in U.S. Industry 812191, Diet and Weight Reducing Centers;
- Establishments primarily engaged in providing personal fitness training services without facilities are classified in Industry 812990, All Other Personal Services;
- Establishments primarily engaged in operating instructional camps (e.g., sports camps) or providing instruction in sports and other recreational activities (e.g., aerobic dance or exercise instruction, yoga instruction) are classified in Sector 61, Educational Services, based on the nature of instruction;
- Establishments primarily engaged in operating health resorts and spas where recreational facilities are combined with accommodations are classified in Industry 721110, Hotels (except Casino Hotels) and Motels; and
- Recreational sports clubs (i.e., sports teams) not operating sports facilities are classified in Industry 713990, All Other Amusement and Recreation Industries.

**71395 Bowling Centers$^{\text{T}}$**
See industry description for 713950.

**713950 Bowling Centers**

This industry comprises establishments engaged in operating bowling centers. These establishments often provide food and beverage services.

**71399 All Other Amusement and Recreation Industries$^{\text{T}}$**
See industry description for 713990.

**713990 All Other Amusement and Recreation Industries**

This industry comprises establishments (except amusement parks and arcades; gambling industries; golf courses and country clubs; skiing facilities; marinas; fitness and recreational sports centers; and bowling centers) primarily engaged in providing recreational and amusement services.

*Illustrative Examples:*

Amusement ride or coin- or card-operated nongambling amusement device concession operators (i.e., supplying and servicing in others' facilities)
Outdoor adventure operations (e.g., white water rafting) without accommodations
Miniature golf courses
Golf driving ranges
Archery or shooting ranges

Recreational day camps (except instructional)
Billiard or pool parlors
Recreational chess or bridge clubs
Boating clubs (without marinas)
Recreational or youth sports clubs (i.e., sports teams) not operating sports facilities
Escape rooms
Riding stables (except boarding horses)

*Cross-References.*

- Establishments primarily engaged in operating amusement parks and arcades are classified in Industry Group 7131, Amusement Parks and Arcades;
- Establishments primarily engaged in operating gambling facilities (except casino hotels) or providing gambling services are classified in Industry Group 7132, Gambling Industries;
- Establishments primarily engaged in operating casino hotels are classified in Industry 721120, Casino Hotels;
- Establishments primarily engaged in operating golf courses (except miniature) and country clubs are classified in Industry 713910, Golf Courses and Country Clubs;

---

T—Canadian, Mexican, and United States industries are comparable.

- Establishments primarily engaged in operating skiing facilities without accommodations are classified in Industry 713920, Skiing Facilities;
- Establishments primarily engaged in operating resorts where recreational facilities are combined with lodging are classified in Industry Group 7211, Traveler Accommodation;
- Establishments primarily engaged in operating marinas are classified in Industry 713930, Marinas;
- Establishments primarily engaged in operating fitness and recreational sports centers are classified in Industry 713940, Fitness and Recreational Sports Centers;
- Establishments primarily engaged in operating bowling centers are classified in Industry 713950, Bowling Centers;
- Establishments primarily engaged in operating instructional camps, such as sports camps, fine arts camps, and computer camps, are classified in Sector 61, Educational Services, based on the nature of instruction;
- Independent athletes engaged in participating in sporting events before a paying audience are classified in U.S. Industry 711219, Other Spectator Sports;
- Independent athletes engaged in providing sports instruction without participating in sporting events before a paying audience are classified in Industry 611620, Sports and Recreation Instruction;
- Independent athletes exclusively engaged in endorsing products or making speeches are classified in Industry 711510, Independent Artists, Writers, and Performers;
- Establishments primarily engaged in providing scenic and sightseeing transportation are classified in Subsector 487, Scenic and Sightseeing Transportation;
- Aviation clubs primarily engaged in providing specialty air and flying services are classified in U.S. Industry 481219, Other Nonscheduled Air Transportation;
- Aviation clubs primarily engaged in advocating social and political causes are classified in U.S. Industry 813319, Other Social Advocacy Organizations; and
- Amateur, semiprofessional, or professional athletic associations or leagues are classified in Industry 813990, Other Similar Organizations (except Business, Professional, Labor, and Political Organizations).

---

T—Canadian, Mexican, and United States industries are comparable.

# Sector 72--Accommodation and Food Services<sup>T</sup>

## The Sector as a Whole

The Accommodation and Food Services sector comprises establishments providing customers with lodging and/or preparing meals, snacks, and beverages for immediate consumption. The sector includes both accommodation and food services establishments because the two activities are often combined at the same establishment.

Some establishments that provide food and beverage services are classified in other sectors. Excluded from this sector are civic and social organizations. These establishments are classified in Sector 81, Other Services (except Public Administration). Amusement and recreation parks, dinner theaters, and other recreation or entertainment facilities are classified in Sector 71, Arts, Entertainment, and Recreation. Motion picture theaters are classified in Sector 51, Information.

### 721     Accommodation<sup>T</sup>

Industries in the Accommodation subsector provide lodging or short-term accommodations for travelers, vacationers, and others. There is a wide range of establishments in these industries. Some provide lodging only, while others provide meals, laundry services, and recreational facilities, as well as lodging. Lodging establishments are classified in this subsector even if the provision of complementary services generates more revenue. The types of complementary services provided vary from establishment to establishment.

The subsector is organized into three groups: (1) traveler accommodation, (2) recreational accommodation, and (3) rooming and boarding houses, dormitories, and workers' camps. The Traveler Accommodation industry group includes establishments that primarily provide traditional types of lodging services. This group includes hotels, motels, and bed-and-breakfast inns. In addition to lodging, these establishments may provide a range of other services to their guests. The RV (Recreational Vehicle) Parks and Recreational Camps industry group includes establishments that operate lodging facilities primarily designed to accommodate outdoor enthusiasts. Included are travel trailer campsites, recreational vehicle parks, and outdoor adventure retreats. The Rooming and Boarding Houses, Dormitories, and Workers' Camps industry group includes establishments providing temporary or longer-term accommodations, that for the period of occupancy, may serve as a principal residence. Board (i.e., meals) may be provided but is not essential.

Establishments that manage short-stay accommodation establishments (e.g., hotels and motels) on a contractual basis are classified in this subsector if they both manage the operation and provide the operating staff. Such establishments are classified based on the type of facility managed and operated.

### 7211     Traveler Accommodation<sup>T</sup>

This industry group comprises establishments primarily engaged in providing short-term lodging in facilities, such as hotels, motels, casino hotels, and bed-and-breakfast inns. In addition to lodging, these establishments may provide a range of other services to their guests.

### 72111     Hotels (except Casino Hotels) and Motels<sup>T</sup>
See industry description for 721110.

### 721110     Hotels (except Casino Hotels) and Motels

This industry comprises establishments primarily engaged in providing short-term lodging in facilities known as hotels, motor hotels, resort hotels, and motels. The establishments in this industry may offer food and beverage services, recreational services, conference rooms, convention services, laundry services, parking, and other services.

*Cross-References.*          Establishments primarily engaged in--

* Providing short-term lodging with a casino on the premises--are classified in Industry 721120, Casino Hotels; and

---

T—Canadian, Mexican, and United States industries are comparable.

- Providing short-term lodging in facilities known as bed-and-breakfast inns, youth hostels, housekeeping cabins and cottages, and tourist homes--are classified in Industry 72119, Other Traveler Accommodation.

**72112   Casino Hotels[T]**
See industry description for 721120.

**721120  Casino Hotels**

This industry comprises establishments primarily engaged in providing short-term lodging in hotel facilities with a casino on the premises. The casino on premises includes table wagering games and may include other gambling activities, such as slot machines and sports betting. These establishments generally offer a range of services and amenities, such as food and beverage services, entertainment, valet parking, swimming pools, and conference and convention facilities. Included in this industry are casino hotels with racetracks.

*Cross-References.*          Establishments primarily engaged in--

- Providing short-term lodging in facilities known as hotels and motels that provide limited gambling activities, such as slot machines, without a casino on the premises--are classified in Industry 721110, Hotels (except Casino Hotels) and Motels; and
- Operating stand-alone casinos--are classified in Industry 713210, Casinos (except Casino Hotels).

**72119   Other Traveler Accommodation[T]**

This industry comprises establishments primarily engaged in providing short-term lodging (except hotels, motels, and casino hotels).

*Illustrative Examples:*

Bed-and-breakfast inns                          Hostels
Tourist homes                                   Housekeeping cabins and cottages
Guest houses

*Cross-References.*          Establishments primarily engaged in--

- Providing short-term lodging in facilities known as hotels without a casino on the premises--are classified in Industry 72111, Hotels (except Casino Hotels) and Motels;
- Providing short-term lodging in facilities known as hotels with a casino on the premises--are classified in Industry 72112, Casino Hotels;
- Operating recreational vehicle parks and campgrounds and recreational and vacation camps that provide accommodation facilities, such as cabins--are classified in Industry 72121, RV (Recreational Vehicle) Parks and Recreational Camps; and
- Acting as lessors of buildings used as residences or dwellings--are classified in Industry 53111, Lessors of Residential Buildings and Dwellings.

**721191  Bed-and-Breakfast Inns**

This U.S. industry comprises establishments primarily engaged in providing short-term lodging in facilities known as bed-and-breakfast inns. These establishments provide short-term lodging in private homes or small buildings converted for this purpose. Bed-and-breakfast inns are characterized by a highly personalized service and inclusion of a full breakfast in the room rate.

**721199  All Other Traveler Accommodation**

This U.S. industry comprises establishments primarily engaged in providing short-term lodging (except hotels, motels, casino hotels, and bed-and-breakfast inns).

---

T—Canadian, Mexican, and United States industries are comparable.

*Illustrative Examples:*

| | |
|---|---|
| Guest houses | Housekeeping cabins and cottages |
| Tourist homes | Hostels |

*Cross-References.*    Establishments primarily engaged in--

- Providing short-term lodging in facilities known as hotels without a casino on the premises--are classified in Industry 721110, Hotels (except Casino Hotels) and Motels;
- Providing short-term lodging in facilities known as hotels with a casino on the premises--are classified in Industry 721120, Casino Hotels;
- Providing short-term lodging in establishments known as bed-and-breakfast inns--are classified in U.S. Industry 721191, Bed-and-Breakfast Inns;
- Operating recreational vehicle parks and campgrounds and recreational and vacation camps that provide accommodation facilities, such as cabins--are classified in Industry 72121, RV (Recreational Vehicle) Parks and Recreational Camps; and
- Acting as lessors of buildings used as residences or dwellings--are classified in Industry 531110, Lessors of Residential Buildings and Dwellings.

## 7212    RV (Recreational Vehicle) Parks and Recreational Camps<sup>T</sup>

## 72121    RV (Recreational Vehicle) Parks and Recreational Camps<sup>T</sup>

This industry comprises establishments primarily engaged in operating recreational vehicle parks and campgrounds and recreational and vacation camps. These establishments cater to outdoor enthusiasts and are characterized by the type of accommodation and by the nature and the range of recreational facilities and activities provided to their clients.

*Illustrative Examples:*

| | |
|---|---|
| Campgrounds | Outdoor adventure retreats |
| Fishing and hunting camps | Vacation camps (except instructional, day) |
| Travel trailer campsites | Recreational vehicle parks |

*Cross-References.*    Establishments primarily engaged in--

- Operating recreational facilities without accommodations--are classified in Subsector 713, Amusement, Gambling, and Recreation Industries;
- Operating instructional camps, such as sports camps, fine arts camps, and computer camps--are classified in Sector 61, Educational Services, based on the nature of instruction;
- Operating children's day camps (except instructional)--are classified in Industry 71399, All Other Amusement and Recreation Industries; and
- Acting as lessors of residential mobile home sites (i.e., trailer parks)--are classified in Industry 53119, Lessors of Other Real Estate Property.

## 721211  RV (Recreational Vehicle) Parks and Campgrounds

This U.S. industry comprises establishments primarily engaged in operating sites to accommodate campers and their equipment, including tents, tent trailers, travel trailers, and RVs (recreational vehicles). These establishments may provide access to facilities, such as washrooms, laundry rooms, recreation halls, playgrounds, stores, and snack bars.

---

T—Canadian, Mexican, and United States industries are comparable.

*Cross-References.*          Establishments primarily engaged in--

- Operating recreational facilities without accommodations--are classified in Subsector 713, Amusement, Gambling, and Recreation Industries; and
- Acting as lessors of residential mobile home sites (i.e., trailer parks)--are classified in Industry 531190, Lessors of Other Real Estate Property.

## 721214  Recreational and Vacation Camps (except Campgrounds)

This U.S. industry comprises establishments primarily engaged in operating overnight recreational camps, such as children's camps, family vacation camps, hunting and fishing camps, and outdoor adventure retreats, that offer trail riding, white water rafting, hiking, and similar activities. These establishments provide accommodation facilities, such as cabins and fixed campsites, and other amenities, such as food services, recreational facilities and equipment, and organized recreational activities.

*Illustrative Examples:*

Fishing camps with accommodation facilities
Dude ranches
Vacation camps (except campgrounds, day, instructional)

Hunting camps with accommodation facilities
Wilderness camps
Outdoor adventure retreats with accommodation facilities

*Cross-References.*          Establishments primarily engaged in--

- Operating instructional camps, such as sports camps, fine arts camps, and computer camps--are classified in Sector 61, Educational Services, based on the nature of instruction; and
- Operating children's day camps (except instructional)--are classified in Industry 713990, All Other Amusement and Recreation Industries.

## 7213     Rooming and Boarding Houses, Dormitories, and Workers' Camps[T]

## 72131    Rooming and Boarding Houses, Dormitories, and Workers' Camps[T]
See industry description for 721310.

## 721310  Rooming and Boarding Houses, Dormitories, and Workers' Camps

This industry comprises establishments primarily engaged in operating rooming and boarding houses and similar facilities, such as fraternity houses, sorority houses, off campus dormitories, residential clubs, and workers' camps. These establishments provide temporary or longer-term accommodations, which, for the period of occupancy, may serve as a principal residence. These establishments also may provide complementary services, such as housekeeping, meals, and laundry services.

*Illustrative Examples*:

Dormitories (off campus)
Sorority houses
Fraternity houses

Workers' camps
Rooming houses

## 722     Food Services and Drinking Places[T]

Industries in the Food Services and Drinking Places subsector prepare meals, snacks, and beverages to customer order for immediate on-premises and off-premises consumption. There is a wide range of establishments in these industries. Some provide food and drink only, while others provide various combinations of seating space, waiter/waitress services, and incidental amenities, such as limited entertainment. The industries in the subsector are grouped based on the type and level of services provided. The industry groups are Special Food Services, such as

---

T—Canadian, Mexican, and United States industries are comparable.

food service contractors, caterers, and mobile food services; Drinking Places (Alcoholic Beverages); and Restaurants and Other Eating Places.

Food and beverage services at hotels and motels, amusement parks, theaters, casinos, country clubs, similar recreational facilities, and civic and social organizations are included in this subsector only if these services are provided by a separate establishment primarily engaged in providing food and beverage services.

Excluded from this subsector are establishments operating dinner cruises. These establishments are classified in Subsector 487, Scenic and Sightseeing Transportation, because they utilize transportation equipment to provide scenic recreational entertainment.

## 7223 Special Food Services[T]

This industry group comprises establishments primarily engaged in providing food services at one or more of the following locations: (1) the customer's location; (2) a location designated by the customer; or (3) from motorized vehicles or nonmotorized carts.

### 72231 Food Service Contractors[T]
See industry description for 722310.

### 722310 Food Service Contractors

This industry comprises establishments primarily engaged in providing food services at institutional, governmental, commercial, or industrial locations of others based on contractual arrangements with these types of organizations for a specified period of time. The establishments of this industry provide food services for the convenience of the contracting organization or the contracting organization's customers. The contractual arrangement of these establishments with contracting organizations may vary by type of facility operated (e.g., cafeteria, restaurant, fast-food eating place), revenue sharing, cost structure, and personnel provided. Management staff is always provided by food service contractors.

*Illustrative Examples:*

Airline food service contractors
Food concession contractors (e.g., at sporting, entertainment, convention facilities)

Cafeteria food service contractors (e.g., at schools, hospitals, government offices)

*Cross-References.* Establishments primarily engaged in--

- Providing food services on a single-event basis--are classified in Industry 722320, Caterers; and
- Supplying and servicing food vending machines--are classified in U.S. Industry 445132, Vending Machine Operators.

### 72232 Caterers[T]
See industry description for 722320.

### 722320 Caterers

This industry comprises establishments primarily engaged in providing single event-based food services. These establishments generally have equipment and vehicles to transport meals and snacks to events and/or prepare food at an off-premise site. Banquet halls with catering staff are included in this industry. Examples of events catered by establishments in this industry are graduation parties, wedding receptions, business or retirement luncheons, and trade shows.

*Cross-References.* Establishments primarily engaged in--

- Preparing and serving meals and snacks for immediate consumption from motorized vehicles or nonmotorized carts--are classified in Industry 722330, Mobile Food Services;

---

T—Canadian, Mexican, and United States industries are comparable.

- Providing food services at institutional, governmental, commercial, or industrial locations of others (e.g., airline contractors, industrial caterers) based on contractual arrangements for a specified period of time--are classified in Industry 722310, Food Service Contractors; and
- Renting out facilities without providing catering staff--are classified in Industry 531120, Lessors of Nonresidential Buildings (except Miniwarehouses).

**72233  Mobile Food Services**[T]
See industry description for 722330.

**722330  Mobile Food Services**

This industry comprises establishments primarily engaged in preparing and serving meals and snacks for immediate consumption from motorized vehicles or nonmotorized carts.  The establishment is the central location from which the caterer route is serviced, not each vehicle or cart.  Included in this industry are establishments primarily engaged in providing food services from vehicles, such as hot dog carts and ice cream trucks.

*Illustrative Examples*:

Ice cream truck vendors                     Mobile refreshment stands
Mobile food concession stands               Mobile food carts and trucks
Mobile canteens                             Mobile snack stands

*Cross-References.*        Establishments primarily engaged in--

- Selling a specialty snack (e.g., ice cream, frozen yogurt, cookies, popcorn) or nonalcoholic beverages, except from mobile vehicles, for consumption on or near the premises--are classified in U.S. Industry 722515, Snack and Nonalcoholic Beverage Bars;
- Providing food services or selling food specialties, such as hamburgers, hot dogs, chicken, pizza, or specialty cuisines, except from mobile vehicles--are classified based on the type of food service provided to patrons; and
- Operating as street vendors (except food) or retailing food (except food prepared and served for immediate consumption)--are classified in Sector 44-45, Retail Trade.

**7224  Drinking Places (Alcoholic Beverages)**[T]

**72241  Drinking Places (Alcoholic Beverages)**[T]
See industry description for 722410.

**722410  Drinking Places (Alcoholic Beverages)**

This industry comprises establishments known as bars, taverns, nightclubs, or drinking places primarily engaged in preparing and serving alcoholic beverages for immediate consumption.  These establishments may also provide limited food services.

*Cross-References.*        Establishments primarily engaged in--

- Preparing and serving alcoholic beverages (i.e., not known as bars or taverns) and providing food services to patrons--are classified in Industry 72251, Restaurants and Other Eating Places;
- Operating a civic or social association with a bar for their members--are classified in Industry 813410, Civic and Social Organizations;
- Retailing packaged alcoholic beverages not for immediate consumption on the premises--are classified in Industry 445320, Beer, Wine, and Liquor Retailers;
- Operating nightclubs or dance clubs without selling alcoholic beverages--are classified in Industry 713990, All Other Amusement and Recreation Industries; and

---

T—Canadian, Mexican, and United States industries are comparable.

- Manufacturing brewery, winery, and distillery products--are classified in Industry Group 3121, Beverage Manufacturing.

## 7225    Restaurants and Other Eating Places[T]

## 72251    Restaurants and Other Eating Places[T]

This industry comprises establishments primarily engaged in one of the following: (1) providing food services to patrons who order and are served while seated (i.e., waiter/waitress service) and pay after eating; (2) providing food services to patrons who generally order or select items (e.g., at a counter, in a buffet line) and pay before eating; or (3) preparing and/or serving a specialty snack (e.g., ice cream, frozen yogurt, cookies) and/or nonalcoholic beverages (e.g., coffee, juices, sodas) for consumption on or near the premises.

*Cross-References.*          Establishments primarily engaged in--

- Preparing and serving alcoholic beverages and known as bars, taverns, or nightclubs--are classified in Industry 72241, Drinking Places (Alcoholic Beverages);
- Preparing and serving snacks and nonalcoholic beverages from mobile vehicles for immediate consumption--are classified in Industry 72233, Mobile Food Services;
- Presenting live theatrical productions and providing food and beverages for consumption on the premises-- are classified in Industry 71111, Theater Companies and Dinner Theaters;
- Operating a civic or social association with a restaurant for their members--are classified in Industry 81341, Civic and Social Organizations;
- Operating as street vendors (except food) or retailing food (except food prepared and served for immediate consumption)--are classified in Sector 44-45, Retail Trade; and
- Restaurant meals order and delivery services (i.e., independent order and delivery services)--are classified in Industry 49221, Local Messengers and Local Delivery.

## 722511  Full-Service Restaurants

This U.S. industry comprises establishments primarily engaged in providing food services to patrons who order and are served while seated (i.e., waiter/waitress service) and pay after eating. These establishments may provide this type of food service to patrons in combination with selling alcoholic beverages, providing carryout services, or presenting live nontheatrical entertainment.

*Cross-References.*          Establishments primarily engaged in--

- Providing food services where patrons generally order or select items and pay before eating, other than mobile food services, cafeterias, grill buffets, buffets, and snack and nonalcoholic beverage bars--are classified in U.S. Industry 722513, Limited-Service Restaurants;
- Preparing and serving meals for immediate consumption using cafeteria-style or buffet serving equipment, known as cafeterias, grill buffets, or buffets--are classified in U.S. Industry 722514, Cafeterias, Grill Buffets, and Buffets;
- Selling a specialty snack (e.g., ice cream, frozen yogurt, cookies, popcorn) or nonalcoholic beverage, except from mobile vehicles, for consumption on or near the premises--are classified in U.S. Industry 722515, Snack and Nonalcoholic Beverage Bars;
- Preparing and serving alcoholic beverages and known as bars, taverns, or nightclubs--are classified in Industry 722410, Drinking Places (Alcoholic Beverages);
- Operating a civic or social association with a restaurant for their members--are classified in Industry 813410, Civic and Social Organizations;
- Presenting live theatrical productions and providing food and beverages for consumption on the premises-- are classified in Industry 711110, Theater Companies and Dinner Theaters; and
- Restaurant meals order and delivery services (i.e., independent order and delivery services)--are classified in Industry 492210, Local Messengers and Local Delivery.

---

T—Canadian, Mexican, and United States industries are comparable.

## 722513 Limited-Service Restaurants

This U.S. industry comprises establishments primarily engaged in providing food services (except snack and nonalcoholic beverage bars) where patrons generally order or select items and pay before eating. Food and drink may be consumed on premises, taken out, or delivered to the customer's location. Some establishments in this industry may provide these food services in combination with selling alcoholic beverages.

*Illustrative Examples:*

Delicatessen restaurants
Pizza delivery shops
Family restaurants, limited-service
Takeout eating places

Fast-food restaurants
Fast casual restaurants
Takeout sandwich shops
Limited-service pizza parlors

*Cross-References.*　　　Establishments primarily engaged in--

- Preparing and serving meals for immediate consumption using cafeteria-style serving equipment, known as cafeterias--are classified in U.S. Industry 722514, Cafeterias, Grill Buffets, and Buffets;
- Providing food services to patrons who order and are served while seated and pay after eating--are classified in U.S. Industry 722511, Full-Service Restaurants;
- Selling a specialty snack (e.g., ice cream, frozen yogurt, candy, cookies) or nonalcoholic beverage, except from mobile vehicles, for consumption on or near the premises--are classified in U.S. Industry 722515, Snack and Nonalcoholic Beverage Bars;
- Retailing confectionery goods and nuts not packaged for immediate consumption--are classified in U.S. Industry 445292, Confectionery and Nut Retailers;
- Retailing baked goods (e.g., pretzels, doughnuts, cookies, and bagels) not baked on the premises and not for immediate consumption--are classified in U.S. Industry 445291, Baked Goods Retailers;
- Preparing and serving alcoholic beverages, known as bars, taverns, or nightclubs--are classified in Industry 722410, Drinking Places (Alcoholic Beverages); and
- Restaurant meals order and delivery services (i.e., independent order and delivery services)--are classified in Industry 492210, Local Messengers and Local Delivery.

## 722514 Cafeterias, Grill Buffets, and Buffets

This U.S. industry comprises establishments, known as cafeterias, grill buffets, or buffets, primarily engaged in preparing and serving meals for immediate consumption using cafeteria-style or buffet serving equipment, such as steam tables, refrigerated areas, display grills, and self-service nonalcoholic beverage dispensing equipment. Patrons select from food and drink items on display in a continuous cafeteria line or from buffet stations.

*Cross-References.*　　　Establishments primarily engaged in--

- Providing food services to patrons who order and are served while seated and pay after eating--are classified in U.S. Industry 722511, Full-Service Restaurants;
- Providing food services where patrons generally order or select items and pay before eating, other than mobile food services, cafeterias, grill buffets, buffets, and snack and nonalcoholic beverage bars--are classified in U.S. Industry 722513, Limited-Service Restaurants; and
- Selling a specialty snack (e.g., ice cream, frozen yogurt, cookies, popcorn) or nonalcoholic beverage, except from mobile vehicles, for consumption on or near the premises--are classified in U.S. Industry 722515, Snack and Nonalcoholic Beverage Bars.

## 722515 Snack and Nonalcoholic Beverage Bars

This U.S. industry comprises establishments primarily engaged in (1) preparing and/or serving a specialty snack, such as ice cream, frozen yogurt, cookies, or popcorn, or (2) serving nonalcoholic beverages, such as coffee, juices, or sodas for consumption on or near the premises. These establishments may carry and sell a combination of snack,

---

T—Canadian, Mexican, and United States industries are comparable.

nonalcoholic beverage, and other related products (e.g., coffee beans, mugs, coffee makers) but generally promote and sell a unique snack or nonalcoholic beverage.

*Illustrative Examples:*

| | |
|---|---|
| Beverage bars, nonalcoholic, fixed location | Cookie shops, on premise baking and carryout service |
| Doughnut shops, on premise baking and carryout service | |
| | Coffee shops, on premise brewing |
| Bagel shops, on premise baking and carryout service | Ice cream parlors |
| Pretzel shops, on premise baking and carryout service | Juice bars, nonalcoholic, fixed location |

*Cross-References.*          Establishments primarily engaged in--

- Selling one or more of the following food specialties (except from mobile vehicles): hamburgers, hot dogs, pizza, chicken, specialty cuisines--are classified based on the type of food service provided to patrons;
- Preparing and serving snacks and nonalcoholic beverages from mobile vehicles for immediate consumption--are classified in Industry 722330, Mobile Food Services; and
- Operating as street vendors (except food) or retailing food (except food prepared and served for immediate consumption)--are classified in Sector 44-45, Retail Trade.

---

T—Canadian, Mexican, and United States industries are comparable.

# Sector 81--Other Services (except Public Administration)<sup>T</sup>

## The Sector as a Whole

The Other Services (except Public Administration) sector comprises establishments engaged in providing services not specifically provided for elsewhere in the classification system. Establishments in this sector are primarily engaged in activities such as equipment and machinery repairing, promoting or administering religious activities, grantmaking, advocacy, and providing drycleaning and laundry services, personal care services, death care services, pet care (except veterinary) services, photofinishing services, temporary parking services, and dating services.

Private households that engage in employing workers on or about the premises in activities primarily concerned with the operation of the household are included in this sector.

Excluded from this sector are establishments primarily engaged in retailing new equipment and also performing repairs and general maintenance on equipment. These establishments are classified in Sector 44-45, Retail Trade.

## 811    Repair and Maintenance<sup>T</sup>

Industries in the Repair and Maintenance subsector restore machinery, equipment, and other products to working order. These establishments also typically provide general or routine maintenance (i.e., servicing) on such products to ensure they work efficiently and to prevent breakdown and unnecessary repairs.

The NAICS structure for this subsector brings together most types of repair and maintenance establishments and categorizes them based on production processes (i.e., on the type of repair and maintenance activity performed, and the necessary skills, expertise, and processes that are found in different repair and maintenance establishments). This NAICS classification does not delineate between repair services provided to businesses versus those that serve households. Although some industries primarily serve either businesses or households, separation by class of customer is limited by the fact that many establishments serve both. Establishments repairing computers and consumer electronics products are two examples of such overlap.

The Repair and Maintenance subsector does not include all establishments that do repair and maintenance. For example, a substantial amount of repair is done by establishments that also manufacture machinery, equipment, and other goods. These establishments are included in the Manufacturing sector in NAICS. In addition, repair of transportation equipment is often provided by or based at transportation facilities, such as airports and seaports, and these activities are included in the Transportation and Warehousing sector. A particularly unique situation exists with repair of buildings. Plumbing, electrical installation and repair, painting and decorating, and other construction-related establishments are often involved in performing installation or other work on new construction as well as providing repair services on existing structures. While some specialize in repair, it is difficult to distinguish between the two types and all are included in the Construction sector.

Excluded from this subsector are establishments primarily engaged in rebuilding or remanufacturing machinery and equipment. These are classified in Sector 31-33, Manufacturing. Also excluded are retail establishments that provide after-sale services and repair. These are classified in Sector 44-45, Retail Trade.

## 8111    Automotive Repair and Maintenance<sup>T</sup>

This industry group comprises establishments involved in providing repair and maintenance services for automotive vehicles, such as passenger cars, trucks, and vans, and all trailers. Establishments in this industry group employ mechanics with specialized technical skills to diagnose and repair the mechanical and electrical systems for automotive vehicles, repair automotive interiors, and paint or repair automotive exteriors.

## 81111    Automotive Mechanical and Electrical Repair and Maintenance<sup>T</sup>

This industry comprises establishments primarily engaged in providing mechanical or electrical repair and maintenance services for automotive vehicles, such as passenger cars, trucks, and vans, and all trailers. These establishments may specialize in a single service or may provide a wide range of these services.

---

T—Canadian, Mexican, and United States industries are comparable.

*Cross-References.*        Establishments primarily engaged in--

- Retailing automotive vehicles and automotive parts and accessories and also providing automotive vehicle repair services--are classified in Subsector 441, Motor Vehicle and Parts Dealers;
- Retailing motor fuels and also providing automotive vehicle repair services--are classified in Industry Group 4571, Gasoline Stations;
- Rebuilding motor vehicle gasoline engines and engine parts--are classified in Industry 33631, Motor Vehicle Gasoline Engine and Engine Parts Manufacturing;
- Changing motor oil and lubricating the chassis of automotive vehicles--are classified in Industry 81119, Other Automotive Repair and Maintenance;
- Providing automotive vehicle air-conditioning repair--are classified in Industry 81119, Other Automotive Repair and Maintenance; and
- Motorcycle repair and maintenance services--are classified in Industry 81149, Other Personal and Household Goods Repair and Maintenance.

### 811111  General Automotive Repair

  This U.S. industry comprises establishments primarily engaged in providing (1) a wide range of mechanical and electrical repair and maintenance services for automotive vehicles, such as passenger cars, trucks, and vans, and all trailers or (2) engine repair and replacement.

*Illustrative Examples:*

Automobile repair garages (except gasoline service stations)

General automotive repair shops
Automotive engine repair and replacement shops

*Cross-References.*        Establishments primarily engaged in--

- Retailing new automotive parts and accessories and also providing automotive vehicle repair services--are classified in Industry 441330, Automotive Parts and Accessories Retailers;
- Changing motor oil and lubricating the chassis of automotive vehicles--are classified in U.S. Industry 811191, Automotive Oil Change and Lubrication Shops;
- Providing specialized mechanical or electrical automotive vehicle repair and maintenance services (except engine repair and replacement)--are classified in U.S. Industry 811114, Specialized Automotive Repair;
- Rebuilding motor vehicle gasoline engines and engine parts--are classified in Industry 336310, Motor Vehicle Gasoline Engine and Engine Parts Manufacturing;
- Retailing motor fuels and also providing automotive vehicle repair services--are classified in Industry Group 4571, Gasoline Stations;
- Retailing automobiles and light trucks for highway use and also providing automotive vehicle repair services--are classified in Industry Group 4411, Automobile Dealers; and
- Motorcycle repair and maintenance services--are classified in Industry 811490, Other Personal and Household Goods Repair and Maintenance.

### 811114  Specialized Automotive Repair

  This U.S. industry comprises establishments primarily engaged in providing specialized mechanical or electrical repair and maintenance services (except engine repair and replacement) for automotive vehicles, such as passenger cars, trucks, and vans, and all trailers.

*Illustrative Examples:*

Automotive brake repair shops
Automotive suspension repair shops
Automotive exhaust system replacement and repair shops

Automotive electrical repair shops
Automotive transmission repair shops
Automotive tune-up shops

---

T—Canadian, Mexican, and United States industries are comparable.

**census.gov/naics**

*Cross-References.*        Establishments primarily engaged in--

- Providing a wide range of mechanical and electrical automotive vehicle repair or specializing in engine repair or replacement--are classified in U.S. Industry 811111, General Automotive Repair;
- Changing motor oil and lubricating the chassis of automotive vehicles--are classified in U.S. Industry 811191, Automotive Oil Change and Lubrication Shops;
- Providing automotive vehicle air-conditioning repair--are classified in U.S. Industry 811198, All Other Automotive Repair and Maintenance; and
- Motorcycle repair and maintenance services--are classified in Industry 811490, Other Personal and Household Goods Repair and Maintenance.

## 81112   Automotive Body, Paint, Interior, and Glass Repair[T]

This industry comprises establishments primarily engaged in providing one or more of the following: (1) repairing or customizing automotive vehicle and trailer bodies and interiors; (2) painting automotive vehicle and trailer bodies; (3) replacing, repairing, and/or tinting automotive vehicle glass; and (4) customizing automobile, truck, and van interiors for the physically disabled or other customers with special requirements.

*Illustrative Examples:*

| | |
|---|---|
| Automotive body shops | Automotive glass shops |
| Automotive paint shops | Restoration shops, antique and classic automotive |

*Cross-References.*        Establishments primarily engaged in--

- Automotive rustproofing and undercoating services--are classified in Industry 81119, Other Automotive Repair and Maintenance;
- Manufacturing automotive vehicles and trailers or customizing these vehicles on an assembly line basis--are classified in Subsector 336, Transportation Equipment Manufacturing; and
- Motorcycle repair and maintenance services--are classified in Industry 81149, Other Personal and Household Goods Repair and Maintenance.

## 811121  Automotive Body, Paint, and Interior Repair and Maintenance

This U.S. industry comprises establishments primarily engaged in repairing or customizing automotive vehicle and trailer bodies and interiors; and/or painting automotive vehicles and trailer bodies.

*Illustrative Examples:*

| | |
|---|---|
| Automotive body shops | Restoration shops, antique and classic automotive |
| Automotive body conversion services | Automotive paint shops |

*Cross-References.*        Establishments primarily engaged in--

- Automotive glass replacement, repair, and/or tinting--are classified in U.S. Industry 811122, Automotive Glass Replacement Shops;
- Automotive rustproofing and undercoating services--are classified in U.S. Industry 811198, All Other Automotive Repair and Maintenance;
- Manufacturing automotive vehicles and trailers or customizing these vehicles on an assembly line basis--are classified in Subsector 336, Transportation Equipment Manufacturing; and
- Motorcycle repair and maintenance services--are classified in Industry 811490, Other Personal and Household Goods Repair and Maintenance.

---

T—Canadian, Mexican, and United States industries are comparable.

**811122 Automotive Glass Replacement Shops**

This U.S. industry comprises establishments primarily engaged in replacing, repairing, and/or tinting automotive vehicle glass, such as passenger car, truck, and van glass.

*Cross-References.*

Establishments primarily engaged in motorcycle repair and maintenance services are classified in Industry 811490, Other Personal and Household Goods Repair and Maintenance.

**81119 Other Automotive Repair and Maintenance[T]**

This industry comprises establishments primarily engaged in providing automotive repair and maintenance services (except mechanical and electrical repair and maintenance and body, paint, interior, and glass repair) for automotive vehicles, such as passenger cars, trucks, and vans, and all trailers.

*Illustrative Examples:*

Automotive air-conditioning repair shops
Automotive tire repair (except retreading) shops
Automotive oil change and lubrication shops

Car washes
Automotive rustproofing and undercoating shops

*Cross-References.*   Establishments primarily engaged in--

- Tire retreading or recapping--are classified in Industry 32621, Tire Manufacturing;
- Automotive vehicle mechanical and electrical repair and maintenance--are classified in Industry 81111, Automotive Mechanical and Electrical Repair and Maintenance;
- Automotive body, paint, interior, and glass repair--are classified in Industry 81112, Automotive Body, Paint, Interior, and Glass Repair;
- Motorcycle repair and maintenance services--are classified in Industry 81149, Other Personal and Household Goods Repair and Maintenance;
- Retailing and installing automotive audio equipment--are classified in Industry 44133, Automotive Parts and Accessories Retailers; and
- Retailing new tires in combination with tire repair services--are classified in Industry 44134, Tire Dealers.

**811191 Automotive Oil Change and Lubrication Shops**

This U.S. industry comprises establishments primarily engaged in changing motor oil and lubricating the chassis of automotive vehicles, such as passenger cars, trucks, and vans.

*Cross-References.*

Establishments primarily engaged in motorcycle repair and maintenance services are classified in Industry 811490, Other Personal and Household Goods Repair and Maintenance.

**811192 Car Washes**

This U.S. industry comprises establishments primarily engaged in cleaning, washing, and/or waxing automotive vehicles, such as passenger cars, trucks, and vans, and trailers.

*Illustrative Examples:*

Automotive detail shops
Mobile car and truck washes

Car washes
Self-service car washes

---

T—Canadian, Mexican, and United States industries are comparable.

**811198   All Other Automotive Repair and Maintenance**

This U.S. industry comprises establishments primarily engaged in providing automotive repair and maintenance services (except mechanical and electrical repair and maintenance; body, paint, interior, and glass repair; motor oil change and lubrication; and car washing) for automotive vehicles, such as passenger cars, trucks, and vans, and all trailers.

*Illustrative Examples:*

Automotive air-conditioning repair shops
Automotive tire repair (except retreading) shops
                                Automotive rustproofing and undercoating shops

*Cross-References.*      Establishments primarily engaged in--

- Tire retreading or recapping--are classified in U.S. Industry 326212, Tire Retreading;
- Providing a range of mechanical and electrical automotive vehicle repair or specializing in engine repair or replacement--are classified in U.S. Industry 811111, General Automotive Repair;
- Providing specialized mechanical or electrical automotive vehicle repair and maintenance services (except engine repair and replacement)--are classified in U.S. Industry 811114, Specialized Automotive Repair;
- Repairing or customizing automotive vehicle bodies and interiors--are classified in U.S. Industry 811121, Automotive Body, Paint, and Interior Repair and Maintenance;
- Replacing, repairing, and/or tinting automotive glass--are classified in U.S. Industry 811122, Automotive Glass Replacement Shops;
- Changing motor oil and lubricating the chassis of automotive vehicles--are classified in U.S. Industry 811191, Automotive Oil Change and Lubrication Shops;
- Cleaning, washing, and/or waxing automotive vehicles and trailers--are classified in U.S. Industry 811192, Car Washes;
- Motorcycle repair and maintenance services--are classified in Industry 811490, Other Personal and Household Goods Repair and Maintenance;
- Retailing and installing automotive audio equipment--are classified in Industry 441330, Automotive Parts and Accessories Retailers; and
- Retailing new tires in combination with tire repair services--are classified in Industry 441340, Tire Dealers.

**8112   Electronic and Precision Equipment Repair and Maintenance**<sup>T</sup>

**81121   Electronic and Precision Equipment Repair and Maintenance**<sup>T</sup>
See industry description for 811210.

**811210   Electronic and Precision Equipment Repair and Maintenance**

This industry comprises establishments primarily engaged in repairing and maintaining one or more of the following: (1) consumer electronic equipment; (2) computers; (3) office machines; (4) communication equipment; and (5) other electronic and precision equipment and instruments, without retailing these products as new. Establishments in this industry repair items, such as microscopes, radar and sonar equipment, televisions, stereos, video recorders, computers, fax machines, photocopying machines, two-way radios, cellular telephones, and other communications equipment, scientific instruments, and medical equipment.

*Cross-References.*      Establishments primarily engaged in--

- Selling, installing, and monitoring home security systems--are classified in U.S. Industry 561621, Security Systems Services (except Locksmiths);
- Installing alarm systems (e.g., fire, burglar), without selling or monitoring services--are classified in Industry 238210, Electrical Contractors and Other Wiring Installation Contractors;
- Retailing new computers, computer peripherals, televisions, and other consumer electronics and also providing repair services--are classified in Industry 449210, Electronics and Appliance Retailers;

---

T—Canadian, Mexican, and United States industries are comparable.

- Selling wireless communication service plans and cellular telephones, as agents for wireless telecommunications carriers and resellers, and also providing repair services--are classified in U.S. Industry 517122, Agents for Wireless Telecommunications Services;
- Rewinding armatures and rebuilding electric motors on a factory basis--are classified in U.S. Industry 335312, Motor and Generator Manufacturing; and
- Factory rebuilding or overhauling of electronic and precision equipment--are classified in the Manufacturing sector by type of equipment.

**8113 Commercial and Industrial Machinery and Equipment (except Automotive and Electronic) Repair and Maintenance[T]**

**81131 Commercial and Industrial Machinery and Equipment (except Automotive and Electronic) Repair and Maintenance[T]**
See industry description for 811310.

**811310 Commercial and Industrial Machinery and Equipment (except Automotive and Electronic) Repair and Maintenance**

This industry comprises establishments primarily engaged in the repair and maintenance of commercial and industrial machinery and equipment. Establishments in this industry either sharpen/install commercial and industrial machinery blades and saws or provide welding (e.g., automotive, general) repair services; or repair agricultural and other heavy and industrial machinery and equipment (e.g., forklifts and other material handling equipment, machine tools, commercial refrigeration equipment, construction equipment, and mining machinery).

*Cross-References.* Establishments primarily engaged in--

- Automotive repair (except welding) and maintenance--are classified in Industry Group 8111, Automotive Repair and Maintenance;
- Repairing and maintaining electronic and precision equipment--are classified in Industry 811210, Electronic and Precision Equipment Repair and Maintenance;
- Oil well rig building, repairing, and dismantling, on a contract basis--are classified in U.S. Industry 213112, Support Activities for Oil and Gas Operations;
- On-site welding for building foundations and structures--are classified in Industry 238190, Other Foundation, Structure, and Building Exterior Contractors;
- Oil and gas pipeline and related structures construction and repair--are classified in Industry 237120, Oil and Gas Pipeline and Related Structures Construction;
- Repairing and servicing aircraft--are classified in Industry 488190, Other Support Activities for Air Transportation;
- Converting, rebuilding, and overhauling aircraft--are classified in Industry 33641, Aerospace Product and Parts Manufacturing;
- Repairing and servicing railroad cars and engines--are classified in Industry 488210, Support Activities for Rail Transportation;
- Rebuilding or remanufacturing railroad engines and cars--are classified in Industry 336510, Railroad Rolling Stock Manufacturing;
- Repairing and overhauling ships at floating drydocks--are classified in Industry 488390, Other Support Activities for Water Transportation;
- Repairing and overhauling ships at shipyards--are classified in U.S. Industry 336611, Ship Building and Repairing;
- Rewinding armatures or rebuilding electric motors on a factory basis--are classified in U.S. Industry 335312, Motor and Generator Manufacturing; and
- Repairing and maintaining home and garden equipment (e.g., sharpening or installing blades and saws)--are classified in U.S. Industry 811411, Home and Garden Equipment Repair and Maintenance.

---

T—Canadian, Mexican, and United States industries are comparable.

## 8114    Personal and Household Goods Repair and Maintenance[T]

This industry group comprises establishments primarily engaged in home and garden equipment and appliance repair and maintenance; reupholstery and furniture repair; footwear and leather goods repair; and other personal and household goods repair and maintenance.

## 81141    Home and Garden Equipment and Appliance Repair and Maintenance[T]

This industry comprises establishments primarily engaged in repairing and servicing home and garden equipment and/or household-type appliances without retailing new equipment or appliances. Establishments in this industry repair and maintain items, such as lawnmowers, edgers, snowblowers, leaf blowers, washing machines, clothes dryers, and refrigerators.

*Cross-References.*          Establishments primarily engaged in--

- Retailing new outdoor power equipment and also providing repair services--are classified in Industry 44423, Outdoor Power Equipment Retailers;
- Retailing an array of new appliances and also providing repair services--are classified in Industry 44921, Electronics and Appliance Retailers;
- Repairing, servicing, or installing central heating and air-conditioning equipment--are classified in Industry 23822, Plumbing, Heating, and Air-Conditioning Contractors; and
- Repairing commercial refrigeration equipment--are classified in Industry 81131, Commercial and Industrial Machinery and Equipment (except Automotive and Electronic) Repair and Maintenance.

## 811411   Home and Garden Equipment Repair and Maintenance

This U.S. industry comprises establishments primarily engaged in repairing and servicing home and garden equipment without retailing new home and garden equipment, such as lawnmowers, handheld power tools, edgers, snowblowers, leaf blowers, and trimmers.

*Cross-References.*

Establishments primarily engaged in retailing new outdoor power equipment and also providing repair services are classified in Industry 444230, Outdoor Power Equipment Retailers.

## 811412   Appliance Repair and Maintenance

This U.S. industry comprises establishments primarily engaged in repairing and servicing household appliances without retailing new appliances, such as refrigerators, stoves, washing machines, clothes dryers, and room air-conditioners.

*Cross-References.*          Establishments primarily engaged in--

- Repairing, servicing, or installing central heating and air-conditioning equipment--are classified in Industry 238220, Plumbing, Heating, and Air-Conditioning Contractors;
- Repairing commercial refrigeration equipment--are classified in Industry 811310, Commercial and Industrial Machinery and Equipment (except Automotive and Electronic) Repair and Maintenance; and
- Retailing an array of new appliances and also providing repair services--are classified in Industry 449210, Electronics and Appliance Retailers.

## 81142    Reupholstery and Furniture Repair[T]
See industry description for 811420.

---

T—Canadian, Mexican, and United States industries are comparable.

## 811420 Reupholstery and Furniture Repair

This industry comprises establishments primarily engaged in one or more of the following: (1) reupholstering furniture; (2) refinishing furniture; (3) repairing furniture; and (4) repairing and restoring furniture.

*Cross-References.* Establishments primarily engaged in--

- Automotive vehicle and trailer upholstery repair--are classified in U.S. Industry 811121, Automotive Body, Paint, and Interior Repair and Maintenance; and
- The restoration of museum pieces by independent conservators--are classified in Industry 711510, Independent Artists, Writers, and Performers.

## 81143 Footwear and Leather Goods Repair[T]
See industry description for 811430.

## 811430 Footwear and Leather Goods Repair

This industry comprises establishments primarily engaged in repairing footwear and/or repairing other leather or leather-like goods without retailing new footwear and leather or leather-like goods, such as handbags and briefcases.

*Cross-References.* Establishments primarily engaged in--

- Retailing new luggage and leather goods and also providing repair services--are classified in Industry 458320, Luggage and Leather Goods Retailers;
- Shining shoes--are classified in Industry 812990, All Other Personal Services; and
- Repairing leather clothing--are classified in Industry 811490, Other Personal and Household Goods Repair and Maintenance.

## 81149 Other Personal and Household Goods Repair and Maintenance[T]
See industry description for 811490.

## 811490 Other Personal and Household Goods Repair and Maintenance

This industry comprises establishments primarily engaged in repairing and servicing personal or household-type goods without retailing new personal or household-type goods (except home and garden equipment, appliances, furniture, and footwear and leather goods). Establishments in this industry repair items, such as garments; watches; jewelry; musical instruments; bicycles and motorcycles; and motorboats, canoes, sailboats, and other recreational boats.

*Cross-References.* Establishments primarily engaged in--

- Repairing home and garden equipment--are classified in U.S. Industry 811411, Home and Garden Equipment Repair and Maintenance;
- Repairing appliances--are classified in U.S. Industry 811412, Appliance Repair and Maintenance;
- Reupholstering and repairing furniture--are classified in Industry 811420, Reupholstery and Furniture Repair;
- Repairing footwear and leather goods--are classified in Industry 811430, Footwear and Leather Goods Repair;
- Operating marinas and providing a range of other services including boat cleaning and repair--are classified in Industry 713930, Marinas; and
- Drycleaning garments--are classified in Industry Group 8123, Drycleaning and Laundry Services.

T—Canadian, Mexican, and United States industries are comparable.

**812    Personal and Laundry Services[T]**

Industries in the Personal and Laundry Services subsector group establishments that provide personal and laundry services to individuals, households, and businesses. Services performed include: personal care services; death care services; laundry and drycleaning services; and a wide range of other personal services, such as pet care (except veterinary) services, photofinishing services, temporary parking services, and dating services.

The Personal and Laundry Services subsector is by no means all-inclusive of the services that could be termed personal services (i.e., those provided to individuals rather than businesses). There are many other subsectors, as well as sectors, that provide services to persons. Establishments providing legal, accounting, tax preparation, architectural, portrait photography, and similar professional services are classified in Sector 54, Professional, Scientific, and Technical Services; those providing job placement, travel arrangement, home security, interior and exterior house cleaning, exterminating, lawn and garden care, and similar support services are classified in Sector 56, Administrative and Support and Waste Management and Remediation Services; those providing health and social services are classified in Sector 62, Health Care and Social Assistance; those providing amusement and recreation services are classified in Sector 71, Arts, Entertainment, and Recreation; those providing educational instruction are classified in Sector 61, Educational Services; those providing repair services are classified in Subsector 811, Repair and Maintenance; and those providing spiritual, civic, and advocacy services are classified in Subsector 813, Religious, Grantmaking, Civic, Professional, and Similar Organizations.

**8121    Personal Care Services**

This industry group comprises establishments, such as barber and beauty shops, that provide appearance care services to individual consumers.

**81211    Hair, Nail, and Skin Care Services**

This industry comprises establishments primarily engaged in one or more of the following: (1) providing hair care services; (2) providing nail care services; and (3) providing facials or applying makeup (except permanent makeup).

*Illustrative Examples:*

Barber shops
Hair stylist shops
Beauty salons

Nail salons
Cosmetology salons

*Cross-References.*    Establishments primarily engaged in--

- Offering training in barbering, hair styling, or the cosmetic arts--are classified in Industry 61151, Technical and Trade Schools;
- Providing massage (except offices of massage therapists), electrolysis (i.e., hair removal), permanent makeup, or tanning services--are classified in Industry 81219, Other Personal Care Services; and
- Providing medical skin care services (e.g., cosmetic surgery, dermatology)--are classified in Sector 62, Health Care and Social Assistance.

**812111  Barber Shops**

This U.S. industry comprises establishments known as barber shops or men's hair stylist shops primarily engaged in cutting, trimming, and styling men's and boys' hair; and/or shaving and trimming men's beards.

*Cross-References.*    Establishments primarily engaged in--

- Offering training in barbering--are classified in U.S. Industry 611511, Cosmetology and Barber Schools; and
- Providing hair care services (except establishments known as barber shops or men's hair stylist shops)--are classified in U.S. Industry 812112, Beauty Salons.

T—Canadian, Mexican, and United States industries are comparable.

### 812112  Beauty Salons

This U.S. industry comprises establishments (except those known as barber shops or men's hair stylist shops) primarily engaged in one or more of the following: (1) cutting, trimming, shampooing, coloring, waving, or styling hair; (2) providing facials; and (3) applying makeup (except permanent makeup).

*Illustrative Examples:*

| | |
|---|---|
| Beauty parlors or shops | Hairdressing salons or shops |
| Facial salons or shops | Cosmetology salons or shops |
| Combined beauty and barber shops | Unisex or women's hair stylist shops |

*Cross-References.*          Establishments primarily engaged in--

- Cutting, trimming, and styling men's and boys' hair (known as barber shops or men's hair stylist shops)--are classified in U.S. Industry 812111, Barber Shops;
- Offering training in hair styling or the cosmetic arts--are classified in U.S. Industry 611511, Cosmetology and Barber Schools;
- Providing nail care services--are classified in U.S. Industry 812113, Nail Salons;
- Providing massage (except offices of massage therapists), electrolysis (i.e., hair removal), permanent makeup, or tanning services--are classified in U.S. Industry 812199, Other Personal Care Services; and
- Providing medical skin care services (e.g., cosmetic surgery, dermatology)--are classified in Sector 62, Health Care and Social Assistance.

### 812113  Nail Salons

This U.S. industry comprises establishments primarily engaged in providing nail care services, such as manicures, pedicures, and nail extensions.

### 81219  Other Personal Care Services

This industry comprises establishments primarily engaged in providing personal care services (except hair, nail, facial, or nonpermanent makeup services).

*Illustrative Examples:*

| | |
|---|---|
| Day spas | Hair replacement (except by offices of physicians) or |
| Depilatory or electrolysis (i.e., hair removal) salons | weaving services |
| Permanent makeup salons | Tanning salons |
| Ear piercing services | Tattoo parlors |
| Steam baths | Non-medical diet and weight reducing centers |

*Cross-References.*          Establishments primarily engaged in--

- Providing hair, nail, facial, or nonpermanent makeup services--are classified in Industry 81211, Hair, Nail, and Skin Care Services;
- Operating physical fitness facilities--are classified in Industry 71394, Fitness and Recreational Sports Centers;
- Providing personal fitness training services without operating a fitness facility--are classified in Industry 81299, All Other Personal Services;
- Operating health resorts and spas that provide lodging--are classified in Industry 72111, Hotels (except Casino Hotels) and Motels; and
- Providing medical or surgical hair replacement, weight reduction, or massage therapy services--are classified in Sector 62, Health Care and Social Assistance.

---

T—Canadian, Mexican, and United States industries are comparable.

## 812191　Diet and Weight Reducing Centers

This U.S. industry comprises establishments primarily engaged in providing non-medical services to assist clients in attaining or maintaining a desired weight. The sale of weight reduction products, such as food supplements, may be an integral component of the program. These services typically include individual or group counseling, menu and exercise planning, and weight and body measurement monitoring.

*Cross-References.*　　　Establishments primarily engaged in--

- Operating physical fitness facilities--are classified in Industry 713940, Fitness and Recreational Sports Centers;
- Providing personal fitness training services without operating a fitness facility--are classified in Industry 812990, All Other Personal Services;
- Operating health resorts and spas that provide lodging--are classified in Industry 721110, Hotels (except Casino Hotels) and Motels; and
- Providing medical or surgical weight reduction--are classified in Sector 62, Health Care and Social Assistance.

## 812199　Other Personal Care Services

This U.S. industry comprises establishments primarily engaged in providing personal care services (except hair, nail, facial, nonpermanent makeup, or non-medical diet and weight reducing services).

*Illustrative Examples:*

Day spas
Depilatory or electrolysis (i.e., hair removal) salons
Saunas
Ear piercing services
Steam baths

Hair replacement (except by offices of physicians) or weaving services
Tanning salons
Tattoo parlors
Permanent makeup salons

*Cross-References.*　　　Establishments primarily engaged in--

- Cutting, trimming, and styling men's and boys' hair (known as barber shops or men's hair stylist shops)--are classified in U.S. Industry 812111, Barber Shops;
- Providing hair, facial, or nonpermanent makeup services (except establishments known as barber shops or men's hair stylist shops)--are classified in U.S. Industry 812112, Beauty Salons;
- Nail care services--are classified in U.S. Industry 812113, Nail Salons;
- Providing non-medical diet and weight reducing services--are classified in U.S. Industry 812191, Diet and Weight Reducing Centers;
- Operating health resorts and spas that provide lodging--are classified in Industry 721110, Hotels (except Casino Hotels) and Motels; and
- Providing medical or surgical hair replacement, weight reduction, or massage therapy services--are classified in Sector 62, Health Care and Social Assistance.

## 8122　Death Care Services

This industry group comprises establishments primarily engaged in preparing the dead for burial or interment, conducting funerals, operating sites or structures reserved for the interment of human or animals remains, and/or cremating the dead.

## 81221　Funeral Homes and Funeral Services
See industry description for 812210.

---

T—Canadian, Mexican, and United States industries are comparable.

### 812210  Funeral Homes and Funeral Services

This industry comprises establishments primarily engaged in preparing the dead for burial or interment and conducting funerals (i.e., providing facilities for wakes, arranging transportation for the dead, selling caskets and related merchandise).  Funeral homes combined with crematories are included in this industry.

*Cross-References.*

Establishments (except funeral homes) primarily engaged in cremating the dead are classified in Industry 812220, Cemeteries and Crematories.

### 81222  Cemeteries and Crematories
See industry description for 812220.

### 812220  Cemeteries and Crematories

This industry comprises establishments primarily engaged in operating sites or structures reserved for the interment of human or animal remains and/or cremating the dead.

*Illustrative Examples:*

Cemetery associations (i.e., operators of cemeteries)
Memorial gardens (i.e., burial places)
Pet cemeteries

Crematories (except combined with funeral homes)
Mausoleums

*Cross-References.*

- Crematories combined with funeral homes are classified in Industry 812210, Funeral Homes and Funeral Services; and
- Cemetery memorial dealers (e.g., headstones, markers, vaults) are classified in U.S. Industry 459999, All Other Miscellaneous Retailers.

### 8123  Drycleaning and Laundry Services

This industry group comprises establishments primarily engaged in operating coin- or card-operated or similar self-service laundries and drycleaners; providing drycleaning and laundry services (except coin- or card-operated); and supplying, on a rental or contract basis, laundered items (e.g., uniforms, gowns, shop towels, etc.).  Included in this industry group are establishments primarily engaged in supplying and servicing coin- or card-operated laundry and drycleaning equipment in places of business operated by others, such as apartments and dormitories.

### 81231  Coin-Operated Laundries and Drycleaners
See industry description for 812310.

### 812310  Coin-Operated Laundries and Drycleaners

This industry comprises establishments primarily engaged in (1) operating facilities with coin- or card-operated or similar self-service laundry and drycleaning equipment for customer use on the premises and/or (2) supplying and servicing coin- or card-operated or similar self-service laundry and drycleaning equipment for customer use in places of business operated by others, such as apartments and dormitories.

### 81232  Drycleaning and Laundry Services (except Coin-Operated)
See industry description for 812320.

---

T—Canadian, Mexican, and United States industries are comparable.

## 812320  Drycleaning and Laundry Services (except Coin-Operated)

This industry comprises establishments primarily engaged in one or more of the following: (1) providing drycleaning services (except coin- or card-operated); (2) providing laundering services (except linen and uniform supply or coin- or card-operated); (3) providing drop-off and pick-up sites for laundries and/or drycleaners; and (4) providing specialty cleaning services for specific types of garments and other textile items (except carpets and upholstery), such as fur, leather, or suede garments; wedding gowns; hats; draperies; and pillows. These establishments may provide all, a combination of, or none of the cleaning services on the premises.

*Cross-References.*          Establishments primarily engaged in--

- Supplying laundered linens and uniforms on a rental or contract basis--are classified in Industry 81233, Linen and Uniform Supply;
- Operating coin- or card-operated or similar self-service laundry or drycleaning facilities--are classified in Industry 812310, Coin-Operated Laundries and Drycleaners; and
- Cleaning used carpets and upholstery--are classified in Industry 561740, Carpet and Upholstery Cleaning Services.

## 81233   Linen and Uniform Supply

This industry comprises establishments primarily engaged in supplying, on a rental or contract basis, laundered items, such as uniforms, gowns and coats, table linens, bed linens, towels, clean room apparel, and treated mops or shop towels.

## 812331  Linen Supply

This U.S. industry comprises establishments primarily engaged in supplying, on a rental or contract basis, laundered items, such as table and bed linens; towels; diapers; and uniforms, gowns, or coats of the type used by doctors, nurses, barbers, beauticians, and waitresses.

*Cross-References.*

Establishments primarily engaged in supplying, on a rental or contract basis, laundered industrial work uniforms and related work clothing are classified in U.S. Industry 812332, Industrial Launderers.

## 812332  Industrial Launderers

This U.S. industry comprises establishments primarily engaged in supplying, on a rental or contract basis, laundered industrial work uniforms and related work clothing, such as protective apparel (flame and heat resistant) and clean room apparel; dust control items, such as treated mops, rugs, mats, dust tool covers, cloths, and shop or wiping towels.

*Cross-References.*

Establishments primarily engaged in supplying, on a rental or contract basis, laundered uniforms, gowns, or coats of the type used by doctors, nurses, barbers, beauticians, and waitresses are classified in U.S. Industry 812331, Linen Supply.

## 8129    Other Personal Services

This industry group comprises establishments primarily engaged in providing personal services (except personal care services, death care services, or drycleaning and laundry services).

## 81291   Pet Care (except Veterinary) Services
See industry description for 812910.

---

T—Canadian, Mexican, and United States industries are comparable.

## 812910  Pet Care (except Veterinary) Services

This industry comprises establishments primarily engaged in providing pet care services (except veterinary), such as boarding, grooming, sitting, walking, and training pets.

*Cross-References.*          Establishments primarily engaged in--

- Practicing veterinary medicine--are classified in Industry 541940, Veterinary Services;
- Boarding horses--are classified in Industry 115210, Support Activities for Animal Production; and
- Transporting pets--are classified in U.S. Industry 485991, Special Needs Transportation.

## 81292  Photofinishing

This industry comprises establishments primarily engaged in developing film and/or making photographic slides, prints, and enlargements.

*Cross-References.*

Establishments primarily engaged in processing motion picture film for the motion picture and television industries are classified in Industry 51219, Postproduction Services and Other Motion Picture and Video Industries.

## 812921  Photofinishing Laboratories (except One-Hour)

This U.S. industry comprises establishments (except those known as "one-hour" photofinishing labs) primarily engaged in developing film and/or making photographic slides, prints, and enlargements.

*Cross-References.*

- Establishments primarily engaged in processing motion picture film for the motion picture and television industries are classified in U.S. Industry 512199, Other Motion Picture and Video Industries; and
- Establishments known as "one-hour" photofinishing labs are classified in U.S. Industry 812922, One-Hour Photofinishing.

## 812922  One-Hour Photofinishing

This U.S. industry comprises establishments known as "one-hour" photofinishing labs primarily engaged in developing film and/or making photographic slides, prints, and enlargements on a short turnaround or while-you-wait basis.

*Cross-References.*

Photofinishing laboratories (except those known as "one-hour" photofinishing labs) are classified in U.S. Industry 812921, Photofinishing Laboratories (except One-Hour).

## 81293  Parking Lots and Garages
See industry description for 812930.

## 812930  Parking Lots and Garages

This industry comprises establishments primarily engaged in providing parking space for motor vehicles, usually on an hourly, daily, or monthly basis and/or valet parking services.

---

T—Canadian, Mexican, and United States industries are comparable.

*Cross-References.*

Establishments primarily engaged in providing extended or dead storage of motor vehicles are classified in Industry 493190, Other Warehousing and Storage.

## 81299   All Other Personal Services
See industry description for 812990.

## 812990   All Other Personal Services

This industry comprises establishments primarily engaged in providing personal services (except personal care services, death care services, drycleaning and laundry services, pet care services, photofinishing services, or parking space and/or valet parking services).

*Illustrative Examples:*

| | |
|---|---|
| Bail bonding or bondsperson services | Social escort services |
| Shoeshine services | Consumer buying services |
| Coin- or card-operated personal services | Wedding planning services |
| machine (e.g., blood pressure, locker, photographic, | Dating services |
| scale, shoeshine) concession operators | Personal fitness training services |

*Cross-References.*          Establishments primarily engaged in--

- Providing personal care services--are classified in Industry Group 8121, Personal Care Services;
- Providing death care services--are classified in Industry Group 8122, Death Care Services;
- Providing drycleaning and laundry services--are classified in Industry Group 8123, Drycleaning and Laundry Services;
- Providing pet care (except veterinary) services--are classified in Industry 812910, Pet Care (except Veterinary) Services;
- Practicing veterinary medicine--are classified in Industry 541940, Veterinary Services;
- Providing photofinishing services--are classified in Industry 81292, Photofinishing;
- Providing parking space for motor vehicles and/or valet parking services--are classified in Industry 812930, Parking Lots and Garages; and
- Providing non-medical home care or homemaker services for the elderly or persons with disabilities--are classified in Industry 624120, Services for the Elderly and Persons with Disabilities.

## 813     Religious, Grantmaking, Civic, Professional, and Similar Organizations[T]

Industries in the Religious, Grantmaking, Civic, Professional, and Similar Organizations subsector group establishments that organize and promote religious activities; support various causes through grantmaking; advocate various social and political causes; and promote and defend the interests of their members.

The industry groups within the subsector are defined in terms of their activities, such as establishments that provide funding for specific causes or for a variety of charitable causes; establishments that advocate and actively promote causes and beliefs for the public good; and establishments that have an active membership structure to promote causes and represent the interests of their members.  Establishments in this subsector may publish newsletters, books, and periodicals for distribution to their members.

## 8131    Religious Organizations

## 81311    Religious Organizations
See industry description for 813110.

---

T—Canadian, Mexican, and United States industries are comparable.

## 813110  Religious Organizations

This industry comprises (1) establishments primarily engaged in operating religious organizations, such as churches, religious temples, mosques, and monasteries, and/or (2) establishments primarily engaged in administering an organized religion or promoting religious activities.

*Illustrative Examples:*

| | |
|---|---|
| Churches | Synagogues |
| Shrines, religious | Mosques, religious |
| Monasteries (except schools) | Temples, religious |

*Cross-References.*

- Schools, colleges, or universities operated by religious organizations are classified in Sector 61, Educational Services;
- Radio and television stations operated by religious organizations are classified in Industry Group 5161, Radio and Television Broadcasting Stations;
- Publishing houses operated by religious organizations are classified in Subsector 513, Publishing Industries;
- Establishments operated by religious organizations primarily engaged in health and social assistance for individuals are classified in Sector 62, Health Care and Social Assistance; and
- Used merchandise retail establishments operated by religious organizations are classified in Industry 459510, Used Merchandise Retailers.

## 8132    Grantmaking and Giving Services

## 81321   Grantmaking and Giving Services

This industry comprises (1) establishments known as grantmaking foundations or charitable trusts and (2) establishments primarily engaged in raising funds for a wide range of social welfare activities, such as health, educational, scientific, and cultural activities.

*Cross-References.*          Establishments primarily engaged in--

- Providing trust management or administration services for others--are classified in Industry Group 5239, Other Financial Investment Activities;
- Organizing and conducting charitable fundraising campaigns on a contract or fee basis--are classified in Industry 56149, Other Business Support Services;
- Providing telemarketing services--are classified in Industry 56142, Telephone Call Centers;
- Raising funds for political purposes--are classified in Industry 81394, Political Organizations;
- Advocating social causes or issues--are classified in Industry 81331, Social Advocacy Organizations; and
- Conducting health research--are classified in Industry 54171, Research and Development in the Physical, Engineering, and Life Sciences.

## 813211  Grantmaking Foundations

This U.S. industry comprises establishments known as grantmaking foundations or charitable trusts. Establishments in this industry award grants from trust funds based on a competitive selection process or the preferences of the foundation managers and grantors; or fund a single entity, such as a museum or university.

*Illustrative Examples:*

| | |
|---|---|
| Community foundations | Philanthropic trusts |

---

T—Canadian, Mexican, and United States industries are comparable.

Corporate foundations, awarding grants          Grantmaking foundations
Scholarship trusts

*Cross-References.*

- Community chest fundraising organizations are classified in U.S. Industry 813219, Other Grantmaking and Giving Services; and
- Establishments primarily engaged in providing trust management or administration services for others are classified in Industry Group 5239, Other Financial Investment Activities.

## 813212  Voluntary Health Organizations

   This U.S. industry comprises establishments primarily engaged in raising funds for health related research, such as disease (e.g., heart, cancer, diabetes) prevention, health education, and patient services.

*Illustrative Examples:*

Disease awareness fundraising organizations          Disease research (e.g., heart, cancer) fundraising
Health research fundraising organizations          organizations
Voluntary health organizations

*Cross-References.*

- Establishments primarily engaged in raising funds for a wide range of social welfare activities, such as educational, scientific, cultural, or health, are classified in U.S. Industry 813219, Other Grantmaking and Giving Services;
- Establishments primarily engaged in organizing and conducting charitable fundraising campaigns on a contract or fee basis are classified in U.S. Industry 561499, All Other Business Support Services;
- Establishments primarily engaged in providing telemarketing services are classified in U.S. Industry 561422, Telemarketing Bureaus and Other Contact Centers;
- Establishments known as grantmaking foundations or charitable trusts are classified in U.S. Industry 813211, Grantmaking Foundations; and
- Establishments primarily engaged in conducting health research are classified in Industry 54171, Research and Development in the Physical, Engineering, and Life Sciences.

## 813219  Other Grantmaking and Giving Services

   This U.S. industry comprises establishments (except voluntary health organizations) primarily engaged in raising funds for a wide range of social welfare activities, such as educational, scientific, cultural, and health.

*Illustrative Examples:*

Community chest fundraising organizations          Federated charities
United fund councils          United funds for colleges

*Cross-References.*

- Establishments primarily engaged in raising funds for health related research are classified in U.S. Industry 813212, Voluntary Health Organizations;
- Establishments known as grantmaking foundations or charitable trusts are classified in U.S. Industry 813211, Grantmaking Foundations;
- Establishments primarily engaged in organizing and conducting charitable fundraising campaigns on a contract or fee basis are classified in U.S. Industry 561499, All Other Business Support Services;
- Establishments primarily engaged in providing telemarketing services are classified in U.S. Industry 561422, Telemarketing Bureaus and Other Contact Centers;

T—Canadian, Mexican, and United States industries are comparable.

- Establishments primarily engaged in raising funds for political purposes are classified in Industry 813940, Political Organizations; and
- Establishments primarily engaged in advocating social causes or issues are classified in Industry 81331, Social Advocacy Organizations.

**8133     Social Advocacy Organizations**

**81331     Social Advocacy Organizations**

This industry comprises establishments primarily engaged in promoting a particular cause or working for the realization of a specific social or political goal to benefit a broad or specific constituency.  These organizations may solicit contributions and offer memberships to support these goals.

*Illustrative Examples:*

Community action advocacy organizations
Firearms advocacy organizations
Conservation advocacy organizations

Human rights advocacy organizations
Environmental advocacy organizations
Wildlife preservation organizations

*Cross-References.*

- Establishments primarily engaged in promoting the civic and social interests of their members are classified in Industry 81341, Civic and Social Organizations;
- Establishments primarily engaged in promoting the interests of organized labor and union employees are classified in Industry 81393, Labor Unions and Similar Labor Organizations;
- Establishments primarily engaged in operating animal shelters are classified in Industry 81291, Pet Care (except Veterinary) Services;
- Establishments primarily engaged in providing legal services for social advocacy organizations are classified in Industry Group 5411, Legal Services;
- Establishments primarily engaged in providing community action services, such as community action services agencies, are classified in Industry 62419, Other Individual and Family Services;
- Nature preserves or conservation areas are classified in Industry 71219, Nature Parks and Other Similar Institutions;
- Government establishments primarily engaged in administering, overseeing, and managing governmental ecological restoration programs are classified in Industry 92411, Administration of Air and Water Resource and Solid Waste Management Programs; and
- Government establishments primarily engaged in administering conservation programs are classified in Industry 92412, Administration of Conservation Programs.

**813311  Human Rights Organizations**

This U.S. industry comprises establishments primarily engaged in promoting causes associated with human rights either for a broad or specific constituency.  Establishments in this industry address issues, such as protecting and promoting the broad constitutional rights and civil liberties of individuals and those suffering from neglect, abuse, or exploitation; promoting the interests of specific groups, such as children, women, senior citizens, or persons with disabilities; improving relations between racial, ethnic, and cultural groups; and promoting voter education and registration.  These organizations may solicit contributions and offer memberships to support these causes.

*Illustrative Examples:*

Civil liberties organizations
Senior citizens' advocacy organizations

Human rights advocacy organizations
Veterans' rights organizations

T—Canadian, Mexican, and United States industries are comparable.

**census.gov/naics**

*Cross-References.* Establishments primarily engaged in--

- Promoting the interests of organized labor and union employees--are classified in Industry 813930, Labor Unions and Similar Labor Organizations; and
- Providing legal services for human rights organizations--are classified in Industry Group 5411, Legal Services.

## 813312  Environment, Conservation and Wildlife Organizations

This U.S. industry comprises establishments primarily engaged in promoting the preservation and protection of the environment and wildlife.  Establishments in this industry address issues, such as clean air and water; global warming; conserving and developing natural resources, including land, plant, water, and energy resources; and protecting and preserving wildlife and endangered species.  These organizations may solicit contributions and offer memberships to support these causes.

*Illustrative Examples:*

Animal rights organizations
Natural resource preservation organizations
Conservation advocacy organizations

Wildlife preservation organizations
Humane societies without animal shelters

*Cross-References.*

- Establishments primarily engaged in operating animal shelters are classified in Industry 812910, Pet Care (except Veterinary) Services;
- Establishments primarily engaged in providing legal services for environment, conservation, and wildlife organizations are classified in Industry Group 5411, Legal Services;
- Nature preserves or conservation areas are classified in Industry 712190, Nature Parks and Other Similar Institutions;
- Government establishments primarily engaged in administering, overseeing, and managing governmental ecological restoration programs are classified in Industry 924110, Administration of Air and Water Resource and Solid Waste Management Programs; and
- Government establishments primarily engaged in administering conservation programs are classified in Industry 924120, Administration of Conservation Programs.

## 813319  Other Social Advocacy Organizations

This U.S. industry comprises establishments primarily engaged in social advocacy (except human rights and environmental protection, conservation, and wildlife preservation).  Establishments in this industry address issues, such as peace and international understanding; community action (excluding civic organizations); or advancing social causes, such as firearms safety, drunk driving prevention, or drug abuse awareness.  These organizations may solicit contributions and offer memberships to support these causes.

*Illustrative Examples:*

Community action advocacy organizations
Substance abuse prevention advocacy organizations
Firearms advocacy organizations

Taxpayers' advocacy organizations
Peace advocacy organizations

*Cross-References.* Establishments primarily engaged in--

- Advocating human rights issues--are classified in U.S. Industry 813311, Human Rights Organizations;
- Promoting the preservation and protection of the environment and wildlife--are classified in U.S. Industry 813312, Environment, Conservation and Wildlife Organizations;

---

T—Canadian, Mexican, and United States industries are comparable.

- Promoting the civic and social interests of their members--are classified in Industry 813410, Civic and Social Organizations;
- Providing legal services for social advocacy organizations--are classified in Industry Group 5411, Legal Services; and
- Providing community action services, such as community action service agencies--are classified in Industry 624190, Other Individual and Family Services.

## 8134    Civic and Social Organizations

## 81341    Civic and Social Organizations
See industry description for 813410.

## 813410  Civic and Social Organizations

This industry comprises establishments primarily engaged in promoting the civic and social interests of their members. Establishments in this industry may operate bars and restaurants for their members.

*Illustrative Examples:*

Alumni associations
Granges
Automobile clubs (except travel)
Parent-teacher associations
Booster clubs

Scouting organizations
Ethnic associations
Social clubs
Fraternal lodges
Veterans' membership organizations

*Cross-References.*

- Establishments of insurance offices operated by fraternal benefit organizations are classified in Subsector 524, Insurance Carriers and Related Activities;
- Establishments primarily engaged in operating residential fraternity and sorority houses are classified in Industry 721310, Rooming and Boarding Houses, Dormitories, and Workers' Camps; and
- Establishments primarily engaged in providing travel arrangements and reservation services, such as automobile travel clubs or motor travel clubs, are classified in U.S. Industry 561599, All Other Travel Arrangement and Reservation Services.

## 8139    Business, Professional, Labor, Political, and Similar Organizations

This industry group comprises establishments primarily engaged in promoting the interests of their members (except religious organizations, social advocacy organizations, and civic and social organizations). Examples of establishments in this industry are business associations, professional organizations, labor unions, and political organizations.

## 81391    Business Associations
See industry description for 813910.

## 813910  Business Associations

This industry comprises establishments primarily engaged in promoting the business interests of their members. These establishments may conduct research on new products and services; develop market statistics; sponsor quality and certification standards; lobby public officials; or publish newsletters, books, or periodicals for distribution to their members.

---

T—Canadian, Mexican, and United States industries are comparable.

*Illustrative Examples:*

Agricultural organizations (except youth farming          Chambers of commerce
organizations, farm granges)                              Trade associations
Real estate boards                                        Manufacturers' associations

*Cross-References.*

- Establishments owned by their members but organized to perform a specific business function, such as common marketing of crops, joint advertising, or buying cooperatives, are classified according to their primary activity;
- Establishments primarily engaged in promoting the professional interests of their members and the profession as a whole are classified in Industry 813920, Professional Organizations;
- Establishments primarily engaged in promoting the interests of organized labor and union employees, such as trade unions, are classified in Industry 813930, Labor Unions and Similar Labor Organizations; and
- Establishments primarily engaged in lobbying public officials (i.e., lobbyists) are classified in Industry 541820, Public Relations Agencies.

**81392    Professional Organizations**
See industry description for 813920.

**813920  Professional Organizations**

This industry comprises establishments primarily engaged in promoting the professional interests of their members and the profession as a whole.  These establishments may conduct research; develop statistics; sponsor quality and certification standards; lobby public officials; or publish newsletters, books, or periodicals for distribution to their members.

*Illustrative Examples:*

Bar associations                                          Engineers' associations
Learned societies                                         Professional standards review boards
Dentists' associations                                    Health professionals' associations
Peer review boards                                        Scientists' associations

*Cross-References.*          Establishments primarily engaged in--

- Promoting the business interests of their members--are classified in Industry 813910, Business Associations; and
- Lobbying public officials (i.e., lobbyists)--are classified in Industry 541820, Public Relations Agencies.

**81393    Labor Unions and Similar Labor Organizations**
See industry description for 813930.

**813930  Labor Unions and Similar Labor Organizations**

This industry comprises establishments primarily engaged in promoting the interests of organized labor and union employees.

*Cross-References.*

Establishments primarily engaged in offering apprenticeship training programs are classified in U.S. Industry 611513, Apprenticeship Training.

---

T—Canadian, Mexican, and United States industries are comparable.

**81394    Political Organizations**
    See industry description for 813940.

**813940  Political Organizations**

  This industry comprises establishments primarily engaged in promoting the interests of national, state, or local political parties or candidates.  Included are political groups organized to raise funds for a political party or individual candidates.

*Illustrative Examples:*

Campaign organizations, political                    Political parties
Political organizations or clubs                     Political campaign organizations
Political action committees (PACs)

*Cross-References.*          Establishments primarily engaged in--

   •   Organizing and conducting charitable fundraising campaigns on a contract or fee basis--are classified in
       U.S. Industry 561499, All Other Business Support Services; and
   •   Providing telemarketing services--are classified in U.S. Industry 561422, Telemarketing Bureaus and Other
       Contact Centers.

**81399    Other Similar Organizations (except Business, Professional, Labor, and Political Organizations)**
    See industry description for 813990.

**813990  Other Similar Organizations (except Business, Professional, Labor, and Political Organizations)**

  This industry comprises establishments (except religious organizations, social advocacy organizations, civic and social organizations, business associations, professional organizations, labor unions, and political organizations) primarily engaged in promoting the interests of their members.

*Illustrative Examples:*

Athletic associations and leagues, regulatory        Tenants' associations (except advocacy)
Property owners' associations                        Cooperative owners' associations
Condominium and homeowners' associations

*Cross-References.*          Establishments primarily engaged in--

   •   Operating religious organizations, such as churches, religious temples, mosques, and monasteries--are
       classified in Industry 813110, Religious Organizations;
   •   Raising funds for a wide range of social welfare activities and establishments known as grantmaking
       foundations or charitable trusts--are classified in Industry 81321, Grantmaking and Giving Services;
   •   Advocating social causes or issues--are classified in Industry 81331, Social Advocacy Organizations;
   •   Promoting the civic and social interests of their members--are classified in Industry 813410, Civic and
       Social Organizations;
   •   Promoting the business interests of their members--are classified in Industry 813910, Business
       Associations;
   •   Promoting the professional interests of their members and the profession as a whole--are classified in
       Industry 813920, Professional Organizations;
   •   Promoting the interests of organized labor and union employees--are classified in Industry 813930, Labor
       Unions and Similar Labor Organizations;
   •   Promoting the interests of national, state, or local political parties or candidates--are classified in Industry
       813940, Political Organizations; and

_____

T—Canadian, Mexican, and United States industries are comparable.

- Providing recreational and amusement services, such as recreational or youth sports league teams--are classified in Industry 713990, All Other Amusement and Recreation Industries.

## 814     Private Households[T]

The Private Households subsector includes private households that engage in employing workers on or about the premises in activities primarily concerned with the operation of the household. These private households may employ individuals, such as cooks, maids, nannies, butlers, non-medical personal care aides, and outside workers, such as gardeners, caretakers, and other maintenance workers.

## 8141    Private Households[T]

## 81411   Private Households[T]
See industry description for 814110.

## 814110  Private Households

This industry comprises private households primarily engaged in employing workers on or about the premises in activities primarily concerned with the operation of the household. These private households may employ individuals, such as cooks, maids, nannies, butlers, non-medical personal care aides, and outside workers, such as gardeners, caretakers, and other maintenance workers.

*Cross-References.*          Establishments primarily engaged in--

- Providing non-medical personal care services for the elderly or persons with disabilities (except private households)--are classified in Industry 624120, Services for the Elderly and Persons with Disabilities; and
- Providing care and early learning opportunities for infants and children (except private households)--are classified in Industry 624410, Child Care Services.

---

T—Canadian, Mexican, and United States industries are comparable.

# Sector 92--Public Administration[T]

## The Sector as a Whole

The Public Administration sector consists of establishments of federal, state, and local government agencies that administer, oversee, and manage public programs and have executive, legislative, or judicial authority over other institutions within a given area. These agencies also set policy, create laws, adjudicate civil and criminal legal cases, and provide for public safety and for national defense. In general, government establishments in the Public Administration sector oversee governmental programs and activities that are not performed by private establishments. Establishments in this sector typically are engaged in the organization and financing of the production of public goods and services, most of which are provided for free or at prices that are not economically significant.

Government establishments also engage in a wide range of productive activities covering not only public goods and services but also individual goods and services similar to those produced in sectors typically identified with private-sector establishments. In general, ownership is not a criterion for classification in NAICS. Therefore, government establishments engaged in the production of private-sector-like goods and services should be classified in the same industry as private-sector establishments engaged in similar activities.

As a practical matter, it is difficult to identify separate establishment detail for many government agencies. To the extent that separate establishment records are available, the administration of governmental programs is classified in Sector 92, Public Administration, while the operation of governmental programs is classified elsewhere in NAICS based on the activities performed. For example, the governmental administrative authority for an airport is classified in Industry 92612, Regulation and Administration of Transportation Programs, while operating the airport is classified in Industry 48811, Airport Operations. When separate records for multi-establishment companies are not available to distinguish between the administration of a governmental program and the operation of it, the establishment is classified in Sector 92, Public Administration.

Examples of government-provided goods and services that are classified in sectors other than Public Administration include: schools, classified in Sector 61, Educational Services; health care facilities, classified in Sector 62, Health Care and Social Assistance; establishments operating transportation facilities, classified in Sector 48-49, Transportation and Warehousing; the operation of utilities, classified in Sector 22, Utilities; and the Government Printing Office, classified in Subsector 323, Printing and Related Support Activities.

## 921 Executive, Legislative, and Other General Government Support

The Executive, Legislative, and Other General Government Support subsector groups offices of government executives, legislative bodies, public finance, and general government support.

## 9211 Executive, Legislative, and Other General Government Support

## 92111 Executive Offices
See industry description for 921110.

## 921110 Executive Offices

This industry comprises government establishments serving as offices of chief executives and their advisory committees and commissions. This industry includes offices of the president, governors, and mayors, in addition to executive advisory commissions.

## 92112 Legislative Bodies
See industry description for 921120.

---

T—Canadian, Mexican, and United States industries are comparable.

**921120  Legislative Bodies**

This industry comprises government establishments serving as legislative bodies and their advisory committees and commissions.  Included in this industry are legislative bodies, such as Congress, state legislatures, and advisory and study legislative commissions.

**92113   Public Finance Activities**
See industry description for 921130.

**921130  Public Finance Activities**

This industry comprises government establishments primarily engaged in public finance, taxation, and monetary policy.  Included are financial administration activities, such as monetary policy; tax administration and collection; custody and disbursement of funds; debt and investment administration; auditing activities; and government employee retirement trust fund administration.

*Cross-References.*          Establishments primarily engaged in--

- Administering income maintenance programs--are classified in Industry 923130, Administration of Human Resource Programs (except Education, Public Health, and Veterans' Affairs Programs);
- Regulating insurance and banking institutions--are classified in Industry 926150, Regulation, Licensing, and Inspection of Miscellaneous Commercial Sectors; and
- Performing central banking functions, such as issuing currency and acting as the fiscal agent for the central government--are classified in Industry 521110, Monetary Authorities-Central Bank.

**92114   Executive and Legislative Offices, Combined**
See industry description for 921140.

**921140  Executive and Legislative Offices, Combined**

This industry comprises government establishments serving as councils and boards of commissioners or supervisors and such bodies where the chief executive (e.g., county executive or city mayor) is a member of the legislative body (e.g., county or city council) itself.

*Cross-References.*          Government establishments primarily engaged in--

- Serving as offices of chief executives--are classified in Industry 921110, Executive Offices; and
- Serving as legislative bodies--are classified in Industry 921120, Legislative Bodies.

**92115   American Indian and Alaska Native Tribal Governments**
See industry description for 921150.

**921150  American Indian and Alaska Native Tribal Governments**

This industry comprises American Indian and Alaska Native governing bodies.  Establishments in this industry perform legislative, judicial, and administrative functions for their American Indian and Alaska Native lands.  Included in this industry are American Indian and Alaska Native councils, courts, and law enforcement bodies.

*Cross-References.*

- Establishments primarily engaged in providing funding for American Indian and Alaska Native tribal programs through commercial activities, such as gaming, are classified in the industry of the commercial activity; and
- Government establishments providing public administration of American Indian and Alaska Native affairs are classified in Industry 921190, Other General Government Support.

T—Canadian, Mexican, and United States industries are comparable.

**92119 Other General Government Support**
See industry description for 921190.

**921190 Other General Government Support**

This industry comprises government establishments primarily engaged in providing general support for government. Such support services include personnel services, election boards, and other general government support establishments that are not classified elsewhere in public administration.

*Illustrative Examples:*

Civil rights commissions
Personnel offices, government
Civil service commissions

Supply agencies, government
General services departments, government

*Cross-References.*

- Government establishments primarily engaged in serving as offices of chief executives and their advisory committees and commissions are classified in Industry 921110, Executive Offices;
- Government establishments primarily engaged in serving as legislative bodies and their advisory committees and commissions are classified in Industry 921120, Legislative Bodies;
- Government establishments primarily engaged in providing administration of public finance, tax collection, and monetary policy programs are classified in Industry 921130, Public Finance Activities;
- Government establishments primarily engaged in serving as combined executive and legislative offices are classified in Industry 921140, Executive and Legislative Offices, Combined; and
- Establishments primarily engaged in serving as American Indian or Alaska Native tribal leadership are classified in Industry 921150, American Indian and Alaska Native Tribal Governments.

**922 Justice, Public Order, and Safety Activities**

The Justice, Public Order, and Safety Activities subsector groups government establishments engaged in the administration of justice, public order, and safety programs.

**9221 Justice, Public Order, and Safety Activities**

**92211 Courts**
See industry description for 922110.

**922110 Courts**

This industry comprises civilian courts of law (except American Indian and Alaska Native tribal courts). Included in this industry are civilian courts, courts of law, and sheriffs' offices conducting court functions only.

*Cross-References.*

- Government establishments primarily engaged in operating military courts are classified in Industry 928110, National Security; and
- Establishments primarily engaged in operating American Indian or Alaska Native tribal courts are classified in Industry 921150, American Indian and Alaska Native Tribal Governments.

**92212 Police Protection**
See industry description for 922120.

T—Canadian, Mexican, and United States industries are comparable.

### 922120  Police Protection

   This industry comprises government establishments primarily engaged in criminal and civil law enforcement, police, traffic safety, and other activities related to the enforcement of the law and preservation of order.  Combined police and fire departments are included in this industry.

*Cross-References.*

- Government establishments primarily engaged in prosecution are classified in Industry 922130, Legal Counsel and Prosecution;
- Government establishments primarily engaged in collection of law enforcement statistics are classified in Industry 922190, Other Justice, Public Order, and Safety Activities;
- Government establishments primarily engaged in providing police service for the military or National Guard are classified in Industry 928110, National Security;
- Government establishments primarily engaged in providing police service for tribal governments are classified in Industry 921150, American Indian and Alaska Native Tribal Governments;
- Government establishments primarily engaged in enforcing immigration laws are classified in Industry 928120, International Affairs;
- Sheriffs' offices conducting court functions only are classified in Industry 922110, Courts; and
- Private establishments primarily engaged in providing security, police, and investigation services are classified in Industry 56161, Investigation, Guard, and Armored Car Services.

### 92213   Legal Counsel and Prosecution
   See industry description for 922130.

### 922130  Legal Counsel and Prosecution

   This industry comprises government establishments primarily engaged in providing legal counsel or prosecution services for the government.

*Illustrative Examples:*

Attorney generals' offices                                District attorneys' offices
Public defenders' offices                                 Public prosecutors' offices

*Cross-References.*

   Government establishments primarily engaged in collecting criminal justice statistics are classified in Industry 922190, Other Justice, Public Order, and Safety Activities.

### 92214   Correctional Institutions
   See industry description for 922140.

### 922140  Correctional Institutions

   This industry comprises government establishments primarily engaged in managing and operating correctional institutions.  The facility is generally designed for the confinement, correction, and rehabilitation of adult and/or juvenile offenders sentenced by a court.

*Illustrative Examples:*

Correctional institutions, public administration              Prisons, public administration
Penitentiaries, public administration                        Jails, public administration
Detention centers, public administration

---

T—Canadian, Mexican, and United States industries are comparable.

*Cross-References.*

- Government establishments primarily engaged in operating halfway houses for ex-criminal offenders and delinquent youths are classified in Industry 623990, Other Residential Care Facilities; and
- Establishments primarily engaged in managing or operating correctional facilities on a contract or fee basis are classified in Industry 561210, Facilities Support Services.

**92215  Parole Offices and Probation Offices**
See industry description for 922150.

**922150  Parole Offices and Probation Offices**

This industry comprises government establishments primarily engaged in judicially administering probation offices, parole offices and boards, and pardon boards.

*Cross-References.*

- Private establishments primarily engaged in providing parole or probation services are classified in Industry 624190, Other Individual and Family Services; and
- Government establishments primarily engaged in providing probation, parole, and pardon activities as an integral part of a central administrative corrections' office are classified in Industry 922140, Correctional Institutions.

**92216  Fire Protection**
See industry description for 922160.

**922160  Fire Protection**

This industry comprises government establishments primarily engaged in firefighting and other related fire protection activities. Government establishments providing combined fire protection and ambulance or rescue services are classified in this industry.

*Cross-References.*        Establishments primarily engaged in--

- Forest firefighting--are classified in Industry 115310, Support Activities for Forestry;
- Providing combined police and fire protection services--are classified in Industry 922120, Police Protection;
- Providing firefighting services as a commercial activity--are classified in Industry 561990, All Other Support Services; and
- Providing ambulance services without fire protection service--are classified in Industry 621910, Ambulance Services.

**92219  Other Justice, Public Order, and Safety Activities**
See industry description for 922190.

**922190  Other Justice, Public Order, and Safety Activities**

This industry comprises government establishments primarily engaged in public order and safety (except courts, police protection, legal counsel and prosecution, correctional institutions, parole offices, probation offices, pardon boards, and fire protection). These establishments include the general administration of public order and safety programs. Government establishments responsible for the collection of statistics on public safety are included in this industry.

---

T—Canadian, Mexican, and United States industries are comparable.

*Illustrative Examples:*

Consumer product safety commissions, public administration

Emergency planning and management offices, government

Disaster preparedness and management offices, government

Public safety bureaus and statistics centers, government

*Cross-References.*

- Government establishments primarily engaged in serving as civilian courts of law (except American Indian and Alaska Native tribal courts) are classified in Industry 922110, Courts;
- Establishments primarily engaged in operating American Indian or Alaska Native tribal courts are classified in Industry 921150, American Indian and Alaska Native Tribal Governments;
- Government establishments primarily engaged in criminal and civil law enforcement, police, traffic safety, and similar activities related to the enforcement of law are classified in Industry 922120, Police Protection;
- Government establishments primarily engaged in providing legal counsel to or prosecution services for their governments are classified in Industry 922130, Legal Counsel and Prosecution;
- Government establishments primarily engaged in the confinement, correction, and rehabilitation of adult and juvenile offenders sentenced by a court are classified in Industry 922140, Correctional Institutions;
- Government establishments primarily engaged in judicially administering probation offices, parole offices and boards, and pardon boards are classified in Industry 922150, Parole Offices and Probation Offices; and
- Government establishments primarily engaged in firefighting and other related fire protection activities are classified in Industry 922160, Fire Protection.

**923      Administration of Human Resource Programs**

The Administration of Human Resource Programs subsector groups government establishments primarily engaged in the administration of human resource programs.

**9231      Administration of Human Resource Programs**

**92311      Administration of Education Programs**
See industry description for 923110.

**923110      Administration of Education Programs**

This industry comprises government establishments primarily engaged in the central coordination, planning, supervision, and administration of funds, policies, intergovernmental activities, statistical reports and data collection, and centralized programs for educational administration.  Government scholarship programs are included in this industry.

*Illustrative Examples:*

Education offices, nonoperating, public administration

State education departments

Education statistics centers, government

University regents or boards, government

*Cross-References.*

Schools and local school boards are classified in Subsector 611, Educational Services.

**92312      Administration of Public Health Programs**
See industry description for 923120.

---

T—Canadian, Mexican, and United States industries are comparable.

**923120  Administration of Public Health Programs**

This industry comprises government establishments primarily engaged in the planning, administration, and coordination of public health programs and services, including environmental health activities, mental health, categorical health programs, health statistics, and immunization services.  Government establishments primarily engaged in conducting public health-related inspections are included in this industry.

*Illustrative Examples:*

Communicable disease program administration, public administration
Mental health program administration, public administration

Coroners' offices, public administration
Public health program administration, nonoperating, public administration
Health program administration, public administration

*Cross-References.*          Government establishments primarily engaged in--

- Operating hospitals (i.e., government or military)--are classified in Subsector 622, Hospitals;
- Providing health care in a clinical setting (i.e., military or government clinics)--are classified in Subsector 621, Ambulatory Health Care Services; and
- Inspecting food, plants, animals, and other agriculture products--are classified in Industry 926140, Regulation of Agricultural Marketing and Commodities.

**92313  Administration of Human Resource Programs (except Education, Public Health, and Veterans' Affairs Programs)**
See industry description for 923130.

**923130  Administration of Human Resource Programs (except Education, Public Health, and Veterans' Affairs Programs)**

This industry comprises government establishments primarily engaged in the planning, administration, and coordination of programs for public assistance, social work, and welfare activities.  The administration of Social Security, disability insurance, Medicare, unemployment insurance, and workers' compensation programs are included in this industry.

*Cross-References.*          Government establishments primarily engaged in--

- Administering veterans' programs--are classified in Industry 923140, Administration of Veterans' Affairs;
- Operating state employment job service offices--are classified in U.S. Industry 561311, Employment Placement Agencies; and
- Operating programs for public assistance, social work, and welfare--are classified in Subsector 624, Social Assistance.

**92314  Administration of Veterans' Affairs**
See industry description for 923140.

**923140  Administration of Veterans' Affairs**

This industry comprises government establishments primarily engaged in the administration of programs of assistance, training, counseling, and other services to veterans and their dependents, heirs, or survivors.  Included in this industry are Veterans' Affairs offices that maintain liaison and coordinate activities with other service organizations and governmental agencies.

*Cross-References.*

- Government establishments primarily engaged in operating veterans' hospitals or clinics are classified in Sector 62, Health Care and Social Assistance;
- Establishments primarily engaged in underwriting or acting as agents in selling veterans' insurance policies are classified in Subsector 524, Insurance Carriers and Related Activities; and
- Establishments operating civic and social organizations for veterans are classified in Industry 813410, Civic and Social Organizations.

## 924    Administration of Environmental Quality Programs

The Administration of Environmental Quality Programs subsector groups government establishments primarily engaged in the administration of environmental quality.

## 9241    Administration of Environmental Quality Programs

## 92411    Administration of Air and Water Resource and Solid Waste Management Programs
See industry description for 924110.

## 924110  Administration of Air and Water Resource and Solid Waste Management Programs

This industry comprises government establishments primarily engaged in one or more of the following: (1) the administration, regulation, and enforcement of air and water resource programs; (2) the administration and regulation of solid waste management programs; (3) the administration and regulation of water and air pollution control and prevention programs; (4) the administration and regulation of flood control programs; (5) the administration and regulation of drainage development and water resource consumption programs; (6) the administration and regulation of toxic waste removal and cleanup programs; and (7) coordination of these activities at intergovernmental levels.

*Illustrative Examples:*

Environmental protection program administration, public administration
Waste management program (except sanitation districts) administration, public administration

Pollution control program administration, public administration
Water control and quality program administration, public administration

*Cross-References.*        Government establishments primarily engaged in--

- Operating water and irrigation systems--are classified in Industry 221310, Water Supply and Irrigation Systems;
- Administering sanitation districts--are classified in Industry 926130, Regulation and Administration of Communications, Electric, Gas, and Other Utilities;
- Operating sewage treatment facilities--are classified in Industry 221320, Sewage Treatment Facilities; and
- Providing waste collection, treatment, disposal, and/or remediation--are classified in Subsector 562, Waste Management and Remediation Services.

## 92412    Administration of Conservation Programs
See industry description for 924120.

## 924120  Administration of Conservation Programs

This industry comprises government establishments primarily engaged in the administration, regulation, supervision, and control of land use, including recreational areas; conservation and preservation of natural resources; erosion control; geological survey program administration; weather forecasting program administration; and the administration and protection of publicly and privately owned forest lands. Government establishments responsible

---

T—Canadian, Mexican, and United States industries are comparable.

for planning, management, regulation, and conservation of game, fish, and wildlife populations, including wildlife management areas and field stations; and other administrative matters relating to the protection of fish, game, and wildlife are included in this industry.

*Cross-References.*          Government establishments primarily engaged in--

- Operating parks--are classified in Industry 712190, Nature Parks and Other Similar Institutions;
- Operating forest property--are classified in Subsector 113, Forestry and Logging;
- Acting as lessors of public land--are classified in Industry 531190, Lessors of Other Real Estate Property;
- Geophysical surveying and/or mapping--are classified in Industry 541360, Geophysical Surveying and Mapping Services;
- Surveying and/or mapping (except geophysical)--are classified in Industry 541370, Surveying and Mapping (except Geophysical) Services;
- Weather forecasting--are classified in Industry 541990, All Other Professional, Scientific, and Technical Services;
- Operating fish and game preserves--are classified in Industry 712130, Zoos and Botanical Gardens; and
- Serving as urban planning commissions--are classified in Industry 925120, Administration of Urban Planning and Community and Rural Development.

## 925    Administration of Housing Programs, Urban Planning, and Community Development

The Administration of Housing Programs, Urban Planning, and Community Development subsector groups government establishments primarily engaged in the administration of housing, urban planning, and community development.

## 9251    Administration of Housing Programs, Urban Planning, and Community Development

## 92511    Administration of Housing Programs
See industry description for 925110.

## 925110    Administration of Housing Programs

This industry comprises government establishments primarily engaged in the administration and planning of housing programs.

*Cross-References.*          Government establishments primarily engaged in--

- Operating government rental housing--are classified in Subsector 531, Real Estate;
- Operating short-term emergency shelters--are classified in Industry Group 6242, Community Food and Housing, and Emergency and Other Relief Services;
- Conducting building inspections and enforcing building codes and standards--are classified in Industry 926150, Regulation, Licensing, and Inspection of Miscellaneous Commercial Sectors; and
- Buying, pooling, and repackaging mortgages or home loans for sale to others on the secondary market--are classified in U.S. Industry 522299, International, Secondary Market, and All Other Nondepository Credit Intermediation.

## 92512    Administration of Urban Planning and Community and Rural Development
See industry description for 925120.

## 925120    Administration of Urban Planning and Community and Rural Development

This industry comprises government establishments primarily engaged in the administration and planning of the development of urban and rural areas. Included in this industry are government zoning boards and commissions.

T--Canadian, Mexican, and United States industries are comparable.

*Illustrative Examples:*

Land redevelopment agencies, government
Regional planning and development program administration, public administration

Urban planning commissions, government
Zoning boards and commissions, public administration

**926        Administration of Economic Programs**

The Administration of Economic Programs subsector groups government establishments primarily engaged in the administration of economic programs.

**9261        Administration of Economic Programs**

**92611        Administration of General Economic Programs**
See industry description for 926110.

**926110  Administration of General Economic Programs**

This industry comprises government establishments primarily engaged in the administration, promotion, and development of economic resources, including business, industry, and tourism.  Included in this industry are government establishments responsible for the development of general statistical data and analyses and promotion of the general economic well-being of the governed area.

*Illustrative Examples:*

Consumer protection offices, public administration
Small business development agencies, public administration
Economic development agencies, government

Trade commissions, government
General economics statistical agencies, public administration

*Cross-References.*        Government establishments primarily engaged in--

- Operating state employment job service offices--are classified in U.S. Industry 561311, Employment Placement Agencies; and
- Providing job training for the unemployed, underemployed, physically disabled, and persons who have a job market disadvantage because of lack of education or job skills--are classified in Industry 624310, Vocational Rehabilitation Services.

**92612        Regulation and Administration of Transportation Programs**
See industry description for 926120.

**926120  Regulation and Administration of Transportation Programs**

This industry comprises government establishments primarily engaged in the administration, regulation, licensing, planning, inspection, and investigation of transportation services and facilities.  Included in this industry are government establishments responsible for motor vehicle and operator licensing, the Coast Guard (except the Coast Guard Academy), and parking authorities.

*Cross-References.*

- Government establishments primarily engaged in operating airports, railroads, depots, ports, toll roads and bridges, and other transportation facilities and systems are classified in Sector 48-49, Transportation and Warehousing;
- Government establishments primarily engaged in operating parking lots and parking garages are classified in Industry 812930, Parking Lots and Garages;

---

T—Canadian, Mexican, and United States industries are comparable.

- Government establishments primarily engaged in operating automobile safety inspection and emission testing facilities are classified in Industry Group 8111, Automotive Repair and Maintenance;
- Government establishments primarily engaged in building and/or maintaining roads and highways are classified in Industry 237310, Highway, Street, and Bridge Construction;
- Government establishments primarily engaged in providing air traffic control (except military) services are classified in U.S. Industry 488111, Air Traffic Control;
- Establishments of the Armed Forces, including the National Guard, primarily engaged in providing military air traffic control services are classified in Industry 928110, National Security;
- Government establishments primarily engaged in operating college-level military service academies, including the Coast Guard Academy, are classified in Industry 611310, Colleges, Universities, and Professional Schools;
- Establishments primarily engaged in providing motor vehicle license issuing services (except government) are classified in Industry 561990, All Other Support Services; and
- Government establishments primarily engaged in operating weigh stations are classified in Industry 488490, Other Support Activities for Road Transportation.

## 92613 Regulation and Administration of Communications, Electric, Gas, and Other Utilities
See industry description for 926130.

## 926130 Regulation and Administration of Communications, Electric, Gas, and Other Utilities

This industry comprises government establishments primarily engaged in the administration, regulation, licensing, and inspection of utilities, such as communications, electric power (including fossil, nuclear, solar, water, and wind), gas and water supply, and sewerage.

*Cross-References.*   Government establishments primarily engaged in--

- Operating utilities--are classified in Subsector 221, Utilities; and
- Acting as lessors of public land for telecommunications structures (e.g., cellular phone towers)--are classified in Industry 531190, Lessors of Other Real Estate Property.

## 92614 Regulation of Agricultural Marketing and Commodities
See industry description for 926140.

## 926140 Regulation of Agricultural Marketing and Commodities

This industry comprises government establishments primarily engaged in the planning, administration, and coordination of agricultural programs for production, marketing, and utilization, including educational and promotional activities. Included in this industry are government establishments responsible for regulating and controlling the grading and inspection of food, plants, animals, and other agricultural products.

*Cross-References.*   Government establishments primarily engaged in--

- Administering programs for developing economic data about agriculture and trade in agricultural products--are classified in Industry 926110, Administration of General Economic Programs;
- Administering programs for the conservation of natural resources--are classified in Industry Group 9241, Administration of Environmental Quality Programs; and
- Administering food stamp programs--are classified in Industry 923130, Administration of Human Resource Programs (except Education, Public Health, and Veterans' Affairs Programs).

## 92615 Regulation, Licensing, and Inspection of Miscellaneous Commercial Sectors
See industry description for 926150.

---

T—Canadian, Mexican, and United States industries are comparable.

**926150  Regulation, Licensing, and Inspection of Miscellaneous Commercial Sectors**

This industry comprises government establishments primarily engaged in the regulation, licensing, and inspection of commercial sectors, such as retail trade, professional occupations, manufacturing, mining, construction, and services. Included in this industry are government establishments maintaining physical standards, regulating hazardous conditions not elsewhere classified, and enforcing alcoholic beverage control regulations.

*Illustrative Examples:*

Alcoholic beverage control boards, public
administration
Labor management negotiations boards, government
Banking regulatory agencies, public administration
Licensing and permit issuance for business
operations, government

Building inspections, government
Licensing and permit issuance for professional
occupations, government
Insurance commissions, government
Securities regulation commissions, public
administration

*Cross-References.*

- Government establishments primarily engaged in regulating, administering, and inspecting transportation services and facilities are classified in Industry 926120, Regulation and Administration of Transportation Programs;
- Government establishments primarily engaged in regulating, administering, and inspecting communications, electric, gas, and other utilities are classified in Industry 926130, Regulation and Administration of Communications, Electric, Gas, and Other Utilities;
- Government establishments primarily engaged in operating liquor stores are classified in Industry 445320, Beer, Wine, and Liquor Retailers; and
- Establishments primarily engaged in operating as branches or banks of the Federal Reserve are classified in Industry 521110, Monetary Authorities-Central Bank.

**927    Space Research and Technology**

The Space Research and Technology subsector comprises government establishments primarily engaged in the administration and operations of space flights, space research, and space exploration.

**9271    Space Research and Technology**

**92711    Space Research and Technology**
See industry description for 927110.

**927110  Space Research and Technology**

This industry comprises government establishments primarily engaged in the administration and operations of space flights, space research, and space exploration. Included in this industry are government establishments operating space flight centers.

*Cross-References.*

- Private establishments primarily engaged in providing space transportation are classified in Industry 48121, Nonscheduled Air Transportation;
- Government establishments primarily engaged in manufacturing aerospace vehicles and parts are classified in Industry 33641, Aerospace Product and Parts Manufacturing;
- Government establishments primarily engaged in manufacturing space satellites are classified in Industry 334220, Radio and Television Broadcasting and Wireless Communications Equipment Manufacturing; and

T—Canadian, Mexican, and United States industries are comparable.

- Private establishments primarily engaged in aerospace research and development (except prototype production) are classified in U.S. Industry 541715, Research and Development in the Physical, Engineering, and Life Sciences (except Nanotechnology and Biotechnology).

## 928    National Security and International Affairs

The National Security and International Affairs subsector groups government establishments primarily engaged in national security and international affairs.

## 9281    National Security and International Affairs

### 92811    National Security
See industry description for 928110.

### 928110   National Security

This industry comprises government establishments of the Armed Forces, including the National Guard, primarily engaged in national security and related activities.

*Illustrative Examples:*

| | |
|---|---|
| Air Force | Marine Corps |
| Military police | National Guard |
| Army | Military courts |
| Military training schools (except military service academies) | Navy |

*Cross-References.*        Government establishments primarily engaged in--

- Operating college-level military service academies--are classified in Industry 611310, Colleges, Universities, and Professional Schools; and
- Regulating and administering water transportation, such as the U.S. Coast Guard and the Merchant Marine--are classified in Industry 926120, Regulation and Administration of Transportation Programs.

### 92812    International Affairs
See industry description for 928120.

### 928120   International Affairs

This industry comprises establishments of U.S. and foreign governments primarily engaged in international affairs and programs relating to other nations and peoples.

*Cross-References.*

- Establishments primarily engaged in providing international trade financing, such as lending funds to foreign buyers of U.S. goods or lending funds to domestic buyers of imported goods, are classified in U.S. Industry 522299, International, Secondary Market, and All Other Nondepository Credit Intermediation;
- Private establishments primarily engaged in providing refugee settlement services are classified in Industry 624230, Emergency and Other Relief Services;
- Human rights organizations, peace advocacy organizations, and trade associations and councils are classified in Subsector 813, Religious, Grantmaking, Civic, Professional, and Similar Organizations; and
- Government establishments administering international trade, such as trade commissions and councils, are classified in Industry 926110, Administration of General Economic Programs.

---

T—Canadian, Mexican, and United States industries are comparable.

# Part II

# Appendixes

Appendixes A and B map the changes for 2022 NAICS to the 2017 NAICS in 2022 NAICS sequence (Appendix A) and 2017 NAICS sequence (Appendix B). The tables do not provide a comprehensive guide to all economic activities, but rather provide a map for the largest and most important changes from 2017 to 2022.

A full concordance for 2017 NAICS to 2022 NAICS is available on the Census Bureau's Web site at www.census.gov/naics.

# Appendix A

# 2022 NAICS U.S. Matched to 2017 NAICS U.S.

| 2022 NAICS Code | 2022 NAICS U.S. Description | Status Code | 2017 NAICS Code | 2017 NAICS U.S. Description |
|---|---|---|---|---|
| 212114 | Surface Coal Mining | N | 212111 | Bituminous Coal and Lignite Surface Mining |
| | | | *212113 | Anthracite Mining - *anthracite surface mining* |
| 212115 | Underground Coal Mining | N | 212112 | Bituminous Coal Underground Mining |
| | | | *212113 | Anthracite Mining - *anthracite underground mining* |
| 212220 | Gold Ore and Silver Ore Mining | N | 212221 | Gold Ore Mining |
| | | | 212222 | Silver Ore Mining |
| 212290 | Other Metal Ore Mining | N | 212291 | Uranium-Radium-Vanadium Ore Mining |
| | | | 212299 | All Other Metal Ore Mining |
| 212323 | Kaolin, Clay, and Ceramic and Refractory Minerals Mining | N | 212324 | Kaolin and Ball Clay Mining |
| | | | 212325 | Clay and Ceramic and Refractory Minerals Mining |
| 212390 | Other Nonmetallic Mineral Mining and Quarrying | N | 212391 | Potash, Soda, and Borate Mineral Mining |
| | | | 212392 | Phosphate Rock Mining |
| | | | 212393 | Other Chemical and Fertilizer Mineral Mining |
| | | | 212399 | All Other Nonmetallic Mineral Mining |
| 31512 | Apparel Knitting Mills | | | |
| 315120 | Apparel Knitting Mills | N | 315110 | Hosiery and Sock Mills |
| | | | 315190 | Other Apparel Knitting Mills |

N—New NAICS industry/code for 2022; *—Part of 2017 NAICS United States industry;
R—2017 NAICS industry code reused with different content.

| 2022 NAICS Code | 2022 NAICS U.S. Description | Status Code | 2017 NAICS Code | 2017 NAICS U.S. Description |
|---|---|---|---|---|
| 31525 | Cut and Sew Apparel Manufacturing (except Contractors) | | | |
| 315250 | Cut and Sew Apparel Manufacturing (except Contractors) | N | 315220 | Men's and Boys' Cut and Sew Apparel Manufacturing |
| | | | 315240 | Women's, Girls', and Infants' Cut and Sew Apparel Manufacturing |
| | | | 315280 | Other Cut and Sew Apparel Manufacturing |
| 316990 | Other Leather and Allied Product Manufacturing | N | 316992 | Women's Handbag and Purse Manufacturing |
| | | | 316998 | All Other Leather Good and Allied Product Manufacturing |
| 321215 | Engineered Wood Member Manufacturing | N | 321213 | Engineered Wood Member (except Truss) Manufacturing |
| | | | 321214 | Truss Manufacturing |
| 322120 | Paper Mills | N | 322121 | Paper (except Newsprint) Mills |
| | | | 322122 | Newsprint Mills |
| 325314 | Fertilizer (Mixing Only) Manufacturing | R | *325314 | Fertilizer (Mixing Only) Manufacturing - *except compost manufacturing* |
| 325315 | Compost Manufacturing | N | *325314 | Fertilizer (Mixing Only) Manufacturing - *compost manufacturing* |
| 333248 | All Other Industrial Machinery Manufacturing | N | 333244 | Printing Machinery and Equipment Manufacturing |
| | | | 333249 | Other Industrial Machinery Manufacturing |
| 333310 | Commercial and Service Industry Machinery Manufacturing | N | 333314 | Optical Instrument and Lens Manufacturing |
| | | | 333316 | Photographic and Photocopying Equipment Manufacturing |
| | | | 333318 | Other Commercial and Service Industry Machinery Manufacturing |
| 333998 | All Other Miscellaneous General Purpose Machinery Manufacturing | N | 333997 | Scale and Balance Manufacturing |
| | | | 333999 | All Other Miscellaneous General Purpose Machinery Manufacturing |

N—New NAICS industry/code for 2022; *—Part of 2017 NAICS United States industry;
R—2017 NAICS industry code reused with different content.

| 2022 NAICS Code | 2022 NAICS U.S. Description | Status Code | 2017 NAICS Code | 2017 NAICS U.S. Description |
|---|---|---|---|---|
| 334610 | Manufacturing and Reproducing Magnetic and Optical Media | N | 334613 | Blank Magnetic and Optical Recording Media Manufacturing |
| | | | 334614 | Software and Other Prerecorded Compact Disc, Tape, and Record Reproducing |
| 33513 | Electric Lighting Equipment Manufacturing | | | |
| 335131 | Residential Electric Lighting Fixture Manufacturing | N | 335121 | Residential Electric Lighting Fixture Manufacturing |
| 335132 | Commercial, Industrial, and Institutional Electric Lighting Fixture Manufacturing | N | 335122 | Commercial, Industrial, and Institutional Electric Lighting Fixture Manufacturing |
| 335139 | Electric Lamp Bulb and Other Lighting Equipment Manufacturing | N | 335110 | Electric Lamp Bulb and Part Manufacturing |
| | | | 335129 | Other Lighting Equipment Manufacturing |
| 335910 | Battery Manufacturing | N | 335911 | Storage Battery Manufacturing |
| | | | 335912 | Primary Battery Manufacturing |
| 336110 | Automobile and Light Duty Motor Vehicle Manufacturing | N | 336111 | Automobile Manufacturing |
| | | | 336112 | Light Truck and Utility Vehicle Manufacturing |
| 337126 | Household Furniture (except Wood and Upholstered) Manufacturing | N | 337124 | Metal Household Furniture Manufacturing |
| | | | 337125 | Household Furniture (except Wood and Metal) Manufacturing |
| 42435 | Clothing and Clothing Accessories Merchant Wholesalers | | | |
| 424350 | Clothing and Clothing Accessories Merchant Wholesalers | N | 424320 | Men's and Boys' Clothing and Furnishings Merchant Wholesalers |
| | | | 424330 | Women's, Children's, and Infants' Clothing and Accessories Merchant Wholesalers |
| 42512 | Wholesale Trade Agents and Brokers | | | |
| 425120 | Wholesale Trade Agents and Brokers | R | 425110 | Business to Business Electronic Markets |
| | | | 425120 | Wholesale Trade Agents and Brokers |

N—New NAICS industry/code for 2022; *—Part of 2017 NAICS United States industry;
R—2017 NAICS industry code reused with different content.

| 2022 NAICS Code | 2022 NAICS U.S. Description | Status Code | 2017 NAICS Code | 2017 NAICS U.S. Description |
|---|---|---|---|---|
| 441227 | Motorcycle, ATV, and All Other Motor Vehicle Dealers | N | 441228 | Motorcycle, ATV, and All Other Motor Vehicle Dealers |
| | | | *454110 | Electronic Shopping and Mail-Order Houses |
| 4413 | Automotive Parts, Accessories, and Tire Retailers | | | |
| 44133 | Automotive Parts and Accessories Retailers | | | |
| 441330 | Automotive Parts and Accessories Retailers | N | 441310 | Automotive Parts and Accessories Stores |
| | | | *454110 | Electronic Shopping and Mail-Order Houses |
| | | | *454390 | Other Direct Selling Establishments |
| 44134 | Tire Dealers | | | |
| 441340 | Tire Dealers | N | 441320 | Tire Dealers |
| | | | *454110 | Electronic Shopping and Mail-Order Houses |
| | | | *454390 | Other Direct Selling Establishments |
| 44414 | Hardware Retailers | | | |
| 444140 | Hardware Retailers | N | 444130 | Hardware Stores |
| | | | *454110 | Electronic Shopping and Mail-Order Houses |
| | | | *454390 | Other Direct Selling Establishments |
| 44418 | Other Building Material Dealers | | | |
| 444180 | Other Building Material Dealers | N | 444190 | Other Building Material Dealers |
| | | | *454110 | Electronic Shopping and Mail-Order Houses |
| | | | *454390 | Other Direct Selling Establishments |
| 4442 | Lawn and Garden Equipment and Supplies Retailers | | | |
| 44423 | Outdoor Power Equipment Retailers | | | |
| 444230 | Outdoor Power Equipment Retailers | N | 444210 | Outdoor Power Equipment Stores |
| | | | *454110 | Electronic Shopping and Mail-Order Houses |
| | | | *454390 | Other Direct Selling Establishments |

N—New NAICS industry/code for 2022; *—Part of 2017 NAICS United States industry;
R—2017 NAICS industry code reused with different content.

| 2022 NAICS Code | 2022 NAICS U.S. Description | Status Code | 2017 NAICS Code | 2017 NAICS U.S. Description |
|---|---|---|---|---|
| 44424 | Nursery, Garden Center, and Farm Supply Retailers | | | |
| 444240 | Nursery, Garden Center, and Farm Supply Retailers | N | 444220 | Nursery, Garden Center, and Farm Supply Stores |
| | | | *454110 | Electronic Shopping and Mail-Order Houses |
| | | | *454390 | Other Direct Selling Establishments |
| 44513 | Convenience Retailers and Vending Machine Operators | | | |
| 445131 | Convenience Retailers | N | 445120 | Convenience Stores |
| | | | *454110 | Electronic Shopping and Mail-Order Houses |
| | | | *454390 | Other Direct Selling Establishments |
| 445132 | Vending Machine Operators | N | 454210 | Vending Machine Operators |
| 44524 | Meat Retailers | | | |
| 445240 | Meat Retailers | N | 445210 | Meat Markets |
| | | | *454110 | Electronic Shopping and Mail-Order Houses |
| | | | *454390 | Other Direct Selling Establishments |
| 44525 | Fish and Seafood Retailers | | | |
| 445250 | Fish and Seafood Retailers | N | 445220 | Fish and Seafood Markets |
| | | | *454110 | Electronic Shopping and Mail-Order Houses |
| | | | *454390 | Other Direct Selling Establishments |
| 445298 | All Other Specialty Food Retailers | N | 445299 | All Other Specialty Food Stores |
| | | | *454110 | Electronic Shopping and Mail-Order Houses |
| | | | *454390 | Other Direct Selling Establishments |
| 4453 | Beer, Wine, and Liquor Retailers | | | |
| 44532 | Beer, Wine, and Liquor Retailers | | | |
| 445320 | Beer, Wine, and Liquor Retailers | N | 445310 | Beer, Wine, and Liquor Stores |
| | | | *454110 | Electronic Shopping and Mail-Order Houses |
| | | | *454390 | Other Direct Selling Establishments |

N—New NAICS industry/code for 2022; *—Part of 2017 NAICS United States industry;
R—2017 NAICS industry code reused with different content.

| 2022 NAICS Code | 2022 NAICS U.S. Description | Status Code | 2017 NAICS Code | 2017 NAICS U.S. Description |
|---|---|---|---|---|
| 449 | Furniture, Home Furnishings, Electronics, and Appliance Retailers | | | |
| 4491 | Furniture and Home Furnishings Retailers | | | |
| 44911 | Furniture Retailers | | | |
| 449110 | Furniture Retailers | N | 442110 | Furniture Stores |
| | | | *454110 | Electronic Shopping and Mail-Order Houses |
| | | | *454390 | Other Direct Selling Establishments |
| 44912 | Home Furnishings Retailers | | | |
| 449121 | Floor Covering Retailers | N | 442210 | Floor Covering Stores |
| | | | *454110 | Electronic Shopping and Mail-Order Houses |
| | | | *454390 | Other Direct Selling Establishments |
| 449122 | Window Treatment Retailers | N | 442291 | Window Treatment Stores |
| | | | *454110 | Electronic Shopping and Mail-Order Houses |
| | | | *454390 | Other Direct Selling Establishments |
| 449129 | All Other Home Furnishings Retailers | N | 442299 | All Other Home Furnishings Stores |
| | | | *454110 | Electronic Shopping and Mail-Order Houses |
| | | | *454390 | Other Direct Selling Establishments |
| 4492 | Electronics and Appliance Retailers | | | |
| 44921 | Electronics and Appliance Retailers | | | |
| 449210 | Electronics and Appliance Retailers | N | 443141 | Household Appliance Stores |
| | | | 443142 | Electronics Stores |
| | | | *454110 | Electronic Shopping and Mail-Order Houses |
| | | | *454390 | Other Direct Selling Establishments |

N—New NAICS industry/code for 2022; *—Part of 2017 NAICS United States industry;
R—2017 NAICS industry code reused with different content.

| 2022 NAICS Code | 2022 NAICS U.S. Description | Status Code | 2017 NAICS Code | 2017 NAICS U.S. Description |
|---|---|---|---|---|
| 455 | General Merchandise Retailers | | | |
| 4551 | Department Stores | | | |
| 45511 | Department Stores | | | |
| 455110 | Department Stores | N | 452210 | Department Stores |
| | | | *454110 | Electronic Shopping and Mail-Order Houses |
| 4552 | Warehouse Clubs, Supercenters, and Other General Merchandise Retailers | | | |
| 45521 | Warehouse Clubs, Supercenters, and Other General Merchandise Retailers | | | |
| 455211 | Warehouse Clubs and Supercenters | N | 452311 | Warehouse Clubs and Supercenters |
| | | | *454110 | Electronic Shopping and Mail-Order Houses |
| 455219 | All Other General Merchandise Retailers | N | 452319 | All Other General Merchandise Stores |
| | | | *453998 | All Other Miscellaneous Store Retailers (except Tobacco Stores) - *general merchandise auction houses* |
| | | | *454110 | Electronic Shopping and Mail-Order Houses |
| | | | *454390 | Other Direct Selling Establishments |
| 456 | Health and Personal Care Retailers | | | |
| 4561 | Health and Personal Care Retailers | | | |
| 45611 | Pharmacies and Drug Retailers | | | |
| 456110 | Pharmacies and Drug Retailers | N | 446110 | Pharmacies and Drug Stores |
| | | | *454110 | Electronic Shopping and Mail-Order Houses |
| | | | *454390 | Other Direct Selling Establishments |
| 45612 | Cosmetics, Beauty Supplies, and Perfume Retailers | | | |
| 456120 | Cosmetics, Beauty Supplies, and Perfume Retailers | N | 446120 | Cosmetics, Beauty Supplies, and Perfume Stores |
| | | | *454110 | Electronic Shopping and Mail-Order Houses |
| | | | *454390 | Other Direct Selling Establishments |

N—New NAICS industry/code for 2022; *—Part of 2017 NAICS United States industry;
R—2017 NAICS industry code reused with different content.

| 2022 NAICS Code | 2022 NAICS U.S. Description | Status Code | 2017 NAICS Code | 2017 NAICS U.S. Description |
|---|---|---|---|---|
| 45613 | Optical Goods Retailers | | | |
| 456130 | Optical Goods Retailers | N | 446130 | Optical Goods Stores |
| | | | *454110 | Electronic Shopping and Mail-Order Houses |
| | | | *454390 | Other Direct Selling Establishments |
| 45619 | Other Health and Personal Care Retailers | | | |
| 456191 | Food (Health) Supplement Retailers | N | 446191 | Food (Health) Supplement Stores |
| | | | *454110 | Electronic Shopping and Mail-Order Houses |
| | | | *454390 | Other Direct Selling Establishments |
| 456199 | All Other Health and Personal Care Retailers | N | 446199 | All Other Health and Personal Care Stores |
| | | | *454110 | Electronic Shopping and Mail-Order Houses |
| | | | *454390 | Other Direct Selling Establishments |
| 457 | Gasoline Stations and Fuel Dealers | | | |
| 4571 | Gasoline Stations | | | |
| 45711 | Gasoline Stations with Convenience Stores | | | |
| 457110 | Gasoline Stations with Convenience Stores | N | 447110 | Gasoline Stations with Convenience Stores |
| 45712 | Other Gasoline Stations | | | |
| 457120 | Other Gasoline Stations | N | 447190 | Other Gasoline Stations |
| 4572 | Fuel Dealers | | | |
| 45721 | Fuel Dealers | | | |
| 457210 | Fuel Dealers | N | 454310 | Fuel Dealers |

N—New NAICS industry/code for 2022; *—Part of 2017 NAICS United States industry;
R—2017 NAICS industry code reused with different content.

| 2022 NAICS Code | 2022 NAICS U.S. Description | Status Code | 2017 NAICS Code | 2017 NAICS U.S. Description |
|---|---|---|---|---|
| 458 | Clothing, Clothing Accessories, Shoe, and Jewelry Retailers | | | |
| 4581 | Clothing and Clothing Accessories Retailers | | | |
| 45811 | Clothing and Clothing Accessories Retailers | | | |
| 458110 | Clothing and Clothing Accessories Retailers | N | 448110 | Men's Clothing Stores |
| | | | 448120 | Women's Clothing Stores |
| | | | 448130 | Children's and Infants' Clothing Stores |
| | | | 448140 | Family Clothing Stores |
| | | | 448150 | Clothing Accessories Stores |
| | | | 448190 | Other Clothing Stores |
| | | | *454110 | Electronic Shopping and Mail-Order Houses |
| | | | *454390 | Other Direct Selling Establishments |
| 4582 | Shoe Retailers | | | |
| 45821 | Shoe Retailers | | | |
| 458210 | Shoe Retailers | N | 448210 | Shoe Stores |
| | | | *454110 | Electronic Shopping and Mail-Order Houses |
| | | | *454390 | Other Direct Selling Establishments |
| 4583 | Jewelry, Luggage, and Leather Goods Retailers | | | |
| 45831 | Jewelry Retailers | | | |
| 458310 | Jewelry Retailers | N | 448310 | Jewelry Stores |
| | | | *454110 | Electronic Shopping and Mail-Order Houses |
| | | | *454390 | Other Direct Selling Establishments |
| 45832 | Luggage and Leather Goods Retailers | | | |
| 458320 | Luggage and Leather Goods Retailers | N | 448320 | Luggage and Leather Goods Stores |
| | | | *454110 | Electronic Shopping and Mail-Order Houses |
| | | | *454390 | Other Direct Selling Establishments |

N—New NAICS industry/code for 2022; *—Part of 2017 NAICS United States industry;
R—2017 NAICS industry code reused with different content.

| 2022 NAICS Code | 2022 NAICS U.S. Description | Status Code | 2017 NAICS Code | 2017 NAICS U.S. Description |
|---|---|---|---|---|
| 459 | Sporting Goods, Hobby, Musical Instrument, Book, and Miscellaneous Retailers | | | |
| 4591 | Sporting Goods, Hobby, and Musical Instrument Retailers | | | |
| 45911 | Sporting Goods Retailers | | | |
| 459110 | Sporting Goods Retailers | N | 451110 | Sporting Goods Stores |
| | | | *454110 | Electronic Shopping and Mail-Order Houses |
| | | | *454390 | Other Direct Selling Establishments |
| 45912 | Hobby, Toy, and Game Retailers | | | |
| 459120 | Hobby, Toy, and Game Retailers | N | 451120 | Hobby, Toy, and Game Stores |
| | | | *454110 | Electronic Shopping and Mail-Order Houses |
| | | | *454390 | Other Direct Selling Establishments |
| 45913 | Sewing, Needlework, and Piece Goods Retailers | | | |
| 459130 | Sewing, Needlework, and Piece Goods Retailers | N | 451130 | Sewing, Needlework, and Piece Goods Stores |
| | | | *454110 | Electronic Shopping and Mail-Order Houses |
| | | | *454390 | Other Direct Selling Establishments |
| 45914 | Musical Instrument and Supplies Retailers | | | |
| 459140 | Musical Instrument and Supplies Retailers | N | 451140 | Musical Instrument and Supplies Stores |
| | | | *454110 | Electronic Shopping and Mail-Order Houses |
| | | | *454390 | Other Direct Selling Establishments |
| 4592 | Book Retailers and News Dealers | | | |
| 45921 | Book Retailers and News Dealers | | | |
| 459210 | Book Retailers and News Dealers | N | 451211 | Book Stores |
| | | | 451212 | News Dealers and Newsstands |
| | | | *454110 | Electronic Shopping and Mail-Order Houses |
| | | | *454390 | Other Direct Selling Establishments |

N—New NAICS industry/code for 2022; *—Part of 2017 NAICS United States industry;
R—2017 NAICS industry code reused with different content.

| 2022 NAICS Code | 2022 NAICS U.S. Description | Status Code | 2017 NAICS Code | 2017 NAICS U.S. Description |
|---|---|---|---|---|
| 4593 | Florists | | | |
| 45931 | Florists | | | |
| 459310 | Florists | N | 453110 | Florists |
| | | | *454110 | Electronic Shopping and Mail-Order Houses |
| | | | *454390 | Other Direct Selling Establishments |
| 4594 | Office Supplies, Stationery, and Gift Retailers | | | |
| 45941 | Office Supplies and Stationery Retailers | | | |
| 459410 | Office Supplies and Stationery Retailers | N | 453210 | Office Supplies and Stationery Stores |
| | | | *454110 | Electronic Shopping and Mail-Order Houses |
| | | | *454390 | Other Direct Selling Establishments |
| 45942 | Gift, Novelty, and Souvenir Retailers | | | |
| 459420 | Gift, Novelty, and Souvenir Retailers | N | 453220 | Gift, Novelty, and Souvenir Stores |
| | | | *454110 | Electronic Shopping and Mail-Order Houses |
| | | | *454390 | Other Direct Selling Establishments |
| 4595 | Used Merchandise Retailers | | | |
| 45951 | Used Merchandise Retailers | | | |
| 459510 | Used Merchandise Retailers | N | 453310 | Used Merchandise Stores |
| | | | *454110 | Electronic Shopping and Mail-Order Houses |
| | | | *454390 | Other Direct Selling Establishments |
| 4599 | Other Miscellaneous Retailers | | | |
| 45991 | Pet and Pet Supplies Retailers | | | |
| 459910 | Pet and Pet Supplies Retailers | N | 453910 | Pet and Pet Supplies Stores |
| | | | *454110 | Electronic Shopping and Mail-Order Houses |
| | | | *454390 | Other Direct Selling Establishments |

N—New NAICS industry/code for 2022; *—Part of 2017 NAICS United States industry;
R—2017 NAICS industry code reused with different content.

| 2022 NAICS Code | 2022 NAICS U.S. Description | Status Code | 2017 NAICS Code | 2017 NAICS U.S. Description |
|---|---|---|---|---|
| 45992 | Art Dealers | | | |
| 459920 | Art Dealers | N | 453920 | Art Dealers |
| | | | *454110 | Electronic Shopping and Mail-Order Houses |
| | | | *454390 | Other Direct Selling Establishments |
| 45993 | Manufactured (Mobile) Home Dealers | | | |
| 459930 | Manufactured (Mobile) Home Dealers | N | 453930 | Manufactured (Mobile) Home Dealers |
| 45999 | All Other Miscellaneous Retailers | | | |
| 459991 | Tobacco, Electronic Cigarette, and Other Smoking Supplies Retailers | N | 453991 | Tobacco Stores |
| | | | *453998 | All Other Miscellaneous Store Retailers (except Tobacco Stores) - *electronic cigarette stores and marijuana stores, medical or recreational* |
| | | | *454110 | Electronic Shopping and Mail-Order Houses |
| | | | *454390 | Other Direct Selling Establishments |
| 459999 | All Other Miscellaneous Retailers | N | *453998 | All Other Miscellaneous Store Retailers (except Tobacco Stores) - *except general merchandise auction houses, electronic cigarette stores, and marijuana stores, medical or recreational* |
| | | | *454110 | Electronic Shopping and Mail-Order Houses |
| | | | *454390 | Other Direct Selling Establishments |
| 513 | Publishing Industries | | | |
| 5131 | Newspaper, Periodical, Book, and Directory Publishers | | | |
| 51311 | Newspaper Publishers | | | |
| 513110 | Newspaper Publishers | N | 511110 | Newspaper Publishers |
| | | | *519130 | Internet Publishing and Broadcasting and Web Search Portals - *Internet newspaper publishers* |

N—New NAICS industry/code for 2022; *—Part of 2017 NAICS United States industry;
R—2017 NAICS industry code reused with different content.

| 2022 NAICS Code | 2022 NAICS U.S. Description | Status Code | 2017 NAICS Code | 2017 NAICS U.S. Description |
|---|---|---|---|---|
| 51312 | Periodical Publishers | | | |
| 513120 | Periodical Publishers | N | 511120 *519130 | Periodical Publishers<br>Internet Publishing and Broadcasting and Web Search Portals - *Internet periodical publishers* |
| 51313 | Book Publishers | | | |
| 513130 | Book Publishers | N | 511130 *519130 | Book Publishers<br>Internet Publishing and Broadcasting and Web Search Portals - *Internet book publishers* |
| 51314 | Directory and Mailing List Publishers | | | |
| 513140 | Directory and Mailing List Publishers | N | 511140 *519130 | Directory and Mailing List Publishers<br>Internet Publishing and Broadcasting and Web Search Portals - *Internet directory and mailing list publishers* |
| 51319 | Other Publishers | | | |
| 513191 | Greeting Card Publishers | N | 511191 *519130 | Greeting Card Publishers<br>Internet Publishing and Broadcasting and Web Search Portals - *Internet greeting card publishers* |
| 513199 | All Other Publishers | N | 511199 *519130 | All Other Publishers<br>Internet Publishing and Broadcasting and Web Search Portals - *all other Internet publishers* |
| 5132 | Software Publishers | | | |
| 51321 | Software Publishers | | | |
| 513210 | Software Publishers | N | 511210 | Software Publishers |
| 516 | Broadcasting and Content Providers | | | |
| 5161 | Radio and Television Broadcasting Stations | | | |
| 51611 | Radio Broadcasting Stations | | | |
| 516110 | Radio Broadcasting Stations | N | 515112 | Radio Stations |

N—New NAICS industry/code for 2022; *—Part of 2017 NAICS United States industry;
R—2017 NAICS industry code reused with different content.

| 2022 NAICS Code | 2022 NAICS U.S. Description | Status Code | 2017 NAICS Code | 2017 NAICS U.S. Description |
|---|---|---|---|---|
| 51612 | Television Broadcasting Stations | | | |
| 516120 | Television Broadcasting Stations | N | *515120 | Television Broadcasting - *television broadcasting stations* |
| 5162 | Media Streaming Distribution Services, Social Networks, and Other Media Networks and Content Providers | | | |
| 51621 | Media Streaming Distribution Services, Social Networks, and Other Media Networks and Content Providers | | | |
| 516210 | Media Streaming Distribution Services, Social Networks, and Other Media Networks and Content Providers | N | 515111 *515120  515210  519110 *519130 | Radio Networks Television Broadcasting - *television networks* Cable and Other Subscription Programming News Syndicates Internet Publishing and Broadcasting and Web Search Portals - *Internet broadcasting* |
| 5171 | Wired and Wireless Telecommunications (except Satellite) | | | |
| 51711 | Wired and Wireless Telecommunications Carriers (except Satellite) | | | |
| 517111 | Wired Telecommunications Carriers | N | 517311 | Wired Telecommunications Carriers |
| 517112 | Wireless Telecommunications Carriers (except Satellite) | N | *517312 | Wireless Telecommunications Carriers (except Satellite) - *except agents for wireless telecommunications carriers* |
| 51712 | Telecommunications Resellers and Agents for Wireless Telecommunication Services | | | |
| 517121 | Telecommunications Resellers | N | *517911 | Telecommunications Resellers - *except agents for wireless telecommunications resellers* |

N—New NAICS industry/code for 2022; *—Part of 2017 NAICS United States industry;
R—2017 NAICS industry code reused with different content.

| 2022 NAICS Code | 2022 NAICS U.S. Description | Status Code | 2017 NAICS Code | 2017 NAICS U.S. Description |
|---|---|---|---|---|
| 517122 | Agents for Wireless Telecommunications Services | N | *517312 | Wireless Telecommunications Carriers (except Satellite) - *agents for wireless telecommunications carriers* |
| | | | *517911 | Telecommunications Resellers - *agents for wireless telecommunications resellers* |
| 5178 | All Other Telecommunications | | | |
| 51781 | All Other Telecommunications | | | |
| 517810 | All Other Telecommunications | N | 517919 | All Other Telecommunications |
| 519 | Web Search Portals, Libraries, Archives, and Other Information Services | R | *519 | Other Information Services - *except news syndicates and Internet publishing and broadcasting* |
| 5192 | Web Search Portals, Libraries, Archives, and Other Information Services | | | |
| 51921 | Libraries and Archives | | | |
| 519210 | Libraries and Archives | N | 519120 | Libraries and Archives |
| 51929 | Web Search Portals and All Other Information Services | | | |
| 519290 | Web Search Portals and All Other Information Services | N | *519130 | Internet Publishing and Broadcasting and Web Search Portals - *web search portals* |
| | | | 519190 | All Other Information Services |
| 52218 | Savings Institutions and Other Depository Credit Intermediation | | | |
| 522180 | Savings Institutions and Other Depository Credit Intermediation | N | 522120 | Savings Institutions |
| | | | 522190 | Other Depository Credit Intermediation |
| 522299 | International, Secondary Market, and All Other Nondepository Credit Intermediation | N | 522293 | International Trade Financing |
| | | | 522294 | Secondary Market Financing |
| | | | 522298 | All Other Nondepository Credit Intermediation |

N—New NAICS industry/code for 2022; *—Part of 2017 NAICS United States industry;
R—2017 NAICS industry code reused with different content.

| 2022 NAICS Code | 2022 NAICS U.S. Description | Status Code | 2017 NAICS Code | 2017 NAICS U.S. Description |
|---|---|---|---|---|
| 52315 | Investment Banking and Securities Intermediation | | | |
| 523150 | Investment Banking and Securities Intermediation | N | 523110 | Investment Banking and Securities Dealing |
| | | | 523120 | Securities Brokerage |
| 52316 | Commodity Contracts Intermediation | | | |
| 523160 | Commodity Contracts Intermediation | N | 523130 | Commodity Contracts Dealing |
| | | | 523140 | Commodity Contracts Brokerage |
| 52394 | Portfolio Management and Investment Advice | | | |
| 523940 | Portfolio Management and Investment Advice | N | 523920 | Portfolio Management |
| | | | 523930 | Investment Advice |
| 811114 | Specialized Automotive Repair | N | 811112 | Automotive Exhaust System Repair |
| | | | 811113 | Automotive Transmission Repair |
| | | | 811118 | Other Automotive Mechanical and Electrical Repair and Maintenance |
| 811210 | Electronic and Precision Equipment Repair and Maintenance | N | 811211 | Consumer Electronics Repair and Maintenance |
| | | | 811212 | Computer and Office Machine Repair and Maintenance |
| | | | 811213 | Communication Equipment Repair and Maintenance |
| | | | 811219 | Other Electronic and Precision Equipment Repair and Maintenance |

N—New NAICS industry/code for 2022; *—Part of 2017 NAICS United States industry;
R—2017 NAICS industry code reused with different content.

# Appendix B

# 2017 NAICS U.S. Matched to 2022 NAICS U.S.

| 2017 NAICS Code | 2017 NAICS U.S. Description | Status Code | 2022 NAICS Code | 2022 NAICS U.S. Description |
|---|---|---|---|---|
| 212111 | Bituminous Coal and Lignite Surface Mining | pt. | 212114 | Surface Coal Mining |
| 212112 | Bituminous Coal Underground Mining | pt. | 212115 | Underground Coal Mining |
| 212113 | Anthracite Mining | | | |
| | *anthracite surface mining* | pt. | 212114 | Surface Coal Mining |
| | *anthracite underground mining* | pt. | 212115 | Underground Coal Mining |
| 212221 | Gold Ore Mining | pt. | 212220 | Gold Ore and Silver Ore Mining |
| 212222 | Silver Ore Mining | pt. | 212220 | Gold Ore and Silver Ore Mining |
| 212291 | Uranium-Radium-Vanadium Ore Mining | pt. | 212290 | Other Metal Ore Mining |
| 212299 | All Other Metal Ore Mining | pt. | 212290 | Other Metal Ore Mining |
| 212324 | Kaolin and Ball Clay Mining | pt. | 212323 | Kaolin, Clay, and Ceramic and Refractory Minerals Mining |
| 212325 | Clay and Ceramic and Refractory Minerals Mining | pt. | 212323 | Kaolin, Clay, and Ceramic and Refractory Minerals Mining |
| 212391 | Potash, Soda, and Borate Mineral Mining | pt. | 212390 | Other Nonmetallic Mineral Mining and Quarrying |
| 212392 | Phosphate Rock Mining | pt. | 212390 | Other Nonmetallic Mineral Mining and Quarrying |
| 212393 | Other Chemical and Fertilizer Mineral Mining | pt. | 212390 | Other Nonmetallic Mineral Mining and Quarrying |
| 212399 | All Other Nonmetallic Mineral Mining | pt. | 212390 | Other Nonmetallic Mineral Mining and Quarrying |
| 315110 | Hosiery and Sock Mills | pt. | 315120 | Apparel Knitting Mills |
| 315190 | Other Apparel Knitting Mills | pt. | 315120 | Apparel Knitting Mills |

pt.—Part of 2022 NAICS United States industry.

| 2017 NAICS Code | 2017 NAICS U.S. Description | Status Code | 2022 NAICS Code | 2022 NAICS U.S. Description |
|---|---|---|---|---|
| 315220 | Men's and Boys' Cut and Sew Apparel Manufacturing | pt. | 315250 | Cut and Sew Apparel Manufacturing (except Contractors) |
| 315240 | Women's, Girls', and Infants' Cut and Sew Apparel Manufacturing | pt. | 315250 | Cut and Sew Apparel Manufacturing (except Contractors) |
| 315280 | Other Cut and Sew Apparel Manufacturing | pt. | 315250 | Cut and Sew Apparel Manufacturing (except Contractors) |
| 316992 | Women's Handbag and Purse Manufacturing | pt. | 316990 | Other Leather and Allied Product Manufacturing |
| 316998 | All Other Leather Good and Allied Product Manufacturing | pt. | 316990 | Other Leather and Allied Product Manufacturing |
| 321213 | Engineered Wood Member (except Truss) Manufacturing | pt. | 321215 | Engineered Wood Member Manufacturing |
| 321214 | Truss Manufacturing | pt. | 321215 | Engineered Wood Member Manufacturing |
| 322121 | Paper (except Newsprint) Mills | pt. | 322120 | Paper Mills |
| 322122 | Newsprint Mills | pt. | 322120 | Paper Mills |
| 325314 | Fertilizer (Mixing Only) Manufacturing<br>　*compost manufacturing*<br>　*except compost manufacturing* | | 325315<br>325314 | Compost Manufacturing<br>Fertilizer (Mixing Only) Manufacturing |
| 333244 | Printing Machinery and Equipment Manufacturing | pt. | 333248 | All Other Industrial Machinery Manufacturing |
| 333249 | Other Industrial Machinery Manufacturing | pt. | 333248 | All Other Industrial Machinery Manufacturing |
| 333314 | Optical Instrument and Lens Manufacturing | pt. | 333310 | Commercial and Service Industry Machinery Manufacturing |
| 333316 | Photographic and Photocopying Equipment Manufacturing | pt. | 333310 | Commercial and Service Industry Machinery Manufacturing |
| 333318 | Other Commercial and Service Industry Machinery Manufacturing | pt. | 333310 | Commercial and Service Industry Machinery Manufacturing |
| 333997 | Scale and Balance Manufacturing | pt. | 333998 | All Other Miscellaneous General Purpose Machinery Manufacturing |
| 333999 | All Other Miscellaneous General Purpose Machinery Manufacturing | pt. | 333998 | All Other Miscellaneous General Purpose Machinery Manufacturing |

pt.—Part of 2022 NAICS United States industry.

| 2017 NAICS Code | 2017 NAICS U.S. Description | Status Code | 2022 NAICS Code | 2022 NAICS U.S. Description |
|---|---|---|---|---|
| 334613 | Blank Magnetic and Optical Recording Media Manufacturing | pt. | 334610 | Manufacturing and Reproducing Magnetic and Optical Media |
| 334614 | Software and Other Prerecorded Compact Disc, Tape, and Record Reproducing | pt. | 334610 | Manufacturing and Reproducing Magnetic and Optical Media |
| 335110 | Electric Lamp Bulb and Part Manufacturing | pt. | 335139 | Electric Lamp Bulb and Other Lighting Equipment Manufacturing |
| 335121 | Residential Electric Lighting Fixture Manufacturing | | 335131 | Residential Electric Lighting Fixture Manufacturing |
| 335122 | Commercial, Industrial, and Institutional Electric Lighting Fixture Manufacturing | | 335132 | Commercial, Industrial, and Institutional Electric Lighting Fixture Manufacturing |
| 335129 | Other Lighting Equipment Manufacturing | pt. | 335139 | Electric Lamp Bulb and Other Lighting Equipment Manufacturing |
| 335911 | Storage Battery Manufacturing | pt. | 335910 | Battery Manufacturing |
| 335912 | Primary Battery Manufacturing | pt. | 335910 | Battery Manufacturing |
| 336111 | Automobile Manufacturing | pt. | 336110 | Automobile and Light Duty Motor Vehicle Manufacturing |
| 336112 | Light Truck and Utility Vehicle Manufacturing | pt. | 336110 | Automobile and Light Duty Motor Vehicle Manufacturing |
| 337124 | Metal Household Furniture Manufacturing | pt. | 337126 | Household Furniture (except Wood and Upholstered) Manufacturing |
| 337125 | Household Furniture (except Wood and Metal) Manufacturing | pt. | 337126 | Household Furniture (except Wood and Upholstered) Manufacturing |
| 424320 | Men's and Boys' Clothing and Furnishings Merchant Wholesalers | pt. | 424350 | Clothing and Clothing Accessories Merchant Wholesalers |
| 424330 | Women's, Children's, and Infants' Clothing and Accessories Merchant Wholesalers | pt. | 424350 | Clothing and Clothing Accessories Merchant Wholesalers |
| 425110 | Business to Business Electronic Markets | pt. | 425120 | Wholesale Trade Agents and Brokers |
| 425120 | Wholesale Trade Agents and Brokers | pt. | 425120 | Wholesale Trade Agents and Brokers |

pt.—Part of 2022 NAICS United States industry.

| 2017 NAICS Code | 2017 NAICS U.S. Description | Status Code | 2022 NAICS Code | 2022 NAICS U.S. Description |
|---|---|---|---|---|
| 441228 | Motorcycle, ATV, and All Other Motor Vehicle Dealers | pt. | 441227 | Motorcycle, ATV, and All Other Motor Vehicle Dealers |
| 441310 | Automotive Parts and Accessories Stores | pt. | 441330 | Automotive Parts and Accessories Retailers |
| 441320 | Tire Dealers | pt. | 441340 | Tire Dealers |
| 442110 | Furniture Stores | pt. | 449110 | Furniture Retailers |
| 442210 | Floor Covering Stores | pt. | 449121 | Floor Covering Retailers |
| 442291 | Window Treatment Stores | pt. | 449122 | Window Treatment Retailers |
| 442299 | All Other Home Furnishings Stores | pt. | 449129 | All Other Home Furnishings Retailers |
| 443141 | Household Appliance Stores | pt. | 449210 | Electronics and Appliance Retailers |
| 443142 | Electronics Stores | pt. | 449210 | Electronics and Appliance Retailers |
| 444130 | Hardware Stores | pt. | 444140 | Hardware Retailers |
| 444190 | Other Building Material Dealers | pt. | 444180 | Other Building Material Dealers |
| 444210 | Outdoor Power Equipment Stores | pt. | 444230 | Outdoor Power Equipment Retailers |
| 444220 | Nursery, Garden Center, and Farm Supply Stores | pt. | 444240 | Nursery, Garden Center, and Farm Supply Retailers |
| 445120 | Convenience Stores | pt. | 445131 | Convenience Retailers |
| 445210 | Meat Markets | pt. | 445240 | Meat Retailers |
| 445220 | Fish and Seafood Markets | pt. | 445250 | Fish and Seafood Retailers |
| 445299 | All Other Specialty Food Stores | pt. | 445298 | All Other Specialty Food Retailers |
| 445310 | Beer, Wine, and Liquor Stores | pt. | 445320 | Beer, Wine, and Liquor Retailers |
| 446110 | Pharmacies and Drug Stores | pt. | 456110 | Pharmacies and Drug Retailers |
| 446120 | Cosmetics, Beauty Supplies, and Perfume Stores | pt. | 456120 | Cosmetics, Beauty Supplies, and Perfume Retailers |
| 446130 | Optical Goods Stores | pt. | 456130 | Optical Goods Retailers |
| 446191 | Food (Health) Supplement Stores | pt. | 456191 | Food (Health) Supplement Retailers |
| 446199 | All Other Health and Personal Care Stores | pt. | 456199 | All Other Health and Personal Care Retailers |

pt.—Part of 2022 NAICS United States industry.

| 2017 NAICS Code | 2017 NAICS U.S. Description | Status Code | 2022 NAICS Code | 2022 NAICS U.S. Description |
|---|---|---|---|---|
| 447110 | Gasoline Stations with Convenience Stores | | 457110 | Gasoline Stations with Convenience Stores |
| 447190 | Other Gasoline Stations | | 457120 | Other Gasoline Stations |
| 448110 | Men's Clothing Stores | pt. | 458110 | Clothing and Clothing Accessories Retailers |
| 448120 | Women's Clothing Stores | pt. | 458110 | Clothing and Clothing Accessories Retailers |
| 448130 | Children's and Infants' Clothing Stores | pt. | 458110 | Clothing and Clothing Accessories Retailers |
| 448140 | Family Clothing Stores | pt. | 458110 | Clothing and Clothing Accessories Retailers |
| 448150 | Clothing Accessories Stores | pt. | 458110 | Clothing and Clothing Accessories Retailers |
| 448190 | Other Clothing Stores | pt. | 458110 | Clothing and Clothing Accessories Retailers |
| 448210 | Shoe Stores | pt. | 458210 | Shoe Retailers |
| 448310 | Jewelry Stores | pt. | 458310 | Jewelry Retailers |
| 448320 | Luggage and Leather Goods Stores | pt. | 458320 | Luggage and Leather Goods Retailers |
| 451110 | Sporting Goods Stores | pt. | 459110 | Sporting Goods Retailers |
| 451120 | Hobby, Toy, and Game Stores | pt. | 459120 | Hobby, Toy, and Game Retailers |
| 451130 | Sewing, Needlework, and Piece Goods Stores | pt. | 459130 | Sewing, Needlework, and Piece Goods Retailers |
| 451140 | Musical Instrument and Supplies Stores | pt. | 459140 | Musical Instrument and Supplies Retailers |
| 451211 | Book Stores | pt. | 459210 | Book Retailers and News Dealers |
| 451212 | News Dealers and Newsstands | pt. | 459210 | Book Retailers and News Dealers |
| 452210 | Department Stores | pt. | 455110 | Department Stores |
| 452311 | Warehouse Clubs and Supercenters | pt. | 455211 | Warehouse Clubs and Supercenters |
| 452319 | All Other General Merchandise Stores | pt. | 455219 | All Other General Merchandise Retailers |

pt.—Part of 2022 NAICS United States industry.

| 2017 NAICS Code | 2017 NAICS U.S. Description | Status Code | 2022 NAICS Code | 2022 NAICS U.S. Description |
|---|---|---|---|---|
| 453110 | Florists | pt. | 459310 | Florists |
| 453210 | Office Supplies and Stationery Stores | pt. | 459410 | Office Supplies and Stationery Retailers |
| 453220 | Gift, Novelty, and Souvenir Stores | pt. | 459420 | Gift, Novelty, and Souvenir Retailers |
| 453310 | Used Merchandise Stores | pt. | 459510 | Used Merchandise Retailers |
| 453910 | Pet and Pet Supplies Stores | pt. | 459910 | Pet and Pet Supplies Retailers |
| 453920 | Art Dealers | pt. | 459920 | Art Dealers |
| 453930 | Manufactured (Mobile) Home Dealers | | 459930 | Manufactured (Mobile) Home Dealers |
| 453991 | Tobacco Stores | pt. | 459991 | Tobacco, Electronic Cigarette, and Other Smoking Supplies Retailers |
| 453998 | All Other Miscellaneous Store Retailers (except Tobacco Stores) | | | |
| | *general merchandise auction houses* | pt. | 455219 | All Other General Merchandise Retailers |
| | *electronic cigarette stores and marijuana stores, medical or recreational* | pt. | 459991 | Tobacco, Electronic Cigarette, and Other Smoking Supplies Retailers |
| | *except general merchandise auction houses, electronic cigarette stores, and marijuana stores, medical or recreational* | pt. | 459999 | All Other Miscellaneous Retailers |
| 454110 | Electronic Shopping and Mail-Order Houses | pt. | 441227 | Motorcycle, ATV, and All Other Motor Vehicle Dealers |
| | | pt. | 441330 | Automotive Parts and Accessories Retailers |
| | | pt. | 441340 | Tire Dealers |
| | | pt. | 444140 | Hardware Retailers |
| | | pt. | 444180 | Other Building Material Dealers |
| | | pt. | 444230 | Outdoor Power Equipment Retailers |
| | | pt. | 444240 | Nursery, Garden Center, and Farm Supply Retailers |
| | | pt. | 445131 | Convenience Retailers |
| | | pt. | 445240 | Meat Retailers |
| | | pt. | 445250 | Fish and Seafood Retailers |
| | | pt. | 445298 | All Other Specialty Food Retailers |
| | | pt. | 445320 | Beer, Wine, and Liquor Retailers |
| | | pt. | 449110 | Furniture Retailers |
| | | pt. | 449121 | Floor Covering Retailers |
| | | pt. | 449122 | Window Treatment Retailers |
| | | pt. | 449129 | All Other Home Furnishings Retailers |

pt.—Part of 2022 NAICS United States industry.

| 2017 NAICS Code | 2017 NAICS U.S. Description | Status Code | 2022 NAICS Code | 2022 NAICS U.S. Description |
|---|---|---|---|---|
| | | pt. | 449210 | Electronics and Appliance Retailers |
| | | pt. | 455110 | Department Stores |
| | | pt. | 455211 | Warehouse Clubs and Supercenters |
| | | pt. | 455219 | All Other General Merchandise Retailers |
| | | pt. | 456110 | Pharmacies and Drug Retailers |
| | | pt. | 456120 | Cosmetics, Beauty Supplies, and Perfume Retailers |
| | | pt. | 456130 | Optical Goods Retailers |
| | | pt. | 456191 | Food (Health) Supplement Retailers |
| | | pt. | 456199 | All Other Health and Personal Care Retailers |
| | | pt. | 458110 | Clothing and Clothing Accessories Retailers |
| | | pt. | 458210 | Shoe Retailers |
| | | pt. | 458310 | Jewelry Retailers |
| | | pt. | 458320 | Luggage and Leather Goods Retailers |
| | | pt. | 459110 | Sporting Goods Retailers |
| | | pt. | 459120 | Hobby, Toy, and Game Retailers |
| | | pt. | 459130 | Sewing, Needlework, and Piece Goods Retailers |
| | | pt. | 459140 | Musical Instrument and Supplies Retailers |
| | | pt. | 459210 | Book Retailers and News Dealers |
| | | pt. | 459310 | Florists |
| | | pt. | 459410 | Office Supplies and Stationery Retailers |
| | | pt. | 459420 | Gift, Novelty, and Souvenir Retailers |
| | | pt. | 459510 | Used Merchandise Retailers |
| | | pt. | 459910 | Pet and Pet Supplies Retailers |
| | | pt. | 459920 | Art Dealers |
| | | pt. | 459991 | Tobacco, Electronic Cigarette, and Other Smoking Supplies Retailers |
| | | pt. | 459999 | All Other Miscellaneous Retailers |
| 454210 | Vending Machine Operators | | 445132 | Vending Machine Operators |
| 454310 | Fuel Dealers | | 457210 | Fuel Dealers |
| 454390 | Other Direct Selling Establishments | pt. | 441330 | Automotive Parts and Accessories Retailers |
| | | pt. | 441340 | Tire Dealers |
| | | pt. | 444140 | Hardware Retailers |
| | | pt. | 444180 | Other Building Material Dealers |
| | | pt. | 444230 | Outdoor Power Equipment Retailers |
| | | pt. | 444240 | Nursery, Garden Center, and Farm Supply Retailers |
| | | pt. | 445131 | Convenience Retailers |
| | | pt. | 445240 | Meat Retailers |
| | | pt. | 445250 | Fish and Seafood Retailers |
| | | pt. | 445298 | All Other Specialty Food Retailers |

pt.—Part of 2022 NAICS United States industry.

| 2017 NAICS Code | 2017 NAICS U.S. Description | Status Code | 2022 NAICS Code | 2022 NAICS U.S. Description |
|---|---|---|---|---|
| | | pt. | 445320 | Beer, Wine, and Liquor Retailers |
| | | pt. | 449110 | Furniture Retailers |
| | | pt. | 449121 | Floor Covering Retailers |
| | | pt. | 449122 | Window Treatment Retailers |
| | | pt. | 449129 | All Other Home Furnishings Retailers |
| | | pt. | 449210 | Electronics and Appliance Retailers |
| | | pt. | 455219 | All Other General Merchandise Retailers |
| | | pt. | 456110 | Pharmacies and Drug Retailers |
| | | pt. | 456120 | Cosmetics, Beauty Supplies, and Perfume Retailers |
| | | pt. | 456130 | Optical Goods Retailers |
| | | pt. | 456191 | Food (Health) Supplement Retailers |
| | | pt. | 456199 | All Other Health and Personal Care Retailers |
| | | pt. | 458110 | Clothing and Clothing Accessories Retailers |
| | | pt. | 458210 | Shoe Retailers |
| | | pt. | 458310 | Jewelry Retailers |
| | | pt. | 458320 | Luggage and Leather Goods Retailers |
| | | pt. | 459110 | Sporting Goods Retailers |
| | | pt. | 459120 | Hobby, Toy, and Game Retailers |
| | | pt. | 459130 | Sewing, Needlework, and Piece Goods Retailers |
| | | pt. | 459140 | Musical Instrument and Supplies Retailers |
| | | pt. | 459210 | Book Retailers and News Dealers |
| | | pt. | 459310 | Florists |
| | | pt. | 459410 | Office Supplies and Stationery Retailers |
| | | pt. | 459420 | Gift, Novelty, and Souvenir Retailers |
| | | pt. | 459510 | Used Merchandise Retailers |
| | | pt. | 459910 | Pet and Pet Supplies Retailers |
| | | pt. | 459920 | Art Dealers |
| | | pt. | 459991 | Tobacco, Electronic Cigarette, and Other Smoking Supplies Retailers |
| | | pt. | 459999 | All Other Miscellaneous Retailers |
| 511110 | Newspaper Publishers | pt. | 513110 | Newspaper Publishers |
| 511120 | Periodical Publishers | pt. | 513120 | Periodical Publishers |
| 511130 | Book Publishers | pt. | 513130 | Book Publishers |
| 511140 | Directory and Mailing List Publishers | pt. | 513140 | Directory and Mailing List Publishers |
| 511191 | Greeting Card Publishers | pt. | 513191 | Greeting Card Publishers |
| 511199 | All Other Publishers | pt. | 513199 | All Other Publishers |

pt.—Part of 2022 NAICS United States industry.

| 2017 NAICS Code | 2017 NAICS U.S. Description | Status Code | 2022 NAICS Code | 2022 NAICS U.S. Description |
|---|---|---|---|---|
| 511210 | Software Publishers | | 513210 | Software Publishers |
| 515111 | Radio Networks | pt. | 516210 | Media Streaming Distribution Services, Social Networks, and Other Media Networks and Content Providers |
| 515112 | Radio Stations | | 516110 | Radio Broadcasting Stations |
| 515120 | Television Broadcasting | | | |
| | *television broadcasting stations* | | 516120 | Television Broadcasting Stations |
| | *television networks* | pt. | 516210 | Media Streaming Distribution Services, Social Networks, and Other Media Networks and Content Providers |
| 515210 | Cable and Other Subscription Programming | pt. | 516210 | Media Streaming Distribution Services, Social Networks, and Other Media Networks and Content Providers |
| 517311 | Wired Telecommunications Carriers | | 517111 | Wired Telecommunications Carriers |
| 517312 | Wireless Telecommunications Carriers (except Satellite) | | | |
| | *except agents for wireless telecommunications carriers* | | 517112 | Wireless Telecommunications Carriers (except Satellite) |
| | *agents for wireless telecommunications carriers* | pt. | 517122 | Agents for Wireless Telecommunications Services |
| 517911 | Telecommunications Resellers | | | |
| | *except agents for wireless telecommunications resellers* | | 517121 | Telecommunications Resellers |
| | *agents for wireless telecommunications resellers* | pt. | 517122 | Agents for Wireless Telecommunications Services |
| 517919 | All Other Telecommunications | | 517810 | All Other Telecommunications |
| 519110 | News Syndicates | pt. | 516210 | Media Streaming Distribution Services, Social Networks, and Other Media Networks and Content Providers |
| 519120 | Libraries and Archives | | 519210 | Libraries and Archives |

pt.—Part of 2022 NAICS United States industry.

| 2017 NAICS Code | 2017 NAICS U.S. Description | Status Code | 2022 NAICS Code | 2022 NAICS U.S. Description |
|---|---|---|---|---|
| 519130 | Internet Publishing and Broadcasting and Web Search Portals | | | |
| | *Internet newspaper publishers* | pt. | 513110 | Newspaper Publishers |
| | *Internet periodical publishers* | pt. | 513120 | Periodical Publishers |
| | *Internet book publishers* | pt. | 513130 | Book Publishers |
| | *Internet directory and mailing list publishers* | pt. | 513140 | Directory and Mailing List Publishers |
| | *Internet greeting card publishers* | pt. | 513191 | Greeting Card Publishers |
| | *all other Internet publishers* | pt. | 513199 | All Other Publishers |
| | *Internet broadcasting* | pt. | 516210 | Media Streaming Distribution Services, Social Networks, and Other Media Networks and Content Providers |
| | *web search portals* | pt. | 519290 | Web Search Portals and All Other Information Services |
| 519190 | All Other Information Services | pt. | 519290 | Web Search Portals and All Other Information Services |
| 522120 | Savings Institutions | pt. | 522180 | Savings Institutions and Other Depository Credit Intermediation |
| 522190 | Other Depository Credit Intermediation | pt. | 522180 | Savings Institutions and Other Depository Credit Intermediation |
| 522293 | International Trade Financing | pt. | 522299 | International, Secondary Market, and All Other Nondepository Credit Intermediation |
| 522294 | Secondary Market Financing | pt. | 522299 | International, Secondary Market, and All Other Nondepository Credit Intermediation |
| 522298 | All Other Nondepository Credit Intermediation | pt. | 522299 | International, Secondary Market, and All Other Nondepository Credit Intermediation |
| 523110 | Investment Banking and Securities Dealing | pt. | 523150 | Investment Banking and Securities Intermediation |
| 523120 | Securities Brokerage | pt. | 523150 | Investment Banking and Securities Intermediation |
| 523130 | Commodity Contracts Dealing | pt. | 523160 | Commodity Contracts Intermediation |
| 523140 | Commodity Contracts Brokerage | pt. | 523160 | Commodity Contracts Intermediation |

pt.—Part of 2022 NAICS United States industry.

| 2017 NAICS Code | 2017 NAICS U.S. Description | Status Code | 2022 NAICS Code | 2022 NAICS U.S. Description |
|---|---|---|---|---|
| 523920 | Portfolio Management | pt. | 523940 | Portfolio Management and Investment Advice |
| 523930 | Investment Advice | pt. | 523940 | Portfolio Management and Investment Advice |
| 811112 | Automotive Exhaust System Repair | pt. | 811114 | Specialized Automotive Repair |
| 811113 | Automotive Transmission Repair | pt. | 811114 | Specialized Automotive Repair |
| 811118 | Other Automotive Mechanical and Electrical Repair and Maintenance | pt. | 811114 | Specialized Automotive Repair |
| 811211 | Consumer Electronics Repair and Maintenance | pt. | 811210 | Electronic and Precision Equipment Repair and Maintenance |
| 811212 | Computer and Office Machine Repair and Maintenance | pt. | 811210 | Electronic and Precision Equipment Repair and Maintenance |
| 811213 | Communication Equipment Repair and Maintenance | pt. | 811210 | Electronic and Precision Equipment Repair and Maintenance |
| 811219 | Other Electronic and Precision Equipment Repair and Maintenance | pt. | 811210 | Electronic and Precision Equipment Repair and Maintenance |

pt.—Part of 2022 NAICS United States industry.

# Part III

# Alphabetic Index

# Alphabetic Index

| | |
|---|---|
| 311611 | Abattoirs |
| 621410 | Abortion clinics |
| 334519 | Abrasion testing machines manufacturing |
| 339114 | Abrasive points, wheels, and disks, dental, manufacturing |
| 327910 | Abrasive products manufacturing |
| 212322 | Abrasive sand quarrying and/or beneficiating |
| 212390 | Abrasive stones (e.g., emery, grindstones, hones, pumice) mining and/or beneficiating |
| 423840 | Abrasives merchant wholesalers |
| 212390 | Abrasives, natural (except sand), mining and/or beneficiating |
| 322120 | Absorbent paper stock manufacturing |
| 332420 | Absorbers, gas, heavy gauge metal, manufacturing |
| 334513 | Absorption analyzers, industrial process type (e.g., infrared), manufacturing |
| 237310 | Abutment construction |
| 611691 | Academic tutoring services |
| 611310 | Academies, college or university |
| 611110 | Academies, elementary or secondary |
| 611210 | Academies, junior college |
| 611310 | Academies, military service (college) |
| 611620 | Academies, riding instruction |
| 334511 | Acceleration indicators and systems components, aerospace type, manufacturing |
| 325199 | Accelerators (i.e., basic synthetic chemical) manufacturing |
| 334519 | Accelerometers (except aerospace type) manufacturing |
| 238330 | Access flooring installation |
| 424350 | Accessories, clothing, men's and boy's, merchant wholesalers |
| 813319 | Accident prevention associations |
| 524130 | Accidental and health reinsurance carriers |
| 524113 | Accidental death and dismemberment insurance carriers, direct |
| 524113 | Accidental death and dismemberment insurance underwriting, direct |
| 339992 | Accordions and parts manufacturing |
| 561440 | Account collection services |
| 541219 | Accountants' (except CPAs) offices |
| 541219 | Accountants' (except CPAs) private practices |
| 541211 | Accountants' (i.e., CPAs) offices, certified public |
| 541211 | Accountants' (i.e., CPAs) private practices, certified public |
| 813920 | Accountants' associations |
| 541211 | Accounting (i.e., CPAs) services, certified public |
| 423420 | Accounting machines merchant wholesalers |
| 541219 | Accounting services (except CPAs) |
| 332420 | Accumulators, industrial pressure vessels, heavy gauge metal, manufacturing |
| 325211 | Acetal resins manufacturing |
| 325199 | Acetaldehyde manufacturing |
| 325220 | Acetate fibers and filaments manufacturing |
| 325194 | Acetate of lime, natural, made by distillation of wood |
| 313110 | Acetate spun yarns made from purchased fiber |
| 325199 | Acetates, not specified elsewhere by process, manufacturing |
| 325199 | Acetic acid manufacturing |
| 325199 | Acetic anhydride manufacturing |
| 325199 | Acetin manufacturing |
| 325194 | Acetone, natural, manufacturing |
| 325199 | Acetone, synthetic, manufacturing |
| 332420 | Acetylene cylinders, heavy gauge metal, manufacturing |
| 325120 | Acetylene manufacturing |
| 325411 | Acetylsalicylic acid manufacturing |
| 325130 | Acid dyes, synthetic organic, manufacturing |
| 325199 | Acid esters, not specified elsewhere by process, manufacturing |
| 324110 | Acid oils made in petroleum refineries |
| 236210 | Acid plant construction |
| 562211 | Acid waste disposal facilities |
| 562211 | Acid waste treatment facilities |
| 334513 | Acidity (i.e., pH) instruments, industrial process type, manufacturing |
| 334516 | Acidity (i.e., pH) measuring equipment, laboratory analysis-type, manufacturing |

| | |
|---|---|
| 213112 | Acidizing oil and gas field wells on a contract basis |
| 311511 | Acidophilus milk manufacturing |
| 424690 | Acids merchant wholesalers |
| 325199 | Acids, organic, not specified elsewhere by process, manufacturing |
| 111219 | Acorn squash farming, field, bedding plant and seed production |
| 238310 | Acoustical ceiling tile and panel installation |
| 541330 | Acoustical engineering consulting services |
| 238310 | Acoustical foam (i.e., sound barrier) installation |
| 332323 | Acoustical suspension systems, metal, manufacturing |
| 541330 | Acoustical system engineering design services |
| 541380 | Acoustics testing laboratories or services |
| 325199 | Acrolein manufacturing |
| 325212 | Acrylate rubber manufacturing |
| 325212 | Acrylate-butadiene rubber manufacturing |
| 313110 | Acrylic and modacrylic filament yarn throwing, twisting, texturizing, or winding of purchased yarn |
| 325220 | Acrylic fibers and filaments manufacturing |
| 326113 | Acrylic film and unlaminated sheet (except packaging) manufacturing |
| 325211 | Acrylic resins manufacturing |
| 325212 | Acrylic rubber manufacturing |
| 313110 | Acrylic spun yarns made from purchased fiber |
| 325220 | Acrylonitrile fibers and filaments manufacturing |
| 325199 | Acrylonitrile manufacturing |
| 325211 | Acrylonitrile-butadiene-styrene (ABS) resins manufacturing |
| 334519 | Actinometers, meteorological, manufacturing |
| 339930 | Action figures manufacturing |
| 325998 | Activated carbon or charcoal manufacturing |
| 624120 | Activity centers for disabled persons and the elderly |
| 711510 | Actors, independent |
| 711510 | Actresses, independent |
| 541612 | Actuarial consulting services (except insurance actuarial services) |
| 524298 | Actuarial services, insurance |
| 333995 | Actuators, fluid power, manufacturing |
| 423830 | Actuators, fluid power, merchant wholesalers |
| 611519 | Acupuncture training |
| 621399 | Acupuncturists' (except MDs or DOs) offices (e.g., centers, clinics) |
| 621111 | Acupuncturists' (MDs or DOs) offices (e.g., centers, clinics) |
| 325110 | Acyclic hydrocarbons (e.g., butene, ethylene, propene) (except acetylene) made from refined petroleum or liquid hydrocarbons |
| 332993 | Adapters, bombcluster, manufacturing |
| 333310 | Adding machines manufacturing |
| 236118 | Addition, alteration and renovation (i.e., construction), multifamily building |
| 236118 | Addition, alteration and renovation (i.e., construction), residential building |
| 236118 | Addition, alteration and renovation of single-family dwellings |
| 236220 | Addition, alteration and renovation, commercial and institutional building |
| 236220 | Addition, alteration and renovation, commercial warehouse |
| 236220 | Addition, alteration and renovation, for-sale builders, commercial and institutional building |
| 236220 | Addition, alteration and renovation, for-sale builders, commercial warehouse |
| 236220 | Addition, alteration and renovation, for-sale builders, hotel and motel |
| 236210 | Addition, alteration and renovation, for-sale builders, industrial building (except warehouses) |
| 236220 | Addition, alteration and renovation, for-sale builders, industrial warehouse |
| 236220 | Addition, alteration and renovation, general contractors, commercial and institutional building |
| 236220 | Addition, alteration and renovation, general contractors, commercial warehouse |
| 236220 | Addition, alteration and renovation, general contractors, hotel and motel |
| 236210 | Addition, alteration and renovation, general contractors, industrial building (except warehouses) |
| 236220 | Addition, alteration and renovation, general contractors, industrial warehouse |
| 236220 | Addition, alteration and renovation, hotel and motel |
| 236210 | Addition, alteration and renovation, industrial building (except warehouses) |
| 236220 | Addition, alteration and renovation, industrial warehouse |

| | |
|---|---|
| 236118 | Addition, alteration and renovation, multifamily building, for-sale builders |
| 236118 | Addition, alteration and renovation, multifamily building, general contractors |
| 236118 | Addition, alteration and renovation, residential building, for-sale builders |
| 236118 | Addition, alteration and renovation, residential building, general contractors |
| 236118 | Addition, alteration and renovation, single-family housing, for-sale builders |
| 236118 | Addition, alteration and renovation, single-family housing, general contractors |
| 333248 | Additive manufacturing machinery manufacturing |
| 325998 | Additive preparations for gasoline (e.g., antiknock preparations, detergents, gum inhibitors) manufacturing |
| 561499 | Address bar coding services |
| 513140 | Address list publishers |
| 513140 | Address list publishers (except exclusive Internet publishing) |
| 513140 | Address list publishers and printing combined |
| 323111 | Address lists commercial printing (except screen) without publishing |
| 323113 | Address lists screen printing without publishing |
| 423420 | Addressing machines merchant wholesalers |
| 322220 | Adhesive tape (except medical) made from purchased materials |
| 339113 | Adhesive tape, medical, manufacturing |
| 325520 | Adhesives (except asphalt, dental, gypsum base) manufacturing |
| 424690 | Adhesives and sealants merchant wholesalers |
| 325199 | Adipic acid esters or amines manufacturing |
| 325199 | Adipic acid manufacturing |
| 325199 | Adiponitrile manufacturing |
| 561440 | Adjustment agencies (except insurance) |
| 236220 | Administration building construction |
| 922110 | Administrative courts |
| 541611 | Administrative management consulting services |
| 561110 | Administrative management services |
| 523991 | Administrators of private estates |
| 327120 | Adobe bricks manufacturing |
| 624110 | Adoption agencies |
| 624110 | Adoption services, child |
| 325411 | Adrenal derivatives, uncompounded, manufacturing |
| 325412 | Adrenal medicinal preparations manufacturing |
| 624120 | Adult day care centers |
| 611691 | Adult literacy instruction |
| 327110 | Advanced and technical ceramic products manufacturing |
| 621399 | Advanced practicing registered nurses' (APRNs) offices (e.g., centers, clinics) |
| 541810 | Advertising agencies |
| 541810 | Advertising agency consulting services |
| 541870 | Advertising material (e.g., coupons, flyers, samples) direct distribution services |
| 541860 | Advertising material preparation services for mailing or other direct distribution |
| 323111 | Advertising materials (e.g., coupons, flyers) commercial printing (except screen) without publishing |
| 541840 | Advertising media representatives (i.e., independent of media owners) |
| 513120 | Advertising periodical publishers |
| 513120 | Advertising periodical publishers (except exclusive Internet publishing) |
| 513120 | Advertising periodical publishers and printing combined |
| 513120 | Advertising periodical publishers, exclusively on Internet |
| 516110 | Advertising sales offices of independent and public radio broadcast stations |
| 541850 | Advertising services, indoor or outdoor display |
| 541890 | Advertising specialty (e.g., keychain, magnet, pen) distribution services |
| 541850 | Advertising, aerial |
| 921110 | Advisory commissions, executive government |
| 921120 | Advisory commissions, legislative |
| 487990 | Aerial cable car, scenic and sightseeing, operation |
| 333310 | Aerial cameras manufacturing |
| 115112 | Aerial crop dusting or spraying (i.e., using specialized or dedicated aircraft) |
| 115310 | Aerial forest firefighting |
| 115310 | Aerial forest mulching or seeding |
| 541360 | Aerial geophysical surveying services |
| 238910 | Aerial or picker truck, construction, rental with operator |
| 541370 | Aerial surveying (except geophysical) services |

| | |
|---|---|
| 487990 | Aerial tramway, scenic and sightseeing, operation |
| 115310 | Aerial wildland firefighting |
| 333923 | Aerial work platforms manufacturing |
| 713940 | Aerobic dance and exercise centers |
| 611620 | Aerobic dance and exercise instruction |
| 423860 | Aeronautical equipment and supplies merchant wholesalers |
| 334511 | Aeronautical systems and instruments manufacturing |
| 334511 | Aeronautical systems and instruments overhauling, conversion, or rebuilding |
| 325998 | Aerosol can filling on a job-order or contract basis |
| 332431 | Aerosol cans, light gauge metal, manufacturing |
| 325998 | Aerosol packaging services |
| 332919 | Aerosol valves manufacturing |
| 423860 | Aerospace equipment and supplies merchant wholesalers |
| 541715 | Aerospace research and development (except prototype production) |
| 332410 | Aftercoolers (i.e., heat exchangers) manufacturing |
| 423120 | Aftermarket parts, automotive, merchant wholesalers |
| 325620 | After-shave preparations manufacturing |
| 325414 | Agar culture media manufacturing |
| 325411 | Agar-agar manufacturing |
| 212390 | Agate mining and/or beneficiating |
| 111998 | Agave farming |
| 522299 | Agencies of foreign banks (i.e., trade financing) |
| 524210 | Agencies, insurance |
| 522310 | Agencies, loan |
| 531210 | Agencies, real estate |
| 531390 | Agencies, real estate escrow |
| 425120 | Agents and brokers, durable goods, wholesale trade |
| 425120 | Agents and brokers, nondurable goods, wholesale trade |
| 517122 | Agents for mobile virtual network operators (MVNOs) |
| 517122 | Agents for wireless telecommunications carriers |
| 531390 | Agents' offices, real estate escrow |
| 711410 | Agents, artists' |
| 711410 | Agents, authors' |
| 711410 | Agents, celebrities' |
| 711410 | Agents, entertainers' |
| 812320 | Agents, laundry and drycleaning |
| 711410 | Agents, modeling |
| 711410 | Agents, public figures' |
| 531210 | Agents, real estate |
| 488510 | Agents, shipping |
| 711410 | Agents, sports figures' |
| 711410 | Agents, talent |
| 711410 | Agents, theatrical talent |
| 212210 | Agglomerates, iron ore, beneficiating |
| 333120 | Aggregate spreaders manufacturing |
| 325414 | Aggressins (except in-vitro) manufacturing |
| 551112 | Agreement corporation (except international trade financing) |
| 522299 | Agreement corporations (i.e., international trade financing) |
| 524126 | Agricultural (i.e., crop, livestock) insurance carriers, direct |
| 424910 | Agricultural chemicals merchant wholesalers |
| 541690 | Agricultural consulting services |
| 926140 | Agricultural cooperative extension program administration |
| 522299 | Agricultural credit institutions, making loans or extending credit (except real estate, sales financing) |
| 711320 | Agricultural fair managers without facilities |
| 711320 | Agricultural fair organizers without facilities |
| 711320 | Agricultural fair promoters without facilities |
| 332216 | Agricultural handtools (e.g., hay forks, hoes, rakes, spades), nonpowered, manufacturing |
| 423820 | Agricultural implements merchant wholesalers |
| 522299 | Agricultural lending (except real estate, sales financing) |
| 327410 | Agricultural lime manufacturing |
| 424910 | Agricultural limestone merchant wholesalers |
| 212312 | Agricultural limestone mining and/or beneficiating |
| 423820 | Agricultural machinery and equipment merchant wholesalers |
| 532490 | Agricultural machinery and equipment rental or leasing |
| 811310 | Agricultural machinery and equipment repair and maintenance services |
| 513120 | Agricultural magazine and periodical publishers |

513120 Agricultural magazine and periodical publishers (except exclusive Internet publishing)

513120 Agricultural magazine and periodical publishers and printing combined

513120 Agricultural magazine and periodical publishers, exclusively on Internet

323111 Agricultural magazines and periodicals commercial printing (except screen) without publishing

323113 Agricultural magazines and periodicals screen printing without publishing

926140 Agricultural marketing services government

813910 Agricultural organizations (except youth farming organizations, farm granges)

926140 Agricultural pest and weed regulation, government

484220 Agricultural products trucking, local

531190 Agricultural property rental or leasing

926140 Agriculture fair boards administration

115115 Agriculture production or harvesting crews

541715 Agriculture research and development laboratories or services (except biotechnology and nanotechnology research and development)

541690 Agrology consulting services

541690 Agronomy consulting services

624110 Aid to families with dependent children (AFDC)

621910 Air ambulance services

336390 Air bag assemblies manufacturing

336390 Air bag initiators manufacturing

336612 Air boat building

336340 Air brake systems and parts, automotive, truck, and bus, manufacturing

481212 Air cargo carriers (except air couriers), nonscheduled

481112 Air cargo carriers (except air couriers), scheduled

332439 Air cargo containers, light gauge metal, manufacturing

335313 Air circuit breakers manufacturing

481111 Air commuter carriers, scheduled

333912 Air compressors (except air-conditioning, refrigeration) manufacturing

423830 Air compressors (except air-conditioning, refrigeration) merchant wholesalers

492110 Air courier services (except establishments operating under a universal service obligation)

332322 Air cowls, sheet metal (except stampings), manufacturing

336390 Air filters, automotive, truck, and bus, manufacturing

334512 Air flow controllers (except valves), air-conditioning and refrigeration, manufacturing

928110 Air Force

325612 Air fresheners manufacturing

313230 Air laid nonwoven fabrics manufacturing

481211 Air passenger carriers, nonscheduled

481111 Air passenger carriers, scheduled

423730 Air pollution control equipment and supplies merchant wholesalers

335210 Air purification equipment, portable, manufacturing

333413 Air purification equipment, stationary, manufacturing

332420 Air receiver tanks, heavy gauge metal, manufacturing

333413 Air scrubbing systems manufacturing

711310 Air show managers with facilities

711320 Air show managers without facilities

711310 Air show organizers with facilities

711320 Air show organizers without facilities

711310 Air show promoters with facilities

711320 Air show promoters without facilities

238220 Air system balancing and testing

481211 Air taxi services

334511 Air traffic control radar systems and equipment manufacturing

611519 Air traffic control schools

488111 Air traffic control services (except military)

928110 Air traffic control, military

238220 Air vent installation

333413 Air washers (i.e., air scrubbers) manufacturing

487210 Airboat (i.e., swamp buggy) operation

334511 Airborne navigational systems manufacturing

334220 Airborne radio communications equipment manufacturing

532210 Air-conditioner rental

811412 Air-conditioner, window, repair and maintenance services

| | |
|---|---|
| 336390 | Air-conditioners, motor vehicle, manufacturing |
| 423620 | Air-conditioners, room, merchant wholesalers |
| 333415 | Air-conditioners, unit (e.g., motor home, travel trailer, window), manufacturing |
| 333415 | Air-conditioning and warm air heating combination units manufacturing |
| 333415 | Air-conditioning compressors (except motor vehicle) manufacturing |
| 333415 | Air-conditioning condensers and condensing units manufacturing |
| 333415 | Air-conditioning equipment (except motor vehicle) manufacturing |
| 423730 | Air-conditioning equipment (except room units) merchant wholesalers |
| 221330 | Air-conditioning supply |
| 238220 | Air-conditioning system (except window) installation |
| 331491 | Aircraft and automotive wire and cable (except aluminum, copper) made from purchased nonferrous metals (except aluminum, copper) in wire drawing plants |
| 331420 | Aircraft and automotive wire or cable made from purchased copper in wire drawing plants |
| 332994 | Aircraft artillery manufacturing |
| 336413 | Aircraft assemblies, subassemblies, and parts (except engines) manufacturing |
| 336413 | Aircraft auxiliary parts (e.g., crop dusting, external fuel tanks, inflight refueling equipment) manufacturing |
| 336413 | Aircraft brakes manufacturing |
| 333998 | Aircraft carrier catapults manufacturing |
| 481219 | Aircraft charter services (i.e., general purpose aircraft used for a variety of specialty air and flying services) |
| 481211 | Aircraft charter services, passenger |
| 336413 | Aircraft control surface assemblies manufacturing |
| 336411 | Aircraft conversions (i.e., major modifications to system) |
| 441227 | Aircraft dealers |
| 336412 | Aircraft engine and engine parts (except carburetors, pistons, piston rings, valves) manufacturing |
| 333924 | Aircraft engine cradles manufacturing |
| 334519 | Aircraft engine instruments manufacturing |
| 336412 | Aircraft engine overhauling |
| 336412 | Aircraft engine rebuilding |
| 423860 | Aircraft engines and parts merchant wholesalers |
| 423860 | Aircraft equipment and supplies merchant wholesalers |
| 488190 | Aircraft ferrying services |
| 334511 | Aircraft flight instruments (except engine instruments) manufacturing |
| 336413 | Aircraft fuselage wing tail and similar assemblies manufacturing |
| 488119 | Aircraft hangar rental |
| 332510 | Aircraft hardware, metal, manufacturing |
| 488190 | Aircraft inspection services |
| 926120 | Aircraft inspection, government |
| 561720 | Aircraft janitorial services |
| 336320 | Aircraft lighting fixtures manufacturing |
| 333924 | Aircraft loading hoists manufacturing |
| 488190 | Aircraft maintenance and repair services (except factory conversion, factory overhaul, factory rebuilding) |
| 336411 | Aircraft manufacturing |
| 423860 | Aircraft merchant wholesalers |
| 336411 | Aircraft overhauling |
| 488119 | Aircraft parking service |
| 336413 | Aircraft propellers and parts manufacturing |
| 336411 | Aircraft rebuilding (i.e., restoration to original design specifications) |
| 532411 | Aircraft rental or leasing without operator |
| 336360 | Aircraft seats manufacturing |
| 488190 | Aircraft testing services |
| 314999 | Aircraft tie-down strap assemblies (except leather) manufacturing |
| 326211 | Aircraft tire manufacturing |
| 336412 | Aircraft turbines manufacturing |
| 811420 | Aircraft upholstery repair |
| 336413 | Aircraft wheels manufacturing |
| 333413 | Aircurtains manufacturing |
| 336413 | Airframe assemblies (except for guided missiles) manufacturing |
| 336419 | Airframe assemblies for guided missiles manufacturing |
| 334511 | Airframe equipment instruments manufacturing |
| 722310 | Airline food services contractors |
| 561599 | Airline reservation services |
| 561599 | Airline ticket offices |
| 332313 | Airlocks, fabricated metal plate work, manufacturing |

481112 Airmail carriers, scheduled

532411 Airplane rental or leasing without operator

488119 Airport baggage handling services

236220 Airport building construction

488119 Airport cargo handling services

531190 Airport leasing, not operating airport, rental or leasing

335311 Airport lighting transformers manufacturing

485999 Airport limousine services (i.e., shuttle)

488119 Airport operators (e.g., civil, international, national)

488190 Airport passenger screening security services

237310 Airport runway construction

238210 Airport runway lighting contractors

237310 Airport runway line painting (e.g., striping)

488119 Airport runway maintenance services

485999 Airport shuttle services

236220 Airport terminal construction

488119 Airports, civil, operation and maintenance

334511 Airspeed instruments (aeronautical) manufacturing

212390 Alabaster mining and/or beneficiating

423610 Alarm apparatus, electric, merchant wholesalers

334519 Alarm clocks manufacturing

238210 Alarm system (e.g., fire, burglar), electric, installation only

334290 Alarm system central monitoring equipment manufacturing

561621 Alarm system monitoring services

334290 Alarm systems and equipment manufacturing

561621 Alarm systems sales combined with installation, repair, or monitoring services

323111 Albums (e.g., photo, scrap) and refills manufacturing

424120 Albums, photo, merchant wholesalers

424690 Alcohol, industrial, merchant wholesalers

922120 Alcohol, tobacco, and firearms control

926150 Alcoholic beverage control boards

492210 Alcoholic beverage delivery service

722410 Alcoholic beverage drinking places

312140 Alcoholic beverages (except brandy) distilling

424810 Alcoholic beverages (except distilled spirits, wine) merchant wholesalers

312130 Alcoholic beverages, brandy, distilling

424820 Alcoholic beverages, wine, and distilled spirits merchant wholesalers

624190 Alcoholism and drug addiction self-help organizations

624190 Alcoholism counseling (except medical treatment), nonresidential

623220 Alcoholism rehabilitation facilities (except licensed hospitals), residential

622210 Alcoholism rehabilitation hospitals

624190 Alcoholism self-help organizations

621420 Alcoholism treatment centers and clinics (except hospitals), outpatient

325199 Aldehydes manufacturing

312120 Ale brewing

424810 Ale merchant wholesalers

111940 Alfalfa hay farming

311119 Alfalfa meal, dehydrated, manufacturing

424910 Alfalfa merchant wholesalers

311119 Alfalfa prepared as feed for animals

111998 Alfalfa seed farming

111419 Alfalfa sprout farming, grown under cover

311119 Alfalfa, cubed, manufacturing

112519 Algae farming

325199 Alginates (e.g., calcium, potassium, sodium) manufacturing

325199 Alginic acid manufacturing

334519 Alidades, surveying, manufacturing

333310 Alignment equipment, motor vehicle, manufacturing

325110 Aliphatic (e.g., hydrocarbons) (except acetylene) made from refined petroleum or liquid hydrocarbons

324110 Aliphatic chemicals (i.e., acyclic) made in petroleum refineries

325180 Alkalies manufacturing

424690 Alkalies merchant wholesalers

335910 Alkaline cell primary batteries manufacturing

335910 Alkaline cell storage batteries (i.e., nickel-cadmium, nickel-iron, silver oxide-zinc) manufacturing

335910 Alkaline manganese primary batteries manufacturing

325211 Alkyd resins manufacturing

| | |
|---|---|
| 324110 | Alkylates made in petroleum refineries |
| 325414 | Allergenic extracts (except diagnostic substances) manufacturing |
| 325414 | Allergens manufacturing |
| 621111 | Allergists' offices (e.g., centers, clinics) |
| 112519 | Alligator production, farm raising |
| 331513 | Alloy steel castings (except investment), unfinished, manufacturing |
| 331314 | Alloying purchased aluminum metals |
| 331420 | Alloying purchased copper |
| 331420 | Alloying purchased copper metals |
| 331492 | Alloying purchased nonferrous metals (except aluminum, copper) |
| 441227 | All-terrain vehicle (ATV) dealers |
| 423110 | All-terrain vehicles (ATVs) merchant wholesalers |
| 336999 | All-terrain vehicles (ATVs), wheeled or tracked, manufacturing |
| 325211 | Allyl resins manufacturing |
| 323120 | Almanac binding without printing |
| 513130 | Almanac publishers |
| 513130 | Almanac publishers (except exclusive Internet publishing) |
| 513130 | Almanac publishers and printing combined |
| 513130 | Almanac publishers, exclusively on Internet |
| 323117 | Almanacs printing and binding without publishing |
| 323117 | Almanacs printing without publishing |
| 111335 | Almond farming |
| 115114 | Almond hulling and shelling |
| 311511 | Almond milk manufacturing |
| 311999 | Almond pastes manufacturing |
| 111998 | Aloe farming |
| 112990 | Alpaca production |
| 721110 | Alpine skiing facilities with accommodations (i.e., ski resorts) |
| 713920 | Alpine skiing facilities without accommodations |
| 237130 | Alternative energy (e.g., geothermal, ocean wave, solar, wind) structure construction |
| 424710 | Alternative fuels, blended with petroleum, bulk stations and terminals, merchant wholesalers |
| 424720 | Alternative fuels, blended with petroleum, merchant wholesalers (except bulk stations, terminals) |
| 457210 | Alternative fuels, direct selling |
| 424690 | Alternative fuels, not blended with petroleum, merchant wholesalers |
| 334515 | Alternator and generator testers manufacturing |
| 336320 | Alternators and generators for internal combustion engines manufacturing |
| 334511 | Altimeters, aeronautical, manufacturing |
| 212390 | Alum, natural, mining and/or beneficiating |
| 327120 | Alumina fused refractories manufacturing |
| 327110 | Alumina porcelain insulators manufacturing |
| 331313 | Alumina refining |
| 327120 | Aluminous refractory cement manufacturing |
| 331313 | Aluminum alloys made from bauxite or alumina producing primary aluminum and manufacturing |
| 331314 | Aluminum alloys made from scrap or dross |
| 423510 | Aluminum and aluminum alloy primary forms merchant wholesalers |
| 331318 | Aluminum bar made by extruding purchased aluminum |
| 331318 | Aluminum bar made in integrated secondary smelting and extruding mills |
| 331314 | Aluminum billet made from purchased aluminum |
| 331314 | Aluminum billet made in integrated secondary smelting and rolling mills |
| 332431 | Aluminum cans, light gauge metal, manufacturing |
| 331524 | Aluminum castings (except die-castings), unfinished, manufacturing |
| 325180 | Aluminum chloride manufacturing |
| 332812 | Aluminum coating of metal products for the trade |
| 325180 | Aluminum compounds, not specified elsewhere by process, manufacturing |
| 331523 | Aluminum die-casting foundries |
| 331523 | Aluminum die-castings, unfinished, manufacturing |
| 238350 | Aluminum door and window, residential-type, installation |
| 331314 | Aluminum extrusion ingot (i.e., billet), secondary |
| 331314 | Aluminum flakes made from purchased aluminum |
| 331315 | Aluminum foil made by flat rolling purchased aluminum |
| 331315 | Aluminum foil made in integrated secondary smelting and flat rolling mills |
| 423510 | Aluminum foil, plate, sheet, coil, and roll products merchant wholesalers |

| | |
|---|---|
| 332112 | Aluminum forgings made from purchased metals, unfinished |
| 331524 | Aluminum foundries (except die-casting) |
| 332999 | Aluminum freezer foil not made in rolling mills |
| 325180 | Aluminum hydroxide (i.e., alumina trihydrate) manufacturing |
| 331313 | Aluminum ingot and other primary aluminum production shapes made from bauxite or alumina |
| 331314 | Aluminum ingot made from purchased aluminum |
| 331314 | Aluminum ingot, secondary smelting of aluminum and manufacturing |
| 331314 | Aluminum ingot, secondary, manufacturing |
| 332999 | Aluminum ladders manufacturing |
| 327910 | Aluminum oxide (fused) abrasives manufacturing |
| 331313 | Aluminum oxide refining |
| 331318 | Aluminum pipe made by extruding purchased aluminum |
| 331318 | Aluminum pipe made in integrated secondary smelting and extruding mills |
| 236210 | Aluminum plant construction |
| 331315 | Aluminum plate made by continuous casting purchased aluminum |
| 331315 | Aluminum plate made by flat rolling purchased aluminum |
| 331315 | Aluminum plate made in integrated secondary smelting and continuous casting mills |
| 331315 | Aluminum plate made in integrated secondary smelting and flat rolling mills |
| 331313 | Aluminum producing from alumina |
| 331314 | Aluminum recovering from scrap and making ingot and billet (except by rolling) |
| 331318 | Aluminum rod made by extruding purchased aluminum |
| 331318 | Aluminum rod made in integrated secondary smelting and extruding mills |
| 331313 | Aluminum shapes (e.g., bar, ingot, rod, sheet) made by producing primary aluminum and manufacturing |
| 331315 | Aluminum sheet made by flat rolling purchased aluminum |
| 331315 | Aluminum sheet made in integrated secondary smelting and flat rolling mills |
| 238170 | Aluminum siding installation |
| 331314 | Aluminum smelting, secondary, and making ingot and billet (except by rolling) |

| | |
|---|---|
| 325180 | Aluminum sulfate manufacturing |
| 331318 | Aluminum tube blooms made by extruding purchased aluminum |
| 331318 | Aluminum tube blooms made in integrated secondary smelting and extruding mills |
| 331318 | Aluminum tube made by drawing or extruding purchased aluminum |
| 331318 | Aluminum tube made in integrated secondary smelting and drawing plants |
| 331318 | Aluminum tube made in integrated secondary smelting and extruding mills |
| 331315 | Aluminum welded tube made by flat rolling purchased aluminum |
| 331315 | Aluminum welded tube made in integrated secondary smelting and flat rolling mills |
| 813410 | Alumni associations |
| 813410 | Alumni clubs |
| 325180 | Alums (e.g., aluminum ammonium sulfate, aluminum potassium sulfate) manufacturing |
| 212390 | Alunite mining and/or beneficiating |
| 516110 | AM radio stations |
| 333131 | Amalgamators (i.e., metallurgical and mining machinery) manufacturing |
| 339114 | Amalgams, dental, manufacturing |
| 111998 | Amaranth farming |
| 713990 | Amateur sports teams, recreational |
| 325920 | Amatols manufacturing |
| 212390 | Amblygonite mining and/or beneficiating |
| 922160 | Ambulance and fire service combined |
| 336211 | Ambulance bodies manufacturing |
| 423110 | Ambulance merchant wholesalers |
| 621910 | Ambulance services, air or ground |
| 336211 | Ambulances assembling on purchased chassis |
| 621493 | Ambulatory surgical centers and clinics, freestanding |
| 921150 | American Indian or Alaska Native tribal councils |
| 921150 | American Indian or Alaska Native tribal courts |
| 921150 | American Indian or Alaska Native, tribal chief's or chairman's office |
| 212390 | Amethyst mining and/or beneficiating |
| 334516 | Amino acid analyzers, laboratory-type, manufacturing |
| 325211 | Amino resins manufacturing |
| 325211 | Amino-aldehyde resins manufacturing |

| | |
|---|---|
| 325194 | Aminoanthraquinone manufacturing |
| 325194 | Aminoazobenzene manufacturing |
| 325194 | Aminoazotoluene manufacturing |
| 325194 | Aminophenol manufacturing |
| 424690 | Ammonia (except fertilizer material) merchant wholesalers |
| 325311 | Ammonia, anhydrous and aqueous, manufacturing |
| 424910 | Ammonia, fertilizer material, merchant wholesalers |
| 325612 | Ammonia, household-type, manufacturing |
| 325180 | Ammonium chloride manufacturing |
| 325180 | Ammonium compounds, not specified elsewhere by process, manufacturing |
| 325180 | Ammonium hydroxide manufacturing |
| 325180 | Ammonium molybdate manufacturing |
| 325311 | Ammonium nitrate manufacturing |
| 325180 | Ammonium perchlorate manufacturing |
| 325312 | Ammonium phosphates manufacturing |
| 236210 | Ammonium plant construction |
| 325311 | Ammonium sulfate manufacturing |
| 325180 | Ammonium thiosulfate manufacturing |
| 423990 | Ammunition (except sporting) merchant wholesalers |
| 332993 | Ammunition (i.e., more than 30 mm., more than 1.18 inch) manufacturing |
| 332439 | Ammunition boxes, light gauge metal, manufacturing |
| 321920 | Ammunition boxes, wood, manufacturing |
| 332994 | Ammunition carts manufacturing |
| 332993 | Ammunition loading and assembling plants |
| 332992 | Ammunition, small arms (i.e., 30 mm. or less, 1.18 inch or less), manufacturing |
| 423910 | Ammunition, sporting, merchant wholesalers |
| 334515 | Ampere-hour meters manufacturing |
| 325411 | Amphetamines, uncompounded, manufacturing |
| 334310 | Amplifiers (e.g., auto, home, musical instrument, public address) manufacturing |
| 334220 | Amplifiers (e.g., RF power and IF), broadcast and studio equipment, manufacturing |
| 423690 | Amplifiers, audio (except household-type), merchant wholesalers |
| 335999 | Amplifiers, magnetic, pulse, and maser, manufacturing |

| | |
|---|---|
| 713120 | Amusement arcades |
| 713990 | Amusement device (except gambling) concession operators (i.e., supplying and servicing in others' facilities) |
| 713120 | Amusement device (except gambling) parlors, coin- or card-operated |
| 713120 | Amusement devices (except gambling) operated in own facilities |
| 236220 | Amusement facility construction |
| 531120 | Amusement facility rental or leasing |
| 339999 | Amusement machines, coin- or card-operated, manufacturing |
| 423850 | Amusement park equipment merchant wholesalers |
| 713110 | Amusement parks (e.g., theme, water) |
| 713990 | Amusement ride concession operators (i.e., supplying and servicing in others' facilities) |
| 325199 | Amyl acetate manufacturing |
| 325412 | Analgesic preparations manufacturing |
| 334111 | Analog computers manufacturing |
| 423490 | Analytical instruments (e.g., chromatographic, photometers, spectrographs) merchant wholesalers |
| 334515 | Analyzers for testing electrical characteristics manufacturing |
| 334513 | Analyzers, industrial process control type, manufacturing |
| 237990 | Anchored earth retention contractors |
| 114111 | Anchovy fishing |
| 212323 | Andalusite mining and/or beneficiating |
| 332999 | Andirons manufacturing |
| 339112 | Anesthesia apparatus manufacturing |
| 621111 | Anesthesiologists' offices (e.g., centers, clinics) |
| 325412 | Anesthetic preparations manufacturing |
| 325411 | Anesthetics, uncompounded, manufacturing |
| 325412 | Angiourographic diagnostic preparations manufacturing |
| 332999 | Angle irons, metal, manufacturing |
| 333515 | Angle rings (i.e., a machine tool accessory) manufacturing |
| 332911 | Angle valves, industrial-type, manufacturing |
| 334511 | Angle-of-attack instrumentation manufacturing |
| 334511 | Angle-of-yaw instrumentation manufacturing |
| 112420 | Angora goat farming |
| 325311 | Anhydrous ammonia manufacturing |

| | |
|---|---|
| 311512 | Anhydrous butterfat manufacturing |
| 325220 | Anidex fibers and filaments manufacturing |
| 325194 | Aniline manufacturing |
| 112519 | Animal aquaculture (except finfish, shellfish) |
| 325180 | Animal black manufacturing |
| 813910 | Animal breeders' associations |
| 812220 | Animal cemeteries |
| 712130 | Animal exhibits, live |
| 311611 | Animal fats (except poultry and small game) produced in slaughtering plants |
| 311613 | Animal fats rendering |
| 311119 | Animal feed mills (except dog and cat) manufacturing |
| 311111 | Animal feed mills, dog and cat, manufacturing |
| 424910 | Animal feeds (except pet food) merchant wholesalers |
| 311119 | Animal feeds, prepared (except dog and cat), manufacturing |
| 311111 | Animal feeds, prepared, dog and cat, manufacturing |
| 313110 | Animal fiber yarn twisting or winding of purchased yarn |
| 812910 | Animal grooming services |
| 424590 | Animal hair, wool, or mohair merchant wholesalers |
| 541940 | Animal hospitals |
| 311613 | Animal oil rendering |
| 926140 | Animal quarantine service, government |
| 813312 | Animal rights organizations |
| 712130 | Animal safari parks |
| 115210 | Animal semen banks |
| 236220 | Animal shelter and clinic construction |
| 812910 | Animal shelters |
| 114210 | Animal trapping, commercial |
| 332999 | Animal traps, metal (except wire), manufacturing |
| 813312 | Animal welfare associations or leagues |
| 336999 | Animal-drawn vehicles and parts manufacturing |
| 711510 | Animated cartoon artists, independent |
| 512120 | Animated cartoon distribution |
| 512110 | Animated cartoon production |
| 512110 | Animated cartoon production and distribution |
| 325998 | Anise oil manufacturing |

| | |
|---|---|
| 315120 | Anklets, sheer hosiery or socks, knitting or knitting and finishing |
| 325194 | Annatto extract manufacturing |
| 332811 | Annealing metals and metal products for the trade |
| 332420 | Annealing vats, heavy gauge metal, manufacturing |
| 711510 | Announcers, independent radio and television |
| 524113 | Annuities underwriting |
| 332991 | Annular ball bearings manufacturing |
| 334513 | Annunciators, relay and solid-state types, industrial display, manufacturing |
| 333248 | Anodizing equipment manufacturing |
| 332813 | Anodizing metals and metal products for the trade |
| 561421 | Answering services, telephone |
| 325320 | Ant poisons manufacturing |
| 325412 | Antacid preparations manufacturing |
| 238290 | Antenna, household-type, installation |
| 423690 | Antennas merchant wholesalers |
| 334220 | Antennas, satellite, manufacturing |
| 334220 | Antennas, transmitting and receiving, manufacturing |
| 325412 | Anthelmintic preparations manufacturing |
| 325194 | Anthracene manufacturing |
| 213113 | Anthracite mine tunneling on a contract basis |
| 213113 | Anthracite mining services on a contract basis (except geophysical surveying and mapping, site preparation, construction, and transportation activities) |
| 325130 | Anthraquinone dyes manufacturing |
| 332994 | Antiaircraft artillery manufacturing |
| 325412 | Antibacterial preparations manufacturing |
| 325412 | Antibiotic preparations manufacturing |
| 424210 | Antibiotics merchant wholesalers |
| 325411 | Antibiotics, uncompounded, manufacturing |
| 325411 | Anticholinergics, uncompounded, manufacturing |
| 325411 | Anticonvulsants, uncompounded, manufacturing |
| 325412 | Antidepressant preparations manufacturing |
| 325411 | Antidepressants, uncompounded, manufacturing |
| 424690 | Antifreeze merchant wholesalers |
| 325998 | Antifreeze preparations manufacturing |

| | |
|---|---|
| 325414 | Antigens manufacturing |
| 325412 | Antihistamine preparations manufacturing |
| 325130 | Antimony based pigments manufacturing |
| 212290 | Antimony concentrates beneficiating |
| 212290 | Antimony ores mining and/or beneficiating |
| 325180 | Antimony oxide (except pigments) manufacturing |
| 331410 | Antimony refining, primary |
| 325412 | Antineoplastic preparations manufacturing |
| 325620 | Antiperspirants, personal, manufacturing |
| 813319 | Antipoverty advocacy organizations |
| 325412 | Antipyretic preparations manufacturing |
| 811121 | Antique and classic automotive restoration |
| 441120 | Antique auto dealers |
| 424920 | Antique book merchant wholesalers |
| 459510 | Antique dealers (except motor vehicles) |
| 423210 | Antique furniture merchant wholesalers |
| 811420 | Antique furniture repair and restoration shops |
| 423220 | Antique home furnishings merchant wholesalers |
| 423220 | Antique houseware merchant wholesalers |
| 423940 | Antique jewelry merchant wholesalers |
| 459510 | Antique shops |
| 332913 | Antiscald bath and shower valves, plumbing, manufacturing |
| 325998 | Antiscaling compounds manufacturing |
| 325412 | Antiseptic preparations manufacturing |
| 424210 | Antiseptics merchant wholesalers |
| 325414 | Antiserums manufacturing |
| 325412 | Antispasmodic preparations manufacturing |
| 332994 | Antisubmarine projectors manufacturing |
| 332994 | Antitank rocket launchers manufacturing |
| 325414 | Antitoxins manufacturing |
| 325414 | Antivenoms manufacturing |
| 236116 | Apartment building construction general contractors |
| 236117 | Apartment building for-sale builders |
| 531110 | Apartment building rental or leasing |
| 531110 | Apartment hotel rental or leasing |
| 531311 | Apartment managers' offices |

| | |
|---|---|
| 531110 | Apartment rental or leasing |
| 212390 | Apatite mining and/or beneficiating |
| 212323 | Aplite mining and/or beneficiating |
| 456110 | Apothecaries |
| 331491 | Apparatus wire and cord (except aluminum, copper) made from purchased nonferrous metals (except aluminum, copper) in wire drawing plants |
| 331420 | Apparatus wire or cord made from purchased copper in wire drawing plants |
| 331318 | Apparatus wire or cord made in aluminum wire drawing plants |
| 458110 | Apparel accessory stores |
| 315210 | Apparel cut and sew contractors |
| 314999 | Apparel fillings (e.g., cotton mill waste, kapok) manufacturing |
| 315990 | Apparel findings and trimmings cut and sewn from purchased fabric (except apparel contractors) |
| 561910 | Apparel folding and packaging services |
| 812320 | Apparel pressing services |
| 458110 | Apparel stores, children's and infants' clothing |
| 458110 | Apparel stores, men's and boys' clothing |
| 459510 | Apparel stores, used clothing |
| 458110 | Apparel stores, women's and girls' clothing |
| 315210 | Apparel trimmings and findings cut and sew apparel contractors |
| 424310 | Apparel trimmings merchant wholesalers |
| 313220 | Apparel webbings manufacturing |
| 315250 | Apparel, fur (except apparel contractors), manufacturing |
| 315210 | Apparel, fur, cut and sew apparel contractors |
| 111331 | Apple orchards |
| 312130 | Applejack distilling |
| 334512 | Appliance controls manufacturing |
| 335999 | Appliance cords made from purchased insulated wire |
| 423710 | Appliance hardware merchant wholesalers |
| 332510 | Appliance hardware, metal, manufacturing |
| 334512 | Appliance regulators (except switches) manufacturing |
| 532210 | Appliance rental |
| 459510 | Appliance stores, household, used |
| 449210 | Appliance stores, household-type |

| | |
|---|---|
| 334519 | Appliance timers manufacturing |
| 811412 | Appliance, household-type, repair and maintenance services without retailing new appliances |
| 423620 | Appliances, household-type (except water heaters, heating stoves (i.e., noncooking)), gas and electric, merchant wholesalers |
| 423450 | Appliances, surgical, merchant wholesalers |
| 518210 | Application hosting (excluding software publishing) |
| 513210 | Applications development and publishing, except on a custom basis |
| 541511 | Applications software programming services, custom computer |
| 513210 | Applications software, computer, packaged |
| 321999 | Applicators, wood, manufacturing |
| 315210 | Appliqueing on apparel |
| 314999 | Appliqueing on textile products (except apparel) |
| 323111 | Appointment books and refills manufacturing |
| 541990 | Appraisal (except real estate) services |
| 531320 | Appraisal services, real estate |
| 531320 | Appraisers' offices, real estate |
| 611513 | Apprenticeship training programs |
| 111339 | Apricot farming |
| 812331 | Apron supply services |
| 316990 | Aprons for textile machinery, leather, manufacturing |
| 316990 | Aprons, leather (e.g., blacksmith's, welder's), manufacturing |
| 315990 | Aprons, waterproof (e.g., plastics, rubberized fabric), rubberizing fabric and manufacturing aprons |
| 315210 | Aprons, waterproof (including rubberized fabric, plastics), cut and sew apparel contractors |
| 315990 | Aprons, waterproof (including rubberized fabric, plastics), cut and sewn from purchased fabric (except apparel contractors) |
| 315210 | Aprons, work (except leather), cut and sew apparel contractors |
| 315250 | Aprons, work (except leather, waterproof), men's and boys', cut and sewn from purchased fabric (except apparel contractors) |
| 315250 | Aprons, work (except waterproof, leather), women's and girls', cut and |

| | |
|---|---|
| | sewn from purchased fabric (except apparel contractors) |
| 812199 | Aqua therapy services, non-medical |
| 332999 | Aquarium accessories, metal, manufacturing |
| 424990 | Aquarium fish and supplies merchant wholesalers |
| 712130 | Aquariums |
| 327215 | Aquariums made from purchased glass |
| 237110 | Aqueduct construction |
| 541990 | Arbitration and conciliation services (except by attorney, paralegal) |
| 333517 | Arbor presses, metalworking, manufacturing |
| 712130 | Arboreta |
| 712130 | Arboretums |
| 561730 | Arborist services |
| 333515 | Arbors (i.e., a machine tool accessory) manufacturing |
| 334510 | Arc lamp units, electrotherapeutic (except infrared, ultraviolet), manufacturing |
| 335139 | Arc lighting fixtures (except electrotherapeutic), electric, manufacturing |
| 713120 | Arcades, amusement |
| 339113 | Arch supports, orthopedic, manufacturing |
| 541720 | Archeological research and development services |
| 712120 | Archeological sites (i.e., public display) |
| 339920 | Archery equipment manufacturing |
| 423910 | Archery equipment merchant wholesalers |
| 713990 | Archery ranges |
| 321215 | Arches, glue laminated or pre-engineered wood, manufacturing |
| 541310 | Architects' (except landscape) offices |
| 541310 | Architects' (except landscape) private practices |
| 813920 | Architects' associations |
| 423490 | Architects' equipment and supplies merchant wholesalers |
| 541320 | Architects' offices, landscape |
| 541320 | Architects' private practices, landscape |
| 541310 | Architectural (except landscape) consultants' offices |
| 541310 | Architectural (except landscape) design services |
| 541310 | Architectural (except landscape) services |

| | |
|---|---|
| 327331 | Architectural block, concrete (e.g., fluted, ground face, screen, slump, split), manufacturing |
| 325510 | Architectural coatings (i.e., paint) manufacturing |
| 541310 | Architectural construction specifications consulting services |
| 332323 | Architectural metalwork manufacturing |
| 423390 | Architectural metalwork merchant wholesalers |
| 459510 | Architectural salvage dealers |
| 327110 | Architectural sculptures, clay, manufacturing |
| 327991 | Architectural sculptures, stone, manufacturing |
| 541320 | Architectural services, landscape |
| 459999 | Architectural supply stores |
| 327120 | Architectural terra cotta manufacturing |
| 327390 | Architectural wall panels, precast concrete, manufacturing |
| 337212 | Architectural woodwork and fixtures (i.e., custom designed interiors) manufacturing |
| 519210 | Archives |
| 316210 | Arctics, plastics or plastics soled fabric upper, manufacturing |
| 316210 | Arctics, rubber or rubber soled fabric, manufacturing |
| 333992 | Arc-welding equipment manufacturing |
| 335311 | Arc-welding transformers, separate solid-state, manufacturing |
| 335139 | Area and sports luminaries (e.g., stadium lighting fixtures), electric, manufacturing |
| 236220 | Arena construction |
| 711310 | Arena operators |
| 531120 | Arena, no promotion of events, rental or leasing |
| 212311 | Argillite mining or quarrying |
| 325120 | Argon manufacturing |
| 315210 | Arm bands cut and sew apparel contractors |
| 315990 | Arm bands, elastic, cut and sewn from purchased fabric (except apparel contractors) |
| 335314 | Armature relays manufacturing |
| 335312 | Armature rewinding on a factory basis |
| 811310 | Armature rewinding services (except on an assembly line or factory basis) |
| 335312 | Armatures, industrial, manufacturing |
| 928110 | Armed forces |
| 332993 | Arming and fusing devices, missile, manufacturing |
| 331110 | Armor plate made in iron and steel mills |
| 331420 | Armored cable made from purchased copper in wire drawing plants |
| 331420 | Armored cable, copper, made in integrated secondary smelting and drawing plants |
| 561613 | Armored car services |
| 336992 | Armored military vehicles (except tanks) and parts manufacturing |
| 236220 | Armory construction |
| 928110 | Army |
| 424690 | Aromatic chemicals merchant wholesalers |
| 325110 | Aromatic petrochemicals made from refined petroleum or liquid hydrocarbons |
| 113210 | Aromatic wood gathering |
| 488999 | Arrangement of car pools and vanpools (except ridesharing arrangement services) |
| 488999 | Arrangement of nonemergency medical transportation, without providing social assistance services |
| 335931 | Arrestors and coils, lighting, manufacturing |
| 325320 | Arsenate insecticides manufacturing |
| 325180 | Arsenates (except insecticides) manufacturing |
| 325130 | Arsenic based pigments manufacturing |
| 325180 | Arsenic compounds, not specified elsewhere by process, manufacturing |
| 212390 | Arsenic mineral mining and/or beneficiating |
| 325320 | Arsenite insecticides manufacturing |
| 325180 | Arsenites (except insecticides) manufacturing |
| 611610 | Art (except commercial or graphic) instruction |
| 459920 | Art auctions |
| 459920 | Art dealers |
| 712110 | Art galleries (except retail) |
| 459920 | Art galleries retailing art |
| 327420 | Art goods (e.g., gypsum, plaster of paris) manufacturing |
| 424990 | Art goods merchant wholesalers |
| 712110 | Art museums |
| 314999 | Art needlework contractors on apparel |
| 314999 | Art needlework on clothing for the trade |

| | |
|---|---|
| 513199 | Art print (except exclusive Internet publishing) publishers |
| 513199 | Art print publishers |
| 513199 | Art print publishers and printing combined |
| 323111 | Art prints commercial printing (except screen) without publishing |
| 323113 | Art prints screen printing without publishing |
| 513199 | Art publishers |
| 513199 | Art publishers (except exclusive Internet publishing) |
| 513199 | Art publishers, exclusively on Internet |
| 711510 | Art restorers, independent |
| 611610 | Art schools (except academic), fine |
| 611519 | Art schools, commercial or graphic |
| 541430 | Art services, commercial |
| 541430 | Art services, graphic |
| 541430 | Art studios, commercial |
| 459999 | Art supply stores |
| 621340 | Art therapists' offices (e.g., centers, clinics) |
| 237110 | Artesian well construction |
| 111219 | Artichoke farming, field, bedding plant and seed production |
| 311421 | Artichokes, canned, manufacturing |
| 424990 | Artificial Christmas trees merchant wholesalers |
| 339999 | Artificial flower arrangements assembled from purchased components |
| 424930 | Artificial flowers and plants merchant wholesalers |
| 334511 | Artificial horizon instrumentation manufacturing |
| 115210 | Artificial insemination services for livestock |
| 115210 | Artificial insemination services for pets |
| 541715 | Artificial intelligence research and development laboratories or services |
| 339113 | Artificial limbs manufacturing |
| 423450 | Artificial limbs merchant wholesalers |
| 238990 | Artificial turf installation |
| 312111 | Artificially carbonated waters manufacturing |
| 332993 | Artillery ammunition (i.e., more than 30 mm., more than 1.18 inch) manufacturing |
| 711510 | Artists (except musical, commercial, medical), independent |
| 711510 | Artists (i.e., painters), independent |

| | |
|---|---|
| 711410 | Artists' agents or managers |
| 339940 | Artist's paint manufacturing |
| 339940 | Artist's supplies (except paper) manufacturing |
| 424990 | Artists' supplies merchant wholesalers |
| 541430 | Artists, independent commercial |
| 541430 | Artists, independent graphic |
| 541430 | Artists, independent medical |
| 926110 | Arts and cultural program administration, government |
| 711310 | Arts event managers with facilities |
| 711320 | Arts event managers without facilities |
| 711310 | Arts event organizers with facilities |
| 711320 | Arts event organizers without facilities |
| 711310 | Arts event promoters with facilities |
| 711320 | Arts event promoters without facilities |
| 711310 | Arts festival managers with facilities |
| 711320 | Arts festival managers without facilities |
| 711310 | Arts festival organizers with facilities |
| 711320 | Arts festival organizers without facilities |
| 711310 | Arts festival promoters with facilities |
| 711320 | Arts festival promoters without facilities |
| 562910 | Asbestos abatement services |
| 212390 | Asbestos mining and/or beneficiating |
| 327999 | Asbestos products (except brake shoes and clutches) manufacturing |
| 562910 | Asbestos removal contractors |
| 325411 | Ascorbic acid (i.e., vitamin C), uncompounded, manufacturing |
| 315210 | Ascots cut and sew apparel contractors |
| 315990 | Ascots, men's and boys', cut and sewn from purchased fabric (except apparel contractors) |
| 562111 | Ash collection services |
| 562111 | Ash hauling, local |
| 484220 | Ash, garbage, recyclable material, refuse, rubbish, trash, or waste hauling (except collection or disposal) |
| 212390 | Ash, volcanic, mining and/or beneficiating |
| 327215 | Ashtrays made from purchased glass |
| 327212 | Ashtrays, glass, made in glass making plants |
| 327110 | Ashtrays, pottery, manufacturing |
| 111219 | Asparagus farming, field, bedding plant and seed production |
| 324110 | Asphalt and asphaltic materials made in petroleum refineries |

| | |
|---|---|
| 423320 | Asphalt and concrete mixtures merchant wholesalers |
| 424710 | Asphalt binder bulk stations and terminals, merchant wholesalers |
| 424720 | Asphalt binder merchant wholesalers (except bulk stations, terminals) |
| 238990 | Asphalt coating and sealing, residential and commercial parking lot and driveway |
| 327999 | Asphalt concrete crushing and grinding (except at construction site) |
| 423330 | Asphalt felts and coatings merchant wholesalers |
| 238330 | Asphalt flooring, installation only |
| 322120 | Asphalt paper made in paper mills |
| 237310 | Asphalt paving (i.e., highway, road, street, public sidewalk) |
| 324121 | Asphalt paving blocks made from purchased asphaltic materials |
| 324121 | Asphalt paving mixtures made from purchased asphaltic materials |
| 324110 | Asphalt paving mixtures made in petroleum refineries |
| 324121 | Asphalt road compounds made from purchased asphaltic materials |
| 212390 | Asphalt rock mining and/or beneficiating |
| 238160 | Asphalt roof shingle installation |
| 324122 | Asphalt roofing cements made from purchased asphaltic materials |
| 324122 | Asphalt roofing coatings made from purchased asphaltic materials |
| 333120 | Asphalt roofing construction machinery manufacturing |
| 423330 | Asphalt roofing shingles merchant wholesalers |
| 324122 | Asphalt saturated boards made from purchased asphaltic materials |
| 324122 | Asphalt saturated mats and felts made from purchased asphaltic materials and paper |
| 324122 | Asphalt shingles made from purchased asphaltic materials |
| 424710 | Asphalt, liquid, bulk stations and terminals, merchant wholesalers |
| 424720 | Asphalt, liquid, merchant wholesalers (except bulk stations, terminals) |
| 212390 | Asphalt, native, mining and/or beneficiating |
| 238990 | Asphalting, residential and commercial driveway and parking area |
| 541380 | Assaying services |
| 336213 | Assembly line conversions of purchased vans and minivans |
| 336310 | Assembly line rebuilding of automotive and truck gasoline engines |
| 336350 | Assembly line rebuilding of automotive, truck, and bus transmissions |
| 333519 | Assembly machines (i.e., wire making equipment) manufacturing |
| 236210 | Assembly plant construction |
| 336120 | Assembly plants, heavy trucks, and buses on chassis of own manufacture |
| 336110 | Assembly plants, light trucks on chassis of own manufacture |
| 336110 | Assembly plants, minivans on chassis of own manufacture |
| 336110 | Assembly plants, passenger car on chassis of own manufacture |
| 336110 | Assembly plants, sport utility vehicles on chassis of own manufacture |
| 921130 | Assessor's offices, tax |
| 325613 | Assistants, textile and leather finishing, manufacturing |
| 623110 | Assisted living facilities (without nursing facilities) for the elderly with nursing care |
| 623312 | Assisted living facilities for the elderly without nursing care |
| 623311 | Assisted living facilities with on-site nursing facilities |
| 813311 | Associations for retired persons, advocacy |
| 522180 | Associations, savings and loan |
| 325412 | Astringent preparations manufacturing |
| 812990 | Astrology services |
| 711219 | Athletes, amateur, independent |
| 711219 | Athletes, independent (i.e., participating in live sports events) |
| 813990 | Athletic associations, regulatory |
| 315210 | Athletic clothing cut and sew apparel contractors |
| 315120 | Athletic clothing made in apparel knitting mills |
| 315250 | Athletic clothing, men's, boys' and unisex (i.e., sized without regard to gender), cut and sewn from purchased fabric (except apparel contractors) |
| 315250 | Athletic clothing, women's and girls', cut and sewn from purchased fabric (except apparel contractors) |
| 713940 | Athletic club facilities, physical fitness |
| 713990 | Athletic clubs (i.e., sports teams) not operating sports facilities, recreational |
| 236220 | Athletic court, indoor, construction |
| 459110 | Athletic equipment and supply stores (including uniforms) |

| | |
|---|---|
| 237990 | Athletic field (except stadium) construction |
| 424340 | Athletic footwear (except specialty athletic footwear) merchant wholesalers |
| 339920 | Athletic goods (except ammunition, clothing, footwear, small arms) manufacturing |
| 423910 | Athletic goods (except apparel, footwear, nonspecialty) merchant wholesalers |
| 813990 | Athletic leagues (i.e., regulating bodies) |
| 458210 | Athletic shoe (except bowling, golf, cleated) stores |
| 316210 | Athletic shoes manufacturing |
| 316210 | Athletic shoes, plastics or plastics soled fabric upper, manufacturing |
| 316210 | Athletic shoes, rubber or rubber soled fabric upper, manufacturing |
| 315120 | Athletic socks knitting or knitting and finishing |
| 423910 | Athletic uniforms merchant wholesalers |
| 315210 | Athletic uniforms, team, cut and sew apparel contractors |
| 315250 | Athletic uniforms, team, cut and sewn from purchased fabric (except apparel contractors) |
| 513130 | Atlas publishers |
| 513130 | Atlas publishers (except exclusive Internet publishing) |
| 513130 | Atlas publishers and printing combined |
| 513130 | Atlas publishers, exclusively on Internet |
| 323111 | Atlases commercial printing (except screen) without publishing |
| 424920 | Atlases merchant wholesalers |
| 323113 | Atlases screen printing without publishing |
| 238290 | ATMs (automated teller machines) installation |
| 334118 | ATMs (automated teller machines) manufacturing |
| 335999 | Atom smashers (i.e., particle accelerators) manufacturing |
| 334516 | Atomic force microscopes manufacturing |
| 339999 | Atomizers (e.g., perfumes) manufacturing |
| 325411 | Atropine and derivatives manufacturing |
| 316990 | Attache cases, all materials, manufacturing |
| 333112 | Attachments, powered lawn and garden equipment, manufacturing |
| 333413 | Attic fans manufacturing |
| 238310 | Attic space insulating |

| | |
|---|---|
| 922130 | Attorney generals' offices |
| 541110 | Attorneys' offices |
| 541110 | Attorneys' private practices |
| 424520 | Auction markets, livestock (except horses, mules), merchant wholesalers |
| 424590 | Auction markets, tobacco, horses, mules, merchant wholesalers |
| 561990 | Auctioneers, independent |
| 531210 | Auctioning real estate for others (i.e., agents, brokers) |
| 455219 | Auctions, general merchandise (new and used), Internet retail |
| 459510 | Auctions, general merchandise (used), Internet retail |
| 423990 | Audio and video tapes and disks, prerecorded, merchant wholesalers |
| 321999 | Audio cabinets (i.e., housings), wood, manufacturing |
| 238210 | Audio equipment installation (except automotive) contractors |
| 449210 | Audio equipment stores (except automotive) |
| 423620 | Audio equipment, household-type, merchant wholesalers |
| 512290 | Audio recording of meetings or conferences |
| 512240 | Audio recording postproduction services |
| 512240 | Audio recording restoration services |
| 541512 | Audio visual and IT (information technology) systems integration design services |
| 238210 | Audio visual equipment installation |
| 532490 | Audio visual equipment rental or leasing |
| 541330 | Audio visual system engineering design services |
| 334515 | Audiofrequency oscillators manufacturing |
| 334510 | Audiological equipment, electromedical, manufacturing |
| 621340 | Audiologists' offices (e.g., centers, clinics) |
| 334515 | Audiometers (except medical) manufacturing |
| 334610 | Audiotape, blank, manufacturing |
| 423690 | Audiotapes, blank, merchant wholesalers |
| 541211 | Auditing accountants' (i.e., CPAs) offices |
| 541211 | Auditing accountants' (i.e., CPAs) private practices |
| 541211 | Auditing services (i.e., CPA services), accounts |
| 236220 | Auditorium construction |

| | |
|---|---|
| 531120 | Auditorium rental or leasing |
| 541211 | Auditors' (i.e., CPAs) offices, accounts |
| 541211 | Auditors' (i.e., CPAs) private practices, accounts |
| 921190 | Auditor's offices, government |
| 213113 | Auger coal mining services on a contract basis (except geophysical surveying and mapping, site preparation, construction, and transportation activities) |
| 333120 | Augers (except mining-type) manufacturing |
| 333131 | Augers, mining-type, manufacturing |
| 332216 | Augers, nonpowered, manufacturing |
| 711410 | Authors' agents or managers |
| 711510 | Authors, independent |
| 423120 | Auto body shop supplies merchant wholesalers |
| 721110 | Auto courts, lodging |
| 441330 | Auto supply stores |
| 339114 | Autoclaves, dental, manufacturing |
| 332420 | Autoclaves, industrial-type, heavy gauge metal, manufacturing |
| 339113 | Autoclaves, laboratory-type (except dental), manufacturing |
| 336411 | Autogiros manufacturing |
| 238290 | Automated and revolving door installation |
| 334510 | Automated blood and body fluid analyzers (except laboratory) manufacturing |
| 522320 | Automated clearinghouses, bank or check (except central bank) |
| 518210 | Automated data processing services |
| 522320 | Automated Teller Machine (ATM) or Automated Loan Machine (ALM) network operation |
| 334118 | Automated teller machines (ATM) manufacturing |
| 423420 | Automated teller machines (ATM) merchant wholesalers |
| 332911 | Automatic (i.e., controlling-type, regulating) valves, industrial-type, manufacturing |
| 423690 | Automatic call distributors merchant wholesalers |
| 334516 | Automatic chemical analyzers, laboratory-type, manufacturing |
| 238290 | Automatic gate (e.g., garage, parking lot) installation |
| 812310 | Automatic laundries, coin-operated |
| 445132 | Automatic merchandising machine operators |

| | |
|---|---|
| 333517 | Automatic screw machines, metal cutting type, manufacturing |
| 336350 | Automatic transmissions, automotive, truck, and bus, manufacturing |
| 423120 | Automobile accessories (except tires, tubes) merchant wholesalers |
| 314110 | Automobile and aircraft carpet and rug manufacturing |
| 334220 | Automobile antennas manufacturing |
| 425120 | Automobile auction agents and brokers, wholesale trade |
| 423110 | Automobile auction merchant wholesalers |
| 336211 | Automobile bodies, passenger car, manufacturing |
| 484220 | Automobile carrier trucking, local |
| 484230 | Automobile carrier trucking, long-distance |
| 813410 | Automobile clubs (except road and travel services) |
| 561599 | Automobile clubs, road and travel services |
| 721110 | Automobile courts, lodging |
| 493190 | Automobile dead storage |
| 441110 | Automobile dealers, new only or new and used |
| 441120 | Automobile dealers, used only |
| 611692 | Automobile driving schools |
| 522220 | Automobile finance leasing companies |
| 522220 | Automobile financing |
| 423120 | Automobile glass merchant wholesalers |
| 332510 | Automobile hardware, metal, manufacturing |
| 541420 | Automobile industrial design services |
| 524126 | Automobile insurance carriers, direct |
| 532112 | Automobile leasing |
| 333921 | Automobile lifts (i.e., garage-type, service station) manufacturing |
| 423110 | Automobile merchant wholesalers |
| 812930 | Automobile parking garages or lots |
| 441330 | Automobile parts dealers |
| 325612 | Automobile polishes and cleaners manufacturing |
| 541380 | Automobile proving and testing grounds |
| 711212 | Automobile racetracks |
| 611620 | Automobile racing schools |
| 711219 | Automobile racing teams |
| 334310 | Automobile radio receivers manufacturing |
| 532111 | Automobile rental |

485320 Automobile rental with driver (except shuttle service, taxis)

561491 Automobile repossession services

336360 Automobile seat covers manufacturing

336360 Automobile seat frames, metal, manufacturing

423120 Automobile service station equipment merchant wholesalers

561920 Automobile show managers

561920 Automobile show organizers

561920 Automobile show promoters

332618 Automobile skid chains made from purchased wire

335910 Automobile storage batteries manufacturing

332613 Automobile suspension springs, heavy gauge metal, manufacturing

336212 Automobile transporter trailers, multi-car, manufacturing

336214 Automobile transporter trailers, single car, manufacturing

336360 Automobile trimmings, textile, manufacturing

333923 Automobile wrecker (i.e., tow truck) hoists manufacturing

336211 Automobile wrecker truck bodies manufacturing

336211 Automobile wreckers assembling on purchased chassis

336110 Automobiles assembling on chassis of own manufacture

339930 Automobiles, children's, manufacturing

423730 Automotive air-conditioners merchant wholesalers

811198 Automotive air-conditioning repair shops

334515 Automotive ammeters and voltmeters manufacturing

441330 Automotive audio equipment stores

811121 Automotive body shops

811114 Automotive brake repair shops

423120 Automotive brakes merchant wholesalers

424690 Automotive chemicals (except lubricating greases, lubrication oils) merchant wholesalers

811192 Automotive detail shops

811192 Automotive detailing services (i.e., cleaning, polishing)

334515 Automotive electrical engine diagnostic equipment manufacturing

811114 Automotive electrical repair shops

335931 Automotive electrical switches manufacturing

334519 Automotive emissions testing equipment manufacturing

811198 Automotive emissions testing services

811111 Automotive engine repair and replacement shops

811114 Automotive exhaust system repair and replacement shops

424310 Automotive fabrics merchant wholesalers

811111 Automotive fleet repair and maintenance services

811114 Automotive front end alignment shops

811122 Automotive glass shops

336320 Automotive harness and ignition sets manufacturing

335139 Automotive light bulbs manufacturing

336320 Automotive lighting fixtures manufacturing

332710 Automotive machine shops

336390 Automotive mirrors, framed, manufacturing

811191 Automotive oil change and lubrication shops

331318 Automotive or aircraft wire and cable made in aluminum wire drawing plants

314999 Automotive pad and upholstery filling (except foam rubber and plastics) manufacturing

811121 Automotive paint shops

424950 Automotive paints merchant wholesalers

441330 Automotive parts and supply stores

441330 Automotive parts dealers, used

423120 Automotive parts, new, merchant wholesalers

423140 Automotive parts, used, merchant wholesalers

811114 Automotive radiator repair shops

423620 Automotive radios merchant wholesalers

811111 Automotive repair and replacement shops, general

811198 Automotive rustproofing and undercoating shops

811198 Automotive safety inspection services

423120 Automotive stampings merchant wholesalers

811114 Automotive suspension repair shops

334290 Automotive theft alarm systems manufacturing

441340 Automotive tire dealers

| | |
|---|---|
| 811198 | Automotive tire repair (except retreading) shops |
| 811114 | Automotive transmission repair shops |
| 811114 | Automotive tune-up shops |
| 811121 | Automotive upholstery shops |
| 811192 | Automotive washing and polishing |
| 336330 | Automotive, truck and bus steering assemblies and parts manufacturing |
| 336330 | Automotive, truck and bus suspension assemblies and parts (except springs) manufacturing |
| 339992 | Autophones (organs with perforated music rolls) manufacturing |
| 335311 | Autotransformers for switchboards (except telephone switchboards) manufacturing |
| 335311 | Autotransformers manufacturing |
| 237990 | Avalanche, rockslide, mudslide, or roadside protection construction |
| 712130 | Aviaries |
| 112990 | Aviaries (i.e., raising birds for sale) |
| 813319 | Aviation advocacy organizations |
| 481219 | Aviation clubs providing a variety of air transportation activities to the general public |
| 488119 | Aviation clubs, primarily providing flying field services to the general public |
| 713990 | Aviation clubs, recreational |
| 324110 | Aviation fuels manufacturing |
| 611512 | Aviation schools |
| 111339 | Avocado farming |
| 332216 | Awls manufacturing |
| 238190 | Awning installation |
| 423390 | Awnings (except canvas) merchant wholesalers |
| 314910 | Awnings and canopies, outdoor, made from purchased fabrics |
| 424990 | Awnings, canvas, merchant wholesalers |
| 326199 | Awnings, rigid plastics or fiberglass, manufacturing |
| 332322 | Awnings, sheet metal (except stampings), manufacturing |
| 713990 | Axe throwing clubs |
| 332216 | Axes manufacturing |
| 336350 | Axle bearings, automotive, truck, and bus, manufacturing |
| 331110 | Axles, rolled or forged, made in iron and steel mills |
| 111421 | Azalea farming |
| 325920 | Azides explosive materials manufacturing |
| 325130 | Azine dyes manufacturing |
| 325130 | Azo dyes manufacturing |
| 325194 | Azobenzene manufacturing |
| 424350 | Baby and infant car seats merchant wholesalers |
| 424350 | Baby and infant high chairs merchant wholesalers |
| 424350 | Baby bottles merchant wholesalers |
| 424350 | Baby clothing merchant wholesalers |
| 458110 | Baby clothing shops |
| 311422 | Baby foods (including meats) canning |
| 424490 | Baby foods, canned, merchant wholesalers |
| 311514 | Baby formula, fresh, processed, and bottled, manufacturing |
| 423210 | Baby furniture merchant wholesalers |
| 325620 | Baby powder and baby oil manufacturing |
| 333998 | Baby scales manufacturing |
| 812990 | Baby shoe bronzing services |
| 561311 | Babysitting bureaus (i.e., registries) |
| 624410 | Babysitting services in provider's own home, child care |
| 624410 | Babysitting services, child care |
| 238910 | Backfilling, construction |
| 332913 | Backflow preventers, plumbing, manufacturing |
| 561611 | Background check services |
| 112111 | Backgrounding, cattle |
| 238910 | Backhoe rental with operator |
| 333120 | Backhoes manufacturing |
| 424990 | Backpacks, textile, merchant wholesalers |
| 311612 | Bacon, slab and sliced, made from purchased carcasses |
| 311611 | Bacon, slab and sliced, produced in slaughtering plants |
| 325414 | Bacterial vaccines manufacturing |
| 325414 | Bacterins (i.e., bacterial vaccines) manufacturing |
| 621511 | Bacteriological laboratories, diagnostic |
| 621511 | Bacteriological laboratories, medical |
| 424210 | Bacteriological medicines merchant wholesalers |

541715 Bacteriological research and development laboratories or services (except biotechnology and nanotechnology research and development)

314999 Badges, fabric, manufacturing

332999 Badges, metal, manufacturing

326199 Badges, plastics, manufacturing

339920 Badminton equipment manufacturing

332313 Baffles, fabricated metal plate work, manufacturing

316110 Bag leather manufacturing

332993 Bag loading plants, ammunition, manufacturing

333993 Bag opening, filling, and closing machines manufacturing

722511 Bagel shops, full service

722515 Bagel shops, on premise baking and carryout service

311812 Bagels made in commercial bakeries

322220 Bags (except plastics only) made by laminating or coating combinations of purchased plastics, foil and paper

316990 Bags (i.e., luggage), all materials, manufacturing

313240 Bags and bagging fabrics made in warp or weft knitting mills

316990 Bags, athletic, manufacturing

322220 Bags, coated paper, made from purchased paper

322220 Bags, foil, made from purchased foil

339920 Bags, golf, manufacturing

313110 Bags, hemp, made from purchased fiber

322220 Bags, multiwall, made from purchased uncoated paper

424130 Bags, paper and disposable plastics, merchant wholesalers

322220 Bags, paper, uncoated, made from purchased paper

326111 Bags, plastics film, single wall or multiwall, manufacturing

314910 Bags, plastics, made from purchased woven plastics

339920 Bags, punching, manufacturing

423930 Bags, reclaimed, merchant wholesalers

314910 Bags, rubberized fabric, manufacturing

314999 Bags, sleeping, manufacturing

314910 Bags, textile, made from purchased woven or knitted materials

424990 Bags, textile, merchant wholesalers

322220 Bags, uncoated paper, made from purchased paper

812990 Bail bonding services

423390 Bailey bridges merchant wholesalers

339920 Bait, artificial, fishing, manufacturing

423910 Bait, artificial, merchant wholesalers

424990 Bait, live, merchant wholesalers

112511 Baitfish production, farm raising

311422 Baked beans canning

311813 Baked goods (except bread, bread-type rolls), frozen, manufacturing

445291 Baked goods (not made on premises) stores

445240 Baked ham stores

311811 Bakeries with baking from flour on the premises, retailing not for immediate consumption

315210 Bakers' service apparel, washable, cut and sew apparel contractors

315250 Bakers' service apparel, washable, men's and boys', cut and sewn from purchased fabric (except apparel contractors)

315250 Bakers' service apparel, washable, women's and girls', cut and sewn from purchased fabric (except apparel contractors)

722515 Bakery cafes, on premise baking and selling for immediate consumption

333241 Bakery machinery and equipment manufacturing

423830 Bakery machinery and equipment merchant wholesalers

333241 Bakery ovens manufacturing

424490 Bakery products (except frozen) merchant wholesalers

311821 Bakery products, dry (e.g., biscuits, cookies, crackers), manufacturing

311812 Bakery products, fresh (i.e., bread, cakes, doughnuts, pastries), made in commercial bakeries

424420 Bakery products, frozen, merchant wholesalers

311351 Baking chocolate made from cacao beans

311352 Baking chocolate made from purchased chocolate

311999 Baking powder manufacturing

423440 Balances and scales (except laboratory) merchant wholesalers

423490 Balances and scales, laboratory (except dental, medical), merchant wholesalers

333998 Balances, including laboratory-type, manufacturing

| | |
|---|---|
| 333310 | Balancing equipment, motor vehicle, manufacturing |
| 423120 | Balancing equipment, motor vehicle, merchant wholesalers |
| 423830 | Balancing machines (except automotive) merchant wholesalers |
| 332323 | Balcony railings, metal, manufacturing |
| 238190 | Balcony, metal, installation |
| 238120 | Balcony, precast concrete, installation |
| 333111 | Bale throwers manufacturing |
| 332618 | Bale ties made from purchased wire |
| 333111 | Balers, farm-type (e.g., cotton, hay, straw), manufacturing |
| 333998 | Baling machinery (e.g., paper, scrap metal) manufacturing |
| 332991 | Ball bearings manufacturing |
| 212323 | Ball clay mining and/or beneficiating |
| 333613 | Ball joints (except aircraft, motor vehicle) manufacturing |
| 339940 | Ball point pens manufacturing |
| 332911 | Ball valves, industrial-type, manufacturing |
| 335311 | Ballasts (i.e., transformers) manufacturing |
| 711120 | Ballet companies |
| 711510 | Ballet dancers, independent |
| 711120 | Ballet productions, live theatrical |
| 611610 | Ballet schools (except academic) |
| 316210 | Ballet slippers manufacturing |
| 459420 | Balloon shops |
| 812990 | Balloon-o-gram services |
| 326199 | Balloons, plastics, manufacturing |
| 326299 | Balloons, rubber, manufacturing |
| 713990 | Ballrooms |
| 339920 | Balls, baseball, basketball, football, golf, tennis, pool, and bowling, manufacturing |
| 339930 | Balls, rubber (except athletic equipment), manufacturing |
| 331110 | Balls, steel, made in iron and steel mills |
| 113210 | Balsam needles gathering |
| 321918 | Bamboo flooring manufacturing |
| 337126 | Bamboo furniture (except upholstered), household-type, manufacturing |
| 337920 | Bamboo window blinds and shades manufacturing |
| 111339 | Banana farming |
| 115114 | Banana ripening |
| 315210 | Band uniforms cut and sew apparel contractors |
| 315250 | Band uniforms cut and sewn from purchased fabric (except apparel contractors) |
| 424210 | Bandages (except surgical) merchant wholesalers |
| 339113 | Bandages and dressings, surgical and orthopedic, manufacturing |
| 315210 | Bandeaux cut and sew apparel contractors |
| 315250 | Bandeaux, women's and girls', cut and sewn from purchased fabric (except apparel contractors) |
| 711130 | Bands |
| 711130 | Bands, dance |
| 711130 | Bands, musical |
| 333243 | Bandsaws, woodworking-type, manufacturing |
| 339992 | Banjos and parts manufacturing |
| 334511 | Bank and turn indicators and components (aeronautical instruments) manufacturing |
| 236220 | Bank building construction |
| 531120 | Bank building rental or leasing |
| 332999 | Bank chests, metal, manufacturing |
| 522320 | Bank clearinghouse associations |
| 524128 | Bank deposit insurance carriers, direct |
| 423420 | Bank equipment merchant wholesalers |
| 332323 | Bank fixtures, ornamental metal, manufacturing |
| 551111 | Bank holding companies (except managing) |
| 523991 | Bank trust offices |
| 813910 | Bankers' associations |
| 926150 | Banking regulatory agencies |
| 611519 | Banking schools (training in banking) |
| 521110 | Banking, central |
| 523150 | Banking, investment |
| 525920 | Bankruptcy estates |
| 522110 | Banks, commercial |
| 522210 | Banks, credit card |
| 521110 | Banks, Federal Reserve |
| 522180 | Banks, industrial (i.e., known as), depository |
| 522299 | Banks, industrial (i.e., known as), nondepository |
| 522180 | Banks, private (i.e., unincorporated) |
| 522180 | Banks, savings |

| | |
|---|---|
| 522299 | Banks, trade (i.e., international trade financing) |
| 314999 | Banners made from purchased fabrics (except banner printing) |
| 332323 | Bannisters, metal, manufacturing |
| 531120 | Banquet hall rental or leasing |
| 722320 | Banquet halls with catering staff |
| 327991 | Baptismal fonts, cut stone, manufacturing |
| 813920 | Bar associations |
| 561499 | Bar code imprinting services |
| 334118 | Bar code scanners manufacturing |
| 423440 | Bar equipment merchant wholesalers |
| 331318 | Bar made by extruding purchased aluminum |
| 331318 | Bar made by rolling purchased aluminum |
| 333519 | Bar mill machinery, metalworking, manufacturing |
| 325611 | Bar soaps manufacturing |
| 331318 | Bar, aluminum, made in integrated secondary smelting and extruding mills |
| 331318 | Bar, aluminum, made in integrated secondary smelting and rolling mills |
| 331420 | Bar, copper and copper alloy, made from purchased copper or in integrated secondary smelting and rolling, drawing or extruding plants |
| 331491 | Bar, nonferrous metals (except aluminum, copper), made from purchased metals in wire drawing plants or in integrated secondary smelting and rolling, drawing, or extruding plants |
| 311421 | Barbecue sauce manufacturing |
| 335220 | Barbecues, grills, and braziers manufacturing |
| 331222 | Barbed and twisted wire made in wire drawing plants |
| 332618 | Barbed wire made from purchased wire |
| 611511 | Barber colleges |
| 236220 | Barber shop construction |
| 423850 | Barber shop equipment and supplies merchant wholesalers |
| 812111 | Barber shops |
| 332215 | Barber's scissors, manufacturing |
| 315210 | Barbers' service apparel, washable, cut and sew apparel contractors |
| 315250 | Barbers' service apparel, washable, men's and boys', cut and sewn from purchased fabric (except apparel contractors) |

| | |
|---|---|
| 325412 | Barbiturate preparations manufacturing |
| 325411 | Barbiturates, uncompounded, manufacturing |
| 325411 | Barbituric acid manufacturing |
| 336611 | Barge building |
| 532411 | Barge rental or leasing without crew |
| 332312 | Barge sections, prefabricated metal, manufacturing |
| 483211 | Barge transportation, canal (freight) |
| 483113 | Barge transportation, coastal or Great Lakes (including St. Lawrence Seaway) |
| 212390 | Barite mining and/or beneficiating |
| 327992 | Barite processing beyond beneficiation |
| 325180 | Barium compounds, not specified elsewhere by process, manufacturing |
| 325180 | Barium hydroxide manufacturing |
| 325412 | Barium in-vivo diagnostic substances manufacturing |
| 212390 | Barium ores mining and/or beneficiating |
| 327992 | Barium processing beyond beneficiation |
| 113210 | Bark gathering |
| 111199 | Barley farming, field and seed production |
| 311119 | Barley feed, chopped, crushed or ground, manufacturing |
| 311211 | Barley flour manufacturing |
| 311213 | Barley, malt, manufacturing |
| 332323 | Barn stanchions and standards manufacturing |
| 334519 | Barographs manufacturing |
| 334519 | Barometers manufacturing |
| 423490 | Barometers merchant wholesalers |
| 332410 | Barometric condensers manufacturing |
| 236220 | Barrack construction |
| 321920 | Barrel heading and staves manufacturing |
| 332994 | Barrels, gun, manufacturing |
| 332439 | Barrels, light gauge metal, manufacturing |
| 423840 | Barrels, new and reconditioned, merchant wholesalers |
| 321920 | Barrels, wood, coopered, manufacturing |
| 332999 | Barricades, metal, manufacturing |
| 541110 | Barristers' offices |
| 541110 | Barristers' private practices |
| 722410 | Bars (i.e., drinking places), alcoholic beverage |
| 331410 | Bars made in primary copper smelting and refining mills |

| | |
|---|---|
| 331110 | Bars, concrete reinforcing (rebar) made in steel mills |
| 331221 | Bars, concrete reinforcing (rebar), made from purchased steel in steel rolling mills |
| 332312 | Bars, concrete reinforcing, manufacturing |
| 331110 | Bars, iron, made in iron and steel mills |
| 423510 | Bars, metal (except precious), merchant wholesalers |
| 331221 | Bars, steel, made from purchased steel in cold rolling mills |
| 331110 | Bars, steel, made in iron and steel mills |
| 722320 | Bartender services including supply of equipment and alcohol |
| 722320 | Bartender services on own account (serving only) |
| 611519 | Bartending schools |
| 561990 | Bartering services |
| 325130 | Barytes based pigments manufacturing |
| 212390 | Barytes mining and/or beneficiating |
| 212319 | Basalt crushed and broken stone mining and/or beneficiating |
| 212311 | Basalt mining or quarrying |
| 561210 | Base facilities operation support services |
| 315210 | Baseball caps (except plastics) cut and sew apparel contractors |
| 315990 | Baseball caps cut and sewn from purchased fabric (except apparel contractors) |
| 711211 | Baseball clubs, professional or semiprofessional |
| 713990 | Baseball clubs, recreational |
| 339920 | Baseball equipment and supplies (except footwear, uniforms) manufacturing |
| 423910 | Baseball equipment and supplies merchant wholesalers |
| 611620 | Baseball instruction, camps or schools |
| 711211 | Baseball teams, professional or semiprofessional |
| 315210 | Baseball uniforms cut and sew apparel contractors |
| 315250 | Baseball uniforms cut and sewn from purchased fabric (except apparel contractors) |
| 423730 | Baseboard heaters, electric, nonportable, merchant wholesalers |
| 333414 | Baseboard heating equipment manufacturing |
| 321918 | Baseboards, floor, wood, manufacturing |
| 332321 | Baseboards, metal, manufacturing |
| 711211 | Basketball clubs, professional or semiprofessional |
| 713990 | Basketball clubs, recreational |
| 339920 | Basketball equipment and supplies (except footwear, uniforms) manufacturing |
| 611620 | Basketball instruction, camps or schools |
| 711211 | Basketball teams, professional or semiprofessional |
| 315210 | Basketball uniforms cut and sew apparel contractors |
| 315250 | Basketball uniforms cut and sewn from purchased fabric (except apparel contractors) |
| 424990 | Baskets merchant wholesalers |
| 331222 | Baskets, iron or steel, made in wire drawing plants |
| 332618 | Baskets, metal, made from purchased wire |
| 321920 | Baskets, wood (e.g., round stave, veneer), manufacturing |
| 337126 | Bassinets, reed and rattan, manufacturing |
| 339992 | Bassoons manufacturing |
| 212290 | Bastnaesite mining and/or beneficiating |
| 335210 | Bath fans with integral lighting fixture, residential, manufacturing |
| 335210 | Bath fans, residential, manufacturing |
| 314110 | Bath mats and bath sets made in carpet mills |
| 326299 | Bath mats, rubber, manufacturing |
| 325620 | Bath salts manufacturing |
| 449129 | Bath shops |
| 713990 | Bathing beaches |
| 315990 | Bathing caps, rubber, manufacturing |
| 315210 | Bathing suits cut and sew apparel contractors |
| 315120 | Bathing suits made in apparel knitting mills |
| 315250 | Bathing suits, men's and boys', cut and sewn from purchased fabric (except apparel contractors) |
| 315250 | Bathing suits, women's, girls', and infants', cut and sewn from purchased fabric (except apparel contractors) |
| 315210 | Bathrobes cut and sew apparel contractors |
| 315120 | Bathrobes made in apparel knitting mills |
| 315250 | Bathrobes, men's and boys', cut and sewn from purchased fabric (except apparel contractors) |

| | |
|---|---|
| 315250 | Bathrobes, women's, girls', and infants', cut and sewn from purchased fabric (except apparel contractors) |
| 423220 | Bathroom accessories merchant wholesalers |
| 327110 | Bathroom accessories, vitreous china and earthenware, manufacturing |
| 326199 | Bathroom and toilet accessories, plastics, manufacturing |
| 332999 | Bathroom fixtures, metal, manufacturing |
| 238220 | Bathroom plumbing fixture and sanitary ware installation |
| 333998 | Bathroom scales manufacturing |
| 337110 | Bathroom vanities (except freestanding), stock or custom wood, manufacturing |
| 812199 | Baths, steam or turkish |
| 238390 | Bathtub refinishing, on-site |
| 423720 | Bathtubs merchant wholesalers |
| 332999 | Bathtubs, metal, manufacturing |
| 326191 | Bathtubs, plastics, manufacturing |
| 611620 | Baton instruction |
| 624221 | Battered women's shelters |
| 423610 | Batteries (except automotive) merchant wholesalers |
| 441330 | Batteries, automotive, dealers |
| 423120 | Batteries, automotive, merchant wholesalers |
| 459999 | Batteries, except automotive, dealers |
| 335910 | Batteries, primary, dry or wet, manufacturing |
| 335910 | Batteries, rechargeable, manufacturing |
| 335910 | Batteries, storage, manufacturing |
| 311824 | Batters, prepared, made from purchased flour |
| 311211 | Batters, prepared, made in flour mills |
| 335999 | Battery chargers, solid-state, manufacturing |
| 334515 | Battery testers, electrical, manufacturing |
| 712120 | Battlefields |
| 314999 | Batts and batting (except nonwoven fabrics) manufacturing |
| 327120 | Bauxite brick manufacturing |
| 423520 | Bauxite merchant wholesalers |
| 212290 | Bauxite mining and/or beneficiating |
| 325998 | Bay oil manufacturing |
| 332994 | BB guns manufacturing |
| 332992 | BB shot manufacturing |
| 532284 | Beach chair rental |
| 713990 | Beach clubs, recreational |

| | |
|---|---|
| 562998 | Beach maintenance and cleaning services |
| 316210 | Beach sandals, plastics or plastics soled fabric upper, manufacturing |
| 316210 | Beach sandals, rubber or rubber soled fabric upper, manufacturing |
| 532284 | Beach umbrella rental |
| 339999 | Beach umbrellas manufacturing |
| 713990 | Beaches, bathing |
| 315210 | Beachwear cut and sew apparel contractors |
| 315120 | Beachwear made in apparel knitting mills |
| 315250 | Beachwear, men's and boys', cut and sewn from purchased fabric (except apparel contractors) |
| 315250 | Beachwear, women's, girls', and infants', cut and sewn from purchased fabric (except apparel contractors) |
| 333517 | Beader machines, metalworking, manufacturing |
| 314999 | Beading on textile products (except apparel) for the trade |
| 333248 | Beaming machinery for yarn manufacturing |
| 313110 | Beaming yarn |
| 321113 | Beams, wood, made from logs or bolts |
| 111219 | Bean (except dry) farming, field and seed production |
| 115114 | Bean cleaning |
| 111130 | Bean farming, dry, field and seed production |
| 111419 | Bean sprout farming, grown under cover |
| 311422 | Beans, baked, canning |
| 424490 | Beans, dry edible, merchant wholesalers |
| 424510 | Beans, dry inedible, merchant wholesalers |
| 423510 | Bearing piles, metal, merchant wholesalers |
| 332216 | Bearing pullers, handtools, manufacturing |
| 336310 | Bearings (e.g., camshaft, crankshaft, connecting rod), automotive and truck gasoline engine, manufacturing |
| 423840 | Bearings merchant wholesalers |
| 332991 | Bearings, ball and roller, manufacturing |
| 333613 | Bearings, plain (except internal combustion engine), manufacturing |
| 812112 | Beautician services |
| 333310 | Beauty and barber shop equipment (except chairs) manufacturing |

| | |
|---|---|
| 812112 | Beauty and barber shops, combined |
| 711310 | Beauty pageant managers with facilities |
| 711320 | Beauty pageant managers without facilities |
| 711310 | Beauty pageant organizers with facilities |
| 711320 | Beauty pageant organizers without facilities |
| 711310 | Beauty pageant promoters with facilities |
| 711320 | Beauty pageant promoters without facilities |
| 423850 | Beauty parlor equipment and supplies merchant wholesalers |
| 812112 | Beauty parlors |
| 424210 | Beauty preparations merchant wholesalers |
| 236220 | Beauty salon construction |
| 812112 | Beauty salons |
| 611511 | Beauty schools |
| 812112 | Beauty shops |
| 424210 | Beauty supplies merchant wholesalers |
| 456120 | Beauty supply stores |
| 721191 | Bed and breakfast inns |
| 337122 | Bed frames, wood household-type, manufacturing |
| 812331 | Bed linen supply services |
| 449110 | Bed stores, retail |
| 335210 | Bedcoverings, electric, manufacturing |
| 111422 | Bedding plant growing (except vegetable and melon bedding plants) |
| 424930 | Bedding plants merchant wholesalers |
| 315210 | Bedjackets cut and sew apparel contractors |
| 315250 | Bedjackets, women's and girls', cut and sewn from purchased fabric (except apparel contractors) |
| 337122 | Bedroom furniture (except upholstered), wood household-type, manufacturing |
| 423210 | Beds (except hospital) merchant wholesalers |
| 337122 | Beds (except hospital), wood household-type, manufacturing |
| 337126 | Beds (including cabinet and folding), metal household-type (except hospital), manufacturing |
| 339113 | Beds, hospital, manufacturing |
| 423450 | Beds, hospital, merchant wholesalers |
| 337910 | Beds, sleep-system ensembles (i.e., flotation, adjustable), manufacturing |
| 337122 | Beds, wood dormitory-type, manufacturing |
| 337122 | Beds, wood hotel-type, manufacturing |
| 314120 | Bedspreads and bed sets made from purchased fabrics |
| 313240 | Bedspreads and bed sets made in lace mills |
| 313240 | Bedspreads and bed sets made in warp or weft knitting mills |
| 112910 | Bee pollen collection |
| 112910 | Bee production (i.e., apiculture) |
| 311611 | Beef carcasses, half carcasses, primal and sub-primal cuts, produced in slaughtering plants |
| 112112 | Beef cattle feedlots (except stockyards for transportation) |
| 112111 | Beef cattle ranching or farming |
| 311611 | Beef produced in slaughtering plants |
| 311612 | Beef stew made from purchased carcasses |
| 311612 | Beef, primal and sub-primal cuts, made from purchased carcasses |
| 424910 | Beekeeping supplies merchant wholesalers |
| 517112 | Beeper (i.e., radio pager) communication carriers |
| 327213 | Beer bottles, glass, manufacturing |
| 312120 | Beer brewing |
| 332431 | Beer cans, light gauge metal, manufacturing |
| 333415 | Beer cooling and dispensing equipment manufacturing |
| 332439 | Beer kegs, light gauge metal, manufacturing |
| 459999 | Beer making supply stores |
| 424810 | Beer merchant wholesalers |
| 445320 | Beer stores, packaged |
| 424590 | Bees merchant wholesalers |
| 325612 | Beeswax polishes and waxes manufacturing |
| 112910 | Beeswax production |
| 111219 | Beet farming (except sugar beets), field, bedding plant and seed production |
| 311313 | Beet pulp, dried, manufacturing |
| 311313 | Beet sugar refining |
| 624410 | Before-school and after-school educational programs, separate from schools |
| 541720 | Behavioral research and development services |
| 325412 | Belladonna preparations manufacturing |
| 332999 | Bellows, hand, manufacturing |
| 333998 | Bellows, industrial-type, manufacturing |

| | |
|---|---|
| 339992 | Bells (musical instruments) manufacturing |
| 335999 | Bells, electric, manufacturing |
| 424310 | Belt and buckle assembly kits merchant wholesalers |
| 333922 | Belt conveyor systems manufacturing |
| 316990 | Belt laces, leather, manufacturing |
| 316110 | Belting butts, curried or rough, manufacturing |
| 313220 | Belting fabrics, narrow woven |
| 316990 | Belting for machinery, leather, manufacturing |
| 316110 | Belting leather, manufacturing |
| 314999 | Belting made from purchased fabrics |
| 423840 | Belting, industrial, merchant wholesalers |
| 326220 | Belting, rubber (e.g., conveyor, elevator, transmission), manufacturing |
| 482112 | Beltline railroads |
| 315210 | Belts, apparel (e.g., fabric, leather, vinyl), cut and sew apparel contractors |
| 315990 | Belts, apparel (e.g., fabric, leather, vinyl), cut and sewn from purchased fabric (except apparel contractors) |
| 332618 | Belts, conveyor, made from purchased wire |
| 332618 | Belts, drying, made from purchased wire |
| 316990 | Belts, leather safety, manufacturing |
| 332994 | Belts, machine gun, manufacturing |
| 315210 | Belts, money, any material, cut and sew apparel contractors |
| 315990 | Belts, money, any material, cut and sewn from purchased fabric (except apparel contractors) |
| 337127 | Benches, park-type (except concrete, stone), manufacturing |
| 337127 | Benches, public building-type, manufacturing |
| 337127 | Benches, work, manufacturing |
| 333517 | Bending and forming machines, metalworking, manufacturing |
| 332996 | Bends, pipe, made from purchased metal pipe |
| 541612 | Benefit consulting services |
| 111998 | Bentgrass seed farming |
| 212323 | Bentonite mining and/or beneficiating |
| 321999 | Bentwood (steam bent) products (except furniture) manufacturing |
| 325194 | Benzaldehyde manufacturing |
| 325320 | Benzene hexachloride (BHC) insecticides manufacturing |
| 325110 | Benzene made from refined petroleum or liquid hydrocarbons |
| 324110 | Benzene made in petroleum refineries |
| 325194 | Benzoic acid manufacturing |
| 311421 | Berries, canned, manufacturing |
| 424480 | Berries, fresh, merchant wholesalers |
| 115113 | Berries, machine harvesting |
| 111334 | Berry (except strawberry) farming |
| 321920 | Berry crates, wood, wirebound, manufacturing |
| 321920 | Berry cups, veneer and splint, manufacturing |
| 333111 | Berry harvesting machines manufacturing |
| 212290 | Beryl mining and/or beneficiating |
| 327110 | Beryllia porcelain insulators manufacturing |
| 331529 | Beryllium castings (except die-castings), unfinished manufacturing |
| 212290 | Beryllium concentrates beneficiating |
| 331523 | Beryllium die-castings, unfinished, manufacturing |
| 212290 | Beryllium ores mining and/or beneficiating |
| 325180 | Beryllium oxide manufacturing |
| 331410 | Beryllium refining, primary |
| 334517 | Beta-ray irradiation equipment manufacturing |
| 335999 | Betatrons manufacturing |
| 813910 | Better business bureaus |
| 713290 | Betting information services |
| 722515 | Beverage (e.g., coffee, juice, soft drink) bars, nonalcoholic, fixed location |
| 311930 | Beverage bases manufacturing |
| 424490 | Beverage bases merchant wholesalers |
| 423830 | Beverage bottling machinery merchant wholesalers |
| 424490 | Beverage concentrates merchant wholesalers |
| 327213 | Beverage containers, glass, manufacturing |
| 423740 | Beverage coolers, mechanical, merchant wholesalers |
| 311930 | Beverage flavorings (except coffee based) manufacturing |
| 423830 | Beverage processing machinery merchant wholesalers |
| 722330 | Beverage stands, nonalcoholic, mobile |
| 311930 | Beverage syrups (except coffee based) manufacturing |

| | |
|---|---|
| 424810 | Beverages, alcoholic (except distilled spirits, wine), merchant wholesalers |
| 312120 | Beverages, beer, ale, and malt liquors, manufacturing |
| 311514 | Beverages, dietary, dairy and nondairy based |
| 312111 | Beverages, fruit and vegetable drinks, cocktails, and ades, manufacturing |
| 311421 | Beverages, fruit and vegetable juice, manufacturing |
| 312140 | Beverages, liquors (except brandies), manufacturing |
| 311511 | Beverages, milk based (except dietary), manufacturing |
| 312112 | Beverages, naturally carbonated bottled water, manufacturing |
| 312111 | Beverages, soft drink (including artificially carbonated waters), manufacturing |
| 424820 | Beverages, wine and distilled spirits, merchant wholesalers |
| 312130 | Beverages, wines and brandies, manufacturing |
| 314999 | Bias bindings made from purchased fabrics |
| 313220 | Bias bindings, woven, manufacturing |
| 611310 | Bible colleges offering baccalaureate degrees |
| 611699 | Bible schools (except degree granting) |
| 813110 | Bible societies |
| 315210 | Bibs and aprons, waterproof (e.g., plastics, rubber, similar materials), cut and sew apparel contractors |
| 315990 | Bibs and aprons, waterproof (e.g., plastics, rubber, similar materials), cut and sewn from purchased fabric (except apparel contractors) |
| 315990 | Bibs and aprons, waterproof (e.g., plastics, rubber, similar materials), rubberizing fabric and manufacturing bibs and aprons |
| 459110 | Bicycle (except motorized) shops |
| 459510 | Bicycle (except motorized) shops, used |
| 492210 | Bicycle courier |
| 333912 | Bicycle pumps manufacturing |
| 532284 | Bicycle rental |
| 811490 | Bicycle repair and maintenance shops without retailing new bicycles |
| 532284 | Bicycle sharing services |
| 441227 | Bicycle shops, motorized |
| 423910 | Bicycle tires and tubes merchant wholesalers |
| 423110 | Bicycle, motorized, merchant wholesalers |
| 423910 | Bicycles (except motorized) merchant wholesalers |
| 336991 | Bicycles and parts manufacturing |
| 327110 | Bidets, vitreous china, manufacturing |
| 561440 | Bill collection services |
| 541850 | Billboard display advertising services |
| 238990 | Billboard erection |
| 339950 | Billboards manufacturing |
| 423990 | Billboards merchant wholesalers |
| 333519 | Billet mill machinery, metalworking, manufacturing |
| 423510 | Billets, metal, merchant wholesalers |
| 331110 | Billets, steel, made in iron and steel mills |
| 316990 | Billfolds (except metal) manufacturing |
| 339920 | Billiard equipment and supplies manufacturing |
| 423910 | Billiard equipment and supplies merchant wholesalers |
| 713990 | Billiard parlors |
| 713990 | Billiard rooms |
| 541219 | Billing services |
| 322130 | Binder's board manufacturing |
| 424120 | Binders, looseleaf, merchant wholesalers |
| 333248 | Bindery machinery manufacturing |
| 314999 | Binding carpets and rugs for the trade |
| 333310 | Binding equipment (i.e., plastics or tape binding), office-type, manufacturing |
| 424310 | Binding, textile, merchant wholesalers |
| 314999 | Bindings, bias, made from purchased fabrics |
| 313220 | Bindings, narrow woven, manufacturing |
| 713290 | Bingo halls |
| 713290 | Bingo parlors |
| 316990 | Binocular cases manufacturing |
| 459999 | Binocular stores |
| 333310 | Binoculars manufacturing |
| 423460 | Binoculars merchant wholesalers |
| 332313 | Bins, fabricated metal plate work, manufacturing |
| 332439 | Bins, light gauge metal, manufacturing |
| 423390 | Bins, storage, merchant wholesalers |
| 324110 | Biodiesel fuels made in petroleum refineries |

324199 Biodiesel fuels not made in petroleum refineries and blended with purchased refined petroleum

325199 Biodiesel fuels not made in petroleum refineries and not blended with petroleum

424710 Biodiesel, blended with petroleum, bulk stations and terminals, merchant wholesalers

424720 Biodiesel, blended with petroleum, merchant wholesalers (except bulk stations, terminals)

424690 Biodiesel, not blended with petroleum, merchant wholesalers

621498 Biofeedback centers and clinics, outpatient

324199 Biofuels not made in petroleum refineries and blended with purchased refined petroleum

325199 Biofuels not made in petroleum refineries and not blended with petroleum

424710 Biofuels, blended with petroleum, bulk stations and terminals, merchant wholesalers

424720 Biofuels, blended with petroleum, merchant wholesalers (except bulk stations, terminals)

424690 Biofuels, not blended with petroleum, merchant wholesalers

325120 Biogases, industrial (i.e., compressed, liquefied, solid), manufacturing

562910 Biohazard cleanup services

339113 Biohazard protective clothing and accessories manufacturing

541380 Biological (except medical, veterinary) testing laboratories or services

541690 Biological consulting services

621511 Biological laboratories, diagnostic

424210 Biologicals and allied products merchant wholesalers

541715 Biology research and development laboratories or services (except biotechnology and nanotechnology research and development)

221117 Biomass electric power generation

334118 Biometrics system input devices (e.g., retinal scan, iris pattern recognition, hand geometry) manufacturing

541714 Biotechnology research and development laboratories or services (except nanobiotechnology research and development)

541714 Biotechnology research and development laboratories or services in agriculture (except nanobiotechnology research and development)

541714 Biotechnology research and development laboratories or services in bacteriology (except nanobiotechnology research and development)

541714 Biotechnology research and development laboratories or services in biology (except nanobiotechnology research and development)

541714 Biotechnology research and development laboratories or services in botany (except nanobiotechnology research and development)

541714 Biotechnology research and development laboratories or services in chemical sciences (except nanobiotechnology research and development)

541714 Biotechnology research and development laboratories or services in entomology (except nanobiotechnology research and development)

541714 Biotechnology research and development laboratories or services in environmental science (except nanobiotechnology research and development)

541714 Biotechnology research and development laboratories or services in food science (except nanobiotechnology research and development)

541714 Biotechnology research and development laboratories or services in genetics (except nanobiotechnology research and development)

541714 Biotechnology research and development laboratories or services in health sciences (except nanobiotechnology research and development)

541714 Biotechnology research and development laboratories or services in industrial research (except nanobiotechnology research and development)

541714 Biotechnology research and development laboratories or services in the medical sciences (except nanobiotechnology research and development)

| | |
|---|---|
| 541714 | Biotechnology research and development laboratories or services in the physical sciences (except nanobiotechnology research and development) |
| 541714 | Biotechnology research and development laboratories or services in the veterinary sciences (except nanobiotechnology research and development) |
| 423690 | Bipolar transistors merchant wholesalers |
| 311119 | Bird feed, prepared, manufacturing |
| 112990 | Bird production (e.g., canaries, love birds, parakeets, parrots) |
| 561710 | Bird proofing services |
| 712190 | Bird sanctuaries |
| 621410 | Birth control clinics |
| 326299 | Birth control devices (i.e., diaphragms, prophylactics) manufacturing |
| 325412 | Birth control pills manufacturing |
| 311812 | Biscuits, bread-type, made in commercial bakeries |
| 331410 | Bismuth refining, primary |
| 112990 | Bison production |
| 333515 | Bits and knives for metalworking lathes, planers, and shapers manufacturing |
| 333515 | Bits, drill, metalworking, manufacturing |
| 332216 | Bits, edge tool, woodworking, manufacturing |
| 333120 | Bits, rock drill, construction and surface mining-type, manufacturing |
| 333132 | Bits, rock drill, oil and gas field-type, manufacturing |
| 333131 | Bits, rock drill, underground mining-type, manufacturing |
| 213113 | Bituminous coal mining services on a contract basis (except geophysical surveying and mapping, site preparation, construction, and transportation activities) |
| 212115 | Bituminous coal or anthracite underground mine site development for own account |
| 212115 | Bituminous coal or anthracite underground mining |
| 213113 | Bituminous coal or lignite surface mine site development (except site preparation and related construction contractor activities) on a contract basis |
| 213113 | Bituminous coal stripping service on a contract basis |

| | |
|---|---|
| 212114 | Bituminous coal, lignite, or anthracite beneficiating (e.g., cleaning, crushing, screening, washing, sizing) |
| 212114 | Bituminous coal, lignite, or anthracite surface mine site development for own account |
| 212114 | Bituminous coal, lignite, or anthracite surface mining and/or beneficiating |
| 212319 | Bituminous limestone mining and/or beneficiating |
| 213113 | Bituminous or lignite auger mining service on a contract basis |
| 212319 | Bituminous sandstone mining and/or beneficiating |
| 325130 | Black pigments (except carbon black, bone black, lamp black) manufacturing |
| 423510 | Black plate merchant wholesalers |
| 111334 | Blackberry farming |
| 423490 | Blackboards merchant wholesalers |
| 339940 | Blackboards, framed, manufacturing |
| 327991 | Blackboards, unframed, slate, manufacturing |
| 331110 | Blackplate made in iron and steel mills |
| 316990 | Blacksmith's aprons, leather, manufacturing |
| 311314 | Blackstrap molasses manufacturing |
| 238990 | Blacktop work, residential and commercial driveway and parking area |
| 811310 | Blade sharpening, commercial and industrial machinery and equipment |
| 423710 | Blades (e.g., knife, saw) merchant wholesalers |
| 333120 | Blades for graders, scrapers, bulldozers, and snowplows manufacturing |
| 332215 | Blades, knife and razor, manufacturing |
| 424210 | Blades, razor, merchant wholesalers |
| 332216 | Blades, saw, all types, manufacturing |
| 325130 | Blanc fixe (i.e., barium sulfate, precipitated) manufacturing |
| 332992 | Blank cartridges (i.e., 30 mm. or less, 1.18 inch or less) manufacturing |
| 423690 | Blank CDs and DVDs merchant wholesalers |
| 423690 | Blank diskettes merchant wholesalers |
| 334610 | Blank tapes, audio and video, manufacturing |
| 423690 | Blank tapes, audio and video, merchant wholesalers |
| 323111 | Blankbooks and refills manufacturing |
| 424120 | Blankbooks merchant wholesalers |
| 314910 | Blanket bags manufacturing |

| | |
|---|---|
| 314120 | Blankets (except electric) made from purchased fabrics or felts |
| 423220 | Blankets (except electric) merchant wholesalers |
| 313210 | Blankets and bedspreads made in broadwoven fabric mills |
| 335210 | Blankets, electric, manufacturing |
| 423620 | Blankets, electric, merchant wholesalers |
| 313230 | Blankets, nonwoven fabric, manufacturing |
| 327212 | Blanks for electric light bulbs, glass, made in glass making plants |
| 333515 | Blanks, cutting tool, manufacturing |
| 327215 | Blanks, ophthalmic lens and optical glass, made from purchased glass |
| 327212 | Blanks, ophthalmic lens and optical glass, made in glass making plants |
| 423830 | Blanks, tips, and inserts merchant wholesalers |
| 321912 | Blanks, wood (e.g., bowling pins, handles, textile machinery accessories), manufacturing |
| 311411 | Blast freezing on a contract basis |
| 236210 | Blast furnace construction |
| 327992 | Blast furnace slag processing |
| 331110 | Blast furnaces |
| 238910 | Blast hole drilling (except mining) |
| 212322 | Blast sand quarrying and/or beneficiating |
| 325920 | Blasting accessories (e.g., caps, fuses, ignitors, squibbs) manufacturing |
| 325920 | Blasting powders manufacturing |
| 213113 | Blasting services, coal mining, on a contract basis |
| 213114 | Blasting services, metal mining, on a contract basis |
| 213115 | Blasting services, nonmetallic minerals mining (except fuels) on a contract basis |
| 238910 | Blasting, building demolition |
| 238910 | Blasting, construction site |
| 238390 | Bleacher installation |
| 337127 | Bleacher seating manufacturing |
| 424690 | Bleaches merchant wholesalers |
| 325612 | Bleaches, formulated for household use, manufacturing |
| 325180 | Bleaching agents, inorganic, manufacturing |
| 325199 | Bleaching agents, organic, manufacturing |
| 212323 | Bleaching clay mining and/or beneficiating |

| | |
|---|---|
| 333248 | Bleaching machinery for textiles manufacturing |
| 313310 | Bleaching textile products, apparel, and fabrics |
| 212230 | Blende (zinc) mining and/or beneficiating |
| 311211 | Blended flour made in flour mills |
| 335210 | Blenders, household-type electric, manufacturing |
| 325620 | Blending and compounding perfume bases |
| 311119 | Blending animal feed |
| 312130 | Blending brandy |
| 312140 | Blending distilled beverages (except brandy) |
| 312130 | Blending wines |
| 336411 | Blimps (i.e., aircraft) manufacturing |
| 337920 | Blinds (e.g., mini, venetian, vertical), all materials, manufacturing |
| 423220 | Blinds and shades, window, merchant wholesalers |
| 331410 | Blister copper manufacturing |
| 561910 | Blister packaging services |
| 333923 | Block and tackle manufacturing |
| 312113 | Block ice manufacturing |
| 324121 | Blocks, asphalt paving, made from purchased asphaltic materials |
| 327331 | Blocks, concrete and cinder, manufacturing |
| 327120 | Blocks, fire clay, manufacturing |
| 327212 | Blocks, glass, made in glass making plants |
| 321999 | Blocks, tackle, wood, manufacturing |
| 321999 | Blocks, tailors' pressing wood, manufacturing |
| 516210 | Blog sites, Internet |
| 621511 | Blood analysis laboratories |
| 334516 | Blood bank process equipment manufacturing |
| 621991 | Blood banks |
| 325413 | Blood derivative in-vitro diagnostic substances manufacturing |
| 325414 | Blood derivatives manufacturing |
| 424210 | Blood derivatives merchant wholesalers |
| 621991 | Blood donor stations |
| 325414 | Blood fractions manufacturing |
| 325413 | Blood glucose test kits manufacturing |
| 424210 | Blood plasma merchant wholesalers |
| 339112 | Blood pressure apparatus manufacturing |

| | |
|---|---|
| 621999 | Blood pressure screening facilities |
| 621999 | Blood pressure screening services |
| 812990 | Blood pressure testing machine concession operators, coin- or card-operated |
| 339113 | Blood testing apparatus, laboratory-type, manufacturing |
| 339112 | Blood transfusion equipment manufacturing |
| 333519 | Blooming and slabbing mill machinery, metalworking, manufacturing |
| 423510 | Blooms, metal, merchant wholesalers |
| 331110 | Blooms, steel, made in iron and steel mills |
| 315210 | Blouses cut and sew apparel contractors |
| 315120 | Blouses made in apparel knitting mills |
| 315250 | Blouses, women's, girls', and infants', cut and sewn from purchased fabric (except apparel contractors) |
| 335210 | Blow dryers, household-type electric, manufacturing |
| 333248 | Blow molding machinery for plastics manufacturing |
| 332216 | Blow torches manufacturing |
| 333413 | Blower filter units manufacturing |
| 238220 | Blower or fan, cooling and dry heating, installation |
| 333111 | Blowers, forage, manufacturing |
| 423830 | Blowers, industrial, merchant wholesalers |
| 333112 | Blowers, leaf, manufacturing |
| 423820 | Blowers, snow and leaf, merchant wholesalers |
| 238310 | Blown-in insulation (e.g., cellulose, vermiculite) installation |
| 221210 | Blue gas, carbureted, distribution |
| 111334 | Blueberry farming |
| 114111 | Bluefish fishing |
| 111998 | Bluegrass-Kentucky seed farming |
| 541340 | Blueprint drafting services |
| 333310 | Blueprint equipment manufacturing |
| 423420 | Blueprinting equipment merchant wholesalers |
| 561439 | Blueprinting services |
| 212311 | Bluestone mining or quarrying |
| 325620 | Blushes, face, manufacturing |
| 423920 | Board games merchant wholesalers |
| 921130 | Board of Governors, Federal Reserve |
| 321219 | Board, bagasse, manufacturing |
| 327420 | Board, gypsum, manufacturing |
| 321219 | Board, particle, manufacturing |
| 115210 | Boarding horses (except racehorses) |
| 721310 | Boarding houses |
| 611110 | Boarding schools, elementary or secondary |
| 812910 | Boarding services, pet |
| 921120 | Boards of supervisors, county and local |
| 813910 | Boards of trade |
| 324122 | Boards, asphalt saturated, made from purchased asphaltic materials |
| 321999 | Boards, bulletin, wood and cork, manufacturing |
| 321999 | Boards, wood (e.g., clip, ironing, meat, pastry), manufacturing |
| 321113 | Boards, wood, made from logs or bolts |
| 321912 | Boards, wood, resawing purchased lumber |
| 336320 | Boat and ship lighting fixtures manufacturing |
| 441222 | Boat dealers, new and used |
| 541330 | Boat engineering design services |
| 484220 | Boat hauling, truck, local |
| 484230 | Boat hauling, truck, long-distance |
| 238990 | Boat lift installation |
| 333923 | Boat lifts manufacturing |
| 532411 | Boat rental (except pleasure) without crew |
| 532411 | Boat rental or leasing, commercial |
| 532284 | Boat rental, pleasure |
| 332312 | Boat sections, prefabricated metal, manufacturing |
| 423910 | Boat supplies, pleasure, merchant wholesalers |
| 441222 | Boat trailer dealers |
| 336212 | Boat transporter trailers, multi-unit, manufacturing |
| 336214 | Boat transporter trailers, single-unit, manufacturing |
| 336612 | Boat yards (i.e., boat manufacturing facilities) |
| 487210 | Boat, fishing charter, operation |
| 811490 | Boat, pleasure, repair and maintenance services without retailing new boats |
| 713930 | Boating clubs with marinas |
| 713990 | Boating clubs without marinas |
| 336612 | Boats (e.g., motorboats, rowboats, canoes, kayaks) manufacturing |
| 423860 | Boats (except pleasure) merchant wholesalers |

336612 Boats (i.e., suitable or intended for personal use) manufacturing

336612 Boats, inflatable plastics (except toy-type), manufacturing

423910 Boats, pleasure (e.g., canoes, motorboats, sailboats), merchant wholesalers

321912 Bobbin blocks and blanks, wood, manufacturing

322219 Bobbins, fiber, made from purchased paperboard

333248 Bobbins, textile machinery, manufacturing

339920 Bobsleds manufacturing

812320 Bobtailers, laundry and drycleaning

713990 Boccie ball courts

423110 Bodies, motor vehicle, merchant wholesalers

713940 Body building studios, physical fitness

811121 Body conversion services, automotive

561612 Body guard services

811121 Body shops, automotive

315210 Body stockings cut and sew apparel contractors

315120 Body stockings made in apparel knitting mills

315250 Body stockings, women's and girls', cut and sewn from purchased fabric (except apparel contractors)

332994 Bofors guns manufacturing

238290 Boiler and pipe insulation installation

332410 Boiler casings manufacturing

238220 Boiler chipping, cleaning and scaling

334513 Boiler controls, industrial, power, and marine-type, manufacturing

332919 Boiler couplings and drains, plumbing and heating-type, manufacturing

238290 Boiler covering installation

332911 Boiler gauge cocks, industrial-type, manufacturing

331210 Boiler tubes, wrought, made from purchased iron

238220 Boiler, heating, installation

423720 Boilers (e.g., heating, hot water, power, steam) merchant wholesalers

333414 Boilers, heating, manufacturing

332410 Boilers, power, manufacturing

311612 Bologna made from purchased carcasses

332722 Bolts, metal, manufacturing

326199 Bolts, nuts, and rivets, plastics, manufacturing

423710 Bolts, nuts, rivets, screws, and other fasteners merchant wholesalers

333924 Bomb lifts manufacturing

332993 Bomb loading and assembling plants

332993 Bombcluster adapters manufacturing

332993 Bombs manufacturing

523150 Bond brokerages

523150 Bond dealing (i.e., acting as a principal in dealing securities to investors)

322230 Bond paper made from purchased paper

322120 Bond paper made in paper mills

493190 Bonded warehousing (except farm products, general merchandise, refrigerated)

493130 Bonded warehousing, farm products (except refrigerated)

493110 Bonded warehousing, general merchandise

493120 Bonded warehousing, refrigerated

313230 Bonded-fiber fabrics manufacturing

332812 Bonderizing metal and metal products for the trade

524126 Bonding, fidelity or surety insurance, direct

812990 Bondsperson services

325180 Bone black manufacturing

327110 Bone china manufacturing

339112 Bone drills manufacturing

311119 Bone meal prepared as feed for animals and fowls

339999 Bone novelties manufacturing

339112 Bone plates and screws manufacturing

339112 Bone rongeurs manufacturing

311613 Bones, fat, rendering

513130 Book (e.g., hardback, paperback, audio) publishers

513130 Book (e.g., hardback, paperback, audio) publishers (except exclusive Internet publishing)

459210 Book clubs, not publishing, new books, mail-order

459510 Book clubs, not publishing, used books, mail-order

813410 Book discussion clubs

332999 Book ends, metal, manufacturing

322220 Book paper made by coating purchased paper

322220 Book paper, coated, made from purchased paper

322120 Book paper, coated, made in paper mills

| | |
|---|---|
| 513130 | Book publishers and printing combined |
| 513130 | Book publishers, exclusively on Internet |
| 513130 | Book publishers, university press |
| 513130 | Book publishers, university press (except exclusive Internet publishing) |
| 459210 | Book stores |
| 459510 | Book stores, used |
| 316110 | Bookbinder's leather manufacturing |
| 333248 | Bookbinding machines manufacturing |
| 323120 | Bookbinding shops |
| 323120 | Bookbinding without printing |
| 337126 | Bookcases (except wood), household-type, manufacturing |
| 337214 | Bookcases (except wood), office-type, manufacturing |
| 337122 | Bookcases, wood household-type, manufacturing |
| 337211 | Bookcases, wood office-type, manufacturing |
| 713290 | Bookies |
| 561599 | Booking (e.g., airline, car rental, hotel, restaurant) services |
| 512199 | Booking agencies, motion picture |
| 512199 | Booking agencies, motion picture or video productions |
| 711320 | Booking agencies, theatrical (except motion picture) |
| 541219 | Bookkeepers' offices |
| 541219 | Bookkeepers' private practices |
| 423420 | Bookkeeping machines merchant wholesalers |
| 541219 | Bookkeeping services |
| 713290 | Bookmakers |
| 519210 | Bookmobiles |
| 424920 | Books merchant wholesalers |
| 323117 | Books printing and binding without publishing |
| 323117 | Books printing without publishing |
| 424120 | Books, sales or receipt, merchant wholesalers |
| 323111 | Books, sales, manifold, printing |
| 339920 | Boomerangs manufacturing |
| 813410 | Booster clubs |
| 486990 | Booster pumping station (except natural gas, petroleum) |
| 486110 | Booster pumping station, crude oil transportation |
| 486210 | Booster pumping station, natural gas transportation |
| 486910 | Booster pumping station, refined petroleum products transportation |
| 424350 | Booster seats merchant wholesalers |
| 332993 | Boosters and bursters, artillery, manufacturing |
| 335311 | Boosters, feeder voltage (i.e., electrical transformers), manufacturing |
| 423850 | Boot and shoe cut stock and findings merchant wholesalers |
| 316990 | Boot and shoe cut stock and findings, leather, manufacturing |
| 321999 | Boot and shoe lasts, all materials, manufacturing |
| 623990 | Boot camps for delinquent youth |
| 333248 | Boot making and repairing machinery manufacturing |
| 811430 | Boot repair shops without retailing new boots |
| 424340 | Boots (e.g., hiking, western, work) merchant wholesalers |
| 316210 | Boots, dress and casual, children's and infants', manufacturing |
| 316210 | Boots, dress and casual, men's, manufacturing |
| 316210 | Boots, dress and casual, women's, manufacturing |
| 316210 | Boots, hiking, children's and infants', manufacturing |
| 316210 | Boots, hiking, men's, manufacturing |
| 316210 | Boots, hiking, women's, manufacturing |
| 316210 | Boots, plastics or plastics soled fabric upper, manufacturing |
| 316210 | Boots, rubber or rubber soled fabric upper, manufacturing |
| 212390 | Borate, natural, mining and/or beneficiating |
| 325180 | Borax (i.e., sodium borate) manufacturing |
| 212390 | Borax, crude, ground or pulverized, mining and/or beneficiating |
| 325320 | Bordeaux mixture insecticides manufacturing |
| 325180 | Boric acid manufacturing |
| 333517 | Boring machines, metalworking, manufacturing |
| 213114 | Boring test holes for metal mining on a contract basis |
| 213115 | Boring test holes for nonmetallic minerals mining (except fuels) on a contract basis |
| 333517 | Boring, drilling, and milling machine combinations, metalworking, manufacturing |
| 238910 | Boring, for building construction |

| | |
|---|---|
| 212390 | Boron compounds prepared at beneficiating plants |
| 325180 | Boron compounds, not specified elsewhere by process, manufacturing |
| 212390 | Boron mineral mining and/or beneficiating |
| 325180 | Borosilicate manufacturing |
| 424210 | Botanical drugs and herbs merchant wholesalers |
| 325412 | Botanical extract preparations (except in-vitro diagnostics) manufacturing |
| 712130 | Botanical gardens |
| 325320 | Botanical insecticides manufacturing |
| 424210 | Botanicals merchant wholesalers |
| 541715 | Botany research and development laboratories or services (except biotechnology and nanotechnology research and development) |
| 326199 | Bottle caps and lids, plastics, manufacturing |
| 332119 | Bottle caps and tops, metal, stamping |
| 321999 | Bottle corks manufacturing |
| 321999 | Bottle covers, willow, rattan, and reed, manufacturing |
| 561990 | Bottle exchanges |
| 335210 | Bottle warmers, household-type electric, manufacturing |
| 333993 | Bottle washers, packaging machinery, manufacturing |
| 457210 | Bottled gas dealers, direct selling |
| 424490 | Bottled water (except water treating) merchant wholesalers |
| 445298 | Bottled water providers, direct selling |
| 423840 | Bottles (except waste) merchant wholesalers |
| 327213 | Bottles (i.e., bottling, canning, packaging), glass, manufacturing |
| 326160 | Bottles, plastics, manufacturing |
| 332439 | Bottles, vacuum, light gauge metal, manufacturing |
| 423930 | Bottles, waste, merchant wholesalers |
| 333993 | Bottling machinery (e.g., capping, filling, labeling, sterilizing, washing) manufacturing |
| 423830 | Bottling machinery and equipment merchant wholesalers |
| 335131 | Boudoir lamp fixtures manufacturing |
| 311422 | Bouillon canning |
| 311423 | Bouillon made in dehydration plants |
| 212319 | Boulder crushed and broken mining and/or beneficiating |

| | |
|---|---|
| 324199 | Boulets (i.e., fuel bricks) made from refined petroleum |
| 561611 | Bounty hunting services |
| 424590 | Bovine semen merchant wholesalers |
| 315210 | Bow ties cut and sew apparel contractors |
| 315990 | Bow ties, men's and boys', cut and sewn from purchased fabric (except apparel contractors) |
| 238290 | Bowling alley equipment installation |
| 713950 | Bowling alleys |
| 337127 | Bowling center furniture manufacturing |
| 713950 | Bowling centers |
| 423910 | Bowling equipment and supplies merchant wholesalers |
| 459110 | Bowling equipment and supply stores |
| 611620 | Bowling instruction |
| 713990 | Bowling leagues or teams, recreational |
| 321912 | Bowling pin blanks manufacturing |
| 339920 | Bowling pin machines, automatic, manufacturing |
| 326199 | Bowls and bowl covers, plastics, manufacturing |
| 321999 | Bowls, wood, turned and shaped, manufacturing |
| 314999 | Bows made from purchased fabrics |
| 339920 | Bows, archery, manufacturing |
| 316990 | Bows, shoe, leather, manufacturing |
| 321920 | Box cleats, wood, manufacturing |
| 311991 | Box lunches (for sale off premises) manufacturing |
| 321920 | Box shook manufacturing |
| 423840 | Box shooks merchant wholesalers |
| 337215 | Box spring frames manufacturing |
| 423210 | Box springs merchant wholesalers |
| 337910 | Box springs, assembled, made from purchased spring |
| 316990 | Box toes (i.e., shoe cut stock), leather, manufacturing |
| 311612 | Boxed beef made from purchased carcasses |
| 311611 | Boxed beef produced in slaughtering plants |
| 311612 | Boxed meat produced from purchased carcasses |
| 311611 | Boxed meats produced in slaughtering plants |
| 711219 | Boxers, independent professional |
| 423840 | Boxes and crates, industrial (except disposable plastics, paperboard, waste), merchant wholesalers |

| | |
|---|---|
| 423610 | Boxes and fittings, electrical, merchant wholesalers |
| 321920 | Boxes, cigar, wood or part wood, manufacturing |
| 322211 | Boxes, corrugated and solid fiber, made from purchased paper or paperboard |
| 335932 | Boxes, electrical wiring (e.g., junction, outlet, switch), manufacturing |
| 322212 | Boxes, folding (except corrugated), made from purchased paperboard |
| 316990 | Boxes, hat (except paper or paperboard), manufacturing |
| 321920 | Boxes, jewelry, wood or part wood, manufacturing |
| 316990 | Boxes, leather, manufacturing |
| 332439 | Boxes, light gauge metal, manufacturing |
| 424130 | Boxes, paperboard and disposable plastics, merchant wholesalers |
| 322219 | Boxes, sanitary food (except folding), made from purchased paper or paperboard |
| 322219 | Boxes, setup (i.e., not shipped flat), made from purchased paperboard |
| 322211 | Boxes, shipping, laminated paper and paperboard, made from purchased paperboard |
| 336211 | Boxes, truck (e.g., cargo, dump, utility, van), assembled on purchased chassis |
| 423930 | Boxes, waste, merchant wholesalers |
| 321920 | Boxes, wood, manufacturing |
| 321920 | Boxes, wood, plain or fabric covered, nailed or lock corner, manufacturing |
| 711211 | Boxing clubs, professional or semiprofessional |
| 713990 | Boxing clubs, recreational |
| 339920 | Boxing equipment manufacturing |
| 711310 | Boxing event managers with facilities |
| 711320 | Boxing event managers without facilities |
| 711310 | Boxing event organizers with facilities |
| 711320 | Boxing event organizers without facilities |
| 711310 | Boxing event promoters with facilities |
| 711320 | Boxing event promoters without facilities |
| 813410 | Boy guiding organizations |
| 623990 | Boys' and girls' residential facilities (e.g., homes, ranches, villages) |
| 721214 | Boys' camps (except day, instructional) |
| 611620 | Boys' camps, sports instruction |
| 611620 | Boys' camps, sports instructor |
| 713990 | Boys' day camps (except instructional) |

| | |
|---|---|
| 315120 | Boys' socks manufacturing |
| 111334 | Boysenberry farming |
| 339910 | Bracelets, precious metal, manufacturing |
| 115112 | Bracing of orchard trees and vines |
| 332510 | Brackets (i.e., builder's hardware-type), metal, manufacturing |
| 332618 | Brackets made from purchased wire |
| 321918 | Brackets, wood, manufacturing |
| 423710 | Brads merchant wholesalers |
| 331222 | Brads, iron or steel, wire or cut, made in wire drawing plants |
| 332618 | Brads, metal, made from purchased wire |
| 333248 | Braiding machinery for textiles manufacturing |
| 313220 | Braiding narrow fabrics |
| 336340 | Brake and brake parts, automotive, truck, and bus, manufacturing |
| 336340 | Brake caliper assemblies, automotive, truck, and bus, manufacturing |
| 336340 | Brake cylinders, master and wheel, automotive, truck, and bus, manufacturing |
| 336340 | Brake discs (rotor), automotive, truck, and bus, manufacturing |
| 336340 | Brake drums, automotive, truck, and bus, manufacturing |
| 325998 | Brake fluid, synthetic, manufacturing |
| 324191 | Brake fluids, petroleum, made from refined petroleum |
| 336340 | Brake hose assemblies manufacturing |
| 336340 | Brake linings, automotive, truck, and bus, manufacturing |
| 336340 | Brake pads and shoes, automotive, truck, and bus, manufacturing |
| 811114 | Brake repair shops, automotive |
| 333310 | Brake service equipment (except mechanic's handtools), motor vehicle, manufacturing |
| 336340 | Brake shoes and pads, asbestos, manufacturing |
| 335314 | Brakes and clutches, electromagnetic, manufacturing |
| 336510 | Brakes and parts for railroad rolling stock manufacturing |
| 335314 | Brakes, electromagnetic, manufacturing |
| 333517 | Brakes, press, metalworking, manufacturing |
| 311212 | Bran and other residues of milling rice |
| 522110 | Branches of foreign banks |
| 521110 | Branches, Federal Reserve Bank |
| 533110 | Brand name licensing |

| | |
|---|---|
| 115210 | Branding |
| 339940 | Branding irons (i.e., marking irons) manufacturing |
| 424820 | Brandy and brandy spirits merchant wholesalers |
| 312130 | Brandy distilling |
| 315210 | Bra-slips cut and sew apparel contractors |
| 315250 | Bra-slips, women's and girls', cut and sewn from purchased fabric (except apparel contractors) |
| 331523 | Brass die-castings, unfinished, manufacturing |
| 331529 | Brass foundries (except die-casting) |
| 423720 | Brass goods, plumbers', merchant wholesalers |
| 325612 | Brass polishes manufacturing |
| 331420 | Brass products, rolling, drawing, or extruding, made from purchased copper or in integrated secondary smelting and rolling, drawing or extruding plants |
| 315210 | Brassieres cut and sew apparel contractors |
| 315250 | Brassieres cut and sewn from purchased fabric (except apparel contractors) |
| 332323 | Brasswork, ornamental, manufacturing |
| 335220 | Braziers, barbecue, manufacturing |
| 111335 | Brazil nut farming |
| 325194 | Brazilwood extract manufacturing |
| 332811 | Brazing (i.e., hardening) metals and metal products for the trade |
| 311824 | Bread and bread-type roll mixes made from purchased flour |
| 311812 | Bread and bread-type rolls made in commercial bakeries |
| 311999 | Bread crumbs not made in bakeries |
| 335210 | Bread machines, household-type electric, manufacturing |
| 333241 | Bread slicing machinery manufacturing |
| 333993 | Bread wrapping machines manufacturing |
| 424490 | Bread, packaged (except frozen), merchant wholesalers |
| 333131 | Breakers, coal, manufacturing |
| 332919 | Breakers, vacuum, plumbing, manufacturing |
| 311340 | Breakfast bars, nonchocolate covered, manufacturing |
| 311230 | Breakfast cereals manufacturing |
| 424490 | Breakfast cereals merchant wholesalers |
| 237990 | Breakwater construction |

| | |
|---|---|
| 334519 | Breath alcohol testing devices manufacturing |
| 334519 | Breathalyzers manufacturing |
| 332313 | Breechings, fabricated metal plate work, manufacturing |
| 112990 | Breeding of butterflies |
| 112990 | Breeding of pets (e.g., birds, cats, dogs) |
| 115210 | Breeding, animal, services |
| 722511 | Brew pub restaurants, primarily serving meals, full service |
| 722410 | Brew pubs, primarily serving alcoholic beverages for immediate consumption |
| 312120 | Breweries |
| 311211 | Brewers' and distillers' flakes and grits, corn, manufacturing |
| 311213 | Brewers' malt manufacturing |
| 325194 | Brewers' pitch made by distillation of wood |
| 311212 | Brewers' rice manufacturing |
| 424490 | Brewers' yeast merchant wholesalers |
| 333241 | Brewery machinery manufacturing |
| 238990 | Brick driveway contractors |
| 238990 | Brick paver (e.g., driveways, patios, sidewalks) installation |
| 238140 | Brick veneer, installation |
| 238140 | Bricklaying contractors |
| 423320 | Bricks (except refractory) merchant wholesalers |
| 327120 | Bricks (i.e., common, face, glazed, hollow, vitrified), clay, manufacturing |
| 327120 | Bricks, adobe, manufacturing |
| 327120 | Bricks, clay refractory, manufacturing |
| 327331 | Bricks, concrete, manufacturing |
| 327215 | Bricks, glass, made from purchased glass |
| 327212 | Bricks, glass, made in glass making plants |
| 327120 | Bricks, nonclay refractory, manufacturing |
| 315210 | Bridal dresses or gowns cut and sew apparel contractors |
| 315250 | Bridal dresses or gowns, custom made |
| 315250 | Bridal dresses or gowns, women's and girls', cut and sewn from purchased fabric (except apparel contractors) |
| 458110 | Bridal gown shops (except custom) |
| 532281 | Bridal wear rental |
| 333998 | Bridge and gate lifting machinery manufacturing |
| 611699 | Bridge and other card game instruction |

| | |
|---|---|
| 321114 | Bridge and trestle parts, wood, treating |
| 237310 | Bridge approach construction |
| 713990 | Bridge clubs, recreational |
| 237310 | Bridge construction |
| 237310 | Bridge decking construction |
| 238320 | Bridge painting |
| 332312 | Bridge sections, prefabricated metal, manufacturing |
| 488490 | Bridge, tunnel, and highway operations |
| 339116 | Bridges, custom made in dental laboratories |
| 334515 | Bridges, electrical (e.g., Kelvin, megohm, vacuum tube, Wheatstone), manufacturing |
| 316110 | Bridle leather manufacturing |
| 237990 | Bridle path construction |
| 423990 | Briefcases merchant wholesalers |
| 316990 | Briefcases, all materials, manufacturing |
| 315210 | Briefs cut and sew apparel contractors |
| 315120 | Briefs, underwear, made in apparel knitting mills |
| 315250 | Briefs, underwear, men's and boys', cut and sewn from purchased fabric (except apparel contractors) |
| 315250 | Briefs, underwear, women's, girls', and infants', cut and sewn from purchased fabric (except apparel contractors) |
| 212390 | Brimstone mining and/or beneficiating |
| 311421 | Brining of fruits and vegetables |
| 212210 | Briquets, iron, mining and/or beneficiating |
| 324199 | Briquettes, petroleum, made from refined petroleum |
| 424590 | Bristles merchant wholesalers |
| 322130 | Bristols board stock manufacturing |
| 322120 | Bristols paper stock manufacturing |
| 333515 | Broaches (i.e., a machine tool accessory) manufacturing |
| 423830 | Broaches (i.e., a machine tool accessory) merchant wholesalers |
| 333517 | Broaching machines, metalworking, manufacturing |
| 334220 | Broadcast equipment (including studio), for radio and television, manufacturing |
| 811210 | Broadcast equipment repair and maintenance services |
| 541910 | Broadcast media rating services |
| 423690 | Broadcasting equipment merchant wholesalers |

| | |
|---|---|
| 516210 | Broadcasting exclusively on Internet, audio |
| 516210 | Broadcasting exclusively on Internet, video |
| 516210 | Broadcasting networks, radio |
| 516210 | Broadcasting networks, television |
| 611519 | Broadcasting schools |
| 236220 | Broadcasting station construction |
| 516110 | Broadcasting stations (except exclusively on Internet), radio |
| 516120 | Broadcasting stations, television |
| 516110 | Broadcasting studio, radio station |
| 711110 | Broadway theaters |
| 313210 | Broadwoven fabrics (except rugs, tire fabrics) weaving |
| 313310 | Broadwoven fabrics finishing |
| 313210 | Brocades weaving |
| 111219 | Broccoli farming, field, bedding plant and seed production |
| 424920 | Brochures merchant wholesalers |
| 112320 | Broiler chicken production |
| 523160 | Brokerages, commodity contracts |
| 524210 | Brokerages, insurance |
| 522310 | Brokerages, loan |
| 522310 | Brokerages, mortgage |
| 531210 | Brokerages, real estate |
| 523150 | Brokerages, securities |
| 524210 | Brokers' offices, insurance |
| 522310 | Brokers' offices, loan |
| 522310 | Brokers' offices, mortgage |
| 531210 | Brokers' offices, real estate |
| 325180 | Bromine manufacturing |
| 325199 | Bromochloromethane manufacturing |
| 339112 | Bronchoscopes (except electromedical) manufacturing |
| 334510 | Bronchoscopes, electromedical, manufacturing |
| 331523 | Bronze die-castings, unfinished, manufacturing |
| 331529 | Bronze foundries (except die-casting) |
| 325910 | Bronze printing inks manufacturing |
| 331420 | Bronze products, rolling, drawing, or extruding, made from purchased copper or in integrated secondary smelting and rolling, drawing or extruding plants |
| 111199 | Broomcorn farming |
| 424590 | Broomcorn merchant wholesalers |

| | |
|---|---|
| 423850 | Brooms (except household-type) merchant wholesalers |
| 423220 | Brooms and brushes, household-type, merchant wholesalers |
| 339994 | Brooms, hand and machine, manufacturing |
| 311422 | Broth (except seafood) canning |
| 311313 | Brown beet sugar refining |
| 212114 | Brown coal mining and/or beneficiating |
| 212210 | Brown ore mining and/or beneficiating |
| 311313 | Brown sugar made from beet sugar |
| 311314 | Brown sugar manufacturing |
| 325411 | Brucine manufacturing |
| 212323 | Brucite mining and/or beneficiating |
| 335991 | Brush blocks, carbon or molded graphite, manufacturing |
| 321912 | Brush blocks, wood, turned and shaped |
| 562119 | Brush collection services |
| 562119 | Brush hauling, local |
| 562119 | Brush removal services |
| 335991 | Brushes and brush stock contacts, electric, carbon and graphite, manufacturing |
| 339940 | Brushes, artists', manufacturing |
| 424990 | Brushes, artists', merchant wholesalers |
| 339994 | Brushes, household-type and industrial, manufacturing |
| 423840 | Brushes, industrial, merchant wholesalers |
| 339994 | Brushes, paint (except artists'), manufacturing |
| 326299 | Brushes, rubber, manufacturing |
| 333517 | Brushing machines, metalworking, manufacturing |
| 335991 | Brushplates, carbon or graphite, manufacturing |
| 111219 | Brussel sprout farming, field, bedding plant and seed production |
| 325620 | Bubble bath preparations manufacturing |
| 326199 | Bubble packaging materials, plastics, manufacturing |
| 333120 | Bucket and scarifier teeth manufacturing |
| 333922 | Buckets, elevator or conveyor, manufacturing |
| 333120 | Buckets, excavating (e.g., clamshell, concrete, drag scraper, dragline, shovel), manufacturing |
| 321920 | Buckets, wood, coopered, manufacturing |
| 339993 | Buckles and buckle parts (including shoe) manufacturing |

| | |
|---|---|
| 111199 | Buckwheat farming |
| 311211 | Buckwheat flour manufacturing |
| 921130 | Budget agencies, government |
| 112990 | Buffalo production |
| 722514 | Buffet eating places |
| 337122 | Buffets (furniture), wood, manufacturing |
| 333517 | Buffing and polishing machines, metalworking, manufacturing |
| 327910 | Buffing and polishing wheels, abrasive and nonabrasive, manufacturing |
| 325612 | Buffing compounds manufacturing |
| 333991 | Buffing machines, handheld power-driven, manufacturing |
| 332813 | Buffing metals and metal products for the trade |
| 316110 | Buffings, russet, manufacturing |
| 332510 | Builder's hardware, metal, manufacturing |
| 541310 | Building architectural design services |
| 238210 | Building automation system installation contractors |
| 423320 | Building blocks (e.g., cinder, concrete) merchant wholesalers |
| 423310 | Building board (e.g., fiber, flake, particle) merchant wholesalers |
| 561720 | Building cleaning services, interior |
| 561720 | Building cleaning services, janitorial |
| 238910 | Building demolition |
| 541690 | Building envelope consulting services |
| 561790 | Building exterior cleaning services (except sandblasting, window cleaning) |
| 238310 | Building fireproofing contractors |
| 238390 | Building fixture and fitting (except mechanical equipment) installation |
| 238130 | Building framing (except structural steel) |
| 561790 | Building gas systems conversion (e.g., from manufactured to natural gas) services |
| 541350 | Building inspection bureaus |
| 541350 | Building inspection services |
| 926150 | Building inspections, government |
| 238310 | Building insulation contractors |
| 238910 | Building interior gutting and stripping |
| 237210 | Building lot subdividing |
| 326199 | Building materials (e.g., fascia, panels, siding, soffit), plastics, manufacturing |
| 444180 | Building materials supply dealers |

| | |
|---|---|
| 423390 | Building materials, fiberglass (except insulation, roofing, siding), merchant wholesalers |
| 213112 | Building oil and gas well foundations on a contract basis |
| 326199 | Building panels, corrugated and flat, plastics, manufacturing |
| 423390 | Building paper merchant wholesalers |
| 322120 | Building paper stock manufacturing |
| 334512 | Building services monitoring controls, automatic, manufacturing |
| 925110 | Building standards agencies, government |
| 423320 | Building stone merchant wholesalers |
| 327120 | Building tile, clay, manufacturing |
| 531110 | Building, apartment, rental or leasing |
| 213112 | Building, erecting, repairing, and dismantling oil and gas field rigs and derricks on a contract basis |
| 531120 | Building, nonresidential (except miniwarehouse), rental or leasing |
| 236118 | Building, residential, addition, alteration and renovation |
| 531110 | Building, residential, rental or leasing |
| 321991 | Buildings, mobile, commercial use, manufacturing |
| 332311 | Buildings, prefabricated metal, manufacturing |
| 423390 | Buildings, prefabricated nonwood, merchant wholesalers |
| 423310 | Buildings, prefabricated wood, merchant wholesalers |
| 321992 | Buildings, prefabricated, wood, manufacturing |
| 238350 | Built-in wood cabinets constructed on site |
| 327999 | Built-up mica manufacturing |
| 335139 | Bulbs, electric light, complete, manufacturing |
| 311211 | Bulgur (flour) manufacturing |
| 424710 | Bulk gasoline stations, merchant wholesalers |
| 484220 | Bulk liquids trucking, local |
| 484230 | Bulk liquids trucking, long-distance |
| 484110 | Bulk mail truck transportation, contract, local |
| 484121 | Bulk mail truck transportation, contract, long-distance (TL) |
| 493190 | Bulk petroleum storage |
| 424710 | Bulk stations, petroleum, merchant wholesalers |
| 332420 | Bulk storage tanks, heavy gauge metal, manufacturing |
| 237990 | Bulkhead wall or embankment construction |
| 115210 | Bull testing stations |
| 532412 | Bulldozer rental or leasing without operator |
| 238910 | Bulldozer rental with operator |
| 333120 | Bulldozers manufacturing |
| 332992 | Bullet jackets and cores (i.e., 30 mm. or less, 1.18 inch or less) manufacturing |
| 321999 | Bulletin boards, wood and cork, manufacturing |
| 339113 | Bulletproof vests manufacturing |
| 423990 | Bulletproof vests merchant wholesalers |
| 212220 | Bullion, gold, produced at the mine |
| 212220 | Bullion, silver, produced at the mine |
| 336390 | Bumpers and bumperettes assembled, automotive, truck, and bus, manufacturing |
| 333310 | Bundling machinery (e.g., box strapping, mail, newspaper) manufacturing |
| 321999 | Bungs, wood, manufacturing |
| 236220 | Bunkhouse construction |
| 339113 | Bunsen burners manufacturing |
| 315210 | Buntings cut and sew apparel contractors |
| 315250 | Buntings, infants', cut and sewn from purchased fabric (except apparel contractors) |
| 334513 | Buoyancy instruments, industrial process-type, manufacturing |
| 321999 | Buoys, cork, manufacturing |
| 332313 | Buoys, fabricated plate work metal, manufacturing |
| 561621 | Burglar alarm monitoring services |
| 561621 | Burglar alarm sales combined with installation, repair, or monitoring services |
| 238210 | Burglar alarm system, electric, installation only |
| 334290 | Burglar alarm systems and equipment manufacturing |
| 524126 | Burglary and theft insurance carriers, direct |
| 339995 | Burial caskets and cases manufacturing |
| 423850 | Burial caskets merchant wholesalers |
| 315210 | Burial garments cut and sew apparel contractors |
| 315250 | Burial garments cut and sewn from purchased fabric (except apparel contractors) |

| | |
|---|---|
| 524128 | Burial insurance carriers, direct |
| 339995 | Burial vaults (except concrete, stone) manufacturing |
| 327390 | Burial vaults, concrete and precast terrazzo, manufacturing |
| 327991 | Burial vaults, stone, manufacturing |
| 424990 | Burlap merchant wholesalers |
| 711110 | Burlesque companies |
| 212323 | Burley mining and/or beneficiating |
| 313310 | Burling and mending fabrics |
| 335311 | Burner ignition transformers manufacturing |
| 423720 | Burners, fuel oil and distillate oil, merchant wholesalers |
| 333414 | Burners, heating, manufacturing |
| 423830 | Burners, industrial, merchant wholesalers |
| 332811 | Burning metals and metal products for the trade |
| 333517 | Burnishing machines, metalworking, manufacturing |
| 321999 | Burnt wood articles manufacturing |
| 314999 | Burnt-out laces manufacturing |
| 112920 | Burro production |
| 212390 | Burrstones, natural, mining and/or beneficiating |
| 335313 | Bus bar structures, switchgear-type, manufacturing |
| 423610 | Bus bars and trolley ducts merchant wholesalers |
| 335931 | Bus bars, electrical conductors (except switchgear-type), manufacturing |
| 336211 | Bus bodies assembling on purchased chassis |
| 336211 | Bus bodies manufacturing |
| 541850 | Bus card advertising services |
| 485510 | Bus charter services (except scenic, sightseeing) |
| 541850 | Bus display advertising services |
| 611519 | Bus driver training |
| 485210 | Bus line operation, intercity |
| 485113 | Bus line, local (except mixed mode) |
| 423110 | Bus merchant wholesalers |
| 485410 | Bus operation, school and employee |
| 532120 | Bus rental or leasing |
| 485113 | Bus services, urban and suburban (except mixed mode) |
| 236220 | Bus shelter construction |
| 236220 | Bus terminal construction |
| 488490 | Bus terminal operation, independent |
| 561599 | Bus ticket offices |
| 485113 | Bus transit systems (except mixed mode) |
| 336120 | Buses (except trackless trolley) assembling on chassis of own manufacture |
| 487110 | Buses, scenic and sightseeing operation |
| 336510 | Buses, trackless trolley, manufacturing |
| 333613 | Bushings, plain (except internal combustion engine), manufacturing |
| 326199 | Bushings, plastics, manufacturing |
| 321999 | Bushings, wood, manufacturing |
| 813910 | Business associations |
| 541990 | Business brokers (except real estate brokers) |
| 611410 | Business colleges or schools not offering academic degrees |
| 611310 | Business colleges or schools offering baccalaureate or graduate degrees |
| 323111 | Business directories commercial printing (except screen) without publishing |
| 323113 | Business directories screen printing without publishing |
| 513140 | Business directory publishers |
| 513140 | Business directory publishers (except exclusive Internet publishing) |
| 513140 | Business directory publishers and printing combined |
| 513140 | Business directory publishers, exclusively on Internet |
| 323113 | Business forms (except manifold) screen printing without publishing |
| 323111 | Business forms commercial printing (except screen) without publishing |
| 323111 | Business forms, manifold, printing |
| 423420 | Business machines and equipment (except computers) merchant wholesalers |
| 541611 | Business management consulting services |
| 561110 | Business management services |
| 541720 | Business research and development services |
| 611410 | Business schools not offering academic degrees |
| 561439 | Business service centers (except private mail centers) |
| 561439 | Business service centers (except private mail centers) providing range of office support services (except printing) |
| 541611 | Business start-up consulting services |

| | |
|---|---|
| 523999 | Business start-up fundraising using a crowdfunding platform |
| 425120 | Business to business electronic markets, durable goods, wholesale trade |
| 425120 | Business to business electronic markets, nondurable goods, wholesale trade |
| 325211 | Butadiene copolymers containing less than 50 percent butadiene manufacturing |
| 325212 | Butadiene copolymers containing more than 50 percent butadiene manufacturing |
| 325199 | Butadiene made from alcohol |
| 325110 | Butadiene made from refined petroleum or liquid hydrocarbons |
| 325212 | Butadiene rubber (i.e., polybutadiene) manufacturing |
| 424720 | Butane gas merchant wholesalers (except bulk stations, terminals) |
| 325110 | Butane made from refined petroleum or liquid hydrocarbons |
| 211130 | Butane, natural, mining |
| 445240 | Butcher shops |
| 332215 | Butcher's knives manufacturing |
| 311512 | Butter manufacturing |
| 424430 | Butter merchant wholesalers |
| 333241 | Butter processing machinery manufacturing |
| 311225 | Butter substitutes made from purchased oils |
| 424490 | Butter substitutes merchant wholesalers |
| 311512 | Butter, creamery and whey, manufacturing |
| 332911 | Butterfly valves, industrial-type, manufacturing |
| 311511 | Buttermilk manufacturing |
| 424430 | Buttermilk merchant wholesalers |
| 111219 | Butternut squash farming, field, bedding plant and seed production |
| 335910 | Button cells, primary batteries, manufacturing |
| 333248 | Buttonhole and eyelet machinery manufacturing |
| 315210 | Buttonhole making apparel contractors |
| 315210 | Buttonhole making, fur goods, cut and sew apparel contractors |
| 315210 | Buttonholing and button covering apparel contractors |
| 339993 | Buttons (except precious metal, precious stones, semiprecious stones) manufacturing |
| 424310 | Buttons merchant wholesalers |
| 339910 | Buttons, precious metal, precious stones, semiprecious stones, manufacturing |
| 325199 | Butyl acetate manufacturing |
| 325212 | Butyl rubber manufacturing |
| 324110 | Butylene (i.e., butene) made in petroleum refineries |
| 325110 | Butylene made from refined petroleum or liquid hydrocarbons |
| 531210 | Buyers' agents, real estate, offices |
| 531210 | Buying agencies, real estate |
| 531210 | Buying real estate for others (i.e., agents, brokers) |
| 485310 | Cab (i.e., taxi) services |
| 336110 | Cab and chassis, light trucks and vans, manufacturing |
| 111219 | Cabbage farming, field, bedding plant and seed production |
| 236115 | Cabin construction general contractors |
| 336612 | Cabin cruiser building |
| 334511 | Cabin environment indicators, transmitters, and sensors manufacturing |
| 236117 | Cabin for-sale builders |
| 423710 | Cabinet hardware and fittings merchant wholesalers |
| 332510 | Cabinet hardware, metal, manufacturing |
| 444180 | Cabinet stores, kitchen (except custom), to be installed |
| 238350 | Cabinet work performed at the construction site |
| 238350 | Cabinetry work performed at the construction site |
| 337214 | Cabinets (except wood), office-type, freestanding, manufacturing |
| 321999 | Cabinets (i.e., housings), wood (e.g., sewing machines, stereo, television), manufacturing |
| 337110 | Cabinets, kitchen (except freestanding), stock or custom wood, manufacturing |
| 423310 | Cabinets, kitchen, built-in, merchant wholesalers |
| 423210 | Cabinets, kitchen, freestanding, merchant wholesalers |
| 337126 | Cabinets, metal (i.e., bathroom, kitchen), manufacturing |
| 337126 | Cabinets, metal household-type, freestanding, manufacturing |
| 337126 | Cabinets, metal, radio and television, manufacturing |
| 238350 | Cabinets, wood built-in, constructed on site |
| 337122 | Cabinets, wood household-type, freestanding, manufacturing |
| 337211 | Cabinets, wood office-type, freestanding, manufacturing |
| 721199 | Cabins, housekeeping |

| | |
|---|---|
| 516210 | Cable broadcasting networks |
| 485119 | Cable car systems (except mixed mode), commuter |
| 487110 | Cable car, land, scenic and sightseeing operation |
| 334220 | Cable decoders manufacturing |
| 237130 | Cable laying (e.g., fiber optic, electricity, marine, telephone, cable television), including underground |
| 517111 | Cable program distribution operators |
| 238990 | Cable splicing (except electrical or fiber optic) |
| 238210 | Cable splicing, electrical or fiber optic |
| 517111 | Cable television distribution services |
| 238210 | Cable television hookup contractors |
| 516210 | Cable television networks |
| 334220 | Cable television transmission and receiving equipment manufacturing |
| 517111 | Cable TV providers (except networks) |
| 331420 | Cable, copper (e.g., armored, bare, insulated), made from purchased copper in wire drawing plants |
| 331420 | Cable, copper (e.g., armored, bare, insulated), made in integrated secondary smelting and wire drawing plants |
| 331222 | Cable, iron or steel, insulated or armored, made in wire drawing plants |
| 335929 | Cable, nonferrous, insulated, or armored, made from purchased nonferrous wire |
| 332618 | Cable, noninsulated wire, made from purchased wire |
| 423510 | Cable, wire (except insulated), merchant wholesalers |
| 333111 | Cabs for agricultural machinery manufacturing |
| 333120 | Cabs for construction machinery manufacturing |
| 333924 | Cabs for industrial trucks manufacturing |
| 111339 | Cactus fruit farming |
| 541512 | CAD (computer-aided design) systems integration design services |
| 541370 | Cadastral surveying services |
| 339920 | Caddy carts manufacturing |
| 331410 | Cadmium refining, primary |
| 541512 | CAE (computer-aided engineering) systems integration design services |
| 722513 | Cafes, limited-service |
| 337215 | Cafeteria fixtures manufacturing |
| 722310 | Cafeteria food services contractors (e.g., government office cafeterias, hospital cafeterias, school cafeterias) |
| 337127 | Cafeteria furniture manufacturing |
| 337127 | Cafeteria tables and benches manufacturing |
| 722514 | Cafeterias |
| 325411 | Caffeine and derivatives (i.e., basic chemicals) manufacturing |
| 315210 | Caftans cut and sew apparel contractors |
| 315250 | Caftans, men's and boys', cut and sewn from purchased fabric (except apparel contractors) |
| 315250 | Caftans, women's, girls', and infants', cut and sewn from purchased fabric (except apparel contractors) |
| 332618 | Cages made from purchased wire |
| 238910 | Caisson (i.e., drilled building foundations) construction |
| 237990 | Caisson (i.e., marine or pneumatic structures) construction |
| 332420 | Caissons, underwater work, heavy gauge metal, manufacturing |
| 459999 | Cake decorating supply stores |
| 311999 | Cake frosting manufacturing |
| 311942 | Cake frosting mixes manufacturing |
| 311824 | Cake mixes made from purchased flour |
| 311340 | Cake ornaments, confectionery, manufacturing |
| 311813 | Cake, frozen, manufacturing |
| 311812 | Cakes, baking (except frozen), made in commercial bakeries |
| 212230 | Calamine mining and/or beneficiating |
| 212220 | Calaverite mining and/or beneficiating |
| 212312 | Calcareous tufa crushed and broken stone mining and/or beneficiating |
| 212311 | Calcareous tufa mining or quarrying |
| 325510 | Calcimines manufacturing |
| 424950 | Calcimines merchant wholesalers |
| 212390 | Calcined phosphate rock mining and/or beneficiating |
| 324199 | Calcining petroleum coke from refined petroleum |
| 212390 | Calcite mining and/or beneficiating |
| 325180 | Calcium carbide, chloride, and hypochlorite manufacturing |
| 325199 | Calcium citrate manufacturing |
| 327410 | Calcium hydroxide (i.e., hydrated lime) manufacturing |
| 325180 | Calcium hypochlorite manufacturing |

| | |
|---|---|
| 325180 | Calcium inorganic compounds, not specified elsewhere by process, manufacturing |
| 325199 | Calcium organic compounds, not specified elsewhere by process, manufacturing |
| 325199 | Calcium oxalate manufacturing |
| 327410 | Calcium oxide (i.e., quicklime) manufacturing |
| 423420 | Calculators and calculating machines merchant wholesalers |
| 333310 | Calculators manufacturing |
| 513199 | Calendar publishers |
| 513199 | Calendar publishers (except exclusive Internet publishing) |
| 513199 | Calendar publishers and printing combined |
| 513199 | Calendar publishers, exclusively on Internet |
| 459999 | Calendar shops |
| 323111 | Calendars commercial printing (except screen) without publishing |
| 323113 | Calendars screen printing without publishing |
| 333248 | Calendering machinery for plastics manufacturing |
| 333248 | Calendering machinery for textiles manufacturing |
| 313310 | Calendering textile products, apparel, and fabrics |
| 112111 | Calf (e.g., feeder, stocker, veal) production |
| 315120 | Calf high sheer hosiery knitting or knitting and finishing |
| 541380 | Calibration and certification testing laboratories or services |
| 332216 | Calipers and dividers, machinists' precision tools, manufacturing |
| 336340 | Calipers, brake, automotive, truck, and bus, manufacturing |
| 339992 | Calliopes (steam organs) manufacturing |
| 541512 | CAM (computer-aided manufacturing) systems integration design services |
| 532210 | Camcorder rental |
| 423410 | Camcorders (except household-type) merchant wholesalers |
| 334310 | Camcorders manufacturing |
| 326211 | Camelback (i.e., retreading material) manufacturing |
| 333248 | Camelback (i.e., retreading materials) machinery manufacturing |
| 316990 | Camera carrying bags, all materials, manufacturing |
| 423410 | Camera equipment and supplies, photographic, merchant wholesalers |
| 333310 | Camera lenses manufacturing |
| 811210 | Camera repair shops without retailing new cameras |
| 449210 | Camera shops, photographic |
| 711510 | Cameramen, independent (freelance) |
| 333310 | Cameras (except television, video) manufacturing |
| 334220 | Cameras, television, manufacturing |
| 423410 | Cameras, television, merchant wholesalers |
| 423410 | Cameras, video (except household-type), merchant wholesalers |
| 315210 | Camisoles cut and sew apparel contractors |
| 315250 | Camisoles, women's and girls', cut and sewn from purchased fabric (except apparel contractors) |
| 337126 | Camp furniture, metal, manufacturing |
| 337126 | Camp furniture, reed and rattan, manufacturing |
| 337122 | Camp furniture, wood, manufacturing |
| 813940 | Campaign organizations, political |
| 441210 | Camper dealers, recreational |
| 441210 | Camper parts and accessories stores |
| 532120 | Camper rental |
| 336214 | Camper units, slide-in, for pick-up trucks, manufacturing |
| 721211 | Campgrounds |
| 325194 | Camphor, natural, manufacturing |
| 325199 | Camphor, synthetic, manufacturing |
| 459110 | Camping and hiking equipment stores |
| 423910 | Camping equipment and supplies merchant wholesalers |
| 423110 | Camping trailer merchant wholesalers |
| 336214 | Camping trailers and chassis manufacturing |
| 721214 | Camps (except day, instructional) |
| 713990 | Camps (except instructional), day |
| 623990 | Camps, boot or disciplinary (except correctional), for delinquent youth |
| 611620 | Camps, sports instruction |
| 721211 | Campsites |
| 333515 | Cams (i.e., a machine tool accessory) manufacturing |
| 333517 | Can forming machines, metalworking, manufacturing |
| 332618 | Can keys made from purchased wire |

| | |
|---|---|
| 332431 | Can lids and ends, light gauge metal, manufacturing |
| 332216 | Can openers (except electric) manufacturing |
| 335210 | Can openers, household-type electric, manufacturing |
| 483211 | Canal barge transportation (freight) |
| 237990 | Canal construction |
| 488310 | Canal maintenance services (except dredging) |
| 488310 | Canal operation |
| 483212 | Canal passenger transportation |
| 221310 | Canal, irrigation |
| 333310 | Canceling machinery, postal office-type, manufacturing |
| 923120 | Cancer detection program administration |
| 622310 | Cancer hospitals |
| 311340 | Candied fruits and fruit peel manufacturing |
| 713950 | Candle pin bowling alleys |
| 713950 | Candle pin bowling centers |
| 459999 | Candle shops |
| 339999 | Candles manufacturing |
| 424990 | Candles merchant wholesalers |
| 311351 | Candy bars, chocolate (including chocolate covered), made from cacao beans |
| 311340 | Candy bars, nonchocolate, manufacturing |
| 424450 | Candy merchant wholesalers |
| 311352 | Candy stores, chocolate, candy made on premises not for immediate consumption |
| 311340 | Candy stores, nonchocolate, candy made on premises, not for immediate consumption |
| 445292 | Candy stores, packaged, retailing only |
| 311351 | Candy, chocolate, made from cacao beans |
| 111930 | Cane farming, sugar, field production |
| 311314 | Cane sugar manufacturing |
| 424490 | Cane sugar, refined, merchant wholesalers |
| 311314 | Cane syrup manufacturing |
| 339999 | Canes (except orthopedic) manufacturing |
| 332993 | Canisters, ammunition, manufacturing |
| 325998 | Cannabidiol (CBD oil) manufacturing |
| 424690 | Cannabidiol (CBD oil) merchant wholesalers |
| 459999 | Cannabidiol (CBD oil) retailers |

| | |
|---|---|
| 424590 | Cannabis merchant wholesalers |
| 111998 | Cannabis, grown in an open field |
| 111419 | Cannabis, grown under cover |
| 424490 | Canned foods (e.g., fish, meat, seafood, soups) merchant wholesalers |
| 311611 | Canned meats (except poultry) produced in slaughtering plants |
| 311911 | Canned nuts manufacturing |
| 236210 | Cannery construction |
| 311710 | Cannery, seafood |
| 311421 | Canning fruits and vegetables |
| 311421 | Canning jams and jellies |
| 333993 | Canning machinery manufacturing |
| 311615 | Canning poultry (except baby and pet food) |
| 311422 | Canning soups (except seafood) |
| 423840 | Canning supplies merchant wholesalers |
| 311710 | Canning, fish, crustacea, and mollusks |
| 332994 | Cannons manufacturing |
| 339112 | Cannulae manufacturing |
| 532284 | Canoe rental |
| 713990 | Canoeing, recreational |
| 311225 | Canola (rapeseed) oil, cake and meal, made from purchased oils |
| 311224 | Canola (rapeseed) oil, cake and meal, made in crushing mills |
| 111120 | Canola farming, field and seed production |
| 332322 | Canopies, sheet metal (except stampings), manufacturing |
| 332431 | Cans, aluminum, light gauge metal, manufacturing |
| 332431 | Cans, light gauge metal, manufacturing |
| 332431 | Cans, steel, light gauge metal, manufacturing |
| 111219 | Cantaloupe farming, field, bedding plant and seed production |
| 722515 | Canteens, fixed location |
| 722330 | Canteens, mobile |
| 321912 | Cants, resawed (lumber), manufacturing |
| 314910 | Canvas bags manufacturing |
| 339940 | Canvas board, artist's, manufacturing |
| 314910 | Canvas products made from purchased canvas or canvas substitutes |
| 424990 | Canvas products merchant wholesalers |
| 316210 | Canvas shoes, plastics soled fabric upper, manufacturing |
| 316210 | Canvas shoes, rubber soled fabric upper, manufacturing |

| | |
|---|---|
| 339940 | Canvas, artist's, prepared on frames, manufacturing |
| 313210 | Canvases weaving |
| 423610 | Capacitors (except electronic) merchant wholesalers |
| 335999 | Capacitors (except electronic), fixed and variable, manufacturing |
| 334416 | Capacitors, electronic, fixed and variable, manufacturing |
| 423690 | Capacitors, electronic, merchant wholesalers |
| 315210 | Capes cut and sew apparel contractors |
| 315250 | Capes, fur (except apparel contractors), manufacturing |
| 315250 | Capes, waterproof (e.g., plastics, rubber, similar materials), cut and sewn from purchased fabric (except apparel contractors) |
| 315250 | Capes, women's and girls', cut and sewn from purchased fabric (except apparel contractors) |
| 237110 | Capping of water wells |
| 333993 | Capping, sealing, and lidding packaging machinery manufacturing |
| 325199 | Caprolactam manufacturing |
| 315990 | Caps (except fur, leather) cut and sewn from purchased fabric (except apparel contractors) |
| 315210 | Caps (i.e., apparel accessory) cut and sew apparel contractors |
| 315990 | Caps (i.e., apparel accessory) cut and sewn from purchased fabric (except fur, leather, apparel contractors) |
| 315210 | Caps and gowns, academic, cut and sew apparel contractors |
| 315250 | Caps and gowns, academic, cut and sewn from purchased fabric (except apparel contractors) |
| 335931 | Caps and plugs, attachment, electric, manufacturing |
| 332119 | Caps and tops, bottle, metal, stamping |
| 336214 | Caps for pick-up trucks manufacturing |
| 325998 | Caps for toy pistols manufacturing |
| 315120 | Caps made in apparel knitting mills |
| 325920 | Caps, blasting and detonating, manufacturing |
| 332993 | Caps, bomb, manufacturing |
| 315250 | Caps, fur (except apparel contractors), manufacturing |
| 316990 | Caps, heel and toe, leather, manufacturing |
| 315250 | Caps, leather (except apparel contractors), manufacturing |
| 315210 | Caps, textiles, straw, fur-felt, and wool-felt, cut and sew apparel contractors |
| 315990 | Caps, textiles, straw, fur-felt, and wool-felt, cut and sewn from purchased fabric (except apparel contractors) |
| 325998 | Capsules, gelatin, empty, manufacturing |
| 334290 | Car alarm manufacturing |
| 336211 | Car bodies, kit, manufacturing |
| 811192 | Car detailers |
| 532112 | Car leasing |
| 483212 | Car lighters (i.e., ferries), inland waters (except on Great Lakes system) |
| 485999 | Car pool operation (except ridesharing and ridesharing arrangement services) |
| 488999 | Car pools, arrangement of (except ridesharing arrangement services) |
| 532111 | Car rental |
| 532111 | Car rental agencies |
| 561599 | Car rental reservation services |
| 811111 | Car repair shops, general |
| 332999 | Car seals, metal, manufacturing |
| 337126 | Car seats, infant, manufacturing |
| 334310 | Car stereos manufacturing |
| 522299 | Car title lending |
| 423850 | Car wash equipment and supplies merchant wholesalers |
| 811192 | Car washes |
| 333310 | Car washing machinery manufacturing |
| 331110 | Car wheels, rolled steel, made in iron and steel mills |
| 325180 | Carbides (e.g., boron, calcium, silicon, tungsten) manufacturing |
| 332994 | Carbines manufacturing |
| 325199 | Carbinol manufacturing |
| 325211 | Carbohydrate plastics manufacturing |
| 423510 | Carbon and alloy steel primary forms merchant wholesalers |
| 334510 | Carbon arc lamp units, electrotherapeutic (except infrared and ultraviolet), manufacturing |
| 325180 | Carbon black manufacturing |
| 424690 | Carbon black merchant wholesalers |
| 327120 | Carbon brick manufacturing |
| 325120 | Carbon dioxide manufacturing |
| 325180 | Carbon disulfide manufacturing |
| 335991 | Carbon electrodes and contacts, electric, manufacturing |
| 325180 | Carbon inorganic compounds manufacturing |

334290 Carbon monoxide detectors manufacturing

423690 Carbon monoxide detectors, electronic, merchant wholesalers

325199 Carbon organic compounds, not specified elsewhere by process, manufacturing

339940 Carbon paper manufacturing

335991 Carbon specialties for aerospace use (except gaskets) manufacturing

335991 Carbon specialties for electrical use manufacturing

335991 Carbon specialties for mechanical use (except gaskets) manufacturing

325199 Carbon tetrachloride manufacturing

325998 Carbon, activated, manufacturing

424490 Carbonated beverages merchant wholesalers

312111 Carbonated soda manufacturing

312111 Carbonated soft drinks manufacturing

325180 Carbonic acid manufacturing

333248 Carbonizing equipment for processing wool manufacturing

313310 Carbonizing textile fibers

335991 Carbons, electric, manufacturing

335991 Carbons, lighting, manufacturing

325998 Carburetor cleaners manufacturing

336310 Carburetors, all types, manufacturing

316990 Card cases (except metal) manufacturing

339910 Card cases, precious metal, manufacturing

423920 Card games merchant wholesalers

713290 Card rooms (e.g., poker rooms)

459420 Card shops, greeting

337122 Card table sets (furniture), wood, manufacturing

337126 Card table sets, metal, manufacturing

424130 Cardboard products merchant wholesalers

322130 Cardboard stock manufacturing

322220 Cardboard, laminated or surface coated, made from purchased paperboard

313230 Carded nonwoven fabrics manufacturing

313110 Carded yarn manufacturing

325412 Cardiac preparations manufacturing

333248 Carding machinery for textiles manufacturing

313310 Carding textile fibers

334510 Cardiodynameter manufacturing

334510 Cardiographs manufacturing

621111 Cardiologists' offices (e.g., centers, clinics)

334510 Cardiophone, electric, manufacturing

334510 Cardioscope manufacturing

334510 Cardiotachometer manufacturing

323111 Cards (e.g., business, greeting, playing, postcards, trading) commercial printing (except screen) without publishing

323113 Cards (e.g., business, greeting, playing, postcards, trading) screen printing without publishing

322299 Cards, die-cut (except office supply) made from purchased paper or paperboard

322230 Cards, die-cut office supply (e.g., index, library, time recording), made from purchased paper or paperboard

424120 Cards, greeting, merchant wholesalers

****** Cards, publishing -- see specific product

611710 Career and vocational counseling services (except rehabilitative)

481112 Cargo carriers, air, scheduled

488390 Cargo checkers, marine

811310 Cargo container repair and maintenance services

488330 Cargo salvaging, marine

336611 Cargo ship building

488390 Cargo surveyors, marine

488490 Cargo surveyors, truck transportation

423110 Cargo van merchant wholesalers

333310 Carnival and amusement park rides manufacturing

333310 Carnival and amusement park shooting gallery machinery manufacturing

423850 Carnival equipment merchant wholesalers

713990 Carnival ride concession operators (i.e., supplying and servicing in others' facilities)

711190 Carnival traveling shows

212290 Carnotite mining and/or beneficiating

333922 Carousel conveyors (e.g., luggage) manufacturing

333310 Carousels (i.e., merry-go-rounds) manufacturing

238350 Carpenters (except framing)

611513 Carpenters' apprenticeship training

332216 Carpenter's handtools, nonelectric, manufacturing

| | |
|---|---|
| 423710 | Carpenters' tools merchant wholesalers |
| 532490 | Carpentry equipment rental or leasing |
| 238350 | Carpentry work (except framing) |
| 238130 | Carpentry, framing |
| 333310 | Carpet and floor cleaning equipment, electric commercial-type, manufacturing |
| 335210 | Carpet and floor cleaning equipment, household-type electric, manufacturing |
| 532490 | Carpet and rug cleaning equipment rental or leasing |
| 313110 | Carpet and rug yarn spinning |
| 532289 | Carpet and rug, residential, rental |
| 423850 | Carpet cleaning equipment and supplies merchant wholesalers |
| 561740 | Carpet cleaning on customers' premises |
| 561740 | Carpet cleaning plants |
| 561740 | Carpet cleaning services |
| 314999 | Carpet cutting and binding |
| 313210 | Carpet linings (except felt) weaving |
| 423220 | Carpet merchant wholesalers |
| 313230 | Carpet paddings, nonwoven, manufacturing |
| 449121 | Carpet stores |
| 333310 | Carpet sweepers, mechanical, manufacturing |
| 238330 | Carpet, installation only |
| 314110 | Carpets and rugs made from textile materials |
| 321999 | Carpets, cork, manufacturing |
| 332311 | Carports, prefabricated metal, manufacturing |
| 487110 | Carriage, horse-drawn, operation |
| 339930 | Carriages, baby, manufacturing |
| 339930 | Carriages, doll, manufacturing |
| 334210 | Carrier equipment (i.e., analog, digital), telephone, manufacturing |
| 111219 | Carrot farming, field, bedding plant and seed production |
| 311991 | Carrots, cut, peeled or sliced fresh, manufacturing |
| 722513 | Carryout restaurants |
| 336110 | Cars, electric, for highway use, assembling on chassis of own manufacture |
| 333131 | Cars, mining, manufacturing |
| 541370 | Cartographic surveying services |
| 333993 | Carton filling machinery manufacturing |
| 423840 | Cartons (except paper and paperboard) merchant wholesalers |
| 322299 | Cartons, egg, molded pulp manufacturing |
| 322212 | Cartons, folding (except milk), made from purchased paperboard |
| 322219 | Cartons, milk, made from purchased paper or paperboard |
| 424130 | Cartons, paper and paperboard, merchant wholesalers |
| 711510 | Cartoonists, independent |
| 333991 | Cartridge (i.e., powder) handheld power-driven tools manufacturing |
| 332992 | Cartridge cases for ammunition (i.e., 30 mm. or less, 1.18 inch or less) manufacturing |
| 331420 | Cartridge cups, discs, and sheets, copper and copper alloy, made from purchased copper or in integrated secondary smelting and rolling, drawing or extruding plants |
| 424120 | Cartridge toner merchant wholesalers |
| 332992 | Cartridges (i.e., 30 mm. or less, 1.18 inch or less) manufacturing |
| 339920 | Carts, caddy, manufacturing |
| 423860 | Carts, golf, motorized passenger merchant wholesalers |
| 333924 | Carts, grocery, made from purchased wire |
| 333112 | Carts, lawn and garden-type, manufacturing |
| 332215 | Carving sets manufacturing |
| 111219 | Casaba melon farming, field, bedding plant and seed production |
| 316110 | Case leather manufacturing |
| 325220 | Casein fibers and filaments manufacturing |
| 325211 | Casein plastics manufacturing |
| 311514 | Casein, dry and wet, manufacturing |
| 332321 | Casements, metal, manufacturing |
| 316990 | Cases, jewelry (except metal), manufacturing |
| 339910 | Cases, jewelry, metal, manufacturing |
| 316990 | Cases, luggage, manufacturing |
| 316990 | Cases, musical instrument, manufacturing |
| 321920 | Cases, shipping, wood, wirebound, manufacturing |
| 321920 | Cases, wood packing, nailed or lock corner, manufacturing |
| 321920 | Cases, wood shipping, nailed or lock corner, manufacturing |
| 332439 | Cash boxes, light gauge metal, manufacturing |
| 532420 | Cash register rental or leasing |

333310 Cash registers (except point of sales terminals) manufacturing

423420 Cash registers merchant wholesalers

111335 Cashew farming

211130 Casing-head butane and propane production

326121 Casings, sausage, nonrigid plastics, manufacturing

332313 Casings, scroll, fabricated metal plate work, manufacturing

332322 Casings, sheet metal (except stampings), manufacturing

236220 Casino construction

721120 Casino hotels

423910 Casino supplies merchant wholesalers

713210 Casinos (except casino hotels)

713210 Casinos (except casino hotels) with racetrack

332510 Casket hardware, metal, manufacturing

339995 Caskets, burial, manufacturing

423850 Caskets, burial, merchant wholesalers

321920 Casks, wood, coopered, manufacturing

111219 Cassava farming, field and seed production

335210 Casseroles, household-type electric, manufacturing

334610 Cassette tapes, prerecorded audio, mass reproducing

532282 Cassette, prerecorded video, rental

423990 Cassettes, prerecorded audio and video, merchant wholesalers

331511 Cast iron brake shoes, railroad, manufacturing

331511 Cast iron pipe and pipe fittings manufacturing

423510 Cast iron pipe merchant wholesalers

331511 Cast iron railroad car wheels manufacturing

331513 Cast steel railroad car wheels, unfinished, manufacturing

327390 Cast stone, concrete (except structural), manufacturing

327120 Castable refractories, clay, manufacturing

327120 Castable refractories, nonclay, manufacturing

332510 Casters, furniture, metal manufacturing

332510 Casters, industrial, metal, manufacturing

561311 Casting agencies (i.e., motion picture, theatrical, video)

561311 Casting agencies, motion picture or video

561311 Casting agencies, theatrical

561311 Casting bureaus (e.g., motion picture, theatrical, video)

561311 Casting bureaus, motion picture or video

561311 Casting bureaus, theatrical

331529 Castings (except die-castings), nonferrous metals (except aluminum), unfinished, manufacturing

331524 Castings (except die-castings), unfinished, aluminum, manufacturing

331511 Castings, compacted graphite iron, unfinished, manufacturing

331511 Castings, malleable iron, unfinished, manufacturing

423510 Castings, metal, merchant wholesalers

331513 Castings, steel (except investment), unfinished, manufacturing

331511 Castings, unfinished iron (e.g., ductile, gray, malleable, semisteel), manufacturing

311224 Castor oil and pomace made in crushing mills

316210 Casual shoes, children's and infants', manufacturing

316210 Casual shoes, men's, manufacturing

316210 Casual shoes, women's, manufacturing

524126 Casualty insurance carriers, direct

621512 CAT (computerized axial tomography) scanner centers

311111 Cat food manufacturing

325998 Cat litter manufacturing

112990 Cat production

513199 Catalog (i.e., mail-order, store merchandise) publishers

513199 Catalog (i.e., mail-order, store merchandise) publishers (except exclusive Internet publishing)

513199 Catalog (i.e., mail-order, store merchandise) publishers and printing combined

513140 Catalog of collections publishers

513140 Catalog of collections publishers (except exclusive Internet publishing)

513140 Catalog of collections publishers and printing combined

513140 Catalog of collections publishers, exclusively on Internet

323111 Catalogs commercial printing (except screen) without publishing

323111 Catalogs of collections commercial printing (except screen) without publishing

| | |
|---|---|
| 323113 | Catalogs of collections screen printing without publishing |
| 323113 | Catalogs screen printing without publishing |
| 336390 | Catalytic converters, engine exhaust, automotive, truck, and bus, manufacturing |
| 332994 | Catapult guns manufacturing |
| 562998 | Catch basin cleaning services |
| 722320 | Caterers |
| 722320 | Catering services, social |
| 112511 | Catfish production, farm raising |
| 325412 | Cathartic preparations manufacturing |
| 339112 | Catheters manufacturing |
| 334419 | Cathode ray tubes (CRT) manufacturing |
| 335999 | Cathodic protection equipment manufacturing |
| 238190 | Cathodic protection, installation |
| 212390 | Catlinite mining and/or beneficiating |
| 424990 | Cats merchant wholesalers |
| 311421 | Catsup manufacturing |
| 112111 | Cattle conditioning operations |
| 112111 | Cattle farming or ranching |
| 333111 | Cattle feeding and watering equipment manufacturing |
| 112112 | Cattle feedlots (except stockyards for transportation) |
| 311119 | Cattle feeds, supplements, concentrates, and premixes, manufacturing |
| 424520 | Cattle merchant wholesalers |
| 115210 | Cattle spraying |
| 111219 | Cauliflower farming, field, bedding plant and seed production |
| 238390 | Caulking (i.e., waterproofing) contractors |
| 325520 | Caulking compounds (except gypsum base) manufacturing |
| 332216 | Caulking guns, nonpowered, manufacturing |
| 424690 | Caulking materials merchant wholesalers |
| 524291 | Cause-of-loss investigators, insurance |
| 237310 | Causeway construction |
| 325180 | Caustic potash manufacturing |
| 325180 | Caustic soda (i.e., sodium hydroxide) manufacturing |
| 424690 | Caustic soda merchant wholesalers |
| 712190 | Caverns (i.e., natural wonder tourist attractions) |
| 334220 | CB (citizens' band) radios manufacturing |
| 332216 | C-clamps manufacturing |
| 334112 | CD-ROM drives manufacturing |
| 334610 | CD-ROM, software, mass reproducing |
| 337122 | Cedar chests manufacturing |
| 325998 | Cedar oil manufacturing |
| 238130 | Ceiling beam, wood, installation |
| 444180 | Ceiling fan stores |
| 335210 | Ceiling fans with integral lighting fixture, residential, manufacturing |
| 335210 | Ceiling fans, residential, manufacturing |
| 335132 | Ceiling lighting fixtures, commercial, industrial, and institutional, manufacturing |
| 335131 | Ceiling lighting fixtures, residential, manufacturing |
| 321912 | Ceiling lumber, dressed, resawing purchased lumber |
| 321113 | Ceiling lumber, made from logs or bolts |
| 238310 | Ceiling tile installation |
| 423390 | Ceiling tile merchant wholesalers |
| 238390 | Ceiling, metal, installation |
| 334519 | Ceilometers manufacturing |
| 711410 | Celebrities' agents or managers |
| 711510 | Celebrity spokespersons, independent |
| 111219 | Celery farming, field, bedding plant and seed production |
| 212390 | Celestite mining and/or beneficiating |
| 325220 | Cellophane film or sheet manufacturing |
| 424120 | Cellophane tape merchant wholesalers |
| 339992 | Cellos and parts manufacturing |
| 237130 | Cellular phone tower construction |
| 449210 | Cellular telephone accessories stores |
| 517112 | Cellular telephone communication carriers |
| 811210 | Cellular telephone repair and maintenance services without retailing new cellular telephones |
| 517112 | Cellular telephone service carriers |
| 517122 | Cellular telephone stores, selling cellular phone service plans on an agent basis |
| 334220 | Cellular telephones (new and rebuilt) manufacturing |
| 423690 | Cellular telephones merchant wholesalers |
| 325199 | Cellulose acetate (except resins) manufacturing |
| 325211 | Cellulose acetate resins manufacturing |

| | |
|---|---|
| 424610 | Cellulose film merchant wholesalers |
| 325211 | Cellulose nitrate resins manufacturing |
| 325211 | Cellulose propionate resins manufacturing |
| 325211 | Cellulose resins manufacturing |
| 325211 | Cellulose xanthate (viscose) manufacturing |
| 238310 | Cellulosic fiber insulation installation |
| 325220 | Cellulosic fibers and filaments manufacturing |
| 325220 | Cellulosic filament yarn manufacturing |
| 326113 | Cellulosic plastics film and unlaminated sheet (except packaging) manufacturing |
| 325220 | Cellulosic staple fibers manufacturing |
| 327310 | Cement (e.g., hydraulic, masonry, Portland, pozzolana) manufacturing |
| 238140 | Cement block laying |
| 327310 | Cement clinker manufacturing |
| 333248 | Cement kilns manufacturing |
| 423830 | Cement making machinery merchant wholesalers |
| 423320 | Cement merchant wholesalers |
| 236210 | Cement plant construction |
| 212312 | Cement rock crushed and broken stone mining and/or beneficiating |
| 327120 | Cement, clay refractory, manufacturing |
| 327420 | Cement, Keene's (i.e., tiling plaster), manufacturing |
| 325520 | Cement, rubber, manufacturing |
| 213112 | Cementing oil and gas well casings on a contract basis |
| 324122 | Cements, asphalt roofing, made from purchased asphaltic materials |
| 339114 | Cements, dental, manufacturing |
| 812220 | Cemeteries |
| 812220 | Cemetery associations (i.e., operators) |
| 812220 | Cemetery management services |
| 459999 | Cemetery memorial dealers (e.g., headstones, markers, vaults) |
| 561730 | Cemetery plot care services |
| 812220 | Cemetery subdividers |
| 333517 | Centering machines, metalworking, manufacturing |
| 519210 | Centers for documentation (i.e., archives) |
| 624120 | Centers, senior citizens' |
| 238220 | Central air-conditioning equipment installation |
| 521110 | Central bank, monetary authorities |

| | |
|---|---|
| 238220 | Central cooling equipment and piping installation |
| 238220 | Central heating equipment and piping installation |
| 423730 | Central heating equipment, warm air, merchant wholesalers |
| 325412 | Central nervous system stimulant preparations manufacturing |
| 334210 | Central office and switching equipment, telephone, manufacturing |
| 522320 | Central reserve financial institutions (except central bank) |
| 333310 | Central vacuuming systems, commercial-type, manufacturing |
| 335210 | Central vacuuming systems, household-type, manufacturing |
| 551114 | Centralized administrative offices |
| 327320 | Central-mixed concrete manufacturing |
| 333914 | Centrifugal pumps manufacturing |
| 333998 | Centrifuges, industrial and laboratory-type, manufacturing |
| 325411 | Cephalosporin, uncompounded, manufacturing |
| 423330 | Ceramic and clay roofing materials merchant wholesalers |
| 325130 | Ceramic colors manufacturing |
| 423320 | Ceramic construction materials (except refractory and ceramic roofing tile) merchant wholesalers |
| 327999 | Ceramic fiber manufacturing |
| 333994 | Ceramic kilns and furnaces manufacturing |
| 238340 | Ceramic tile installation |
| 444180 | Ceramic tile stores |
| 327120 | Ceramic tiles, floor and wall, manufacturing |
| 423220 | Ceramic wall (except structural) and floor tile merchant wholesalers |
| 611610 | Ceramics instruction |
| 311211 | Cereal grain flour manufacturing |
| 311211 | Cereal grain germ manufacturing |
| 424490 | Cereal products merchant wholesalers |
| 212290 | Cerium concentrates beneficiating |
| 212290 | Cerium ores mining and/or beneficiating |
| 325180 | Cerium salts manufacturing |
| 523150 | Certificate of deposit (CD) brokers' offices |
| 923110 | Certification of schools and teachers |
| 541211 | Certified accountants' offices |
| 523940 | Certified financial planners, customized, fees paid by client |

| | |
|---|---|
| 541211 | Certified public accountants' (CPAs) offices |
| 621399 | Certified registered nurse anesthetists' (CRNAs) offices (e.g., centers, clinics) |
| 212230 | Cerussite mining and/or beneficiating |
| 339113 | Cervical collars manufacturing |
| 325180 | Cesium and cesium compounds, not specified elsewhere by process, manufacturing |
| 562991 | Cesspool cleaning services |
| 238910 | Cesspool construction |
| 325199 | Cetyl alcohol manufacturing |
| 335210 | Chafing dishes, household-type electric, manufacturing |
| 332999 | Chain fittings manufacturing |
| 333923 | Chain hoists manufacturing |
| 332323 | Chain ladders, metal, manufacturing |
| 238990 | Chain link fence installation |
| 332618 | Chain link fencing and fence gates made from purchased wire |
| 331222 | Chain link fencing, iron or steel, made in wire drawing plants |
| 332618 | Chain made from purchased wire |
| 332216 | Chain saw blades manufacturing |
| 333991 | Chain saws, handheld power-driven, manufacturing |
| 332618 | Chain, welded, made from purchased wire |
| 339910 | Chains or necklace, precious metal, manufacturing |
| 333613 | Chains, power transmission, manufacturing |
| 334519 | Chains, surveyor's, manufacturing |
| 423830 | Chainsaws merchant wholesalers |
| 337121 | Chair and couch springs, assembled, manufacturing |
| 337215 | Chair glides manufacturing |
| 337215 | Chair seats for furniture manufacturing |
| 337122 | Chairs (except upholstered), wood household-type, manufacturing |
| 337214 | Chairs (except wood), office-type, manufacturing |
| 337127 | Chairs, barber, beauty shop (i.e., hydraulic), manufacturing |
| 337126 | Chairs, cane, household-type, manufacturing |
| 339114 | Chairs, dentist's, manufacturing |
| 423850 | Chairs, hydraulic, beauty and barber shop, merchant wholesalers |
| 337126 | Chairs, metal household-type (except upholstered), manufacturing |
| 337127 | Chairs, portable folding, auditorium-type, manufacturing |
| 337127 | Chairs, stacking, auditorium-type, manufacturing |
| 337121 | Chairs, upholstered household-type (except dining room, kitchen), manufacturing |
| 337211 | Chairs, wood office-type, manufacturing |
| 212230 | Chalcocite mining and/or beneficiating |
| 212230 | Chalcopyrite mining and/or beneficiating |
| 339940 | Chalk (e.g., artist's, blackboard, carpenter's, marking, tailor's), manufacturing |
| 212312 | Chalk crushed and broken stone mining and/or beneficiating |
| 212312 | Chalk, ground or otherwise treated, mining and/or beneficiating |
| 339940 | Chalkboards, framed, manufacturing |
| 711130 | Chamber musical groups |
| 711130 | Chamber orchestras |
| 813910 | Chambers of commerce |
| 313210 | Chambrays weaving |
| 333517 | Chamfering machines, metalworking, manufacturing |
| 316110 | Chamois leather manufacturing |
| 424990 | Chamois, leather, merchant wholesalers |
| 312130 | Champagne method sparkling wine, manufacturing |
| 335132 | Chandeliers, commercial, industrial, and institutional electric, manufacturing |
| 335131 | Chandeliers, residential, manufacturing |
| 333310 | Change making machines manufacturing |
| 325180 | Channel black manufacturing |
| 237990 | Channel construction |
| 332323 | Channels, furring metal, manufacturing |
| 325194 | Charcoal (except activated) manufacturing |
| 325194 | Charcoal briquettes, wood, manufacturing |
| 424990 | Charcoal merchant wholesalers |
| 325998 | Charcoal, activated, manufacturing |
| 522210 | Charge card issuing |
| 423410 | Charged coupled devices (CCD) merchant wholesalers |
| 561499 | Charitable fundraising campaign organization services on a contract or fee basis |
| 813219 | Charitable fundraising using a crowdfunding platform (except on a contract or fee basis) |

| | |
|---|---|
| 561499 | Charitable fundraising using a crowdfunding platform, on a contract or fee basis |
| 813211 | Charitable trusts, awarding grants |
| 611699 | Charm schools |
| 481212 | Charter air freight services |
| 481211 | Charter air passenger services |
| 485510 | Charter bus services (except scenic, sightseeing) |
| 487210 | Charter fishing boat operation |
| 611110 | Charter schools |
| 333515 | Chasers (i.e., a machine tool accessory) manufacturing |
| 212390 | Chasers mining and/or beneficiating |
| 332812 | Chasing metals and metal products (except printing plates) for the trade |
| 336110 | Chassis, automobile, manufacturing |
| 336120 | Chassis, heavy truck, with or without cabs, manufacturing |
| 336110 | Chassis, light truck and utility, manufacturing |
| 423110 | Chassis, motor vehicle, merchant wholesalers |
| 561311 | Chauffeur registries |
| 611519 | Chauffeur training |
| 315210 | Chauffeurs' hats and caps cut and sew apparel contractors |
| 315990 | Chauffeurs' hats and caps cut and sewn from purchased fabric (except apparel contractors) |
| 522390 | Check cashing services |
| 521110 | Check clearing activities of the central bank |
| 522320 | Check clearing services (except central banks) |
| 522320 | Check clearinghouse services (except central banks) |
| 423420 | Check handling machines merchant wholesalers |
| 812990 | Check room services |
| 522320 | Check validation services |
| 332911 | Check valves, industrial-type, manufacturing |
| 333310 | Check writing machines manufacturing |
| 316990 | Checkbook covers (except metal) manufacturing |
| 339910 | Checkbook covers, precious metal, manufacturing |
| 323111 | Checkbooks and refills printing |
| 339930 | Checkers and checkerboards manufacturing |

| | |
|---|---|
| 611620 | Cheerleading instruction, camps or schools |
| 311513 | Cheese (except cottage cheese) manufacturing |
| 311513 | Cheese analogs manufacturing |
| 311941 | Cheese based salad dressing manufacturing |
| 424450 | Cheese confections (e.g., curls, puffs) merchant wholesalers |
| 311919 | Cheese curls and puffs manufacturing |
| 424430 | Cheese merchant wholesalers |
| 333241 | Cheese processing machinery manufacturing |
| 311513 | Cheese products, imitation or substitute, manufacturing |
| 311513 | Cheese spreads manufacturing |
| 311511 | Cheese, cottage, manufacturing |
| 311513 | Cheese, imitation or substitute, manufacturing |
| 424490 | Cheese, imitation or substitute, merchant wholesalers |
| 311513 | Cheese, natural (except cottage cheese), manufacturing |
| 313210 | Cheesecloths weaving |
| 236210 | Chemical (except petrochemical process-type) plant construction |
| 424690 | Chemical additives (e.g., concrete, food, fuel, oil) merchant wholesalers |
| 423490 | Chemical and technical pottery products merchant wholesalers |
| 541690 | Chemical consulting services |
| 541330 | Chemical engineering services |
| 313310 | Chemical finishing (e.g., fire, mildew, water resistance) fabrics |
| 424690 | Chemical gases merchant wholesalers |
| 423830 | Chemical industries machinery and equipment merchant wholesalers |
| 333248 | Chemical kilns manufacturing |
| 332710 | Chemical milling job shops |
| 333517 | Chemical milling machines, metalworking, manufacturing |
| 333248 | Chemical processing machinery and equipment manufacturing |
| 541715 | Chemical research and development laboratories or services (except biotechnology and nanotechnology research and development) |
| 327110 | Chemical stoneware (i.e., pottery products) manufacturing |
| 326191 | Chemical toilets, plastics, manufacturing |
| 115112 | Chemical treatment of soil for crops |

| | |
|---|---|
| 213112 | Chemically treating oil and gas wells (e.g., acidizing, bailing, swabbing) on a contract basis |
| 424690 | Chemicals (except agriculture) (e.g., automotive, household, industrial, photographic) merchant wholesalers |
| 424910 | Chemicals, agricultural, merchant wholesalers |
| 315210 | Chemises cut and sew apparel contractors |
| 315120 | Chemises made in apparel knitting mills |
| 315250 | Chemises, women's and girls', cut and sewn from purchased fabric (except apparel contractors) |
| 111339 | Cherry farming |
| 113210 | Cherry gum, gathering |
| 611699 | Chess instruction |
| 713990 | Chess or bridge clubs, recreational |
| 339930 | Chessmen and chessboards manufacturing |
| 325194 | Chestnut extract manufacturing |
| 113210 | Chestnut gum, gathering |
| 321920 | Chests for tools, wood, manufacturing |
| 332999 | Chests, fire or burglary resistive, metal, manufacturing |
| 332999 | Chests, money, metal, manufacturing |
| 332999 | Chests, safe deposit, metal, manufacturing |
| 311340 | Chewing gum base manufacturing |
| 333241 | Chewing gum machinery manufacturing |
| 311340 | Chewing gum manufacturing |
| 424450 | Chewing gum merchant wholesalers |
| 312230 | Chewing tobacco manufacturing |
| 424940 | Chewing tobacco merchant wholesalers |
| 424440 | Chicken and chicken products (except canned and packaged frozen) merchant wholesalers |
| 333111 | Chicken brooders manufacturing |
| 321920 | Chicken coops (i.e., crates), wood, wirebound for shipping poultry, manufacturing |
| 321992 | Chicken coops, prefabricated, wood, manufacturing |
| 112310 | Chicken egg production |
| 112310 | Chicken eggs (table, hatching) production |
| 333111 | Chicken feeders manufacturing |
| 311119 | Chicken feeds, prepared, manufacturing |
| 112340 | Chicken hatcheries |
| 332618 | Chicken netting made from purchased wire |
| 112320 | Chicken production (except egg laying) |
| 311615 | Chickens, processing, fresh, frozen, canned, or cooked (except baby and pet food) |
| 311615 | Chickens, slaughtering and dressing |
| 424590 | Chicks, live, merchant wholesalers |
| 111998 | Chicory farming |
| 624410 | Child care babysitting services |
| 624410 | Child care services |
| 624410 | Child care services in provider's own home |
| 624410 | Child care, before or after school, separate from schools |
| 624410 | Child day care centers |
| 623990 | Child group foster homes |
| 624110 | Child guidance agencies |
| 624110 | Child welfare services |
| 621410 | Childbirth preparation classes |
| 721214 | Children's camps (except day, instructional) |
| 424350 | Children's clothing merchant wholesalers |
| 513199 | Children's coloring book publishers |
| 513199 | Children's coloring book publishers (except exclusive Internet publishing) |
| 513199 | Children's coloring book publishers, exclusively on Internet |
| 622110 | Children's hospitals, general |
| 622210 | Children's hospitals, psychiatric or substance abuse |
| 622310 | Children's hospitals, specialty (except psychiatric, substance abuse) |
| 458210 | Children's shoe stores |
| 316210 | Children's shoes (except orthopedic extension) manufacturing |
| 315120 | Children's socks manufacturing |
| 423920 | Children's vehicles (except bicycles) merchant wholesalers |
| 623990 | Children's villages |
| 311422 | Chili con carne canning |
| 311942 | Chili pepper or powder manufacturing |
| 311421 | Chili sauce manufacturing |
| 238220 | Chilled water system installation |
| 339992 | Chimes and parts (musical instruments) manufacturing |
| 335999 | Chimes, electric, manufacturing |
| 327390 | Chimney caps, concrete, manufacturing |

| | |
|---|---|
| 561790 | Chimney cleaning services |
| 238220 | Chimney liner installation |
| 561790 | Chimney sweep (i.e., cleaning) services |
| 238140 | Chimney, brick, block or stone, contractors |
| 238110 | Chimney, concrete, construction |
| 212323 | China clay mining and/or beneficiating |
| 337122 | China closets, wood, manufacturing |
| 327110 | China cooking ware manufacturing |
| 811490 | China repair services |
| 327110 | China tableware, vitreous, manufacturing |
| 449129 | Chinaware stores |
| 423440 | Chinaware, commercial, merchant wholesalers |
| 423220 | Chinaware, household-type, merchant wholesalers |
| 112930 | Chinchilla production |
| 311422 | Chinese foods canning |
| 311999 | Chinese noodles, fried, manufacturing |
| 111219 | Chinese pea farming, bedding plant and seed production |
| 313210 | Chintzes weaving |
| 333248 | Chip placement machinery manufacturing |
| 322130 | Chipboard (i.e., paperboard) stock manufacturing |
| 321219 | Chipboard (i.e., particle core, wood chip face) manufacturing |
| 322220 | Chipboard, laminated or surface coated, made from purchased paperboard |
| 321113 | Chipper mills (except portable) |
| 333112 | Chippers (i.e., shredders), lawn and garden-type, manufacturing |
| 333120 | Chippers, portable, commercial (e.g., brush, limb, log), manufacturing |
| 333243 | Chippers, stationary (e.g., log), manufacturing |
| 424450 | Chips (e.g., corn, potato) merchant wholesalers |
| 621310 | Chiropractors' offices (e.g., centers, clinics) |
| 332216 | Chisels manufacturing |
| 333991 | Chisels, handheld power-driven, manufacturing |
| 111219 | Chive farming, field, bedding plant and seed production |
| 325199 | Chloral manufacturing |
| 325320 | Chlordane insecticides manufacturing |
| 325180 | Chloride of lime manufacturing |

| | |
|---|---|
| 325212 | Chlorinated rubber, synthetic, manufacturing |
| 325180 | Chlorine compounds, not specified elsewhere by process, manufacturing |
| 325180 | Chlorine dioxide manufacturing |
| 325180 | Chlorine manufacturing |
| 424690 | Chlorine merchant wholesalers |
| 325199 | Chloroacetic acid manufacturing |
| 325194 | Chlorobenzene manufacturing |
| 325120 | Chlorodifluoromethane manufacturing |
| 325120 | Chlorofluorocarbon (CFC) gases manufacturing |
| 325199 | Chloroform manufacturing |
| 325194 | Chloronaphthalene manufacturing |
| 325194 | Chlorophenol manufacturing |
| 325199 | Chloropicrin manufacturing |
| 325212 | Chloroprene rubber manufacturing |
| 325212 | Chlorosulfonated polyethylenes manufacturing |
| 325180 | Chlorosulfonic acid manufacturing |
| 325194 | Chlorotoluene manufacturing |
| 311352 | Chocolate (coating, instant, liquor, syrups) made from purchased chocolate |
| 311351 | Chocolate (e.g., coatings, instant, liquor, syrups) made from cacao beans |
| 424490 | Chocolate (except candy) merchant wholesalers |
| 311351 | Chocolate bars made from cocoa beans |
| 424450 | Chocolate candy merchant wholesalers |
| 311352 | Chocolate coatings and syrups made from purchased chocolate |
| 424490 | Chocolate coatings merchant wholesalers |
| 311352 | Chocolate covered candy bars made from purchased chocolate |
| 311352 | Chocolate covered granola bars made from purchased chocolate |
| 311511 | Chocolate drink (milk based) manufacturing |
| 311511 | Chocolate milk manufacturing |
| 333241 | Chocolate processing machinery manufacturing |
| 424490 | Chocolate syrups (except fountain) merchant wholesalers |
| 311351 | Chocolate, confectionery, made from cacao beans |
| 711130 | Choirs |
| 334416 | Chokes for electronic circuitry manufacturing |
| 325414 | Cholera serums manufacturing |

| | |
|---|---|
| 325320 | Cholinesterase inhibitors used as insecticides manufacturing |
| 311412 | Chop suey, frozen, manufacturing |
| 115113 | Chopping and silo filling |
| 711510 | Choreographers, independent |
| 311412 | Chow mein, frozen, manufacturing |
| 311710 | Chowders, seafood, manufacturing |
| 621399 | Christian Science practitioners' offices (e.g., centers, clinics) |
| 424990 | Christmas ornaments merchant wholesalers |
| 459420 | Christmas stores |
| 333132 | Christmas tree assemblies, oil and gas field-type, manufacturing |
| 111421 | Christmas tree growing |
| 335139 | Christmas tree light bulbs manufacturing |
| 335139 | Christmas tree lighting sets, electric, manufacturing |
| 339999 | Christmas tree ornaments (except electric, glass) manufacturing |
| 327215 | Christmas tree ornaments made from purchased glass |
| 327212 | Christmas tree ornaments, glass, made in glass making plants |
| 424990 | Christmas trees (e.g., artificial, cut) merchant wholesalers |
| 339999 | Christmas trees, artificial, manufacturing |
| 444240 | Christmas trees, cut, direct selling |
| 334516 | Chromatographic instruments, laboratory-type, manufacturing |
| 334513 | Chromatographs, industrial process-type, manufacturing |
| 325130 | Chrome pigments (e.g., chrome green, chrome orange, chrome yellow) manufacturing |
| 332813 | Chrome plating metals and metal products for the trade |
| 325180 | Chromic acid manufacturing |
| 212290 | Chromite mining and/or beneficiating |
| 325180 | Chromium compounds, not specified elsewhere by process, manufacturing |
| 212290 | Chromium concentrates beneficiating |
| 212290 | Chromium ore mining and/or beneficiating |
| 325180 | Chromium oxide manufacturing |
| 331410 | Chromium refining, primary |
| 325180 | Chromium salts manufacturing |
| 622310 | Chronic disease hospitals |
| 334519 | Chronographs manufacturing |
| 334519 | Chronometers manufacturing |

| | |
|---|---|
| 334516 | Chronoscopes manufacturing |
| 333517 | Chucking machines, automatic, metalworking, manufacturing |
| 333515 | Chucks (i.e., a machine tool accessory) manufacturing |
| 112390 | Chukar partridge production |
| 238290 | Church bell and tower clock installation |
| 337127 | Church furniture (except concrete, stone) manufacturing |
| 423490 | Church supplies (except plated ware, silverware) merchant wholesalers |
| 813110 | Churches |
| 332313 | Chutes, fabricated metal plate work, manufacturing |
| 333241 | Cider presses manufacturing |
| 311941 | Cider vinegar manufacturing |
| 312130 | Cider, alcoholic, manufacturing |
| 311941 | Cider, nonalcoholic, manufacturing |
| 326199 | Cigar and cigarette holders, plastics, manufacturing |
| 321920 | Cigar boxes, wood and part wood, manufacturing |
| 316990 | Cigar cases (except metal) manufacturing |
| 339910 | Cigar cases, precious metal, manufacturing |
| 312230 | Cigar manufacturing |
| 459991 | Cigar stores |
| 316990 | Cigarette cases (except metal) manufacturing |
| 339910 | Cigarette cases, precious metal, manufacturing |
| 339999 | Cigarette holders manufacturing |
| 339999 | Cigarette lighter flints manufacturing |
| 339999 | Cigarette lighters (except precious metal) manufacturing |
| 424990 | Cigarette lighters merchant wholesalers |
| 333248 | Cigarette making machinery manufacturing |
| 322299 | Cigarette paper made from purchased paper |
| 322120 | Cigarette paper made in paper mills |
| 322299 | Cigarette paper, book, made from purchased paper |
| 459991 | Cigarette stands, permanent |
| 459991 | Cigarette stands, temporary |
| 325220 | Cigarette tow, cellulosic fiber, manufacturing |
| 333310 | Cigarette vending machines manufacturing |
| 312230 | Cigarettes manufacturing |

| | |
|---|---|
| 424940 | Cigarettes merchant wholesalers |
| 424940 | Cigars merchant wholesalers |
| 325411 | Cinchona and derivatives (i.e., basic chemicals) manufacturing |
| 327331 | Cinder (clinker) block, concrete, manufacturing |
| 238140 | Cinder block installation |
| 236220 | Cinema construction |
| 512131 | Cinemas |
| 711510 | Cinematographers, independent |
| 212290 | Cinnabar mining and/or beneficiating |
| 333248 | Circuit board making machinery manufacturing |
| 423690 | Circuit boards merchant wholesalers |
| 334412 | Circuit boards, printed, bare, manufacturing |
| 423610 | Circuit breakers merchant wholesalers |
| 335313 | Circuit breakers, air, manufacturing |
| 335313 | Circuit breakers, power, manufacturing |
| 922110 | Circuit courts |
| 334515 | Circuit testers manufacturing |
| 423690 | Circuits, integrated, merchant wholesalers |
| 313240 | Circular (i.e., weft) fabrics knitting |
| 541870 | Circular direct distribution services |
| 333248 | Circular knitting machinery manufacturing |
| 333991 | Circular saws, handheld power-driven, manufacturing |
| 333243 | Circular saws, woodworking-type, stationary, manufacturing |
| 519210 | Circulating libraries |
| 711190 | Circus companies |
| 711190 | Circuses |
| 449210 | Citizens' band (CB) radio stores |
| 334220 | Citizens' band (CB) radios manufacturing |
| 423690 | Citizens' band (CB) radios merchant wholesalers |
| 325199 | Citral manufacturing |
| 325199 | Citrates, not specified elsewhere by process, manufacturing |
| 325199 | Citric acid manufacturing |
| 325998 | Citronella oil manufacturing |
| 325199 | Citronellal manufacturing |
| 115112 | Citrus grove cultivation services |
| 111320 | Citrus groves (except orange) |
| 311119 | Citrus pulp, cattle feed, manufacturing |
| 311411 | Citrus pulp, frozen, manufacturing |
| 921120 | City and town councils |
| 921110 | City and town managers' offices |
| 485113 | City bus services (except mixed mode) |
| 922110 | City or county courts |
| 541320 | City planning services |
| 813410 | Civic associations |
| 236220 | Civic center construction |
| 541330 | Civil engineering services |
| 813311 | Civil liberties organizations |
| 921190 | Civil rights commissions |
| 921190 | Civil service commissions |
| 524291 | Claims adjusting, insurance |
| 524292 | Claims processing services, insurance, third party |
| 114112 | Clam digging |
| 112512 | Clam production, farm raising |
| 333515 | Clamps (i.e., a machine tool accessory) manufacturing |
| 339112 | Clamps, surgical, manufacturing |
| 339992 | Clarinets and parts manufacturing |
| 316990 | Clasps, shoe (leather), manufacturing |
| 813410 | Classic car clubs |
| 711120 | Classical dance companies |
| 711130 | Classical musical artists, independent |
| 711130 | Classical musical groups |
| 327110 | Clay and ceramic statuary manufacturing |
| 212323 | Clay bleaching |
| 423320 | Clay construction materials (except refractory and clay roofing tile) merchant wholesalers |
| 212323 | Clay mining and/or beneficiating |
| 327120 | Clay refractories (e.g., mortar, brick, tile, block) manufacturing |
| 212323 | Clay, ball, mining and/or beneficiating |
| 212323 | Clay, ceramic and refractory minerals, mining and/or beneficiating |
| 212323 | Clay, fire, mining and/or beneficiating |
| 339940 | Clay, modeling, manufacturing |
| 212323 | Clay, natural, mining and/or beneficiating |
| 333248 | Clayworking and tempering machinery manufacturing |
| 812332 | Clean room apparel supply services |
| 236210 | Clean room construction |

| | |
|---|---|
| 339113 | Clean room suits and accessories manufacturing |
| 812320 | Cleaners, drycleaning and laundry service (except coin-operated) |
| 335210 | Cleaners, household-type electric vacuum, manufacturing |
| 561790 | Cleaning (e.g., power sweeping, washing) driveways and parking lots |
| 332813 | Cleaning and descaling metals and metal products for the trade |
| 812320 | Cleaning and dyeing plants (except rug cleaning plants) |
| 311212 | Cleaning and polishing rice |
| 561790 | Cleaning building exteriors (except sandblasting, window cleaning) |
| 561740 | Cleaning carpets |
| 424690 | Cleaning compounds and preparations merchant wholesalers |
| 335999 | Cleaning equipment, ultrasonic (except dental, medical), manufacturing |
| 561720 | Cleaning homes |
| 333131 | Cleaning machinery, mining-type, manufacturing |
| 561720 | Cleaning offices |
| 213112 | Cleaning oil and gas field lease tanks on a contract basis |
| 213112 | Cleaning out (e.g., bailing out, steam cleaning, swabbing) wells on a contract basis |
| 561740 | Cleaning plants, carpet and rug |
| 115210 | Cleaning poultry houses |
| 561740 | Cleaning rugs |
| 561740 | Cleaning services, carpet and rug |
| 561720 | Cleaning shopping centers |
| 561790 | Cleaning swimming pools |
| 213112 | Cleaning wells on a contract basis |
| 213112 | Cleaning, repairing, and dismantling oil and gas field lease tanks on a contract basis |
| 321918 | Clear and finger joint wood moldings manufacturing |
| 522320 | Clearinghouses, bank or check |
| 523999 | Clearinghouses, commodity exchange or securities exchange |
| 316210 | Cleated athletic shoes manufacturing |
| 332215 | Cleavers manufacturing |
| 611410 | Clerical schools |
| 315210 | Clerical vestments cut and sew apparel contractors |
| 315250 | Clerical vestments cut and sewn from purchased fabric (except apparel contractors) |
| 315120 | Clerical vestments made in apparel knitting mills |
| 316210 | Climbing shoes, plastics or plastics soled fabric upper, manufacturing |
| 316210 | Climbing shoes, rubber or rubber soled fabric upper, manufacturing |
| 236220 | Clinic construction |
| 621399 | Clinical nurse specialists' (CNSs) offices (e.g., centers, clinics) |
| 621111 | Clinical pathologists' offices (e.g., centers, clinics) |
| 621399 | Clinical pharmacists' offices (e.g., centers, clinics) |
| 621330 | Clinical psychologists' offices (e.g., centers, clinics) |
| ****** | Clinics, medical -- see type |
| 621498 | Clinics/centers of health practitioners from more than one industry practicing within the same establishment |
| 621498 | Clinics/centers of health practitioners with multi-industry degrees |
| 321999 | Clipboards, wood, manufacturing |
| 332216 | Clippers for animal use, nonelectric, manufacturing |
| 332215 | Clippers, fingernail and toenail, manufacturing |
| 519290 | Clipping services, news |
| 332994 | Clips, gun, manufacturing |
| 334519 | Clock materials and parts (except crystals) manufacturing |
| 334519 | Clock or watch springs, precision, made from purchased wire |
| 334310 | Clock radios manufacturing |
| 811490 | Clock repair shops without retailing new clocks |
| 458310 | Clock shops |
| 334519 | Clocks assembling |
| 334519 | Clocks assembling from purchased components |
| 423940 | Clocks merchant wholesalers |
| 541714 | Cloning research and experimental development laboratories |
| 561492 | Closed captioning services, real-time (i.e., simultaneous) |
| 512191 | Closed captioning services, taped material |
| 517111 | Closed-circuit television (CCTV) services |
| 334220 | Closed-circuit television equipment manufacturing |

| | |
|---|---|
| 525990 | Closed-end investment funds |
| 423220 | Closet accessories merchant wholesalers |
| 459999 | Closet organizer stores |
| 238390 | Closet organizer system installation |
| 423840 | Closures, industrial, merchant wholesalers |
| 332119 | Closures, metal, stamping |
| 424130 | Closures, paper and disposable plastics, merchant wholesalers |
| 327910 | Cloth (e.g., aluminum oxide, garnet, emery, silicon carbide), abrasive-coated, made from purchased cloth |
| 333248 | Cloth spreading machinery manufacturing |
| 321999 | Cloth winding reels, wood, manufacturing |
| 332618 | Cloth, woven wire, made from purchased wire |
| 334512 | Clothes dryer controls, including dryness controls, manufacturing |
| 811412 | Clothes dryer, household-type, repair and maintenance services without retailing new clothes dryers |
| 321999 | Clothes dryers (clothes horses), wood, manufacturing |
| 423850 | Clothes dryers (except household-type) merchant wholesalers |
| 423620 | Clothes dryers merchant wholesalers |
| 424990 | Clothes hangers merchant wholesalers |
| 326199 | Clothes hangers, plastics, manufacturing |
| 321999 | Clothes poles, wood, manufacturing |
| 326199 | Clothespins, plastics, manufacturing |
| 321999 | Clothespins, wood, manufacturing |
| 458110 | Clothing accessories stores |
| 424350 | Clothing accessories, women's, children's, and infants', merchant wholesalers |
| 541490 | Clothing design services |
| 532281 | Clothing rental (except industrial launderer, linen supply) |
| 811490 | Clothing repair shops, alterations only |
| 458110 | Clothing stores, children's and infants' |
| 458110 | Clothing stores, family |
| 458110 | Clothing stores, men's and boys' |
| 459510 | Clothing stores, used |
| 458110 | Clothing stores, women's and girls' |
| 339930 | Clothing, doll, manufacturing |
| 315250 | Clothing, fur (except apparel contractors), manufacturing |
| 315210 | Clothing, fur, cut and sew apparel contractors |
| 315250 | Clothing, leather or sheep-lined (except apparel contractors), manufacturing |
| 315210 | Clothing, leather or sheep-lined, cut and sew apparel contractors |
| 424350 | Clothing, men's and boys', merchant wholesalers |
| 315210 | Clothing, water resistant, cut and sew apparel contractors |
| 315250 | Clothing, water resistant, men's and boys', cut and sewn from purchased fabric (except apparel contractors) |
| 315250 | Clothing, water resistant, women's, girls', and infants', cut and sewn from purchased fabric (except apparel contractors) |
| 315210 | Clothing, waterproof, cut and sew apparel contractors |
| 315250 | Clothing, waterproof, cut and sewn from purchased fabric (except apparel contractors) |
| 315210 | Clothing, water-repellent, cut and sew apparel contractors |
| 315250 | Clothing, water-repellent, men's and boys', cut and sewn from purchased fabric (except apparel contractors) |
| 315250 | Clothing, water-repellent, women's, girls', and infants', cut and sewn from purchased fabric (except apparel contractors) |
| 424350 | Clothing, women's, children's, and infants', merchant wholesalers |
| 325612 | Cloths, dusting and polishing, chemically treated, manufacturing |
| 518210 | Cloud computing services (except software publishing and computer systems design) |
| 518210 | Cloud storage services |
| 325998 | Clove oil manufacturing |
| 111940 | Clover hay farming |
| 111998 | Clover seed farming |
| 721310 | Clubs, residential |
| 339920 | Clubs, sporting goods (e.g., golf, Indian), manufacturing |
| 336350 | Clutches and clutch discs, asbestos, manufacturing |
| 525990 | CMOs (collateralized mortgage obligations) |
| 325413 | Coagulation in-vitro diagnostic substances manufacturing |
| 325412 | Coagulation in-vivo diagnostic substances manufacturing |
| 333922 | Coal and ore conveyors manufacturing |

| | |
|---|---|
| 212114 | Coal beneficiating plants (e.g., cleaning, crushing, screening, washing) |
| 333131 | Coal breakers, cutters, and pulverizers manufacturing |
| 332322 | Coal chutes, sheet metal (except stampings), manufacturing |
| 457210 | Coal dealers, direct selling |
| 423520 | Coal dust merchant wholesalers |
| 211130 | Coal gasification at mine site |
| 484220 | Coal hauling, truck, local |
| 211130 | Coal liquefaction at mine site |
| 423520 | Coal merchant wholesalers |
| 213113 | Coal mining services on a contract basis (except geophysical surveying and mapping, site preparation, construction, and transportation activities) |
| 213113 | Coal mining support services on a contract basis (e.g., tunneling, blasting, training, overburden removal) (except geophysical surveying and mapping, site preparation, construction, and transportation activities) |
| 486990 | Coal pipeline transportation |
| 211130 | Coal pyrolysis |
| 212114 | Coal stripping (except on a contract, fee, or other basis) |
| 424690 | Coal tar distillates and resins merchant wholesalers |
| 325194 | Coal tar distillates manufacturing |
| 324121 | Coal tar paving materials made from purchased coal tar |
| 423320 | Coal tar paving materials merchant wholesalers |
| 424690 | Coal tar products, primary and intermediate, merchant wholesalers |
| 325211 | Coal tar resins manufacturing |
| 212115 | Coal, bituminous or anthracite, underground mining |
| 212114 | Coal, bituminous, lignite, or anthracite, surface mining and/or beneficiating |
| 212114 | Coal, brown, mining and/or beneficiating |
| 926120 | Coast Guard (except academy) |
| 611310 | Coast Guard Academy |
| 483113 | Coastal freight transportation to and from domestic ports |
| 483114 | Coastal passenger transportation to and from domestic ports |
| 483113 | Coastal shipping of freight to and from domestic ports |
| 812331 | Coat (e.g., barber's, beautician's, doctor's, nurse's) supply services |

| | |
|---|---|
| 332618 | Coat hangers made from purchased wire |
| 315250 | Coat linings, fur (except apparel contractors), manufacturing |
| 315210 | Coat linings, fur, cut and sew apparel contractors |
| 458110 | Coat stores |
| 315990 | Coat trimmings fabric cut and sewn from purchased fabric (except apparel contractors) |
| 315210 | Coat trimmings, fabric, cut and sew apparel contractors |
| 322220 | Coated board made from purchased paperboard |
| 322130 | Coated board made in paperboard mills |
| 324122 | Coating compounds, tar, made from purchased asphaltic materials |
| 238390 | Coating concrete structures with plastics |
| 332812 | Coating metals and metal products for the trade |
| 332812 | Coating of metal and metal products with plastics for the trade |
| 335139 | Coating purchased light bulbs |
| 322220 | Coating purchased papers for nonpackaging applications (except photosensitive paper) |
| 322220 | Coating purchased papers for packaging applications |
| 311351 | Coatings, chocolate, made from cacao beans |
| 315210 | Coats (e.g., tailored, fur, artificial leather, leather, sheep-lined), cut and sew apparel contractors |
| 315250 | Coats (including tailored), leather or sheep-lined (except apparel contractors), manufacturing |
| 315250 | Coats, artificial leather, cut and sewn from purchased fabric (except apparel contractors) |
| 315250 | Coats, fur (except apparel contractors), manufacturing |
| 315250 | Coats, leather (except apparel contractors), manufacturing |
| 315250 | Coats, men's and boys', cut and sewn from purchased fabric (except apparel contractors) |
| 424350 | Coats, men's and boys', merchant wholesalers |
| 315250 | Coats, nontailored service apparel (e.g., laboratory, mechanics', medical), men's and boys', cut and sewn from purchased fabric (except apparel contractors) |
| 315210 | Coats, nontailored service apparel (e.g., laboratory, medical, mechanics'), cut and sew apparel contractors |

| | |
|---|---|
| 315250 | Coats, nontailored service apparel (e.g., laboratory, medical, mechanics'), women's and girls', cut and sewn from purchased fabric (except apparel contractors) |
| 315250 | Coats, tailored, men's and boys', cut and sewn from purchased fabric (except apparel contractors) |
| 315250 | Coats, tailored, women's and girls', cut and sewn from purchased fabric |
| 315250 | Coats, waterproof (e.g., plastics, rubberized fabric, similar materials), cut and sewn from purchased fabric (except apparel contractors) |
| 315250 | Coats, waterproof (e.g., plastics, rubberized fabric, similar materials), rubberizing fabric and manufacturing coats |
| 315210 | Coats, waterproof (i.e., plastics, rubberized fabric, similar materials), cut and sew apparel contractors |
| 424350 | Coats, women's, children's, and infants', merchant wholesalers |
| 315250 | Coats, women's, girls', and infants', cut and sewn from purchased fabric (except apparel contractors) |
| 331318 | Coaxial cable made in aluminum wire drawing plants |
| 423610 | Coaxial cable merchant wholesalers |
| 331420 | Coaxial cable, copper, made from purchased copper in wire drawing plants |
| 331491 | Coaxial cable, nonferrous metals (except aluminum, copper), made from purchased nonferrous metals (except aluminum, copper) in wire drawing plants |
| 335929 | Coaxial cable, nonferrous, made from purchased nonferrous wire |
| 334417 | Coaxial connectors manufacturing |
| 339991 | Coaxial mechanical face seals manufacturing |
| 325180 | Cobalt 60 (i.e., radioactive cobalt) manufacturing |
| 325180 | Cobalt chloride manufacturing |
| 325180 | Cobalt compounds, not specified elsewhere by process, manufacturing |
| 212290 | Cobalt concentrates beneficiating |
| 212290 | Cobalt ores mining and/or beneficiating |
| 331410 | Cobalt refining, primary |
| 325180 | Cobalt sulfate manufacturing |
| 325411 | Cocaine and derivatives (i.e., basic chemicals) manufacturing |
| 332913 | Cocks, drain, plumbing, manufacturing |

| | |
|---|---|
| 722410 | Cocktail lounges |
| 311999 | Cocktail mixes, dry, manufacturing |
| 424820 | Cocktails, alcoholic, premixed, merchant wholesalers |
| 311351 | Cocoa (e.g., instant, mix, mixed with other ingredients, powder drink, powdered) made from cacao beans |
| 424590 | Cocoa beans merchant wholesalers |
| 311351 | Cocoa butter made from cocoa beans |
| 311352 | Cocoa, powdered drink, prepared, made from purchased chocolate |
| 311352 | Cocoa, powdered, made from purchased chocolate |
| 311352 | Cocoa, powdered, mixed with other ingredients, made from purchased chocolate |
| 311225 | Coconut oil made from purchased oils |
| 311224 | Coconut oil made in crushing mills |
| 111339 | Coconut tree farming |
| 311999 | Coconut, desiccated and shredded, manufacturing |
| 114111 | Cod catching |
| 114111 | Cod fishing |
| 311710 | Cod liver oil extraction, crude, processing |
| 325411 | Cod liver oil, medicinal, uncompounded, manufacturing |
| 325411 | Codeine and derivatives (i.e., basic chemicals) manufacturing |
| 333993 | Coding, dating, and imprinting packaging machinery manufacturing |
| 561330 | Co-employment staffing services |
| 445298 | Coffee and tea (i.e., packaged) stores |
| 722330 | Coffee carts, mobile |
| 311920 | Coffee concentrates (i.e., instant coffee) manufacturing |
| 311920 | Coffee extracts manufacturing |
| 111339 | Coffee farming |
| 322299 | Coffee filters made from purchased paper |
| 311920 | Coffee flavoring and syrups (i.e., made from coffee) manufacturing |
| 333310 | Coffee makers and urns, commercial-type, manufacturing |
| 423440 | Coffee makers, commercial, merchant wholesalers |
| 335210 | Coffee makers, household-type electric, manufacturing |
| 423620 | Coffee makers, household-type, merchant wholesalers |
| 424490 | Coffee merchant wholesalers |

| | |
|---|---|
| 311920 | Coffee roasting |
| 333241 | Coffee roasting and grinding machinery (i.e., food manufacturing-type) manufacturing |
| 722515 | Coffee shops, on premise brewing |
| 311920 | Coffee substitute manufacturing |
| 337122 | Coffee tables, wood, manufacturing |
| 311920 | Coffee, blended, manufacturing |
| 312111 | Coffee, iced, manufacturing |
| 311920 | Coffee, instant and freeze-dried, manufacturing |
| 237990 | Cofferdam construction |
| 423850 | Coffins merchant wholesalers |
| 487110 | Cog railway, scenic and sightseeing, operation |
| 237130 | Co-generation plant construction |
| 541720 | Cognitive research and development services |
| 811310 | Coil rewinding (except on an assembly line or factory basis) |
| 333519 | Coil winding and cutting machinery, metalworking, manufacturing |
| 423830 | Coil winding machines, spring, merchant wholesalers |
| 332613 | Coiled springs (except clock, watch), light gauge, made from purchased wire or strip, manufacturing |
| 332613 | Coiled springs, heavy gauge metal, manufacturing |
| 335312 | Coils for motors and generators manufacturing |
| 423690 | Coils, electronic, merchant wholesalers |
| 336320 | Coils, ignition, internal combustion engines, manufacturing |
| 332996 | Coils, pipe, made from purchased metal pipe |
| 333310 | Coin counting machinery manufacturing |
| 339999 | Coin- or card-operated amusement machines (except jukebox) manufacturing |
| 713290 | Coin- or card-operated gambling device concession operators (i.e., supplying and servicing in others' facilities) |
| 423990 | Coin- or card-operated game machines merchant wholesalers |
| 334310 | Coin- or card-operated jukebox manufacturing |
| 423440 | Coin- or card-operated merchandising machine merchant wholesalers |
| 713990 | Coin- or card-operated nongambling amusement device concession operators (i.e., supplying and servicing in others' facilities) |
| 812990 | Coin- or card-operated personal service machine (e.g., blood pressure, locker, photographic, scale, shoeshine) concession operators |
| 423440 | Coin- or card-operated phonographs and vending machines merchant wholesalers |
| 333310 | Coin- or card-operated vending machines manufacturing |
| 561990 | Coin pick-up services, parking meter |
| 316990 | Coin purses (except metal) manufacturing |
| 339910 | Coin purses, precious metal, manufacturing |
| 423420 | Coin sorting machines merchant wholesalers |
| 333310 | Coin wrapping machines manufacturing |
| 812310 | Coin-operated drycleaners and laundries |
| 812310 | Coin-operated laundry and drycleaning routes (i.e., concession operators) |
| 339999 | Coin-or card-operated gambling devices manufacturing |
| 423940 | Coins merchant wholesalers |
| 423520 | Coke merchant wholesalers |
| 221210 | Coke oven gas distribution |
| 324199 | Coke oven products (e.g., coke, gases, tars) made in coke oven establishments |
| 331110 | Coke oven products made in iron and steel mills |
| 324110 | Coke, petroleum, made in petroleum refineries |
| 335139 | Cold cathode fluorescent lamp tubes manufacturing |
| 332111 | Cold forgings made from purchased iron or steel, unfinished |
| 332112 | Cold forgings made from purchased nonferrous metals, unfinished |
| 325412 | Cold remedies manufacturing |
| 333519 | Cold rolling mill machinery, metalworking, manufacturing |
| 331221 | Cold rolling steel shapes (e.g., bar, plate, rod, sheet, strip) made from purchased steel |
| 493120 | Cold storage locker services |
| 423740 | Cold storage machinery merchant wholesalers |
| 236220 | Cold storage plant construction |
| 493120 | Cold storage warehousing |
| 332811 | Cold treating metals for the trade |
| 311991 | Cole slaw, fresh, manufacturing |
| 212390 | Colemanite mining and/or beneficiating |
| 311612 | Collagen sausage casings made from purchased hides |

| | |
|---|---|
| 332439 | Collapsible tubes (e.g., toothpaste, glue), light gauge metal, manufacturing |
| 315210 | Collar and cuff sets cut and sew apparel contractors |
| 315120 | Collar and cuff sets made in apparel knitting mills |
| 315250 | Collar and cuff sets, women's and girls', cut and sewn from purchased fabric (except apparel contractors) |
| 316110 | Collar leather, manufacturing |
| 111219 | Collard farming, field, bedding plant and seed production |
| 333515 | Collars (i.e., a machine tool accessory) manufacturing |
| 316990 | Collars and collar pads (i.e., harness) manufacturing |
| 316990 | Collars, dog, manufacturing |
| 333613 | Collars, shaft for power transmission equipment, manufacturing |
| 522299 | Collateralized mortgage obligation (CMO) issuing, private |
| 525990 | Collateralized mortgage obligations (CMOs) |
| 333248 | Collating machinery for printing and bookbinding manufacturing |
| 333310 | Collating machinery, office-type, manufacturing |
| 459420 | Collectible gift shops (e.g., crystal, pewter, porcelain) |
| 812320 | Collecting and distributing agents, laundry and drycleaning |
| 561440 | Collection agencies |
| 561440 | Collection agencies, accounts |
| 221320 | Collection, treatment, and disposal of waste through a sewer system |
| 813930 | Collective bargaining units |
| 335312 | Collector rings for motors and generators manufacturing |
| 459999 | Collectors' items (e.g., autograph, card, coin, stamp) shops (except used rare items) |
| 459510 | Collectors' items (e.g., autograph, card, coin, stamp), mail-order houses (except used rare items) |
| 611691 | College board preparation centers |
| 611691 | College entrance exam preparation instruction |
| 611710 | College selection services |
| 611310 | Colleges (except junior colleges) |
| 611511 | Colleges, barber and beauty |
| 611210 | Colleges, community |
| 611210 | Colleges, junior |

| | |
|---|---|
| 611310 | Colleges, universities, and professional schools |
| 333515 | Collets (i.e., a machine tool accessory) manufacturing |
| 518210 | Colocation services (i.e., rental of server and networking space in data centers) |
| 325620 | Colognes manufacturing |
| 424210 | Colognes merchant wholesalers |
| 334510 | Colonscopes, electromedical, manufacturing |
| 812199 | Color consulting services (i.e., personal care services) |
| 325130 | Color pigments, inorganic (except bone black, carbon black, lamp black), manufacturing |
| 325130 | Color pigments, organic (except animal black, bone black), manufacturing |
| 323120 | Color separation services, for the printing trade |
| 334516 | Colorimeters, laboratory-type, manufacturing |
| 423920 | Coloring books merchant wholesalers |
| 316110 | Coloring leather |
| 332813 | Coloring metals and metal products (except coating) for the trade |
| 339113 | Colostomy appliances manufacturing |
| 812220 | Columbariums |
| 212290 | Columbite mining and/or beneficiating |
| 212290 | Columbium ores mining and/or beneficiating |
| 327420 | Columns, architectural or ornamental plaster work, manufacturing |
| 332420 | Columns, fractionating, heavy gauge metal, manufacturing |
| 321918 | Columns, porch, wood, manufacturing |
| 316990 | Comb cases (except metal) manufacturing |
| 339910 | Comb cases, precious metal, manufacturing |
| 334512 | Combination limit and fan controls manufacturing |
| 112990 | Combination livestock farming (except dairy, poultry) |
| 334512 | Combination oil and hydronic controls manufacturing |
| 333111 | Combines (i.e., harvester-threshers) manufacturing |
| 423820 | Combines merchant wholesalers |
| 313310 | Combing and converting top |
| 333248 | Combing machinery for textiles manufacturing |
| 313310 | Combing textile fibers |

| | |
|---|---|
| 115113 | Combining, agricultural |
| 332999 | Combs, metal, manufacturing |
| 326199 | Combs, plastics, manufacturing |
| 326299 | Combs, rubber, manufacturing |
| 334513 | Combustion control instruments (except commercial, household furnace-type) manufacturing |
| 541330 | Combustion engineering consulting services |
| 562211 | Combustors, hazardous waste |
| 562213 | Combustors, nonhazardous solid waste |
| 711510 | Comedians, independent |
| 711110 | Comedy troupes |
| 812990 | Comfort station operation |
| 314120 | Comforters made from purchased fabrics |
| 513120 | Comic book publishers |
| 513120 | Comic book publishers (except exclusive Internet publishing) |
| 513120 | Comic book publishers and printing combined |
| 513120 | Comic book publishers, exclusively on Internet |
| 459210 | Comic book stores |
| 323111 | Comic books commercial printing (except screen) without publishing |
| 323113 | Comic books screen printing without publishing |
| 811310 | Commercial and industrial machinery repair and maintenance services |
| 522220 | Commercial and inventory financing (except international trade financing) |
| 541430 | Commercial art services |
| 541430 | Commercial artists, independent |
| 311812 | Commercial bakeries |
| 522110 | Commercial banking |
| 522110 | Commercial banks |
| 236220 | Commercial building construction |
| 236220 | Commercial building construction for-sale builders |
| 236220 | Commercial building construction general contractors |
| 531120 | Commercial building rental or leasing |
| 561450 | Commercial credit reporting bureaus |
| 323111 | Commercial digital printing (except books) |
| 323111 | Commercial engraving printing (except books) |
| 541922 | Commercial event videography services |
| 423830 | Commercial fishing equipment and supplies (except boats, ships) merchant wholesalers |
| 323111 | Commercial flexographic printing (except books) |
| 238220 | Commercial freezer installation |
| 811310 | Commercial gaming machine repair and maintenance services |
| 323111 | Commercial gravure printing (except books) |
| 541430 | Commercial illustration services |
| 541430 | Commercial illustrators, independent |
| 561790 | Commercial kitchen exhaust hood cleaning services |
| 238290 | Commercial kitchen food preparation equipment (e.g., mixers, ovens, stoves) installation |
| 323111 | Commercial letterpress printing (except books) |
| 335132 | Commercial lighting fixtures, electric, manufacturing |
| 323111 | Commercial lithographic (offset) printing (except books) |
| 523150 | Commercial note brokers' offices |
| 523150 | Commercial paper dealing (i.e., acting as a principal in dealing securities to investors) |
| 541922 | Commercial photography services |
| 323111 | Commercial printing (except screen, books) |
| 531312 | Commercial property managing |
| 323111 | Commercial quick printing (except books) |
| 531210 | Commercial real estate agencies |
| 531210 | Commercial real estate agents' offices |
| 531312 | Commercial real estate property managers' offices |
| 811310 | Commercial refrigeration equipment repair and maintenance services |
| 238220 | Commercial refrigeration system installation |
| 323113 | Commercial screen printing (except books, manifold business forms, grey goods) |
| 424120 | Commercial stationery supplies merchant wholesalers |
| 334519 | Commercial timing mechanisms manufacturing |
| 512110 | Commercials, television, production |
| 238290 | Commercial-type door installation |
| 445110 | Commissaries, primarily groceries |
| 523160 | Commodity contract pool operators |

| | |
|---|---|
| 523160 | Commodity contract trading companies |
| 523160 | Commodity contracts brokerages |
| 523160 | Commodity contracts brokers' offices |
| 523160 | Commodity contracts dealing (i.e., acting as a principal in dealing commodities to investors) |
| 523210 | Commodity contracts exchanges |
| 523160 | Commodity contracts floor brokers |
| 523160 | Commodity contracts floor traders (i.e., acting as a principal in dealing commodities to investors) |
| 523160 | Commodity contracts floor trading (i.e., acting as a principal in dealing commodities to investors) |
| 523160 | Commodity contracts options brokerages |
| 523160 | Commodity contracts options dealing (i.e., acting as a principal in dealing commodities to investors) |
| 523160 | Commodity contracts traders (i.e., acting as a principal in dealing commodities to investors) |
| 522299 | Commodity Credit Corporation |
| 523160 | Commodity futures brokerages |
| 541990 | Commodity inspection services |
| 212323 | Common clay mining and/or beneficiating |
| 212321 | Common sand quarrying and/or beneficiating |
| 212323 | Common shale mining and/or beneficiating |
| 923120 | Communicable disease program administration |
| 237130 | Communication antenna construction |
| 541430 | Communication design services, visual |
| 238210 | Communication equipment installation |
| 811210 | Communication equipment repair and maintenance services |
| 237130 | Communication tower construction |
| 926130 | Communications commissions |
| 423690 | Communications equipment merchant wholesalers |
| 334220 | Communications equipment, mobile and microwave, manufacturing |
| 334210 | Communications headgear, telephone, manufacturing |
| 926130 | Communications licensing commissions and agencies |
| 334515 | Communications signal testing and evaluation equipment manufacturing |
| 335929 | Communications wire and cable, nonferrous, made from purchased nonferrous wire |
| 331318 | Communications wire or cable made in aluminum wire drawing plants |
| 331420 | Communications wire or cable, copper, made from purchased copper in wire drawing plants |
| 331491 | Communications wire or cable, nonferrous metals (except aluminum, copper), made from purchased nonferrous metals (except aluminum, copper) in wire drawing plants |
| 311812 | Communion wafer manufacturing |
| 813319 | Community action advocacy organizations |
| 624190 | Community action service agencies |
| 624120 | Community centers (except recreational only), adult |
| 624110 | Community centers (except recreational only), youth |
| 813219 | Community chest fundraising organizations |
| 611210 | Community colleges |
| 611210 | Community colleges offering a wide variety of academic and technical training |
| 925120 | Community development agencies, government |
| 813211 | Community foundations |
| 621498 | Community health centers and clinics, outpatient |
| 624190 | Community health education services (except health care services) |
| 923120 | Community health programs administration |
| 624210 | Community meals, social services |
| 712110 | Community museums |
| 924120 | Community recreation programs, government |
| 923130 | Community social service program administration |
| 711110 | Community theaters |
| 335312 | Commutators, electric motor, manufacturing |
| 481111 | Commuter air carriers, scheduled |
| 485113 | Commuter bus operation (except mixed mode) |
| 485112 | Commuter rail systems (except mixed mode) |
| 485111 | Commuter transit systems, mixed mode (e.g., bus, commuter rail, subway combination) |

| | |
|---|---|
| 334310 | Compact disc players (e.g., automotive, household-type) manufacturing |
| 423620 | Compact disc players merchant wholesalers |
| 423990 | Compact discs (CDs), prerecorded, merchant wholesalers |
| 334610 | Compact discs (i.e., CD-ROM), software, mass reproducing |
| 334610 | Compact discs, prerecorded audio, mass reproducing |
| 334610 | Compact discs, recordable or rewritable, blank, manufacturing |
| 335139 | Compact fluorescent light bulbs manufacturing |
| 423830 | Compactors, trash, industrial, merchant wholesalers |
| 339910 | Compacts, precious metal, manufacturing |
| 316990 | Compacts, solid leather, manufacturing |
| 112990 | Companion animals production (e.g., cats, dogs, parakeets, parrots) |
| 624120 | Companion services for disabled persons and the elderly |
| 333310 | Comparators, optical, manufacturing |
| 334511 | Compasses, gyroscopic and magnetic (except portable), manufacturing |
| 334519 | Compasses, portable magnetic-type, manufacturing |
| 541612 | Compensation consulting services |
| 541612 | Compensation planning services |
| 525190 | Compensation, workers, insurance funds |
| 311119 | Complete feed, livestock, manufacturing |
| 711510 | Composers, independent |
| 322219 | Composite cans (i.e., foil-fiber and other combinations) manufacturing |
| 562219 | Compost dumps |
| 325315 | Compost manufacturing |
| 325120 | Compressed and liquefied industrial gas manufacturing |
| 332911 | Compressed gas cylinder valves manufacturing |
| 424690 | Compressed gases (except LP gas) merchant wholesalers |
| 424710 | Compressed liquefied petroleum gas (LPG) bulk stations and terminals, merchant wholesalers |
| 321219 | Compression modified wood manufacturing |
| 333248 | Compression molding machinery for plastics manufacturing |
| 339991 | Compression packings manufacturing |
| 532490 | Compressor, air and gas, rental or leasing |
| 237120 | Compressor, metering and pumping station, gas and oil pipeline, construction |
| 423830 | Compressors (except air-conditioning, refrigeration) merchant wholesalers |
| 333912 | Compressors, air and gas, general purpose-type, manufacturing |
| 423730 | Compressors, air-conditioning, merchant wholesalers |
| 336390 | Compressors, motor vehicle air-conditioning, manufacturing |
| 423740 | Compressors, refrigeration, merchant wholesalers |
| 238210 | Computer and network cable installation |
| 541715 | Computer and related hardware research and development laboratories or services (except nanotechnology research and development) |
| 423430 | Computer boards, loaded, merchant wholesalers |
| 423690 | Computer boards, unloaded, merchant wholesalers |
| 334419 | Computer cable sets (e.g., monitor, printer) manufacturing |
| 423690 | Computer chips merchant wholesalers |
| 423430 | Computer data storage devices merchant wholesalers |
| 518210 | Computer data storage services |
| 541519 | Computer disaster recovery services |
| 813410 | Computer enthusiasts clubs |
| 449210 | Computer equipment stores |
| 238330 | Computer flooring installation |
| 323111 | Computer forms (manifold or continuous) printing |
| 337126 | Computer furniture, metal household-type, manufacturing |
| 337122 | Computer furniture, wood household-type, manufacturing |
| 541512 | Computer hardware consulting services or consultants |
| 518210 | Computer input preparation services |
| 334118 | Computer input/output equipment manufacturing |
| 611420 | Computer operator training |
| 424120 | Computer paper supplies merchant wholesalers |
| 322230 | Computer paper, die-cut, made from purchased paper |
| 423430 | Computer peripheral equipment merchant wholesalers |
| 532420 | Computer peripheral equipment rental or leasing |

| | |
|---|---|
| 811210 | Computer peripheral equipment repair and maintenance, without retailing new computer peripheral equipment |
| 325992 | Computer printer toner cartridges manufacturing |
| 423430 | Computer printers merchant wholesalers |
| 541511 | Computer program or software development, custom |
| 611420 | Computer programming schools |
| 541511 | Computer programming services, custom |
| 611420 | Computer programming, software, and systems training, online (through a website or mobile application) |
| 611420 | Computer programming, software, and systems training, online learning marketplace services (through a website or mobile application) |
| 532420 | Computer rental or leasing |
| 811210 | Computer repair and maintenance services, without retailing new computers |
| 611519 | Computer repair training |
| 334111 | Computer servers manufacturing |
| 541511 | Computer software analysis and design services, custom |
| 541512 | Computer software consulting services or consultants |
| 541511 | Computer software programming services, custom |
| 513210 | Computer software publishers, packaged |
| 513210 | Computer software publishing and reproduction |
| 541511 | Computer software support services, custom |
| 334610 | Computer software tapes and disks, blank, rigid and floppy, manufacturing |
| 611420 | Computer software training |
| 423430 | Computer software, packaged, merchant wholesalers |
| 449210 | Computer software, prepackaged, new, mail-order houses |
| 459510 | Computer software, prepackaged, used, mail-order houses |
| 449210 | Computer stores |
| 541513 | Computer systems facilities (i.e., clients' facilities) management and operation services |
| 541512 | Computer systems integration analysis and design services |
| 541512 | Computer systems integration design consulting services |
| 541512 | Computer systems integrator services |

| | |
|---|---|
| 334118 | Computer terminals manufacturing |
| 423430 | Computer terminals merchant wholesalers |
| 518210 | Computer time leasing |
| 518210 | Computer time rental |
| 518210 | Computer time sharing services |
| 621512 | Computer tomography (CT-SCAN) centers |
| 611420 | Computer training (except repair) |
| 532282 | Computer video game rental |
| 541512 | Computer-aided design (CAD) systems integration design services |
| 541340 | Computer-aided design drafting (CADD) services |
| 541512 | Computer-aided engineering (CAE) systems integration design services |
| 541512 | Computer-aided manufacturing (CAM) systems integration design services |
| 334517 | Computerized axial tomography (CT/CAT) scanners manufacturing |
| 334512 | Computerized environmental control systems for buildings manufacturing |
| 334111 | Computers manufacturing |
| 423430 | Computers merchant wholesalers |
| 518210 | Computing infrastructure provision |
| 518210 | Computing platform infrastructure provision |
| 325411 | Concentrated medicinal chemicals, uncompounded, manufacturing |
| 311930 | Concentrates, drink (except frozen fruit juice), manufacturing |
| 311930 | Concentrates, flavoring (except coffee based), manufacturing |
| 424450 | Concentrates, fountain (except soft drink), merchant wholesalers |
| 311411 | Concentrates, frozen fruit juice, manufacturing |
| 423520 | Concentrates, metallic, merchant wholesalers |
| 333131 | Concentration machinery, mining-type, manufacturing |
| 711130 | Concert artists, independent |
| 711320 | Concert booking agencies |
| 711310 | Concert hall operators |
| 531120 | Concert hall, no promotion of events, rental or leasing |
| 711310 | Concert managers with facilities |
| 711320 | Concert managers without facilities |
| 711310 | Concert organizers with facilities |
| 711320 | Concert organizers without facilities |
| 711310 | Concert promoters with facilities |

| | |
|---|---|
| 711320 | Concert promoters without facilities |
| 561599 | Concert ticket offices |
| 713990 | Concession operators, amusement device (except gambling) and ride |
| 722330 | Concession snack stands, mobile |
| 812990 | Concierge services |
| 926150 | Conciliation and mediation services, government |
| 325998 | Concrete additive preparations (e.g., curing, hardening) manufacturing |
| 424690 | Concrete additives merchant wholesalers |
| 327320 | Concrete batch plants (including temporary) |
| 238140 | Concrete block laying |
| 238910 | Concrete breaking and cutting for demolition |
| 423320 | Concrete building products merchant wholesalers |
| 238390 | Concrete coating, glazing or sealing |
| 327999 | Concrete crushing and grinding (except at construction site) |
| 238110 | Concrete finishing |
| 333120 | Concrete finishing machinery manufacturing |
| 238110 | Concrete floor surfacing |
| 238190 | Concrete form contractors |
| 332322 | Concrete forms, sheet metal (except stampings), manufacturing |
| 327390 | Concrete furniture (e.g., benches, tables) manufacturing |
| 333120 | Concrete gunning equipment manufacturing |
| 333120 | Concrete mixing machinery, portable, manufacturing |
| 423320 | Concrete mixtures merchant wholesalers |
| 238990 | Concrete patio construction |
| 237310 | Concrete paving (i.e., highway, road, street, public sidewalk) |
| 238990 | Concrete paving, residential and commercial driveway and parking area |
| 238110 | Concrete pouring |
| 423810 | Concrete processing equipment merchant wholesalers |
| 238120 | Concrete product (e.g., structural precast, structural prestressed) installation |
| 333248 | Concrete products forming machinery manufacturing |
| 327390 | Concrete products, precast (except block, brick and pipe), manufacturing |
| 238110 | Concrete pumping (i.e., placement) |
| 238120 | Concrete reinforcement placement |
| 332312 | Concrete reinforcing bar (rebar) assemblies, fabrication |
| 331110 | Concrete reinforcing bar (rebar) made in iron and steel mills |
| 331221 | Concrete reinforcing bar (rebar), made from purchased steel in cold rolling mills |
| 331221 | Concrete reinforcing bar (rebar), made from purchased steel in steel rolling mills |
| 423510 | Concrete reinforcing bars merchant wholesalers |
| 332618 | Concrete reinforcing mesh made from purchased wire |
| 238110 | Concrete repair |
| 238110 | Concrete resurfacing |
| 238990 | Concrete sawing and drilling (except demolition) |
| 327390 | Concrete tanks manufacturing |
| 327999 | Concrete, dry mixture, manufacturing |
| 211130 | Condensate, cycle, natural gas production |
| 333241 | Condensed and evaporated milk machinery manufacturing |
| 311514 | Condensed milk manufacturing |
| 311514 | Condensed, evaporated or powdered whey, manufacturing |
| 332410 | Condenser boxes, metal, manufacturing |
| 335999 | Condensers (except electronic), fixed and variable, manufacturing |
| 334416 | Condensers, electronic, manufacturing |
| 423690 | Condensers, electronic, merchant wholesalers |
| 332410 | Condensers, steam, manufacturing |
| 335312 | Condensers, synchronous, electric, manufacturing |
| 423830 | Condensing units (except air-conditioning, refrigeration) merchant wholesalers |
| 423730 | Condensing units, air-conditioning, merchant wholesalers |
| 423740 | Condensing units, refrigeration, merchant wholesalers |
| 326299 | Condom manufacturing |
| 813990 | Condominium corporations |
| 236117 | Condominium for-sale builders |
| 531312 | Condominium managers' offices, commercial |
| 531311 | Condominium managers' offices, residential |
| 813990 | Condominium owners' associations |

561599  Condominium time-share exchange services

236116  Condominium, multifamily, construction general contractors

236115  Condominium, single-family, construction general contractors

335931  Conductor connectors, solderless connectors, sleeves, or soldering lugs, manufacturing

711510  Conductors, independent

423320  Conduit and pipe, concrete, merchant wholesalers

423610  Conduit, electric wire and cable, merchant wholesalers

327120  Conduit, vitrified clay, manufacturing

331210  Conduit, welded and lock joint, made from purchased iron or steel

335932  Conduits and fittings, electrical, manufacturing

423610  Conduits and raceways, electrical, merchant wholesalers

327332  Conduits, concrete, manufacturing

322219  Cones (e.g., winding yarn, string, ribbon, cloth), fiber, made from purchased paperboard

311821  Cones, ice cream, manufacturing

327110  Cones, pyrometric, earthenware, manufacturing

311313  Confectioner's beet sugar manufacturing

311314  Confectioner's powdered sugar manufacturing

311351  Confectionery chocolate made from cacao beans

333241  Confectionery machinery manufacturing

424450  Confectionery merchant wholesalers

722515  Confectionery snack shops, made on premises with carryout services

445292  Confectionery stores, packaged, retailing only

311340  Confectionery, nonchocolate, manufacturing

531120  Conference center, no promotion of events, rental or leasing

322299  Confetti made from purchased paper

921120  Congress of the United States

336310  Connecting rods, automotive and truck gasoline engine, manufacturing

335931  Connectors and terminals for electrical devices manufacturing

335931  Connectors, electric cord, manufacturing

423610  Connectors, electrical, merchant wholesalers

334417  Connectors, electronic (e.g., coaxial, cylindrical, printed circuit, rack and panel), manufacturing

423690  Connectors, electronic, merchant wholesalers

335313  Connectors, power, manufacturing

335931  Connectors, solderless (wiring devices), manufacturing

335931  Connectors, twist on wire (i.e., nuts), manufacturing

813312  Conservation advocacy organizations

924120  Conservation and reclamation agencies

712190  Conservation areas

611310  Conservatories of music (colleges or universities)

712130  Conservatories, botanical

711510  Conservators (i.e., art, artifact restorers), independent

611610  Conservatory of music (except academic)

459510  Consignment shops, used merchandise

336350  Constant velocity joints, automotive, truck, and bus, manufacturing

813940  Constituencies' associations, political party

325520  Construction adhesives (except asphalt, gypsum base) manufacturing

813910  Construction associations

238990  Construction elevator (i.e., temporary use during construction) erection and dismantling

541330  Construction engineering services

238910  Construction equipment (except crane) rental with operator

541990  Construction estimation services

532412  Construction form rental

561320  Construction labor supply services

522292  Construction lending

423810  Construction machinery and equipment merchant wholesalers

532412  Construction machinery and equipment rental or leasing without operator

811310  Construction machinery and equipment repair and maintenance services

333120  Construction machinery manufacturing

236220  Construction management, commercial and institutional building

237990  Construction management, dam

237310  Construction management, highway, road, street and bridge

236210  Construction management, industrial building (except warehouses)

| | |
|---|---|
| 237990 | Construction management, marine structure |
| 237990 | Construction management, mass transit |
| 236116 | Construction management, multifamily building |
| 237120 | Construction management, oil and gas pipeline |
| 237120 | Construction management, oil refinery and petrochemical complex |
| 237990 | Construction management, outdoor recreation facility |
| 237130 | Construction management, power and communication transmission line |
| 236118 | Construction management, residential remodeling |
| 236115 | Construction management, single-family building |
| 237990 | Construction management, tunnel |
| 237110 | Construction management, water and sewage treatment plant |
| 237110 | Construction management, water and sewer line |
| 423610 | Construction materials, electrical, merchant wholesalers |
| 322230 | Construction paper, school and art, made from purchased paper |
| 322120 | Construction paper, school and art, made in paper mills |
| 212321 | Construction sand and gravel beneficiating (e.g., grinding, screening, washing) |
| 212321 | Construction sand or gravel dredging |
| 541370 | Construction surveying services |
| 333120 | Construction-type tractors and attachments manufacturing |
| 928120 | Consulates |
| ****** | Consultants -- see specific activity |
| 813920 | Consultants' associations |
| 531390 | Consultants', real estate (except appraisers), offices |
| 541330 | Consulting engineers' offices |
| 541330 | Consulting engineers' private practices |
| 812990 | Consumer buying services |
| 541990 | Consumer credit counseling services |
| 561450 | Consumer credit reporting bureaus |
| 423620 | Consumer electronics merchant wholesalers |
| 532210 | Consumer electronics rental |
| 811210 | Consumer electronics repair and maintenance services without retailing new consumer electronics |

| | |
|---|---|
| 522291 | Consumer finance companies (i.e., unsecured cash loans) |
| 522291 | Consumer lending |
| 922190 | Consumer product safety commissions |
| 926110 | Consumer protection offices |
| 449210 | Consumer-type electronic stores (e.g., televisions, computers, cameras) |
| 334514 | Consumption meters (e.g., gas, water) manufacturing |
| 524128 | Contact lens insurance, direct |
| 339115 | Contact lenses manufacturing |
| 423460 | Contact lenses merchant wholesalers |
| 335931 | Contacts, electrical (except carbon and graphite), manufacturing |
| 335991 | Contacts, electrical, carbon and graphite, manufacturing |
| 322130 | Container board stock manufacturing |
| 336611 | Container ship building |
| 484110 | Container trucking services, local |
| 484121 | Container trucking services, long-distance (TL) |
| 327213 | Containers for packaging, bottling, and canning, glass, manufacturing |
| 332439 | Containers, air cargo, light gauge metal, manufacturing |
| 332999 | Containers, foil (except bags), manufacturing |
| 423220 | Containers, household (except paper and disposable plastics), merchant wholesalers |
| 423840 | Containers, industrial, merchant wholesalers |
| 332439 | Containers, light gauge metal (except cans), manufacturing |
| 424130 | Containers, paper and disposable plastics, merchant wholesalers |
| 321920 | Containers, wood, manufacturing |
| 712110 | Contemporary art museums |
| 711120 | Contemporary dance companies |
| 623311 | Continuing care retirement communities |
| 611430 | Continuing education online learning marketplace services (through a website or mobile application) |
| 611430 | Continuing education seminars or conferences |
| 611430 | Continuing education training, online (through a website or mobile application) |
| 325412 | Contraceptive preparations manufacturing |

| | |
|---|---|
| 213112 | Contract services (except geophysical surveying and mapping, site preparation, construction, and transportation activities) for oil and gas fields |
| 561320 | Contract staffing services |
| ****** | Contractors -- see specific activity |
| 813910 | Contractors' associations |
| 315210 | Contractors, cut and sew apparel |
| 325412 | Contrast media in-vivo diagnostic substances (e.g., iodine, barium) manufacturing |
| 335314 | Control circuit devices, magnet and solid-state, manufacturing |
| 335314 | Control circuit relays, industrial, manufacturing |
| 335314 | Control equipment, electric, manufacturing |
| 335313 | Control panels, electric power distribution, manufacturing |
| 238210 | Control system (e.g., environmental, humidity, temperature) installation |
| 335311 | Control transformers manufacturing |
| 332912 | Control valves, fluid power, manufacturing |
| 332911 | Control valves, industrial-type, manufacturing |
| 921130 | Controllers' and comptrollers' offices, government |
| 334513 | Controllers for process variables (e.g., electric, electronic, mechanical, pneumatic operation) manufacturing |
| 334290 | Controlling equipment, street light, manufacturing |
| 335314 | Controls and control accessories, industrial, manufacturing |
| 335314 | Controls for adjustable speed drives manufacturing |
| 334514 | Controls, revolution and timing instruments, manufacturing |
| 623110 | Convalescent homes or convalescent hospitals (except psychiatric) |
| 623220 | Convalescent homes or hospitals for psychiatric patients |
| 456199 | Convalescent supply stores |
| 335220 | Convection ovens (including portable), household-type, manufacturing |
| 423720 | Convectors merchant wholesalers |
| 445131 | Convenience food stores (except those with fuel pumps) |
| 457110 | Convenience food with gasoline stations |
| 335931 | Convenience outlets, electric, manufacturing |
| 561591 | Convention and visitors bureaus |

| | |
|---|---|
| 561591 | Convention bureaus |
| 531120 | Convention center, no promotion of events, rental or leasing |
| 561920 | Convention managers |
| 561920 | Convention or trade show event planners |
| 561920 | Convention organizers |
| 561920 | Convention promoters |
| 561920 | Convention services |
| 813110 | Convents (except schools) |
| 424130 | Converted paper (except stationery and office supplies) merchant wholesalers |
| 316110 | Converters, leather |
| 335312 | Converters, phase and rotary, electrical equipment, manufacturing |
| 313310 | Converters, piece goods |
| 337121 | Convertible sofas (except futons) manufacturing |
| 336390 | Convertible tops for automotive, truck, and bus, manufacturing |
| 313310 | Converting textiles |
| 423830 | Conveying equipment (except farm) merchant wholesalers |
| 423820 | Conveying equipment, farm, merchant wholesalers |
| 326220 | Conveyor belts, rubber, manufacturing |
| 238290 | Conveyor system installation |
| 333922 | Conveyors and conveying equipment manufacturing |
| 311612 | Cooked meats made from purchased carcasses |
| 311824 | Cookie dough made from purchased flour |
| 722515 | Cookie shops, on premise baking and carryout service |
| 311821 | Cookies manufacturing |
| 424490 | Cookies merchant wholesalers |
| 311821 | Cookies, filled, manufacturing |
| 311225 | Cooking and baking oil sprays made from purchased oils |
| 335210 | Cooking appliances (except convection, microwave ovens), household-type electric portable, manufacturing |
| 311351 | Cooking chocolate made from cacao beans |
| 333310 | Cooking equipment (i.e., fryers, microwave ovens, ovens, ranges), commercial-type, manufacturing |
| 423440 | Cooking equipment, commercial, merchant wholesalers |
| 423620 | Cooking equipment, gas and electric, household-type, merchant wholesalers |

| | |
|---|---|
| 424490 | Cooking oils merchant wholesalers |
| 611519 | Cooking schools |
| 331511 | Cooking utensils, cast iron, manufacturing |
| 332215 | Cooking utensils, fabricated metal, manufacturing |
| 327212 | Cooking utensils, glass and glass ceramic, made in glass making plants |
| 423220 | Cooking utensils, household-type, merchant wholesalers |
| 327110 | Cooking ware (e.g., stoneware, coarse earthenware, pottery), manufacturing |
| 327215 | Cooking ware made from purchased glass |
| 327212 | Cooking ware made in glass making plants |
| 327110 | Cooking ware, china, manufacturing |
| 327110 | Cooking ware, fine earthenware, manufacturing |
| 332215 | Cookware, fabricated metal, manufacturing |
| 221330 | Cooled air distribution |
| 326199 | Coolers or ice chests, plastics (except foam), manufacturing |
| 326140 | Coolers or ice chests, polystyrene foam, manufacturing |
| 423740 | Coolers, mechanical, merchant wholesalers |
| 333415 | Coolers, refrigeration, manufacturing |
| 333415 | Coolers, water, manufacturing |
| 423730 | Cooling equipment and supplies merchant wholesalers |
| 238220 | Cooling tower installation |
| 333415 | Cooling towers manufacturing |
| 321920 | Cooperage manufacturing |
| 321920 | Cooperage stock (e.g., heading, hoops, staves) manufacturing |
| 423840 | Cooperage stock merchant wholesalers |
| 321920 | Cooperage stock mills |
| 236117 | Cooperative apartment for-sale builders |
| 531311 | Cooperative apartment managers' offices |
| 236116 | Cooperative apartment, construction general contractors |
| 812331 | Cooperative hospital laundries (i.e., linen supply services) |
| 524113 | Cooperative life insurance organizations |
| 813990 | Cooperative owners' associations |
| 321920 | Coopered tubs manufacturing |
| 332216 | Coordinate and contour measuring machines, machinists' precision tools, manufacturing |

| | |
|---|---|
| 532420 | Copier rental or leasing |
| 327120 | Coping, wall, clay, manufacturing |
| 327390 | Copings, concrete, manufacturing |
| 331529 | Copper alloy castings (except die-castings), unfinished, manufacturing |
| 331420 | Copper alloys (e.g., brass, bronze) made from purchased metal or scrap |
| 331410 | Copper alloys made in primary copper smelting and refining mills |
| 423510 | Copper and copper alloy primary forms merchant wholesalers |
| 331420 | Copper and copper-based shapes (e.g., cake, ingot, slag, wire bar) made from purchased metal or scrap |
| 325130 | Copper base pigments manufacturing |
| 212230 | Copper beneficiating plants |
| 325180 | Copper chloride manufacturing |
| 325612 | Copper cleaners manufacturing |
| 325180 | Copper compounds, not specified elsewhere by process, manufacturing |
| 331410 | Copper concentrate refining |
| 331523 | Copper die-casting foundries |
| 331523 | Copper die-castings, unfinished, manufacturing |
| 331420 | Copper foil made from purchased metal or scrap |
| 332999 | Copper foil not made in rolling mills |
| 332112 | Copper forgings made from purchased metals, unfinished |
| 331529 | Copper foundries (except die-casting) |
| 325180 | Copper iodide manufacturing |
| 212230 | Copper ore concentrates recovery |
| 212230 | Copper ore mine site development for own account |
| 212230 | Copper ores mining and/or beneficiating |
| 331420 | Copper powder, flakes, and paste made from purchased copper |
| 331420 | Copper products made by drawing purchased copper |
| 331420 | Copper products made by rolling, drawing, or extruding purchased copper |
| 331420 | Copper products made in integrated secondary smelting and extruding mills |
| 331420 | Copper products made in integrated secondary smelting mills and drawing plants |
| 238160 | Copper roofing installation |
| 331420 | Copper secondary smelting and alloying |
| 331420 | Copper secondary smelting and refining from purchased metal or scrap |

331410 Copper shapes (e.g., bar, billet, ingot, plate, sheet) made in primary copper smelting and refining mills

331410 Copper smelting and refining, primary

325180 Copper sulfate manufacturing

212230 Copper-water precipitates

561439 Copy centers (except combined with printing services)

561439 Copy shops (except combined with printing services)

423420 Copying machines merchant wholesalers

314994 Cord (except wire) manufacturing

335931 Cord connectors, electric, manufacturing

314994 Cord for reinforcing rubber tires, industrial belting, and fuel cells manufacturing

331420 Cord sets, flexible, made from purchased copper in wire drawing plants

331318 Cord sets, flexible, made in aluminum wire drawing plants

331491 Cord sets, flexible, nonferrous metals (except aluminum, copper), made from purchased nonferrous metals (except aluminum, copper) in wire drawing plants

314994 Cordage (except wire) manufacturing

333248 Cordage and rope (except wire) making machines manufacturing

423840 Cordage merchant wholesalers

325920 Cordite explosive materials manufacturing

334210 Cordless telephones (except cellular) manufacturing

313220 Cords and braids, narrow woven, manufacturing

313210 Corduroys weaving

333994 Core baking and mold drying ovens manufacturing

213112 Core cutting in oil and gas wells, on a contract basis

238910 Core drilling and test boring for construction

213112 Core drilling, exploration services, oil and gas field

333131 Core drills, underground mining-type, manufacturing

322219 Cores (i.e., all-fiber, nonfiber ends of any material), fiber, made from purchased paperboard

332992 Cores, bullet (i.e., 30 mm. or less, 1.18 inch or less), manufacturing

332999 Cores, sand foundry, manufacturing

423840 Cork merchant wholesalers

321999 Cork products (except gaskets) manufacturing

321999 Corks, bottle, manufacturing

111421 Corms farming

311230 Corn breakfast foods manufacturing

311919 Corn chips and related corn snacks manufacturing

424450 Corn chips and related corn snacks merchant wholesalers

311340 Corn confections manufacturing

321992 Corn cribs, prefabricated, wood, manufacturing

311221 Corn dextrin manufacturing

115114 Corn drying

111150 Corn farming (except sweet corn), field and seed production

311211 Corn flour manufacturing

311221 Corn gluten feed manufacturing

311221 Corn gluten meal manufacturing

333111 Corn heads for combines manufacturing

311211 Corn meal made in flour mills

424490 Corn milling products (except pet and livestock feeds) merchant wholesalers

311221 Corn oil cake and meal manufacturing

311225 Corn oil made from purchased oils

311221 Corn oil mills

311221 Corn oil, crude and refined, made by wet milling corn

333111 Corn pickers and shellers manufacturing

335210 Corn poppers, household-type electric, manufacturing

333241 Corn popping machinery (i.e., food manufacturing-type) manufacturing

333310 Corn popping machines, commercial-type, manufacturing

339113 Corn remover and bunion pad manufacturing

115114 Corn shelling

311221 Corn starch manufacturing

311221 Corn sweeteners (e.g., dextrose, fructose, glucose) made by wet milling corn

311999 Corn syrups made from purchased sweeteners

311213 Corn, malt, manufacturing

424510 Corn, raw (except seed corn), merchant wholesalers

339112 Corneal microscopes manufacturing

311612 Corned meats made from purchases carcasses

| | |
|---|---|
| 316990 | Corners, luggage, leather, manufacturing |
| 339992 | Cornets and parts manufacturing |
| 332322 | Cornices, sheet metal (except stampings), manufacturing |
| 321918 | Cornices, wood, manufacturing |
| 112320 | Cornish hen production |
| 424490 | Cornmeal, edible, merchant wholesalers |
| 212323 | Cornwall stone mining and/or beneficiating |
| 923120 | Coroners' offices |
| 522130 | Corporate credit unions |
| 813211 | Corporate foundations, awarding grants |
| 541430 | Corporate identification (i.e., logo) design services |
| 541110 | Corporate law offices |
| 551114 | Corporate offices |
| 721310 | Corporate rooming and boarding houses |
| 115210 | Corralling, drovers |
| 332323 | Corrals, metal, manufacturing |
| 325998 | Correction fluids (i.e., typewriter) manufacturing |
| 922140 | Correctional boot camps (except private operation of) |
| 561210 | Correctional facilities, privately operated |
| 561210 | Correctional facility operation on a contract or fee basis |
| 922140 | Correctional institutions (except private operation of) |
| 237120 | Corrosion protection, underground pipeline and oil storage tank |
| 322211 | Corrugated and solid fiber boxes made from purchased paper or paperboard |
| 322211 | Corrugated and solid fiberboard pads made from purchased paper or paperboard |
| 238160 | Corrugated metal roofing installation |
| 322211 | Corrugated paper made from purchased paper or paperboard |
| 424130 | Corrugated paper merchant wholesalers |
| 331221 | Corrugating iron or steel in cold rolling mills made from purchased iron or steel |
| 315210 | Corselets cut and sew apparel contractors |
| 315250 | Corselets, women's and girls', cut and sewn from purchased fabric (except apparel contractors) |
| 315210 | Corsets and allied garments (except surgical) cut and sew apparel contractors |
| 315250 | Corsets and allied garments (except surgical), women's and girls', cut and |

| | |
|---|---|
| | sewn from purchased fabric (except apparel contractors) |
| 339113 | Corsets, surgical, manufacturing |
| 325411 | Cortisone, uncompounded, manufacturing |
| 212390 | Corundum mining and/or beneficiating |
| 611511 | Cosmetic art schools (e.g., makeup, skin care) |
| 316990 | Cosmetic bags (except metal) manufacturing |
| 339910 | Cosmetic bags, precious metal, manufacturing |
| 325620 | Cosmetic creams, lotions, and oils manufacturing |
| 561910 | Cosmetic kit assembling and packaging services |
| 424210 | Cosmetics merchant wholesalers |
| 456120 | Cosmetics stores |
| 812112 | Cosmetology salons or shops |
| 611511 | Cosmetology schools |
| 541490 | Costume design services (except independent theatrical costume designers) |
| 711510 | Costume designers, independent theatrical |
| 339910 | Costume jewelry manufacturing |
| 423940 | Costume jewelry merchant wholesalers |
| 458110 | Costume jewelry stores |
| 532281 | Costume rental |
| 458110 | Costume stores (including theatrical) |
| 315210 | Costumes (e.g., lodge, masquerade, theatrical) cut and sew apparel contractors |
| 315250 | Costumes (e.g., lodge, masquerade, theatrical) cut and sewn from purchased fabric (except apparel contractors) |
| 424350 | Costumes, clothing, men's and boys', merchant wholesalers |
| 424350 | Costumes, women's, children's, and infants', merchant wholesalers |
| 337121 | Cot springs, assembled, manufacturing |
| 337126 | Cots, metal household-type, manufacturing |
| 337122 | Cots, wood household-type, manufacturing |
| 311511 | Cottage cheese manufacturing |
| 236115 | Cottage construction general contractors |
| 236117 | Cottage for-sale builders |
| 531110 | Cottage rental or leasing |
| 721199 | Cottages, housekeeping |

| | |
|---|---|
| 332722 | Cotter pins, metal, manufacturing |
| 424990 | Cotton (except raw) merchant wholesalers |
| 339113 | Cotton and cotton balls, absorbent, manufacturing |
| 333111 | Cotton balers and presses manufacturing |
| 314999 | Cotton battings (except nonwoven batting) manufacturing |
| 313110 | Cotton cordage spun yarns made from purchased fiber |
| 313210 | Cotton fabrics, broadwoven, weaving |
| 313220 | Cotton fabrics, narrow woven weaving |
| 111920 | Cotton farming, field and seed production |
| 322120 | Cotton fiber paper stock manufacturing |
| 115111 | Cotton ginning |
| 333111 | Cotton ginning machinery manufacturing |
| 333111 | Cotton picker and stripper harvesting machinery manufacturing |
| 313110 | Cotton spun yarns made from purchased fiber |
| 313110 | Cotton thread manufacturing |
| 339113 | Cotton tipped applicators manufacturing |
| 115113 | Cotton, machine harvesting |
| 424590 | Cotton, raw, merchant wholesalers |
| 111920 | Cottonseed farming |
| 311225 | Cottonseed oil made from purchased oils |
| 311224 | Cottonseed oil, cake and meal, made in crushing mills |
| 337121 | Couch springs, assembled, manufacturing |
| 337121 | Couches, upholstered, manufacturing |
| 311340 | Cough drops (except medicated) manufacturing |
| 325412 | Cough drops, medicated, manufacturing |
| 325412 | Cough medicines manufacturing |
| 334513 | Coulometric analyzers, industrial process-type, manufacturing |
| 334516 | Coulometric analyzers, laboratory-type, manufacturing |
| 325199 | Coumarin manufacturing |
| 325211 | Coumarone-indene resins manufacturing |
| 926110 | Councils of Economic Advisers |
| 624190 | Counseling services (except by psychiatrists, psychoanalysts, or psychotherapists) |
| 621410 | Counseling services, family planning |
| 541110 | Counselors' at law offices |

| | |
|---|---|
| 541110 | Counselors' at law private practices |
| 334519 | Count rate meters, nuclear radiation, manufacturing |
| 334514 | Counter type registers manufacturing |
| 337215 | Counter units (except refrigerated) manufacturing |
| 333515 | Counterbores (i.e., a machine tool accessory), metalworking, manufacturing |
| 332216 | Counterbores and countersinking bits, woodworking, manufacturing |
| 334511 | Countermeasure sets (e.g., active countermeasures, jamming equipment) manufacturing |
| 334514 | Counters (e.g., electrical, electronic, mechanical), totalizing, manufacturing |
| 316990 | Counters (i.e., shoe cut stock), leather, manufacturing |
| 333415 | Counters and display cases, refrigerated, manufacturing |
| 334514 | Counters, revolution, manufacturing |
| 333515 | Countersinks (i.e., a machine tool accessory) manufacturing |
| 238340 | Countertop (ceramic tile, stone), residential-type, installation |
| 238350 | Countertop (except ceramic tile or stone), residential-type, installation |
| 238390 | Countertop and cabinet, metal (except residential-type), installation |
| 337215 | Countertops (except kitchen and bathroom), wood or plastics laminated on wood, manufacturing |
| 423390 | Countertops (except wood, wood fiber, stone, concrete) merchant wholesalers |
| 337110 | Countertops (i.e., kitchen, bathroom), wood or plastics laminated on wood, manufacturing |
| 326199 | Countertops, plastics, manufacturing |
| 423320 | Countertops, stone and concrete, merchant wholesalers |
| 327991 | Countertops, stone, manufacturing |
| 423310 | Countertops, wood and wood fiber, merchant wholesalers |
| 337110 | Countertops, wood, manufacturing |
| 334514 | Counting devices manufacturing |
| 713910 | Country clubs |
| 711130 | Country musical artists, independent |
| 711130 | Country musical groups |
| 921120 | County commissioners |
| 925120 | County development agencies |
| 921110 | County supervisors' and executives' offices |

| | |
|---|---|
| 923110 | County supervisors of education (except school boards) |
| 332919 | Couplings, hose, metal (except fluid power), manufacturing |
| 333613 | Couplings, mechanical power transmission, manufacturing |
| 332996 | Couplings, pipe, made from purchased metal pipe |
| 541870 | Coupon direct distribution services |
| 561990 | Coupon processing services |
| 561990 | Coupon redemption services (i.e., clearinghouse) |
| 492110 | Courier services (i.e., intercity network) (except establishments operating under a universal service obligation) |
| 611410 | Court reporting schools |
| 561492 | Court reporting services |
| 922110 | Courts of law, civilian (except American Indian or Alaska Native) |
| 921150 | Courts, American Indian or Alaska Native |
| 922110 | Courts, civilian (except American Indian or Alaska Native) |
| 928110 | Courts, military |
| 922110 | Courts, small claims |
| 315210 | Coveralls, work, cut and sew apparel contractors |
| 315250 | Coveralls, work, men's and boys', cut and sewn from purchased fabric (except apparel contractors) |
| 315250 | Coveralls, work, women's and girls', cut and sewn from purchased fabric (except apparel contractors) |
| 314910 | Covers (e.g., boat, swimming pool, truck) made from purchased fabrics |
| 332313 | Covers, annealing, fabricated metal plate work, manufacturing |
| 321999 | Covers, bottle and demijohn, willow, rattan, and reed, manufacturing |
| 332313 | Covers, floating, fabricated metal plate work, manufacturing |
| 332322 | Cowls, sheet metal (except stampings), manufacturing |
| 531120 | Coworking space rental or leasing |
| 111219 | Cowpea (except dry) farming, field and seed production |
| 111130 | Cowpea farming, dry, field and seed production |
| 541211 | CPAs' (certified public accountants) offices |
| 611699 | CPR (cardiopulmonary resuscitation) training and certification |
| 332618 | Crab traps made from purchased wire |

| | |
|---|---|
| 114112 | Crabbing |
| 333241 | Cracker making machinery manufacturing |
| 311821 | Crackers (e.g., graham, soda) manufacturing |
| 424490 | Crackers merchant wholesalers |
| 333519 | Cradle assembly machinery (i.e., wire making equipment) manufacturing |
| 337122 | Cradles, wood, manufacturing |
| 459420 | Craft (except craft supply) stores |
| 339930 | Craft and hobby kits and sets manufacturing |
| 561920 | Craft fair managers |
| 561920 | Craft fair organizers |
| 561920 | Craft fair promoters |
| 423920 | Craft kits merchant wholesalers |
| 459120 | Craft supply stores (except needlecraft) |
| 611513 | Craft union apprenticeship training programs |
| 111334 | Cranberry farming |
| 335314 | Crane and hoist controls, including metal mill, manufacturing |
| 532412 | Crane rental or leasing without operator |
| 238990 | Crane rental with operator |
| 423810 | Cranes (except industrial) merchant wholesalers |
| 333120 | Cranes, construction-type, manufacturing |
| 333924 | Cranes, industrial truck, manufacturing |
| 423830 | Cranes, industrial, merchant wholesalers |
| 423810 | Cranes, mining, merchant wholesalers |
| 333923 | Cranes, overhead traveling, manufacturing |
| 325998 | Crankcase additive preparations manufacturing |
| 336310 | Crankshaft assemblies, automotive and truck gasoline engine, manufacturing |
| 333517 | Crankshaft grinding machines metal cutting type, manufacturing |
| 321920 | Crates (e.g., berry, butter, fruit, vegetable) made of wood, wirebound, manufacturing |
| 424130 | Crates, paperboard and disposable plastics, merchant wholesalers |
| 488991 | Crating goods for shipping |
| 112512 | Crawfish production, farm raising |
| 238910 | Crawler tractor rental with operator |
| 114112 | Crayfish fishing |
| 339940 | Crayons manufacturing |

| | |
|---|---|
| 311511 | Cream manufacturing |
| 424430 | Cream merchant wholesalers |
| 325199 | Cream of tartar manufacturing |
| 333111 | Cream separators, farm-type, manufacturing |
| 333241 | Cream separators, industrial, manufacturing |
| 424430 | Cream stations merchant wholesalers |
| 311514 | Cream, dried and powdered, manufacturing |
| 311512 | Creamery butter manufacturing |
| 424430 | Creamery products (except canned) merchant wholesalers |
| 424490 | Creamery products, canned, merchant wholesalers |
| 313310 | Crease resistant finishing of fabrics |
| 561450 | Credit agencies |
| 323111 | Credit and identification card imprinting, embossing, and encoding |
| 326199 | Credit and identification card stock, plastics, manufacturing |
| 524126 | Credit and other financial responsibility insurance carriers, direct |
| 561440 | Credit arrears collection services |
| 561450 | Credit bureaus |
| 522210 | Credit card banks |
| 522210 | Credit card issuing |
| 812990 | Credit card notification services (i.e., lost or stolen card reporting) |
| 522320 | Credit card processing services |
| 561450 | Credit clearinghouses |
| 561450 | Credit investigation services |
| 524113 | Credit life insurance carriers, direct |
| 561450 | Credit rating services |
| 541990 | Credit repair (i.e., counseling) services, consumer |
| 561450 | Credit reporting bureaus |
| 522130 | Credit unions |
| 333998 | Cremating ovens manufacturing |
| 812220 | Crematories (except combined with funeral homes) |
| 111219 | Crenshaw melon farming, field, bedding plant and seed production |
| 325194 | Creosote made by distillation of coal tar |
| 325194 | Creosote made by distillation of wood tar |
| 321114 | Creosoting of wood |
| 322299 | Crepe paper made from purchased paper |
| 325211 | Cresol resins manufacturing |
| 325211 | Cresol-furfural resins manufacturing |
| 325194 | Cresols made by distillation of coal tar |
| 325194 | Cresylic acids made from refined petroleum or natural gas |
| 115115 | Crew leaders, farm labor |
| 315120 | Crew socks knitting or knitting and finishing |
| 237990 | Cribbing (i.e., shore protection), construction |
| 337126 | Cribs (i.e., baby beds), metal, manufacturing |
| 337122 | Cribs (i.e., baby beds), wood, manufacturing |
| 112990 | Cricket production |
| 562910 | Crime scene cleanup services |
| 922120 | Criminal investigation offices, government |
| 922190 | Criminal justice statistics centers, government |
| 541110 | Criminal law offices |
| 111998 | Crimson cloves seed farming |
| 624190 | Crisis intervention centers |
| 114111 | Croaker fishing |
| 313110 | Crochet spun yarns (e.g., cotton, manmade fiber, silk, wool) made from purchased fiber |
| 314999 | Crochet ware made from purchased materials |
| 335210 | Crock pots, household-type electric, manufacturing |
| 327110 | Crockery manufacturing |
| 311812 | Croissants, baking, made in commercial bakeries |
| 115114 | Crop cleaning |
| 333111 | Crop driers manufacturing |
| 115112 | Crop dusting |
| 524126 | Crop insurance carrier, direct |
| 423820 | Crop preparation machinery (e.g., cleaning, conditioning, drying) merchant wholesalers |
| 115112 | Crop spraying |
| 316990 | Crops, riding, manufacturing |
| 339920 | Croquet sets manufacturing |
| 713920 | Cross country skiing facilities without accommodations |
| 332911 | Cross valves, industrial-type, manufacturing |
| 321114 | Crossties, treating |
| 311812 | Croutons and bread crumbs made in commercial bakeries |

| | |
|---|---|
| 423840 | Crowns and closures, metal, merchant wholesalers |
| 332119 | Crowns, metal (e.g., bottle, can), stamping |
| 334419 | CRT (cathode ray tube) manufacturing |
| 327120 | Crucibles, fire clay, manufacturing |
| 327120 | Crucibles, graphite, magnesite, chrome, silica, or other nonclay materials, manufacturing |
| 311221 | Crude corn oil manufacturing |
| 424720 | Crude oil merchant wholesalers (except bulk stations, terminals) |
| 486110 | Crude oil pipeline transportation |
| 324110 | Crude oil refining |
| 424710 | Crude oil terminals, merchant wholesalers |
| 211120 | Crude petroleum from oil sand |
| 211120 | Crude petroleum from oil shale |
| 211120 | Crude petroleum lease condensate production |
| 211120 | Crude petroleum production |
| 324110 | Crude petroleum refineries |
| 424990 | Crude rubber merchant wholesalers |
| 336320 | Cruise control mechanisms, electronic, automotive, truck, and bus, manufacturing |
| 483114 | Cruise lines (i.e., deep sea passenger transportation to and from domestic ports, including Puerto Rico) |
| 483112 | Cruise lines (i.e., deep sea passenger transportation to or from foreign ports) |
| 561599 | Cruise reservation services |
| 561599 | Cruise ship ticket offices |
| 713210 | Cruises, gambling |
| 115310 | Cruising timber |
| 311812 | Crullers (except frozen) made in commercial bakeries |
| 311813 | Crullers, frozen, made in a commercial bakery |
| 423320 | Crushed stone merchant wholesalers |
| 333120 | Crushing machinery, portable, manufacturing |
| 333131 | Crushing machinery, stationary, manufacturing |
| 423810 | Crushing, pulverizing, and screening machinery, construction and mining, merchant wholesalers |
| 423830 | Crushing, pulverizing, and screening machinery, industrial, merchant wholesalers |

| | |
|---|---|
| 333120 | Crushing, pulverizing, and screening machinery, portable, manufacturing |
| 112512 | Crustacean production, farm raising |
| 339113 | Crutches and walkers manufacturing |
| 423450 | Crutches merchant wholesalers |
| 532283 | Crutches, invalid, rental |
| 423830 | Cryogenic cooling devices merchant wholesalers |
| 332420 | Cryogenic tanks, heavy gauge metal, manufacturing |
| 332811 | Cryogenic treating metals for the trade |
| 212390 | Cryolite mining and/or beneficiating |
| 311340 | Crystallized fruits and fruit peel manufacturing |
| 334419 | Crystals and crystal assemblies, electronic, manufacturing |
| 334517 | CT/CAT (computerized axial tomography) scanners manufacturing |
| 621512 | CT-SCAN (computer tomography) centers |
| 335313 | Cubicles (i.e., electric switchboard equipment) manufacturing |
| 111219 | Cucumber farming (except under cover), field, bedding plant and seed production |
| 111419 | Cucumber farming, grown under cover |
| 339993 | Cuff links (except precious) manufacturing |
| 339910 | Cuff links, precious metal, manufacturing |
| 332999 | Cuffs, leg, iron, manufacturing |
| 611519 | Culinary arts schools |
| 112310 | Cull hen production |
| 213113 | Culm bank recovery, anthracite, on a contract basis |
| 212114 | Culm bank recovery, bituminous coal, lignite, or anthracite (except on a contract basis) |
| 213113 | Culm bank recovery, coal, on a contract basis |
| 315210 | Culottes cut and sew apparel contractors |
| 315250 | Culottes, women's and girls', cut and sewn from purchased fabric (except apparel contractors) |
| 111422 | Cultivated florist greens growing |
| 423820 | Cultivating machinery and equipment merchant wholesalers |
| 115112 | Cultivation services |
| 333111 | Cultivators, farm-type, manufacturing |
| 333112 | Cultivators, powered, lawn and garden-type, manufacturing |
| 926110 | Cultural and arts development support program administration |

| | |
|---|---|
| 325414 | Culture media manufacturing |
| 326191 | Cultured marble plumbing fixtures manufacturing |
| 326199 | Cultured marble products (except plumbing fixtures) manufacturing |
| 112512 | Cultured pearl production, farm raising |
| 326199 | Cultured stone products (except plumbing fixtures) manufacturing |
| 238910 | Culvert or bridge removal |
| 327332 | Culvert pipe, concrete, manufacturing |
| 423320 | Culvert pipe, concrete, merchant wholesalers |
| 423390 | Culvert pipe, metal and plastics, merchant wholesalers |
| 238990 | Culvert, concrete, residential and commercial paved area |
| 332313 | Culverts, fabricated metal plate work, manufacturing |
| 237310 | Culverts, highway, road and street, construction |
| 332322 | Culverts, sheet metal (except stampings), manufacturing |
| 325110 | Cumene made from refined petroleum or liquid hydrocarbons |
| 324110 | Cumene made in petroleum refineries |
| 315210 | Cummerbunds cut and sew apparel contractors |
| 315990 | Cummerbunds cut and sewn from purchased fabric (except apparel contractors) |
| 332313 | Cupolas, fabricated metal plate work, manufacturing |
| 212230 | Cuprite mining and/or beneficiating |
| 423440 | Cups, commercial (except paper and disposable plastics), merchant wholesalers |
| 322299 | Cups, molded pulp, manufacturing |
| 424130 | Cups, paper and disposable plastics, merchant wholesalers |
| 423220 | Cups, plastics (except disposable), merchant wholesalers |
| 326199 | Cups, plastics (except foam), manufacturing |
| 326140 | Cups, polystyrene foam, manufacturing |
| 238990 | Curb and gutter construction, residential and commercial driveway and parking area, concrete |
| 327991 | Curbing, granite and stone, manufacturing |
| 237310 | Curbs and street gutters, highway, road and street, construction |
| 311513 | Curds, cheese, made in a cheese plant, manufacturing |
| 424460 | Cured fish merchant wholesalers |
| 311611 | Cured hides and skins produced in slaughtering plants |
| 311612 | Cured meats (e.g., brined, dried, and salted) made from purchased carcasses |
| 333111 | Curers, tobacco, manufacturing |
| 311710 | Curing fish and seafood |
| 459420 | Curio shops |
| 424990 | Curios merchant wholesalers |
| 326299 | Curlers, hair, rubber, manufacturing |
| 713990 | Curling facilities |
| 423620 | Curling irons, electric, merchant wholesalers |
| 335210 | Curling irons, household-type electric, manufacturing |
| 111334 | Currant farming |
| 333310 | Currency counting machinery manufacturing |
| 423420 | Currency handling machines merchant wholesalers |
| 335311 | Current limiting reactors, electrical, manufacturing |
| 334515 | Current measuring equipment manufacturing |
| 335931 | Current taps, attachment plug and screw shell types, manufacturing |
| 423610 | Current-carrying wiring devices merchant wholesalers |
| 316110 | Currying furs |
| 316110 | Currying leather |
| 449122 | Curtain and drapery stores, packaged |
| 812320 | Curtain cleaning services |
| 337920 | Curtain or drapery fixtures (e.g., poles, rods, rollers) manufacturing |
| 337920 | Curtain rods and fittings manufacturing |
| 321999 | Curtain stretchers, wood, manufacturing |
| 238150 | Curtain wall, glass, installation |
| 238190 | Curtain wall, metal, installation |
| 332323 | Curtain wall, metal, manufacturing |
| 238120 | Curtain wall, precast concrete, installation |
| 313210 | Curtains and draperies made in broadwoven fabric mills |
| 314120 | Curtains and draperies, window, made from purchased fabrics |
| 313240 | Curtains made in lace mills |
| 313240 | Curtains made in warp or weft knitting mills |
| 423220 | Curtains merchant wholesalers |

| | |
|---|---|
| 337121 | Cushion springs, assembled, manufacturing |
| 314120 | Cushions (except carpet, springs) made from purchased fabrics |
| 326150 | Cushions, carpet and rug, urethane and other foam plastics (except polystyrene), manufacturing |
| 311520 | Custard, frozen, manufacturing |
| 561720 | Custodial services |
| 337212 | Custom architectural millwork and fixtures, manufacturing on a job shop basis |
| 236116 | Custom builders (except for-sale), multifamily buildings |
| 236115 | Custom builders (except for-sale), single-family home |
| 236117 | Custom builders, for-sale builders, multifamily buildings |
| 236117 | Custom builders, for-sale builders, single-family home |
| 325991 | Custom compounding (i.e., blending and mixing) of purchased plastics resins |
| 337212 | Custom design interiors (i.e., coordinated furniture, architectural woodwork, fixtures), manufacturing |
| 311119 | Custom milling of animal feed |
| 449129 | Custom picture frame shops |
| 333517 | Custom roll forming machines, metalworking, manufacturing |
| 332114 | Custom roll forming metal products |
| 321113 | Custom sawmills |
| 311611 | Custom slaughtering |
| 315250 | Custom tailors, men's and boys' dress shirts, cut and sewn from purchased fabric |
| 315250 | Custom tailors, men's and boys' suits, cut and sewn from purchased fabric |
| 315250 | Custom tailors, women's and girls' dresses cut and sewn from purchased fabric (except apparel contractors) |
| 561422 | Customer service call centers |
| 541613 | Customer service management consulting services |
| 488510 | Customs brokers |
| 921130 | Customs bureaus |
| 541614 | Customs consulting services |
| 327215 | Cut and engraved glassware made from purchased glass |
| 315210 | Cut and sew apparel contractors |
| 111422 | Cut flower growing |
| 111422 | Cut rose growing |
| 316990 | Cut stock for boots and shoes manufacturing |
| 321912 | Cut stock manufacturing |
| 327991 | Cut stone bases (e.g., desk sets pedestals, lamps, plaques and similar small particles) manufacturing |
| 327991 | Cut stone products (e.g., blocks, statuary) manufacturing |
| 811490 | Cutlery (e.g., knives, scissors) sharpening, household-type |
| 423710 | Cutlery merchant wholesalers |
| 332215 | Cutlery, nonprecious and precious plated metal, manufacturing |
| 339910 | Cutlery, precious metal (except precious plated), manufacturing |
| 333517 | Cut-off machines, metalworking, manufacturing |
| 335931 | Cutouts, switch and fuse, manufacturing |
| 333131 | Cutters, coal, manufacturing |
| 332216 | Cutters, glass, manufacturing |
| 333515 | Cutters, metal milling, manufacturing |
| 113310 | Cutting and transporting timber |
| 213112 | Cutting cores in oil and gas wells on a contract basis |
| 332216 | Cutting dies (e.g., paper, leather, textile) manufacturing |
| 332216 | Cutting dies (except metal cutting) manufacturing |
| 333514 | Cutting dies, metalworking, manufacturing |
| 315210 | Cutting fabric owned by others for apparel |
| 339114 | Cutting instruments, dental, manufacturing |
| 333517 | Cutting machines, metalworking, manufacturing |
| 238910 | Cutting new rights of way |
| 316110 | Cutting of leather |
| 424470 | Cutting of purchased carcasses (except boxed meat cut on an assembly line basis) merchant wholesalers |
| 324191 | Cutting oils made from refined petroleum |
| 325998 | Cutting oils, synthetic, manufacturing |
| 113310 | Cutting timber |
| 327215 | Cutting, engraving, etching, painting or polishing purchased glass |
| 111422 | Cuttings farming |
| 325180 | Cyanides manufacturing |
| 212323 | Cyanite mining and/or beneficiating |
| 211130 | Cycle condensate production |

325110 Cyclic aromatic hydrocarbons made from refined petroleum or liquid hydrocarbons

324110 Cyclic aromatic hydrocarbons made in petroleum refineries

424690 Cyclic crudes and intermediates merchant wholesalers

325194 Cyclic crudes made by distillation of coal tar

325194 Cyclic intermediates made from refined petroleum or natural gas (except aromatic petrochemicals)

325212 Cyclo rubber, synthetic, manufacturing

325194 Cyclohexane manufacturing

332313 Cyclones, industrial, fabricated metal plate work, manufacturing

325194 Cyclopentane made from refined petroleum or natural gas

325194 Cyclopropane made from refined petroleum or natural gas

325412 Cyclopropane medicinal preparations manufacturing

325194 Cycloterpenes manufacturing

335999 Cyclotrons manufacturing

333517 Cylinder boring machines metal cutting type, manufacturing

336310 Cylinder heads, automotive and truck gasoline engine, manufacturing

327332 Cylinder pipe, prestressed concrete, manufacturing

332618 Cylinder wire cloth made from purchased wire

332994 Cylinders and clips, gun, manufacturing

333995 Cylinders, fluid power, manufacturing

336340 Cylinders, master brake (new and rebuilt), manufacturing

332420 Cylinders, pressure, heavy gauge metal, manufacturing

334417 Cylindrical connectors, electronic, manufacturing

332991 Cylindrical roller bearings manufacturing

339992 Cymbals and parts manufacturing

339112 Cystoscopes (except electromedical) manufacturing

334510 Cystoscopes, electromedical, manufacturing

325413 Cytology and histology in-vitro diagnostic substances manufacturing

621511 Cytology health laboratories

112120 Dairy cattle farming

311119 Dairy cattle feeds, supplements, concentrates, and premixes, manufacturing

424430 Dairy depots merchant wholesalers

311514 Dairy food canning

112420 Dairy goat farming

112111 Dairy heifer replacement production

541690 Dairy herd consulting services

115210 Dairy herd improvement associations

333241 Dairy product plant machinery and equipment

445298 Dairy product stores

424430 Dairy products (except canned, dried) merchant wholesalers

424490 Dairy products, dried or canned, merchant wholesalers

424430 Dairy products, frozen, merchant wholesalers

112410 Dairy sheep farming

237990 Dam construction

332312 Dam gates, metal plate, manufacturing

334512 Damper operators (e.g., electric, pneumatic, thermostatic) manufacturing

332322 Dampers, sheet metal (except stampings), manufacturing

238390 Dampproofing contractors

711130 Dance bands

713940 Dance centers, aerobic

711120 Dance companies

711310 Dance festival managers with facilities

711320 Dance festival managers without facilities

711310 Dance festival organizers with facilities

711320 Dance festival organizers without facilities

711310 Dance festival promoters with facilities

711320 Dance festival promoters without facilities

531120 Dance hall rental or leasing

713990 Dance halls

611610 Dance instruction

711120 Dance productions, live theatrical

611610 Dance schools

611610 Dance studios

711120 Dance theaters

621340 Dance therapists' offices (e.g., centers, clinics)

711120 Dance troupes

| | |
|---|---|
| 711510 | Dancers, independent |
| 313110 | Darning thread (e.g., cotton, manmade fibers, silk, wool) manufacturing |
| 332994 | Dart guns manufacturing |
| 339930 | Darts and dart games manufacturing |
| 518210 | Data capture imaging services |
| 236220 | Data center construction |
| 334210 | Data communications equipment (e.g., bridges, gateways, routers) manufacturing |
| 518210 | Data entry services |
| 423430 | Data keying equipment merchant wholesalers |
| 334513 | Data loggers, industrial process-type, manufacturing |
| 518210 | Data processing computer services |
| 541513 | Data processing facilities (i.e., clients' facilities) management and operation services |
| 423430 | Data processing machines, computer, merchant wholesalers |
| 518210 | Data processing services (except payroll services, financial transaction processing services) |
| 323111 | Databases commercial printing (except screen) without publishing |
| 323113 | Databases screen printing without publishing |
| 111339 | Date farming |
| 339940 | Date stamps, hand operated, manufacturing |
| 311423 | Dates, dried, made in dehydration plants |
| 311340 | Dates, sugared and stuffed, manufacturing |
| 334519 | Dating devices and machines (except rubber stamps) manufacturing |
| 812990 | Dating services |
| 333923 | Davits manufacturing |
| ****** | Day camps, instructional -- see type of instruction |
| 624120 | Day care centers for disabled persons and the elderly |
| 624120 | Day care centers, adult |
| 624410 | Day care centers, child or infant |
| 624410 | Day care services, child or infant |
| 812199 | Day spas |
| 621310 | DCs' (doctors of chiropractic) offices (e.g., centers, clinics) |
| 621210 | DDSs' (doctors of dental surgery) offices (e.g., centers, clinics) |

| | |
|---|---|
| 325320 | DDT (dichlorodiphenyltrichloroethane) insecticides manufacturing |
| 922120 | DEA (Drug Enforcement Administration) |
| 332510 | Dead bolts, metal, manufacturing |
| ****** | Dealers -- see type |
| 562119 | Debris removal services |
| 561440 | Debt collection services |
| 333517 | Deburring machines, metalworking, manufacturing |
| 334515 | Decade boxes (i.e., capacitance, inductance, resistance) manufacturing |
| 325199 | Decahydronaphthalene manufacturing |
| 327110 | Decalcomania on china and glass for the trade |
| 339999 | Decalcomania work (except on china, glass) |
| 111339 | Deciduous tree fruit (except apples, citrus) farming |
| 238190 | Deck and grate (except roof), metal, installation |
| 238350 | Deck construction, residential-type |
| 327215 | Decorated glassware made from purchased glass |
| 327110 | Decorating china (e.g., encrusting gold, silver, other metal on china) for the trade |
| 541410 | Decorating consulting services, interior |
| 541410 | Decoration services for special events |
| 335139 | Decorative area lighting fixtures (except residential) manufacturing |
| 335131 | Decorative area lighting fixtures, residential, manufacturing |
| 712110 | Decorative art museums |
| 238150 | Decorative glass and mirror installation |
| 327212 | Decorative glassware made in glass making plants |
| 335139 | Decorative lamp bulbs manufacturing |
| 238190 | Decorative steel and wrought iron work installation |
| 314999 | Decorative stitching contractors on apparel |
| 314999 | Decorative stitching on textile articles and apparel |
| 321918 | Decorative wood moldings (e.g., base, chair rail, crown, shoe) manufacturing |
| 115114 | Decorticating flax |
| 483113 | Deep sea freight transportation to or from domestic ports (including Puerto Rico) |
| 483111 | Deep sea freight transportation to or from foreign ports |

| | |
|---|---|
| 483114 | Deep sea passenger transportation to and from domestic ports (including Puerto Rico) |
| 483112 | Deep sea passenger transportation to or from foreign ports |
| 333310 | Deep-fat fryers, commercial-type, manufacturing |
| 335210 | Deep-fat fryers, household-type electric, manufacturing |
| 112990 | Deer production |
| 334510 | Defibrillators manufacturing |
| 325312 | Defluorinated phosphates manufacturing |
| 325998 | Defoamers and antifoaming agents manufacturing |
| 325320 | Defoliants manufacturing |
| 325998 | Degreasing preparations for machinery parts manufacturing |
| 325612 | Degreasing preparations, household-type, manufacturing |
| 333415 | Dehumidifiers (except portable electric) manufacturing |
| 335210 | Dehumidifiers, portable electric, manufacturing |
| 311514 | Dehydrated milk manufacturing |
| 311423 | Dehydrating fruits and vegetables |
| 311423 | Dehydrating potato products (e.g., flakes, granules) |
| 325998 | Deicing preparations manufacturing |
| 322110 | Deinking plants |
| 322110 | Deinking recovered paper |
| 424470 | Deli meats (except poultry) merchant wholesalers |
| 424440 | Deli meats, poultry, merchant wholesalers |
| 722513 | Delicatessen restaurants |
| 333998 | Delicatessen scales manufacturing |
| 445240 | Delicatessens (except grocery store, restaurants) |
| 445110 | Delicatessens primarily retailing a range of grocery items and meats |
| 561440 | Delinquent account collection services |
| 623990 | Delinquent youth halfway group homes |
| 115114 | Delinting cottonseed |
| 332618 | Delivery cases made from purchased wire |
| 492210 | Delivery service (except as part of intercity courier network, U.S. Postal Service) |
| 334515 | Demand meters, electric, manufacturing |
| 541720 | Demographic research and development services |
| 238910 | Demolition contractor |
| 238910 | Demolition, building and structure |
| 541890 | Demonstration services, merchandise |
| 336212 | Demountable cargo containers manufacturing |
| 325193 | Denatured alcohol manufacturing |
| 313210 | Denims weaving |
| 321219 | Densified wood manufacturing |
| 333310 | Densitometers (except laboratory analytical) manufacturing |
| 334516 | Densitometers, laboratory analytical, manufacturing |
| 334513 | Density and specific gravity instruments, industrial process-type, manufacturing |
| 339114 | Dental alloys for amalgams manufacturing |
| 424210 | Dental care preparations merchant wholesalers |
| 339114 | Dental chairs manufacturing |
| 423450 | Dental chairs merchant wholesalers |
| 339114 | Dental equipment and instruments manufacturing |
| 423450 | Dental equipment and supplies merchant wholesalers |
| 811210 | Dental equipment repair and maintenance services |
| 325620 | Dental floss manufacturing |
| 339114 | Dental glues and cements manufacturing |
| 339114 | Dental hand instruments (e.g., forceps) manufacturing |
| 611519 | Dental hygienist schools |
| 621399 | Dental hygienists' offices (e.g., centers, clinics) |
| 339114 | Dental impression materials manufacturing |
| 339114 | Dental instrument delivery systems manufacturing |
| 524114 | Dental insurance carriers, direct |
| 339116 | Dental laboratories |
| 339114 | Dental laboratory equipment manufacturing |
| 541715 | Dental research and development laboratories or services |
| 611310 | Dental schools |
| 621210 | Dental surgeons' offices (e.g., centers, clinics) |
| 611519 | Dental technician schools |
| 339114 | Dental wax manufacturing |
| 621512 | Dental X-ray laboratories |
| 325611 | Dentifrices manufacturing |

| | |
|---|---|
| 424210 | Dentifrices merchant wholesalers |
| 813920 | Dentists' associations |
| 621210 | Dentists' offices (e.g., centers, clinics) |
| 423450 | Dentists' professional supplies merchant wholesalers |
| 325620 | Denture adhesives manufacturing |
| 325620 | Denture cleaners, effervescent, manufacturing |
| 339114 | Denture materials manufacturing |
| 339116 | Dentures, custom made in dental laboratories |
| 621399 | Denturists' offices (e.g., centers, clinics) |
| 561720 | Deodorant servicing of rest rooms |
| 325612 | Deodorants (except personal) manufacturing |
| 424690 | Deodorants (except personal) merchant wholesalers |
| 325620 | Deodorants, personal, manufacturing |
| 424210 | Deodorants, personal, merchant wholesalers |
| 238290 | Deodorization (i.e., air filtration) system installation |
| 561720 | Deodorizing services |
| 455110 | Department stores |
| 812199 | Depilatory (i.e., hair removal) salons |
| 325620 | Depilatory preparations manufacturing |
| 332813 | Depolishing metals and metal products for the trade |
| 523999 | Deposit brokers |
| 524128 | Deposit or share insurance carriers, direct |
| 561492 | Deposition services |
| 522110 | Depository trust companies |
| 339113 | Depressors, tongue, manufacturing |
| 332994 | Depth charge projectors manufacturing |
| 332993 | Depth charges manufacturing |
| 424210 | Dermatological medicines merchant wholesalers |
| 325412 | Dermatological preparations manufacturing |
| 621111 | Dermatologists' offices (e.g., centers, clinics) |
| 213112 | Derrick building, repairing, and dismantling at oil and gas fields on a contract basis |
| 333132 | Derricks, oil and gas field-type, manufacturing |
| 325998 | Desalination kits manufacturing |
| 327992 | Desiccants, activated clay, manufacturing |

| | |
|---|---|
| 424120 | Desk accessories, office, merchant wholesalers |
| 335210 | Desk fans, electric, manufacturing |
| 335132 | Desk lamps, commercial, electric, manufacturing |
| 335131 | Desk lamps, residential, electric, manufacturing |
| 316990 | Desk sets, leather, manufacturing |
| 337214 | Desks (except wood), office-type, manufacturing |
| 337122 | Desks, wood household-type, manufacturing |
| 337211 | Desks, wood office-type, manufacturing |
| 561410 | Desktop publishing services (i.e., document preparation services) |
| 424490 | Dessert powders merchant wholesalers |
| 424430 | Desserts, dairy, merchant wholesalers |
| 311520 | Desserts, frozen (except bakery), manufacturing |
| 311813 | Desserts, frozen bakery, manufacturing |
| 811192 | Detailing services (i.e., cleaning and polishing), automotive |
| 115112 | Detasseling corn |
| 561611 | Detective agencies |
| 334519 | Detectors, scintillation, manufacturing |
| 922140 | Detention centers (except private operation of) |
| 325611 | Detergents (e.g., dishwashing, industrial, laundry) manufacturing |
| 424690 | Detergents merchant wholesalers |
| 331492 | Detinning scrap (e.g., cans) |
| 325920 | Detonating caps, cord, fuses, and primers manufacturing |
| 325920 | Detonators (except ammunition) manufacturing |
| 424690 | Detonators (except ammunition) merchant wholesalers |
| 332993 | Detonators, ammunition (i.e., more than 30 mm., more than 1.18 inch), manufacturing |
| 621420 | Detoxification centers and clinics (except hospitals), outpatient |
| 622210 | Detoxification hospitals |
| 325180 | Deuterium oxide (i.e., heavy water) manufacturing |
| 325992 | Developers, prepared photographic, manufacturing |
| 336411 | Developing and producing prototypes for aircraft |
| 336412 | Developing and producing prototypes for aircraft engines and engine parts |

336413 Developing and producing prototypes for aircraft parts (except engines) and auxiliary equipment

336414 Developing and producing prototypes for complete guided missiles and space vehicles

336419 Developing and producing prototypes for guided missile and space vehicle components

336415 Developing and producing prototypes for guided missile and space vehicle engines

423410 Developing apparatus, photographic, merchant wholesalers

333310 Developing equipment, film, manufacturing

926110 Development assistance program administration

813311 Developmentally disabled advocacy organizations

238910 Dewatering contractors

111334 Dewberry farming

325520 Dextrin glues manufacturing

311221 Dextrin made by wet milling corn

212319 Diabase crushed and broken stone mining and/or beneficiating

212311 Diabase mining or quarrying

325412 Diagnostic biological preparations (except in-vitro) manufacturing

811198 Diagnostic centers without repair, automotive

334510 Diagnostic equipment, electromedical, manufacturing

423450 Diagnostic equipment, medical, merchant wholesalers

334510 Diagnostic equipment, MRI (magnetic resonance imaging), manufacturing

621512 Diagnostic imaging centers (medical)

811210 Diagnostic imaging equipment repair and maintenance services

424210 Diagnostic reagents merchant wholesalers

325413 Diagnostic substances, in-vitro, manufacturing

424210 Diagnostics, in-vitro and in-vivo, merchant wholesalers

332216 Dial indicators, machinists' precision tools, manufacturing

517810 Dial-up Internet service providers, using client-supplied telecommunications connections

621492 Dialysis centers and clinics

334510 Dialysis equipment, electromedical, manufacturing

325312 Diammonium phosphates manufacturing

332618 Diamond cloths made from purchased wire

339910 Diamond cutting and polishing

333514 Diamond dies, metalworking, manufacturing

327910 Diamond dressing wheels manufacturing

423940 Diamonds (except industrial) merchant wholesalers

423840 Diamonds, industrial, merchant wholesalers

212390 Diamonds, industrial, mining and/or beneficiating

315250 Diaper covers, infants', cut and sewn from purchased fabric (except apparel contractors)

315210 Diaper covers, water resistant and waterproof, cut and sew apparel contractors

812331 Diaper supply services

314999 Diapers (except disposable) made from purchased fabrics

424350 Diapers (except disposable) merchant wholesalers

322291 Diapers, disposable, made from purchased paper or textile fiber

322120 Diapers, disposable, made in paper mills

424130 Diapers, disposable, merchant wholesalers

326299 Diaphragms (i.e., birth control device), rubber, manufacturing

323111 Diaries manufacturing

513199 Diary and time scheduler publishers

513199 Diary and time scheduler publishers (except exclusive Internet publishing)

513199 Diary and time scheduler publishers, exclusively on Internet

212323 Diaspore mining and/or beneficiating

334510 Diathermy apparatus, electromedical, manufacturing

334510 Diathermy units manufacturing

212390 Diatomaceous earth mining and/or beneficiating

327992 Diatomaceous earth processing beyond beneficiation

212390 Diatomite mining and/or beneficiating

325992 Diazo (i.e., whiteprint) paper and cloth, sensitized, manufacturing

325120 Dichlorodifluoromethane manufacturing

325180 Dichromates manufacturing

315210 Dickeys cut and sew apparel contractors

| | |
|---|---|
| 315250 | Dickeys, women's and girls', cut and sewn from purchased fabric (except apparel contractors) |
| 333310 | Dictating machines manufacturing |
| 423420 | Dictating machines merchant wholesalers |
| 561410 | Dictation services |
| 611699 | Diction schools |
| 323117 | Dictionaries printing and binding without publishing |
| 323117 | Dictionaries printing without publishing |
| 323120 | Dictionary binding without printing |
| 513130 | Dictionary publishers |
| 513130 | Dictionary publishers (except exclusive Internet publishing) |
| 513130 | Dictionary publishers and printing combined |
| 513130 | Dictionary publishers, exclusively on Internet |
| 325211 | Dicyandiamine resins manufacturing |
| 333514 | Die sets for metal stamping presses manufacturing |
| 333517 | Die sinking machines, metalworking, manufacturing |
| 333511 | Die-casting dies manufacturing |
| 333517 | Die-casting machines, metalworking, manufacturing |
| 331523 | Die-castings, aluminum, unfinished, manufacturing |
| 331523 | Die-castings, nonferrous metals, unfinished, manufacturing |
| 322299 | Die-cut paper products (except for office use) made from purchased paper or paperboard |
| 322230 | Die-cut paper products for office use made from purchased paper or paperboard |
| 333994 | Dielectric industrial heating equipment manufacturing |
| 333514 | Dies and die holders for metal cutting and forming (except threading) manufacturing |
| 333515 | Dies and taps (i.e., a machine tool accessory) manufacturing |
| 332216 | Dies, cutting (except metal cutting), manufacturing |
| 333514 | Dies, metalworking (except threading), manufacturing |
| 423830 | Dies, metalworking, merchant wholesalers |
| 333514 | Dies, plastics forming, manufacturing |
| 332216 | Dies, steel rule (except metal cutting), manufacturing |
| 333514 | Dies, steel rule, metal cutting, manufacturing |
| 333618 | Diesel and semidiesel engines manufacturing |
| 811111 | Diesel engine repair shops, automotive |
| 423830 | Diesel engines and parts, industrial, merchant wholesalers |
| 424710 | Diesel fuel bulk stations and terminals, merchant wholesalers |
| 424720 | Diesel fuel merchant wholesalers (except bulk stations, terminals) |
| 324110 | Diesel fuels made in petroleum refineries |
| 812191 | Diet centers, non-medical |
| 812191 | Diet workshops |
| 311514 | Dietary drinks, dairy and nondairy based, manufacturing |
| 424210 | Dietary supplements merchant wholesalers |
| 325412 | Dietary supplements, compounded, manufacturing |
| 325411 | Dietary supplements, uncompounded, manufacturing |
| 325194 | Diethylcyclohexane manufacturing |
| 325199 | Diethylene glycol manufacturing |
| 813920 | Dietitians' associations |
| 621399 | Dietitians' offices (e.g., centers, clinics) |
| 336350 | Differential and rear axle assemblies, automotive, truck, and bus, manufacturing |
| 334513 | Differential pressure instruments, industrial process-type, manufacturing |
| 334516 | Differential thermal analysis instruments, laboratory-type, manufacturing |
| 332420 | Digesters, industrial-type, heavy gauge metal, manufacturing |
| 325412 | Digestive system preparations manufacturing |
| 238910 | Digging foundations |
| 541810 | Digital advertising agencies |
| 333310 | Digital cameras manufacturing |
| 334111 | Digital computers manufacturing |
| 334513 | Digital displays of process variables manufacturing |
| 334515 | Digital panel meters, electricity measuring, manufacturing |
| 323111 | Digital printing (e.g., billboards, other large format graphic materials, high resolution) (except books) |
| 333248 | Digital printing presses manufacturing |

| | |
|---|---|
| 334515 | Digital test equipment (e.g., electronic and electrical circuits and equipment testing) manufacturing |
| 423620 | Digital video disc (DVD) players merchant wholesalers |
| 334310 | Digital video disc players manufacturing |
| 423990 | Digital video discs (DVDs), prerecorded, merchant wholesalers |
| 325412 | Digitalis medicinal preparations manufacturing |
| 423430 | Digitizer and light pen tables merchant wholesalers |
| 325411 | Digitoxin, uncompounded, manufacturing |
| 325211 | Diisocyanate resins manufacturing |
| 237990 | Dike and other flood control structure construction |
| 111219 | Dill farming, field and seed production |
| 321113 | Dimension lumber, hardwood, made from logs or bolts |
| 321912 | Dimension lumber, hardwood, resawing purchased lumber |
| 321113 | Dimension lumber, made from logs or bolts |
| 321912 | Dimension lumber, resawing purchased lumber |
| 321113 | Dimension lumber, softwood, made from logs or bolts |
| 321912 | Dimension lumber, softwood, resawing purchased lumber |
| 321912 | Dimension stock, hardwood, manufacturing |
| 321912 | Dimension stock, softwood, manufacturing |
| 321912 | Dimension stock, wood, manufacturing |
| 327991 | Dimension stone dressing and manufacturing |
| 327991 | Dimension stone for buildings manufacturing |
| 212311 | Dimension stone mining or quarrying |
| 325199 | Dimethyl divinyl acetylene (di-isopropenyl acetylene) manufacturing |
| 325199 | Dimethylhydrazine manufacturing |
| 335931 | Dimmer switches, outlet box mounting-type, manufacturing |
| 722511 | Diners, full service |
| 722513 | Diners, limited-service |
| 337126 | Dinette sets, metal household-type, manufacturing |
| 336612 | Dinghies manufacturing |
| 337126 | Dining room chairs (including upholstered), metal, manufacturing |
| 337126 | Dining room chairs (including upholstered), plastics, manufacturing |
| 337122 | Dining room chairs (including upholstered), wood, manufacturing |
| 337126 | Dining room furniture, metal household-type, manufacturing |
| 337122 | Dining room furniture, wood household-type, manufacturing |
| 487210 | Dinner cruises |
| 711110 | Dinner theaters |
| 311412 | Dinners, frozen (except seafood-based), manufacturing |
| 311710 | Dinners, frozen seafood, manufacturing |
| 424420 | Dinners, frozen, merchant wholesalers |
| 326199 | Dinnerware, plastics (except polystyrene foam), manufacturing |
| 326140 | Dinnerware, polystyrene foam, manufacturing |
| 334515 | Diode and transistor testers manufacturing |
| 423690 | Diodes merchant wholesalers |
| 334413 | Diodes, solid-state (e.g., germanium, silicon), manufacturing |
| 212313 | Diorite crushed and broken stone mining and/or beneficiating |
| 212311 | Diorite mining or quarrying |
| 325194 | Diphenylamine manufacturing |
| 928120 | Diplomatic services |
| 311941 | Dips (except cheese and sour cream based) manufacturing |
| 325320 | Dips (i.e., pesticides), cattle and sheep, manufacturing |
| 311513 | Dips, cheese based, manufacturing |
| 311511 | Dips, sour cream based, manufacturing |
| 334112 | Direct access storage devices manufacturing |
| 517111 | Direct broadcast satellite (DBS) services |
| 325130 | Direct dyes manufacturing |
| 541860 | Direct mail advertising services |
| 541860 | Direct mail or other direct distribution advertising campaign services |
| 331110 | Direct reduction of iron ore |
| 213111 | Directional drilling of oil and gas wells on a contract basis |
| 812210 | Director services, funeral |
| 323111 | Directories commercial printing (except screen) without publishing |
| 323113 | Directories screen printing without publishing |
| 711510 | Directors (i.e., film, motion picture, music, theatrical), independent |

| | |
|---|---|
| 711510 | Directors, independent motion picture |
| 711510 | Directors, independent music |
| 513140 | Directory and mailing list publishers |
| 513140 | Directory and mailing list publishers (except exclusive Internet publishing) |
| 513140 | Directory and mailing list publishers and printing combined |
| 513140 | Directory publishers |
| 513140 | Directory publishers (except exclusive Internet publishing) |
| 513140 | Directory publishers and printing combined |
| 513140 | Directory publishers, exclusively on Internet |
| 541870 | Directory, telephone, distribution on a contract basis |
| 517111 | Direct-to-home satellite system (DTH) services |
| 238910 | Dirt moving for construction |
| 524113 | Disability insurance carriers, direct |
| 524113 | Disability insurance underwriting, direct |
| 624120 | Disability support groups |
| 485991 | Disabled or elderly passenger transportation services |
| 922190 | Disaster preparedness and management offices, government |
| 562998 | Disaster recovery services (i.e., cleanup, salvaging), without providing remediation services |
| 624230 | Disaster relief services |
| 711510 | Disc jockeys, independent |
| 623990 | Disciplinary camps for delinquent youth |
| 713990 | Discotheques (except those serving alcoholic beverages) |
| 722410 | Discotheques, alcoholic beverage |
| 812990 | Discount buying services, including medical cards and similar negotiated discount plans for individuals |
| 513199 | Discount coupon book publishers |
| 513199 | Discount coupon book publishers (except exclusive Internet publishing) |
| 513199 | Discount coupon book publishers and printing combined |
| 513199 | Discount coupon book publishers, exclusively on Internet |
| 323111 | Discount coupon books commercial printing (except screen) without publishing |
| 323113 | Discount coupon books screen printing without publishing |
| 523150 | Discount securities brokerages |

| | |
|---|---|
| 813212 | Disease awareness fundraising organizations |
| 115112 | Disease control for crops |
| 813212 | Disease research (e.g., cancer, heart) fundraising organizations |
| 541940 | Disease testing services, veterinary |
| 313240 | Dishcloths made in warp or weft knitting mills |
| 423440 | Dishes, commercial (except paper and disposable plastics), merchant wholesalers |
| 423220 | Dishes, household-type (except disposable plastics, paper), merchant wholesalers |
| 424130 | Dishes, paper and disposable plastics, merchant wholesalers |
| 327110 | Dishes, pottery, manufacturing |
| 339930 | Dishes, toy, manufacturing |
| 321999 | Dishes, wood, manufacturing |
| 325611 | Dishwasher detergents manufacturing |
| 811412 | Dishwasher, household-type, repair and maintenance services without retailing new dishwashers |
| 335220 | Dishwashers, household-type, manufacturing |
| 423620 | Dishwashers, household-type, merchant wholesalers |
| 423440 | Dishwashing equipment, commercial-type, merchant wholesalers |
| 333310 | Dishwashing machines, commercial-type, manufacturing |
| 335220 | Dishwashing machines, household-type, manufacturing |
| 424690 | Disinfectants (except agricultural) merchant wholesalers |
| 325612 | Disinfectants, household-type and industrial, manufacturing |
| 561720 | Disinfecting services |
| 518210 | Disk and diskette conversion services |
| 518210 | Disk and diskette recertification services |
| 332613 | Disk and ring springs, heavy gauge metal, manufacturing |
| 334112 | Disk drives, computer, manufacturing |
| 423430 | Disk drives, computer, merchant wholesalers |
| 423430 | Diskettes, blank computer, merchant wholesalers |
| 334610 | Diskettes, blank, manufacturing |
| 423690 | Diskettes, blank, merchant wholesalers |
| 238910 | Dismantling engineering structures (e.g., oil storage tank) |

| | |
|---|---|
| 238290 | Dismantling large-scale machinery and equipment |
| 213112 | Dismantling of oil well rigs on a contract basis |
| 333914 | Dispensing and measuring pumps (e.g., gasoline, lubricants) manufacturing |
| 325130 | Disperse dyes manufacturing |
| 325510 | Dispersions, pigment, manufacturing |
| 423440 | Display cases (except refrigerated) merchant wholesalers |
| 337215 | Display cases and fixtures (except refrigerated) manufacturing |
| 333415 | Display cases, refrigerated, manufacturing |
| 423740 | Display cases, refrigerated, merchant wholesalers |
| 334513 | Display instruments, industrial process control-type, manufacturing |
| 541890 | Display lettering services |
| 339950 | Displays (e.g., counter, floor, point-of-purchase) manufacturing |
| 335910 | Disposable flashlight batteries manufacturing |
| 424130 | Disposable plastics products (e.g., boxes, cups, cutlery, dishes, sanitary food containers) merchant wholesalers |
| 334511 | Distance measuring equipment (DME), aeronautical, manufacturing |
| 325194 | Distillates, wood, manufacturing |
| 333994 | Distillation ovens, charcoal and coke, manufacturing |
| 424820 | Distilled alcoholic beverages merchant wholesalers |
| 325998 | Distilled water manufacturing |
| 312140 | Distilleries |
| 311213 | Distiller's malt manufacturing |
| 423830 | Distillery machinery merchant wholesalers |
| 312140 | Distilling alcoholic beverages (except brandy) |
| 312130 | Distilling brandy |
| 333248 | Distilling equipment (except beverage), including laboratory-type, manufacturing |
| 333241 | Distilling equipment, beverage, manufacturing |
| 312140 | Distilling potable liquor (except brandy) |
| 334515 | Distortion meters and analyzers manufacturing |
| 335313 | Distribution boards, electric, manufacturing |
| 335313 | Distribution cutouts manufacturing |
| 423610 | Distribution equipment, electrical, merchant wholesalers |
| 237120 | Distribution line, gas and oil, construction |
| 237110 | Distribution line, sewer and water, construction |
| 221330 | Distribution of cooled air |
| 221122 | Distribution of electric power |
| 221330 | Distribution of heated air |
| 221210 | Distribution of manufactured gas |
| 221210 | Distribution of natural gas |
| 221210 | Distribution of renewable natural gas (RNG) |
| 221330 | Distribution of steam heat |
| 335311 | Distribution transformers, electric, manufacturing |
| 336320 | Distributor cap and rotor for internal combustion engines manufacturing |
| 813910 | Distributors' associations |
| 336320 | Distributors for internal combustion engines manufacturing |
| 551114 | District and regional offices |
| 922130 | District attorneys' offices |
| 333120 | Ditchers and trenchers, self-propelled, manufacturing |
| 325412 | Diuretic preparations manufacturing |
| 332216 | Dividers, machinists' precision tools, manufacturing |
| 459110 | Diving equipment stores |
| 561990 | Diving services on a contract or fee basis |
| 621210 | DMDs' (doctors of dental medicine) offices (e.g., centers, clinics) |
| 541714 | DNA technologies (e.g., microarrays) research and experimental development laboratories |
| 621511 | DNA testing laboratories |
| 531120 | Dock and associated building rental or leasing |
| 237990 | Dock construction |
| 488330 | Docking and undocking marine vessel services |
| 488310 | Docking facility operations |
| 621310 | Doctors of chiropractic (DCs) offices (e.g., centers, clinics) |
| 621210 | Doctors of dental medicine (DMDs) offices (e.g., centers, clinics) |
| 621210 | Doctors of dental surgery (DDSs) offices (e.g., centers, clinics) |
| 621320 | Doctors of optometry (ODs) offices (e.g., centers, clinics) |

| | |
|---|---|
| 621112 | Doctors of osteopathic medicine (DOs), mental health, offices (e.g., centers, clinics) |
| 621111 | Doctors of osteopathic medicine (DOs, except mental health) offices (e.g., centers, clinics) |
| 621391 | Doctors of podiatry (DPs) offices (e.g., centers, clinics) |
| 621330 | Doctors of psychology offices (e.g., centers, clinics) |
| 561439 | Document copying services (except combined with printing services) |
| 561439 | Document duplicating services (except combined with printing services) |
| 561410 | Document preparation services |
| 561990 | Document shredding services |
| 493190 | Document storage and warehousing |
| 561410 | Document transcription services |
| 325110 | Dodecene made from refined petroleum or liquid hydrocarbons |
| 311111 | Dog and cat food (e.g., canned, dry, frozen, semimoist), manufacturing |
| 311111 | Dog food manufacturing |
| 316990 | Dog furnishings (e.g., collars, harnesses, leashes, muzzles) manufacturing |
| 711219 | Dog owners, race (i.e., racing dogs) |
| 812910 | Dog pounds |
| 112990 | Dog production |
| 711212 | Dog racetracks |
| 711219 | Dog racing kennels |
| 424990 | Dogs merchant wholesalers |
| 322299 | Doilies, paper, made from purchased paper |
| 339930 | Doll carriages and carts manufacturing |
| 339930 | Doll clothing manufacturing |
| 455219 | Dollar stores |
| 333924 | Dollies manufacturing |
| 423920 | Dolls merchant wholesalers |
| 339930 | Dolls, doll parts, and doll clothing (except wigs) manufacturing |
| 212312 | Dolomite crushed and broken stone mining and/or beneficiating |
| 212311 | Dolomite mining or quarrying |
| 327410 | Dolomite, dead-burned, manufacturing |
| 327410 | Dolomitic lime manufacturing |
| 212319 | Dolomitic marble crushed and broken stone mining and/or beneficiating |
| 212311 | Dolomitic marble mining or quarrying |
| 114111 | Dolphin fishing |

| | |
|---|---|
| 112920 | Donkey production |
| 332321 | Door and jamb assemblies, metal, manufacturing |
| 238350 | Door and window frame construction |
| 238350 | Door and window, prefabricated, installation |
| 332321 | Door frames and sash, metal, manufacturing |
| 321911 | Door frames and sash, wood and covered wood, manufacturing |
| 332322 | Door hoods, sheet metal (except stampings), manufacturing |
| 321911 | Door jambs, wood, manufacturing |
| 332510 | Door locks, metal, manufacturing |
| 332510 | Door opening and closing devices (except electrical), metal, manufacturing |
| 335999 | Door opening and closing devices, electrical, manufacturing |
| 321918 | Door shutters, wood, manufacturing |
| 444180 | Door stores |
| 321918 | Door trim, wood molding, manufacturing |
| 321911 | Door units, prehung, wood and covered wood, manufacturing |
| 238290 | Door, commercial- or industrial-type, installation |
| 238350 | Door, folding, installation |
| 314110 | Doormats, all materials (except entirely of rubber or plastics), manufacturing |
| 326199 | Doormats, plastics, manufacturing |
| 326299 | Doormats, rubber, manufacturing |
| 423310 | Doors and door frames merchant wholesalers |
| 326199 | Doors and door frames, plastics, manufacturing |
| 321911 | Doors, combination screen-storm, wood, manufacturing |
| 332321 | Doors, metal, manufacturing |
| 332999 | Doors, safe and vault, metal, manufacturing |
| 327215 | Doors, unframed glass, made from purchased glass |
| 321911 | Doors, wood and covered wood, manufacturing |
| 541870 | Door-to-door distribution of advertising materials (e.g., coupons, flyers, samples) |
| 325510 | Dopes, paint, and lacquer manufacturing |
| 336612 | Dories building |
| 721310 | Dormitories, off campus |
| 236220 | Dormitory construction |

621112 DOs' (doctors of osteopathic medicine), mental health, offices (e.g., centers, clinics)

621111 DOs' (doctors of osteopathic medicine, except mental health) offices (e.g., centers, clinics)

334519 Dosimetry devices manufacturing

333241 Dough mixing machinery (i.e., food manufacturing-type) manufacturing

722511 Doughnut shops, full service

722515 Doughnut shops, on premise baking and carryout service

311812 Doughnuts (except frozen) made in commercial bakeries

311813 Doughnuts, frozen, manufacturing

424420 Doughs, frozen, merchant wholesalers

311211 Doughs, prepared, made in flour mills

311824 Doughs, refrigerated or frozen, made from purchased flour

812990 Doula services (providing coaching and support during childbirth)

333243 Dovetailing machines, woodworking-type, manufacturing

332722 Dowel pins, metal, manufacturing

321999 Dowels, wood, manufacturing

315210 Down-filled clothing cut and sew apparel contractors

315250 Down-filled clothing, men's and boys', cut and sewn from purchased fabric (except apparel contractors)

315250 Down-filled clothing, women's, girls', and infants', cut and sewn from purchased fabric (except apparel contractors)

713920 Downhill skiing facilities without accommodations

238170 Downspout, gutter, and gutter guard installation

332322 Downspouts, sheet metal (except stampings), manufacturing

621391 DPs' (doctors of podiatry) offices (e.g., centers, clinics)

334513 Draft gauges, industrial process-type, manufacturing

334519 Drafting instruments manufacturing

423490 Drafting instruments merchant wholesalers

339940 Drafting materials (except instruments and tables) manufacturing

541340 Drafting services

337127 Drafting tables and boards manufacturing

423490 Drafting tables merchant wholesalers

541340 Draftsmen's offices

711212 Drag strips

333120 Draglines, crawler, manufacturing

423860 Draglines, ship, merchant wholesalers

325194 Dragon's blood manufacturing

333111 Drags, farm-type equipment, manufacturing

333120 Drags, road construction and road maintenance equipment, manufacturing

212390 Dragstones mining and/or beneficiating

561790 Drain cleaning services

332913 Drain cocks, plumbing, manufacturing

325612 Drain pipe cleaners manufacturing

332999 Drain plugs, magnetic, metal, manufacturing

327120 Drain tile, clay, manufacturing

238220 Drain, waste and vent system installation

237990 Drainage canal and ditch construction

237990 Drainage project construction

238910 Drainage system (e.g., cesspool, septic tank) installation

337110 Drainboards, wood or plastics laminated on wood, manufacturing

213113 Draining or pumping coal mines on a contract basis

213114 Draining or pumping of metal mines on a contract basis

213115 Draining or pumping of nonmetallic mineral mines (except fuels) on a contract basis

611610 Drama schools (except academic)

314120 Draperies made from purchased fabrics or sheet goods

423220 Draperies merchant wholesalers

812320 Drapery cleaning services

238390 Drapery fixture (e.g., hardware, rods, tracks) installation

423710 Drapery hardware merchant wholesalers

424310 Drapery material merchant wholesalers

339113 Drapes, surgical, disposable, manufacturing

333519 Draw bench machines manufacturing

315210 Drawers cut and sew apparel contractors

315120 Drawers, apparel, made in apparel knitting mills

315250 Drawers, men's and boys', cut and sewn from purchased fabric (except apparel contractors)

| | |
|---|---|
| 315250 | Drawers, women's and girls', cut and sewn from purchased fabric (except apparel contractors) |
| 325998 | Drawing inks manufacturing |
| 331222 | Drawing iron or steel wire from purchased iron or steel |
| 331222 | Drawing iron or steel wire from purchased iron or steel and fabricating wire products |
| 333248 | Drawing machinery for textiles manufacturing |
| 337127 | Drawing tables and boards, artist's, manufacturing |
| 332216 | Drawknives manufacturing |
| 336611 | Dredge building |
| 423810 | Dredges (except ships') merchant wholesalers |
| 423860 | Dredges, ship, merchant wholesalers |
| 237990 | Dredging (e.g., canal, channel, ditch, waterway) |
| 333120 | Dredging machinery manufacturing |
| 315210 | Dress and semidress gloves cut and sew apparel contractors |
| 315990 | Dress and semidress gloves cut and sewn from purchased fabric (except apparel contractors) |
| 315120 | Dress and semidress gloves made in apparel knitting mills |
| 316210 | Dress shoes, children's and infants', manufacturing |
| 316210 | Dress shoes, men's, manufacturing |
| 316210 | Dress shoes, women's, manufacturing |
| 458110 | Dress shops |
| 532281 | Dress suit rental |
| 315210 | Dress trimmings cut and sew apparel contractors |
| 315990 | Dress trimmings cut and sewn from purchased fabric (except apparel contractors) |
| 424990 | Dressed furs and skins merchant wholesalers |
| 337126 | Dressers, metal, manufacturing |
| 337122 | Dressers, wood, manufacturing |
| 315210 | Dresses cut and sew apparel contractors |
| 315120 | Dresses made in apparel knitting mills |
| 424350 | Dresses merchant wholesalers |
| 315120 | Dresses, hand-knit, manufacturing |
| 315250 | Dresses, women's, girls', and infants', cut and sewn from purchased fabric (except apparel contractors) |
| 316110 | Dressing (i.e., bleaching, blending, currying, scraping, tanning) furs |
| 315210 | Dressing gowns cut and sew apparel contractors |
| 315250 | Dressing gowns, women's and girls', cut and sewn from purchased fabric (except apparel contractors) |
| 316110 | Dressing hides |
| 311615 | Dressing small game |
| 337126 | Dressing tables, metal, manufacturing |
| 337122 | Dressing tables, wood, manufacturing |
| 423450 | Dressings, medical, merchant wholesalers |
| 339113 | Dressings, surgical, manufacturing |
| 424490 | Dried foods (e.g., fruits, milk, vegetables) merchant wholesalers |
| 311612 | Dried meats made from purchased carcasses |
| 212390 | Dried phosphate rock mining and/or beneficiating |
| 325510 | Driers, paint and varnish, manufacturing |
| 325992 | Driers, photographic chemical, manufacturing |
| 333310 | Driers, photographic, manufacturing |
| 334511 | Driftmeters, aeronautical, manufacturing |
| 333515 | Drill bits, metalworking, manufacturing |
| 332216 | Drill bits, woodworking, manufacturing |
| 333517 | Drill presses, metalworking, manufacturing |
| 333243 | Drill presses, woodworking-type, manufacturing |
| 332999 | Drill stands, metal, manufacturing |
| 238910 | Drilled pier (i.e., for building foundations) contractors |
| 238910 | Drilled shaft (i.e., drilled building foundations) construction |
| 336611 | Drilling and production platforms, floating, oil and gas, building |
| 213111 | Drilling directional oil and gas field wells on a contract basis |
| 333132 | Drilling equipment, oil and gas field-type, manufacturing |
| 333131 | Drilling equipment, underground mining-type, manufacturing |
| 213111 | Drilling for gas on a contract basis |
| 213111 | Drilling for oil on a contract basis |
| 213111 | Drilling gas and oil field wells on a contract basis |
| 333517 | Drilling machines, metalworking, manufacturing |

325998 Drilling mud compounds, conditioners, and additives (except bentonites) manufacturing

424690 Drilling muds merchant wholesalers

213111 Drilling oil and gas field service wells on a contract basis

339910 Drilling pearls

213112 Drilling rat holes and mouse holes at oil and gas fields on a contract basis

333132 Drilling rigs, oil and gas field-type, manufacturing

213113 Drilling services for coal mining on a contract basis

213114 Drilling services for metal mining on a contract basis

213115 Drilling services for nonmetallic mineral (except fuels) mining on a contract basis

213112 Drilling shot holes at oil and gas fields on a contract basis

213112 Drilling site preparation at oil and gas fields on a contract basis

213111 Drilling water intake wells, oil and gas field on a contract basis

237110 Drilling water wells (except water intake wells in oil and gas fields)

313210 Drills weaving

333131 Drills, core, underground mining-type, manufacturing

339114 Drills, dental, manufacturing

333991 Drills, handheld power-driven (except heavy construction and mining-type), manufacturing

332216 Drills, handheld, nonelectric, manufacturing

333131 Drills, rock, underground mining-type, manufacturing

213112 Drill-stem testing in oil, gas, dry, and service well drilling on a contract basis

311999 Drink powder mixes (except chocolate, coffee, milk based, tea) manufacturing

311351 Drink powdered mixes, cocoa, made from cacao

311352 Drink powdered mixes, cocoa, made from purchased cocoa

311511 Drink, chocolate milk, manufacturing

238220 Drinking fountain installation

332999 Drinking fountains (except mechanically refrigerated), metal, manufacturing

326191 Drinking fountains (except mechanically refrigerated), plastics, manufacturing

423720 Drinking fountains (except refrigerated) merchant wholesalers

333415 Drinking fountains, refrigerated, manufacturing

423740 Drinking fountains, refrigerated, merchant wholesalers

327110 Drinking fountains, vitreous china, non-refrigerated, manufacturing

722410 Drinking places (i.e., bars, lounges, taverns), alcoholic

312111 Drinks, fruit (except juice), manufacturing

333613 Drive chains, bicycle and motorcycle, manufacturing

811114 Drive shaft repair shops, automotive

336350 Drive shafts and half shafts, automotive, truck, and bus, manufacturing

512132 Drive-in motion picture theaters

237990 Drive-in movie facility construction

722513 Drive-in restaurants

611692 Driver education

611692 Driver training schools (except bus, heavy equipment, truck)

711219 Drivers, harness or race car

423840 Drives and gears merchant wholesalers

333612 Drives, high-speed industrial (except hydrostatic), manufacturing

561790 Driveway cleaning (e.g., power sweeping, washing) services

238990 Driveway paving or sealing

713990 Driving ranges, golf

488490 Driving services, independent (e.g., automobile, truck delivery)

238310 Drop ceiling installation

332111 Drop forgings made from purchased iron or steel, unfinished

333517 Drop hammers, metal forging and shaping, manufacturing

812320 Drop-off and pick-up sites for laundries and drycleaners

813319 Drug abuse prevention advocacy organizations

623220 Drug addiction rehabilitation facilities (except licensed hospitals), residential

622210 Drug addiction rehabilitation hospitals

624190 Drug addiction self-help organizations

621420 Drug addiction treatment centers and clinics (except hospitals), outpatient

922120 Drug enforcement agencies and offices

424210 Drug proprietaries merchant wholesalers

456110 Drug stores

424210 Druggists' sundries merchant wholesalers

424210 Drugs merchant wholesalers

711130 Drum and bugle corps (i.e., drill teams)

| | |
|---|---|
| 333924 | Drum cradles manufacturing |
| 339992 | Drums (musical instruments), parts, and accessories manufacturing |
| 332439 | Drums, light gauge metal, manufacturing |
| 423840 | Drums, new and reconditioned, merchant wholesalers |
| 326199 | Drums, plastics (i.e., containers), manufacturing |
| 321920 | Drums, plywood, manufacturing |
| 321920 | Drums, shipping, wood, wirebound, manufacturing |
| 813319 | Drunk driving prevention advocacy organizations |
| 311422 | Dry beans canning |
| 424510 | Dry beans, inedible, merchant wholesalers |
| 484230 | Dry bulk carrier, truck, long-distance |
| 484220 | Dry bulk trucking (except garbage collection, garbage hauling), local |
| 335910 | Dry cell primary batteries, single and multiple cell, manufacturing |
| 335910 | Dry cells, primary (e.g., AAA, AA, C, D, 9V), manufacturing |
| 238220 | Dry heating equipment installation |
| 325120 | Dry ice (i.e., solid carbon dioxide) manufacturing |
| 424690 | Dry ice merchant wholesalers |
| 311514 | Dry milk manufacturing |
| 333241 | Dry milk processing machinery manufacturing |
| 311514 | Dry milk products and mixture manufacturing |
| 311514 | Dry milk products for animal feed manufacturing |
| 327999 | Dry mix concrete manufacturing |
| 311824 | Dry mixes made from purchased flour |
| 311824 | Dry pasta manufacturing |
| 311824 | Dry pasta packaged with other ingredients made in dry pasta plants |
| 335210 | Dry shavers (i.e., electric razors) manufacturing |
| 238910 | Dry well construction |
| 812320 | Drycleaner drop-off and pick-up sites |
| 812320 | Drycleaners (except coin-operated) |
| 335220 | Drycleaning and laundry machines, household-type, manufacturing |
| 333310 | Drycleaning equipment and machinery manufacturing |
| 423850 | Drycleaning equipment and supplies merchant wholesalers |
| 812310 | Drycleaning machine routes (i.e., concession operators), coin-operated or similar self-service |
| 236220 | Drycleaning plant construction |
| 812320 | Drycleaning plants (except rug cleaning plants) |
| 325612 | Drycleaning preparations manufacturing |
| 812320 | Drycleaning services (except coin-operated) |
| 812310 | Drycleaning services, coin-operated or similar self-service |
| 424690 | Drycleaning solvents and chemicals merchant wholesalers |
| 336611 | Drydock, floating, building |
| 488390 | Drydocks, floating (i.e., routine repair and maintenance of ships) |
| 532210 | Dryer, clothes, rental |
| 335220 | Dryers, clothes, household-type, gas and electric, manufacturing |
| 423620 | Dryers, clothes, merchant wholesalers |
| 423620 | Dryers, hair, merchant wholesalers |
| 335220 | Dryers, household-type laundry, manufacturing |
| 339113 | Dryers, laboratory-type, manufacturing |
| 333310 | Dryers, laundry (except household-type), manufacturing |
| 311710 | Drying fish and seafood |
| 333248 | Drying kilns, lumber, manufacturing |
| 333248 | Drying machinery for textiles manufacturing |
| 423310 | Drywall board merchant wholesalers |
| 238310 | Drywall contractors |
| 238310 | Drywall finishing (e.g., sanding, spackling, stippling, taping, texturing) |
| 238310 | Drywall hanging |
| 238310 | Drywall installation |
| 423320 | Drywall joint compounds merchant wholesalers |
| 713950 | Duck pin bowling alleys |
| 713950 | Duck pin bowling centers |
| 112390 | Duck production |
| 313210 | Ducks weaving |
| 311615 | Ducks, processing, fresh, frozen, canned, or cooked |
| 311615 | Ducks, slaughtering and dressing |
| 561790 | Duct cleaning services |
| 238290 | Duct insulation installation |
| 322220 | Duct tape made from purchased materials |

238220 Duct work (e.g., cooling, dust collection, exhaust, heating, ventilation) installation

331511 Ductile iron castings, unfinished, manufacturing

331511 Ductile iron foundries

332313 Ducting, fabricated metal plate work, manufacturing

423730 Ductless heating and air-conditioning system equipment merchant wholesalers

335313 Ducts for electrical switchboard apparatus manufacturing

332322 Ducts, sheet metal, manufacturing

721214 Dude ranches

339920 Dumbbells manufacturing

238290 Dumbwaiter installation

333921 Dumbwaiters manufacturing

212323 Dumortierite mining and/or beneficiating

336212 Dump trailers manufacturing

532120 Dump truck rental or leasing without operator

484220 Dump trucking (e.g., gravel, sand, top-soil)

562119 Dump trucking of rubble or brush with collection or disposal

333131 Dumpers, mining car, manufacturing

562219 Dumps, compost

562212 Dumps, nonhazardous solid waste (e.g., trash)

336211 Dump-truck lifting mechanisms manufacturing

315210 Dungarees cut and sew apparel contractors

315250 Dungarees, men's and boys', cut and sewn from purchased fabric (except apparel contractors)

315250 Dungarees, women's, girls', and infants', cut and sewn from purchased fabric (except apparel contractors)

423860 Dunnage, marine supplies, merchant wholesalers

236116 Duplex (i.e., one unit above the other), construction general contractors

236115 Duplex (i.e., side-by-side) construction general contractors

236117 Duplex for-sale builders

531110 Duplex houses (i.e., single-family) rental or leasing

335931 Duplex receptacles, electrical, manufacturing

325910 Duplicating inks manufacturing

532420 Duplicating machine (e.g., copier) rental or leasing

333517 Duplicating machines (e.g., key cutting), metalworking, manufacturing

425120 Durable goods agents and brokers, wholesale trade

425120 Durable goods business to business electronic markets, wholesale trade

311211 Durum flour manufacturing

333413 Dust and fume collecting equipment manufacturing

314999 Dust cloths made from purchased fabrics

238220 Dust collecting and bag house equipment installation

423730 Dust collection equipment merchant wholesalers

812332 Dust control textile item (e.g., cloths, mats, mops, rugs, shop towels) supply services

315210 Dusters (i.e., apparel) cut and sew apparel contractors

315250 Dusters (i.e., apparel), women's and girls', cut and sewn from purchased fabric (except apparel contractors)

333111 Dusters, farm-type, manufacturing

115112 Dusting crops

445320 Duty free liquor shops

334112 DVD (digital video disc) drives, computer peripheral equipment, manufacturing

334310 DVD (digital video disc) players manufacturing

531110 Dwelling rental or leasing

332311 Dwellings, prefabricated metal, manufacturing

325998 Dye preparations, clothing, household-type, manufacturing

316110 Dyeing furs

313310 Dyeing gloves, woven or knit, for the trade

316110 Dyeing leather

333248 Dyeing machinery for textiles manufacturing

423830 Dyeing machinery, textile, merchant wholesalers

313310 Dyeing textile products and fabrics

424690 Dyes, industrial, merchant wholesalers

325130 Dyes, inorganic, manufacturing

325194 Dyes, natural, manufacturing

325130 Dyes, synthetic organic, manufacturing

424690 Dyestuffs merchant wholesalers

325920 Dynamite manufacturing

424690 Dynamite merchant wholesalers

| | |
|---|---|
| 334519 | Dynamometers manufacturing |
| 335312 | Dynamos, electric (except automotive), manufacturing |
| 335312 | Dynamotors manufacturing |
| 812199 | Ear piercing services |
| 237990 | Earth retention system construction |
| 334220 | Earth station communications equipment manufacturing |
| 517810 | Earth stations (except satellite telecommunication carriers) |
| 517410 | Earth stations for satellite communication carriers |
| 212390 | Earth, diatomaceous, mining and/or beneficiating |
| 212323 | Earth, fuller's (e.g., all natural bleaching clays), mining and/or beneficiating |
| 327110 | Earthenware table and kitchen articles, coarse, manufacturing |
| 327110 | Earthenware, commercial and household, semivitreous, manufacturing |
| 237990 | Earth-filled dam construction |
| 532412 | Earthmoving equipment rental or leasing without operator |
| 311119 | Earthworm food and bedding manufacturing |
| 112990 | Earthworm hatcheries |
| 339940 | Easels, artists', manufacturing |
| 424130 | Eating utensils, disposable plastics, merchant wholesalers |
| 332322 | Eaves, sheet metal (except stampings), manufacturing |
| 238170 | Eavestrough installation |
| 423330 | Eavestroughing merchant wholesalers |
| 334310 | E-book readers (i.e., dedicated) manufacturing |
| 327110 | Ecclesiastical statuary, clay, manufacturing |
| 327420 | Ecclesiastical statuary, gypsum, manufacturing |
| 327999 | Ecclesiastical statuary, papier-mache, manufacturing |
| 327991 | Ecclesiastical statuary, stone, manufacturing |
| 332999 | Ecclesiastical ware, precious plated metal, manufacturing |
| 459991 | E-cigarette stores |
| 541620 | Ecological restoration consulting services |
| 541690 | Economic consulting services |
| 926110 | Economic development agencies, government |
| 928120 | Economic development assistance (i.e., international), government |
| 541720 | Economic research and development services |
| 332410 | Economizers (i.e., power boiler accessory) manufacturing |
| 522299 | Edge Act corporations |
| 332216 | Edge tools, woodworking (e.g., augers, bits, countersinks), manufacturing |
| 333310 | Editing equipment, motion picture (e.g., rewinders, splicers, titlers, viewers), manufacturing |
| 561410 | Editing services |
| 923110 | Education offices, nonoperating |
| 923110 | Education program administration |
| 923110 | Education statistics centers, government |
| 236220 | Educational building construction |
| 611710 | Educational consultants |
| 611710 | Educational curriculum development services |
| 611710 | Educational guidance counseling services |
| 611710 | Educational support services |
| 611710 | Educational testing evaluation services |
| 611710 | Educational testing services |
| 813211 | Educational trusts, awarding grants |
| 813920 | Educators' associations |
| 114111 | Eel fishing |
| 325412 | Effervescent salts manufacturing |
| 541614 | Efficiency management (i.e., efficiency expert) consulting services |
| 424130 | Egg cartons, paper and disposable plastics, merchant wholesalers |
| 321920 | Egg cases, wood, manufacturing |
| 335210 | Egg cookers, household-type electric, manufacturing |
| 112340 | Egg hatcheries, poultry |
| 311824 | Egg noodles, dry, manufacturing |
| 311991 | Egg noodles, fresh, manufacturing |
| 112310 | Egg production, chicken |
| 112330 | Egg production, turkey |
| 311999 | Egg substitutes manufacturing |
| 424490 | Egg substitutes merchant wholesalers |
| 312140 | Eggnog, alcoholic, manufacturing |
| 311514 | Eggnog, canned, nonalcoholic, manufacturing |
| 311511 | Eggnog, fresh, nonalcoholic, manufacturing |
| 311511 | Eggnog, nonalcoholic (except canned), manufacturing |

| | |
|---|---|
| 111219 | Eggplant farming (except under cover), field, bedding plant and seed production |
| 111419 | Eggplant farming, grown under cover |
| 424440 | Eggs merchant wholesalers |
| 112310 | Eggs, chicken (table, hatching) production |
| 311999 | Eggs, processed, manufacturing |
| 334515 | Elapsed time meters, electronic, manufacturing |
| 313210 | Elastic fabrics, more than 12 inches in width, weaving |
| 313220 | Elastic fabrics, narrow woven, manufacturing |
| 339113 | Elastic hosiery, orthopedic, manufacturing |
| 325220 | Elastomeric fibers and filaments manufacturing |
| 325211 | Elastomers (except synthetic rubber) manufacturing |
| 325212 | Elastomers, synthetic rubber, manufacturing |
| 332322 | Elbows for conductor pipe, hot air ducts, and stovepipe, sheet metal (except stampings), manufacturing |
| 332919 | Elbows, pipe, metal (except made from purchased pipe), manufacturing |
| 921190 | Election boards |
| 334512 | Electric air cleaner controls, automatic, manufacturing |
| 334513 | Electric and electronic controllers, industrial process-type, manufacturing |
| 336110 | Electric automobiles for highway use manufacturing |
| 335999 | Electric bells manufacturing |
| 336991 | Electric bicycles manufacturing |
| 335210 | Electric blankets manufacturing |
| 423620 | Electric blankets merchant wholesalers |
| 335210 | Electric comfort heating equipment, portable, manufacturing |
| 238210 | Electric contracting |
| 335999 | Electric fence chargers manufacturing |
| 335311 | Electric furnace transformers manufacturing |
| 334512 | Electric heat proportioning controls, modulating controls, manufacturing |
| 335139 | Electric lamp bulb parts (except glass blanks and light emitting diodes (LEDs)) manufacturing |
| 335139 | Electric lamps (i.e., light bulbs) manufacturing |
| 237130 | Electric light and power plant (except hydroelectric) construction |

| | |
|---|---|
| 335139 | Electric light bulbs, complete, manufacturing |
| 423610 | Electric light fixtures merchant wholesalers |
| 333995 | Electric linear actuators manufacturing |
| 811310 | Electric motor repair and maintenance services, commercial or industrial |
| 423610 | Electric motors, wiring supplies, and lighting fixtures merchant wholesalers |
| 339992 | Electric musical instruments manufacturing |
| 333618 | Electric outboard motors manufacturing |
| 221122 | Electric power brokers |
| 221121 | Electric power control |
| 238210 | Electric power control panel and outlet installation |
| 221122 | Electric power distribution systems |
| 221117 | Electric power generation, biomass |
| 221112 | Electric power generation, fossil fuel (e.g., coal, oil, gas) |
| 221116 | Electric power generation, geothermal |
| 221111 | Electric power generation, hydroelectric |
| 221113 | Electric power generation, nuclear |
| 221114 | Electric power generation, solar |
| 221118 | Electric power generation, tidal |
| 221115 | Electric power generation, wind |
| 237130 | Electric power transmission line and tower construction |
| 221121 | Electric power transmission systems |
| 423610 | Electric prime movers merchant wholesalers |
| 334512 | Electric space heater controls, automatic, manufacturing |
| 335210 | Electric space heaters, portable, manufacturing |
| 333415 | Electric warm air (i.e., forced air) furnaces manufacturing |
| 423610 | Electrical apparatus merchant wholesalers |
| 238210 | Electrical contractors |
| 336320 | Electrical control chips (modules), motor vehicle, manufacturing |
| 541330 | Electrical engineering services |
| 238210 | Electrical equipment and appliance installation |
| 811310 | Electrical generating and transmission equipment repair and maintenance services |
| 541360 | Electrical geophysical surveying services |

| | |
|---|---|
| 336320 | Electrical ignition cable sets for internal combustion engines manufacturing |
| 327110 | Electrical insulators, ceramic, manufacturing |
| 811210 | Electrical measuring instrument repair and maintenance services |
| 335932 | Electrical metallic tube (EMTs) manufacturing |
| 561990 | Electrical meter reading services, contract |
| 334515 | Electrical network analyzers manufacturing |
| 334515 | Electrical power measuring equipment manufacturing |
| 811114 | Electrical repair shops, automotive |
| 339950 | Electrical signs manufacturing |
| 423440 | Electrical signs merchant wholesalers |
| 327110 | Electrical supplies, ceramic, manufacturing |
| 444180 | Electrical supply stores |
| 541380 | Electrical testing laboratories or services |
| 238210 | Electrical wiring contractors |
| 238210 | Electrical work |
| 238210 | Electrical, electrical wiring, and low voltage electrical work |
| 335210 | Electrically heated bed coverings manufacturing |
| 238210 | Electrician |
| 611513 | Electricians' apprenticeship training |
| 334515 | Electricity and electrical signal measuring instruments manufacturing |
| 334515 | Electricity and electrical signal testing equipment manufacturing |
| 237130 | Electricity generating plant (except hydroelectric) construction |
| 237990 | Electricity generating plant, hydroelectric, construction |
| 334510 | Electrocardiographs manufacturing |
| 335999 | Electrochemical generators (i.e., fuel cells) manufacturing |
| 333517 | Electrochemical milling machines, metalworking, manufacturing |
| 333517 | Electrode discharge metal cutting machines manufacturing |
| 333992 | Electrode holders, welding, manufacturing |
| 335991 | Electrodes for thermal and electrolytic uses, carbon and graphite, manufacturing |
| 334513 | Electrodes used in industrial process measurement manufacturing |
| 335139 | Electrodes, cold cathode fluorescent lamp, manufacturing |

| | |
|---|---|
| 333992 | Electrodes, welding, manufacturing |
| 334510 | Electroencephalographs manufacturing |
| 334510 | Electrogastrograph manufacturing |
| 332912 | Electrohydraulic servo valves, fluid power, manufacturing |
| 812199 | Electrolysis (i.e., hair removal) salons |
| 325412 | Electrolyte in-vivo diagnostic substances manufacturing |
| 334513 | Electrolytic conductivity instruments, industrial process-type, manufacturing |
| 334516 | Electrolytic conductivity instruments, laboratory-type, manufacturing |
| 333517 | Electrolytic metal cutting machines manufacturing |
| 334513 | Electromagnetic flowmeters manufacturing |
| 541360 | Electromagnetic geophysical surveying services |
| 334514 | Electromechanical counters manufacturing |
| 334510 | Electromedical diagnostic equipment manufacturing |
| 334510 | Electromedical equipment manufacturing |
| 423450 | Electromedical equipment merchant wholesalers |
| 334510 | Electromedical therapy equipment manufacturing |
| 331110 | Electrometallurgical ferroalloy manufacturing |
| 331110 | Electrometallurgical steel manufacturing |
| 334510 | Electromyographs manufacturing |
| 333992 | Electron beam welding equipment manufacturing |
| 335999 | Electron linear accelerators manufacturing |
| 334516 | Electron microprobes, laboratory-type, manufacturing |
| 334516 | Electron microscopes manufacturing |
| 334516 | Electron paramagnetic spin-type apparatus manufacturing |
| 333248 | Electron tube machinery manufacturing |
| 334419 | Electron tube parts (e.g., bases, getters, guns) (except glass blanks) manufacturing |
| 327215 | Electron tube parts, glass blanks, made from purchased glass |
| 327212 | Electron tube parts, glass blanks, made in glass making plants |
| 334515 | Electron tube test equipment manufacturing |
| 334419 | Electron tubes manufacturing |

| | |
|---|---|
| 333517 | Electron-discharge metal cutting machines manufacturing |
| 423690 | Electronic aircraft instruments merchant wholesalers |
| 455219 | Electronic auctions, general merchandise (new and used), retail |
| 459510 | Electronic auctions, general merchandise (used), retail |
| 459991 | Electronic cigarette stores |
| 424690 | Electronic cigarette vapor liquids merchant wholesalers |
| 325998 | Electronic cigarette vapor liquids, including closed refills, manufacturing |
| 339999 | Electronic cigarettes manufacturing |
| 424940 | Electronic cigarettes merchant wholesalers |
| 541990 | Electronic communication content verification services |
| 423690 | Electronic communications equipment merchant wholesalers |
| 238210 | Electronic containment fencing for pets, installation |
| 238210 | Electronic control installation and service |
| 238210 | Electronic control system installation |
| 518210 | Electronic data processing services |
| 513140 | Electronic directory publishers |
| 513140 | Electronic directory publishers (except exclusive Internet publishing) |
| 513140 | Electronic directory publishers, exclusively on Internet |
| 611519 | Electronic equipment repair training |
| 522320 | Electronic financial payment services |
| 522320 | Electronic funds transfer services, including peer-to-peer payment services |
| 713120 | Electronic game arcades |
| 423920 | Electronic games merchant wholesalers |
| 334511 | Electronic guidance systems and equipment manufacturing |
| 425120 | Electronic markets, durable goods, business to business, wholesale trade |
| 425120 | Electronic markets, nondurable goods, business to business, wholesale trade |
| 449210 | Electronic part and component stores |
| 423690 | Electronic parts (e.g., condensers, connectors, switches) merchant wholesalers |
| 323120 | Electronic prepress services for the printing trade |
| 541715 | Electronic research and development laboratories or services (except nanotechnology research and development) |
| 423690 | Electronic sound equipment (except household-type and automotive) merchant wholesalers |
| 334515 | Electronic test equipment for testing electrical characteristics manufacturing |
| 541380 | Electronic testing laboratories or services |
| 334514 | Electronic totalizing counters manufacturing |
| 339930 | Electronic toys and games manufacturing |
| 423690 | Electronic tubes (e.g., industrial, receiving, transmitting) merchant wholesalers |
| 339930 | Electronic video games, handheld, manufacturing |
| 423930 | Electronics parts, recyclable, merchant wholesalers |
| 334516 | Electrophoresis instruments manufacturing |
| 333248 | Electroplating machinery and equipment manufacturing |
| 332813 | Electroplating metals and formed products for the trade |
| 238320 | Electrostatic painting, on-site, contractors |
| 335999 | Electrostatic particle accelerators manufacturing |
| 333413 | Electrostatic precipitation equipment manufacturing |
| 334510 | Electrosurgical units manufacturing |
| 334510 | Electrotherapeutic apparatus manufacturing |
| 335139 | Electrotherapeutic lamp bulbs for ultraviolet and infrared radiation manufacturing |
| 334510 | Electrotherapy units manufacturing |
| 323120 | Electrotype plate preparation services |
| 333248 | Electrotyping machinery manufacturing |
| 334516 | Elemental analyzers manufacturing |
| 611110 | Elementary and secondary schools |
| 611110 | Elementary schools |
| 237310 | Elevated highway construction |
| 332323 | Elevator guide rails, metal, manufacturing |
| 238290 | Elevator installation |
| 423830 | Elevators merchant wholesalers |
| 333922 | Elevators, farm, manufacturing |
| 333921 | Elevators, passenger and freight, manufacturing |
| 112990 | Elk production |
| 325998 | Embalming fluids manufacturing |

| | |
|---|---|
| 812210 | Embalming services |
| 237990 | Embankment construction |
| 928120 | Embassies |
| 316110 | Embossing leather |
| 323120 | Embossing plate preparation services |
| 339940 | Embossing stamps manufacturing |
| 313310 | Embossing textile products and fabrics |
| 313220 | Embroideries, Schiffli machine, manufacturing |
| 314999 | Embroidering contractors on apparel |
| 314999 | Embroidering on textile products or apparel for the trade |
| 339930 | Embroidery kits manufacturing |
| 333248 | Embroidery machinery manufacturing |
| 424310 | Embroidery products merchant wholesalers |
| 313110 | Embroidery spun yarns (e.g., cotton, manmade fiber, silk, wool) made from purchased fiber |
| 313110 | Embroidery thread (e.g., cotton, manmade fibers, silk, wool) manufacturing |
| 335132 | Emergency lighting (i.e., battery backup) manufacturing |
| 621493 | Emergency medical centers and clinics, freestanding |
| 621910 | Emergency medical transportation services, air or ground |
| 922190 | Emergency planning and management offices, government |
| 459999 | Emergency preparedness supply stores |
| 624230 | Emergency relief services |
| 488410 | Emergency road services (i.e., tow service) |
| 624221 | Emergency shelters (except for victims of domestic or international disasters or conflicts) |
| 624230 | Emergency shelters for victims of domestic or international disasters or conflicts |
| 561421 | Emergency telephone dispatch (i.e., contractor) services |
| 212390 | Emery mining and/or beneficiating |
| 811198 | Emissions testing without repair, automotive |
| 541612 | Employee assessment consulting services |
| 541612 | Employee benefit consulting services |
| 525110 | Employee benefit pension plans |
| 525120 | Employee benefit plans (except pension) |
| 524292 | Employee benefit plans, third party administrative processing services |
| 485410 | Employee bus services |
| 541612 | Employee compensation consulting services |
| 621999 | Employee drug testing services |
| 561330 | Employee leasing services |
| 561311 | Employee recruitment services (non-executive) |
| 813930 | Employees' associations for improvement of wages and working conditions |
| 561311 | Employment agencies |
| 561311 | Employment agencies, motion picture or video |
| 561311 | Employment agencies, radio or television |
| 561311 | Employment agencies, theatrical |
| 561311 | Employment placement agencies or services |
| 561311 | Employment referral agencies or services |
| 561311 | Employment registries |
| 335932 | EMTs (electrical metallic tube) manufacturing |
| 112390 | Emu production |
| 325613 | Emulsifiers (i.e., surface active agents) manufacturing |
| 325510 | Enamel paints manufacturing |
| 212322 | Enamel sand quarrying and/or beneficiating |
| 332215 | Enameled metal cutting utensils |
| 332812 | Enameling metals and metal products for the trade |
| 333994 | Enameling ovens manufacturing |
| 424950 | Enamels merchant wholesalers |
| 339114 | Enamels, dental, manufacturing |
| 323120 | Encyclopedia binding without printing |
| 513130 | Encyclopedia publishers |
| 513130 | Encyclopedia publishers (except exclusive Internet publishing) |
| 513130 | Encyclopedia publishers and printing combined |
| 513130 | Encyclopedia publishers, exclusively on Internet |
| 323117 | Encyclopedias printing and binding without publishing |
| 323117 | Encyclopedias printing without publishing |
| 337126 | End tables, metal, manufacturing |
| 337122 | End tables, wood, manufacturing |

111219 Endive farming (except under cover), field, bedding plant and seed production

111419 Endive farming, grown under cover

325411 Endocrine products, uncompounded, manufacturing

424210 Endocrine substances merchant wholesalers

621210 Endodontists' offices (e.g., centers, clinics)

334510 Endoscopic equipment, electromedical (e.g., bronchoscopes, colonoscopes, cystoscopes), manufacturing

325320 Endrin insecticides manufacturing

624229 Energy assistance programs

541690 Energy consulting services

334512 Energy cutoff controls, residential and commercial types, manufacturing

926110 Energy development and conservation agencies, nonoperating

926130 Energy development and conservation programs, government

541350 Energy efficiency inspection services

334515 Energy measuring equipment, electrical, manufacturing

926110 Energy program administration

331318 Energy wire or cable made in aluminum wire drawing plants

331420 Energy wire or cable, copper, made from purchased copper in wire drawing plants

331491 Energy wire or cable, nonferrous metals (except aluminum, copper), made from purchased nonferrous metals (except aluminum, copper) in wire drawing plants

924110 Enforcement of environmental and pollution control regulations

336310 Engine block assemblies, automotive and truck gasoline, manufacturing

325998 Engine degreasers manufacturing

336310 Engine intake and exhaust valves manufacturing

811310 Engine repair (except automotive, small engine)

811111 Engine repair and replacement shops, automotive

811411 Engine repair, small

325998 Engine starting fluids manufacturing

423120 Engine testing equipment, motor vehicle, merchant wholesalers

541330 Engineering consulting services

541330 Engineering design services

541715 Engineering research and development laboratories or services (except nanotechnology research and development)

541330 Engineering services

238320 Engineering structure (e.g., oil storage tank, water tower) painting

813920 Engineers' associations

423490 Engineers' equipment and supplies merchant wholesalers

541330 Engineers' offices

541330 Engineers' private practices

336412 Engines and engine parts, aircraft (except carburetors, pistons, piston rings, valves), manufacturing

336310 Engines and parts (except diesel), automotive and truck, manufacturing

423860 Engines and parts, aircraft, merchant wholesalers

423120 Engines and parts, automotive, new, merchant wholesalers

423860 Engines and turbines, marine, merchant wholesalers

333618 Engines, diesel and semidiesel, manufacturing

333618 Engines, diesel locomotive, manufacturing

423830 Engines, internal combustion (except aircraft, automotive), merchant wholesalers

333618 Engines, internal combustion (except aircraft, nondiesel automotive), manufacturing

333618 Engines, natural gas, manufacturing

111219 English pea farming (except under cover), field, bedding plant and seed production

111419 English pea farming, grown under cover

332216 Engraver's handtools, nonpowered, manufacturing

339910 Engraving and etching precious metal flatware

339910 Engraving and etching precious metal jewelry

339910 Engraving and/or etching costume jewelry

423830 Engraving machinery merchant wholesalers

332812 Engraving metals and metal products (except printing plates) for the trade

323120 Engraving printing plate, for the printing trade

333310 Enlargers, photographic, manufacturing

| | |
|---|---|
| 315210 | Ensemble dresses cut and sew apparel contractors |
| 315120 | Ensemble dresses made in apparel knitting mills |
| 315250 | Ensemble dresses, women's and girls', cut and sewn from purchased fabric (except apparel contractors) |
| 711130 | Ensembles, musical |
| 926110 | Enterprise development program administration |
| 711410 | Entertainers' agents or managers |
| 711510 | Entertainers, independent |
| 516210 | Entertainment broadcasting sites, Internet |
| 541715 | Entomological research and development laboratories or services (except biotechnology and nanotechnology research and development) |
| 115112 | Entomological service, agricultural |
| 541690 | Entomology consulting services |
| 333243 | Envelope making machinery manufacturing |
| 424110 | Envelope paper, bulk, merchant wholesalers |
| 333310 | Envelope stuffing, sealing, and addressing machinery manufacturing |
| 322230 | Envelopes (i.e., mailing, stationery) made from any material |
| 424120 | Envelopes merchant wholesalers |
| 813312 | Environmental advocacy organizations |
| 541620 | Environmental consulting services |
| 238210 | Environmental control system installation |
| 423830 | Environmental controlling instruments and equipment merchant wholesalers |
| 541330 | Environmental engineering services |
| 923120 | Environmental health program administration |
| 924110 | Environmental protection program administration |
| 541620 | Environmental reclamation planning services |
| 562910 | Environmental remediation services |
| 541715 | Environmental research and development laboratories or services (except biotechnology and nanotechnology research and development) |
| 541380 | Environmental testing laboratories or services |
| 325413 | Enzyme and isoenzyme in-vitro diagnostic substances manufacturing |

| | |
|---|---|
| 325199 | Enzyme proteins (i.e., basic synthetic chemicals) (except pharmaceutical use) manufacturing |
| 325411 | Enzyme proteins (i.e., basic synthetic chemicals), pharmaceutical use, manufacturing |
| 325130 | Eosin dyes manufacturing |
| 325411 | Ephedrine and derivatives (i.e., basic chemicals) manufacturing |
| 325211 | Epichlorohydrin bisphenol manufacturing |
| 325211 | Epichlorohydrin diphenol manufacturing |
| 325212 | Epichlorohydrin elastomers manufacturing |
| 325520 | Epoxy adhesives manufacturing |
| 238190 | Epoxy application contractors |
| 325510 | Epoxy coatings made from purchased resins |
| 325211 | Epoxy resins manufacturing |
| 923130 | Equal employment opportunity offices |
| 621340 | Equestrian physical therapists' offices (e.g., centers, clinics) |
| 115210 | Equine boarding |
| 522220 | Equipment finance leasing |
| 238910 | Equipment rental (except crane), construction, with operator |
| 531130 | Equity real estate investment trusts (REITs), primarily leasing miniwarehouses and self-storage units |
| 531120 | Equity real estate investment trusts (REITs), primarily leasing nonresidential buildings (except miniwarehouses) |
| 531190 | Equity real estate investment trusts (REITs), primarily leasing real estate (except residential buildings and dwellings, nonresidential buildings, miniwarehouses, and self-storage units) |
| 531110 | Equity real estate investment trusts (REITs), primarily leasing residential buildings and dwellings |
| 326299 | Erasers, rubber or rubber and abrasive combined, manufacturing |
| 238120 | Erecting structural steel |
| 238190 | Erection and dismantling, poured concrete form |
| 325411 | Ergot alkaloids (i.e., basic chemicals) manufacturing |
| 541330 | Erosion control engineering services |
| 238290 | Escalator installation |
| 333921 | Escalators manufacturing |
| 423830 | Escalators merchant wholesalers |

| | |
|---|---|
| 713990 | Escape game rooms |
| 713990 | Escape rooms |
| 111219 | Escarole farming (except under cover), field, bedding plant and seed production |
| 111419 | Escarole farming, grown under cover |
| 812990 | Escort services, social |
| 523991 | Escrow agencies (except real estate) |
| 531390 | Escrow agencies, real estate |
| 711211 | Esports video gaming clubs or teams, professional or semiprofessional |
| 713990 | Esports video gaming clubs, teams, or leagues, recreational |
| 325998 | Essential oils manufacturing |
| 424690 | Essential oils merchant wholesalers |
| 325199 | Essential oils, synthetic, manufacturing |
| 541990 | Estate assessment (i.e., appraisal) services |
| 541110 | Estate law offices |
| 325211 | Ester gum manufacturing |
| 325199 | Esters, not specified elsewhere by process, manufacturing |
| 812112 | Esthetician (i.e., skin care) services |
| 115310 | Estimating timber |
| 333242 | Etching equipment, semiconductor, manufacturing |
| 332812 | Etching metals and metal products (except printing plates) for the trade |
| 325110 | Ethane made from refined petroleum or liquid hydrocarbons |
| 211130 | Ethane recovered from oil and gas field gases |
| 424710 | Ethanol, blended with petroleum, bulk stations and terminals, merchant wholesalers |
| 424720 | Ethanol, blended with petroleum, merchant wholesalers (except bulk stations, terminals) |
| 325193 | Ethanol, nonpotable, manufacturing |
| 424690 | Ethanol, not blended with petroleum, merchant wholesalers |
| 813410 | Ethnic associations |
| 711510 | Ethnic dancers, independent |
| 711320 | Ethnic festival managers without facilities |
| 711320 | Ethnic festival organizers without facilities |
| 711310 | Ethnic festival promoters with facilities |
| 711320 | Ethnic festival promoters without facilities |
| 325194 | Ethyl acetate, natural, manufacturing |

| | |
|---|---|
| 325199 | Ethyl acetate, synthetic, manufacturing |
| 424820 | Ethyl alcohol merchant wholesalers |
| 325193 | Ethyl alcohol, nonpotable, manufacturing |
| 312140 | Ethyl alcohol, potable, manufacturing |
| 325199 | Ethyl butyrate manufacturing |
| 325199 | Ethyl cellulose (except resins) manufacturing |
| 325199 | Ethyl chloride manufacturing |
| 325199 | Ethyl ether manufacturing |
| 325199 | Ethyl formate manufacturing |
| 325199 | Ethyl nitrite manufacturing |
| 325199 | Ethyl perhydrophenanthrene manufacturing |
| 325110 | Ethylbenzene made from refined petroleum or liquid hydrocarbons |
| 325211 | Ethylcellulose plastics manufacturing |
| 325199 | Ethylene glycol ether manufacturing |
| 325199 | Ethylene glycol manufacturing |
| 325110 | Ethylene made from refined petroleum or liquid hydrocarbons |
| 324110 | Ethylene made in petroleum refineries |
| 325199 | Ethylene oxide manufacturing |
| 325212 | Ethylene-propylene rubber manufacturing |
| 325212 | Ethylene-propylene-nonconjugated diene (EPDM) rubber manufacturing |
| 325211 | Ethylene-vinyl acetate resins manufacturing |
| 325998 | Eucalyptus oil manufacturing |
| 311514 | Evaporated milk manufacturing |
| 334519 | Evaporation meters manufacturing |
| 333415 | Evaporative condensers (i.e., heat transfer equipment) manufacturing |
| 561920 | Event and meeting planning services |
| 611691 | Exam preparation and tutoring online learning marketplace services (through a website or mobile application) |
| 611691 | Exam preparation and tutoring services, online (through a website or mobile application) |
| 611691 | Exam preparation services |
| 423810 | Excavating machinery and equipment merchant wholesalers |
| 213112 | Excavating mud pits, slush pits, and cellars at oil and gas fields on a contract basis |

| | |
|---|---|
| 238910 | Excavating, earthmoving or land clearing, mining (except overburden removal at open pit mine sites or quarries) |
| 238910 | Excavating, earthmoving, or land clearing contractors |
| 238910 | Excavation contractors |
| 333120 | Excavators (e.g., power shovels) manufacturing |
| 321999 | Excelsior (e.g., pads, wrappers) manufacturing |
| 423840 | Excelsior (e.g., pads, wrappers) merchant wholesalers |
| 523999 | Exchange clearinghouses, commodities or securities |
| 332410 | Exchangers, heat, manufacturing |
| 523210 | Exchanges, commodity contracts |
| 523210 | Exchanges, securities |
| 335312 | Exciter assemblies, motor and generator, manufacturing |
| 531210 | Exclusive buyers' agencies |
| 531210 | Exclusive buyers' agents, offices of |
| 487210 | Excursion boat operation |
| 921140 | Executive and legislative office combinations |
| 561110 | Executive management services |
| 921110 | Executive offices, federal, state, and local (e.g., governor, mayor, president) |
| 561312 | Executive placement consulting services |
| 561312 | Executive placement services |
| 561312 | Executive search consulting services |
| 561312 | Executive search services |
| 531120 | Executive suites (i.e., full service office space provision) |
| 811490 | Exercise and athletic equipment repair and maintenance services without retailing new exercise and athletic equipment |
| 713940 | Exercise centers |
| 532284 | Exercise equipment rental |
| 459110 | Exercise equipment stores |
| 339920 | Exercise machines manufacturing |
| 621340 | Exercise physiologists' offices (e.g., centers, clinics) |
| 336390 | Exhaust and tail pipes, automotive, truck, and bus, manufacturing |
| 333413 | Exhaust fans, industrial and commercial-type, manufacturing |
| 238220 | Exhaust system (e.g., kitchens, industrial work areas) installation |
| 811114 | Exhaust system repair and replacement shops, automotive |
| 336390 | Exhaust systems and parts, automotive, truck, and bus, manufacturing |
| 531120 | Exhibition hall, no promotion of events, rental or leasing |
| 624190 | Ex-offender rehabilitation agencies |
| 624190 | Ex-offender self-help organizations |
| 316110 | Exotic leathers manufacturing |
| 332312 | Expansion joints, metal, manufacturing |
| 541715 | Experimental farms |
| 213113 | Exploration services for coal (except geophysical surveying and mapping) on a contract basis |
| 213114 | Exploration services for metal (except geophysical surveying and mapping) on a contract basis |
| 213115 | Exploration services for nonmetallic minerals (except geophysical surveying and mapping) on a contract basis |
| 213112 | Exploration services for oil and gas (except geophysical surveying and mapping) on a contract basis |
| 424690 | Explosives (except ammunition, fireworks) merchant wholesalers |
| 325920 | Explosives manufacturing |
| 522299 | Export trading companies (i.e., international trade financing) |
| 522299 | Export-Import banks |
| 333310 | Exposure meters, photographic, manufacturing |
| 492110 | Express delivery services (except establishments operating under a universal service obligation) |
| 622310 | Extended care hospitals (except mental, substance abuse) |
| 335999 | Extension cords made from purchased insulated wire |
| 321999 | Extension ladders, wood, manufacturing |
| 321999 | Extension planks, wood, manufacturing |
| 238910 | Exterior demolition contractors |
| 238310 | Exterior insulation finish system installation |
| 321918 | Exterior wood shutters manufacturing |
| 325320 | Exterminating chemical products (e.g., fungicides, insecticides, pesticides) manufacturing |
| 561710 | Exterminating services |
| 423990 | Extinguishers, fire, merchant wholesalers |
| 333120 | Extractors, piling, manufacturing |

| | |
|---|---|
| 311920 | Extracts, essences and preparations, coffee, manufacturing |
| 311920 | Extracts, essences and preparations, tea, manufacturing |
| 311942 | Extracts, food (except coffee, meat), manufacturing |
| 311942 | Extracts, malt, manufacturing |
| 325194 | Extracts, natural dyeing and tanning, manufacturing |
| 326291 | Extruded, molded or lathe-cut rubber goods manufacturing |
| 333248 | Extruding machinery for plastics and rubber manufacturing |
| 333248 | Extruding machinery for yarn manufacturing |
| 333517 | Extruding machines, metalworking, manufacturing |
| 331318 | Extrusion billet made by rolling purchased aluminum |
| 331318 | Extrusion billet, aluminum, made in integrated secondary smelting and rolling mills |
| 333514 | Extrusion dies for use with all materials manufacturing |
| 331318 | Extrusion ingot made by rolling purchased aluminum |
| 331318 | Extrusion ingot, aluminum, made in integrated secondary smelting and rolling mills |
| 331313 | Extrusion ingot, primary aluminum, manufacturing |
| 325412 | Eye and ear preparations manufacturing |
| 621991 | Eye banks |
| 339112 | Eye examining instruments and apparatus manufacturing |
| 325620 | Eye makeup (e.g., eye shadow, eyebrow pencil, mascara) manufacturing |
| 622310 | Eye, ear, nose, and throat hospitals |
| 812199 | Eyebrow threading services |
| 316990 | Eyeglass cases (except metal) manufacturing |
| 339115 | Eyeglass frames (i.e., fronts and temples), ophthalmic, manufacturing |
| 423460 | Eyeglasses merchant wholesalers |
| 315210 | Eyelet making contractors on apparel |
| 339993 | Eyelets, metal, manufacturing |
| 339115 | Eyes, glass and plastics, manufacturing |
| 313310 | Fabric finishing |
| 313310 | Fabric mercerizing |
| 459130 | Fabric shops |
| 325612 | Fabric softeners manufacturing |
| 424690 | Fabric softeners merchant wholesalers |
| 238310 | Fabric wall system, noise insulating, installation |
| 332312 | Fabricated bar joists manufacturing |
| 332996 | Fabricated pipe and pipe fittings made from purchased pipe |
| 332313 | Fabricated plate work manufacturing |
| 314994 | Fabricated rope products (e.g., nets, slings) made in cordage or twine mills |
| 332312 | Fabricated structural metal manufacturing |
| 321215 | Fabricated structural wood members manufacturing |
| 238390 | Fabrication, metal cabinet or countertop, on site |
| 313210 | Fabrics (except rug, tire fabrics), broadwoven, weaving |
| 314994 | Fabrics for reinforcing rubber tires, industrial belting, and fuel cells manufacturing |
| 313240 | Fabrics, knit, made in warp or weft knit fabric mills |
| 313240 | Fabrics, lace, made in lace mills |
| 313220 | Fabrics, narrow woven, weaving |
| 313230 | Fabrics, nonwoven, manufacturing |
| 424310 | Fabrics, textile (except burlap, felt), merchant wholesalers |
| 332618 | Fabrics, woven wire, made from purchased wire |
| 325620 | Face creams (e.g., cleansing, moisturizing) manufacturing |
| 335932 | Face plates (i.e., outlet or switch covers) manufacturing |
| 525990 | Face-amount certificate funds |
| 812112 | Facial salons |
| 424130 | Facial tissue merchant wholesalers |
| 322291 | Facial tissues made from purchased paper |
| 322120 | Facial tissues made in paper mills |
| 561210 | Facilities (except computer operation) support services |
| 541513 | Facilities (i.e., clients' facilities) management and operation services, computer systems or data processing |
| 541513 | Facilities (i.e., clients' facilities) support services, computer systems or data processing |
| 333517 | Facing machines, metalworking, manufacturing |
| 334210 | Facsimile equipment, stand-alone, manufacturing |
| 532420 | Facsimile machine rental or leasing |
| 811210 | Facsimile machine repair and maintenance services |

| | |
|---|---|
| 423690 | Facsimile machines merchant wholesalers |
| 325992 | Facsimile toner cartridges manufacturing |
| 522299 | Factoring accounts receivable |
| 236210 | Factory construction |
| 711310 | Fair managers with facilities, agricultural |
| 711320 | Fair managers without facilities, agricultural |
| 711310 | Fair organizers with facilities, agricultural |
| 711320 | Fair organizers without facilities, agricultural |
| 711310 | Fair promoters with facilities |
| 711310 | Fair promoters with facilities, agricultural |
| 711320 | Fair promoters without facilities |
| 711320 | Fair promoters without facilities, agricultural |
| 238190 | Falsework construction |
| 624410 | Family child care homes (excluding private households employing nannies) |
| 458110 | Family clothing stores |
| 621210 | Family dentists' offices (e.g., centers, clinics) |
| 713120 | Family fun centers |
| 541110 | Family law offices |
| 621111 | Family physicians' offices (e.g., centers, clinics) |
| 621410 | Family planning centers |
| 621410 | Family planning counseling services |
| 722511 | Family restaurants, full service |
| 722513 | Family restaurants, limited-service |
| 624190 | Family social service agencies |
| 624190 | Family welfare services |
| 326220 | Fan belts, rubber or plastics, manufacturing |
| 813410 | Fan clubs |
| 334512 | Fan controls, temperature responsive, manufacturing |
| 316110 | Fancy leathers manufacturing |
| 335210 | Fans (except attic), household-type electric, manufacturing |
| 336320 | Fans, electric cooling, automotive, truck, and bus, manufacturing |
| 335210 | Fans, household-type kitchen, manufacturing |
| 423620 | Fans, household-type, merchant wholesalers |
| 333413 | Fans, industrial and commercial-type, manufacturing |
| 423830 | Fans, industrial, merchant wholesalers |
| 423850 | Fare boxes, public transit vehicle, merchant wholesalers |
| 334514 | Fare collection equipment manufacturing |
| 311211 | Farina (except breakfast food) made in flour mills |
| 311230 | Farina, breakfast cereal, manufacturing |
| 236220 | Farm building construction |
| 332311 | Farm buildings, prefabricated metal, manufacturing |
| 321992 | Farm buildings, prefabricated wood, manufacturing |
| 237990 | Farm drainage tile installation |
| 532490 | Farm equipment rental or leasing |
| 813410 | Farm granges |
| 115115 | Farm labor contractors |
| 423820 | Farm machinery and equipment merchant wholesalers |
| 811310 | Farm machinery and equipment repair and maintenance services |
| 115116 | Farm management services |
| 522292 | Farm mortgage lending |
| 493130 | Farm product warehousing and storage (except refrigerated) |
| 493120 | Farm product warehousing and storage, refrigerated |
| 484220 | Farm products hauling, local |
| 484230 | Farm products trucking, long-distance |
| 332420 | Farm storage tanks, heavy gauge metal, manufacturing |
| 424910 | Farm supplies merchant wholesalers |
| 444240 | Farm supply stores |
| 532490 | Farm tractor rental or leasing |
| 333111 | Farm tractors and attachments manufacturing |
| 333111 | Farm wagons manufacturing |
| 813910 | Farmers' associations |
| 813910 | Farmers' unions |
| ****** | Farming -- see type |
| 531190 | Farmland rental or leasing |
| 333922 | Farm-type conveyors manufacturing |
| 115210 | Farriers |
| 112210 | Farrow-to-finish operations |
| 238170 | Fascia and soffit installation |
| 423330 | Fascia, building (except wood), merchant wholesalers |

| | |
|---|---|
| 541490 | Fashion design services |
| 541490 | Fashion designer services |
| 722513 | Fast casual restaurants |
| 423710 | Fasteners (e.g., bolts, nuts, rivets, screws) merchant wholesalers |
| 339993 | Fasteners (e.g., glove, hook and eye, slide, snap) manufacturing |
| 424310 | Fasteners, clothing, merchant wholesalers |
| 423610 | Fastening devices, electrical, merchant wholesalers |
| 722513 | Fast-food restaurants |
| 334511 | Fathometers manufacturing |
| 334519 | Fatigue testing machines, industrial, mechanical, manufacturing |
| 311611 | Fats, animal (except poultry, small game), produced in slaughtering plants |
| 311613 | Fats, animal, rendering |
| 112112 | Fattening cattle |
| 325199 | Fatty acid esters and amines manufacturing |
| 325199 | Fatty acids (e.g., margaric, oleic, stearic) manufacturing |
| 325199 | Fatty alcohols manufacturing |
| 327110 | Faucet handles, vitreous china and earthenware, manufacturing |
| 332913 | Faucets, plumbing, manufacturing |
| 532420 | Fax machine rental or leasing |
| 811210 | Fax machine repair and maintenance services |
| 339999 | Feather dusters manufacturing |
| 315210 | Feather-filled clothing cut and sew apparel contractors |
| 315250 | Feather-filled clothing, jackets, and vests, women's, girls', and infants', cut and sewn from purchased fabric (except apparel contractors) |
| 315250 | Feather-filled clothing, men's and boys', cut and sewn from purchased fabric (except apparel contractors) |
| 424590 | Feathers merchant wholesalers |
| 339999 | Feathers, preparing (i.e., for use in apparel and textile products) |
| 516210 | Feature syndicates (i.e., advice columns, comic, news) |
| 522299 | Federal Agricultural Mortgage Corporation |
| 926120 | Federal Aviation Administration (except air traffic control) |
| 922120 | Federal Bureau of Investigation (FBI) |
| 926130 | Federal Communications Commission (FCC) |
| 522130 | Federal credit unions |
| 522299 | Federal Home Loan Banks (FHLB) |
| 522299 | Federal Home Loan Mortgage Corporation (FHLMC) |
| 522299 | Federal Intermediate Credit Bank |
| 522292 | Federal Land Banks |
| 522299 | Federal National Mortgage Association (FNMA) |
| 922120 | Federal police services |
| 521110 | Federal Reserve Banks or Branches |
| 921130 | Federal Reserve Board of Governors |
| 522180 | Federal savings and loan associations (S&L) |
| 522180 | Federal savings banks |
| 813219 | Federated charities |
| 813930 | Federation of workers, labor organizations |
| 813930 | Federations of labor |
| 424910 | Feed additives merchant wholesalers |
| 316990 | Feed bags for horses manufacturing |
| 314910 | Feed bags made from purchased woven or knitted materials |
| 311119 | Feed concentrates, animal, manufacturing |
| 311514 | Feed grade dry milk products manufacturing |
| 311119 | Feed premixes, animal, manufacturing |
| 333111 | Feed processing equipment, farm-type, manufacturing |
| 444240 | Feed stores (except pet) |
| 459910 | Feed stores, pet |
| 311119 | Feed supplements, animal (except cat, dog), manufacturing |
| 311111 | Feed supplements, dog and cat, manufacturing |
| 112112 | Feed yards (except stockyards for transportation), cattle |
| 112111 | Feeder calf production |
| 112210 | Feeder pig farming |
| 335311 | Feeder voltage regulators and boosters (i.e., electrical transformers) manufacturing |
| 423820 | Feeders, animal, merchant wholesalers |
| 333131 | Feeders, mineral beneficiating-type, manufacturing |
| 112112 | Feedlots (except stockyards for transportation), cattle |
| 112210 | Feedlots (except stockyards for transportation), hog |

| | |
|---|---|
| 112410 | Feedlots (except stockyards for transportation), lamb |
| 424910 | Feeds (except pet) merchant wholesalers |
| 311111 | Feeds, prepared for dog and cat, manufacturing |
| 311119 | Feeds, prepared, for animals (except cat, dog) manufacturing |
| 311119 | Feeds, specialty (e.g., guinea pig, mice, mink), manufacturing |
| 212323 | Feldspar mining and/or beneficiating |
| 327992 | Feldspar processing beyond beneficiation |
| 424990 | Felt merchant wholesalers |
| 339940 | Felt tip markers manufacturing |
| 322120 | Felts, asphalt, made in paper mills |
| 313210 | Felts, broadwoven, weaving |
| 313230 | Felts, nonwoven, manufacturing |
| 331222 | Fence gates, posts, and fittings, iron or steel, made in wire drawing plants |
| 238990 | Fence installation (except electronic containment fencing for pets) |
| 331110 | Fence posts, iron or steel, made in iron and steel mills |
| 332323 | Fences and gates (except wire), metal, manufacturing |
| 332618 | Fencing and fence gates made from purchased wire |
| 423390 | Fencing and fencing accessories (except wood) merchant wholesalers |
| 238990 | Fencing contractors (except electronic containment fencing for pets) |
| 444180 | Fencing dealers |
| 339920 | Fencing equipment (sporting goods) manufacturing |
| 321999 | Fencing, prefabricated sections, wood, manufacturing |
| 321999 | Fencing, wood (except rough pickets, poles, and rails), manufacturing |
| 423310 | Fencing, wood, merchant wholesalers |
| 212290 | Ferberite ores and concentrates mining and/or beneficiating |
| 333248 | Fermentation equipment, chemical, manufacturing |
| 332420 | Fermentation tanks, heavy gauge metal, manufacturing |
| 424810 | Fermented malt beverages merchant wholesalers |
| 325180 | Ferric chloride manufacturing |
| 325180 | Ferric oxide manufacturing |
| 325130 | Ferric oxide pigments manufacturing |
| 333310 | Ferris wheels manufacturing |

| | |
|---|---|
| 212290 | Ferroalloy ores (e.g., chromium, columbium, molybdenum, tungsten) mining and/or beneficiating |
| 331110 | Ferroalloys manufacturing |
| 423510 | Ferroalloys merchant wholesalers |
| 331110 | Ferrochromium manufacturing |
| 325180 | Ferrocyanides manufacturing |
| 331110 | Ferromanganese manufacturing |
| 331110 | Ferromolybdenum manufacturing |
| 331110 | Ferrophosphorus manufacturing |
| 331110 | Ferrosilicon manufacturing |
| 331110 | Ferrotitanium manufacturing |
| 331110 | Ferrotungsten manufacturing |
| 332111 | Ferrous forgings made from purchased iron or steel, unfinished |
| 331221 | Ferrous metal powder, paste, and flake made from purchased iron or steel |
| 423510 | Ferrous metals merchant wholesalers |
| 331110 | Ferrovanadium manufacturing |
| 483114 | Ferry passenger transportation, Great Lakes (including St. Lawrence Seaway) |
| 336611 | Ferryboat building |
| 621410 | Fertility clinics |
| 424910 | Fertilizer and fertilizer materials merchant wholesalers |
| 115112 | Fertilizer application for crops |
| 212390 | Fertilizer minerals, natural, mining and/or beneficiating |
| 325314 | Fertilizers, mixed, made in plants not manufacturing fertilizer materials |
| 325311 | Fertilizers, mixed, made in plants producing nitrogenous fertilizer materials |
| 325312 | Fertilizers, mixed, made in plants producing phosphatic fertilizer materials |
| 325311 | Fertilizers, natural organic (except compost), manufacturing |
| 325311 | Fertilizers, of animal waste origin, manufacturing |
| 325311 | Fertilizers, of sewage origin, manufacturing |
| 561730 | Fertilizing lawns |
| 333111 | Fertilizing machinery, farm-type, manufacturing |
| 111998 | Fescue seed farming |
| 711310 | Festival managers with facilities |
| 711320 | Festival managers without facilities |
| 711310 | Festival of arts managers with facilities |
| 711320 | Festival of arts managers without facilities |

| | |
|---|---|
| 711310 | Festival of arts organizers with facilities |
| 711320 | Festival of arts organizers without facilities |
| 711310 | Festival of arts promoters with facilities |
| 711320 | Festival of arts promoters without facilities |
| 711310 | Festival organizers with facilities |
| 711320 | Festival organizers without facilities |
| 711310 | Festival promoters with facilities |
| 711320 | Festival promoters without facilities |
| 325412 | Fever remedy preparations manufacturing |
| 522299 | FHLMC (Federal Home Loan Mortgage Corporation) |
| 322219 | Fiber cans and drums (i.e., all-fiber, nonfiber ends of any material) made from purchased paperboard |
| 424130 | Fiber cans and drums merchant wholesalers |
| 322219 | Fiber drums made from purchased paperboard |
| 337126 | Fiber furniture (except upholstered), household-type, manufacturing |
| 238210 | Fiber optic cable (except transmission lines) installation |
| 335921 | Fiber optic cable made from purchased fiber optic strand |
| 237130 | Fiber optic cable transmission line construction |
| 334417 | Fiber optic connectors manufacturing |
| 322219 | Fiber spools, reels, blocks made from purchased paperboard |
| 322219 | Fiber tubes made from purchased paperboard |
| 314999 | Fiber, textile recovery from textile mill waste and rags |
| 321219 | Fiberboard manufacturing |
| 423310 | Fiberboard merchant wholesalers |
| 423390 | Fiberglass building materials (except insulation, roofing, siding) merchant wholesalers |
| 424310 | Fiberglass fabrics merchant wholesalers |
| 313210 | Fiberglass fabrics weaving |
| 327993 | Fiberglass insulation products manufacturing |
| 313220 | Fiberglasses, narrow woven, weaving |
| 325220 | Fibers and filaments, cellulosic, manufacturing and texturizing |
| 325220 | Fibers and filaments, noncellulosic, manufacturing and texturizing |
| 335991 | Fibers, carbon and graphite, manufacturing |

| | |
|---|---|
| 327212 | Fibers, glass, textile, made in glass making plants |
| 424690 | Fibers, manmade, merchant wholesalers |
| 424590 | Fibers, vegetable, merchant wholesalers |
| 513130 | Fiction book publishers |
| 513130 | Fiction book publishers (except exclusive Internet publishing) |
| 513130 | Fiction book publishers and printing combined |
| 513130 | Fiction book publishers, exclusively on Internet |
| 323120 | Fiction bookbinding without printing |
| 323117 | Fiction books printing and binding without publishing |
| 323117 | Fiction books printing without publishing |
| 524126 | Fidelity insurance carriers, direct |
| 531390 | Fiduciaries', real estate, offices |
| 523991 | Fiduciary agencies (except real estate) |
| 332994 | Field artillery manufacturing |
| 315210 | Field jackets, military, cut and sew apparel contractors |
| 315250 | Field jackets, military, men's and boys', cut and sewn from purchased fabric (except apparel contractors) |
| 111421 | Field nurseries (i.e., growing of flowers and shrubbery) |
| 238140 | Field stone (i.e., masonry) installation |
| 334515 | Field strength and intensity measuring equipment, electrical, manufacturing |
| 336211 | Fifth-wheel assemblies manufacturing |
| 111339 | Fig farming |
| 711219 | Figure skaters, independent |
| 335139 | Filaments for electric lamp bulbs manufacturing |
| 111335 | Filbert farming |
| 115114 | Filbert hulling and shelling |
| 424120 | File cards and folders merchant wholesalers |
| 322230 | File folders (e.g., accordion, expanding, hanging, manila) made from purchased paper and paperboard |
| 333515 | Files (i.e., a machine tool accessory) manufacturing |
| 332216 | Files, handheld, manufacturing |
| 337214 | Filing cabinets (except wood), office-type, manufacturing |
| 337211 | Filing cabinets, wood, office-type, manufacturing |
| 333517 | Filing machines, metalworking, manufacturing |

| | |
|---|---|
| 212390 | Fill dirt pits mining and/or beneficiating |
| 424120 | Filler paper, looseleaf, merchant wholesalers |
| 325510 | Fillers, wood (e.g., dry, liquid, paste), manufacturing |
| 314999 | Filling (except nonwoven textile), upholstery, manufacturing |
| 311999 | Fillings, cake or pie (except fruits, meat, vegetables), manufacturing |
| 711510 | Film actors, independent |
| 519210 | Film archives |
| 541380 | Film badge testing (i.e., radiation testing) laboratories or services |
| 812921 | Film developing and printing (except motion picture, one-hour) |
| 812922 | Film developing and printing, one-hour |
| 333310 | Film developing equipment manufacturing |
| 423410 | Film developing equipment merchant wholesalers |
| 512120 | Film distribution agencies |
| 512120 | Film distribution, motion picture and video |
| 512131 | Film festivals exhibitors |
| 423410 | Film finishing equipment merchant wholesalers |
| 512120 | Film libraries, commercial distribution |
| 512199 | Film libraries, motion picture or video, stock footage |
| 512191 | Film or tape closed captioning |
| 512191 | Film or video transfer services |
| 512199 | Film preservation services |
| 512199 | Film processing laboratories, motion picture |
| 711510 | Film producers, independent |
| 512199 | Film restoration services |
| 512110 | Film studios producing films |
| 423410 | Film, camera, merchant wholesalers |
| 423410 | Film, photographic, merchant wholesalers |
| 326113 | Film, plastics (except packaging), manufacturing |
| 326112 | Film, plastics, packaging, manufacturing |
| 325992 | Film, sensitized (e.g., camera, motion picture, X-ray), manufacturing |
| 512110 | Films, motion picture production |
| 512110 | Films, motion picture production and distribution |
| 424130 | Filter papers merchant wholesalers |
| 327110 | Filtering media, pottery, manufacturing |
| 336390 | Filters (e.g., air, engine oil, fuel) automotive, truck, and bus, manufacturing |
| 333413 | Filters, air-conditioner, manufacturing |
| 334419 | Filters, electronic component-type, manufacturing |
| 333413 | Filters, furnace, manufacturing |
| 333998 | Filters, industrial and general purpose-type (except internal combustion engine, warm air furnace), manufacturing |
| 322299 | Filters, paper, made from purchased paper |
| 221310 | Filtration plant, water |
| 212322 | Filtration sand quarrying and/or beneficiating |
| 332993 | Fin assemblies, mortar, manufacturing |
| 332993 | Fin assemblies, torpedo and bomb, manufacturing |
| 522291 | Finance companies (i.e., unsecured cash loans) |
| 523160 | Financial futures brokerages |
| 551112 | Financial holding companies |
| 523940 | Financial investment advice services, customized, fees paid by client |
| 513120 | Financial magazine and periodical publishers |
| 513120 | Financial magazine and periodical publishers (except exclusive Internet publishing) |
| 513120 | Financial magazine and periodical publishers and printing combined |
| 513120 | Financial magazine and periodical publishers, exclusively on Internet |
| 323111 | Financial magazines and periodicals commercial printing (except screen) without publishing |
| 323113 | Financial magazines and periodicals screen printing without publishing |
| 541611 | Financial management consulting (except investment advice) services |
| 523940 | Financial planning services, customized, fees paid by client |
| 522320 | Financial transactions processing (except central bank) |
| 521110 | Financial transactions processing of the central bank |
| 522220 | Financing, sales |
| 522299 | Financing, secondary market |
| 316990 | Findings, boot and shoe, manufacturing |
| 339910 | Findings, jeweler's, manufacturing |
| 315210 | Findings, suit and coat (e.g., coat fronts, pockets), cut and sew apparel contractors |

| | |
|---|---|
| 315990 | Findings, suit and coat (e.g., coat fronts, pockets), cut and sewn from purchased fabric (except apparel contractors) |
| 712110 | Fine arts museums |
| 611610 | Fine arts schools (except academic) |
| 722511 | Fine dining restaurants, full service |
| 424110 | Fine paper, bulk, merchant wholesalers |
| 114111 | Finfish fishing (e.g., flounder, salmon, trout) |
| 112511 | Finfish production, farm raising |
| 112511 | Finfish, hatcheries |
| 321215 | Finger joint lumber manufacturing |
| 561611 | Fingerprint services |
| 238350 | Finish carpentry |
| 314110 | Finishing (e.g., dyeing) rugs and carpets |
| 325613 | Finishing agents, textile and leather, manufacturing |
| 238310 | Finishing drywall contractors |
| 316110 | Finishing hides and skins on a contract basis |
| 316110 | Finishing leather |
| 333248 | Finishing machinery for textile manufacturing |
| 611110 | Finishing schools, secondary |
| 561621 | Fire alarm monitoring services |
| 561621 | Fire alarm sales combined with installation, repair, or monitoring services |
| 238210 | Fire alarm system, electric, installation only |
| 236220 | Fire and flood restoration of commercial and institutional buildings |
| 236118 | Fire and flood restoration, multifamily building, general contractors |
| 236118 | Fire and flood restoration, single-family housing, general contractors |
| 922160 | Fire and rescue service |
| 212323 | Fire clay mining and/or beneficiating |
| 922160 | Fire departments (e.g., government, volunteer (except private)) |
| 334290 | Fire detection and alarm systems manufacturing |
| 334519 | Fire detector systems, nonelectric, manufacturing |
| 332321 | Fire doors, metal, manufacturing |
| 238190 | Fire escape installation |
| 332323 | Fire escapes, metal, manufacturing |
| 325998 | Fire extinguisher chemical preparations manufacturing |
| 238220 | Fire extinguisher installation |

| | |
|---|---|
| 238220 | Fire extinguisher installation and repair |
| 424690 | Fire extinguisher preparations merchant wholesalers |
| 811310 | Fire extinguisher repair and maintenance, without installation |
| 423990 | Fire extinguisher sales combined with rental and/or service, merchant wholesalers |
| 541990 | Fire extinguisher testing and/or inspection, without sales, service, or installation |
| 423990 | Fire extinguishers merchant wholesalers |
| 339999 | Fire extinguishers, portable, manufacturing |
| 314999 | Fire hose, textile, made from purchased materials |
| 237110 | Fire hydrant installation |
| 332911 | Fire hydrant valves manufacturing |
| 423840 | Fire hydrants merchant wholesalers |
| 332911 | Fire hydrants, complete, manufacturing |
| 524126 | Fire insurance carriers, direct |
| 541380 | Fire insurance underwriters' laboratories |
| 524291 | Fire investigators |
| 922160 | Fire marshals' offices |
| 922160 | Fire prevention offices, government |
| 115310 | Fire prevention, forest |
| 325998 | Fire retardant chemical preparations manufacturing |
| 238220 | Fire sprinkler system installation |
| 236220 | Fire station construction |
| 423990 | Firearms (except sporting) merchant wholesalers |
| 813319 | Firearms advocacy organizations |
| 611699 | Firearms training |
| 332994 | Firearms, small, manufacturing |
| 423910 | Firearms, sporting, merchant wholesalers |
| 336611 | Fireboat building |
| 327120 | Firebrick, clay refractories, manufacturing |
| 611519 | Firefighter training schools |
| 315210 | Firefighters' dress uniforms cut and sew apparel contractors |
| 315250 | Firefighters' dress uniforms, men's, cut and sewn from purchased fabric (except apparel contractors) |
| 315250 | Firefighters' dress uniforms, women's, cut and sewn from purchased fabric (except apparel contractors) |

| | |
|---|---|
| 922160 | Firefighting (except forest), government and volunteer (except private) |
| 423850 | Firefighting equipment and supplies merchant wholesalers |
| 922160 | Firefighting services (except forest and private) |
| 561990 | Firefighting services as a commercial activity |
| 339113 | Firefighting suits and accessories manufacturing |
| 115310 | Firefighting, forest |
| 332999 | Fireplace fixtures and equipment manufacturing |
| 333414 | Fireplace inserts (i.e., heat directing) manufacturing |
| 423320 | Fireplace linings merchant wholesalers |
| 335139 | Fireplace logs, electric, manufacturing |
| 238140 | Fireplace, masonry, installation |
| 238220 | Fireplace, natural gas, installation |
| 423720 | Fireplaces, gas, merchant wholesalers |
| 423220 | Fireplaces, prefabricated (except gas), merchant wholesalers |
| 423720 | Fireplaces, prefabricated gas, merchant wholesalers |
| 238310 | Fireproof flooring installation |
| 238310 | Fireproofing buildings |
| 238310 | Firestop contractors |
| 321999 | Firewood and fuel wood containing fuel binder manufacturing |
| 457210 | Firewood dealers, direct selling |
| 423990 | Firewood merchant wholesalers |
| 713990 | Fireworks display services |
| 325998 | Fireworks manufacturing |
| 423920 | Fireworks merchant wholesalers |
| 459999 | Fireworks shops (i.e., permanent location) |
| 327110 | Firing china for the trade |
| 321920 | Firkins and kits, wood, coopered, manufacturing |
| 611699 | First-aid instruction |
| 423450 | First-aid kits (except household) merchant wholesalers |
| 424210 | First-aid kits, household, merchant wholesalers |
| 424210 | First-aid supplies, household, merchant wholesalers |
| 339113 | First-aid, snake bite, or burn kits manufacturing |
| 424460 | Fish (except canned, packaged frozen) merchant wholesalers |
| 924120 | Fish and game agencies |
| 311710 | Fish and marine animal oils processing |
| 924120 | Fish and wildlife conservation program administration |
| 311710 | Fish egg bait canning |
| 112511 | Fish farms, finfish |
| 112512 | Fish farms, shellfish |
| 334511 | Fish finders (i.e., sonar) manufacturing |
| 311119 | Fish food for feeding fish manufacturing |
| 311710 | Fish freezing (e.g., blocks, fillets, ready-to-serve products) |
| 325411 | Fish liver oils, medicinal, uncompounded, manufacturing |
| 311710 | Fish manufacturing |
| 445250 | Fish markets |
| 311710 | Fish meal processing |
| 236210 | Fish processing plant construction |
| 332216 | Fish wire (i.e., electrical wiring tool) manufacturing |
| 424490 | Fish, canned, merchant wholesalers |
| 311710 | Fish, curing, drying, pickling, salting, and smoking |
| 424420 | Fish, packaged frozen, merchant wholesalers |
| 424460 | Fish, salted or preserved (except canned), merchant wholesalers |
| 424990 | Fish, tropical, merchant wholesalers |
| 541715 | Fisheries research and development laboratories or services |
| 114111 | Fisheries, finfish |
| 114112 | Fisheries, shellfish |
| 487210 | Fishing boat charter operation |
| 336611 | Fishing boat, commercial, building |
| 721214 | Fishing camps with accommodation facilities |
| 713990 | Fishing clubs, recreational |
| 423910 | Fishing equipment and supplies (except commercial) merchant wholesalers |
| 213112 | Fishing for tools at oil and gas fields on a contract basis |
| 713990 | Fishing guide services |
| 332215 | Fishing knives manufacturing |
| 314999 | Fishing nets made from purchased materials |
| 713990 | Fishing piers |
| 114210 | Fishing preserves |
| 459110 | Fishing supply stores (e.g., bait) |
| 339920 | Fishing tackle and equipment (except lines, nets, seines) manufacturing |
| 713940 | Fitness centers |

| | |
|---|---|
| 423910 | Fitness equipment and supplies merchant wholesalers |
| 339920 | Fitness equipment manufacturing |
| 713940 | Fitness salons |
| 713940 | Fitness spas without accommodations |
| 326122 | Fittings and unions, rigid plastics pipe, manufacturing |
| 423720 | Fittings and valves, plumbers', merchant wholesalers |
| 423610 | Fittings, electrical, merchant wholesalers |
| 423840 | Fittings, industrial, merchant wholesalers |
| 326122 | Fittings, rigid plastics pipe, manufacturing |
| 331511 | Fittings, soil and pressure pipe, cast iron, manufacturing |
| 713950 | Five pin bowling centers |
| 445298 | Fix-and-freeze meal stores |
| 488119 | Fixed base operators |
| 722515 | Fixed location refreshment stands |
| 325992 | Fixers, prepared photographic, manufacturing |
| 337920 | Fixtures (e.g., poles, rods, rollers), curtain and drapery, manufacturing |
| 423610 | Fixtures, electric lighting, merchant wholesalers |
| 423740 | Fixtures, refrigerated, merchant wholesalers |
| 423440 | Fixtures, store (except refrigerated), merchant wholesalers |
| 337215 | Fixtures, store display, manufacturing |
| 459999 | Flag and banner shops |
| 561990 | Flagging (i.e., traffic control) services |
| 238990 | Flagpole installation |
| 332323 | Flagpoles, metal, manufacturing |
| 321999 | Flagpoles, wood, manufacturing |
| 314999 | Flags, textile (e.g., banners, bunting, emblems, pennants), made from purchased fabrics |
| 212311 | Flagstone mining or quarrying |
| 327991 | Flagstones cutting |
| 321219 | Flakeboard manufacturing |
| 331221 | Flakes made from purchased iron or steel |
| 331314 | Flakes, aluminum, made from purchased aluminum |
| 331110 | Flakes, iron or steel, made in iron and steel mills |
| 334516 | Flame photometers manufacturing |
| 812332 | Flame resistant clothing supply services |
| 334512 | Flame safety controls for furnaces and boilers manufacturing |
| 332994 | Flame throwers manufacturing |
| 333517 | Flange facing machines, metalworking, manufacturing |
| 332991 | Flange units, ball or roller bearing, manufacturing |
| 332919 | Flanges and flange unions, pipe, metal, manufacturing |
| 315210 | Flannel shirts cut and sew apparel contractors |
| 315250 | Flannel shirts, men's and boys', cut and sewn from purchased fabric (except apparel contractors) |
| 315250 | Flannel shirts, women's, girls', and infants', cut and sewn from purchased fabric (except apparel contractors) |
| 313210 | Flannels, broadwoven, weaving |
| 325998 | Flares manufacturing |
| 333310 | Flash apparatus, photographic, manufacturing |
| 335139 | Flash bulbs, photographic, manufacturing |
| 238170 | Flashing contractors |
| 335910 | Flashlight batteries, disposable, manufacturing |
| 335139 | Flashlight bulb manufacturing |
| 335139 | Flashlights manufacturing |
| 423610 | Flashlights merchant wholesalers |
| 313240 | Flat (i.e., warp) fabrics knitting |
| 331221 | Flat bright steel strip made in cold rolling mills made from purchased steel |
| 327211 | Flat glass (e.g., float, plate) manufacturing |
| 423390 | Flat glass merchant wholesalers |
| 334118 | Flat panel displays (i.e., complete units), computer peripheral equipment, manufacturing |
| 332613 | Flat springs (except clock, watch), light gauge, made from purchased wire or strip, manufacturing |
| 332613 | Flat springs, heavy gauge metal, manufacturing |
| 336212 | Flatbed trailers, commercial, manufacturing |
| 484220 | Flatbed trucking, local |
| 484230 | Flatbed trucking, long-distance |
| 331110 | Flats, iron or steel, made in iron and steel mills |
| 321920 | Flats, wood, greenhouse, manufacturing |
| 423220 | Flatware (except plated, precious) merchant wholesalers |

| | |
|---|---|
| 332215 | Flatware, nonprecious and precious plated metal, manufacturing |
| 423940 | Flatware, precious and plated, merchant wholesalers |
| 311942 | Flavor extracts (except coffee) manufacturing |
| 311511 | Flavored milk drinks manufacturing |
| 312111 | Flavored water manufacturing |
| 311930 | Flavoring concentrates (except coffee based) manufacturing |
| 424490 | Flavoring extracts (except for fountain use) merchant wholesalers |
| 325199 | Flavoring materials (i.e., basic synthetic chemicals such as coumarin) manufacturing |
| 311930 | Flavoring pastes, powders, and syrups for soft drink manufacturing |
| 313110 | Flax spun yarns made from purchased fiber |
| 111120 | Flaxseed farming, field and seed production |
| 311225 | Flaxseed oil made from purchased oils |
| 311224 | Flaxseed oil made in crushing mills |
| 531190 | Flea market space (except under roof) rental or leasing |
| 531120 | Flea market space, under roof, rental or leasing |
| 459510 | Flea markets, used merchandise, permanent |
| 325320 | Flea powders or sprays manufacturing |
| 532112 | Fleet leasing, passenger vehicle |
| 316110 | Fleshers, leather (i.e., flesh side of split leather), manufacturing |
| 334112 | Flexible (i.e., floppy) magnetic disk drives manufacturing |
| 332999 | Flexible metal hose and tubing manufacturing |
| 322220 | Flexible packaging sheet materials made by coating or laminating purchased paper |
| 322220 | Flexible packaging sheet materials made by laminating purchased foil |
| 326112 | Flexible packaging, plastics film, manufacturing |
| 334412 | Flexible wiring boards, bare, manufacturing |
| 325910 | Flexographic inks manufacturing |
| 323120 | Flexographic plate preparation services |
| 323111 | Flexographic printing (except books, grey goods) |
| 333248 | Flexographic printing presses manufacturing |
| 339920 | Flies, artificial fishing, manufacturing |

| | |
|---|---|
| 334511 | Flight and navigation sensors, transmitters, and displays manufacturing |
| 611519 | Flight attendant schools |
| 334511 | Flight recorders (i.e., black boxes) manufacturing |
| 333310 | Flight simulation machinery manufacturing |
| 611512 | Flight simulation training |
| 611512 | Flight training schools |
| 212323 | Flint clay mining and/or beneficiating |
| 327992 | Flint processing beyond beneficiation |
| 339999 | Flints, lighter, manufacturing |
| 321113 | Flitches (i.e., veneer stock) made in sawmills |
| 334512 | Float controls, residential and commercial types, manufacturing |
| 561990 | Float decorating services |
| 541490 | Float design services |
| 327120 | Floaters, glasshouse, clay, manufacturing |
| 713210 | Floating casinos (i.e., gambling cruises, riverboat casinos) |
| 332313 | Floating covers, fabricated metal plate work, manufacturing |
| 311710 | Floating factory ships, seafood processing |
| 332812 | Flocking metals and metal products for the trade |
| 237990 | Flood control project construction |
| 332312 | Flood gates, metal plate, manufacturing |
| 335139 | Floodlights (i.e., lighting fixtures) manufacturing |
| 237990 | Floodway canal and ditch construction |
| 321918 | Floor baseboards, wood, manufacturing |
| 449121 | Floor covering stores (except hardwood or ceramic tile only) |
| 444180 | Floor covering stores, hardwood or ceramic tile only |
| 423220 | Floor coverings merchant wholesalers |
| 326199 | Floor coverings, linoleum, manufacturing |
| 326199 | Floor coverings, resilient, manufacturing |
| 326199 | Floor coverings, rubber, manufacturing |
| 326199 | Floor coverings, vinyl, manufacturing |
| 332312 | Floor jacks, metal, manufacturing |
| 335131 | Floor lamps (i.e., lighting fixtures), residential, manufacturing |
| 238330 | Floor laying, scraping, finishing and refinishing |
| 423850 | Floor maintenance equipment merchant wholesalers |

| | |
|---|---|
| 326299 | Floor mats (e.g., bath, door), rubber, manufacturing |
| 325612 | Floor polishes and waxes manufacturing |
| 332312 | Floor posts, adjustable metal, manufacturing |
| 532490 | Floor sanding machine rental or leasing |
| 333310 | Floor sanding, washing, and polishing machines, commercial-type, manufacturing |
| 335210 | Floor scrubbing and shampooing machines, household-type electric, manufacturing |
| 335210 | Floor standing fans, household-type electric, manufacturing |
| 238330 | Floor tile and sheets, installation only |
| 327120 | Floor tile, ceramic, manufacturing |
| 321215 | Floor trusses, wood, manufacturing |
| 335210 | Floor waxers and polishers, household-type electric, manufacturing |
| 532490 | Floor waxing equipment rental or leasing |
| 332323 | Flooring, open steel (i.e., grating), manufacturing |
| 332322 | Flooring, sheet metal (except stampings), manufacturing |
| 321114 | Flooring, wood block, treating |
| 321918 | Flooring, wood, manufacturing |
| 423310 | Flooring, wood, merchant wholesalers |
| 334112 | Floppy disk drives manufacturing |
| 561422 | Floral wire services (i.e., telemarketing services) |
| 459310 | Florists |
| 327110 | Florists' articles, red earthenware, manufacturing |
| 424930 | Florist's supplies merchant wholesalers |
| 333131 | Flotation machinery, mining-type, manufacturing |
| 114111 | Flounder fishing |
| 314910 | Flour bags made from purchased woven or knitted materials |
| 424490 | Flour merchant wholesalers |
| 333241 | Flour milling machinery manufacturing |
| 311230 | Flour mills, breakfast cereal, manufacturing |
| 311211 | Flour mills, cereals grains (except breakfast cereals, rice) |
| 311211 | Flour mixes made in flour mills |
| 311824 | Flour, blended or self-rising, made from purchased flour |
| 311211 | Flour, blended, prepared, or self-rising (except rice), made in flour mills |

| | |
|---|---|
| 311213 | Flour, malt, manufacturing |
| 311212 | Flour, rice, manufacturing |
| 321999 | Flour, wood, manufacturing |
| 335314 | Flow actuated electrical switches manufacturing |
| 334513 | Flow instruments, industrial process-type, manufacturing |
| 327420 | Flower boxes, plaster of paris, manufacturing |
| 111421 | Flower bulb growing |
| 424910 | Flower bulbs merchant wholesalers |
| 111422 | Flower growing |
| 327110 | Flower pots, red earthenware, manufacturing |
| 111422 | Flower seed production |
| 459999 | Flower shops, artificial or dried |
| 459310 | Flower shops, fresh |
| 561920 | Flower show managers |
| 561920 | Flower show organizers |
| 561920 | Flower show promoters |
| 424930 | Flowers merchant wholesalers |
| 339999 | Flowers, artificial (except glass, plastics), manufacturing |
| 327120 | Flue lining, clay, manufacturing |
| 423320 | Flue pipe and linings merchant wholesalers |
| 332322 | Flues, stove and furnace, sheet metal (except stampings), manufacturing |
| 423830 | Fluid meters, industrial, merchant wholesalers |
| 332439 | Fluid milk shipping containers, light gauge metal, manufacturing |
| 311511 | Fluid milk substitutes processing |
| 333995 | Fluid power actuators manufacturing |
| 332912 | Fluid power aircraft subassemblies manufacturing |
| 333995 | Fluid power cylinders manufacturing |
| 332912 | Fluid power hose assemblies manufacturing |
| 333996 | Fluid power motors manufacturing |
| 333996 | Fluid power pumps manufacturing |
| 423830 | Fluid power transmission equipment merchant wholesalers |
| 332912 | Fluid power valves and hose fittings manufacturing |
| 334513 | Fluidic devices, circuits, and systems for process control, manufacturing |
| 332313 | Flumes, fabricated metal plate work, manufacturing |

| | |
|---|---|
| 332322 | Flumes, sheet metal (except stampings), manufacturing |
| 325180 | Fluoboric acid manufacturing |
| 335311 | Fluorescent ballasts (i.e., transformers) manufacturing |
| 325130 | Fluorescent dyes manufacturing |
| 335139 | Fluorescent lamp electrodes, cold cathode, manufacturing |
| 335139 | Fluorescent lamp tubes, electric, manufacturing |
| 335132 | Fluorescent lighting fixtures, commercial, institutional, and industrial electric, manufacturing |
| 335131 | Fluorescent lighting fixtures, residential, manufacturing |
| 335311 | Fluorescent lighting transformers manufacturing |
| 325120 | Fluorinated hydrocarbon gases manufacturing |
| 325180 | Fluorine manufacturing |
| 212390 | Fluorite mining and/or beneficiating |
| 325212 | Fluoro rubbers manufacturing |
| 325212 | Fluorocarbon derivative rubbers manufacturing |
| 325220 | Fluorocarbon fibers and filaments manufacturing |
| 325120 | Fluorocarbon gases manufacturing |
| 325211 | Fluorohydrocarbon resins manufacturing |
| 325211 | Fluoro-polymer resins manufacturing |
| 334517 | Fluoroscopes manufacturing |
| 334517 | Fluoroscopic X-ray apparatus and tubes manufacturing |
| 212390 | Fluorspar mining and/or beneficiating |
| 332999 | Flush tanks, metal, manufacturing |
| 332913 | Flush valves, plumbing, manufacturing |
| 332911 | Flushing hydrant manufacturing |
| 339992 | Flutes and parts manufacturing |
| 325998 | Fluxes (e.g., brazing, galvanizing, soldering, welding) manufacturing |
| 423930 | Fly ash merchant wholesalers |
| 325320 | Fly sprays manufacturing |
| 339999 | Fly swatters manufacturing |
| 541870 | Flyer direct distribution (except direct mail) services |
| 713990 | Flying clubs, recreational |
| 488119 | Flying field operators |
| 611512 | Flying instruction |
| 335139 | Flytraps, electrical, manufacturing |
| 336310 | Flywheels and ring gears, automotive and truck gasoline engine, manufacturing |
| 516110 | FM radio stations |
| 522299 | FNMA (Federal National Mortgage Association) |
| 238310 | Foam insulation installation |
| 424130 | Foam plastic trays merchant wholesalers |
| 326150 | Foam plastics products (except polystyrene) manufacturing |
| 326140 | Foam polystyrene products manufacturing |
| 424990 | Foam rubber merchant wholesalers |
| 424610 | Foam, plastics, resins and shapes, merchant wholesalers |
| 322220 | Foil bags made from purchased foil |
| 332999 | Foil containers (except bags) manufacturing |
| 332999 | Foil not made in rolling mills |
| 322220 | Foil sheet, laminating purchased foil sheets for packaging applications |
| 331315 | Foil, aluminum, made by flat rolling purchased aluminum |
| 331315 | Foil, aluminum, made in integrated secondary smelting and flat rolling mills |
| 331420 | Foil, copper, made from purchased metal or scrap |
| 331491 | Foil, gold, made by rolling purchased metals or scrap |
| 331491 | Foil, nickel, made by rolling purchased metals or scrap |
| 331491 | Foil, silver, made by rolling purchased metals or scrap |
| 424120 | Folders, file, merchant wholesalers |
| 561910 | Folding and packaging services, textile and apparel |
| 322130 | Folding boxboard stock manufacturing |
| 322212 | Folding boxes (except corrugated) made from purchased paperboard |
| 322212 | Folding paper and paperboard containers (except corrugated) made from purchased paperboard |
| 111422 | Foliage growing |
| 711120 | Folk dance companies |
| 711510 | Folk dancers, independent |
| 423430 | Font cartridges merchant wholesalers |
| 445110 | Food (i.e., groceries) stores |
| 336999 | Food (vendor) carts on wheels manufacturing |
| 424690 | Food additives, chemical, merchant wholesalers |
| 624210 | Food banks |

| | |
|---|---|
| 722330 | Food carts and trucks, mobile |
| 333241 | Food choppers, grinders, mixers, and slicers (i.e., food manufacturing-type) manufacturing |
| 311942 | Food coloring, natural, manufacturing |
| 325130 | Food coloring, synthetic, manufacturing |
| 722310 | Food concession contractors (e.g., convention facilities, entertainment facilities, sporting facilities) |
| 722330 | Food concession stands, mobile |
| 322299 | Food containers made from molded pulp |
| 326140 | Food containers, polystyrene foam, manufacturing |
| 322219 | Food containers, sanitary (except folding), made from purchased paper or paperboard |
| 322212 | Food containers, sanitary, folding, made from purchased paperboard |
| 333241 | Food dehydrating equipment (except household-type) manufacturing |
| 923130 | Food distribution program administration, government |
| 311942 | Food extracts (except coffee, meat) manufacturing |
| 926140 | Food inspection agencies |
| 811310 | Food machinery repair and maintenance services |
| 335210 | Food mixers, household-type electric, manufacturing |
| 333993 | Food packaging machinery manufacturing |
| 327213 | Food packaging, glass, manufacturing |
| 624210 | Food pantries |
| 423830 | Food processing machinery and equipment merchant wholesalers |
| 236210 | Food processing plant construction |
| 333241 | Food product machinery manufacturing |
| 541715 | Food research and development laboratories or services (except biotechnology and nanotechnology research and development) |
| 722310 | Food service contractors, airline |
| 722310 | Food service contractors, cafeteria |
| 722310 | Food service contractors, concession operators (e.g., convention facilities, entertainment facilities, sporting facilities) |
| 722310 | Food service contractors, industrial |
| 722310 | Food service contractors, institutional |
| 423440 | Food service equipment (except refrigerated), commercial, merchant wholesalers |

| | |
|---|---|
| 923120 | Food service health inspections |
| 326111 | Food storage bags, plastics film, single wall or multiwall, manufacturing |
| 541380 | Food testing laboratories or services |
| 322299 | Food trays, molded pulp, manufacturing |
| 333310 | Food warming equipment, commercial-type, manufacturing |
| 335220 | Food waste disposal units, household-type, manufacturing |
| 424410 | Food, general-line, merchant wholesalers |
| 311991 | Food, prepared, perishable, packaged for individual resale |
| 424420 | Foods, prepared, packaged frozen, merchant wholesalers |
| 339113 | Foot appliances, orthopedic, manufacturing |
| 621391 | Foot specialists' (podiatry) offices (e.g., centers, clinics) |
| 711211 | Football clubs, professional or semiprofessional |
| 713990 | Football clubs, recreational |
| 339920 | Football equipment and supplies (except footwear, uniforms) manufacturing |
| 423910 | Football equipment and supplies merchant wholesalers |
| 611620 | Football instruction, camps or schools |
| 711211 | Football teams, professional or semiprofessional |
| 316210 | Footholds, plastics or plastics soled fabric upper, manufacturing |
| 316210 | Footholds, rubber or rubber soled fabric upper, manufacturing |
| 315120 | Footies, sheer, knitting or knitting and finishing |
| 238110 | Footing and foundation concrete contractors |
| 459110 | Footwear (e.g., bowling, golf, cleated), specialty sports, stores |
| 333248 | Footwear making or repairing machinery manufacturing |
| 424340 | Footwear merchant wholesalers |
| 326199 | Footwear parts (e.g., heels, soles), plastics, manufacturing |
| 326299 | Footwear parts (e.g., heels, soles, soling strips), rubber, manufacturing |
| 316210 | Footwear, athletic, manufacturing |
| 316210 | Footwear, children's (except orthopedic extension), manufacturing |
| 316210 | Footwear, children's, leather or vinyl upper with rubber or plastics soles, manufacturing |
| 316210 | Footwear, men's (except orthopedic extension), manufacturing |

| | |
|---|---|
| 316210 | Footwear, men's leather or vinyl upper with rubber or plastics soles, manufacturing |
| 316210 | Footwear, plastics or plastics soled fabric uppers, manufacturing |
| 316210 | Footwear, women's (except orthopedic extension), manufacturing |
| 316210 | Footwear, women's leather or vinyl upper with rubber or plastics soles, manufacturing |
| 339112 | Forceps, surgical, manufacturing |
| 523160 | Foreign currency exchange brokering services |
| 523160 | Foreign currency exchange dealing (i.e., acting as a principal in dealing commodities to investors) |
| 523160 | Foreign currency exchange services (i.e., selling to the public) |
| 928120 | Foreign economic and social development services, government |
| 928120 | Foreign government service |
| 611630 | Foreign language schools |
| 928120 | Foreign missions |
| 541380 | Forensic (except medical) laboratories or services |
| 621511 | Forensic laboratories, medical |
| 621111 | Forensic pathologists' offices |
| 531190 | Forest land rental or leasing |
| 115310 | Forest management plans preparation |
| 113210 | Forest nurseries for reforestation, growing trees |
| 423990 | Forest products (except lumber) merchant wholesalers |
| 484230 | Forest products trucking, long-distance |
| 115310 | Forest thinning |
| 423810 | Forestry machinery and equipment merchant wholesalers |
| 532412 | Forestry machinery and equipment rental or leasing |
| 811310 | Forestry machinery and equipment repair and maintenance services |
| 541715 | Forestry research and development laboratories or services |
| 115310 | Forestry services |
| 333517 | Forging machinery and hammers manufacturing |
| 332111 | Forgings made from purchased iron or steel, unfinished |
| 331110 | Forgings, iron or steel, made in iron and steel mills |
| 423510 | Forgings, metal, merchant wholesalers |
| 811310 | Forklift repair and maintenance services |
| 423830 | Forklift trucks (except log) merchant wholesalers |
| 333924 | Forklifts manufacturing |
| 332216 | Forks, handtools (e.g., garden, hay, manure), manufacturing |
| 332215 | Forks, table, nonprecious and precious plated metal, manufacturing |
| 331222 | Form ties made in wire drawing plants |
| 315210 | Formal jackets cut and sew apparel contractors |
| 315250 | Formal jackets, men's and boys', cut and sewn from purchased fabric (except apparel contractors) |
| 532281 | Formal wear rental |
| 325199 | Formaldehyde manufacturing |
| 325199 | Formalin manufacturing |
| 325199 | Formic acid manufacturing |
| 238190 | Forming contractor |
| 333517 | Forming machines (except drawing), metalworking, manufacturing |
| 327110 | Forms for dipped rubber products, pottery, manufacturing |
| 238190 | Forms for poured concrete, erecting and dismantling |
| 423420 | Forms handling machines merchant wholesalers |
| 332322 | Forms, concrete, sheet metal (except stampings), manufacturing |
| 321999 | Forms, display, boot and shoe, all materials, manufacturing |
| 424120 | Forms, paper (e.g., business, office, sales), merchant wholesalers |
| 236220 | For-sale builders (i.e., building on own land, for sale), commercial and institutional building |
| 236210 | For-sale builders (i.e., building on own land, for sale), industrial building (except warehouses) |
| 236117 | For-sale builders (i.e., building on own land, for sale), residential |
| 236117 | For-sale builders (i.e., building on own land, for sale), single-family housing |
| 312130 | Fortified wines manufacturing |
| 812990 | Fortune-telling services |
| 624110 | Foster care placement agencies |
| 624110 | Foster home placement services |
| 238140 | Foundation (e.g., brick, block, stone), building, contractors |
| 238390 | Foundation dampproofing (including installing rigid foam insulation) |
| 238910 | Foundation digging (i.e., excavation) |
| 238910 | Foundation drilling contractors |

| | |
|---|---|
| 315210 | Foundation garments cut and sew apparel contractors |
| 315250 | Foundation garments, women's and girls', cut and sewn from purchased fabric (except apparel contractors) |
| 238110 | Foundation, building, poured concrete, contractors |
| 238130 | Foundation, building, wood, contractors |
| 325620 | Foundations (i.e., makeup) manufacturing |
| 331529 | Foundries (except die-casting), nonferrous metals (except aluminum) |
| 331524 | Foundries, aluminum (except die-casting) |
| 331523 | Foundries, die-casting, aluminum |
| 331523 | Foundries, die-casting, nonferrous metals |
| 331511 | Foundries, iron (i.e., ductile, gray, malleable, semisteel) |
| 331513 | Foundries, steel (except investment) |
| 331512 | Foundries, steel investment |
| 333511 | Foundry casting molds manufacturing |
| 236210 | Foundry construction |
| 325998 | Foundry core oil, wash, and wax manufacturing |
| 332999 | Foundry cores manufacturing |
| 423830 | Foundry machinery and equipment merchant wholesalers |
| 811310 | Foundry machinery and equipment repair and maintenance services |
| 332999 | Foundry pattern making |
| 423510 | Foundry products merchant wholesalers |
| 212322 | Foundry sand quarrying and/or beneficiating |
| 424450 | Fountain fruits and syrups (except soft drink) merchant wholesalers |
| 335139 | Fountain lighting fixtures manufacturing |
| 339940 | Fountain pens manufacturing |
| 424450 | Fountain syrups (except soft drink) merchant wholesalers |
| 332999 | Fountains (except drinking), metal, manufacturing |
| 332999 | Fountains, drinking (except mechanically refrigerated), metal, manufacturing |
| 423720 | Fountains, drinking (except refrigerated), merchant wholesalers |
| 423740 | Fountains, drinking, refrigerated, merchant wholesalers |
| 327420 | Fountains, plaster of paris, manufacturing |
| 333415 | Fountains, refrigerated drinking, manufacturing |
| 713920 | Four season ski resorts without accommodations |
| 333243 | Fourdrinier machinery manufacturing |
| 332618 | Fourdrinier wire cloth made from purchased wire |
| 112930 | Fox production |
| 335312 | Fractional horsepower electric motors manufacturing |
| 333248 | Fractionating equipment, chemical, manufacturing |
| 211130 | Fractionating natural gas liquids |
| 333310 | Frame and body alignment equipment, motor vehicle, manufacturing |
| 332999 | Frames and handles, handbag and luggage, metal, manufacturing |
| 423220 | Frames and pictures merchant wholesalers |
| 339940 | Frames for artist's canvases (i.e., stretchers) manufacturing |
| 333248 | Frames for textile making machinery manufacturing |
| 332321 | Frames, door and window, metal, manufacturing |
| 321911 | Frames, door and window, wood, manufacturing |
| 332999 | Frames, metal, lamp shade, manufacturing |
| 332999 | Frames, metal, umbrella and parasol, manufacturing |
| 339999 | Frames, mirror and picture, all materials, manufacturing |
| 423460 | Frames, ophthalmic, merchant wholesalers |
| 238130 | Framework, house, contractors |
| 238130 | Framing contractors |
| 533110 | Franchise agreements, leasing, selling or licensing, without providing other services |
| 813410 | Fraternal associations or lodges, social or civic |
| 524113 | Fraternal life insurance organizations |
| 813410 | Fraternal lodges |
| 813410 | Fraternal organizations |
| 813410 | Fraternities (except residential) |
| 721310 | Fraternity houses |
| 621493 | Freestanding ambulatory surgical centers and clinics |
| 621498 | Freestanding birth centers, outpatient |
| 621493 | Freestanding emergency medical centers and clinics |
| 311423 | Freeze-dried, food processing, fruits and vegetables |

| | |
|---|---|
| 811310 | Freezer, commercial, repair and maintenance services |
| 335220 | Freezers, chest and upright household-type, manufacturing |
| 423740 | Freezers, commercial-type, merchant wholesalers |
| 423620 | Freezers, household-type, merchant wholesalers |
| 333415 | Freezing equipment, industrial and commercial-type, manufacturing |
| 311710 | Freezing fish (e.g., blocks, fillets, ready-to-serve products) |
| 488210 | Freight car cleaning services |
| 481112 | Freight carriers (except air couriers), air, scheduled |
| 481212 | Freight charter services, air |
| 488510 | Freight forwarding |
| 482111 | Freight railways, line-haul |
| 482112 | Freight railways, short-line or beltline |
| 541614 | Freight rate auditor services |
| 541614 | Freight rate consulting services |
| 483113 | Freight shipping on the Great Lakes system (including St. Lawrence Seaway) |
| 541614 | Freight traffic consulting services |
| 481212 | Freight transportation, air, charter services |
| 481212 | Freight transportation, air, nonscheduled |
| 483113 | Freight transportation, deep sea, to and from domestic ports |
| 483111 | Freight transportation, deep sea, to or from foreign ports |
| 483211 | Freight transportation, inland waters (except on Great Lakes system) |
| 311411 | French fries, frozen, pre-cooked, manufacturing |
| 311412 | French toast, frozen, manufacturing |
| 335312 | Frequency converters (i.e., electric generators) manufacturing |
| 334515 | Frequency meters (e.g., electrical, electronic, mechanical) manufacturing |
| 334515 | Frequency synthesizers manufacturing |
| 238310 | Fresco (i.e., decorative plaster finishing) contractors |
| 424460 | Fresh fish merchant wholesalers |
| 424480 | Fresh fruits, vegetables, and berries merchant wholesalers |
| 424470 | Fresh meats merchant wholesalers |
| 424440 | Fresh poultry merchant wholesalers |
| 424460 | Fresh seafood merchant wholesalers |
| 339992 | Fretted instruments and parts manufacturing |

| | |
|---|---|
| 313220 | Fringes weaving |
| 325510 | Frit manufacturing |
| 114119 | Frog fishing |
| 112519 | Frog production, farm raising |
| 331110 | Frogs, iron or steel, made in iron and steel mills |
| 811114 | Front end alignment shops, automotive |
| 423820 | Frost protection machinery merchant wholesalers |
| 311999 | Frosting, prepared, manufacturing |
| 311411 | Frozen ades, drinks and cocktail mixes, manufacturing |
| 311812 | Frozen bread and bread-type rolls, made in commercial bakeries |
| 311813 | Frozen cake manufacturing |
| 311411 | Frozen citrus pulp manufacturing |
| 311520 | Frozen custard manufacturing |
| 722515 | Frozen custard stands, fixed location |
| 311520 | Frozen dairy product substitutes manufacturing |
| 311520 | Frozen desserts (except bakery) manufacturing |
| 311412 | Frozen dinners (except seafood-based) manufacturing |
| 311824 | Frozen doughs made from purchased flour |
| 424460 | Frozen fish (except packaged) merchant wholesalers |
| 445298 | Frozen food and freezer meal plan providers, direct selling |
| 326111 | Frozen food bags, plastics film, single wall or multiwall, manufacturing |
| 311412 | Frozen food entrees (except seafood-based), packaged, manufacturing |
| 424420 | Frozen foods, packaged (except dairy products), merchant wholesalers |
| 311411 | Frozen fruit and vegetable processing |
| 311411 | Frozen fruits, fruit juices, and vegetables, manufacturing |
| 311612 | Frozen meat pies (i.e., tourtiere) made from purchased carcasses |
| 445240 | Frozen meat stores |
| 424470 | Frozen meats (except packaged) merchant wholesalers |
| 311412 | Frozen pizza manufacturing |
| 311412 | Frozen pot pies manufacturing |
| 424440 | Frozen poultry (except packaged) merchant wholesalers |
| 311412 | Frozen rice dishes manufacturing |
| 424460 | Frozen seafood (except packaged) merchant wholesalers |

| | |
|---|---|
| 311412 | Frozen side dishes manufacturing |
| 311412 | Frozen soups (except seafood) manufacturing |
| 311412 | Frozen waffles manufacturing |
| 424430 | Frozen yogurt merchant wholesalers |
| 722515 | Frozen yogurt shops |
| 111336 | Fruit and tree nut combination farming |
| 445230 | Fruit and vegetable stands, permanent |
| 311423 | Fruit and vegetables, dehydrating, manufacturing |
| 459420 | Fruit basket or fruit bouquet stores |
| 321920 | Fruit baskets, veneer and splint, manufacturing |
| 311421 | Fruit brining |
| 311421 | Fruit butters manufacturing |
| 424450 | Fruit concentrates, fountain, merchant wholesalers |
| 321920 | Fruit crates, wood, wirebound, manufacturing |
| 312111 | Fruit drinks (except juice), manufacturing |
| 311942 | Fruit extracts manufacturing |
| 111419 | Fruit farming, grown under cover |
| 311211 | Fruit flour, meal, and powders, manufacturing |
| 333111 | Fruit harvesting machines manufacturing |
| 311421 | Fruit juice canning |
| 311411 | Fruit juice concentrates, frozen, manufacturing |
| 311421 | Fruit juices, fresh, manufacturing |
| 445230 | Fruit markets |
| 311340 | Fruit peel products (e.g., candied, crystallized, glace, glazed) manufacturing |
| 311421 | Fruit pickling |
| 311421 | Fruit pie fillings, canning |
| 311520 | Fruit pops, frozen, manufacturing |
| 115114 | Fruit precooling |
| 115114 | Fruit sorting, grading, and packing |
| 445230 | Fruit stands, permanent |
| 445230 | Fruit stands, temporary |
| 111421 | Fruit stock (e.g., plants, seedlings, trees) growing |
| 311930 | Fruit syrups, flavoring, manufacturing |
| 311991 | Fruit, cut or peeled, fresh, manufacturing |
| 115113 | Fruit, machine harvesting |
| 115114 | Fruit, sun drying |

| | |
|---|---|
| 115114 | Fruit, vacuum cooling |
| 311340 | Fruits (e.g., candied, crystallized, glazed) manufacturing |
| 326199 | Fruits and vegetables, artificial, plastics, manufacturing |
| 311423 | Fruits dehydrating (except sun drying) |
| 311421 | Fruits pickling |
| 339999 | Fruits, artificial (except glass, plastics), manufacturing |
| 327215 | Fruits, artificial, made from purchased glass |
| 327212 | Fruits, artificial, made in glass making plants |
| 311421 | Fruits, canned, bottled, and jarred, manufacturing |
| 424490 | Fruits, canned, merchant wholesalers |
| 424480 | Fruits, fresh, merchant wholesalers |
| 311411 | Fruits, frozen, manufacturing |
| 424420 | Fruits, frozen, merchant wholesalers |
| 112320 | Fryer chicken production |
| 335210 | Fryers, household-type electric, manufacturing |
| 311351 | Fudge, chocolate, made from cacao beans |
| 311352 | Fudge, chocolate, made from purchased chocolate |
| 311340 | Fudge, nonchocolate, manufacturing |
| 424690 | Fuel additives merchant wholesalers |
| 326299 | Fuel bladders, rubber, manufacturing |
| 324199 | Fuel briquettes or boulets made from refined petroleum |
| 335999 | Fuel cells, electrochemical generators, manufacturing |
| 334413 | Fuel cells, solid-state, manufacturing |
| 334519 | Fuel densitometers, aircraft engine, manufacturing |
| 336310 | Fuel injection systems and parts, automotive and truck gasoline engine, manufacturing |
| 334519 | Fuel mixture indicators, aircraft engine, manufacturing |
| 457210 | Fuel oil (i.e., heating) dealers, direct selling |
| 424710 | Fuel oil bulk stations and terminals, merchant wholesalers |
| 238220 | Fuel oil burner installation |
| 424720 | Fuel oil merchant wholesalers (except bulk stations, terminals) |
| 424720 | Fuel oil truck jobbers |
| 324110 | Fuel oils manufacturing |

| | |
|---|---|
| 325180 | Fuel propellants, solid inorganic, not specified elsewhere by process, manufacturing |
| 325199 | Fuel propellants, solid organic, not specified elsewhere by process, manufacturing |
| 336320 | Fuel pumps, electric, automotive, truck, and bus, manufacturing |
| 336310 | Fuel pumps, mechanical, automotive and truck gasoline engine, manufacturing |
| 334519 | Fuel system instruments, aircraft, manufacturing |
| 334519 | Fuel totalizers, aircraft engine, manufacturing |
| 424720 | Fuel, aircraft, merchant wholesalers (except bulk stations, terminals) |
| 423520 | Fuel, coal and coke, merchant wholesalers |
| 424720 | Fueling aircraft (except on contract basis), merchant wholesalers |
| 488190 | Fueling aircraft on a contract or fee basis |
| 324110 | Fuels, jet, manufacturing |
| 531120 | Full service office space provision |
| 722511 | Full service restaurants |
| 423520 | Fuller's earth merchant wholesalers |
| 212323 | Fuller's earth mining and/or beneficiating |
| 327992 | Fuller's earth processing beyond beneficiating |
| 332313 | Fumigating chambers, fabricated metal plate work, manufacturing |
| 115114 | Fumigating grain |
| 561710 | Fumigating services (except crop fumigating) |
| 334515 | Function generators manufacturing |
| 334118 | Funds transfer devices manufacturing |
| 525110 | Funds, employee benefit pension |
| 525120 | Funds, health and welfare |
| 525990 | Funds, mutual, closed-end |
| 525910 | Funds, mutual, open-ended |
| 525110 | Funds, pension |
| 525190 | Funds, self-insurance (except employee benefit funds) |
| 812210 | Funeral director services |
| 423850 | Funeral home supplies merchant wholesalers |
| 812210 | Funeral homes |
| 812210 | Funeral homes combined with crematories |
| 524128 | Funeral insurance carriers, direct |
| 812210 | Funeral parlors |
| 325320 | Fungicides manufacturing |
| 424910 | Fungicides, agricultural, merchant wholesalers |
| 315250 | Fur accessories and trimmings (except apparel contractors) manufacturing |
| 315210 | Fur accessories and trimmings cut and sew apparel contractors |
| 315250 | Fur apparel (e.g., capes, coats, hats, jackets, neckpieces) (except apparel contractors) manufacturing |
| 315210 | Fur apparel (e.g., capes, coats, hats, jackets, neckpieces) cut and sew apparel contractors |
| 458110 | Fur apparel stores |
| 315250 | Fur clothing (except apparel contractors) manufacturing |
| 315210 | Fur clothing cut and sew apparel contractors |
| 424350 | Fur clothing merchant wholesalers |
| 423930 | Fur cuttings and scraps merchant wholesalers |
| 541490 | Fur design services |
| 315210 | Fur finishers, liners, and buttonhole makers cut and sew apparel contractors |
| 812320 | Fur garment cleaning services |
| 811490 | Fur garment repair shops without retailing new fur garments |
| 315250 | Fur plates and trimmings (except apparel contractors) manufacturing |
| 315210 | Fur plates and trimmings cut and sew apparel contractors |
| 532281 | Fur rental |
| 493120 | Fur storage warehousing for the trade |
| 316110 | Fur stripping |
| 112930 | Fur-bearing animal production |
| 236210 | Furnace (i.e., industrial plant structure) construction |
| 325180 | Furnace black manufacturing |
| 332322 | Furnace casings, sheet metal (except stampings), manufacturing |
| 238220 | Furnace conversion (i.e., from one fuel to another) |
| 333413 | Furnace filters manufacturing |
| 332322 | Furnace flues, sheet metal (except stampings), manufacturing |
| 238220 | Furnace humidifier installation |
| 238220 | Furnace installation |
| 238220 | Furnace, forced air, installation |
| 333414 | Furnaces (except forced air), heating, manufacturing |

423720 Furnaces (except forced air), heating, merchant wholesalers

333994 Furnaces and ovens for drying and redrying, industrial process-type, manufacturing

333994 Furnaces and ovens, semiconductor wafer, manufacturing

339114 Furnaces, dental laboratory, manufacturing

333414 Furnaces, floor and wall, manufacturing

333994 Furnaces, industrial and laboratory-type (except dental), manufacturing

423830 Furnaces, industrial process, merchant wholesalers

333415 Furnaces, warm air (i.e., forced air), manufacturing

423730 Furnaces, warm air (i.e., forced air), merchant wholesalers

424350 Furnishings (except shoes), men's and boys', merchant wholesalers

424350 Furnishings (except shoes), women's, girls', and infants', merchant wholesalers

458110 Furnishings stores, men's and boys'

458110 Furnishings stores, women's and girls'

423210 Furniture (except drafting tables, hospital beds, medical furniture) merchant wholesalers

337214 Furniture (except wood), office-type, padded, upholstered, or plain, manufacturing

337126 Furniture (except wood, upholstered), indoor and outdoor (e.g., beach, garden, lawn, porch) household-type, manufacturing

532289 Furniture (i.e., residential) rental centers

449110 Furniture and appliance stores (i.e., primarily retailing furniture)

561740 Furniture cleaning on customers' premises

561740 Furniture cleaning services

423220 Furniture coverings and protectors merchant wholesalers

541420 Furniture design services

321912 Furniture dimension stock, hardwood, unfinished, manufacturing

321912 Furniture dimension stock, softwood, unfinished, manufacturing

321912 Furniture dimension stock, unfinished wood, manufacturing

337215 Furniture frames and parts, metal, manufacturing

337215 Furniture frames, wood, manufacturing

332510 Furniture hardware, metal, manufacturing

321999 Furniture inlays manufacturing

484210 Furniture moving, used

423210 Furniture parts merchant wholesalers

337215 Furniture parts, finished metal, manufacturing

337215 Furniture parts, finished plastics, manufacturing

337215 Furniture parts, finished wood, manufacturing

325612 Furniture polishes and waxes manufacturing

811420 Furniture refinishing shops

811420 Furniture repair shops

811420 Furniture reupholstering shops

332613 Furniture springs, light gauge, unassembled, made from purchased wire or strip

321912 Furniture squares, unfinished hardwood, manufacturing

449110 Furniture stores (e.g., household, office, outdoor)

459510 Furniture stores, used

327215 Furniture tops, glass (e.g., beveled, cut, polished), made from purchased glass

314999 Furniture trimmings made from purchased fabrics

327991 Furniture, cut stone (i.e., benches, tables, church), manufacturing

337127 Furniture, factory-type (e.g., cabinets, stools, tool stands, work benches), manufacturing

532283 Furniture, home health, rental

339113 Furniture, hospital, specialized (e.g., hospital beds, operating room furniture), manufacturing

337121 Furniture, household-type, upholstered on frames of any material, manufacturing

532490 Furniture, institutional (i.e. public building), rental or leasing

337127 Furniture, institutional, manufacturing

337127 Furniture, laboratory-type (e.g., benches, cabinets, stools, tables), manufacturing

532420 Furniture, office, rental or leasing

337211 Furniture, office-type, padded, upholstered, or plain wood, manufacturing

337122 Furniture, outdoor wood household-type (e.g., beach, garden, lawn, porch), manufacturing

337127 Furniture, public building (e.g., church, library, school, theater), manufacturing

532289 Furniture, residential, rental or leasing

| | |
|---|---|
| 337127 | Furniture, restaurant-type, manufacturing |
| 337122 | Furniture, unassembled or knock-down wood household-type, manufacturing |
| 337122 | Furniture, unfinished wood household-type, manufacturing |
| 337122 | Furniture, wood household-type, not upholstered (except TV and radio housings, and sewing machine cabinets), manufacturing |
| 458110 | Furriers |
| 423850 | Furriers equipment and supplies merchant wholesalers |
| 332323 | Furring channels, sheet metal, manufacturing |
| 316110 | Furs, dressed (e.g., bleached, curried, dyed, scraped, tanned), manufacturing |
| 424990 | Furs, dressed, merchant wholesalers |
| 424590 | Furs, raw, merchant wholesalers |
| 335313 | Fuse clips and blocks, electric, manufacturing |
| 335931 | Fuse cutouts manufacturing |
| 335313 | Fuse mountings, electric power, manufacturing |
| 332993 | Fuses ammunition (i.e., more than 30 mm., more than 1.18 inch) manufacturing |
| 423610 | Fuses, electric, merchant wholesalers |
| 335313 | Fuses, electrical, manufacturing |
| 325194 | Fustic wood extract manufacturing |
| 337122 | Futon frames manufacturing |
| 337121 | Futons with frames manufacturing |
| 523160 | Futures commodity contracts brokerages |
| 523160 | Futures commodity contracts brokers' offices |
| 523160 | Futures commodity contracts dealing (i.e., acting as a principal in dealing commodities to investors) |
| 523210 | Futures commodity contracts exchanges |
| 212319 | Gabbro crushed and broken stone mining and/or beneficiating |
| 212311 | Gabbro mining or quarrying |
| 237990 | Gabion construction |
| 316210 | Gaiters, plastics or plastics soled fabric upper, manufacturing |
| 316210 | Gaiters, rubber or rubber soled fabric upper, manufacturing |
| 212230 | Galena mining and/or beneficiating |
| 712110 | Galleries, art (except retail) |
| 459920 | Galleries, art, retail |
| 713990 | Galleries, shooting |

| | |
|---|---|
| 316210 | Galoshes, plastics or plastics soled fabric upper, manufacturing |
| 316210 | Galoshes, rubber, or rubber soled fabric upper, manufacturing |
| 423510 | Galvanized iron and steel products merchant wholesalers |
| 238160 | Galvanized iron roofing installation |
| 333519 | Galvanizing machinery manufacturing |
| 331110 | Galvanizing metals and metal formed products made in iron and steel mills |
| 332812 | Galvanizing metals and metal products for the trade |
| 334515 | Galvanometers (except geophysical) manufacturing |
| 334519 | Galvanometers, geophysical, manufacturing |
| 325194 | Gambier extract manufacturing |
| 921130 | Gambling control boards, nonoperating |
| 713290 | Gambling control boards, operating gambling activities |
| 713210 | Gambling cruises |
| 713290 | Gambling device arcades or parlors, coin- or card-operated |
| 713290 | Gambling device concession operators (i.e., supplying and servicing in others' facilities), coin- or card-operated |
| 924120 | Game and inland fish agencies |
| 334610 | Game cartridge software, mass reproducing |
| 114210 | Game preserves, commercial |
| 114210 | Game propagation |
| 114210 | Game retreats |
| 713120 | Game rooms (except gambling) |
| 518210 | Game server hosting providers |
| 423430 | Game software merchant wholesalers |
| 924120 | Game wardens |
| 423920 | Games (except coin- or card-operated) merchant wholesalers |
| 339930 | Games (except coin- or card-operated), children's and adult, manufacturing |
| 339999 | Games, coin- or card-operated, manufacturing |
| 423990 | Games, coin- or card-operated, merchant wholesalers |
| 334610 | Games, computer software, mass reproducing |
| 513210 | Games, computer software, publishing |
| 339930 | Gaming consoles manufacturing |
| 423920 | Gaming consoles merchant wholesalers |
| 513210 | Gaming site publishers |

| | |
|---|---|
| 516210 | Gaming sites, Internet (except publishers) |
| 334517 | Gamma-ray irradiation equipment manufacturing |
| 212319 | Ganister crushed and broken stone mining and/or beneficiating |
| 236220 | Garage and service station, commercial, construction |
| 444180 | Garage door dealers |
| 335999 | Garage door openers manufacturing |
| 238290 | Garage door, commercial- or industrial-type, installation |
| 238350 | Garage door, residential-type, installation |
| 332321 | Garage doors, metal, manufacturing |
| 321911 | Garage doors, wood, manufacturing |
| 812930 | Garages, automobile parking |
| 811198 | Garages, do-it-yourself automotive repair |
| 811111 | Garages, general automotive repair (except gasoline service stations) |
| 332311 | Garages, prefabricated metal, manufacturing |
| 321992 | Garages, prefabricated wood, manufacturing |
| 332439 | Garbage cans, light gauge metal, manufacturing |
| 562111 | Garbage collection services |
| 562213 | Garbage disposal combustors or incinerators |
| 562212 | Garbage disposal landfills |
| 236210 | Garbage disposal plant construction |
| 333310 | Garbage disposal units, commercial-type, manufacturing |
| 423440 | Garbage disposal units, commercial-type, merchant wholesalers |
| 335220 | Garbage disposal units, household-type, manufacturing |
| 423620 | Garbage disposal units, household-type, merchant wholesalers |
| 562212 | Garbage dumps |
| 562111 | Garbage hauling, local |
| 333994 | Garbage incinerators (except precast concrete) manufacturing |
| 327390 | Garbage incinerators, precast concrete, manufacturing |
| 562111 | Garbage pick-up services |
| 336211 | Garbage truck bodies manufacturing |
| 336120 | Garbage trucks assembling on chassis of own manufacture |
| 336211 | Garbage trucks assembling on purchased chassis |
| 111130 | Garbanzo farming, dry, field and seed production |
| 236116 | Garden apartment construction general contractors |
| 236117 | Garden apartment for-sale builders |
| 444240 | Garden centers |
| 813410 | Garden clubs |
| 811411 | Garden equipment repair and maintenance services without retailing new garden equipment |
| 327390 | Garden furniture, precast concrete, manufacturing |
| 327991 | Garden furniture, stone, manufacturing |
| 337122 | Garden furniture, wood, manufacturing |
| 326220 | Garden hose, rubber or plastics, manufacturing |
| 423820 | Garden machinery and equipment merchant wholesalers |
| 333112 | Garden machinery and equipment, powered, manufacturing |
| 561730 | Garden maintenance services |
| 541320 | Garden planning services |
| 327110 | Garden pottery manufacturing |
| 444230 | Garden power equipment stores |
| 424910 | Garden supplies (e.g., fertilizers, pesticides) merchant wholesalers |
| 811411 | Garden tool sharpening and repair services |
| 532490 | Garden tractor rental or leasing |
| 339999 | Garden umbrellas manufacturing |
| 712130 | Gardens, zoological or botanical |
| 111219 | Garlic farming (except under cover), field, bedding plant and seed production |
| 111419 | Garlic farming, grown under cover |
| 811490 | Garment alteration and/or repair shops without retailing new garments |
| 812320 | Garment cleaning (e.g., fur, leather, suede) services |
| 321999 | Garment hangers, wood, manufacturing |
| 316110 | Garment leather manufacturing |
| 314910 | Garment storage bags manufacturing |
| 315250 | Garments, leather or sheep-lined (except apparel contractors), manufacturing |
| 315210 | Garments, leather or sheep-lined, cut and sew apparel contractors |
| 313320 | Garments, oiling (i.e., waterproofing) |
| 212390 | Garnet mining and/or beneficiating |
| 333248 | Garnetting machinery for textiles manufacturing |
| 314999 | Garnetting of textile waste and rags |

| | |
|---|---|
| 315210 | Garter belts cut and sew apparel contractors |
| 315250 | Garter belts cut and sewn from purchased fabric (except apparel contractors) |
| 315210 | Garters cut and sew apparel contractors |
| 315250 | Garters, women's and girls', cut and sewn from purchased fabric (except apparel contractors) |
| 334513 | Gas analyzers, industrial process-type, manufacturing |
| 334516 | Gas analyzers, laboratory-type, manufacturing |
| 334513 | Gas and liquid analysis instruments, industrial process-type, manufacturing |
| 334512 | Gas burner automatic controls (except valves) manufacturing |
| 333414 | Gas burners, heating, manufacturing |
| 334513 | Gas chromatographic instruments, industrial process-type, manufacturing |
| 334516 | Gas chromatographic instruments, laboratory-type, manufacturing |
| 423830 | Gas detecting equipment and supplies (except household-type) merchant wholesalers |
| 211130 | Gas field development for own account |
| 211130 | Gas field exploration for own account |
| 333414 | Gas fireplaces manufacturing |
| 423720 | Gas fireplaces merchant wholesalers |
| 238220 | Gas fitting contractor |
| 334513 | Gas flow instrumentation, industrial process-type, manufacturing |
| 333998 | Gas generating machinery, general purpose-type, manufacturing |
| 423720 | Gas hot water heaters merchant wholesalers |
| 334519 | Gas leak detectors manufacturing |
| 523999 | Gas lease brokers' offices |
| 335139 | Gas lighting fixtures manufacturing |
| 423990 | Gas lighting fixtures merchant wholesalers |
| 238220 | Gas line installation, individual hookup, contractors |
| 333248 | Gas liquefying machinery manufacturing |
| 237120 | Gas main construction |
| 339113 | Gas masks manufacturing |
| 561990 | Gas meter reading services, contract |
| 333310 | Gas ranges, commercial-type, manufacturing |
| 335220 | Gas ranges, household-type, manufacturing |
| 333998 | Gas separating machinery manufacturing |
| 333414 | Gas space heaters manufacturing |
| 333995 | Gas spring cylinders manufacturing |
| 332420 | Gas storage tanks, heavy gauge metal, manufacturing |
| 336390 | Gas tanks assembled, automotive, truck, and bus, manufacturing |
| 333611 | Gas turbine generator set units manufacturing |
| 333611 | Gas turbines (except aircraft) manufacturing |
| 336412 | Gas turbines, aircraft, manufacturing |
| 332911 | Gas valves, industrial-type, manufacturing |
| 333992 | Gas welding equipment manufacturing |
| 333992 | Gas welding rods, coated or cored, manufacturing |
| 213111 | Gas well drilling on a contract basis |
| 333132 | Gas well machinery and equipment manufacturing |
| 213112 | Gas well rig building, repairing, and dismantling on a contract basis |
| 213112 | Gas, compressing natural, in the field on a contract basis |
| 221210 | Gas, manufactured, distribution |
| 221210 | Gas, mixed natural and manufactured, distribution |
| 211130 | Gas, natural liquefied petroleum, extraction |
| 221210 | Gas, natural, distribution |
| 211130 | Gas, natural, extraction |
| 211130 | Gas, natural, liquids, extraction |
| 486210 | Gas, natural, pipeline operation |
| 211130 | Gas, residue, extraction |
| 424690 | Gases, compressed and liquefied (except liquefied petroleum gas), merchant wholesalers |
| 325120 | Gases, industrial (i.e., compressed, liquefied, solid), manufacturing |
| 211130 | Gases, petroleum, liquefied, extraction |
| 339991 | Gasket, packing, and sealing devices manufacturing |
| 339991 | Gaskets manufacturing |
| 423840 | Gaskets merchant wholesalers |
| 334514 | Gasmeters, consumption registering, manufacturing |
| 334514 | Gasmeters, large capacity, domestic and industrial, manufacturing |
| 424710 | Gasohol bulk stations and terminals, merchant wholesalers |

424720  Gasohol merchant wholesalers (except bulk stations, terminals)

333414  Gas-oil burners, combination, manufacturing

424710  Gasoline bulk stations and terminals, merchant wholesalers

334514  Gasoline dispensing meters (except pumps) manufacturing

336412  Gasoline engine parts (except carburetors, pistons, piston rings, valves), aircraft, manufacturing

336310  Gasoline engine parts, mechanical, automotive and truck, manufacturing

333618  Gasoline engines (except aircraft, automotive, truck) manufacturing

336310  Gasoline engines for hybrid automotive vehicles manufacturing

336412  Gasoline engines, aircraft, manufacturing

336310  Gasoline engines, automotive and truck, manufacturing

324110  Gasoline made in petroleum refineries

423120  Gasoline marketing equipment merchant wholesalers

333914  Gasoline measuring and dispensing pumps manufacturing

423120  Gasoline measuring and dispensing pumps merchant wholesalers

424720  Gasoline merchant wholesalers (except bulk stations, terminals)

486910  Gasoline pipeline transportation

238290  Gasoline pump, service station, installation

423120  Gasoline service station equipment merchant wholesalers

457110  Gasoline stations with convenience stores

457120  Gasoline stations without convenience stores

211130  Gasoline, natural, production

313310  Gassing yarn (i.e., singeing)

621111  Gastroenterologists' offices (e.g., centers, clinics)

339112  Gastroscopes (except electromedical) manufacturing

334510  Gastroscopes, electromedical, manufacturing

333998  Gate and bridge lifting machinery manufacturing

423390  Gate and fence hardware merchant wholesalers

332911  Gate valves, industrial-type, manufacturing

332323  Gates, holding, sheet metal, manufacturing

332323  Gates, metal (except wire), manufacturing

237120  Gathering line, gas and oil field, construction

113210  Gathering of forest products (e.g., barks, gums, needles, seeds)

113210  Gathering, extracting, and selling tree seeds

332216  Gauge blocks, machinists' precision tools, manufacturing

334514  Gauges (e.g., oil pressure, water temperature, speedometer, tachometer), motor vehicle, manufacturing

334513  Gauges (i.e., analog, digital), industrial process-type, manufacturing

334514  Gauges for computing pressure-temperature corrections manufacturing

333310  Gauges, machinist's precision tool, optical, manufacturing

332216  Gauges, machinists' precision tools (except optical), manufacturing

424210  Gauze merchant wholesalers

339113  Gauze, surgical, made from purchased fabric

313210  Gauzes, surgical, made in broadwoven fabric mills

321999  Gavels, wood, manufacturing

333517  Gear cutting and finishing machines, metalworking, manufacturing

332216  Gear pullers, handtools, manufacturing

333517  Gear rolling machines, metalworking, manufacturing

333612  Gearmotors (i.e., power transmission equipment) manufacturing

336350  Gears (e.g., crown, pinion, spider), automotive, truck, and bus, manufacturing

423840  Gears merchant wholesalers

333612  Gears, power transmission (except aircraft, motor vehicle), manufacturing

112390  Geese production

311615  Geese, processing, fresh, frozen, canned, or cooked

311615  Geese, slaughtering and dressing

334519  Geiger counters manufacturing

325998  Gelatin (except dessert preparations) manufacturing

325998  Gelatin capsules, empty, manufacturing

311999  Gelatin dessert preparations manufacturing

311999  Gelatin for cooking manufacturing

424490  Gelatin, edible, merchant wholesalers

424690  Gelatin, inedible, merchant wholesalers

| | |
|---|---|
| 212390 | Gem stone (e.g., amethyst, garnet, agate, ruby, sapphire, jade) mining and/or beneficiating |
| 333248 | Gem stone processing machinery manufacturing |
| 458310 | Gem stone shops, precious and semiprecious |
| 423940 | Gem stones merchant wholesalers |
| 325414 | Gene therapy preparations manufacturing |
| 812990 | Genealogical investigation services |
| 921190 | General accounting offices, government |
| 811111 | General automotive repair shops |
| 112990 | General combination animal farming |
| 111998 | General combination crop farming (except fruit and nut combinations, oilseed and grain, vegetable) |
| 926110 | General economics statistical agencies |
| 484110 | General freight trucking, local |
| 484122 | General freight trucking, long-distance, less-than-truckload (LTL) |
| 484121 | General freight trucking, long-distance, truckload (TL) |
| 541611 | General management consulting services |
| 622110 | General medical and surgical hospitals |
| 455219 | General merchandise (new and used) auction houses |
| 459510 | General merchandise (used) auction houses |
| 423990 | General merchandise, durable goods, merchant wholesalers |
| 424990 | General merchandise, nondurable goods, merchant wholesalers |
| 921190 | General public administration |
| 423830 | General purpose industrial machinery and equipment merchant wholesalers |
| 532310 | General rental centers |
| 921190 | General services departments, government |
| 455219 | General stores |
| 493110 | General warehousing and storage |
| 424210 | General-line drugs merchant wholesalers |
| 424410 | General-line groceries merchant wholesalers |
| 423840 | General-line industrial supplies merchant wholesalers |
| 423930 | General-line scrap merchant wholesalers |
| 336320 | Generating apparatus and parts for internal combustion engines manufacturing |

| | |
|---|---|
| 335312 | Generating apparatus and parts, electrical (except internal combustion engine and welding), manufacturing |
| 333992 | Generating apparatus and parts, welding, electrical, manufacturing |
| 335313 | Generator control and metering panels, switchgear-type, manufacturing |
| 532490 | Generator rental or leasing |
| 335312 | Generator sets, prime mover (except turbine generator sets), manufacturing |
| 333611 | Generator sets, turbine (e.g., gas, hydraulic, steam), manufacturing |
| 335311 | Generator voltage regulators, electric induction and step-type (except engine electrical equipment), manufacturing |
| 335312 | Generators and sets, electric (except internal combustion engine, welding, turbine generator sets), manufacturing |
| 335312 | Generators for gas-electric and oil-electric vehicles, manufacturing |
| 336320 | Generators for internal combustion engines manufacturing |
| 335312 | Generators for storage battery chargers (except internal combustion engine and aircraft) manufacturing |
| 423610 | Generators, electrical (except motor vehicle), merchant wholesalers |
| 423120 | Generators, motor vehicle electrical, new, merchant wholesalers |
| 423140 | Generators, motor vehicle electrical, used, merchant wholesalers |
| 332994 | Generators, smoke, manufacturing |
| 334517 | Generators, X-ray, manufacturing |
| 621511 | Genetic testing laboratories |
| 541715 | Genetics research and development laboratories or services (except biotechnology and nanotechnology research and development) |
| 541690 | Geochemical consulting services |
| 321992 | Geodesic domes, prefabricated, wood, manufacturing |
| 541370 | Geodetic surveying services |
| 541370 | Geographic information system (GIS) base mapping services |
| 541330 | Geological engineering services |
| 213112 | Geological exploration (except surveying) for oil and gas on a contract basis |
| 541715 | Geological research and development laboratories or services (except nanotechnology research and development) |
| 924120 | Geological research program administration |

| | |
|---|---|
| 541360 | Geological surveying services |
| 541330 | Geophysical engineering services |
| 213112 | Geophysical exploration (except surveying) for oil and gas on a contract basis |
| 334519 | Geophysical instruments manufacturing |
| 541360 | Geophysical mapping services |
| 541360 | Geophysical surveying services |
| 541370 | Geospatial mapping services |
| 541380 | Geotechnical testing laboratories or services |
| 237110 | Geothermal drilling |
| 221116 | Geothermal electric power generation |
| 221330 | Geothermal steam production |
| 325199 | Geraniol manufacturing |
| 331492 | Germanium recovering from scrap and/or alloying purchased metals |
| 331410 | Germanium refining, primary |
| 335931 | GFCI (ground fault circuit interrupters) manufacturing |
| 711510 | Ghost writers, independent |
| 459420 | Gift shops |
| 459420 | Gift stands, permanent location |
| 322220 | Gift wrap made from purchased materials |
| 424120 | Gift wrapping paper merchant wholesalers |
| 561910 | Gift wrapping services |
| 212390 | Gilsonite mining and/or beneficiating |
| 111219 | Gingerroot farming (except under cover), field, bedding plant and seed production |
| 111419 | Gingerroot farming, grown under cover |
| 115111 | Ginning cotton |
| 111219 | Ginseng farming (except under cover), field, bedding plant and seed production |
| 111419 | Ginseng farming, grown under cover |
| 113210 | Ginseng gathering |
| 327390 | Girders and beams, prestressed concrete, manufacturing |
| 327390 | Girders, prestressed concrete, manufacturing |
| 315120 | Girdles and other foundation garments made in apparel knitting mills |
| 315210 | Girdles cut and sew apparel contractors |
| 315250 | Girdles, women's and girls', cut and sewn from purchased fabric (except apparel contractors) |
| 813410 | Girl guiding organizations |
| 721214 | Girls' camps (except day, instructional) |
| 611620 | Girls' camps, sports instruction |
| 713990 | Girls' day camps (except instructional) |
| 315120 | Girls' hosiery, sheer, full-length and knee-length, knitting or knitting and finishing |
| 315120 | Girls' socks manufacturing |
| 325411 | Glandular derivatives, uncompounded, manufacturing |
| 325412 | Glandular medicinal preparations manufacturing |
| 444180 | Glass (except automotive) stores |
| 325612 | Glass and tile cleaning preparations manufacturing |
| 327215 | Glass blanks for electric light bulbs made from purchased glass |
| 327212 | Glass blanks for electric light bulbs made in glass making plants |
| 238140 | Glass block laying |
| 334290 | Glass breakage detection and signaling devices |
| 313210 | Glass broadwoven fabrics weaving |
| 238150 | Glass cladding (i.e., curtain wall), installation |
| 238150 | Glass coating and tinting (except automotive) contractors |
| 313220 | Glass fabrics, narrow woven weaving |
| 238310 | Glass fiber insulation installation |
| 327212 | Glass fiber, optical, made in glass making plants |
| 327212 | Glass fiber, textile type, made in glass making plants |
| 327212 | Glass fiber, unsheathed, made in glass making plants |
| 238150 | Glass installation (except automotive) contractors |
| 811122 | Glass installation, automotive repair |
| 327212 | Glass making and blowing by hand |
| 333248 | Glass making machinery (e.g., blowing, forming, molding) manufacturing |
| 327213 | Glass packaging containers manufacturing |
| 238150 | Glass partitions, installation |
| 327215 | Glass products (except packaging containers) made from purchased glass |
| 327212 | Glass products (except packaging containers) made in a glass making plants |
| 212322 | Glass sand quarrying and/or beneficiating |
| 423930 | Glass scrap merchant wholesalers |
| 811122 | Glass shops, automotive |

| | |
|---|---|
| 811122 | Glass tinting, automotive |
| 238140 | Glass unit (i.e., glass block) masonry |
| 811122 | Glass work, automotive |
| 327215 | Glass, automotive, made from purchased glass |
| 327212 | Glass, automotive, made in glass making plants |
| 423120 | Glass, automotive, merchant wholesalers |
| 423390 | Glass, block and brick, merchant wholesalers |
| 327211 | Glass, plate, made in glass making plants |
| 423390 | Glass, plate, merchant wholesalers |
| 333310 | Glasses, field or opera, manufacturing |
| 423460 | Glasses, optical, merchant wholesalers |
| 327120 | Glasshouse refractories manufacturing |
| 322299 | Glassine wrapping paper made from purchased paper |
| 322120 | Glassine wrapping paper made in paper mills |
| 327215 | Glassware for industrial, scientific, and technical use made from purchased glass |
| 327212 | Glassware for industrial, scientific, and technical use made in glass making plants |
| 327215 | Glassware for lighting fixtures made from purchased glass |
| 327212 | Glassware for lighting fixtures made in glass making plants |
| 449129 | Glassware stores |
| 327215 | Glassware, art decorative and novelty, made from purchased glass |
| 327212 | Glassware, art, decorative, and novelty made in glass making plants |
| 327215 | Glassware, cutting and engraving, made from purchased glass |
| 423220 | Glassware, household-type, merchant wholesalers |
| 423450 | Glassware, medical, merchant wholesalers |
| 325180 | Glauber's salt manufacturing |
| 212390 | Glauber's salt mining and/or beneficiating |
| 325510 | Glaziers' putty manufacturing |
| 238150 | Glazing contractors |
| 315250 | Glazing furs |
| 332812 | Glazing metals and metal products for the trade |
| 334511 | Glide slope instrumentation manufacturing |
| 487990 | Glider excursions |
| 336411 | Gliders (i.e., aircraft) manufacturing |
| 334220 | Global positioning system (GPS) equipment manufacturing |
| 513130 | Globe cover publishers |
| 513130 | Globe cover publishers and printing combined |
| 323111 | Globe covers and maps commercial printing (except screen) without publishing |
| 323113 | Globe covers and maps screen printing without publishing |
| 332911 | Globe valves, industrial-type, manufacturing |
| 339999 | Globes, geographical, manufacturing |
| 316110 | Glove leather manufacturing |
| 315990 | Glove linings (except fur) manufacturing |
| 315250 | Glove linings, fur (except apparel contractors), manufacturing |
| 315210 | Glove linings, fur, cut and sew apparel contractors |
| 315210 | Gloves and mittens (except athletic), leather, fabric, fur, or combinations, cut and sew apparel contractors |
| 315990 | Gloves and mittens (except athletic), leather, fabric, fur, or combinations, cut and sewn from purchased fabric (except apparel contractors) |
| 315210 | Gloves and mittens, woven or knit, cut and sew apparel contractors |
| 315990 | Gloves and mittens, woven or knit, cut and sewn from purchased fabric (except apparel contractors), manufacturing |
| 315120 | Gloves, knit, made in apparel knitting mills |
| 315990 | Gloves, leather (except athletic, cut and sewn apparel contractors), manufacturing |
| 424350 | Gloves, men's and boys', merchant wholesalers |
| 326199 | Gloves, plastics, manufacturing |
| 339113 | Gloves, rubber (e.g., electrician's, examination, household-type, surgeon's), manufacturing |
| 339920 | Gloves, sport and athletic (e.g., baseball, boxing, racquetball, handball), manufacturing |
| 424350 | Gloves, women's, children's, and infants', merchant wholesalers |
| 335139 | Glow lamp bulbs manufacturing |
| 339114 | Glue, dental, manufacturing |
| 325520 | Glues (except dental) manufacturing |
| 424690 | Glues merchant wholesalers |

| | |
|---|---|
| 311221 | Gluten feed, flour, and meal, made by wet milling corn |
| 311221 | Gluten manufacturing |
| 325611 | Glycerin (i.e., glycerol), natural, manufacturing |
| 325199 | Glycerin (i.e., glycerol), synthetic, manufacturing |
| 325411 | Glycosides, uncompounded, manufacturing |
| 212313 | Gneiss crushed and broken stone mining and/or beneficiating |
| 212311 | Gneiss mining or quarrying |
| 522299 | GNMA (Government National Mortgage Association) |
| 112420 | Goat farming (e.g., meat, milk, mohair production) |
| 424520 | Goats merchant wholesalers |
| 713990 | Gocart raceways (i.e., amusement rides) |
| 713990 | Gocart tracks (i.e., amusement rides) |
| 336999 | Gocarts (except children's) manufacturing |
| 423910 | Gocarts merchant wholesalers |
| 339930 | Gocarts, children's, manufacturing |
| 339115 | Goggles (e.g., industrial, safety, sun, underwater) manufacturing |
| 331491 | Gold and gold alloy bar, sheet, strip, and tubing made from purchased metals or scrap |
| 332813 | Gold and silver plating metals and metal products for the trade |
| 332999 | Gold beating (i.e., foil, leaf) |
| 331410 | Gold bullion or dore bar produced at primary metal refineries |
| 332999 | Gold foil and leaf not made in rolling mills |
| 331491 | Gold foil made by rolling purchased metals or scrap |
| 212220 | Gold lode mining and/or beneficiating |
| 212220 | Gold ore mine site development for own account |
| 212220 | Gold ore mining and/or beneficiating plants |
| 212220 | Gold ores, concentrates, bullion, and/or precipitates mining and/or beneficiating |
| 212220 | Gold placer mining and/or beneficiating |
| 325910 | Gold printing inks manufacturing |
| 331492 | Gold recovering from scrap and/or alloying purchased metals |
| 331410 | Gold refining, primary |
| 331491 | Gold rolling and drawing purchased metals or scrap |
| 323120 | Gold stamping books for the trade |

| | |
|---|---|
| 813410 | Golden age clubs |
| 112511 | Goldfish production, farm raising |
| 713910 | Golf and country clubs |
| 441227 | Golf cart dealers, powered |
| 532284 | Golf cart rental |
| 423910 | Golf carts (except motorized passenger) merchant wholesalers |
| 336999 | Golf carts and similar motorized passenger carriers manufacturing |
| 423860 | Golf carts, motorized passenger, merchant wholesalers |
| 336999 | Golf carts, powered, manufacturing |
| 237990 | Golf course construction |
| 541320 | Golf course design services |
| 713910 | Golf courses (except miniature, pitch-n-putt) |
| 713990 | Golf courses, miniature |
| 713990 | Golf courses, pitch-n-putt |
| 713990 | Golf driving ranges |
| 423910 | Golf equipment and supplies merchant wholesalers |
| 611620 | Golf instruction, camps or schools |
| 713990 | Golf practice ranges |
| 459110 | Golf pro shops |
| 316210 | Golf shoes, men's cleated, manufacturing |
| 316210 | Golf shoes, women's cleated, manufacturing |
| 711219 | Golfers, independent professional (i.e., participating in sports events) |
| 339920 | Golfing equipment (e.g., bags, balls, caddy carts, clubs, tees) manufacturing |
| 335999 | Gongs, electric, manufacturing |
| 111334 | Gooseberry farming |
| 332216 | Gouges, woodworking, manufacturing |
| 445298 | Gourmet food stores |
| 561210 | Government base facilities operation support services |
| 522299 | Government National Mortgage Association (GNMA) |
| 522299 | Government-sponsored enterprises providing secondary market financing |
| 336310 | Governors for automotive gasoline engines manufacturing |
| 921110 | Governors' offices |
| 333618 | Governors, diesel engine, manufacturing |
| 333618 | Governors, gasoline engine (except automotive), manufacturing |
| 333611 | Governors, steam, manufacturing |

| | |
|---|---|
| 812331 | Gown (e.g., doctors, nurses, hospital, beauticians) supply services |
| 532281 | Gown rental |
| 315210 | Gowns (e.g., academic, choir, clerical) cut and sew apparel contractors |
| 315250 | Gowns (e.g., academic, choir, clerical) cut and sewn from purchased fabric (except apparel contractors) |
| 315210 | Gowns, formal, cut and sew apparel contractors |
| 315250 | Gowns, formal, women's and girls', cut and sewn from purchased fabric (except apparel contractors) |
| 315210 | Gowns, hospital, surgical and patient, cut and sew apparel contractors |
| 315250 | Gowns, hospital, surgical and patient, cut and sewn from purchased fabric (except apparel contractors) |
| 315210 | Gowns, wedding, cut and sew apparel contractors |
| 315250 | Gowns, wedding, women's and girls', cut and sewn from purchased fabric (except apparel contractors) |
| 334220 | GPS (global positioning system) equipment manufacturing |
| 333120 | Grader attachments manufacturing |
| 333120 | Graders, road, manufacturing |
| 238910 | Grading construction sites |
| 333241 | Grading, cleaning, and sorting machinery (i.e., food manufacturing-type) manufacturing |
| 333111 | Grading, cleaning, and sorting machinery, farm-type, manufacturing |
| 237310 | Grading, highway, road, street and airport runway |
| 334512 | Gradual switches, pneumatic, manufacturing |
| 532281 | Graduation cap and gown rental |
| 315210 | Graduation caps and gowns cut and sew apparel contractors |
| 315250 | Graduation caps and gowns cut and sewn from purchased fabric (except apparel contractors) |
| 311211 | Graham flour manufacturing |
| 311821 | Graham wafers manufacturing |
| 212390 | Grahamite mining and/or beneficiating |
| 312140 | Grain alcohol, beverage, manufacturing |
| 325193 | Grain alcohol, nonpotable, manufacturing |
| 236220 | Grain bin construction |
| 115114 | Grain cleaning |
| 333111 | Grain drills manufacturing |
| 115114 | Grain drying |
| 236220 | Grain elevator construction |
| 424510 | Grain elevators merchant wholesalers |
| 493130 | Grain elevators, storage only |
| 115114 | Grain fumigation |
| 115114 | Grain grinding (except custom grinding for animal feed) |
| 311119 | Grain grinding, custom, for animal feed |
| 484220 | Grain hauling, local |
| 484230 | Grain hauling, long-distance |
| 488210 | Grain leveling and trimming in railroad cars |
| 321999 | Grain measures, wood, turned and shaped, manufacturing |
| 424510 | Grain merchant wholesalers |
| 333241 | Grain milling machinery manufacturing |
| 311211 | Grain mills (except animal feed, breakfast cereal, rice) |
| 311119 | Grain mills, animal feed |
| 311230 | Grain mills, breakfast cereal |
| 311212 | Grain mills, rice |
| 333111 | Grain stackers manufacturing |
| 311230 | Grain, breakfast cereal, manufacturing |
| 312120 | Grain, brewers' spent, manufacturing |
| 115113 | Grain, machine harvesting |
| 327910 | Grains, abrasive, natural and artificial, manufacturing |
| 813410 | Granges |
| 212313 | Granite beneficiating plants (e.g., grinding or pulverizing) |
| 212313 | Granite crushed and broken stone mining and/or beneficiating |
| 212311 | Granite mining or quarrying |
| 238140 | Granite, exterior, contractors |
| 238340 | Granite, interior, installation |
| 311351 | Granola bars and clusters, chocolate, made from cacao beans |
| 311352 | Granola bars and clusters, chocolate, made from purchased chocolate |
| 311340 | Granola bars and clusters, nonchocolate, manufacturing |
| 311230 | Granola, cereal (except bars and clusters), manufacturing |
| 813211 | Grantmaking foundations |
| 311313 | Granulated beet sugar manufacturing |
| 311314 | Granulated cane sugar manufacturing |
| 333248 | Granulator and pelletizer machinery for plastics manufacturing |

| | |
|---|---|
| 212319 | Granules, slate, mining and/or beneficiating |
| 312130 | Grape farming and making wine |
| 111332 | Grape farming without making wine |
| 111320 | Grapefruit groves |
| 325998 | Grapefruit oil manufacturing |
| 311423 | Grapes, artificially drying |
| 541430 | Graphic art and related design services |
| 541430 | Graphic artists, independent |
| 325992 | Graphic arts plates, sensitized, manufacturing |
| 611519 | Graphic arts schools |
| 541430 | Graphic design services |
| 513130 | Graphic novel publishers |
| 334515 | Graphic recording meters, electric, manufacturing |
| 335991 | Graphite electrodes and contacts, electric, manufacturing |
| 212390 | Graphite mining and/or beneficiating |
| 335991 | Graphite specialties for aerospace use (except gaskets) manufacturing |
| 335991 | Graphite specialties for electrical use manufacturing |
| 335991 | Graphite specialties for mechanical use (except gaskets) manufacturing |
| 327992 | Graphite, natural (e.g., ground, pulverized, refined, blended), manufacturing |
| 111940 | Grass hay farming |
| 333111 | Grass mowing equipment (except lawn and garden) manufacturing |
| 332216 | Grass mowing equipment, nonpowered lawn and garden, manufacturing |
| 333112 | Grass mowing equipment, powered lawn and garden, manufacturing |
| 111998 | Grass seed farming |
| 332323 | Gratings (i.e., open steel flooring) manufacturing |
| 333310 | Gratings, diffraction, manufacturing |
| 238910 | Grave excavation contractors |
| 484220 | Gravel hauling, local |
| 484230 | Gravel hauling, long-distance |
| 212321 | Gravel quarrying and/or beneficiating |
| 423320 | Gravel, construction, merchant wholesalers |
| 541360 | Gravity geophysical surveying services |
| 325910 | Gravure inks manufacturing |
| 323120 | Gravure plate and cylinder preparation services |
| 323111 | Gravure printing (except books, grey goods) |
| 333248 | Gravure printing presses manufacturing |
| 311422 | Gravy canning |
| 311942 | Gravy mixes, dry, manufacturing |
| 331511 | Gray iron foundries |
| 531190 | Grazing land rental or leasing |
| 311613 | Grease rendering |
| 339991 | Grease seals manufacturing |
| 562998 | Grease trap cleaning |
| 311225 | Grease, inedible, animal and vegetable, refining and blending purchased oils |
| 424990 | Greases, inedible animal and vegetable, merchant wholesalers |
| 324191 | Greases, petroleum lubricating, made from refined petroleum |
| 325998 | Greases, synthetic lubricating, manufacturing |
| 483113 | Great Lakes freight transportation (including St. Lawrence Seaway) |
| 483114 | Great Lakes passenger transportation (including St. Lawrence Seaway) |
| 111219 | Green bean farming, field and seed production |
| 111219 | Green cowpea farming, field and seed production |
| 111219 | Green lima bean farming, field and seed production |
| 111219 | Green pea farming, field and seed production |
| 332311 | Greenhouses, prefabricated metal, manufacturing |
| 212390 | Greensand mining and/or beneficiating |
| 212311 | Greenstone mining or quarrying |
| 513191 | Greeting card publishers |
| 513191 | Greeting card publishers (except exclusive Internet publishing) |
| 513191 | Greeting card publishers and printing combined |
| 513191 | Greeting card publishers, exclusively on Internet |
| 459420 | Greeting card shops |
| 323111 | Greeting cards (e.g., birthday, holiday, sympathy) commercial printing (except screen) without publishing |
| 323113 | Greeting cards (e.g., birthday, holiday, sympathy) screen printing without publishing |
| 424120 | Greeting cards merchant wholesalers |
| 332994 | Grenade launchers manufacturing |
| 332993 | Grenades, hand or projectile, manufacturing |

| | |
|---|---|
| 711212 | Greyhound dog racetracks |
| 335210 | Griddles and grills, household-type portable electric, manufacturing |
| 332618 | Grilles and grillwork made from purchased wire |
| 332323 | Grills and grillwork, sheet metal, manufacturing |
| 332323 | Grillwork, ornamental metal, manufacturing |
| 333991 | Grinders, handheld power-driven, manufacturing |
| 325411 | Grinding and milling botanicals (i.e., for medicinal or dietary supplement use) |
| 423510 | Grinding balls merchant wholesalers |
| 327910 | Grinding balls, ceramic, manufacturing |
| 333517 | Grinding machines, metalworking, manufacturing |
| 324191 | Grinding oils, petroleum, made from refined petroleum |
| 212390 | Grinding pebbles mining and/or beneficiating |
| 212322 | Grinding sand quarrying and/or beneficiating |
| 311942 | Grinding spices |
| 327910 | Grinding wheels manufacturing |
| 212390 | Grindstones mining and/or beneficiating |
| 326299 | Grips and handles, rubber, manufacturing |
| 311211 | Grits and flakes, corn brewer's, manufacturing |
| 212319 | Grits crushed and broken stone mining and/or beneficiating |
| 424410 | Groceries, general-line, merchant wholesalers |
| 322220 | Grocers' bags and sacks made from purchased uncoated paper |
| 326111 | Grocery bags, plastics film, single wall or multiwall, manufacturing |
| 333924 | Grocery carts made from purchased wire |
| 492210 | Grocery delivery services (i.e., independent service from grocery store) |
| 445110 | Grocery stores |
| 423840 | Grommets merchant wholesalers |
| 326299 | Grommets, rubber, manufacturing |
| 812910 | Grooming services, animal |
| 335931 | Ground clamps (i.e., electric wiring devices) manufacturing |
| 335931 | Ground fault circuit interrupters (GFCI) manufacturing |
| 335312 | Ground Power Units (GPU) manufacturing |
| 238910 | Ground thawing for construction site digging |
| 322120 | Groundwood paper products (e.g., publication and printing paper, tablet stock, wallpaper base) made in newsprint mills |
| 424110 | Groundwood paper, bulk, merchant wholesalers |
| 322120 | Groundwood paper, coated, laminated, or treated in paper mills |
| 322220 | Groundwood paper, coated, made from purchased paper |
| 322120 | Groundwood paper, coated, made in paper mills |
| 322120 | Groundwood paper, newsprint, made in paper mills |
| 322110 | Groundwood pulp manufacturing |
| 624410 | Group day care centers, child or infant |
| 623990 | Group foster homes for children |
| 623110 | Group homes for the disabled with nursing care |
| 623990 | Group homes for the hearing impaired |
| 623990 | Group homes for the visually impaired |
| 623210 | Group homes, intellectual and developmental disability |
| 621491 | Group hospitalization plans providing health care services |
| 524114 | Group hospitalization plans without providing health care services |
| 425120 | Group purchasing organizations (acting as agents for goods distribution) |
| 114111 | Grouper fishing |
| 238110 | Grouting (i.e., reinforcing with concrete) |
| 335132 | Grow light fixtures (except residential) manufacturing |
| 335131 | Grow light fixtures, residential, electric, manufacturing |
| 813910 | Growers' associations |
| 212390 | Guano mining and/or beneficiating |
| 111998 | Guar farming |
| 524126 | Guaranteeing international trade loans |
| 524127 | Guaranteeing titles |
| 561612 | Guard dog services |
| 812910 | Guard dog training services |
| 561612 | Guard services |
| 237310 | Guardrail construction |
| 332322 | Guardrails, highway, sheet metal (except stampings), manufacturing |
| 332323 | Guards, bannisters, and railings, sheet metal, manufacturing |
| 332618 | Guards, wire, made from purchased wire |
| 111339 | Guava farming |

| | |
|---|---|
| 721199 | Guest houses |
| 721214 | Guest ranches with accommodation facilities |
| 812910 | Guide dog training services |
| 713990 | Guide services (i.e., fishing, hunting, tourist) |
| 713990 | Guide services, fishing |
| 713990 | Guide services, hunting |
| 713990 | Guide services, tourist |
| 513130 | Guide, street map, publishers |
| 513130 | Guide, street map, publishers (except exclusive Internet publishing) |
| 513130 | Guide, street map, publishers and printing combined |
| 513130 | Guide, street map, publishers, exclusively on Internet |
| 336415 | Guided missile and space vehicle engine manufacturing |
| 541715 | Guided missile and space vehicle engine research and development |
| 336414 | Guided missile and space vehicle manufacturing |
| 336419 | Guided missile and space vehicle parts (except engines) manufacturing |
| 541715 | Guided missile and space vehicle parts (except engines) research and development |
| 423860 | Guided missiles and space vehicles merchant wholesalers |
| 336414 | Guided missiles, complete, assembling |
| 323111 | Guides, street map, commercial printing (except screen) without publishing |
| 323113 | Guides, street map, screen printing without publishing |
| 339992 | Guitars and parts, electric and nonelectric, manufacturing |
| 113210 | Gum (i.e., forest product) gathering |
| 325194 | Gum and wood chemicals manufacturing |
| 424690 | Gum and wood chemicals merchant wholesalers |
| 311340 | Gum, chewing, manufacturing |
| 424450 | Gum, chewing, merchant wholesalers |
| 322220 | Gummed paper products (e.g., labels, sheets, tapes) made from purchased paper |
| 424130 | Gummed tapes (except cellophane) merchant wholesalers |
| 424120 | Gummed tapes, cellophane, merchant wholesalers |
| 332994 | Gun barrels manufacturing |
| 332994 | Gun cleaning kits manufacturing |
| 325612 | Gun cleaning preparations |
| 713990 | Gun clubs, recreational |
| 813319 | Gun control organizations |
| 332111 | Gun forgings made from purchased iron or steel, unfinished |
| 331110 | Gun forgings made in iron and steel mills |
| 332994 | Gun magazines manufacturing |
| 811490 | Gun repair and maintenance shops without retailing new guns |
| 459110 | Gun shops |
| 333310 | Gun sighting and fire control equipment and instruments, optical, manufacturing |
| 333310 | Gun sights, optical, manufacturing |
| 332613 | Gun springs, light gauge, made from purchased wire or strip, manufacturing |
| 321912 | Gun stock blanks manufacturing |
| 332510 | Gun trigger locks, metal, manufacturing |
| 332994 | Gun turrets manufacturing |
| 238110 | Gunite contractors |
| 334413 | Gunn effect devices manufacturing |
| 238110 | Gunning shotcrete |
| 325920 | Gunpowder manufacturing |
| 423990 | Guns (except sporting) merchant wholesalers |
| 332994 | Guns manufacturing |
| 332994 | Guns, BB and pellet, manufacturing |
| 332216 | Guns, caulking, nonpowered, manufacturing |
| 423910 | Guns, sporting equipment, merchant wholesalers |
| 811490 | Gunsmith shops without retailing new guns |
| 238170 | Gutter and downspout contractors |
| 561790 | Gutter cleaning services |
| 423330 | Gutters and down spouts (except wood) merchant wholesalers |
| 332114 | Gutters and down spouts sheet metal, custom roll formed, manufacturing |
| 326199 | Gutters and down spouts, plastics, manufacturing |
| 238170 | Gutters, seamless roof, formed and installed on site |
| 332322 | Gutters, sheet metal (except custom roll formed), manufacturing |
| 339920 | Gymnasium and playground equipment, manufacturing |
| 423910 | Gymnasium equipment merchant wholesalers |
| 713940 | Gymnasiums |

| | |
|---|---|
| 611620 | Gymnastics instruction, camps or schools |
| 713940 | Gyms, physical fitness |
| 339113 | Gynecological supplies and appliances manufacturing |
| 621111 | Gynecologists' offices (e.g., centers, clinics) |
| 212390 | Gypsite mining and/or beneficiating |
| 238310 | Gypsum board installation |
| 327420 | Gypsum building products manufacturing |
| 423390 | Gypsum building products merchant wholesalers |
| 212390 | Gypsum mining and/or beneficiating |
| 327420 | Gypsum products (e.g., block, board, plaster, lath, rock, tile) manufacturing |
| 327420 | Gypsum statuary manufacturing |
| 334511 | Gyrocompasses manufacturing |
| 334511 | Gyrogimbals manufacturing |
| 334511 | Gyroscopes manufacturing |
| 624310 | Habilitation job counseling and training, vocational |
| 114111 | Haddock fishing |
| 212290 | Hafnium mining and/or beneficiating |
| 424310 | Hair accessories merchant wholesalers |
| 326299 | Hair care products (e.g., combs, curlers), rubber, manufacturing |
| 424210 | Hair care products merchant wholesalers |
| 333111 | Hair clippers for animal use, electric, manufacturing |
| 332216 | Hair clippers for animal use, nonelectric, manufacturing |
| 335210 | Hair clippers for human use, electric, manufacturing |
| 332215 | Hair clippers for human use, nonelectric, manufacturing |
| 325620 | Hair coloring preparations manufacturing |
| 335210 | Hair curlers, household-type electric, manufacturing |
| 332999 | Hair curlers, metal, manufacturing |
| 333310 | Hair dryers, beauty parlor-type, manufacturing |
| 335210 | Hair dryers, electric (except equipment designed for beauty parlor use), manufacturing |
| 423620 | Hair dryers, personal, merchant wholesalers |
| 339999 | Hair nets made from purchased netting |
| 325620 | Hair preparations (e.g., conditioners, dyes, rinses, shampoos) manufacturing |

| | |
|---|---|
| 424210 | Hair preparations (except professional) merchant wholesalers |
| 423850 | Hair preparations, professional, merchant wholesalers |
| 812199 | Hair removal (i.e., depilatory, electrolysis, laser, waxing) services |
| 812199 | Hair replacement services (except by offices of physicians) |
| 325620 | Hair sprays manufacturing |
| 812112 | Hair stylist salons or shops, unisex or women's |
| 812111 | Hair stylist services, men's |
| 812112 | Hair stylist services, unisex or women's |
| 812111 | Hair stylist shops, men's |
| 812199 | Hair weaving services |
| 339994 | Hairbrushes manufacturing |
| 424990 | Hairbrushes merchant wholesalers |
| 812112 | Hairdresser services |
| 812112 | Hairdressing salons or shops, unisex or women's |
| 339999 | Hairpieces (e.g., toupees, wigs, wiglets) manufacturing |
| 424990 | Hairpieces (e.g., toupees, wigs, wiglets) merchant wholesalers |
| 339993 | Hairpins (except rubber) manufacturing |
| 326299 | Hairpins, rubber, manufacturing |
| 332613 | Hairsprings (except clock, watch), light gauge, made from purchased wire or strip, manufacturing |
| 114111 | Hake fishing |
| 623990 | Halfway group homes for delinquents and ex-offenders |
| 623220 | Halfway houses for patients with mental health illnesses |
| 623220 | Halfway houses, substance abuse (e.g., alcoholism, drug addiction) |
| 114111 | Halibut fishing |
| 531120 | Hall and banquet room, nonresidential, rental or leasing |
| 334413 | Hall effect devices manufacturing |
| 531120 | Hall, nonresidential, rental or leasing |
| 712110 | Halls of fame |
| 335139 | Halogen light bulbs manufacturing |
| 325194 | Halogenated aromatic hydrocarbon derivatives manufacturing |
| 325199 | Halogenated hydrocarbon derivatives (except aromatic) manufacturing |
| 311340 | Halvah manufacturing |
| 332111 | Hammer forgings made from purchased iron or steel, unfinished |

| | |
|---|---|
| 332112 | Hammer forgings made from purchased nonferrous metals, unfinished |
| 333120 | Hammer mill machinery (i.e., rock and ore crushing machines), portable, manufacturing |
| 333131 | Hammer mill machinery (i.e., rock and ore crushing machines), stationary, manufacturing |
| 332216 | Hammers, handtools, manufacturing |
| 339992 | Hammers, piano, manufacturing |
| 321999 | Hammers, wood, meat, manufacturing |
| 314999 | Hammocks, fabric, manufacturing |
| 337126 | Hammocks, metal framed, manufacturing |
| 337122 | Hammocks, wood framed, manufacturing |
| 326199 | Hampers, laundry, plastics, manufacturing |
| 337126 | Hampers, laundry, reed, wicker, rattan, manufacturing |
| 332322 | Hampers, laundry, sheet metal (except stampings), manufacturing |
| 311611 | Hams (except poultry) produced in slaughtering plants |
| 311612 | Hams, canned, made from purchased carcasses |
| 311615 | Hams, poultry, manufacturing |
| 311612 | Hams, preserved (except poultry), made from purchased carcasses |
| 327215 | Hand blowing purchased glass |
| 313240 | Hand knitting lace or warp fabric products |
| 812320 | Hand laundries |
| 325620 | Hand lotions manufacturing |
| 339940 | Hand operated stamps (e.g., canceling, postmark, shoe, textile marking) manufacturing |
| 325611 | Hand sanitizers manufacturing |
| 424210 | Hand sanitizers merchant wholesalers |
| 325611 | Hand soaps (e.g., hard, liquid, soft) manufacturing |
| 334519 | Hand stamps (e.g., date, time), timing mechanism operated, manufacturing |
| 333924 | Hand trucks manufacturing |
| 313220 | Hand weaving fabric, 12 inches or less (30cm) |
| 313210 | Hand weaving fabrics, more than 12 inches (30 cm) in width |
| 316110 | Handbag leather manufacturing |
| 458110 | Handbag stores |
| 424350 | Handbags merchant wholesalers |
| 316990 | Handbags, all materials (except precious metal), manufacturing |
| 339910 | Handbags, precious metal, manufacturing |
| 713940 | Handball club facilities |
| 541870 | Handbill direct distribution services |
| 332999 | Handcuffs manufacturing |
| 332216 | Handheld edge tools (except scissors-type), nonelectric, manufacturing |
| 611610 | Handicrafts instruction |
| 315210 | Handkerchiefs (except paper) cut and sew apparel contractors |
| 315990 | Handkerchiefs (except paper) cut and sewn from purchased fabric |
| 322291 | Handkerchiefs, paper, made from purchased paper |
| 321912 | Handle blanks, wood, manufacturing |
| 321912 | Handle stock, sawed or planed, manufacturing |
| 321999 | Handles (e.g., broom, mop, handtool), wood, manufacturing |
| 424990 | Handles (e.g., broom, mop, paint) merchant wholesalers |
| 326199 | Handles (e.g., brush, tool, umbrella), plastics, manufacturing |
| 316990 | Handles (e.g., luggage, whip), leather, manufacturing |
| 332999 | Handles (e.g., parasol, umbrella), metal, manufacturing |
| 327110 | Handles, faucet, vitreous china and earthenware, manufacturing |
| 541420 | Handtool industrial design services |
| 332216 | Handtool metal blades (e.g., putty knives, scrapers, screwdrivers) manufacturing |
| 423710 | Handtools (except motor vehicle mechanics', machinists' precision) merchant wholesalers |
| 332216 | Handtools, machinists' precision, manufacturing |
| 423830 | Handtools, machinists' precision, merchant wholesalers |
| 332216 | Handtools, motor vehicle mechanics', manufacturing |
| 423120 | Handtools, motor vehicle mechanics', merchant wholesalers |
| 333991 | Handtools, power-driven, manufacturing |
| 811411 | Handtools, power-driven, repair and maintenance services without retailing new power-driven handtools |
| 444140 | Handtools, power-driven, stores |
| 541990 | Handwriting analysis services |
| 541990 | Handwriting expert services |

| | |
|---|---|
| 236220 | Handyman construction service, commercial and institutional building |
| 236118 | Handyman construction service, residential building |
| 336411 | Hang gliders manufacturing |
| 236220 | Hangar construction |
| 332321 | Hangar doors, metal, manufacturing |
| 488119 | Hangar rental, aircraft |
| 321999 | Hangers, wooden, garment, manufacturing |
| 111422 | Hanging basket plant growing |
| 423610 | Hanging devices, electrical, merchant wholesalers |
| 237990 | Harbor construction |
| 488310 | Harbor maintenance services (except dredging) |
| 488310 | Harbor operation |
| 487210 | Harbor sightseeing tours |
| 488330 | Harbor tugboat services |
| 213112 | Hard banding oil and gas field service on a contract basis |
| 311340 | Hard candies manufacturing |
| 424820 | Hard cider merchant wholesalers |
| 212114 | Hard coal (i.e., anthracite) surface mining and/or beneficiating |
| 212115 | Hard coal (i.e., anthracite) underground mining |
| 334112 | Hard disk drives, computer peripheral equipment, manufacturing |
| 334610 | Hard drive media (disk drive platters) manufacturing |
| 313210 | Hard fiber fabrics, broadwoven, weaving |
| 313110 | Hard fiber spun yarns made from purchased fiber |
| 313110 | Hard fiber thread manufacturing |
| 313220 | Hard fiber, narrow woven, weaving |
| 339113 | Hard hats manufacturing |
| 321219 | Hardboard manufacturing |
| 332811 | Hardening (i.e., heat treating) metals and metal products for the trade |
| 334519 | Hardness testing equipment manufacturing |
| 423710 | Hardware (except motor vehicle) merchant wholesalers |
| 332618 | Hardware cloth, woven wire, made from purchased wire |
| 444140 | Hardware stores |
| 423120 | Hardware, motor vehicle, merchant wholesalers |
| 326199 | Hardware, plastics, manufacturing |

| | |
|---|---|
| 335932 | Hardware, transmission pole and line, manufacturing |
| 423610 | Hardware, transmission pole and line, merchant wholesalers |
| 321912 | Hardwood dimension lumber and stock, resawing purchased lumber |
| 325194 | Hardwood distillates manufacturing |
| 444180 | Hardwood flooring dealers |
| 238330 | Hardwood flooring, installation only |
| 321211 | Hardwood plywood composites manufacturing |
| 321211 | Hardwood veneer or plywood manufacturing |
| 339992 | Harmonicas manufacturing |
| 334419 | Harness assemblies for electronic use manufacturing |
| 711219 | Harness drivers |
| 424910 | Harness equipment merchant wholesalers |
| 316110 | Harness leather manufacturing |
| 332999 | Harness parts, metal, manufacturing |
| 711212 | Harness racetracks |
| 316990 | Harnesses and harness parts, leather, manufacturing |
| 316990 | Harnesses, dog, manufacturing |
| 339992 | Harps and parts manufacturing |
| 339992 | Harpsichords manufacturing |
| 333111 | Harrows (e.g., disc, spring, tine) manufacturing |
| 315990 | Harvest hats, straw, manufacturing |
| 113210 | Harvesting berries or nuts from native and non-cultivated plants |
| 333111 | Harvesting machinery and equipment, agriculture, manufacturing |
| 423820 | Harvesting machinery and equipment, agriculture, merchant wholesalers |
| 335210 | Hassock fans, electric, manufacturing |
| 424310 | Hat and cap materials merchant wholesalers |
| 458110 | Hat and cap stores |
| 339999 | Hat blocks manufacturing |
| 315210 | Hat bodies (e.g., fur-felt, straw, wool-felt) cut and sew apparel contractors |
| 315990 | Hat bodies (e.g., fur-felt, straw, wool-felt) cut and sewn from purchased fabric (except apparel contractors) |
| 812320 | Hat cleaning services |
| 315210 | Hat findings cut and sew apparel contractors |

| | |
|---|---|
| 315990 | Hat findings cut and sewn from purchased fabric (except apparel contractors) |
| 315210 | Hat linings and trimmings cut and sew apparel contractors |
| 315990 | Hat linings and trimmings cut and sewn from purchased fabric (except apparel contractors) |
| 112511 | Hatcheries, finfish |
| 112340 | Hatcheries, poultry |
| 112512 | Hatcheries, shellfish |
| 236220 | Hatchery construction |
| 332216 | Hatchets manufacturing |
| 315210 | Hats (e.g., cloth, fur, fur-felt, leather, straw, wool-felt) cut and sew apparel contractors |
| 315990 | Hats (except fur, knitting mill products, leather) cut and sewn from purchased fabric (except apparel contractors) |
| 424350 | Hats and caps, men's and boys', merchant wholesalers |
| 424350 | Hats and caps, women's, girls', and infants', merchant wholesalers |
| 322299 | Hats made from purchased paper |
| 315120 | Hats made in apparel knitting mills |
| 315990 | Hats, cloth, cut and sewn from purchased fabric (except apparel contractors) |
| 315250 | Hats, fur (except apparel contractors), manufacturing |
| 315990 | Hats, fur-felt, straw, and wool-felt, cut and sewn from purchased fabric (except apparel contractors) |
| 315250 | Hats, leather (except apparel contractors), manufacturing |
| 315210 | Hats, trimmed, cut and sew apparel contractors |
| 315990 | Hats, trimmed, cut and sewn from purchased fabric (except apparel contractors) |
| 713990 | Haunted houses and similar fright attractions, concession operators (i.e., supplying and servicing in others' facilities) |
| 333111 | Hay balers and presses manufacturing |
| 111940 | Hay farming (e.g., alfalfa hay, clover hay, grass hay) |
| 424910 | Hay merchant wholesalers |
| 115113 | Hay mowing, raking, baling, and chopping |
| 111998 | Hay seed farming |
| 311119 | Hay, cubed, manufacturing |
| 333111 | Haying machines manufacturing |
| 423820 | Haying machines merchant wholesalers |
| 562910 | Hazardous material storage tank removal and disposal services |
| 562112 | Hazardous waste collection services |
| 562211 | Hazardous waste disposal facilities |
| 562211 | Hazardous waste disposal facilities combined with collection and/or local hauling of hazardous waste |
| 562211 | Hazardous waste material disposal facilities |
| 562211 | Hazardous waste material treatment facilities |
| 562211 | Hazardous waste treatment facilities |
| 562211 | Hazardous waste treatment facilities combined with collection and/or local hauling of hazardous waste |
| 111335 | Hazelnut farming |
| 334610 | Head cleaners for magnetic tape equipment, manufacturing |
| 621999 | Head lice removal services (except by offices of health practitioners) |
| 551114 | Head offices |
| 311212 | Head rice manufacturing |
| 624410 | Head Start and Early Head Start programs, separate from schools |
| 315210 | Headbands cut and sew apparel contractors |
| 315990 | Headbands, women's and girls', cut and sewn from purchased fabric (except apparel contractors) |
| 337122 | Headboards, wood, manufacturing |
| 321920 | Heading, barrel (i.e., cooperage stock), wood, manufacturing |
| 551114 | Headquarters offices |
| 334419 | Heads (e.g., recording, read/write) manufacturing |
| 334511 | Heads-up display (HUD) systems, aeronautical, manufacturing |
| 236220 | Health and athletic club construction |
| 525120 | Health and welfare funds |
| 713940 | Health club facilities, physical fitness |
| 424490 | Health foods (except fresh fruits, vegetables) merchant wholesalers |
| 424480 | Health foods, fresh fruits and vegetables, merchant wholesalers |
| 524114 | Health insurance carriers, direct |
| 335139 | Health lamp bulbs, infrared and ultraviolet radiation, manufacturing |
| 621491 | Health maintenance organization (HMO) medical centers and clinics |

| | |
|---|---|
| 923120 | Health planning and development agencies, government |
| 813920 | Health professionals' associations |
| 926150 | Health professions licensure agencies |
| 923120 | Health program administration |
| 541715 | Health research and development laboratories or services (except biotechnology and nanotechnology research and development) |
| 813212 | Health research fundraising organizations |
| 813212 | Health research fundraising using a crowdfunding platform (except on a contract or fee basis) |
| 621999 | Health screening services (except by offices of health practitioners) |
| 621111 | Health screening services in physicians' offices |
| 721110 | Health spas (i.e., physical fitness facilities) with accommodations |
| 713940 | Health spas without accommodations, physical fitness |
| 923120 | Health statistics centers, government |
| 713940 | Health studios, physical fitness |
| 456199 | Hearing aid stores (except offices of audiologists) |
| 423450 | Hearing aids merchant wholesalers |
| 334510 | Hearing aids, electronic, manufacturing |
| 621999 | Hearing testing services (except by offices of audiologists) |
| 621340 | Hearing testing services by offices of audiologists |
| 336211 | Hearse bodies manufacturing |
| 485320 | Hearse rental with driver |
| 532111 | Hearse rental without driver |
| 336110 | Hearses assembling on chassis of own manufacture |
| 336211 | Hearses assembling on purchased chassis |
| 334510 | Heart-lung machine manufacturing |
| 423830 | Heat exchange equipment, industrial, merchant wholesalers |
| 332410 | Heat exchangers manufacturing |
| 323111 | Heat press printing apparel and textile products (e.g., caps, napkins, placemats, T-shirts, towels) (except grey goods and T-shirt shops) |
| 238220 | Heat pump installation |
| 333415 | Heat pumps manufacturing |
| 423730 | Heat pumps merchant wholesalers |
| 325992 | Heat sensitized (i.e., thermal) paper made from purchased paper |
| 335991 | Heat shields, carbon or graphite, manufacturing |
| 332811 | Heat treating metals and metal products for the trade |
| 333994 | Heat treating ovens, industrial process-type, manufacturing |
| 221330 | Heat, steam, distribution |
| 221330 | Heated air distribution |
| 335210 | Heaters, portable electric space, manufacturing |
| 423620 | Heaters, portable electric, merchant wholesalers |
| 333414 | Heaters, space (except portable electric), manufacturing |
| 333414 | Heaters, swimming pool, manufacturing |
| 335210 | Heaters, tape, manufacturing |
| 333415 | Heating and air-conditioning combination units manufacturing |
| 238220 | Heating and cooling duct work installation |
| 334512 | Heating and cooling system controls, residential and commercial, manufacturing |
| 238220 | Heating and ventilation system component (e.g., air registers, diffusers, filters, grilles, sound attenuators) installation |
| 238220 | Heating boiler installation |
| 423720 | Heating boilers, steam and hot water, merchant wholesalers |
| 238220 | Heating contractors |
| 541330 | Heating engineering consulting services |
| 238220 | Heating equipment installation |
| 333414 | Heating equipment, hot water (except hot water heaters), manufacturing |
| 423720 | Heating equipment, hot water, merchant wholesalers |
| 423730 | Heating equipment, warm air (i.e. forced air), merchant wholesalers |
| 333415 | Heating equipment, warm air (i.e., forced air), manufacturing |
| 424710 | Heating oil bulk stations and terminals, merchant wholesalers |
| 457210 | Heating oil dealers, direct selling |
| 324110 | Heating oils made in petroleum refineries |
| 335210 | Heating pads, electric, manufacturing |
| 334512 | Heating regulators manufacturing |
| 221330 | Heating steam (suppliers of heat) providers |

335210 Heating units for electric appliances manufacturing

333414 Heating units, baseboard, manufacturing

238220 Heating, ventilation and air-conditioning (HVAC) contractors

532412 Heavy construction equipment rental without operator

611519 Heavy equipment operation schools

611519 Heavy equipment repair training

811310 Heavy machinery and equipment repair and maintenance services

423130 Heavy truck tires and tubes merchant wholesalers

336120 Heavy trucks assembling on chassis of own manufacture

336211 Heavy trucks assembling on purchased chassis

325180 Heavy water (i.e., deuterium oxide) manufacturing

332216 Hedge shears and trimmers, nonelectric, manufacturing

333112 Hedge trimmers, powered, manufacturing

316990 Heel caps, leather or metal, manufacturing

316990 Heel lifts, leather, manufacturing

321999 Heels, boot and shoe, finished wood, manufacturing

316990 Heels, boot and shoe, leather, manufacturing

238910 Helical pier (i.e., drilled building foundations) construction

237990 Helical pier (i.e., marine or pneumatic structures) construction

332613 Helical springs, hot wound heavy gauge metal, manufacturing

332613 Helical springs, light gauge, made from purchased wire or strip, manufacturing

481212 Helicopter carriers, freight, nonscheduled

481112 Helicopter freight carriers, scheduled

481211 Helicopter passenger carriers (except scenic, sightseeing), nonscheduled

481111 Helicopter passenger carriers, scheduled

487990 Helicopter ride, scenic and sightseeing, operation

336411 Helicopters manufacturing

325120 Helium manufacturing

325120 Helium recovery from natural gas

339113 Helmets (except athletic), safety (e.g., motorized vehicle crash helmets, space helmets), manufacturing

339920 Helmets, athletic (except motorized vehicle crash helmets), manufacturing

561320 Help supply services

212210 Hematite mining and/or beneficiating

334516 Hematology instruments manufacturing

325413 Hematology in-vitro diagnostic substances manufacturing

325412 Hematology in-vivo diagnostic substances manufacturing

325414 Hematology products (except diagnostic substances) manufacturing

325194 Hemlock extract manufacturing

113210 Hemlock gum gathering

621492 Hemodialysis centers and clinics

313110 Hemp bags made from purchased fiber

424590 Hemp merchant wholesalers

313110 Hemp ropes made from purchased fiber

313110 Hemp spun yarns made from purchased fiber

111998 Hemp, grown in an open field

111419 Hemp, grown under cover

315210 Hemstitching apparel contractors on apparel

325110 Heptanes made from refined petroleum or liquid hydrocarbons

325110 Heptenes made from refined petroleum or liquid hydrocarbons

111419 Herb farming, grown under cover

111998 Herb farming, open field

111421 Herbaceous perennial growing

456191 Herbal supplement stores

424210 Herbal supplements merchant wholesalers

325412 Herbal supplements, compounded, manufacturing

325411 Herbal supplements, uncompounded, manufacturing

621399 Herbalists' offices (e.g., centers, clinics)

712110 Herbariums

325320 Herbicides manufacturing

424910 Herbicides merchant wholesalers

711310 Heritage festival managers with facilities

711320 Heritage festival managers without facilities

711310 Heritage festival organizers with facilities

711320 Heritage festival organizers without facilities

| | |
|---|---|
| 711310 | Heritage festival promoters with facilities |
| 711320 | Heritage festival promoters without facilities |
| 712120 | Heritage villages |
| 238150 | Hermetically sealed window unit, commercial-type, installation |
| 238350 | Hermetically sealed window unit, residential-type, installation |
| 114111 | Herring fishing |
| 325199 | Heterocyclic chemicals, not specified elsewhere by process, manufacturing |
| 325199 | Hexadecanol manufacturing |
| 325199 | Hexamethylenediamine manufacturing |
| 325199 | Hexamethylenetetramine manufacturing |
| 325199 | Hexanol manufacturing |
| 311221 | HFCS (high fructose corn syrup) manufacturing |
| 311611 | Hides and skins produced in slaughtering plants |
| 316110 | Hides and skins, finishing on a contract basis |
| 424590 | Hides merchant wholesalers |
| 316110 | Hides, tanning, currying, dressing, and finishing |
| 337122 | High chairs, wood, children's, manufacturing |
| 311221 | High fructose corn syrup (HFCS) manufacturing |
| 335139 | High intensity lamp bulbs manufacturing |
| 331110 | High percentage nonferrous alloying elements (i.e., ferroalloys) manufacturing |
| 611691 | High school equivalency (e.g., GED) exam instruction |
| 611110 | High schools |
| 611110 | High schools offering both academic and technical courses |
| 611110 | High schools offering both academic and vocational courses |
| 236116 | High-rise apartment construction general contractors |
| 236117 | High-rise apartment for-sale builders |
| 332312 | Highway bridge sections, prefabricated metal, manufacturing |
| 237310 | Highway construction |
| 332322 | Highway guardrails, sheet metal (except stampings), manufacturing |
| 333120 | Highway line marking machinery manufacturing |
| 237310 | Highway line painting |

| | |
|---|---|
| 922120 | Highway patrols, police |
| 336120 | Highway tractors assembled on chassis of own manufacture |
| 336211 | Highway tractors assembling on purchased chassis |
| 238210 | Highway, street and bridge lighting and electrical signal installation |
| 423710 | Hinges merchant wholesalers |
| 332510 | Hinges, metal, manufacturing |
| 541720 | Historic and cultural preservation research and development services |
| 813410 | Historical clubs |
| 712120 | Historical forts |
| 712110 | Historical museums |
| 712120 | Historical ships |
| 712120 | Historical sites |
| 336390 | Hitches, trailer, automotive, truck, and bus, manufacturing |
| 325413 | HIV test kits manufacturing |
| 621491 | HMO (health maintenance organization) medical centers and clinics |
| 423920 | Hobby craft kits merchant wholesalers |
| 459120 | Hobby shops |
| 339930 | Hobbyhorses manufacturing |
| 423920 | Hobbyists' supplies merchant wholesalers |
| 333515 | Hobs (i.e., metal gear cutting tool) manufacturing |
| 711211 | Hockey clubs, professional or semiprofessional |
| 713990 | Hockey clubs, recreational |
| 339920 | Hockey equipment (except apparel) manufacturing |
| 423910 | Hockey equipment and supplies merchant wholesalers |
| 611620 | Hockey instruction, camps or schools |
| 339920 | Hockey skates manufacturing |
| 711211 | Hockey teams, professional or semiprofessional |
| 713990 | Hockey teams, recreational |
| 115112 | Hoeing |
| 332216 | Hoes, garden and mason's handtools, manufacturing |
| 112210 | Hog and pig (including breeding, farrowing, nursery, and finishing activities) farming |
| 333111 | Hog feeding and watering equipment manufacturing |
| 112210 | Hog feedlots (except stockyards for transportation) |

| | |
|---|---|
| 424520 | Hogs merchant wholesalers |
| 321920 | Hogsheads, coopered wood, manufacturing |
| 238290 | Hoisting and placement of large-scale apparatus |
| 333923 | Hoists (except aircraft loading) manufacturing |
| 423830 | Hoists (except automotive) merchant wholesalers |
| 333924 | Hoists, aircraft loading, manufacturing |
| 423120 | Hoists, automotive, merchant wholesalers |
| 551112 | Holding companies (except bank, managing) |
| 551114 | Holding companies that manage |
| 551111 | Holding companies, bank (except managing) |
| 333310 | Holepunchers (except hand operated), office-type, manufacturing |
| 339940 | Holepunchers, hand operated, manufacturing |
| 423220 | Hollowware (except precious metal) merchant wholesalers |
| 339910 | Hollowware, precious metal, manufacturing |
| 423940 | Hollowware, precious metal, merchant wholesalers |
| 332999 | Hollowware, precious plated metal, manufacturing |
| 316990 | Holsters, leather, manufacturing |
| 455219 | Home and auto supply stores |
| 532310 | Home and garden equipment rental centers |
| 238210 | Home automation system installation |
| 236116 | Home builders (except for-sale), multifamily |
| 236115 | Home builders (except for-sale), single-family |
| 236117 | Home builders, for-sale |
| 332119 | Home canning lids and rings, metal stamping |
| 621610 | Home care of elderly, medical |
| 624120 | Home care of elderly, non-medical |
| 444110 | Home centers, building materials |
| 624229 | Home construction organizations, work (sweat) equity |
| 459210 | Home delivery newspaper routes, direct selling |
| 337126 | Home entertainment centers, metal, manufacturing |
| 337122 | Home entertainment centers, wood, manufacturing |
| 522292 | Home equity credit lending |
| 423220 | Home furnishings merchant wholesalers |
| 449129 | Home furnishings stores |
| 621610 | Home health agencies |
| 611519 | Home health aid schools |
| 621610 | Home health care agencies |
| 423450 | Home health care supplies merchant wholesalers |
| 456199 | Home health equipment stores |
| 532283 | Home health furniture and equipment rental |
| 236118 | Home improvement (e.g., adding on, remodeling, renovating) |
| 236118 | Home improvement (e.g., adding on, remodeling, renovating), multifamily building, for-sale builders |
| 236118 | Home improvement (e.g., adding on, remodeling, renovating), multifamily building, general contractors |
| 236118 | Home improvement (e.g., adding on, remodeling, renovating), single-family housing, for-sale builders |
| 236118 | Home improvement (e.g., adding on, remodeling, renovating), single-family housing, general contractors |
| 444110 | Home improvement centers |
| 621610 | Home infusion therapy services |
| 541350 | Home inspection services |
| 621610 | Home nursing services (except private practices) |
| 621399 | Home nursing services, private practice |
| 236118 | Home renovation |
| 459999 | Home security equipment stores |
| 561920 | Home show managers |
| 561920 | Home show organizers |
| 561920 | Home show promoters |
| 238210 | Home standby power generator installation |
| 334310 | Home stereo systems manufacturing |
| 334310 | Home tape recorders and players (e.g., cartridge, cassette, reel) manufacturing |
| 334310 | Home theater audio and video equipment manufacturing |
| 238210 | Home theater installation |
| 333517 | Home workshop metal cutting machine tools (except handtools, welding equipment) manufacturing |
| 624221 | Homeless shelters |
| 624120 | Homemaker's service for elderly or disabled persons, non-medical |

| | |
|---|---|
| 621399 | Homeopaths' offices (e.g., centers, clinics) |
| 813990 | Homeowners' associations |
| 813990 | Homeowners' associations, condominium |
| 524126 | Homeowners' insurance carriers, direct |
| 524128 | Homeowners' warranty insurance carriers, direct |
| 623990 | Homes for children with health care incidental |
| 623220 | Homes for emotionally disturbed adults or children |
| 623110 | Homes for the aged with nursing care |
| 623312 | Homes for the aged without nursing care |
| 623110 | Homes for the elderly with nursing care |
| 623312 | Homes for the elderly without nursing care |
| 623990 | Homes for unwed mothers |
| 623210 | Homes with or without health care, intellectual and developmental disability |
| 623220 | Homes, psychiatric convalescent |
| 311211 | Hominy grits (except breakfast food), manufacturing |
| 311230 | Hominy grits, prepared as cereal breakfast food, manufacturing |
| 311421 | Hominy, canned, manufacturing |
| 333241 | Homogenizing machinery, food, manufacturing |
| 311511 | Homogenizing milk |
| 212390 | Hones mining and/or beneficiating |
| 112910 | Honey bee production |
| 424490 | Honey merchant wholesalers |
| 311999 | Honey processing |
| 111219 | Honeydew melon farming, field, bedding plant and seed production |
| 333517 | Honing and lapping machines, metal cutting type, manufacturing |
| 333515 | Honing heads (i.e., a machine tool accessory) manufacturing |
| 922140 | Honor camps, correctional (except private operation of) |
| 332313 | Hoods, industrial, fabricated metal plate work, manufacturing |
| 332322 | Hoods, range (except household-type), sheet metal (except stampings), manufacturing |
| 335210 | Hoods, range, household-type, manufacturing |
| 115210 | Hoof trimming |
| 339993 | Hook and eye fasteners (i.e., sewing accessories) manufacturing |
| 332722 | Hook and eye latches, metal, manufacturing |
| 313220 | Hook and loop fastener fabric manufacturing |
| 713990 | Hookah lounges (except primarily selling food and beverages) |
| 332722 | Hooks (i.e., general purpose fasteners), metal, manufacturing |
| 339920 | Hooks, fishing, manufacturing |
| 332216 | Hooks, handtools (e.g., baling, bush, grass, husking), manufacturing |
| 332722 | Hooks, metal screw, manufacturing |
| 331110 | Hoops made in iron and steel mills |
| 331110 | Hoops, galvanized, made in iron and steel mills |
| 332999 | Hoops, metal (except wire), fabricated from purchased metal |
| 321920 | Hoops, sawed or split wood for tight or slack cooperage, manufacturing |
| 311942 | Hop extract manufacturing |
| 424490 | Hop extract merchant wholesalers |
| 111998 | Hop farming |
| 333515 | Hopper feed devices (i.e., a machine tool accessory) manufacturing |
| 332313 | Hoppers, fabricated metal plate work, manufacturing |
| 332439 | Hoppers, light gauge metal, manufacturing |
| 424590 | Hops merchant wholesalers |
| 334511 | Horizon situation instrumentation manufacturing |
| 237990 | Horizontal drilling (e.g., underground cable, pipeline, sewer installation) |
| 325413 | Hormone in-vitro diagnostic substances manufacturing |
| 325412 | Hormone preparations (except in-vitro diagnostics) manufacturing |
| 325411 | Hormones and derivatives, uncompounded, manufacturing |
| 112920 | Horse (including thoroughbreds) production |
| 332999 | Horse bits manufacturing |
| 316990 | Horse boots and muzzles manufacturing |
| 711212 | Horse racetracks |
| 711219 | Horse racing stables |
| 713990 | Horse rental services, recreational saddle |
| 711310 | Horse show managers with facilities |
| 711320 | Horse show managers without facilities |
| 711310 | Horse show organizers with facilities |
| 711320 | Horse show organizers without facilities |
| 711310 | Horse show promoters with facilities |

| | |
|---|---|
| 711320 | Horse show promoters without facilities |
| 711190 | Horse shows |
| 441227 | Horse trailer dealers |
| 336214 | Horse trailers (except fifth-wheel-type) manufacturing |
| 336212 | Horse trailers, fifth-wheel-type, manufacturing |
| 713990 | Horseback riding, recreational |
| 487110 | Horse-drawn carriage operation |
| 311611 | Horsemeat produced in slaughtering plants |
| 311111 | Horsemeat, processing, for dog and cat food |
| 311421 | Horseradish (except sauce) canning |
| 311941 | Horseradish, prepared sauce, manufacturing |
| 115210 | Horses (except racehorses), boarding |
| 424590 | Horses merchant wholesalers |
| 115210 | Horses, training (except racehorses) |
| 331222 | Horseshoe nails, iron or steel, made in wire drawing plants |
| 115210 | Horseshoeing |
| 332111 | Horseshoes, ferrous forged, made from purchased iron or steel |
| 541690 | Horticultural consulting services |
| 424910 | Horticultural products merchant wholesalers |
| 332912 | Hose assemblies for fluid power systems manufacturing |
| 332722 | Hose clamps, metal, manufacturing |
| 332912 | Hose couplings and fittings, fluid power, manufacturing |
| 332919 | Hose couplings, metal (except fluid power), manufacturing |
| 313220 | Hose fabrics, tubular, weaving |
| 332999 | Hose, flexible metal, manufacturing |
| 423840 | Hose, industrial, merchant wholesalers |
| 326220 | Hoses, reinforced, rubber or plastics, manufacturing |
| 326220 | Hoses, rubberized fabric, manufacturing |
| 333248 | Hosiery machines manufacturing |
| 458110 | Hosiery stores |
| 424350 | Hosiery, men's and boys', merchant wholesalers |
| 339113 | Hosiery, orthopedic support, manufacturing |
| 315120 | Hosiery, sheer, women's, misses', and girls' full-length and knee-length, knitting or knitting and finishing |
| 424350 | Hosiery, women's and girls', merchant wholesalers |
| 424350 | Hosiery, women's, children's, and infants', merchant wholesalers |
| 315120 | Hosiery, women's, girls', and infants', manufacturing |
| 621610 | Hospice care services, in-home |
| 623110 | Hospices, inpatient care |
| 813920 | Hospital administrators' associations |
| 524114 | Hospital and medical service plans, direct, without providing health care services |
| 813910 | Hospital associations |
| 532283 | Hospital bed rental and leasing (i.e., home use) |
| 339113 | Hospital beds manufacturing |
| 423450 | Hospital beds merchant wholesalers |
| 236220 | Hospital construction |
| 423450 | Hospital equipment and supplies merchant wholesalers |
| 532283 | Hospital equipment rental (i.e. home use) |
| 532283 | Hospital furniture and equipment rental (i.e. home use) |
| 423450 | Hospital furniture merchant wholesalers |
| 339113 | Hospital furniture, specialized (e.g., hospital beds, operating room furniture) |
| 423450 | Hospital gowns merchant wholesalers |
| 926150 | Hospital licensure agencies |
| 611519 | Hospital management schools (except academic) |
| 611310 | Hospital management schools offering baccalaureate or graduate degrees |
| 315210 | Hospital service apparel, washable, cut and sew apparel contractors |
| 315250 | Hospital service apparel, washable, men's and boys', cut and sewn from purchased fabric (except apparel contractors) |
| 315250 | Hospital service apparel, washable, women's and girls', cut and sewn from purchased fabric (except apparel contractors) |
| 611519 | Hospitality management schools (except academic) |
| 611310 | Hospitality management schools offering baccalaureate or graduate degrees |
| 524114 | Hospitalization insurance carriers, direct, without providing health care services |
| ****** | Hospitals -- see type |

| | |
|---|---|
| 622210 | Hospitals for alcoholics |
| 622210 | Hospitals, addiction |
| 541940 | Hospitals, animal |
| 622110 | Hospitals, general medical and surgical |
| 622110 | Hospitals, general pediatric |
| 623210 | Hospitals, intellectual and developmental disability |
| 622210 | Hospitals, mental (except intellectual and developmental disability) |
| 622210 | Hospitals, psychiatric (except convalescent) |
| 623220 | Hospitals, psychiatric convalescent |
| 622210 | Hospitals, psychiatric pediatric |
| 622310 | Hospitals, specialty (except psychiatric, substance abuse) |
| 622210 | Hospitals, substance abuse |
| 721199 | Hostels |
| 487990 | Hot air balloon ride, scenic and sightseeing, operation |
| 333310 | Hot beverage vending machines manufacturing |
| 332812 | Hot dip galvanizing metals and metal products for the trade |
| 311612 | Hot dogs (except poultry) made from purchased carcasses |
| 311611 | Hot dogs (except poultry) produced in slaughtering plants |
| 311615 | Hot dogs, poultry, manufacturing |
| 332111 | Hot forgings made from purchased iron or steel, unfinished |
| 332112 | Hot forgings made from purchased nonferrous metals, unfinished |
| 213112 | Hot oil treating of oil field tanks on a contract basis |
| 213112 | Hot shot oil field services (on- and off-road) on a contract basis |
| 333519 | Hot strip mill machinery, metalworking, manufacturing |
| 459999 | Hot tub stores |
| 423910 | Hot tubs merchant wholesalers |
| 321920 | Hot tubs, coopered, manufacturing |
| 326191 | Hot tubs, plastics or fiberglass, manufacturing |
| 326299 | Hot water bottles, rubber, manufacturing |
| 335220 | Hot water heaters (including nonelectric), household-type, manufacturing |
| 238220 | Hot water heating system installation |
| 238220 | Hot water tank installation |
| 531120 | Hotel building rental or leasing, not operating hotel |
| 236220 | Hotel construction |
| 423440 | Hotel equipment and supplies (except furniture) merchant wholesalers |
| 423210 | Hotel furniture merchant wholesalers |
| 561110 | Hotel management services (except complete operation of client's business) |
| 721110 | Hotel management services (i.e., providing management and operating staff to run hotel) |
| 561599 | Hotel reservation services |
| 327110 | Hotel tableware and kitchen articles, vitreous china, manufacturing |
| 721110 | Hotels (except casino hotels) |
| 721110 | Hotels (except casino hotels) with golf courses, tennis courts, and/or other health spa facilities (i.e., resorts) |
| 721120 | Hotels, casino |
| 721110 | Hotels, membership |
| 721120 | Hotels, resort, with casinos |
| 721110 | Hotels, resort, without casinos |
| 721120 | Hotels, seasonal, with casinos |
| 721110 | Hotels, seasonal, without casinos |
| 624190 | Hotline centers |
| 333310 | Hotplates, commercial-type, manufacturing |
| 335210 | Hotplates, household-type electric, manufacturing |
| 331110 | Hot-rolling iron or steel products in iron and steel mills |
| 333519 | Hot-rolling mill machinery, metalworking, manufacturing |
| 331221 | Hot-rolling purchased steel |
| 238910 | House demolishing |
| 238130 | House framing |
| 238990 | House moving (i.e., raising from one site, moving, and placing on a new foundation) |
| 238320 | House painting |
| 111422 | House plant growing |
| 238910 | House razing |
| 812990 | House sitting services |
| 316210 | House slippers manufacturing |
| 316210 | House slippers, plastics or plastics soled fabric upper, manufacturing |
| 316210 | House slippers, rubber or rubber soled fabric upper, manufacturing |
| 423330 | House wrapping insulation materials merchant wholesalers |
| 532284 | Houseboat rental |

| | |
|---|---|
| 315210 | Housecoats cut and sew apparel contractors |
| 315120 | Housecoats made in apparel knitting mills |
| 315250 | Housecoats, women's, girls', and infants', cut and sewn from purchased fabric (except apparel contractors) |
| 315210 | Housedresses cut and sew apparel contractors |
| 315250 | Housedresses, women's and girls', cut and sewn from purchased fabric (except apparel contractors) |
| 238220 | Household oil storage tank installation |
| 814110 | Households, private, employing (e.g., cooks, maids, chauffeurs, gardeners) |
| 814110 | Households, private, employing domestic personnel |
| 449210 | Household-type appliance stores |
| 423620 | Household-type appliances (except water heaters, heating stoves (i.e., noncooking)), gas and electric, merchant wholesalers |
| 327110 | Household-type earthenware, semivitreous, manufacturing |
| 423210 | Household-type furniture merchant wholesalers |
| 337121 | Household-type furniture, upholstered, manufacturing |
| 337122 | Household-type furniture, wood, not upholstered (except TV and radio housings and sewing machine cabinets), manufacturing |
| 325320 | Household-type insecticides manufacturing |
| 423620 | Household-type laundry equipment (e.g., dryers, washers) merchant wholesalers |
| 327110 | Household-type tableware and kitchen articles, vitreous china, manufacturing |
| 334519 | Household-type timing mechanisms manufacturing |
| 321999 | Household-type woodenware manufacturing |
| 721199 | Housekeeping cabins |
| 721199 | Housekeeping cottages |
| 561720 | Housekeeping services (i.e., cleaning services) |
| 922140 | Houses of correction (except private operation of) |
| 531110 | Houses rental or leasing |
| 332311 | Houses, prefabricated metal, manufacturing |
| 321991 | Houses, prefabricated mobile homes, manufacturing |

| | |
|---|---|
| 321992 | Houses, prefabricated, wood (except mobile homes), manufacturing |
| 423220 | Housewares (except electric) merchant wholesalers |
| 449129 | Housewares stores |
| 423620 | Housewares, gas and electric, merchant wholesalers |
| 624229 | Housing assistance agencies |
| 531110 | Housing authorities owning and operating residential buildings |
| 925110 | Housing authorities, nonoperating |
| 236117 | Housing construction, for-sale builder |
| 236117 | Housing construction, merchant builder |
| 922120 | Housing police, government |
| 925110 | Housing programs, planning and development, government |
| 624229 | Housing repair organizations, volunteer |
| 236116 | Housing, multifamily, construction general contractors |
| 236115 | Housing, single-family, construction general contractors |
| 336612 | Hovercraft building |
| 487210 | Hovercraft sightseeing operation |
| 332994 | Howitzers manufacturing |
| 321999 | Hubs, wood, manufacturing |
| 111334 | Huckleberry farming |
| 113210 | Huckleberry greens, gathering of |
| 334511 | HUD (heads-up display) systems, aeronautical, manufacturing |
| 212290 | Huebnerite mining and/or beneficiating |
| 115114 | Hulling and shelling of nuts |
| 333111 | Hulling machinery, farm-type, manufacturing |
| 621991 | Human egg or ova banks |
| 621991 | Human embryo storage services |
| 712110 | Human history museums |
| 812210 | Human remains transportation services |
| 541612 | Human resource consulting services |
| 813311 | Human rights advocacy organizations |
| 921190 | Human rights commissions, government |
| 813312 | Humane societies without animal shelters |
| 541720 | Humanities research and development services |
| 423730 | Humidifiers and dehumidifiers (except portable) merchant wholesalers |
| 423620 | Humidifiers and dehumidifiers, portable, merchant wholesalers |

| | |
|---|---|
| 335210 | Humidifiers, portable electric, manufacturing |
| 333415 | Humidifying equipment (except portable) manufacturing |
| 334512 | Humidistats (e.g., duct, skeleton, wall) manufacturing |
| 238210 | Humidity control system installation |
| 334512 | Humidity controls, air-conditioning-type, manufacturing |
| 334519 | Humidity instruments (except industrial process and air-conditioning type) manufacturing |
| 334513 | Humidity instruments, industrial process-type, manufacturing |
| 212390 | Humus, peat, mining and/or beneficiating |
| 112390 | Hungarian partridge production |
| 721214 | Hunting camps with accommodation facilities |
| 713990 | Hunting clubs, recreational |
| 315210 | Hunting coats and vests cut and sew apparel contractors |
| 315250 | Hunting coats and vests, men's and boys', cut and sewn from purchased fabric (except apparel contractors) |
| 423910 | Hunting equipment and supplies merchant wholesalers |
| 459110 | Hunting equipment stores |
| 713990 | Hunting guide services |
| 332215 | Hunting knives manufacturing |
| 114210 | Hunting preserves |
| 813319 | Hunting, fishing, and sport shooting advocacy organizations |
| 238220 | HVAC (heating, ventilation and air-conditioning) contractors |
| 423730 | HVAC equipment merchant wholesalers |
| 334111 | Hybrid computers manufacturing |
| 334413 | Hybrid integrated circuits manufacturing |
| 112511 | Hybrid striped bass production |
| 237110 | Hydrant and flushing hydrant installation |
| 327410 | Hydrated lime (i.e., calcium hydroxide) manufacturing |
| 332912 | Hydraulic aircraft subassemblies manufacturing |
| 333995 | Hydraulic cylinders, fluid power, manufacturing |
| 811310 | Hydraulic equipment repair and maintenance services |
| 324110 | Hydraulic fluids made in petroleum refineries |
| 324191 | Hydraulic fluids, petroleum, made from refined petroleum |

| | |
|---|---|
| 325998 | Hydraulic fluids, synthetic, manufacturing |
| 213112 | Hydraulic fracturing wells on a contract basis |
| 332912 | Hydraulic hose fittings, fluid power, manufacturing |
| 326220 | Hydraulic hoses (without fitting), rubber or plastics, manufacturing |
| 423830 | Hydraulic power transmission equipment merchant wholesalers |
| 423830 | Hydraulic pumps and parts merchant wholesalers |
| 333996 | Hydraulic pumps, fluid power, manufacturing |
| 336340 | Hydraulic slave cylinders, automotive, truck, and bus clutch, manufacturing |
| 333611 | Hydraulic turbine generator set units manufacturing |
| 333611 | Hydraulic turbines manufacturing |
| 332912 | Hydraulic valves, fluid power, manufacturing |
| 325180 | Hydrazine manufacturing |
| 325180 | Hydrochloric acid manufacturing |
| 325120 | Hydrochlorofluorocarbon (HCFC) gases manufacturing |
| 325180 | Hydrocyanic acid manufacturing |
| 238910 | Hydrodemolition (i.e., demolition with pressurized water) contractors |
| 237990 | Hydroelectric generating facility construction |
| 221111 | Hydroelectric power generation |
| 325180 | Hydrofluoric acid manufacturing |
| 325120 | Hydrofluorocarbon (HFC) gases manufacturing |
| 325180 | Hydrofluosilicic acid manufacturing |
| 336611 | Hydrofoil vessel building and repairing in shipyard |
| 325120 | Hydrogen manufacturing |
| 325180 | Hydrogen peroxide manufacturing |
| 325180 | Hydrogen sulfide manufacturing |
| 311225 | Hydrogenating purchased oil |
| 541370 | Hydrographic mapping services |
| 323111 | Hydrographic printing |
| 541370 | Hydrographic surveying services |
| 541690 | Hydrology consulting services |
| 334519 | Hydrometers (except industrial process-type) manufacturing |
| 334513 | Hydrometers, industrial process-type, manufacturing |
| 334512 | Hydronic circulator control, automatic, manufacturing |

| | |
|---|---|
| 423720 | Hydronic heating equipment and supplies merchant wholesalers |
| 333414 | Hydronic heating equipment manufacturing |
| 238220 | Hydronic heating system installation |
| 334512 | Hydronic limit control manufacturing |
| 334512 | Hydronic limit, pressure, and temperature controls, manufacturing |
| 334511 | Hydrophones manufacturing |
| 111419 | Hydroponic crop farming |
| 325194 | Hydroquinone manufacturing |
| 561730 | Hydroseeding services (e.g., decorative, erosion control purposes) |
| 333996 | Hydrostatic drives manufacturing |
| 541380 | Hydrostatic testing laboratories or services |
| 333996 | Hydrostatic transmissions manufacturing |
| 325180 | Hydrosulfites manufacturing |
| 339113 | Hydrotherapy equipment manufacturing |
| 424210 | Hygiene products, oral, merchant wholesalers |
| 334519 | Hygrometers (except industrial process-type) manufacturing |
| 334513 | Hygrometers, industrial process-type, manufacturing |
| 334519 | Hygrothermographs manufacturing |
| 621399 | Hypnotherapists' offices (e.g., centers, clinics) |
| 325411 | Hypnotic drugs, uncompounded, manufacturing |
| 325180 | Hypochlorites manufacturing |
| 339112 | Hypodermic needles and syringes manufacturing |
| 325180 | Hypophosphites manufacturing |
| 312113 | Ice (except dry ice) manufacturing |
| 424990 | Ice (except dry ice) merchant wholesalers |
| 238170 | Ice apron, roof, installation |
| 334512 | Ice bank controls manufacturing |
| 335220 | Ice boxes, household-type, manufacturing |
| 326199 | Ice buckets, plastics (except foam), manufacturing |
| 326140 | Ice buckets, polystyrene foam, manufacturing |
| 326150 | Ice buckets, urethane or other plastics foam (except polystyrene), manufacturing |
| 332439 | Ice chests or coolers, light gauge metal, manufacturing |

| | |
|---|---|
| 326199 | Ice chests or coolers, plastics (except plastics foam), manufacturing |
| 326140 | Ice chests or coolers, polystyrene foam, manufacturing |
| 326150 | Ice chests or coolers, urethane or other plastics foam (except polystyrene) manufacturing |
| 445298 | Ice cream (i.e., packaged) stores |
| 424430 | Ice cream and ices merchant wholesalers |
| 311821 | Ice cream cones manufacturing |
| 424490 | Ice cream cones merchant wholesalers |
| 333241 | Ice cream making machinery manufacturing |
| 311520 | Ice cream manufacturing |
| 424430 | Ice cream merchant wholesalers |
| 311514 | Ice cream mix manufacturing |
| 722515 | Ice cream parlors |
| 311520 | Ice cream specialties manufacturing |
| 722330 | Ice cream truck vendors |
| 333310 | Ice cream vending machines manufacturing |
| 335210 | Ice crushers, household-type electric, manufacturing |
| 333998 | Ice crushers, industrial and commercial-type, manufacturing |
| 711211 | Ice hockey clubs, professional or semiprofessional |
| 713990 | Ice hockey clubs, recreational |
| 334512 | Ice maker controls manufacturing |
| 333415 | Ice making machinery manufacturing |
| 423740 | Ice making machines merchant wholesalers |
| 311520 | Ice milk manufacturing |
| 424430 | Ice milk merchant wholesalers |
| 311514 | Ice milk mix manufacturing |
| 311520 | Ice milk specialties manufacturing |
| 237990 | Ice rink (except indoor) construction |
| 236220 | Ice rink, indoor, construction |
| 339920 | Ice skates manufacturing |
| 711190 | Ice skating companies |
| 713940 | Ice skating rinks |
| 711190 | Ice skating shows |
| 312130 | Ice wine |
| 325120 | Ice, dry, manufacturing |
| 424690 | Ice, dry, merchant wholesalers |
| 312111 | Iced coffee manufacturing |
| 312111 | Iced tea manufacturing |

| | |
|---|---|
| 212390 | Iceland spar (i.e., optical grade calcite), mining and/or beneficiating |
| 311520 | Ices, flavored sherbets, manufacturing |
| 332999 | Identification plates, metal, manufacturing |
| 423410 | Identity recorders merchant wholesalers |
| 812990 | Identity theft protection services |
| 332993 | Igniters, ammunition tracer (i.e., more than 30 mm., more than 1.18 inch), manufacturing |
| 811114 | Ignition and battery repair shops, automotive |
| 334512 | Ignition controls for gas appliances and furnaces, automatic, manufacturing |
| 336320 | Ignition points and condensers for internal combustion engines manufacturing |
| 334515 | Ignition testing instruments manufacturing |
| 336320 | Ignition wiring harness for internal combustion engines manufacturing |
| 321215 | I-joists, wood, fabricating |
| 335132 | Illuminated indoor lighting fixtures (e.g., directional, exit) manufacturing |
| 541430 | Illustrators, independent commercial |
| 212290 | Ilmenite ores mining and/or beneficiating |
| 327420 | Images, small gypsum, manufacturing |
| 327999 | Images, small papier-mache, manufacturing |
| 323120 | Imagesetting services, prepress |
| 312230 | Imitation tobacco cigarettes, manufacturing |
| 335210 | Immersion heaters, household-type electric, manufacturing |
| 624230 | Immigrant resettlement services |
| 928120 | Immigration services |
| 923120 | Immunization program administration |
| 621111 | Immunologists' offices (e.g., centers, clinics) |
| 334516 | Immunology instruments, laboratory, manufacturing |
| 333991 | Impact wrenches, handheld power-driven, manufacturing |
| 334515 | Impedance measuring equipment manufacturing |
| 334514 | Impeller and counter driven flow meters manufacturing |
| 339113 | Implants, surgical, manufacturing |
| 213112 | Impounding and storing salt water in connection with petroleum production |
| 221310 | Impounding reservoirs, irrigation |
| 339114 | Impression material, dental, manufacturing |
| 711110 | Improvisational theaters |
| 334512 | In-built thermostats, filled system and bimetal types, manufacturing |
| 335139 | Incandescent filament lamp bulbs, complete, manufacturing |
| 325998 | Incense manufacturing |
| 334512 | Incinerator control systems, residential and commercial-type, manufacturing |
| 236210 | Incinerator, mass-burn type, construction |
| 236210 | Incinerator, municipal waste disposal, construction |
| 333994 | Incinerators (except precast concrete) manufacturing |
| 238290 | Incinerators, building equipment type, installation |
| 562211 | Incinerators, hazardous waste, operating |
| 562213 | Incinerators, nonhazardous solid waste |
| 327390 | Incinerators, precast concrete, manufacturing |
| 541213 | Income tax compilation services |
| 541213 | Income tax return preparation services |
| 333310 | Incoming mail handling equipment (e.g., opening, scanning, sorting) manufacturing |
| 339113 | Incubators, infant, manufacturing |
| 339113 | Incubators, laboratory-type, manufacturing |
| 333111 | Incubators, poultry, manufacturing |
| 325998 | Indelible inks manufacturing |
| 711510 | Independent museum exhibit designers |
| 488190 | Independent pilot, air (except owner-operators) |
| 711510 | Independent technical writers |
| 488490 | Independent truck driver (except owner-operators) |
| 333515 | Indexing, rotary tables (i.e., a machine tool accessory) manufacturing |
| 325998 | India inks manufacturing |
| 921190 | Indian affairs programs, government |
| 334515 | Indicating instruments, electric, manufacturing |
| 334519 | Indicator testers, turntable, manufacturing |
| 334513 | Indicators, industrial process control-type, manufacturing |
| 325180 | Indium chloride manufacturing |
| 624190 | Individual and family social services, multi-purpose |

| | |
|---|---|
| 523910 | Individuals investing in financial contracts on own account |
| 541850 | Indoor display advertising services |
| 713120 | Indoor play areas |
| 236220 | Indoor swimming pool construction |
| 333994 | Induction heating equipment, industrial process-type, manufacturing |
| 334416 | Inductors, electronic component-type (e.g., chokes, coils, transformers), manufacturing |
| 813910 | Industrial associations |
| 522180 | Industrial banks (i.e., known as), depository |
| 522299 | Industrial banks (i.e., known as), nondepository |
| 314994 | Industrial belting reinforcement, cord and fabric, manufacturing |
| 236210 | Industrial building (except warehouses) construction |
| 236210 | Industrial building (except warehouses) construction, for-sale builders |
| 236210 | Industrial building (except warehouses) construction, general contractors |
| 531120 | Industrial building rental or leasing |
| 722310 | Industrial caterers (i.e., providing food services on a contractual arrangement (except single-event basis)) |
| 424690 | Industrial chemicals merchant wholesalers |
| 423840 | Industrial containers merchant wholesalers |
| 335314 | Industrial controls (e.g., pushbutton, selector, and pilot switches) manufacturing |
| 423610 | Industrial controls, electrical, merchant wholesalers |
| 541420 | Industrial design consulting services |
| 533110 | Industrial design licensing |
| 541420 | Industrial design services |
| 926110 | Industrial development program administration |
| 423840 | Industrial diamonds merchant wholesalers |
| 541330 | Industrial engineering services |
| 811310 | Industrial equipment and machinery repair and maintenance services |
| 315210 | Industrial garments cut and sew apparel contractors |
| 315250 | Industrial garments, men's and boys', cut and sewn from purchased fabric (except apparel contractors) |
| 315250 | Industrial garments, women's and girls', cut and sewn from purchased fabric (except apparel contractors) |
| 325120 | Industrial gases manufacturing |
| 424690 | Industrial gases merchant wholesalers |
| 327212 | Industrial glassware and glass products, pressed or blown, made in glass making plants |
| 327215 | Industrial glassware made from purchased glass |
| 813930 | Industrial labor unions |
| 541320 | Industrial land use planning services |
| 812332 | Industrial launderers |
| 423840 | Industrial leather products merchant wholesalers |
| 335132 | Industrial lighting fixtures, electric, manufacturing |
| 522299 | Industrial loan companies, nondepository |
| 336510 | Industrial locomotives and parts manufacturing |
| 423830 | Industrial machinery and equipment (except electrical) merchant wholesalers |
| 561110 | Industrial management services |
| 335132 | Industrial mercury lighting fixtures, electric, manufacturing |
| 333511 | Industrial molds (except steel ingot) manufacturing |
| 331511 | Industrial molds, steel ingot, manufacturing |
| 332999 | Industrial pattern manufacturing |
| 423840 | Industrial pottery products merchant wholesalers |
| 334513 | Industrial process control instruments manufacturing |
| 238220 | Industrial process piping installation |
| 325510 | Industrial product finishes and coatings (i.e., paint) manufacturing |
| 541715 | Industrial research and development laboratories or services (except biotechnology and nanotechnology research and development) |
| 541511 | Industrial robot automation applications/software design and development services |
| 333998 | Industrial robot cells manufacturing |
| 541511 | Industrial robot programming services |
| 423830 | Industrial robotics equipment merchant wholesalers |
| 333998 | Industrial robots manufacturing |
| 423830 | Industrial robots merchant wholesalers |

| | |
|---|---|
| 325998 | Industrial salt manufacturing |
| 424690 | Industrial salts merchant wholesalers |
| 212322 | Industrial sand beneficiating (e.g., screening, washing) |
| 212322 | Industrial sand sandpits and dredging |
| 333998 | Industrial scales manufacturing |
| 423840 | Industrial supplies (except disposable plastics, paper) merchant wholesalers |
| 424130 | Industrial supplies, disposable plastics, paper, merchant wholesalers |
| 541380 | Industrial testing laboratories or services |
| 621340 | Industrial therapists' offices (e.g., centers, clinics) |
| 811310 | Industrial truck (e.g., forklifts) repair and maintenance services |
| 532490 | Industrial truck rental or leasing |
| 333924 | Industrial trucks and tractors manufacturing |
| 423830 | Industrial trucks, tractors, or trailers merchant wholesalers |
| 812332 | Industrial uniform supply services |
| 423930 | Industrial wastes to be reclaimed merchant wholesalers |
| 311611 | Inedible products (e.g., hides, skins, pulled wool, wool grease) produced in slaughtering plants |
| 334511 | Inertial navigation systems, aeronautical, manufacturing |
| 311422 | Infant and junior food canning |
| 624410 | Infant care services |
| 311230 | Infant cereals, dry, manufacturing |
| 624410 | Infant day care centers |
| 339113 | Infant incubators manufacturing |
| 315250 | Infants' apparel cut and sewn from purchased fabric (except apparel contractors) |
| 424350 | Infants' clothing merchant wholesalers |
| 315210 | Infants' cut and sew apparel contractors |
| 311514 | Infant's formulas manufacturing |
| 316210 | Infant's shoes manufacturing |
| 315250 | Infants' water resistant outerwear cut and sewn from purchased fabric (except apparel contractors) |
| 336612 | Inflatable plastic boats, heavy-duty, manufacturing |
| 336612 | Inflatable rubber boats, heavy-duty, manufacturing |
| 541512 | Information management computer systems integration design services |
| 334516 | Infrared analytical instruments, laboratory-type, manufacturing |

| | |
|---|---|
| 334511 | Infrared homing systems, aeronautical, manufacturing |
| 334513 | Infrared instruments, industrial process-type, manufacturing |
| 335139 | Infrared lamp bulbs manufacturing |
| 335139 | Infrared lamp fixtures manufacturing |
| 333994 | Infrared ovens, industrial, manufacturing |
| 334413 | Infrared sensors, solid-state, manufacturing |
| 518210 | Infrastructure as a service (IaaS) |
| 621498 | Infusion therapy centers and clinics, outpatient |
| 331318 | Ingot made by rolling purchased aluminum |
| 331110 | Ingot made in iron and steel mills |
| 331318 | Ingot, aluminum, made in integrated secondary smelting and rolling mills |
| 331492 | Ingot, nonferrous metals (except aluminum, copper), secondary smelting and refining |
| 331313 | Ingot, primary aluminum, manufacturing |
| 331410 | Ingot, primary, nonferrous metals (except aluminum), manufacturing |
| 423510 | Ingots (except precious) merchant wholesalers |
| 423940 | Ingots, precious, merchant wholesalers |
| 621399 | Inhalation therapists' offices (e.g., centers, clinics) |
| 339112 | Inhalation therapy equipment manufacturing |
| 339112 | Inhalators, surgical and medical, manufacturing |
| 325998 | Inhibitors (e.g., corrosion, oxidation, polymerization) manufacturing |
| 333248 | Injection molding machinery for plastics manufacturing |
| 325612 | Ink eradicators manufacturing |
| 424120 | Ink, writing, merchant wholesalers |
| 339940 | Inked ribbons manufacturing |
| 424120 | Inked ribbons merchant wholesalers |
| 325910 | Inkjet cartridges manufacturing |
| 325910 | Inkjet inks manufacturing |
| 424120 | Inks, pastes, and solvents, office, merchant wholesalers |
| 325910 | Inks, printing, manufacturing |
| 423840 | Inks, printing, merchant wholesalers |
| 325998 | Inks, writing, manufacturing |
| 316990 | Inner soles, leather, manufacturing |
| 326211 | Inner tubes manufacturing |
| 337910 | Innerspring cushions manufacturing |

| | |
|---|---|
| 721191 | Inns, bed and breakfast |
| 424690 | Inorganic chemicals merchant wholesalers |
| 325130 | Inorganic pigments (except bone black, carbon black, lamp black) manufacturing |
| 334118 | Input/output equipment, computer, manufacturing |
| 423620 | Insect control devices, electric, merchant wholesalers |
| 115112 | Insect control for crops |
| 335139 | Insect lamps, electric, manufacturing |
| 332618 | Insect screening made from purchased wire |
| 424690 | Insecticides (except lawn and agricultural) merchant wholesalers |
| 325320 | Insecticides manufacturing |
| 424910 | Insecticides, agricultural, merchant wholesalers |
| 333515 | Inserts, cutting tool, manufacturing |
| 541350 | Inspection bureaus, building |
| 926150 | Inspection for labor standards |
| 488490 | Inspection or weighing services, truck transportation |
| 488190 | Inspection services, aircraft |
| 541350 | Inspection services, building or home |
| 238210 | Installation of photovoltaic panels |
| 213112 | Installing production equipment at the oil or gas field on a contract basis |
| 522220 | Installment sales financing |
| 311920 | Instant coffee manufacturing |
| 311230 | Instant hot cereals manufacturing |
| 323111 | Instant printing (i.e., quick printing) (except books) |
| 311920 | Instant tea manufacturing |
| 236220 | Institutional building construction |
| 236220 | Institutional building construction for-sale builders |
| 236220 | Institutional building construction general contractors |
| 337127 | Institutional furniture manufacturing |
| 335132 | Institutional lighting fixtures, electric, manufacturing |
| 456110 | Institutional pharmacies, off-site, exclusively on Internet |
| 456110 | Institutional pharmacies, off-site, mail-order |
| 456110 | Institutional pharmacies, on-site |
| 522180 | Institutions, savings |
| ****** | Instruction -- see type of training |

| | |
|---|---|
| 512110 | Instructional video production |
| 336320 | Instrument control panels (i.e., assembling purchased gauges), automotive, truck, and bus, manufacturing |
| 334511 | Instrument landing system instrumentation, airborne or airport, manufacturing |
| 333310 | Instrument lenses manufacturing |
| 334514 | Instrument panels, assembling gauges made in the same establishment |
| 334515 | Instrument shunts manufacturing |
| 332613 | Instrument springs, precision (except clock, watch), light gauge, made from purchased wire or strip, manufacturing |
| 335311 | Instrument transformers (except complete instruments) for metering or protective relaying use manufacturing |
| 334519 | Instrumentation for reactor controls, auxiliary, manufacturing |
| 423830 | Instruments (except electrical) (e.g., controlling, indicating, recording) merchant wholesalers |
| 334513 | Instruments for industrial process control manufacturing |
| 334515 | Instruments for measuring electrical quantities manufacturing |
| 334511 | Instruments, aeronautical, manufacturing |
| 423450 | Instruments, dental and medical, merchant wholesalers |
| 334515 | Instruments, electric (i.e., testing electrical characteristics), manufacturing |
| 423610 | Instruments, electric measuring, merchant wholesalers |
| 339112 | Instruments, mechanical microsurgical, manufacturing |
| 339992 | Instruments, musical, manufacturing |
| 423990 | Instruments, musical, merchant wholesalers |
| 423490 | Instruments, professional and scientific, merchant wholesalers |
| 331420 | Insulated wire or cable made from purchased copper in wire drawing plants |
| 331318 | Insulated wire or cable made in aluminum wire drawing plants |
| 423610 | Insulated wire or cable merchant wholesalers |
| 331420 | Insulated wire or cable, copper, made in integrated secondary smelting and wire drawing plants |
| 322299 | Insulating batts, fills, or blankets made from purchased paper |
| 327993 | Insulating batts, fills, or blankets, fiberglass, manufacturing |

| | |
|---|---|
| 327120 | Insulating firebrick and shapes, clay, manufacturing |
| 327215 | Insulating glass, sealed units, made from purchased glass |
| 327211 | Insulating glass, sealed units, made in glass making plants |
| 321999 | Insulating materials, cork, manufacturing |
| 325998 | Insulating oils manufacturing |
| 335929 | Insulating purchased nonferrous wire |
| 326150 | Insulation and cushioning, foam plastics (except polystyrene), manufacturing |
| 326140 | Insulation and cushioning, polystyrene foam plastics, manufacturing |
| 321219 | Insulation board, cellular fiber or hard pressed wood, manufacturing |
| 238310 | Insulation contractors |
| 423330 | Insulation materials (except wood) merchant wholesalers |
| 238290 | Insulation, boiler, duct and pipe, installation |
| 335932 | Insulators, electrical (except glass, porcelain), manufacturing |
| 327110 | Insulators, electrical porcelain, manufacturing |
| 327215 | Insulators, electrical, glass, made from purchased glass |
| 327212 | Insulators, electrical, glass, made in glass making plants |
| 423610 | Insulators, electrical, merchant wholesalers |
| 325412 | Insulin preparations manufacturing |
| 325411 | Insulin, uncompounded, manufacturing |
| 524298 | Insurance actuarial services |
| 524298 | Insurance advisory services |
| 524210 | Insurance agencies |
| 524210 | Insurance brokerages |
| 531120 | Insurance building rental or leasing |
| 524113 | Insurance carriers, disability, direct |
| 524126 | Insurance carriers, fidelity, direct |
| 524114 | Insurance carriers, health, direct |
| 524113 | Insurance carriers, life, direct |
| 524126 | Insurance carriers, property and casualty, direct |
| 524126 | Insurance carriers, surety, direct |
| 524127 | Insurance carriers, title, direct |
| 524291 | Insurance claims adjusting |
| 524291 | Insurance claims investigation services |
| 524292 | Insurance claims processing services, third party |

| | |
|---|---|
| 926150 | Insurance commissions, government |
| 524298 | Insurance coverage consulting services |
| 524298 | Insurance exchanges |
| 524292 | Insurance fund, third party administrative services (except claims adjusting only) |
| 551112 | Insurance holding companies |
| 524298 | Insurance investigation services (except claims investigation) |
| 524298 | Insurance loss prevention services |
| 524292 | Insurance plan administrative services (except claims adjusting only), third party |
| 522220 | Insurance premium financing |
| 524298 | Insurance ratemaking services |
| 524298 | Insurance reporting services |
| 524291 | Insurance settlement offices |
| 524298 | Insurance underwriters laboratories and standards services |
| 524113 | Insurance underwriting, disability, direct |
| 524114 | Insurance underwriting, health and medical, direct |
| 524113 | Insurance underwriting, life, direct |
| 524126 | Insurance underwriting, property and casualty, direct |
| 524127 | Insurance underwriting, title, direct |
| 813910 | Insurers' associations |
| 323111 | Intaglio printing (except books) |
| 335312 | Integral horsepower electric motors manufacturing |
| 423690 | Integrated circuits merchant wholesalers |
| 334413 | Integrated microcircuits manufacturing |
| 512250 | Integrated record companies (i.e., releasing, promoting, distributing) |
| 512250 | Integrated record production and distribution |
| 334515 | Integrated-circuit testers manufacturing |
| 334515 | Integrating electricity meters manufacturing |
| 334514 | Integrating meters, nonelectric, manufacturing |
| 623210 | Intellectual and developmental disability facilities (e.g., homes, hospitals, intermediate care facilities), residential |
| 623210 | Intellectual and developmental disability homes |
| 623210 | Intellectual and developmental disability hospitals |
| 623210 | Intellectual and developmental disability intermediate care facilities |

| | |
|---|---|
| 813311 | Intellectually and developmentally disabled advocacy groups |
| 712110 | Interactive museums |
| 485210 | Intercity bus line operation |
| 483113 | Intercoastal freight transportation to and from domestic ports |
| 483114 | Intercoastal transportation of passengers to and from domestic ports |
| 334290 | Intercom systems and equipment manufacturing |
| 238210 | Intercommunication (intercom) system installation |
| 332410 | Intercooler shells manufacturing |
| 333310 | Interferometers manufacturing |
| 541410 | Interior decorating consultant services |
| 541410 | Interior decorating consulting services |
| 238910 | Interior demolition contractors |
| 541410 | Interior design consulting services |
| 541410 | Interior design services |
| 541410 | Interior designer services |
| 561730 | Interior landscaping services |
| 811121 | Interior repair shops, automotive |
| 238990 | Interlocking brick and block installation |
| 623210 | Intermediate care facilities, intellectual and developmental disability |
| 334515 | Internal combustion engine analyzers (i.e., testing electrical characteristics) manufacturing |
| 333618 | Internal combustion engines (except aircraft, nondiesel automotive, nondiesel truck) manufacturing |
| 423830 | Internal combustion engines (except aircraft, nondiesel automotive, nondiesel truck) merchant wholesalers |
| 333618 | Internal combustion engines for hybrid drive systems (except automotive) manufacturing |
| 336412 | Internal combustion engines, aircraft, manufacturing |
| 336310 | Internal combustion engines, automotive and truck gasoline, manufacturing |
| 921130 | Internal Revenue Service |
| 928120 | International Monetary Fund |
| 522299 | International trade financing |
| 541810 | Internet advertising agencies |
| 455219 | Internet auctions, general merchandise (new and used), retail |
| 459510 | Internet auctions, general merchandise (used), retail |
| 513130 | Internet book publishers |

| | |
|---|---|
| 516210 | Internet broadcasting |
| 561439 | Internet cafes (i.e., not serving food and beverages) |
| 513120 | Internet comic book publishing |
| 455110 | Internet department store sites |
| 516210 | Internet entertainment broadcasting sites |
| 561311 | Internet job listing services, including intermediary platform services |
| 513120 | Internet magazine publishing |
| 541910 | Internet media audience research services |
| 513120 | Internet newsletter publishing |
| 513110 | Internet newspaper publishing |
| 513120 | Internet periodical publishers |
| 516210 | Internet radio stations |
| 561311 | Internet resume listing services, including intermediary platform services |
| 455219 | Internet retail sales sites (except department store, warehouse club, and supercenter sites), new general merchandise |
| 459510 | Internet retail sales sites, used general merchandise |
| 519290 | Internet search portals |
| 519290 | Internet search Web sites |
| 517810 | Internet service providers, using client-supplied telecommunications (e.g., dial-up ISPs) |
| 517111 | Internet service providers, using own operated wired telecommunications infrastructure (e.g., cable, DSL) |
| 516210 | Internet sports broadcasting sites |
| 455211 | Internet supercenter sites |
| 541910 | Internet traffic monitoring research services |
| 516210 | Internet video broadcast sites |
| 455211 | Internet warehouse club sites |
| 621111 | Internists' offices (e.g., centers, clinics) |
| 541940 | Internists' offices, veterinary |
| 541930 | Interpretation services, language |
| 712190 | Interpretive centers, nature |
| 711120 | Interpretive dance companies |
| 711510 | Interpretive dancers, independent |
| 485210 | Interstate bus line operation |
| 485210 | Interurban bus line operation |
| 483211 | Intracoastal transportation of freight |
| 483212 | Intracoastal transportation of passengers |
| 339113 | Intraocular lenses manufacturing |

| | |
|---|---|
| 339113 | Intrauterine devices manufacturing |
| 325412 | Intravenous (IV) solution preparations manufacturing |
| 812990 | Introduction services, social |
| 532283 | Invalid equipment rental (i.e., home use) |
| 561990 | Inventory computing services |
| 541614 | Inventory planning and control management consulting services |
| 561990 | Inventory taking services |
| 311314 | Invert sugar manufacturing |
| 335312 | Inverters, rotating electrical, manufacturing |
| 335999 | Inverters, solid-state, manufacturing |
| 561611 | Investigation services (except credit), private |
| 561450 | Investigation services, credit |
| 561611 | Investigators, private |
| 523940 | Investment advice consulting services, customized, fees paid by client |
| 523940 | Investment advice counseling services, customized, fees paid by client |
| 523940 | Investment advisory services, customized, fees paid by client |
| 523150 | Investment banking |
| 331524 | Investment castings, aluminum, unfinished, manufacturing |
| 331529 | Investment castings, nonferrous metal (except aluminum), unfinished, manufacturing |
| 331512 | Investment castings, steel, unfinished, manufacturing |
| 523910 | Investment clubs |
| 525990 | Investment funds, closed-end |
| 525910 | Investment funds, open-ended |
| 523940 | Investment management |
| 325413 | In-vitro diagnostic substances manufacturing |
| 325412 | In-vivo diagnostic substances manufacturing |
| 325180 | Iodides manufacturing |
| 325412 | Iodinated in-vivo diagnostic substances manufacturing |
| 325180 | Iodine, crude or resublimed, manufacturing |
| 334519 | Ion chambers manufacturing |
| 325211 | Ion exchange resins manufacturing |
| 325211 | Ionomer resins manufacturing |
| 325199 | Ionone manufacturing |
| 331491 | Iridium bar, rod, sheet, strip and tubing made from purchased metals or scrap |

| | |
|---|---|
| 212290 | Iridium mining and/or beneficiating |
| 331492 | Iridium recovering from scrap and/or alloying purchased metals |
| 331410 | Iridium refining, primary |
| 423390 | Iron and steel architectural shapes merchant wholesalers |
| 325130 | Iron based pigments manufacturing |
| 331511 | Iron castings, unfinished, manufacturing |
| 325180 | Iron compounds, not specified elsewhere by process, manufacturing |
| 332111 | Iron forgings made from purchased iron, unfinished |
| 331511 | Iron foundries |
| 212210 | Iron ore (e.g., hematite, magnetite, siderite, taconite) mining and/or beneficiating |
| 212210 | Iron ore agglomerates mining and/or beneficiating |
| 212210 | Iron ore beneficiating plants (e.g., agglomeration, sintering) |
| 212210 | Iron ore mine site development for own account |
| 331110 | Iron ore recovery from open hearth slag |
| 212210 | Iron ore, blocked, mining and/or beneficiating |
| 331110 | Iron sinter made in iron and steel mills |
| 325180 | Iron sulphate manufacturing |
| 238120 | Iron work, structural, contractors |
| 331110 | Iron, pig, manufacturing |
| 335220 | Ironers and mangles, household-type (except portable irons), manufacturing |
| 423220 | Ironing boards merchant wholesalers |
| 332999 | Ironing boards, metal, manufacturing |
| 321999 | Ironing boards, wood, manufacturing |
| 335210 | Irons, household-type electric, manufacturing |
| 423620 | Irons, household-type, electric, merchant wholesalers |
| 334517 | Irradiation apparatus and tubes (e.g., industrial, medical diagnostic, medical therapeutic, research, scientific), manufacturing |
| 334517 | Irradiation equipment manufacturing |
| 115114 | Irradiation of fruits and vegetables |
| 926130 | Irrigation districts, nonoperating |
| 423820 | Irrigation equipment merchant wholesalers |
| 333111 | Irrigation equipment, agriculture, manufacturing |
| 327332 | Irrigation pipe, concrete, manufacturing |

| | |
|---|---|
| 332322 | Irrigation pipe, sheet metal (except stampings), manufacturing |
| 237110 | Irrigation project construction (except lawn) |
| 221310 | Irrigation system operation |
| 325110 | Isobutane made from refined petroleum or liquid hydrocarbons |
| 211130 | Isobutane recovered from oil and gas field gases |
| 325110 | Isobutene made from refined petroleum or liquid hydrocarbons |
| 325211 | Isobutylene polymer resins manufacturing |
| 325212 | Isobutylene-isoprene rubber manufacturing |
| 325212 | Isocyanate rubber manufacturing |
| 325194 | Isocyanates manufacturing |
| 335311 | Isolation transformers manufacturing |
| 211130 | Isopentane recovered from oil and gas field gases |
| 325110 | Isoprene made from refined petroleum or liquid hydrocarbons |
| 325199 | Isopropyl alcohol manufacturing |
| 522210 | Issuing, credit card |
| 311422 | Italian foods canning |
| 339112 | IV apparatus manufacturing |
| 333120 | Jack hammers manufacturing |
| 315210 | Jackets cut and sew apparel contractors |
| 315120 | Jackets made in apparel knitting mills |
| 332992 | Jackets, bullet (i.e., 30 mm. or less, 1.18 inch or less), manufacturing |
| 315250 | Jackets, fur (except apparel contractors), manufacturing |
| 315210 | Jackets, fur, cut and sew apparel contractors |
| 332313 | Jackets, industrial, fabricated metal plate work, manufacturing |
| 315250 | Jackets, leather (except welders') or sheep-lined (except apparel contractors), manufacturing |
| 315210 | Jackets, leather (except welders') or sheep-lined, cut and sew apparel contractors |
| 315250 | Jackets, men's and boys', cut and sewn from purchased fabric (except apparel contractors) |
| 315210 | Jackets, service apparel (e.g., laboratory, medical), cut and sew apparel contractors |
| 315250 | Jackets, service apparel (e.g., laboratory, medical), men's and boys', cut and sewn from purchased fabric (except apparel contractors) |
| 315250 | Jackets, service apparel (e.g., laboratory, medical), women's and girls', cut and sewn from purchased fabric (except apparel contractors) |
| 315210 | Jackets, ski, cut and sew apparel contractors |
| 315250 | Jackets, ski, men's and boys', cut and sewn from purchased fabric (except apparel contractors) |
| 315250 | Jackets, ski, women's, girls', and infants', cut and sewn from purchased fabric (except apparel contractors) |
| 315250 | Jackets, tailored, men's and boys', cut and sewn from purchased fabric (except apparel contractors) |
| 316990 | Jackets, welder's, leather, manufacturing |
| 315250 | Jackets, women's, girls', and infants', cut and sewn from purchased fabric (except apparel contractors) |
| 332216 | Jacks (except hydraulic, pneumatic) manufacturing |
| 333998 | Jacks, hydraulic and pneumatic, manufacturing |
| 333248 | Jacquard card cutting machinery manufacturing |
| 313210 | Jacquard woven fabrics weaving |
| 212390 | Jade mining and/or beneficiating |
| 611620 | Jai alai instruction, camps or schools |
| 711211 | Jai alai teams, professional or semiprofessional |
| 236220 | Jail construction |
| 561210 | Jail operation on a contract or fee basis |
| 922140 | Jails (except private operation of) |
| 561210 | Jails, privately operated |
| 332321 | Jalousies, metal, manufacturing |
| 424690 | Janitorial chemicals merchant wholesalers |
| 423850 | Janitorial equipment and supplies merchant wholesalers |
| 459999 | Janitorial equipment and supplies stores |
| 561720 | Janitorial services |
| 561720 | Janitorial services, aircraft |
| 332812 | Japanning metals and metal products for the trade |
| 316110 | Japanning of leather |
| 333994 | Japanning ovens manufacturing |
| 327213 | Jars for packaging, bottling, and canning, glass, manufacturing |
| 326199 | Jars, plastics, manufacturing |
| 711120 | Jazz dance companies |
| 711510 | Jazz dancers, independent |

| | |
|---|---|
| 711130 | Jazz musical artists, independent |
| 711130 | Jazz musical groups |
| 315210 | Jean-cut casual slacks cut and sew apparel contractors |
| 315250 | Jean-cut casual slacks, men's and boys', cut and sewn from purchased fabric (except apparel contractors) |
| 315250 | Jean-cut casual slacks, women's and girls', cut and sewn from purchased fabric (except apparel contractors) |
| 315210 | Jeans cut and sew apparel contractors |
| 315250 | Jeans, women's, girls', and infants', cut and sewn from purchased fabric (except apparel contractors) |
| 311421 | Jellies and jams manufacturing |
| 424490 | Jellies and jams merchant wholesalers |
| 311340 | Jelly candies manufacturing |
| 315210 | Jerseys cut and sew apparel contractors |
| 315120 | Jerseys made in apparel knitting mills |
| 315250 | Jerseys, men's and boys', cut and sewn from purchased fabric (except apparel contractors) |
| 315250 | Jerseys, women's and girls', cut and sewn from purchased fabric (except apparel contractors) |
| 424710 | Jet fuel bulk stations and terminals, merchant wholesalers |
| 457210 | Jet fuel bulk stations, selling for consumption |
| 324110 | Jet fuels manufacturing |
| 336412 | Jet propulsion and internal combustion engines and parts, aircraft, manufacturing |
| 332993 | Jet propulsion projectiles (except guided missiles) manufacturing |
| 423910 | Jet skis merchant wholesalers |
| 237990 | Jetty construction |
| 339910 | Jewel settings and mountings, precious metal, manufacturing |
| 339910 | Jeweler's findings and materials manufacturing |
| 423940 | Jewelers' findings merchant wholesalers |
| 332216 | Jeweler's handtools, nonelectric, manufacturing |
| 424990 | Jewelry boxes merchant wholesalers |
| 541490 | Jewelry design services |
| 423940 | Jewelry merchant wholesalers |
| 811490 | Jewelry repair shops without retailing new jewelry |
| 458110 | Jewelry stores, costume |
| 458310 | Jewelry stores, precious |
| 339910 | Jewelry, costume, manufacturing |
| 339910 | Jewelry, natural or cultured pearls, manufacturing |
| 339910 | Jewelry, precious metal, manufacturing |
| 333514 | Jigs (e.g., checking, gauging, inspection) manufacturing |
| 333514 | Jigs and fixtures for use with machine tools manufacturing |
| 423830 | Jigs merchant wholesalers |
| 333991 | Jigsaws, handheld power-driven, manufacturing |
| 333243 | Jigsaws, woodworking-type, stationary, manufacturing |
| 624310 | Job counseling, vocational rehabilitation or habilitation |
| 323111 | Job printing (except screen, books) |
| 323111 | Job printing, engraving (except books) |
| 323111 | Job printing, flexographic (except books) |
| 323111 | Job printing, gravure (except books) |
| 323111 | Job printing, letterpress (except books) |
| 323111 | Job printing, lithographic (except books) |
| 323111 | Job printing, offset (except books) |
| 323113 | Job printing, screen |
| 336370 | Job stampings, automotive, metal, manufacturing |
| 624310 | Job training, vocational rehabilitation or habilitation |
| 711219 | Jockeys, horse racing |
| 339920 | Jogging machines, manufacturing |
| 315210 | Jogging suits cut and sew apparel contractors |
| 315120 | Jogging suits made in apparel knitting mills |
| 315250 | Jogging suits, men's and boys', cut and sewn from purchased fabric (except apparel contractors) |
| 315250 | Jogging suits, women's, girls', and infants', cut and sewn from purchased fabric (except apparel contractors) |
| 325520 | Joint compounds (except gypsum base) manufacturing |
| 327420 | Joint compounds, gypsum based, manufacturing |
| 333243 | Jointers, woodworking-type, manufacturing |
| 333613 | Joints, swivel (except aircraft, motor vehicle), manufacturing |
| 333613 | Joints, universal (except aircraft, motor vehicle), manufacturing |
| 336413 | Joints, universal, aircraft, manufacturing |

| | |
|---|---|
| 336350 | Joints, universal, automotive, truck, and bus, manufacturing |
| 332312 | Joists, fabricated bar, manufacturing |
| 332322 | Joists, sheet metal (except stampings), manufacturing |
| 111998 | Jojoba farming |
| 711510 | Journalists, independent (freelance) |
| 334118 | Joystick devices manufacturing |
| 611620 | Judo instruction, camps or schools |
| 326150 | Jugs, vacuum, foam plastics (except polystyrene), manufacturing |
| 332439 | Jugs, vacuum, light gauge metal, manufacturing |
| 326140 | Jugs, vacuum, polystyrene foam plastics, manufacturing |
| 722515 | Juice bars, nonalcoholic, fixed location |
| 333241 | Juice extractors (i.e., food manufacturing-type) manufacturing |
| 335210 | Juice extractors, household-type electric, manufacturing |
| 311520 | Juice pops, frozen, manufacturing |
| 424490 | Juices, canned or fresh, merchant wholesalers |
| 424420 | Juices, frozen, merchant wholesalers |
| 311411 | Juices, fruit or vegetable concentrates, frozen, manufacturing |
| 311421 | Juices, fruit or vegetable, canned manufacturing |
| 311421 | Juices, fruit or vegetable, fresh, manufacturing |
| 311411 | Juices, fruit or vegetable, frozen, manufacturing |
| 713990 | Jukebox concession operators (i.e., supplying and servicing in others' facilities) |
| 334310 | Jukeboxes manufacturing |
| 315210 | Jumpsuits cut and sew apparel contractors |
| 315250 | Jumpsuits, women's and girls', cut and sewn from purchased fabric (except apparel contractors) |
| 335932 | Junction boxes, electrical wiring, manufacturing |
| 813910 | Junior chambers of commerce |
| 611210 | Junior colleges |
| 611210 | Junior colleges offering a wide variety of academic and technical training |
| 611110 | Junior high schools |
| 423140 | Junk yards, auto, merchant wholesalers |
| 541199 | Jury consulting services |
| 313210 | Jute bags made in broadwoven mills |
| 424310 | Jute piece goods (except burlap) merchant wholesalers |
| 337122 | Juvenile furniture (except upholstered), wood, manufacturing |
| 337126 | Juvenile furniture (except wood, upholstered) manufacturing |
| 337126 | Juvenile furniture, rattan and reed, manufacturing |
| 337121 | Juvenile furniture, upholstered, manufacturing |
| 623990 | Juvenile halfway group homes |
| 513120 | Juvenile magazine and periodical publishers |
| 513120 | Juvenile magazine and periodical publishers (except exclusive Internet publishing) |
| 513120 | Juvenile magazine and periodical publishers and printing combined |
| 513120 | Juvenile magazine and periodical publishers, exclusively on Internet |
| 323111 | Juvenile magazines and periodicals commercial printing (except screen) without publishing |
| 323113 | Juvenile magazines and periodicals screen printing without publishing |
| 111219 | Kale farming, field, bedding plant and seed production |
| 212323 | Kaolin mining and/or beneficiating |
| 327992 | Kaolin, processing beyond beneficiation |
| 611620 | Karate instruction, camps or schools |
| 713990 | Kayaking, recreational |
| 327420 | Keene's cement manufacturing |
| 321920 | Kegs, wood, coopered, manufacturing |
| 311119 | Kelp meal and pellets, animal feed manufacturing |
| 334515 | Kelvin bridges (i.e., electrical measuring instruments) manufacturing |
| 111998 | Kenaf farming |
| 112990 | Kennels, breeding and raising stock for sale |
| 711219 | Kennels, dog racing |
| 812910 | Kennels, pet boarding |
| 212390 | Kernite mining and/or beneficiating |
| 211120 | Kerogen processing |
| 424710 | Kerosene bulk stations and terminals, merchant wholesalers |
| 324110 | Kerosene manufacturing |
| 424720 | Kerosene merchant wholesalers (except bulk stations, terminals) |
| 333414 | Kerosene space heaters manufacturing |
| 311421 | Ketchup manufacturing |

| | |
|---|---|
| 325199 | Ketone compounds, not specified elsewhere by process, manufacturing |
| 332420 | Kettles, heavy gauge metal, manufacturing |
| 332510 | Key blanks, metal, manufacturing |
| 316990 | Key cases (except metal) manufacturing |
| 339910 | Key cases, precious metal, manufacturing |
| 333517 | Key cutting machines, metal cutting type, manufacturing |
| 811490 | Key duplicating shops |
| 332618 | Key rings made from purchased wire |
| 334118 | Keyboards, computer peripheral equipment, manufacturing |
| 423430 | Keyboards, computer, merchant wholesalers |
| 339992 | Keyboards, piano or organ, manufacturing |
| 336320 | Keyless entry systems, automotive, truck, and bus, manufacturing |
| 423710 | Keys and locks merchant wholesalers |
| 334210 | Keysets, telephone, manufacturing |
| 621492 | Kidney dialysis centers and clinics |
| 236210 | Kiln construction |
| 321999 | Kiln drying lumber |
| 327120 | Kiln furniture, clay, manufacturing |
| 333994 | Kilns (except cement, chemical, wood) manufacturing |
| 333248 | Kilns (i.e., cement, chemical, wood) manufacturing |
| 423830 | Kilns, industrial, merchant wholesalers |
| 611110 | Kindergartens |
| 611110 | Kindergartens, combined with preschools |
| 334519 | Kinematic test and measuring equipment manufacturing |
| 561910 | Kit assembling and packaging services |
| 336211 | Kit car bodies manufacturing |
| 423440 | Kitchen appliances, commercial (except refrigerated), merchant wholesalers |
| 423620 | Kitchen appliances, household-type, gas and electric, merchant wholesalers |
| 327110 | Kitchen articles, coarse earthenware, manufacturing |
| 444180 | Kitchen cabinet (except custom) stores |
| 337110 | Kitchen cabinets (except freestanding), stock or custom wood, manufacturing |
| 238350 | Kitchen cabinets and counters, constructed on site |
| 423310 | Kitchen cabinets, built-in, merchant wholesalers |

| | |
|---|---|
| 337122 | Kitchen chairs (e.g., upholstered), wood, manufacturing |
| 337126 | Kitchen chairs (including upholstered), metal, manufacturing |
| 337126 | Kitchen chairs (including upholstered), plastics, manufacturing |
| 332215 | Kitchen cutlery, nonprecious and precious plated metal, manufacturing |
| 325612 | Kitchen degreasing and cleaning preparations manufacturing |
| 337126 | Kitchen furniture, household-type, metal, manufacturing |
| 337126 | Kitchen furniture, metal household-type, manufacturing |
| 337122 | Kitchen furniture, wood household-type, manufacturing |
| 238220 | Kitchen sink and hardware installation |
| 423440 | Kitchen utensils, commercial, merchant wholesalers |
| 332215 | Kitchen utensils, fabricated metal (e.g., colanders, garlic presses, ice cream scoops, spatulas), manufacturing |
| 423220 | Kitchen utensils, household-type, merchant wholesalers |
| 326199 | Kitchen utensils, plastics, manufacturing |
| 449129 | Kitchenware stores |
| 327110 | Kitchenware, commercial and household-type, vitreous china, manufacturing |
| 327110 | Kitchenware, semivitreous earthenware, manufacturing |
| 321999 | Kitchenware, wood, manufacturing |
| 339930 | Kites manufacturing |
| 111339 | Kiwi fruit farming |
| 334419 | Klystron tubes manufacturing |
| 423690 | Klystron tubes merchant wholesalers |
| 314910 | Knapsacks (e.g., backpacks, book bags) manufacturing |
| 314910 | Knapsacks, made from purchased woven or knitted materials |
| 315210 | Knickers cut and sew apparel contractors |
| 315250 | Knickers, men's and boys', cut and sewn from purchased fabric (except apparel contractors) |
| 315250 | Knickers, women's, girls', and infants', cut and sewn from purchased fabric (except apparel contractors) |
| 337122 | Knickknack shelves, wood, manufacturing |
| 332215 | Knife blades manufacturing |
| 332215 | Knife blanks manufacturing |

| | |
|---|---|
| 335313 | Knife switches, electric power switchgear-type, manufacturing |
| 311812 | Knishes (except frozen) made in commercial bakeries |
| 311813 | Knishes, frozen, manufacturing |
| 315210 | Knit gloves cut and sew apparel contractors |
| 315990 | Knit gloves cut and sewn from purchased fabric (except apparel contractors) |
| 315120 | Knit gloves made in apparel knitting mills |
| 313110 | Knitting and crocheting thread manufacturing |
| 313240 | Knitting and finishing lace |
| 313240 | Knitting and finishing warp or weft fabric |
| 313240 | Knitting lace |
| 333248 | Knitting machinery manufacturing |
| 313110 | Knitting spun yarns (e.g., cotton, manmade fiber, silk, wool) made from purchased fiber |
| 313240 | Knitting warp or weft fabric |
| 332215 | Knives (e.g., hunting, pocket, table nonprecious, table precious plated) manufacturing |
| 423710 | Knives (except disposable plastics) merchant wholesalers |
| 333515 | Knives and bits for metalworking lathes, planers, and shapers manufacturing |
| 332216 | Knives and bits for woodworking lathes, planers, and shapers manufacturing |
| 424130 | Knives, disposable plastics, merchant wholesalers |
| 335210 | Knives, household-type electric carving, manufacturing |
| 339112 | Knives, surgical, manufacturing |
| 339992 | Knobs, organ, manufacturing |
| 321999 | Knobs, wood, manufacturing |
| 333248 | Knot tying machinery for textiles manufacturing |
| 333517 | Knurling machines, metalworking, manufacturing |
| 322130 | Kraft linerboard manufacturing |
| 322120 | Kraft paper stock manufacturing |
| 212323 | Kyanite mining and/or beneficiating |
| 339940 | Label making equipment, handheld, manufacturing |
| 333993 | Labeling (i.e., packaging) machinery manufacturing |
| 423420 | Labeling machines merchant wholesalers |
| 561910 | Labeling services |
| 313220 | Labels weaving |
| 323111 | Labels, commercial printing (except screen), on a job-order basis |
| 424310 | Labels, textile, merchant wholesalers |
| 561320 | Labor (except farm) contractors (i.e., personnel suppliers) |
| 561320 | Labor (except farm) pools |
| 115115 | Labor contractors, farm |
| 813930 | Labor federations |
| 561330 | Labor leasing services |
| 926150 | Labor management negotiations boards, government |
| 541612 | Labor relations consulting services |
| 926110 | Labor statistics agencies |
| 813930 | Labor unions (except apprenticeship programs) |
| ****** | Laboratories -- see specific type |
| 621512 | Laboratories, dental X-ray |
| 621511 | Laboratories, medical (except radiological, X-ray) |
| 621512 | Laboratories, medical radiological or X-ray |
| 334516 | Laboratory analytical instruments (except optical) manufacturing |
| 333310 | Laboratory analytical optical instruments (e.g., microscopes) manufacturing |
| 311119 | Laboratory animal feed manufacturing |
| 112990 | Laboratory animal production (e.g., guinea pigs, mice, rats) |
| 315210 | Laboratory coats cut and sew apparel contractors |
| 315250 | Laboratory coats, men's and boys', cut and sewn from purchased fabric (except apparel contractors) |
| 315250 | Laboratory coats, women's and girls', cut and sewn from purchased fabric (except apparel contractors) |
| 236220 | Laboratory construction |
| 423490 | Laboratory equipment (except dental, medical, ophthalmic) merchant wholesalers |
| 423450 | Laboratory equipment, dental and medical, merchant wholesalers |
| 238390 | Laboratory furniture and equipment installation |
| 327215 | Laboratory glassware (e.g., beakers, test tubes, vials) made from purchased glass |
| 327212 | Laboratory glassware (e.g., beakers, test tubes, vials) made in glass making plants |

| | |
|---|---|
| 811210 | Laboratory instrument repair and maintenance services |
| 512199 | Laboratory services, motion picture |
| 334515 | Laboratory standards testing instruments (e.g., capacitance, electrical resistance, inductance) manufacturing |
| 541380 | Laboratory testing (except medical, veterinary) services |
| 621511 | Laboratory testing services, medical (except radiological, X-ray) |
| 621512 | Laboratory testing services, medical radiological or X-ray |
| 541940 | Laboratory testing services, veterinary |
| 339113 | Laboratory-type evaporation apparatus manufacturing |
| 333415 | Laboratory-type freezers manufacturing |
| 337127 | Laboratory-type furniture (e.g., benches, cabinets, stools, tables) (except dental) manufacturing |
| 339113 | Laboratory-type sample preparation apparatus manufacturing |
| 333248 | Lace and net making machinery manufacturing |
| 316110 | Lace leather manufacturing |
| 313240 | Lace manufacturing |
| 313240 | Lace products (except apparel) made in lace mills |
| 314999 | Lace, burnt-out, manufacturing |
| 316990 | Laces (e.g., shoe), leather, manufacturing |
| 313220 | Laces (e.g., shoe), textile, manufacturing |
| 332812 | Lacquering metals and metal products for the trade |
| 333994 | Lacquering ovens manufacturing |
| 325510 | Lacquers manufacturing |
| 424950 | Lacquers merchant wholesalers |
| 325199 | Lactic acid manufacturing |
| 311514 | Lactose manufacturing |
| 332999 | Ladder jacks, metal, manufacturing |
| 321999 | Ladder jacks, wood, manufacturing |
| 321912 | Ladder rounds or rungs, hardwood, manufacturing |
| 423830 | Ladders merchant wholesalers |
| 321999 | Ladders, extension, wood, manufacturing |
| 326199 | Ladders, fiberglass, manufacturing |
| 332323 | Ladders, metal chain, manufacturing |
| 332323 | Ladders, permanently installed, metal, manufacturing |
| 332999 | Ladders, portable metal, manufacturing |
| 332313 | Ladle bails, fabricated metal plate work, manufacturing |
| 332313 | Ladles, fabricated metal plate work, manufacturing |
| 312120 | Lager brewing |
| 237110 | Lagoon, sewage treatment construction |
| 483211 | Lake freight transportation (except on Great Lakes system) |
| 483113 | Lake freight transportation, Great Lakes (including St. Lawrence Seaway) |
| 562998 | Lake maintenance and cleaning services |
| 483212 | Lake passenger transportation (except on Great Lakes system) |
| 483114 | Lake passenger transportation, Great Lakes (including St. Lawrence Seaway) |
| 325130 | Lakes (i.e., organic pigments) manufacturing |
| 311611 | Lamb carcasses, half carcasses, primal and sub-primal cuts, produced in slaughtering plants |
| 112410 | Lamb feedlots (except stockyards for transportation) |
| 311612 | Lamb, primal and sub-primal cuts, made from purchased carcasses |
| 327215 | Laminated glass made from purchased glass |
| 327211 | Laminated glass made in glass making plants |
| 326130 | Laminated plastics plate, rod, and sheet, manufacturing |
| 321215 | Laminated structural wood members manufacturing |
| 321215 | Laminated veneer lumber (LVL) manufacturing |
| 423310 | Laminates, wood, merchant wholesalers |
| 322220 | Laminating foil for flexible packaging applications |
| 332813 | Laminating metals and metal formed products without fabricating |
| 322220 | Laminating purchased foil sheets for nonpackaging applications |
| 322220 | Laminating purchased paperboard |
| 322220 | Laminating purchased papers for nonpackaging applications |
| 322220 | Laminating purchased papers for packaging applications |
| 313320 | Laminating purchased textiles |
| 335311 | Lamp ballasts manufacturing |
| 327110 | Lamp bases, pottery, manufacturing |
| 325180 | Lamp black manufacturing |
| 335139 | Lamp bulb parts (except glass blanks and light emitting diodes (LEDs)), electric, manufacturing |

335139   Lamp bulbs and tubes, electric (i.e., fluorescent, incandescent filament, vapor), manufacturing

335139   Lamp bulbs and tubes, health, infrared and ultraviolet radiation, manufacturing

332618   Lamp frames, wire, made from purchased wire

335931   Lamp holders manufacturing

332999   Lamp shade frames, metal, manufacturing

335131   Lamp shades (except glass, plastics), residential, manufacturing

327215   Lamp shades made from purchased glass

327212   Lamp shades made in glass making plants

326199   Lamp shades, plastics, manufacturing

449129   Lamp shops, electric

335931   Lamp sockets and receptacles (i.e., electric wiring devices) manufacturing

423220   Lamps (i.e., lighting fixtures) merchant wholesalers

335132   Lamps (i.e., lighting fixtures), commercial, industrial, and institutional, manufacturing

335131   Lamps (i.e., lighting fixtures), residential, electric, manufacturing

335139   Lamps, insect, electric fixture, manufacturing

334517   Lamps, X-ray, manufacturing

237210   Land (except cemeteries) subdividers

237210   Land acquisition, assembling and subdividing

238910   Land clearing

237210   Land developers (i.e., subdividing and installing infrastructure)

237990   Land drainage contractors

238910   Land leveling contractors

924120   Land management program administration

423820   Land preparation machinery, agricultural, merchant wholesalers

333120   Land preparation machinery, construction, manufacturing

423810   Land preparation machinery, construction, merchant wholesalers

925120   Land redevelopment agencies, government

531190   Land rental or leasing

237210   Land subdividing and utility installation (e.g., electric, sewer and water)

541370   Land surveying services

335312   Land transportation motors and generators manufacturing

541320   Land use design services

541320   Land use planning services

562212   Landfills

332312   Landing mats, aircraft, metal, manufacturing

531390   Landman services

541320   Landscape architects' offices

541320   Landscape architects' private practices

541320   Landscape architectural services

561730   Landscape care and maintenance services

541320   Landscape consulting services

561730   Landscape contractors (except construction)

541320   Landscape design services

561730   Landscape installation services

541320   Landscape planning services

561730   Landscaping services (except planning)

541930   Language interpretation services

541720   Language research and development services

611630   Language schools

541930   Language services (e.g., interpretation, sign, translation)

541930   Language translation services

335139   Lanterns (e.g., carbide, electric, gas, gasoline, kerosene) manufacturing

423840   Lapidary equipment, industrial, merchant wholesalers

339910   Lapidary work manufacturing

334111   Laptop computers manufacturing

811210   Laptop repair and maintenance services, without retailing new laptops

311613   Lard made from purchased fat

424470   Lard merchant wholesalers

311611   Lard produced in slaughtering plants

333517   Laser boring, drilling, and cutting machines, metalworking, manufacturing

334413   Laser diodes manufacturing

532282   Laser disc, video, rental

334610   Laser disks, prerecorded video, mass reproducing

334510   Laser equipment, electromedical, manufacturing

621493   Laser surgery centers, freestanding

334510   Laser systems and equipment, medical, manufacturing

333992   Laser welding equipment manufacturing

| | |
|---|---|
| 316990 | Lashes (i.e., whips) manufacturing |
| 321999 | Last sole patterns, all materials, manufacturing |
| 212323 | Laterite mining and/or beneficiating |
| 326299 | Latex foam rubber manufacturing |
| 326299 | Latex foam rubber products manufacturing |
| 325510 | Latex paint (i.e., water based) manufacturing |
| 325212 | Latex rubber, synthetic, manufacturing |
| 332323 | Lath, expanded metal, manufacturing |
| 321219 | Lath, fiber, manufacturing |
| 327420 | Lath, gypsum, manufacturing |
| 321912 | Lath, wood, manufacturing |
| 333517 | Lathes, metalworking, manufacturing |
| 333243 | Lathes, woodworking-type, manufacturing |
| 238310 | Lathing contractors |
| 321912 | Lathmills, wood |
| 316110 | Latigo leather manufacturing |
| 812332 | Laundered mat and rug supply services |
| 812332 | Launderers, industrial |
| 812310 | Launderettes |
| 812320 | Laundries (except coin-operated, linen supply, uniform supply) |
| 812310 | Laundries, coin-operated or similar self-service |
| 812331 | Laundries, linen and uniform supply |
| 812310 | Laundromats |
| 812320 | Laundry and drycleaning agents |
| 314910 | Laundry bags made from purchased woven or knitted materials |
| 325612 | Laundry bluing manufacturing |
| 812320 | Laundry drop-off and pick-up sites |
| 335220 | Laundry equipment (e.g., dryers, washers), household-type, manufacturing |
| 333310 | Laundry extractors manufacturing |
| 332439 | Laundry hampers, light gauge metal, manufacturing |
| 337126 | Laundry hampers, rattan, reed, wicker or willow, manufacturing |
| 812310 | Laundry machine routes (i.e., concession operators), coin-operated or similar self-service |
| 333310 | Laundry machinery and equipment (except household-type) manufacturing |
| 423620 | Laundry machinery and equipment, household-type (e.g., dryers, washers), merchant wholesalers |
| 423850 | Laundry machinery, equipment, and supplies, commercial, merchant wholesalers |
| 314999 | Laundry nets made from purchased materials |
| 333310 | Laundry pressing machines (except household-type) manufacturing |
| 812320 | Laundry services (except coin-operated, linen supply, uniform supply) |
| 812310 | Laundry services, coin-operated or similar self-service |
| 812332 | Laundry services, industrial |
| 812331 | Laundry services, linen supply |
| 325611 | Laundry soap, chips, and powder manufacturing |
| 424690 | Laundry soap, chips, and powder, merchant wholesalers |
| 332999 | Laundry tubs, metal, manufacturing |
| 326191 | Laundry tubs, plastics, manufacturing |
| 325199 | Lauric acid esters and amines manufacturing |
| 332999 | Lavatories, metal, manufacturing |
| 327110 | Lavatories, vitreous china, manufacturing |
| 423720 | Lavatory fixtures merchant wholesalers |
| 423850 | Law enforcement equipment (except safety) merchant wholesalers |
| 922190 | Law enforcement statistics centers, government |
| 541110 | Law firms |
| 541110 | Law offices |
| 541110 | Law practices |
| 611310 | Law schools |
| 333112 | Lawn and garden equipment manufacturing |
| 811411 | Lawn and garden equipment repair and maintenance services without retailing new lawn and garden equipment |
| 713990 | Lawn bowling clubs |
| 561730 | Lawn care services (e.g., fertilizing, mowing, seeding, spraying) |
| 424910 | Lawn care supplies (e.g., chemicals, fertilizers, pesticides) merchant wholesalers |
| 332216 | Lawn edgers, nonpowered, manufacturing |
| 333112 | Lawn edgers, powered, manufacturing |

| | |
|---|---|
| 561730 | Lawn fertilizing services |
| 337126 | Lawn furniture (except concrete, stone, wood) manufacturing |
| 337122 | Lawn furniture, wood, manufacturing |
| 332919 | Lawn hose nozzles and lawn sprinklers manufacturing |
| 561730 | Lawn irrigation services |
| 423820 | Lawn maintenance machinery and equipment merchant wholesalers |
| 561730 | Lawn maintenance services |
| 561730 | Lawn mowing services |
| 561730 | Lawn mulching services |
| 444230 | Lawn power equipment stores |
| 561730 | Lawn seeding services |
| 561730 | Lawn spraying services |
| 238220 | Lawn sprinkler system installation |
| 444240 | Lawn supply stores |
| 562219 | Lawn waste disposal facilities |
| 532490 | Lawnmower rental or leasing |
| 811411 | Lawnmower repair and maintenance shops without retailing new lawnmowers |
| 333112 | Lawnmowers (except agricultural-type), powered, manufacturing |
| 423820 | Lawnmowers merchant wholesalers |
| 333111 | Lawnmowers, agricultural-type, powered, manufacturing |
| 332216 | Lawnmowers, nonpowered, manufacturing |
| 541110 | Lawyers' offices |
| 541110 | Lawyers' private practices |
| 325412 | Laxative preparations manufacturing |
| 112310 | Layer-type chicken production |
| 334419 | LCD (liquid crystal display) unit screens manufacturing |
| 212290 | Leaching of uranium, radium, or vanadium ores |
| 335910 | Lead acid storage batteries manufacturing |
| 331491 | Lead and lead alloy bar, pipe, plate, rod, sheet, strip, and tubing made from purchased metals or scrap |
| 325130 | Lead based pigments manufacturing |
| 331529 | Lead castings (except die-castings), unfinished, manufacturing |
| 331523 | Lead die-castings, unfinished, manufacturing |
| 332999 | Lead foil not made in rolling mills |
| 238390 | Lead lining walls for X-ray room contractors |
| 212230 | Lead ore mine site development for own account |
| 212230 | Lead ore mining and/or beneficiating |
| 325180 | Lead oxides (except pigments) manufacturing |
| 562910 | Lead paint abatement services |
| 562910 | Lead paint removal contractors |
| 325130 | Lead pigments manufacturing |
| 423510 | Lead primary forms merchant wholesalers |
| 331492 | Lead recovering from scrap and/or alloying purchased metals |
| 331491 | Lead rolling, drawing, or extruding purchased metals or scrap |
| 325180 | Lead silicate manufacturing |
| 331410 | Lead smelting and refining, primary |
| 327992 | Lead, black (i.e., natural graphite), ground, refined, or blended, manufacturing |
| 335139 | Lead-in wires, electric lamp, made from purchased wire |
| 212230 | Lead-zinc ore mining and/or beneficiating |
| 333112 | Leaf blowers manufacturing |
| 332216 | Leaf skimmers and rakes, nonpowered swimming pool, manufacturing |
| 332613 | Leaf springs, heavy gauge metal, manufacturing |
| 424590 | Leaf tobacco merchant wholesalers |
| 332999 | Leaf, metal, manufacturing |
| 334519 | Leak detectors, water, manufacturing |
| 813920 | Learned societies |
| 611691 | Learning centers offering remedial courses |
| 541720 | Learning disabilities research and development services |
| 213112 | Lease tank cleaning and repairing on a contract basis |
| 316990 | Leashes, dog, manufacturing |
| ****** | Leasing -- see type of property or article being leased |
| 522220 | Leasing in combination with sales financing |
| 315250 | Leather apparel (e.g., capes, coats, hats, jackets) (except apparel contractors) manufacturing |
| 315210 | Leather apparel (e.g., capes, coats, hats, jackets) cut and sew apparel contractors |
| 316990 | Leather belting manufacturing |
| 315250 | Leather clothing (except apparel contractors) manufacturing |

| | |
|---|---|
| 315210 | Leather clothing cut and sew apparel contractors |
| 458110 | Leather coat stores |
| 316110 | Leather coloring, cutting, embossing, and japanning |
| 316110 | Leather converters |
| 424990 | Leather cut stock (except boot, shoe) merchant wholesalers |
| 316990 | Leather cut stock for shoe and boot manufacturing |
| 424340 | Leather cut stock for shoe and boot merchant wholesalers |
| 316210 | Leather footwear manufacturing |
| 316210 | Leather footwear, men's, manufacturing |
| 316210 | Leather footwear, slippers, manufacturing |
| 316210 | Leather footwear, women's, manufacturing |
| 812320 | Leather garment cleaning services |
| 315210 | Leather gloves or mittens (except athletic) cut and sew apparel contractors |
| 315990 | Leather gloves or mittens (except athletic, cut and sewn apparel contractors) manufacturing |
| 339920 | Leather gloves, athletic, manufacturing |
| 424990 | Leather goods (except belting, footwear, handbags, gloves, luggage) merchant wholesalers |
| 811430 | Leather goods repair shops without retailing new leather goods |
| 458320 | Leather goods stores |
| 316990 | Leather goods, small personal (e.g., coin purses, eyeglass cases, key cases), manufacturing |
| 316990 | Leather handbags and purses manufacturing |
| 316210 | Leather house slippers manufacturing |
| 316990 | Leather luggage manufacturing |
| 316110 | Leather tanning, currying, and finishing |
| 316210 | Leather upper athletic footwear manufacturing |
| 316990 | Leather welting manufacturing |
| 333248 | Leather working machinery manufacturing |
| 313320 | Leather, artificial, made from purchased fabric |
| 322220 | Leatherboard (i.e., paperboard based) made from purchased paperboard |
| 322130 | Leatherboard (i.e., paperboard based) made in paperboard mills |
| 311225 | Lecithin made from purchased oils |

| | |
|---|---|
| 311224 | Lecithin, cottonseed, made in crushing mills |
| 311224 | Lecithin, soybean, made in crushing mills |
| 711410 | Lecture bureaus |
| 711510 | Lecturers, independent |
| 335139 | LED (light emitting diode) light bulbs manufacturing |
| 334413 | LED (light emitting diode) manufacturing |
| 111219 | Leek farming, field, bedding plant and seed production |
| 541110 | Legal aid services |
| 922130 | Legal counsel offices, government |
| 315210 | Leggings cut and sew apparel contractors |
| 315120 | Leggings knitting or knitting and finishing |
| 316990 | Leggings, welder's, leather, manufacturing |
| 315250 | Leggings, women's, girls', and infants', cut and sewn from purchased fabric (except apparel contractors) |
| 921140 | Legislative and executive office combinations |
| 921120 | Legislative assemblies |
| 921120 | Legislative bodies (e.g., federal, local, and state) |
| 921120 | Legislative commissions |
| 111320 | Lemon groves |
| 325998 | Lemon oil manufacturing |
| 519210 | Lending libraries |
| 423460 | Lens blanks, ophthalmic, merchant wholesalers |
| 327215 | Lens blanks, optical and ophthalmic, made from purchased glass |
| 327212 | Lens blanks, optical and ophthalmic, made in glass making plants |
| 326199 | Lens blanks, plastics ophthalmic or optical, manufacturing |
| 333310 | Lens coating (except ophthalmic) |
| 339115 | Lens coating, ophthalmic |
| 333310 | Lens grinding (except ophthalmic) |
| 339115 | Lens grinding, ophthalmic (except in retail stores) |
| 456130 | Lens grinding, ophthalmic, in retail stores |
| 333310 | Lens hoods, camera, manufacturing |
| 333310 | Lens mounting (except ophthalmic) |
| 339115 | Lens mounts, ophthalmic, manufacturing |

| | |
|---|---|
| 333310 | Lens polishing (except ophthalmic) |
| 339115 | Lens polishing, ophthalmic |
| 333310 | Lenses (except ophthalmic) manufacturing |
| 339115 | Lenses, ophthalmic, manufacturing |
| 423460 | Lenses, optical, merchant wholesalers |
| 111130 | Lentil farming, dry, field and seed production |
| 315210 | Leotards cut and sew apparel contractors |
| 315120 | Leotards made in apparel knitting mills |
| 315250 | Leotards, women's and girls', cut and sewn from purchased fabric (except apparel contractors) |
| 212390 | Lepidolite mining and/or beneficiating |
| 622310 | Leprosy hospitals |
| ****** | Lessors -- see specific type of asset or property being rented or leased |
| 531130 | Lessors of miniwarehouses |
| 531120 | Lessors of nonresidential buildings (except miniwarehouses) |
| 531110 | Lessors of residential buildings and dwellings |
| 531130 | Lessors of self-storage units |
| 423420 | Letter and envelope handling machines merchant wholesalers |
| 333310 | Letter folding, stuffing, and sealing machinery manufacturing |
| 333515 | Letter pins (e.g., gauging, measuring) manufacturing |
| 561410 | Letter writing services |
| 325910 | Letterpress inks manufacturing |
| 323120 | Letterpress plate preparation services |
| 333248 | Letterpress printing presses manufacturing |
| 339950 | Letters for signs manufacturing |
| 322230 | Letters, die-cut, made from purchased cardboard |
| 111219 | Lettuce farming, field, bedding plant and seed production |
| 237990 | Levee construction |
| 334513 | Level and bulk measuring instruments, industrial process-type, manufacturing |
| 334519 | Level gauges, radiation-type, manufacturing |
| 334519 | Levels and tapes, surveying, manufacturing |
| 332216 | Levels, carpenter's, manufacturing |
| 524126 | Liability insurance carriers, direct |
| 519210 | Libraries (except motion picture stock footage, motion picture commercial distribution) |
| 512199 | Libraries, motion picture stock footage film |
| 512199 | Libraries, video tape, stock footage |
| 236220 | Library construction |
| 561990 | License issuing services (except government), motor vehicle |
| 621399 | Licensed practical nurses' (LPNs) offices (e.g., centers, clinics) |
| 926130 | Licensing and inspecting of utilities |
| 926150 | Licensing and permit issuance for business operations, government |
| 926150 | Licensing and permit issuance for professional occupations, government |
| 926120 | Licensing of transportation equipment, facilities, and services |
| 311340 | Licorice candy manufacturing |
| 332431 | Lids and ends, can, light gauge metal, manufacturing |
| 332119 | Lids, jar, metal, stamping |
| 561611 | Lie detection services |
| 334519 | Lie detectors manufacturing |
| 611699 | Life guard training |
| 524210 | Life insurance agencies |
| 524113 | Life insurance carriers, direct |
| 339113 | Life preservers manufacturing |
| 336612 | Life rafts, inflatable, manufacturing |
| 524130 | Life reinsurance carriers |
| 541715 | Life sciences research and development laboratories or services (except biotechnology and nanotechnology research and development) |
| 423830 | Lift trucks, industrial, merchant wholesalers |
| 316990 | Lifts, heel, leather, manufacturing |
| 333248 | Light bulb and tube (i.e., electric lamp) machinery manufacturing |
| 335139 | Light bulbs manufacturing |
| 423610 | Light bulbs merchant wholesalers |
| 335139 | Light bulbs, sealed beam automotive, manufacturing |
| 334413 | Light emitting diodes (LED) manufacturing |
| 333310 | Light meters, photographic, manufacturing |
| 336510 | Light rail cars and equipment manufacturing |
| 237990 | Light rail system construction |
| 485119 | Light rail systems (except mixed mode), commuter |
| 334511 | Light reconnaissance and surveillance systems and equipment manufacturing |

| | |
|---|---|
| 334512 | Light responsive appliance controls manufacturing |
| 441110 | Light utility truck dealers, new only or new and used |
| 441120 | Light utility truck dealers, used only |
| 336110 | Light utility trucks assembling on chassis of own manufacture |
| 325998 | Lighter fluids (e.g., charcoal, cigarette) manufacturing |
| 483211 | Lighterage (i.e., freight transportation except vessel supply services) |
| 339999 | Lighters, cigar and cigarette (except motor vehicle, precious metal), manufacturing |
| 339910 | Lighters, cigar and cigarette, clad with precious metal, manufacturing |
| 424990 | Lighters, cigar and cigarette, merchant wholesalers |
| 488310 | Lighthouse operation |
| 335991 | Lighting carbons manufacturing |
| 541490 | Lighting design services |
| 423990 | Lighting equipment, gas, merchant wholesalers |
| 444180 | Lighting fixture (except electric lamps) stores |
| 335139 | Lighting fixtures, airport (e.g., approach, ramp, runway, taxi), manufacturing |
| 335132 | Lighting fixtures, commercial electric, manufacturing |
| 423610 | Lighting fixtures, electric, merchant wholesalers |
| 335132 | Lighting fixtures, industrial electric, manufacturing |
| 335132 | Lighting fixtures, institutional electric, manufacturing |
| 335139 | Lighting fixtures, nonelectric (e.g., propane, kerosene, carbide), manufacturing |
| 335131 | Lighting fixtures, residential electric, manufacturing |
| 561790 | Lighting maintenance services (e.g., bulb and fuse replacement and cleaning) |
| 238210 | Lighting system installation |
| 711510 | Lighting technicians, theatrical, independent |
| 335311 | Lighting transformers manufacturing |
| 335311 | Lighting transformers, street and airport, manufacturing |
| 335931 | Lightning arrestors and coils manufacturing |
| 423610 | Lightning arrestors merchant wholesalers |
| 238290 | Lightning protection equipment (e.g., lightning rod) installation |
| 335931 | Lightning protection equipment manufacturing |
| 238290 | Lightning rod and conductor installation |
| 325211 | Lignin plastics manufacturing |
| 213113 | Lignite mining services on a contract basis (except geophysical surveying and mapping, site preparation, construction, and transportation activities) |
| 212114 | Lignite surface mining and/or beneficiating |
| 111130 | Lima bean farming, dry, field and seed production |
| 339113 | Limbs, artificial, manufacturing |
| 423320 | Lime (except agricultural) merchant wholesalers |
| 111320 | Lime groves |
| 325998 | Lime oil manufacturing |
| 327410 | Lime production |
| 212312 | Lime rock, ground, mining and/or beneficiating |
| 424910 | Lime, agricultural, merchant wholesalers |
| 212312 | Limestone (except bituminous) crushed and broken stone mining and/or beneficiating |
| 212312 | Limestone beneficiating plants (e.g., grinding or pulverizing) |
| 212311 | Limestone mining or quarrying |
| 212319 | Limestone, bituminous, mining and/or beneficiating |
| 325320 | Lime-sulfur fungicides manufacturing |
| 334512 | Limit controls (e.g., air-conditioning, appliance, heating) manufacturing |
| 513199 | Limited editions art print publishers |
| 513199 | Limited editions art print publishers (except exclusive Internet publishing) |
| 455219 | Limited price variety stores |
| 212210 | Limonite mining and/or beneficiating |
| 532111 | Limousine rental without driver |
| 485320 | Limousine services (except shuttle services) |
| 485320 | Limousines for hire with driver (except taxis) |
| 325320 | Lindane pesticides manufacturing |
| 334512 | Line or limit control for electric heat manufacturing |
| 561730 | Line slash (i.e., rights of way) maintenance services |
| 238910 | Line slashing or cutting (except maintenance) |
| 335311 | Line voltage regulators (i.e., electric transformers) manufacturing |

335999 Linear accelerators manufacturing

332991 Linear ball bearings manufacturing

334514 Linear counters manufacturing

325220 Linear esters fibers and filaments manufacturing

332991 Linear roller bearings manufacturing

449129 Linen stores

812331 Linen supply services

423220 Linens (e.g., bath, bed, table) merchant wholesalers

314120 Linens made from purchased materials

327120 Liner brick and plates, vitrified clay, manufacturing

332313 Liners, industrial, fabricated metal plate work, manufacturing

114111 Lingcod fishing

315210 Lingerie cut and sew apparel contractors

424350 Lingerie merchant wholesalers

458110 Lingerie stores

315250 Lingerie, women's and girls', cut and sewn from purchased fabric (except apparel contractors)

316110 Lining leather manufacturing

316990 Linings, boot and shoe, leather, manufacturing

314999 Linings, casket, manufacturing

315210 Linings, hat, cut and sew apparel contractors

315990 Linings, hat, men's, cut and sewn from purchased fabric (except apparel contractors)

314999 Linings, luggage, manufacturing

332999 Linings, metal safe and vault, manufacturing

332994 Links, ammunition, manufacturing

325199 Linoleic acid esters and amines manufacturing

326199 Linoleum floor coverings manufacturing

238330 Linoleum, installation only

333248 Linotype machines manufacturing

311225 Linseed oil made from purchased oils

311224 Linseed oil, cake and meal, made in crushing mills

327390 Lintels, concrete, manufacturing

325412 Lip balms manufacturing

325620 Lipsticks manufacturing

424690 Liquefied gases (except LP) merchant wholesalers

488999 Liquefied natural gas (LNG) terminals (liquefaction and regasification)

424710 Liquefied petroleum gas (LPG) bulk stations and terminals, merchant wholesalers

332420 Liquefied petroleum gas (LPG) cylinders manufacturing

457210 Liquefied petroleum gas (LPG) dealers, direct selling

221210 Liquefied petroleum gas (LPG) distribution through mains

324110 Liquefied petroleum gas (LPG) made in refineries

424720 Liquefied petroleum gas (LPG) merchant wholesalers (except bulk stations, terminals)

211130 Liquefied petroleum gases (LPG), natural

325120 Liquid air manufacturing

334513 Liquid analysis instruments, industrial process-type, manufacturing

311313 Liquid beet syrup manufacturing

334516 Liquid chromatographic instruments, laboratory-type, manufacturing

334513 Liquid concentration instruments, industrial process-type, manufacturing

423690 Liquid crystal displays merchant wholesalers

334514 Liquid flow meters manufacturing

211130 Liquid hydrocarbons recovered from oil and gas field gases

334512 Liquid level controls, residential and commercial heating-type, manufacturing

334513 Liquid level instruments, industrial process-type, manufacturing

332420 Liquid oxygen tanks manufacturing

311313 Liquid sugar made from beet sugar

311314 Liquid sugar manufacturing

211130 Liquids, natural gas (e.g., ethane, isobutane, natural gasoline, propane) recovered from oil and gas field gases

445320 Liquor stores, package

311351 Liquor, chocolate, made from cacao beans

311352 Liquor, chocolate, made from purchased chocolate

424820 Liquors merchant wholesalers

312130 Liquors, brandy, distilling and blending

424820 Liquors, distilled, merchant wholesalers

312140 Liquors, distilling and blending (except brandy)

339940 List finders and roledex address files manufacturing

| | |
|---|---|
| 531390 | Listing services, real estate |
| 711410 | Literary agents |
| 325130 | Litharge manufacturing |
| 335910 | Lithium batteries manufacturing |
| 325180 | Lithium compounds, not specified elsewhere by process, manufacturing |
| 212390 | Lithium mineral mining and/or beneficiating |
| 325910 | Lithographic inks manufacturing |
| 323120 | Lithographic plate preparation services |
| 323111 | Lithographic printing (except books, grey goods) |
| 333248 | Lithographic printing presses manufacturing |
| 325130 | Lithopone manufacturing |
| 334510 | Lithotripters manufacturing |
| 711310 | Live arts center operators |
| 424990 | Live bait merchant wholesalers |
| 711310 | Live theater operators |
| 332994 | Livens projectors (i.e., ordnance) manufacturing |
| 424520 | Livestock (except horses, mules, and feedlots) merchant wholesalers |
| 541690 | Livestock breeding consulting services |
| 115210 | Livestock breeding services (except consulting) |
| 424910 | Livestock feeds merchant wholesalers |
| 311119 | Livestock feeds, supplements, concentrates and premixes, manufacturing |
| 541940 | Livestock inspecting and testing services, veterinary |
| 115210 | Livestock spraying |
| 484220 | Livestock trucking, local |
| 484230 | Livestock trucking, long-distance |
| 541940 | Livestock veterinary services |
| 337126 | Living room furniture (except upholstered), metal, manufacturing |
| 337122 | Living room furniture (except upholstered), wood, manufacturing |
| 337121 | Living room furniture, upholstered, manufacturing |
| 112990 | Llama production |
| 334418 | Loaded computer boards manufacturing |
| 423430 | Loaded computer boards merchant wholesalers |
| 423810 | Loaders merchant wholesalers |
| 333120 | Loaders, shovel, manufacturing |
| 332993 | Loading and assembling bombs |
| 488490 | Loading and unloading at truck terminals |
| 488320 | Loading and unloading services at ports and harbors |
| 488210 | Loading and unloading services at rail terminals |
| 333131 | Loading machines, underground mining, manufacturing |
| 334418 | Loading printed circuit boards |
| 522310 | Loan brokerages |
| 522310 | Loan brokers' or agents' offices (i.e., independent) |
| 522291 | Loan companies (i.e., consumer, personal, small, student) |
| 522292 | Loan correspondents (i.e., lending funds with real estate as collateral) |
| 522390 | Loan servicing |
| 541820 | Lobbying services |
| 541820 | Lobbyists' offices |
| 114112 | Lobster fishing |
| 334210 | Local area network (LAN) communications equipment (e.g., bridges, gateways, routers) manufacturing |
| 541512 | Local area network (LAN) computer systems integration design services |
| 611420 | Local area network (LAN) management training |
| 485113 | Local bus services (except mixed mode) |
| 561421 | Local call centers (e.g., answering services, message services) |
| 492210 | Local letter and parcel delivery services (except as part of intercity courier network, U.S. Postal Service) |
| 492110 | Local letter and parcel delivery services as part of intercity courier network |
| 485112 | Local passenger rail systems (except mixed mode) |
| 813940 | Local political organizations |
| 517111 | Local telephone carriers, wired |
| 485111 | Local transit systems, mixed mode (e.g., bus, commuter rail, subway combinations) |
| 561990 | Locating underground utility lines prior to digging |
| 237990 | Lock and waterway construction |
| 561622 | Lock rekeying services |
| 332722 | Lock washers, metal, manufacturing |
| 445240 | Locker meat provisioners, direct selling |
| 337215 | Lockers (except refrigerated) manufacturing |

423440 Lockers (except refrigerated) merchant wholesalers

812990 Lockers, coin- or card-operated, rental

333415 Lockers, refrigerated, manufacturing

423740 Lockers, refrigerated, merchant wholesalers

332510 Locks (except coin- or card-operated, time locks), metal, manufacturing

333310 Locks, coin- or card-operated, manufacturing

423710 Locks, security, merchant wholesalers

423850 Locksmith equipment and supplies merchant wholesalers

561622 Locksmith services

561622 Locksmith services with or without sales of locking devices, safes, and security vaults

561622 Locksmith shops

488210 Locomotive and rail car repair (except factory conversion, factory overhaul, factory rebuilding)

336320 Locomotive and railroad car light fixtures manufacturing

333923 Locomotive cranes manufacturing

333618 Locomotive diesel engines manufacturing

336510 Locomotives manufacturing

423860 Locomotives merchant wholesalers

336510 Locomotives rebuilding

212220 Lode gold mining and/or beneficiating

321992 Log cabins, prefabricated wood, manufacturing

333120 Log debarking machinery, portable, manufacturing

333243 Log debarking machinery, stationary, manufacturing

113310 Log harvesting

484220 Log hauling, local

484230 Log hauling, long-distance

236115 Log home construction general contractors

236117 Log home for-sale builders

333120 Log splitters, portable, manufacturing

333243 Log splitters, stationary, manufacturing

111334 Loganberry farming

113310 Logging

236220 Logging camp construction

541330 Logging engineering services

423810 Logging equipment merchant wholesalers

532412 Logging equipment rental or leasing without operator

482112 Logging railroads

237310 Logging road construction

336212 Logging trailers manufacturing

213112 Logging wells on a contract basis

334515 Logic circuit testers manufacturing

541614 Logistics and integrated supply chain management consulting services

541614 Logistics management consulting services

423990 Logs merchant wholesalers

333414 Logs, gas fireplace, manufacturing

325194 Logwood extract manufacturing

517121 Long-distance telecommunication resellers (except satellite telecommunications)

517111 Long-distance telephone carriers, wired

517410 Long-distance telephone satellite communication carriers

488320 Longshoremen services

333248 Loom bobbins manufacturing

333248 Loom reeds manufacturing

333248 Looms for textiles manufacturing

333248 Loopers for textiles manufacturing

323111 Looseleaf binders and devices manufacturing

424120 Looseleaf binders merchant wholesalers

322230 Looseleaf fillers and paper made from purchased paper

322120 Looseleaf fillers and paper made in paper mills

524291 Loss control consultants

325620 Lotions (e.g., body, face, hand) manufacturing

713290 Lottery control boards (i.e., operating lotteries)

921130 Lottery control boards, nonoperating

713290 Lottery corporations

713290 Lottery ticket sales agents (except retail stores)

334118 Lottery ticket sales terminals manufacturing

713290 Lottery ticket vendors (except retail stores)

334310 Loudspeakers manufacturing

722410 Lounges, cocktail

315210 Lounging robes and dressing gowns cut and sew apparel contractors

| | |
|---|---|
| 315120 | Lounging robes and dressing gowns made in apparel knitting mills |
| 315250 | Lounging robes and dressing gowns, men's and boys', cut and sewn from purchased fabric (except apparel contractors) |
| 315250 | Lounging robes and dressing gowns, women's, girls', and infants', cut and sewn from purchased fabric (except apparel contractors) |
| 333310 | Loupes (e.g., jewelers) manufacturing |
| 321911 | Louver windows and doors, made from purchased glass with wood frame |
| 332321 | Louver windows, metal, manufacturing |
| 332322 | Louvers, sheet metal (except stampings), manufacturing |
| 236117 | Low income housing construction for-sale builders |
| 236116 | Low income housing, multifamily, construction general contractors |
| 236115 | Low income housing, single-family, construction general contractors |
| 238160 | Low slope roofing installation |
| 238210 | Low voltage electrical work |
| 335131 | Low voltage lighting equipment, residential, electric, manufacturing |
| 236116 | Low-rise apartment construction general contractors |
| 236117 | Low-rise apartment for-sale builders |
| 311340 | Lozenges, nonmedicated, candy, manufacturing |
| 621399 | LPNs' (licensed practical nurses) offices (e.g., centers, clinics) |
| 484122 | LTL (less-than-truckload) long-distance freight trucking |
| 424710 | Lubricating oils and greases bulk stations and terminals, merchant wholesalers |
| 324110 | Lubricating oils and greases made in petroleum refineries |
| 424720 | Lubricating oils and greases merchant wholesalers (except bulk stations, terminals) |
| 324191 | Lubricating oils and greases, petroleum, made from refined petroleum |
| 325998 | Lubricating oils and greases, synthetic, manufacturing |
| 811191 | Lubrication shops, automotive |
| 336510 | Lubrication systems, locomotive (except pumps), manufacturing |
| 332510 | Luggage hardware, metal, manufacturing |
| 314999 | Luggage linings manufacturing |
| 423990 | Luggage merchant wholesalers |
| 336390 | Luggage racks, car top, automotive, truck, and bus, manufacturing |
| 811430 | Luggage repair shops without retailing new luggage |
| 458320 | Luggage stores |
| 316990 | Luggage, all materials, manufacturing |
| 335931 | Lugs and connectors, electrical, manufacturing |
| 423610 | Lugs and connectors, electrical, merchant wholesalers |
| 423310 | Lumber (e.g., dressed, finished, rough) merchant wholesalers |
| 321113 | Lumber (i.e., rough, dressed) made from logs or bolts |
| 561990 | Lumber grading services |
| 444180 | Lumber retailing yards |
| 493190 | Lumber storage terminals |
| 321113 | Lumber, hardwood dimension, made from logs or bolts |
| 321912 | Lumber, hardwood dimension, resawing purchased lumber |
| 321999 | Lumber, kiln drying |
| 321215 | Lumber, parallel strand, manufacturing |
| 321113 | Lumber, softwood dimension, made from logs or bolts |
| 321912 | Lumber, softwood dimension, resawing purchased lumber |
| 335132 | Luminous panel ceilings, electric, manufacturing |
| 335311 | Luminous tube transformers manufacturing |
| 332439 | Lunch boxes, light gauge metal, manufacturing |
| 722330 | Lunch wagons |
| 311612 | Luncheon meat (except poultry) made from purchased carcasses |
| 311611 | Luncheon meat (except poultry) produced in slaughtering plants |
| 311615 | Luncheon meat, poultry, manufacturing |
| 337127 | Lunchroom tables and chairs manufacturing |
| 532111 | Luxury automobile rental without driver |
| 485320 | Luxury automobiles for hire with driver (except taxis) |
| 321215 | LVL (laminated veneer lumber) manufacturing |
| 325612 | Lye, household-type, manufacturing |
| 111335 | Macadamia farming |
| 424490 | Macaroni merchant wholesalers |
| 311824 | Macaroni, dry, manufacturing |

311991 Macaroni, fresh, manufacturing

311412 Macaroni, frozen, manufacturing

332216 Machetes manufacturing

332999 Machine bases, metal, manufacturing

332322 Machine guards, sheet metal (except stampings), manufacturing

332994 Machine gun belts manufacturing

332994 Machine guns manufacturing

332722 Machine keys, metal, manufacturing

332216 Machine knives (except metal cutting) manufacturing

333515 Machine knives, metal cutting, manufacturing

238290 Machine rigging

332710 Machine shops

333515 Machine tool attachments and accessories manufacturing

335311 Machine tool transformers manufacturing

423830 Machine tools and accessories merchant wholesalers

811310 Machine tools repair and maintenance services

333517 Machine tools, metal cutting, manufacturing

333517 Machine tools, metal forming, manufacturing

541511 Machine vision software design and development services

238290 Machinery and equipment, large-scale, installation

522220 Machinery finance leasing

238910 Machinery, construction (except cranes), rental with operator

423420 Machines, office, merchant wholesalers

332216 Machinists' precision measuring tools (except optical) manufacturing

423830 Machinists' precision measuring tools merchant wholesalers

334511 Machmeters manufacturing

114111 Mackerel fishing

315210 Mackinaws cut and sew apparel contractors

315250 Mackinaws, men's and boys', cut and sewn from purchased fabric (except apparel contractors)

315250 Mackinaws, women's, girls', and infants', cut and sewn from purchased fabric (except apparel contractors)

541840 Magazine advertising representatives (i.e., independent of media owners)

513120 Magazine publishers

513120 Magazine publishers (except exclusive Internet publishing)

513120 Magazine publishers and printing combined

513120 Magazine publishers, exclusively on Internet

337122 Magazine racks, wood, manufacturing

459210 Magazine stands (i.e., permanent)

323111 Magazines and periodicals commercial printing (except screen) without publishing

323113 Magazines and periodicals screen printing without publishing

424920 Magazines merchant wholesalers

711190 Magic shows

459120 Magic supply stores

711510 Magicians, independent

327120 Magnesia refractory cement manufacturing

325411 Magnesia, medicinal, uncompounded, manufacturing

212323 Magnesite mining and/or beneficiating

327992 Magnesite, crude (e.g., calcined, dead-burned, ground), manufacturing

331491 Magnesium and magnesium alloy bar, rod, shape, sheet, strip, and tubing made from purchased metals or scrap

325180 Magnesium carbonate manufacturing

331529 Magnesium castings (except die-castings), unfinished, manufacturing

325180 Magnesium chloride manufacturing

325180 Magnesium compounds, not specified elsewhere by process, manufacturing

331523 Magnesium die-castings, unfinished, manufacturing

331491 Magnesium foil made by rolling purchased metals or scrap

332999 Magnesium foil not made in rolling mills

423520 Magnesium ores merchant wholesalers

331492 Magnesium recovering from scrap and/or alloying purchased metals

331410 Magnesium refining, primary

331491 Magnesium rolling, drawing, or extruding purchased metals or scrap

331420 Magnet wire, insulated, made from purchased copper in wire drawing plants

331318 Magnet wire, insulated, made in aluminum wire drawing plants

331491 Magnet wire, nonferrous metals (except aluminum, copper), made from purchased nonferrous metals (except aluminum, copper) in wire drawing plants

| | |
|---|---|
| 334610 | Magnetic and optical media, blank, manufacturing |
| 423690 | Magnetic bubble memories merchant wholesalers |
| 334514 | Magnetic counters manufacturing |
| 334513 | Magnetic flow meters, industrial process-type, manufacturing |
| 333517 | Magnetic forming machines, metalworking, manufacturing |
| 541360 | Magnetic geophysical surveying services |
| 334118 | Magnetic ink recognition devices, computer peripheral equipment, manufacturing |
| 334610 | Magnetic recording media for tapes, cassettes, and disks, manufacturing |
| 621512 | Magnetic resonance imaging (MRI) centers |
| 334510 | Magnetic resonance imaging (MRI) medical diagnostic equipment manufacturing |
| 334516 | Magnetic resonance imaging (MRI) type apparatus (except medical diagnostic) manufacturing |
| 334610 | Magnetic tapes, cassettes and disks, blank, manufacturing |
| 423690 | Magnetic tapes, cassettes, and disks, blank, merchant wholesalers |
| 334112 | Magnetic/optical combination storage units for computers manufacturing |
| 334519 | Magnetometers manufacturing |
| 334419 | Magnetron tubes manufacturing |
| 327110 | Magnets, permanent, ceramic or ferrite, manufacturing |
| 332999 | Magnets, permanent, metallic, manufacturing |
| 339115 | Magnifiers, corrective vision-type, manufacturing |
| 333310 | Magnifying glasses (except corrective vision-type) manufacturing |
| 423460 | Magnifying glasses merchant wholesalers |
| 333310 | Magnifying instruments, optical, manufacturing |
| 114111 | Mahimahi fishing |
| 561311 | Maid registries |
| 561720 | Maid services (i.e., cleaning services) |
| 238990 | Mail box units, outdoor, multiple box-type, erection |
| 337215 | Mail carrier cases and tables, wood, manufacturing |
| 332322 | Mail chutes, sheet metal (except stampings), manufacturing |
| 561499 | Mail consolidation services |
| 333310 | Mail handling machinery, post office-type, manufacturing |
| 561499 | Mail presorting services |
| 561431 | Mailbox rental centers, private |
| 561431 | Mailbox rental services combined with one or more other office support services, private |
| 423990 | Mailboxes merchant wholesalers |
| 332439 | Mailboxes, light gauge metal, manufacturing |
| 322219 | Mailing cases and tubes, paper fiber (i.e., all-fiber, nonfiber ends of any material), made from purchased paperboard |
| 532420 | Mailing equipment rental or leasing |
| 513140 | Mailing list publishers |
| 513140 | Mailing list publishers (except exclusive Internet publishing) |
| 423420 | Mailing machines merchant wholesalers |
| 334111 | Mainframe computers manufacturing |
| 488190 | Maintenance and repair services, aircraft (except factory conversion, factory overhaul, factory rebuilding) |
| 561730 | Maintenance of plants and shrubs in buildings |
| 488210 | Maintenance of rights of way and structures, railway |
| 488119 | Maintenance services, runway |
| 488310 | Maintenance services, waterfront terminal (except dredging) |
| 711211 | Major league baseball clubs |
| 812112 | Makeup (except permanent) salons |
| 325620 | Makeup (i.e., cosmetics) manufacturing |
| 812199 | Makeup salons, permanent |
| 523150 | Making markets for securities |
| 337126 | Malacca furniture (except upholstered), household-type, manufacturing |
| 325320 | Malathion insecticides manufacturing |
| 325194 | Maleic anhydride manufacturing |
| 531120 | Mall property operation (i.e., not operating contained businesses) rental or leasing |
| 331511 | Malleable iron foundries |
| 332216 | Mallets (e.g., rubber, wood) manufacturing |
| 321999 | Mallets, wood, manufacturing |
| 325199 | Malonic dinitrile manufacturing |
| 524126 | Malpractice insurance carriers, direct |
| 311942 | Malt extract and syrups manufacturing |

| | |
|---|---|
| 424490 | Malt extract merchant wholesalers |
| 311213 | Malt flour manufacturing |
| 312120 | Malt liquor brewing |
| 424810 | Malt liquor merchant wholesalers |
| 311213 | Malt manufacturing |
| 424490 | Malt merchant wholesalers |
| 333241 | Malt milling machinery manufacturing |
| 311213 | Malt sprouts manufacturing |
| 311514 | Malted milk manufacturing |
| 311213 | Malting (germinating and drying grains) |
| 311221 | Maltodextrins manufacturing |
| 621512 | Mammogram (i.e., breast imaging) centers |
| 711410 | Management agencies for artists, entertainers, and other public figures |
| 611430 | Management development training |
| 525910 | Management investment offices, open-ended |
| 561110 | Management services (except complete operation of client's business) |
| 115116 | Management services, farm |
| 711310 | Managers of agricultural fairs with facilities |
| 711320 | Managers of agricultural fairs without facilities |
| 711310 | Managers of arts events with facilities |
| 711320 | Managers of arts events without facilities |
| 711310 | Managers of festivals with facilities |
| 711320 | Managers of festivals without facilities |
| 711310 | Managers of live performing arts productions (e.g., concerts) with facilities |
| 711320 | Managers of live performing arts productions (e.g., concerts) without facilities |
| 711310 | Managers of sports events with facilities |
| 711320 | Managers of sports events without facilities |
| 531312 | Managers' offices, commercial condominium |
| 531312 | Managers' offices, commercial real estate |
| 531312 | Managers' offices, nonresidential real estate |
| 531311 | Managers' offices, residential condominium |
| 531311 | Managers' offices, residential real estate |
| 711410 | Managers, authors' |
| 711410 | Managers, celebrities' |
| 561920 | Managers, convention |
| 711410 | Managers, entertainers' |
| 711410 | Managers, public figures' |
| 711410 | Managers, sports figures' |
| 561920 | Managers, trade fair or show |
| 531312 | Managing commercial condominiums |
| 531312 | Managing commercial real estate |
| 531311 | Managing cooperative apartments |
| 523940 | Managing investment funds |
| 523940 | Managing mutual funds |
| 561110 | Managing offices of dentists |
| 561110 | Managing offices of physicians and surgeons |
| 561110 | Managing offices of professionals (e.g., dentists, physicians, surgeons) |
| 523940 | Managing personal investment trusts |
| 531311 | Managing residential condominiums |
| 531311 | Managing residential real estate |
| 523940 | Managing trusts |
| 111320 | Mandarin groves |
| 339992 | Mandolins manufacturing |
| 333515 | Mandrels (i.e., a machine tool accessory) manufacturing |
| 212290 | Manganese concentrates beneficiating |
| 325180 | Manganese dioxide manufacturing |
| 331110 | Manganese metal ferroalloys manufacturing |
| 212290 | Manganese ores mining and/or beneficiating |
| 212290 | Manganiferous ores (not valued for iron content) mining and/or beneficiating |
| 212210 | Manganiferous ores valued for iron content, mining and/or beneficiating |
| 212290 | Manganite mining and/or beneficiating |
| 111339 | Mango farming |
| 325194 | Mangrove extract manufacturing |
| 331511 | Manhole covers, cast iron, manufacturing |
| 237120 | Manhole, oil and gas, construction |
| 812113 | Manicure and pedicure salons |
| 611511 | Manicure and pedicure schools |
| 325620 | Manicure preparations manufacturing |
| 812113 | Manicurist services |
| 423850 | Manicurists supplies merchant wholesalers |
| 424120 | Manifold business forms merchant wholesalers |

| | |
|---|---|
| 323111 | Manifold business forms printing |
| 336310 | Manifolds (i.e., intake and exhaust), automotive and truck gasoline engine, manufacturing |
| 332996 | Manifolds, pipe, made from purchased metal pipe |
| 322230 | Manila folders, die-cut, made from purchased paper or paperboard |
| 327999 | Manmade and engineered proppants (e.g., resin-coated sand, ceramic materials) manufacturing |
| 325220 | Manmade cellulosic fibers manufacturing |
| 313220 | Manmade fabric, narrow woven, weaving |
| 313210 | Manmade fabrics, broadwoven, weaving |
| 313110 | Manmade fiber thread manufacturing |
| 424690 | Manmade fibers merchant wholesalers |
| 325220 | Manmade noncellulosic fibers and filaments manufacturing |
| 313110 | Manmade staple spun yarns made from purchased fiber |
| 541890 | Mannequin decorating services |
| 339999 | Mannequins manufacturing |
| 423440 | Mannequins merchant wholesalers |
| 325920 | Mannitol hexanitrate explosive materials manufacturing |
| 334513 | Manometers, industrial process-type, manufacturing |
| 561320 | Manpower pools |
| 238340 | Mantel, marble or stone, installation |
| 621399 | Manual-arts therapists' offices (e.g., centers, clinics) |
| 423390 | Manufactured (i.e., mobile) homes merchant wholesalers |
| 321991 | Manufactured (mobile) buildings for commercial use (e.g., banks, offices) manufacturing |
| 321991 | Manufactured (mobile) classrooms manufacturing |
| 459930 | Manufactured (mobile) home dealers |
| 531190 | Manufactured (mobile) home parks |
| 238990 | Manufactured (mobile) home set up and tie-down work |
| 531190 | Manufactured (mobile) home sites rental or leasing |
| 321991 | Manufactured (mobile) homes manufacturing |
| 221210 | Manufactured gas distribution |
| 813910 | Manufacturers' associations |
| 236210 | Manufacturing building construction |
| 531120 | Manufacturing building rental or leasing |
| 532490 | Manufacturing machinery and equipment rental or leasing |
| 423830 | Manufacturing machinery and equipment, industrial, merchant wholesalers |
| 541614 | Manufacturing management consulting services |
| 541614 | Manufacturing operations improvement consulting services |
| 513130 | Map publishers |
| 513130 | Map publishers (except exclusive Internet publishing) |
| 513130 | Map publishers and printing combined |
| 513130 | Map publishers, exclusively on Internet |
| 111998 | Maple sap concentrating (i.e., producing pure maple syrup in the field) |
| 111998 | Maple sap gathering |
| 111998 | Maple syrup (i.e., maple sap reducing) |
| 424490 | Maple syrup merchant wholesalers |
| 311999 | Maple syrup mixing into other products |
| 541370 | Mapping (except geophysical) services |
| 541360 | Mapping services, geophysical |
| 424920 | Maps (except globe, school, wall) merchant wholesalers |
| 323111 | Maps commercial printing (except screen) without publishing |
| 323113 | Maps screen printing without publishing |
| 212319 | Marble crushed and broken stone mining and/or beneficiating |
| 212311 | Marble mining or quarrying |
| 238140 | Marble, granite and slate, exterior, contractors |
| 238340 | Marble, granite, and slate, interior installation contractors |
| 339930 | Marbles manufacturing |
| 212390 | Marcasite mining and/or beneficiating |
| 325199 | Margaric acid manufacturing |
| 311221 | Margarine and other corn oils made by wet milling corn |
| 424490 | Margarine merchant wholesalers |
| 311225 | Margarine-butter blend made from purchased fats and oils |
| 311225 | Margarines (including imitation) made from purchased fats and oils |
| 424590 | Marijuana merchant wholesalers |
| 459991 | Marijuana stores, medical or recreational |
| 111998 | Marijuana, grown in an open field |
| 111419 | Marijuana, grown under cover |

| | |
|---|---|
| 713930 | Marinas |
| 335314 | Marine and navy auxiliary controls, manufacturing |
| 713930 | Marine basins, operation of |
| 488390 | Marine cargo checkers and surveyors |
| 488320 | Marine cargo handling services |
| 237990 | Marine construction |
| 928110 | Marine Corps |
| 541330 | Marine engineering services |
| 333618 | Marine engines manufacturing |
| 541990 | Marine forecasting services |
| 332510 | Marine hardware, metal, manufacturing |
| 332999 | Marine horns, compressed air or steam, metal, manufacturing |
| 524126 | Marine insurance carriers, direct |
| 712110 | Marine museums |
| 611519 | Marine navigational schools |
| 325510 | Marine paints manufacturing |
| 332410 | Marine power boilers manufacturing |
| 334220 | Marine radio communications equipment manufacturing |
| 524130 | Marine reinsurance carriers |
| 488330 | Marine salvaging services |
| 457120 | Marine service stations |
| 488510 | Marine shipping agency |
| 335910 | Marine storage batteries manufacturing |
| 423860 | Marine supplies (except pleasure) merchant wholesalers |
| 423910 | Marine supplies, pleasure, merchant wholesalers |
| 441222 | Marine supply dealers |
| 541990 | Marine surveyor (i.e., ship appraiser) services |
| 488330 | Marine vessel traffic reporting services |
| 339999 | Marionettes (i.e., puppets) manufacturing |
| 541330 | Maritime technology engineering services |
| 339940 | Marker boards (i.e., whiteboards) manufacturing |
| 523150 | Market making for securities |
| 541910 | Marketing analysis services |
| 541613 | Marketing consulting services |
| 541613 | Marketing management consulting services |
| 541910 | Marketing research services |
| 339940 | Marking devices manufacturing |

| | |
|---|---|
| 424120 | Marking devices merchant wholesalers |
| 333519 | Marking machines, metal, manufacturing |
| 212312 | Marl crushed and broken stone mining and/or beneficiating |
| 311421 | Marmalade manufacturing |
| 424490 | Marmalade merchant wholesalers |
| 321999 | Marquetry, wood, manufacturing |
| 624190 | Marriage counseling services (except by offices of mental health practitioners) |
| 922120 | Marshals' offices |
| 311340 | Marshmallow creme manufacturing |
| 311340 | Marshmallows manufacturing |
| 611620 | Martial arts instruction, camps or schools |
| 311340 | Marzipan (i.e., candy) manufacturing |
| 335999 | Maser (i.e., microwave amplification by stimulated emission of radiation) amplifiers manufacturing |
| 321999 | Mashers, potato, wood, manufacturing |
| 322220 | Masking tape made from purchased paper |
| 444180 | Masonry (e.g., block, brick, stone) dealers |
| 238140 | Masonry contractors |
| 238140 | Masonry pointing, cleaning or caulking |
| 332216 | Mason's handtools manufacturing |
| 423320 | Mason's materials merchant wholesalers |
| 334516 | Mass spectrometers manufacturing |
| 334516 | Mass spectroscopy instrumentation manufacturing |
| 423850 | Massage equipment merchant wholesalers |
| 335210 | Massage machines, electric (except designed for beauty and barber shop use), manufacturing |
| 611519 | Massage therapist instruction |
| 621399 | Massage therapists' offices (e.g., centers, clinics) |
| 812199 | Massage wellness spas/centers |
| 512250 | Master recording leasing and licensing |
| 424690 | Mastics (except construction) merchant wholesalers |
| 423390 | Mastics, construction, merchant wholesalers |
| 321999 | Masts, wood, manufacturing |
| 812332 | Mat and rug supply services |
| 325998 | Matches and match books manufacturing |

| | |
|---|---|
| 424990 | Matches and match books merchant wholesalers |
| 238290 | Material handling equipment installation |
| 811310 | Material handling equipment repair and maintenance services |
| 423830 | Material handling machinery and equipment merchant wholesalers |
| 532490 | Material handling machinery and equipment rental or leasing |
| 541511 | Material handling robot applications/software design and development services |
| 541614 | Materials management consulting services |
| 562920 | Materials recovery facilities (MRF) |
| 236210 | Materials recovery facility construction |
| 923120 | Maternity and child health program administration |
| 315210 | Maternity bras and corsets cut and sew apparel contractors |
| 315250 | Maternity bras and corsets, women's and girls', cut and sewn from purchased fabric (except apparel contractors) |
| 622310 | Maternity hospitals |
| 458110 | Maternity shops |
| 541715 | Mathematics research and development laboratories or services |
| 332618 | Mats and matting made from purchased wire |
| 332216 | Mattocks (i.e., handtools) manufacturing |
| 326299 | Mattress protectors, rubber, manufacturing |
| 332613 | Mattress springs and spring units, light gauge, made from purchased wire or strip |
| 449110 | Mattress stores (including waterbeds) |
| 337910 | Mattresses (i.e., box spring, innerspring, noninnerspring) manufacturing |
| 337910 | Mattresses made from felt, foam rubber, urethane and similar materials |
| 423210 | Mattresses merchant wholesalers |
| 326199 | Mattresses, air, plastics, manufacturing |
| 326299 | Mattresses, air, rubber, manufacturing |
| 311812 | Matzo baking made in commercial bakeries |
| 332216 | Mauls, metal, manufacturing |
| 321999 | Mauls, wood, manufacturing |
| 236220 | Mausoleum (i.e., building) construction |
| 812220 | Mausoleums |
| 311941 | Mayonnaise manufacturing |

| | |
|---|---|
| 311941 | Mayonnaise, imitation or substitute, manufacturing |
| 921110 | Mayor's offices |
| 321219 | MDF (medium density fiberboard) manufacturing |
| 621112 | MDs' (medical doctors), mental health, offices (e.g., centers, clinics) |
| 621111 | MDs' (medical doctors, except mental health) offices (e.g., centers, clinics) |
| 445298 | Meal assembly retailers |
| 624210 | Meal delivery programs |
| 311119 | Meal, alfalfa, manufacturing |
| 311119 | Meal, bone, prepared as feed for animals and fowls, manufacturing |
| 311211 | Meal, corn, for human consumption made in flour mills |
| 423830 | Measuring and testing equipment (except electric measuring and automotive) merchant wholesalers |
| 333515 | Measuring attachments (e.g., sine bars) for machine tool manufacturing |
| 334515 | Measuring equipment for electronic and electrical circuits and equipment manufacturing |
| 811210 | Measuring instrument repair and maintenance services |
| 334515 | Measuring instruments and meters, electric, manufacturing |
| 334513 | Measuring instruments, industrial process control-type, manufacturing |
| 332216 | Measuring tools, machinist's (except optical), manufacturing |
| 334514 | Measuring wheels manufacturing |
| 311613 | Meat and bone meal and tankage, produced in rendering plant |
| 333241 | Meat and poultry processing and preparation machinery |
| 311612 | Meat canning (except baby food, pet food, poultry), made from purchased carcasses |
| 311611 | Meat canning (except poultry) produced in slaughtering plants |
| 311422 | Meat canning, baby food, manufacturing |
| 311111 | Meat canning, dog and cat, pet food, made from purchased carcasses |
| 311615 | Meat canning, poultry (except baby and pet food), manufacturing |
| 311612 | Meat extracts made from purchased carcasses |
| 333241 | Meat grinders, food-type, manufacturing |
| 445240 | Meat markets |
| 424420 | Meat product substitutes, frozen, merchant wholesalers |

| | |
|---|---|
| 311615 | Meat products (e.g., hot dogs, luncheon meats, sausages) made from a combination of poultry and other meats |
| 311612 | Meat products canning (except baby food, pet food, poultry) made from purchased carcasses |
| 311111 | Meat products, dog and cat, pet food, canning, made from purchased carcasses |
| 424420 | Meat substitutes, frozen, merchant wholesalers |
| 311412 | Meatless patties, frozen, manufacturing |
| 424420 | Meatless patties, frozen, merchant wholesalers |
| 311612 | Meats (except poultry), cured or smoked, made from purchased carcasses |
| 424470 | Meats and meat products (except canned, packaged frozen) merchant wholesalers |
| 311611 | Meats fresh, chilled or frozen (except poultry and small game), produced in slaughtering plants |
| 424490 | Meats, canned, merchant wholesalers |
| 424470 | Meats, cured or smoked, merchant wholesalers |
| 311611 | Meats, cured or smoked, produced in slaughtering plants |
| 311612 | Meats, fresh or chilled (except poultry and small game), frozen, made from purchased carcasses |
| 424470 | Meats, fresh, merchant wholesalers |
| 424470 | Meats, frozen (except packaged), merchant wholesalers |
| 424420 | Meats, packaged frozen, merchant wholesalers |
| 238220 | Mechanical contractors |
| 541330 | Mechanical engineering services |
| 238290 | Mechanical equipment insulation |
| 313310 | Mechanical finishing of fabrics |
| 316110 | Mechanical leather manufacturing |
| 334513 | Mechanical measuring instruments, industrial process-type, manufacturing |
| 339940 | Mechanical pencil refills manufacturing |
| 339940 | Mechanical pencils manufacturing |
| 811310 | Mechanical power transmission equipment repair and maintenance services |
| 423840 | Mechanical power transmission supplies (e.g., gears, pulleys, sprockets) merchant wholesalers |
| 326291 | Mechanical rubber goods (i.e., extruded, lathe-cut, molded) manufacturing |
| 423840 | Mechanical rubber goods merchant wholesalers |
| 541380 | Mechanical testing laboratories or services |
| 611513 | Mechanic's apprenticeship training |
| 333924 | Mechanic's creepers manufacturing |
| 325611 | Mechanic's hand soaps and pastes manufacturing |
| 332216 | Mechanic's handtools, nonpowered, manufacturing |
| 611519 | Mechanic's schools (except apprenticeship) |
| 423120 | Mechanic's tools merchant wholesalers |
| 333310 | Mechanisms for coin- or card-operated machines manufacturing |
| 334519 | Mechanisms, clockwork operated device, manufacturing |
| 423940 | Medallions merchant wholesalers |
| 516210 | Media (e.g., audio, video) streaming distribution services |
| 541840 | Media advertising representatives (i.e., independent of media owners) |
| 541830 | Media buying agencies |
| 541830 | Media buying services |
| 541840 | Media representatives (i.e., independent of media owners) |
| 518210 | Media streaming data storage services |
| 518210 | Media streaming technical support services |
| 926150 | Mediation and conciliation services, government |
| 541990 | Mediation product services (except by lawyer, attorney, paralegal offices, family and social services) |
| 624190 | Mediation, social service, family, agencies |
| 811210 | Medical and surgical equipment repair and maintenance services |
| 541430 | Medical art services |
| 541430 | Medical artists, independent |
| 923130 | Medical assistance programs administration, government |
| 813920 | Medical associations |
| 531120 | Medical building rental or leasing |
| 621999 | Medical care management services |
| 621999 | Medical case management services |
| 334510 | Medical cleaning equipment, ultrasonic, manufacturing |
| 541219 | Medical coding services combined with accounting services (except CPA services) |
| 561499 | Medical coding services, not combined with accounting services |
| 524298 | Medical cost evaluation services |

| | |
|---|---|
| 621112 | Medical doctors' (MDs), mental health, offices (e.g., centers, clinics) |
| 621111 | Medical doctors' (MDs, except mental health) offices (e.g., centers, clinics) |
| 532490 | Medical equipment (except home health furniture and equipment) rental or leasing |
| 456199 | Medical equipment and supplies stores |
| 423450 | Medical equipment merchant wholesalers |
| 423450 | Medical furniture merchant wholesalers |
| 424690 | Medical gases merchant wholesalers |
| 327215 | Medical glassware made from purchased glass |
| 327212 | Medical glassware made in glass making plants |
| 423450 | Medical glassware merchant wholesalers |
| 541430 | Medical illustration services |
| 541430 | Medical illustrators, independent |
| 423450 | Medical instruments merchant wholesalers |
| 524114 | Medical insurance carriers, direct |
| 513120 | Medical journal and periodical publishers |
| 513120 | Medical journal and periodical publishers (except exclusive Internet publishing) |
| 513120 | Medical journal and periodical publishers and printing combined |
| 513120 | Medical journal and periodical publishers, exclusively on Internet |
| 621511 | Medical laboratories (except radiological, X-ray) |
| 621512 | Medical laboratories, radiological or X-ray |
| 541611 | Medical office management consulting services or consultants |
| 561110 | Medical office management services |
| 621511 | Medical pathology laboratories |
| 541922 | Medical photography services |
| 334517 | Medical radiation therapy equipment manufacturing |
| 621512 | Medical radiological laboratories |
| 524130 | Medical reinsurance carriers |
| 541715 | Medical research and development laboratories or services (except biotechnology and nanotechnology research and development) |
| 611310 | Medical schools |
| 315210 | Medical service apparel cut and sew apparel contractors |
| 315250 | Medical service apparel, men's and boys', cut and sewn from purchased fabric (except apparel contractors) |
| 315250 | Medical service apparel, women's and girls', cut and sewn from purchased fabric (except apparel contractors) |
| 524114 | Medical service plans without providing health care services |
| 424210 | Medical sundries, rubber, merchant wholesalers |
| 423450 | Medical supplies (except household first-aid kits and nonsurgical bandages) merchant wholesalers |
| 611519 | Medical technician schools |
| 339112 | Medical thermometers manufacturing |
| 334510 | Medical ultrasound equipment manufacturing |
| 562211 | Medical waste treatment facilities, hazardous |
| 621512 | Medical X-ray laboratories |
| 923130 | Medicare and Medicaid administration |
| 325411 | Medicinal chemicals, uncompounded, manufacturing |
| 325411 | Medicinal gelatins manufacturing |
| 337110 | Medicine cabinets (except freestanding), wood household-type, manufacturing |
| 337126 | Medicine cabinets, metal household-type, manufacturing |
| 321219 | Medium density fiberboard (MDF) manufacturing |
| 212390 | Meerschaum mining and/or beneficiating |
| 531120 | Meeting hall and room rental or leasing |
| 325211 | Melamine resins manufacturing |
| 111219 | Melon farming (e.g., cantaloupe, casaba, honeydew, watermelon), field, bedding plant and seed production |
| 111419 | Melon farming, grown under cover |
| 313230 | Melt blown nonwoven fabrics manufacturing |
| 315210 | Melton jackets cut and sew apparel contractors |
| 315250 | Melton jackets, men's and boys', cut and sewn from purchased fabric (except apparel contractors) |
| 315250 | Melton jackets, women's, girls', and infants', cut and sewn from purchased fabric (except apparel contractors) |
| 813410 | Membership associations, civic or social |
| 721110 | Membership hotels |
| 812220 | Memorial gardens (i.e., burial places) |
| 334418 | Memory boards manufacturing |

423430 Memory boards merchant wholesalers

334413 Memory chip, semiconductor, manufacturing

712130 Menageries

114111 Menhaden fishing

424350 Men's and boys' clothing merchant wholesalers

424350 Men's and boys' furnishings (except shoes) merchant wholesalers

315120 Men's socks knitting or knitting and finishing

622210 Mental (except intellectual and developmental disability) hospitals

621420 Mental health centers and clinics (except hospitals), outpatient

623220 Mental health facilities, residential

623220 Mental health halfway houses

622210 Mental health hospitals

621112 Mental health physicians' offices (e.g., centers, clinics)

923120 Mental health program administration

561450 Mercantile credit reporting bureaus

333248 Mercerizing machinery manufacturing

313310 Mercerizing textile products and fabrics

326111 Merchandise bags, plastics film, single wall or multiwall, manufacturing

423440 Merchandising machines, coin- or card-operated, merchant wholesalers

236117 Merchant builders (i.e., building on own land, for sale), residential

926120 Merchant Marine (except academy)

813910 Merchants' associations

335910 Mercuric oxide batteries manufacturing

212290 Mercury (quicksilver) mining and/or beneficiating

335999 Mercury arc rectifiers (i.e., electrical apparatus) manufacturing

325180 Mercury chloride manufacturing

325180 Mercury compounds, not specified elsewhere by process, manufacturing

325920 Mercury fulminate explosive materials manufacturing

335139 Mercury halide lamp bulbs manufacturing

212290 Mercury ores mining and/or beneficiating

325180 Mercury oxide manufacturing

332618 Mesh made from purchased wire

331420 Mesh, wire, made from purchased copper in wire drawing plants

331318 Mesh, wire, made in aluminum wire drawing plants

331110 Mesh, wire, made in iron and steel mills

331222 Mesh, wire, made in wire drawing mills

331491 Mesh, wire, nonferrous metals (except aluminum, copper), made from purchased nonferrous metals (except aluminum, copper) in wire drawing plants

561421 Message services, telephone answering

492210 Messenger service

325412 Metabolite in-vivo diagnostic substances manufacturing

423390 Metal buildings merchant wholesalers

332431 Metal cans, light gauge metal, manufacturing

333248 Metal casting machinery and equipment manufacturing

333517 Metal cutting machine tools manufacturing

332216 Metal cutting saw blades manufacturing

424690 Metal cyanides merchant wholesalers

333517 Metal deposit forming machines manufacturing

334519 Metal detectors manufacturing

339113 Metal fabric and mesh safety gloves manufacturing

332999 Metal foil containers (except bags) manufacturing

333517 Metal forming machine tools manufacturing

337121 Metal framed furniture, household-type, upholstered, manufacturing

238190 Metal furring contractors

339940 Metal hand stamps manufacturing

333994 Metal melting furnaces, industrial, manufacturing

213114 Metal mining support services on a contract basis (e.g., shaft sinking, tunneling, blasting) (except geophysical surveying and mapping, site preparation, construction, and transportation activities)

336370 Metal motor vehicle body parts stamping

423520 Metal ores merchant wholesalers

334413 Metal oxide silicon (MOS) devices manufacturing

423510 Metal pipe merchant wholesalers

325612 Metal polishes (i.e., tarnish removers) manufacturing

| | |
|---|---|
| 331314 | Metal powder and flake made from purchased aluminum |
| 331420 | Metal powder and flake made from purchased copper |
| 331221 | Metal powder and flake made from purchased iron or steel |
| 331492 | Metal powder and flake nonferrous (except aluminum, copper) made from purchased metal |
| 236210 | Metal processing plant construction |
| 423510 | Metal products (e.g., bars, ingots, plates, rods, shapes, sheets) merchant wholesalers |
| 423930 | Metal scrap and waste merchant wholesalers |
| 238170 | Metal siding installation |
| 332119 | Metal stampings (except automotive, cans, coins), unfinished, manufacturing |
| 335991 | Metal-graphite products manufacturing |
| 423520 | Metallic concentrates merchant wholesalers |
| 325130 | Metallic pigments, inorganic, manufacturing |
| 325199 | Metallic soap manufacturing |
| 313320 | Metallizing purchased textiles |
| 541380 | Metallurgical testing laboratories or services |
| 423510 | Metals sales offices |
| 423510 | Metals service centers |
| 423510 | Metals, ferrous and nonferrous, merchant wholesalers |
| 423940 | Metals, precious, merchant wholesalers |
| 424690 | Metalworking compounds merchant wholesalers |
| 333517 | Metalworking lathes manufacturing |
| 423830 | Metalworking machinery and equipment merchant wholesalers |
| 532490 | Metalworking machinery and equipment rental or leasing |
| 423830 | Metalworking tools (drills, taps, dies, grinding wheels) merchant wholesalers |
| 334519 | Meteorologic tracking systems manufacturing |
| 811210 | Meteorological instrument repair and maintenance services |
| 334519 | Meteorological instruments manufacturing |
| 541990 | Meteorological services |
| 561990 | Meter reading services, contract |
| 334514 | Metering devices (except electrical and industrial process control) manufacturing |

| | |
|---|---|
| 335313 | Metering panels, electric, manufacturing |
| 334514 | Meters (except electrical and industrial process control) manufacturing |
| 423830 | Meters (except electrical, parking) merchant wholesalers |
| 334515 | Meters, electrical (i.e., graphic recording, panelboard, pocket, portable), manufacturing |
| 423610 | Meters, electrical, merchant wholesalers |
| 334513 | Meters, industrial process control-type, manufacturing |
| 334514 | Meters, parking, manufacturing |
| 423850 | Meters, parking, merchant wholesalers |
| 334515 | Meters, power factor and phase angle, manufacturing |
| 325320 | Methoxychlor insecticides manufacturing |
| 325194 | Methyl acetone manufacturing |
| 325211 | Methyl acrylate resins manufacturing |
| 325199 | Methyl alcohol (i.e., methanol), synthetic, manufacturing |
| 325194 | Methyl alcohol (methanol), natural, manufacturing |
| 325211 | Methyl cellulose resins manufacturing |
| 325199 | Methyl chloride manufacturing |
| 325211 | Methyl methacrylate resins manufacturing |
| 325199 | Methyl perhydrofluorine manufacturing |
| 325199 | Methyl salicylate manufacturing |
| 325130 | Methyl violet toners manufacturing |
| 325199 | Methylamine manufacturing |
| 325199 | Methylene chloride manufacturing |
| 311422 | Mexican foods canning |
| 311412 | Mexican foods, frozen, manufacturing |
| 212390 | Mica mining and/or beneficiating |
| 327992 | Mica processing beyond beneficiation |
| 327999 | Mica products manufacturing |
| 212319 | Mica schist crushed and broken stone mining and/or beneficiating |
| 212311 | Mica schist mining or quarrying |
| 311119 | Micro and macro premixes, livestock, manufacturing |
| 334516 | Microbiology instruments manufacturing |
| 325413 | Microbiology, virology, and serology in-vitro diagnostic substances manufacturing |
| 812199 | Microblading tattoo services |
| 312120 | Microbreweries without restaurant or bar |

| | |
|---|---|
| 334111 | Microcomputers manufacturing |
| 334413 | Microcontroller chip manufacturing |
| 333310 | Microfiche equipment (e.g., cameras, projectors, readers) manufacturing |
| 518210 | Microfiche recording and imaging services |
| 333310 | Microfilm equipment (e.g., cameras, projectors, readers) manufacturing |
| 423420 | Microfilm equipment and supplies merchant wholesalers |
| 518210 | Microfilm recording and imaging services |
| 622110 | Micro-hospitals |
| 212290 | Microlite mining and/or beneficiating |
| 333242 | Micro-lithography equipment, semiconductor, manufacturing |
| 332216 | Micrometers, machinist's precision tools, manufacturing |
| 334310 | Microphones (except broadcast and studio equipment) manufacturing |
| 334220 | Microphones, broadcast and studio equipment, manufacturing |
| 334516 | Microprobes (e.g., electron, ion, laser, X-ray) manufacturing |
| 334413 | Microprocessor chip manufacturing |
| 423430 | Microprocessors merchant wholesalers |
| 333310 | Microscopes (except electron, proton) manufacturing |
| 334516 | Microscopes, electron and proton, manufacturing |
| 237990 | Microtunneling contractors |
| 334220 | Microwave communications equipment manufacturing |
| 334419 | Microwave components manufacturing |
| 811412 | Microwave oven, household-type, repair and maintenance services, without retailing new microwave ovens |
| 335220 | Microwave ovens (including portable), household-type, manufacturing |
| 423440 | Microwave ovens, commercial, merchant wholesalers |
| 333310 | Microwave ovens, commercial-type, manufacturing |
| 423620 | Microwave ovens, household-type, merchant wholesalers |
| 237130 | Microwave relay tower construction |
| 517121 | Microwave telecommunication resellers |
| 334515 | Microwave test equipment manufacturing |
| 326199 | Microwaveware, plastics, manufacturing |
| 315210 | Middies cut and sew apparel contractors |
| 315250 | Middies, women's, girls', and infants', cut and sewn from purchased fabric (except apparel contractors) |
| 611110 | Middle schools |
| 621399 | Midwives' offices (e.g., clinics) |
| 721310 | Migrant workers' camps |
| 611310 | Military academies, college-level |
| 611110 | Military academies, elementary or secondary |
| 561210 | Military base support services |
| 928110 | Military bases and camps |
| 315210 | Military dress uniforms cut and sew apparel contractors |
| 315250 | Military dress uniforms, men's and boys', cut and sewn from purchased fabric (except apparel contractors) |
| 315250 | Military dress uniforms, tailored, women's and girls', cut and sewn from purchased fabric (except apparel contractors) |
| 611512 | Military flight instruction training |
| 332999 | Military insignia, metal, manufacturing |
| 314999 | Military insignia, textile, manufacturing |
| 712110 | Military museums |
| 928110 | Military police |
| 928110 | Military reserve armories and bases |
| 611310 | Military service academies (college) |
| 928110 | Military training schools (except academies) |
| 423860 | Military vehicles (except trucks) merchant wholesalers |
| 311511 | Milk based drinks (except dietary) manufacturing |
| 311514 | Milk based drinks, dietary, manufacturing |
| 322130 | Milk carton board made in paperboard mills |
| 322220 | Milk carton board stock made from purchased paperboard |
| 322219 | Milk cartons made from purchased paper or paperboard |
| 311511 | Milk drink, chocolate, manufacturing |
| 484220 | Milk hauling, local |
| 311511 | Milk pasteurizing |
| 311511 | Milk processing (e.g., bottling, homogenizing, pasteurizing, vitaminizing) manufacturing |
| 333241 | Milk processing (except farm-type) machinery manufacturing |
| 112120 | Milk production, dairy cattle |

| | |
|---|---|
| 311511 | Milk substitutes manufacturing |
| 424490 | Milk substitutes merchant wholesalers |
| 115210 | Milk testing for butterfat and milk solids |
| 311511 | Milk, acidophilus, manufacturing |
| 424490 | Milk, canned or dried, merchant wholesalers |
| 311514 | Milk, concentrated, condensed, dried, evaporated, and powdered, manufacturing |
| 311511 | Milk, fluid (except canned), manufacturing |
| 424430 | Milk, fluid (except canned), merchant wholesalers |
| 311514 | Milk, malted, manufacturing |
| 311514 | Milk, powdered, manufacturing |
| 311514 | Milk, ultra high temperature, manufacturing |
| 112120 | Milking dairy cattle |
| 112420 | Milking dairy goat |
| 112410 | Milking dairy sheep |
| 423820 | Milking machinery and equipment merchant wholesalers |
| 333111 | Milking machines manufacturing |
| 311514 | Milkshake mixes manufacturing |
| 314999 | Mill menders, contract, woven fabrics |
| 316990 | Mill strapping for textile mills, leather, manufacturing |
| 423840 | Mill supplies merchant wholesalers |
| 315210 | Millinery cut and sew apparel contractors |
| 315990 | Millinery cut and sewn from purchased fabric (except apparel contractors) |
| 424350 | Millinery merchant wholesalers |
| 424310 | Millinery supplies merchant wholesalers |
| 315210 | Millinery trimmings cut and sew apparel contractors |
| 315990 | Millinery trimmings cut and sewn from purchased fabric (except apparel contractors) |
| 333517 | Milling machines, metalworking, manufacturing |
| 311212 | Milling rice |
| 212390 | Millstones mining and/or beneficiating |
| 238350 | Millwork installation |
| 423310 | Millwork merchant wholesalers |
| 337212 | Millwork, custom architectural, manufacturing |
| 321114 | Millwork, treating |
| 238290 | Millwrights |
| 111199 | Milo farming, field and seed production |
| 711110 | Mime theaters |
| 333922 | Mine conveyors manufacturing |
| 213114 | Mine development (except site preparation and related construction contractor activities) for metal mining on a contract basis |
| 236210 | Mine loading and discharging station construction |
| 321114 | Mine props, treating |
| 562910 | Mine reclamation services, integrated (e.g., demolition, hazardous material removal, soil remediation, revegetation) |
| 213113 | Mine shaft sinking services for coal mining on a contract basis |
| 213114 | Mine shaft sinking services for metal mining on a contract basis |
| 213115 | Mine shaft sinking services for nonmetallic minerals (except fuels) on a contract basis |
| 238910 | Mine site preparation and related construction activities, construction contractors |
| 321114 | Mine ties, wood, treated, manufacturing |
| 213113 | Mine tunneling services for coal mining on a contract basis |
| 213114 | Mine tunneling services for metal mining on a contract basis |
| 213115 | Mine tunneling services for nonmetallic minerals (except fuels) on a contract basis |
| 325130 | Mineral colors and pigments manufacturing |
| 311119 | Mineral feed supplements (except cat, dog) manufacturing |
| 212390 | Mineral pigments, natural, mining and/or beneficiating |
| 333131 | Mineral processing and beneficiating machinery manufacturing |
| 523910 | Mineral royalties or leases dealing (i.e., acting as a principal in dealing royalties or leases to investors) |
| 311119 | Mineral supplements, animal (except cat, dog), manufacturing |
| 424910 | Mineral supplements, animal, merchant wholesalers |
| 238310 | Mineral wool insulation installation |
| 327993 | Mineral wool insulation materials manufacturing |
| 327993 | Mineral wool products (e.g., board, insulation, tile) manufacturing |
| 423520 | Minerals (except construction materials, petroleum) merchant wholesalers |
| 335139 | Miner's lamps manufacturing |

| | |
|---|---|
| 332993 | Mines, ammunition, manufacturing |
| 713990 | Miniature golf courses |
| 337920 | Miniblinds manufacturing |
| 334111 | Minicomputers manufacturing |
| 331110 | Mini-mills, steel |
| 926150 | Minimum wage program administration |
| ****** | Mining -- see type |
| 813910 | Mining associations |
| 333131 | Mining cars manufacturing |
| 423810 | Mining cranes merchant wholesalers |
| 541330 | Mining engineering services |
| 336510 | Mining locomotives and parts manufacturing |
| 423810 | Mining machinery and equipment (except petroleum) merchant wholesalers |
| 532412 | Mining machinery and equipment rental or leasing |
| 811310 | Mining machinery and equipment repair and maintenance services |
| 423830 | Mining machinery and equipment, petroleum, merchant wholesalers |
| 531190 | Mining property leasing |
| 813110 | Ministries, religious |
| 423110 | Minivan merchant wholesalers |
| 336110 | Minivans assembling on chassis of own manufacture |
| 531130 | Miniwarehouse rental or leasing |
| 112930 | Mink production |
| 112511 | Minnow production, farm raising |
| 711211 | Minor league baseball clubs |
| 111998 | Mint farming |
| 238150 | Mirror installation |
| 423220 | Mirrors (except automotive) merchant wholesalers |
| 423120 | Mirrors, automotive, merchant wholesalers |
| 327215 | Mirrors, framed (except automotive) or unframed, made from purchased glass |
| 333310 | Mirrors, optical, manufacturing |
| 237990 | Missile facility construction |
| 332993 | Missile warheads manufacturing |
| 561611 | Missing person tracing services |
| 813110 | Missions, religious organization |
| 332216 | Miter boxes manufacturing |
| 315210 | Mittens (e.g., leather, woven or knit) cut and sew apparel contractors |

| | |
|---|---|
| 315990 | Mittens cut and sewn from purchased fabric (except apparel contractors) |
| 315120 | Mittens, knit, made in apparel knitting mills |
| 315990 | Mittens, leather (except apparel contractors), manufacturing |
| 315990 | Mittens, woven or knit, cut and sewn from purchased fabric (except apparel contractors) |
| 311230 | Mix grain breakfast manufacturing |
| 311514 | Mix, ice cream, manufacturing |
| 312140 | Mixed drinks, alcoholic, manufacturing |
| 111940 | Mixed hay farming |
| 711219 | Mixed martial artists, independent professional |
| 485111 | Mixed mode transit systems (e.g., bus, commuter rail, subway combinations) |
| 333120 | Mixers, concrete, portable, manufacturing |
| 423810 | Mixers, construction and mining, merchant wholesalers |
| 424490 | Mixes (e.g., cake, dessert, pie) merchant wholesalers |
| 311211 | Mixes, flour (e.g., biscuit, cake, doughnut, pancake) made in flour mills |
| 311824 | Mixes, flour (e.g., biscuit, cake, doughnut, pancake), made from purchased flour |
| 325314 | Mixing purchased fertilizer materials |
| 531190 | Mobile (manufactured) home parks |
| 531110 | Mobile (manufactured) home rental or leasing, on-site |
| 531190 | Mobile (manufactured) home sites rental or leasing |
| 513210 | Mobile applications development and publishing, except on a custom basis |
| 811111 | Mobile automotive and truck repair services |
| 621512 | Mobile breast imaging centers |
| 811192 | Mobile car and truck washes |
| 334220 | Mobile communications equipment manufacturing |
| 311119 | Mobile feed mill |
| 722330 | Mobile food stands |
| 459930 | Mobile home dealers, manufactured |
| 532120 | Mobile home rental, off-site |
| 484220 | Mobile home towing services, local |
| 484230 | Mobile home towing services, long-distance |
| 321991 | Mobile homes manufacturing |
| 712110 | Mobile museums |

| | |
|---|---|
| 532490 | Mobile office building rental or leasing, off-site |
| 531120 | Mobile office building rental or leasing, on-site |
| 517122 | Mobile phone stores, selling mobile phone service plans on an agent basis |
| 624210 | Mobile soup kitchens |
| 333924 | Mobile straddle carriers manufacturing |
| 517112 | Mobile telephone communication carriers (except satellite) |
| 517121 | Mobile virtual network operators (MVNOs) (except agents) |
| 621512 | Mobile X-ray facilities (medical) |
| 316210 | Moccasins manufacturing |
| 325220 | Modacrylic fibers and filaments manufacturing |
| 313110 | Modacrylic spun yarns made from purchased fiber |
| 339930 | Model kits manufacturing |
| 423920 | Model kits merchant wholesalers |
| 339930 | Model railroad manufacturing |
| 561311 | Model registries |
| 561320 | Model supply services |
| 711410 | Modeling agents |
| 339940 | Modeling clay manufacturing |
| 611519 | Modeling schools |
| 711410 | Models' agents or managers |
| 339999 | Models, anatomical, manufacturing |
| 711510 | Models, independent |
| 339930 | Models, toy and hobby (e.g., airplane, boat, ship), manufacturing |
| 423690 | Modems merchant wholesalers |
| 334210 | Modems, carrier equipment, manufacturing |
| 711120 | Modern dance companies |
| 532490 | Modular building rental or leasing, off-site |
| 238390 | Modular furniture system attachment and installation |
| 337214 | Modular furniture systems (except wood frame), office-type, manufacturing |
| 337211 | Modular furniture systems, wood frame office-type, manufacturing |
| 236117 | Modular housing, residential, assembled on site by for-sale builders |
| 236115 | Modular single-family housing assembled on site by general contractors |
| 334519 | Modules for clocks and watches manufacturing |
| 112420 | Mohair farming |
| 313110 | Mohair yarn twisting or winding of purchased yarn |
| 424590 | Mohair, raw, merchant wholesalers |
| 334516 | Moisture analyzers, laboratory-type, manufacturing |
| 334513 | Moisture meters, industrial process-type, manufacturing |
| 311313 | Molasses made from sugar beets |
| 311314 | Molasses manufacturing |
| 424490 | Molasses merchant wholesalers |
| 311314 | Molasses, blackstrap, manufacturing |
| 562910 | Mold remediation services |
| 339991 | Molded packings and seals manufacturing |
| 322299 | Molded pulp products (e.g., egg cartons, food containers, food trays) manufacturing |
| 423310 | Molding (e.g., sheet metal, wood) merchant wholesalers |
| 332321 | Molding and trim (except motor vehicle), metal, manufacturing |
| 238350 | Molding or trim, wood or plastic, installation |
| 212322 | Molding sand quarrying and/or beneficiating |
| 336370 | Moldings and trim, motor vehicle, stamping |
| 321918 | Moldings, clear and finger joint wood, manufacturing |
| 321918 | Moldings, wood and covered wood, manufacturing |
| 333511 | Molds (except steel ingot), industrial, manufacturing |
| 331511 | Molds for casting steel ingots manufacturing |
| 333511 | Molds for forming materials (e.g., glass, plastics, rubber) manufacturing |
| 333511 | Molds for metal casting (except steel ingot) manufacturing |
| 333511 | Molds for plastics and rubber working machinery manufacturing |
| 331511 | Molds, steel ingot, industrial, manufacturing |
| 112512 | Mollusk production, farm raising |
| 212290 | Molybdenite mining and/or beneficiating |
| 331491 | Molybdenum and molybdenum alloy bar, plate, pipe, rod, sheet, tubing, and wire made from purchased metals or scrap |
| 212290 | Molybdenum ores mining and/or beneficiating |
| 331491 | Molybdenum rolling, drawing, or extruding purchased metals or scrap |

| | |
|---|---|
| 331110 | Molybdenum silicon ferroalloys manufacturing |
| 212290 | Molybdite mining and/or beneficiating |
| 813110 | Monasteries (except schools) |
| 212290 | Monazite mining and/or beneficiating |
| 521110 | Monetary authorities, central bank |
| 332999 | Money chests, metal, manufacturing |
| 525990 | Money market mutual funds, closed-end |
| 525910 | Money market mutual funds, open-ended |
| 522390 | Money order issuance services |
| 522390 | Money transmission services |
| 423430 | Monitor screen projection devices merchant wholesalers |
| 334118 | Monitors, computer peripheral equipment, manufacturing |
| 423430 | Monitors, computer, merchant wholesalers |
| 325120 | Monochlorodifluoromethane manufacturing |
| 334516 | Monochrometers, laboratory-type, manufacturing |
| 334413 | Monolithic integrated circuits (solid-state) manufacturing |
| 325199 | Monomethylparaminophenol sulfate manufacturing |
| 237990 | Monorail construction |
| 333923 | Monorail systems (except passenger-type) manufacturing |
| 485119 | Monorail transit systems (except mixed mode), commuter |
| 487110 | Monorail, scenic and sightseeing, operation |
| 325199 | Monosodium glutamate manufacturing |
| 611110 | Montessori schools, elementary or secondary |
| 236220 | Monument (i.e., building) construction |
| 459999 | Monument (i.e., burial marker) dealers |
| 423990 | Monuments and grave markers merchant wholesalers |
| 327991 | Monuments and tombstones, cut stone, manufacturing |
| 333310 | Mop wringers manufacturing |
| 441227 | Moped dealers |
| 423110 | Moped merchant wholesalers |
| 532284 | Moped rental |
| 336991 | Mopeds and parts manufacturing |
| 339994 | Mops, floor and dust, manufacturing |
| 423220 | Mops, household, merchant wholesalers |
| 423850 | Mops, industrial, merchant wholesalers |

| | |
|---|---|
| 325130 | Mordant dyes manufacturing |
| 325613 | Mordants manufacturing |
| 325411 | Morphine and derivatives (i.e., basic chemicals) manufacturing |
| 522180 | Morris Plans (i.e., known as), depository |
| 522299 | Morris Plans (i.e., known as), nondepository |
| 333120 | Mortar mixers, portable, manufacturing |
| 332993 | Mortar shells manufacturing |
| 327120 | Mortar, nonclay refractory, manufacturing |
| 332994 | Mortars manufacturing |
| 327120 | Mortars, clay refractory, manufacturing |
| 522292 | Mortgage banking (i.e., nondepository mortgage lending) |
| 522310 | Mortgage brokerages |
| 522310 | Mortgage brokers' or agents' offices (i.e., independent) |
| 522292 | Mortgage companies |
| 523910 | Mortgage dealers, buying and selling |
| 524126 | Mortgage guaranty insurance carriers, direct |
| 525990 | Mortgage real estate investment trusts (REITs) |
| 525990 | Mortgage-backed securities |
| 812210 | Mortician services |
| 333243 | Mortisers, woodworking-type, manufacturing |
| 812210 | Mortuaries |
| 334413 | MOS (metal oxide silicon) devices manufacturing |
| 327120 | Mosaic tile, ceramic, manufacturing |
| 238340 | Mosaic work |
| 813110 | Mosques, religious |
| 926130 | Mosquito eradication districts |
| 561710 | Mosquito eradication services |
| 113210 | Moss gathering |
| 531120 | Motel building rental or leasing, not operating motel |
| 236220 | Motel construction |
| 561110 | Motel management services (except complete operation of client's business) |
| 721110 | Motels |
| 325320 | Moth repellents manufacturing |
| 423430 | Motherboards, loaded, merchant wholesalers |
| 334290 | Motion alarms (e.g., swimming pool, perimeter) manufacturing |

| | |
|---|---|
| 334290 | Motion detectors, security system, manufacturing |
| 512110 | Motion picture and video production |
| 512110 | Motion picture and video production and distribution |
| 512191 | Motion picture animation, postproduction |
| 512199 | Motion picture booking agencies |
| 333310 | Motion picture cameras manufacturing |
| 423410 | Motion picture cameras, equipment, and supplies merchant wholesalers |
| 541690 | Motion picture consulting services |
| 711510 | Motion picture directors, independent |
| 512120 | Motion picture distribution exclusive of production |
| 532490 | Motion picture equipment rental or leasing |
| 512131 | Motion picture exhibition |
| 512131 | Motion picture exhibitors for airlines |
| 512131 | Motion picture exhibitors, itinerant |
| 512120 | Motion picture film distributors |
| 512199 | Motion picture film laboratories |
| 519210 | Motion picture film libraries, archives |
| 512120 | Motion picture film libraries, commercial distribution |
| 512199 | Motion picture film libraries, stock footage |
| 325992 | Motion picture film manufacturing |
| 512199 | Motion picture film reproduction for theatrical distribution |
| 512199 | Motion picture laboratories |
| 512191 | Motion picture or video editing services |
| 512191 | Motion picture or video postproduction services |
| 512191 | Motion picture or video titling |
| 711510 | Motion picture producers, independent |
| 512110 | Motion picture production |
| 512110 | Motion picture production and distribution |
| 512110 | Motion picture production payroll agents |
| 541214 | Motion picture production payroll services |
| 512191 | Motion picture production special effects, postproduction |
| 512110 | Motion picture studios, producing motion pictures |
| 333310 | Motion picture theater projectors manufacturing |
| 512132 | Motion picture theaters, drive-in |
| 512131 | Motion picture theaters, indoor |
| 532281 | Motion picture wardrobe and costume rental |
| 711510 | Motivational speakers, independent |
| 926120 | Motor carrier licensing and inspection offices |
| 485210 | Motor coach operation, interurban and rural |
| 335314 | Motor control accessories (including overload relays) manufacturing |
| 335314 | Motor control centers, manufacturing |
| 335314 | Motor controls, electric, manufacturing |
| 423610 | Motor controls, electric, merchant wholesalers |
| 721110 | Motor courts |
| 484110 | Motor freight carrier, general, local |
| 484122 | Motor freight carrier, general, long-distance, less-than-truckload (LTL) |
| 484121 | Motor freight carrier, general, long-distance, truckload (TL) |
| 484210 | Motor freight carrier, used household goods |
| 335312 | Motor generator sets (except automotive, turbine generator sets) manufacturing |
| 333611 | Motor generator sets, turbo generators, manufacturing |
| 441210 | Motor home dealers |
| 423110 | Motor home merchant wholesalers |
| 532120 | Motor home rental, off-site |
| 336213 | Motor homes, self-contained, assembling on purchased chassis |
| 336120 | Motor homes, self-contained, mounted on heavy truck chassis of own manufacture |
| 336110 | Motor homes, self-contained, mounted on light duty truck chassis of own manufacture |
| 721110 | Motor hotels without casinos |
| 721110 | Motor inns |
| 721110 | Motor lodges |
| 324191 | Motor oils, petroleum, made from refined petroleum |
| 325998 | Motor oils, synthetic, manufacturing |
| 811310 | Motor repair and maintenance services, commercial or industrial |
| 441227 | Motor scooters dealers |
| 336991 | Motor scooters manufacturing |
| 335314 | Motor starters, contactors, and controllers, industrial, manufacturing |
| 561599 | Motor travel clubs |

| | |
|---|---|
| 333998 | Motor truck scales manufacturing |
| 236210 | Motor vehicle assembly plant construction |
| 326220 | Motor vehicle belts, rubber or plastics, manufacturing |
| 238290 | Motor vehicle garage and service station mechanical equipment (e.g., gasoline pumps, hoists) installation |
| 332510 | Motor vehicle hardware, metal, manufacturing |
| 326220 | Motor vehicle hoses, rubber or plastics, manufacturing |
| 334514 | Motor vehicle instruments (e.g., fuel level gauges, oil pressure, speedometers, tachometers, water temperature) manufacturing |
| 423120 | Motor vehicle instruments, electric, merchant wholesalers |
| 336360 | Motor vehicle interior systems (e.g., headliners, panels, seats, trims) manufacturing |
| 561990 | Motor vehicle license issuing services, private franchise |
| 926120 | Motor vehicle licensing offices, government |
| 423110 | Motor vehicle merchant wholesalers |
| 336370 | Motor vehicle metal bumper stampings |
| 336370 | Motor vehicle metal parts stamping |
| 336370 | Motor vehicle metal stampings (e.g., body parts, fenders, hub caps, tops, trim) manufacturing |
| 326199 | Motor vehicle moldings and extrusions, plastics, manufacturing |
| 325510 | Motor vehicle paints manufacturing |
| 423120 | Motor vehicle parts and accessories, new, merchant wholesalers |
| 423140 | Motor vehicle parts, used, merchant wholesalers |
| 336360 | Motor vehicle seats manufacturing |
| 336360 | Motor vehicle seats, metal framed, manufacturing |
| 423130 | Motor vehicle tire and tube merchant wholesalers |
| 326211 | Motor vehicle tires manufacturing |
| 488410 | Motor vehicle towing services |
| 336360 | Motor vehicle trimmings manufacturing |
| 441227 | Motorbike dealers |
| 811490 | Motorboat (i.e., inboard and outboard) repair and maintenance services |
| 336612 | Motorboat, inboard or outboard, building |
| 441227 | Motorcycle dealers |
| 611692 | Motorcycle driving schools |
| 423110 | Motorcycle merchant wholesalers |
| 441227 | Motorcycle parts and accessories dealers |
| 423120 | Motorcycle parts, new, merchant wholesalers |
| 711212 | Motorcycle racetracks |
| 711219 | Motorcycle racing teams |
| 532284 | Motorcycle rental |
| 811490 | Motorcycle repair shops without retailing new motorcycles |
| 336991 | Motorcycles and parts manufacturing |
| 423860 | Motorized passenger golf carts merchant wholesalers |
| 335312 | Motors, electric (except engine starting motors, gearmotors, outboard), manufacturing |
| 423610 | Motors, electric, merchant wholesalers |
| 333996 | Motors, fluid power, manufacturing |
| 333612 | Motors, gear, manufacturing |
| 333618 | Motors, outboard, manufacturing |
| 423910 | Motors, outboard, merchant wholesalers |
| 336320 | Motors, starter, for internal combustion engines, manufacturing |
| 713990 | Mountain hiking, recreational |
| 561910 | Mounting merchandise on cards |
| 334118 | Mouse devices, computer peripheral equipment, manufacturing |
| 213112 | Mouse hole and rat hole drilling at oil and gas fields on a contract basis |
| 339116 | Mouth guards and protectors, custom made in dental laboratories |
| 339992 | Mouthpieces for musical instruments manufacturing |
| 325620 | Mouthwashes (except medicinal) manufacturing |
| 325412 | Mouthwashes, medicated, manufacturing |
| 334519 | Movements, watch or clock, manufacturing |
| 423620 | Movie apparatus, home, merchant wholesalers |
| 512110 | Movie production and distribution |
| 512131 | Movie theaters (except drive-in) |
| 512132 | Movie theaters, drive-in |
| 238290 | Moving sidewalk installation |
| 561730 | Mowing services (e.g., highway, lawn, road strip) |
| 562920 | MRF (materials recovery facilities) |
| 621512 | MRI (magnetic resonance imaging) centers |

| | |
|---|---|
| 334510 | MRI (magnetic resonance imaging) medical diagnostic equipment manufacturing |
| 325520 | Mucilage adhesives manufacturing |
| 213112 | Mud service for oil field drilling on a contract basis |
| 238110 | Mud-jacking contractors |
| 811114 | Muffler repair and replacement shops |
| 336390 | Mufflers and resonators, automotive, truck, and buses manufacturing |
| 315210 | Mufflers cut and sew apparel contractors |
| 315990 | Mufflers cut and sewn from purchased fabric (except apparel contractors) |
| 315120 | Mufflers made in apparel knitting mills |
| 423120 | Mufflers, exhaust, merchant wholesalers |
| 424910 | Mulch merchant wholesalers |
| 333112 | Mulchers, lawn and garden-type, manufacturing |
| 112920 | Mule production |
| 424590 | Mules merchant wholesalers |
| 114111 | Mullet fishing |
| 517111 | Multichannel multipoint distribution services (MMDS) |
| 712110 | Multidisciplinary museums |
| 236116 | Multifamily building construction general contractors |
| 236117 | Multifamily building for-sale builders |
| 334515 | Multimeters manufacturing |
| 334210 | Multiplex equipment, telephone, manufacturing |
| 624190 | Multiservice centers, neighborhood |
| 212390 | Muriate of potash, mining |
| 325412 | Muscle relaxant preparations manufacturing |
| 212390 | Muscovite mining and/or beneficiating |
| 561990 | Museum cataloging services |
| 236220 | Museum construction |
| 238390 | Museum exhibit installation and dismantling contractors |
| 712110 | Museums |
| 111411 | Mushroom farming |
| 111411 | Mushroom spawn farming |
| 311421 | Mushrooms canning |
| 519210 | Music archives |
| 711510 | Music arrangers, independent |
| 512230 | Music book (i.e., bound sheet music) publishers |
| 512230 | Music book (i.e., bound sheet music) publishers and printing combined |

| | |
|---|---|
| 323117 | Music books printing or printing and binding without publishing |
| 339999 | Music boxes manufacturing |
| 512230 | Music copyright authorizing use |
| 512230 | Music copyright buying and licensing |
| 711510 | Music directors, independent |
| 711310 | Music festival managers with facilities |
| 711320 | Music festival managers without facilities |
| 711310 | Music festival organizers with facilities |
| 711320 | Music festival organizers without facilities |
| 711310 | Music festival promoters with facilities |
| 711320 | Music festival promoters without facilities |
| 611610 | Music instruction (e.g., guitar, piano) |
| 516110 | Music program distribution, broadcasting stations (except exclusively on Internet), radio |
| 512230 | Music publishers |
| 449210 | Music retailers (e.g., downloadable digital music files (without production or publishing)) |
| 339992 | Music rolls, perforated, manufacturing |
| 611610 | Music schools (except academic) |
| 449210 | Music stores (e.g., cassette, compact disc, record, tape) |
| 459510 | Music stores (e.g., cassette, instrument, record, tape), used |
| 459140 | Music stores (i.e., instrument) |
| 621340 | Music therapists' offices (e.g., centers, clinics) |
| 512110 | Music video production |
| 512110 | Music video production and distribution |
| 323111 | Music, sheet, commercial printing (except screen) without publishing |
| 424990 | Music, sheet, merchant wholesalers |
| 512230 | Music, sheet, publishers and printing combined |
| 323113 | Music, sheet, screen printing without publishing |
| 711130 | Musical artists, independent |
| 711130 | Musical groups (except musical theater groups) |
| 339992 | Musical instrument accessories (e.g., mouthpieces, reeds, stands, traps) manufacturing |
| 423990 | Musical instrument accessories and supplies merchant wholesalers |
| 316990 | Musical instrument cases, all materials, manufacturing |

| | |
|---|---|
| 532289 | Musical instrument rental |
| 811490 | Musical instrument repair shops without retailing new musical instruments |
| 459140 | Musical instrument stores |
| 339992 | Musical instruments (except toy) manufacturing |
| 423990 | Musical instruments merchant wholesalers |
| 339930 | Musical instruments, toy, manufacturing |
| 711130 | Musical productions (except musical theater productions), live |
| 512250 | Musical recording, releasing, promoting, and distributing |
| 423990 | Musical recordings (e.g., compact discs, records, tapes) merchant wholesalers |
| 711110 | Musical theater companies or groups |
| 711110 | Musical theater productions, live |
| 711130 | Musicians, independent |
| 111219 | Muskmelon farming, field, bedding plant and seed production |
| 114112 | Mussel fishing |
| 112512 | Mussel production, farm raising |
| 111120 | Mustard seed farming, field and seed production |
| 311941 | Mustard, prepared, manufacturing |
| 523150 | Mutual fund agencies (i.e., brokerages) |
| 523150 | Mutual fund agents' (i.e., brokers') offices |
| 523940 | Mutual fund managing |
| 525990 | Mutual funds, closed-end |
| 525910 | Mutual funds, open-ended |
| 522180 | Mutual savings banks |
| 621511 | Mycology health laboratories |
| 325194 | Myrobalans extract manufacturing |
| 333991 | Nail guns, handheld power-driven, manufacturing |
| 333517 | Nail heading machines manufacturing |
| 325620 | Nail polish remover manufacturing |
| 325620 | Nail polishes manufacturing |
| 812113 | Nail salons |
| 333991 | Nailers and staplers, handheld power-driven, manufacturing |
| 423510 | Nails merchant wholesalers |
| 331318 | Nails, aluminum, made in wire drawing plants |
| 332618 | Nails, brads, and staples made from purchased wire |
| 331222 | Nails, iron or steel, made in wire drawing plants |
| 331491 | Nails, nonferrous metals (except aluminum, copper), made from purchased nonferrous metals (except aluminum, copper) in wire drawing plants |
| 332999 | Name plate blanks, metal, manufacturing |
| 541713 | Nanobiotechnologies research and experimental development laboratories |
| 334513 | Nanofluidic measurement and control devices manufacturing |
| 333242 | Nanoindentation equipment, semiconductor, manufacturing |
| 334516 | Nanomanipulator equipment manufacturing |
| 334516 | Nanosensor instruments manufacturing |
| 541713 | Nanotechnology research and development laboratories or services, all fields of science |
| 325998 | Napalm manufacturing |
| 325194 | Naphtha made by distillation of coal tar |
| 324110 | Naphtha made in petroleum refineries |
| 325194 | Naphtha, solvent, made by distillation of coal tar |
| 325194 | Naphthalene made from refined petroleum or natural gas |
| 325194 | Naphthalenesulfonic acid manufacturing |
| 325199 | Naphthenic acid soaps manufacturing |
| 325194 | Naphthenic acids made from refined petroleum or natural gas |
| 324110 | Naphthenic acids made in petroleum refineries |
| 325194 | Naphthol sulfonic acids manufacturing |
| 325194 | Naphthol, alpha and beta, manufacturing |
| 423220 | Napkins (except paper) merchant wholesalers |
| 314120 | Napkins made from purchased fabrics |
| 424130 | Napkins, paper, merchant wholesalers |
| 322291 | Napkins, table, made from purchased paper |
| 322120 | Napkins, table, made in paper mills |
| 333248 | Napping machinery for textiles manufacturing |
| 313310 | Napping textile products and fabrics |
| 313220 | Narrow fabrics weaving |
| 927110 | National Aeronautics and Space Administration |
| 522110 | National commercial banks |
| 522299 | National Credit Union Administration (NCUA) |
| 928110 | National Guard |

| | |
|---|---|
| 712190 | National parks |
| 926120 | National Transportation Safety Board |
| 311422 | Nationality specialty foods canning, bottling, and jarring |
| 311412 | Nationality specialty foods, frozen, manufacturing |
| 212390 | Native asphalt mining and/or beneficiating |
| 327310 | Natural (i.e., calcined earth) cement manufacturing |
| 212390 | Natural abrasives (e.g., emery, grindstones, hones, pumice) (except sand) mining and/or beneficiating |
| 313110 | Natural fiber (i.e., hemp, linen, ramie) thread manufacturing |
| 313210 | Natural fiber fabrics (i.e., jute, linen, hemp, ramie), broadwoven, weaving |
| 313220 | Natural fiber fabrics (i.e., jute, linen, hemp, ramie), narrow woven, weaving |
| 313110 | Natural fiber spun yarns (i.e., hemp, jute, ramie, flax) made from purchased fiber |
| 221210 | Natural gas brokers |
| 423690 | Natural gas detectors, electronic, merchant wholesalers |
| 221210 | Natural gas distribution systems |
| 221210 | Natural gas distribution with transmission |
| 333618 | Natural gas engines manufacturing |
| 211130 | Natural gas liquid lease condensate production |
| 211130 | Natural gas liquids (e.g., ethane, isobutane, natural gasoline, propane) recovered from oil and gas field gases |
| 486910 | Natural gas liquids pipeline transportation |
| 221210 | Natural gas marketers |
| 237120 | Natural gas pipeline construction |
| 486210 | Natural gas pipeline transportation |
| 238220 | Natural gas piping installation |
| 237120 | Natural gas processing plant construction |
| 211130 | Natural gas production |
| 486210 | Natural gas transmission (i.e., processing plants to local distribution systems) |
| 211130 | Natural gas, offshore production |
| 211130 | Natural gasoline recovered from oil and gas field gases |
| 712110 | Natural history museums |
| 325199 | Natural nonfood coloring manufacturing |
| 813312 | Natural resource preservation organizations |
| 712110 | Natural science museums |
| 712190 | Natural wonder tourist attractions (e.g., caverns, waterfalls) |
| 312112 | Naturally carbonated water, purifying and bottling |
| 712190 | Nature centers |
| 712190 | Nature parks |
| 712190 | Nature preserves |
| 712190 | Nature reserves |
| 621399 | Naturopaths' offices (e.g., centers, clinics) |
| 334511 | Nautical systems and instruments manufacturing |
| 332994 | Naval artillery manufacturing |
| 336611 | Naval ship building |
| 325194 | Naval stores, gum or wood, manufacturing |
| 811210 | Navigational instruments (e.g., radar, sonar) repair and maintenance services |
| 423860 | Navigational instruments (except electronic) merchant wholesalers |
| 334511 | Navigational instruments manufacturing |
| 423690 | Navigational instruments, electronic (e.g., radar, sonar), merchant wholesalers |
| 928110 | Navy |
| 312120 | Near beer brewing |
| 311613 | Neatsfoot oil rendering |
| 315250 | Neckpieces, fur (except apparel contractors), manufacturing |
| 315210 | Neckpieces, fur, cut and sew apparel contractors |
| 315210 | Neckties cut and sew apparel contractors |
| 315990 | Neckties cut and sewn from purchased fabric (except apparel contractors) |
| 315120 | Neckties made in apparel knitting mills |
| 424350 | Neckties, men's and boys', merchant wholesalers |
| 315210 | Neckwear cut and sew apparel contractors |
| 315990 | Neckwear cut and sewn from purchased fabric (except apparel contractors) |
| 315120 | Neckwear made in apparel knitting mills |
| 458110 | Neckwear stores |
| 111339 | Nectarine farming |
| 332991 | Needle roller bearings manufacturing |
| 459130 | Needlecraft sewing supply stores |

| | |
|---|---|
| 339993 | Needles (except hypodermic, phonograph, styli) manufacturing |
| 333248 | Needles for knitting machinery manufacturing |
| 339112 | Needles, hypodermic and suture, manufacturing |
| 334419 | Needles, phonograph and styli, manufacturing |
| 424310 | Needles, sewing, merchant wholesalers |
| 314999 | Needlework art contractors on apparel |
| 315210 | Negligees cut and sew apparel contractors |
| 315120 | Negligees made in apparel knitting mills |
| 315250 | Negligees, women's and girls', cut and sewn from purchased fabric (except apparel contractors) |
| 813319 | Neighborhood development advocacy organizations |
| 325120 | Neon manufacturing |
| 339950 | Neon signs manufacturing |
| 325212 | Neoprene manufacturing |
| 212323 | Nepheline syenite mining and/or beneficiating |
| 334516 | Nephelometers (except meteorological) manufacturing |
| 334519 | Nephoscopes manufacturing |
| 621111 | Nephrologists' offices (e.g., centers, clinics) |
| 333248 | Net and lace making machinery manufacturing |
| 424310 | Net goods merchant wholesalers |
| 313210 | Nets and nettings, more than 12 inches in width, weaving |
| 313240 | Netting made in warp or weft knitting mills |
| 313240 | Netting made on a lace or net machine |
| 326199 | Netting, plastics, manufacturing |
| 332618 | Netting, woven, made from purchased wire |
| 516210 | Network broadcasting service, radio |
| 516210 | Network radio broadcasting |
| 541512 | Network systems integration design services, computer |
| 516210 | Network television broadcasting |
| 516210 | Networks, cable television |
| 622310 | Neurological hospitals |
| 621111 | Neurologists' offices (e.g., centers, clinics) |
| 621111 | Neuropathologists' offices (e.g., centers, clinics) |
| 312140 | Neutral spirit, beverages (except fruit), manufacturing |
| 424820 | Neutral spirits merchant wholesalers |
| 334516 | Neutron activation analysis instruments manufacturing |
| 441110 | New car dealers |
| 541613 | New product development consulting services |
| 321918 | Newel posts, wood, manufacturing |
| 519290 | News clipping services |
| 711510 | News correspondents, independent (freelance) |
| 459210 | News dealers |
| 516210 | News picture gathering and distributing services |
| 516210 | News reporting services |
| 516210 | News service syndicates |
| 516210 | News ticker services |
| 513120 | Newsletter publishers |
| 513120 | Newsletter publishers (except exclusive Internet publishing) |
| 513120 | Newsletter publishers and printing combined |
| 513120 | Newsletter publishers, exclusively on Internet |
| 323111 | Newsletters commercial printing (except screen) without publishing |
| 323113 | Newsletters screen printing without publishing |
| 541840 | Newspaper advertising representatives (i.e., independent of media owners) |
| 424920 | Newspaper agencies merchant wholesalers |
| 513110 | Newspaper branch offices |
| 711510 | Newspaper columnists, independent (freelance) |
| 516210 | Newspaper feature syndicates |
| 333248 | Newspaper inserting equipment manufacturing |
| 513110 | Newspaper publishers |
| 513110 | Newspaper publishers (except exclusive Internet publishing) |
| 513110 | Newspaper publishers and printing combined |
| 513110 | Newspaper publishing, exclusively on Internet |
| 323111 | Newspapers commercial printing (except screen) without publishing |
| 424920 | Newspapers merchant wholesalers |
| 323113 | Newspapers screen printing without publishing |
| 424110 | Newsprint merchant wholesalers |

| | |
|---|---|
| 322120 | Newsprint mills |
| 322120 | Newsprint paper, manufacturing |
| 459210 | Newsstands (i.e., permanent) |
| 339940 | Nibs (i.e., pen points) manufacturing |
| 331523 | Nickel alloy die-castings, unfinished, manufacturing |
| 325180 | Nickel ammonium sulfate manufacturing |
| 331491 | Nickel and nickel alloy pipe, plate, sheet, strip, and tubing made from purchased metals or scrap |
| 423510 | Nickel and nickel alloy primary forms merchant wholesalers |
| 325180 | Nickel carbonate manufacturing |
| 331529 | Nickel castings (except die-castings), unfinished, manufacturing |
| 325180 | Nickel compounds, not specified elsewhere by process, manufacturing |
| 212230 | Nickel concentrates recovery |
| 331523 | Nickel die-castings, unfinished, manufacturing |
| 332999 | Nickel foil not made in rolling mills |
| 212230 | Nickel ore beneficiating plants |
| 212230 | Nickel ore mine site development for own account |
| 212230 | Nickel ores mining and/or beneficiating |
| 331492 | Nickel recovering from scrap and/or alloying purchased metals |
| 331410 | Nickel refining, primary |
| 331491 | Nickel rolling, drawing, or extruding purchased metals or scrap |
| 325180 | Nickel sulfate manufacturing |
| 335910 | Nickel-cadmium storage batteries manufacturing |
| 325411 | Nicotine and derivatives (i.e., basic chemicals) manufacturing |
| 325320 | Nicotine insecticides manufacturing |
| 337122 | Night stands, wood, manufacturing |
| 333310 | Night vision optical devices manufacturing |
| 713990 | Nightclubs without alcoholic beverages |
| 722410 | Nightclubs, alcoholic beverage |
| 315210 | Nightgowns cut and sew apparel contractors |
| 315120 | Nightgowns made in apparel knitting mills |
| 315250 | Nightgowns, men's and boys', cut and sewn from purchased fabric (except apparel contractors) |
| 315250 | Nightgowns, women's, girls', and infants', cut and sewn from purchased fabric (except apparel contractors) |
| 315210 | Nightshirts cut and sew apparel contractors |
| 315120 | Nightshirts made in apparel knitting mills |
| 315250 | Nightshirts, men's and boys', cut and sewn from purchased fabric (except apparel contractors) |
| 315250 | Nightshirts, women's, girls', and infants', cut and sewn from purchased fabric (except contractors) |
| 315210 | Nightwear cut and sew apparel contractors |
| 315120 | Nightwear made in apparel knitting mills |
| 315250 | Nightwear, men's and boys', cut and sewn from purchased fabric (except apparel contractors) |
| 424350 | Nightwear, men's and boys', merchant wholesalers |
| 424350 | Nightwear, women's, children's, and infants', merchant wholesalers |
| 315250 | Nightwear, women's, girls', and infants', cut and sewn from purchased fabric (except apparel contractors) |
| 331410 | Niobium refining, primary |
| 326299 | Nipples and teething rings, rubber, manufacturing |
| 332996 | Nipples, metal, made from purchased pipe |
| 325194 | Nitrated hydrocarbon derivatives manufacturing |
| 325311 | Nitric acid manufacturing |
| 325212 | Nitrile rubber manufacturing |
| 325212 | Nitrile-butadiene rubber manufacturing |
| 325212 | Nitrile-chloroprene rubbers manufacturing |
| 325194 | Nitroaniline manufacturing |
| 325194 | Nitrobenzene manufacturing |
| 325211 | Nitrocellulose (i.e., pyroxylin) resins manufacturing |
| 325920 | Nitrocellulose explosive materials manufacturing |
| 325220 | Nitrocellulose fibers manufacturing |
| 325120 | Nitrogen manufacturing |
| 325311 | Nitrogenous fertilizer materials manufacturing |
| 325314 | Nitrogenous fertilizers made by mixing purchased materials |
| 325920 | Nitroglycerin explosive materials manufacturing |

| | |
|---|---|
| 325194 | Nitrophenol manufacturing |
| 325194 | Nitrosated hydrocarbon derivatives manufacturing |
| 325130 | Nitroso dyes manufacturing |
| 325920 | Nitrostarch explosive materials manufacturing |
| 325199 | Nitrous ether manufacturing |
| 325120 | Nitrous oxide manufacturing |
| 325411 | N-methylpiperazine manufacturing |
| 924110 | NOAA (National Oceanic and Atmospheric Administration) |
| 339113 | Noise protectors, personal, manufacturing |
| 312120 | Nonalcoholic beer brewing |
| 312130 | Nonalcoholic wines manufacturing |
| 551112 | Nonbank holding companies (except managing) |
| 325220 | Noncellulosic fibers and filaments manufacturing |
| 325220 | Noncellulosic filament yarn manufacturing |
| 325220 | Noncellulosic staple fibers and filaments manufacturing |
| 111339 | Noncitrus fruit farming |
| 327120 | Nonclay refractories (e.g., block, brick, mortar, tile) manufacturing |
| 311225 | Nondairy butter made from purchased oils |
| 311513 | Nondairy cheese manufacturing |
| 311513 | Nondairy cheese products manufacturing |
| 424490 | Nondairy creamers merchant wholesalers |
| 311514 | Nondairy creamers, dry, manufacturing |
| 311511 | Nondairy creamers, liquid, manufacturing |
| 311520 | Nondairy frozen desserts (except bakery) manufacturing |
| 311520 | Nondairy frozen yogurt manufacturing |
| 311520 | Nondairy ice cream manufacturing |
| 424490 | Nondairy milk merchant wholesalers |
| 311511 | Nondairy yogurt (except frozen) manufacturing |
| 424490 | Nondairy yogurt merchant wholesalers |
| 541380 | Nondestructive testing laboratories or services |
| 425120 | Nondurable goods agents and brokers, wholesale trade |
| 425120 | Nondurable goods business to business electronic markets, wholesale trade |
| 485991 | Nonemergency medical transportation services (except ambulance services) |

| | |
|---|---|
| 325110 | Nonene made from refined petroleum or liquid hydrocarbons |
| 311514 | Nonfat dry milk manufacturing |
| 331492 | Nonferrous alloys (except aluminum, copper) made from purchased nonferrous metals |
| 331492 | Nonferrous alloys (except aluminum, copper) made in integrated secondary smelting and alloying plants |
| 331523 | Nonferrous die-casting foundries |
| 331410 | Nonferrous metal (except aluminum) shapes made in primary nonferrous metal smelting and refining mills |
| 331491 | Nonferrous metal shapes (except aluminum, copper) made by rolling, drawing, or extruding purchased nonferrous metal |
| 331491 | Nonferrous metal shapes (except aluminum, copper) made in integrated secondary smelting and extruding mills |
| 331491 | Nonferrous metal shapes (except aluminum, copper) made in integrated secondary smelting and rolling mills |
| 331491 | Nonferrous metal shapes (except aluminum, copper) made in integrated secondary smelting mills and wire drawing plants |
| 331529 | Nonferrous metals (except aluminum) foundries (except die-casting) |
| 331410 | Nonferrous metals (except aluminum) made in primary nonferrous metal smelting and refining mills |
| 331410 | Nonferrous metals (except aluminum) smelting and refining, primary |
| 331529 | Nonferrous metals (except aluminum) unfinished castings (except die-castings) manufacturing |
| 331492 | Nonferrous metals (except aluminum, copper) secondary smelting and refining |
| 423510 | Nonferrous metals (except precious) merchant wholesalers |
| 331491 | Nonferrous wire (except aluminum, copper) made from purchased nonferrous metals (except aluminum, copper) in wire drawing plants |
| 331491 | Nonferrous wire (except aluminum, copper) made in integrated secondary smelting mills and wire drawing plants |
| 513130 | Nonfiction book publishers |
| 513130 | Nonfiction book publishers (except exclusive Internet publishing) |
| 513130 | Nonfiction book publishers and printing combined |
| 513130 | Nonfiction book publishers, exclusively on Internet |

| | | | |
|---|---|---|---|
| 323120 | Nonfiction bookbinding without printing | 541199 | Notary publics' private practices |
| 323117 | Nonfiction books printing and binding without publishing | 334111 | Notebook computers manufacturing |
| 323117 | Nonfiction books printing without publishing | 322230 | Notebooks (including mechanically bound by wire, or plastics) made from purchased paper |
| 562219 | Nonhazardous waste treatment and disposal facilities (except combustors, incinerators, landfills, sewer systems, sewage treatment facilities) | 424120 | Notebooks merchant wholesalers |
| | | 424310 | Notions merchant wholesalers |
| 423510 | Noninsulated wire merchant wholesalers | 332999 | Novelties and specialties, nonprecious metal and precious plated, manufacturing |
| 423520 | Nonmetallic minerals (except precious and semiprecious stones and minerals used in construction, such as sand and gravel) | 424990 | Novelties merchant wholesalers |
| | | 316990 | Novelties, leather (e.g., cigarette lighter covers, key fobs), manufacturing |
| 213115 | Nonmetallic minerals mine development on a contract basis (except site preparation and related construction activities) | 339999 | Novelties, not specified elsewhere, manufacturing |
| | | 339910 | Novelties, precious metal (except precious plated), manufacturing |
| 213115 | Nonmetallic minerals mining support services on a contract basis (e.g., blasting, shaft sinking, tunneling) (except geophysical surveying and mapping, site preparation, construction, and transportation activities) | 321999 | Novelties, wood fiber, manufacturing |
| | | 459420 | Novelty shops |
| | | 314999 | Novelty stitching contractors on apparel |
| | | 326199 | Nozzles, aerosol spray, plastics, manufacturing |
| 423520 | Nonmetallic ores merchant wholesalers | 332919 | Nozzles, firefighting, manufacturing |
| 325412 | Nonprescription drug preparations manufacturing | 332919 | Nozzles, lawn hose, manufacturing |
| | | 325212 | N-type rubber manufacturing |
| 424210 | Nonprescription drugs merchant wholesalers | 332911 | Nuclear application valves manufacturing |
| 531120 | Nonresidential building (except miniwarehouse) rental or leasing | 332410 | Nuclear control drive mechanisms manufacturing |
| 531312 | Nonresidential property managing | 541690 | Nuclear energy consulting services |
| 481212 | Nonscheduled air freight transportation | 926130 | Nuclear energy inspection and regulation offices |
| 481211 | Nonscheduled air passenger transportation | 325180 | Nuclear fuel scrap reprocessing |
| | | 325180 | Nuclear fuels, inorganic, manufacturing |
| 332215 | Nonstick metal cooking utensils | 334519 | Nuclear instrument modules manufacturing |
| 337122 | Nonupholstered, household-type, custom wood furniture, manufacturing | 334517 | Nuclear irradiation equipment manufacturing |
| 313230 | Nonwoven fabric tapes manufacturing | 325412 | Nuclear medicine (e.g., radioactive isotopes) preparations manufacturing |
| 313230 | Nonwoven fabrics manufacturing | 237130 | Nuclear power plant construction |
| 313230 | Nonwoven felts manufacturing | 332410 | Nuclear reactor steam supply systems manufacturing |
| 311999 | Noodle mixes made from purchased dry ingredients | 332410 | Nuclear reactors control rod drive mechanisms manufacturing |
| 311423 | Noodle mixes made in dehydration plants | 332410 | Nuclear reactors manufacturing |
| 311824 | Noodle mixes made in dry pasta plants | 332313 | Nuclear shielding, fabricated metal plate work, manufacturing |
| 311824 | Noodles, dry, manufacturing | 332420 | Nuclear waste casks, heavy gauge metal, manufacturing |
| 311991 | Noodles, fresh, manufacturing | | |
| 311999 | Noodles, fried, manufacturing | 237990 | Nuclear waste disposal site construction |
| 339113 | Nose and ear plugs manufacturing | | |
| 541199 | Notary public services | | |

541714 Nucleic acid chemistry research and experimental development laboratories

721214 Nudist camps with accommodation facilities

713990 Nudist camps without accommodations

335314 Numerical controls, manufacturing

333517 Numerically controlled metal cutting machine tools manufacturing

812990 Numerology services

423940 Numismatic goods merchant wholesalers

621610 Nurse associations, visiting

621399 Nurse practitioners' offices (e.g., centers, clinics)

561311 Nurse registries

113210 Nurseries for reforestation growing trees

444240 Nurseries, retail, stock primarily grown off premises

444240 Nursery and garden centers without tree production

337122 Nursery furniture (except upholstered), wood, manufacturing

337126 Nursery furniture, metal, manufacturing

624410 Nursery schools

424930 Nursery stock (except plant bulbs, seeds) merchant wholesalers

111421 Nursery stock growing

111421 Nursery with tree production (except for reforestation)

611519 Nurse's aides schools

813920 Nurses' associations

621399 Nurses', licensed practical or registered, offices (e.g., centers, clinics)

621610 Nursing agencies, primarily providing home nursing services

621399 Nursing call centers

623110 Nursing homes

611519 Nursing schools (except academic)

445292 Nut (i.e., packaged) stores

115114 Nut hulling and shelling

331221 Nut rods, iron or steel, made in cold rolling mills

331110 Nut rods, iron or steel, made in iron and steel mills

333111 Nut shellers, farm-type, manufacturing

456191 Nutrition (i.e., food supplement) stores

621399 Nutritionists' offices (e.g., centers, clinics)

424450 Nuts (e.g., canned, roasted, salted) merchant wholesalers

311351 Nuts, chocolate covered, made from cacao beans

311352 Nuts, chocolate covered, made from purchased chocolate

311340 Nuts, covered (except chocolate covered), manufacturing

311911 Nuts, kernels and seeds, roasting and processing

115113 Nuts, machine harvesting

332722 Nuts, metal, manufacturing

311911 Nuts, salted, roasted, cooked, canned, manufacturing

424590 Nuts, unprocessed or shelled only, merchant wholesalers

325220 Nylon fibers and filaments manufacturing

424690 Nylon fibers merchant wholesalers

315120 Nylon hosiery, sheer, women's, misses', and girls' full-length and knee-length, knitting or knitting and finishing

325211 Nylon resins manufacturing

424610 Nylon resins merchant wholesalers

313110 Nylon spun yarns made from purchased fiber

313110 Nylon thread manufacturing

313110 Nylon yarn twisting or winding of purchased yarn

315120 Nylons, sheer, women's, misses', and girls' full-length and knee-length, knitting or knitting and finishing

325194 Oak extract manufacturing

321999 Oars, wood, manufacturing

111199 Oat farming, field and seed production

311211 Oat flour manufacturing

311511 Oat milk manufacturing

311230 Oatmeal (i.e., cereal breakfast food) manufacturing

311230 Oats, breakfast cereal, manufacturing

311230 Oats, rolled (i.e., cereal breakfast food), manufacturing

812910 Obedience training services, pet

339992 Oboes manufacturing

713990 Observation towers

712110 Observatories (except research institutions)

541715 Observatories, research institutions

622310 Obstetrical hospital

621111 Obstetricians' offices (e.g., centers, clinics)

339992 Ocarinas manufacturing

| | |
|---|---|
| 926150 | Occupational safety and health administration |
| 926150 | Occupational safety and health standards agencies |
| 813920 | Occupational therapists' associations |
| 621340 | Occupational therapists' offices (e.g., centers, clinics) |
| 541715 | Oceanographic research and development laboratories or services |
| 212390 | Ocher mining and/or beneficiating |
| 325130 | Ocher pigments manufacturing |
| 339992 | Octophones manufacturing |
| 114112 | Octopus fishing |
| 621399 | Ocularists' offices (e.g., centers, clinics) |
| 621320 | ODs' (doctors of optometry) offices (e.g., centers, clinics) |
| 332994 | Oerlikon guns manufacturing |
| 721310 | Off campus dormitories |
| 624190 | Offender self-help organizations |
| 336999 | Off-highway tracked vehicles (except construction, armored military) manufacturing |
| 333120 | Off-highway trucks manufacturing |
| 561110 | Office administration services |
| 541512 | Office automation computer systems integration design services |
| 236220 | Office building construction |
| 531120 | Office building rental or leasing |
| 561720 | Office cleaning services |
| 423420 | Office equipment merchant wholesalers |
| 337214 | Office furniture (except wood), padded, upholstered, or plain (except wood), manufacturing |
| 423210 | Office furniture merchant wholesalers |
| 532420 | Office furniture rental or leasing |
| 449110 | Office furniture stores |
| 238390 | Office furniture, modular system, installation |
| 337211 | Office furniture, padded, upholstered, or plain wood, manufacturing |
| 561320 | Office help supply services |
| 811210 | Office machine repair and maintenance services |
| 532420 | Office machinery and equipment rental or leasing |
| 423420 | Office machines merchant wholesalers |
| 561110 | Office management services |

| | |
|---|---|
| 322120 | Office paper (e.g., computer printer, photocopy, plain paper) made in paper mills |
| 322230 | Office paper (e.g., computer printer, photocopy, plain paper), cut sheet, made from purchased paper |
| 424120 | Office supplies (except furniture, machines) merchant wholesalers |
| 322230 | Office supplies, die-cut paper, made from purchased paper or paperboard |
| 561320 | Office supply pools |
| 459410 | Office supply stores |
| 551111 | Offices of bank holding companies |
| 441227 | Off-road all-terrain vehicles (ATVs), wheeled or tracked, dealers |
| 336999 | Off-road all-terrain vehicles (ATVs), wheeled or tracked, manufacturing |
| 325910 | Offset inks manufacturing |
| 323120 | Offset plate preparation services |
| 323111 | Offset printing (except books, grey goods) |
| 333248 | Offset printing presses manufacturing |
| 211120 | Offshore crude petroleum production |
| 211130 | Offshore natural gas production |
| 713290 | Off-track betting parlors |
| 334515 | Ohmmeters manufacturing |
| 324110 | Oil (i.e., petroleum) refineries |
| 325998 | Oil additive preparations manufacturing |
| 324110 | Oil additives made in petroleum refineries |
| 424690 | Oil additives merchant wholesalers |
| 237120 | Oil and gas field distribution line construction |
| 484220 | Oil and gas field equipment trucking, local |
| 484230 | Oil and gas field equipment trucking, long-distance |
| 811310 | Oil and gas field machinery and equipment repair and maintenance services |
| 213112 | Oil and gas field services on a contract basis (except geophysical surveying and mapping, site preparation, construction, and transportation activities) |
| 333132 | Oil and gas field-type drilling machinery and equipment (except offshore floating platforms) manufacturing |
| 336611 | Oil and gas offshore floating platforms manufacturing |
| 213111 | Oil and gas well drilling services (redrilling, spudding, tailing) on a contract basis |

| | |
|---|---|
| 238220 | Oil burner installation |
| 333414 | Oil burners, heating, manufacturing |
| 423720 | Oil burners, heating, merchant wholesalers |
| 811191 | Oil change and lubrication shops, automotive |
| 424690 | Oil drilling muds merchant wholesalers |
| 211120 | Oil field development for own account |
| 423830 | Oil field equipment merchant wholesalers |
| 213112 | Oil field exploration (except surveying) on a contract basis |
| 211120 | Oil field exploration for own account |
| 532412 | Oil field machinery and equipment rental or leasing |
| 237310 | Oil field road construction |
| 423120 | Oil filters, automotive, merchant wholesalers |
| 336390 | Oil filters, automotive, truck, and bus, manufacturing |
| 424590 | Oil kernels merchant wholesalers |
| 523999 | Oil lease brokers' offices |
| 211130 | Oil line drip, natural gas liquid |
| 333914 | Oil measuring and dispensing pumps manufacturing |
| 424590 | Oil nuts merchant wholesalers |
| 237120 | Oil pipeline construction |
| 237120 | Oil refinery construction |
| 533110 | Oil royalty companies |
| 523910 | Oil royalty dealing (i.e., acting as a principal in dealing royalties to investors) |
| 533110 | Oil royalty leasing |
| 533110 | Oil royalty traders (except for own account) |
| 213112 | Oil sampling services on a contract basis |
| 339991 | Oil seals manufacturing |
| 211120 | Oil shale mining and/or beneficiating |
| 562910 | Oil spill cleanup services |
| 332420 | Oil storage tanks, heavy gauge metal, manufacturing |
| 333310 | Oil water separators manufacturing |
| 333914 | Oil well and oil field pumps manufacturing |
| 532412 | Oil well drilling machinery and equipment rental or leasing |
| 213111 | Oil well drilling on a contract basis |
| 213112 | Oil well logging on a contract basis |
| 423830 | Oil well machinery and equipment merchant wholesalers |
| 213112 | Oil well rig building, repairing, and dismantling, on a contract basis |
| 423830 | Oil well supply houses merchant wholesalers |
| 311613 | Oil, animal, rendering |
| 311221 | Oil, corn crude and refined, made by wet milling corn |
| 311225 | Oil, olive, made from purchased oils |
| 424710 | Oil, petroleum, bulk stations and terminals, merchant wholesalers |
| 424720 | Oil, petroleum, merchant wholesalers (except bulk stations, terminals) |
| 311225 | Oil, vegetable stearin, made from purchased oils |
| 423930 | Oil, waste, merchant wholesalers |
| 324199 | Oil-based additives made from refined petroleum |
| 313320 | Oilcloth manufacturing |
| 313320 | Oiling of purchased textiles and apparel |
| 325998 | Oils (e.g., cutting, lubricating), synthetic, manufacturing |
| 325194 | Oils made by distillation of coal tar |
| 424490 | Oils, cooking and salad, merchant wholesalers |
| 324110 | Oils, fuel, manufacturing |
| 424990 | Oils, inedible, animal or vegetable, merchant wholesalers |
| 324191 | Oils, lubricating petroleum, made from refined petroleum |
| 325998 | Oils, lubricating, synthetic, manufacturing |
| 324191 | Oils, petroleum lubricating, re-refining used |
| 325613 | Oils, soluble (i.e., textile finishing assistants), manufacturing |
| 325411 | Oils, vegetable and animal, medicinal, uncompounded, manufacturing |
| 325194 | Oils, wood, made by distillation of wood |
| 111191 | Oilseed and grain combination farming, field and seed production |
| 424990 | Oilseed cake and meal merchant wholesalers |
| 333241 | Oilseed crushing and extracting machinery manufacturing |
| 111120 | Oilseed farming (except soybean), field and seed production |
| 424590 | Oilseeds merchant wholesalers |
| 212390 | Oilstones mining and/or beneficiating |
| 111219 | Okra farming, field, bedding plant and seed production |
| 623312 | Old age homes without nursing care |

| | |
|---|---|
| 923130 | Old age survivors and disability programs |
| 623312 | Old soldiers' homes without nursing care |
| 325220 | Olefin fibers and filaments manufacturing |
| 325110 | Olefins made from refined petroleum or liquid hydrocarbons |
| 325199 | Oleic acid (i.e., red oil) manufacturing |
| 325199 | Oleic acid esters manufacturing |
| 325180 | Oleum (i.e., fuming sulfuric acid) manufacturing |
| 111339 | Olive farming |
| 311225 | Olive oil made from purchased oils |
| 311224 | Olive oil made in crushing mills |
| 311421 | Olives brined |
| 311423 | Olives, dried, made in dehydration plants |
| 212323 | Olivine, non-gem, mining and/or beneficiating |
| 334511 | Omnibearing instrumentation manufacturing |
| 621111 | Oncologists' offices (e.g., centers, clinics) |
| 812922 | One-hour photofinishing services |
| 111219 | Onion farming, field, bedding plant and seed production |
| 311421 | Onions pickled |
| 517810 | Online access service providers, using client-supplied telecommunications (e.g., dial-up ISPs) |
| 517111 | Online access service providers, using own operated wired telecommunications infrastructure |
| 561599 | Online accommodations reservation services (through a website or mobile application) |
| 541810 | Online advertising agencies |
| 561599 | Online airline reservation services (through a website or mobile application) |
| 561599 | Online cruise reservation services (through a website or mobile application) |
| 561422 | Online customer service centers |
| 812990 | Online dating services (through a website or mobile application) |
| 561311 | Online employment registries or listing services, including intermediary platform services |
| 713290 | Online gambling sites |
| 561599 | Online motor vehicle rental reservation services (through a website or mobile application) |
| 523150 | Online securities brokerages |
| 713290 | Online sports betting sites |
| 561320 | Online temporary staffing services, including intermediary platform services |
| 561599 | Online ticket (e.g., airline, bus, cruise ship, sports, theatrical) agencies (through a website or mobile application) |
| 561510 | Online travel agencies |
| 212319 | Onyx marble crushed and broken stone mining and/or beneficiating |
| 212311 | Onyx marble mining or quarrying |
| 512132 | Open air motion picture theaters |
| 711110 | Opera companies |
| 315210 | Opera hats cut and sew apparel contractors |
| 315990 | Opera hats cut and sewn from purchased fabric (except apparel contractors) |
| 711130 | Opera singers, independent |
| 927110 | Operating and launching government satellites |
| 213112 | Operating condensate gasoline field gathering lines on a contract basis |
| 211120 | Operating crude petroleum field gathering lines, except on a contract basis |
| 211130 | Operating natural gas liquid field gathering lines, except on a contract basis |
| 339113 | Operating room tables manufacturing |
| 513210 | Operating systems software, computer, packaged |
| 541614 | Operations research consulting services |
| 325411 | Ophthalmic agents, uncompounded, manufacturing |
| 423460 | Ophthalmic goods (except cameras) merchant wholesalers |
| 339112 | Ophthalmic instruments and apparatus (except laser surgical) manufacturing |
| 621111 | Ophthalmologists' offices (e.g., centers, clinics) |
| 339112 | Ophthalmometers and ophthalmoscopes manufacturing |
| 541910 | Opinion research services |
| 325411 | Opium and opium derivatives (i.e., basic chemicals) manufacturing |
| 333310 | Optical alignment and display instruments manufacturing |
| 334112 | Optical disk drives manufacturing |

| | |
|---|---|
| 423460 | Optical goods (except cameras) merchant wholesalers |
| 456130 | Optical goods stores (except offices of optometrists, ophthalmologists) |
| 212390 | Optical grade calcite mining and/or beneficiating |
| 333310 | Optical gun sighting and fire control equipment and instruments manufacturing |
| 811210 | Optical instrument repair and maintenance services (e.g., microscopes, telescopes) |
| 333248 | Optical lens making and grinding machinery manufacturing |
| 334118 | Optical readers and scanners manufacturing |
| 518210 | Optical scanning services |
| 333310 | Optical test and inspection equipment manufacturing |
| 334413 | Optoelectronic devices manufacturing |
| 339112 | Optometers manufacturing |
| 423460 | Optometric equipment and supplies merchant wholesalers |
| 813920 | Optometrists' associations |
| 621320 | Optometrists' offices (e.g., centers, clinics) |
| 621210 | Oral and maxillofacial surgeons' offices (e.g., centers, clinics) |
| 325412 | Oral contraceptive preparations manufacturing |
| 621210 | Oral pathologists' offices (e.g., centers, clinics) |
| 111310 | Orange groves |
| 325998 | Orange oil manufacturing |
| 115112 | Orchard cultivation services (e.g., bracing, planting, pruning, removal, spraying, surgery) |
| 111998 | Orchard grass seed farming |
| 711510 | Orchestra conductors, independent |
| 711130 | Orchestras |
| 423990 | Ordnance and accessories merchant wholesalers |
| 236210 | Ore and metal refinery construction |
| 423520 | Ore concentrates merchant wholesalers |
| 333131 | Ore crushing, washing, screening, and loading machinery manufacturing |
| 423520 | Ores (e.g., gold, iron, lead, silver, zinc) merchant wholesalers |
| 621991 | Organ banks, body |
| 621991 | Organ donor centers, body |
| 424690 | Organic chemicals merchant wholesalers |

| | |
|---|---|
| 325220 | Organic noncellulosic fibers and filaments manufacturing |
| 325130 | Organic pigments, dyes, lakes, and toners manufacturing |
| 541612 | Organization development consulting services |
| 928120 | Organization for Economic Cooperation and Development |
| 928120 | Organization of American States |
| 812990 | Organizer services, personal |
| 326199 | Organizers for closets, drawers, and shelves, plastics, manufacturing |
| 711310 | Organizers of agricultural fairs with facilities |
| 711320 | Organizers of agricultural fairs without facilities |
| 711310 | Organizers of arts events with facilities |
| 711320 | Organizers of arts events without facilities |
| 711310 | Organizers of festivals with facilities |
| 711320 | Organizers of festivals without facilities |
| 711310 | Organizers of live performing arts productions (e.g., concerts) with facilities |
| 711320 | Organizers of live performing arts productions (e.g., concerts) without facilities |
| 711310 | Organizers of sports events with facilities |
| 711320 | Organizers of sports events without facilities |
| 325199 | Organo-inorganic compound manufacturing |
| 325320 | Organo-phosphate based insecticides manufacturing |
| 321219 | Oriented strandboard (OSB) manufacturing |
| 327420 | Ornamental and architectural plaster work (e.g., columns, mantels, molding) manufacturing |
| 327390 | Ornamental and statuary precast concrete products manufacturing |
| 112511 | Ornamental fish production, farm raising |
| 423390 | Ornamental ironwork merchant wholesalers |
| 238190 | Ornamental metal work installation |
| 332323 | Ornamental metalwork manufacturing |
| 111422 | Ornamental plant growing |
| 424930 | Ornamental plants and flowers merchant wholesalers |
| 561730 | Ornamental tree and shrub services |
| 321918 | Ornamental woodwork (e.g., cornices, mantels) manufacturing |

| | |
|---|---|
| 339999 | Ornaments, Christmas tree (except electric, glass), manufacturing |
| 335139 | Ornaments, Christmas tree, electric, manufacturing |
| 327212 | Ornaments, Christmas tree, glass, made in glass making plants |
| 327215 | Ornaments, Christmas tree, made from purchased glass |
| 623990 | Orphanages |
| 325998 | Orris oil manufacturing |
| 325194 | Orthodichlorobenzene manufacturing |
| 339116 | Orthodontic appliance, custom made in dental laboratories |
| 339114 | Orthodontic appliances manufacturing |
| 621210 | Orthodontists' offices (e.g., centers, clinics) |
| 339113 | Orthopedic canes manufacturing |
| 339113 | Orthopedic device manufacturing and sale in retail environment |
| 339113 | Orthopedic devices manufacturing |
| 423450 | Orthopedic equipment and supplies merchant wholesalers |
| 339113 | Orthopedic extension shoes manufacturing |
| 339113 | Orthopedic hosiery, elastic, manufacturing |
| 622310 | Orthopedic hospitals |
| 621111 | Orthopedic physicians' offices (e.g., centers, clinics) |
| 327420 | Orthopedic plaster, gypsum, manufacturing |
| 316210 | Orthopedic shoes (except extension shoes), children's, manufacturing |
| 316210 | Orthopedic shoes (except extension shoes), men's, manufacturing |
| 316210 | Orthopedic shoes (except extension shoes), women's, manufacturing |
| 458210 | Orthopedic shoes stores |
| 621111 | Orthopedic surgeons' offices (e.g., centers, clinics) |
| 621399 | Orthotists' offices (e.g., centers, clinics) |
| 321219 | OSB (oriented strandboard) manufacturing |
| 334515 | Oscillators (e.g., instrument type audiofrequency and radiofrequency) manufacturing |
| 334515 | Oscilloscopes manufacturing |
| 212290 | Osmium mining and/or beneficiating |
| 334516 | Osmometers manufacturing |
| 325998 | Ossein manufacturing |
| 622110 | Osteopathic hospitals |

| | |
|---|---|
| 621111 | Osteopathic physicians' (except mental health) offices (e.g., centers, clinics) |
| 112390 | Ostrich production |
| 621111 | Otolaryngologists' offices (e.g., centers, clinics) |
| 334510 | Otoscopes, electromedical, manufacturing |
| 337121 | Ottomans, upholstered, manufacturing |
| 441222 | Outboard motor dealers |
| 811490 | Outboard motor repair shops |
| 333618 | Outboard motors manufacturing |
| 423910 | Outboard motors merchant wholesalers |
| 713990 | Outdoor adventure operations (e.g., white water rafting) without accommodations |
| 721214 | Outdoor adventure retreats with accommodation facilities |
| 541850 | Outdoor display advertising services |
| 423210 | Outdoor furniture merchant wholesalers |
| 423620 | Outdoor grills merchant wholesalers |
| 237990 | Outdoor recreation facility construction |
| 459110 | Outdoor sporting equipment stores |
| 315120 | Outerwear handknitted for the trade |
| 424350 | Outerwear, men's and boys', merchant wholesalers |
| 424350 | Outerwear, women's, children's, and infants', merchant wholesalers |
| 713990 | Outfitters (i.e., providing trips and equipment) |
| 335932 | Outlet boxes, electrical wiring, manufacturing |
| 335931 | Outlets (i.e., receptacles), electrical, manufacturing |
| 335931 | Outlets, convenience, electrical, manufacturing |
| 541850 | Out-of-home media (i.e., display) advertising services |
| 621420 | Outpatient mental health centers and clinics (except hospitals) |
| 621420 | Outpatient treatment centers and clinics (except hospitals) for substance abuse (i.e., alcoholism, drug addiction) |
| 621420 | Outpatient treatment centers and clinics for alcoholism |
| 621420 | Outpatient treatment centers and clinics for drug addiction |
| 561320 | Outplacement consulting services |
| 561320 | Outplacement services |
| 325612 | Oven cleaners manufacturing |
| 334512 | Oven temperature controls, nonindustrial, manufacturing |

811412 Oven, household-type, repair and maintenance services without retailing new ovens

236210 Oven, industrial plant, construction

333241 Ovens, bakery, manufacturing

333310 Ovens, commercial-type, manufacturing

423440 Ovens, commercial-type, merchant wholesalers

335220 Ovens, freestanding household-type, manufacturing

423620 Ovens, gas and electric, household-type, merchant wholesalers

333994 Ovens, industrial process and laboratory-type, manufacturing

423830 Ovens, industrial, merchant wholesalers

335210 Ovens, portable household-type (except microwave and convection ovens), manufacturing

335220 Ovens, portable household-type convection and microwave, manufacturing

327215 Ovenware made from purchased glass

327212 Ovenware, glass, made in glass making plants

315210 Overall jackets, work, cut and sew apparel contractors

315250 Overall jackets, work, men's and boys', cut and sewn from purchased fabric (except apparel contractors)

315210 Overalls, work, cut and sew apparel contractors

315250 Overalls, work, men's and boys', cut and sewn from purchased fabric (except apparel contractors)

213113 Overburden removal for coal mining on a contract basis

213114 Overburden removal for metal mining on a contract basis

213115 Overburden removal for nonmetallic minerals mining (except fuels) on a contract basis

315210 Overcoats cut and sew apparel contractors

315250 Overcoats, men's and boys', cut and sewn from purchased fabric (except apparel contractors)

315250 Overcoats, women's and girls', cut and sewn from purchased fabric (except apparel contractors)

333922 Overhead conveyors manufacturing

238290 Overhead door, commercial- or industrial-type, installation

238350 Overhead door, residential-type, installation

333310 Overhead projectors (except computer peripheral) manufacturing

334118 Overhead projectors, computer peripheral-type, manufacturing

333923 Overhead traveling cranes manufacturing

237310 Overpass construction

316210 Overshoes, plastics or plastics soled fabric upper, manufacturing

316210 Overshoes, rubber, or rubber soled fabric, manufacturing

325199 Oxalates (e.g., ammonium oxalate, ethyl oxalate, sodium oxalate) manufacturing

325199 Oxalic acid manufacturing

532283 Oxygen equipment rental (i.e., home use)

325120 Oxygen manufacturing

339112 Oxygen tents manufacturing

114112 Oyster dredging

112512 Oyster production, farm raising

212390 Ozokerite mining and/or beneficiating

333310 Ozone machines for water purification manufacturing

621999 Pacemaker monitoring services

334510 Pacemakers manufacturing

326299 Pacifiers, rubber, manufacturing

713990 Pack trains (i.e., trail riding), recreational

445320 Package stores (i.e., liquor)

513210 Packaged computer software publishers

424440 Packaged poultry (except canned and frozen) merchant wholesalers

326112 Packaging film, plastics, single-web or multiweb, manufacturing

115114 Packaging fresh or farm-dried fruits and vegetables

541420 Packaging industrial design services

333993 Packaging machinery manufacturing

423840 Packaging materials merchant wholesalers

561910 Packaging services (except packing and crating for transportation)

326150 Packaging, foam plastics (except polystyrene), manufacturing

326199 Packaging, plastics (e.g., blister, bubble), manufacturing

325998 Packer's fluids manufacturing

488991 Packing and preparing goods for shipping

321920 Packing cases, wood, nailed or lock corner, manufacturing

| | |
|---|---|
| 321920 | Packing crates, wood, manufacturing |
| 115114 | Packing fruits and vegetables |
| 423830 | Packing machinery and equipment merchant wholesalers |
| 423840 | Packing materials merchant wholesalers |
| 813940 | PACs (Political Action Committees) |
| 316210 | Pacs, plastics or plastics soled fabric upper, manufacturing |
| 316210 | Pacs, rubber or rubber soled fabric upper, manufacturing |
| 322230 | Padded envelopes manufacturing |
| 314999 | Padding and wadding (except nonwoven fabric) manufacturing |
| 423850 | Padding, upholstery filling, merchant wholesalers |
| 424310 | Paddings, apparel, merchant wholesalers |
| 321999 | Paddles, wood, manufacturing |
| 332510 | Padlocks, metal, manufacturing |
| 314120 | Pads and protectors (e.g., ironing board, mattress, table), textile, made from purchased fabrics or felts |
| 313230 | Pads and wadding, nonwoven, manufacturing |
| 322211 | Pads, corrugated and solid fiberboard, made from purchased paper or paperboard |
| 322230 | Pads, desk, made from purchased paper |
| 321999 | Pads, excelsior, wood, manufacturing |
| 322291 | Pads, incontinent and bed, manufacturing |
| 332999 | Pads, soap impregnated scouring, manufacturing |
| 321999 | Pads, table, rattan, reed, and willow, manufacturing |
| 334220 | Pagers manufacturing |
| 517112 | Paging services (except satellite) |
| 321920 | Pails, coopered wood, manufacturing |
| 326199 | Pails, plastics, manufacturing |
| 321920 | Pails, plywood, manufacturing |
| 321920 | Pails, wood, manufacturing |
| 621498 | Pain therapy centers and clinics, outpatient |
| 325510 | Paint and varnish removers manufacturing |
| 238320 | Paint and wallpaper stripping |
| 333994 | Paint baking and drying ovens manufacturing |
| 424950 | Paint removers merchant wholesalers |
| 339994 | Paint rollers manufacturing |
| 424950 | Paint rollers merchant wholesalers |

| | |
|---|---|
| 811121 | Paint shops, automotive |
| 333991 | Paint spray guns, handheld pneumatic, manufacturing |
| 333912 | Paint sprayers (i.e., compressor and spray gun unit) manufacturing |
| 332999 | Paint sticks, metal, manufacturing |
| 326199 | Paint sticks, plastics, manufacturing |
| 321999 | Paint sticks, wood, manufacturing |
| 444120 | Paint stores |
| 325510 | Paint thinner and reducer preparations manufacturing |
| 424950 | Paint thinners merchant wholesalers |
| 713990 | Paintball, laser tag, and similar fields and arenas |
| 325510 | Paintbrush cleaners manufacturing |
| 339994 | Paintbrushes manufacturing |
| 424950 | Paintbrushes merchant wholesalers |
| 711510 | Painters (i.e., artists), independent |
| 424950 | Painter's supplies (except artists', turpentine) merchant wholesalers |
| 238320 | Painting (except roof) contractors |
| 238320 | Painting and wallpapering |
| 611610 | Painting instruction |
| 237310 | Painting lines on highways, streets and bridges |
| 332812 | Painting metals and metal products for the trade |
| 711510 | Painting restorers, independent |
| 237310 | Painting traffic lanes or parking lots |
| 238160 | Painting, spraying, or coating, roof |
| 325510 | Paints (except artist's) manufacturing |
| 424950 | Paints (except artists') merchant wholesalers |
| 339940 | Paints, artist's, manufacturing |
| 424990 | Paints, artist's, merchant wholesalers |
| 325510 | Paints, emulsion (i.e., latex paint), manufacturing |
| 325510 | Paints, oil and alkyd vehicle, manufacturing |
| 315210 | Pajamas cut and sew apparel contractors |
| 315120 | Pajamas made in apparel knitting mills |
| 315250 | Pajamas, men's and boys', cut and sewn from purchased fabric (except apparel contractors) |
| 315250 | Pajamas, women's, girls', and infants', cut and sewn from purchased fabric (except apparel contractors) |
| 339940 | Palettes, artist's, manufacturing |
| 212290 | Palladium mining and/or beneficiating |

| | |
|---|---|
| 321920 | Pallet containers, wood or wood and metal combination, manufacturing |
| 333924 | Pallet movers manufacturing |
| 333924 | Pallet or skid jacks manufacturing |
| 332999 | Pallet parts, metal, manufacturing |
| 321920 | Pallet parts, wood, manufacturing |
| 532490 | Pallet rental or leasing |
| 423830 | Pallets and skids merchant wholesalers |
| 322211 | Pallets, corrugated and solid fiber, made from purchased paper or paperboard |
| 332999 | Pallets, metal, manufacturing |
| 321920 | Pallets, wood or wood and metal combination, manufacturing |
| 812990 | Palm reading services |
| 325199 | Palmitic acid esters and amines manufacturing |
| 311225 | Palm-kernel oil made from purchased oils |
| 311224 | Palm-kernel oil, cake, and meal made in crushing mills |
| 323120 | Pamphlet binding without printing |
| 513130 | Pamphlet publishers |
| 513130 | Pamphlet publishers (except exclusive Internet publishing) |
| 513130 | Pamphlet publishers and printing combined |
| 513130 | Pamphlet publishers, exclusively on Internet |
| 424920 | Pamphlets merchant wholesalers |
| 323117 | Pamphlets printing and binding without publishing |
| 323117 | Pamphlets printing without publishing |
| 315210 | Panama hats cut and sew apparel contractors |
| 315990 | Panama hats cut and sewn from purchased fabric (except apparel contractors) |
| 311824 | Pancake mixes made from purchased flour |
| 311999 | Pancake syrups (except pure maple) manufacturing |
| 311412 | Pancakes, frozen, manufacturing |
| 238310 | Panel or rigid board insulation installation |
| 321918 | Panel work, wood millwork, manufacturing |
| 238390 | Panel, metal, installation |
| 334513 | Panelboard indicators, recorders, and controllers, receiver industrial process-type, manufacturing |
| 335313 | Panelboards, electric power distribution, manufacturing |

| | |
|---|---|
| 423610 | Panelboards, electric power distribution, merchant wholesalers |
| 238350 | Paneling installation |
| 423310 | Paneling merchant wholesalers |
| 236117 | Panelized housing, residential, assembled on site by for-sale builders |
| 236117 | Panelized multifamily housing assembled on site by for-sale builders |
| 236116 | Panelized multifamily housing assembled on site by general contractors |
| 236115 | Panelized single-family housing assembled on site by general contractors |
| 335313 | Panels, generator control and metering, manufacturing |
| 321211 | Panels, hardwood plywood, manufacturing |
| 332311 | Panels, prefabricated metal building, manufacturing |
| 321992 | Panels, prefabricated wood building, manufacturing |
| 321212 | Panels, softwood plywood, manufacturing |
| 423440 | Pans, commercial, merchant wholesalers |
| 315210 | Panties cut and sew apparel contractors |
| 315120 | Panties made in apparel knitting mills |
| 315250 | Panties, women's, girls', and infants', cut and sewn from purchased fabric (except apparel contractors) |
| 315210 | Pants (e.g., athletic, dress, leather, sweat, waterproof outerwear, work) cut and sew apparel contractors |
| 315250 | Pants (e.g., athletic, dress, sweat, work), men's and boys', cut and sewn from purchased fabric (except apparel contractors) |
| 315210 | Pants outfits cut and sew apparel contractors |
| 315250 | Pants outfits, women's and girls', cut and sewn from purchased fabric (except apparel contractors) |
| 315120 | Pants, athletic, made in apparel knitting mills |
| 315250 | Pants, athletic, women's, girls', and infants', cut and sewn from purchased fabric (except apparel contractors) |
| 315250 | Pants, leather (except apparel contractors), manufacturing |
| 315120 | Pants, outerwear, made in apparel knitting mills |
| 315250 | Pants, rubber and rubberized fabric, made in the same establishment as the basic material |

| | |
|---|---|
| 315250 | Pants, sweat, women's, girls', and infants', cut and sewn from purchased fabric (except apparel contractors) |
| 315250 | Pants, vulcanized rubber, manufacturing |
| 315250 | Pants, waterproof outerwear, cut and sewn from purchased fabric (except apparel contractors) |
| 315250 | Pants, women's, girls', and infants', cut and sewn from purchased fabric (except apparel contractors) |
| 315210 | Pantsuits cut and sew apparel contractors |
| 315250 | Pantsuits, women's, girls', and infants', cut and sewn from purchased fabric (except apparel contractors) |
| 315210 | Panty girdles cut and sew apparel contractors |
| 315250 | Panty girdles, women's and girls', cut and sewn from purchased fabric (except apparel contractors) |
| 315120 | Panty hose, women's and girls', knitting or knitting and finishing |
| 111339 | Papaya farming |
| 327910 | Paper (e.g., aluminum oxide, emery, garnet, silicon carbide), abrasive-coated, made from purchased paper |
| 424110 | Paper (e.g., fine, printing, writing), bulk, merchant wholesalers |
| 424130 | Paper (except office supplies, printing paper, stationery, writing paper) merchant wholesalers |
| 333243 | Paper and paperboard coating and finishing machinery manufacturing |
| 333243 | Paper and paperboard converting machinery manufacturing |
| 333243 | Paper and paperboard corrugating machinery manufacturing |
| 333243 | Paper and paperboard cutting and folding machinery manufacturing |
| 333243 | Paper and paperboard die-cutting and stamping machinery manufacturing |
| 423830 | Paper and pulp industries manufacturing machinery merchant wholesalers |
| 333243 | Paper bag making machinery manufacturing |
| 424130 | Paper bags merchant wholesalers |
| 322220 | Paper bags, coated, made from purchased paper |
| 322220 | Paper bags, uncoated, made from purchased paper |
| 212323 | Paper clay mining and/or beneficiating |
| 332618 | Paper clips made from purchased wire |
| 331222 | Paper clips, iron or steel, made in wire drawing plants |
| 322219 | Paper cups made from purchased paper or paperboard |
| 339940 | Paper cutters, office-type, manufacturing |
| 322299 | Paper dishes (e.g., cups, plates) made from molded pulp |
| 322219 | Paper dishes (e.g., cups, plates) made from purchased paper or paperboard |
| 315210 | Paper dresses cut and sew apparel contractors |
| 315250 | Paper dresses, women's and girls', cut and sewn from purchased fabric (except apparel contractors) |
| 313220 | Paper fabric, narrow woven, weaving |
| 313210 | Paper fabrics, broadwoven, weaving |
| 332618 | Paper machine wire cloth made from purchased wire |
| 333243 | Paper making machinery manufacturing |
| 811310 | Paper making machinery repair and maintenance services |
| 322120 | Paper manufacturing |
| 322120 | Paper mills |
| 322120 | Paper mills, newsprint |
| 322120 | Paper mills, uncoated groundwood |
| 322291 | Paper napkins and tablecloths made from purchased paper |
| 322299 | Paper novelties made from purchased paper |
| 236210 | Paper or pulp mill construction |
| 322219 | Paper plates made from purchased paper or paperboard |
| 322299 | Paper products (except office supply), die-cut, made from purchased paper or paperboard |
| 322120 | Paper products made in paper mills |
| 322230 | Paper products, die-cut office supply, made from purchased paper or paperboard |
| 332992 | Paper shells (i.e., 30 mm. or less, 1.18 inch or less) manufacturing |
| 423420 | Paper shredders merchant wholesalers |
| 322120 | Paper stock for conversion into paper products (e.g., bag and sack stock, envelope stock, tissue stock, wallpaper stock) manufacturing |
| 322291 | Paper towels made from purchased paper |
| 322120 | Paper towels made in paper mills |
| 424130 | Paper towels merchant wholesalers |
| 313110 | Paper yarn manufacturing |
| 322120 | Paper, asphalt, made in paper mills |
| 423390 | Paper, building, merchant wholesalers |

| | |
|---|---|
| 339940 | Paper, carbon, manufacturing |
| 322120 | Paper, coated, laminated or treated, made in paper mills |
| 322211 | Paper, corrugated, made from purchased paper or paperboard |
| 523150 | Paper, dealing of commercial (i.e., acting as a principal in dealing securities to investors) |
| 322120 | Paper, newsprint and uncoated groundwood, manufacturing |
| 424120 | Paper, office (e.g., printer, copier), merchant wholesalers |
| 325992 | Paper, photographic sensitized, manufacturing |
| 423930 | Paper, scrap, merchant wholesalers |
| 339940 | Paper, stencil, manufacturing |
| 322130 | Paperboard (e.g., can/drum stock, container board, corrugating medium, folding carton stock, linerboard, tube) manufacturing |
| 424130 | Paperboard and paperboard products (except office supplies) merchant wholesalers |
| 333243 | Paperboard box making machinery manufacturing |
| 322130 | Paperboard coating, laminating, or treating in paperboard mills |
| 333243 | Paperboard making machinery manufacturing |
| 322130 | Paperboard mills |
| 322130 | Paperboard products (e.g., containers) made in paperboard mills |
| 322220 | Paperboard, pasted, lined, laminated, or surface coated, made from purchased paperboard |
| 238320 | Paperhanging and removal contractors |
| 238320 | Paperhanging or removal contractors |
| 327999 | Papier-mache statuary and related art goods (e.g., urns, vases) manufacturing |
| 314999 | Parachutes manufacturing |
| 213112 | Paraffin services, oil and gas field, on a contract basis |
| 324110 | Paraffin waxes made in petroleum refineries |
| 325110 | Paraffins made from refined petroleum or liquid hydrocarbons |
| 541199 | Paralegal services |
| 321215 | Parallel strand lumber manufacturing |
| 621399 | Paramedics' offices (e.g., centers, clinics) |
| 325130 | Pararosaniline dyes manufacturing |
| 713990 | Parasailing, recreational |

| | |
|---|---|
| 621511 | Parasitology health laboratories |
| 339999 | Parasols manufacturing |
| 325320 | Parathion insecticides manufacturing |
| 485991 | Paratransit transportation services |
| 561431 | Parcel mailing services combined with one or more other office support services, private |
| 561431 | Parcel mailing services, private |
| 561910 | Parcel packing services |
| 333998 | Parcel post scales manufacturing |
| 316110 | Parchment leather manufacturing |
| 922150 | Pardon boards and offices |
| 624190 | Parenting support services |
| 813410 | Parent-teachers' associations |
| 325320 | Paris green insecticides manufacturing |
| 237990 | Park and recreational open space improvement construction |
| 922120 | Park police |
| 332812 | Parkerizing metals and metal products for the trade |
| 236220 | Parking garage construction |
| 812930 | Parking garages, automobile |
| 561790 | Parking lot cleaning (e.g., power sweeping, washing) services |
| 237310 | Parking lot marking and line painting |
| 238990 | Parking lot paving and sealing |
| 812930 | Parking lots, automobile |
| 334514 | Parking meters manufacturing |
| 561612 | Parking security services |
| 488119 | Parking services, aircraft |
| 812930 | Parking services, valet |
| 713110 | Parks (e.g., theme, water), amusement |
| 924120 | Parks and recreation commission, government |
| 712190 | Parks, national |
| 712190 | Parks, nature |
| 712130 | Parks, wild animal |
| 237310 | Parkway construction |
| 611310 | Parochial schools, college-level |
| 611110 | Parochial schools, elementary or secondary |
| 624190 | Parole offices, privately operated |
| 922150 | Parole offices, publicly administered |
| 238330 | Parquet flooring installation |
| 321918 | Parquet flooring, hardwood, manufacturing |

| | |
|---|---|
| 321918 | Parquetry, hardwood, manufacturing |
| 111219 | Parsley farming, field, bedding plant and seed production |
| 111219 | Parsnip farming, field, bedding plant and seed production |
| 335999 | Particle accelerators, high-voltage, manufacturing |
| 334516 | Particle beam excitation instruments, laboratory-type, manufacturing |
| 334516 | Particle size analyzers manufacturing |
| 321219 | Particleboard manufacturing |
| 423310 | Particleboard merchant wholesalers |
| 238390 | Partition (e.g., office, washroom), metal, installation |
| 238390 | Partition, moveable and/or demountable, installation |
| 337215 | Partitions for floor attachment, prefabricated, manufacturing |
| 423440 | Partitions merchant wholesalers |
| 322211 | Partitions, corrugated and solid fiber, made from purchased paper or paperboard |
| 337215 | Partitions, freestanding, prefabricated, manufacturing |
| 332323 | Partitions, ornamental metal, manufacturing |
| 112390 | Partridge production |
| 441330 | Parts and accessories dealers, automotive |
| 423120 | Parts, new, motor vehicle, merchant wholesalers |
| 423140 | Parts, used, motor vehicle, merchant wholesalers |
| 532289 | Party (i.e., banquet) equipment rental |
| 459420 | Party goods (e.g., paper supplies, decorations, novelties) stores |
| 812990 | Party planning services |
| 532289 | Party rental supply centers |
| 481211 | Passenger air transportation, nonscheduled |
| 481111 | Passenger air transportation, scheduled |
| 333922 | Passenger baggage belt loaders (except industrial truck) manufacturing |
| 532112 | Passenger car leasing |
| 532111 | Passenger car rental |
| 481211 | Passenger carriers, air, nonscheduled |
| 481111 | Passenger carriers, air, scheduled |
| 485320 | Passenger limousine rental with driver (except shuttle service, taxi) |
| 482111 | Passenger railways, line-haul |
| 336611 | Passenger ship building |
| 483114 | Passenger transportation, coastal or Great Lakes (including St. Lawrence Seaway) |
| 483114 | Passenger transportation, deep sea, to and from domestic ports (including Puerto Rico) |
| 483112 | Passenger transportation, deep sea, to or from foreign ports |
| 483212 | Passenger transportation, inland waters (except on Great Lakes system) |
| 532112 | Passenger truck (light duty) leasing |
| 532111 | Passenger truck (light duty) rental |
| 532112 | Passenger van leasing |
| 532111 | Passenger van rental |
| 532111 | Passenger van rental agencies |
| 485320 | Passenger van rental with driver (except shuttle service, taxi) |
| 532112 | Passenger vehicle fleet leasing |
| 111339 | Passion fruit farming |
| 928120 | Passport issuing services |
| 541921 | Passport photography services |
| 311422 | Pasta based products canning |
| 333241 | Pasta making machinery (i.e., food manufacturing-type) manufacturing |
| 311999 | Pasta mixes made from purchased dry ingredients |
| 311824 | Pasta, dry, manufacturing |
| 311991 | Pasta, fresh, manufacturing |
| 331314 | Paste made from purchased aluminum |
| 331420 | Paste made from purchased copper |
| 331221 | Paste made from purchased iron or steel |
| 331110 | Paste, iron or steel, made in iron and steel mills |
| 331492 | Paste, nonferrous metals (except aluminum, copper), made from purchased metal |
| 325520 | Pastes, adhesive, manufacturing |
| 311421 | Pastes, fruit and vegetable, canning |
| 333241 | Pasteurizing equipment, food, manufacturing |
| 311511 | Pasteurizing milk |
| 311612 | Pastrami made from purchased carcasses |
| 311812 | Pastries (e.g., Danish, French), fresh, made in commercial bakeries |
| 311813 | Pastries (e.g., Danish, French), frozen, manufacturing |
| 311824 | Pastries, uncooked, manufacturing |
| 321999 | Pastry boards, wood, manufacturing |

| | |
|---|---|
| 541199 | Patent agent services (i.e., patent filing and searching services) |
| 541110 | Patent attorneys' offices |
| 541110 | Patent attorneys' private practices |
| 541990 | Patent broker services (i.e., patent marketing services) |
| 533110 | Patent buying and licensing |
| 533110 | Patent leasing |
| 316110 | Patent leather manufacturing |
| 325412 | Patent medicine preparations manufacturing |
| 621511 | Pathological analysis laboratories |
| 621111 | Pathologists' (except oral, speech, voice) offices (e.g., centers, clinics) |
| 621111 | Pathologists', forensic, offices (e.g., centers, clinics) |
| 621111 | Pathologists', neuropathological, offices (e.g., centers, clinics) |
| 621210 | Pathologists', oral, offices (e.g., centers, clinics) |
| 621340 | Pathologists', speech or voice, offices (e.g., centers, clinics) |
| 621111 | Pathologists', surgical, offices (e.g., centers, clinics) |
| 621511 | Pathology laboratories, medical |
| 334510 | Patient monitoring equipment (e.g., intensive care, coronary care unit) manufacturing |
| 423450 | Patient monitoring equipment merchant wholesalers |
| 327331 | Patio block, concrete, manufacturing |
| 238990 | Patio construction |
| 336611 | Patrol boat building |
| 561612 | Patrol services, security |
| 541990 | Patrolling (i.e., visual inspection) of electric transmission or gas lines |
| 513199 | Pattern and plan (e.g., clothing patterns) publishers |
| 513199 | Pattern and plan (e.g., clothing patterns) publishers (except exclusive Internet publishing) |
| 513199 | Pattern and plan (e.g., clothing patterns) publishers and printing combined |
| 513199 | Pattern and plan (e.g., clothing patterns) publishers, exclusively on Internet |
| 332999 | Patterns (except shoe), industrial, manufacturing |
| 423830 | Patterns (except shoe), industrial, merchant wholesalers |
| 323111 | Patterns and plans (e.g., clothing patterns) commercial printing (except blueprinting, screen) without publishing |
| 323113 | Patterns and plans (e.g., clothing patterns) screen printing without publishing |
| 339999 | Patterns, shoe, manufacturing |
| 423850 | Patterns, shoe, merchant wholesalers |
| 237310 | Pavement, highway, road, street, bridge or airport runway, construction |
| 238990 | Paver, brick (e.g., driveway, patio, sidewalk), installation |
| 423810 | Pavers merchant wholesalers |
| 212390 | Pavers mining and/or beneficiating |
| 324121 | Paving blocks and mixtures made from purchased asphaltic materials |
| 327331 | Paving blocks, concrete, manufacturing |
| 327120 | Paving brick, clay, manufacturing |
| 333120 | Paving machinery manufacturing |
| 423320 | Paving mixtures merchant wholesalers |
| 238990 | Paving, residential and commercial driveway and parking lot |
| 522299 | Pawnshops |
| 812990 | Pay telephone equipment concession operators |
| 516210 | Pay television networks |
| 522390 | Payday lending services |
| 516210 | Pay-per-view cable programming |
| 541214 | Payroll processing services |
| 334210 | PBX (private branch exchange) equipment manufacturing |
| 111219 | Pea (except dry) farming, field and seed production |
| 111130 | Pea farming, dry, field and seed production |
| 813319 | Peace advocacy organizations |
| 928120 | Peace Corps |
| 111339 | Peach farming |
| 325130 | Peacock blue lake manufacturing |
| 311911 | Peanut butter blended with jelly manufacturing |
| 311911 | Peanut butter manufacturing |
| 311224 | Peanut cake, meal, and oil made in crushing mills |
| 333111 | Peanut combines (i.e., diggers, packers, threshers) manufacturing |
| 111992 | Peanut farming |
| 311225 | Peanut oil made from purchased oils |
| 333241 | Peanut roasting machines (i.e., food manufacturing-type) manufacturing |
| 115114 | Peanut shelling |
| 115113 | Peanut, machine harvesting |

| | |
|---|---|
| 424590 | Peanuts, bulk, unprocessed, merchant wholesalers |
| 111339 | Pear farming |
| 339910 | Pearl drilling, peeling, or sawing |
| 325130 | Pearl essence pigment, synthetic, manufacturing |
| 331511 | Pearlitic castings, malleable iron, unfinished, manufacturing |
| 423940 | Pearls merchant wholesalers |
| 339910 | Pearls, costume, manufacturing |
| 212390 | Peat grinding |
| 212390 | Peat humus mining and/or beneficiating |
| 212390 | Peat mining and/or beneficiating |
| 327999 | Peat pots, molded pulp, manufacturing |
| 212321 | Pebbles (except grinding) mining and/or beneficiating |
| 212390 | Pebbles grinding |
| 111335 | Pecan farming |
| 115114 | Pecan hulling and shelling |
| 311942 | Pectin manufacturing |
| 621111 | Pediatricians' (except mental health) offices (e.g., centers, clinics) |
| 621112 | Pediatricians', mental health, offices (e.g., centers, clinics) |
| 812113 | Pedicure and manicure salons |
| 812113 | Pedicurist services |
| 115210 | Pedigree (i.e., livestock, pets, poultry) record services |
| 812910 | Pedigree record services, pet |
| 334514 | Pedometers manufacturing |
| 621399 | Pedorthics' offices (e.g., centers, clinics) |
| 813920 | Peer review boards |
| 212323 | Pegmatite, feldspar, mining and/or beneficiating |
| 316990 | Pegs, leather shoe, manufacturing |
| 332994 | Pellet guns manufacturing |
| 333131 | Pellet mills machinery, mining-type, manufacturing |
| 332992 | Pellets, air rifle and pistol, manufacturing |
| 316110 | Pelts bleaching, currying, dyeing, scraping, and tanning |
| 424590 | Pelts, raw, merchant wholesalers |
| 339112 | Pelvimeters manufacturing |
| 339940 | Pen refills and cartridges manufacturing |
| 339940 | Pencil leads manufacturing |
| 339940 | Pencil sharpeners manufacturing |
| 321999 | Pencil slats, wood, manufacturing |

| | |
|---|---|
| 339940 | Pencils manufacturing |
| 424120 | Pencils merchant wholesalers |
| 335132 | Pendant lamps (except residential), electric, manufacturing |
| 335131 | Pendant lamps fixtures, residential electric, manufacturing |
| 325613 | Penetrants manufacturing |
| 325998 | Penetrating fluids, synthetic, manufacturing |
| 325412 | Penicillin preparations manufacturing |
| 325411 | Penicillin, uncompounded, manufacturing |
| 922140 | Penitentiaries (except private operation of) |
| 236220 | Penitentiary construction |
| 339940 | Pens manufacturing |
| 424120 | Pens, writing, merchant wholesalers |
| 523940 | Pension fund managing |
| 524292 | Pension fund, third party administrative services |
| 525110 | Pension funds |
| 525110 | Pension plans (e.g., employee benefit, retirement) |
| 332313 | Penstocks, fabricated metal plate, manufacturing |
| 325194 | Pentachlorophenol manufacturing |
| 325199 | Pentaerythritol manufacturing |
| 325110 | Pentanes made from refined petroleum or liquid hydrocarbons |
| 325110 | Pentenes made from refined petroleum or liquid hydrocarbons |
| 325920 | Pentolite explosive materials manufacturing |
| 561330 | PEO (professional employer organizations) |
| 111219 | Pepper (e.g., bell, chili, green, hot, red, sweet) farming |
| 311942 | Pepper (i.e., spice) manufacturing |
| 325998 | Peppermint oil manufacturing |
| 313210 | Percales weaving |
| 114111 | Perch fishing |
| 325180 | Perchloric acid manufacturing |
| 325199 | Perchloroethylene manufacturing |
| 335210 | Percolators, household-type electric, manufacturing |
| 332992 | Percussion caps (i.e., 30 mm. or less, 1.18 inch or less), ammunition, manufacturing |
| 339992 | Percussion musical instruments manufacturing |

| | |
|---|---|
| 423420 | Perforating machines merchant wholesalers |
| 213112 | Perforating oil and gas well casings on a contract basis |
| 533110 | Performance rights, licensing of |
| 711510 | Performers (i.e., entertainers), independent |
| 711510 | Performing artists, independent |
| 711310 | Performing arts center operators |
| 611610 | Performing arts schools (except academic) |
| 561599 | Performing arts ticket offices |
| 325199 | Perfume materials (i.e., basic synthetic chemicals, such as terpineol) manufacturing |
| 456120 | Perfume stores |
| 325620 | Perfumes manufacturing |
| 424210 | Perfumes merchant wholesalers |
| 513120 | Periodical publishers |
| 513120 | Periodical publishers (except exclusive Internet publishing) |
| 513120 | Periodical publishers and printing combined |
| 513120 | Periodical publishers, exclusively on Internet |
| 323111 | Periodicals commercial printing (except screen) without publishing |
| 424920 | Periodicals merchant wholesalers |
| 323113 | Periodicals screen printing without publishing |
| 621210 | Periodontists' offices (e.g., centers, clinics) |
| 334418 | Peripheral controller boards manufacturing |
| 423430 | Peripheral equipment, computer, merchant wholesalers |
| 333310 | Periscopes manufacturing |
| 327992 | Perlite aggregates manufacturing |
| 212390 | Perlite mining and/or beneficiating |
| 327992 | Perlite, expanded, manufacturing |
| 331524 | Permanent mold castings, aluminum, unfinished, manufacturing |
| 331529 | Permanent mold castings, nonferrous metal (except aluminum), unfinished, manufacturing |
| 325620 | Permanent wave preparations manufacturing |
| 238130 | Permanent wood foundation installation |
| 325180 | Peroxides, inorganic, manufacturing |
| 325199 | Peroxides, organic, manufacturing |
| 325130 | Persian orange lake manufacturing |

| | |
|---|---|
| 111339 | Persimmon farming |
| 334310 | Personal audio and video headsets, including virtual reality headsets, manufacturing |
| 423620 | Personal care appliances, electric, merchant wholesalers |
| 812990 | Personal chef services |
| 334418 | Personal computer modems manufacturing |
| 334111 | Personal computers manufacturing |
| 522291 | Personal credit institutions (i.e., unsecured cash loans) |
| 611699 | Personal development schools |
| 525920 | Personal estates (i.e., managing assets) |
| 522291 | Personal finance companies (i.e., unsecured cash loans) |
| 611519 | Personal fitness instructor training |
| 812990 | Personal fitness training services |
| 339910 | Personal goods, metal, manufacturing |
| 551112 | Personal holding companies |
| 525920 | Personal investment trusts |
| 523991 | Personal investments trust administration |
| 523940 | Personal investments trusts, managing |
| 316990 | Personal leather goods (e.g., coin purses, eyeglass cases, key cases), small, manufacturing |
| 456199 | Personal mobility scooter dealers |
| 812990 | Personal organizer services |
| 561612 | Personal protection services (except security systems services) |
| 423990 | Personal safety devices and supplies (e.g., eye shields, face shields, nonelectric respirators) merchant wholesalers |
| 339113 | Personal safety devices, not specified elsewhere, manufacturing |
| 424130 | Personal sanitary paper products merchant wholesalers |
| 812990 | Personal shopping services |
| 525920 | Personal trusts |
| 441227 | Personal watercraft dealers |
| 336999 | Personal watercraft manufacturing |
| 532284 | Personal watercraft rental |
| 561320 | Personnel (e.g., industrial, office, health care, legal, construction) suppliers |
| 813920 | Personnel management associations |
| 541612 | Personnel management consulting services |
| 921190 | Personnel offices, government |

| | |
|---|---|
| 325320 | Pest (e.g., ant, rat, roach, rodent) control poison manufacturing |
| 561710 | Pest (e.g., termite) inspection services |
| 561710 | Pest control (except agricultural, forestry) services |
| 926140 | Pest control programs, agriculture, government |
| 115112 | Pest control services, agricultural |
| 115310 | Pest control services, forestry |
| 424690 | Pesticides (except agricultural) merchant wholesalers |
| 325320 | Pesticides manufacturing |
| 424910 | Pesticides, agricultural, merchant wholesalers |
| 334510 | PET (positron emission tomography) scanners manufacturing |
| 812910 | Pet boarding services |
| 812220 | Pet cemeteries |
| 812220 | Pet crematories |
| 311119 | Pet food (except cat, dog) manufacturing |
| 424490 | Pet food merchant wholesalers |
| 311111 | Pet food, dog and cat, manufacturing |
| 812910 | Pet grooming services |
| 524128 | Pet health insurance carriers, direct |
| 541940 | Pet hospitals |
| 926150 | Pet licensing |
| 459910 | Pet shops |
| 812910 | Pet sitting services |
| 424990 | Pet supplies (except pet food) merchant wholesalers |
| 459910 | Pet supply stores |
| 812910 | Pet training services |
| 485991 | Pet transportation services |
| 812910 | Pet walking services |
| 324110 | Petrochemical feedstocks made in petroleum refineries |
| 237120 | Petrochemical plant construction |
| 324110 | Petrochemicals made in petroleum refineries |
| 424710 | Petroleum and petroleum products bulk stations and terminals, merchant wholesalers |
| 424720 | Petroleum and petroleum products merchant wholesalers (except bulk stations, terminals) |
| 425120 | Petroleum brokers |
| 324110 | Petroleum coke made in petroleum refineries |
| 424720 | Petroleum coke merchant wholesalers |
| 324110 | Petroleum cracking and reforming |
| 324110 | Petroleum distillation |
| 541330 | Petroleum engineering services |
| 211130 | Petroleum gases, liquefied, recovering from oil and gas field gases |
| 324199 | Petroleum jelly made from refined petroleum |
| 324110 | Petroleum jelly made in petroleum refineries |
| 324191 | Petroleum lubricating oils made from refined petroleum |
| 324110 | Petroleum lubricating oils made in petroleum refineries |
| 486110 | Petroleum pipelines, crude |
| 486910 | Petroleum pipelines, refined |
| 325211 | Petroleum polymer resins manufacturing |
| 423830 | Petroleum production machinery and equipment merchant wholesalers |
| 324110 | Petroleum refineries |
| 237120 | Petroleum refinery construction |
| 333248 | Petroleum refining machinery manufacturing |
| 332420 | Petroleum storage tanks, heavy gauge metal, manufacturing |
| 324199 | Petroleum waxes made from refined petroleum |
| 211120 | Petroleum, crude, production (i.e., extraction) |
| 424990 | Pets merchant wholesalers |
| 712130 | Petting zoos |
| 337127 | Pews, church, manufacturing |
| 339910 | Pewter ware manufacturing |
| 236210 | Pharmaceutical manufacturing plant construction |
| 325412 | Pharmaceutical preparations (e.g., capsules, liniments, ointments, tablets) manufacturing |
| 424210 | Pharmaceuticals merchant wholesalers |
| 456110 | Pharmacies |
| 813920 | Pharmacists' associations |
| 524292 | Pharmacy Benefit Management (PBM) services |
| 334515 | Phase angle meters manufacturing |
| 335312 | Phase converters (i.e., electrical equipment) manufacturing |
| 112390 | Pheasant production |
| 325194 | Phenol manufacturing |
| 325211 | Phenol-formaldehyde resins manufacturing |
| 325211 | Phenol-furfural resins manufacturing |

| | |
|---|---|
| 325211 | Phenolic resins manufacturing |
| 325211 | Phenoxy resins manufacturing |
| 813211 | Philanthropic trusts, awarding grants |
| 212390 | Phlogopite mining and/or beneficiating |
| 334510 | Phonocardiographs manufacturing |
| 334610 | Phonograph records manufacturing |
| 423990 | Phonograph records merchant wholesalers |
| 423440 | Phonographs, coin- or card-operated, merchant wholesalers |
| 325199 | Phosgene manufacturing |
| 212390 | Phosphate rock mining and/or beneficiating |
| 424910 | Phosphate rock, ground, merchant wholesalers |
| 325312 | Phosphatic fertilizer materials manufacturing |
| 325314 | Phosphatic fertilizers made by mixing purchased materials |
| 325130 | Phosphomolybdic acid lakes and toners manufacturing |
| 325199 | Phosphoric acid esters manufacturing |
| 325312 | Phosphoric acid manufacturing |
| 325180 | Phosphorus compounds, not specified elsewhere by process, manufacturing |
| 325180 | Phosphorus oxychloride manufacturing |
| 325130 | Phosphotungstic acid lakes and toners manufacturing |
| 323111 | Photo albums and refills manufacturing |
| 424120 | Photo albums merchant wholesalers |
| 323120 | Photocomposition services, for the printing trade |
| 424120 | Photocopy supplies merchant wholesalers |
| 811210 | Photocopying machine repair and maintenance services without retailing new photocopying machines |
| 333310 | Photocopying machines manufacturing |
| 561439 | Photocopying services (except combined with printing services) |
| 325992 | Photocopying toner cartridges manufacturing |
| 334413 | Photoelectric cells, solid-state (e.g., electronic eye), manufacturing |
| 333248 | Photoengraving machinery manufacturing |
| 323120 | Photoengraving plate preparation services |
| 423410 | Photofinishing equipment merchant wholesalers |
| 812921 | Photofinishing labs (except one-hour) |

| | |
|---|---|
| 812922 | Photofinishing labs, one-hour |
| 812921 | Photofinishing services (except one-hour) |
| 812922 | Photofinishing services, one-hour |
| 335139 | Photoflash and photoflood lamp bulbs and tubes manufacturing |
| 333310 | Photoflash equipment manufacturing |
| 541370 | Photogrammetric mapping services |
| 322299 | Photograph folders, mats, and mounts manufacturing |
| 541922 | Photographers specializing in aerial photography |
| 711510 | Photographers, independent artistic |
| 325992 | Photographic chemicals manufacturing |
| 423410 | Photographic equipment and supplies merchant wholesalers |
| 333310 | Photographic equipment manufacturing |
| 532210 | Photographic equipment rental |
| 811210 | Photographic equipment repair shops without retailing new photographic equipment |
| 423410 | Photographic film and plates merchant wholesalers |
| 325992 | Photographic film, cloth, paper, and plate, sensitized, manufacturing |
| 333310 | Photographic lenses manufacturing |
| 812990 | Photographic machine concession operators, coin- or card-operated |
| 449210 | Photographic supply stores |
| 326113 | Photographic, micrographic, and X-ray plastics, sheet, and film (except sensitized), manufacturing |
| 611610 | Photography schools, art |
| 611519 | Photography schools, commercial |
| 541922 | Photography services, commercial |
| 541921 | Photography services, portrait (e.g., still, video) |
| 541922 | Photography studios, commercial |
| 541921 | Photography studios, portrait |
| 711510 | Photojournalists, independent (freelance) |
| 327212 | Photomask blanks, glass, made in glass making plants |
| 325992 | Photomasks manufacturing |
| 334516 | Photometers (except photographic exposure meters) manufacturing |
| 334516 | Photonexcitation analyzers manufacturing |
| 334413 | Photonic integrated circuits manufacturing |

| | |
|---|---|
| 541715 | Photonics research and development services (except nanotechnology research and development) |
| 325992 | Photosensitized paper manufacturing |
| 323120 | Phototypesetting services |
| 334413 | Photovoltaic cells manufacturing |
| 334413 | Photovoltaic devices, solid-state, manufacturing |
| 335999 | Photovoltaic panels made from purchased cells |
| 325199 | Phthalate acid manufacturing |
| 325211 | Phthalic alkyd resins manufacturing |
| 325194 | Phthalic anhydride manufacturing |
| 325211 | Phthalic anhydride resins manufacturing |
| 325130 | Phthalocyanine pigments manufacturing |
| 541614 | Physical distribution consulting services |
| 713940 | Physical fitness centers |
| 621999 | Physical fitness evaluation services (except by offices of health practitioners) |
| 713940 | Physical fitness facilities |
| 713940 | Physical fitness studios |
| 334519 | Physical properties testing and inspection equipment manufacturing |
| 622310 | Physical rehabilitation hospitals |
| 541715 | Physical science research and development laboratories or services (except biotechnology and nanotechnology research and development) |
| 621340 | Physical therapists' offices (e.g., centers, clinics) |
| 621340 | Physical therapy offices (e.g., centers, clinics) |
| 621340 | Physical-integration practitioners' offices (e.g., centers, clinics) |
| 621111 | Physicians' (except mental health) offices (e.g., centers, clinics) |
| 621399 | Physicians' assistants' offices (e.g., centers, clinics) |
| 423450 | Physicians' equipment and supplies merchant wholesalers |
| 621112 | Physicians', mental health, offices (e.g., centers, clinics) |
| 541690 | Physics consulting services |
| 541715 | Physics research and development laboratories or services (except nanotechnology research and development) |
| 621340 | Physiotherapists' offices (e.g., centers, clinics) |
| 339112 | Physiotherapy equipment (except electrotherapeutic) manufacturing |
| 325411 | Physostigmine and derivatives (i.e., basic chemicals) manufacturing |
| 332510 | Piano hardware, metal, manufacturing |
| 339992 | Piano parts and materials (except piano hardware) manufacturing |
| 532289 | Piano rental |
| 459140 | Piano stores |
| 339992 | Piccolos and parts manufacturing |
| 333248 | Picker machinery for textiles manufacturing |
| 333248 | Picker sticks for looms manufacturing |
| 311710 | Picking crab meat |
| 713990 | Pickleball clubs, recreational |
| 333519 | Picklers and pickling machinery, metalworking, manufacturing |
| 311421 | Pickles manufacturing |
| 311421 | Pickling fruits and vegetables |
| 332813 | Pickling metals and metal products for the trade |
| 332216 | Picks (i.e., handtools) manufacturing |
| 812320 | Pick-up and drop-off sites for drycleaners and laundries |
| 336214 | Pick-up canopies, caps, or covers manufacturing |
| 336110 | Pick-up trucks, light duty, assembling on chassis of own manufacture |
| 713990 | Picnic grounds |
| 326199 | Picnic jugs, plastics (except foam), manufacturing |
| 325920 | Picric acid explosive materials manufacturing |
| 334511 | Pictorial situation instrumentation manufacturing |
| 449129 | Picture frame shops, custom |
| 311824 | Pie crust shells, uncooked, made from purchased flour |
| 424310 | Piece goods (except burlap, felt) merchant wholesalers |
| 459130 | Piece goods stores |
| 424990 | Piece goods, burlap and felt, merchant wholesalers |
| 237990 | Pier construction |
| 531120 | Piers and associated building rental or leasing |
| 713110 | Piers, amusement |
| 424420 | Pies (e.g., fruit, meat, poultry), frozen, merchant wholesalers |
| 311812 | Pies, fresh, made in commercial bakeries |
| 311813 | Pies, frozen, manufacturing |

| | |
|---|---|
| 334419 | Piezoelectric crystals manufacturing |
| 334419 | Piezoelectric devices manufacturing |
| 112210 | Pig farming |
| 331110 | Pig iron manufacturing |
| 423510 | Pig iron merchant wholesalers |
| 325130 | Pigment, scarlet lake, manufacturing |
| 325130 | Pigments (except animal black, bone black), organic, manufacturing |
| 325130 | Pigments (except bone black, carbon black, lamp black), inorganic, manufacturing |
| 212390 | Pigments, natural, mineral, mining and/or beneficiating |
| 424950 | Pigments, paint, merchant wholesalers |
| 311612 | Pig's feet, cooked and pickled, made from purchased carcasses |
| 713940 | Pilates fitness studios or centers |
| 611699 | Pilates instruction, camps or schools |
| 114111 | Pilchard fishing |
| 238910 | Pile driving, building foundation |
| 237990 | Pile driving, marine |
| 313240 | Pile fabrics made in warp or weft knitting mills |
| 332313 | Pile shells, fabricated metal plate, manufacturing |
| 332322 | Pile shells, sheet metal (except stampings), manufacturing |
| 333120 | Pile-driving equipment manufacturing |
| 238910 | Piling (i.e., bored, cast-in-place, drilled), building foundation, contractors |
| 321114 | Pilings, foundation and marine construction, treating |
| 331110 | Pilings, iron or steel plain sheet, made in iron and steel mills |
| 423510 | Pilings, metal, merchant wholesalers |
| 321114 | Pilings, round wood, cutting and treating |
| 321114 | Pilings, wood, treating |
| 332991 | Pillow blocks with ball or roller bearings manufacturing |
| 812320 | Pillow cleaning services |
| 314120 | Pillowcases, bed, made from purchased fabrics |
| 314120 | Pillows made from purchased materials |
| 488490 | Pilot car services (i.e., wide load warning services) |
| 488330 | Piloting services, water transportation |
| 713120 | Pinball arcades |
| 713990 | Pinball machine concession operators (i.e., supplying and servicing in others' facilities) |
| 339999 | Pinball machines, coin- or card-operated, manufacturing |
| 113210 | Pine gum extracting |
| 325194 | Pine oil manufacturing |
| 111339 | Pineapple farming |
| 325194 | Pinene manufacturing |
| 713990 | Ping pong parlors |
| 212323 | Pinite mining and/or beneficiating |
| 339993 | Pins (except precious) manufacturing |
| 339910 | Pins and brooches, precious metal, manufacturing |
| 712120 | Pioneer villages |
| 331210 | Pipe (e.g., heavy riveted, lock joint, seamless, welded) made from purchased iron or steel |
| 423720 | Pipe and boiler coverings merchant wholesalers |
| 332996 | Pipe and pipe fittings made from purchased metal pipe |
| 331511 | Pipe and pipe fittings, cast iron, manufacturing |
| 333519 | Pipe and tube rolling mill machinery, metalworking, manufacturing |
| 332323 | Pipe bannisters, metal, manufacturing |
| 326299 | Pipe bits and stems, tobacco, hard rubber, manufacturing |
| 339999 | Pipe cleaners manufacturing |
| 332996 | Pipe couplings made from purchased metal pipe |
| 331511 | Pipe couplings, cast iron, manufacturing |
| 238290 | Pipe covering |
| 333517 | Pipe cutting and threading machines, metalworking, manufacturing |
| 332996 | Pipe fabricating (i.e., bending, cutting, threading) made from purchased metal pipe |
| 238220 | Pipe fitting contractors |
| 423840 | Pipe fittings and valves (except plumbing) merchant wholesalers |
| 423720 | Pipe fittings and valves, plumbers', merchant wholesalers |
| 326122 | Pipe fittings, rigid plastics, manufacturing |
| 332323 | Pipe guards, metal, manufacturing |
| 332999 | Pipe hangers and supports, metal, manufacturing |
| 332996 | Pipe headers made from purchased metal pipe |
| 237120 | Pipe lining (except thermal insulating) contractors |
| 331318 | Pipe made by extruding purchased aluminum |

| | |
|---|---|
| 332323 | Pipe railings, metal, manufacturing |
| 325520 | Pipe sealing compounds manufacturing |
| 213112 | Pipe testing services, oil and gas field, on a contract basis |
| 424940 | Pipe tobacco merchant wholesalers |
| 312230 | Pipe tobacco, prepared, manufacturing |
| 331318 | Pipe, aluminum, made in integrated secondary smelting and extruding mills |
| 327332 | Pipe, concrete, manufacturing |
| 238290 | Pipe, duct and boiler insulation |
| 331420 | Pipe, extruded and drawn, brass, bronze, and copper, made from purchased copper or in integrated secondary smelting and rolling, drawing or extruding plants |
| 332313 | Pipe, fabricated metal plate, manufacturing |
| 331110 | Pipe, iron or steel, made in iron and steel mills |
| 423510 | Pipe, metal, merchant wholesalers |
| 331491 | Pipe, nonferrous metals (except aluminum, copper), made from purchased metals or scrap |
| 326122 | Pipe, rigid plastics, manufacturing |
| 332322 | Pipe, sheet metal (except stampings), manufacturing |
| 516110 | Piped-in music services, radio transmitted |
| 237990 | Pipe-jacking contractors |
| 237120 | Pipeline construction on oil and gas field gathering lines to point of distribution on a contract basis |
| 541990 | Pipeline inspection (i.e., visual) services |
| 423830 | Pipeline machinery and equipment merchant wholesalers |
| 237120 | Pipeline rehabilitation contractors |
| 488999 | Pipeline terminal facilities, independently operated |
| 486990 | Pipeline transportation (except crude oil, natural gas, refined petroleum products) |
| 486110 | Pipeline transportation, crude oil |
| 486910 | Pipeline transportation, gasoline and other refined petroleum products |
| 486210 | Pipeline transportation, natural gas |
| 237120 | Pipeline wrapping contractors |
| 237120 | Pipeline, gas and oil, construction |
| 339992 | Pipes, organ, manufacturing |
| 339999 | Pipes, smoker's, manufacturing |
| 212390 | Pipestones mining and/or beneficiating |
| 111335 | Pistachio farming |

| | |
|---|---|
| 332994 | Pistols manufacturing |
| 336310 | Pistons and piston rings manufacturing |
| 423120 | Pistons and valves, automotive, merchant wholesalers |
| 423840 | Pistons and valves, industrial, merchant wholesalers |
| 423830 | Pistons, hydraulic and pneumatic, merchant wholesalers |
| 325194 | Pitch made by distillation of coal tar |
| 324122 | Pitch, roofing, made from purchased asphaltic materials |
| 325194 | Pitch, wood, manufacturing |
| 212290 | Pitchblende mining and/or beneficiating |
| 334519 | Pitometers manufacturing |
| 325411 | Pituitary gland derivatives, uncompounded, manufacturing |
| 325412 | Pituitary gland preparations manufacturing |
| 722513 | Pizza delivery shops |
| 311824 | Pizza doughs made from purchased flour |
| 722511 | Pizza parlors, full service |
| 722513 | Pizza parlors, limited-service |
| 424490 | Pizzas (except frozen) merchant wholesalers |
| 311991 | Pizzas, fresh, manufacturing |
| 311412 | Pizzas, frozen, manufacturing |
| 424420 | Pizzas, frozen, merchant wholesalers |
| 722511 | Pizzerias, full service |
| 722513 | Pizzerias, limited-service (e.g., takeout) |
| 314120 | Placemats, all materials, made from purchased materials |
| 561311 | Placement agencies or services, employment |
| 621991 | Placenta banks |
| 212220 | Placer gold mining and/or beneficiating |
| 212220 | Placer silver mining and/or beneficiating |
| 813110 | Places of worship |
| 238120 | Placing and tying reinforcing rod at a construction site |
| 334417 | Planar cable connectors manufacturing |
| 333243 | Planers woodworking-type, stationary, manufacturing |
| 333120 | Planers, bituminous, manufacturing |
| 333991 | Planers, handheld power-driven, manufacturing |
| 333517 | Planers, metalworking, manufacturing |
| 332216 | Planes, handheld, nonpowered, manufacturing |
| 712110 | Planetariums |

| | |
|---|---|
| 321912 | Planing mills (except millwork) |
| 321918 | Planing mills, millwork |
| 321912 | Planing purchased lumber |
| 525120 | Plans, health- and welfare-related employee benefit |
| 522180 | Plans, Morris (i.e., known as), depository |
| 522299 | Plans, Morris (i.e., known as), nondepository |
| 525110 | Plans, pension |
| 561730 | Plant and shrub maintenance in buildings |
| 112519 | Plant aquaculture |
| 424910 | Plant bulbs merchant wholesalers |
| 424990 | Plant food merchant wholesalers |
| 325311 | Plant foods, mixed, made in plants producing nitrogenous fertilizer materials |
| 325312 | Plant foods, mixed, made in plants producing phosphatic fertilizer materials |
| 325320 | Plant growth regulants manufacturing |
| 561730 | Plant maintenance services |
| 111422 | Plant, ornamental, growing |
| 111422 | Plant, potted flower and foliage, growing |
| 111339 | Plantain farming |
| 115112 | Planting crops |
| 423820 | Planting machinery and equipment, farm-type, merchant wholesalers |
| 333111 | Planting machines, farm-type, manufacturing |
| 424930 | Plants, potted, merchant wholesalers |
| 621991 | Plasma collection services |
| 333517 | Plasma jet spray metal forming machines manufacturing |
| 333517 | Plasma process metal cutting machines (except welding equipment) manufacturing |
| 333992 | Plasma welding equipment manufacturing |
| 621991 | Plasmapheresis centers |
| 325414 | Plasmas manufacturing |
| 424210 | Plasmas, blood, merchant wholesalers |
| 327420 | Plaster and plasterboard, gypsum, manufacturing |
| 423320 | Plaster merchant wholesalers |
| 327420 | Plaster of paris manufacturing |
| 327420 | Plaster of paris products (e.g., columns, statuary, urns) manufacturing |
| 327420 | Plaster, gypsum, manufacturing |
| 238310 | Plastering (i.e., ornamental, plain) contractors |
| 212323 | Plastic fire clay mining and/or beneficiating |
| 621111 | Plastic surgeons' offices (e.g., centers, clinics) |
| 325510 | Plastic wood fillers manufacturing |
| 332813 | Plastic, glass, or other media blasting services |
| 325199 | Plasticizers (i.e., basic synthetic chemicals) manufacturing |
| 424610 | Plasticizers merchant wholesalers |
| 337126 | Plastics (including fiberglass) furniture (except upholstered), household-type, manufacturing |
| 326220 | Plastics and rubber belts and hoses (without fittings) manufacturing |
| 325211 | Plastics and synthetic resins regenerating, precipitating, and coagulating |
| 424130 | Plastics bags merchant wholesalers |
| 424610 | Plastics basic shapes (e.g., film, rod, sheet, sheeting, tubing) merchant wholesalers |
| 313320 | Plastics coating of textiles and apparel |
| 326113 | Plastics film and unlaminated sheet (except packaging) manufacturing |
| 424610 | Plastics foam merchant wholesalers |
| 423840 | Plastics foam packing and packaging materials merchant wholesalers |
| 424990 | Plastics foam products (except disposable and packaging) merchant wholesalers |
| 424130 | Plastics foam products, disposable (except packaging, packing), merchant wholesalers |
| 315210 | Plastics gowns cut and sew apparel contractors |
| 315250 | Plastics gowns cut and sewn from purchased fabric (except apparel contractors) |
| 423830 | Plastics industries machinery, equipment, and supplies merchant wholesalers |
| 337110 | Plastics laminated over particleboard (e.g., fixture tops) manufacturing |
| 424610 | Plastics materials merchant wholesalers |
| 315210 | Plastics rainwear cut and sew apparel contractors |
| 315250 | Plastics rainwear cut and sewn from purchased fabric (except apparel contractors) |
| 325991 | Plastics resins compounding from recycled materials |

| | |
|---|---|
| 424610 | Plastics resins merchant wholesalers |
| 325991 | Plastics resins, custom compounding of purchased |
| 423930 | Plastics scrap merchant wholesalers |
| 333248 | Plastics working machinery manufacturing |
| 325510 | Plastisol coating compounds manufacturing |
| 524126 | Plate glass insurance carriers, direct |
| 423390 | Plate glass merchant wholesalers |
| 333519 | Plate rolling mill machinery, metalworking, manufacturing |
| 332313 | Plate work (e.g., bending, cutting, punching, shaping, welding), fabricated metal, manufacturing |
| 331315 | Plate, aluminum, made by continuous casting purchased aluminum |
| 331315 | Plate, aluminum, made by flat rolling purchased aluminum |
| 331315 | Plate, aluminum, made in integrated secondary smelting and continuous casting mills |
| 331315 | Plate, aluminum, made in integrated secondary smelting and flat rolling mills |
| 331420 | Plate, copper and copper alloy, made from purchased copper or in integrated secondary smelting and rolling, drawing or extruding plants |
| 331110 | Plate, iron or steel, made in iron and steel mills |
| 326130 | Plate, laminated plastics, manufacturing |
| 331491 | Plate, nonferrous metals (except aluminum, copper), made from purchased metals or scrap |
| 332215 | Plated metal cutlery manufacturing |
| 423940 | Plated metal cutlery or flatware merchant wholesalers |
| 332215 | Plated metal flatware manufacturing |
| 332999 | Plated ware (e.g., ecclesiastical ware, hollowware, toilet ware) manufacturing |
| 335932 | Plates (i.e., outlet or switch covers), face, manufacturing |
| 322299 | Plates, molded pulp, manufacturing |
| 326140 | Plates, polystyrene foam, manufacturing |
| 518210 | Platform as a service (PaaS) |
| 332813 | Plating metals and metal products for the trade |
| 331491 | Platinum and platinum alloy rolling, drawing, or extruding from purchased metals or scrap |
| 331491 | Platinum and platinum alloy sheet and tubing made from purchased metals or scrap |

| | |
|---|---|
| 332999 | Platinum foil and leaf not made in rolling mills |
| 212290 | Platinum mining and/or beneficiating |
| 331492 | Platinum recovering from scrap and/or alloying purchased metals |
| 331410 | Platinum refining, primary |
| 237990 | Playground construction |
| 423910 | Playground equipment and supplies merchant wholesalers |
| 238990 | Playground equipment installation |
| 423920 | Playing cards merchant wholesalers |
| 337126 | Playpens, children's metal, manufacturing |
| 337122 | Playpens, children's wood, manufacturing |
| 315210 | Playsuits cut and sew apparel contractors |
| 315250 | Playsuits, women's, girls', and infants', cut and sewn from purchased fabric (except apparel contractors) |
| 711510 | Playwrights, independent |
| 811490 | Pleasure boat maintenance services (e.g., cleaning, scaling, waxing) |
| 532284 | Pleasure boat rental |
| 336612 | Pleasure boats manufacturing |
| 423910 | Pleasure boats merchant wholesalers |
| 315210 | Pleating contractors on apparel |
| 332216 | Pliers, handtools, manufacturing |
| 327331 | Plinth blocks, precast terrazzo, manufacturing |
| 334418 | Plotter controller boards manufacturing |
| 423430 | Plotters merchant wholesalers |
| 334118 | Plotters, computer, manufacturing |
| 115112 | Plowing |
| 333120 | Plows, construction (e.g., excavating, grading), manufacturing |
| 423820 | Plows, farm, merchant wholesalers |
| 333111 | Plows, farm-type, manufacturing |
| 111422 | Plug (i.e., floriculture products) growing |
| 332911 | Plug valves, industrial-type, manufacturing |
| 213112 | Plugging and abandoning wells on a contract basis |
| 335931 | Plugs, electric cord, manufacturing |
| 332999 | Plugs, magnetic metal drain, manufacturing |
| 321999 | Plugs, wood, manufacturing |
| 111339 | Plum farming |
| 238220 | Plumbers |

| | |
|---|---|
| 611513 | Plumbers' apprenticeship training |
| 423720 | Plumbers' brass goods merchant wholesalers |
| 332216 | Plumbers' handtools, nonpowered, manufacturing |
| 325520 | Plumbers' putty manufacturing |
| 423710 | Plumbers' tools and equipment merchant wholesalers |
| 238220 | Plumbing and heating contractors |
| 332919 | Plumbing and heating inline valves (e.g., check, cutoffs, stop) manufacturing |
| 423720 | Plumbing and heating valves merchant wholesalers |
| 238220 | Plumbing contractors |
| 423720 | Plumbing equipment merchant wholesalers |
| 532490 | Plumbing equipment rental or leasing |
| 332913 | Plumbing fittings and couplings (e.g., compression fittings, metal elbows, metal unions) manufacturing |
| 332913 | Plumbing fixture fittings and trim, all materials, manufacturing |
| 238220 | Plumbing fixture installation |
| 326191 | Plumbing fixtures (e.g., shower stalls, toilets, urinals), plastics or fiberglass, manufacturing |
| 423720 | Plumbing fixtures merchant wholesalers |
| 332999 | Plumbing fixtures, metal, manufacturing |
| 327110 | Plumbing fixtures, vitreous china, manufacturing |
| 423720 | Plumbing supplies merchant wholesalers |
| 444180 | Plumbing supply stores |
| 423310 | Plywood merchant wholesalers |
| 321211 | Plywood, faced with nonwood materials, hardwood, manufacturing |
| 321212 | Plywood, faced with nonwood materials, softwood, manufacturing |
| 321211 | Plywood, hardwood faced, manufacturing |
| 321211 | Plywood, hardwood, manufacturing |
| 321212 | Plywood, softwood faced, manufacturing |
| 321212 | Plywood, softwood, manufacturing |
| 332912 | Pneumatic aircraft subassemblies manufacturing |
| 334513 | Pneumatic controllers, industrial process type, manufacturing |
| 333995 | Pneumatic cylinders, fluid power, manufacturing |
| 326220 | Pneumatic hose (without fittings), rubber or plastics, manufacturing |

| | |
|---|---|
| 332912 | Pneumatic hose fittings, fluid power, manufacturing |
| 423830 | Pneumatic pumps and parts merchant wholesalers |
| 333996 | Pneumatic pumps, fluid power, manufacturing |
| 334512 | Pneumatic relays, air-conditioning-type, manufacturing |
| 238290 | Pneumatic tube conveyor system installation |
| 333922 | Pneumatic tube conveyors manufacturing |
| 332912 | Pneumatic valves, fluid power, manufacturing |
| 322230 | Pocket folders made from purchased paper or paperboard |
| 332215 | Pocket knives manufacturing |
| 339910 | Pocketbooks, precious metal, men's or women's, manufacturing |
| 315210 | Pockets (e.g., coat, suit) cut and sew apparel contractors |
| 621391 | Podiatrists' offices (e.g., centers, clinics) |
| 813410 | Poetry clubs |
| 711510 | Poets, independent |
| 334118 | Point of sale terminals manufacturing |
| 423420 | Point of sale terminals merchant wholesalers |
| 334118 | Pointing devices, computer peripheral equipment, manufacturing |
| 315250 | Pointing furs |
| 339114 | Points, abrasive dental, manufacturing |
| 334516 | Polariscopes manufacturing |
| 334516 | Polarizers manufacturing |
| 334516 | Polarographic equipment manufacturing |
| 238990 | Pole (e.g., telephone) removal |
| 237130 | Pole line construction |
| 423610 | Pole line hardware merchant wholesalers |
| 327390 | Poles, concrete, manufacturing |
| 423510 | Poles, metal, merchant wholesalers |
| 321114 | Poles, round wood, cutting and treating |
| 321113 | Poles, wood, made from log or bolts |
| 321114 | Poles, wood, treating |
| 922120 | Police academies |
| 922120 | Police and fire departments, combined |
| 315210 | Police caps and hats (except protective head gear) cut and sew apparel contractors |

| | |
|---|---|
| 315990 | Police caps and hats (except protective head gear) cut and sewn from purchased fabric (except apparel contractors) |
| 922120 | Police departments (except American Indian or Alaska Native) |
| 315250 | Police dress uniforms, men's, cut and sewn from purchased fabric (except apparel contractors) |
| 315250 | Police dress uniforms, women's, cut and sewn from purchased fabric (except apparel contractors) |
| 459999 | Police supply stores |
| 611519 | Police training schools |
| 315210 | Police uniforms cut and sew apparel contractors |
| 921150 | Police, American Indian or Alaska Native tribal |
| 311212 | Polished rice manufacturing |
| 333991 | Polishers, handheld power-driven, manufacturing |
| 325612 | Polishes (e.g., automobile, furniture, metal, shoe) manufacturing |
| 424690 | Polishes (e.g., automobile, furniture, metal, shoe, stove) merchant wholesalers |
| 333517 | Polishing and buffing machines, metalworking, manufacturing |
| 332813 | Polishing metals and metal products for the trade |
| 325612 | Polishing preparations manufacturing |
| 327910 | Polishing wheels manufacturing |
| 813940 | Political action committees (PACs) |
| 813940 | Political campaign organizations |
| 711510 | Political cartoonists, independent |
| 541820 | Political consulting services |
| 541910 | Political opinion polling services |
| 813940 | Political organizations or clubs |
| 813940 | Political parties |
| 115112 | Pollinating |
| 114111 | Pollock fishing |
| 423830 | Pollution control equipment (except air) merchant wholesalers |
| 423730 | Pollution control equipment, air, merchant wholesalers |
| 924110 | Pollution control program administration |
| 541380 | Pollution testing (except automotive emissions testing) services |
| 315210 | Polo shirts cut and sew apparel contractors |
| 315120 | Polo shirts made in apparel knitting mills |
| 315250 | Polo shirts, men's and boys', cut and sewn from purchased fabric (except apparel contractors) |
| 315250 | Polo shirts, women's and girls', cut and sewn from purchased fabric (except apparel contractors) |
| 325211 | Polyacrylonitrile resins manufacturing |
| 325211 | Polyamide resins manufacturing |
| 325211 | Polycarbonate resins manufacturing |
| 325220 | Polyester fibers and filaments manufacturing |
| 424690 | Polyester fibers merchant wholesalers |
| 313110 | Polyester filament yarn throwing, twisting, texturizing, or winding of purchased yarn |
| 326113 | Polyester film and unlaminated sheet (except packaging) manufacturing |
| 325211 | Polyester resins manufacturing |
| 424610 | Polyester resins merchant wholesalers |
| 313110 | Polyester spun yarns made from purchased fiber |
| 313110 | Polyester thread manufacturing |
| 326113 | Polyethylene film and unlaminated sheet (except packaging) manufacturing |
| 325211 | Polyethylene resins manufacturing |
| 325212 | Polyethylene rubber manufacturing |
| 325220 | Polyethylene terephthalate (PET) fibers and filaments manufacturing |
| 325211 | Polyethylene terephthalate (PET) resins manufacturing |
| 334519 | Polygraph machines manufacturing |
| 561611 | Polygraph services |
| 325211 | Polyhexamethylenediamine adipamide resins manufacturing |
| 325199 | Polyhydric alcohol esters and amines manufacturing |
| 325199 | Polyhydric alcohols manufacturing |
| 325211 | Polyisobutylene resins manufacturing |
| 325212 | Polyisobutylene rubber manufacturing |
| 325212 | Polyisobutylene-isoprene rubber manufacturing |
| 325211 | Polymethacrylate resins manufacturing |
| 325212 | Polymethylene rubber manufacturing |
| 325220 | Polyolefin fibers and filaments manufacturing |
| 313110 | Polypropylene filament yarn throwing, twisting, texturizing, or winding of purchased yarn |
| 326113 | Polypropylene film and unlaminated sheet (except packaging) manufacturing |
| 325211 | Polypropylene resins manufacturing |

| | |
|---|---|
| 313110 | Polypropylene spun yarns made from purchased fiber |
| 238310 | Polystyrene board insulation installation |
| 326140 | Polystyrene foam packaging manufacturing |
| 325211 | Polystyrene resins manufacturing |
| 325212 | Polysulfide rubber manufacturing |
| 325211 | Polytetrafluoroethylene resins manufacturing |
| 325510 | Polyurethane coatings manufacturing |
| 326150 | Polyurethane foam products manufacturing |
| 325211 | Polyurethane resins manufacturing |
| 325211 | Polyvinyl alcohol resins manufacturing |
| 325211 | Polyvinyl chloride (PVC) resins manufacturing |
| 325220 | Polyvinyl ester fibers and filaments manufacturing |
| 326113 | Polyvinyl film and unlaminated sheet (except packaging) manufacturing |
| 325211 | Polyvinyl halide resins manufacturing |
| 325211 | Polyvinyl resins manufacturing |
| 325220 | Polyvinylidene chloride (i.e., saran) fibers and filaments manufacturing |
| 111339 | Pomegranate farming |
| 315210 | Ponchos and similar waterproof raincoats cut and sew apparel contractors |
| 315250 | Ponchos and similar waterproof raincoats cut and sewn from purchased fabric (except apparel contractors) |
| 562998 | Pond maintenance and cleaning services |
| 112920 | Pony production |
| 423910 | Pool (billiards) tables and supplies merchant wholesalers |
| 423910 | Pool (swimming) and equipment merchant wholesalers |
| 713990 | Pool halls |
| 713990 | Pool parlors |
| 713990 | Pool rooms |
| 525990 | Pooled investment vehicle (PIV) funds, closed-end |
| 312111 | Pop, soda, manufacturing |
| 311919 | Popcorn (except candy covered), popped, manufacturing |
| 311999 | Popcorn (except popped) manufacturing |
| 311340 | Popcorn balls manufacturing |
| 111150 | Popcorn farming, field and seed production |
| 424450 | Popcorn merchant wholesalers |

| | |
|---|---|
| 335210 | Popcorn poppers, household-type electric, manufacturing |
| 311340 | Popcorn, candy covered popped, manufacturing |
| 313210 | Poplins weaving |
| 621391 | Popopediatricians' offices (e.g., centers, clinics) |
| 711130 | Popular musical artists, independent |
| 711130 | Popular musical groups |
| 532120 | Popup camper rental |
| 327110 | Porcelain parts, electrical and electronic device, molded, manufacturing |
| 327110 | Porcelain, chemical, manufacturing |
| 236118 | Porch construction, residential-type |
| 337122 | Porch furniture (except upholstered), wood, manufacturing |
| 337920 | Porch shades, wood slat, manufacturing |
| 337126 | Porch swings, metal, manufacturing |
| 321918 | Porch work (e.g., columns, newels, rails, trellises), wood, manufacturing |
| 114111 | Porgy fishing |
| 311422 | Pork and beans canning |
| 311611 | Pork carcasses, half carcasses, and primal and sub-primal cuts produced in slaughtering plants |
| 311919 | Pork rinds manufacturing |
| 311612 | Pork, primal and sub-primal cuts, made from purchased carcasses |
| 926120 | Port authorities and districts, nonoperating |
| 237990 | Port facility construction |
| 488310 | Port facility operation |
| 332311 | Portable buildings, prefabricated metal, manufacturing |
| 332999 | Portable chemical toilets, metal, manufacturing |
| 334111 | Portable computers manufacturing |
| 335210 | Portable cooking appliances (except convection, microwave ovens), household-type electric, manufacturing |
| 335210 | Portable electric space heaters manufacturing |
| 335210 | Portable hair dryers, electric, manufacturing |
| 335210 | Portable humidifiers and dehumidifiers manufacturing |
| 334290 | Portable intrusion detection and signaling devices manufacturing |
| 334310 | Portable stereo systems manufacturing |
| 334515 | Portable test meters manufacturing |

| | |
|---|---|
| 562991 | Portable toilet pumping (i.e., cleaning) services |
| 562991 | Portable toilet renting and/or servicing |
| 326191 | Portable toilets, plastics, manufacturing |
| 519290 | Portals, web search |
| 312120 | Porter brewing |
| 424810 | Porter merchant wholesalers |
| 812990 | Porter services |
| 523940 | Portfolio fund managing |
| 541921 | Portrait photography services |
| 541921 | Portrait photography studios |
| 334511 | Position indicators (e.g., for landing gear, stabilizers), airframe equipment, manufacturing |
| 336310 | Positive crankcase ventilation (PCV) valves, engine, manufacturing |
| 334514 | Positive displacement meters manufacturing |
| 621512 | Positron emission tomography (PET) scanner centers |
| 334510 | Positron emission tomography (PET) scanners manufacturing |
| 238130 | Post framing contractors |
| 332216 | Post hole diggers, nonpowered, manufacturing |
| 333120 | Post hole diggers, powered, manufacturing |
| 236220 | Post office construction |
| 333998 | Post office-type scales manufacturing |
| 333310 | Postage meters manufacturing |
| 423420 | Postage meters merchant wholesalers |
| 333310 | Postage stamp vending machines manufacturing |
| 491110 | Postal delivery services, local, operated by U.S. Postal Service |
| 491110 | Postal delivery services, local, operated on a contract basis |
| 337215 | Postal service lock boxes manufacturing |
| 491110 | Postal services operated by U.S. Postal Service |
| 491110 | Postal stations operated by U.S. Postal Service |
| 491110 | Postal stations operated on a contract basis |
| 513199 | Postcard publishers |
| 513199 | Postcard publishers (except exclusive Internet publishing) |
| 513199 | Postcard publishers and printing combined |
| 513199 | Postcard publishers, exclusively on Internet |
| 323111 | Postcards commercial printing (except screen) without publishing |
| 424120 | Postcards merchant wholesalers |
| 323113 | Postcards screen printing without publishing |
| 513199 | Poster publishers |
| 513199 | Poster publishers (except exclusive Internet publishing) |
| 513199 | Poster publishers and printing combined |
| 513199 | Poster publishers, exclusively on Internet |
| 323111 | Posters commercial printing (except screen) without publishing |
| 323113 | Posters screen printing without publishing |
| 238990 | Posthole digging |
| 323120 | Postpress services (e.g., beveling, bronzing, folding, gluing, edging, foil stamping, gilding) on printed materials |
| 512191 | Postproduction facilities, motion picture or video |
| 327390 | Posts, concrete, manufacturing |
| 423510 | Posts, metal, merchant wholesalers |
| 321114 | Posts, round wood, cutting and treating |
| 321114 | Posts, wood, treating |
| 512191 | Post-synchronization sound dubbing |
| 311412 | Pot pies, frozen, manufacturing |
| 212390 | Potash mining and/or beneficiating |
| 325314 | Potassic fertilizers made by mixing purchased materials |
| 325180 | Potassium aluminum sulfate manufacturing |
| 325180 | Potassium bichromate and chromate manufacturing |
| 325199 | Potassium bitartrate manufacturing |
| 325180 | Potassium bromide manufacturing |
| 212390 | Potassium bromide, natural, mining and/or beneficiating |
| 325180 | Potassium carbonate manufacturing |
| 325180 | Potassium chlorate manufacturing |
| 325180 | Potassium chloride manufacturing |
| 212390 | Potassium chloride mining and/or beneficiating |
| 212390 | Potassium compounds prepared at beneficiating plants |
| 212390 | Potassium compounds, natural, mining and/or beneficiating |
| 325180 | Potassium cyanide manufacturing |
| 325180 | Potassium hydroxide (i.e., caustic potash) manufacturing |

| | |
|---|---|
| 325180 | Potassium hypochlorate manufacturing |
| 325180 | Potassium inorganic compounds, not specified elsewhere by process, manufacturing |
| 325180 | Potassium iodide manufacturing |
| 325180 | Potassium nitrate manufacturing |
| 325199 | Potassium organic compounds, not specified elsewhere by process, manufacturing |
| 325180 | Potassium permanganate manufacturing |
| 325180 | Potassium salts manufacturing |
| 212390 | Potassium salts, natural, mining and/or beneficiating |
| 325180 | Potassium sulfate manufacturing |
| 424450 | Potato chips and related snacks merchant wholesalers |
| 311919 | Potato chips manufacturing |
| 115114 | Potato curing |
| 333111 | Potato diggers, harvesters, and planters manufacturing |
| 111211 | Potato farming, field and seed potato production |
| 311211 | Potato flour manufacturing |
| 332215 | Potato mashers manufacturing |
| 311999 | Potato mixes made from purchased dry ingredients |
| 311423 | Potato products (e.g., flakes, granules) dehydrating |
| 311221 | Potato starches manufacturing |
| 311919 | Potato sticks manufacturing |
| 311991 | Potatoes, peeled or cut, manufacturing |
| 334515 | Potentiometric instruments (except industrial process-type) manufacturing |
| 334513 | Potentiometric instruments (except X-Y recorders), industrial process-type, manufacturing |
| 237310 | Pothole filling, highway, road, street or bridge |
| 339999 | Potpourri manufacturing |
| 332420 | Pots (e.g., annealing, melting, smelting), heavy gauge metal, manufacturing |
| 332215 | Pots and pans, fabricated metal, manufacturing |
| 327120 | Pots, glasshouse, clay refractory, manufacturing |
| 311612 | Potted meats made from purchased carcasses |
| 459120 | Pottery (unfinished pottery to be painted by customer on premises) stores |
| 327110 | Pottery made and sold on site |
| 327110 | Pottery products manufacturing |
| 424990 | Pottery, novelty, merchant wholesalers |
| 325314 | Potting soil manufacturing |
| 311615 | Poultry (e.g., canned, cooked, fresh, frozen) manufacturing |
| 311615 | Poultry (e.g., canned, cooked, fresh, frozen) processing |
| 424440 | Poultry and poultry products (except canned, packaged frozen) merchant wholesalers |
| 333111 | Poultry brooders, feeders, and waterers manufacturing |
| 311615 | Poultry canning (except baby and pet food) |
| 115210 | Poultry catching services |
| 445240 | Poultry dealers |
| 423820 | Poultry equipment merchant wholesalers |
| 311119 | Poultry feeds, supplements, and concentrates manufacturing |
| 112340 | Poultry hatcheries |
| 332618 | Poultry netting made from purchased wire |
| 424440 | Poultry pies (except packaged frozen) merchant wholesalers |
| 423830 | Poultry processing machinery merchant wholesalers |
| 311615 | Poultry slaughtering, dressing, and packing |
| 424490 | Poultry, canned, merchant wholesalers |
| 424440 | Poultry, live and dressed, merchant wholesalers |
| 424420 | Poultry, packaged frozen, merchant wholesalers |
| 333991 | Powder actuated handheld power tools manufacturing |
| 332812 | Powder coating metals and metal products for the trade |
| 325510 | Powder coatings manufacturing |
| 331314 | Powder made from purchased aluminum |
| 331420 | Powder made from purchased copper |
| 331221 | Powder made from purchased iron or steel |
| 333517 | Powder metal forming presses manufacturing |
| 332117 | Powder metallurgy products manufactured on a job or order basis |
| 314999 | Powder puffs and mitts manufacturing |
| 331110 | Powder, iron or steel, made in iron and steel mills |
| 331492 | Powder, nonferrous metals (except aluminum, copper), made from purchased metal |

| | |
|---|---|
| 311999 | Powdered drink mixes (except chocolate, coffee, tea, milk based) manufacturing |
| 311514 | Powdered milk manufacturing |
| 325620 | Powders (e.g., baby, body, face, talcum, toilet) manufacturing |
| 311999 | Powders, baking, manufacturing |
| 333912 | Power (i.e., pressure) washer units manufacturing |
| 441222 | Power boat dealers |
| 238290 | Power boiler, installation only |
| 332410 | Power boilers manufacturing |
| 335313 | Power circuit breakers manufacturing |
| 335313 | Power connectors manufacturing |
| 335999 | Power converter units (i.e., AC to DC), static, manufacturing |
| 444230 | Power equipment stores, outdoor |
| 334515 | Power factor meters manufacturing |
| 335313 | Power fuses (i.e., 600 volts and over) manufacturing |
| 238290 | Power generating equipment (except home standby power generator) installation |
| 221117 | Power generation, biomass |
| 221112 | Power generation, fossil fuel (e.g., coal, gas, oil), electric |
| 221116 | Power generation, geothermal |
| 221111 | Power generation, hydroelectric |
| 562213 | Power generation, nonhazardous solid waste combustor or incinerator electric |
| 221113 | Power generation, nuclear electric |
| 221114 | Power generation, solar electric |
| 221118 | Power generation, tidal electric |
| 221115 | Power generation, wind electric |
| 335312 | Power generators manufacturing |
| 423710 | Power handtools (e.g., drills, sanders, saws) merchant wholesalers |
| 812320 | Power laundries, family |
| 541990 | Power line inspection (i.e., visual) services |
| 237130 | Power line stringing |
| 334515 | Power measuring equipment, electrical, manufacturing |
| 237130 | Power plant (except hydroelectric) construction |
| 423830 | Power plant machinery (except electrical) merchant wholesalers |
| 237990 | Power plant, hydroelectric, construction |
| 238910 | Power shovel, construction, rental with operator |
| 336330 | Power steering hose assemblies manufacturing |
| 336330 | Power steering pumps manufacturing |
| 335999 | Power supplies, regulated and unregulated, manufacturing |
| 335313 | Power switchboards manufacturing |
| 335313 | Power switching equipment manufacturing |
| 335311 | Power transformers, electric, manufacturing |
| 423610 | Power transmission equipment, electrical, merchant wholesalers |
| 423840 | Power transmission supplies (e.g., gears, pulleys, sprockets), mechanical, merchant wholesalers |
| 333310 | Power washer cleaning equipment manufacturing |
| 532490 | Power washer rental or leasing |
| 561790 | Power washing building exteriors |
| 336320 | Power window and door lock systems, automotive, truck, and bus, manufacturing |
| 238910 | Power, communication and pipe line right of way clearance (except maintenance) |
| 333991 | Power-driven handtools manufacturing |
| 212390 | Pozzolana mining and/or beneficiating |
| 621399 | Practical nurses' offices (e.g., centers, clinics), licensed |
| 315210 | Prayer shawls cut and sew apparel contractors |
| 315250 | Prayer shawls cut and sewn from purchased fabric (except apparel contractors) |
| 315120 | Prayer shawls made in apparel knitting mills |
| 327331 | Precast concrete block and brick manufacturing |
| 238120 | Precast concrete panel, slab, or form installation |
| 327332 | Precast concrete pipe manufacturing |
| 327390 | Precast concrete products (except brick, block, pipe) manufacturing |
| 423940 | Precious and semiprecious stones merchant wholesalers |
| 331491 | Precious metal bar, rod, sheet, strip, and tubing made from purchased metals or scrap |
| 423520 | Precious metal ores merchant wholesalers |
| 423940 | Precious metals merchant wholesalers |
| 331492 | Precious metals recovering from scrap and/or alloying purchased metals |

| | |
|---|---|
| 331410 | Precious metals refining, primary |
| 212390 | Precious stones mining and/or beneficiating |
| 811210 | Precision equipment calibration |
| 332216 | Precision tools, machinist's (except optical), manufacturing |
| 332721 | Precision turned product manufacturing |
| 488999 | Precooling of fruits and vegetables in connection with transportation |
| 236117 | Precut housing, residential, assembled on site by for-sale builders |
| 236116 | Precut multifamily housing assembled on site by general contractors |
| 236115 | Precut single-family housing assembled on site by general contractors |
| 334514 | Predetermined counters manufacturing |
| 444180 | Prefabricated building (except manufactured home) dealers |
| 423390 | Prefabricated buildings (except wood) merchant wholesalers |
| 332311 | Prefabricated buildings, metal, manufacturing |
| 326199 | Prefabricated buildings, plastics, manufacturing |
| 423310 | Prefabricated buildings, wood, merchant wholesalers |
| 236220 | Prefabricated commercial building erection |
| 321992 | Prefabricated homes (except mobile homes), wood, manufacturing |
| 332311 | Prefabricated homes, metal, manufacturing |
| 236210 | Prefabricated industrial building (except warehouses) erection |
| 236220 | Prefabricated institutional building erection |
| 238350 | Prefabricated kitchen and bath cabinet, residential-type, installation |
| 236116 | Prefabricated residential building erection, multifamily |
| 236115 | Prefabricated residential building erection, single-family |
| 238350 | Prefabricated sash and door installation |
| 444180 | Prefabricated shed dealers |
| 321992 | Prefabricated wood buildings manufacturing |
| 238130 | Prefabricated wood frame component (e.g., trusses) installation |
| 321211 | Prefinished hardwood plywood manufacturing |
| 321212 | Prefinished softwood plywood manufacturing |
| 621410 | Pregnancy counseling centers |
| 325413 | Pregnancy test kits manufacturing |
| 624410 | Pre-kindergarten centers (except part of elementary school system) |
| 236117 | Premanufactured housing assembled on site by for-sale builders |
| 236115 | Premanufactured single-family housing assembled on site by general contractors |
| 334610 | Prepackaged software, mass reproducing |
| 424990 | Pre-paid calling card distribution, merchant wholesalers |
| 517121 | Pre-paid calling cards, telecommunications resellers |
| 213112 | Preparation of oil and gas field drilling sites (except site preparation and related construction contractor activities) on a contract basis |
| 212114 | Preparation plants, coal |
| 611110 | Preparatory schools, elementary or secondary |
| 311824 | Prepared flour mixes made from purchased flour |
| 311211 | Prepared flour mixes made in flour mills |
| 424490 | Prepared foods (except frozen) merchant wholesalers |
| 424420 | Prepared foods, frozen (except dairy products), merchant wholesalers |
| 424430 | Prepared foods, frozen dairy, merchant wholesalers |
| 311991 | Prepared meals, perishable, packaged for individual resale |
| 311941 | Prepared sauces (except gravy, tomato-based) manufacturing |
| 237210 | Preparing and subdividing land for sale |
| 488991 | Preparing goods for transportation (i.e., crating, packing) |
| 323120 | Prepress printing services (e.g., color separation, imagesetting, photocomposition, typesetting) |
| 541350 | Prepurchase home inspection services |
| 423990 | Prerecorded audio and video tapes and discs merchant wholesalers |
| 512250 | Prerecorded audio tapes and compact discs integrated manufacture, release, and distribution |
| 334610 | Prerecorded magnetic audio tapes and cassettes mass reproducing |
| 449210 | Prerecorded tape, compact disc, and record, new, mail-order houses |
| 459510 | Prerecorded tape, compact disc, and record, used, mail-order houses |
| 624410 | Preschool centers |
| 424210 | Prescription drugs merchant wholesalers |
| 111421 | Preseeded mat farming |

| | |
|---|---|
| 311421 | Preserves (e.g., imitation) canning |
| 321114 | Preserving purchased wood and wood products |
| 313310 | Preshrinking textile products and fabrics |
| 921110 | President's office, United States |
| 325611 | Presoaks manufacturing |
| 333517 | Press brakes, metalworking, manufacturing |
| 519290 | Press clipping services |
| 332111 | Press forgings made from purchased iron or steel, unfinished |
| 332112 | Press forgings made from purchased nonferrous metals, unfinished |
| 424130 | Pressed and molded pulp goods (e.g., egg cartons, shipping supplies) merchant wholesalers |
| 313230 | Pressed felts manufacturing |
| 321999 | Pressed logs of sawdust and other wood particles, nonpetroleum binder, manufacturing |
| 333517 | Presses (e.g., bending, punching, shearing, stamping), metal forming, manufacturing |
| 333241 | Presses (i.e., food manufacturing-type) manufacturing |
| 333243 | Presses for making composite woods (e.g., hardboard, medium density fiberboard (MDF), particleboard, plywood) manufacturing |
| 333111 | Presses, farm-type, manufacturing |
| 333998 | Presses, metal baling, manufacturing |
| 333248 | Presses, printing, manufacturing |
| 321999 | Pressing blocks, wood, tailor's, manufacturing |
| 336350 | Pressure and clutch plate assemblies, automotive, truck, and bus, manufacturing |
| 334519 | Pressure and vacuum indicators, aircraft engine, manufacturing |
| 332911 | Pressure control valves (except fluid power), industrial-type, manufacturing |
| 332912 | Pressure control valves, fluid power, manufacturing |
| 334512 | Pressure controllers, air-conditioning system-type, manufacturing |
| 332215 | Pressure cookers, household-type, manufacturing |
| 334513 | Pressure gauges (e.g., dial, digital), industrial process-type, manufacturing |
| 334513 | Pressure instruments, industrial process-type, manufacturing |
| 327332 | Pressure pipe, reinforced concrete, manufacturing |
| 322220 | Pressure sensitive paper and tape (except medical) made from purchased materials |
| 334519 | Pressure transducers manufacturing |
| 321113 | Pressure treated lumber made from logs or bolts and treated |
| 321114 | Pressure treated lumber made from purchased lumber |
| 423850 | Pressure washers merchant wholesalers |
| 561790 | Pressure washing (e.g., buildings, decks, fences) |
| 334512 | Pressurestats manufacturing |
| 238120 | Prestressed concrete beam, slab or other component installation |
| 327331 | Prestressed concrete blocks or bricks manufacturing |
| 327332 | Prestressed concrete pipes manufacturing |
| 327390 | Prestressed concrete products (except blocks, bricks, pipes) manufacturing |
| 722515 | Pretzel shops, on premise baking and carryout service |
| 424490 | Pretzels (except frozen) merchant wholesalers |
| 311919 | Pretzels (except soft) manufacturing |
| 424420 | Pretzels, frozen, merchant wholesalers |
| 311812 | Pretzels, soft, manufacturing |
| 335139 | Prewired poles, brackets, and accessories for electric lighting, manufacturing |
| 926150 | Price control agencies |
| 111339 | Prickly pear farming |
| 331313 | Primary aluminum production and manufacturing aluminum alloys |
| 331313 | Primary aluminum production and manufacturing aluminum shapes (e.g., bar, ingot, rod, sheet) |
| 335910 | Primary batteries manufacturing |
| 334513 | Primary elements for process flow measurement (i.e., orifice plates) manufacturing |
| 334512 | Primary oil burner controls (e.g., cadmium cells, stack controls) manufacturing |
| 334513 | Primary process temperature sensors manufacturing |
| 331313 | Primary refining of aluminum |
| 331410 | Primary refining of copper |
| 331410 | Primary refining of nonferrous metals (except aluminum) |
| 611110 | Primary schools |
| 331313 | Primary smelting of aluminum |
| 331410 | Primary smelting of copper |

| | |
|---|---|
| 331410 | Primary smelting of nonferrous metals (except aluminum) |
| 335312 | Prime mover generator sets (except turbine generator sets) manufacturing |
| 332993 | Primers (i.e., more than 30 mm., more than 1.18 inch), ammunition, manufacturing |
| 325510 | Primers, paint, manufacturing |
| 323111 | Print shops, digital (except printing books) |
| 323111 | Print shops, engraving (except printing books) |
| 323111 | Print shops, flexographic (except printing books) |
| 323111 | Print shops, gravure (except printing books) |
| 323111 | Print shops, letterpress (except printing books) |
| 323111 | Print shops, lithographic (offset) (except printing books) |
| 323111 | Print shops, quick (except printing books) |
| 323113 | Print shops, screen |
| 334418 | Printed circuit assemblies manufacturing |
| 334418 | Printed circuit boards loading |
| 423690 | Printed circuit boards merchant wholesalers |
| 334412 | Printed circuit boards, bare, manufacturing |
| 334419 | Printed circuit laminates manufacturing |
| 333248 | Printer machinery, 3D, manufacturing |
| 334118 | Printers, computer, manufacturing |
| 423430 | Printers, computer, merchant wholesalers |
| 323117 | Printing and binding books without publishing |
| 323111 | Printing apparel (except screen printing) |
| 323117 | Printing books without publishing |
| 561990 | Printing brokers |
| 313310 | Printing fabric grey goods |
| 325910 | Printing inks manufacturing |
| 423840 | Printing inks merchant wholesalers |
| 333248 | Printing machinery for textiles manufacturing |
| 323111 | Printing manifold business forms |
| 424120 | Printing paper (except bulk) merchant wholesalers |
| 424110 | Printing paper, bulk, merchant wholesalers |
| 236210 | Printing plant construction |

| | |
|---|---|
| 333248 | Printing plate engraving machinery manufacturing |
| 323120 | Printing plate preparation services |
| 333248 | Printing plates, blank (except photosensitive), manufacturing |
| 323120 | Printing postpress services (e.g., beveling, bronzing, folding, gluing, edging, foil stamping) to printed products (e.g., books, cards, paper) |
| 323120 | Printing prepress services (e.g., color separation, imagesetting, photocomposition, typesetting) |
| 333248 | Printing press rollers manufacturing |
| 333248 | Printing presses manufacturing |
| 313310 | Printing textile banners (except screen printing) |
| 313310 | Printing textile products (except screen and apparel printing) |
| 811310 | Printing trade machinery repair and maintenance services |
| 423830 | Printing trade machinery, equipment, and supplies merchant wholesalers |
| 323111 | Printing, digital (e.g., billboards, other large format graphical materials, high resolution) (except books, grey goods) |
| 323111 | Printing, engraving, on paper products |
| 323111 | Printing, flexographic (except books, grey goods) |
| 323111 | Printing, gravure (except books, grey goods) |
| 323111 | Printing, letterpress (except books, grey goods) |
| 323111 | Printing, lithographic (except books, grey goods) |
| 323111 | Printing, photo-offset (except books, grey goods) |
| 323111 | Printing, quick (except books, grey goods) |
| 323113 | Printing, screen (except books, manifold business forms, grey goods) |
| 423410 | Printmaking apparatus, photographic, merchant wholesalers |
| 333310 | Prisms, optical, manufacturing |
| 337127 | Prison bed manufacturing |
| 236220 | Prison construction |
| 922140 | Prison farms (except private operation of) |
| 561210 | Prison operation on a contract or fee basis |
| 922140 | Prisons (except private operation of) |
| 561210 | Prisons, privately operated |
| 522180 | Private banks (i.e., unincorporated) |

| | |
|---|---|
| 334210 | Private branch exchange (PBX) equipment manufacturing |
| 611310 | Private colleges (except community or junior college) |
| 561611 | Private detective services |
| 238210 | Private driveway or parking area lighting contractors |
| 523940 | Private equity fund managing |
| 525920 | Private estates (i.e., administering on behalf of beneficiaries) |
| 814110 | Private households employing domestic personnel |
| 814110 | Private households with employees |
| 561611 | Private investigation services (except credit) |
| 561431 | Private mail centers |
| 561431 | Private mailbox rental centers |
| 561612 | Private police services |
| 611110 | Private schools, elementary or secondary |
| 561990 | Private volunteer firefighting |
| 493190 | Private warehousing and storage (except farm products, general merchandise, refrigerated) |
| 493130 | Private warehousing and storage, farm products (except refrigerated) |
| 493110 | Private warehousing and storage, general merchandise |
| 493120 | Private warehousing and storage, refrigerated |
| 459110 | Pro shops (e.g., golf, skiing, tennis) |
| 624190 | Probation offices, privately operated |
| 922150 | Probation offices, publicly administered |
| 212390 | Probertite mining and/or quarrying |
| 334510 | Probes, electric medical, manufacturing |
| 339112 | Probes, surgical, manufacturing |
| 325411 | Procaine and derivatives (i.e., basic chemicals) manufacturing |
| 334513 | Process control instruments, industrial, manufacturing |
| 238220 | Process piping installation |
| 541199 | Process server services |
| 541199 | Process serving services |
| 311513 | Processed cheeses manufacturing |
| 424470 | Processed meats (e.g., luncheon, sausage) merchant wholesalers |
| 311612 | Processed meats manufacturing |
| 424440 | Processed poultry (e.g., luncheon) merchant wholesalers |
| 311615 | Processed poultry manufacturing |

| | |
|---|---|
| 423410 | Processing and finishing equipment, photographic, merchant wholesalers |
| 522320 | Processing financial transactions |
| 314999 | Processing of textile mill waste and recovering fibers |
| 621111 | Proctologists' offices (e.g., centers, clinics) |
| 424910 | Produce containers merchant wholesalers |
| 445230 | Produce markets |
| 445230 | Produce stands, permanent |
| 445230 | Produce stands, temporary |
| 424480 | Produce, fresh, merchant wholesalers |
| 813910 | Producers' associations |
| 711510 | Producers, independent |
| 512290 | Producers, recorded radio shows (except independent producers) |
| 561910 | Product sterilization and packaging services |
| 541380 | Product testing laboratories or services |
| 524128 | Product warranty insurance carriers, direct |
| 334514 | Production counters manufacturing |
| 541614 | Production planning and control consulting services |
| 541614 | Productivity improvement consulting services |
| 813920 | Professional associations |
| 711219 | Professional athletes, independent (i.e., participating in sports events) |
| 711211 | Professional baseball clubs |
| 513130 | Professional book publishers |
| 513130 | Professional book publishers (except exclusive Internet publishing) |
| 513130 | Professional book publishers and printing combined |
| 513130 | Professional book publishers, exclusively on Internet |
| 323120 | Professional bookbinding without printing |
| 323117 | Professional books printing and binding without publishing |
| 323117 | Professional books printing without publishing |
| 611430 | Professional development training |
| 561330 | Professional employer organizations (PEO) |
| 423490 | Professional equipment and supplies (except dental, medical, ophthalmic) merchant wholesalers |
| 423460 | Professional equipment and supplies, optical, merchant wholesalers |

611691 Professional examination review instruction

711211 Professional football clubs

423490 Professional furniture (except dental, metal, ophthalmic, and school) merchant wholesalers

423490 Professional instruments merchant wholesalers

513120 Professional magazine and periodical publishers

513120 Professional magazine and periodical publishers (except exclusive Internet publishing)

513120 Professional magazine and periodical publishers and printing combined

513120 Professional magazine and periodical publishers, exclusively on Internet

323111 Professional magazines and periodicals commercial printing (except screen) without publishing

323113 Professional magazines and periodicals screen printing without publishing

813920 Professional membership associations

531120 Professional office building rental or leasing

611310 Professional schools (e.g., business administration, dental, law, medical)

315210 Professional service apparel, washable, cut and sew apparel contractors

315250 Professional service apparel, washable, men's and boys', cut and sewn from purchased fabric (except apparel contractors)

315250 Professional service apparel, washable, women's and girls', cut and sewn from purchased fabric (except apparel contractors)

611620 Professional sports (e.g., golf, skiing, swimming, tennis) instructors (i.e., not participating in sporting events)

711211 Professional sports clubs

711310 Professional sports promoters with facilities

711320 Professional sports promoters without facilities

813920 Professional standards review boards

326130 Profile shapes (e.g., plate, rod, sheet), laminated plastics, manufacturing

326121 Profile shapes (e.g., rod, tube), nonrigid plastics, manufacturing

525990 Profit-sharing funds

512110 Program producing, television

334513 Programmers, process-type, manufacturing

513210 Programming language and compiler software publishers, packaged

541511 Programming services, custom computer

332993 Projectiles (except guided missile), jet propulsion, manufacturing

333310 Projection equipment (e.g., motion picture, slide), photographic, manufacturing

423410 Projection equipment (e.g., motion picture, slide), photographic, merchant wholesalers

333310 Projection lenses manufacturing

333310 Projection screens (i.e., motion picture, overhead, slide) manufacturing

334310 Projection television manufacturing

332994 Projectors (e.g., antisub, depth charge release, grenade, livens, rocket), ordnance, manufacturing

711310 Promoters of agricultural fairs with facilities

711320 Promoters of agricultural fairs without facilities

711310 Promoters of arts events with facilities

711320 Promoters of arts events without facilities

561920 Promoters of conventions with or without facilities

711310 Promoters of festivals with facilities

711320 Promoters of festivals without facilities

711310 Promoters of live performing arts productions (e.g., concerts) with facilities

711320 Promoters of live performing arts productions (e.g., concerts) without facilities

711310 Promoters of sports events with facilities

711320 Promoters of sports events without facilities

561920 Promoters of trade fairs or shows with or without facilities

561410 Proofreading services

111421 Propagation material farming

424710 Propane bulk stations and terminals, merchant wholesalers

324110 Propane gases made in petroleum refineries

424720 Propane merchant wholesalers (except bulk stations, terminals)

211130 Propane recovered from oil and gas field gases

333519 Propeller straightening presses manufacturing

| | |
|---|---|
| 334514 | Propeller type meters with registers manufacturing |
| 332999 | Propellers, ship and boat, made from purchased metal |
| 524126 | Property and casualty insurance carriers, direct |
| 524130 | Property and casualty reinsurance carriers |
| 524126 | Property damage insurance carriers, direct |
| 531312 | Property managers' offices, commercial real estate |
| 531312 | Property managers' offices, nonresidential real estate |
| 531311 | Property managers' offices, residential real estate |
| 531312 | Property managing, commercial real estate |
| 531312 | Property managing, nonresidential real estate |
| 531311 | Property managing, residential real estate |
| 813990 | Property owners' associations |
| 561612 | Property protection services (except armored car, security systems) |
| 921130 | Property tax assessors' offices |
| 326299 | Prophylactics manufacturing |
| 112910 | Propolis production, bees |
| 423860 | Propulsion systems, marine, merchant wholesalers |
| 336415 | Propulsion units and parts, guided missile and space vehicle, manufacturing |
| 325199 | Propylcarbinol manufacturing |
| 324110 | Propylene (i.e., propene) made in petroleum refineries |
| 325199 | Propylene glycol manufacturing |
| 325110 | Propylene made from refined petroleum or liquid hydrocarbons |
| 325211 | Propylene resins manufacturing |
| 213113 | Prospect and test drilling services for coal mining on contract basis |
| 213114 | Prospect and test drilling services for metal mining on contract basis |
| 213115 | Prospect and test drilling services for nonmetallic mineral mining (except fuels) on a contract basis |
| 339113 | Prosthetic appliances and supplies manufacturing |
| 423450 | Prosthetic appliances and supplies merchant wholesalers |
| 456199 | Prosthetic stores (except offices of prosthetists) |

| | |
|---|---|
| 621399 | Prosthetists' offices (e.g., centers, clinics) |
| 621210 | Prosthodontists' offices (e.g., centers, clinics) |
| 561612 | Protection services (except armored car, security systems), personal or property |
| 812332 | Protective apparel supply services |
| 523999 | Protective committees, security holders |
| 316210 | Protective footwear, plastics or plastics soled fabric upper, manufacturing |
| 316210 | Protective footwear, rubber or rubber soled fabric upper, manufacturing |
| 561612 | Protective guard services |
| 339920 | Protectors, sports (e.g., baseball, basketball, hockey), manufacturing |
| 334516 | Protein analyzers, laboratory-type, manufacturing |
| 541714 | Protein engineering research and experimental development laboratories |
| 325220 | Protein fibers and filaments manufacturing |
| 325211 | Protein plastics manufacturing |
| 712190 | Provincial parks |
| 334511 | Proximity warning (i.e., collision avoidance) equipment manufacturing |
| 111339 | Prune farming |
| 332216 | Pruners manufacturing |
| 311423 | Prunes, dried, made in dehydration plants |
| 115112 | Pruning of orchard trees and vines |
| 561730 | Pruning services, ornamental tree and shrub |
| 325130 | Prussian blue pigments manufacturing |
| 332216 | Pry (i.e., crow) bars manufacturing |
| 212290 | Psilomelane mining and/or beneficiating |
| 621420 | Psychiatric centers and clinics (except hospitals), outpatient |
| 623220 | Psychiatric convalescent homes or hospitals |
| 622210 | Psychiatric hospitals (except convalescent) |
| 621112 | Psychiatrists' offices (e.g., centers, clinics) |
| 812990 | Psychic services |
| 621330 | Psychoanalysts' (except MDs or DOs) offices (e.g., centers, clinics) |
| 621112 | Psychoanalysts' (MDs or DOs) offices (e.g., centers, clinics) |
| 813920 | Psychologists' associations |
| 621330 | Psychologists' offices (e.g., centers, clinics), clinical |

| | |
|---|---|
| 541720 | Psychology research and development services |
| 621330 | Psychotherapists' (except MDs or DOs) offices (e.g., centers, clinics) |
| 621112 | Psychotherapists' (MDs or DOs) offices (e.g., centers, clinics) |
| 541211 | Public accountants' (CPAs) offices, certified |
| 541211 | Public accountants' (CPAs) private practices, certified |
| 541219 | Public accountants' (except CPAs) offices |
| 541219 | Public accountants' (except CPAs) private practices |
| 238210 | Public address system installation |
| 532490 | Public address system rental or leasing |
| 811210 | Public address system repair and maintenance services |
| 334310 | Public address systems and equipment manufacturing |
| 423690 | Public address systems and equipment merchant wholesalers |
| 423210 | Public building furniture merchant wholesalers |
| 922130 | Public defenders' offices |
| 711410 | Public figures' agents or managers |
| 923120 | Public health program administration, nonoperating |
| 541910 | Public opinion polling services |
| 541910 | Public opinion research services |
| 922150 | Public parole offices |
| 922150 | Public probation offices |
| 921190 | Public property management services, government |
| 922130 | Public prosecutors' offices |
| 541820 | Public relations agencies |
| 541820 | Public relations consulting services |
| 541820 | Public relations services |
| 813319 | Public safety advocacy organizations |
| 922190 | Public safety bureaus and statistics centers, government |
| 922190 | Public safety statistics centers, government |
| 611110 | Public schools, elementary or secondary |
| 926130 | Public service (except transportation) commissions, nonoperating |
| 813410 | Public speaking improvement clubs |
| 611699 | Public speaking training |
| 561492 | Public stenography services |
| 926120 | Public transportation commissions, nonoperating |

| | |
|---|---|
| 926130 | Public utility (except transportation) commissions, nonoperating |
| 813910 | Public utility associations |
| 551112 | Public utility holding companies |
| 236220 | Public warehouse construction |
| 493190 | Public warehousing and storage (except farm products, general merchandise, refrigerated, self-storage) |
| 493110 | Public warehousing and storage (except self-storage), general merchandise |
| 493130 | Public warehousing and storage, farm products (except refrigerated) |
| 493120 | Public warehousing and storage, refrigerated |
| ****** | Publishers -- see specific type |
| 513130 | Publishers (except exclusive Internet publishing), book |
| 513140 | Publishers (except exclusive Internet publishing), directory |
| 513191 | Publishers (except exclusive Internet publishing), greeting card |
| 513120 | Publishers (except exclusive Internet publishing), magazine |
| 513130 | Publishers (except exclusive Internet publishing), map |
| 513120 | Publishers (except exclusive Internet publishing), periodical |
| 513199 | Publishers (except exclusive Internet publishing), racing form |
| 541840 | Publishers' advertising representatives (i.e., independent of media owners) |
| ****** | Publishers and printing combined -- see specific type of publisher |
| ****** | Publishers or publishing -- see specific type |
| 513130 | Publishers, book |
| 513130 | Publishers, book, combined with printing |
| 513140 | Publishers, directory |
| 513191 | Publishers, greeting card |
| 513191 | Publishers, greeting card, combined with printing |
| 513191 | Publishers, Internet greeting card |
| 513130 | Publishers, Internet map |
| 513199 | Publishers, Internet racing form |
| 513120 | Publishers, magazine |
| 513120 | Publishers, magazine, combined with printing |
| 513130 | Publishers, map |
| 512230 | Publishers, music |
| 513110 | Publishers, newspaper |

| | |
|---|---|
| 513110 | Publishers, newspaper (except exclusive Internet publishing) |
| 513110 | Publishers, newspaper, combined with printing |
| 513210 | Publishers, packaged computer software |
| 513120 | Publishers, periodical |
| 513120 | Publishers, periodical, combined with printing |
| 513199 | Publishers, racing form |
| 311520 | Pudding pops, frozen, manufacturing |
| 311999 | Puddings, canned dessert, manufacturing |
| 311999 | Puddings, dessert, manufacturing |
| 333923 | Pulleys (except power transmission), metal, manufacturing |
| 333613 | Pulleys, power transmission, manufacturing |
| 321999 | Pulleys, wood, manufacturing |
| 213112 | Pulling oil and gas field casings, tubes, or rods on a contract basis |
| 621111 | Pulmonary specialists' offices (e.g., centers, clinics) |
| 322120 | Pulp and newsprint combined manufacturing |
| 322120 | Pulp and paper combined manufacturing |
| 322130 | Pulp and paperboard combined manufacturing |
| 333243 | Pulp making machinery manufacturing |
| 322110 | Pulp manufacturing (i.e., chemical, mechanical, or semichemical processes) without making paper |
| 322110 | Pulp manufacturing (made from bagasse, linters, rags, straw, wastepaper, or wood) without making paper |
| 322120 | Pulp mills and groundwood paper, uncoated and untreated, manufacturing |
| 322110 | Pulp mills not making paper or paperboard |
| 322120 | Pulp mills producing newsprint paper |
| 322120 | Pulp mills producing paper |
| 322130 | Pulp mills producing paperboard |
| 322299 | Pulp products, molded, manufacturing |
| 333243 | Pulp, paper, and paperboard molding machinery manufacturing |
| 212390 | Pulpstones, natural, mining and/or beneficiating |
| 113310 | Pulpwood logging camps |
| 423990 | Pulpwood merchant wholesalers |
| 334515 | Pulse (i.e., signal) generators manufacturing |
| 334519 | Pulse analyzers, nuclear monitoring, manufacturing |

| | |
|---|---|
| 423830 | Pulverizing machinery and equipment, industrial, merchant wholesalers |
| 327992 | Pumice (except abrasives) processing beyond beneficiation |
| 327910 | Pumice and pumicite abrasives manufacturing |
| 212390 | Pumice mining and/or beneficiating |
| 212390 | Pumicite mining and/or beneficiating |
| 562991 | Pumping (i.e., cleaning) cesspools and septic tanks |
| 562991 | Pumping (i.e., cleaning) portable toilets |
| 213112 | Pumping oil and gas wells on a contract basis |
| 213113 | Pumping or draining coal mines on a contract basis |
| 213114 | Pumping or draining metal mines on a contract basis |
| 213115 | Pumping or draining nonmetallic mineral mines (except fuel) on a contract basis |
| 237120 | Pumping station, gas and oil transmission, construction |
| 237110 | Pumping station, water and sewage system, construction |
| 238220 | Pumping system, water, installation |
| 111219 | Pumpkin farming, field and seed production |
| 423120 | Pumps (e.g., fuel, oil, power steering, water), automotive, merchant wholesalers |
| 336310 | Pumps (e.g., fuel, oil, water), mechanical, automotive and truck gasoline engine (except power steering), manufacturing |
| 333914 | Pumps (except fluid power), general purpose, manufacturing |
| 316210 | Pumps (i.e., dress shoes) manufacturing |
| 423830 | Pumps and pumping equipment, industrial-type, merchant wholesalers |
| 333914 | Pumps for railroad equipment lubrication systems manufacturing |
| 333996 | Pumps, fluid power, manufacturing |
| 333914 | Pumps, industrial and commercial-type, general purpose, manufacturing |
| 333914 | Pumps, measuring and dispensing (e.g., gasoline), manufacturing |
| 333914 | Pumps, oil field or well, manufacturing |
| 333914 | Pumps, sump or water, residential-type, manufacturing |
| 313230 | Punched felts manufacturing |
| 332216 | Punches (except paper), nonpowered handtool, manufacturing |

| | |
|---|---|
| 333514 | Punches for use with machine tools manufacturing |
| 333517 | Punching machines, metalworking, manufacturing |
| 711110 | Puppet theaters |
| 339999 | Puppets manufacturing |
| 921190 | Purchasing and supply agencies, government |
| 522299 | Purchasing of accounts receivable |
| 332323 | Purlins, metal, manufacturing |
| 316990 | Purses (except precious metal) manufacturing |
| 424350 | Purses merchant wholesalers |
| 339910 | Purses, precious metal or clad with precious metal, manufacturing |
| 333515 | Pushers (i.e., a machine tool accessory) manufacturing |
| 332216 | Putty knives manufacturing |
| 423920 | Puzzles merchant wholesalers |
| 326122 | PVC pipe manufacturing |
| 325320 | Pyrethrin insecticides manufacturing |
| 334519 | Pyrheliometers manufacturing |
| 212390 | Pyrite concentrates mining and/or beneficiating |
| 212390 | Pyrite mining and/or beneficiating |
| 325194 | Pyroligneous acids manufacturing |
| 212290 | Pyrolusite mining and/or beneficiating |
| 327110 | Pyrometer tubes manufacturing |
| 334513 | Pyrometers, industrial process-type, manufacturing |
| 327110 | Pyrometric cones, earthenware, manufacturing |
| 212390 | Pyrophyllite mining and/or beneficiating |
| 327992 | Pyrophyllite processing beyond beneficiation |
| 332994 | Pyrotechnic pistols and projectors manufacturing |
| 325998 | Pyrotechnics (e.g., flares, flashlight bombs, signals) manufacturing |
| 325211 | Pyroxylin (i.e., nitrocellulose) resins manufacturing |
| 212390 | Pyrrhotite mining and/or beneficiating |
| 112390 | Quail production |
| 611430 | Quality assurance training |
| 541990 | Quantity surveyor services |
| 327120 | Quarry tiles, clay, manufacturing |
| 333131 | Quarrying machinery and equipment manufacturing |
| 423810 | Quarrying machinery and equipment merchant wholesalers |
| 316990 | Quarters (i.e., shoe cut stock), leather, manufacturing |
| 212390 | Quartz crystal, pure, mining and/or beneficiating |
| 334419 | Quartz crystals, electronic application, manufacturing |
| 212319 | Quartzite crushed and broken stone mining and/or beneficiating |
| 212311 | Quartzite dimension stone mining or quarrying |
| 325194 | Quebracho extracts manufacturing |
| 112910 | Queen bee production |
| 325194 | Quercitron extracts manufacturing |
| 323111 | Quick printing (except books) |
| 327410 | Quicklime (i.e., calcium oxide) manufacturing |
| 811191 | Quick-lube shops |
| 212290 | Quicksilver ores and metal mining and/or beneficiating |
| 314999 | Quilting of textiles |
| 459130 | Quilting supply stores |
| 314120 | Quilts made from purchased materials |
| 111339 | Quince farming |
| 325411 | Quinine and derivatives (i.e., basic chemicals) manufacturing |
| 523999 | Quotation services, securities |
| 523999 | Quotation services, stock |
| 311119 | Rabbit food manufacturing |
| 112930 | Rabbit production |
| 311615 | Rabbits processing (i.e., canned, cooked, fresh, frozen) |
| 311615 | Rabbits slaughtering and dressing |
| 711219 | Race car drivers |
| 711219 | Race car owners (i.e., racing cars) |
| 336999 | Race cars manufacturing |
| 711219 | Race dog owners (i.e., racing dogs) |
| 711219 | Racehorse owners (i.e., racing horses) |
| 711219 | Racehorse trainers |
| 711219 | Racehorse training |
| 332991 | Races, ball or roller bearings, manufacturing |
| 513199 | Racetrack program publishers |
| 513199 | Racetrack program publishers and printing combined |
| 513199 | Racetrack program publishers, exclusively on Internet |
| 323111 | Racetrack programs commercial printing (except screen) without publishing |

| | |
|---|---|
| 323113 | Racetrack programs screen printing without publishing |
| 711212 | Racetracks (e.g., automobile, dog, horse) |
| 713990 | Racetracks, slot car (i.e., amusement devices) |
| 335932 | Raceways manufacturing |
| 713990 | Raceways, gocart (i.e., amusement rides) |
| 513199 | Racing form publishers |
| 513199 | Racing form publishers (except exclusive Internet publishing) |
| 513199 | Racing form publishers and printing combined |
| 513199 | Racing form publishers, exclusively on Internet |
| 323111 | Racing forms commercial printing (except screen) without publishing |
| 323113 | Racing forms screen printing without publishing |
| 711219 | Racing stables, horse |
| 711219 | Racing teams (e.g., automobile, motorcycle, snowmobile) |
| 334417 | Rack and panel connectors manufacturing |
| 336330 | Rack and pinion steering assemblies manufacturing |
| 336390 | Racks (e.g., bicycle, luggage, ski, tire), automotive, truck, and buses manufacturing |
| 332313 | Racks (e.g., trash), fabricated metal plate, manufacturing |
| 332618 | Racks, household-type, made from purchased wire |
| 713940 | Racquetball club facilities |
| 811210 | Radar and sonar equipment repair and maintenance services |
| 334511 | Radar detectors manufacturing |
| 423690 | Radar equipment merchant wholesalers |
| 517810 | Radar station operations |
| 334511 | Radar systems and equipment manufacturing |
| 334515 | Radar testing instruments, electric, manufacturing |
| 334519 | RADIAC (radioactivity detection, identification, and computation) equipment manufacturing |
| 238220 | Radiant floor heating equipment installation |
| 334519 | Radiation detection and monitoring instruments manufacturing |
| 541380 | Radiation dosimetry (i.e., radiation testing) laboratories or services |

| | |
|---|---|
| 812332 | Radiation protection garment supply services |
| 339113 | Radiation shielding aprons, gloves, and sheeting manufacturing |
| 541380 | Radiation testing laboratories or services |
| 325998 | Radiator additive preparations manufacturing |
| 326220 | Radiator and heater hoses, rubber or plastics, manufacturing |
| 811114 | Radiator repair shops, automotive |
| 332322 | Radiator shields and enclosures, sheet metal (except stampings), manufacturing |
| 333414 | Radiators (except motor vehicle, portable electric) manufacturing |
| 336390 | Radiators and cores manufacturing |
| 423720 | Radiators, heating, nonelectric, merchant wholesalers |
| 423120 | Radiators, motor vehicle, merchant wholesalers |
| 335210 | Radiators, portable electric, manufacturing |
| 541840 | Radio advertising representatives (i.e., independent of media owners) |
| 236220 | Radio and television broadcast studio construction |
| 449210 | Radio and television stores |
| 332312 | Radio and television tower sections, fabricated structural metal, manufacturing |
| 488330 | Radio beacon (i.e., ship navigation) services |
| 516110 | Radio broadcasting (except exclusively on Internet) stations (e.g., AM, FM, shortwave) |
| 516210 | Radio broadcasting network services |
| 516210 | Radio broadcasting networks |
| 516210 | Radio broadcasting syndicates |
| 711510 | Radio commentators, independent |
| 541690 | Radio consulting services |
| 334419 | Radio frequency identification (RFID) devices manufacturing |
| 423690 | Radio frequency identification (RFID) equipment merchant wholesalers |
| 513120 | Radio guide publishers |
| 513120 | Radio guide publishers (except exclusive Internet publishing) |
| 513120 | Radio guide publishers and printing combined |
| 513120 | Radio guide publishers, exclusively on Internet |
| 323111 | Radio guides commercial printing (except screen) without publishing |

| | |
|---|---|
| 323113 | Radio guides screen printing without publishing |
| 334310 | Radio headphones manufacturing |
| 326199 | Radio housings, plastics, manufacturing |
| 334511 | Radio magnetic instrumentation (RMI) manufacturing |
| 517112 | Radio paging services communications carriers |
| 423690 | Radio parts and accessories (e.g., transistors, tubes) merchant wholesalers |
| 512290 | Radio program recording production (except independent producers) |
| 334310 | Radio receiving sets manufacturing |
| 811210 | Radio repair and maintenance services without retailing new radios |
| 811210 | Radio repair, automotive, without retailing new |
| 513120 | Radio schedule publishers |
| 513120 | Radio schedule publishers (except exclusive Internet publishing) |
| 513120 | Radio schedule publishers and printing combined |
| 513120 | Radio schedule publishers, exclusively on Internet |
| 323111 | Radio schedules commercial printing (except screen) without publishing |
| 323113 | Radio schedules screen printing without publishing |
| 236220 | Radio station construction |
| 516110 | Radio stations (except exclusively on Internet) |
| 561410 | Radio transcription services |
| 334220 | Radio transmitting antennas and ground equipment manufacturing |
| 237130 | Radio transmitting tower construction |
| 325180 | Radioactive elements manufacturing |
| 541360 | Radioactive geophysical surveying services |
| 325412 | Radioactive in-vivo diagnostic substances manufacturing |
| 325180 | Radioactive isotopes manufacturing |
| 424210 | Radioactive pharmaceutical isotopes merchant wholesalers |
| 562112 | Radioactive waste collecting and/or local hauling |
| 562211 | Radioactive waste collecting and/or local hauling in combination with disposal and/or treatment facilities |
| 562211 | Radioactive waste disposal facilities |
| 484230 | Radioactive waste hauling, long-distance |
| 562211 | Radioactive waste treatment facilities |
| 334519 | Radioactivity detection, identification, and computation (RADIAC) equipment manufacturing |
| 334515 | Radiofrequency measuring equipment manufacturing |
| 334515 | Radiofrequency oscillators manufacturing |
| 541380 | Radiographic testing laboratories or services |
| 541380 | Radiographing welded joints on pipes and fittings |
| 541380 | Radiography inspection services |
| 621512 | Radiological laboratories, medical |
| 621512 | Radiological laboratory services, medical |
| 621111 | Radiologists' offices (e.g., centers, clinics) |
| 424210 | Radiopharmaceuticals merchant wholesalers |
| 423690 | Radios (except household-type) merchant wholesalers |
| 423620 | Radios, household-type, merchant wholesalers |
| 111219 | Radish farming, field and seed production |
| 325180 | Radium chloride manufacturing |
| 334517 | Radium equipment manufacturing |
| 325180 | Radium luminous compounds manufacturing |
| 212290 | Radium ores mining and/or beneficiating |
| 238990 | Radon gas alleviation contractors |
| 562910 | Radon remediation cleanup services |
| 541380 | Radon testing laboratories or services |
| 326299 | Rafts, swimming pool-type, rubber inflatable, manufacturing |
| 423930 | Rags merchant wholesalers |
| 335931 | Rail bonds, propulsion and signal circuit electric, manufacturing |
| 331110 | Rail joints and fastenings made in iron and steel mills |
| 336510 | Rail laying and tamping equipment manufacturing |
| 485112 | Rail transportation (except mixed mode), commuter |
| 332323 | Railings, metal, manufacturing |
| 321918 | Railings, wood stair, manufacturing |
| 423310 | Railings, wood, merchant wholesalers |
| 926120 | Railroad and warehouse commissions, nonoperating |
| 333613 | Railroad car journal bearings, plain, manufacturing |

| | |
|---|---|
| 532411 | Railroad car rental or leasing |
| 336510 | Railroad cars and car equipment manufacturing |
| 423860 | Railroad cars merchant wholesalers |
| 336510 | Railroad cars, self-propelled, manufacturing |
| 237990 | Railroad construction |
| 331110 | Railroad crossings, iron or steel, made in iron and steel mills |
| 423860 | Railroad equipment and supplies merchant wholesalers |
| 551112 | Railroad holding companies |
| 336510 | Railroad locomotives and parts (except diesel engines) manufacturing |
| 339930 | Railroad models, hobby and toy, manufacturing |
| 923130 | Railroad Retirement Board |
| 531190 | Railroad right of way leasing |
| 336510 | Railroad rolling stock manufacturing |
| 336360 | Railroad seating manufacturing |
| 238210 | Railroad signaling equipment installation |
| 334290 | Railroad signaling equipment manufacturing |
| 488210 | Railroad switching services |
| 488210 | Railroad terminals, independent operation |
| 561599 | Railroad ticket offices |
| 321114 | Railroad ties (i.e., bridge, cross, switch) treating |
| 423990 | Railroad ties, wood, merchant wholesalers |
| 333998 | Railroad track scales manufacturing |
| 482111 | Railroad transportation, line-haul |
| 487110 | Railroad transportation, scenic and sightseeing |
| 482112 | Railroad transportation, short-line or beltline |
| 487110 | Railroad, scenic and sightseeing, operation |
| 482111 | Railroads, line-haul |
| 482112 | Railroads, short-line or beltline |
| 321999 | Rails (except rough), wood fence, manufacturing |
| 423510 | Rails and accessories, metal, merchant wholesalers |
| 331318 | Rails made by rolling or drawing purchased aluminum |
| 331110 | Rails rerolled or renewed in iron and steel mills |
| 331318 | Rails, aluminum, made in integrated secondary smelting and drawing plants |
| 331318 | Rails, aluminum, made in integrated secondary smelting and rolling mills |
| 331110 | Rails, iron or steel, made in iron and steel mills |
| 113310 | Rails, rough wood, manufacturing |
| 332312 | Railway bridge sections, prefabricated metal, manufacturing |
| 237990 | Railway construction (e.g., interlocker, roadbed, signal, track) |
| 335312 | Railway motors and control equipment, electric, manufacturing |
| 237990 | Railway roadbed construction |
| 236220 | Railway station construction |
| 485112 | Railway systems (except mixed mode), commuter |
| 488210 | Railway terminals, independent operation |
| 482111 | Railway transportation, line-haul |
| 487110 | Railway transportation, scenic and sightseeing |
| 482112 | Railway transportation, short-line or beltline |
| 334519 | Rain gauges manufacturing |
| 315210 | Raincoats (e.g., water resistant, waterproof, water-repellent) cut and sew apparel contractors |
| 313320 | Raincoats waterproofing (i.e., oiling) |
| 315250 | Raincoats, rubber or rubberized fabric, manufacturing |
| 315250 | Raincoats, water resistant, men's and boys', cut and sewn from purchased fabric (except apparel contractors) |
| 315250 | Raincoats, water resistant, women's, girls', and infants', cut and sewn from purchased fabric (except apparel contractors) |
| 315250 | Raincoats, waterproof, cut and sewn from purchased fabric (except apparel contractors) |
| 315250 | Raincoats, water-repellent, men's and boys', cut and sewn from purchased fabric (except apparel contractors) |
| 315250 | Raincoats, water-repellent, women's, girls', and infants', cut and sewn from purchased fabric (except apparel contractors) |
| 111332 | Raisin farming |
| 112990 | Raising swans, peacocks, flamingos, or other adornment birds |
| 311423 | Raisins made in dehydration plants |
| 333111 | Rakes, hay, manufacturing |
| 332216 | Rakes, nonpowered handtool, manufacturing |

| | |
|---|---|
| 313110 | Ramie spun yarns made from purchased fiber |
| 423690 | Random access memory (RAM) chips merchant wholesalers |
| 316990 | Rands (i.e., shoe cut stock), leather, manufacturing |
| 333310 | Range finders, photographic, manufacturing |
| 335210 | Range hoods with integral lighting fixtures, household-type, manufacturing |
| 335210 | Range hoods, household-type, manufacturing |
| 333310 | Ranges, commercial-type, manufacturing |
| 423620 | Ranges, gas and electric, merchant wholesalers |
| 335220 | Ranges, household-type cooking, manufacturing |
| 624190 | Rape crisis centers |
| 311225 | Rapeseed (i.e., canola) oil made from purchased oils |
| 311224 | Rapeseed (i.e., canola) oil made in crushing mills |
| 111120 | Rapeseed farming, field and seed production |
| 336510 | Rapid transit cars and equipment manufacturing |
| 325180 | Rare earth compounds, not specified elsewhere by process, manufacturing |
| 212290 | Rare earth metal concentrates beneficiating |
| 212290 | Rare earth metal ores mining and/or beneficiating |
| 325180 | Rare earth salts manufacturing |
| 459510 | Rare manuscript stores |
| 111334 | Raspberry farming |
| 332216 | Rasps, handheld, manufacturing |
| 332216 | Ratchets, nonpowered, manufacturing |
| 524298 | Ratemaking services, insurance |
| 334511 | Rate-of-climb instrumentation manufacturing |
| 213112 | Rathole and mousehole drilling at oil and gas fields on a contract basis |
| 112390 | Ratite production |
| 337126 | Rattan furniture, household-type, manufacturing |
| 321999 | Rattan ware (except furniture) manufacturing |
| 112990 | Rattlesnake production |
| 311313 | Raw beet sugar manufacturing |
| 424590 | Raw farm products (except field beans, grains) merchant wholesalers |
| 424430 | Raw milk merchant wholesalers |

| | |
|---|---|
| 325199 | Raw organic waxes manufacturing |
| 316110 | Rawhide manufacturing |
| 114111 | Ray fishing |
| 325220 | Rayon fibers and filaments manufacturing |
| 313110 | Rayon spun yarns made from purchased fiber |
| 313110 | Rayon thread manufacturing |
| 313110 | Rayon yarn throwing, twisting, texturizing, or winding purchased filament |
| 331221 | Razor blade strip steel made in cold rolling mills |
| 332215 | Razor blades manufacturing |
| 424210 | Razor blades merchant wholesalers |
| 316990 | Razor strops manufacturing |
| 332215 | Razors (except electric) manufacturing |
| 424210 | Razors (except electric) merchant wholesalers |
| 335210 | Razors, electric, manufacturing |
| 423620 | Razors, electric, merchant wholesalers |
| 332313 | Reactor containment vessels, fabricated metal plate, manufacturing |
| 332410 | Reactors, nuclear, manufacturing |
| 333310 | Readers, microfilm or microfiche, manufacturing |
| 327320 | Ready-mix concrete manufacturing and distributing |
| 336211 | Ready-mix concrete trucks assembling on purchased chassis |
| 531190 | Real estate (except building) rental or leasing |
| 237210 | Real estate (except cemeteries) subdividers |
| 531210 | Real estate agencies |
| 531210 | Real estate agents' offices |
| 531320 | Real estate appraisal services |
| 531320 | Real estate appraisers' offices |
| 531390 | Real estate asset management services (except property management) |
| 813910 | Real estate boards |
| 531210 | Real estate brokerages |
| 531210 | Real estate brokers' offices |
| 531390 | Real estate consultants' (except agents, appraisers) offices |
| 522292 | Real estate credit lending |
| 531390 | Real estate escrow agencies |
| 531390 | Real estate escrow agents' offices |
| 531390 | Real estate fiduciaries' offices |

| | |
|---|---|
| 541110 | Real estate law offices |
| 531390 | Real estate listing services |
| 525990 | Real estate mortgage investment conduits (REMICs) |
| 522299 | Real estate mortgage investment conduits (REMICs) issuing, private |
| 531312 | Real estate property managers' offices, commercial |
| 531311 | Real estate property managers' offices, residential |
| 531130 | Real estate rental or leasing of miniwarehouses and self-storage units |
| 531120 | Real estate rental or leasing of nonresidential building (except miniwarehouse) |
| 531110 | Real estate rental or leasing of residential building |
| 611519 | Real estate schools |
| 524127 | Real estate title insurance carriers, direct |
| 237210 | Real property (except cemeteries) subdivision |
| 561492 | Real-time (i.e., simultaneous) closed captioning of live television performances, meetings, conferences, and so forth |
| 333515 | Reamers (i.e., a machine tool accessory) manufacturing |
| 333517 | Reaming machines, metalworking, manufacturing |
| 238120 | Rebar contractors |
| 323120 | Rebinding books, magazines, or pamphlets |
| 516110 | Rebroadcast radio stations (except exclusively on Internet) |
| 336310 | Rebuilding automotive and truck gasoline engines |
| 326212 | Rebuilding tires |
| 423130 | Recapped tires merchant wholesalers |
| 423830 | Recapping machinery, tire, merchant wholesalers |
| 326212 | Recapping tires |
| 424120 | Receipt books merchant wholesalers |
| 334220 | Receiver-transmitter units (i.e., transceivers) manufacturing |
| 335931 | Receptacles (i.e., outlets), electrical, manufacturing |
| 423610 | Receptacles, electrical, merchant wholesalers |
| 531120 | Reception hall rental or leasing |
| 335132 | Recessed lighting housings and trim (except residential), electric, manufacturing |
| 335131 | Recessed lighting housings and trim, residential electric, manufacturing |
| 335910 | Rechargeable battery packs made from purchased battery cells and housings |
| 335910 | Rechargeable nickel-cadmium (NICAD) batteries manufacturing |
| 314999 | Reclaimed wool processing |
| 326299 | Reclaiming rubber from waste or scrap |
| 337121 | Recliners, upholstered, manufacturing |
| 332994 | Recoil mechanisms, gun, manufacturing |
| 332994 | Recoilless rifles manufacturing |
| 541714 | Recombinant DNA research and experimental development laboratories |
| 423840 | Reconditioned barrels and drums merchant wholesalers |
| 213111 | Reconditioning oil and gas field wells on a contract basis |
| 811310 | Reconditioning shipping barrels and drums |
| 321211 | Reconstituted hardwood veneer manufacturing |
| 321219 | Reconstituted wood panels manufacturing |
| 321219 | Reconstituted wood sheets and boards manufacturing |
| 312230 | Reconstituting tobacco |
| 512250 | Record producers (except independent) |
| 711510 | Record producers, independent |
| 512250 | Record production (except independent record producers) without duplication or distribution |
| 512250 | Record releasing, promoting, and distributing combined with mass duplication |
| 449210 | Record stores, new |
| 459510 | Record stores, used |
| 423620 | Recorders (e.g., tape, video), household-type, merchant wholesalers |
| 334513 | Recorders, industrial process control-type, manufacturing |
| 334515 | Recorders, oscillographic, manufacturing |
| 512290 | Recording books on tape or disc (except publishers) |
| 512290 | Recording seminars and conferences, audio |
| 512240 | Recording studios, sound, operating on a contract or fee basis |
| 711510 | Recording technicians, independent |
| 541611 | Records management consulting services |
| 314999 | Recovered fibers processing |

| | |
|---|---|
| 331492 | Recovering and refining of nonferrous metals (except aluminum, copper) from scrap |
| 331492 | Recovering silver from used photographic film or X-ray plates |
| 237990 | Recreation area, open space, construction |
| 621340 | Recreational (e.g., art, dance, music) therapists' offices (e.g., centers, clinics) |
| 721214 | Recreational camps with accommodation facilities (except campgrounds) |
| 713990 | Recreational camps without accommodations |
| 713990 | Recreational day camps (except instructional) |
| 423910 | Recreational equipment and supplies (except vehicles) merchant wholesalers |
| 236220 | Recreational facility building construction |
| 532284 | Recreational goods rental |
| 924120 | Recreational programs administration, government |
| 713940 | Recreational sports club facilities |
| 713990 | Recreational sports clubs (i.e., sports teams) not operating sports facilities |
| 713990 | Recreational sports teams and leagues |
| 532120 | Recreational trailer rental |
| 441210 | Recreational vehicle (RV) dealers |
| 441210 | Recreational vehicle (RV) parts and accessories stores |
| 532120 | Recreational vehicle (RV) rental or leasing |
| 811111 | Recreational vehicle (RV) repair and maintenance services, general |
| 423110 | Recreational vehicle merchant wholesalers |
| 237990 | Recreational vehicle park construction |
| 721211 | Recreational vehicle parks |
| 335999 | Rectifiers (except electronic component-type, semiconductor) manufacturing |
| 334419 | Rectifiers, electronic component-type (except semiconductor), manufacturing |
| 423690 | Rectifiers, electronic, merchant wholesalers |
| 334413 | Rectifiers, semiconductor, manufacturing |
| 333248 | Rectifying equipment, chemical, manufacturing |
| 423930 | Recyclable inkjet cartridges merchant wholesalers |
| 562111 | Recyclable material collection services |
| 562111 | Recyclable material hauling, local |
| 484230 | Recyclable material hauling, long-distance |
| 423930 | Recyclable materials (e.g., glass, metal, paper) merchant wholesalers |
| 562920 | Recyclable materials recovery facilities |
| 325612 | Recycling drycleaning fluids |
| 325998 | Recycling services for degreasing solvents (e.g., engine, machinery) manufacturing |
| 333248 | Recycling sorting machinery manufacturing |
| 325199 | Red oil (i.e., oleic acid) manufacturing |
| 925120 | Redevelopment land agencies, government |
| 334516 | Redox (i.e., oxidation-reduction potential) instruments manufacturing |
| 333612 | Reducers, speed, manufacturing |
| 333612 | Reduction gears and gear units (except aircraft power transmission equipment, automotive) manufacturing |
| 337126 | Reed furniture (except upholstered), household-type, manufacturing |
| 212390 | Reed peat mining and/or beneficiating |
| 321999 | Reed ware (except furniture) manufacturing |
| 339992 | Reeds, musical instrument, manufacturing |
| 339920 | Reels, fishing, manufacturing |
| 332999 | Reels, metal, manufacturing |
| 326199 | Reels, plastics, manufacturing |
| 321999 | Reels, plywood, manufacturing |
| 321999 | Reels, wood, manufacturing |
| 711219 | Referees and umpires |
| 519210 | Reference libraries |
| 561311 | Referral agencies or services, employment |
| 624190 | Referral services for personal and social problems |
| 486910 | Refined petroleum products pipeline transportation |
| 324110 | Refineries, petroleum |
| 324110 | Refinery gases made in petroleum refineries |
| 423830 | Refinery machinery and equipment merchant wholesalers |
| 237120 | Refinery, petroleum, construction |
| 331313 | Refining aluminum, primary |
| 331314 | Refining aluminum, secondary |
| 331410 | Refining copper, primary |
| 331420 | Refining copper, secondary |

| | |
|---|---|
| 331410 | Refining nonferrous metals and alloys (except aluminum), primary |
| 331492 | Refining nonferrous metals and alloys (except aluminum, copper), secondary |
| 335139 | Reflectors for lighting equipment, metal, manufacturing |
| 333310 | Reflectors, optical, manufacturing |
| 326199 | Reflectors, plastics, manufacturing |
| 115310 | Reforestation (except forest nurseries) |
| 922140 | Reformatories (except private operation of) |
| 325991 | Reformulating plastics resins from recycled plastics products |
| 334513 | Refractometers, industrial process-type, manufacturing |
| 334516 | Refractometers, laboratory-type, manufacturing |
| 327120 | Refractories (e.g., block, brick, mortar, tile), clay, manufacturing |
| 327120 | Refractories (e.g., block, brick, mortar, tile), nonclay, manufacturing |
| 238140 | Refractory brick contractors |
| 327120 | Refractory cement, nonclay, manufacturing |
| 423840 | Refractory materials (e.g., block, brick, mortar, tile) merchant wholesalers |
| 212323 | Refractory minerals mining and/or beneficiating |
| 722515 | Refreshment stands, fixed location |
| 722330 | Refreshment stands, mobile |
| 325199 | Refrigerant mixtures and blends manufacturing |
| 424690 | Refrigerants merchant wholesalers |
| 423740 | Refrigerated display cases merchant wholesalers |
| 311824 | Refrigerated doughs made from purchased flour |
| 333415 | Refrigerated lockers manufacturing |
| 484220 | Refrigerated products trucking, local |
| 484230 | Refrigerated products trucking, long-distance |
| 493120 | Refrigerated warehousing |
| 333415 | Refrigeration compressors manufacturing |
| 334512 | Refrigeration controls, residential and commercial-type, manufacturing |
| 423740 | Refrigeration equipment and supplies, commercial-type, merchant wholesalers |
| 811310 | Refrigeration equipment repair and maintenance services, industrial and commercial-type |
| 333415 | Refrigeration equipment, industrial and commercial-type, manufacturing |
| 238220 | Refrigeration system (e.g., commercial, industrial, scientific) installation |
| 334512 | Refrigeration thermostats manufacturing |
| 423740 | Refrigeration units, motor vehicle, merchant wholesalers |
| 333415 | Refrigeration units, truck-type, manufacturing |
| 334512 | Refrigeration/air-conditioning defrost controls manufacturing |
| 532210 | Refrigerator rental |
| 811412 | Refrigerator, household-type, repair and maintenance services without retailing new refrigerators |
| 335220 | Refrigerator/freezer combinations, household-type, manufacturing |
| 335220 | Refrigerators (e.g., absorption, mechanical), household-type, manufacturing |
| 423740 | Refrigerators (e.g., reach-in, walk-in), commercial-type, merchant wholesalers |
| 423620 | Refrigerators, household-type, merchant wholesalers |
| 624230 | Refugee settlement services |
| 562212 | Refuse collecting and operating solid waste landfills |
| 562111 | Refuse collection services |
| 562213 | Refuse disposal combustors or incinerators |
| 562212 | Refuse disposal landfills |
| 236210 | Refuse disposal plant (except sewage treatment) construction |
| 562111 | Refuse hauling, local |
| 484230 | Refuse hauling, long-distance |
| 325220 | Regenerated cellulosic fibers manufacturing |
| 925120 | Regional planning and development program administration |
| 621399 | Registered nurses' (RNs) offices (e.g., centers, clinics) |
| 334514 | Registers, linear tallying, manufacturing |
| 332323 | Registers, metal air, manufacturing |
| 561311 | Registries, employment |
| 561311 | Registries, teacher |
| 335311 | Regulating transformers, power system-type, manufacturing |
| 926140 | Regulation and inspection of agricultural products |
| 926130 | Regulation of utilities |
| 335311 | Regulators (i.e., electric transformers), feeder voltage, manufacturing |

| | |
|---|---|
| 336320 | Regulators, motor vehicle voltage for internal combustion engines manufacturing |
| 335313 | Regulators, power, manufacturing |
| 423610 | Regulators, voltage (except motor vehicle), merchant wholesalers |
| 624190 | Rehabilitation agencies for offenders |
| 622310 | Rehabilitation hospitals (except alcoholism, drug addiction) |
| 622210 | Rehabilitation hospitals, alcoholism and drug addiction |
| 624310 | Rehabilitation job counseling and training, vocational |
| 922150 | Rehabilitation services, correctional, government |
| 423510 | Reinforcement mesh and wire merchant wholesalers |
| 332618 | Reinforcing mesh, concrete, made from purchased wire |
| 238120 | Reinforcing rod, bar, mesh and cage installation |
| 238120 | Reinforcing steel contractors |
| 524130 | Reinsurance carriers |
| 334515 | Relays (except electrical, electronic), instrument, manufacturing |
| 423610 | Relays merchant wholesalers |
| 335314 | Relays, electrical and electronic, manufacturing |
| 624230 | Relief services, disaster |
| 624230 | Relief services, emergency |
| 513130 | Religious book publishers |
| 513130 | Religious book publishers (except exclusive Internet publishing) |
| 513130 | Religious book publishers and printing combined |
| 513130 | Religious book publishers, exclusively on Internet |
| 459210 | Religious book stores |
| 323120 | Religious bookbinding without printing |
| 323117 | Religious books printing and binding without publishing |
| 323117 | Religious books printing without publishing |
| 236220 | Religious building (e.g., church, synagogue, mosque, temple) construction |
| 337127 | Religious furniture manufacturing |
| 423210 | Religious furniture merchant wholesalers |
| 459999 | Religious goods (except books) stores |
| 513120 | Religious magazine and periodical publishers |
| 513120 | Religious magazine and periodical publishers (except exclusive Internet publishing) |
| 513120 | Religious magazine and periodical publishers and printing combined |
| 513120 | Religious magazine and periodical publishers, exclusively on Internet |
| 323111 | Religious magazines and periodicals commercial printing (except screen) without publishing |
| 323113 | Religious magazines and periodicals screen printing without publishing |
| 813110 | Religious organizations |
| 423490 | Religious supplies merchant wholesalers |
| 311421 | Relishes canning |
| 562910 | Remediation and cleanup of contaminated buildings, mine sites, soil, or ground water |
| 562910 | Remediation services, environmental |
| 525990 | REMICs (real estate mortgage investment conduits) |
| 522299 | REMICs (real estate mortgage investment conduits) issuing, private |
| 424310 | Remnants, piece goods, merchant wholesalers |
| 236118 | Remodeling and renovating for-sale builders |
| 236118 | Remodeling and renovating general contractors, multifamily building |
| 236118 | Remodeling and renovating general contractors, residential |
| 236118 | Remodeling and renovating general contractors, single-family housing |
| 236118 | Remodeling and renovating single-family housing |
| 236118 | Remodeling and renovating, residential building |
| 334290 | Remote control units (e.g., garage door, television) manufacturing |
| 541360 | Remote sensing geophysical surveying services |
| 238910 | Removal of dams, dikes, and other heavy and civil engineering constructions |
| 213113 | Removal of overburden for coal mining on a contract basis |
| 213114 | Removal of overburden for metal mining on a contract basis |
| 213115 | Removal of overburden for nonmetallic minerals mining (except fuels) on a contract basis |
| 562920 | Removal of recyclable materials from a waste stream |
| 621492 | Renal dialysis centers and clinics |

| | |
|---|---|
| 311613 | Rendering animals (carrion) for feed |
| 311613 | Rendering fats |
| 311613 | Rendering plants |
| 424990 | Rennets merchant wholesalers |
| 926150 | Rent control agencies |
| ****** | Rental -- see type of article or property being rented |
| 532310 | Rent-all centers |
| 532490 | Renting coin- or card-operated amusement devices (except concession operators) |
| 531210 | Renting real estate for others (i.e., agents, brokers) |
| 541611 | Reorganizational consulting services |
| 522299 | Repackaging loans for sale to others (i.e., private conduits) |
| ****** | Repair -- see type of article being repaired |
| 237310 | Repair, highway, road, street, bridge or airport runway |
| 323120 | Repairing books |
| 334210 | Repeater and transceiver equipment, carrier line, manufacturing |
| 711110 | Repertory companies, theatrical |
| 322230 | Report covers made from purchased paper or paperboard |
| 711510 | Reporters, independent (freelance) |
| 561491 | Repossession services |
| 512199 | Reproduction of motion picture films for theatrical distribution |
| 115210 | Reproductive flushing services for animals |
| 621410 | Reproductive health services centers |
| 561439 | Reprographic services |
| 712130 | Reptile exhibits, live |
| 324191 | Re-refining used petroleum lubricating oils |
| 321912 | Resawing purchased lumber |
| 621910 | Rescue services, air |
| 621910 | Rescue services, medical |
| 517410 | Resellers, satellite telecommunication |
| 517121 | Resellers, telecommunication (except satellite telecommunications and agents for wireless telecommunications services) |
| 325411 | Reserpines (i.e., basic chemicals) manufacturing |
| 561599 | Reservation (e.g., airline, car rental, hotel, restaurant) services |

| | |
|---|---|
| 522320 | Reserve and liquidity services (except central bank) |
| 237110 | Reservoir construction |
| 562998 | Reservoir maintenance and cleaning services |
| 721310 | Residence clubs, organizational |
| 531110 | Residential building rental or leasing |
| 561720 | Residential cleaning services |
| 721310 | Residential clubs |
| 236116 | Residential construction, multifamily, general contractors |
| 236115 | Residential construction, single-family, general contractors |
| 236117 | Residential for-sale builders |
| 623220 | Residential group homes for the emotionally disturbed |
| 531110 | Residential hotel rental or leasing |
| 531311 | Residential property managing |
| 531210 | Residential real estate agencies |
| 531210 | Residential real estate agents' offices |
| 531210 | Residential real estate brokerages |
| 531210 | Residential real estate brokers' offices |
| 531311 | Residential real estate property managers' offices |
| 531190 | Residential trailer parks |
| 211130 | Residue gas production |
| 326199 | Resilient floor coverings (e.g., sheet, tile) manufacturing |
| 238330 | Resilient floor tile or sheet (e.g., linoleum, rubber, vinyl), installation only |
| 325211 | Resins, plastics (except custom compounding purchased resins), manufacturing |
| 424610 | Resins, plastics, merchant wholesalers |
| 424690 | Resins, synthetic rubber, merchant wholesalers |
| 334515 | Resistance measuring equipment manufacturing |
| 334513 | Resistance thermometers and bulbs, industrial process-type, manufacturing |
| 333992 | Resistance welding equipment manufacturing |
| 334416 | Resistors, electronic, manufacturing |
| 423690 | Resistors, electronic, merchant wholesalers |
| 335312 | Resolvers manufacturing |
| 334516 | Resonance instruments (i.e., laboratory-type) manufacturing |
| 334419 | Resonant reed devices, electronic, manufacturing |

| | |
|---|---|
| 325194 | Resorcinol manufacturing |
| 721120 | Resort hotels with casinos |
| 721110 | Resort hotels without casinos |
| 531311 | Resort or vacation property managers' offices |
| 334510 | Respiratory analysis equipment, electromedical, manufacturing |
| 339113 | Respiratory protection mask manufacturing |
| 621399 | Respiratory therapists' offices (e.g., centers, clinics) |
| 623110 | Rest homes with nursing care |
| 623312 | Rest homes without nursing care |
| 561720 | Rest room cleaning services |
| 812990 | Rest room operation |
| 813910 | Restaurant associations |
| 236220 | Restaurant construction |
| 423440 | Restaurant equipment (except furniture) merchant wholesalers |
| 811310 | Restaurant fryer equipment cleaning services |
| 337127 | Restaurant furniture (e.g., carts, chairs, foodwagons, tables) manufacturing |
| 423210 | Restaurant furniture merchant wholesalers |
| 561720 | Restaurant kitchen cleaning services |
| 611519 | Restaurant management schools (except academic) |
| 492210 | Restaurant meals order and delivery services (i.e., independent order and delivery services) |
| 722513 | Restaurants, carryout |
| 722513 | Restaurants, fast-food |
| 722511 | Restaurants, full service |
| 811420 | Restoration and repair of antique furniture |
| 811121 | Restoration shops, antique and classic automotive |
| 339113 | Restraints, patient, manufacturing |
| 561410 | Resume writing services |
| 238330 | Resurfacing hardwood flooring |
| 237310 | Resurfacing, highway, road, street, bridge or airport runway |
| ****** | Retail -- see type of dealer, shop, or store |
| 333998 | Retail scales (e.g., butcher, delicatessen, produce) manufacturing |
| 813910 | Retailers' associations |
| 238110 | Retaining wall (except anchored earth), poured concrete, construction |

| | |
|---|---|
| 238140 | Retaining wall, masonry (i.e., block, brick, stone), construction |
| 237990 | Retaining walls, anchored (e.g., with piles, soil nails, tieback anchors), construction |
| 325998 | Retarders (e.g., flameproofing agents, mildewproofing agents) manufacturing |
| 339112 | Retinoscopes (except electromedical) manufacturing |
| 334510 | Retinoscopes, electromedical, manufacturing |
| 813410 | Retirement associations, social |
| 623311 | Retirement communities, continuing care |
| 623110 | Retirement homes with nursing care |
| 623312 | Retirement homes without nursing care |
| 531110 | Retirement hotel rental or leasing |
| 525110 | Retirement pension plans |
| 332420 | Retorts, heavy gauge metal, manufacturing |
| 339112 | Retractors, medical, manufacturing |
| 326211 | Retreading materials, tire, manufacturing |
| 326212 | Retreading tires |
| 813110 | Retreat houses, religious |
| 115114 | Retting flax |
| 811420 | Reupholstery shops, furniture |
| 522292 | Reverse mortgage lending |
| 237990 | Revetment construction |
| 332994 | Revolvers manufacturing |
| 238290 | Revolving door installation |
| 811310 | Rewinding armatures (except on an assembly line or factory basis) |
| 213111 | Reworking oil and gas wells on a contract basis |
| 331410 | Rhenium refining, primary |
| 335931 | Rheostats (i.e., dimmer switches), current-carrying wiring device, manufacturing |
| 334419 | Rheostats, electronic, manufacturing |
| 335314 | Rheostats, industrial control, manufacturing |
| 212290 | Rhodium mining and/or beneficiating |
| 212290 | Rhodochrosite mining and/or beneficiating |
| 111219 | Rhubarb farming, field and seed production |
| 111419 | Rhubarb, grown under cover |
| 339940 | Ribbons (e.g., cash register, printer, typewriter), inked, manufacturing |

| | |
|---|---|
| 314999 | Ribbons made from purchased fabrics |
| 313220 | Ribbons made in narrow woven fabric mills |
| 313230 | Ribbons made in nonwoven fabric mills |
| 339940 | Ribbons, inked, manufacturing |
| 424120 | Ribbons, inked, merchant wholesalers |
| 424310 | Ribbons, textile, merchant wholesalers |
| 111160 | Rice (except wild rice) farming, field and seed production |
| 311212 | Rice bran, flour, and meals, manufacturing |
| 311230 | Rice breakfast foods manufacturing |
| 311212 | Rice cleaning and polishing |
| 115114 | Rice drying |
| 311212 | Rice flour manufacturing |
| 311213 | Rice malt manufacturing |
| 311212 | Rice meal manufacturing |
| 311511 | Rice milk manufacturing |
| 311212 | Rice milling |
| 311999 | Rice mixes (i.e., uncooked and packaged with other ingredients) made from purchased rice and dry ingredients |
| 311423 | Rice mixes (i.e., uncooked and packaged with other ingredients) made in dehydration plants |
| 311212 | Rice mixes (i.e., uncooked and packaged with other ingredients) made in rice mills |
| 311221 | Rice starches manufacturing |
| 311212 | Rice, brewer's, manufacturing |
| 311212 | Rice, brown, manufacturing |
| 424490 | Rice, polished, merchant wholesalers |
| 424510 | Rice, unpolished, merchant wholesalers |
| 485310 | Ride hailing arrangement services |
| 485310 | Ride hailing services |
| 485310 | Ridesharing arrangement services |
| 485310 | Ridesharing services |
| 315210 | Riding clothes cut and sew apparel contractors |
| 315250 | Riding clothes, men's and boys', cut and sewn from purchased fabric (except apparel contractors) |
| 315250 | Riding clothes, women's and girls', cut and sewn from purchased fabric (except apparel contractors) |
| 713990 | Riding clubs, recreational |
| 316990 | Riding crops manufacturing |
| 611620 | Riding instruction academies or schools |
| 713990 | Riding stables (except boarding horses) |
| 713990 | Rifle clubs, recreational |
| 332994 | Rifles (except toy) manufacturing |
| 332994 | Rifles, BB and pellet, manufacturing |
| 332994 | Rifles, pneumatic, manufacturing |
| 332994 | Rifles, recoilless, manufacturing |
| 339930 | Rifles, toy, manufacturing |
| 333517 | Rifling machines, metalworking, manufacturing |
| 213112 | Rig skidding, oil and gas field, on a contract basis |
| 238290 | Rigging large-scale equipment |
| 238910 | Right of way cutting (except maintenance) |
| 336612 | Rigid inflatable boats (RIBs) manufacturing |
| 336390 | Rims, automotive, truck, and bus wheel, manufacturing |
| 336310 | Rings, piston, manufacturing |
| 713940 | Rinks, ice or roller skating |
| 212319 | Riprap (except granite, limestone) preparation plants |
| 212319 | Riprap (except limestone and granite) mining or quarrying |
| 237990 | Riprap installation |
| 212313 | Riprap, granite, mining or quarrying |
| 212313 | Riprap, granite, preparation plants |
| 212312 | Riprap, limestone, mining or quarrying |
| 212312 | Riprap, limestone, preparation plants |
| 483211 | River freight transportation |
| 483212 | River passenger transportation |
| 713990 | River rafting, recreational |
| 713210 | Riverboat casinos |
| 333991 | Riveting guns, handheld power-driven, manufacturing |
| 333517 | Riveting machines, metalworking, manufacturing |
| 332722 | Rivets, metal, manufacturing |
| 621399 | RNs' (registered nurses) offices (e.g., centers, clinics) |
| 325320 | Roach poisons manufacturing |
| 711110 | Road companies, theatrical |
| 237310 | Road construction |
| 423810 | Road construction and maintenance machinery merchant wholesalers |
| 238910 | Road decommissioning |
| 324199 | Road oils made from refined petroleum |
| 324110 | Road oils made in petroleum refineries |

| | |
|---|---|
| 516210 | Road traffic reporting services |
| 311911 | Roasted nuts and seeds manufacturing |
| 112320 | Roaster chicken production |
| 335210 | Roasters (i.e., cooking appliances), household-type electric, manufacturing |
| 311920 | Roasting coffee |
| 333241 | Roasting machinery manufacturing |
| 315210 | Robes, lounging, cut and sew apparel contractors |
| 315120 | Robes, lounging, made in apparel knitting mills |
| 315250 | Robes, lounging, men's and boys', cut and sewn from purchased fabric (except apparel contractors) |
| 315250 | Robes, lounging, women's, girls', and infants', cut and sewn from purchased fabric (except apparel contractors) |
| 541511 | Robotics applications/software design and development services |
| 541330 | Robotics automation engineering services |
| 541330 | Robotics engineering design and integration services |
| 541511 | Robotics process automation software design and development services |
| 541715 | Robotics research and development laboratories or services |
| 333120 | Rock crushing machinery, portable, manufacturing |
| 333131 | Rock crushing machinery, stationary, manufacturing |
| 333132 | Rock drill bits, oil and gas field-type, manufacturing |
| 333120 | Rock drills, construction and surface mining-type, manufacturing |
| 333131 | Rock drills, underground mining-type, manufacturing |
| 711130 | Rock musical artists, independent |
| 711130 | Rock musical groups |
| 237990 | Rock removal, underwater |
| 212390 | Rock salt mining and/or beneficiating |
| 336310 | Rocker arms and parts, automotive and truck gasoline engine, manufacturing |
| 337122 | Rockers (except upholstered), wood, manufacturing |
| 337121 | Rockers, upholstered, manufacturing |
| 332313 | Rocket casings, fabricated metal work, manufacturing |
| 336412 | Rocket engines, aircraft, manufacturing |
| 336415 | Rocket engines, guided missile, manufacturing |
| 332994 | Rocket launchers manufacturing |

| | |
|---|---|
| 336414 | Rockets (guided missiles), space and military, complete, manufacturing |
| 332993 | Rockets, ammunition (except guided missiles, pyrotechnic), manufacturing |
| 114111 | Rockfish fishing |
| 339930 | Rocking horses manufacturing |
| 331318 | Rod made by extruding purchased aluminum |
| 331318 | Rod made by rolling purchased aluminum |
| 333519 | Rod rolling mill machinery, metalworking, manufacturing |
| 331318 | Rod, aluminum, made in integrated secondary smelting and extruding mills |
| 331318 | Rod, aluminum, made in integrated secondary smelting and rolling mills |
| 331420 | Rod, copper and copper alloy, made from purchased copper or in integrated secondary smelting and rolling, drawing or extruding plants |
| 326130 | Rod, laminated plastics, manufacturing |
| 331491 | Rod, nonferrous metals (except aluminum, copper), made from purchased metals or scrap |
| 326121 | Rod, nonrigid plastics, manufacturing |
| 325320 | Rodent poisons manufacturing |
| 325320 | Rodenticides manufacturing |
| 711310 | Rodeo managers with facilities |
| 711320 | Rodeo managers without facilities |
| 711310 | Rodeo organizers with facilities |
| 711320 | Rodeo organizers without facilities |
| 711310 | Rodeo promoters with facilities |
| 711320 | Rodeo promoters without facilities |
| 339920 | Rods and rod parts, fishing, manufacturing |
| 326299 | Rods, hard rubber, manufacturing |
| 331110 | Rods, iron or steel, made in iron and steel mills |
| 423510 | Rods, metal (except precious), merchant wholesalers |
| 334519 | Rods, surveyor's, manufacturing |
| 238160 | Roll roofing installation |
| 332991 | Roller bearings manufacturing |
| 711211 | Roller hockey clubs, professional or semiprofessional |
| 316110 | Roller leather manufacturing |
| 339920 | Roller skates manufacturing |
| 713940 | Roller skating rinks |
| 333120 | Rollers, road construction and maintenance machinery, manufacturing |

| | |
|---|---|
| 321999 | Rollers, wood, manufacturing |
| 332321 | Rolling doors for industrial buildings and warehouses, metal, manufacturing |
| 333519 | Rolling mill machinery and equipment, metalworking, manufacturing |
| 423830 | Rolling mill machinery merchant wholesalers |
| 333519 | Rolling mill roll machines, metalworking, manufacturing |
| 331511 | Rolling mill rolls, iron, manufacturing |
| 331513 | Rolling mill rolls, steel, manufacturing |
| 321999 | Rolling pins, wood, manufacturing |
| 336510 | Rolling stock, railroad, rebuilding |
| 311812 | Rolls and buns (including frozen) made in commercial bakeries |
| 326299 | Rolls and roll coverings, rubber (e.g., industrial, papermill, painters', steelmill) manufacturing |
| 111219 | Romaine lettuce farming, field and seed production |
| 315210 | Rompers cut and sew apparel contractors |
| 315250 | Rompers, infants', cut and sewn from purchased fabric (except apparel contractors) |
| 541690 | Roof consulting services |
| 332322 | Roof deck, sheet metal (except stampings), manufacturing |
| 238310 | Roof insulation contractor |
| 238160 | Roof membrane installation |
| 238160 | Roof painting, spraying, or coating |
| 238130 | Roof truss (wood) installation |
| 321215 | Roof trusses, wood, manufacturing |
| 332322 | Roof ventilators, sheet metal (except stampings), manufacturing |
| 326299 | Roofing (i.e., single ply rubber membrane) manufacturing |
| 324122 | Roofing cements, asphalt, made from purchased asphaltic materials |
| 324122 | Roofing coatings made from purchased asphaltic materials |
| 238160 | Roofing contractors |
| 324122 | Roofing felts made from purchased asphaltic materials |
| 444180 | Roofing material dealers |
| 423330 | Roofing materials (except wood) merchant wholesalers |
| 423310 | Roofing materials, wood, merchant wholesalers |
| 327120 | Roofing tile, clay, manufacturing |
| 327390 | Roofing tile, concrete, manufacturing |
| 238160 | Roofing, built-up tar and gravel, installation |
| 332322 | Roofing, sheet metal (except stampings), manufacturing |
| 333415 | Room air-conditioners manufacturing |
| 423620 | Room air-conditioners merchant wholesalers |
| 337122 | Room dividers, wood household-type, manufacturing |
| 333414 | Room heaters (except portable electric) manufacturing |
| 335210 | Room heaters, portable electric, manufacturing |
| 334512 | Room thermostats manufacturing |
| 721310 | Rooming and boarding houses |
| 325320 | Root removing chemicals manufacturing |
| 311221 | Root starches manufacturing |
| 332999 | Rope fittings manufacturing |
| 332618 | Rope, wire, made from purchased wire |
| 314994 | Ropes (except wire rope) manufacturing |
| 423840 | Ropes (except wire rope) merchant wholesalers |
| 423510 | Ropes, wire (except insulated), merchant wholesalers |
| 339910 | Rosaries and other small religious articles, precious metal, manufacturing |
| 212290 | Roscoelite (vanadium hydromica) mining and/or beneficiating |
| 111421 | Rose bush growing |
| 325211 | Rosins (i.e., modified resins) manufacturing |
| 325194 | Rosins made by distillation of pine gum or pine wood |
| 424690 | Rosins merchant wholesalers |
| 333111 | Rotary hoes manufacturing |
| 333111 | Rotary tillers, farm-type, manufacturing |
| 334514 | Rotary type meters, consumption registering, manufacturing |
| 325320 | Rotenone insecticides manufacturing |
| 323111 | Rotogravure printing (except books) |
| 323120 | Rotogravure printing plates and cylinders preparation services |
| 335312 | Rotor retainers and housings manufacturing |
| 335312 | Rotors (i.e., for motors) manufacturing |
| 325620 | Rouge, cosmetic, manufacturing |
| 321920 | Round stave baskets (e.g., fruit, vegetable) manufacturing |
| 321912 | Rounds or rungs, furniture, hardwood, manufacturing |

| | |
|---|---|
| 331110 | Rounds, tube, steel, made in iron and steel mills |
| 423990 | Roundwood merchant wholesalers |
| 213112 | Roustabout mining services, on a contract basis |
| 423690 | Routers merchant wholesalers |
| 333991 | Routers, handheld power-driven, manufacturing |
| 333248 | Roving machinery for textiles manufacturing |
| 236115 | Row house (i.e., single-family type) construction general contractors |
| 236117 | Row house construction for-sale builders |
| 532284 | Rowboat rental |
| 713990 | Rowing clubs, recreational |
| 112910 | Royal jelly production, bees |
| 326220 | Rubber and plastics belts and hoses (without fittings) manufacturing |
| 326299 | Rubber bands manufacturing |
| 325520 | Rubber cements manufacturing |
| 212323 | Rubber clay mining and/or beneficiating |
| 238290 | Rubber door installation |
| 326199 | Rubber floor coverings manufacturing |
| 326291 | Rubber goods, mechanical (i.e., extruded, lathe-cut, molded), manufacturing |
| 423840 | Rubber goods, mechanical (i.e., extruded, lathe-cut, molded), merchant wholesalers |
| 424210 | Rubber goods, medical, merchant wholesalers |
| 325998 | Rubber processing preparations (e.g., accelerators, stabilizers) manufacturing |
| 423930 | Rubber scrap and scrap tires merchant wholesalers |
| 339940 | Rubber stamps manufacturing |
| 424120 | Rubber stamps merchant wholesalers |
| 313220 | Rubber thread and yarns, fabric covered, manufacturing |
| 326299 | Rubber tubing manufacturing |
| 333248 | Rubber working machinery manufacturing |
| 424990 | Rubber, crude, merchant wholesalers |
| 325212 | Rubber, synthetic, manufacturing |
| 313320 | Rubberizing purchased capes |
| 313320 | Rubberizing purchased cloaks |
| 313320 | Rubberizing purchased clothing |
| 313320 | Rubberizing purchased coats |

| | |
|---|---|
| 313320 | Rubberizing purchased textiles and apparel |
| 212390 | Rubbing stones mining and/or beneficiating |
| 562111 | Rubbish (i.e., nonhazardous solid waste) hauling, local |
| 562111 | Rubbish collection services |
| 562213 | Rubbish disposal combustors or incinerators |
| 562212 | Rubbish disposal landfills |
| 484230 | Rubbish hauling without collection or disposal, truck, long-distance |
| 562119 | Rubble hauling, local |
| 562119 | Rubble removal services |
| 212390 | Ruby mining and/or beneficiating |
| 532289 | Rug and carpet rental |
| 561740 | Rug cleaning plants |
| 325612 | Rug cleaning preparations manufacturing |
| 561740 | Rug cleaning services |
| 449121 | Rug stores |
| 314110 | Rugs and carpets made from textile materials |
| 423220 | Rugs merchant wholesalers |
| 321999 | Rulers and rules (except slide), wood, manufacturing |
| 332216 | Rulers, metal, manufacturing |
| 326199 | Rulers, plastics, manufacturing |
| 334519 | Rules, slide, manufacturing |
| 624221 | Runaway youth shelters |
| 488119 | Runway maintenance services |
| 237310 | Runway, airport, line painting (e.g., striping) |
| 485210 | Rural bus services |
| 324191 | Rust arresting petroleum compounds made from refined petroleum |
| 325998 | Rust preventive preparations manufacturing |
| 325612 | Rust removers manufacturing |
| 238320 | Rustproofing (except automotive) |
| 332812 | Rustproofing metals and metal products for the trade |
| 811198 | Rustproofing shops, automotive |
| 111219 | Rutabaga farming, field and seed production |
| 212290 | Ruthenium ore mining and/or beneficiating |
| 212290 | Rutile mining and/or beneficiating |
| 721211 | RV (recreational vehicle) parks |

| | |
|---|---|
| 532120 | RV (recreational vehicle) rental or leasing |
| 441210 | RV dealers |
| 111199 | Rye farming, field and seed production |
| 311211 | Rye flour manufacturing |
| 311213 | Rye malt manufacturing |
| 111998 | Ryegrass seed farming |
| 114111 | Sablefish fishing |
| 325199 | Saccharin manufacturing |
| 325620 | Sachet, scented, manufacturing |
| 322220 | Sacks, multiwall, made from purchased uncoated paper |
| 424130 | Sacks, paper, merchant wholesalers |
| 713990 | Saddle horse rental services, recreational |
| 325612 | Saddle soaps manufacturing |
| 321999 | Saddle trees, wood, manufacturing |
| 316110 | Saddlery leather manufacturing |
| 424910 | Saddlery merchant wholesalers |
| 332999 | Saddlery parts, metal, manufacturing |
| 811430 | Saddlery repair shops without retailing new saddlery |
| 459110 | Saddlery stores |
| 316990 | Saddles and parts, leather, manufacturing |
| 332999 | Safe deposit boxes and chests, metal, manufacturing |
| 332999 | Safe doors and linings, metal, manufacturing |
| 332999 | Safes, metal, manufacturing |
| 423420 | Safes, security, merchant wholesalers |
| 332911 | Safety (i.e., pop-off) valves, industrial-type, manufacturing |
| 316990 | Safety belts, leather, manufacturing |
| 541690 | Safety consulting services |
| 423990 | Safety deposit boxes merchant wholesalers |
| 325920 | Safety fuses, blasting, manufacturing |
| 327215 | Safety glass (including motor vehicle) made from purchased glass |
| 238990 | Safety net system, erecting and dismantling at construction site |
| 339993 | Safety pins manufacturing |
| 332215 | Safety razor blades manufacturing |
| 332215 | Safety razors manufacturing |
| 111120 | Safflower farming, field and seed production |
| 311225 | Safflower oil made from purchased oils |
| 311224 | Safflower oil made in crushing mills |

| | |
|---|---|
| 339920 | Sailboards manufacturing |
| 336612 | Sailboat building, not done in shipyards |
| 441222 | Sailboat dealers |
| 532284 | Sailboat rental |
| 713930 | Sailing clubs with marinas |
| 713990 | Sailing clubs without marinas |
| 336611 | Sailing ships, commercial, manufacturing |
| 314910 | Sails made from purchased fabrics |
| 312130 | Sake manufacturing |
| 325180 | Sal soda (i.e., washing soda) manufacturing |
| 311423 | Salad dressing mixes, dry, made in dehydration plants |
| 311942 | Salad dressing mixes, dry, manufacturing |
| 311941 | Salad dressings manufacturing |
| 424490 | Salad dressings merchant wholesalers |
| 424490 | Salad oils merchant wholesalers |
| 311991 | Salads, fresh or refrigerated, manufacturing |
| 424480 | Salads, prepackaged, merchant wholesalers |
| 424120 | Sales books merchant wholesalers |
| 323111 | Sales books, manifold, printing |
| 522220 | Sales financing |
| 541613 | Sales management consulting services |
| 325199 | Salicylic acid (except medicinal) manufacturing |
| 325411 | Salicylic acid, medicinal, uncompounded, manufacturing |
| 212390 | Salines mining and/or beneficiating |
| 114111 | Salmon fishing |
| 236220 | Salon construction |
| 311421 | Salsa canning |
| 325998 | Salt (except table) manufacturing |
| 311942 | Salt substitute manufacturing |
| 213112 | Salt water disposal systems, oil and gas field, on a contract basis |
| 212390 | Salt, common, mining and/or beneficiating |
| 212390 | Salt, rock, mining and/or beneficiating |
| 311942 | Salt, table, manufacturing |
| 424490 | Salt, table, merchant wholesalers |
| 311612 | Salted meats made from purchased carcasses |
| 311821 | Saltines manufacturing |
| 424210 | Salts, bath, merchant wholesalers |

424690 Salts, industrial, merchant wholesalers

423930 Salvage, scrap, merchant wholesalers

334516 Sample analysis instruments (except medical) manufacturing

316990 Sample cases, all materials, manufacturing

334519 Sample changers, nuclear radiation, manufacturing

541870 Sample direct distribution services

323120 Samples mounting

541910 Sampling services, statistical

423320 Sand (except industrial) merchant wholesalers

212321 Sand and gravel quarrying (i.e., construction grade) and/or beneficiating

331524 Sand castings, aluminum, unfinished, manufacturing

331529 Sand castings, nonferrous metals (except aluminum), unfinished, manufacturing

484220 Sand hauling, local

484230 Sand hauling, long-distance

333120 Sand mixers manufacturing

212322 Sand, blast, quarrying and/or beneficiating

212321 Sand, construction grade, quarrying and/or beneficiating

212322 Sand, industrial (e.g., engine, filtration, glass grinding, proppant), quarrying and/or beneficiating

423840 Sand, industrial, merchant wholesalers

316210 Sandals, children's, manufacturing

316210 Sandals, men's footwear, manufacturing

316210 Sandals, plastics or plastics soled fabric upper, manufacturing

316210 Sandals, rubber or rubber soled fabric upper, manufacturing

316210 Sandals, women's footwear, manufacturing

332813 Sandblasting metals and metal products for the trade

213112 Sandblasting pipelines on lease, oil and gas field, on a contract basis

238990 Sandblasting, building exterior

333991 Sanders, handheld power-driven, manufacturing

333310 Sanding machines, floor, manufacturing

333243 Sanding machines, woodworking-type, stationary, manufacturing

333243 Sandpaper making machines manufacturing

327910 Sandpaper manufacturing

212319 Sandstone crushed and broken stone mining

212311 Sandstone mining or quarrying

722513 Sandwich shops, limited-service

311612 Sandwich spreads, meat, made from purchased carcasses

311941 Sandwich spreads, salad dressing based, manufacturing

335210 Sandwich toasters and grills, household-type electric, manufacturing

424490 Sandwiches merchant wholesalers

311991 Sandwiches, fresh (i.e., assembled and packaged for wholesale market), manufacturing

322212 Sanitary food container, folding, made from purchased paperboard

424130 Sanitary food containers (e.g., disposable plastics, paper, paperboard) merchant wholesalers

322219 Sanitary food containers (except folding) made from purchased paper or paperboard

562212 Sanitary landfills

322291 Sanitary napkins and tampons made from purchased paper or textile fiber

322120 Sanitary napkins and tampons made in paper mills

322120 Sanitary paper products made in paper mills

424130 Sanitary paper products merchant wholesalers

322120 Sanitary paper stock manufacturing

322291 Sanitary products made from purchased sanitary paper stock

322120 Sanitary products made in paper mills

237110 Sanitary sewer construction

332999 Sanitary ware (e.g., bathtubs, lavatories, sinks), metal, manufacturing

238220 Sanitary ware installation

423720 Sanitary ware, china or enameled iron, merchant wholesalers

541620 Sanitation consulting services

926130 Sanitation districts, nonoperating

924110 Sanitation engineering agencies, government

212390 Sapphire mining and/or beneficiating

325220 Saran (i.e., polyvinylidene chloride) fibers and filaments manufacturing

332613 Sash balance springs, light gauge, made from purchased wire or strip

332321 Sash, door and window, metal, manufacturing

| | |
|---|---|
| 321911 | Sash, door and window, wood and covered wood, manufacturing |
| 316990 | Satchels, all materials, manufacturing |
| 334220 | Satellite antennas manufacturing |
| 334220 | Satellite communications equipment manufacturing |
| 238290 | Satellite dish, household-type, installation |
| 517111 | Satellite master antenna television service (SMATV) |
| 516210 | Satellite radio networks |
| 237130 | Satellite receiving station construction |
| 517410 | Satellite telecommunication carriers |
| 517410 | Satellite telecommunication resellers |
| 517810 | Satellite telemetry operations on a contract or fee basis |
| 517111 | Satellite television distribution systems |
| 516210 | Satellite television networks |
| 517810 | Satellite tracking stations |
| 325130 | Satin white pigments manufacturing |
| 335311 | Saturable transformers manufacturing |
| 324122 | Saturated felts made from purchased paper |
| 322120 | Saturated felts made in paper mills |
| 311423 | Sauce mixes, dry, made in dehydration plants |
| 311942 | Sauce mixes, dry, manufacturing |
| 311941 | Sauces (except tomato-based) manufacturing |
| 311941 | Sauces for meat (except tomato-based) manufacturing |
| 311941 | Sauces for seafood (except tomato-based) manufacturing |
| 311941 | Sauces for vegetable (except tomato-based) manufacturing |
| 311421 | Sauces, tomato-based, canning |
| 311421 | Sauerkraut manufacturing |
| 335210 | Sauna heaters, electric, manufacturing |
| 321992 | Sauna rooms, prefabricated, wood, manufacturing |
| 812199 | Saunas |
| 311612 | Sausage and similar cased products made from purchased carcasses |
| 424490 | Sausage casings merchant wholesalers |
| 311612 | Sausage casings, collagen, made from purchased hides |
| 311611 | Sausage casings, natural, produced in slaughtering plant |
| 326121 | Sausage casings, plastics, manufacturing |
| 522180 | Savings and loan associations (S&L) |

| | |
|---|---|
| 551112 | Savings and loan holding companies |
| 524113 | Savings bank life insurance carriers, direct |
| 522180 | Savings banks |
| 522180 | Savings institutions |
| 332216 | Saw blades, all types, manufacturing |
| 811411 | Saw repair and maintenance (except sawmills) without retailing new saws |
| 321113 | Sawdust and shavings (i.e., sawmill byproducts) manufacturing |
| 424990 | Sawdust merchant wholesalers |
| 321999 | Sawdust, regrinding |
| 321113 | Sawed lumber made in sawmills |
| 321912 | Sawed lumber, resawing purchased lumber |
| 333517 | Sawing machines, metalworking, manufacturing |
| 333243 | Sawmill equipment manufacturing |
| 532490 | Sawmill machinery rental or leasing |
| 423830 | Sawmill machinery, equipment, and supplies merchant wholesalers |
| 321113 | Sawmills |
| 333243 | Saws, bench and table, power-driven, woodworking-type, manufacturing |
| 332216 | Saws, hand, nonpowered, manufacturing |
| 333991 | Saws, handheld power-driven, manufacturing |
| 423830 | Saws, industrial, merchant wholesalers |
| 339112 | Saws, surgical, manufacturing |
| 339992 | Saxophones and parts manufacturing |
| 238990 | Scaffold erecting and dismantling |
| 423810 | Scaffolding merchant wholesalers |
| 532490 | Scaffolding rental or leasing |
| 332323 | Scaffolds, metal, manufacturing |
| 334519 | Scalers, nuclear radiation, manufacturing |
| 333998 | Scales, including laboratory-type, manufacturing |
| 423490 | Scales, laboratory (except dental and medical), merchant wholesalers |
| 114112 | Scallop fishing |
| 812199 | Scalp treating services |
| 423430 | Scanners, computer, merchant wholesalers |
| 518210 | Scanning services, optical |
| 334516 | Scanning tunneling microscopes manufacturing |
| 333243 | Scarfing machines, woodworking-type, manufacturing |

| | |
|---|---|
| 333519 | Scarfing units, rolling mill machinery, metalworking, manufacturing |
| 333120 | Scarifiers, road, manufacturing |
| 325130 | Scarlet 2 R lake manufacturing |
| 315210 | Scarves cut and sew apparel contractors |
| 315990 | Scarves cut and sewn from purchased fabric (except apparel contractors) |
| 315120 | Scarves made in apparel knitting mills |
| 336350 | Scattershield, engine, manufacturing |
| 711510 | Scenery designers, independent theatrical |
| 532490 | Scenery, theatrical, rental or leasing |
| 487990 | Scenic and sightseeing excursions, aerial |
| 487110 | Scenic and sightseeing excursions, land |
| 487210 | Scenic and sightseeing excursions, water |
| 481112 | Scheduled air freight carriers |
| 481112 | Scheduled air freight transportation |
| 481111 | Scheduled air passenger carriers |
| 481111 | Scheduled air passenger transportation |
| 212290 | Scheelite mining and/or beneficiating |
| 313220 | Schiffli machine embroideries manufacturing |
| 333248 | Schiffli machinery manufacturing |
| 212319 | Schist, mica, crushed and broken stone, mining and/or beneficiating |
| 212311 | Schist, mica, mining or quarrying |
| 513120 | Scholarly journal publishers |
| 513120 | Scholarly journal publishers (except exclusive Internet publishing) |
| 513120 | Scholarly journal publishers and printing combined |
| 513120 | Scholarly journal publishers, exclusively on Internet |
| 323111 | Scholarly journals commercial printing (except screen) without publishing |
| 323113 | Scholarly journals screen printing without publishing |
| 813211 | Scholarship trusts (i.e., grantmaking, charitable trust foundations) |
| 513120 | Scholastic magazine and periodical publishers |
| 513120 | Scholastic magazine and periodical publishers (except exclusive Internet publishing) |
| 513120 | Scholastic magazine and periodical publishers and printing combined |
| 513120 | Scholastic magazine and periodical publishers, exclusively on Internet |
| 323111 | Scholastic magazines and periodicals commercial printing (except screen) without publishing |
| 323113 | Scholastic magazines and periodicals screen printing without publishing |
| 611110 | School boards, elementary and secondary |
| 513130 | School book publishers |
| 513130 | School book publishers (except exclusive Internet publishing) |
| 513130 | School book publishers and printing combined |
| 513130 | School book publishers, exclusively on Internet |
| 323117 | School books printing and binding without publishing |
| 323117 | School books printing without publishing |
| 236220 | School building construction |
| 611710 | School bus attendant services |
| 423110 | School bus merchant wholesalers |
| 532120 | School bus rental or leasing |
| 485410 | School bus services |
| 336211 | School buses assembling on purchased chassis |
| 611110 | School districts, elementary or secondary |
| 423490 | School equipment and supplies (except books, furniture) merchant wholesalers |
| 337127 | School furniture manufacturing |
| 423210 | School furniture merchant wholesalers |
| 485410 | School or employee bus transportation for the disabled or elderly |
| 541921 | School photography (i.e., portrait photography) services |
| 459410 | School supply stores |
| 513130 | School textbook publishers |
| 513130 | School textbook publishers (except exclusive Internet publishing) |
| 513130 | School textbook publishers and printing combined |
| 513130 | School textbook publishers, exclusively on Internet |
| 323120 | School textbooks binding without printing |
| 458110 | School uniform stores |
| 611110 | Schools for the intellectually and developmentally disabled (except preschool, job training, vocational rehabilitation) |
| 611110 | Schools for the physically disabled, elementary or secondary |
| 611512 | Schools, aviation |
| 611511 | Schools, barber |
| 611511 | Schools, beauty |

| | |
|---|---|
| 611410 | Schools, business, not offering academic degrees |
| 611310 | Schools, correspondence, college-level |
| 611511 | Schools, cosmetology |
| 611610 | Schools, drama (except academic) |
| 611110 | Schools, elementary |
| 611210 | Schools, junior college |
| 611210 | Schools, junior college vocational |
| 611630 | Schools, language |
| 611310 | Schools, medical |
| 611310 | Schools, music (colleges or universities) |
| 611610 | Schools, music (except academic) |
| 611310 | Schools, online, college-level (through a website or mobile application) |
| 611110 | Schools, online, elementary- or secondary-level (through a website or mobile application) |
| 611210 | Schools, online, junior college-level (through a website or mobile application) |
| 611310 | Schools, professional (colleges or universities) |
| 611110 | Schools, secondary |
| 611620 | Schools, sports instruction |
| 712110 | Science and technology museums |
| 339930 | Science kits (e.g., chemistry sets, microscopes, natural science sets) manufacturing |
| 423920 | Science kits and sets merchant wholesalers |
| 327215 | Scientific apparatus glassware made from purchased glass |
| 813920 | Scientific associations |
| 327215 | Scientific glassware made from purchased glass |
| 327212 | Scientific glassware, pressed or blown, made in glass making plants |
| 423490 | Scientific instruments merchant wholesalers |
| 513120 | Scientific journal and periodical publishers |
| 513120 | Scientific journal and periodical publishers (except exclusive Internet publishing) |
| 513120 | Scientific journal and periodical publishers and printing combined |
| 513120 | Scientific journal and periodical publishers, exclusively on Internet |
| 423490 | Scientific laboratory equipment merchant wholesalers |
| 334519 | Scintillation detectors manufacturing |

| | |
|---|---|
| 335210 | Scissors, electric, manufacturing |
| 332215 | Scissors, nonelectric, manufacturing |
| 332216 | Scoops, metal (except kitchen-type), manufacturing |
| 321999 | Scoops, wood, manufacturing |
| 339930 | Scooters, children's, manufacturing |
| 339950 | Scoreboards manufacturing |
| 212390 | Scoria mining and/or beneficiating |
| 313310 | Scouring and combing textile fibers |
| 325611 | Scouring cleansers (e.g., pastes, powders) manufacturing |
| 332999 | Scouring pads, soap impregnated, manufacturing |
| 813410 | Scouting organizations |
| 423930 | Scrap materials (e.g., automotive, industrial) merchant wholesalers |
| 323111 | Scrapbooks and refills manufacturing |
| 424120 | Scrapbooks merchant wholesalers |
| 333131 | Scraper loaders, underground mining-type, manufacturing |
| 333120 | Scrapers, construction-type, manufacturing |
| 332321 | Screen doors, metal frame, manufacturing |
| 323120 | Screen for printing, preparation services |
| 323113 | Screen printing (except books, manifold business forms, grey goods) |
| 323113 | Screen printing apparel and textile products (e.g., caps, napkins, placemats, T-shirts, towels) (except grey goods and T-shirt shops) |
| 313310 | Screen printing fabric grey goods |
| 323113 | Screen printing textile banners |
| 325910 | Screen process inks manufacturing |
| 333998 | Screening and sifting machinery for general industrial use manufacturing |
| 423830 | Screening machinery and equipment, industrial, merchant wholesalers |
| 333120 | Screening machinery, portable, manufacturing |
| 333131 | Screening machinery, stationary, manufacturing |
| 212390 | Screening peat |
| 326199 | Screening, window, plastics, manufacturing |
| 711510 | Screenplay writers, independent |
| 334419 | Screens for liquid crystal display (LCD) manufacturing |
| 332321 | Screens, door and window, metal frame, manufacturing |

| | |
|---|---|
| 321911 | Screens, door and window, wood framed, manufacturing |
| 333310 | Screens, projection (i.e., motion picture, overhead, slide), manufacturing |
| 423310 | Screens, window and door, merchant wholesalers |
| 333517 | Screw and nut slotting machines, metalworking, manufacturing |
| 333922 | Screw conveyors manufacturing |
| 332722 | Screw eyes, metal, manufacturing |
| 333519 | Screwdowns and boxes machinery, metal, manufacturing |
| 333991 | Screwdrivers and nut drivers, handheld power-driven, manufacturing |
| 332216 | Screwdrivers, nonelectric, manufacturing |
| 333519 | Screwdriving machines manufacturing |
| 332216 | Screwjacks manufacturing |
| 332722 | Screws, metal, manufacturing |
| 711510 | Script writers, independent |
| 238220 | Scrubber, air purification, installation |
| 339920 | Scuba diving equipment manufacturing |
| 611620 | Scuba instruction, camps or schools |
| 711510 | Sculptors, independent |
| 611610 | Sculpture instruction |
| 327420 | Sculptures (e.g., gypsum, plaster of paris) manufacturing |
| 327110 | Sculptures, architectural, clay, manufacturing |
| 332216 | Scythes manufacturing |
| 212390 | Scythestones mining and/or beneficiating |
| 114111 | Sea bass fishing |
| 114111 | Sea herring fishing |
| 713990 | Sea kayaking, recreational |
| 112519 | Sea plant agriculture |
| 114111 | Sea trout fishing |
| 114112 | Sea urchin fishing |
| 424460 | Seafood (except canned, packaged frozen) merchant wholesalers |
| 311710 | Seafood and seafood products canning |
| 311710 | Seafood and seafood products curing |
| 311710 | Seafood and seafood products manufacturing |
| 311710 | Seafood dinners, frozen, manufacturing |
| 445250 | Seafood markets |
| 424490 | Seafood, canned, merchant wholesalers |
| 424420 | Seafoods, packaged frozen, merchant wholesalers |
| 339940 | Seal presses (e.g., notary), hand operated, manufacturing |
| 424690 | Sealants merchant wholesalers |
| 335139 | Sealed beam automotive light bulbs manufacturing |
| 325520 | Sealing compounds for pipe threads and joints manufacturing |
| 423840 | Seals merchant wholesalers |
| 339991 | Seals, grease or oil, manufacturing |
| 333992 | Seam welding equipment manufacturing |
| 334511 | Search and detection systems and instruments manufacturing |
| 541511 | Search engine optimization (SEO) services, custom (except hosting and infrastructure support services) |
| 519290 | Search portals, Internet |
| 335139 | Searchlights, electric and nonelectric, manufacturing |
| 459420 | Seasonal and holiday decoration stores |
| 721110 | Seasonal hotels without casinos |
| 561730 | Seasonal property maintenance services (i.e., snow plowing in winter, landscaping during other seasons) |
| 311942 | Seasoning salt manufacturing |
| 336360 | Seat belts, motor vehicle and aircraft, manufacturing |
| 423120 | Seat belts, motor vehicle, merchant wholesalers |
| 423120 | Seat covers, automotive, merchant wholesalers |
| 321999 | Seat covers, rattan, manufacturing |
| 326150 | Seat cushions, foam plastics (except polystyrene), manufacturing |
| 316990 | Seatbelts, leather, manufacturing |
| 336360 | Seats for public conveyances, manufacturing |
| 336360 | Seats, railroad, manufacturing |
| 321999 | Seats, toilet, wood, manufacturing |
| 237990 | Seawall, wave protection, construction |
| 488310 | Seaway operation |
| 112519 | Seaweed farming |
| 114119 | Seaweed gathering |
| 311710 | Seaweed processing (e.g., dulse) |
| 325199 | Sebacic acid esters manufacturing |
| 325199 | Sebacic acid manufacturing |
| 611630 | Second language instruction |
| 522299 | Secondary market financing (i.e., buying, pooling, repackaging loans for sale to others) |

| | |
|---|---|
| 331492 | Secondary refining of nonferrous metals (except aluminum, copper) |
| 611110 | Secondary schools offering both academic and technical courses |
| 331492 | Secondary smelting of nonferrous metals (except aluminum, copper) |
| 459510 | Secondhand merchandise stores |
| 611410 | Secretarial schools |
| 561410 | Secretarial services |
| 332311 | Sections for prefabricated metal buildings manufacturing |
| 321992 | Sections, prefabricated wood building, manufacturing |
| 523150 | Securities brokerages |
| 523150 | Securities brokers' offices |
| 523991 | Securities custodians |
| 523150 | Securities dealers (i.e., acting as a principal in dealing securities to investors) |
| 523150 | Securities dealing (i.e., acting as a principal in dealing securities to investors) |
| 523150 | Securities distributing (i.e., acting as a principal in dealing securities to investors) |
| 523210 | Securities exchanges |
| 523150 | Securities floor brokers |
| 523150 | Securities floor traders (i.e., acting as a principal in dealing securities to investors) |
| 523150 | Securities flotation companies |
| 523999 | Securities holders' protective services |
| 523150 | Securities originating (i.e., acting as a principal in dealing securities to investors) |
| 926150 | Securities regulation commissions |
| 523910 | Securities speculators for own account |
| 523150 | Securities trading (i.e., acting as a principal in dealing securities to investors) |
| 523999 | Securities transfer agencies |
| 523150 | Securities underwriting |
| 561621 | Security alarm systems sales combined with installation, repair, or monitoring services |
| 238210 | Security and fire system, installation only |
| 541690 | Security consulting services |
| 561612 | Security guard services |
| 611519 | Security guard training |

| | |
|---|---|
| 561612 | Security patrol services |
| 423420 | Security safes merchant wholesalers |
| 561621 | Security system monitoring services |
| 423610 | Security systems merchant wholesalers |
| 325412 | Sedative preparations manufacturing |
| 212390 | Sedge peat mining and/or beneficiating |
| 237990 | Sediment control system construction |
| 333131 | Sedimentary mineral machinery manufacturing |
| 314910 | Seed bags made from purchased woven or knitted materials |
| 115112 | Seed bed preparing |
| 115114 | Seed cleaning |
| 322230 | Seed packets made from purchased paper |
| 115114 | Seed processing, postharvest for propagation |
| 541380 | Seed testing laboratories or services |
| 325320 | Seed treatment preparations manufacturing |
| 333111 | Seeders, farm-type, manufacturing |
| 333112 | Seeders, lawn and garden-type, manufacturing |
| 115112 | Seeding crops |
| 561730 | Seeding lawns |
| 424450 | Seeds (e.g., canned, roasted, salted) merchant wholesalers |
| 424910 | Seeds (e.g., field, flower, garden) merchant wholesalers |
| 311911 | Seeds, snack (e.g., canned, cooked, roasted, salted) manufacturing |
| 541360 | Seismic geophysical surveying services |
| 213112 | Seismograph exploration (except surveying) for oil and gas on a contract basis |
| 334519 | Seismographs manufacturing |
| 334519 | Seismometers manufacturing |
| 334519 | Seismoscopes manufacturing |
| 212390 | Selenite mining and/or beneficiating |
| 331491 | Selenium bar, rod, sheet, strip, and tubing made from purchased metals or scrap |
| 325180 | Selenium compounds, not specified elsewhere by process, manufacturing |
| 325180 | Selenium dioxide manufacturing |
| 331492 | Selenium recovering from scrap and/or alloying purchased metals |
| 331410 | Selenium refining, primary |
| 611699 | Self defense (except martial arts) instruction |

| | |
|---|---|
| 624190 | Self-help organizations (except for disabled persons, the elderly) |
| 624120 | Self-help organizations for disabled persons and the elderly |
| 624110 | Self-help organizations, youth |
| 525190 | Self-insurance funds (except employee benefit funds) |
| 811192 | Self-service car washes |
| 812310 | Self-service drycleaners and laundries |
| 236220 | Self-storage facility construction |
| 531130 | Self-storage unit rental or leasing |
| 531130 | Self-storage warehousing |
| 531210 | Selling real estate for others (i.e., agents, brokers) |
| 531210 | Selling time-share condominiums for others (i.e., agents, brokers) |
| 115210 | Semen collection |
| 424590 | Semen, bovine, merchant wholesalers |
| 212114 | Semianthracite surface mining and/or beneficiating |
| 212115 | Semianthracite underground mining |
| 212114 | Semibituminous coal surface mining and/or beneficiating |
| 212115 | Semibituminous coal underground mining |
| 333242 | Semiconductor assembly and packaging machinery manufacturing |
| 335999 | Semiconductor battery chargers manufacturing |
| 334413 | Semiconductor circuit networks (i.e., solid-state integrated circuits) manufacturing |
| 334413 | Semiconductor devices manufacturing |
| 423690 | Semiconductor devices merchant wholesalers |
| 334413 | Semiconductor dice and wafers manufacturing |
| 335999 | Semiconductor high-voltage power supplies manufacturing |
| 333242 | Semiconductor making machinery manufacturing |
| 334413 | Semiconductor memory chips manufacturing |
| 334515 | Semiconductor test equipment manufacturing |
| 333618 | Semidiesel engines manufacturing |
| 423510 | Semi-finished metal products merchant wholesalers |
| 611110 | Seminaries, below university grade |
| 611310 | Seminaries, theological, offering baccalaureate or graduate degrees |

| | |
|---|---|
| 212390 | Semiprecious stones mining and/or beneficiating |
| 711211 | Semiprofessional baseball clubs |
| 711211 | Semiprofessional football clubs |
| 711211 | Semiprofessional sports clubs |
| 331511 | Semisteel foundries |
| 532120 | Semi-trailer rental or leasing |
| 336212 | Semi-trailers manufacturing |
| 311211 | Semolina flour manufacturing |
| 624120 | Senior citizens activity centers |
| 813311 | Senior citizens advocacy organizations |
| 813410 | Senior citizens' associations, social |
| 624120 | Senior citizens centers |
| 623312 | Senior citizens' homes without nursing care |
| 485991 | Senior citizens transportation services |
| 561312 | Senior executive search services |
| 325992 | Sensitized cloth or paper (e.g., blueprint, photographic) manufacturing |
| 333310 | Sensitometers, photographic, manufacturing |
| 334510 | Sentinel, cardiac, manufacturing |
| 238910 | Septic system contractors |
| 238910 | Septic tank and weeping tile installation |
| 562991 | Septic tank cleaning services |
| 562991 | Septic tank pumping (i.e., cleaning) services |
| 423390 | Septic tanks (except concrete) merchant wholesalers |
| 423320 | Septic tanks, concrete, merchant wholesalers |
| 332420 | Septic tanks, heavy gauge metal, manufacturing |
| 326199 | Septic tanks, plastics or fiberglass, manufacturing |
| 334512 | Sequencing controls for electric heating equipment manufacturing |
| 335999 | Series capacitors (except electronic) manufacturing |
| 212319 | Serpentine crushed and broken stone mining and/or beneficiating |
| 212311 | Serpentine mining or quarrying |
| 325414 | Serums (except diagnostic substances) manufacturing |
| 315210 | Service apparel, washable, cut and sew apparel contractors |
| 315250 | Service apparel, washable, men's and boys', cut and sewn from purchased fabric (except apparel contractors) |

| | |
|---|---|
| 315250 | Service apparel, washable, women's and girls', cut and sewn from purchased fabric (except apparel contractors) |
| 423850 | Service establishment equipment and supplies merchant wholesalers |
| 813910 | Service industries associations |
| 237120 | Service line, gas and oil, construction |
| 811310 | Service machinery and equipment repair and maintenance services |
| 561720 | Service station cleaning and degreasing services |
| 236220 | Service station construction |
| 457120 | Service stations, gasoline |
| 213111 | Service well drilling on a contract basis |
| 213112 | Servicing oil and gas wells on a contract basis |
| 337126 | Serving carts, metal household-type, manufacturing |
| 337122 | Serving carts, wood household-type, manufacturing |
| 335312 | Servomotors manufacturing |
| 111120 | Sesame farming, field and seed production |
| 711510 | Set designers, independent theatrical |
| 541191 | Settlement offices, real estate |
| 525920 | Settlement trust funds |
| 322219 | Setup (i.e., not shipped flat) boxes made from purchased paperboard |
| 322130 | Setup boxboard stock manufacturing |
| 325315 | Sewage and animal waste compost manufacturing |
| 237110 | Sewage collection and disposal line construction |
| 237110 | Sewage disposal plant construction |
| 221320 | Sewage disposal plants |
| 333310 | Sewage treatment equipment manufacturing |
| 237110 | Sewage treatment plant construction |
| 221320 | Sewage treatment plants or facilities |
| 562998 | Sewer cleaning and rodding services |
| 562998 | Sewer cleanout services |
| 237110 | Sewer construction |
| 238220 | Sewer hookup and connection, building |
| 237110 | Sewer main, pipe and connection, construction |
| 327120 | Sewer pipe and fittings, clay, manufacturing |
| 331511 | Sewer pipe, cast iron, manufacturing |
| 423320 | Sewer pipe, clay (except refractory), merchant wholesalers |
| 327332 | Sewer pipe, concrete, manufacturing |
| 423510 | Sewer pipe, metal, merchant wholesalers |
| 221320 | Sewer systems |
| 424310 | Sewing accessories merchant wholesalers |
| 339999 | Sewing and mending kits assembling |
| 316990 | Sewing cases (except metal) manufacturing |
| 339910 | Sewing cases, precious metal, manufacturing |
| 315210 | Sewing fabric owned by others for apparel |
| 321999 | Sewing machine cabinets, wood, manufacturing |
| 449210 | Sewing machine stores, household-type |
| 811412 | Sewing machine, household-type, repair shops without retailing new sewing machines |
| 333248 | Sewing machines (including household-type) manufacturing |
| 423620 | Sewing machines, household-type, merchant wholesalers |
| 423830 | Sewing machines, industrial, merchant wholesalers |
| 459130 | Sewing supply stores |
| 313110 | Sewing threads manufacturing |
| 115210 | Sexing services for poultry (e.g., separating males/females) |
| 334511 | Sextants (except surveying) manufacturing |
| 334519 | Sextants, surveying, manufacturing |
| 337920 | Shade pulls, window, manufacturing |
| 335131 | Shades, lamp (except glass, plastics), residential-type, manufacturing |
| 337920 | Shades, window (except outdoor canvas awnings), manufacturing |
| 213113 | Shaft sinking for coal mines on a contract basis |
| 213114 | Shaft sinking for metal mines on a contract basis |
| 238160 | Shake and shingle, roof, installation |
| 321113 | Shakes (i.e., hand split shingles) manufacturing |
| 212323 | Shale (except oil shale) mining and/or beneficiating |
| 327992 | Shale, expanded, manufacturing |
| 211120 | Shale, oil, mining and/or beneficiating |
| 111219 | Shallot farming, field and seed production |
| 325620 | Shampoos and conditioners, hair, manufacturing |
| 316990 | Shanks, shoe, leather, manufacturing |

| | |
|---|---|
| 333243 | Shapers, woodworking-type, manufacturing |
| 531120 | Shared workspace provision |
| 114111 | Shark fishing |
| 339994 | Shaving brushes manufacturing |
| 333517 | Shaving machines, metalworking, manufacturing |
| 325620 | Shaving preparations (e.g., creams, gels, lotions, powders) manufacturing |
| 424210 | Shaving preparations merchant wholesalers |
| 333517 | Shearing machines, metal forming, manufacturing |
| 316110 | Shearling (i.e., prepared sheepskin) manufacturing |
| 333991 | Shears and nibblers, handheld power-driven, manufacturing |
| 332215 | Shears, nonelectric, household-type (e.g., kitchen, barber, tailor) manufacturing |
| 332216 | Shears, nonelectric, tool-type (e.g., garden, pruners, tinsnip), manufacturing |
| 333111 | Shears, powered, for use on animals, manufacturing |
| 322120 | Sheathing paper made in paper mills |
| 324122 | Sheathing, asphalt saturated, made from refined petroleum |
| 238130 | Sheathing, wood, installation |
| 333613 | Sheaves, mechanical power transmission, manufacturing |
| 332311 | Sheds (e.g., garden, storage, utility), prefabricated metal, manufacturing |
| 321992 | Sheds (e.g., garden, storage, utility), prefabricated wood, manufacturing |
| 115210 | Sheep dipping and shearing |
| 112410 | Sheep farming (e.g., meat, milk, wool production) |
| 424520 | Sheep merchant wholesalers |
| 333111 | Sheep shears, powered, manufacturing |
| 326140 | Sheet (i.e., board), polystyrene foam insulation, manufacturing |
| 423730 | Sheet metal duct work (heating and air-conditioning) merchant wholesalers |
| 238220 | Sheet metal duct work installation |
| 333517 | Sheet metal forming machines manufacturing |
| 238160 | Sheet metal roofing installation |
| 423330 | Sheet metal roofing materials merchant wholesalers |
| 332322 | Sheet metal work (except stampings) manufacturing |
| 611513 | Sheet metal workers' apprenticeship training |
| 323111 | Sheet music commercial printing (except screen) without publishing |
| 424990 | Sheet music merchant wholesalers |
| 512230 | Sheet music publishers |
| 512230 | Sheet music publishers and printing combined |
| 323113 | Sheet music screen printing without publishing |
| 459140 | Sheet music stores |
| 331110 | Sheet pilings, plain, iron or steel, made in iron and steel mills |
| 331315 | Sheet, aluminum, made by flat rolling purchased aluminum |
| 331315 | Sheet, aluminum, made in integrated secondary smelting and flat rolling mills |
| 331420 | Sheet, copper and copper alloy, made from purchased copper or in integrated secondary smelting and rolling, drawing or extruding plants |
| 326130 | Sheet, laminated plastics (except flexible packaging), manufacturing |
| 326113 | Sheet, plastics, unlaminated (except packaging), manufacturing |
| 326299 | Sheeting, rubber, manufacturing |
| 314120 | Sheets and pillowcases made from purchased fabrics |
| 313210 | Sheets and pillowcases made in broadwoven fabric mills |
| 331110 | Sheets, steel, made in iron and steel mills |
| 311119 | Shell crushing and grinding for animal feed |
| 311119 | Shell crushing for feed |
| 332993 | Shell loading and assembly plants |
| 212390 | Shell mining and/or beneficiating |
| 339999 | Shell novelties |
| 331110 | Shell slugs, steel, made in iron and steel mills |
| 325510 | Shellac manufacturing |
| 424950 | Shellac merchant wholesalers |
| 311710 | Shellfish and shellfish products canning |
| 311710 | Shellfish and shellfish products manufacturing |
| 311710 | Shellfish curing |
| 114112 | Shellfish fishing (e.g., clam, crab, oyster, shrimp) |
| 112512 | Shellfish hatcheries |
| 332993 | Shells, artillery, manufacturing |
| 332992 | Shells, small arms (i.e., 30 mm. or less, 1.18 inch or less), manufacturing |
| 624310 | Sheltered workshops (i.e., work experience centers) |

| | |
|---|---|
| 624221 | Shelters (except for victims of domestic or international disasters or conflicts), emergency |
| 624230 | Shelters for victims of domestic or international disasters or conflicts, emergency |
| 624221 | Shelters, battered women's |
| 624221 | Shelters, homeless |
| 624221 | Shelters, runaway youth |
| 624221 | Shelters, temporary (e.g., battered women's, homeless, runaway youth) |
| 337215 | Shelving (except wire) manufacturing |
| 423440 | Shelving, commercial, merchant wholesalers |
| 423830 | Shelving, industrial, merchant wholesalers |
| 238390 | Shelving, metal, constructed on site |
| 332618 | Shelving, wire, made from purchased wire |
| 238350 | Shelving, wood, constructed on site |
| 332812 | Sherardizing of metals and metal products for the trade |
| 311520 | Sherbets manufacturing |
| 922120 | Sheriffs' offices (except court functions only) |
| 922110 | Sheriffs' offices, court functions only |
| 332999 | Shims, metal, manufacturing |
| 321113 | Shingle mills, wood |
| 423330 | Shingles (except wood) merchant wholesalers |
| 324122 | Shingles made from purchased asphaltic materials |
| 423310 | Shingles, wood, merchant wholesalers |
| 321113 | Shingles, wood, sawed or hand split, manufacturing |
| 331529 | Ship and boat propellers, cast brass, bronze and copper (except die-casting), unfinished, manufacturing |
| 424990 | Ship chandler merchant wholesalers |
| 483113 | Ship chartering with crew, coastal or Great Lakes freight transportation (including St. Lawrence Seaway) |
| 483114 | Ship chartering with crew, coastal or Great Lakes passenger transportation (including St. Lawrence Seaway) |
| 483111 | Ship chartering with crew, deep sea freight transportation to or from foreign ports |
| 483112 | Ship chartering with crew, deep sea passenger transportation to or from foreign ports |
| 483211 | Ship chartering with crew, freight transportation, inland waters (except on Great Lakes system) |
| 483212 | Ship chartering with crew, passenger transportation, inland waters (except on Great Lakes system) |
| 333923 | Ship cranes and derricks manufacturing |
| 561311 | Ship crew employment agencies |
| 561311 | Ship crew registries |
| 423930 | Ship dismantling (except at floating drydocks and shipyards) merchant wholesalers |
| 488390 | Ship dismantling at floating drydock |
| 336611 | Ship dismantling at shipyards |
| 337127 | Ship furniture manufacturing |
| 488320 | Ship hold cleaning services |
| 238350 | Ship joinery contractors |
| 238320 | Ship painting contractors |
| 532411 | Ship rental or leasing without crew |
| 336611 | Ship repair done in a shipyard |
| 336611 | Ship scaling services done at a shipyard |
| 488390 | Ship scaling services not done at a shipyard |
| 332312 | Ship sections, prefabricated metal, manufacturing |
| 331420 | Shipboard cable made from purchased copper in wire drawing plants |
| 331318 | Shipboard cable made in aluminum wire drawing plants |
| 488510 | Shipping agents (freight forwarding) |
| 314910 | Shipping bags made from purchased woven or knitted materials |
| 332439 | Shipping barrels, drums, kegs, and pails, light gauge metal, manufacturing |
| 321920 | Shipping cases and drums, wood, wirebound, manufacturing |
| 321920 | Shipping cases, wood, nailed or lock corner, manufacturing |
| 813910 | Shipping companies' associations |
| 423840 | Shipping containers (except disposable plastics, paper) merchant wholesalers |
| 322211 | Shipping containers made from purchased paperboard |
| 322211 | Shipping containers, corrugated, made from purchased paper or paperboard |
| 321920 | Shipping crates, wood, manufacturing |
| 483113 | Shipping freight to and from domestic ports (i.e., coastal, deep sea (including Puerto Rico), Great Lakes system (including St. Lawrence Seaway)) |

| | |
|---|---|
| 483111 | Shipping freight to or from foreign ports, deep sea |
| 483211 | Shipping freight, inland waters (except on Great Lakes system) |
| 326150 | Shipping pads and shaped cushioning, foam plastics (except polystyrene), manufacturing |
| 326140 | Shipping pads and shaped cushioning, polystyrene foam, manufacturing |
| 423840 | Shipping pails, metal, merchant wholesalers |
| 323111 | Shipping registers commercial printing (except screen) without publishing |
| 323113 | Shipping registers screen printing without publishing |
| 424130 | Shipping supplies, paper and disposable plastics, merchant wholesalers |
| 336611 | Ships (i.e., not suitable or intended for personal use) manufacturing |
| 423860 | Ships merchant wholesalers |
| 517112 | Ship-to-shore broadcasting communication carriers (except satellite) |
| 336611 | Shipyard (i.e., facility capable of building ships) |
| 315210 | Shirts, outerwear, cut and sew apparel contractors |
| 315120 | Shirts, outerwear, made in apparel knitting mills |
| 315250 | Shirts, outerwear, men's and boys', cut and sewn from purchased fabric (except apparel contractors) |
| 315250 | Shirts, outerwear, unisex (i.e., sized without regard to gender), cut and sewn from purchased fabric (except apparel contractors) |
| 315250 | Shirts, outerwear, women's, girls', and infants', cut and sewn from purchased fabric (except apparel contractors) |
| 315210 | Shirts, underwear, cut and sew apparel contractors |
| 315120 | Shirts, underwear, made in apparel knitting mills |
| 315250 | Shirts, underwear, men's and boys', cut and sewn from purchased fabric (except apparel contractors) |
| 315250 | Shirts, underwear, women's, girls', and infants', cut and sewn from purchased fabric (except apparel contractors) |
| 111411 | Shitake mushroom farming |
| 336330 | Shock absorbers, automotive, truck, and bus, manufacturing |
| 458210 | Shoe (except bowling, golf, cleated) stores |
| 424340 | Shoe accessories merchant wholesalers |
| 326299 | Shoe and boot parts (e.g., heels, soles, soling strips), rubber, manufacturing |
| 322212 | Shoe boxes, folding, made from purchased paperboard |
| 322219 | Shoe boxes, setup, made from purchased paperboard |
| 541490 | Shoe design services |
| 321999 | Shoe display forms, all materials, manufacturing |
| 316990 | Shoe kits (i.e., cases), all materials, manufacturing |
| 333248 | Shoe making and repairing machinery manufacturing |
| 423830 | Shoe manufacturing and repairing machinery merchant wholesalers |
| 326199 | Shoe parts (e.g., heels, soles), plastics, manufacturing |
| 335210 | Shoe polishers, household-type electric, manufacturing |
| 325612 | Shoe polishes and cleaners manufacturing |
| 423850 | Shoe repair materials merchant wholesalers |
| 811430 | Shoe repair shops without retailing new shoes |
| 316990 | Shoe soles, leather, manufacturing |
| 458210 | Shoe stores, orthopedic |
| 459110 | Shoe stores, specialty sports footwear (e.g., bowling, golf, cleated) |
| 321999 | Shoe stretchers manufacturing |
| 321999 | Shoe trees manufacturing |
| 424340 | Shoes merchant wholesalers |
| 316210 | Shoes, athletic, manufacturing |
| 316210 | Shoes, ballet, manufacturing |
| 316210 | Shoes, children's and infant's (except orthopedic extension), manufacturing |
| 316210 | Shoes, cleated or spiked, all materials, manufacturing |
| 316210 | Shoes, men's (except orthopedic extension), manufacturing |
| 339113 | Shoes, orthopedic extension, manufacturing |
| 316210 | Shoes, plastics or plastics soled fabric upper, manufacturing |
| 316210 | Shoes, rubber or rubber soled fabric upper, manufacturing |
| 316210 | Shoes, theatrical, manufacturing |
| 316210 | Shoes, women's (except orthopedic extension), manufacturing |
| 316210 | Shoes, wooden, manufacturing |
| 812990 | Shoeshine parlors |
| 812990 | Shoeshine services |

| | |
|---|---|
| 321920 | Shook, box, manufacturing |
| 713990 | Shooting clubs, recreational |
| 713990 | Shooting galleries |
| 713990 | Shooting ranges |
| 423120 | Shop equipment, service station, merchant wholesalers |
| 424130 | Shopping bags, paper and plastics, merchant wholesalers |
| 531120 | Shopping center (i.e., not operating contained businesses) rental or leasing |
| 236220 | Shopping center construction |
| 236220 | Shopping mall construction |
| 812990 | Shopping services, personal |
| ****** | Shops -- see type |
| 238990 | Shoring, construction |
| 111421 | Short rotation woody tree growing (i.e., growing and harvesting cycle ten years or less) |
| 311225 | Shortening made from purchased fats and oils |
| 311224 | Shortening made in crushing mills |
| 424490 | Shortening, vegetable, merchant wholesalers |
| 482112 | Short-line railroads |
| 315210 | Shorts, outerwear, cut and sew apparel contractors |
| 315120 | Shorts, outerwear, made in apparel knitting mills |
| 315250 | Shorts, outerwear, men's and boys', cut and sewn from purchased fabric (except apparel contractors) |
| 315250 | Shorts, outerwear, women's, girls', and infants', cut and sewn from purchased fabric (except apparel contractors) |
| 315210 | Shorts, underwear, cut and sew apparel contractors |
| 315120 | Shorts, underwear, made in apparel knitting mills |
| 315250 | Shorts, underwear, men's and boys', cut and sewn from purchased fabric (except apparel contractors) |
| 522299 | Short-term inventory credit lending |
| 213112 | Shot hole drilling, oil and gas field, on a contract basis |
| 332811 | Shot peening metal and metal products for the trade |
| 332992 | Shot, BB, manufacturing |
| 332992 | Shot, lead, manufacturing |
| 332992 | Shot, pellet, manufacturing |
| 332992 | Shot, steel, manufacturing |
| 238110 | Shotcrete contractors |
| 332992 | Shotgun shells manufacturing |
| 332994 | Shotguns manufacturing |
| 333120 | Shovel loaders manufacturing |
| 332216 | Shovels, handheld, manufacturing |
| 333120 | Shovels, power, manufacturing |
| 423810 | Shovels, power, merchant wholesalers |
| 337215 | Showcases (except refrigerated) manufacturing |
| 423440 | Showcases (except refrigerated) merchant wholesalers |
| 333415 | Showcases, refrigerated, manufacturing |
| 423740 | Showcases, refrigerated, merchant wholesalers |
| 314120 | Shower and bath curtains, all materials, made from purchased fabric or sheet goods |
| 332913 | Shower heads, plumbing, manufacturing |
| 332999 | Shower receptors, metal, manufacturing |
| 332999 | Shower rods, metal, manufacturing |
| 316210 | Shower sandals or slippers, rubber, manufacturing |
| 332999 | Shower stalls, metal, manufacturing |
| 326191 | Shower stalls, plastics or fiberglass, manufacturing |
| 115210 | Showing of cattle, hogs, sheep, goats, and poultry |
| 333111 | Shredders, farm-type, manufacturing |
| 212390 | Shredding peat mining and/or beneficiating |
| 114112 | Shrimp fishing |
| 112512 | Shrimp production, farm raising |
| 813110 | Shrines, religious |
| 561910 | Shrink wrapping services |
| 313310 | Shrinking textile products and fabrics |
| 561730 | Shrub services (e.g., bracing, planting, pruning, removal, spraying, surgery, trimming) |
| 111421 | Shrubbery farming |
| 311710 | Shucking and packing fresh shellfish |
| 488490 | Shunting of trailers in truck terminals |
| 488210 | Shunting trailers in rail terminals |
| 334515 | Shunts, instrument, manufacturing |
| 238190 | Shutter installation |
| 332321 | Shutters, door and window, metal, manufacturing |
| 321918 | Shutters, door and window, wood and covered wood, manufacturing |
| 326199 | Shutters, plastics, manufacturing |

| | |
|---|---|
| 321918 | Shutters, wood, manufacturing |
| 485999 | Shuttle services (except employee bus) |
| 333248 | Shuttles for textile weaving machinery manufacturing |
| 456199 | Sick room supply stores |
| 332216 | Sickles manufacturing |
| 212210 | Siderite mining and/or beneficiating |
| 238990 | Sidewalk construction, residential and commercial |
| 237310 | Sidewalk, public, construction |
| 238170 | Siding (e.g., vinyl, wood, aluminum) installation |
| 423330 | Siding (except wood) merchant wholesalers |
| 238170 | Siding contractors |
| 444180 | Siding dealers |
| 324122 | Siding made from purchased asphaltic materials |
| 321113 | Siding mills, wood |
| 321113 | Siding, dressed lumber, manufacturing |
| 326199 | Siding, plastics, manufacturing |
| 332322 | Siding, sheet metal (except stampings), manufacturing |
| 423310 | Siding, wood, merchant wholesalers |
| 212390 | Sienna mining and/or beneficiating |
| 325130 | Sienna pigment manufacturing |
| 333241 | Sieves and screening equipment (i.e., food manufacturing-type) manufacturing |
| 333248 | Sieves and screening equipment, chemical preparation-type, manufacturing |
| 333998 | Sieves and screening equipment, general purpose-type, manufacturing |
| 333131 | Sieves and screening equipment, mineral beneficiating, manufacturing |
| 332618 | Sieves, made from purchased wire, manufacturing |
| 333241 | Sifting machine (i.e., food manufacturing-type) manufacturing |
| 333310 | Sights, telescopic, manufacturing |
| 487210 | Sightseeing boat operation |
| 487110 | Sightseeing bus operation |
| 487110 | Sightseeing operation, human-drawn vehicle |
| 238990 | Sign (except on highways, streets, bridges and tunnels) erection |
| 237310 | Sign erection, highway, road, street, or bridge |
| 611630 | Sign language instruction |
| 611630 | Sign language schools |
| 541930 | Sign language services |
| 541890 | Sign lettering and painting services |
| 238990 | Sign, building, erection |
| 331420 | Signal and control cable made from purchased copper in wire drawing plants |
| 331318 | Signal and control cable made in aluminum wire drawing plants |
| 334515 | Signal generators and averagers manufacturing |
| 423610 | Signal systems and devices merchant wholesalers |
| 335311 | Signaling transformers, electric, manufacturing |
| 334290 | Signals (e.g., highway, pedestrian, railway, traffic) manufacturing |
| 423990 | Signs (except electrical) merchant wholesalers |
| 339950 | Signs and signboards (except paper, paperboard) manufacturing |
| 423440 | Signs, electrical, merchant wholesalers |
| 325180 | Silica gel manufacturing |
| 212322 | Silica mining and/or beneficiating |
| 212322 | Silica sand quarrying and/or beneficiating |
| 325180 | Silica, amorphous, manufacturing |
| 325180 | Silicofluorides manufacturing |
| 331110 | Silicomanganese ferroalloys manufacturing |
| 327910 | Silicon carbide abrasives manufacturing |
| 334413 | Silicon wafers, chemically doped, manufacturing |
| 334413 | Silicon wave guides manufacturing |
| 327992 | Silicon, ultra high purity, manufacturing |
| 325199 | Silicone (except resins) manufacturing |
| 325211 | Silicone resins manufacturing |
| 325212 | Silicone rubber manufacturing |
| 313210 | Silk fabrics, broadwoven, weaving |
| 541430 | Silk screen design services |
| 333248 | Silk screens for textile fabrics manufacturing |
| 313110 | Silk spun yarns made from purchased fiber |
| 313110 | Silk thread manufacturing |
| 313110 | Silk throwing, spooling, twisting, or winding of purchased yarn |
| 424590 | Silk, raw, merchant wholesalers |
| 212323 | Sillimanite mining and/or beneficiating |
| 327390 | Sills, concrete, manufacturing |
| 236220 | Silo construction |

| | |
|---|---|
| 327390 | Silos, prefabricated concrete, manufacturing |
| 332311 | Silos, prefabricated metal, manufacturing |
| 423390 | Silt fence and other fabrics (e.g., for erosion control) merchant wholesalers |
| 331491 | Silver and silver alloy bar, rod, sheet, strip, and tubing made from purchased metals or scrap |
| 332999 | Silver beating (i.e., foil, leaf) |
| 325180 | Silver bromide manufacturing |
| 331410 | Silver bullion or dore bar produced at primary metal refineries |
| 325180 | Silver chloride manufacturing |
| 325180 | Silver compounds, not specified elsewhere by process, manufacturing |
| 332999 | Silver foil and leaf not made in rolling mills |
| 331491 | Silver foil made by rolling purchased metals or scrap |
| 325180 | Silver nitrate manufacturing |
| 212220 | Silver ore mine site development for own account |
| 212220 | Silver ores mining and/or beneficiating |
| 325612 | Silver polishes manufacturing |
| 331492 | Silver recovering from scrap and/or alloying purchased metals |
| 331492 | Silver recovering from used photographic film or X-ray plates |
| 331410 | Silver refining, primary |
| 331491 | Silver rolling, drawing, or extruding purchased metals or scrap |
| 532289 | Silverware rental |
| 423940 | Silverware, precious and plated, merchant wholesalers |
| 333515 | Sine bars (i.e., a machine tool accessory) manufacturing |
| 711130 | Singers, independent |
| 611610 | Singing instruction |
| 813410 | Singing societies |
| 812990 | Singing telegram services |
| 621512 | Single photon emission computerized tomography (SPECT) centers |
| 236115 | Single-family attached housing construction general contractors |
| 236115 | Single-family detached housing construction general contractors |
| 236115 | Single-family homes built on land owned by others, general contractors of |
| 236115 | Single-family house construction by general contractors |
| 531110 | Single-family house rental or leasing |

| | |
|---|---|
| 236117 | Single-family housing built on own land for sale (i.e., for-sale builders) |
| 236117 | Single-family housing construction for-sale builders |
| 213113 | Sinking shafts for coal mining on a contract basis |
| 213114 | Sinking shafts for metal mining on a contract basis |
| 423720 | Sinks merchant wholesalers |
| 332999 | Sinks, metal, manufacturing |
| 326191 | Sinks, plastics, manufacturing |
| 327110 | Sinks, vitreous china, manufacturing |
| 212210 | Sintered iron ore produced at the mine |
| 212390 | Sintered phosphate rock mining and/or beneficiating |
| 334290 | Sirens (e.g., air raid, industrial, marine, vehicle) manufacturing |
| 541611 | Site location consulting services |
| 541620 | Site remediation consulting services |
| 562910 | Site remediation services |
| 541611 | Site selection consulting services |
| 812990 | Sitting services, house |
| 812910 | Sitting services, pet |
| 313310 | Sizing of fabrics |
| 339920 | Skateboards manufacturing |
| 339920 | Skates and parts, ice and roller, manufacturing |
| 713990 | Skeet shooting facilities |
| 331110 | Skelp, iron or steel, made in iron and steel mills |
| 711510 | Sketch artists, independent |
| 321999 | Skewers, wood, manufacturing |
| 541320 | Ski area design services |
| 541320 | Ski area planning services |
| 532284 | Ski equipment rental |
| 713920 | Ski lift and tow operators |
| 721110 | Ski lodges and resorts with accommodations |
| 315210 | Ski pants cut and sew apparel contractors |
| 315120 | Ski pants made in apparel knitting mills |
| 315250 | Ski pants, men's and boys', cut and sewn from purchased fabric (except apparel contractors) |
| 315250 | Ski pants, women's, girls', and infants', cut and sewn from purchased fabric (except apparel contractors) |
| 713920 | Ski resorts without accommodations |
| 315210 | Ski suits cut and sew apparel contractors |

| | |
|---|---|
| 315120 | Ski suits made in apparel knitting mills |
| 315250 | Ski suits, men's and boys', cut and sewn from purchased fabric (except apparel contractors) |
| 315250 | Ski suits, women's, girls', and infants', cut and sewn from purchased fabric (except apparel contractors) |
| 237990 | Ski tow construction |
| 532490 | Skid rental or leasing |
| 213112 | Skidding of rigs, oil and gas field, on a contract basis |
| 321920 | Skids and pallets, wood or wood and metal combination, manufacturing |
| 423830 | Skids merchant wholesalers |
| 332999 | Skids, metal, manufacturing |
| 711219 | Skiers, independent (i.e., participating in sports events) |
| 423910 | Skiing equipment and supplies merchant wholesalers |
| 713920 | Skiing facilities, cross country, without accommodations |
| 713920 | Skiing facilities, downhill, without accommodations |
| 611620 | Skiing instruction, camps or schools |
| 623110 | Skilled nursing facilities |
| 561910 | Skin blister packaging services |
| 424210 | Skin care preparations merchant wholesalers |
| 611620 | Skin diving instruction, camps or schools |
| 339112 | Skin grafting equipment manufacturing |
| 424990 | Skins, dressed, merchant wholesalers |
| 424590 | Skins, raw, merchant wholesalers |
| 316110 | Skins, tanning, currying and finishing |
| 561611 | Skip tracing services |
| 316110 | Skirting leather manufacturing |
| 315210 | Skirts cut and sew apparel contractors |
| 315120 | Skirts made in apparel knitting mills |
| 315250 | Skirts, tennis, women's and girls', cut and sewn from purchased fabric (except apparel contractors) |
| 315250 | Skirts, women's, girls', and infants', cut and sewn from purchased fabric (except apparel contractors) |
| 339920 | Skis and skiing equipment (except apparel) manufacturing |
| 316110 | Skivers, leather, manufacturing |
| 611620 | Sky diving instruction, camps or schools |
| 238160 | Skylight installation |
| 332321 | Skylights, metal, manufacturing |

| | |
|---|---|
| 331410 | Slab, nonferrous metals (except aluminum) primary |
| 331313 | Slab, primary aluminum, manufacturing |
| 331110 | Slab, steel, made in iron and steel mills |
| 315210 | Slacks cut and sew apparel contractors |
| 315120 | Slacks made in apparel knitting mills |
| 315210 | Slacks, jean-cut casual, cut and sew apparel contractors |
| 315120 | Slacks, jean-cut casual, made in apparel knitting mills |
| 315250 | Slacks, jean-cut casual, men's and boys', cut and sewn from purchased fabric (except apparel contractors) |
| 315250 | Slacks, jean-cut casual, women's, girls', and infants', cut and sewn from purchased fabric (except apparel contractors) |
| 315250 | Slacks, men's and boys', cut and sewn from purchased fabric (except apparel contractors) |
| 315250 | Slacks, women's, girls', and infants', cut and sewn from purchased fabric (except apparel contractors) |
| 333120 | Slag mixers, portable, manufacturing |
| 238140 | Slate (i.e., masonry) contractors |
| 423320 | Slate and slate products merchant wholesalers |
| 212319 | Slate crushed and broken stone mining and/or beneficiating |
| 212311 | Slate mining or quarrying |
| 327991 | Slate products manufacturing |
| 238340 | Slate, interior, installation |
| 311611 | Slaughtering, custom |
| 311991 | Slaw, cole, fresh, manufacturing |
| 332216 | Sledgehammers manufacturing |
| 339930 | Sleds, children's, manufacturing |
| 621498 | Sleep disorder centers and clinics, outpatient |
| 337215 | Sleeper mechanisms, convertible bed, manufacturing |
| 314999 | Sleeping bags manufacturing |
| 424350 | Sleepwear, men's and boys', merchant wholesalers |
| 424350 | Sleepwear, women's, children's, and infants', merchant wholesalers |
| 316990 | Sleeves, welder's, leather, manufacturing |
| 333241 | Slicing machinery (i.e., food manufacturing-type) manufacturing |
| 339993 | Slide fasteners (i.e., zippers) manufacturing |

| | |
|---|---|
| 332618 | Slings, lifting, made from purchased wire |
| 212323 | Slip clay mining and/or beneficiating |
| 335312 | Slip rings for motors and generators manufacturing |
| 423220 | Slipcovers merchant wholesalers |
| 314120 | Slipcovers, all materials, made from purchased materials |
| 316210 | Slipper socks made from purchased socks |
| 315120 | Slipper socks made in sock mills |
| 424340 | Slippers merchant wholesalers |
| 316210 | Slippers, ballet, manufacturing |
| 316210 | Slippers, house, manufacturing |
| 315210 | Slips cut and sew apparel contractors |
| 315120 | Slips made in apparel knitting mills |
| 315250 | Slips, women's and girls', cut and sewn from purchased fabric (except apparel contractors) |
| 322220 | Slitting adhesive-type tapes other than medical types for the trade |
| 316110 | Slitting leather for the trade |
| 339113 | Slitting medical adhesive tapes for the trade |
| 522299 | SLMA (Student Loan Marketing Association) |
| 713990 | Slot car racetracks (i.e., amusement devices) |
| 713290 | Slot machine concession operators (i.e., supplying and servicing in others' facilities) |
| 713290 | Slot machine parlors |
| 339999 | Slot machines manufacturing |
| 333517 | Slotting machines, metalworking, manufacturing |
| 562212 | Sludge disposal sites |
| 333998 | Sludge tables manufacturing |
| 327331 | Slumped brick manufacturing |
| 486990 | Slurry pipeline transportation |
| 213112 | Slush pits and cellars, excavation of, on a contract basis |
| 541940 | Small animal veterinary services |
| 332992 | Small arms ammunition (i.e., 30 mm. or less, 1.18 inch or less) manufacturing |
| 332994 | Small arms manufacturing |
| 926110 | Small business development agencies |
| 811411 | Small engine repair and maintenance shops |
| 311615 | Small game, processing, fresh, frozen, canned or cooked |

| | |
|---|---|
| 311615 | Small game, slaughtering, dressing and packing |
| 522291 | Small loan companies (i.e., unsecured cash loans) |
| 334118 | Smart card readers manufacturing |
| 423490 | Smartboards merchant wholesalers |
| 334220 | Smartphones (new and rebuilt) manufacturing |
| 423690 | Smartphones merchant wholesalers |
| 334220 | Smartwatches manufacturing |
| 423690 | Smartwatches merchant wholesalers |
| 236210 | Smelter construction |
| 331492 | Smelting and refining of nonferrous metals (except aluminum, copper), secondary |
| 423830 | Smelting machinery and equipment merchant wholesalers |
| 331492 | Smelting nonferrous metals (except aluminum, copper), secondary |
| 331410 | Smelting of nonferrous metals (except aluminum), primary |
| 333994 | Smelting ovens manufacturing |
| 332420 | Smelting pots and retorts manufacturing |
| 212230 | Smithsonite mining and/or beneficiating |
| 238210 | Smoke detection system, installation only |
| 334290 | Smoke detectors manufacturing |
| 423620 | Smoke detectors, household-type, merchant wholesalers |
| 332994 | Smoke generators manufacturing |
| 311612 | Smoked meats made from purchased carcasses |
| 424990 | Smokers' supplies merchant wholesalers |
| 459991 | Smokers' supply stores |
| 332313 | Smokestacks, fabricated metal boiler plate, manufacturing |
| 621999 | Smoking cessation programs |
| 312230 | Smoking tobacco (e.g., cigarette, pipe) manufacturing |
| 722515 | Smoothie shops |
| 333310 | Snack and confection vending machines manufacturing |
| 722515 | Snack bars (e.g., cookies, popcorn, pretzels), fixed location |
| 722330 | Snack stands, mobile |
| 111219 | Snap bean farming (i.e., bush and pole), field and seed production |
| 335931 | Snap switches (i.e., electric wiring devices) manufacturing |
| 114111 | Snapper fishing |

| | |
|---|---|
| 488490 | Snow clearing, highways and bridges, road transportation |
| 321912 | Snow fence lath manufacturing |
| 321999 | Snow fence, sections or rolls, manufacturing |
| 333415 | Snow making machinery manufacturing |
| 238210 | Snow melting cable, electric, installation |
| 238220 | Snow melting system (e.g., hot water, glycol) installation |
| 111219 | Snow pea farming, field and seed production |
| 333120 | Snow plow attachments (except lawn, garden-type) manufacturing |
| 333112 | Snow plow attachments, lawn and garden-type, manufacturing |
| 561790 | Snow plowing driveways and parking lots (i.e., not combined with any other service) |
| 561730 | Snow plowing services combined with landscaping services (i.e., seasonal property maintenance services) |
| 423810 | Snow plows merchant wholesalers |
| 488490 | Snow removal, highway |
| 532284 | Snow ski equipment rental |
| 423810 | Snowblowers (except household-type) merchant wholesalers |
| 333112 | Snowblowers and throwers, residential-type, manufacturing |
| 423820 | Snowblowers, household-type, merchant wholesalers |
| 441227 | Snowmobile dealers |
| 423110 | Snowmobile merchant wholesalers |
| 711212 | Snowmobile racetracks |
| 711219 | Snowmobile racing teams |
| 336999 | Snowmobiles and parts manufacturing |
| 713990 | Snowmobiling, recreational |
| 339920 | Snowshoes manufacturing |
| 315210 | Snowsuits cut and sew apparel contractors |
| 315120 | Snowsuits made in apparel knitting mills |
| 315250 | Snowsuits, men's and boys', cut and sewn from purchased fabric (except apparel contractors) |
| 315250 | Snowsuits, women's, girls, and infants', cut and sewn from purchased fabric (except apparel contractors) |
| 312230 | Snuff manufacturing |
| 424940 | Snuff merchant wholesalers |
| 327110 | Soap dishes, vitreous china and earthenware, manufacturing |
| 332999 | Soap dispensers, metal, manufacturing |

| | |
|---|---|
| 325611 | Soaps (e.g., bar, chip, powder) manufacturing |
| 212390 | Soapstone mining and/or beneficiating |
| 327992 | Soapstone processing beyond beneficiation |
| 711211 | Soccer clubs, professional or semiprofessional |
| 713990 | Soccer clubs, recreational |
| 611620 | Soccer instruction, camps or schools |
| 711211 | Soccer teams, professional or semiprofessional |
| 923130 | Social assistance cost-sharing, government |
| 813319 | Social change advocacy organizations |
| 813410 | Social clubs |
| 812990 | Social escort services |
| 516210 | Social network sites, Internet |
| 813410 | Social organizations, civic and fraternal |
| 541720 | Social science research and development services |
| 923130 | Social Security Administration (SSA), federal |
| 813319 | Social service advocacy organizations |
| 624190 | Social service agencies, family |
| 624190 | Social service centers, multi-purpose |
| 424120 | Social stationery merchant wholesalers |
| 813920 | Social workers' associations |
| 621330 | Social workers', mental health, offices (e.g., centers, clinics) |
| 541720 | Sociological research and development services |
| 541720 | Sociology research and development services |
| 458110 | Sock shops |
| 332216 | Sockets and socket sets manufacturing |
| 335931 | Sockets, electric, manufacturing |
| 315120 | Socks knitting or knitting and finishing |
| 315120 | Socks, men's and boy's, manufacturing |
| 424350 | Socks, men's and boys', merchant wholesalers |
| 316210 | Socks, slipper, made from purchased socks |
| 315120 | Socks, slipper, made in sock mills |
| 424350 | Socks, women's, children's, and infants', merchant wholesalers |
| 111421 | Sod farming |
| 333111 | Sod harvesting machines manufacturing |
| 561730 | Sod laying services |
| 424590 | Sod merchant wholesalers |

| | |
|---|---|
| 325180 | Soda ash manufacturing |
| 212390 | Soda ash mining and/or beneficiating |
| 212390 | Soda ash, natural, mining and/or beneficiating |
| 327213 | Soda bottles, glass, manufacturing |
| 312111 | Soda carbonated, manufacturing |
| 311821 | Soda crackers manufacturing |
| 333415 | Soda fountain cooling and dispensing equipment manufacturing |
| 423440 | Soda fountain fixtures (except refrigerated) merchant wholesalers |
| 423740 | Soda fountain fixtures, refrigerated, merchant wholesalers |
| 311930 | Soda fountain syrups manufacturing |
| 312111 | Soda pop manufacturing |
| 325199 | Sodium acetate manufacturing |
| 325199 | Sodium alginate manufacturing |
| 325180 | Sodium aluminate manufacturing |
| 325180 | Sodium aluminum sulfate manufacturing |
| 325180 | Sodium antimoniate manufacturing |
| 325180 | Sodium arsenite (except insecticides) manufacturing |
| 325320 | Sodium arsenite insecticides manufacturing |
| 325199 | Sodium benzoate manufacturing |
| 325180 | Sodium bicarbonate manufacturing |
| 325180 | Sodium bichromate and chromate manufacturing |
| 325180 | Sodium borate manufacturing |
| 212390 | Sodium borates, natural, mining and/or beneficiating |
| 325180 | Sodium borohydride manufacturing |
| 325180 | Sodium bromide manufacturing |
| 325180 | Sodium carbonate (i.e., soda ash) manufacturing |
| 212390 | Sodium carbonates, natural, mining and/or beneficiating |
| 325180 | Sodium chlorate manufacturing |
| 325412 | Sodium chloride pharmaceutical preparations manufacturing |
| 212390 | Sodium chloride, rock salt, mining and/or beneficiating |
| 212390 | Sodium compounds prepared at beneficiating plants |
| 212390 | Sodium compounds, natural, mining and/or beneficiating |
| 325180 | Sodium cyanide manufacturing |
| 325199 | Sodium glutamate manufacturing |
| 325180 | Sodium hydrosulfite manufacturing |
| 325180 | Sodium hydroxide (i.e., caustic soda) manufacturing |
| 325180 | Sodium hypochlorite manufacturing |
| 325180 | Sodium inorganic compounds, not specified elsewhere by process, manufacturing |
| 325180 | Sodium molybdate manufacturing |
| 325199 | Sodium organic compounds, not specified elsewhere by process, manufacturing |
| 325199 | Sodium pentachlorophenate manufacturing |
| 325180 | Sodium perborate manufacturing |
| 325180 | Sodium peroxide manufacturing |
| 325180 | Sodium phosphate manufacturing |
| 325180 | Sodium polyphosphate manufacturing |
| 325412 | Sodium salicylate preparations manufacturing |
| 325180 | Sodium silicate (i.e., water glass) manufacturing |
| 325180 | Sodium silicofluoride manufacturing |
| 325180 | Sodium stannate manufacturing |
| 325180 | Sodium sulfate manufacturing |
| 212390 | Sodium sulfate, natural, mining and/or beneficiating |
| 325199 | Sodium sulfoxalate formaldehyde manufacturing |
| 325180 | Sodium tetraborate manufacturing |
| 325180 | Sodium thiosulfate manufacturing |
| 325180 | Sodium tungstate manufacturing |
| 325180 | Sodium uranate manufacturing |
| 335139 | Sodium vapor lamp bulbs manufacturing |
| 337121 | Sofa beds and chair beds, upholstered, manufacturing |
| 337121 | Sofas, convertible (except futons), manufacturing |
| 337121 | Sofas, upholstered, manufacturing |
| 423330 | Soffit, building (except wood), merchant wholesalers |
| 722515 | Soft drink beverage bars, nonalcoholic, fixed location |
| 332431 | Soft drink cans manufacturing |
| 311930 | Soft drink concentrates (i.e., syrup) manufacturing |
| 445298 | Soft drink stores, bottled |
| 333310 | Soft drink vending machines manufacturing |
| 312111 | Soft drinks manufacturing |
| 424490 | Soft drinks merchant wholesalers |

| | |
|---|---|
| 311812 | Soft pretzels made in a commercial bakery |
| 325613 | Softeners, leather or textile, manufacturing |
| 541511 | Software analysis and design services, custom computer |
| 611420 | Software application training |
| 513210 | Software computer, packaged, publishers |
| 541519 | Software installation services, computer |
| 541511 | Software programming services, custom computer |
| 513210 | Software publishers |
| 513210 | Software publishers, packaged |
| 449210 | Software retailers (e.g., downloadable computer software (without publishing)) |
| 449210 | Software stores, computer |
| 423430 | Software, computer, packaged, merchant wholesalers |
| 334610 | Software, packaged, mass reproducing |
| 321912 | Softwood dimension lumber and stock, resawing purchased lumber |
| 325194 | Softwood distillates manufacturing |
| 321212 | Softwood plywood composites manufacturing |
| 321212 | Softwood veneer or plywood manufacturing |
| 238910 | Soil compacting |
| 924120 | Soil conservation services, government |
| 331511 | Soil pipe, cast iron, manufacturing |
| 562910 | Soil remediation services |
| 238910 | Soil test drilling |
| 325998 | Soil testing kits manufacturing |
| 541380 | Soil testing laboratories or services |
| 424930 | Soil, top and potting, merchant wholesalers |
| 334413 | Solar cells manufacturing |
| 423690 | Solar cells merchant wholesalers |
| 926130 | Solar energy regulation |
| 333414 | Solar energy heating equipment manufacturing |
| 221114 | Solar farms |
| 238220 | Solar heating equipment installation |
| 423720 | Solar heating panels and equipment merchant wholesalers |
| 333414 | Solar heating systems manufacturing |
| 335132 | Solar lighting fixtures (except residential), electric, manufacturing |
| 335131 | Solar lighting fixtures, residential, electric, manufacturing |
| 238210 | Solar panel installation |
| 237130 | Solar power structure construction |
| 238160 | Solar reflecting coating, roof, application |
| 423330 | Solar reflective film merchant wholesalers |
| 334519 | Solarimeters manufacturing |
| 331491 | Solder wire, nonferrous metals (except aluminum, copper), made from purchased metals or scrap |
| 333992 | Soldering equipment (except handheld) manufacturing |
| 332216 | Soldering guns and irons, handheld (including electric), manufacturing |
| 332216 | Soldering iron tips and tiplets manufacturing |
| 335931 | Solderless connectors (electric wiring devices) manufacturing |
| 316110 | Sole leather manufacturing |
| 335314 | Solenoid switches, industrial, manufacturing |
| 332911 | Solenoid valves (except fluid power), industrial-type, manufacturing |
| 332912 | Solenoid valves, fluid power, manufacturing |
| 334419 | Solenoids for electronic applications manufacturing |
| 316990 | Soles, boot and shoe, leather, manufacturing |
| 922130 | Solicitors' offices, government |
| 541110 | Solicitors' offices, private |
| 541110 | Solicitors' private practices |
| 325180 | Solid fuel propellants, inorganic, not specified elsewhere by process, manufacturing |
| 562213 | Solid waste combustors or incinerators, nonhazardous |
| 562212 | Solid waste landfills combined with collection and/or local hauling of nonhazardous waste materials |
| 562212 | Solid waste landfills, nonhazardous |
| 711130 | Soloists, independent musical |
| 325130 | Solvent dyes manufacturing |
| 324110 | Solvents made in petroleum refineries |
| 334511 | Sonabuoys manufacturing |
| 423690 | Sonar equipment merchant wholesalers |
| 334511 | Sonar fish finders manufacturing |
| 334511 | Sonar systems and equipment manufacturing |
| 512230 | Song publishers |
| 512230 | Song publishers and printing combined |

| | |
|---|---|
| 711510 | Song writers, independent |
| 325612 | Soot removing chemicals manufacturing |
| 325199 | Sorbitol manufacturing |
| 111199 | Sorghum farming, field and seed production |
| 311211 | Sorghum flour manufacturing |
| 111998 | Sorghum sudan seed farming |
| 311999 | Sorghum syrup manufacturing |
| 813410 | Sororities (except residential) |
| 721310 | Sorority houses |
| 115114 | Sorting, grading, cleaning, and packing of fruits and vegetables |
| 532490 | Sound and lighting equipment rental or leasing |
| 423430 | Sound boards, computer, merchant wholesalers |
| 512191 | Sound dubbing services, motion picture |
| 238210 | Sound equipment installation |
| 423620 | Sound equipment, household-type, merchant wholesalers |
| 423330 | Sound insulation merchant wholesalers |
| 512240 | Sound recording studios (except integrated record companies) |
| 512250 | Sound recording, integrated production, reproduction, release, and distribution |
| 512250 | Sound recording, releasing, promoting, and distributing |
| 238310 | Soundproofing contractors |
| 332431 | Soup cans, light gauge metal, manufacturing |
| 624210 | Soup kitchens |
| 311423 | Soup mixes made in dehydration plants |
| 311999 | Soup mixes, dry, made from purchased dry ingredients |
| 424490 | Soups (except frozen) merchant wholesalers |
| 311422 | Soups (except seafood) canning |
| 311412 | Soups, frozen (except seafood), manufacturing |
| 424420 | Soups, frozen, merchant wholesalers |
| 311710 | Soups, seafood, manufacturing |
| 311511 | Sour cream manufacturing |
| 311511 | Sour cream substitutes manufacturing |
| 459420 | Souvenir shops |
| 311511 | Soy milk manufacturing |
| 311941 | Soy sauce manufacturing |
| 311224 | Soybean cakes and meal manufacturing |
| 311225 | Soybean cooking oil made from purchased oils |
| 111110 | Soybean farming, field and seed production |
| 325220 | Soybean fibers and filaments manufacturing |
| 311224 | Soybean flour and grits manufacturing |
| 311224 | Soybean millfeed made in oil mills |
| 311224 | Soybean oil mills |
| 311224 | Soybean oil, cake, and meal, made in crushing mills |
| 311224 | Soybean oil, crude, manufacturing |
| 311224 | Soybean oil, deodorized, made in oil mills |
| 311224 | Soybean oil, refined, made in crushing mills |
| 325211 | Soybean plastics manufacturing |
| 311224 | Soybean protein concentrates made in crushing mills |
| 311224 | Soybean protein isolates made in crushing mills |
| 424510 | Soybeans merchant wholesalers |
| 423720 | Spa equipment merchant wholesalers |
| 336419 | Space capsules manufacturing |
| 927110 | Space flight operations, government |
| 928110 | Space Force |
| 333414 | Space heaters (except portable electric) manufacturing |
| 423860 | Space propulsion units and parts merchant wholesalers |
| 927110 | Space research services, government |
| 334220 | Space satellites, communications, manufacturing |
| 332313 | Space simulation chambers, fabricated metal plate work, manufacturing |
| 339113 | Space suits manufacturing |
| 481212 | Space transportation, freight, nonscheduled |
| 481211 | Space transportation, passenger, nonscheduled |
| 334511 | Space vehicle guidance systems and equipment manufacturing |
| 336414 | Space vehicles, complete, manufacturing |
| 332216 | Spades and shovels, handheld, manufacturing |
| 311422 | Spaghetti canning |
| 424490 | Spaghetti merchant wholesalers |
| 311421 | Spaghetti sauce canning |
| 111219 | Spaghetti squash farming, field, bedding plant and seed production |
| 311824 | Spaghetti, dry, manufacturing |
| 313210 | Spandex broadwoven fabrics |

| | |
|---|---|
| 325220 | Spandex fiber, filaments, and yarn manufacturing |
| 113210 | Spanish moss gathering |
| 212390 | Spar, iceland, mining and/or beneficiating |
| 327110 | Spark plug insulators, porcelain, manufacturing |
| 334515 | Spark plug testing instruments, electric, manufacturing |
| 336320 | Spark plugs for internal combustion engines manufacturing |
| 312130 | Sparkling wines manufacturing |
| 321999 | Spars, wood, manufacturing |
| 713940 | Spas without accommodations, fitness |
| 316990 | Spats, leather, manufacturing |
| 326299 | Spatulas, rubber, manufacturing |
| 321999 | Speaker cabinets (i.e., housings), wood, manufacturing |
| 334310 | Speaker systems manufacturing |
| 423620 | Speaker systems merchant wholesalers |
| 711410 | Speakers' bureaus |
| 813410 | Speakers' clubs |
| 711510 | Speakers, independent |
| 325998 | Spearmint oil manufacturing |
| 711510 | Special effect technicians, independent |
| 512191 | Special effects for motion picture production, postproduction |
| 485991 | Special needs passenger transportation services |
| 525990 | Special purpose financial vehicles |
| 336211 | Special purpose highway vehicle (e.g., firefighting vehicles) assembling on purchased chassis |
| 336211 | Special purpose highway vehicle (e.g., firefighting vehicles) bodies manufacturing |
| 423110 | Special purpose highway vehicle merchant wholesalers |
| 336120 | Special purpose highway vehicles (e.g., firefighting vehicles) assembling on heavy chassis of own manufacture |
| 423830 | Special purpose industrial machinery and equipment merchant wholesalers |
| 611519 | Specialized military training (except flight instruction, academies, and basic training) |
| 423910 | Specialty athletic footwear (e.g., bowling, golf, cleated) merchant wholesalers |
| 445298 | Specialty food stores |
| 316110 | Specialty leathers manufacturing |
| 516210 | Specialty television (e.g., music, sports, news) cable networks |
| 335311 | Specialty transformers, electric, manufacturing |
| 423710 | Specialty-line hardware merchant wholesalers |
| 424210 | Specialty-line pharmaceuticals merchant wholesalers |
| 334516 | Specific ion measuring instruments, laboratory-type, manufacturing |
| 238390 | Spectator seating installation |
| 334516 | Spectrofluorometers manufacturing |
| 334516 | Spectrographs manufacturing |
| 334516 | Spectrometers (e.g., electron diffraction, mass, NMR, Raman) manufacturing |
| 334519 | Spectrometers (e.g., liquid scintillation, nuclear) manufacturing |
| 334516 | Spectrophotometers (e.g., atomic absorption, atomic emission, flame, fluorescence, infrared, Raman, visible) manufacturing |
| 334515 | Spectrum analyzers manufacturing |
| 236220 | Speculative builders (i.e., building on own land, for sale), commercial and institutional building |
| 236210 | Speculative builders (i.e., building on own land, for sale), industrial building (except warehouses) |
| 236117 | Speculative builders (i.e., building on own land, for sale), multifamily housing |
| 236117 | Speculative builders (i.e., building on own land, for sale), residential |
| 236117 | Speculative builders (i.e., building on own land, for sale), single-family housing |
| 339112 | Speculums manufacturing |
| 541930 | Speech (i.e., language) interpretation services |
| 621340 | Speech clinicians' offices (e.g., centers, clinics) |
| 621340 | Speech defect clinics |
| 621340 | Speech pathologists' offices (e.g., centers, clinics) |
| 621340 | Speech therapists' offices (e.g., centers, clinics) |
| 333612 | Speed changers (i.e., power transmission equipment) manufacturing |
| 423840 | Speed changers merchant wholesalers |
| 611699 | Speed reading instruction |
| 333612 | Speed reducers (i.e., power transmission equipment) manufacturing |
| 334511 | Speed, pitch, and roll navigational instruments and systems manufacturing |

| | |
|---|---|
| 711212 | Speedways |
| 621991 | Sperm banks, human |
| 113210 | Sphagnum moss gathering |
| 212230 | Sphalerite mining and/or beneficiating |
| 339112 | Sphygmomanometers manufacturing |
| 111998 | Spice farming |
| 111419 | Spice farming, grown under cover |
| 311942 | Spice grinding and blending |
| 311942 | Spice mixtures manufacturing |
| 445298 | Spice stores |
| 311942 | Spices and spice mix manufacturing |
| 424490 | Spices merchant wholesalers |
| 424590 | Spices, raw, merchant wholesalers |
| 331110 | Spiegeleisen ferroalloys manufacturing |
| 332913 | Spigots, plumbing fixture fitting, manufacturing |
| 321999 | Spigots, wood, manufacturing |
| 331110 | Spike rods made in iron and steel mills |
| 332618 | Spikes made from purchased wire |
| 331222 | Spikes, iron or steel, made in wire drawing plants |
| 423510 | Spikes, metal, merchant wholesalers |
| 237990 | Spillway, floodwater, construction |
| 111219 | Spinach farming, field, bedding plant and seed production |
| 333248 | Spindles for textile machinery manufacturing |
| 313110 | Spinning carpet and rug yarn from purchased fiber |
| 333248 | Spinning machinery for textiles manufacturing |
| 333517 | Spinning machines, metalworking, manufacturing |
| 332119 | Spinning unfinished metal products |
| 313110 | Spinning yarn from purchased fiber |
| 332618 | Spiral cloth made from purchased wire |
| 312140 | Spirits, distilled (except brandy), manufacturing |
| 424820 | Spirits, distilled, merchant wholesalers |
| 333517 | Spline rolling machines, metalworking, manufacturing |
| 321920 | Splint baskets for fruits and vegetables, manufacturing |
| 339113 | Splints manufacturing |
| 316110 | Splits, leather, manufacturing |
| 212390 | Spodumene mining and/or beneficiating |
| 321999 | Spokes, wood, manufacturing |

| | |
|---|---|
| 114119 | Sponge gathering |
| 331110 | Sponge iron |
| 424990 | Sponges merchant wholesalers |
| 332999 | Sponges, metal scouring, manufacturing |
| 326199 | Sponges, plastics, manufacturing |
| 326299 | Sponges, rubber, manufacturing |
| 313310 | Sponging textile products and fabrics |
| 313110 | Spooling of yarn |
| 313110 | Spooling of yarns for the trade |
| 321999 | Spools (except for textile machinery), wood, manufacturing |
| 333248 | Spools for textile machinery manufacturing |
| 332215 | Spoons, table, nonprecious and precious plated metal, manufacturing |
| 315210 | Sport coats cut and sew apparel contractors |
| 315250 | Sport coats, fur (except apparel contractors), manufacturing |
| 315210 | Sport coats, fur, cut and sew apparel contractors |
| 315250 | Sport coats, leather (including artificial and tailored) (except apparel contractors), manufacturing |
| 315210 | Sport coats, leather (including artificial and tailored), cut and sew apparel contractors |
| 315250 | Sport coats, men's and boys', cut and sewn from purchased fabric (except apparel contractors) |
| 424490 | Sport energy drinks merchant wholesalers |
| 315210 | Sport shirts cut and sew apparel contractors |
| 315250 | Sport shirts, men's and boys', cut and sewn from purchased fabric (except apparel contractors) |
| 532112 | Sport utility vehicle leasing |
| 423110 | Sport utility vehicle merchant wholesalers |
| 532111 | Sport utility vehicle rental |
| 336110 | Sport utility vehicles assembling on chassis of own manufacture |
| 811490 | Sporting equipment repair and maintenance without retailing new sports equipment |
| 423910 | Sporting firearms and ammunition merchant wholesalers |
| 339920 | Sporting goods (except ammunition, clothing, footwear, small arms) manufacturing |
| 423910 | Sporting goods and supplies merchant wholesalers |

| | |
|---|---|
| 532284 | Sporting goods rental |
| 459110 | Sporting goods stores |
| 459510 | Sporting goods stores, used |
| 711510 | Sports announcers, independent |
| 458110 | Sports apparel stores (except uniforms) |
| 711310 | Sports arena operators |
| 611620 | Sports camps (e.g., baseball, basketball, football), instructional |
| 315210 | Sports clothing cut and sew apparel contractors |
| 315120 | Sports clothing made in apparel knitting mills |
| 315250 | Sports clothing, men's and boys', cut and sewn from purchased fabric (except apparel contractors) |
| 315250 | Sports clothing, team uniforms, cut and sewn from purchased fabric (except apparel contractors) |
| 315250 | Sports clothing, women's and girls', cut and sewn from purchased fabric (except apparel contractors) |
| 713940 | Sports club facilities, physical fitness |
| 713990 | Sports clubs (i.e., sports teams) not operating sports facilities, recreational |
| 711211 | Sports clubs, professional or semiprofessional |
| 423910 | Sports equipment and supplies merchant wholesalers |
| 532284 | Sports equipment rental |
| 711310 | Sports event managers with facilities |
| 711320 | Sports event managers without facilities |
| 711310 | Sports event organizers with facilities |
| 711320 | Sports event organizers without facilities |
| 711310 | Sports event promoters with facilities |
| 711320 | Sports event promoters without facilities |
| 237990 | Sports field construction |
| 711410 | Sports figures' agents or managers |
| 459110 | Sports gear stores (e.g., outdoors, scuba, skiing) |
| 813990 | Sports governing bodies |
| 712110 | Sports halls of fame |
| 611620 | Sports instruction, camps or schools |
| 611620 | Sports instructors, independent (i.e., not participating in sporting events) |
| 813990 | Sports leagues (i.e., regulating bodies) |
| 621340 | Sports physical therapists' offices (e.g., centers, clinics) |
| 711219 | Sports professionals, independent (i.e., participating in sports events) |

| | |
|---|---|
| 315120 | Sports shirts made in apparel knitting mills |
| 711310 | Sports stadium operators |
| 711219 | Sports team scouting services, independent |
| 713990 | Sports teams and leagues, recreational or youth |
| 711211 | Sports teams, professional or semiprofessional |
| 561599 | Sports ticket offices |
| 711219 | Sports trainers, independent |
| 424350 | Sportswear, men's and boys', merchant wholesalers |
| 325612 | Spot removers (except laundry presoaks) manufacturing |
| 333992 | Spot welding equipment manufacturing |
| 335139 | Spotlights (except vehicular) manufacturing |
| 336320 | Spotlights, vehicular, manufacturing |
| 332322 | Spouts, sheet metal (except stampings), manufacturing |
| 424950 | Spray painting equipment (except industrial-type) merchant wholesalers |
| 423830 | Spray painting equipment, industrial-type, merchant wholesalers |
| 333111 | Sprayers and dusters, farm-type, manufacturing |
| 423820 | Sprayers, farm-type, merchant wholesalers |
| 333912 | Sprayers, manual pump, general purpose-type, manufacturing |
| 115112 | Spraying crops |
| 561730 | Spraying lawns |
| 811198 | Spray-on bedliner installation for trucks |
| 333111 | Spreaders, farm-type, manufacturing |
| 423820 | Spreaders, fertilizer, merchant wholesalers |
| 333112 | Spreaders, lawn and garden-type, manufacturing |
| 115112 | Spreading lime for crops |
| 311513 | Spreads, cheese, manufacturing |
| 332722 | Spring pins, metal, manufacturing |
| 332722 | Spring washers, metal, manufacturing |
| 312112 | Spring waters, purifying and bottling |
| 333517 | Spring winding and forming machines, metalworking, manufacturing |
| 332613 | Springs and spring units for seats, light gauge, made from purchased wire or strip |
| 337910 | Springs, assembled bed and box, made from purchased springs |

| | |
|---|---|
| 334519 | Springs, clock and watch, made from purchased wire |
| 332613 | Springs, heavy gauge metal, manufacturing |
| 332613 | Springs, light gauge (except clock, watch), made from purchased wire or strip |
| 332613 | Springs, precision (except clock, watch), light gauge, made from purchased wire or strip |
| 423510 | Springs, steel, merchant wholesalers |
| 238220 | Sprinkler system, building, installation |
| 333998 | Sprinkler systems, automatic fire, manufacturing |
| 423850 | Sprinkler systems, fire, merchant wholesalers |
| 423820 | Sprinklers, agricultural, merchant wholesalers |
| 423820 | Sprinklers, garden, merchant wholesalers |
| 332919 | Sprinklers, lawn, manufacturing |
| 423840 | Sprockets merchant wholesalers |
| 333613 | Sprockets, power transmission equipment, manufacturing |
| 113210 | Spruce gum gathering |
| 213111 | Spudding in oil and gas wells on a contract basis |
| 313230 | Spunbonded fabrics manufacturing |
| 332216 | Squares, carpenters', metal, manufacturing |
| 713940 | Squash club facilities |
| 339920 | Squash equipment (except apparel) manufacturing |
| 111219 | Squash farming, field, bedding plant and seed production |
| 114112 | Squid fishing |
| 424610 | Stabilizers, plastic, merchant wholesalers |
| 332999 | Stabilizing bars, cargo, metal, manufacturing |
| 711219 | Stables, horse racing |
| 713990 | Stables, riding |
| 423830 | Stackers, industrial, merchant wholesalers |
| 333924 | Stackers, industrial, truck-type, manufacturing |
| 333924 | Stackers, portable (except farm), manufacturing |
| 236220 | Stadium and arena construction |
| 711310 | Stadium operators |
| 531120 | Stadium rental or leasing without promotion of events |

| | |
|---|---|
| 337127 | Stadium seating manufacturing |
| 561330 | Staff leasing services |
| 335139 | Stage lighting equipment manufacturing |
| 711510 | Stage set (e.g., concert, motion picture, television) erecting and dismantling, independent |
| 327211 | Stained glass and stained glass products made in glass making plants |
| 238150 | Stained glass installation |
| 327215 | Stained glass products made from purchased glass |
| 331513 | Stainless steel castings (except investment), unfinished, manufacturing |
| 331110 | Stainless steel made in iron and steel mills |
| 423510 | Stainless steel merchant wholesalers |
| 325510 | Stains (except biological) manufacturing |
| 424950 | Stains merchant wholesalers |
| 325130 | Stains, biological, manufacturing |
| 332323 | Stair railings, metal, manufacturing |
| 321918 | Stair railings, wood, manufacturing |
| 332323 | Stair treads, metal, manufacturing |
| 326299 | Stair treads, rubber, manufacturing |
| 332323 | Staircases, metal, manufacturing |
| 332323 | Stairs, metal, manufacturing |
| 423310 | Stairs, wood, merchant wholesalers |
| 238190 | Stairway, metal, installation |
| 238120 | Stairway, precast concrete, installation |
| 238350 | Stairway, wood, installation |
| 333921 | Stairways, moving, manufacturing |
| 321918 | Stairwork (e.g., newel posts, railings, staircases, stairs), wood, manufacturing |
| 321999 | Stakes, surveyor's, wood, manufacturing |
| 333111 | Stalk choppers (i.e., shredders) manufacturing |
| 332323 | Stalls, metal, manufacturing |
| 325998 | Stamp pad ink manufacturing |
| 339940 | Stamp pads manufacturing |
| 339910 | Stamping coins |
| 339940 | Stamping devices, hand operated, manufacturing |
| 333517 | Stamping machines, metalworking, manufacturing |
| 336370 | Stamping metal motor vehicle body parts |
| 336370 | Stamping metal motor vehicle moldings and trims |
| 332119 | Stampings (except automotive, cans, coins), metal, unfinished, manufacturing |

| | |
|---|---|
| 423920 | Stamps, philatelist, merchant wholesalers |
| 713210 | Stand-alone casinos (except slot machine parlors) |
| 516210 | Stand-alone streaming services |
| 334515 | Standards and calibration equipment for electrical measuring manufacturing |
| 813920 | Standards review committees, professional |
| 926150 | Standards, setting and management, agencies, government |
| 334515 | Standing wave ratio measuring equipment manufacturing |
| 337215 | Stands (except wire), merchandise display, manufacturing |
| 711510 | Standup comedians, independent |
| 325180 | Stannic and stannous chloride manufacturing |
| 339940 | Staple removers manufacturing |
| 333991 | Staplers and nailers, handheld power-driven, manufacturing |
| 339940 | Staplers manufacturing |
| 332618 | Staples made from purchased wire |
| 423710 | Staples merchant wholesalers |
| 331222 | Staples, iron or steel, made in wire drawing plants |
| 423420 | Stapling machines merchant wholesalers |
| 325520 | Starch glues manufacturing |
| 311221 | Starches (except laundry) manufacturing |
| 325612 | Starches, laundry, manufacturing |
| 112310 | Started pullet production |
| 336320 | Starter and starter parts for internal combustion engines manufacturing |
| 522110 | State commercial banks |
| 522130 | State credit unions |
| 928120 | State Department |
| 923110 | State education departments |
| 561311 | State operated employment job services offices |
| 922120 | State police |
| 522180 | State savings and loan associations |
| 522180 | State savings banks |
| 921130 | State tax commissions |
| 334413 | Static converters, integrated circuits, manufacturing |
| 334512 | Static pressure regulators manufacturing |
| 332410 | Stationary power boilers manufacturing |
| 327110 | Stationery articles, pottery, manufacturing |
| 322230 | Stationery made from purchased paper |
| 459410 | Stationery stores |
| 424120 | Stationery supplies merchant wholesalers |
| 323111 | Stationery, commercial printing (except screen), on a job-order basis |
| 323113 | Stationery, screen printing, on a job-order basis |
| 335312 | Stators for motors manufacturing |
| 327420 | Statuary (e.g., gypsum, plaster of paris) manufacturing |
| 424990 | Statuary (except religious) merchant wholesalers |
| 327110 | Statuary, clay and ceramic, manufacturing |
| 327991 | Statuary, marble, manufacturing |
| 423490 | Statuary, religious, merchant wholesalers |
| 327999 | Statuary, vases, and urns, papier-mache, manufacturing |
| 238990 | Statue erection |
| 212390 | Staurolite mining and/or beneficiating |
| 321920 | Staves, barrel, sawed or split, manufacturing |
| 316990 | Stays, shoe, leather, manufacturing |
| 722511 | Steak houses, full service |
| 722513 | Steak houses, limited-service |
| 812199 | Steam baths |
| 561790 | Steam cleaning building exteriors |
| 213112 | Steam cleaning oil and gas wells on a contract basis |
| 332410 | Steam condensers manufacturing |
| 333310 | Steam cookers, commercial-type, manufacturing |
| 335210 | Steam cookers, household-type, manufacturing |
| 611513 | Steam fitters' apprenticeship training |
| 238220 | Steam fitting contractors |
| 332919 | Steam fittings, metal, manufacturing |
| 221330 | Steam heat distribution |
| 333414 | Steam heating equipment manufacturing |
| 221330 | Steam heating systems (i.e., suppliers of heat) |
| 334512 | Steam pressure controls, residential and commercial heating-type, manufacturing |
| 221330 | Steam production and distribution |
| 333998 | Steam separating machinery manufacturing |
| 221330 | Steam supply systems, including geothermal |

| | |
|---|---|
| 333310 | Steam tables manufacturing |
| 487110 | Steam train excursions |
| 332911 | Steam traps, industrial-type, manufacturing |
| 333611 | Steam turbine generator set units manufacturing |
| 333611 | Steam turbines manufacturing |
| 532411 | Steamship rental or leasing without crew |
| 325199 | Stearic acid esters manufacturing |
| 325199 | Stearic acid manufacturing |
| 325199 | Stearic acid salts manufacturing |
| 311613 | Stearin, animal, rendering |
| 212390 | Steatite mining and/or beneficiating |
| 327110 | Steatite porcelain insulators manufacturing |
| 331110 | Steel balls made in iron and steel mills |
| 332431 | Steel cans, light gauge metal, manufacturing |
| 331513 | Steel castings (except investment), unfinished, manufacturing |
| 332111 | Steel forgings made from purchased steel, unfinished |
| 331513 | Steel foundries (except investment) |
| 238130 | Steel framing contractors |
| 331512 | Steel investment castings, unfinished, manufacturing |
| 331512 | Steel investment foundries |
| 332312 | Steel joists manufacturing |
| 331110 | Steel manufacturing |
| 423510 | Steel merchant wholesalers |
| 236210 | Steel mill construction |
| 331110 | Steel mill products (e.g., bar, plate, rod, sheet, structural shapes) manufacturing |
| 331110 | Steel mills |
| 332312 | Steel railroad car racks manufacturing |
| 238120 | Steel reinforcing contractors |
| 327910 | Steel shot abrasives manufacturing |
| 423510 | Steel wire cloth (screening) merchant wholesalers |
| 332999 | Steel wool manufacturing |
| 423510 | Steel wool merchant wholesalers |
| 331110 | Steel, from pig iron, manufacturing |
| 238160 | Steep slope roofing installation |
| 238990 | Steeplejack work |
| 311221 | Steepwater concentrate manufacturing |
| 336330 | Steering boxes, manual and power assist, manufacturing |
| 336330 | Steering columns, automotive, truck, and bus, manufacturing |
| 336330 | Steering wheels, automotive, truck, and bus, manufacturing |
| 327215 | Stemware made from purchased glass |
| 327212 | Stemware, glass, made in glass making plants |
| 325910 | Stencil inks manufacturing |
| 339940 | Stencil paper manufacturing |
| 339940 | Stencils for painting and marking (e.g., cardboard, metal) manufacturing |
| 561410 | Stenographic services (except court or stenographic reporting) |
| 333310 | Stenography machinery manufacturing |
| 561492 | Stenography services, public |
| 561492 | Stenotype recording services |
| 332999 | Stepladders, metal, manufacturing |
| 321999 | Stepladders, wood, manufacturing |
| 321999 | Stereo cabinets (i.e., housings), wood, manufacturing |
| 423620 | Stereo equipment merchant wholesalers |
| 532210 | Stereo equipment rental |
| 811210 | Stereo equipment repair shops without retailing new stereo equipment |
| 325212 | Stereo rubber manufacturing |
| 449210 | Stereo stores (except automotive) |
| 441330 | Stereo stores, automotive |
| 339114 | Sterilizers, dental, manufacturing |
| 339113 | Sterilizers, hospital and surgical, manufacturing |
| 339113 | Sterilizers, laboratory-type (except dental), manufacturing |
| 332313 | Sterilizing chambers, fabricated metal plate work, manufacturing |
| 325411 | Steroids, uncompounded, manufacturing |
| 339112 | Stethoscopes manufacturing |
| 488320 | Stevedoring services |
| 339920 | Sticks, sports (e.g., hockey, lacrosse), manufacturing |
| 325130 | Stilbene dyes manufacturing |
| 324110 | Still gases made in petroleum refineries |
| 332420 | Stills, heavy gauge metal, manufacturing |
| 333248 | Stitchers and trimmers bookbinding equipment manufacturing |
| 314999 | Stitching, decorative and novelty, contractors on apparel |
| 314999 | Stitching, decorative and novelty, on textile articles and apparel |
| 523150 | Stock brokerages |

| | |
|---|---|
| 523150 | Stock brokers' offices |
| 711212 | Stock car racetracks |
| 711219 | Stock car racing teams |
| 711110 | Stock companies, theatrical |
| 523210 | Stock exchanges |
| 512199 | Stock footage film libraries |
| 512290 | Stock music and other audio services |
| 523150 | Stock options brokerages |
| 523150 | Stock options dealing (i.e., acting as a principal in dealing securities to investors) |
| 523210 | Stock or commodity options exchanges |
| 519290 | Stock photo agencies |
| 523999 | Stock quotation services |
| 512290 | Stock sound library (e.g., general background sounds, stock music) |
| 523999 | Stock transfer agencies |
| 321912 | Stock, chair, unfinished hardwood, manufacturing |
| 112111 | Stocker calf production |
| 315120 | Stockings, sheer, manufacturing |
| 315120 | Stockings, sheer, women's, misses', and girls', full-length and knee-length, knitting or knitting and finishing |
| 488999 | Stockyards (i.e., not for fattening or selling livestock), transportation |
| 212319 | Stone (except limestone and granite) beneficiating plants (e.g., grinding) |
| 333131 | Stone beneficiating machinery manufacturing |
| 332216 | Stone cutting saw blades manufacturing |
| 238340 | Stone flooring installation |
| 313310 | Stone washing textile products, apparel, and fabrics |
| 333248 | Stone working machinery manufacturing |
| 423320 | Stone, building or crushed, merchant wholesalers |
| 212319 | Stone, crushed and broken (except granite or limestone), mining and/or beneficiating |
| 212311 | Stone, dimension, mining or quarrying |
| 332216 | Stonecutters' handtools, nonpowered, manufacturing |
| 212390 | Stones, abrasive (e.g., emery, grindstones, hones, pumice), mining and/or beneficiating |
| 423940 | Stones, precious and semiprecious, merchant wholesalers |
| 327999 | Stones, synthetic, for gem stones and industrial use, manufacturing |
| 327110 | Stoneware (i.e., pottery products) manufacturing |
| 212323 | Stoneware clay mining and/or beneficiating |
| 238140 | Stonework (i.e., masonry) contractors |
| 337126 | Stools, metal household-type (except upholstered), manufacturing |
| 337122 | Stools, wood household-type (except upholstered), manufacturing |
| 621999 | Stop smoking clinics |
| 332911 | Stop valves, industrial-type, manufacturing |
| 332913 | Stopcock drains, plumbing, manufacturing |
| 321999 | Stoppers, cork, manufacturing |
| 326299 | Stoppers, rubber, manufacturing |
| 423610 | Storage batteries (except automotive) merchant wholesalers |
| 335910 | Storage batteries manufacturing |
| 335312 | Storage battery chargers (except internal combustion engine-type) manufacturing |
| 423390 | Storage bins merchant wholesalers |
| 334112 | Storage devices, computer, manufacturing |
| 236220 | Storage elevator construction |
| 486210 | Storage of natural gas |
| 237120 | Storage tank, natural gas or oil, tank farm or field, construction |
| 332420 | Storage tanks, heavy gauge metal, manufacturing |
| 423510 | Storage tanks, metal, merchant wholesalers |
| 236220 | Store construction |
| 541850 | Store display advertising services |
| 337215 | Store display fixtures manufacturing |
| 423440 | Store equipment (except furniture) merchant wholesalers |
| 423440 | Store fixtures (except refrigerated) merchant wholesalers |
| 423210 | Store furniture merchant wholesalers |
| 238190 | Storefront, metal or metal frame, installation |
| ****** | Stores -- see type |
| 562998 | Storm basin cleanout services |
| 332321 | Storm doors and windows, metal, manufacturing |
| 321911 | Storm doors and windows, wood framed, manufacturing |
| 237110 | Storm sewer construction |
| 711510 | Storytellers, independent |
| 312120 | Stout brewing |

| | |
|---|---|
| 332322 | Stove boards, sheet metal (except stampings), manufacturing |
| 327120 | Stove lining, clay, manufacturing |
| 332322 | Stove pipes and flues, sheet metal (except stampings), manufacturing |
| 811412 | Stove, household-type, repair and maintenance services without retailing new stoves |
| 423720 | Stoves (i.e., noncooking), heating, merchant wholesalers |
| 335220 | Stoves, ceramic disk element, household-type, manufacturing |
| 333310 | Stoves, commercial-type, manufacturing |
| 423620 | Stoves, cooking, household-type, merchant wholesalers |
| 335220 | Stoves, household-type cooking, manufacturing |
| 333924 | Straddle carriers, mobile, manufacturing |
| 332215 | Straight razors manufacturing |
| 332911 | Straightway (i.e., Y-type) valves, industrial-type, manufacturing |
| 333998 | Strainers, pipeline, manufacturing |
| 321219 | Strandboard, oriented, manufacturing |
| 332618 | Stranded wire, uninsulated, made from purchased wire |
| 316110 | Strap leather manufacturing |
| 332999 | Strappings, metal, manufacturing |
| 316990 | Straps, leather, manufacturing |
| 316990 | Straps, watch (except metal), manufacturing |
| 339910 | Straps, watch, precious metal, manufacturing |
| 541611 | Strategic planning consulting services |
| 213112 | Stratigraphic drilling, oil and gas field exploration on a contract basis |
| 321999 | Straw baskets manufacturing |
| 315990 | Straw hats manufacturing |
| 424910 | Straw merchant wholesalers |
| 111333 | Strawberry farming |
| 488490 | Street cleaning service |
| 237310 | Street construction |
| 335139 | Street lighting fixtures (except traffic signals) manufacturing |
| 513130 | Street map guide publishers |
| 513130 | Street map guide publishers (except exclusive Internet publishing) |
| 513130 | Street map guide publishers, exclusively on Internet |
| 485119 | Street railway systems (except mixed mode), commuter |
| 423810 | Street sweeping and cleaning equipment merchant wholesalers |
| 722330 | Street vendors, food |
| 238990 | Street, interlocking brick (i.e., not mortared), installation |
| 237990 | Streetcar line construction |
| 485119 | Streetcar systems (except mixed mode), commuter |
| 336510 | Streetcars and car equipment, urban transit, manufacturing |
| 713940 | Strength development centers |
| 336211 | Stretch limousines assembling on purchased chassis |
| 321999 | Stretchers, curtain, wood, manufacturing |
| 339113 | Stretchers, medical, manufacturing |
| 333517 | Stretching machines, metalworking, manufacturing |
| 111219 | String bean farming, field and seed production |
| 314994 | Strings (except musical instrument) manufacturing |
| 339992 | Strings, musical instrument, manufacturing |
| 212114 | Strip mining, bituminous coal, lignite, or anthracite, on own account |
| 331420 | Strip, copper and copper alloy, made from purchased copper or in integrated secondary smelting and rolling, drawing or extruding plants |
| 331110 | Strip, galvanized iron or steel, made in iron and steel mills |
| 331110 | Strip, iron or steel, made in iron and steel mills |
| 331491 | Strip, nonferrous metals (except aluminum, copper), made from purchased metals or scrap |
| 211130 | Stripper gas well production |
| 211120 | Stripper oil well production |
| 213113 | Stripping overburden services for coal mining on a contract basis |
| 213114 | Stripping overburden services for metal mining on a contract basis |
| 213115 | Stripping overburden services for nonmetallic minerals mining (except fuels) on a contract basis |
| 423510 | Strips, metal (except precious), merchant wholesalers |
| 334515 | Stroboscopes manufacturing |
| 335139 | Strobotrons manufacturing |
| 424350 | Strollers merchant wholesalers |
| 339930 | Strollers, baby, manufacturing |
| 212390 | Strontianite mining and/or beneficiating |

| | |
|---|---|
| 325180 | Strontium carbonate manufacturing |
| 325180 | Strontium compounds, not specified elsewhere by process, manufacturing |
| 212390 | Strontium mineral mining and/or beneficiating |
| 325180 | Strontium nitrate manufacturing |
| 423510 | Structural assemblies, metal, merchant wholesalers |
| 423390 | Structural assemblies, prefabricated (except wood), merchant wholesalers |
| 423310 | Structural assemblies, prefabricated wood, merchant wholesalers |
| 423320 | Structural clay tile (except refractory and clay roofing tile) merchant wholesalers |
| 327120 | Structural clay tile manufacturing |
| 321114 | Structural lumber and timber, treating |
| 321215 | Structural members, glue laminated or pre-engineered wood, manufacturing |
| 333519 | Structural rolling mill machinery, metalworking, manufacturing |
| 331318 | Structural shapes made by rolling purchased aluminum |
| 331318 | Structural shapes, aluminum, made in integrated secondary smelting and rolling mills |
| 331110 | Structural shapes, iron or steel, made in iron and steel mills |
| 238120 | Structural steel erecting or iron work contractors |
| 332312 | Structural steel, fabricated, manufacturing |
| 339930 | Structural toy sets manufacturing |
| 321215 | Structural wood members, fabricated, manufacturing |
| 336330 | Struts, automotive, truck, and bus, manufacturing |
| 325411 | Strychnine and derivatives (i.e., basic chemicals) manufacturing |
| 327999 | Stucco and stucco products manufacturing |
| 238140 | Stucco contractors |
| 423320 | Stucco merchant wholesalers |
| 321113 | Stud mills |
| 115210 | Stud services |
| 238130 | Stud wall (e.g., wood, steel) installation |
| 813410 | Student clubs |
| 611710 | Student exchange programs |
| 522291 | Student loan companies |
| 522299 | Student Loan Marketing Association (SLMA) |
| 813410 | Students' associations |
| 813410 | Students' unions |
| 334220 | Studio equipment, radio and television broadcasting, manufacturing |
| 541430 | Studios, commercial art |
| 321912 | Studs, resawing purchased lumber |
| 332322 | Studs, sheet metal (except stampings), manufacturing |
| 611710 | Study abroad programs |
| 921120 | Study commissions, legislative |
| 339930 | Stuffed toys (including animals) manufacturing |
| 333241 | Stuffer, sausage machinery, manufacturing |
| 113310 | Stump removing in the field |
| 325212 | S-type rubber manufacturing |
| 325920 | Styphnic acid explosive materials manufacturing |
| 325110 | Styrene made from refined petroleum or liquid hydrocarbons |
| 324110 | Styrene made in petroleum refineries |
| 325211 | Styrene resins manufacturing |
| 325211 | Styrene-acrylonitrile resins manufacturing |
| 325212 | Styrene-butadiene rubber containing less than 50 percent styrene manufacturing |
| 325212 | Styrene-chloroprene rubber manufacturing |
| 325212 | Styrene-isoprene rubber manufacturing |
| 238310 | Styrofoam insulation installation |
| 722513 | Sub shops, limited-service |
| 212114 | Subbituminous coal surface mining and/or beneficiating |
| 212115 | Subbituminous coal underground mining |
| 237210 | Subdividers, real estate |
| 237210 | Subdividing and preparing land owned by others |
| 237210 | Subdividing real estate |
| 332994 | Submachine guns manufacturing |
| 336611 | Submarine building |
| 333514 | Subpresses, machine tool, manufacturing |
| 334210 | Subscriber loop equipment, telephone, manufacturing |
| 513140 | Subscription directory publishers |
| 516210 | Subscription television networks |
| 516210 | Subscription Video on Demand (SVOD) services |
| 551114 | Subsidiary management offices |

| | |
|---|---|
| 623220 | Substance abuse (i.e., alcoholism, drug addiction) halfway houses |
| 623220 | Substance abuse facilities, residential |
| 813319 | Substance abuse prevention advocacy organizations |
| 621420 | Substance abuse treatment centers and clinics (except hospitals), outpatient |
| 237130 | Substation and switching station, power transmission line, construction |
| 335311 | Substation transformers, electric power distribution, manufacturing |
| 512191 | Subtitling of motion picture film or video |
| 485113 | Suburban bus line services (except mixed mode) |
| 485112 | Suburban commuter rail systems (except mixed mode) |
| 485111 | Suburban transit systems, mixed mode (e.g., bus, commuter rail, subway combinations) |
| 541850 | Subway card display advertising services |
| 336510 | Subway cars manufacturing |
| 423860 | Subway cars merchant wholesalers |
| 237990 | Subway construction |
| 485119 | Subway systems (except mixed mode), commuter |
| 339112 | Suction therapy apparatus manufacturing |
| 812320 | Suede garment cleaning services |
| 313310 | Sueding textile products and fabrics |
| 111991 | Sugar beet farming |
| 115113 | Sugar beets, machine harvesting |
| 311221 | Sugar made by wet milling corn |
| 333241 | Sugar refining machinery manufacturing |
| 325998 | Sugar substitutes (i.e., synthetic sweeteners blended with other ingredients) made from purchased synthetic sweeteners |
| 325199 | Sugar substitutes (i.e., synthetic sweeteners blended with other ingredients) made in synthetic sweetener establishments |
| 311314 | Sugar, cane, manufacturing |
| 311314 | Sugar, clarified, granulated, and raw, manufacturing |
| 311313 | Sugar, confectionery, made from sugar beets |
| 311314 | Sugar, confectionery, manufacturing |
| 311313 | Sugar, granulated, made from sugar beets |
| 311314 | Sugar, granulated, manufacturing |
| 311313 | Sugar, invert, made from sugar beets |
| 311314 | Sugar, invert, manufacturing |
| 311313 | Sugar, liquid, made from sugar beets |
| 311314 | Sugar, raw, manufacturing |
| 424590 | Sugar, raw, merchant wholesalers |
| 311314 | Sugar, refined, manufacturing |
| 424490 | Sugar, refined, merchant wholesalers |
| 111930 | Sugarcane farming, field production |
| 311314 | Sugarcane mills |
| 311314 | Sugarcane refining |
| 115113 | Sugarcane, machine harvesting |
| 624190 | Suicide crisis centers |
| 532281 | Suit rental |
| 315210 | Suit trimmings cut and sew apparel contractors |
| 315990 | Suit trimmings cut and sewn from purchased fabric (except apparel contractors) |
| 332510 | Suitcase hardware, metal, manufacturing |
| 423990 | Suitcases merchant wholesalers |
| 316990 | Suitcases, all materials, manufacturing |
| 315250 | Suits (e.g., jogging, snowsuit, warmup), women's, girls', and infants', cut and sewn from purchased fabric (except apparel contractors) |
| 315210 | Suits (i.e., nontailored, tailored, work) cut and sew apparel contractors |
| 315120 | Suits made in apparel knitting mills |
| 339113 | Suits, firefighting, manufacturing |
| 424350 | Suits, men's and boys', merchant wholesalers |
| 315250 | Suits, nontailored (e.g., jogging, snow, ski, warmup), men's and boys', cut and sewn from purchased fabric (except apparel contractors) |
| 339113 | Suits, space, manufacturing |
| 315250 | Suits, tailored, men's and boys', cut and sewn from purchased fabric (except apparel contractors) |
| 315250 | Suits, tailored, women's and girls', cut and sewn from purchased fabric (except apparel contractors) |
| 325411 | Sulfa drugs, uncompounded, manufacturing |
| 212390 | Sulfate, sodium, mining and/or beneficiating |
| 325180 | Sulfides and sulfites manufacturing |
| 325180 | Sulfocyanides manufacturing |

| | |
|---|---|
| 325411 | Sulfonamides, uncompounded, manufacturing |
| 325194 | Sulfonated naphthalene manufacturing |
| 325180 | Sulfur and sulfur compounds, not specified elsewhere by process, manufacturing |
| 325180 | Sulfur chloride manufacturing |
| 325180 | Sulfur dioxide manufacturing |
| 325180 | Sulfur hexafluoride gas manufacturing |
| 325320 | Sulfur insecticides manufacturing |
| 212390 | Sulfur mining and/or beneficiating |
| 211130 | Sulfur recovered from natural gas |
| 325180 | Sulfur recovering or refining (except from sour natural gas) |
| 212390 | Sulfur, native, mining and/or beneficiating |
| 325180 | Sulfuric acid manufacturing |
| 424690 | Sulfuric acid merchant wholesalers |
| 325194 | Sulphonated derivatives manufacturing |
| 311423 | Sulphured fruits and vegetables manufacturing |
| 325194 | Sumac extract manufacturing |
| 721214 | Summer camps (except day, instructional) |
| 713990 | Summer day camps (except instructional) |
| 721110 | Summer resort hotels without casinos |
| 711110 | Summer theaters |
| 238220 | Sump pump installation |
| 333914 | Sump pumps, residential-type, manufacturing |
| 115114 | Sun drying of dates, prunes, raisins, and olives |
| 115114 | Sun drying of fruits and vegetables |
| 115114 | Sun drying of tomatoes |
| 812199 | Sun tanning salons |
| 111120 | Sunflower farming, field and seed production |
| 311224 | Sunflower seed oil, cake and meal, made in crushing mills |
| 456130 | Sunglass stores |
| 339115 | Sunglasses and goggles manufacturing |
| 423460 | Sunglasses merchant wholesalers |
| 336390 | Sunroofs and parts, automotive, truck, and bus, manufacturing |
| 236118 | Sunroom additions, residential |
| 325620 | Sunscreen lotions and oils manufacturing |

| | |
|---|---|
| 315250 | Sunsuits, infants', cut and sewn from purchased fabric (except apparel contractors) |
| 325620 | Suntan lotions and oils manufacturing |
| 331110 | Superalloys, iron or steel, manufacturing |
| 331492 | Superalloys, nonferrous based, made from purchased metals or scrap |
| 455211 | Supercenters |
| 445110 | Supermarkets |
| 325312 | Superphosphates manufacturing |
| 455211 | Superstores (i.e., food and general merchandise) |
| 921190 | Supply agencies, government |
| 332913 | Supply line assemblies, plumbing (i.e., flexible hose with fittings), manufacturing |
| 624190 | Support group services |
| 339113 | Supports, orthopedic (e.g., abdominal, ankle, arch, kneecap), manufacturing |
| 325412 | Suppositories manufacturing |
| 524126 | Surety insurance carriers, direct |
| 325613 | Surface active agents manufacturing |
| 424690 | Surface active agents merchant wholesalers |
| 334516 | Surface area analyzers manufacturing |
| 334512 | Surface burner controls, temperature, manufacturing |
| 322220 | Surface coating purchased paperboard |
| 333120 | Surface mining machinery (except drilling) manufacturing |
| 333242 | Surface mount machinery for making printed circuit boards manufacturing |
| 237310 | Surfacing, highway, road, street, bridge or airport runway |
| 532284 | Surfboard rental |
| 339920 | Surfboards manufacturing |
| 335999 | Surge suppressors manufacturing |
| 621111 | Surgeons' (except dental) offices (e.g., centers, clinics) |
| 541940 | Surgeons' offices, veterinary |
| 621210 | Surgeons', dental, offices (e.g., centers, clinics) |
| 115112 | Surgery on trees and vines |
| 541940 | Surgery services, veterinary |
| 339113 | Surgical and medical masks manufacturing |
| 423450 | Surgical and medical masks merchant wholesalers |
| 423450 | Surgical appliances merchant wholesalers |

| | |
|---|---|
| 339112 | Surgical clamps manufacturing |
| 339113 | Surgical dressings manufacturing |
| 423450 | Surgical dressings merchant wholesalers |
| 339113 | Surgical implants manufacturing |
| 811210 | Surgical instrument repair and maintenance services |
| 423450 | Surgical instruments and apparatus merchant wholesalers |
| 339112 | Surgical knife blades and handles manufacturing |
| 621111 | Surgical pathologists' offices (e.g., centers, clinics) |
| 339112 | Surgical stapling devices manufacturing |
| 339113 | Surgical supplies (except medical instruments) manufacturing |
| 423450 | Surgical supplies merchant wholesalers |
| 334510 | Surgical support systems, electromedical, manufacturing |
| 423450 | Surgical towels merchant wholesalers |
| 311710 | Surimi manufacturing |
| 238210 | Surveillance system, installation only |
| 213112 | Surveying (except seismographic) oil or gas wells on a contract basis |
| 541370 | Surveying and mapping services (except geophysical) |
| 423490 | Surveying equipment and supplies merchant wholesalers |
| 811210 | Surveying instrument repair and maintenance services |
| 334519 | Surveying instruments manufacturing |
| 541360 | Surveying services, geophysical |
| 321999 | Surveyor's stakes, wood, manufacturing |
| 611699 | Survival training instruction |
| 238310 | Suspended ceiling installation |
| 315210 | Suspenders cut and sew apparel contractors |
| 315990 | Suspenders cut and sewn from purchased fabric (except apparel contractors) |
| 811114 | Suspension repair shops, automotive |
| 339113 | Sutures, surgical, manufacturing |
| 213112 | Swabbing oil or gas wells on a contract basis |
| 333517 | Swaging machines, metalworking, manufacturing |
| 487210 | Swamp buggy operation |
| 323120 | Swatches and samples, mounting for the trade |
| 315210 | Sweat bands cut and sew apparel contractors |

| | |
|---|---|
| 315250 | Sweat bands cut and sewn from purchased fabric (except apparel contractors) |
| 315120 | Sweat bands made in apparel knitting mills |
| 315210 | Sweat pants cut and sew apparel contractors |
| 315120 | Sweat pants made in apparel knitting mills |
| 315250 | Sweat pants, men's, boys', and unisex (i.e., sized without regard to gender), cut and sewn from purchased fabric (except apparel contractors) |
| 315250 | Sweat pants, women's, girls', and infants', cut and sewn from purchased fabric (except apparel contractors) |
| 315210 | Sweat suits cut and sew apparel contractors |
| 315120 | Sweat suits made in apparel knitting mills |
| 315250 | Sweat suits, men's and boys', cut and sewn from purchased fabric (except apparel contractors) |
| 315250 | Sweat suits, women's, girls', and infants', cut and sewn from purchased fabric (except apparel contractors) |
| 316110 | Sweatband leather manufacturing |
| 315210 | Sweater jackets cut and sew apparel contractors |
| 315120 | Sweater jackets made in apparel knitting mills |
| 315250 | Sweater jackets, men's and boys', cut and sewn from purchased fabric (except apparel contractors) |
| 315250 | Sweater jackets, women's, girls', and infants', cut and sewn from purchased fabric (except apparel contractors) |
| 315210 | Sweater vests cut and sew apparel contractors |
| 315120 | Sweater vests made in apparel knitting mills |
| 315250 | Sweater vests, men's and boys', cut and sewn from purchased fabric (except apparel contractors) |
| 315250 | Sweater vests, women's, girls', and infants', cut and sewn from purchased fabric (except apparel contractors) |
| 315210 | Sweaters cut and sew apparel contractors |
| 315120 | Sweaters made in apparel knitting mills |
| 315250 | Sweaters, men's and boys', cut and sewn from purchased fabric (except apparel contractors) |

| | |
|---|---|
| 315250 | Sweaters, women's, girls', and infants', cut and sewn from purchased fabric (except apparel contractors) |
| 315210 | Sweatshirts cut and sew apparel contractors |
| 315120 | Sweatshirts made in apparel knitting mills |
| 315250 | Sweatshirts, men's and boys', cut and sewn from purchased fabric (except apparel contractors) |
| 315250 | Sweatshirts, outerwear, unisex (sized without regard to gender), cut and sewn from purchased fabric (except apparel contractors) |
| 315250 | Sweatshirts, women's, girls', and infants', cut and sewn from purchased fabric (except apparel contractors) |
| 334515 | Sweep generators manufacturing |
| 334515 | Sweep oscillators manufacturing |
| 335210 | Sweepers, household-type electric vacuum, manufacturing |
| 325612 | Sweeping compounds, absorbent, manufacturing |
| 111219 | Sweet corn farming, field and seed production |
| 111219 | Sweet pepper farming, field, bedding plant and seed production |
| 115114 | Sweet potato curing |
| 111211 | Sweet potato farming, field and seed potato production |
| 311812 | Sweet yeast goods (except frozen) manufacturing |
| 311813 | Sweet yeast goods, frozen, manufacturing |
| 311999 | Sweetening syrups (except pure maple) manufacturing |
| 236220 | Swimming facility, indoor, construction |
| 611620 | Swimming instruction |
| 459999 | Swimming pool (above-ground) and supply stores |
| 325998 | Swimming pool chemical preparations manufacturing |
| 561790 | Swimming pool cleaning and maintenance services |
| 326199 | Swimming pool covers and liners, plastics, manufacturing |
| 333310 | Swimming pool filter systems manufacturing |
| 333414 | Swimming pool heaters manufacturing |
| 335139 | Swimming pool lighting fixtures manufacturing |
| 238990 | Swimming pool screen enclosure construction |
| 238990 | Swimming pool, outdoor, construction |

| | |
|---|---|
| 713940 | Swimming pools |
| 423910 | Swimming pools and equipment merchant wholesalers |
| 339920 | Swimming pools, above ground, manufacturing |
| 326199 | Swimming pools, fiberglass, manufacturing |
| 315210 | Swimsuits cut and sew apparel contractors |
| 315120 | Swimsuits made in apparel knitting mills |
| 315250 | Swimsuits, men's and boys', cut and sewn from purchased fabric (except apparel contractors) |
| 315250 | Swimsuits, women's, girls', and infants', cut and sewn from purchased fabric (except apparel contractors) |
| 458110 | Swimwear stores |
| 424350 | Swimwear, men's and boys', merchant wholesalers |
| 424350 | Swimwear, women's, children's, and infants', merchant wholesalers |
| 112210 | Swine farming |
| 311119 | Swine feed, complete, manufacturing |
| 311119 | Swine feed, supplements, concentrates, and premixes, manufacturing |
| 424520 | Swine merchant wholesalers |
| 335932 | Switch boxes, electrical wiring, manufacturing |
| 335931 | Switch cutouts manufacturing |
| 335313 | Switchboards and parts, power, manufacturing |
| 423610 | Switchboards, electrical distribution, merchant wholesalers |
| 335931 | Switches for electrical wiring (e.g., pressure, pushbutton, snap, tumbler) manufacturing |
| 334419 | Switches for electronic applications manufacturing |
| 335313 | Switches, electric power (except pushbutton, snap, solenoid, tumbler), manufacturing |
| 423610 | Switches, electrical, merchant wholesalers |
| 423690 | Switches, electronic, merchant wholesalers |
| 335931 | Switches, outlet box mounting-type, manufacturing |
| 334512 | Switches, pneumatic positioning remote, manufacturing |
| 334512 | Switches, thermostatic, manufacturing |
| 335313 | Switchgear and switchgear accessories manufacturing |

| | |
|---|---|
| 335313 | Switching equipment, power, manufacturing |
| 334210 | Switching equipment, telephone, manufacturing |
| 488210 | Switching services, railroad |
| 114111 | Swordfish fishing |
| 332215 | Swords, nonprecious and precious plated metal, manufacturing |
| 212313 | Syenite (except nepheline) crushed and broken stone mining and/or beneficiating |
| 212311 | Syenite (except nepheline) mining or quarrying |
| 212323 | Syenite, nepheline, mining and/or beneficiating |
| 212220 | Sylvanite mining and/or beneficiating |
| 711130 | Symphony orchestras |
| 813110 | Synagogues |
| 335312 | Synchronous condensers and timing motors, electric, manufacturing |
| 335312 | Synchronous motors manufacturing |
| 334515 | Synchroscopes manufacturing |
| 516210 | Syndicates, news |
| 339992 | Synthesizers, music, manufacturing |
| 311340 | Synthetic chocolate manufacturing |
| 314110 | Synthetic or artificial turf manufacturing |
| 423990 | Synthetic or artificial turf merchant wholesalers |
| 325212 | Synthetic rubber (i.e., vulcanizable elastomers) manufacturing |
| 424690 | Synthetic rubber merchant wholesalers |
| 327999 | Synthetic stones, for gem stones and industrial use, manufacturing |
| 325199 | Synthetic sweeteners (i.e., sweetening agents) manufacturing |
| 339112 | Syringes, hypodermic, manufacturing |
| 424490 | Syrup (except fountain) merchant wholesalers |
| 311313 | Syrup made from sugar beets |
| 311930 | Syrup, beverage, manufacturing |
| 311314 | Syrup, cane, manufacturing |
| 311351 | Syrup, chocolate, made from cacao beans |
| 311352 | Syrup, chocolate, made from purchased chocolate |
| 311999 | Syrup, corn (except wet milled), manufacturing |
| 311221 | Syrup, corn, made by wet milling |
| 311930 | Syrup, flavoring (except coffee based), manufacturing |
| 311920 | Syrup, flavoring, coffee based, manufacturing |
| 111998 | Syrup, pure maple (i.e., maple syrup reducing) |
| 311999 | Syrup, sweetening (except pure maple), manufacturing |
| 311999 | Syrup, table, artificially flavored, manufacturing |
| 424450 | Syrups, fountain (except soft drink), merchant wholesalers |
| 541512 | Systems integration design consulting services, computer |
| 541512 | Systems integration design services, computer |
| 532289 | Table and banquet accessory rental |
| 327110 | Table articles, coarse earthenware, manufacturing |
| 327110 | Table articles, earthenware, manufacturing |
| 327110 | Table articles, fine earthenware (i.e., whiteware), manufacturing |
| 327110 | Table articles, vitreous china, manufacturing |
| 332215 | Table cutlery, nonprecious and precious plated metal, manufacturing |
| 339910 | Table cutlery, precious metal, manufacturing |
| 335131 | Table lamps (i.e., lighting fixtures) manufacturing |
| 812331 | Table linen supply services |
| 311225 | Table oil made from purchased oils |
| 311221 | Table oil, corn, made by wet milling |
| 311942 | Table salt manufacturing |
| 327991 | Table tops, marble, manufacturing |
| 337215 | Table tops, wood, manufacturing |
| 314120 | Tablecloths (except paper) made from purchased materials |
| 313210 | Tablecloths made in broadwoven fabric mills |
| 313240 | Tablecloths made in lace mills |
| 313240 | Tablecloths made in warp or weft knitting mills |
| 322291 | Tablecloths, paper, made from purchased paper |
| 337214 | Tables (except wood), office-type, manufacturing |
| 337126 | Tables, metal household-type, manufacturing |
| 337122 | Tables, wood household-type, manufacturing |
| 337211 | Tables, wood, office-type, manufacturing |
| 334111 | Tablet computers manufacturing |

| | |
|---|---|
| 811210 | Tablet repair and maintenance services, without retailing new tablets |
| 322230 | Tablets (e.g., memo, note, writing) made from purchased paper |
| 322120 | Tablets (e.g., memo, note, writing) made in paper mills |
| 332999 | Tablets, metal, manufacturing |
| 423220 | Tableware (except disposable, plated, precious) merchant wholesalers |
| 327215 | Tableware made from purchased glass |
| 327212 | Tableware made in glass making plants |
| 532289 | Tableware rental |
| 424130 | Tableware, disposable, merchant wholesalers |
| 423940 | Tableware, precious and plated, merchant wholesalers |
| 327110 | Tableware, vitreous china, manufacturing |
| 334515 | Tachometer generators manufacturing |
| 424910 | Tack (e.g., harnesses, saddlery) merchant wholesalers |
| 459110 | Tack (e.g., harnesses, saddlery) shops |
| 321999 | Tackle blocks, wood, manufacturing |
| 459110 | Tackle shops (i.e., fishing) |
| 339920 | Tackle, fishing (except line, nets, seines), manufacturing |
| 423710 | Tacks merchant wholesalers |
| 331222 | Tacks, iron or steel, made in wire drawing plants |
| 332618 | Tacks, metal, made from purchased wire |
| 212210 | Taconite concentrates or agglomerates beneficiating |
| 212210 | Taconite ores mining and/or beneficiating |
| 334511 | Taffrail logs manufacturing |
| 213111 | Tailing in oil and gas field wells on a contract basis |
| 811490 | Tailor shops, alterations only |
| 315210 | Tailored dress and sport coats cut and sew apparel contractors |
| 315250 | Tailored dress and sport coats, men's and boys', cut and sewn from purchased fabric (except apparel contractors) |
| ****** | Tailors -- see specific apparel manufacturing |
| 332215 | Tailors' scissors, nonelectric, manufacturing |
| 423850 | Tailors' supplies merchant wholesalers |
| 445298 | Take-and-bake meal stores |
| 445298 | Take-and-bake pizza shops |
| 722513 | Takeout eating places |

| | |
|---|---|
| 212390 | Talc mining and/or beneficiating |
| 327992 | Talc processing beyond beneficiation |
| 325620 | Talcum powders manufacturing |
| 711410 | Talent agencies |
| 711410 | Talent agents |
| 541214 | Talent payment services |
| 325194 | Tall oil (except skimmings) manufacturing |
| 311611 | Tallow produced in a slaughtering plant |
| 311613 | Tallow produced in rendering plant |
| 334514 | Tally counters manufacturing |
| 334514 | Tallying meters (except clocks, electricity meters, watches) manufacturing |
| 333120 | Tampers, powered, manufacturing |
| 332994 | Tampion guns manufacturing |
| 111320 | Tangelo groves |
| 111320 | Tangerine groves |
| 332994 | Tank artillery manufacturing |
| 336211 | Tank bodies for trucks manufacturing |
| 562998 | Tank cleaning and disposal services, commercial or industrial |
| 562991 | Tank cleaning services, septic |
| 238990 | Tank lining contractors |
| 315210 | Tank tops cut and sew apparel contractors |
| 315120 | Tank tops, outerwear, made in apparel knitting mills |
| 315250 | Tank tops, outerwear, men's and boys', cut and sewn from purchased fabric (except apparel contractors) |
| 315120 | Tank tops, underwear, made in apparel knitting mills |
| 315250 | Tank tops, underwear, men's and boys', cut and sewn from purchased fabric (except apparel contractors) |
| 315250 | Tank tops, women's, girls', and infants', cut and sewn from purchased fabric (except apparel contractors) |
| 336212 | Tank trailers, liquid and dry bulk, manufacturing |
| 334514 | Tank truck meters manufacturing |
| 336211 | Tank trucks (e.g., fuel oil, milk, water) assembling on purchased chassis |
| 532411 | Tanker (boat) rental or leasing without crew |
| 484220 | Tanker trucking (e.g., chemical, juice, milk, petroleum), local |
| 484230 | Tanker trucking (e.g., chemical, juice, milk, petroleum), long-distance |

| | |
|---|---|
| 423860 | Tanks and tank components merchant wholesalers |
| 327390 | Tanks, concrete, manufacturing |
| 327110 | Tanks, flush, vitreous china, manufacturing |
| 332420 | Tanks, heavy gauge metal, manufacturing |
| 336992 | Tanks, military (including factory rebuilding), manufacturing |
| 333310 | Tanks, photographic developing, fixing, and washing, manufacturing |
| 423830 | Tanks, pressure, merchant wholesalers |
| 423510 | Tanks, storage metal, merchant wholesalers |
| 326199 | Tanks, storage, plastics or fiberglass, manufacturing |
| 321920 | Tanks, wood, coopered, manufacturing |
| 316110 | Tannery leather manufacturing |
| 333248 | Tannery machinery manufacturing |
| 325194 | Tannic acid (i.e., tannins) manufacturing |
| 325180 | Tanning agents, inorganic, manufacturing |
| 325199 | Tanning agents, synthetic organic, manufacturing |
| 316110 | Tanning and currying furs |
| 325194 | Tanning extracts and materials, natural, manufacturing |
| 812199 | Tanning salons |
| 212290 | Tantalite mining and/or beneficiating |
| 212290 | Tantalum ores mining and/or beneficiating |
| 331410 | Tantalum refining, primary |
| 711120 | Tap dance companies |
| 722410 | Tap rooms (i.e., drinking places) |
| 339940 | Tape dispensers manufacturing |
| 423420 | Tape dispensing machines merchant wholesalers |
| 512120 | Tape distribution for television |
| 332216 | Tape measures, metal, manufacturing |
| 334310 | Tape players and recorders, household-type, manufacturing |
| 423620 | Tape players and recorders, household-type, merchant wholesalers |
| 532210 | Tape recorder rental |
| 334112 | Tape storage units (e.g., drive backups), computer peripheral equipment, manufacturing |
| 512191 | Tape transfer service |
| 332991 | Tapered roller bearings manufacturing |
| 322230 | Tapes (e.g., adding machine, calculator, cash register) made from purchased paper |
| 313220 | Tapes weaving |
| 423690 | Tapes, blank, audio and video, merchant wholesalers |
| 424120 | Tapes, cellophane, merchant wholesalers |
| 334610 | Tapes, magnetic recording (i.e., audio, data, video), blank, manufacturing |
| 339113 | Tapes, medical adhesive, manufacturing |
| 423450 | Tapes, medical and surgical, merchant wholesalers |
| 313230 | Tapes, nonwoven fabric, manufacturing |
| 423990 | Tapes, prerecorded, audio or video, merchant wholesalers |
| 322220 | Tapes, pressure sensitive (e.g., cellophane, masking), gummed, made from purchased paper or other materials |
| 334519 | Tapes, surveyor's, manufacturing |
| 424310 | Tapes, textile, merchant wholesalers |
| 313320 | Tapes, varnished and coated (except magnetic), made from purchased fabric |
| 238310 | Taping and finishing drywall |
| 311221 | Tapioca manufacturing |
| 333517 | Tapping machines, metalworking, manufacturing |
| 333515 | Taps and dies (i.e., a machine tool accessory) manufacturing |
| 335931 | Taps, current, attachment plug and screw shell types, manufacturing |
| 316990 | Taps, shoe, leather, manufacturing |
| 325211 | Tar acid resins manufacturing |
| 324121 | Tar and asphalt paving mixtures made from purchased asphaltic materials |
| 325194 | Tar and tar oils made by distillation of wood |
| 325194 | Tar made by distillation of coal tar |
| 324110 | Tar made in petroleum refineries |
| 324122 | Tar paper made from purchased asphaltic materials and paper |
| 324122 | Tar paper, building and roofing, made from purchased paper |
| 322120 | Tar paper, building and roofing, made in paper mills |
| 324122 | Tar roofing cements and coatings made from purchased asphaltic materials |
| 211120 | Tar sands mining |
| 336411 | Target drones, aircraft, manufacturing |
| 336413 | Targets, trailer type, aircraft, manufacturing |
| 541614 | Tariff rate consulting services |

| | |
|---|---|
| 541614 | Tariff rate information services |
| 111219 | Taro farming, field and seed production |
| 314910 | Tarpaulins made from purchased fabrics |
| 423330 | Tarred felts merchant wholesalers |
| 237310 | Tarring roads |
| 311941 | Tartar sauce manufacturing |
| 325199 | Tartaric acid manufacturing |
| 325199 | Tartrates, not specified elsewhere by process, manufacturing |
| 314999 | Tassels manufacturing |
| 812199 | Tattoo parlors |
| 722410 | Taverns (i.e., drinking places) |
| 561440 | Tax collection services on a contract or fee basis |
| 541110 | Tax law attorneys' offices |
| 541110 | Tax law attorneys' private practices |
| 523910 | Tax liens dealing (i.e., acting as a principal in dealing tax liens to investors) |
| 541213 | Tax return preparation services |
| 921130 | Taxation departments |
| 541850 | Taxicab card advertising services |
| 485310 | Taxicab dispatch services |
| 485310 | Taxicab fleet operators |
| 423110 | Taxicab merchant wholesalers |
| 485310 | Taxicab organizations |
| 485310 | Taxicab owner-operators |
| 485310 | Taxicab services |
| 711510 | Taxidermists, independent |
| 423850 | Taxidermy supplies merchant wholesalers |
| 334514 | Taximeters manufacturing |
| 813319 | Taxpayers' advocacy organizations |
| 311920 | Tea (except herbal) manufacturing |
| 445298 | Tea and coffee (i.e., packaged) stores |
| 311920 | Tea blending |
| 111998 | Tea farming |
| 424490 | Tea merchant wholesalers |
| 311920 | Tea, herbal, manufacturing |
| 312111 | Tea, iced, manufacturing |
| 311920 | Tea, instant, manufacturing |
| 113210 | Teaberries gathering |
| 923110 | Teacher certification bureaus |
| 561311 | Teacher registries |
| 333310 | Teaching machines (e.g., flight simulators) manufacturing |
| 423490 | Teaching machines (except computers), electronic, merchant wholesalers |
| 332215 | Teakettles and coffee pots, fabricated metal (except electric, glass), manufacturing |
| 335210 | Teakettles, electric, manufacturing |
| 327212 | Teakettles, glass and glass ceramic, made in glass making plants |
| 315210 | Team athletic uniforms cut and sew apparel contractors |
| 315250 | Team athletic uniforms cut and sewn from purchased fabric (except apparel contractors) |
| 325199 | Tear gas manufacturing |
| 313310 | Teaseling fabrics |
| 325412 | Technetium medicinal preparations manufacturing |
| 561410 | Technical editing services |
| 327212 | Technical glassware and glass products, pressed or blown, made in glass making plants |
| 327215 | Technical glassware made from purchased glass |
| 513120 | Technical magazine and periodical publishers |
| 513120 | Technical magazine and periodical publishers (except exclusive Internet publishing) |
| 513120 | Technical magazine and periodical publishers and printing combined |
| 513120 | Technical magazine and periodical publishers, exclusively on Internet |
| 323111 | Technical magazines and periodicals commercial printing (except screen) without publishing |
| 323113 | Technical magazines and periodicals screen printing without publishing |
| 513130 | Technical manual and paperback book publishers |
| 513130 | Technical manual and paperback book publishers (except exclusive Internet publishing) |
| 513130 | Technical manual and paperback book publishers and printing combined |
| 323120 | Technical manual paper (books) binding without printing |
| 513130 | Technical manual publishers |
| 513130 | Technical manual publishers (except exclusive Internet publishing) |
| 513130 | Technical manual publishers, exclusively on Internet |

| | |
|---|---|
| 323117 | Technical manuals and papers (books) printing and binding without publishing |
| 323117 | Technical manuals and papers (books) printing without publishing |
| 711510 | Technical writers, independent |
| 315210 | Teddies cut and sew apparel contractors |
| 315250 | Teddies, women's and girls', cut and sewn from purchased fabric (except apparel contractors) |
| 624110 | Teen outreach services |
| 339114 | Teeth (except customized) manufacturing |
| 325611 | Teeth whiteners (e.g., pastes, gels) manufacturing |
| 339116 | Teeth, custom made in dental laboratories |
| 423450 | Teeth, dental, merchant wholesalers |
| 517112 | Telecommunications carriers, cellular telephone |
| 517111 | Telecommunications carriers, wired |
| 238210 | Telecommunications equipment and wiring (except transmission line) installation contractors |
| 423690 | Telecommunications equipment merchant wholesalers |
| 532490 | Telecommunications equipment rental or leasing |
| 541618 | Telecommunications management consulting services |
| 517121 | Telecommunications resellers (except satellite telecommunications and agents for wireless telecommunications services) |
| 423690 | Teleconferencing equipment, audio or video, merchant wholesalers |
| 561499 | Teleconferencing services |
| 812990 | Telegram services, singing |
| 423690 | Telegraph equipment merchant wholesalers |
| 561422 | Telemarketing bureaus |
| 561422 | Telemarketing services on a contract or fee basis |
| 334513 | Telemetering instruments, industrial process-type, manufacturing |
| 517810 | Telemetry and tracking system operations on a contract or fee basis |
| 334416 | Telephone and telegraph transformers, electronic component-type, manufacturing |
| 334210 | Telephone answering machines manufacturing |
| 423620 | Telephone answering machines merchant wholesalers |
| 561421 | Telephone answering services |
| 337215 | Telephone booths manufacturing |
| 561422 | Telephone call centers (e.g., customer service centers, telemarketing services) |
| 561421 | Telephone call forwarding services |
| 334210 | Telephone carrier line equipment manufacturing |
| 334210 | Telephone carrier switching equipment manufacturing |
| 517410 | Telephone communications carriers, satellite |
| 517112 | Telephone communications carriers, wireless (except satellite) |
| 517121 | Telephone communications resellers (except satellite telecommunications and agents for wireless telecommunications services) |
| 624190 | Telephone counseling services |
| 323111 | Telephone directories commercial printing (except screen) without publishing |
| 323113 | Telephone directories screen printing without publishing |
| 541870 | Telephone directory distribution services, door-to-door |
| 513140 | Telephone directory publishers |
| 513140 | Telephone directory publishers (except exclusive Internet publishing) |
| 513140 | Telephone directory publishers and printing combined |
| 513140 | Telephone directory publishers, exclusively on Internet |
| 238210 | Telephone equipment and building wiring installation |
| 423690 | Telephone equipment merchant wholesalers |
| 811210 | Telephone equipment repair and maintenance services without retailing new telephone equipment |
| 238210 | Telephone installation contractors |
| 237130 | Telephone line construction |
| 237130 | Telephone line stringing |
| 561422 | Telephone solicitation services on a contract or fee basis |
| 519290 | Telephone-based recorded information services |
| 334210 | Telephones (except cellular telephone) manufacturing |
| 423690 | Telephones merchant wholesalers |
| 334220 | Telephones, cellular (new and rebuilt), manufacturing |
| 334210 | Telephones, coin- or card-operated, manufacturing |

| | |
|---|---|
| 334118 | Teleprinters (i.e., computer terminals) manufacturing |
| 512191 | Teleproduction services |
| 333310 | Telescopes manufacturing |
| 334310 | Television (TV) sets manufacturing |
| 541840 | Television advertising representatives (i.e., independent of media owners) |
| 449210 | Television and radio stores |
| 516210 | Television broadcasting networks |
| 516120 | Television broadcasting stations |
| 321999 | Television cabinets (i.e., housings), wood, manufacturing |
| 423410 | Television cameras merchant wholesalers |
| 512110 | Television commercial production |
| 561311 | Television employment agencies |
| 513120 | Television guide publishers |
| 513120 | Television guide publishers (except exclusive Internet publishing) |
| 513120 | Television guide publishers and printing combined |
| 513120 | Television guide publishers, exclusively on Internet |
| 323111 | Television guides commercial printing (except screen) without publishing |
| 323113 | Television guides screen printing without publishing |
| 326199 | Television housings, plastics, manufacturing |
| 517111 | Television operations, closed-circuit |
| 334419 | Television picture tubes manufacturing |
| 711510 | Television producers, independent |
| 532210 | Television rental |
| 811210 | Television repair services without retailing new televisions |
| 423620 | Television sets merchant wholesalers |
| 512110 | Television show production |
| 512120 | Television show syndicators |
| 236220 | Television station construction |
| 516210 | Television subscription services |
| 332312 | Television tower sections, fabricated structural metal, manufacturing |
| 334220 | Television transmitting antennas and ground equipment manufacturing |
| 237130 | Television transmitting tower construction |
| 334220 | Television, closed-circuit equipment, manufacturing |
| 212220 | Telluride (gold) mining and/or beneficiating |
| 331410 | Tellurium refining, primary |
| 813319 | Temperance organizations |
| 238210 | Temperature control system installation |
| 334512 | Temperature controls, automatic, residential and commercial-types, manufacturing |
| 334513 | Temperature instruments, industrial process-type (except glass and bimetal thermometers), manufacturing |
| 334512 | Temperature sensors for motor windings manufacturing |
| 327215 | Tempered glass made from purchased glass |
| 332811 | Tempering metals and metal products for the trade |
| 331110 | Template, made in iron and steel mills, manufacturing |
| 334519 | Templates, drafting, manufacturing |
| 339115 | Temples and fronts (i.e., eyeglass frames), ophthalmic, manufacturing |
| 813110 | Temples, religious |
| 561320 | Temporary employment services |
| 561320 | Temporary help services |
| 624221 | Temporary housing for families of medical patients |
| 624221 | Temporary shelters (e.g., battered women's, homeless, runaway youth) |
| 561320 | Temporary staffing services |
| 713950 | Ten pin bowling alleys |
| 713950 | Ten pin bowling centers |
| 813319 | Tenants' advocacy associations |
| 813990 | Tenants' associations (except advocacy) |
| 813319 | Tenants' associations, advocacy |
| 713940 | Tennis club facilities |
| 236220 | Tennis court, indoor, construction |
| 713940 | Tennis courts |
| 237990 | Tennis courts, outdoor, construction |
| 423910 | Tennis equipment and supplies merchant wholesalers |
| 339920 | Tennis goods (e.g., balls, frames, rackets) manufacturing |
| 611620 | Tennis instruction, camps or schools |
| 711219 | Tennis professionals, independent (i.e., participating in sports events) |
| 315210 | Tennis shirts cut and sew apparel contractors |
| 315120 | Tennis shirts made in apparel knitting mills |

| | |
|---|---|
| 315250 | Tennis shirts, men's and boys', cut and sewn from purchased fabric (except apparel contractors) |
| 315250 | Tennis shirts, women's, girls', and infants', cut and sewn from purchased fabric (except apparel contractors) |
| 315210 | Tennis skirts cut and sew apparel contractors |
| 315120 | Tennis skirts made in apparel knitting mills |
| 315250 | Tennis skirts, women's, girls', and infants', cut and sewn from purchased fabric (except apparel contractors) |
| 334510 | TENS (transcutaneous electrical nerve stimulator) manufacturing |
| 334519 | Tensile strength testing equipment manufacturing |
| 321999 | Tent poles, wood, manufacturing |
| 336214 | Tent trailers (hard top and soft top) manufacturing |
| 532284 | Tent, camping, rental |
| 532289 | Tent, party, rental |
| 424990 | Tents (except camping) merchant wholesalers |
| 314910 | Tents made from purchased fabrics |
| 335931 | Terminals and connectors for electrical devices manufacturing |
| 334118 | Terminals, computer, manufacturing |
| 424710 | Terminals, petroleum, merchant wholesalers |
| 561710 | Termite control services |
| 325320 | Termite poisons manufacturing |
| 331110 | Terneplate made in iron and steel mills |
| 423510 | Terneplate merchant wholesalers |
| 331110 | Ternes, iron or steel, long or short, made in iron and steel mills |
| 325199 | Terpineol manufacturing |
| 423320 | Terra cotta merchant wholesalers |
| 114119 | Terrapin fishing |
| 238340 | Terrazzo and tile refinishing |
| 238340 | Terrazzo contractors |
| 327390 | Terrazzo products, precast (except brick, block and pipe), manufacturing |
| 313210 | Terry broadwoven fabrics weaving |
| 325199 | Tert-butylated bis (p-phenoxyphenyl) ether fluid manufacturing |
| 238910 | Test boring for construction |
| 611710 | Test development and evaluation services, educational |
| 213114 | Test drilling for metal mining on a contract basis |
| 213115 | Test drilling for nonmetallic minerals mining (except fuel) on a contract basis |
| 334515 | Test equipment for electronic and electrical circuits and equipment manufacturing |
| 334515 | Test sets, ignition harness, manufacturing |
| 525920 | Testamentary trusts |
| 334519 | Testers for checking hydraulic controls on aircraft manufacturing |
| 423830 | Testing and measuring equipment, electrical (except automotive), merchant wholesalers |
| 423120 | Testing and measuring equipment, electrical, automotive, merchant wholesalers |
| 334519 | Testing equipment (e.g., abrasion, shearing strength, tensile strength, torsion) manufacturing |
| 541380 | Testing laboratories (except medical, veterinary) |
| 621511 | Testing laboratories, medical |
| 541940 | Testing laboratories, veterinary |
| 541940 | Testing services for veterinarians |
| 488190 | Testing services, aircraft |
| 611710 | Testing services, educational |
| 333993 | Testing, weighing, inspecting, packaging machinery manufacturing |
| 325199 | Tetrachloroethylene manufacturing |
| 325411 | Tetracycline, uncompounded, manufacturing |
| 325199 | Tetraethyl lead manufacturing |
| 325920 | Tetryl explosive materials manufacturing |
| 424920 | Textbooks merchant wholesalers |
| 323117 | Textbooks printing and binding without publishing |
| 323117 | Textbooks printing without publishing |
| 314910 | Textile bags made from purchased woven or knitted materials |
| 424990 | Textile bags merchant wholesalers |
| 313210 | Textile broadwoven fabrics mills |
| 541490 | Textile design services |
| 325613 | Textile finishing assistants manufacturing |
| 333248 | Textile finishing machinery (e.g., bleaching, dyeing, mercerizing, printing) manufacturing |
| 314999 | Textile fire hose made from purchased material |
| 561910 | Textile folding and packaging services |

| | |
|---|---|
| 327212 | Textile glass fibers made in glass making plants |
| 327110 | Textile guides, porcelain, manufacturing |
| 316990 | Textile leathers (e.g., apron picker leather, mill strapping) manufacturing |
| 423830 | Textile machinery and equipment merchant wholesalers |
| 532490 | Textile machinery rental or leasing |
| 811310 | Textile machinery repair and maintenance services |
| 333248 | Textile making machinery manufacturing |
| 236210 | Textile mill construction |
| 313210 | Textile mills, broadwoven fabrics |
| 313220 | Textile mills, narrow woven fabric |
| 313220 | Textile narrow woven fabric mills |
| 325910 | Textile printing inks manufacturing |
| 333248 | Textile printing machinery manufacturing |
| 313210 | Textile products (except apparel) made in broadwoven fabric mills |
| 313240 | Textile products (except apparel) made in lace mills |
| 313220 | Textile products (except apparel) made in narrow woven fabric mills |
| 313240 | Textile products (except apparel) made in warp or weft knitting mills |
| 313310 | Textile products finishing |
| 325613 | Textile scouring agents manufacturing |
| 423930 | Textile waste merchant wholesalers |
| 313320 | Textile waterproofing |
| 424310 | Textiles (except burlap, felt) merchant wholesalers |
| 325220 | Texturizing cellulosic yarn made in the same establishment |
| 333248 | Texturizing machinery for textiles manufacturing |
| 325220 | Texturizing noncellulosic yarn made in the same establishment |
| 313110 | Texturizing purchased yarn |
| 212290 | Thallium mining and/or beneficiating |
| 711110 | Theater companies (except dance) |
| 711110 | Theater companies (except dance), amateur |
| 711120 | Theater companies, dance |
| 236220 | Theater construction |
| 423410 | Theater equipment (except seats) merchant wholesalers |
| 711310 | Theater festival managers with facilities |
| 711320 | Theater festival managers without facilities |

| | |
|---|---|
| 711310 | Theater festival organizers with facilities |
| 711320 | Theater festival organizers without facilities |
| 711310 | Theater festival promoters with facilities |
| 711320 | Theater festival promoters without facilities |
| 711310 | Theater operators |
| 531120 | Theater property rental or leasing, not operating theater |
| 611610 | Theater schools |
| 337127 | Theater seating manufacturing |
| 423210 | Theater seats merchant wholesalers |
| 711120 | Theaters, dance |
| 711110 | Theaters, dinner |
| 711110 | Theaters, live theatrical production (except dance) |
| 512131 | Theaters, motion picture (except drive-in) |
| 512132 | Theaters, motion picture, drive-in |
| 512131 | Theaters, motion picture, indoor |
| 711110 | Theaters, musical |
| 512132 | Theaters, outdoor motion picture |
| 711320 | Theatrical booking agencies (except motion picture) |
| 315210 | Theatrical costumes cut and sew apparel contractors |
| 315250 | Theatrical costumes cut and sewn from purchased fabric (except apparel contractors) |
| 711120 | Theatrical dance productions, live |
| 561311 | Theatrical employment agencies |
| 532490 | Theatrical equipment (except costumes) rental or leasing |
| 711310 | Theatrical production managers with facilities |
| 711320 | Theatrical production managers without facilities |
| 711310 | Theatrical production organizers with facilities |
| 711320 | Theatrical production organizers without facilities |
| 711310 | Theatrical production promoters with facilities |
| 711320 | Theatrical production promoters without facilities |
| 711110 | Theatrical repertory companies |
| 711110 | Theatrical road companies |
| 339999 | Theatrical scenery manufacturing |
| 711110 | Theatrical stock companies |
| 711410 | Theatrical talent agents |

| | |
|---|---|
| 561599 | Theatrical ticket offices |
| 532281 | Theatrical wardrobe and costume rental |
| 334290 | Theft prevention signaling devices (e.g., door entrance annunciation, holdup signaling devices, personal duress signaling devices), manufacturing |
| 713110 | Theme parks, amusement |
| 325411 | Theobromine and derivatives (i.e., basic chemicals) manufacturing |
| 333310 | Theodolites manufacturing |
| 334519 | Theodolites, surveying, manufacturing |
| 611310 | Theological seminaries offering baccalaureate or graduate degrees |
| 334517 | Therapeutic X-ray apparatus and tubes (e.g., medical, industrial, research) manufacturing |
| ****** | Therapists' offices -- see type |
| 423450 | Therapy equipment merchant wholesalers |
| 334516 | Thermal analysis instruments, laboratory-type, manufacturing |
| 334516 | Thermal conductivity instruments and sensors manufacturing |
| 334513 | Thermal conductivity instruments, industrial process-type, manufacturing |
| 326140 | Thermal insulation, polystyrene foam, manufacturing |
| 237130 | Thermal power plant construction |
| 541380 | Thermal testing laboratories or services |
| 423330 | Thermal wrap, house, merchant wholesalers |
| 334416 | Thermistors manufacturing |
| 334513 | Thermistors, industrial process-type, manufacturing |
| 334519 | Thermocouples (except industrial process, aircraft type, glass vacuum) manufacturing |
| 334512 | Thermocouples, glass vacuum, manufacturing |
| 334513 | Thermocouples, industrial process-type, manufacturing |
| 335999 | Thermoelectric generators manufacturing |
| 333993 | Thermoform, blister, and skin packaging machinery manufacturing |
| 333248 | Thermoforming machinery for plastics manufacturing |
| 334516 | Thermogravimetric analyzers manufacturing |
| 334519 | Thermometer, liquid-in-glass and bimetal types (except medical), manufacturing |
| 423450 | Thermometers merchant wholesalers |

| | |
|---|---|
| 334513 | Thermometers, filled system industrial process-type, manufacturing |
| 339112 | Thermometers, medical, manufacturing |
| 325211 | Thermoplastic resins and plastics materials manufacturing |
| 325211 | Thermosetting plastics resins manufacturing |
| 325212 | Thermosetting vulcanizable elastomers manufacturing |
| 332911 | Thermostatic traps, industrial-type, manufacturing |
| 334512 | Thermostats (e.g., air-conditioning, appliance, comfort heating, refrigeration) manufacturing |
| 336390 | Thermostats, automotive, truck, and bus, manufacturing |
| 334519 | Thickness gauging instruments, ultrasonic, manufacturing |
| 332999 | Thimbles for wire rope manufacturing |
| 334413 | Thin film integrated circuits manufacturing |
| 333242 | Thin layer deposition equipment, semiconductor, manufacturing |
| 115112 | Thinning of crops, mechanical and chemical |
| 325180 | Thiocyanate manufacturing |
| 325199 | Thioglycolic acid manufacturing |
| 325212 | Thiol rubber manufacturing |
| 212290 | Thorite mining and/or beneficiating |
| 212290 | Thorium ores mining and/or beneficiating |
| 711212 | Thoroughbred racetracks |
| 424310 | Thread (except industrial) merchant wholesalers |
| 333515 | Thread cutting dies (i.e., a machine tool accessory) manufacturing |
| 313310 | Thread finishing |
| 333248 | Thread making machinery manufacturing |
| 313110 | Thread mills |
| 333517 | Thread rolling machines, metalworking, manufacturing |
| 313110 | Thread, all fibers, manufacturing |
| 423840 | Thread, industrial, merchant wholesalers |
| 326299 | Thread, rubber (except fabric covered), manufacturing |
| 333517 | Threading machines, metalworking, manufacturing |
| 423830 | Threading tools merchant wholesalers |
| 115113 | Threshing service |
| 551112 | Thrift holding companies |

| | |
|---|---|
| 459510 | Thrift shops, used merchandise |
| 333248 | Through-hole machinery, printed circuit board loading, manufacturing |
| 325220 | Throwing cellulosic yarn made in the same establishment |
| 325220 | Throwing noncellulosic yarn made in the same establishment |
| 313110 | Throwing purchased yarn |
| 334519 | Thrust power indicators, aircraft engine, manufacturing |
| 332991 | Thrust roller bearings manufacturing |
| 334413 | Thyristors manufacturing |
| 325412 | Thyroid preparations manufacturing |
| 325320 | Tick powders or sprays manufacturing |
| 561599 | Ticket (e.g., airline, bus, cruise ship, sports, theatrical) offices |
| 561599 | Ticket (e.g., airline, bus, cruise ship, sports, theatrical) sales offices |
| 561599 | Ticket (e.g., amusement, sports, theatrical) agencies |
| 561599 | Ticket (e.g., amusement, sports, theatrical) sales agencies |
| 561599 | Ticket agencies, amusement |
| 561599 | Ticket agencies, sports |
| 561599 | Ticket agencies, theatrical |
| 561599 | Ticket offices for foreign cruise ship companies |
| 331110 | Tie plates, iron or steel, made in iron and steel mills |
| 458110 | Tie shops |
| 331222 | Tie wires made in wire drawing plants |
| 315210 | Ties cut and sew apparel contractors |
| 315120 | Ties made in apparel knitting mills |
| 327390 | Ties, concrete, railroad, manufacturing |
| 315990 | Ties, men's and boys' hand sewn (except apparel contractors), manufacturing |
| 321113 | Ties, railroad, made from logs or bolts |
| 321114 | Ties, wood railroad bridge, cross, and switch, treating |
| 321113 | Ties, wood, made from logs or bolts |
| 423990 | Ties, wood, merchant wholesalers |
| 315120 | Tights knitting or knitting and finishing |
| 112511 | Tilapia production |
| 238340 | Tile (except resilient) contractors |
| 238340 | Tile (except resilient) laying and setting |
| 325520 | Tile adhesives manufacturing |
| 333994 | Tile making kilns manufacturing |
| 333248 | Tile making machinery (except kilns) manufacturing |
| 444180 | Tile stores, ceramic |
| 327120 | Tile, ceramic wall and floor, manufacturing |
| 327120 | Tile, clay, refractory, manufacturing |
| 327120 | Tile, clay, structural, manufacturing |
| 321999 | Tile, cork, manufacturing |
| 327120 | Tile, roofing and drain, clay, manufacturing |
| 327120 | Tile, sewer, clay, manufacturing |
| 423320 | Tile, structural clay (except refractory and clay roofing tile) merchant wholesalers |
| 114111 | Tilefish fishing |
| 326199 | Tiles, floor (i.e., linoleum, rubber, vinyl), manufacturing |
| 423820 | Tillers, farm and garden, merchant wholesalers |
| 333112 | Tillers, lawn and garden-type, manufacturing |
| 423990 | Timber and timber products (except lumber) merchant wholesalers |
| 113310 | Timber piling |
| 113310 | Timber pole cutting |
| 237990 | Timber removal, underwater |
| 113110 | Timber tract operations |
| 115310 | Timber valuation |
| 321114 | Timber, structural, treating |
| 321113 | Timbers, made from logs or bolts |
| 321215 | Timbers, structural, glue laminated or pre-engineered wood, manufacturing |
| 334519 | Time clocks and time recording devices manufacturing |
| 334513 | Time cycle and program controllers, industrial process-type, manufacturing |
| 334519 | Time locks manufacturing |
| 323111 | Time planners/organizers and refills manufacturing |
| 334512 | Time program controls, air-conditioning systems, manufacturing |
| 423420 | Time recording machines merchant wholesalers |
| 334519 | Time stamps containing clock mechanisms manufacturing |
| 335313 | Time switches, electrical switchgear apparatus, manufacturing |
| 334519 | Timers for industrial use, clockwork mechanism, manufacturing |
| 236117 | Time-share condominium construction for-sale builders |
| 236115 | Time-share condominium construction general contractors |

| | |
|---|---|
| 561599 | Time-share exchange services, condominium |
| 326220 | Timing belt, rubber or plastics, manufacturing |
| 335314 | Timing devices, mechanical and solid-state (except clockwork), manufacturing |
| 336310 | Timing gears and chains, automotive and truck gasoline engine, manufacturing |
| 334519 | Timing mechanisms, clockwork, manufacturing |
| 335312 | Timing motors, synchronous, electric, manufacturing |
| 331491 | Tin and tin alloy bar, pipe, rod, sheet, strip, and tubing made from purchased metals or scrap |
| 423510 | Tin and tin alloy primary forms merchant wholesalers |
| 331410 | Tin base alloys made in primary tin smelting and refining mills |
| 325180 | Tin chloride manufacturing |
| 325180 | Tin compounds, not specified elsewhere by process, manufacturing |
| 212290 | Tin metal concentrates beneficiating |
| 212290 | Tin metal ores mining and/or beneficiating |
| 325180 | Tin oxide manufacturing |
| 332431 | Tin plate cans, light gauge metal, manufacturing |
| 423510 | Tin plate merchant wholesalers |
| 331492 | Tin recovering from scrap and/or alloying purchased metals |
| 331410 | Tin refining, primary |
| 331491 | Tin rolling, drawing, or extruding purchased metals or scrap |
| 325180 | Tin salts manufacturing |
| 325412 | Tincture of iodine preparations manufacturing |
| 332999 | Tinfoil not made in rolling mills |
| 331110 | Tin-free steel made in iron and steel mills |
| 332216 | Tinners' snips manufacturing |
| 331110 | Tinplate made in iron and steel mills |
| 339999 | Tinsel manufacturing |
| 325998 | Tint and dye preparations, household-type (except hair), manufacturing |
| 325620 | Tints, dyes, and rinses, hair, manufacturing |
| 212114 | Tipple operation, bituminous coal mining and/or beneficiating |
| 236210 | Tipple, mining, construction |
| 316990 | Tips, shoe, leather, manufacturing |
| 423130 | Tire and tube repair materials merchant wholesalers |
| 332618 | Tire chains made from purchased wire |
| 314994 | Tire cord and fabric, all materials, manufacturing |
| 336360 | Tire covers made from purchased fabric |
| 441340 | Tire dealers, automotive |
| 325998 | Tire inflators, aerosol, manufacturing |
| 333248 | Tire making machinery manufacturing |
| 333310 | Tire mounting machines, motor vehicle, manufacturing |
| 333248 | Tire recapping machinery manufacturing |
| 423830 | Tire recapping machinery merchant wholesalers |
| 326211 | Tire repair materials manufacturing |
| 811198 | Tire repair shops (except retreading), automotive |
| 326212 | Tire retreading, recapping or rebuilding |
| 333248 | Tire shredding machinery manufacturing |
| 423130 | Tire tubes, motor vehicle, merchant wholesalers |
| 326211 | Tires (e.g., pneumatic, semi-pneumatic, solid rubber) manufacturing |
| 423130 | Tires, new, motor vehicle, merchant wholesalers |
| 326199 | Tires, plastics, manufacturing |
| 423930 | Tires, scrap, merchant wholesalers |
| 423130 | Tires, used (except scrap), merchant wholesalers |
| 111421 | Tissue culture farming |
| 322120 | Tissue paper stock manufacturing |
| 424130 | Tissue paper, toilet and facial, merchant wholesalers |
| 327110 | Titania porcelain insulators manufacturing |
| 212290 | Titaniferous-magnetite ores, valued chiefly for titanium content, mining and/or beneficiating |
| 331491 | Titanium and titanium alloy bar, billet, rod, sheet, strip, and tubing made from purchased metals or scrap |
| 325130 | Titanium based pigments manufacturing |
| 331529 | Titanium castings (except die-castings), unfinished, manufacturing |
| 212290 | Titanium concentrates beneficiating |
| 331523 | Titanium die-castings, unfinished, manufacturing |
| 325180 | Titanium dioxide manufacturing |
| 332112 | Titanium forgings made from purchased metals, unfinished |

| | |
|---|---|
| 212290 | Titanium ores mining and/or beneficiating |
| 331410 | Titanium refining, primary |
| 331491 | Titanium rolling, drawing, or extruding purchased metals or scrap |
| 541191 | Title abstract companies, real estate |
| 541191 | Title companies, real estate |
| 524127 | Title insurance carriers, real estate, direct |
| 541191 | Title search companies, real estate |
| 519290 | Title search services (except real estate) |
| 512191 | Titling of motion picture film or video |
| 334516 | Titrimeters manufacturing |
| 325920 | TNT (trinitrotoluene) manufacturing |
| 335210 | Toaster ovens, household-type electric, manufacturing |
| 423620 | Toasters, electric, merchant wholesalers |
| 335210 | Toasters, household-type electric, manufacturing |
| 424940 | Tobacco (except leaf) merchant wholesalers |
| 111910 | Tobacco farming, field and seed production |
| 115114 | Tobacco grading |
| 333111 | Tobacco harvester machines manufacturing |
| 321920 | Tobacco hogshead stock, manufacturing |
| 321920 | Tobacco hogsheads, manufacturing |
| 312230 | Tobacco leaf processing and aging |
| 339999 | Tobacco pipes manufacturing |
| 316990 | Tobacco pouches (except metal) manufacturing |
| 339910 | Tobacco pouches, precious metal, manufacturing |
| 333248 | Tobacco processing machinery (except farm-type) manufacturing |
| 312230 | Tobacco products (e.g., chewing, smoking, snuff) manufacturing |
| 424940 | Tobacco products merchant wholesalers |
| 312230 | Tobacco products, imitation, manufacturing |
| 312230 | Tobacco sheeting services |
| 312230 | Tobacco stemming and redrying |
| 459991 | Tobacco stores |
| 424590 | Tobacco, leaf, merchant wholesalers |
| 339920 | Toboggans manufacturing |
| 316990 | Toe caps, leather, manufacturing |
| 311340 | Toffee manufacturing |
| 311991 | Tofu (i.e., bean curd) (except frozen desserts) manufacturing |
| 311520 | Tofu frozen desserts manufacturing |
| 332722 | Toggle bolts, metal, manufacturing |
| 325612 | Toilet bowl cleaners manufacturing |
| 423720 | Toilet bowls and tanks merchant wholesalers |
| 332999 | Toilet fixtures, metal, manufacturing |
| 326191 | Toilet fixtures, plastics, manufacturing |
| 327110 | Toilet fixtures, vitreous china, manufacturing |
| 316990 | Toilet kits and cases (except metal) manufacturing |
| 339910 | Toilet kits and cases, precious metal, manufacturing |
| 322291 | Toilet paper made from purchased paper |
| 322120 | Toilet paper made in paper mills |
| 325620 | Toilet preparations (e.g., cosmetics, deodorants, perfumes) manufacturing |
| 424210 | Toilet preparations merchant wholesalers |
| 562991 | Toilet renting and/or servicing, portable |
| 321999 | Toilet seats, wood, manufacturing |
| 325611 | Toilet soaps manufacturing |
| 424210 | Toilet soaps merchant wholesalers |
| 424130 | Toilet tissue merchant wholesalers |
| 332999 | Toilet ware, precious plated metal, manufacturing |
| 325620 | Toilet water manufacturing |
| 424210 | Toiletries merchant wholesalers |
| 488490 | Toll road operations, highway |
| 334210 | Toll switching equipment, telephone, manufacturing |
| 325110 | Toluene made from refined petroleum or liquid hydrocarbons |
| 324110 | Toluene made in petroleum refineries |
| 325194 | Toluidines manufacturing |
| 111219 | Tomato farming (except under cover), field, bedding plant and seed production |
| 111419 | Tomato farming, grown under cover |
| 333111 | Tomato harvesting machines manufacturing |
| 423990 | Tombstones merchant wholesalers |
| 325992 | Toner cartridges manufacturing |
| 424120 | Toner cartridges merchant wholesalers |
| 325992 | Toner cartridges rebuilding |
| 325130 | Toners (except electrostatic, photographic) manufacturing |

| | |
|---|---|
| 325992 | Toners, electrostatic and photographic, manufacturing |
| 339113 | Tongue depressors manufacturing |
| 316990 | Tongues, boot and shoe, leather, manufacturing |
| 339112 | Tonometers, medical, manufacturing |
| 332439 | Tool boxes, light gauge metal, manufacturing |
| 321920 | Tool chests, wood, manufacturing |
| 321999 | Tool handles, wood, turned and shaped, manufacturing |
| 541420 | Tool industrial design services |
| 532289 | Tool rental or leasing for home use |
| 337127 | Tool stands, factory, manufacturing |
| 331110 | Tool steel made in iron and steel mills |
| 444140 | Tool stores, power and hand (except outdoor) |
| 811411 | Tool, home and garden, sharpening and repair services without retailing new home and garden tools |
| 333515 | Toolholders (i.e., a machine tool accessory) manufacturing |
| 333515 | Tools and accessories for machine tools manufacturing |
| 423120 | Tools and equipment, motor vehicle, merchant wholesalers |
| 339114 | Tools, dentists', manufacturing |
| 423710 | Tools, hand (except motor vehicle, machinists' precision tools), merchant wholesalers |
| 332216 | Tools, hand, metal blade (e.g., putty knives, scrapers, screwdrivers) |
| 333991 | Tools, handheld power-driven, manufacturing |
| 332216 | Tools, handheld, nonpowered (except kitchen-type), manufacturing |
| 423830 | Tools, machinists' precision, merchant wholesalers |
| 332216 | Tools, woodworking edge (e.g., augers, bits, countersinks), manufacturing |
| 339994 | Toothbrushes (except electric) manufacturing |
| 424210 | Toothbrushes (except electric) merchant wholesalers |
| 335210 | Toothbrushes, electric, manufacturing |
| 423620 | Toothbrushes, electric, merchant wholesalers |
| 424210 | Toothpastes merchant wholesalers |
| 325611 | Toothpastes, gels, and tooth powders manufacturing |
| 321999 | Toothpicks, wood, manufacturing |
| 316990 | Top lifts, boot and shoe, leather, manufacturing |
| 212323 | Topaz, non-gem, mining and/or beneficiating |
| 315210 | Topcoats cut and sew apparel contractors |
| 315250 | Topcoats, men's and boys', cut and sewn from purchased fabric (except apparel contractors) |
| 541370 | Topographic mapping services |
| 541370 | Topographic surveying services |
| 424490 | Toppings (except fountain) merchant wholesalers |
| 424450 | Toppings, fountain, merchant wholesalers |
| 336390 | Tops, convertible automotive, manufacturing |
| 484220 | Top-soil hauling, local |
| 332994 | Torpedo tubes manufacturing |
| 332993 | Torpedoes manufacturing |
| 336350 | Torque converters, automotive, truck, and bus, manufacturing |
| 335312 | Torque motors, electric, manufacturing |
| 332613 | Torsion bar, heavy gauge metal, manufacturing |
| 334519 | Torsion testing equipment manufacturing |
| 311919 | Tortilla chips manufacturing |
| 311830 | Tortillas manufacturing |
| 334514 | Totalizing fluid meters manufacturing |
| 334514 | Totalizing meters (except aircraft), consumption registering, manufacturing |
| 423690 | Touch-screen displays (except computer monitors) merchant wholesalers |
| 339999 | Toupees manufacturing |
| 424990 | Toupees merchant wholesalers |
| 487110 | Tour bus, scenic and sightseeing, operation |
| 561520 | Tour operators (i.e., arranging and assembling tours) |
| 561591 | Tourism bureaus |
| 926110 | Tourism development offices, government |
| 721199 | Tourist courts |
| 713990 | Tourist guide services |
| 721199 | Tourist homes |
| 561591 | Tourist information bureaus |
| 721110 | Tourist lodges |
| 336413 | Tow targets, aircraft, manufacturing |
| 488410 | Tow truck services |
| 336211 | Tow trucks (including tilt and load) assembling on purchased chassis |

| | |
|---|---|
| 336611 | Towboat building and repairing |
| 532411 | Towboat rental or leasing without crew |
| 812331 | Towel (except shop, wiping) supply services |
| 327110 | Towel bar holders, vitreous china and earthenware, manufacturing |
| 812332 | Towel supply services, shop or wiping |
| 325620 | Towelettes, premoistened, manufacturing |
| 313210 | Towels and washcloths made in broadwoven fabric mills |
| 313240 | Towels and washcloths made in warp or weft knitting mills |
| 423220 | Towels and washcloths merchant wholesalers |
| 314120 | Towels or washcloths made from purchased fabrics |
| 423840 | Towels, industrial, merchant wholesalers |
| 322291 | Towels, paper, made from purchased paper |
| 322120 | Towels, paper, made in paper mills |
| 423450 | Towels, surgical, merchant wholesalers |
| 237130 | Tower, power distribution and communication, construction |
| 336390 | Towing bars and systems manufacturing |
| 483211 | Towing service, inland waters (except on Great Lakes system) |
| 488410 | Towing services, motor vehicle |
| 236115 | Town house (i.e., single-family type) construction by general contractors |
| 236117 | Town house construction for-sale builders |
| 531110 | Town house rental or leasing |
| 541320 | Town planners' offices |
| 541320 | Town planning services |
| 562910 | Toxic material abatement services |
| 562910 | Toxic material removal contractors |
| 621511 | Toxicology health laboratories |
| 325414 | Toxoids (e.g., diphtheria, tetanus) manufacturing |
| 339930 | Toy furniture and household-type equipment manufacturing |
| 423920 | Toy furniture merchant wholesalers |
| 459120 | Toy stores |
| 459120 | Toy stores, electronic |
| 423920 | Toys (including electronic) merchant wholesalers |
| 339930 | Toys manufacturing |
| 333515 | Tracer and tapering machine tool attachments manufacturing |
| 332993 | Tracer igniters, ammunition (i.e., more than 30 mm., more than 1.18 inch), manufacturing |
| 339920 | Track and field athletic equipment (except apparel, footwear) manufacturing |
| 335131 | Track lighting fixtures and equipment, residential, electric, manufacturing |
| 484220 | Tracked vehicle freight transportation, local |
| 484230 | Tracked vehicle freight transportation, long-distance |
| 487110 | Tracked vehicle sightseeing operation |
| 339113 | Traction apparatus manufacturing |
| 811310 | Tractor, farm or construction equipment repair and maintenance services |
| 532490 | Tractor, farm, rental or leasing |
| 532490 | Tractor, garden, rental or leasing |
| 811411 | Tractor, lawn and garden, repair and maintenance services without retailing new lawn and garden tractors |
| 333120 | Tractors and attachments, construction-type, manufacturing |
| 333111 | Tractors and attachments, farm-type, manufacturing |
| 333112 | Tractors and attachments, lawn and garden-type, manufacturing |
| 333120 | Tractors, crawler, manufacturing |
| 423820 | Tractors, farm and garden, merchant wholesalers |
| 423110 | Tractors, highway, merchant wholesalers |
| 333924 | Tractors, industrial, manufacturing |
| 423830 | Tractors, industrial, merchant wholesalers |
| 336120 | Tractors, truck for highway use, assembled on chassis of own manufacture |
| 813910 | Trade associations |
| 522299 | Trade banks (i.e., international trade financing) |
| 323120 | Trade binding services |
| 926110 | Trade commissions, government |
| 926110 | Trade development program administration |
| 561920 | Trade fair managers |
| 561920 | Trade fair organizers |
| 561920 | Trade fair promoters |
| 522299 | Trade financing, international |
| 513120 | Trade journal publishers |
| 513120 | Trade journal publishers (except exclusive Internet publishing) |

| | |
|---|---|
| 513120 | Trade journal publishers and printing combined |
| 513120 | Trade journal publishers, exclusively on Internet |
| 323111 | Trade journals commercial printing (except screen) without publishing |
| 323113 | Trade journals screen printing without publishing |
| 513120 | Trade magazine and periodical publishers |
| 513120 | Trade magazine and periodical publishers (except exclusive Internet publishing) |
| 513120 | Trade magazine and periodical publishers and printing combined |
| 513120 | Trade magazine and periodical publishers, exclusively on Internet |
| 323111 | Trade magazines and periodicals commercial printing (except screen) without publishing |
| 323113 | Trade magazines and periodicals screen printing without publishing |
| 238390 | Trade show exhibit installation and dismantling contractors |
| 561920 | Trade show managers |
| 561920 | Trade show organizers |
| 561920 | Trade show promoters |
| 611513 | Trade union apprenticeship training programs |
| 813930 | Trade unions (except apprenticeship programs) |
| 813930 | Trade unions, local |
| 533110 | Trademark licensing |
| 423920 | Trading cards merchant wholesalers |
| 523160 | Trading companies, commodity contracts |
| 455219 | Trading posts, general merchandise |
| 523150 | Trading securities (i.e., acting as a principal in dealing securities to investors) |
| 561990 | Trading stamp promotion and sale to stores |
| 561990 | Trading stamp redemption services |
| 339950 | Traffic (e.g., highway, road, street, bridge) signs manufacturing |
| 334290 | Traffic advisory and signalling systems manufacturing |
| 532490 | Traffic control equipment (e.g., barricades, cones, traffic signs) rental or leasing |
| 922110 | Traffic courts |
| 541330 | Traffic engineering consulting services |
| 237310 | Traffic lane painting |

| | |
|---|---|
| 238210 | Traffic signal installation |
| 334290 | Traffic signals manufacturing |
| 237990 | Trail construction |
| 721214 | Trail riding camps with accommodation facilities |
| 713990 | Trail riding, recreational |
| 423620 | Trail video cameras, household-type, merchant wholesalers |
| 336390 | Trailer hitches, motor vehicle, manufacturing |
| 531190 | Trailer park or court, residential |
| 423120 | Trailer parts, new, merchant wholesalers |
| 532120 | Trailer rental or leasing |
| 336214 | Trailers for transporting horses (except fifth-wheel-type) manufacturing |
| 336214 | Trailers, camping, manufacturing |
| 336212 | Trailers, fifth-wheel-type, for transporting horses, manufacturing |
| 423830 | Trailers, industrial, merchant wholesalers |
| 423110 | Trailers, motor vehicle, merchant wholesalers |
| 115210 | Training horses (except racehorses) |
| 315210 | Training pants (i.e., underwear) cut and sew apparel contractors |
| 315250 | Training pants (i.e., underwear), infants', cut and sewn from purchased fabric (except apparel contractors) |
| 711219 | Training race dogs |
| 711219 | Training racehorses |
| 339930 | Trains and equipment, toy, electric or mechanical, manufacturing |
| 713990 | Trampoline facilities, recreational |
| 485119 | Tramway systems (except mixed mode), commuter |
| 487990 | Tramway, aerial, scenic and sightseeing operation |
| 332994 | Tranquilizer guns, manufacturing |
| 325412 | Tranquilizer preparations manufacturing |
| 336350 | Transaxles, automotive, truck, and bus, manufacturing |
| 334220 | Transceivers (i.e., transmitter-receiver units) manufacturing |
| 561410 | Transcription services |
| 334510 | Transcutaneous electrical nerve stimulators (TENS) manufacturing |
| 334419 | Transducers (except pressure) manufacturing |
| 334519 | Transducers, pressure, manufacturing |
| 325199 | Transesterification of vegetable oils to produce fuels or fuel additives |

| | |
|---|---|
| 484110 | Transfer (trucking) services, general freight, local |
| 523999 | Transfer agencies, securities |
| 237130 | Transformer station and substation, electric power, construction |
| 423610 | Transformers (except electronic) merchant wholesalers |
| 335311 | Transformers, electric power, manufacturing |
| 334416 | Transformers, electronic component-types, manufacturing |
| 423690 | Transformers, electronic, merchant wholesalers |
| 335311 | Transformers, ignition, for use on domestic fuel burners, manufacturing |
| 335311 | Transformers, reactor, manufacturing |
| 335311 | Transformers, separate solid-state arc-welding, manufacturing |
| 335910 | Transistor radio batteries manufacturing |
| 334413 | Transistors manufacturing |
| 423690 | Transistors merchant wholesalers |
| 541850 | Transit advertising services |
| 922120 | Transit police |
| 926120 | Transit systems and authorities, nonoperating |
| 485111 | Transit systems, mixed mode (e.g., bus, commuter rail, subway combinations) |
| 624229 | Transitional housing agencies |
| 327320 | Transit-mixed concrete manufacturing |
| 334519 | Transits, surveying, manufacturing |
| 541930 | Translation services, language |
| 237130 | Transmission and distribution line construction |
| 335311 | Transmission and distribution voltage regulators manufacturing |
| 316990 | Transmission belting, leather, manufacturing |
| 326220 | Transmission belts, rubber, manufacturing |
| 336390 | Transmission coolers manufacturing |
| 423610 | Transmission equipment, electrical, merchant wholesalers |
| 324191 | Transmission fluids, petroleum, made from refined petroleum |
| 325998 | Transmission fluids, synthetic, manufacturing |
| 221121 | Transmission of electric power |
| 486210 | Transmission of natural gas via pipeline (i.e., processing plants to local distribution systems) |
| 335932 | Transmission pole and line hardware manufacturing |

| | |
|---|---|
| 811114 | Transmission repair shops, automotive |
| 332312 | Transmission tower sections, fabricated structural metal, manufacturing |
| 336350 | Transmissions and parts, automotive, truck, and bus, manufacturing |
| 423690 | Transmitters merchant wholesalers |
| 334513 | Transmitters, industrial process control-type, manufacturing |
| 333111 | Transplanters, farm-type, manufacturing |
| 115112 | Transplanting services |
| ****** | Transportation -- see mode |
| 481212 | Transportation by spacecraft, freight |
| 926120 | Transportation departments, nonoperating |
| 423860 | Transportation equipment and supplies (except marine pleasure craft, motor vehicles) merchant wholesalers |
| 336360 | Transportation equipment seating manufacturing |
| 423110 | Transportation equipment, motor vehicle, merchant wholesalers |
| 423860 | Transportation machinery, equipment, and supplies (except marine pleasure craft, motor vehicles) merchant wholesalers |
| 541614 | Transportation management consulting services |
| 926120 | Transportation regulatory agencies |
| 926120 | Transportation safety programs, government |
| 483111 | Transporting freight to or from foreign ports, deep sea |
| 483112 | Transporting passengers to or from foreign ports, deep sea |
| 212319 | Trap rock crushed and broken stone mining and/or beneficiating |
| 212311 | Trap rock mining or quarrying |
| 332618 | Traps, animal and fish, made from purchased wire |
| 332919 | Traps, water, manufacturing |
| 423910 | Trapshooting equipment and supplies merchant wholesalers |
| 713990 | Trapshooting facilities, recreational |
| 333310 | Trash and garbage compactors, commercial-type, manufacturing |
| 335220 | Trash and garbage compactors, household-type, manufacturing |
| 326111 | Trash bags, plastics film, single wall or multiwall, manufacturing |
| 562111 | Trash collection services |
| 423620 | Trash compactors, household-type, merchant wholesalers |

| | |
|---|---|
| 326199 | Trash containers, plastics, manufacturing |
| 562213 | Trash disposal combustors or incinerators |
| 562212 | Trash disposal landfills |
| 562111 | Trash hauling, local |
| 484230 | Trash hauling, long-distance |
| 332313 | Trash racks, fabricated metal plate work, manufacturing |
| 621493 | Trauma centers (except hospitals), freestanding |
| 561510 | Travel agencies |
| 513130 | Travel guide book publishers |
| 513130 | Travel guide book publishers (except exclusive Internet publishing) |
| 513130 | Travel guide book publishers and printing combined |
| 513130 | Travel guide book publishers, exclusively on Internet |
| 323117 | Travel guide books printing and binding without publishing |
| 323117 | Travel guide books printing without publishing |
| 561510 | Travel management services |
| 561520 | Travel tour operators |
| 423110 | Travel trailer (e.g., tent trailers) merchant wholesalers |
| 721211 | Travel trailer campsites |
| 441210 | Travel trailer dealers |
| 336214 | Travel trailers, recreational, manufacturing |
| 624190 | Travelers' aid centers |
| 522390 | Travelers' check issuance services |
| 316990 | Traveling bags, all materials, manufacturing |
| 712110 | Traveling museum exhibits |
| 711190 | Traveling shows, carnival |
| 334419 | Traveling wave tubes manufacturing |
| 212312 | Travertine crushed and broken stone mining and/or beneficiating |
| 212311 | Travertine mining or quarrying |
| 337127 | Tray trucks, restaurant, manufacturing |
| 321920 | Trays, carrier, wood, manufacturing |
| 322299 | Trays, food, molded pulp, manufacturing |
| 333310 | Trays, photographic printing and processing, manufacturing |
| 332618 | Trays, wire, made from purchased wire |
| 321999 | Trays, wood, wicker, and bagasse, manufacturing |
| 326211 | Tread rubber (i.e., camelback) manufacturing |
| 332323 | Treads, metal stair, manufacturing |
| 921130 | Treasurers' offices, government |
| 321114 | Treating purchased wood and wood products |
| 238160 | Treating roofs (by spraying, painting or coating) |
| 321114 | Treating wood products with creosote or other preservatives |
| 561730 | Tree and brush trimming, overhead utility line |
| 113310 | Tree chipping in the field |
| 111421 | Tree crop farming (except forestry), short rotation growing and harvesting cycle |
| 111335 | Tree nut farming |
| 311225 | Tree nut oils (e.g., tung, walnut) made from purchased oils |
| 311224 | Tree nut oils (e.g., tung, walnut) made in crushing mill |
| 561730 | Tree pruning services |
| 561730 | Tree removal services |
| 113210 | Tree seed extracting |
| 113210 | Tree seed gathering |
| 113210 | Tree seed growing for reforestation |
| 561730 | Tree services (e.g., bracing, planting, pruning, removal, spraying, surgery, trimming) |
| 333111 | Tree shakers (e.g., citrus, nut, soft fruit) manufacturing |
| 561730 | Tree surgery services |
| 561730 | Tree trimming services |
| 339999 | Trees and plants, artificial, manufacturing |
| 424930 | Trees merchant wholesalers |
| 321918 | Trellises, wood, manufacturing |
| 238910 | Trenching (except underwater) |
| 333120 | Trenching machines manufacturing |
| 237990 | Trenching, underwater |
| 237310 | Trestle construction |
| 321114 | Trestle parts, wood, treating |
| 325220 | Triacetate fibers and yarns manufacturing |
| 541199 | Trial consulting services |
| 921150 | Tribal chief's or chairman's office, American Indian or Alaska Native |
| 921150 | Tribal councils, American Indian or Alaska Native |

| | |
|---|---|
| 921150 | Tribal courts, American Indian or Alaska Native |
| 325199 | Trichloroethylene manufacturing |
| 325199 | Trichlorophenoxyacetic acid manufacturing |
| 325199 | Tricresyl phosphate manufacturing |
| 339930 | Tricycles (except metal) manufacturing |
| 336991 | Tricycles, metal, adult and children's, manufacturing |
| 325199 | Tridecyl alcohol manufacturing |
| 238350 | Trim and finish carpentry contractors |
| 332321 | Trim and molding (except motor vehicle), metal, manufacturing |
| 332321 | Trim, metal, manufacturing |
| 321918 | Trim, wood and covered wood, manufacturing |
| 333112 | Trimmers, hedge, electric, manufacturing |
| 332216 | Trimmers, hedge, nonelectric, manufacturing |
| 333112 | Trimmers, string, lawn and garden-type, manufacturing |
| 315250 | Trimmings, fur (except apparel contractors), manufacturing |
| 315210 | Trimmings, fur, cut and sew apparel contractors |
| 316990 | Trimmings, shoe, leather, manufacturing |
| 325920 | Trinitrotoluene (TNT) manufacturing |
| 325199 | Triphenyl phosphate manufacturing |
| 333310 | Tripods, camera and projector, manufacturing |
| 212390 | Tripoli mining and/or beneficiating |
| 339112 | Trocars manufacturing |
| 485119 | Trolley systems (except mixed mode), commuter |
| 487110 | Trolley, scenic and sightseeing, operation |
| 339992 | Trombones and parts manufacturing |
| 212390 | Trona mining and/or beneficiating |
| 423940 | Trophies merchant wholesalers |
| 332999 | Trophies, nonprecious and precious plated metal, manufacturing |
| 339910 | Trophies, precious metal (except precious plated), manufacturing |
| 459999 | Trophy (including awards and plaques) shops |
| 321999 | Trophy bases, wood, manufacturing |
| 424990 | Tropical fish merchant wholesalers |
| 112511 | Tropical fish production, farm raising |
| 561730 | Tropical plant maintenance services |

| | |
|---|---|
| 335139 | Trouble lights manufacturing |
| 332322 | Troughs, elevator, sheet metal (except stampings), manufacturing |
| 332313 | Troughs, industrial, fabricated metal plate work, manufacturing |
| 335210 | Trouser pressers, household-type electric, manufacturing |
| 315210 | Trousers cut and sew apparel contractors |
| 315120 | Trousers made in apparel knitting mills |
| 315250 | Trousers, men's and boys', cut and sewn from purchased fabric (except apparel contractors) |
| 114111 | Trout fishing |
| 112511 | Trout production, farm raising |
| 332216 | Trowels manufacturing |
| 532120 | Truck (except industrial, light duty passenger) rental or leasing |
| 811192 | Truck and bus washes |
| 336390 | Truck and trailer liftgates manufacturing |
| 336211 | Truck bodies and cabs manufacturing |
| 336211 | Truck bodies assembling on purchased chassis |
| 336214 | Truck campers (i.e., slide-in campers) manufacturing |
| 441330 | Truck cap stores |
| 611519 | Truck driving schools |
| 111219 | Truck farming, field, bedding plant and seed production |
| 522220 | Truck finance leasing |
| 423120 | Truck parts, new, merchant wholesalers |
| 811310 | Truck refrigeration repair and maintenance services |
| 811111 | Truck repair shops, general |
| 457120 | Truck stops |
| 236220 | Truck terminal construction |
| 441340 | Truck tires and tubes dealers (except heavy truck) |
| 532120 | Truck tractor rental or leasing without driver |
| 336120 | Truck tractors for highway use, assembling on chassis of own manufacture |
| 336211 | Truck tractors for highway use, assembling on purchased chassis |
| 423110 | Truck tractors, road, merchant wholesalers |
| 811121 | Truck trailer body shops |
| 423110 | Truck trailer merchant wholesalers |
| 811121 | Truck trailer paint and body repair |
| 336212 | Truck trailers manufacturing |

| | |
|---|---|
| 488490 | Truck weighing station operation |
| 532490 | Truck, industrial, rental or leasing |
| 488490 | Trucking terminals, independently operated |
| 484210 | Trucking used household, office, or institutional furniture and equipment |
| 484110 | Trucking, general freight, local |
| 484122 | Trucking, general freight, long-distance, less-than-truckload (LTL) |
| 484121 | Trucking, general freight, long-distance, truckload (TL) |
| 484220 | Trucking, specialized freight (except used goods), local |
| 484230 | Trucking, specialized freight (except used goods), long-distance |
| 327320 | Truck-mixed concrete manufacturing |
| 336120 | Trucks, heavy, assembling on chassis of own manufacture |
| 333924 | Trucks, industrial, manufacturing |
| 423830 | Trucks, industrial, merchant wholesalers |
| 336110 | Trucks, light duty, assembling on chassis of own manufacture |
| 333120 | Trucks, off-highway, manufacturing |
| 423110 | Trucks, road, merchant wholesalers |
| 111419 | Truffles farming, grown under cover |
| 113210 | Truffles gathering |
| 339992 | Trumpets and parts manufacturing |
| 316990 | Trunks (i.e., luggage), all materials, manufacturing |
| 332313 | Truss plates, metal, manufacturing |
| 321215 | Trusses, glue laminated or pre-engineered wood, manufacturing |
| 321215 | Trusses, wood roof or floor, manufacturing |
| 321215 | Trusses, wood, glue laminated or metal connected, manufacturing |
| 523991 | Trust administration, personal investment |
| 523991 | Trust companies, nondepository |
| 813211 | Trusts, charitable, awarding grants |
| 813211 | Trusts, educational, awarding grants |
| 525920 | Trusts, estates, and agency accounts |
| 813211 | Trusts, religious, awarding grants |
| 458110 | T-shirt shops |
| 315210 | T-shirts, outerwear, cut and sew apparel contractors |
| 315120 | T-shirts, outerwear, made in apparel knitting mills |

| | |
|---|---|
| 315250 | T-shirts, outerwear, men's and boys', cut and sewn from purchased fabric (except apparel contractors) |
| 315250 | T-shirts, outerwear, unisex (i.e., sized without regard to gender), cut and sewn from purchased fabric (except apparel contractors) |
| 315250 | T-shirts, outerwear, women's, girls', and infants', cut and sewn from purchased fabric (except apparel contractors) |
| 315210 | T-shirts, underwear, cut and sew apparel contractors |
| 315120 | T-shirts, underwear, made in apparel knitting mills |
| 315250 | T-shirts, underwear, men's and boys', cut and sewn from purchased fabric (except apparel contractors) |
| 315250 | T-shirts, underwear, women's, girls', and infants', cut and sewn from purchased fabric (except apparel contractors) |
| 334519 | T-squares (drafting) manufacturing |
| 325612 | Tub and tile cleaning preparations manufacturing |
| 331210 | Tube (e.g., heavy riveted, lock joint, seamless, welded) made from purchased iron or steel |
| 332912 | Tube and hose fittings, fluid power, manufacturing |
| 331318 | Tube blooms made by extruding purchased aluminum |
| 331318 | Tube blooms, aluminum, made in integrated secondary smelting and extruding mills |
| 331318 | Tube made by drawing or extruding purchased aluminum |
| 333519 | Tube rolling mill machinery, metalworking, manufacturing |
| 331110 | Tube rounds, iron or steel, made in iron and steel mills |
| 331318 | Tube, aluminum, made in integrated secondary smelting and drawing plants |
| 331318 | Tube, aluminum, made in integrated secondary smelting and extruding mills |
| 331110 | Tube, iron or steel, made in iron and steel mills |
| 326121 | Tube, nonrigid plastics, manufacturing |
| 331315 | Tube, welded, aluminum, made by flat rolling purchased aluminum |
| 331315 | Tube, welded, aluminum, made in integrated secondary smelting and flat rolling mills |
| 325414 | Tuberculin (i.e., tuberculo-protein derived) manufacturing |
| 622310 | Tuberculosis and other respiratory illness hospitals |

| | |
|---|---|
| 332996 | Tubes made from purchased metal pipe |
| 334419 | Tubes, cathode ray, manufacturing |
| 334419 | Tubes, electron, manufacturing |
| 423690 | Tubes, electronic (e.g., industrial, receiving, transmitting), merchant wholesalers |
| 334419 | Tubes, electronic, manufacturing |
| 334419 | Tubes, klystron, manufacturing |
| 334517 | Tubes, X-ray, manufacturing |
| 331420 | Tubing, copper and copper alloy, made from purchased copper or in integrated secondary smelting and rolling, drawing or extruding plants |
| 332999 | Tubing, flexible metal, manufacturing |
| 331210 | Tubing, mechanical and hypodermic sizes, cold-drawn stainless steel, made from purchased steel |
| 423510 | Tubing, metal, merchant wholesalers |
| 331491 | Tubing, nonferrous metals (except aluminum, copper), made from purchased metals or scrap |
| 331110 | Tubing, seamless steel, made in iron and steel mills |
| 331110 | Tubing, wrought iron or steel, made in iron and steel mills |
| 332999 | Tubs, laundry and bath, metal, manufacturing |
| 238140 | Tuck pointing contractors |
| 212312 | Tufa, calcareous, crushed and broken stone, mining and/or beneficiating |
| 212311 | Tufa, calcareous, mining or quarrying |
| 333248 | Tufting machinery for textiles manufacturing |
| 336611 | Tugboat building |
| 532411 | Tugboat rental or leasing without crew |
| 488330 | Tugboat services, harbor operation |
| 326199 | Tumblers, plastics, manufacturing |
| 332813 | Tumbling (i.e., cleaning and polishing) metal and metal products for the trade |
| 114111 | Tuna fishing |
| 811114 | Tune-up shops, automotive |
| 325180 | Tungstates (e.g., ammonium tungstate, sodium tungstate) manufacturing |
| 331491 | Tungsten bar, rod, sheet, strip, and tubing made by rolling, drawing, or extruding purchased metals or scrap |
| 331492 | Tungsten carbide powder made by metallurgical process |
| 325180 | Tungsten compounds, not specified elsewhere by process, manufacturing |
| 212290 | Tungsten concentrates beneficiating |
| 212290 | Tungsten ores mining and/or beneficiating |
| 811490 | Tuning and repair of musical instruments |
| 339992 | Tuning forks manufacturing |
| 237990 | Tunnel construction |
| 238210 | Tunnel lighting contractors |
| 332313 | Tunnel lining, fabricated metal plate work, manufacturing |
| 213113 | Tunneling services for coal mining on a contract basis |
| 332313 | Tunnels, wind, fabricated metal plate work, manufacturing |
| 334513 | Turbidity instruments, industrial process-type, manufacturing |
| 334516 | Turbidometers, laboratory-type, manufacturing |
| 334513 | Turbine flow meters, industrial process-type, manufacturing |
| 333611 | Turbine generator set units manufacturing |
| 334514 | Turbine meters, consumption registering, manufacturing |
| 333611 | Turbines (except aircraft) manufacturing |
| 423830 | Turbines (except transportation) merchant wholesalers |
| 423860 | Turbines, transportation, merchant wholesalers |
| 561730 | Turf (except artificial) installation services |
| 111421 | Turf farming |
| 238990 | Turf, artificial, installation |
| 424440 | Turkey and turkey products (except canned and packaged frozen) merchant wholesalers |
| 112330 | Turkey egg production |
| 311119 | Turkey feeds, prepared, manufacturing |
| 112340 | Turkey hatcheries |
| 112330 | Turkey production |
| 325613 | Turkey-red oil manufacturing |
| 311615 | Turkeys, processing, fresh, frozen, canned, or cooked |
| 311615 | Turkeys, slaughtering and dressing |
| 812199 | Turkish bathhouses |
| 812199 | Turkish baths |
| 332722 | Turnbuckles, metal, manufacturing |
| 333517 | Turning machines (i.e., lathes), metalworking, manufacturing |
| 321912 | Turnings, furniture, unfinished wood, manufacturing |

| | |
|---|---|
| 111219 | Turnip farming, field, bedding plant and seed production |
| 325194 | Turpentine made by distillation of pine gum or pine wood |
| 424690 | Turpentine merchant wholesalers |
| 212390 | Turquoise mining and/or beneficiating |
| 333517 | Turret lathes, metalworking, manufacturing |
| 332994 | Turrets, gun, manufacturing |
| 114119 | Turtle fishing |
| 112519 | Turtle production, farm raising |
| 611691 | Tutoring, academic |
| 532281 | Tuxedo rental |
| 315210 | Tuxedos cut and sew apparel contractors |
| 315250 | Tuxedos cut and sewn from purchased fabric (except apparel contractors) |
| 334310 | TV (television) sets manufacturing |
| 449210 | TV (television) stores |
| 532490 | TV broadcasting and studio equipment rental or leasing |
| 337126 | TV stands and similar stands for consumer electronics, metal, manufacturing |
| 337126 | TV stands and similar stands for consumer electronics, plastics, manufacturing |
| 337122 | TV stands and similar stands for consumer electronics, wood, manufacturing |
| 313210 | Twills weaving |
| 423840 | Twine merchant wholesalers |
| 314994 | Twines manufacturing |
| 423830 | Twist drills merchant wholesalers |
| 517112 | Two-way paging communication carriers (except satellite) |
| 811210 | Two-way radio repair and maintenance services |
| 323120 | Typesetting (i.e., computer controlled, hand, machine) |
| 333248 | Typesetting machinery manufacturing |
| 424120 | Typewriter paper merchant wholesalers |
| 811210 | Typewriter repair and maintenance services |
| 339940 | Typewriter ribbons manufacturing |
| 333310 | Typewriters manufacturing |
| 423420 | Typewriters merchant wholesalers |
| 561410 | Typing services |
| 212290 | Tyuyamunite mining and/or beneficiating |

| | |
|---|---|
| 922130 | U.S. attorneys' offices |
| 311514 | UHT (ultra high temperature) milk manufacturing |
| 339992 | Ukuleles and parts manufacturing |
| 212390 | Ulexite mining and/or beneficiating |
| 531130 | U-lock storage |
| 336411 | Ultra light aircraft manufacturing |
| 325130 | Ultramarine pigments manufacturing |
| 333517 | Ultrasonic boring, drilling, and cutting machines, metalworking, manufacturing |
| 335999 | Ultrasonic cleaning equipment (except dental, medical) manufacturing |
| 339114 | Ultrasonic dental equipment manufacturing |
| 335999 | Ultrasonic generators sold separately for inclusion in tools and equipment manufacturing |
| 339113 | Ultrasonic medical cleaning equipment manufacturing |
| 334510 | Ultrasonic medical equipment manufacturing |
| 333517 | Ultrasonic metal forming machines manufacturing |
| 334510 | Ultrasonic scanning devices, medical, manufacturing |
| 334519 | Ultrasonic testing equipment (except medical) manufacturing |
| 333992 | Ultrasonic welding equipment manufacturing |
| 423450 | Ultrasound equipment, medical, merchant wholesalers |
| 621512 | Ultrasound imaging centers |
| 335139 | Ultraviolet lamp bulbs manufacturing |
| 335139 | Ultraviolet lamp fixtures manufacturing |
| 334516 | Ultraviolet-type analytical instruments manufacturing |
| 325130 | Umber manufacturing |
| 212390 | Umber mining and/or beneficiating |
| 339999 | Umbrellas manufacturing |
| 424350 | Umbrellas, men's and boys', merchant wholesalers |
| 424350 | Umbrellas, women's and girls', merchant wholesalers |
| 322120 | Uncoated groundwood paper mills |
| 811198 | Undercoating shops, automotive |
| 237130 | Underground cable (e.g., fiber optic, electricity, telephone, cable television) laying |
| 333131 | Underground mining machinery manufacturing |
| 238910 | Underground tank (except hazardous material) removal |

237310 Underpass construction

238990 Underpinning, construction

812210 Undertaker services

423850 Undertakers' equipment and supplies merchant wholesalers

335139 Underwater lighting fixtures manufacturing

334511 Underwater navigational systems manufacturing

336612 Underwater remotely operated vehicles (ROVs) manufacturing in boat yards

336611 Underwater remotely operated vehicles (ROVs) manufacturing in shipyards

315210 Underwear cut and sew apparel contractors

315120 Underwear made in apparel knitting mills

315210 Underwear shirts cut and sew apparel contractors

315120 Underwear shirts made in apparel knitting mills

315250 Underwear shirts, men's and boys', cut and sewn from purchased fabric (except apparel contractors)

315250 Underwear shirts, women's, girls', and infants', cut and sewn from purchased fabric (except apparel contractors)

315210 Underwear shorts cut and sew apparel contractors

315120 Underwear shorts made in apparel knitting mills

315250 Underwear shorts, men's and boys', cut and sewn from purchased fabric (except apparel contractors)

315250 Underwear shorts, women's, girls', and infants', cut and sewn from purchased fabric (except apparel contractors)

315250 Underwear, men's and boys', cut and sewn from purchased fabric (except apparel contractors)

424350 Underwear, men's and boys', merchant wholesalers

424350 Underwear, women's, children's, and infants', merchant wholesalers

315250 Underwear, women's, girls', and infants', cut and sewn from purchased fabric (except apparel contractors)

523150 Underwriting securities

923130 Unemployment insurance program administration

812331 Uniform (except industrial) supply services

315210 Uniform hats and caps cut and sew apparel contractors

315990 Uniform hats and caps cut and sewn from purchased fabric (except apparel contractors)

315210 Uniform shirts cut and sew apparel contractors

315250 Uniform shirts, men's and boys', cut and sewn from purchased fabric (except apparel contractors)

315250 Uniform shirts, team athletic, cut and sewn from purchased fabric (except apparel contractors)

315250 Uniform shirts, women's and girls', cut and sewn from purchased fabric (except apparel contractors)

458110 Uniform stores (except athletic)

459110 Uniform stores, athletic

812332 Uniform supply services, industrial

424350 Uniforms (except athletic), men's and boys', merchant wholesalers

424350 Uniforms (except athletic), women's, children's, and infants', merchant wholesalers

315210 Uniforms, band, cut and sew apparel contractors

315250 Uniforms, band, cut and sewn from purchased fabric (except apparel contractors)

315250 Uniforms, dress (e.g., firefighter, military, police), men's, cut and sewn from purchased fabric (except apparel contractors)

315210 Uniforms, dress (e.g., military, police, firefighter), cut and sew apparel contractors

315250 Uniforms, dress, tailored (e.g., firefighter, military, police), women's and girls', cut and sewn from purchased fabric (except apparel contractors)

315210 Uniforms, nontailored, cut and sew apparel contractors

315120 Uniforms, nontailored, made in apparel knitting mills

315250 Uniforms, nontailored, men's and boys', cut and sewn from purchased fabric (except apparel contractors)

315250 Uniforms, nontailored, women's and girls', cut and sewn from purchased fabric (except apparel contractors)

315210 Uniforms, team athletic, cut and sew apparel contractors

315250 Uniforms, team athletic, cut and sewn from purchased fabric (except apparel contractors)

335999 Uninterruptible power supplies (UPS) manufacturing

| | |
|---|---|
| 525120 | Union health and welfare funds |
| 525110 | Union pension funds |
| 315210 | Union suits cut and sew apparel contractors |
| 315120 | Union suits made in apparel knitting mills |
| 315250 | Union suits, men's and boys', cut and sewn from purchased fabric (except apparel contractors) |
| 315250 | Union suits, women's, girls', and infants', cut and sewn from purchased fabric (except apparel contractors) |
| 813930 | Unions (except apprenticeship programs), labor |
| 522130 | Unions, credit |
| 332919 | Unions, pipe, metal (except made from purchased pipe), manufacturing |
| 424350 | Unisex clothing merchant wholesalers |
| 458110 | Unisex clothing stores |
| 812112 | Unisex hair stylist shops |
| 333414 | Unit heaters (except portable electric) manufacturing |
| 335210 | Unit heaters, portable electric, manufacturing |
| 525990 | Unit investment trust funds |
| 323111 | Unit set forms (e.g., manifold credit card slips) printing |
| 423610 | Unit substations, electrical, merchant wholesalers |
| 813219 | United fund councils |
| 813219 | United funds for colleges |
| 928120 | United Nations |
| 333613 | Universal joints (except aircraft, motor vehicle) manufacturing |
| 336413 | Universal joints, aircraft, manufacturing |
| 336350 | Universal joints, automotive, truck, and bus, manufacturing |
| 611310 | Universities |
| 813410 | University clubs |
| 513130 | University press publishers |
| 513130 | University press publishers (except exclusive Internet publishing) |
| 513130 | University press publishers, exclusively on Internet |
| 923110 | University regents or boards, government |
| 311812 | Unleavened bread made in commercial bakeries |
| 423690 | Unloaded computer boards merchant wholesalers |
| 336411 | Unmanned and robotic aircraft manufacturing |
| 336110 | Unmanned and robotic automobiles manufacturing |
| 333924 | Unmanned and robotic forklifts manufacturing |
| 333924 | Unmanned and robotic pallet loaders and unloaders manufacturing |
| 336612 | Unmanned and robotic watercraft manufacturing in boat yards |
| 336611 | Unmanned and robotic watercraft manufacturing in shipyards |
| 337121 | Upholstered furniture, household-type, custom, manufacturing |
| 337121 | Upholstered furniture, household-type, on frames of any material, manufacturing |
| 423850 | Upholsterers' equipment and supplies (except fabrics) merchant wholesalers |
| 314999 | Upholstering filling (except nonwoven fabric) manufacturing |
| 811420 | Upholstery (except motor vehicle) repair services |
| 561740 | Upholstery cleaning on customers' premises |
| 561740 | Upholstery cleaning services |
| 424310 | Upholstery fabrics merchant wholesalers |
| 316110 | Upholstery leather manufacturing |
| 459130 | Upholstery materials stores |
| 811121 | Upholstery shops, automotive |
| 332613 | Upholstery springs and spring units, light gauge, made from purchased wire or strip |
| 316110 | Upper leather manufacturing |
| 316990 | Uppers (i.e., shoe cut stock), leather, manufacturing |
| 335999 | UPS (uninterruptible power supplies) manufacturing |
| 332111 | Upset forgings made from purchased iron or steel, unfinished |
| 332112 | Upset forgings made from purchased nonferrous metals, unfinished |
| 333517 | Upsetters (i.e., forging machines) manufacturing |
| 212290 | Uraninite (pitchblende) mining and/or beneficiating |
| 325180 | Uranium compounds, not specified elsewhere by process, manufacturing |
| 212290 | Uranium ores mining and/or beneficiating |
| 325180 | Uranium oxide manufacturing |
| 331410 | Uranium refining, primary |
| 325180 | Uranium, enriched, manufacturing |
| 212290 | Uranium-radium-vanadium ore mine site development for own account |

| | |
|---|---|
| 212290 | Uranium-radium-vanadium ores mining and/or beneficiating |
| 485113 | Urban bus line services (except mixed mode) |
| 485112 | Urban commuter rail systems (except mixed mode) |
| 541320 | Urban planners' offices |
| 925120 | Urban planning commissions, government |
| 541320 | Urban planning services |
| 485111 | Urban transit systems, mixed mode (e.g., bus, commuter rail, subway combinations) |
| 325311 | Urea manufacturing |
| 325211 | Urea resins manufacturing |
| 325211 | Urea-formaldehyde resins manufacturing |
| 238310 | Urethane foam insulation application |
| 326150 | Urethane foam products manufacturing |
| 325212 | Urethane rubber manufacturing |
| 238190 | Urethane slabjacking contractors |
| 238190 | Urethane soil stabilization contractors |
| 621493 | Urgent medical care centers and clinics (except hospitals), freestanding |
| 423720 | Urinals merchant wholesalers |
| 332999 | Urinals, metal, manufacturing |
| 326191 | Urinals, plastics, manufacturing |
| 327110 | Urinals, vitreous china, manufacturing |
| 621511 | Urinalysis laboratories |
| 327420 | Urns (e.g., gypsum, plaster of paris) manufacturing |
| 335210 | Urns, household-type electric, manufacturing |
| 621111 | Urologists' offices (e.g., centers, clinics) |
| 334112 | USB flash drives (e.g., thumbdrives, jumpdrives) manufacturing |
| 423430 | USB flash drives (e.g., thumbdrives, jumpdrives) merchant wholesalers |
| 441227 | Used aircraft dealers |
| 441330 | Used automotive parts stores |
| 441340 | Used automotive tire dealers |
| 459510 | Used bicycle (except motorized) shops |
| 441222 | Used boat dealers |
| 441120 | Used car dealers |
| 423110 | Used car merchant wholesalers |
| 484210 | Used household and office goods moving |
| 459930 | Used manufactured (mobile) home dealers |

| | |
|---|---|
| 459510 | Used merchandise dealers (except motor vehicles and parts) |
| 459510 | Used merchandise stores |
| 441227 | Used motorcycle dealers |
| 423140 | Used parts, motor vehicle, merchant wholesalers |
| 459510 | Used rare collectors' items (e.g., autograph, coin, card, stamps) shops |
| 459999 | Used rare collectors' items (e.g., autograph, coin, card, stamps), mail-order houses |
| 441210 | Used recreational vehicle (RV) dealers |
| 441340 | Used tire dealers |
| 423130 | Used tires, motor vehicle, merchant wholesalers |
| 441227 | Used utility trailer dealers |
| 541618 | Utilities management consulting services |
| 332311 | Utility buildings, prefabricated metal, manufacturing |
| 326199 | Utility containers (e.g., baskets, bins, boxes, buckets, dishpans, pails), plastics (except foam), manufacturing |
| 237130 | Utility line (i.e., communication, electric power), construction |
| 237110 | Utility line (i.e., sewer, water), construction |
| 513210 | Utility software, computer, packaged |
| 441227 | Utility trailer dealers |
| 423110 | Utility trailer merchant wholesalers |
| 532120 | Utility trailer rental or leasing |
| 336214 | Utility trailers manufacturing |
| 531190 | Vacant lot rental or leasing |
| 531190 | Vacation and recreation land rental or leasing |
| 721214 | Vacation camps (except campgrounds, day, instructional) |
| 236115 | Vacation home, single-family, construction by general contractors |
| 236117 | Vacation housing construction for-sale builders |
| 115210 | Vaccinating livestock (except by veterinarians) |
| 541940 | Vaccination services, veterinary |
| 325414 | Vaccines (i.e., bacterial, virus) manufacturing |
| 424210 | Vaccines merchant wholesalers |
| 332439 | Vacuum bottles and jugs, light gauge metal, manufacturing |
| 336340 | Vacuum brake booster, automotive, truck, and bus, manufacturing |

| | |
|---|---|
| 326220 | Vacuum cleaner belts, rubber or plastics, manufacturing |
| 449210 | Vacuum cleaner stores, household-type |
| 335210 | Vacuum cleaners (e.g., canister, handheld, upright) household-type electric, manufacturing |
| 335210 | Vacuum cleaners and sweepers, household-type electric, manufacturing |
| 423620 | Vacuum cleaners, household-type, merchant wholesalers |
| 333310 | Vacuum cleaners, industrial and commercial-type, manufacturing |
| 238290 | Vacuum cleaning system, built-in, installation |
| 423850 | Vacuum cleaning systems, commercial, merchant wholesalers |
| 333912 | Vacuum pumps (except laboratory) manufacturing |
| 423830 | Vacuum pumps merchant wholesalers |
| 339113 | Vacuum pumps, laboratory-type, manufacturing |
| 335314 | Vacuum relays manufacturing |
| 332420 | Vacuum tanks, heavy gauge metal, manufacturing |
| 327215 | Vacuum tube blanks, glass, made from purchased glass |
| 327212 | Vacuum tube blanks, glass, made in glass making plants |
| 334419 | Vacuum tubes manufacturing |
| 488119 | Vacuuming of airport runways |
| 333112 | Vacuums, yard, manufacturing |
| 812930 | Valet parking services |
| 316990 | Valises, all materials, manufacturing |
| 325194 | Valonia extract manufacturing |
| 333517 | Valve grinding machines, metalworking, manufacturing |
| 423840 | Valves (except hydraulic, plumbing, pneumatic) merchant wholesalers |
| 332911 | Valves for nuclear applications manufacturing |
| 332911 | Valves for water works and municipal water systems manufacturing |
| 336310 | Valves, engine, intake and exhaust, manufacturing |
| 332912 | Valves, hydraulic and pneumatic, fluid power, manufacturing |
| 423830 | Valves, hydraulic and pneumatic, merchant wholesalers |
| 332911 | Valves, industrial-type (e.g., check, gate, globe, relief, safety), manufacturing |
| 332919 | Valves, inline plumbing and heating (e.g., cutoffs, stop), manufacturing |
| 423720 | Valves, plumbing and heating, merchant wholesalers |
| 316990 | Vamps, leather, manufacturing |
| 532120 | Van (except passenger) rental or leasing without driver |
| 532112 | Van (passenger) leasing |
| 532111 | Van (passenger) rental |
| 336213 | Van and minivan conversions on purchased chassis |
| 811121 | Van conversion shops (except on assembly line or factory basis) |
| 484210 | Van lines, moving and storage services |
| 212290 | Vanadium ores mining and/or beneficiating |
| 325199 | Vanillin, synthetic, manufacturing |
| 337110 | Vanities (except freestanding), stock or custom wood, manufacturing |
| 337122 | Vanities, freestanding, wood, manufacturing |
| 337126 | Vanities, metal household-type, manufacturing |
| 316990 | Vanity cases, leather, manufacturing |
| 337110 | Vanity tops, wood or plastics laminated on wood, manufacturing |
| 485999 | Vanpool operation (except ridesharing and ridesharing arrangement services) |
| 488999 | Vanpools, arrangement of (except ridesharing arrangement services) |
| 336110 | Vans, commercial and passenger light duty, assembling on chassis of own manufacture |
| 459991 | Vape shops |
| 333242 | Vapor deposition equipment, semiconductor, manufacturing |
| 334512 | Vapor heating controls manufacturing |
| 335139 | Vapor lamps, electric, manufacturing |
| 333998 | Vapor separating machinery manufacturing |
| 335210 | Vaporizers, household-type electric, manufacturing |
| 334513 | Variable control instruments, industrial process-type, manufacturing |
| 311612 | Variety meats, edible organs, made from purchased meats |
| 311611 | Variety meats, edible organs, made in slaughtering plants |
| 455219 | Variety stores |
| 334416 | Varistors manufacturing |
| 325510 | Varnishes manufacturing |
| 424950 | Varnishes merchant wholesalers |
| 332812 | Varnishing metals and metal products for the trade |

| | |
|---|---|
| 313320 | Varnishing purchased textiles and apparel |
| 327420 | Vases (e.g., gypsum, plaster of paris) manufacturing |
| 327215 | Vases, glass, made from purchased glass |
| 327212 | Vases, glass, made in glass making plants |
| 327110 | Vases, pottery (e.g., china, earthenware, stoneware), manufacturing |
| 325130 | Vat dyes, synthetic, manufacturing |
| 332420 | Vats, heavy gauge metal, manufacturing |
| 332439 | Vats, light gauge metal, manufacturing |
| 711110 | Vaudeville companies |
| 332999 | Vault doors and linings, metal, manufacturing |
| 238290 | Vault, safe and banking machine installation |
| 332999 | Vaults (except burial), metal, manufacturing |
| 339995 | Vaults (except concrete) manufacturing |
| 326220 | V-belts, rubber or plastics, manufacturing |
| 334310 | VCR (video cassette recorder) manufacturing |
| 112111 | Veal calf production |
| 311611 | Veal carcasses, half carcasses, primal and sub-primal cuts, produced in slaughtering plants |
| 311612 | Veal, primal and sub-primal cuts, made from purchased carcasses |
| 325411 | Vegetable alkaloids (i.e., basic chemicals) (e.g., caffeine, codeine, morphine, nicotine), manufacturing |
| 111211 | Vegetable and melon farming, potato dominant crop, field and seed production |
| 111219 | Vegetable and melon farming, vegetable (except potato) and melon dominant crops, field, bedding plants and seed production |
| 111211 | Vegetable and potato farming, potato dominant crop, field and seed potato production |
| 111219 | Vegetable and potato farming, vegetable (except potato) dominant crops, field, bedding plants and seed production |
| 321920 | Vegetable baskets, veneer and splint, manufacturing |
| 311421 | Vegetable brining |
| 424990 | Vegetable cake and meal merchant wholesalers |
| 311421 | Vegetable canning, bottling, and jarring |
| 321920 | Vegetable crates, wood, wirebound, manufacturing |
| 424910 | Vegetable dusts and sprays merchant wholesalers |
| 111419 | Vegetable farming, grown under cover |
| 311211 | Vegetable flour manufacturing |
| 311211 | Vegetable flour, meal, and powders, made in flour mills |
| 311411 | Vegetable juice concentrates, frozen, manufacturing |
| 311421 | Vegetable juices canning |
| 311421 | Vegetable juices, fresh, manufacturing |
| 445230 | Vegetable markets |
| 333241 | Vegetable oil processing machinery manufacturing |
| 424990 | Vegetable oils (except cooking) merchant wholesalers |
| 311225 | Vegetable oils made from purchased oils |
| 311224 | Vegetable oils made in crushing mills |
| 311412 | Vegetable patties, frozen, manufacturing |
| 424420 | Vegetable patties, frozen, merchant wholesalers |
| 115114 | Vegetable precooling |
| 115114 | Vegetable sorting, grading, and packing |
| 311221 | Vegetable starches manufacturing |
| 115114 | Vegetable sun drying |
| 115114 | Vegetable vacuum cooling |
| 311423 | Vegetables dehydrating |
| 311421 | Vegetables pickling |
| 424490 | Vegetables, canned, merchant wholesalers |
| 311991 | Vegetables, cut or peeled, fresh, manufacturing |
| 424480 | Vegetables, fresh, merchant wholesalers |
| 311411 | Vegetables, frozen, manufacturing |
| 424420 | Vegetables, frozen, merchant wholesalers |
| 115113 | Vegetables, machine harvesting |
| 238290 | Vehicle lift installation |
| 333998 | Vehicle scales manufacturing |
| 321912 | Vehicle stock, hardwood, manufacturing |
| 336991 | Vehicle, children's, metal manufacturing |
| 339930 | Vehicles, children's (except bicycles and metal tricycles), manufacturing |
| 423920 | Vehicles, children's (except bicycles), merchant wholesalers |
| 423110 | Vehicles, recreational, merchant wholesalers |

| | |
|---|---|
| 336320 | Vehicular lighting fixtures manufacturing |
| 316110 | Vellum leather manufacturing |
| 313210 | Velvets, manmade fiber and silk, weaving |
| 238290 | Vending machine installation |
| 445132 | Vending machine merchandisers, sale of products |
| 532490 | Vending machine rental |
| 333310 | Vending machines manufacturing |
| 423440 | Vending machines merchant wholesalers |
| 333243 | Veneer and plywood forming machinery manufacturing |
| 321920 | Veneer baskets, for fruits and vegetables, manufacturing |
| 321211 | Veneer mills, hardwood |
| 321212 | Veneer mills, softwood |
| 321999 | Veneer work, inlaid, manufacturing |
| 423310 | Veneer, wood, merchant wholesalers |
| 561720 | Venetian blind cleaning services |
| 811490 | Venetian blind repair and maintenance shops without retailing new venetian blinds |
| 321918 | Venetian blind slats, wood, manufacturing |
| 337920 | Venetian blinds manufacturing |
| 238390 | Ventilated wire shelving (i.e., closet organizing-type) installation |
| 238220 | Ventilating contractors |
| 423730 | Ventilating equipment and supplies (except household-type fans) merchant wholesalers |
| 333413 | Ventilating fans, industrial and commercial-type, manufacturing |
| 335210 | Ventilating kitchen fans, household-type electric, manufacturing |
| 335210 | Ventilation and exhaust fans (except attic fans), household-type, manufacturing |
| 561790 | Ventilation duct cleaning services |
| 334510 | Ventilators, electromedical, manufacturing |
| 523910 | Venture capital companies |
| 212319 | Verde' antique crushed and broken stone mining and/or beneficiating |
| 212311 | Verde' antique mining or quarrying |
| 212390 | Vermiculite mining and/or beneficiating |
| 327992 | Vermiculite, exfoliated, manufacturing |
| 325412 | Vermifuge preparations manufacturing |
| 325130 | Vermilion pigments manufacturing |
| 312130 | Vermouth manufacturing |
| 337920 | Vertical blinds manufacturing |
| 332420 | Vessels, heavy gauge metal, manufacturing |
| 315210 | Vestments, academic and clerical, cut and sew apparel contractors |
| 315250 | Vestments, academic and clerical, cut and sewn from purchased fabric (except apparel contractors) |
| 423490 | Vestments, religious, merchant wholesalers |
| 315210 | Vests cut and sew apparel contractors |
| 315250 | Vests, leather, fur, or sheep-lined (except apparel contractors), manufacturing |
| 315210 | Vests, leather, fur, or sheep-lined, cut and sew apparel contractors |
| 315250 | Vests, men's and boys', cut and sewn from purchased fabric (except apparel contractors) |
| 315250 | Vests, women's and girls', cut and sewn from purchased fabric (except apparel contractors) |
| 813410 | Veterans' membership organizations |
| 923140 | Veterans' affairs offices |
| 923140 | Veterans' benefits program administration, government |
| 813311 | Veterans' rights organizations |
| 423490 | Veterinarians' equipment and supplies merchant wholesalers |
| 339112 | Veterinarians' instruments and apparatus manufacturing |
| 424210 | Veterinarians' medicines merchant wholesalers |
| 541940 | Veterinarians' offices |
| 541940 | Veterinarians' practices |
| 541940 | Veterinary clinics |
| 541690 | Veterinary consulting services |
| 325412 | Veterinary medicinal preparations manufacturing |
| 541715 | Veterinary research and development laboratories or services (except biotechnology and nanotechnology research and development) |
| 541940 | Veterinary services |
| 541940 | Veterinary services, livestock |
| 541940 | Veterinary services, pets and other animal specialties |
| 541940 | Veterinary testing laboratories |
| 523910 | Viatical settlement companies |
| 339992 | Vibraphones manufacturing |

| | |
|---|---|
| 238390 | Vibration isolation contractors |
| 334519 | Vibration meters, analyzers, and calibrators, manufacturing |
| 541380 | Vibration testing laboratories or services |
| 333120 | Vibrators, concrete, manufacturing |
| 518210 | Video and audio technical streaming support services |
| 423430 | Video boards merchant wholesalers |
| 516210 | Video broadcasting, exclusively on Internet |
| 334220 | Video cameras (except household-type) manufacturing |
| 423410 | Video cameras (except household-type) merchant wholesalers |
| 334310 | Video cameras, household-type, manufacturing |
| 423620 | Video cameras, household-type, merchant wholesalers |
| 811210 | Video cassette recorder (VCR) repair services without retailing new video cassette recorders |
| 532210 | Video cassette recorder rental |
| 334310 | Video cassette recorders (VCR) manufacturing |
| 334610 | Video cassettes, blank, manufacturing |
| 334610 | Video cassettes, prerecorded, mass reproducing |
| 512191 | Video conversion services (i.e., between formats, except technical streaming support services) |
| 532210 | Video disc player rental |
| 532282 | Video disc rental for home electronic equipment (e.g., DVD) |
| 713290 | Video gambling device concession operators (i.e., supplying and servicing in others' facilities) |
| 713120 | Video game arcades (except gambling) |
| 339930 | Video game devices manufacturing |
| 339930 | Video game machines (except coin- or card-operated) manufacturing |
| 532282 | Video game rental |
| 449210 | Video game software stores |
| 423920 | Video games merchant wholesalers |
| 713290 | Video gaming device concession operators (i.e., supplying and servicing in others' facilities) |
| 516210 | Video on Demand (VOD) programming |
| 516210 | Video on Demand (VOD) streaming distribution services |
| 541921 | Video photography services, portrait |
| 512191 | Video postproduction services |
| 512110 | Video production |
| 512110 | Video production and distribution |
| 334220 | Video projectors (except household-type, motion picture theater) manufacturing |
| 334310 | Video projectors, household-type, manufacturing |
| 532210 | Video recorder rental |
| 512191 | Video tape and film stock digitization services (except technical streaming support services) |
| 518210 | Video tape and film stock technical streaming support services |
| 512199 | Video tape libraries, stock footage |
| 334610 | Video tape or disk mass reproducing |
| 532210 | Video tape player rental |
| 532282 | Video tape rental for home electronic equipment (e.g., VCR) |
| 532282 | Video tape rental stores |
| 449210 | Video tape stores |
| 334610 | Video tapes, blank, manufacturing |
| 423690 | Video tapes, blank, merchant wholesalers |
| 423990 | Video tapes, prerecorded, merchant wholesalers |
| 541922 | Video taping services for legal depositions |
| 541921 | Video taping services, special events (e.g., birthdays, weddings) |
| 334290 | Video-based stadium displays manufacturing |
| 561499 | Videoconferencing services |
| 311941 | Vinegar manufacturing |
| 115112 | Vineyard cultivation services |
| 325199 | Vinyl acetate (except resins) manufacturing |
| 325211 | Vinyl acetate resins manufacturing |
| 326113 | Vinyl and vinyl copolymer film and unlaminated sheet (except packaging) manufacturing |
| 325211 | Vinyl chloride resins manufacturing |
| 313320 | Vinyl coated fabrics manufacturing |
| 325220 | Vinyl fibers and filaments manufacturing |
| 326199 | Vinyl floor coverings manufacturing |
| 238330 | Vinyl flooring contractors |
| 325211 | Vinyl resins manufacturing |
| 423330 | Vinyl siding merchant wholesalers |
| 238170 | Vinyl siding, soffit and fascia, installation |

| | |
|---|---|
| 316210 | Vinyl upper athletic footwear manufacturing |
| 325220 | Vinylidene chloride fiber and filament manufacturing |
| 325211 | Vinylidene resins manufacturing |
| 339992 | Violas and parts manufacturing |
| 339992 | Violins and parts manufacturing |
| 325413 | Viral in-vitro diagnostic test substances manufacturing |
| 523160 | Virtual currency (cryptocurrency) brokering |
| 523160 | Virtual currency (cryptocurrency) dealing |
| 518210 | Virtual currency (cryptocurrency) mining |
| 523160 | Virtual currency exchange services (i.e., selling to the public) |
| 523999 | Virtual currency trading exchange clearinghouses |
| 516210 | Virtual Multichannel Video Programming Distributors (vMVPDs) |
| 325414 | Virus vaccines manufacturing |
| 325220 | Viscose fibers, bands, strips, and yarn manufacturing |
| 334519 | Viscosimeters (except industrial process type) manufacturing |
| 334513 | Viscosimeters, industrial process-type, manufacturing |
| 334513 | Viscosity instruments, industrial process-type, manufacturing |
| 332216 | Vises (except machine tool attachments) manufacturing |
| 621610 | Visiting nurse associations |
| 561591 | Visitor information centers |
| 561591 | Visitors bureaus |
| 325412 | Vitamin preparations manufacturing |
| 456191 | Vitamin stores |
| 424210 | Vitamins merchant wholesalers |
| 325411 | Vitamins, uncompounded, manufacturing |
| 711130 | Vocalists, independent |
| 611513 | Vocational apprenticeship training |
| 624310 | Vocational habilitation job counseling |
| 624310 | Vocational habilitation job training facilities (except schools) |
| 624310 | Vocational rehabilitation agencies |
| 624310 | Vocational rehabilitation job counseling |
| 624310 | Vocational rehabilitation job training facilities (except schools) |
| 624310 | Vocational rehabilitation or habilitation services (e.g., job counseling, job training, work experience) |
| 611610 | Voice instruction |
| 561421 | Voice mailbox services |
| 621340 | Voice pathologists' offices (e.g., centers, clinics) |
| 423430 | Voice recognition equipment merchant wholesalers |
| 517810 | VoIP service providers, using client-supplied telecommunications connections |
| 517111 | VoIP service providers, using own operated wired telecommunications infrastructure |
| 212390 | Volcanic ash mining and/or beneficiating |
| 212319 | Volcanic rock crushed and broken stone mining and/or beneficiating |
| 212311 | Volcanic rock, mining or quarrying |
| 335311 | Voltage regulating transformers, electric power, manufacturing |
| 423610 | Voltage regulators (except motor vehicle) merchant wholesalers |
| 336320 | Voltage regulators for internal combustion engines manufacturing |
| 334413 | Voltage regulators, integrated circuits, manufacturing |
| 423120 | Voltage regulators, motor vehicle, merchant wholesalers |
| 335311 | Voltage regulators, transmission and distribution, manufacturing |
| 334515 | Voltmeters manufacturing |
| 813212 | Voluntary health organizations |
| 624229 | Volunteer housing repair organizations |
| 333310 | Voting machines manufacturing |
| 423850 | Voting machines merchant wholesalers |
| 322219 | Vulcanized fiber products made from purchased paperboard |
| 325212 | Vulcanized oils manufacturing |
| 333248 | Vulcanizing machinery manufacturing |
| 332992 | Wads, ammunition, manufacturing |
| 333242 | Wafer processing equipment, semiconductor, manufacturing |
| 321219 | Waferboard manufacturing |
| 334413 | Wafers (semiconductor devices) manufacturing |
| 335210 | Waffle irons, household-type electric, manufacturing |
| 311412 | Waffles, frozen, manufacturing |
| 926150 | Wage control agencies, government |

| | |
|---|---|
| 339930 | Wagons, children's (e.g., coaster, express, and play), manufacturing |
| 333111 | Wagons, farm-type, manufacturing |
| 333112 | Wagons, lawn and garden-type, manufacturing |
| 321918 | Wainscots, wood, manufacturing |
| 561421 | Wakeup call services |
| 532283 | Walker, invalid, rental |
| 339930 | Walkers, baby (vehicles), manufacturing |
| 621111 | Walk-in physicians' offices (e.g., centers, clinics) |
| 333921 | Walkways, moving, manufacturing |
| 238310 | Wall cavity and attic space insulation installation |
| 334519 | Wall clocks manufacturing |
| 238130 | Wall component (i.e., exterior, interior), prefabricated, installation |
| 238320 | Wall covering or removal contractors |
| 424950 | Wall coverings (e.g., fabric, plastics) merchant wholesalers |
| 335132 | Wall lamps (i.e., lighting fixtures), commercial, institutional, and industrial electric, manufacturing |
| 335131 | Wall lamps (i.e., lighting fixtures), residential electric, manufacturing |
| 423490 | Wall maps merchant wholesalers |
| 327120 | Wall tile, ceramic, manufacturing |
| 423310 | Wallboard merchant wholesalers |
| 327420 | Wallboard, gypsum, manufacturing |
| 316990 | Wallets (except metal) manufacturing |
| 339910 | Wallets, precious metal, manufacturing |
| 444120 | Wallpaper and wall coverings stores |
| 325612 | Wallpaper cleaners manufacturing |
| 238320 | Wallpaper hanging and removal contractors |
| 322220 | Wallpaper made from purchased papers or other materials |
| 424950 | Wallpaper merchant wholesalers |
| 238320 | Wallpaper stripping |
| 111335 | Walnut farming |
| 115114 | Walnut hulling and shelling |
| 712110 | War museums |
| 316990 | Wardrobe bags (i.e., luggage) manufacturing |
| 532281 | Wardrobe rental |
| 337126 | Wardrobes, metal household-type, manufacturing |
| 337122 | Wardrobes, wood household-type, manufacturing |

| | |
|---|---|
| 455211 | Warehouse clubs (i.e., food and general merchandise) |
| 236220 | Warehouse construction (e.g., commercial, industrial, manufacturing, private) |
| 238220 | Warehouse refrigeration system installation |
| 236220 | Warehouse, commercial and institutional, construction |
| 236220 | Warehouse, industrial, construction |
| 332311 | Warehouses, prefabricated metal, manufacturing |
| 493190 | Warehousing (except farm products, general merchandise, refrigerated) |
| 493110 | Warehousing (including foreign trade zones), general merchandise |
| 493110 | Warehousing and storage, general merchandise |
| 813910 | Warehousing associations |
| 493130 | Warehousing, farm products (except refrigerated) |
| 493120 | Warehousing, refrigerated |
| 531130 | Warehousing, self-storage |
| 334511 | Warfare countermeasures equipment manufacturing |
| 423730 | Warm air heating equipment merchant wholesalers |
| 238220 | Warm air heating system installation |
| 335210 | Warming trays, electric, manufacturing |
| 315210 | Warmup suits cut and sew apparel contractors |
| 315120 | Warmup suits made in apparel knitting mills |
| 315250 | Warmup suits, men's and boys', cut and sewn from purchased fabric (except apparel contractors) |
| 315250 | Warmup suits, women's, girls', and infants', cut and sewn from purchased fabric (except apparel contractors) |
| 313240 | Warp or weft fabrics knitting |
| 333248 | Warping machinery manufacturing |
| 524128 | Warranty insurance carriers (e.g., appliance, automobile, homeowners', product), direct |
| 333310 | Wash water recycling machinery manufacturing |
| 315210 | Washable service apparel (e.g., barbers', hospital, professional) cut and sew apparel contractors |
| 315250 | Washable service apparel (e.g., barbers', hospital, professional), men's and boys', cut and sewn from purchased fabric (except apparel contractors) |

| | |
|---|---|
| 315250 | Washable service apparel, women's and girls', cut and sewn from purchased fabric (except apparel contractors) |
| 321999 | Washboards, wood and part wood, manufacturing |
| 532210 | Washer, clothes, rental |
| 333131 | Washers, aggregate and sand, stationary, manufacturing |
| 332722 | Washers, metal, manufacturing |
| 236210 | Washery, mining, construction |
| 811412 | Washing machine, household-type, repair and maintenance services without retailing new washing machine |
| 335220 | Washing machines, household-type, manufacturing |
| 423620 | Washing machines, household-type, merchant wholesalers |
| 333310 | Washing machines, laundry (except household-type), manufacturing |
| 561720 | Washroom sanitation services |
| 562219 | Waste (except sewage) treatment facilities, nonhazardous |
| 562119 | Waste (except solid and hazardous) collection services |
| 562119 | Waste (except solid and hazardous) hauling, local |
| 562112 | Waste collection services, hazardous |
| 562111 | Waste collection services, nonhazardous solid |
| 221320 | Waste collection, treatment, and disposal through a sewer system |
| 562213 | Waste disposal combustors or incinerators, nonhazardous solid |
| 562211 | Waste disposal facilities, hazardous |
| 562212 | Waste disposal landfills, nonhazardous solid |
| 236210 | Waste disposal plant (except sewage treatment) construction |
| 484230 | Waste hauling, hazardous, long-distance |
| 562112 | Waste hauling, local, hazardous |
| 562111 | Waste hauling, local, nonhazardous solid |
| 484230 | Waste hauling, nonhazardous, long-distance |
| 924110 | Waste management program administration |
| 423930 | Waste materials merchant wholesalers |
| 562920 | Waste recovery facilities |
| 562112 | Waste transfer stations, hazardous |
| 562111 | Waste transfer stations, nonhazardous solid |
| 562211 | Waste treatment facilities, hazardous |

| | |
|---|---|
| 562211 | Waste treatment plants, hazardous |
| 322219 | Wastebaskets, fiber made from purchased paperboard |
| 316990 | Watch bands (except metal) manufacturing |
| 339910 | Watch bands, metal, manufacturing |
| 335910 | Watch batteries manufacturing |
| 327215 | Watch crystals made from purchased glass |
| 326199 | Watch crystals, plastics, manufacturing |
| 334519 | Watch jewels manufacturing |
| 811490 | Watch repair shops without retailing new watches |
| 458310 | Watch shops |
| 334519 | Watchcase manufacturing |
| 423940 | Watchcases merchant wholesalers |
| 334519 | Watches (except smartwatches) and parts (except crystals) manufacturing |
| 423940 | Watches and parts merchant wholesalers |
| 333415 | Water (i.e., drinking) coolers, mechanical, manufacturing |
| 325412 | Water (i.e., drinking) decontamination or purification tablets manufacturing |
| 337126 | Water bed frames, metal, manufacturing |
| 337122 | Water bed frames, wood, manufacturing |
| 337910 | Water bed mattresses manufacturing |
| 327110 | Water closet bowls, vitreous china, manufacturing |
| 332999 | Water closets, metal, manufacturing |
| 339940 | Water colors, artist's, manufacturing |
| 924110 | Water control and quality program administration |
| 423740 | Water coolers, mechanical, merchant wholesalers |
| 237110 | Water desalination plant construction |
| 221310 | Water distribution (except irrigation) |
| 221310 | Water distribution for irrigation |
| 237110 | Water filtration plant construction |
| 221310 | Water filtration plant operation |
| 334512 | Water heater controls manufacturing |
| 238220 | Water heater installation |
| 811412 | Water heater repair and maintenance services without retailing new water heaters |
| 333310 | Water heaters (except boilers), commercial-type, manufacturing |
| 335220 | Water heaters (including nonelectric), household-type, manufacturing |

| | |
|---|---|
| 423720 | Water heaters, gas and electric, merchant wholesaler |
| 326220 | Water hoses, rubber or plastics, manufacturing |
| 213111 | Water intake well drilling, oil and gas field on a contract basis |
| 334519 | Water leak detectors manufacturing |
| 237110 | Water main and line construction |
| 238220 | Water meter installation |
| 713110 | Water parks, amusement |
| 238290 | Water pipe insulating |
| 331511 | Water pipe, cast iron, manufacturing |
| 335210 | Water pulsating devices, household-type electric, manufacturing |
| 237110 | Water pumping or lift station construction |
| 333310 | Water purification equipment manufacturing |
| 423720 | Water purification equipment, household-type, merchant wholesalers |
| 334513 | Water quality monitoring and control systems manufacturing |
| 315210 | Water resistant apparel cut and sew apparel contractors |
| 315250 | Water resistant jackets and windbreakers, nontailored, men's and boys', cut and sewn from purchased fabric (except apparel contractors) |
| 315250 | Water resistant jackets and windbreakers, nontailored, women's and girls', cut and sewn from purchased fabric (except apparel contractors) |
| 315210 | Water resistant outerwear cut and sew apparel contractors |
| 315250 | Water resistant outerwear, men's and boys', cut and sewn from purchased fabric (except apparel contractors) |
| 315250 | Water resistant outerwear, women's, girls', and infants', cut and sewn from purchased fabric (except apparel contractors) |
| 315250 | Water resistant overcoats, men's and boys', cut and sewn from purchased fabric (except apparel contractors) |
| 315250 | Water resistant overcoats, women's and girls', cut and sewn from purchased fabric (except apparel contractors) |
| 237110 | Water sampling station installation |
| 332911 | Water sampling station manufacturing |
| 316210 | Water shoes, plastics or plastics soled fabric upper, manufacturing |
| 316210 | Water shoes, rubber or rubber soled fabric upper, manufacturing |

| | |
|---|---|
| 483212 | Water shuttle services |
| 532284 | Water ski rental |
| 238220 | Water softener installation |
| 423720 | Water softening and conditioning equipment merchant wholesalers |
| 561990 | Water softening and conditioning services |
| 424690 | Water softening compounds merchant wholesalers |
| 333310 | Water softening equipment manufacturing |
| 445298 | Water stores, bottled |
| 221310 | Water supply systems |
| 238220 | Water system balancing and testing contractors |
| 237110 | Water system storage tank and tower construction |
| 332420 | Water tanks, heavy gauge metal, manufacturing |
| 483212 | Water taxi services |
| 332919 | Water traps manufacturing |
| 221310 | Water treatment and distribution |
| 333310 | Water treatment equipment manufacturing |
| 423830 | Water treatment equipment, industrial, merchant wholesalers |
| 423850 | Water treatment equipment, municipal, merchant wholesalers |
| 237110 | Water treatment plant construction |
| 221310 | Water treatment plants |
| 333611 | Water turbines manufacturing |
| 333132 | Water well drilling machinery manufacturing |
| 237110 | Water well drilling, digging, boring or sinking (except water intake wells in oil and gas fields) |
| 237110 | Water well pump and well piping system installation |
| 312111 | Water, artificially carbonated, manufacturing |
| 424490 | Water, bottled (except water treating), merchant wholesalers |
| 325998 | Water, distilled, manufacturing |
| 312111 | Water, flavored, manufacturing |
| 312112 | Water, naturally carbonated, purifying and bottling |
| 712190 | Waterfalls (i.e., natural wonder tourist attractions) |
| 488310 | Waterfront terminal operation (e.g., docks, piers, wharves) |
| 326199 | Watering cans, plastics, manufacturing |

| | |
|---|---|
| 238220 | Waterless fire suppression system installation |
| 238220 | Waterless fire suppression system installation and repair |
| 811310 | Waterless fire suppression system repair and maintenance, without installation |
| 541990 | Waterless fire suppression system testing and/or inspection, without sales, service, or installation |
| 325611 | Waterless hand soaps manufacturing |
| 111219 | Watermelon farming, field, bedding plant and seed production |
| 334514 | Watermeters, consumption registering, manufacturing |
| 541690 | Waterproof consulting services |
| 424350 | Waterproof garments, men's and boys', merchant wholesalers |
| 424350 | Waterproof garments, women's, children's, and infants', merchant wholesalers |
| 315210 | Waterproof outerwear cut and sew apparel contractors |
| 315250 | Waterproof outerwear cut and sewn from purchased fabric (except apparel contractors) |
| 315250 | Waterproof outerwear, rubberizing fabric and manufacturing outerwear |
| 313320 | Waterproofing apparel, fabrics and textile products (e.g., oiling, rubberizing, waxing, varnishing) |
| 238390 | Waterproofing contractors |
| 325510 | Water-repellent coatings for wood, concrete and masonry manufacturing |
| 315210 | Water-repellent outerwear cut and sew apparel contractors |
| 315250 | Water-repellent outerwear, men's and boys', cut and sewn from purchased fabric (except apparel contractors) |
| 315250 | Water-repellent outerwear, women's, girls', and infants', cut and sewn from purchased fabric (except apparel contractors) |
| 315250 | Water-repellent overcoats, men's and boys', cut and sewn from purchased fabric (except apparel contractors) |
| 315250 | Water-repellent overcoats, women's and girls', cut and sewn from purchased fabric (except apparel contractors) |
| 713990 | Waterslides (i.e., amusement rides) |
| 332911 | Waterworks and municipal water system valves manufacturing |
| 334515 | Watt-hour and demand meters, combined, manufacturing |
| 334515 | Watt-hour and time switch meters, combined, manufacturing |

| | |
|---|---|
| 334515 | Watt-hour meters, electric, manufacturing |
| 325194 | Wattle extract manufacturing |
| 334515 | Wattmeters manufacturing |
| 713940 | Wave pools |
| 334515 | Waveform measuring and/or analyzing equipment manufacturing |
| 713990 | Wax figure exhibitions, amusement |
| 339999 | Wax figures (i.e., mannequins) manufacturing |
| 712110 | Wax museums |
| 325612 | Wax removers manufacturing |
| 322220 | Waxed paper for nonpackaging applications made from purchased paper |
| 322220 | Waxed paper for packaging applications made from purchased paper |
| 424130 | Waxed paper merchant wholesalers |
| 424690 | Waxes (except petroleum) merchant wholesalers |
| 324199 | Waxes, petroleum, made from refined petroleum |
| 324110 | Waxes, petroleum, made in petroleum refineries |
| 325612 | Waxes, polishing (e.g., floor, furniture), manufacturing |
| 313320 | Waxing purchased textiles and apparel |
| 115114 | Waxing, fruits or vegetables |
| 112210 | Weaning pig operations |
| 336992 | Weapons, self-propelled, manufacturing |
| 423410 | Wearable video cameras (except household-type) merchant wholesalers |
| 423620 | Wearable video cameras, household-type, merchant wholesalers |
| 541990 | Weather forecasting services |
| 924120 | Weather research program administration |
| 334519 | Weather tracking equipment manufacturing |
| 333998 | Weather vanes manufacturing |
| 331420 | Weatherproof wire or cable made from purchased copper in wire drawing plants |
| 331318 | Weatherproof wire or cable made in aluminum wire drawing plants |
| 238390 | Weatherproofing concrete |
| 332321 | Weatherstrip, metal, manufacturing |
| 321918 | Weatherstrip, wood, manufacturing |
| 238390 | Weatherstripping installation |
| 314999 | Weatherstripping made from purchased textiles |
| 423330 | Weatherstripping merchant wholesalers |

| | |
|---|---|
| 313220 | Weaving and finishing narrow fabrics |
| 313210 | Weaving and finishing of broadwoven fabrics (except rugs, tire fabric) |
| 313210 | Weaving broadwoven fabrics (except rugs, tire fabrics) |
| 313210 | Weaving broadwoven felts |
| 313220 | Weaving fabric less than 12 inches (30cm) |
| 313210 | Weaving fabrics more than 12 inches (30cm) in width |
| 333248 | Weaving machinery manufacturing |
| 313220 | Weaving narrow fabrics |
| 314110 | Weaving rugs, carpets, and mats |
| 541511 | Web (i.e., Internet) page design services, custom |
| 516210 | Web broadcasting |
| 518210 | Web hosting (excluding software publishing) |
| 519290 | Web search portals |
| 313220 | Webbing weaving |
| 321999 | Webbing, cane, reed, and rattan, manufacturing |
| 812990 | Wedding chapels (except churches) |
| 315210 | Wedding dresses cut and sew apparel contractors |
| 315250 | Wedding dresses, women's and girls', cut and sewn from purchased fabric (except apparel contractors) |
| 541921 | Wedding photography services |
| 812990 | Wedding planning services |
| 561730 | Weed control and fertilizing services (except crop) |
| 115112 | Weed control services for crops |
| 926140 | Weed control, agriculture, government |
| 424910 | Weed killers merchant wholesalers |
| 333111 | Weeding machines, farm-type, manufacturing |
| 238910 | Weeping tile installation |
| 811210 | Weighing equipment (e.g., balance, scales) repair and maintenance services |
| 812191 | Weight loss centers, non-medical |
| 812191 | Weight reducing centers, non-medical |
| 713940 | Weight training centers |
| 541890 | Welcoming services (i.e., advertising services) |
| 331222 | Welded iron or steel wire fabric made in wire drawing plants |
| 316990 | Welders' aprons, leather, manufacturing |
| 339113 | Welder's hoods manufacturing |
| 316990 | Welders' jackets, leggings, and sleeves, leather, manufacturing |
| 333992 | Welding equipment manufacturing |
| 532412 | Welding equipment rental or leasing |
| 424690 | Welding gases merchant wholesalers |
| 423830 | Welding machinery and equipment merchant wholesalers |
| 333514 | Welding positioners (i.e., jigs) manufacturing |
| 811310 | Welding repair services (e.g., automotive, general) |
| 541511 | Welding robot applications/software design and development services |
| 331491 | Welding rod, uncoated, nonferrous metals (except aluminum, copper), made from purchased metals or scrap |
| 423840 | Welding supplies (except welding gases) merchant wholesalers |
| 333992 | Welding wire or rods (i.e., coated, cored) manufacturing |
| 238190 | Welding, on-site, contractors |
| 332313 | Weldments manufacturing |
| 923130 | Welfare administration, nonoperating |
| 923130 | Welfare programs administration |
| 624190 | Welfare service centers, multi-program |
| 213112 | Well casing running, cutting and pulling, oil and gas field on a contract basis |
| 331210 | Well casings (e.g., heavy riveted, lock joint, welded, wrought) made from purchased iron or steel |
| 331110 | Well casings, iron or steel, made in iron and steel mills |
| 213111 | Well drilling (i.e., oil, gas, water intake wells) on a contract basis |
| 532412 | Well drilling machinery and equipment rental or leasing |
| 333132 | Well logging equipment manufacturing |
| 213112 | Well logging, oil and gas field, on a contract basis |
| 213112 | Well plugging, oil and gas field, on a contract basis |
| 213112 | Well pumping, oil and gas field, on a contract basis |
| 213112 | Well servicing, oil and gas field, on a contract basis |
| 213112 | Well surveying, oil and gas field, on a contract basis |
| 332322 | Wells, light, sheet metal (except stampings), manufacturing |
| 316110 | Welting leather manufacturing |
| 458110 | Western wear stores |
| 316110 | Wet blues manufacturing |

| | |
|---|---|
| 313230 | Wet laid nonwoven fabrics manufacturing |
| 322130 | Wet machine board mills |
| 311221 | Wet milling corn and other vegetables |
| 339920 | Wet suits manufacturing |
| 541620 | Wetland restoration planning services |
| 325613 | Wetting agents manufacturing |
| 487210 | Whale watching excursions |
| 237990 | Wharf construction |
| 488310 | Wharf operation |
| 311211 | Wheat bran manufacturing |
| 311230 | Wheat breakfast cereal manufacturing |
| 111140 | Wheat farming, field and seed production |
| 311211 | Wheat flour manufacturing |
| 311211 | Wheat germ manufacturing |
| 311213 | Wheat malt manufacturing |
| 424510 | Wheat merchant wholesalers |
| 334515 | Wheatstone bridges (i.e., electrical measuring instruments) manufacturing |
| 811114 | Wheel alignment shops, automotive |
| 334511 | Wheel position indicators and transmitters, aircraft, manufacturing |
| 332216 | Wheel pullers, handtools, manufacturing |
| 333924 | Wheelbarrows manufacturing |
| 532283 | Wheelchair rental |
| 456199 | Wheelchair stores |
| 339113 | Wheelchairs manufacturing |
| 423450 | Wheelchairs merchant wholesalers |
| 336390 | Wheels (i.e., rims), automotive, truck, and bus, manufacturing |
| 327910 | Wheels, abrasive, manufacturing |
| 331110 | Wheels, car and locomotive, iron or steel, made in iron and steel mills |
| 423120 | Wheels, motor vehicle, new, merchant wholesalers |
| 327910 | Wheels, polishing and grinding, manufacturing |
| 336330 | Wheels, steering, automotive, truck, and bus, manufacturing |
| 327910 | Whetstones manufacturing |
| 212390 | Whetstones mining and/or beneficiating |
| 311512 | Whey butter manufacturing |
| 311514 | Whey, condensed, dried, evaporated, and powdered, manufacturing |
| 311513 | Whey, raw, liquid, manufacturing |
| 311511 | Whipped topping (except dry mix, frozen) manufacturing |

| | |
|---|---|
| 311514 | Whipped topping, dry mix, manufacturing |
| 311412 | Whipped topping, frozen, manufacturing |
| 335210 | Whippers, household-type electric, manufacturing |
| 311511 | Whipping cream manufacturing |
| 316990 | Whips, horse, manufacturing |
| 316990 | Whipstocks manufacturing |
| 339113 | Whirlpool baths (i.e., hydrotherapy equipment) manufacturing |
| 423450 | Whirlpool baths, hospital, merchant wholesalers |
| 493190 | Whiskey warehousing |
| 325130 | White extender pigments (e.g., barytes, blanc fixe, whiting) manufacturing |
| 331529 | White metal castings (except die-castings), unfinished, manufacturing |
| 713990 | White water rafting, recreational |
| 238320 | Whitewashing contractors |
| 212312 | Whiting crushed and broken stone, mining and/or beneficiating |
| 114111 | Whiting fishing |
| 325130 | Whiting manufacturing |
| 334519 | Whole body counters, nuclear, manufacturing |
| 238910 | Whole building deconstruction |
| ****** | Wholesale -- see type of product |
| 561520 | Wholesale tour operators |
| 813910 | Wholesalers' associations |
| 337126 | Wicker furniture (except upholstered), household-type, manufacturing |
| 313220 | Wicks manufacturing |
| 334210 | Wide area network communications equipment (e.g., bridges, gateways, routers) manufacturing |
| 458110 | Wig and hairpiece stores |
| 424990 | Wigs merchant wholesalers |
| 339999 | Wigs, wiglets, toupees, hairpieces, manufacturing |
| 516210 | Wiki sites, Internet |
| 712130 | Wild animal parks |
| 111199 | Wild rice farming, field and seed production |
| 721214 | Wilderness camps |
| 711510 | Wildlife artists, independent |
| 924120 | Wildlife conservation agencies |
| 813312 | Wildlife preservation organizations |
| 712190 | Wildlife sanctuaries |
| 212230 | Willemite mining and/or beneficiating |

| | |
|---|---|
| 337126 | Willow furniture (except upholstered), household-type, manufacturing |
| 321999 | Willow ware (except furniture) manufacturing |
| 333923 | Winches manufacturing |
| 423830 | Winches merchant wholesalers |
| 924120 | Wind and water erosion control agencies, government |
| 334519 | Wind direction indicators manufacturing |
| 926130 | Wind generated electrical power regulation |
| 237130 | Wind power structure construction |
| 333611 | Wind powered turbine generator sets manufacturing |
| 333611 | Wind turbines (i.e., windmill) manufacturing |
| 315210 | Windbreakers cut and sew apparel contractors |
| 315250 | Windbreakers, men's and boys', cut and sewn from purchased fabric (except apparel contractors) |
| 315250 | Windbreakers, women's, girls', and infants', cut and sewn from purchased fabric (except apparel contractors) |
| 333248 | Winding machinery for textiles manufacturing |
| 313110 | Winding purchased yarn |
| 313110 | Winding, spooling, beaming and rewinding of purchased yarn |
| 333611 | Windmills, electric power, generation-type, manufacturing |
| 333111 | Windmills, farm-type, manufacturing |
| 238350 | Window and door (residential-type) of any material, prefabricated, installation |
| 325612 | Window cleaning preparations manufacturing |
| 561720 | Window cleaning services |
| 423440 | Window display equipment merchant wholesalers |
| 541890 | Window dressing or trimming services, store |
| 332321 | Window frames and sash, metal, manufacturing |
| 321911 | Window frames and sash, wood and covered wood, manufacturing |
| 238350 | Window installation |
| 238150 | Window pane or sheet installation |
| 326199 | Window sashes, vinyl, manufacturing |
| 332618 | Window screening, woven, made from purchased wire |
| 332321 | Window screens, metal frame, manufacturing |

| | |
|---|---|
| 321911 | Window screens, wood framed, manufacturing |
| 238390 | Window shade and blind installation |
| 811490 | Window shade repair and maintenance shops |
| 337920 | Window shade rollers and fittings manufacturing |
| 337920 | Window shades (except awnings) manufacturing |
| 423220 | Window shades and blinds merchant wholesalers |
| 444180 | Window stores |
| 811122 | Window tinting, automotive |
| 449122 | Window treatment stores |
| 321918 | Window trim, wood and covered wood moldings, manufacturing |
| 321911 | Window units, wood and covered wood, manufacturing |
| 238350 | Window, metal frame residential-type, installation |
| 238350 | Window, wood, installation |
| 423310 | Windows and window frames merchant wholesalers |
| 326199 | Windows and window frames, plastics, manufacturing |
| 326199 | Windows and window frames, vinyl, manufacturing |
| 321911 | Windows, louver, wood, manufacturing |
| 332321 | Windows, metal, manufacturing |
| 321911 | Windows, wood and covered wood, manufacturing |
| 811122 | Windshield repair shops, automotive |
| 325612 | Windshield washer fluid manufacturing |
| 336320 | Windshield washer pumps, automotive, truck, and bus, manufacturing |
| 336390 | Windshield wiper blades and refills manufacturing |
| 336320 | Windshield wiper systems, automotive, truck, and bus, manufacturing |
| 326199 | Windshields, plastics, manufacturing |
| 312130 | Wine coolers manufacturing |
| 424820 | Wine coolers, alcoholic, merchant wholesalers |
| 459999 | Wine making supply stores |
| 445320 | Wine shops, packaged |
| 312130 | Wineries |
| 312130 | Wines manufacturing |
| 424820 | Wines merchant wholesalers |
| 312130 | Wines, cooking, manufacturing |
| 325998 | Wintergreen oil manufacturing |

| | |
|---|---|
| 336390 | Wipers, windshield, automotive, truck, and bus, manufacturing |
| 313230 | Wipes, nonwoven fabric, manufacturing |
| 423840 | Wiping cloths merchant wholesalers |
| 423510 | Wire (except insulated) merchant wholesalers |
| 423510 | Wire and cable (except electrical) merchant wholesalers |
| 333248 | Wire and cable insulating machinery manufacturing |
| 331222 | Wire cages, iron or steel, made in wire drawing plants |
| 331222 | Wire carts (e.g., grocery, household, industrial), iron or steel, made in wire drawing plants |
| 331420 | Wire cloth made from purchased copper in wire drawing plants |
| 331318 | Wire cloth made in aluminum wire drawing plants |
| 331420 | Wire cloth, copper, made in integrated secondary smelting and wire drawing plants |
| 331222 | Wire cloth, iron or steel, made in wire drawing plants |
| 331491 | Wire cloth, nonferrous metals (except aluminum, copper), made from purchased metals or scrap |
| 333519 | Wire drawing and fabricating machinery and equipment (except dies) manufacturing |
| 333514 | Wire drawing and straightening dies manufacturing |
| 331222 | Wire garment hangers, iron or steel, made in wire drawing plants |
| 516210 | Wire photo services |
| 331110 | Wire products, iron or steel, made in iron and steel mills |
| 331222 | Wire products, iron or steel, made in wire drawing plants |
| 423510 | Wire rope (except insulated) merchant wholesalers |
| 333923 | Wire rope hoists manufacturing |
| 423510 | Wire screening merchant wholesalers |
| 331318 | Wire screening, aluminum, made in integrated secondary smelting and drawing plants |
| 331491 | Wire screening, nonferrous metals (except aluminum, copper), made from purchased nonferrous metals (except aluminum, copper) in wire drawing plants |
| 561422 | Wire services (i.e., telemarketing services), floral |
| 516210 | Wire services, news |
| 331318 | Wire, armored, made in aluminum wire drawing plants |
| 331318 | Wire, bare, made in aluminum wire drawing plants |
| 331420 | Wire, copper (e.g., armored, bare, insulated), made from purchased copper in wire drawing plants |
| 331420 | Wire, copper (e.g., armored, bare, insulated), made in integrated secondary smelting and wire drawing plants |
| 331221 | Wire, flat, rolled strip, made in cold rolling mills |
| 331318 | Wire, insulated, made in aluminum wire drawing plants |
| 423610 | Wire, insulated, merchant wholesalers |
| 331222 | Wire, iron or steel (e.g., armored, bare, insulated), made in wire drawing plants |
| 331420 | Wire, mechanical, copper and copper alloy, made from purchased copper or in integrated secondary smelting and rolling, drawing or extruding plants |
| 331491 | Wire, nonferrous metals (except aluminum, copper), made from purchased nonferrous metals (except aluminum, copper) in wire drawing plants |
| 331491 | Wire, nonferrous metals (except aluminum, copper), made in integrated secondary smelting mills and wire drawing plants |
| 517121 | Wired telecommunication resellers |
| 517112 | Wireless data communication carriers (except satellite) |
| 517112 | Wireless Internet service providers (except satellite) |
| 517122 | Wireless phone service plan sales agents, selling on behalf of wireless telecommunications carriers |
| 517122 | Wireless phone stores, selling wireless phone service plans on an agent basis |
| 517121 | Wireless telecommunications resellers (except satellite telecommunications and agents) |
| 517112 | Wireless telephone communications carriers (except satellite) |
| 213112 | Wireline services, oil and gas field, on a contract basis |
| 336320 | Wiring harness and ignition sets for internal combustion engines manufacturing |
| 423610 | Wiring supplies merchant wholesalers |
| 325194 | Witch hazel extract manufacturing |
| 212290 | Wolframite mining and/or beneficiating |

| | |
|---|---|
| 212390 | Wollastonite mining and/or beneficiating |
| 424350 | Women's and children's clothing accessories merchant wholesalers |
| 813410 | Women's auxiliaries |
| 923130 | Women's bureaus |
| 424350 | Women's clothing merchant wholesalers |
| 813410 | Women's clubs |
| 624221 | Women's shelters, battered |
| 325194 | Wood alcohol, natural, manufacturing |
| 325199 | Wood alcohol, synthetic, manufacturing |
| 424990 | Wood carvings merchant wholesalers |
| 113310 | Wood chipping in the field |
| 321113 | Wood chips made in sawmills |
| 332216 | Wood cutting saw blades manufacturing |
| 325194 | Wood distillates manufacturing |
| 321911 | Wood door frames and sash manufacturing |
| 333248 | Wood drying kilns manufacturing |
| 321114 | Wood fence (i.e., pickets, poling, rails), treating |
| 423310 | Wood fencing merchant wholesalers |
| 325510 | Wood fillers manufacturing |
| 238330 | Wood floor finishing (e.g., coating, sanding) |
| 321918 | Wood flooring (including laminate and wood composite) manufacturing |
| 423310 | Wood flooring merchant wholesalers |
| 238330 | Wood flooring, installation only |
| 321999 | Wood flour manufacturing |
| 238130 | Wood frame component (e.g., truss) fabrication on site |
| 337121 | Wood framed furniture, upholstered, household-type, manufacturing |
| 321999 | Wood heel blocks manufacturing |
| 321999 | Wood heels, finished, manufacturing |
| 321215 | Wood I-joists manufacturing |
| 321918 | Wood moldings (e.g., prefinished, unfinished), clear and finger joint, manufacturing |
| 325194 | Wood oils manufacturing |
| 424950 | Wood paste merchant wholesalers |
| 321999 | Wood pellets manufacturing |
| 423990 | Wood products (e.g., chips, posts, shavings, ties) merchant wholesalers |
| 321114 | Wood products, creosoting purchased wood products |
| 322110 | Wood pulp manufacturing |
| 424990 | Wood pulp merchant wholesalers |
| 423310 | Wood shingles merchant wholesalers |
| 321918 | Wood shutters manufacturing |
| 423310 | Wood siding merchant wholesalers |
| 238170 | Wood siding, installation |
| 333414 | Wood stoves manufacturing |
| 424690 | Wood treating preparations merchant wholesalers |
| 333243 | Wood veneer laminating and gluing machines manufacturing |
| 321911 | Wood window frames and sash manufacturing |
| 321999 | Wood wool (excelsior) manufacturing |
| 449129 | Wood-burning stove stores |
| 423440 | Woodenware, commercial, merchant wholesalers |
| 321999 | Woodenware, kitchen and household, manufacturing |
| 532490 | Woodworking machinery and equipment rental or leasing |
| 423830 | Woodworking machinery merchant wholesalers |
| 333243 | Woodworking machines (except handheld) manufacturing |
| 333248 | Wool and worsted finishing machinery manufacturing |
| 313210 | Wool fabrics, broadwoven, weaving |
| 313220 | Wool fabrics, narrow woven, weaving |
| 313110 | Wool spun yarn made from purchased fiber |
| 313310 | Wool tops and noils manufacturing |
| 424590 | Wool tops and noils merchant wholesalers |
| 314999 | Wool waste processing |
| 313110 | Wool yarn, twisting or winding of purchased yarn |
| 424590 | Wool, raw, merchant wholesalers |
| 311941 | Worcestershire sauce manufacturing |
| 333310 | Word processing equipment, dedicated, manufacturing |
| 561410 | Word processing services |
| 624229 | Work (sweat) equity home construction organizations |
| 337127 | Work benches manufacturing |
| 812332 | Work clothing and uniform supply services, industrial |
| 424350 | Work clothing, men's and boys', merchant wholesalers |
| 315210 | Work coats and jackets cut and sew apparel contractors |

| | |
|---|---|
| 315250 | Work coats and jackets, men's and boys', cut and sewn from purchased fabric (except apparel contractors) |
| 624310 | Work experience centers (i.e., sheltered workshops) |
| 315120 | Work gloves and mittens, knit, made in apparel knitting mills |
| 315990 | Work gloves, leather (except apparel contractors), manufacturing |
| 315210 | Work gloves, leather, cut and sew apparel contractors |
| 315210 | Work pants cut and sew apparel contractors |
| 315250 | Work pants, men's and boys', cut and sewn from purchased fabric (except apparel contractors) |
| 315210 | Work shirts cut and sew apparel contractors |
| 315250 | Work shirts, men's and boys', cut and sewn from purchased fabric (except apparel contractors) |
| 316210 | Work shoes manufacturing |
| 721310 | Workers' camps |
| 525190 | Workers' compensation insurance funds |
| 524126 | Workers' compensation insurance underwriting |
| 923130 | Workers' compensation program administration |
| 721310 | Workers' dormitories |
| 926110 | Workforce Development Boards, nonoperating |
| 812910 | Working, sporting, and service dog training services |
| 213111 | Workover of oil and gas wells on a contract basis |
| 624310 | Workshops for persons with disabilities |
| 334111 | Workstations, computer, manufacturing |
| 928120 | World Bank |
| 813319 | World peace and understanding advocacy organizations |
| 112990 | Worm production |
| 424990 | Worms merchant wholesalers |
| 313210 | Worsted fabrics weaving |
| 321999 | Wrappers, excelsior, manufacturing |
| 333993 | Wrapping (i.e., packaging) machinery manufacturing |
| 424130 | Wrapping paper (except gift wrap) merchant wholesalers |
| 339999 | Wreaths, artificial, manufacturing |
| 488410 | Wrecker services (i.e., towing services), motor vehicle |
| 238910 | Wrecking, building or other structure |
| 332216 | Wrenches, handtools, nonpowered, manufacturing |
| 333991 | Wrenches, impact, handheld power-driven, manufacturing |
| 711219 | Wrestlers, independent professional |
| 711310 | Wrestling event managers with facilities |
| 711320 | Wrestling event managers without facilities |
| 711310 | Wrestling event organizers with facilities |
| 711320 | Wrestling event organizers without facilities |
| 711310 | Wrestling event promoters with facilities |
| 711320 | Wrestling event promoters without facilities |
| 711510 | Writers of advertising copy, independent |
| 711510 | Writers, independent (freelance) |
| 813410 | Writing clubs |
| 325998 | Writing inks manufacturing |
| 424120 | Writing paper (except bulk) merchant wholesalers |
| 322230 | Writing paper and envelopes, boxed sets, made from purchased paper |
| 322120 | Writing paper made in paper mills |
| 322230 | Writing paper, cut sheet, made from purchased paper |
| 332323 | Wrought iron fences manufacturing |
| 337126 | Wrought iron furniture (except upholstered), household-type, manufacturing |
| 332996 | Wrought iron or steel pipe and tubing made from purchased metal pipe |
| 331110 | Wrought iron or steel pipe and tubing made in iron and steel mills |
| 212290 | Wulfenite mining and/or beneficiating |
| 212390 | Wurtzilite mining and/or beneficiating |
| 325320 | Xanthone insecticides manufacturing |
| 334517 | X-ray apparatus and tubes (e.g., control, industrial, medical, research) manufacturing |
| 325992 | X-ray film and plates, sensitized, manufacturing |
| 334517 | X-ray generators manufacturing |
| 541380 | X-ray inspection services |
| 334517 | X-ray irradiation equipment manufacturing |
| 621512 | X-ray laboratories, medical or dental |
| 423450 | X-ray machines and parts, medical and dental, merchant wholesalers |
| 334517 | X-ray tubes manufacturing |

| | |
|---|---|
| 334515 | X-Y recorders (i.e., plotters (except computer peripheral equipment)) manufacturing |
| 325110 | Xylene made from refined petroleum or liquid hydrocarbons |
| 324110 | Xylene made in petroleum refineries |
| 339992 | Xylophones and parts manufacturing |
| 713930 | Yacht basins |
| 336612 | Yacht building, not done in shipyards |
| 713930 | Yacht clubs with marinas |
| 713990 | Yacht clubs without marinas |
| 532284 | Yacht rental without crew |
| 423860 | Yachts (except pleasure) merchant wholesalers |
| 336611 | Yachts built in shipyards |
| 423910 | Yachts, pleasure, merchant wholesalers |
| 111211 | Yam farming, field and seed production |
| 424310 | Yard goods, textile (except burlap, felt), merchant wholesalers |
| 335131 | Yard lights, residential electric, manufacturing |
| 332216 | Yardsticks, metal, manufacturing |
| 321999 | Yardsticks, wood, manufacturing |
| 313110 | Yarn spinning mills |
| 313110 | Yarn spun from purchased fiber |
| 333248 | Yarn texturizing machines manufacturing |
| 313110 | Yarn throwing, twisting, and winding of purchased yarn |
| 313110 | Yarn, carpet and rug, spun from purchased fiber |
| 325220 | Yarn, cellulosic filament, manufacturing |
| 325220 | Yarn, cellulosic filament, manufacturing and texturizing |
| 327212 | Yarn, fiberglass, made in glass making plants |
| 325220 | Yarn, noncellulosic fiber and filament, manufacturing |
| 325220 | Yarn, noncellulosic fiber and filament, manufacturing and texturizing |
| 424310 | Yarns (except industrial) merchant wholesalers |
| 424990 | Yarns, industrial, merchant wholesalers |
| 513199 | Yearbook (e.g., high school, college, university) publishers |
| 513199 | Yearbook (e.g., high school, college, university) publishers (except exclusive Internet publishing) |
| 513199 | Yearbook (e.g., high school, college, university) publishers and printing combined |

| | |
|---|---|
| 513199 | Yearbook (e.g., high school, college, university) publishers, exclusively on Internet |
| 323111 | Yearbooks commercial printing (except screen) without publishing |
| 323113 | Yearbooks screen printing without publishing |
| 311999 | Yeast manufacturing |
| 424490 | Yeast merchant wholesalers |
| 713940 | Yoga fitness studios or centers |
| 611699 | Yoga instruction, camps or schools |
| 611519 | Yoga instructor training |
| 311511 | Yogurt (except frozen) manufacturing |
| 424430 | Yogurt merchant wholesalers |
| 311514 | Yogurt mix manufacturing |
| 311520 | Yogurt, frozen, manufacturing |
| 111334 | Youngberry farming |
| 624110 | Youth centers (except recreational only) |
| 813410 | Youth civic clubs |
| 813410 | Youth clubs (except recreational only) |
| 813410 | Youth farming organizations |
| 624110 | Youth guidance organizations |
| 721199 | Youth hostels |
| 813410 | Youth scouting organizations |
| 624110 | Youth self-help organizations |
| 813410 | Youth social clubs |
| 713990 | Youth sports league teams |
| 325220 | Zein fibers and filaments manufacturing |
| 325180 | Zinc ammonium chloride manufacturing |
| 331491 | Zinc and zinc alloy bar, plate, pipe, rod, sheet, tubing, and wire made from purchased metals or scrap |
| 423510 | Zinc and zinc alloy primary forms merchant wholesalers |
| 325130 | Zinc based pigments manufacturing |
| 335910 | Zinc carbon batteries manufacturing |
| 331529 | Zinc castings (except die-castings), unfinished, manufacturing |
| 325180 | Zinc chloride manufacturing |
| 325180 | Zinc compounds, not specified elsewhere by process, manufacturing |
| 331523 | Zinc die-castings, unfinished, manufacturing |
| 331492 | Zinc dust reclaiming |
| 332999 | Zinc foil and leaf not made in rolling mills |
| 325180 | Zinc hydrosulfite (i.e., zinc dithionite) manufacturing |

| | |
|---|---|
| 212230 | Zinc ore mine site development for own account |
| 212230 | Zinc ores mining and/or beneficiating |
| 325180 | Zinc oxide (except pigments) manufacturing |
| 325412 | Zinc oxide medicinal preparations manufacturing |
| 331492 | Zinc recovering from scrap and/or alloying purchased metals |
| 331410 | Zinc refining, primary |
| 331491 | Zinc rolling, drawing, or extruding purchased metals or scrap |
| 325180 | Zinc sulfide manufacturing |
| 212230 | Zinc-blende (sphalerite) mining and/or beneficiating |
| 212230 | Zincite mining and/or beneficiating |
| 713990 | Zip-line courses (i.e., amusement rides) |
| 333248 | Zipper making machinery manufacturing |
| 313220 | Zipper tape weaving |
| 339993 | Zippers (i.e., slide fasteners) manufacturing |
| 424310 | Zippers merchant wholesalers |
| 331491 | Zirconium and zirconium alloy bar, rod, billet, sheet, strip, and tubing made from purchased metals or scrap |
| 212290 | Zirconium concentrates beneficiating |
| 212290 | Zirconium ores mining and/or beneficiating |
| 331410 | Zirconium refining, primary |
| 331491 | Zirconium rolling, drawing, or extruding purchased metals or scrap |
| 339992 | Zithers and parts manufacturing |
| 925120 | Zoning boards and commissions |
| 712130 | Zoological gardens |
| 712130 | Zoos |
| 111219 | Zucchini farming, field, bedding plant and seed production |

CPSIA information can be obtained
at www.ICGtesting.com
Printed in the USA
BVHW070330100522
636328BV00003B/3